A

I

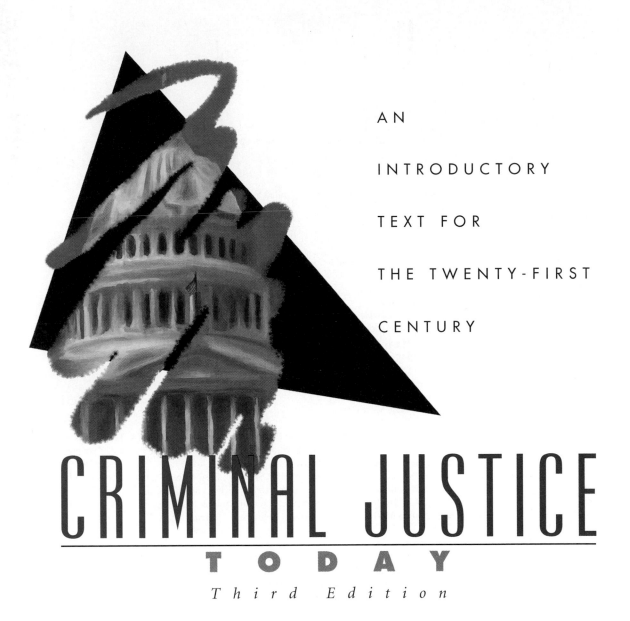

AN

INTRODUCTORY

TEXT FOR

THE TWENTY-FIRST

CENTURY

CRIMINAL JUSTICE
TODAY
Third Edition

FRANK SCHMALLEGER, PH.D.

Pembroke State Uiversity,
Pembroke, North Carolina

FORWARD BY

SAM SOURYAL, PH.D.

PRENTICE HALL CAREER & TECHNOLOGY, ENGLEWOOD CLIFFS, NEW JERSEY 07632

LIBRARY OF CONGRESS CATALOGING-IN-PUBLICATION DATA
Schmalleger, Frank.
    Criminal justice today: an introductory text for the twenty-first
century / Frank Schmalleger; foreword by Sam Souryal,—3rd ed.
        p.   cm.
    Includes index.
    ISBN 0-13-302895-X
    1. Criminal justice, Administration of—United States.   I. Title.
    HV9950.S35   1995   94-6699
    364.973—dc20   CIP

Editorial/production supervision
    and electronic page composition: Janet M. McGillicuddy
Interior design: Patrice Fodero
Cover design: Ruta Kysilewskyj
Cover art: Rolando Corujo
Charts and graphs: Freddy Flake
Electronic photos: Mark LaSalle
Photo research: Chris Pullo
Manufacturing buyer: Ed O'Dougherty
Acquisitions editor: Robin Baliszewski
Marketing manager: Ramona Sherman
Supplements editor: Judy Casillo
Editorial assistant: Rose Mary Florio

Chapter opening photograph for chapter 1: Bob Riha/Gamma Liaison; for chapter 2: Telemundo/Roberts/Sipa
Press; for chapter 3: Bob Daemmrich/Stock Boston; for chapter 4: Alex Branson/Sygma; for chapter 5:
Marlow/Magnum; for chapter 6: Nina Berman/Sipa Press; for chapter 7: Juan Venegez/Sipa Press; for chapter 8:
Bob Daemmrich/Stock Boston; for chapter 9: Stacy Pick/Stock Boston; for chapter 10: Reuters/Bettmann; for
chapter 11: Bob Daemmrich/Stock Boston; for chapter 12: Richard Falco/Black Star; for chapter 13: Armineh
Johannes/Sipa Press; for chapter 14: Lester Sloan/Woodfin Camp & Associates; for chapter 15: Billy
Barnes/Stock Boston; for chapter 16: Mulvehill/The Image Works; for chapter 17: Douglas Burrows/Gamma
Liaison.

©1995, 1993, 1991 by Prentice Hall Career & Technology
Prentice-Hall Inc.
A Paramount Communications Company
Englewood Cliffs, New Jersey 07632

Printed in the United States of America

10 9 8 7 6 5 4 3 2 1

ISBN 0-13-302895-X
ISBN 0-13-302985-9

Prentice-Hall International (UK) Limited, *London*
Prentice-Hall of Australia Pty. Limited, *Sydney*
Prentice-Hall Canada, Inc., *Toronto*
Prentice-Hall Hispanoamericana, S.A., *Mexico*
Prentice-Hall of India Private Limited, *New Delhi*
Prentice-Hall of Japan, Inc., *Tokyo*
Simon & Schuster Asia Pte. Ltd., *Singapore*
Editora Prentice-Hall do Brasil, Ltda., *Rio de Janeiro*

CONTENTS

PREFACE

A great sage of modern times once observed that we live in a world of constant change. The increasing rapidity of change in today's world brings with it challenges to our way of life and requires a continual reexamination of the social institutions with which we make sense out of what happens around us.

One social institution in particular—the criminal justice system—has become the subject of numerous critiques and is now deeply embroiled in change. The powers that are at work in reshaping our American justice system include both formal and institutionalized processes, such as the far-reaching decisions of the U.S. Supreme Court, and other, less predictable forces ranging from organized special interest groups to technological innovations and social exigencies. Among the latter, public concern over what is perceived as a national drug problem and the fear of AIDS are two powerful social issues with the potential to bend the justice system in directions which would have been unimaginable only a decade or two ago.

Any introductory book on criminal justice, if it is to have a place in today's college and university classrooms, must do three things well. First, it must provide a thorough historical coverage of the field by recognizing significant past developments and by acknowledging the individuals who have already contributed to the study of criminal justice. Second, to be relevant and to excite the student, it must focus on contemporary issues. Last, to have value the book must provide a guide for understanding. It must be insightful in a way that will allow readers to reach conclusions about the practice of criminal justice and to apply what they have learned to their own lives as informed citizens of a dynamic society. To meet these goals, *Criminal Justice Today* draws intentionally upon the tensions created in the modern world by criminal activity and efforts at social control. The practice of criminal justice occurs within a web woven of highly valued and hard-won civil rights, on the one hand, and the concerns of society for order, predictability, and safety, on the other— a fact from which the book never strays.

A number of distinctive features set this book apart from others like it. One is timeliness. Information is being produced today at a prodigious rate. In many cases published sources are out of date even before they are published. Textbooks that rely solely on other "hard-copy" works are doubly doomed to untimeliness and social irrelevance. *Criminal Justice Today* is as much a product of the modern world as it is a guide to it. It is one of the first introductory criminal justice texts to take advantage of high-technology information retrieval sources and on-line criminal justice data bases. Well-researched and highly regarded on-line services such as the National Criminal Justice Reference Service, Dialogue, Compuserve, AP Online, the Search Group BBS, and the U.S. Supreme Court's Project HERMES have all contributed to the development of *Criminal Justice Today* in a way that would not have been possible only a few years ago. The statistics, citations, and court cases this book contains are up to date, and the news stories it describes are easily remembered by students.

Another distinguishing feature of this text is its emphasis on the multidimensional environment surrounding the criminal justice system. Legal, technical, social, and international forces are all discussed as major shapers of the American system of justice. In the area of constitutional issues, for example, most other texts discuss search and seizure primarily as they affect police agencies. *Criminal Justice Today* is more comprehensive in its approach. It covers the legal environment in which all agencies of criminal justice must function, from police through courts, corrections, and probation and parole. Criminal Justice Today also recognizes the impact on the justice system of social issues through coverage of American social problems such as child abuse, kiddie porn, and the problems that drugs represent to society today. The multi-national criminal justice chapter and another on the future of criminal justice expand consideration of the web of social forces in which the modern justice system is enmeshed.

Criminal Justice Today brings the study of criminal justice into the modern world through detailed coverage of modern technology and computers in the service of criminal justice and high-technology crime as a major emerging issue in the field. In this edition expanded emphasis is given to the use of visual materials. The charts and graphs, combined with a liberal use of color and photographs, are designed to produce an attractive text-based learning environment for today's visually oriented students.

Even though this book is future directed, it recognizes the debt any future owes to its past. Each section and every chapter begin with a series of thought-provoking quotations from famous philosophers, poets, scientists, and statesmen and stateswomen who have gone before. Quotations from contemporary thinkers are included as well. Some readers may find that here and there a quote will "ring true" with them. To assist students in identifying and researching historical figures, the years in which those people lived are indicated in parentheses where the quotations appear. Contemporary figures have no such dates associated with them.

Criminal Justice Today is intended not as a simple description of what has already taken place in the field, but as a visual guide to criminal justice today, a road map to criminal justice in the twenty-first century, and a bridge between past and future.

Instructions to the Student for Using the Disk That Accompanies Criminal Justice Today

A number of student-oriented disk-based simulations are available for IBM-compatible computers for use with *Criminal Justice Today*. If your instructor has elected to assign the disk provided by Prentice Hall, you should be especially attentive to this symbol:

The symbol, commonly called a "disk icon," signifies that your disk contains a scenario that is relevant to the text material at the point where the icon appears. Your instructor may require you to complete the assignments keyed to text material identified by the icon and may also ask that you turn in your disk at specified intervals or at the completion of the course. The disk also contains a self-administered survey that allows for an assessment of your attitudes along a continuum of social order versus individual rights of advocacy. Take care of your disk, for it maintains an internal record of your progress through whatever scenarios may be assigned!

ACKNOWLEDGMENTS

My thanks to all who assisted in so many different ways in the development of this textbook. The sacrifice of time made by my wife, Harmonie, and daughter Nicole, as I worked endlessly in my study, is heartfelt. Thanks also to Robin Baliszewski, Ramona Sherman, Janet McGillicuddy, Patrick Walsh, Judy Casillo, Rose Mary Florio, Sally Ann Bailey, and all the Prentice Hall Career & Technology staff—true professionals, who make the task of manuscript development enjoyable. My supplements authors, Ted Alleman and Gordon Armstrong, are both extremely talented, and I am grateful to them for using their skills in support of this new edition. This book benefited considerably from the suggestions of Gordon Armstrong, Clem Bartollas, Terry Hutchins, Jess Maghan, and Richard Zevitz and from suggestions made by Herman Woltring of the United Nations' Crime Prevention and Criminal Justice Branch. I am grateful, as well, to manuscript reviewers Larry Bassi, W. Garrett Capune, Armand P. Hernandez, Terry Hutchins, William D. Hyatt, Raymond E. Lloyd II, Michael J. Mahaney, G. Larry Mays, David Neubauer, James S. E. Opolot, Roger L. Pennel, Gary Prawel, Albert Roberts, Robert W. Taylor, Lawrence F. Travis III, Bryan J. Vila, and L. Thomas Winfree, Jr., for holding me to the fire when I might have opted for a less rigorous coverage of some topics—and to George Hernandez, at California's Grossmont College, who sure knows the law! A special thanks goes to Darl Champion of Methodist College for his insightful suggestions.

Writing a textbook is never a solitary act. The author would like to extend a special thanks to the following individuals for their invaluable comments and suggestions along the way: Howard Abadinsky, Z. G. Standing Bear, Michael Blankenship, Kathy Cameron-Hahn, Art Chete, Geary Chlebus, Jon E. Clark, Warren Clark, Mark L. Dantzker, Vicky Doworth, Steve Egger, Michael Gray, Joe Graziano, Alex Greenberg, Ed Heischmidt, P. Ray Kedia, Joan Luxenburg, Michael Lyman, Richard H. Martin, Thomas P. McAninch, Bob J. Meadows, Donald J. Melisi, Jim Mezhir, Rik Michelson, Roslyn Muraskin, Harv Morley, Charles Myles, David F. Owens, Michael J. Palmiotto, William H. Parsonage, Ken Peak,

Phil Purpura, Philip L. Reichel, John Robich, Carl E. Russell, Judith M. Sgarzi, Ira Silverman, John Sinsel, Ted Skotnicki, B. Grant Stitt, Tom Thackery, Joe Trevalino, Howard Tritt, Bill Tyrrell, Tim Veiders, Ron Vogel, John Volman, Jr., David Whelan, and Lois Wims.

Jean E. Sexton and Lucy H. Hartley, both very fine librarians, helped uncover information otherwise irretrievable. Thanks are also due everyone who assisted in artistic arrangements, including Freddy Flake, Ruta Kysilewskyj, Paula Maylahn, Mark LaSalle, photo researcher Chris Pullo, Michael L. Hammond of the Everett (Washington) Police Department, Sgt. Michael Flores of New York City Police Department's Photo Unit, Assistant Chief James M. Lewis of the Bakersfield (California) Police Department, Monique Smith of the National Institute of Justice, and Tonya Matz of the University of Illinois at Chicago—all of whom were especially helpful in providing a wealth of photo resources. I am indebted to special friends Steve Marson, Tom Ross, Robert Reising, and Michael Stratil for their encouragement, by both word and example, when the going got tough, and the hours long.

A special "thank you" to my university secretary Wanda Hammonds, who fielded frequent messages and phone calls; to students Matthew E. Croke, Terre Chipman, and Pamela Monroe; and to my good friend Sam Souryal who has a knack of being able to say more in one or two pages than I can in hundreds. I'd also like to acknowledge J. Harper Wilson, Chief of the FBI's Uniform Crime Reporting Program; Nancy Carnes of the same program; Mark Reading of the Drug Enforcement Administration's Office of Intelligence; Kristina Rose at the National Criminal Justice Reference Service; Wilma M. Grant of the U.S. Supreme Court's Project Hermes; Ken Kerle at the American Jail Association; Lisa Bastian, survey statistician with the National Crime Victimization Survey Program; Steve Shackelton with the U.S. Parks Service; and Bernie Homme of the California Peace Officer Standards and Training Commission for their help in making this book both timely and accurate.

Last, but by no means least, Reed Adams, Gary Colboth, H. R. Delaney, Jannette O. Domingo, Al Garcia, Rodney Hennigsen, David M. Jones, Victor E. Kappeler, Robert O. Lampert, Norman G. Kittel, Robert J. Meadows, Joseph M. Pellicciotti, and Jeff Schrink should know that their writings, contributions, and valuable suggestions at the earliest stages of manuscript development continue to be very much appreciated. Thank you, each and everyone!

Frank Schmalleger, Ph.D.
Hilton Head Island, SC

Criminal Justice Today is the culmination of Frank Schmalleger's years of experience as a writer. The author of two dozen articles and a number of books, Schmalleger is probably best known for his work in founding the referred journal *The Justice Professional*, and for his books *The Social Basis of Criminal Justice: Ethical Issues for the 1980s* and *Ethics in Criminal Justice.* He has recently finished work on a textbook covering the use of computers in criminal justice and is now writing an introductory criminology text.

Frank Schmalleger received his B.A. in the field of operations research from the University of Notre Dame in 1969. The burgeoning social idealism of the late 1960s and early 1970s led him to a graduate career in sociology, specializing in criminology, at the Ohio State University. He received both his Master's degree and Ph.D. degree from OSU. As the war in Vietnam raged, Schmalleger, still a graduate student at OSU, enrolled in ROTC and was commissioned a second lieutenant in the Adjutant General branch of the U.S. Army. He served both on active duty and in the Army reserves until 1980.

In 1975 Schmalleger began his teaching career at Pembroke State University, where he personally taught every course in the department's newly begun criminal justice program. Over the last 20 years the program has increased dramatically in size and Schmalleger now chairs the Department of Sociology, Social Work, and Criminal Justice—a position he has held for the last 14 years.

Schmalleger's commitment to the profession of criminal justice has won for him a university yearbook dedication, in which students described him as "*someone who makes coming to school worthwhile,*" and the 1989–90 Outstanding Criminal Justice Educator Award from the North Carolina Criminal Justice Association. Schmalleger's professional activities keep him busily involved in every meeting of the Academy of Criminal Justice Sciences and the American Society of Criminology. In the spring of 1991 he received his university's award as "Distinguished Professor." Schmalleger is also a member of the American Society for Industrial Security and teaches graduate-level computer security to a military audience.

Schmalleger's philosophy in both teaching and writing can be summed up in these few words: "*In order to teach students, we have to first get—then hold—their interest. A good teacher is fascinating in his or her delivery; a good book can't be put down.*" It is with this philosophy in mind that *Criminal Justice Today* has been written.

FOREWORD

Human knowledge increases with every passing moment, but scholarship can be enhanced only with the enlightenment brought about by new generations of scholars. As academic disciplines mature, external and internal debates usually arise and a dialectic movement toward reform invariably ensues. During such movements the true nature of the discipline is reexamined, its boundaries are reestablished, and its claims are legitimized. The leaders of such reformist movements are usually new-generation scholars who, in addressing the same questions raised to their predecessors, recognize their independent thought, beg to differ with their teachers, and rejoice in formulating new ideas. Consider, for example, Aristotle's concept of *eudaemonia* or the integrated state of mind. It was basically a refinement of Plato's concept of *knowledge of the good*, which, in turn, was a moral adaptation of Socrates' dictum, *know thyself*. The scholarship produced by these three successive thinkers spanned over 75 years and basically presented improved versions of what constituted the "good life." Concerns for criminality, or the "bad life" were nonissues in Greek philosophy. Ironically, they have become constant vexations of contemporary criminal justice thinkers who—rather deservingly—seem to have forgotten the Greek wisdom which obligates society to nurture and preserve the "good life."

Frank Schmalleger's third edition represents the thinking of the new wave of scholars whom Manning calls the *third-generation criminal justice scholars* (i.e., those who were originally the students of, or influenced by, Dinitz, Reiss, Skolnick, Banton, Wilson, and certainly a few others). These scholars, like their mentors, invariably attempt to explain, describe, or account for what constitutes justice in crime-related situations. In a free and a progressive society, that necessitates the tedious task of continuously refining the critical balance that determines the extent of individual freedom, on one hand, and the unavoidable controls to be placed by society—*solely to perpetuate justice*.

In search for that elusive balance, the third edition of *Criminal Justice Today* focuses on the continuing debate between *individual rights advocates* and *public order advocates*. The debate method is critical to the understanding of criminal justice issues, since (1) it can further sharpen our view of what is truly criminal, and what is not, under a *truly* just system; (2) it can expose naturalistic falsities and compel dogmas to be rethought by promoting a more tolerant view of ambiguity and diversity; and (3) it can ultimately lead to the institution of a Rawlsian view of justice rationality, one which operates "under the veil of ignorance," or *without regard to who might be the criminal*. Schmalleger and a few other new-generation criminal justice scholars have certainly made great strides in the continuous process of clarifying the criminal justice issues of the twenty-first century. Schmalleger's work reflects the unique blend of a pragmatic concern for crime victims and substantive support for crime control mechanisms *that work*—without compromising his solid attachment to the principles of liberty and justice in a civilized society.

Criminal justice is a young discipline which continues to experience growing pains in its development. Several features have dominated its traditional thought. It is directed by (1) a legalistic rather than a *justicist perspective*, (2) the *myth of coercive power* rather than by the practice of mutual accommodation, and (3) a *reductionist view of rationality*. Consequently, the discipline continues to be fraught with contradiction: It employs violence to keep the peace, relies on deprivation of freedom to sustain liberty, and treats offenders—but not until their infection by the germs of prisonizaton has become permanent.

First, *the fundamental proposition of justice*—the greatest interest of man on earth without which theories of law, order, and crime make no sense—has been largely ignored to the point of being treated as ancillary to the discipline, or simply a cosmetic trimming of social order. The impartial administration of justice which characterizes the essential nature of a civilized society, and which was enshrined by the Founding Fathers as *the* foundation of liberty, has been imperiled. It has been overtaken by a mentality of "popular *juste-milieu*" computed in bureaucratic formulas and seemingly systematic arrangements of guideline matrices. Subsequently, and sadly so, the radically illuminating views of thinkers such as Quinney, Pepinsky, and Braswell, depicting crime as "suffering," criminology as "peacemaking," and correction as "touching the inner spirit," have been amusingly read, but quietly returned to the shelf.

Two other related symptoms are particularly noteworthy in our present regard for justice. First, the fact that the world today has been experiencing such dramatic change (especially in Eastern Europe, South Africa, and the Middle East), from accepting "justice permitted" to demanding "justice deserved," seems to have gone all but unnoticed in current literature. Second, the fact that still very few professional publications address the issues of ethics and morality speaks for the true extent of our concern for justice in the equation of criminal justice. Criminal justice departments rarely teach courses on justice, and professors appear far more concerned with the minutiae of changes in crime rates than with articulating the benefits of social justice. Certainly, too much time and effort is being spent teaching the criminalization process, criminal and civil liabilities, and the rhetoric of administrative efficiency, rather than articulating and advocating social justice. The moral of that sad state of affairs is: without a valiant effort to uphold the ethic of justice, the discipline will continue to grow into an elaborate temple without a god, an overgrown body without a soul, and a complex theory without a meaning.

Second, the *myth of coercive power* (i.e., state power, judicial power, police power) has traditionally forced the belief in the invincibility of the state and its organs, their ultimate triumph, and the inevitable defeat of all "asocial" elements. For a better appreciation of that myth, one need only to reflect for a moment over the myth of the Berlin Wall—the mighty obstacle which was built and fortified so that "no one can escape oppression," ended up by "everyone who chose freedom" walking freely through it.

In criminal justice, belief in the coercive power of the all-powerful system has led to what A. C. German called the "obedience training" mentality. Over the latter half of the twentieth century, such a mentality has been reinforced by high-minded slogans, such as the "war on crime" in the 1960s and the "war on drugs" in the 1990s. Subsequently, as Manning describes, the processes of criminal justice have been eroded on all sides by worrisome machines said to take the place of human concern—for example, computers, submachine guns, gas, electronic gadgets for monitoring parolees, and the like. Such a "garrison" mentality, which has been much more culturally espoused in the United States than in other civilized nations, has caused considerable embarrassment to the "authorities" and has created what verges on a sovereignty crisis. As Goldstein explains, the requirements are so incongruous, the public expectations are so unrealistic, and the state is so ineffective.

As a result, the efficacy of criminal justice agencies has not significantly improved since the 1960s. It continues to be questioned by the policymakers who authorize their operation, the officials who oversee their management, and the consumers whom the agencies are designed to assist. In essence it can be safely argued that few useful reforms have been accomplished in the area of criminal justice management—the field's most effective instrument of reform.

Third, the *reductionist view of rationality* in traditional criminal justice thought has been widespread. Reference here is not made to myths or superstitions prevalent during the Dark Ages, or even during the latter days of common law England. I am referring to numerous fallacies which have been casually disregarded in modern-day literature. Samuel Walker has been a pioneer in identifying many of these fallacies. It is true that many have been reexamined, albeit under political and/or economic pressure, but many remain conviently unquestioned. For example, the myth of "doing justice" instead of "producing justice," the fairness of the jury system, the deference given testimonies presented under oath, the impartiality of elected prosecutors and judges, the productivity of the police, and the lost art of human relationships in custodial treatment, among others.

As the twentieth century comes to an end, giving way to a new millennium, criminal justice, both as an academic discipline and as a practical field, will continue to grapple with many dilemmas. The least important among these dilemmas will most likely be those of a materialistic nature (i.e., more courtrooms, more prison facilities, more police vehicles, weaponry, and more technological gadgetry). Even the highly visible demand for increased personnel budgets will essentially continue to present a minor obstacle, since the integrity of government—and the reelectibility of its officials—must be sustained "at any price," and the problem of criminality continues to make us less American.

The more serious dilemmas in the twenty-first century will be largely philosophical and will address the more private feelings in our lives. These are the residual products of what Samuel Walker calls the "wildly contradictory attitudes" Americans have toward crime and justice. As a case in point, it has always been particularly difficult for American scholars to explain to their foreign colleagues why, as a nation endowed with all of the ingredients of civilization, the United States continues an unacknowledged tradition of collective and individual law breaking that stands out among all industrial countries. Foreign scholars, on the other hand, never quite understand the *libertarian mind* Americans possess which makes them altogether different from any other nation. Through that unique mind-set, Americans as a society face up to failures, admit unjust acts, and strive to maintain civic righteousness. Historically, it was that *libertarian mind* that rejected the British injustices in the first place, sustained the Union during the Civil War, abolished slavery and attended to the needs of its victims, defeated Hitler and rebuilt the continent he destroyed, and made human rights a global issue.

Regarding the issues of crime and justice, Americans in the twenty-first century will be hard pressed *not* to follow their libertarian mind-set. They will eventually come to terms with themselves and find the solution of the crime problem in the "just society" model, which, instead of exasperating conflict and violence, will bring about further healing and bonding. New-generation criminal justice thinkers will have no *moral alternative* but to continue to humanize the discipline, to treat the social, political, and economic roots of criminality, and to advance the cause of civil righteousness. In essence, they will be looking backward to the lost notion of the *good life* made central to civilized existence by their Greek predecessors two thousand years before them.

On the basis of this culturally moralistic premise, the direction of criminal justice in the twenty-first century will, most likely, focus on:

1. Placing less emphasis on the burgeoning legal–technological complex and more on ameliorating the problems of discrimination, poverty, unemployment, poor education, and bad housing that go hand in hand with crime, simply because that is the decent thing to do.
2. Ridding society of slums, *not* particularly because they are productive of delinquency and crime but because they are a despicable way for people to have to live.
3. Rethinking our "gun culture," doing away with most weapons, *not* because it is unconstitutional to bear them, but because, as a society, they cause more harm than good.
4. Making communities safer by increasing vigilance—rather than vigilantism—through devising coherent policies that can recreate those familial and neighborhood conditions prerequisite for safe and tranquil living.
5. Treating America's crime problem by treating its youth problem. The period between the ages of 11 and 25 are perilous for millions of young Americans who should, and deserve to be, treated "as if they were our children."
6. Dislodging the drug problem by fighting it in the minds of the youth through compassion and caring at home, emphatic instruction at school, and promoting a supportive environment in the workplace. Hitting the "cartel" out there is reminiscent of the Vietnam war and will end the way the Vietnam war ended.

Schmalleger's book certainly presents a well-balanced preview of the issues of criminal justice as they are likely to unfold in the twenty-first century—with their prospects, fears, and hopes. *Quo vadis.*

Sam S. Souryal, Ph.D.
Criminal Justice Center
Sam Houston State University
Huntsville, Texas

CRIMINAL JUSTICE TODAY

Injustice anywhere is a threat to justice everywhere.
—MARTIN LUTHER KING, JR.

The freedom to die before you're a teenager
is not the freedom Martin Luther King lived and died for.
We have to make our people whole again.
—PRESIDENT CLINTON

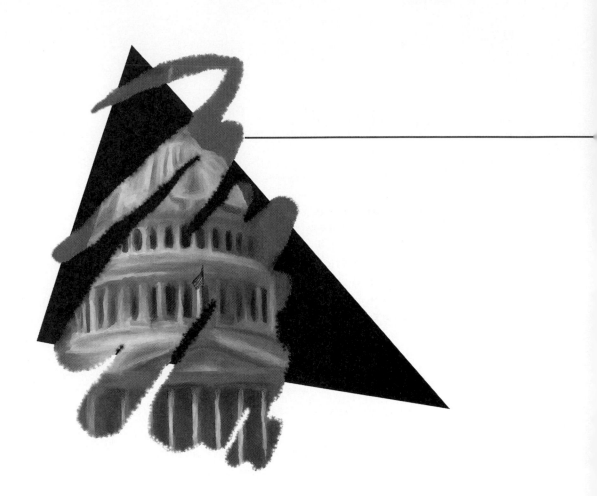

INDIVIDUAL RIGHTS VERSUS SOCIAL CONCERNS

GOALS OF THE CRIMINAL JUSTICE SYSTEM

Common law, constitutional, statutory, and humanitarian rights of the accused:

Justice for the Individual
Personal Liberty
Dignity as a Human Being
The Right to Due Process

The individual rights listed must be effectively balanced against these community concerns:

Social Justice
Equality Before the Law
The Protection of Society
Freedom from Fear

How does our system of justice work toward balance?

CRIME IN AMERICA

Whenever a separation is made between liberty and justice, neither, in my opinion, is safe.
   —EDMUND BURKE (1729–1797)

Justice is the great interest of man on earth. It is the ligament which holds civilized beings and civilized nations together.
   —DANIEL WEBSTER (1782–1852)

Justice is my being allowed to do whatever I like. Injustice is whatever prevents my doing so.
   —SAMUEL JOHNSON (1709–1784)

We do not yet have justice, equal and practical, for the poor, for the members of minority groups, for the criminally accused, for the displaced persons of the technological revolution, for alienated youth, for the urban masses, for the unrepresented consumer...
   —WILLIAM BRENNAN
      FORMER U.S. SUPREME COURT JUSTICE

CHAPTER 1

WHAT IS CRIMINAL JUSTICE?

Citizens are coproducers of justice.
—**BUREAU OF JUSTICE STATISTICS—PRINCETON PROJECT**

Crime does more than expose the weakness in social relationships; it under-mines the social order itself, by destroying the assumptions on which it is based.[1]
—**CHARLES E. SILBERMAN**

Violent crime and the fear it provokes are crippling our society, limiting personal freedom, and fraying the ties that bind us.
—**PRESIDENT BILL CLINTON**
   1994 STATE OF THE UNION ADDRESS

consensus model   due process   crime control model
conflict model   probable cause   individual rights
criminal justice   social control

JUSTICE AND CRIMINAL JUSTICE

Social Control The use of sanctions and rewards available through a group to influence and shape the behavior of individual members of that group. Social control is a primary concern of social groups and communities, and it is the interest that human groups hold in the exercise of social control that leads to the creation of both criminal and civil statutes.

On December 7, 1993 the 5:33 PM Long Island Railroad commuter train from Manhattan's Penn Station to Hicksville, New York, was packed with holiday shoppers and office workers on their way home. Before the short trip was over, two of the train's cars had become a gruesome scene of mass murder. Less than half-way along the train's route, Colin Ferguson, a 35-year-old Jamaican-born immigrant allegedly opened fire on crowded passengers with a 9 mm semi-automatic handgun, pausing at least once during the melee to reload the 15-shot weapon.[2] When the shooting ended, 6 people lay dead, and another 17 were seriously wounded.

Ferguson, whose assault terminated when he was tackled by 3 surviving passengers, had apparently been motivated in the attack by dissatisfaction with the American economy and a hatred of white people. All of the dead and wounded were white or Asian-American. Almost all had been shot in the head or neck. Notes found on Ferguson spoke of racial hatred.

Shortly before Ferguson's rampage, a 16-year-old boy shot 38-year-old Christine Schweiger to death in a robbery attempt outside of a Milwaukee chicken restaurant while the woman's 10-year-old daughter watched. Schweiger had told the boy she had no money. The young man killed her, shooting her in the head with a sawed-off weapon, because, he said, she had an "attitude." "I'm the big man. I got the gun. Why does she have this attitude?"[3] the boy said to detectives following his arrest.

These stories and others like them, appearing daily in the national media, illustrate a new breed of lawlessness sweeping through American society. Responses have come from individuals seeking to protect themselves and their loved ones, and from government officials at all levels.

In early 1994, for example, Ellie Nesler, 40, of Jamestown, California, was sentenced to 10 years in prison for the murder of Daniel Mark Driver. Nesler pumped five bullets into Driver's head and neck during Driver's preliminary hearing on charges he sexually molested Nesler's 10-year-old son.[4] Nesler appeared especially upset by Driver's previous conviction for child molestation, and by the fact that he had never served time in prison. According to locals, Nesler was pushed over the edge during the hearing by a smirking Driver. A few days after the shooting, cars in Jamestown were sporting bumper stickers reading, "Nice Shootin' Ellie," and there was talk of erecting a statue in her honor. "If a few more people around the country would take the law into their own hands like Ellie did, we'd have a lot safer country," commented one townsperson seated in a bar across from the courthouse in which Driver died. Nesler, who suffers from cancer, many not survive her stay in prison.

Government responses to criminal violence include the largest anti-crime bill ever to be proposed at the federal level. As this book goes to press, the U.S. Congress continues debate on a bill aimed at reducing violent crime through gun control, putting more police officers on the street, mandating stiff criminal penalties, and opening more prisons. The 1994 crime bill would authorize over $22 billion for enhanced federal crime fighting measures.

Colin Ferguson, the 35-year-old Jamaican-born gunman who allegedly killed four people and wounded 17 others in a racially motivated attack on a Long Island commuter train in December 1993. *Photo: Dick Yarwood/Newsday.*

Fortunately, the bill would provide assistance to local and state governments which are often hard-pressed to provide needed criminal justice services. In 1993, for example, California announced that it would confiscate $2.6 billion in county property taxes as a way of easing the state budget deficit.[5] The move meant cuts of 50% for the criminal justice system, "funded almost exclusively by local property tax revenues."[6] Local prosecutors threatened to ignore misdemeanors, leaving many citizens to fall back on their own resources. John Meehan, Alameda County District Attorney, found himself left with the prospect of a dramatically reduced staff. "How can I pay attention to anything but the most violent crimes," he asked, suggesting that local businesses would have to deal with shoplifters themselves. "Businessmen might as well put legs on their merchandise," he said. "We'll have to close down our entire misdemeanor operation," said Grover Trask, Riverside County's District Attorney. One California store owner, asked what he would do with shoplifters now that they would no longer be officially prosecuted, responded, "I'll shoot them. ... It's not what I want, but I'm at the point where I have no choice."[7]

THE FOCUS OF THIS BOOK

This book has an orientation which we think is especially valuable for studying criminal justice today. The materials presented in the text are built around the following theme:

> there is a growing realization in contemporary society of the need to balance the respect accorded the rights of the individual with the interests of society. While the personal freedoms guaranteed by the Constitution must be closely guarded, so too the urgent social needs of local communities for controlling unacceptable behavior and protecting law-abiding citizens from harm must be recognized.

Many people today who intelligently consider the criminal justice system assume either one or the other of these two perspectives. We shall refer to those who seek to protect personal freedoms as individual rights advocates. Those who suggest that, under certain circumstances involving criminal threats to public safety, the interests of society should take precedence over individual rights, will be called public order advocates.

Both perspectives have their roots in the values which formed our nation. However, the past 30 years have been especially important in clarifying the differences between the two points of view. The past few decades have seen a burgeoning concern with the rights of ethnic minorities, women, the physically and mentally challenged, and many other groups. The civil rights movement of the 1960s and 1970s emphasized equality of opportunity and respect for individuals regardless of race, color, creed, or personal attributes. As new laws were passed and suits filed, court involvement in the movement grew. Soon a plethora of hard-won individual rights and prerogatives, based upon the U.S. Constitution and the Bill of Rights, were recognized and guaranteed. By the early 1980s the rights movement had profoundly affected all areas of social life—from education, through employment, to the activities of the criminal justice system.

This emphasis on **individual rights** was accompanied by a dramatic increase in criminal activity. "Traditional" crimes such as murder, rape, and assault, as reported by the FBI, increased astronomically during the 1970s. Some analysts of American culture suggested that increased criminality was the result of new-found freedoms which combined with the long pent-up hostilities of the socially and economically deprived to produce social disorganization. Others doubted the accuracy of "official" accounts, claiming that any actual rise in crime was much less than that portrayed in the reports.

By the mid-1980s, however, popular perceptions identified one particularly insidious form of criminal activity—the dramatic increase in the sale and use of illicit drugs—as a threat to the very fabric of American society. Cocaine, in particular, and later laboratory-processed "crack," had spread to every corner of America. The country's borders were inundated with smugglers intent on reaping quick fortunes. Large cities became havens for drug gangs, and many inner-city areas were all but abandoned to highly armed and well-financed racketeers. Some famous personalities succumbed to the allure of drugs, and athletic teams and sporting events became focal points for drug busts. Like wildfire, drugs soon spread to even younger users. Even small-town elementary schools found themselves facing the specter of campus drug dealing and associated violence.

> When you know both the accuser and the accused, as we so often do, the conflict between civil rights and victim's rights is seldom completely black or white. And it is the gray areas in between that make the debate so difficult.
>
> —*Columnist Vicki Williams, writing on crime in a small American town*

Worse still were the seemingly ineffective governmental measures to stem the drug tide. Drug peddlers, because of the huge reserves of money available to them, were often able to escape prosecution, or wrangle plea bargains and avoid imprisonment. Media coverage of such "miscarriages of justice" became epidemic and public anger grew.

By the close of the 1980s neighborhoods and towns felt themselves fighting for their communal lives. City businesses faced dramatic declines in property values, and residents wrestled with the eroding quality of life. Huge rents had been torn in the national social fabric. The American way of life, long taken for granted, was under the gun. Traditional values appeared in danger of going up in smoke along with the "crack" now being smoked openly in some parks and resorts. Looking for a way to stem the tide, many took up the call for "law and order." In response, then-President Reagan initiated a "War on Drugs" and created a "drug czar" cabinet-level post to coordinate the war. Careful thought was given at the

Individual Rights Those rights guaranteed by the U.S. Constitution to criminal defendants (especially as found in the first ten amendments to the Constitution, known as the Bill of Rights) facing formal processing by the criminal justice system. The preservation of the rights of criminal defendants is important to society because it is through the exercise of such rights that the values of our culture are most clearly and directly expressed.

New York City's Guardian Angels on patrol. Communities have a valid interest in safety and order. Where formal mechanisms of the criminal justice system are perceived as inadequate for the purpose of social control, informal mechanisms may arise. *Photo: Costa Manos/Magnum Photos, Inc.*

highest levels to using the military to patrol the sea lanes and air corridors through which many of the illegal drugs entered the country. President Bush, who followed President Reagan into office, quickly embraced and expanded the government's antidrug efforts.

The 1990s began with a focus on police brutality and management effectiveness. In 1992, the videotaped beating of Rodney King, a black motorist, at the hands of Los Angeles–area police officers, splashed across TV screens throughout the country and reintroduced the nation to the concerns of what sociologists now call "underrepresented groups." As the King incident seemed to show, when members of such groups come face to face with agents of the American criminal justice system, something less than justice may be the result. Although initially acquitted by a California jury which contained no black members, two of the officers who beat King were convicted in a 1993 federal courtroom of violating his civil rights.[8]

The year 1993 saw an especially violent encounter in Waco, Texas, between agents of the Bureau of Alcohol, Tobacco, and Firearms, the FBI, and members of cult leader David Koresh's Branch Davidian. The fray, which began when ATF agents assaulted Koresh's fortresslike compound, leaving 4 agents and 6 cultists dead, ended 51 days later with the fiery deaths of Koresh and 71 of his followers. Many of them were children. The assault on Koresh's compound led to a congressional investigation and charges that the ATF and FBI had been ill-prepared to deal successfully with large-scale domestic resistance and had reacted more out of alarm and frustration than wisdom. Janet Reno, Attorney General under President Clinton, refused to blame agents for misjudging Koresh's intentions, although 11 Davidians were later acquitted of charges they murdered the agents.

Later that year James Jordan, father of Chicago Bulls basketball superstar Michael Jordan, was killed in a cold-blooded robbery by two young men with long criminal records—an event that occurred less than a mile from the home of the author as this book was being written. Because Jordan's death seemed the result of a chance encounter, the nation's attention was riveted on the seemingly increasing frequency of random and sense-less violence.

Also in 1993, a powerful bomb ripped apart the basement of one of the twin World Trade Center buildings in New York city. The explosion, which killed five and opened a 100-foot crater through four sublevels of concrete, displaced 50,000 workers, including employees at the commodities exchanges that handle billions of dollars worth of trade in oil, gold, coffee, and sugar. Apparently the product of foreign terrorists, the bombing high-lighted the susceptibility of the American infrastructure to terrorist activity.[9]

The social situation surrounding criminal justice activities today is a result of all these elements and more. Calls for accountability of the justice system continue to echo through government chambers and newspaper columns. Rights advocates carry on the fight for an expansion of civil and criminal rights, seeing both as necessary to an equitable and just social order. The treatment of the accused, they argue, mirrors basic cultural values. The purpose of any civilized society, they claim, should be to secure rights and freedoms for each of its citizens. They fear unnecessarily restrictive government action and view it as an assault upon basic human dignity. In the defense of general principles, criminal rights activists tend to recognize that it is sometimes necessary to sacrifice some degree of public safety and predictability in order to guarantee basic freedoms. Rights advocates are content with a justice system which limits police powers and holds justice agencies accountable to the highest evidentiary standards. A national news story,[10] which showed undercover agents of the Broward County, Florida, Sheriff's Department selling crack manufactured in the police crime lab as a lure to capture drug users, is the kind of activity civil libertarians strongly question.

Another example comes from the case of James Richardson, who served 21 years in a Florida prison for a crime he did not commit.[11] Following perjured testimony, Richardson was convicted in 1968 of the poisoning deaths of his seven children. He was released in 1989 after a babysitter confessed to poisoning the children's last meal because of personal jealousies. The criminal rights perspective allows that it is necessary to see some guilty peo-ple go free in order to reduce the likelihood of convicting the innocent.

On the other hand, calls for system accountability are now often tempered with new demands to unfetter the criminal justice system to make arrests easier and punishments swift and harsh. Advocates of law and order, wanting ever-greater police powers, have mounted a drive to abandon some of the gains made in the rights of criminal defendants during the civil rights era. Citing high rates of recidivism, uncertain punishments, and an inefficient courtroom maze, they claim that the present system coddles the offender and encourages law violation. Society, they say, if it is to survive, can no longer afford to accord too many rights to the individual or place the interests of any one person over that of the group.

This text has two basic purposes: (1) to describe in detail the criminal justice system, while (2) helping students develop an appreciation for the delicacy of the balancing act now facing it. The question for the future will be how to manage a justice system which is as fair to the individual as it is supportive of the needs of society. Is justice for all a reason-able expectation of today's system of criminal justice? As the book will show, this question is complicated by the fact that individual needs and social interests sometimes diverge, while at other times they parallel one another.

SOCIAL JUSTICE

Social justice is a concept that embraces all aspects of civilized life. Social justice extends to relationships between parties, between the rich and the poor, between the sexes, between ethnic groups and minorities, and to social linkages of all sorts. In the abstract, the concept

T H E O R Y   I N T O   P R A C T I C E

INDIVIDUAL RIGHTS VERSUS GROUP INTERESTS: CRACK BABIES

The question of "What is crime?" is intimately connected to cultural conceptions of morality and justice. What makes one form of behavior "wrong" while another is "correct" or proper? The key, more often than not, is social acceptability—a consensus among policymaking social groups that translates into various kinds of regulations and into law. Behavior that society finds unacceptable at a particular time, under a given set of circumstances, can be termed immoral and, if sufficient political power is brought to bear, defined as "criminal." Realistically, however, there are many kinds of behavior which fall though the proverbial cracks. There is little consensus relative to the meaning of such behaviors, which may then become the focus of intense debate and, frequently, subjects of TV talk show disputes.

One such issue concerns the degree of responsibility to which mothers who deliver drug-addicted newborns—commonly referred to a "crack babies"—should be held. The case of Kimberly Hardy, a 24-year-old Muskegon, Michigan, woman is similar to that of many other such mothers. Kimberly, a habitual drug user, admitted smoking crack cocaine less than 13 hours before her premature son was born. The baby was born addicted, and Kimberly was charged with the delivery of a controlled substance to a minor via the umbilical cord. Although, if convicted, she faced the possibility of a $25,000 fine and 20 years in prison, a Michigan court ruled before her trial that she could not be tried on the charges because, under Michigan law, a fetus is not a person. Jennifer Johnson, a 23-year-old Florida mother, was not so lucky. Johnson, a cocaine user, was found guilty by a Florida jury of delivering controlled substances to a minor following the birth of her medically impaired child. Although she faced up to 30 years in prison, Johnson was sentenced to 1 year of house arrest in a drug rehabilitation center and 14 years of supervised probation.

Estimates are that thousands of crack-addicted babies will be born throughout the United States this year. Many of them will face a childhood full of medical problems, while some will never recover from severe neurological damages induced by their mother's drug use. Yet, as the two cases described here show, there is little consensus in American society on whether mothers who expose their unborn children to illegal drugs should be held criminally accountable. Following dismissal of the charges against her, Kimberly Hardy said she was pleased that the court recognized that drug use is a "medical problem and not a criminal problem." Judge Maureen Reilly, who heard Kimberly's case, wrote that courts must "refrain from transforming into a criminal act what is now essentially a moral obligation by the pregnant woman to her developing fetus," and the ACLU called the dismissal "a great victory for fundamental women's rights." Prosecutors, on the other hand, while they agreed that a mother should feel obligations toward her child, claimed that where that obligation is lacking, the legal power of society must be brought to bear in an effort to help the child.

Sources: "Mother Cleared of Giving Cocaine to Child at Birth," *USA Today*, April 3, 1991, p. 2A, and "Now, Parents on Trial," *Newsweek*, October 2, 1989, p. 54.

THEORY INTO PRACTICE

"THE RODNEY KING" TRIALS

Until the summer of 1992 most Americans would probably have agreed that the justice system, though flawed in numerous individual instances, was the most equitable mechanism available for the apprehension of wrongdoers, for determinations of guilt or innocence, and for the imposition of punishment upon criminal offenders in an otherwise imperfect world. At the same time, most probably felt, at least intuitively, that the exercise of criminal justice occurred within a framework that was basically fair and impartial and that embodied our highest cultural ideals of social justice. In short, the symbolism of "blind justice" as equitable justice was, for many Americans, an article of faith.

This is not to say that the system was without its detractors. On the contrary, the voices of the poor, the disenfranchised, the unempowered—in particular ethnic minorities, and what sociologists have come to call "underrepresented groups"— have long appealed to the conscience of the American people, chanting a litany of claimed injustices for over 200 years. The system, they said, understood only one type of justice: justice for the rich and for the powerful, justice for those who make the laws and for those who stand to benefit from them. From time to time, academicians and liberal politicians joined the fray on the side of the disenfranchised, claiming that law enforcement is fundamentally a tool of power, exercised exclusively in the service of the wealthy and the well connected. They, along with a variety of social commentators, portrayed criminal justice as one more aspect of a much broader issue—social *in*justice.

Then came an event that grabbed our nation's attention. In 1991 the videotaped police beating of a black Los Angeles motorist, Rodney King, burst upon the national scene and transfixed the American national conscience via television. And the images wouldn't fade. In 1992 a Simi Valley, California, jury, with but one minority member, found the police officers who had been arrested for assaulting King innocent of the charges brought against them. The nation was aghast—unable to reconcile what it had perceived clearly in the media with the workings of American criminal justice. In an instant Rodney King became, to many, the symbol of justice denied. Within hours Los Angeles was embroiled in social protests, rioting, and looting. Racial tensions increased dramatically. In the spring of 1993 two of the officers, Sergeant Stacey Koon and Officer Laurence Powell, were found guilty by a jury in federal court of depriving King of his constitutional right "not to be deprived of liberty without due process of law, including the right to be ... free from the intentional use of unreasonable force."[1] Officers Theodore Briseno and Timothy Wind were found not guilty of the same charge. Commenting on the differences between the two trials, *Newsweek* magazine said, "Λ ... cynical explanation for the convictions this time is that the 12 jurors knew all too well what a full acquittal could mean. The difference between this case and last year's were the riots," says Harland Braun, Briseno's lawyer.

"The Simi Valley trial surely taught the perils of a criminal justice system that's perceived to be racist. But a system that's perceived as political—one that responds to public pressure as much as evidence—isn't much better."[2] As controversy over the case continued, the American Civil Liberties Union, in heated debate, voted to protest the convictions, claiming that "repeat prosecution by different jurisdictions for the same act amounted to double jeopardy."[3]

The Rodney King "incident" was a transfiguring event in the history of American criminal justice. It brought us to realize that the strokes which paint the canvas of intergroup relations in the United States are broader than the particulars of any one case. There is little denying that minorities are over represented at all stages of criminal justice processing. Similarly, there is little denying that minority youth violate laws with considerably greater frequency than do other youths, and that the violations they commit are often found to be especially socially reprehensible—typified by crimes of violence, drug dealing, and the like. And yet whose laws are these people violating? By whose standards are they being held accountable? Because crime is a social construct arising out of a nexus of legislative action, social conditions, and individual choice, it becomes possible to ask: "Whose crime is it, after all?" From the perspective of those involved in it, drug dealing may seem like a reasonable way out from poverty, and violence a day-to-day necessity rooted in the will to survive. From the perspective of official agents of justice, these same behaviors confer criminal responsibility, and those who engage in them are condemned—arrested and sentenced to be removed from society until such time as they are adjudged fit to return. And therein lies the rub. Return to what? To the social order understood by the lawmakers? Or a society inherently different, and populated by less forgiving foes than criminal justice policymakers and enforcers of official law?

Ultimately we have to ask: "Is there one form of justice for the poor and another for the rich?" "Is there a separate system of justice that embodies the values of the powerful, while condemning the strivings of the underclass?" "Are the felt needs of certain people being denied by the contemporary American criminal justice system?" "Can the scales of justice be balanced?" "In a more fundamental sense, can justice be truly equitable in a society built upon the free pursuit of individual wealth and the often unbridled drive toward personal power?"

Some have suggested creating two systems of criminal justice: one for the rich and one for the poor, one for the socially downtrodden and another for the well connected. After all, they say, isn't it necessary for enforcement agents, judges, juries, and probation/parole officers to understand the backgrounds and values of the criminal justice clients with whom they must deal? Shouldn't the system recognize the harsh realities of life in the inner city, and the desperation of the indigent and the disenfranchised? But, if we lose faith in our existing system's ability to deliver justice, what is left? How do we remake a system which for over 200 years has formed the bedrock of a tenuous social order, and which has held in check the excesses of the criminally compelled?

---

[1] "Cries of Relief," *Time*, April 26, 1993, p. 18.
[2] "King II: What Made the Difference?" *Newsweek*, April 26, 1993, p. 26.
[3] "A.C.L.U.—Not All That Civil," *Time*, April 26, 1993, p. 31.

Violence has become a way of life in some parts of America. Here a Chicago day care center class practices ducking—a skill they will need if a gunfight breaks out on nearby streets. *Photo: Steve Leonard/Black Star.*

of justice embodies the highest cultural ideals. Reality however, typically falls short of the ideal and is severely complicated by the fact that justice seems to wear different guises when viewed from diverse social vantage points.

> Criminal justice cannot be achieved in the absence of social justice…
>
> —*Struggle for Justice, American Friends' Service Committee*

Criminal Justice The criminal law, the law of criminal procedure, and that array of procedures and activities having to do with the enforcement of the criminal law. Criminal justice cannot be separated from social justice because the kind of justice enacted in our nation's criminal courts is a reflection of basic American understandings of right and wrong.

Criminal justice, in its broadest sense, refers to those aspects of social justice which concern violations of the criminal law. Community interests demand apprehension and punishment of the guilty. At the same time, criminal justice ideals extend to the protection of the innocent, the fair treatment of offenders, and fair play by the agencies of law enforcement, including the courts and correctional institutions.

Once again, reality generally falls short of the ideal. To many people the criminal justice system and criminal justice agencies often seem biased in favor of the powerful. The laws they enforce seem to emanate more from well-financed, organized, and vocal interest groups than they do from an idealized sense of social justice. Disenfranchised groups, those who do not feel as though they share in the political and economic power of society, are often wary of the agencies of justice, seeing them more as enemies than as benefactors.

On the other hand, justice practitioners, including police officers, prosecutors, judges, and correctional officials frequently complain of unfair criticism of their efforts to uphold the law. The "realities" of law enforcement, they say, and of justice itself, are often overlooked by critics of the system who have little experience in dealing with offenders and victims.

Whichever side we choose in the ongoing debate over the nature and quality of justice in America, we should recognize that the process of criminal justice is especially important in achieving and maintaining social order. From the perspective of social order, law is an instrument of control. Laws set limits on behavior and define particular forms of social

Kimberly Hardy, charged with delivery of a controlled substance to a minor via the umbilical cord, after her premature baby was born addicted to cocaine. *Photo: Tim Fitzgerald/USA Today.*

interaction as unacceptable. Laws, including whatever inequities they may embody, are a primary device for order creation in any society.

Justice Is a Product

Once a law is created, people who are suspected of violations are apprehended and face handling by the criminal justice system. The system is generally described as composed of the agencies of police, courts, and corrections. There are many actors within the justice system, from the police officer walking a beat, to a Supreme Court justice sitting on the bench in Washington, D.C.

Defendants processed by the system come into contact with numerous justice professionals whose duty it is to enforce the law, but who also have a stake in the agencies which employ them and who hold their own personal interests and values. As they wend their way through the system, defendants may be held accountable to the law, but in the process they will also be buffeted by personal whims as well as by the practical needs of the system. Hence, a complete view of American criminal justice needs to recognize that the final outcome of any encounter with the criminal justice system will be a consequence of decisions made not just at the legislative level, but in the day-to-day activities undertaken by everyone involved in the system.

The Justice Ideal: A Modern Conflict

Most of us agree that laws against murder, rape, assault, and other serious crimes are necessary. Certain other laws, such as those against marijuana use, prostitution, gambling, and some "victimless crimes" rest upon a less certain consensus.

Where a near-consensus exists as to the legitimacy of a particular statute, questions may still be raised as to how specific behavior fits the law under consideration. Even more fundamental questions can center on the process by which justice is achieved. Two cases which received much media attention during the late 1980s illustrate these points. One involved the "subway gunman," Bernhard Goetz.[12] Goetz, a 39-year-old electronics specialist, admitted shooting four young men who, he said, approached him in a threatening manner. Goetz had been mugged previously and carried a concealed weapon. Goetz was white, the young men were black.

Few would disagree that mugging is wrong, and most would grant that some form of self-defense is justifiable under certain circumstances, including robbery. The Goetz situation, however, was complicated by many things, among them the fact that Goetz fled after the shootings; he shot one of the men twice—after telling him, "You don't look too bad. Here's another"; and it was later shown that some of the young men had committed crimes both previous to and after the subway incident. Although no one died, one of the people shot was permanently paralyzed.

Bernhard Goetz finally was convicted of a firearms violation and received a sentence of 6 months in prison. He was also ordered to undergo psychiatric treatment, placed on 5 years' probation, fined $5,000, and made to perform 280 hours of community service.

The "Howard Beach Incident" had some characteristics in common with the "subway gunman" case.[13] Howard Beach is a densely populated white section of New York City. On a night in 1987 two black men were riding through Howard Beach when their car broke down. A gang of white youths, some armed with baseball bats, attacked the men. One was injured in the attack, while another fled onto a busy highway where he was struck by a car and killed. Eventually, manslaughter convictions were returned against three of the youths involved in the incident, and they were sentenced to prison terms which may run for 15 years. A fourth youth was found innocent of all charges.

To most people, the law was clear in both cases. Goetz should not have been carrying a concealed weapon. He should not have shot the young men who surrounded him unless there was an immediate and serious threat to his safety. The white youths in Howard Beach

Bernhard Goetz, shown here under arrest, became known as the "subway gunman" after he shot four youths whom he said were preparing to rob him on New York subway train. *Photo: Joel Landau/AP/Wide World Photos.*

violated the law in assaulting two men. Yet while a considerable consensus existed as to the law and as to the facts of each case, actors in the criminal justice system found themselves embroiled in a raging debate about what an appropriate outcome should be. One famous legal scholar, analyzing the Goetz case relative to the social context of the times, referred to Goetz's actions as "a crime of self-defense."[14]

Basic to both cases was the belief, held by some, including many members of the black community in New York, that minorities historically have not been fairly represented in the justice process. The fact that black men approached a white in New York's subways was said to be automatically interpreted much differently than if the races involved had been reversed. Other critics said that the Howard Beach incident reflected the system's devaluation of the life of a black man.

Both the Howard Beach and the subway gunman cases are illustrative of the fact that any formal resolution of law violations occurs through an elaborate process. Justice, while it can be fine-tuned in order to take into consideration the interests of ever wider numbers of people, rarely pleases everyone. Justice is a social product, and, like any product which is the result of group effort, it is a patchwork quilt of human emotions and concerns. One of the major challenges faced by the justice system today comes in the form of disenfranchised groups who are not convinced that they receive "justice" under current arrangements. Was justice done in the *Howard Beach* or the *Goetz* case? While the question will be debated for years, it is doubtful that an answer acceptable to everyone will ever be found.

AMERICAN CRIMINAL JUSTICE:
SYSTEM OR NONSYSTEM?

To this point we have described the agencies of law enforcement, the courts, and corrections as a **system of criminal justice**.[15] The systems model of criminal justice, however, is more an analytical tool than a reality. Any analytical model, be it in the so-called "hard" sciences or in the social sciences, is simply a convention chosen for its explanatory power. By explaining the actions of criminal justice officials (such as arrest, prosecution, sentencing, etc.) as though they are systematically related, we are able to envision a fairly smooth and predictable process. The advantage we gain from this convention is a reduction in complexity which allows us to describe the totality of criminal justice at a conceptually manageable level.

Those who speak of a system of criminal justice usually define it as consisting of the agencies of police, courts, and corrections. Each of these agencies can, in turn, be described in terms of their subsystems. Corrections, for example, includes jails, prisons, community-based treatment programs such as "halfway houses," and programs for probation and parole. Students of corrections also study the process of sentencing, through which an offender's fate is decided by the justice system.

The systems model has been criticized for implying a greater level of organization and cooperation among the various agencies of justice than actually exists. The word "system" calls to mind a near-perfect form of social organization. The modern mind associates the idea of a system with machinelike precision in which wasted effort, redundancy, and conflicting actions are quickly abandoned and their causes repaired. The justice system has nowhere near this level of perfection. Conflicts among and within agencies are rife, immediate goals are often not shared by individual actors in the system, and the system may move in different directions depending upon political currents, informal arrangements, and personal discretionary decisions.

The Criminal Justice System The aggregate of all operating and administrative or technical support agencies that perform criminal justice functions. The basic divisions of the operational aspect of criminal justice are law enforcement, courts, and corrections.

Consensus Model A perspective on the study of criminal justice which assumes that the system's subcomponents work together harmoniously to achieve that social product we call "justice."

Conflict Model A perspective on the study of criminal justice which assumes that the system's subcomponents function primarily to serve their own interests. According to this theoretical framework, "justice" is more a product of conflicts among agencies within the system than it is the result of cooperation among component agencies.

The systems model of criminal justice is part of a larger point of view called the **consensus model** of justice. The consensus model of the justice system assumes that all parts of the system work together toward a common goal and that the movement of cases and people through the system is smooth due to cooperation between components of the system.

The **conflict model** provides another approach to the study of American criminal justice. The conflict model says that agency interests tend to make actors within the system self-serving. Pressures for success, promotion, pay increases and general accountability, according to this model, fragment the efforts of the system as a whole, leading to a criminal justice nonsystem.[16]

Both models have something to tell us. Agencies of justice are linked closely enough for the term "system" to be meaningfully applied to them. On the other hand, the very size of the criminal justice undertaking makes effective cooperation between component agencies difficult. The police, for example, may have an interest in seeing offenders put behind bars. Prison officials, on the other hand, may be working with extremely overcrowded facilities. They may desire to see early release programs for certain categories of offenders such as those who are judged to be nonviolent. Who wins out in the long run could be just a matter of internal politics. Everyone should be concerned, however, when the goal of justice is impacted, and sometimes even sacrificed, because of conflicts within the system.

THE JUSTICE NONSYSTEM: A CLASSIC CASE

Jerome Skolnick's classic study of clearance rates provides support for the idea of a criminal justice nonsystem.[17] Clearance rates are a measure of crimes solved by the police. The more crimes the police can show they have solved, the happier is the public they serve.

Skolnick discovered an instance in which an individual burglar was caught red-handed during the commission of a burglary. After his arrest, the police suggested that he should confess to many unsolved burglaries which they knew he had not committed. In effect they said, "Help us out, and we will try to help you out!" The burglar did confess—to over 400 other burglaries. Following the confession, the police were satisfied because they could say they had "solved" many burglaries, and the suspect was pleased as well because the police had agreed to speak on his behalf before the judge.

THE DUE PROCESS MODEL

Both the systems and nonsystems models of criminal justice provide a view of agency relationships. Another way to view American criminal justice is in terms of its goals. Two primary goals were identified at the start of this chapter: (1) the need to enforce the law and maintain social order and (2) the need to protect individuals from injustice. The first of these principles values the efficient arrest and conviction of criminal offenders. It is often referred to as the crime control model of justice. The crime control model was first brought to the attention of the academic community in Herbert Packer's cogent analysis of the state of criminal justice in the late 1960s.[18] For that reason it is sometimes referred to as Packer's crime control model.

The second principle is called the due process model for its emphasis on individual rights. Due process is a central and necessary part of American criminal justice. It requires a careful and informed consideration of the facts of each individual case. Under the model, police are required to recognize the rights of suspects during arrest, questioning, and handling. Prosecutors and judges must recognize constitutional and other guarantees during trial and the presentation of evidence. Due process is intended to ensure that innocent people are not convicted of crimes. The due process model became reality following a number of far-reaching Supreme Court decisions affecting criminal procedure which were made during the 1960s. The 1960s were the era of the Warren Court, a Supreme Court which is remembered for its concern with protecting the innocent against the massive power of the state in criminal proceedings.[19]

The guarantee of due process is found throughout the Bill of Rights. Of special importance is the Fourteenth Amendment, which makes due process binding upon the states—that is, it requires individual states in the union to respect the rights of individuals who come under their jurisdiction. The Fourteenth Amendment reads as follows:

> …nor shall any State deprive any person of life, liberty, or property, without due process of law; nor deny to any person within its jurisdiction the equal protection of the laws.

As a result of the tireless efforts of the Warren court to institutionalize the Bill of Rights, the daily practice of modern American criminal justice is set squarely upon the due process standard. Under the due process model rights violations may become the basis for the dismissal of evidence or criminal charges, especially at the appellate level. Not all nations of the world adhere to the same ideal, however. In 1989 a tense international situation arose following the publication of Salman Rushdie's *Satanic Verses*, a book which Iranian leaders condemned for its attack upon Islam. Rushdie's book, defended strongly by free speech advocates in the West, led to a call by Ayatollah Khomeini for Rushdie's assassination. The criminal justice systems of selected nations and their varied approaches to issues of crime control and due process are described in Chapter 16, International Criminal Justice.

INDIVIDUAL RIGHTS

The due process clause of the U.S. Constitution mandates the recognition of individual rights, especially when criminal defendants are faced with prosecution by the states or the federal government. The first ten amendments to the Constitution are known as the "Bill of Rights" and specify the basic rights of all citizens of the United States. These rights have been interpreted and clarified by courts (especially the U.S. Supreme Court) over time. Due process requires that agencies of justice recognize these rights in their enforcement of the law. Table 1–1 outlines the basic rights to which defendants in criminal proceedings are generally entitled.

Individual Rights and the Courts

Although the Constitution deals with many issues, what we have been calling "rights" are often open to interpretation. Many modern rights, although written into the Constitution, would not exist in practice were it not for the fact that the U.S. Supreme Court decided, at some point in history, to recognize them in cases brought before it. The well-known Supreme Court case of *Gideon* v. *Wainwright*[20] (1963), for example (which is discussed in detail in Chapter 9, The Courtroom Work Group) found the Court embracing the Sixth Amendment guarantee of a right to a lawyer for all criminal defendants. Prior to *Gideon*, court-appointed attorneys for defendants unable to afford their own counsel were practically unknown, except in capital cases and some federal courts. After the *Gideon* decision court-appointed counsel became commonplace, and measures were instituted in jurisdictions across the nation to fairly select attorneys for indigent defendants.

Due Process of Law A right guaranteed by the Fifth, Sixth, and Fourteenth Amendments of the U.S. Constitution, and generally understood, in legal contexts, to mean the due course of legal proceedings according to the rules and forms which have been established for the protection of private rights. *Annotation* Due process of law, in criminal proceedings, is generally understood to include the following basic elements: a law creating and defining the offense, an impartial tribunal having jurisdictional authority over the case, accusation in proper form, notice and opportunity to defend, trial according to established procedure, and discharge from all restraints or obligations unless convicted.

Probable Cause A legal criterion residing in a set of facts and circumstances which would cause a reasonable person to believe that a particular other person has committed a specific crime. Probable cause refers to the necessary level of belief which would allow for police seizures (arrests) of individuals and searches of dwellings, vehicles, and possessions.

T A B L E 1 - 1

INDIVIDUAL RIGHTS GUARANTEED BY THE "BILL OF RIGHTS"

A Right to Be Assumed Innocent Until Proven Guilty
A Right Against Unreasonable Searches of Person and Place of Residence
A Right Against Arrest Without Probable Cause
A Right Against Unreasonable Seizures of Personal Property
A Right Against Self-incrimination
A Right to Fair Questioning by the Police
A Right to Protection from Physical Harm Throughout the Justice Process
A Right to an Attorney
A Right to Trial by Jury
A Right to Know the Charges
A Right to Cross-examine Prosecution Witnesses
A Right to Speak and Present Witnesses
A Right Not to Be Tried Twice for the Same Crime
A Right Against Cruel or Unusual Punishment
A Right to Due Process
A Right to a Speedy Trial
A Right Against Excessive Bail
A Right Against Excessive Fines
A Right to Be Treated the Same as Others, Regardless of Race, Sex, Religious Preference, and Other Personal Attributes

Unlike the high courts of many nations, the U.S. Supreme Court is very powerful, and its decisions often have far-reaching consequences. The decisions rendered by the justices in cases like *Gideon* become, in effect, the law of the land. For all practical purposes such decisions often carry as much weight as legislative action. For this reason some writers speak of judge-made law in describing judicial precedents which impact the process of justice.

Rights which have been recognized by Court decision are often subject to continual refinement. New interpretations may broaden or narrow the scope of applicability accorded to constitutional guarantees. Although the process of change is usually very slow, we should recognize that any right is subject to continual interpretation by the courts—and especially by the U.S. Supreme Court.

Any potential whittling away of procedural rights is of considerable concern to a great many people. It was in recognition of just such a possibility that the U.S. Senate held lengthy hearings over Supreme Court candidates nominated by Presidents Reagan and Bush during the 1980s and early 1990s. Senators were concerned that some nominees might have personal agendas which included wanting to eliminate precedents set by the Court in earlier times.

Crime Control Through Due Process

Up until now we have suggested that the dual goals of crime control and due process are in constant and unavoidable opposition to one another. Some critics of American criminal justice have argued that the practice of justice is too often concerned with crime control at the expense of due process. Other conservative analysts of the American scene maintain that our type of justice coddles offenders and does too little to protect the innocent.

Many people worry that Constitutional rights may soon become a casualty of today's war on drugs. Copyright 1989, *USA Today*. Reprinted with permission.

While it is impossible to avoid ideological conflicts such as these, it is also realistic to think of the American system of justice as representative of *crime control through due process*. It is this model, of law enforcement infused with the recognition of individual rights, which provides a conceptual framework for the chapters which follow.

THINGS TO COME: AN OVERVIEW
OF THIS BOOK

This textbook is divided into five parts. Part I, entitled *Crime in America*, provides a general introduction to the study of criminal justice, including crime statistics (Chapter 2), the causes of crime (Chapter 3), and criminal law (Chapter 4).

Part II is called *The Process Begins*. Its three chapters focus on the agencies and activities of law enforcement and on the problems of today's jails. The law enforcement field is described in Chapters 5 and 6, where historical developments are combined with modern studies to depict a dynamic profession. Precedent-setting court cases are introduced in Chapter 7 along with more recent decisions which have refined earlier ones.

Part III, called *Adjudication and Punishment*, includes chapters on the courts (Chapters 8 and 9), sentencing (Chapter 10), and probation and parole (Chapter 11). Special attention is given throughout Part IV, *Prisons*, to the legal issues surrounding jails, sentencing, and the various forms of criminal punishment. Prisons (Chapter 12) and prison life (Chapter 13) are discussed in a special section devoted exclusively to them.

The final section, Part V, *Special Issues*, looks at problems facing the justice system today. Included are "victimless" crimes and drug abuse (Chapter 15) and juvenile delinquency (Chapter 14). Chapter 16 provides a cursory overview of criminal justice in other nations, and points out the need for international understanding. Finally, the challenges and opportunities which the future holds for the practice of criminal justice, including computer crime and emerging investigative technologies, are discussed in the last chapter (Chapter 17).

Although this book covers many issues, its overall structure is sequential. Consecutive chapters provide a tour of criminal justice agencies and practices as they exist in the United States today. The tour begins in Part I with an explanation of how criminal law is created and ends in Part IV with a discussion of problems facing corrections in the future.

A more detailed preview of what is to come can be had by reading the overview of the criminal justice process provided in the few pages which follow. The overview provides a concise picture of criminal justice processing, and it is useful both as a guide to this book, and as a "road map" of the criminal justice system itself.

STAGES IN THE JUSTICE PROCESS

Investigation and Arrest

Warrant Any of a number of writs issued by a judicial officer, which direct a law enforcement officer to perform a specified act and afford him protection from damage if he performs it.

The modern justice process begins with investigation. When a crime has been committed, it is often discovered and reported to the police. On occasion a police officer on routine patrol discovers the crime while it is still in progress. Evidence will be gathered on the scene when possible, and a follow-up investigation will attempt to reconstruct the likely sequence of activities. A few offenders are arrested at the scene of the crime, while some are apprehended only after an extensive investigation. In such cases, arrest warrants issued by magistrates or other judges provide the legal basis for an apprehension by police.

An arrest involves taking a person into custody and limits their freedom. Arrest is a serious step in the process of justice and involves a discretionary decision made by the police seeking to bring criminal sanctions to bear. Most arrests are made peacefully, but some involve force when the suspect tries to resist. Only about 50% of all persons arrested are eventually convicted, and of those, only about 25% are sentenced to a year or more in prison. Beginning with the investigation of reported crimes, Figure 1–1 diagrammatically shows the processing of a criminal case through the federal justice system.

During arrest and prior to questioning defendants are usually advised of their constitutional rights as enumerated in the famous Supreme Court decision of *Miranda* v. *Arizona*.[21] Defendants are told (1) "You have the right to remain silent." (2) "Anything you say can and will be used against you in court." (3) "You have the right to talk to a lawyer for advice before we ask you any questions, and to have him with you during questioning." (4) "If you cannot afford a lawyer, one will be appointed for you before any questioning if you wish." (5) "If you decide to answer questions now without a lawyer present, you will still have the right to stop answering at any time. You also have the right to stop answering at any time and may talk with a lawyer before deciding to speak again." (6) "Do you wish to talk or not?" and (7) "Do you want a lawyer?"[22]

It is important to realize that although popular television programs almost always show a rights advisement at the time of arrest, the *Miranda* decision only requires police personnel to advise a person of his or her rights prior to questioning. An arrest without questioning can occur in the absence of any warning. When an officer interrupts a crime in progress, public safety considerations may make it reasonable for the officer to ask a few questions prior to a rights advisement. Many officers, however, feel on sound legal ground only by immediately following arrest with an advisement of rights. Investigation and arrest are discussed in detail in Chapter 7, Police: The Legal Environment.

Federal Criminal Case Processing

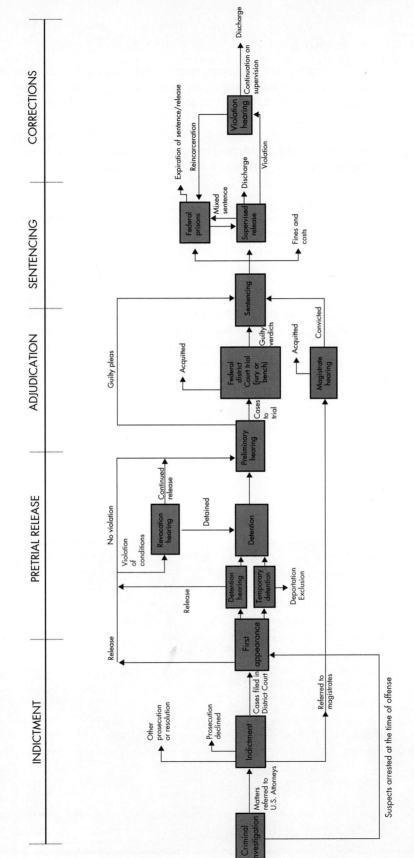

FIGURE 1–1 Federal criminal case processing. *Source:* Adapted from *U.S. Department of Justice, Compendium of Federal Justice Statistics, 1989* (Washington, D.C.: Bureau of Justice Statistics, 1992), p. 3.

Booking A law enforcement or correctional administrative process officially recording an entry into detention after arrest, and identifying the person, the place, time, and reason for the arrest, and the arresting authority.

Booking

During the arrest process suspects are booked: pictures are taken, fingerprints are made, and personal information, such as address, date of birth, weight, and height, are gathered. Details of the charges are recorded, and an administrative record of the arrest is created.

During booking suspects are again advised of their rights, and asked to sign a form on which each right is written. The written form generally contains a statement acknowledging the rights advisement and attesting to the fact that the suspect understands them.

First Appearance

Within hours of arrest suspects must be brought before a magistrate, a judicial officer, for a first appearance. The judge will tell them of the charges against them, will again advise them of their rights, and may sometimes provide the opportunity for bail.

Bail The money or property pledged to the court or actually deposited with the court to effect the release of a person from legal custody.

Most defendants are released on recognizance (into their own care or the care of another) or given the chance to post bond during their first appearance. A bond may take the form of a cash deposit or a property bond in which a house or other property can serve as collateral against flight. Those who flee may be ordered to forfeit the posted cash or property. Suspects who either are not afforded the opportunity for bail because their crimes are very serious, or who do not have the needed financial resources, are taken to jail to await the next stage in the justice process.

If a defendant doesn't have a lawyer, one will be appointed at the first appearance. The defendant may actually have to demonstrate financial hardship or be ordered to pay for counsel. The names of assigned lawyers are usually drawn off the roster of practicing defense attorneys in the county. Some jurisdictions utilize public defenders to represent

The criminal justice process often begins when a suspect is arrested and evidence is seized. Here, members of the Boston Police Department's Special Operations Unit batter down a drug suspect's door. *Photo: Jon Hill/ The Boston Herald.*

indigent defendants. All aspects of the first appearance, including bail bonds and appointed counsel, are discussed in detail in Chapter 8, The Courts.

Preliminary Hearing

The primary purpose of a preliminary hearing is to determine whether or not sufficient evidence exists against a person to continue the justice process. The decision is a judicial one, but the process provides the prosecutor with an opportunity to test the strength of evidence at his or her disposal. In a preliminary hearing, the judge will decide if a crime has indeed been committed, and if it is likely that the person before the court is the one who has committed it.

The preliminary hearing also allows defense counsel the chance to assess the strength of the prosecution's case. As the prosecution presents evidence, the defense is said to "discover" what it is. Hence, the preliminary hearing serves a *discovery* function for the defense. If the defense attorney thinks the evidence is strong, he or she may suggest that a plea bargain be arranged.

Information or Indictment

In some states the prosecutor may seek to continue the case against a defendant by filing an "information" with the court. An information is filed on the basis of the outcome of the preliminary hearing.

Other states require an indictment be returned by a grand jury before prosecution can proceed. The grand jury hears evidence from the prosecutor and decides whether a case should go to trial. In effect, the grand jury is the formal indicting authority. It determines whether or not probable cause exists to charge a defendant formally with a crime. Grand juries can return an indictment on less than a unanimous vote.

The grand jury system has been criticized because it is one-sided. The defense has no opportunity to present evidence; the grand jury is led only by the prosecutor, often through an appeal to emotions or in ways which will not be permitted in a trial.

At the same time, the grand jury is less bound by specific rules than a jury in a trial. For example, one member of a grand jury related to the author that a rape case had been dismissed because the man had taken the woman to dinner first. Personal ignorance and subcultural biases are far more likely to be decisive in grand jury hearings than in criminal trials.

In defense of the grand jury, however, we should recognize that defendants who are clearly innocent will likely not be indicted. A refusal to indict can save considerable time and money by diverting poorly prepared cases from further processing by the system.

Arraignment

At arraignment the accused stands before a judge and hears the information or indictment against him or her as it is read. Defendants will again be notified of their rights and will be asked to enter a plea. Acceptable pleas generally include (1) "Not guilty"; (2) "Guilty"; and (3) "No contest" (*nolo contendere*), which may result in conviction, but which can't be used later as an admission of guilt in civil proceedings. Civil proceedings, while not covered in detail in this book, provide an additional avenue of relief for victims or their survivors. Convicted offenders increasingly find themselves facing suits brought against them by victims seeking to collect monetary damages.

Guilty pleas are not always accepted by the judge. If the judge feels a guilty plea was made under duress, or because of a lack of knowledge on the part of the defendant, the plea

Preliminary Hearing The proceeding before a judicial officer in which three matters must be decided: whether a crime was committed, whether the crime occurred within the territorial jurisdiction of the court, and whether there are reasonable grounds to believe that the defendant committed the crime.

Grand Jury A body of persons who have been selected according to law and sworn to hear the evidence against accused persons and determine whether there is sufficient evidence to bring those persons to trial, to investigate criminal activity generally, and to investigate the conduct of public agencies and officials.

Indictment A formal, written accusation submitted to the court by a grand jury, alleging that a specified person(s) has committed a specified offense(s), usually a felony.

Arraignment I. The hearing before a court having jurisdiction in a criminal case, in which the identity of the defendant is established, the defendant is informed of the charge(s) and of his or her rights, and the defendant is required to enter a plea. II. In some usages, any appearance in court prior to trial in criminal proceedings.

Trial The examination in a court of the issues of fact and law in a case, for the purpose of reaching a judgment of conviction or acquittal of the defendant(s).

will be rejected and a plea of "not guilty" will be substituted for it. Sometimes defendants "stand mute"; that is, they refuse to speak or enter a plea of any kind. In that case, the judge will enter a plea of "not guilty" on their behalf. The arraignment process, including pretrial motions made by the defense, is discussed in detail in Chapter 8, The Courts.

Trial

Every criminal defendant has a right under the Sixth Amendment to the U.S. Constitution to a trail by jury. The U.S. Supreme Court, however, has held that petty offense are not covered by the Sixth Amendment guarantee, and that the seriousness of a case is determined by the way in which "society regards the offense." For the most part, "offenses for which the maximum period of incarceration is six months or less are presumptively petty."[23] In *Blanton* v. *North Las Vegas* (1989),[24] the Court held that "a defendant can overcome this presumption, and become entitled to a jury trial, only by showing that…additional penalties [such as fines and community service] viewed together with the maximum prison term, are so severe that the legislature clearly determined that the offense is a serious one." The *Blanton* decision was further reinforced in the case of *U.S.* v. *Nachtigal* (1993).[25]

In most jurisdictions, many criminal cases never come to trial. The majority are "pled out," or dismissed for a variety of reasons. Some studies have found that as many as 82% of all sentences are imposed in criminal cases because of guilty pleas rather than trials.[26]

In cases which do come to trial the procedures which govern the submission of evidence are tightly controlled by procedural law and precedent. Procedural law specifies what type of evidence may be submitted, what the credentials of those allowed to represent the state or the defendant must be, and what a jury is allowed to hear.

Precedent refers to understandings built up through common usage, and also to decisions rendered by courts in previous cases. Precedent in the courtroom, for example, requires that lawyers request permission from the judge before approaching a witness. It also can mean that excessively gruesome items of evidence may not be used or must be altered in some way so that their factual value is not lost in the strong emotional reactions they may create.

Some states allow trials for less serious offenses to occur before a judge if defendants waive their right to a trial by jury. This is called a bench trial. Other states require a jury trial for all serious criminal offenses.

Trials are expensive and time consuming. They pit defense attorneys against prosecutors. Regulated conflict is the rule, and juries are required to decide the facts and apply the law as it is explained to them by the judge. In some cases, however, a jury may be unable to decide. In such cases, it is said to be deadlocked, resulting in a mistrial being declared. The defendant will be tried again when a new jury is empaneled. The criminal trial and its participants are described fully in Chapter 9.

Sentencing

Once a person is convicted it becomes the responsibility of the judge to impose some form of punishment. The sentence may take the form of supervised probation in the community, a fine, a prison term or some combination of these. Defendants will often be ordered to pay the costs of court or of their own defense if they are able.

Prior to sentencing, a sentencing hearing may be held in which lawyers on both sides present information concerning the defendant. The judge may also request that a presentence report be compiled by a probation or parole officer. The report will contain information on the defendant's family and business situation, emotional state, social background, and criminal history. It will be used to assist the judge in making an appropriate sentencing decision.

Judges usually have considerable discretion in sentencing, although new state and federal laws have placed limits on judicial discretion in some cases and require that a sentence "presumed" by law be imposed. Judges still retain enormous discretion, however, in specifying whether sentences on multiple charges are to run consecutively or concurrently. Offenders found guilty of more than one charge may be ordered to serve one sentence after another is completed (consecutive) or be told that their sentences will run at the same time (concurrent).

Many sentences are appealed. The appeals process can be complex, involving both state and federal judiciaries. It is based upon the defendant's claim that rules of procedure were not properly followed at some earlier stage in the justice process, or that the defendant was denied the rights accorded him by the U.S. Constitution. Chapter 10, Sentencing, outlines modern sentencing practices and describes the many modern alternatives to imprisonment.

Consecutive Sentence A sentence that is one of two or more sentences imposed at the same time, after conviction for more than one offense, and which is served in sequence with the other sentence(s); or a new sentence for a new conviction, imposed upon a person already under sentence(s) for previous offense(s), which is added to a previous sentence(s), thus increasing the maximum time the offender may be confined or under supervision.

Corrections

Once an offender has been sentenced, the stage of "corrections" begins. Some offenders are sentenced to prison where they "do time for their crimes." Once in the correctional system, they are classified according to local procedures and assigned to confinement facilities and treatment programs. Newer prisons today bear little resemblance to the massive bastions of the past which isolated offenders from society behind huge stone walls. Unfortunately, modern prisons still suffer from a "lock psychosis" among many administrators and a lack of significant rehabilitation programs. One of the chapters in this book, Chapter 12, Prisons, discusses the philosophy behind prisons and sketches their historical development. Another chapter, Chapter 13, Prison Life, portrays life on the inside and delineates the social structures which develop as a response to the pains of imprisonment.

JUSTICE IN AMERICAN CONTEXT...
Attitudes Toward the Justice System

In April 1993 *Parade Magazine* released findings from its national survey on law and order. The survey was conducted by the independent firm of Mark Clements Research, Inc., at the request of the magazine. While the survey reports only perceptions, and not actual incidents, it is indicative of American attitudes toward the criminal justice system in this country. Among the findings were the following:

ON EQUAL TREATMENT

> 93% of respondents say affluent people "receive special treatment" from the justice system.
> 77% say "the poor are treated unfairly" by the system.
> 61% say "minorities don't get a fair shake."
> 87% of respondents, overall, say "our judicial system does not treat people equally."

ON THE POLICE

> 85% of white respondents report a "positive attitude toward the police."
> 64% of Hispanic and black Americans report similarly positive attitudes.

14% of white Americans say the police "frequently use excessive force."

42% of black and Hispanic Americans say the police "frequently use excessive force."

76% of black and Hispanic Americans, compared with 44% of whites, feel there are more cases of police brutality against minorities than whites.

77% of "those aged 18 to 34" have positive attitudes towards the police, while 92% of those aged 65 to 75 have positive attitudes.

ON COURTS

23% "believe that juries almost always convict the guilty and free the innocent."

30% "feel that juries are right only about half the time."

62% "do not approve of plea-bargaining."

ON PRISONS

45% of respondents support building more prisons to reduce current overcrowding.

22% "favor paroling more prisoners."

79% suggest "community service as a solution to overcrowded" prisons.

ON SENTENCING OPTIONS

92% "say repeat offenders who commit serious crimes should not be eligible for parole."

83% of respondents say "people who commit certain nonviolent crimes should do community service rather than go to prison." Among the crimes cited, 60% of respondents indicated community service rather than prison was appropriate for tax evaders, 62% chose community service over prison for petty theft, 48% for prostitution, and 42% for forgery (bad check writing).

ON THE DEATH PENALTY

87% of respondents "say the U.S. should have a death penalty."

ON JUVENILE OFFENDERS

71% "say that 13- to 16-year-olds who commit violent crimes should be tried in adult courts."

Source: Parade Magazine, April 18, 1993, pp. 4–7.

Probation and Parole

Not everyone who is convicted of a crime and sentenced ends up in prison. Some offenders are ordered to prison only to have their sentences suspended and a probationary term imposed. They may also be ordered to perform community service activities as a condition of their probation. During the term of probation these offenders are required to submit to supervision by a probation officer and to meet other conditions set by the court. Failure to do so results in revocation of probation and imposition of the original prison sentence. Other offenders, who have served a portion of their prison sentences, may be freed on parole. They will be supervised by a parole officer and assisted in their readjustment to society. Two chapters deal with the practice of probation and parole and with the issues surrounding it. They are Chapter 10, Sentencing, and Chapter 11, Probation and Parole.

CRIMINAL JUSTICE AND CRIMINOLOGY

EARLY BEGINNINGS

The study of criminal justice as an academic discipline began in this country in the 1920s when August Vollmer, the former police chief of Berkeley, California, persuaded the University of California to offer courses on the subject.[27] Vollmer was joined by his student Orlando W. Wilson and by William H. Parker in calling for increased professionalism in police work through better training.[28] Early criminal justice education was practice oriented; it was a kind of extension of on-the-job training for working practitioners.

CRIMINOLOGY

While criminal justice was often seen as a technical subject, **criminology**, on the other hand, had a firm academic base. Criminology is the study of the causes of crime and of criminal motivation. It combines the academic disciplines of sociology and psychology in an effort to explore the mind of the offender. The study of criminology is central to the criminal justice discipline, and courses in criminology are almost always found in criminal justice programs. Victimology is a subfield of criminology which seeks answers to the question of why some people are victimized while others are not.

Criminology The scientific study of crime causation, prevention, and the rehabilitation and punishment of offenders.

LEAA

As a separate field of study, criminal justice had fewer than 1,000 students before 1950.[29] The turbulent 1960s and 1970s brought an increasing concern with social issues and, in particular, justice. Drug use, social protests, and dramatically increasing crime rates turned the nation's attention to the criminal justice system. During the period, Congress passed two significant pieces of legislation: (1) the Law Enforcement Assistance Act of 1965, which created the Law Enforcement Assistance Administration (LEAA), and (2) the Omnibus Crime Control and Safe Streets Act of 1968.

Vast amounts of monies were funneled into fighting crime. Law enforcement agencies received a great deal of technical assistance and new crime-fighting hardware. Students interested in the study of criminal justice often found themselves eligible for financial help under the Law Enforcement Education Program (LEEP).

LEEP

LEEP monies funded a rapid growth in criminal justice offerings nationwide. In the first year of its existence, the LEEP program spent $6.5 million on 20,602 students in 485 schools around the country. By 1975 more than 100,000 students were studying criminal justice at 1,065 schools with assistance from LEEP. The federal government in that year spent in excess of $40 million on criminal justice education.[30]

LEEP funding began to decline in 1979. Meanwhile, criminal justice programs nationwide were undergoing considerable self-examination. The direction of justice studies and the future of the discipline were open to debate. The resultant clarification of criminal justice as a discipline has made the field stronger and more professional than ever before.

SUMMARY

In this chapter the process of American criminal justice and the agencies that contribute to it have been described as a system. As we have warned, however, such a viewpoint is useful primarily for the reduction in complexity it provides. A more realistic approach to understanding criminal justice may be the nonsystem approach. As a nonsystem, criminal justice is depicted as a fragmented activity in which individuals and agencies within the process have interests and goals which at times coincide, but often conflict.

An alternative way of viewing the practice of criminal justice is in terms of its two goals: crime control and due process. The crime control perspective urges rapid and effective law enforcement, and calls for the stiff punishment of law breakers. Due process, on the other hand, requires a recognition of the defendant's rights and holds the agents of justice accountable for any actions which might contravene those rights.

The goals of due process and crime control are often in conflict. Popular opinion may even see them as mutually exclusive. As we describe the agencies of justice in the various chapters which follow, the goals of crime control and due process will appear again and again. As we shall see, the challenge of criminal justice in America is one of achieving efficient enforcement of the laws while recognizing the rights of individuals. The mandate of crime control through due process ensures that criminal justice will remain an exciting and ever-evolving undertaking.

DISCUSSION QUESTIONS

1. What are the two models of the criminal justice process which this chapter describes? Which model do you think is more useful? Which is more accurate?

2. What have we suggested are the two primary goals of the criminal justice system? Do you think one goal is more important than the other? If so, which one? Why?

3. What do we mean when we say that the "primary purpose of law is the maintenance of order?" Why is social order necessary?

4. What might a large, complex society such as our own be like without laws? Without a system of criminal justice? Would you want to live in such a society? Why or why not?

5. A box in this chapter asks: "Is there one form of justice for the poor and another for the rich? Is there a separate system of justice which embodies the values of the powerful, while condemning the strivings of the underclass? Are the felt needs of certain people being denied by the contemporary American criminal justice system? Can the scales of justice be balanced? In a more fundamental sense, can justice be truly equitable in a society built upon the free pursuit of individual wealth and the often unbridled drive toward personal power?" What do you think?

ENDNOTES

1. Charles E. Silberman, *Criminal Violence, Criminal Justice* (New York: Random House, 1978), p. 12.

2. "Shooting Spree on Commuter Train Racially Motivated," Reuters wire services, December 8, 1993.

3. "Teen Shoots Woman Because of Her Attitude," United Press International wire services, central edition, November 19, 1993.

4. "Spirit of Frontier Justice Lives Again," *USA Today*, April 8, 1993, p. 8A.

5. "Crime May Pay Thanks to California Budget Crisis", *USA Today*, May 10, 1993, p. 3A.

6. Ibid.

7. Ibid.

8. See, "Cries of Relief," *Time*, April 26, 1993, p. 18, and "King II: What Made the Difference?" *Newsweek*, April 26, 1993, p. 26.

9. "FBI: Definitely a Bomb," *USA Today*, March 1, 1993, p. 1A.

10. "Some Worry Police 'out of Control,'" *USA Today*, November 15, 1989, pp. 1A–2A.

11. "A Free Man," *USA Today*, April 27, 1989, p. 13A.

12. "The Subway Gunman," *Facts on File* (New York: Facts on File, 1987), p. 792.

13. Ibid., p. 88.

14. George P. Fletcher, *A Crime of Self-defense: Bernhard Goetz and Law on Trial* (New York: The Free Press, 1988).

15. The systems model of criminal justice is often attributed to the frequent use of the term "system" by the 1967 Presidential Commission in its report, *The Challenge of Crime in a Free Society* (Washington, D.C.: U.S. Government Printing Office, 1967).

16. One of the first published works to utilize the nonsystems approach to criminal justice was the American Bar Association's *New Perspective on Urban Crime* (Washington, D.C.: ABA Special Committee on Crime Prevention and Control, 1972).

17. Jerome H. Skolnick, *Justice Without Trial* (New York: John Wiley, 1966), p. 179.

18. Herbert Packer, *The Limits of the Criminal Sanction* (Stanford, CA: Stanford University Press, 1968).

19. For a complete analysis of the impact of decisions made by the Warren Court, see Fred P. Graham, *The Due Process Revolution: The Warren Court's Impact on Criminal Law* (New York: Hayden Press, 1970).

20. *Gideon* v. *Wainwright*, 372 U.S. 353 (1963).

21. *Miranda* v. *Arizona*, 384 U.S. 436 (1966).

22. North Carolina Justice Academy, *Miranda Warning Card* (Salemburg, N.C.).

23. *Blanton* v. *North Las Vegas*, 489 U.S. 538 (1989).

24. Ibid.

25. *U.S.* v. *Nachtigal,* No. 92–609. Decided February 22, 1993.

26. Barbara Borland and Ronald Sones, *Prosecution of Felony Arrests, 1981* (Washington, D.C.: Bureau of Justice Statistics, 1986).

27. For an excellent history of policing in the United States, see Edward A. Farris, "Five Decades of American Policing: 1932–1982," *The Police Chief,* November 1982, pp. 30–36.

28. Gene Edward Carte, "August Vollmer and the Origins of Police Professionalism," *Journal of Police Science and Administration,* Vol. 1, no. 1 (1973), pp. 274–281.

29. Larry L. Gaines, "Criminal Justice Education Marches On!" in Roslyn Muraskin, ed., *The Future of Criminal Justice Education* (New York: Criminal Justice Institute, Long Island University, C. W. Post Campus, 1987).

30. Ibid.

CHAPTER 2

THE CRIME PICTURE

It may turn out that a free society cannot really prevent crime. Perhaps its causes are locked so deeply into the human personality, the intimate processes of family life, and the subtlest aspects of the popular culture that coping is the best that we can hope for...[1]
—JAMES Q. WILSON, UCLA

If people here were not getting killed on the job in homicides, we would have quite a low rate of fatalities.[2]
—SAMUEL EHRENHALT, LABOR DEPARTMENT OFFICIAL COMMENTING ON FINDINGS THAT SHOW MURDER TO BE THE TOP CAUSE OF ON-THE-JOB DEATHS IN NEW YORK CITY.

No one way of describing crime describes it well enough.
—THE PRESIDENT'S COMMISSION ON LAW ENFORCEMENT AND ADMINISTRATION OF JUSTICE

We are the most violent and self-destructive nation on earth....In 1990, no nation had a higher murder rate than the United States. What is worse, no nation was even close.
—FROM A 1991 REPORT RELEASED BY JOSEPH R. BIDEN, JR. U.S. SENATE JUDICIARY COMMITTEE CHAIRMAN

KEY CONCEPTS

Bureau of Justice Statistics	Uniform Crime Reports	clearance rates
victimization surveys	Part I offenses	Part II offenses
major crimes	violent crime	Crime Index
property crime	National Crime	clearance rates
date rape	Victimization Survey	

KEY CASES

R.A.V. v. *City of St. Paul*   *Wisconsin* v. *Mitchell*

INTRODUCTION: SOURCES OF DATA

On June 16, 1991, a well-dressed, silver-haired moustached white man in his forties walked into the 52-story United Bank of Denver wearing sunglasses and a brown derby hat.[3] When he walked out, four bank guards, who had been counting money in the bank's high-security area were dead, and $196,000 of the depositors' money was missing. The guards had been killed execution style—each shot repeatedly. The dead were William McCullom, 33, of Aurora; Philip Mankoff, 41, also of Aurora; Scott McCarthy, 21, of Littleton; and Todd Wilson, 21, of Englewood. McCarthy had wanted to be a police officer and had been married just months before the shooting. Wilson was best man at the wedding. In 1992, following a jury trial, James King, a retired police sergeant and former bank guard, was acquitted on multiple counts of first-degree murder and one charge of aggravated robbery in the case. While each of the dead guards led intricate lives and had families, dreams, and desires, their deaths were reported—like so many other murders—as a statistical count in the FBI's Uniform Crime Reports (UCR) for that year. UCR statistics do not contain details on the personal lives of crime victims but represent an objective statistical compilation of law violations—ranging from murder to petty theft and beyond.

Some, however, question just how "objective" crime statistics are. Social events, including crime, are complex and difficult to quantify. Even the choice of which crimes should be included in statistical reports is itself a judgment which reflects the interests and biases of policymakers. The FBI, for example, classifies certain crimes as "Part I offenses," often called "major crimes." Part I offenses are:

- Murder
- Forcible rape
- Robbery
- Aggravated assault
- Burglary
- Larceny
- Motor vehicle theft
- Arson

Part I offenses do not encompass most large-scale while-collar crimes, such as insider trading in securities, price fixing by corporate executives, and unfair business practices.

Nor are statistics on "victimless" crimes included. Such crimes, however, probably result in far more monetary damage than most of the traditionally classified "major offenses."

Crime statistics are also difficult to interpret because of the way in which they are collected. Most widely quoted numbers come from the FBI's Uniform Crime Reports and depend upon reports to the police by victims of crime. One problem with such summaries is that citizens may not always make official reports, sometimes because they are afraid to report or perhaps because they don't think the police can do anything about the offense. Even when reports are made they are filtered through a number of bureaucratic levels. As Frank Hagan points out, quoting an earlier source, "The government is very keen on amassing statistics. They collect them, add to them, raise them to the nth power, take the cube root and prepare wonderful diagrams. But what you must never forget is that every one of these figures comes in the first instance from the *chowty dar* (village watchman), who puts down what he damn pleases."[4]

Another problem is the fact that certain kinds of crimes are rarely reported and are especially difficult to detect. These include "victimless crimes," or crimes which, by their nature, involve willing participants. Victimless crimes include such things as drug use, prostitution, and gambling. Similarly, white-collar and high-technology offenses such as embezzlement, computer crime, and corporate misdeeds, probably enter the official statistics only rarely. Hence, a large amount of criminal activity goes undetected in the United States, while those types of crimes which are detected may paint a misleading picture of criminal activity by virtue of the publicity accorded to them.

A second data collection format is typified by the Bureau of Justice Statistics' (BJS) National Crime Victimization Survey. It relies upon personal interpretations of what may (or may not) have been criminal events, and upon quasi-confidential surveys which may selectively include data from those most willing to answer interviewer's questions, and excludes information from less gregarious respondents. Some victims are afraid to report

Victimless crimes such as prostitution are rarely reported. As a consequence they are likely to be seriously underrepresented in the FBI's Uniform Crime Reports. Here, teenage prostitutes solicit a "John." *Photo: John Maher/Stock Boston.*

crimes even to nonpolice interviewers. Others may inaccurately interpret their own experiences or may be tempted to invent victimizations for the sake of interviewers. As the first page of the National Crime Victimization Survey (NCVS) admits, "Details about the crimes come directly from the victims, and no attempt is made to validate the information against police records or any other source."[5]

Although the FBI's Uniform Crime Reports and the BJS's National Crime Victimization Survey are the major sources of crime data, other regular publications contribute to our knowledge of crime patterns. Available yearly is the *Sourcebook of Criminal Justice Statistics*, a compilation of national information on crime and on the criminal justice system. The *Sourcebook* is published by the Bureau of Justice Statistics through moneys provided by the Justice System Improvement Act of 1979. A less frequent, but more concise document is the *Report to the Nation on Crime and Justice*, issued in updated editions every few years. The National Institute of Justice, the primary research arm of the U.S. Department of Justice, along with the Office of Juvenile Justice and Delinquency Prevention, the Federal Justice Research Program, and the National Victim's Resource Center, provide still more information on crime patterns.

This chapter describes crime in America through a summation of available data drawn from many of these sources. The fact that such data may be flawed in many ways already mentioned, however, is important to remember in making decisions based on it.

THE UNIFORM CRIME REPORTS

DEVELOPMENT OF THE UCR PROGRAM

In 1930 Congress authorized the attorney general of the United States to survey crime in America, and the FBI was designated to implement the program. The Bureau quickly built upon early efforts by the International Association of Chiefs of Police (IACP) to create a national system of uniform crime statistics. As a practical measure IACP recommendations had utilized readily available information, and so it was that citizen's reports of crimes to the police became the basis of the plan.[6]

During its first year of operation the UCR Program received reports from 400 cities in 43 states. Twenty million people were covered by that first comprehensive survey. Today almost 16,000 law enforcement agencies provide crime information for the program, with data coming from city, state, and county departments. To assure uniformity in reporting, the FBI has developed standardized definitions of offenses and terminologies used in the program. A number of publications, including the *Uniform Crime Reporting Handbook* and *Manual of Law Enforcement Records*, are supplied to participating agencies, and training for effective reporting is made available through FBI-sponsored seminars and instructional literature.

Following IACP recommendations, the original UCR Program was designed to permit comparisons over time through construction of a Crime Index. The Index summed the total of seven major offenses—murder, forcible rape, robbery, aggravated assault, burglary, larceny-theft, and motor vehicle theft—and expressed the result as a crime rate based on population. In 1979, by congressional mandate, an eighth offense—arson—was added to the Index. Although Uniform Crime Report categories today parallel statutory definitions of criminal behavior, they are not legal classifications but only conveniences created for statistical reporting purposes.

Beginning in 1987 the UCR Program discontinued the practice of collecting data on ethnic origin for persons arrested. The last year such data were reported was in 1986.

HISTORICAL TRENDS

Since the UCR Program began there have been two major shifts in crime rates. One occurred during the early 1940s, when crime decreased due to the large number of young men who entered military service during World War II. Young males comprise the most "crime-prone" segment of the population, and their removal to the European and Pacific theaters of war did much to lower crime rates.

The other noteworthy shift in offense statistics—a dramatic increase in most forms of crime beginning in the 1960s—also had a link to World War II. With the end of the war, and the return of millions of young men to civilian life, birth rates skyrocketed during the period 1945–1955, creating a postwar "baby boom." By 1960, "baby boomers" were entering their teenage years. A disproportionate number of young people produced a dramatic increase in most major crimes.

Other factors contributed to the increase in reported crime during the same period. Modified reporting requirements, which reduced the stress associated with filing police reports, and the publicity associated with the rise in crime, sensitized victims to the importance of reporting. Crimes which may have gone undetected in the past began to figure more prominently in official statistics. Similarly, the growing professionalization of some police departments resulted in more accurate and increased data collection, causing some of the most progressive departments to be associated with the largest crime increases.[7]

The 1960s were tumultuous years. The Vietnam war, a vibrant civil rights struggle, the heady growth of secularism, dramatic increases in the divorce rate, diverse forms of "liberation," and the influx of psychedelic and other drugs, all combined to fragment existing institutions. Social norms were blurred, and group control over individual behavior declined substantially. The "normless" quality of American society in the 1960s contributed greatly to the rise in crime. Crime rates continued their upward swing until the late 1970s when the postwar boomers began to age out of the crime-prone years, and American society emerged from the cultural drift which had characterized the previous 20 years. Decreases in most major crimes continued into the 1980s.

UCR TERMINOLOGY

Figure 2–1 shows the UCR crime clock, which is calculated yearly as a short-hand way of diagramming crime severity in the United States. Seven Part I offenses are listed in the right-hand margin of the figure. Arson has been temporarily excluded, although it is now an eighth index offense.

The crime clock distinguishes between two general categories of crime: **violent** (or **personal**) and **property crime**. Violent crimes include murder, forcible rape, robbery, and aggravated assault. Property crimes, as the figure shows, are burglary, larceny, and motor vehicle theft. Other than for the use of such a simple dichotomy, UCR data do not provide a clear measure of the severity of the crimes they cover.

Crime clock data are based, as are most UCR statistics, upon crimes reported to (or discovered by) the police. For a few offenses the numbers reported are probably close to the numbers which actually occur. Murder, for example, is a crime that is difficult to conceal because of its seriousness. Even where the crime is not immediately discovered, the victim

Violent Crime An offense category that, according to the FBI's Uniform Crime reports, includes murder, rape, aggravated assault, and robbery. Because the UCR depends upon *reports* (to the police) of crimes, the "official statistics" on these offenses are apt to reflect inaccurately the actual incidence of such crimes.

Property Crime An offense category that, according to the FBI's UCR program, includes burglary, larceny, auto theft, and arson. Since citizen reports of criminal incidents figure heavily in the compilation of "official statistics," the same critiques apply to tallies of these crimes as to the category of violent crime.

is often quickly missed by friends and associates and a "missing persons" report is filed with the police.

Auto theft is another crime that is reported with a frequency similar to its actual rate of occurrence, probably because insurance companies require that a police report be filed before any claims can be collected. Unfortunately, most crimes other than murder and auto theft appear to be seriously underreported. Victims may not report for various reasons, including (1) the belief that the police can't do anything; (2) a fear of reprisal; (3) embarrassment about the crime itself, or a fear of being embarrassed during the reporting process; and (4) an acceptance of criminal victimization as a normal part of life.

FIGURE 2–1   FBI Crime Clock 1992. The crime clock should be viewed with care. Being the most aggregate representation of UCR data, it is designed to convey the annual reported crime experience by showing the relative frequency of occurrence of Crime Index offenses. This mode of display should not be taken to imply a regularity in the commission of Part I offenses; rather, it represents the annual ratio of crime to fixed time intervals. *Source*: Adapted from Federal Bureau of Investigation, *Uniform Crime Reports for the United States, 1992* (Washington, D.C.: U.S. Government Printing Office, 1993).

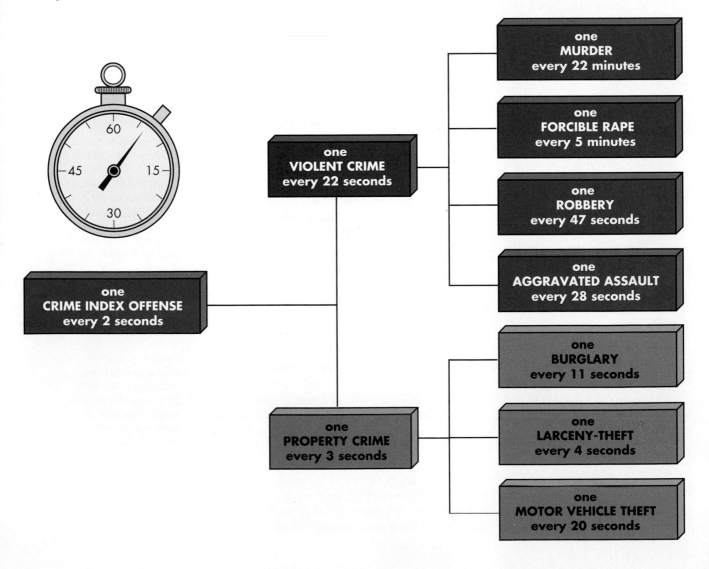

UCR data tend to underestimate the amount of crime which actually occurs for another reason: built into the reporting system is the hierarchy rule—a way of "counting" crime reports such that only the most serious out of a series of events is scored. If a man and woman go on a picnic, for example, and their party is set upon by a criminal who kills the man, rapes the woman, steals the couple's car, and later burns the vehicle, the hierarchy rule dictates that only one crime will be reported in official statistics—that of murder. The offender, if apprehended, may later be charged with each of the offenses listed, but only one report of murder will appear in UCR data.

Most UCR information is reported as a rate of crime. Rates are computed as the number of crimes *per* some unit of population. National reports generally make use of large units of population, such as 100,000 persons. Hence, the rate of rape reported by the UCR for 1992 was 42.8 forcible rapes per every 100,000 inhabitants of the United States.[8] Rates allow for a meaningful comparison over areas and across time. The rate of reported rape for 1975, for example, was about 26 per 100,000.[9] We expect the number of crimes to increase as population grows, but rate increases are cause for concern because they indicate that crimes are increasing faster than the population is growing. Rates, however, require interpretation. Since the FBI definition of rape includes only female victims, for example, the rate of victimization might be more meaningfully expressed in terms of every 100,000 female inhabitants. Similarly, although there is a tendency to judge an individual's risk of victimization based upon rates, such judgments tend to be inaccurate since they are based purely on averages and do not take into consideration individual life circumstances. While rates may tell us about aggregate conditions and trends, we must be very careful in applying them to individual cases. The crime clock, itself a useful diagrammatic tool, is not a rate-based measure of criminal activity and does not allow easy comparisons over time.

A commonly used term in today's UCRs is **clearance rate**. The clearance rate of any crime refers to the proportion of reported crimes which have been "solved." Clearances are judged primarily on the basis of arrests and do not involve judicial disposition. Once an arrest has been made, a crime is regarded as "cleared" for purposes of reporting in the UCR Program. Exceptional clearances (sometimes called clearances by exceptional means) can result when law enforcement authorities believe they know who the perpetrator of a crime is, but cannot make an arrest. The perpetrator may, for example, flee the country, commit suicide, or die.

For data gathering and reporting purposes, the UCR Program divides the country into four geographic regions: the Northeast, West, South, and Midwest. Unfortunately, no real attempt has been made to create divisions with nearly equal populations or similar demographic characteristics, and it is difficult to compare one region of the country with another meaningfully. Table 2–1 summarizes UCR statistics for 1992.

PART I OFFENSES

Murder

UCR statistics on murder include nonnegligent manslaughter or any willful and unlawful homicide. Not included in the court are suicides, justifiable homicides, deaths caused by negligence or accident, and attempts to murder. In 1992, some 23,760 murders came to the attention of police departments across the United States.[10] Murder is the smallest numerical category in the Part I offenses. The 1992 murder rate was 9.3 homicides for every 100,000 persons in the country—a decrease of 5% over the previous year.

Crime Index An inclusive measure of the violent and property crime categories of the UCR, also known as "Part I offenses." The Crime Index has been a useful tool for geographic (state-to-state) and historical (year-to-year) comparative purposes because it employs the concept of a crime rate (the number of crimes *per* unit of population). However, the addition of arson, as an eighth index offense in recent years, and the new Executive Branch requirements with regard to the gathering of "hate crime" statistics, have the potential to result in new crime index measurements which provide less than ideal comparisons.

Clearance Rate A traditional measure of investigative effectiveness that compares the number of crimes reported and/or discovered to the number of crimes solved through arrest or other means (such as the death of a suspect).

Murder The unlawful killing of a human being. Murder is a generic term, which, in common usage may include first- and second-degree murder, as well as "manslaughter," "involuntary manslaughter," and other, similar kinds of offenses.[11]

T A B L E   2 - 1

MAJOR CRIMES KNOWN TO THE POLICE 1992
(PART I OFFENSES FROM THE UCR)

Offense	Number	Rate per 100,000	Clearance Rate
Personal/Violent Crimes			
Murder	23,760	9.3	65%
Forcible rape	109,060	42.8	52
Robbery	672,480	263.6	24
Aggravated assault	1,126,970	441.8	56
Property Crimes			
Burglary	2,979,900	1,168.2	13
Larceny	7,915,200	3,103.0	20
Motor vehicle theft	1,610,800	631.5	14
Arson[1]	86,547	—	15
U.S. total	14,438,200	5,660.2	21

[1] Arson can be classified as either a property crime or a violent crime, depending upon whether or not personal injury or loss of life results from its commission. It is generally classified as a property crime, however. Arson statistics are incomplete for 1922, and do not enter in the "total" tabulations.
Source: Adapted from Federal Bureau of Investigation, *Uniform Crime Reports for the United States, 1992* (Washington, D.C.: U.S. Government Printing Office, 1993).

Murder rates tend to peak annually in the warmest months. In many years, July and August show the highest number of homicides. Typically, in 1992 the month of August showed the highest number of murders.

Geographically, murder is most common in the Southern states. However, because they are the most populous, a meaningful comparison across regions of the country is difficult. Although the 1992 data show a one year decline in the murder rate, 5- and 10-year trends show the 1992 rate was 11 percent higher than in 1988 and 12 percent above the 1983 rate.

Age is no barrier to murder. Statistics for 1992 reveal that 254 infants (under the age of one) were victims of homicide, as were 474 persons aged 75 and over.[12] Persons aged 25–29 were the most likely to be murdered. Murder perpetrators, on the other hand, were most common in the 18- to 24-year-old age group.

Firearms are the weapon of choice in most murders. Our is a well-armed society, and guns accounted for 68% of all killings in 1992. Handguns out-numbered shotguns by 10 to 1 in the murder statistics, while rifles were a distant third. Knives were used in approximately 15% of all murders. Other weapons included explosives, poisons, narcotics overdoses, blunt objects such as clubs, and hands, feet and fists.

Few murders are committed by strangers. Only 14% of all murders in 1992 were perpetrated by persons classified as "strangers." In 39% of all killings the relationship between the parties had not yet been determined. The largest category of killers was officially listed as "acquaintances," which probably includes a large number of former "friends."

Murders may occur in sprees, which "involve killings at two or more locations with almost no time break between murders."[13] Mass murders entail "the killing of four or more victims at one location, within one event."[14] Serial murders happen over time, and are officially defined to "involve the killing of several victims in three or more separate

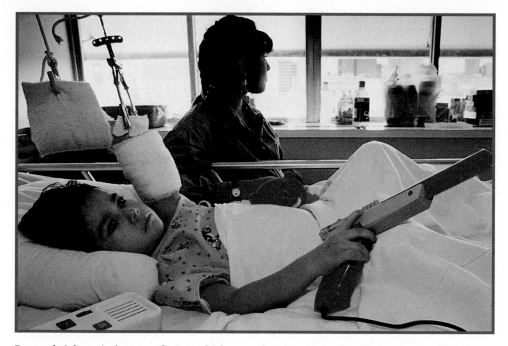

Personal violence is the type of crime which engenders the greatest fear. Here a 3-year-old in San Antonio's Santa Rosa Children's Hospital recovers after becoming the victim of a drive-by shooting. *Photo: Rick Hunter/Sygma.*

events."[15] Days, months, or even years may elapse between the murders. Serial killers have been frequently portrayed in the media. Some of the more infamous in recent years include Jeffrey Dahmer, who received 936 years in prison for the homosexual dismemberment murders of 15 young men; Ted Bundy who killed many college-aged women; Henry Lee Lucas, now on death row in Texas, who was convicted of 11 murders and linked to 140 others; Charles Manson still serving time for ordering followers to kill 7 Californians, including actress Sharon Tate; and David Berkowitz, also known as the "Son of Sam," who killed 6 people and wounded 7 on lover's lanes around New York City. Arguments cause most murders (29%), but murders occur during commission of other crimes, such as robbery, rape, and burglary. Homicides which follow from other crimes are more likely to be impulsive rather than planned.

Murder is a serious crime, and when it occurs it consumes substantial police resources. Consequently, over the years the offense has shown the highest clearance rate of any index crime. 65% of all homicides were cleared in 1992. Figure 2–2 shows clearance rates for all Part I offenses.

Forcible Rape

Forcible rape is the least reported of all violent crimes. Typical estimates are that only one out of every four forcible rapes which actually occur are reported to the police. An even lower figure was reported by a 1992 government-sponsored study which found that only 16% of rapes were reported.[16] The victim's fear of embarrassment has been cited as the reason most often given for nonreports. In the past, reports of rape were usually taken by seemingly hardened desk sergeants or male detectives who may not have been sensitive to the needs of the victim. In addition, the physical examination which victims had to endure was often a traumatizing experience in itself. Finally, many states routinely permitted the

Forcible Rape Unlawful sexual intercourse with a female, by force and against her will, or without legal or factual consent. Statutory rape differs from forcible rape in that it involves sexual intercourse with a female who is under the age of consent—regardless of whether or not she is a willing partner. Date rape, or acquaintance rape, are subcategories of rape which are of special interest today.

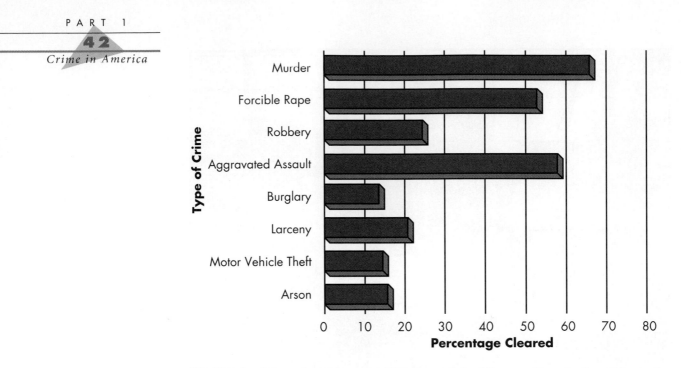

FIGURE 2–2   Crimes cleared by arrest, 1992. *Source*: Federal Bureau of Investigation, *Crime in the United States, 1992* (Washington, D.C.: U.S. Department of Justice, 1993).

Date Rape   Unlawful, forced sexual intercourse with a female against her will which occurs within the context of a dating relationship.

woman's past sexual history to be revealed in detail in the courtroom if a trial ensued. All these practices contributed to a considerable hesitancy on the part of rape victims to report their victimizations.

The last decade has seen many changes designed to facilitate accurate reporting of rape and other sex offenses. Sexual histories are no longer regarded as relevant in most trials, trained female detectives often act as victim interviewers, and physicians have been better educated in handling the psychological needs of victims.

UCR statistics show 109,060 reported rapes for 1992 (Figure 2–3), a slight increase over the number of offenses reported for the previous year. Rape is a crime which has shown a consistent increase in reporting even in years when other personal crimes have been on the decline. By definition, rapes reported under the UCR Program are always of females. Homosexual rape is excluded from the count, but attempts to commit rape by force or the threat of force are included. Statutory rape, where no force is involved, but the female is below the age of consent, is not included in rape statistics.

The offense of rape follows homicide in its seasonal variation. Most rapes in 1992 were reported in the hot summer months, while January, February, and December recorded the lowest number of reports. Most rapes are committed by acquaintances of the victims and often betray a trust or friendship. Date rape, which falls into this category, appears to be far more common than previously believed.

Rape is a complex crime involving strong emotions and injuries to the victim which often go beyond the physical. As a consequence, it is not a well-understood offense. Ronald Barri Flowers[17] has identified many cultural myths which surround the crime of rape. They include:

Fallacy 1: Rape cannot occur if the woman resists.
Fallacy 2: All women secretly desire to be raped.
Fallacy 3: The majority of rapes are triggered by women being out alone at night.

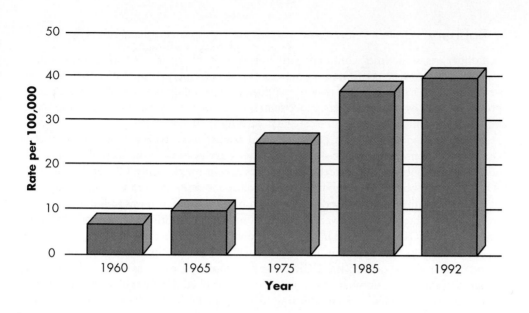

FIGURE 2–3   Rate of reported rape, 1960–1992. *Source:* Federal Bureau of Investigation, *Crime in the United States, 1992* (Washington, D.C.: U.S. Department of Justice, 1993).

Fallacy 4: Rape is a victim-precipitated crime.
Fallacy 5: Only young attractive women are raped.
Fallacy 6: It cannot happen to me.
Fallacy 7: Rape is motivated by the need for sexual gratification.
Fallacy 8: Most rapes are perpetrated by strangers.
Fallacy 9: The rapist looks the part.
Fallacy 10: Rape is an impulsive act.

Rape is often a planned violent crime which serves the offender's need for power rather than sexual gratification.[18] It is frequently committed by a man known to the victim—as in the case of date rape. Victims may be held captive and subjected to repeated assaults.[19] In the crime of heterosexual rape, any female—regardless of age, appearance, or occupation—is a potential victim. Through personal violation, humiliation, and physical battering, rapists seek a sense of personal aggrandizement and feelings of dominance. Victims of rape, on the other hand, often experience a lessened sense of personal worth; increased feelings of despair, helplessness, and vulnerability; a misplaced sense of guilt; and a lack of control over their personal lives.

Rape within marriage is a growing area of concern in American criminal justice, and new laws are being written to recognize it. Some states have redefined their rape statutes to include homosexual rape and marriage rape, although the latter is sometimes classified as sexual battery (indicating that force has been used), a lesser offense than the crime of rape.

Although UCR statistics only report the rape or attempted rape of females, some state statutes, by definition, allow for the rape of a male by a female—although such an offense, when it occurs, is typically of the statutory variety. In late 1993, for example, 24-year-old Fairfax County, Virginia , swimming coach Jean-Michelle Whitiak pleaded guilty to one count of statutory rape, admitting an affair with a 13-year-old boy. When the boy ended the relationship, Whitiak said, she had sex with two of his friends.[20]

Robbery

Robbery is sometimes confused with burglary. Robbery is a personal crime, and involves a face-to-face confrontation between victim and perpetrator. Weapons may be used, or strong-armed robbery may occur through intimidation, especially where gangs threaten victims by sheer numbers. Purse snatching is not classified as robbery by the UCR Program, but is included under the category "larceny-theft."

In 1992 individuals (versus businesses and banks) were typical targets of robbers. Banks, gas stations, convenience stores, and other businesses were the second most common target of robbers, with residential robberies accounting for only 12% of the total. In 1992, 672,480 robberies were reported to the police and 56% of them were highway robberies (meaning that they occurred outdoors, probably as the victim was walking), or muggings. Strong-armed robberies were the most common, accounting for 40% of total robberies reported. Guns were used in 40% of all robberies and knives in 11%.

Armed robbers are dangerous. Guns are actually discharged in 20% of all robberies.[21] Whenever a robbery occurs, the UCR Program scores the event as one robbery, even though there may be a number of victims who were robbed during the occurrence. With the move toward incident-driven reporting (discussed later in this chapter), however, the UCRs will soon make data available on the number of individuals robbed in each instance of robbery. Because statistics on crime show only the most serious offense which occurred during a particular episode, robberies are often hidden when they occur in conjunction with other, more serious, crimes. For example, in a recent year 3% of robbery victims were also raped, and a large number of homicide victims were robbed.[22]

Robbery is primarily an urban offense, and most arrestees are young males who are members of minority groups. The robbery rate in large cities in 1992 was 323 (per every 100,000 inhabitants) while it was only 39 in rural areas. Ninety-two percent of those arrested in 1992 were male, 62% were under the age of 25, and 62% were minorities.[23]

Aggravated Assault

Assaults are of two types: aggravated and simple. Simple assaults may involve pushing and shoving or even fistfights. Aggravated assaults are distinguished from simple assaults by the fact that they either include the use of a weapon, or the individual assaulted requires medical assistance. When deadly weapons are employed, even though no injury may result, aggravated assaults may be chargeable as attempted murder.[24] Hence, because of their potentially serious consequences, the UCR Program scores some cases of attempted assault as aggravated assaults.

In 1992, 1,126,970 cases of aggravated assault were reported to law enforcement agencies in the United States. The summer months evidenced the greatest frequency of assault, while February was once again the month with the lowest number of reports. Most aggravated assaults were committed with blunt objects or objects near at hand (31%), while hands, feet, and fists were also commonly used (26%). Less frequent were knives and firearms (18% and 25%, respectively), as Figure 2–4 shows.

Burglary

Although it may involve personal and even violent confrontations, burglary is primarily a property crime. Burglars are interested in financial gain, and usually fence stolen items in order to recover a fraction of their cash value. About 3 million burglaries were reported to the police in 1992. Dollar losses to burglary victims totaled over $3.8 billion, with an average loss per offense of $1,278.

JUSTICE IN AMERICAN CONTEXT...
The 1994 Federal Anti-Crime Bill

As this book goes to press the U.S. Congress is debating passage of the 1994 Anti-Crime Bill. While there is little doubt that Congress will enact major anti-crime legislation, key provisions of the plan have yet to be finalized. Listed below are ten of the most significant features of the Senate's version of the plan:

1. Overall $22.3 billion has been budgeted directly for crime-fighting. The bill includes $8.9 billion to pay salaries for up to 100,000 additional law enforcement officers.

2. Building on the Brady Law, which took effect in 1994, gun control is an integral part of the proposed legislation. The bill bans the continued manufacture of 19 types of military-style assault weapons and prohibits the sale of many others.

3. Federal application of the death penalty would expand to cover approximately 50 offenses, including murder of a law enforcement officer, drive-by shootings, terrorist bombings, and carjackings in which death results.

4. Under the now famous "three strikes and you're out" provision, the bill would impose mandatory life sentences on those convicted in federal court of a third violent crime or major drug felony.

5. New prisons are planned under the law, which earmarks $6 billion for construction of state, regional, and federal correctional facilities.

6. The bill authorizes $1.8 billion to aid police, prosecutors and victim advocates in fighting crimes against women.

7. Sexual violence would be curtailed through proposals to develop a national criminal background check for caregivers working with children, the elderly, or the disabled.

8. Victims' assistance is built into the bill which allows wider use of victims' impact statements and requires that some criminals pay restitution to their victims.

9. The bill furthers anti-drug efforts by creating $1.2 billion in grants to states over three years for 1.) drug court programs, 2.) the provision of drug testing and treatment services, 3.) alternative punishments, and 4.) job training and the counseling of drug-dependent offenders.

10. The issue of gang violence is addressed in the bill through proposals which would make several gang activities federal offenses. Such activities would range from conspiring to join a criminal street gang to gang-related murders.

While these provisions form the crux of a get-tough approach to crime, analysts concede that it is likely a somewhat "watered-down" version of the proposed bill will finally pass. By April of 1994 the House Judiciary Committee presented its version of the bill which mandated freeing from prison non-violent drug offenders lacking extensive criminal records. The House version would also authorize the death penalty for many additional federal crimes. However, a portion of the law, known as the Racially Discriminatory Capital Sentencing law, would reprieve those sentenced to death if they could show that "race was a statistically significant factor" in sentencing.

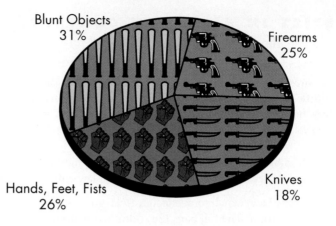

Blunt Objects
31%

Firearms
25%

Knives
18%

Hands, Feet, Fists
26%

FIGURE 2–4   Aggravated assault—weapons used, 1992. *Source:* Federal Bureau of Investigation, *Crime in the United States, 1992* (Washington, D.C.: U.S. Department of Justice, 1993).

Burglary The unlawful entry of any fixed structure, vehicle or vessel used for regular residence, industry, or business, with or without force, with intent to commit a felony, or larceny. For UCR purposes, the crime of burglary can be reported if (1) an unlawful entry of an unlocked structure has occurred, (2) a breaking and entering (of a secured structure) has taken place, or (3) a burglary has been attempted.

Many people fear nighttime burglary of their residence. They imagine themselves asleep in bed as a stranger breaks into their home and then conjure up visions of a violent confrontation. While such scenarios do occur, daytime burglary is also common. Many families now have two or more breadwinners, and since children are in school during the day, some homes—and even entire neighborhoods—are virtually unoccupied during daylight hours. This shift in patterns of social activity has led to a growing burglary threat against residences during daytime.

The UCR Program employs three classifications of burglary: (1) forcible entry, (2) unlawful entry where no force is used, and (3) attempted forcible entry. In most

Nancy Kerrigan—this Olympic ice skater may have been 1994's most famous assault victim when she was clubbed on the knee prior to the winter games. *Photo: Gary Hershorn Reuters/Bettmann.*

jurisdictions force need not be employed for a crime to be classified as burglary. Unlocked doors and open windows are invitations to burglars, and the crime of burglary consists not so much in a forcible entry as it does in the intent of the offender to trespass and steal. In a ten-year period analyzed by the Bureau of Justice Statistics, 23% of all burglaries were unlawful entries, 69% were forcible entries, and 8% were attempted forcible entries.[25] The most dangerous burglaries were those in which a household member was home (about 10% of all burglaries).[26] Residents who were home during a burglary suffered a greater than 30% chance of becoming the victim of a violent crime.[27]

Property crimes generally involve low rates of clearance. Burglary is no exception. The clearance rate for burglary in 1992 was only 13%. Burglars are usually unknown to their victims, and even if known, they conceal their identity by committing their crime when the victim is not present.

Larceny

Larceny is another name for theft. Some states distinguish between simple larceny and grand larceny. Grand larceny is usually defined as theft of valuables in excess of a certain set dollar amount, such as $200. Categorizing the crime by dollar amount can present unique problems, as during the high fiscal inflation periods of the 1970s, when legislatures found themselves unable to enact statutory revisions fast enough to keep pace with inflation.

Larceny, as defined by the UCR Program, includes thefts of any amount. The reports specifically list the following offenses as types of larceny:

- Shoplifting
- Pocket picking
- Purse snatching
- Thefts from motor vehicles
- Thefts of motor vehicle parts and accessories
- Bicycle thefts
- Thefts from coin-operated machines

Larceny The unlawful taking or attempted taking of property other than a motor vehicle from the possession of another, by stealth, without force and without deceit, with intent to permanently deprive the owner of the property. Larceny is the most common of the eight major offenses—although probably only a small percentage of all larcenies which occur are actually reported to the police because of the small dollar amounts involved.

Thefts of farm animals, or rustling, and thefts of most types of farm machinery also fall into the larceny category. In fact, larceny is such a broad category that it serves as a kind of "catch all" in the Uniform Crime Reports. Technically, reported thefts can involve amounts that range anywhere from pocket change to the stealing of a $100 million aircraft. Specifically excluded from the count of larceny for reporting purposes, however, are crimes of embezzlement, "con" games, forgery, and worthless checks. Larceny is thought of as a crime which requires physical possession of the item appropriated. Hence, most high-technology crimes, including thefts engineered through the use of computers or thefts of technology itself, are not scored as larcenies—unless electronic circuitry, disks, or machines themselves are actually stolen.

Reports to the police in 1992 showed 7,915,200 larcenies nationwide, with the total value of property stolen placed at $3.8 billion. The most common form of larceny in recent years has been theft of motor vehicle parts, accessories, and contents. The theft of tires, wheels, stereos, hubcaps, radar detectors, CB radios, cassette tapes, compact discs, and cellular phones account for many of the items reported stolen.

Larceny is the most frequent major crime according to the UCRs. It may also be the UCR's most underreported crime category, because small thefts rarely come to the attention of the police. The average value of items reported stolen in 1992 was about $480.

Motor Vehicle Theft The unlawful taking or attempted taking, of a self-propelled road vehicle owned by another, with the intent to deprive him or her of it permanently or temporarily. The stealing of trains, plains, boats, snowmobiles, and farm machinery is classified as larceny under the UCR reporting program, *not* as motor vehicle theft.

Motor Vehicle Theft

The UCR Program defines motor vehicles as self-propelled vehicles which run on the ground and not on rails. Included in the definition are automobiles, motorcycles, trucks, buses, and some farm machinery. Excluded are trains, airplanes, ships, boats, and spacecraft—whose theft would be scored as larceny. Vehicles that are temporarily taken by individuals who have lawful access to them are not scored as thefts. Hence, spouses who jointly own most property may drive the family car, even though one spouse may think of the vehicle as their exclusive personal property.

As mentioned earlier, motor vehicle theft is a crime in which most occurrences are reported to law enforcement agencies. Insurance companies require police reports before they will reimburse car owners for their losses. Some reports of motor vehicle thefts, however, may be false. People who have damaged their own vehicles in solitary crashes, or who have been unable to sell them, may try to force insurance companies to "buy" them through reports of theft.

In 1992 more than 1.6 million motor vehicles were reported stolen. The average value per vehicle stolen was $4,713, making motor vehicle theft a $7.6 billion crime. The clearance rate for motor vehicle theft was only 14% in 1992. City agencies reported the lowest rates of clearance (13%), while rural counties had the highest rate (32%). Many stolen vehicles are routinely and quickly disassembled, with parts being resold through chop shops. Auto parts are, of course, much more difficult to identify and trace than are intact vehicles. In some parts of the country, chop shops operate like big business, and one shop may strip a dozen or more cars per day.

Motor vehicle theft can turn violent in cases of "carjacking"—a crime in which offenders force the occupants of a car onto the street before stealing the vehicle. In an incident that brought carjacking to national prominence, Pamela Basu of Savage, Maryland, was dragged 2 miles to her death when she became entangled in her seat belt after being pushed

Fear of crime is pervasive in America. Here a purse snatcher finds a new target as the camera looks on. *Photo: Marc Anderson.*

from her car as the carjackers drove off. The thieves had to sideswipe a chain-link fence in order to finally dislodge her. Her 2-year-old daughter, still strapped into her carseat was apparently later tossed from the vehicle. The FBI estimates that carjackings account for slightly more than 1% of all motor vehicle thefts.[28]

Arrest reports for motor vehicle theft show that the typical offender is a young male. Sixty-two percent of all arrestees in 1990 were under the age of 21, and 90% were male.

Arson

The crime of arson exists in a kind of statistical limbo. In 1979 Congress ordered that it be added as an eighth Index offense. To date, however, the UCR Program has been unable to integrate statistics on arson successfully into the yearly Crime Index. The problem is twofold: (1) many law enforcement agencies have not yet begun making regular reports to the FBI on arson offenses which come under their jurisdiction, and (2) any change in the number of index offenses produces a Crime Index which will not permit meaningful comparisons to earlier crime data. The Crime Index is a composite offense rate which provides for useful comparisons over time and between jurisdictions, so long as it retains definitional consistency. Adding a new offense to the Index, or substantially changing the definition of any of its categories, still provides a measure of "crime," but it changes the meaning of the term.

The UCR Program received crime reports from 16,314 law enforcement agencies in 1992.[29] Of these, only 9,054 submitted arson reports for all 12 months of the year. Few agencies provided complete data as to the type of arson (nature of the item burned), the estimated monetary value of the property damaged, ownership of the property, and so on.

Some of these difficulties may soon be resolved through the Special Arson Program, authorized by Congress in 1982. The FBI, in conjunction with the National Fire Data Center, now operates a Special Arson Reporting System which focuses upon fire departments across the nation. The Arson Reporting system is designed to provide data which will supplement the yearly UCRs.[30]

Current arson data include only those fires which, through investigation, are determined to have been willfully or maliciously set. Fires of unknown or suspicious origin are excluded from arson statistics.[31]

The intentional and unlawful burning of structures (houses, storage buildings, manufacturing facilities, etc.), was the type of arson most often reported in 1992 (46,615 instances). The arson of vehicles was the second most common category, with 22,976 such burnings reported. The average dollar loss per instance of arson in 1992 was $16,649, and total property damage was placed at over $1 billion.[32] As with most property crimes, the clearance rate for arson was low—only 15% nationally.

Part II Offenses

The Uniform Crime Reports also include information on what the FBI calls Part II offenses. Part II offenses are generally less serious than those that make up the Crime Index, and include a number of victimless crimes. The statistics on Part II offenses are for recorded arrests, not crimes reported to the police. The logic inherent in this form of scoring is that most Part II offenses would never come to the attention of the police were it not for arrests. Included in the Part II category are the crimes shown in Table 2–2 with the number of arrests reported in each category for 1992.

Part II arrests are counted each time a person is taken into custody. As a result, the statistics in Table 2–2 do not measure the number of persons arrested, but rather the number of arrests made. Some persons were arrested more than once.

Arson The unlawful, willful, or malicious burning or attempted burning of property with or without intent to defraud. Some instances of arson are the result of malicious mischief, while others involve attempts to claim insurance moneys. Still others are committed in an effort to disguise other crimes, such as murder, burglary, and larceny.

PROPOSED CHANGES IN THE UCR

Changes are coming in the Uniform Crime Reports. From 1985 to 1992 the UCR Program was comprehensively evaluated under federal contract by ABT Associates, Inc., of Cambridge, Massachusetts. The final report of the UCR study group, entitled *A Blueprint for the Future of the Uniform Crime Reporting System,* recommended a number of sweeping changes. Among them are

- Each category of offense should clearly distinguish statistics on attempts versus actual commissions.
- The rape category should be broadened to include all forcible sex offenses. Sexual battery, sodomy, and oral copulation—accomplished though the use of force—should be counted.
- The "hierarchy rule" should be modified so as to count the most serious offense for each individual victim during an incident.[33]
- Crimes against individuals, households, and businesses should be more clearly distinguished in most categories.
- Aggravated assault should be more clearly defined in terms of the weapons used and the degree of injury suffered.

TABLE 2-2
UCR PART II OFFENSES, 1992

Offense Category	Number of Arrests
Simple assault	912,517
Forgery and counterfeiting	88,649
Fraud	346,314
Embezzlement	11,707
Stolen property (receiving, etc.)	136,765
Vandalism	262,477
Weapons (carrying, etc.)	204,116
Prostitution and related offenses	86,988
Sex offenses (statutory rape, etc.)	91,560
Drug law violations	920,424
Gambling	15,029
Offenses against the family (nonsupport, etc.)	84,328
Driving under the influence	1,319,583
Liquor law violations	442,985
Public drunkenness	664,236
Disorderly conduct	605,367
Vagrancy	29,004
Curfew/loitering	74,619
Runaways	146,170
All other violations of state and local laws (except traffic law violations)	2,954,440
Total	9,397,278

Source: Federal Bureau of Investigation, *Uniform Crime Reports for the United States, 1992* (Washington, D.C.: U.S. Government Printing Office, 1993).

- A code of professional standards should be developed for reporting agencies and for the system as a whole.
- The UCR should be modified so as to permit easier and more meaningful comparisons with the National Crime Victimization Survey and with Offender-Based Transaction Statistics (OBTS).

A pilot study to test some of these recommendations, and to integrate computerized scoring and reporting more fully into the UCR Program, was initiated in 1987 by the South Carolina Law Enforcement Division (SLED). Following the SLED pilot program, law enforcement experts from around the country met to discuss the results. They recommended[34] (1) establishment of a new incident-driven national crime reporting system, (2) FBI management of the new program, and (3) the creation of an advisory policy board composed of law enforcement executives to assist in implementation of the new program.

Whereas the original UCR system was "summary based," the new "enhanced" Uniform Crime Reports, to be called the National Incident-Based Reporting System, or NIBRS, will be incident driven. The old system depended upon statistical tabulations of crime data which were often little more than frequency counts. Under the new system many details will be gathered about each criminal incident. Included among them will be information on place of occurrence, weapon used, type and value of property damaged or stolen, the personal characteristics of the offender and the victim, the nature of any relationship between the two, nature of the disposition of the complaint, and so on. The new reporting system will replace the old Part I and Part II offenses with 22 general offenses, to include arson, assault, bribery, burglary, counterfeiting, vandalism, narcotic offenses, embezzlement, extortion, fraud, gambling, homicide, kidnapping, larceny, motor vehicle theft, pornography, prostitution, robbery, forcible sex offenses, nonforcible sex offenses, receiving stolen property, and weapons violations. Other offenses on which data will be gathered are bad checks, vagrancy, disorderly conduct, driving under the influence, drunkenness,

Young black males are more likely to be victims of violent crime than are members of any other group. Here a shooting victim receives paramedic services. *Photo: P. Chauvel/Sygma.*

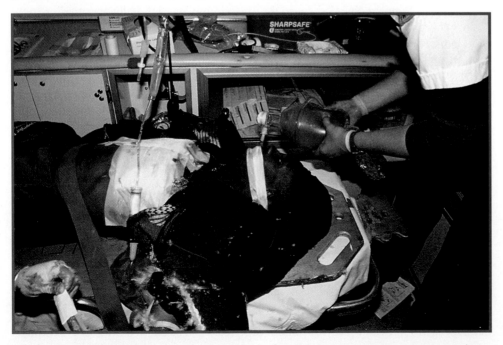

nonviolent family offenses, liquor law violations, "peeping Tom"-activity, runaway, trespass, and a general category of all "other" criminal law violations. The FBI began accepting crime data in the NIBRS format in January 1989. The system is intended to be fully in place by 1999.

The 1990 Crime Awareness and Campus Security Act, which required college campuses to commence publishing annual "security reports" beginning in September 1992, has the potential to additionally affect crime rates reported through the UCR Program. Although campuses are not required by the law to share crime data with the FBI, it is expected that many will—increasing the reported incidence of a variety of offenses.

Hate Crimes Criminal offenses in which there is evidence of prejudice based on race, religion, sexual orientation, or ethnicity.

A final change in reporting practices will no doubt follow from the Hate Crime Statistics Act, signed into law by President Bush in April 1990. The act mandates a statistical tally of "hate crimes," and data collection under the law began in January 1991, Hate crimes are defined by the law as offenses in which there is "evidence of prejudice based on race, religion, sexual orientation, or ethnicity."

In 1991 police agencies reported a total of 4,755 hate crime incidents, including 12 murders, across the country. Sixty-five percent of reported incidents were committed by whites, 30% by blacks and 2% by persons of other races. The remainder were committed by groups of mixed race.[35]

THE NATIONAL CRIME VICTIMIZATION SURVEY

A second major source of statistical data about crime in the United States is the National Crime Victimization Survey (NCVS), which uses victim self-reports in place of crimes reported to the police. The NCVS began operation in 1972 and built upon earlier efforts by both the National Opinion Research Center and the President's Commission on Law Enforcement and the Administration of Justice in the late 1960s.

Early data from the NCVS changed the way criminologists thought about crime in the United States. The use of victim self-reports led to the discovery that crime of all types was more prevalent than the UCR statistics indicated. Many cities were shown to have victimization rates more than twice the rate of reported offenses. Others, such as St. Louis, Missouri, and Newark, New Jersey, were found to have rates of victimization which very nearly approximated reported crime. New York, often thought of as a "high-crime" city, was discovered to have one of the lowest rates of self-reported victimization.

National Crime Victimization Survey data are gathered by the Bureau of Justice Statistics through a cooperative arrangement with the U.S. Census Bureau.[36] NCVS interviewers work with a national sample of about 42,000 households which are interviewed twice each year. Household lists are completely revised at the end of every three-year period. BJS statistics are published as research briefs called "Crime and the Nation's Households" and "Criminal Victimization" and annual reports entitled *Criminal Victimization in the United States.*

Crimes covered by the NCVS include rape, robbery, assault, burglary, personal and household larceny, and motor vehicle theft. Not included are murder, kidnapping, and victimless crimes. Commercial robbery and the burglary of businesses were dropped from NCVS reports in 1977. Definitions of crime categories are generally similar to those used by the UCR Program. The NCVS employs a hierarchical counting system similar to that of the UCR: It counts only the most "serious" incident in any series of criminal events perpetrated against the same individual. Both completed and attempted offenses are counted, although only persons 12 years of age and older are included in household surveys. Highlights of the NCVS statistics for the early 1990s revealed that[37]

- Approximately 23 million American households per year were touched by crime—or 25% of all households.
- Nearly 35 million victimizations were reported to the NCVS per year.
- City residents were about twice as likely as rural residents to be victims of crime.
- About half of all violent crimes, two-fifths of all household crimes, and slightly more than one-fourth of all crimes of personal theft were reported to police.[38]
- The total "personal cost" of crime to victims was about $13 billion per year for the United States as a whole.
- Victims of crime are more often men than women.
- Younger people are more likely than the elderly to be victims of crime.
- Blacks are more likely than whites or members of other racial groups to be victims of violent crimes.[39]
- Violent victimization rates are higher among people in lower-income families.
- Young males have the highest violent victimization rates; elderly females have the lowest.
- The chance of violent criminal victimization was much higher for young black males than for any other segment of the population. (The life chances of murder ran from a high of 1 in 21 for a black male to a low of 1 in 369 for a white female.)[40]

A comparison of NCVS and UCR data for the year 1992 can be found in Table 2–3.

TABLE 2 - 3
A COMPARISON OF UCR AND NCVS DATA, 1992

Offense	UCR Number	NCVS[1] Number
Violent Crime		
Homicide[2]	23,760	—
Rape	109,060	149,000
Robbery	672,480	998,000
Assault	1,126,970	3,975,000
Property Crime		
Burglary	2,979,900	4,116,000
Larceny	7,915,200	15,343,000
Motor vehicle theft	1,610,800	1,947,000
Arson[3]	86,547	—

[1] NCVS data covers "households touched by crime," not absolute numbers of crime occurrences. More than one victimization may occur per household, but only the number of households in which victimizations occur enter the tabulations.

[2] Homicide statistics are not maintained by the NCVS.

[3] Arson data are incomplete in the UCR and not reported by NCVS.

Sources: Compiled from the U.S. Department of Justice, *Crime in the Nation's Households 1992* (Washington, D.C.: Bureau of Justice Statistics, 1993), and Federal Bureau of Investigation, *Crime in the United States 1992* (Washington, D.C.: U.S. Government Printing Office, 1993).

PROBLEMS WITH THE NCVS

The tendency among researchers today seems to be to accept NCVS data in preference to that of the UCR. The National Crime Victimization Survey, however, is not without its problems. Primary among them is the potential for false or exaggerated reports. False reports may be generated by overzealous interviewers or self-aggrandizing respondents and are difficult to filter out. There are no reliable estimates as to the proportion of such responses which make up NCVS totals. Unintentional inaccuracies create other problems. Respondents may suffer from faulty memories, they may misinterpret events, and they may ascribe criminal intent to accidents and mistakes. Likewise, the lapse of time between the event itself and the conduct of the interview may cause some crimes to be forgotten and others to be inaccurately reported.

COMING CHANGES IN THE NCVS

Just as the Uniform Crime Reports are undergoing change, so too is the National Crime Victimization Survey. In 1986 the Bureau of Justice Statistics implemented the first phase in a massive overhaul of the NCVS.[41] With that implementation, the NCVS began to gather information in three new areas:[42]

1. Victim's perceptions of drug and alcohol use by violent offenders
2. Protective actions taken by victims and bystanders
3. The response of the police and other criminal justice agencies to reported crimes

The most recent NCVS household survey data indicate that 33% of victims of violent crimes believed their assailants to be under the influence of drugs or alcohol. In cases of rape, the proportion of assailants believed under the influenced jumped to 45%, the highest reported by the survey.

71% of violent crime victims reported taking some self-protective measure. Self-protective measures included struggling or fighting with the assailant, threats, running away, efforts at appeasement, or pleading. 60% of victims who took self-protective measures reported that their actions reduced the severity of their victimization.

Justice agency response, as measured by the survey, shows that the police came to see the victim in 70% of violent crimes, 68% of household crimes (such as burglary and motor vehicle theft), and 51% of all larcenies. Police response was fastest in violent crimes, averaging under 10 minutes, and slowest where household crimes were involved.

Plans for additional changes in the NCVS are in the works. A new survey form which will require the gradual retraining of interviewers is being developed.[43] The new form will (1) utilize questions designed to prod victim's memories, (2) reduce complexity in terminology, and (3) include questions dealing with ecological factors, victim characteristics, lifestyle, and protective or preventive measures undertaken by all victims. Victimizations will be classified according to various life "domains," such as work or leisure, in which they occur. The new form was implemented in July 1991.[44] Finalized data from the new NCVS survey instrument are now becoming available.

COMPARIONS OF THE UCR AND NCVS

Table 2–4 summarizes the differences between the UCR and the NCVS. Both provide estimates of crime in America. Both are limited by the type of crimes they choose to measure,

by those they exclude from measurement, and by the methods they use to gather crime data. Figure 2–5 provides a graphical representation of the differences in data gathered by the UCR and the NCVS.

Crime statistics from the UCR and NCVS are often used in building explanations of crime. Unfortunately, however, researchers too often forget that descriptive statistics can be weak in explanatory power. For example, NCVS data show that "household crime rates" are highest for households (1) headed by blacks, (2) headed by younger people, (3) with six or more members, (4) headed by renters, and (5) in central cities.[45] Such findings, combined with statistics which show that most crime occurs among members of the same race, have led some researches to conclude that values among black subcultural group members propel them into crime and make them targets of criminal victimization. Annual rates of victimization, by race, for both violent and property crimes are shown in Figure 2–6. The truth may be, however, that crime is more a function of geography (inner-city location) than of culture. The next chapter examines explanations for crime, some of which began as attempts to explain the statistics we have examined in this chapter.

TABLE 2 - 4

HOW DO THE UCR AND NCVS COMPARE?

	Uniform Crime Reports	National Crime Victimization Survey
Offenses measured	Homicide Rape Robbery (personal and commercial) Assault (aggravated) Burglary (commercial and household) Larceny (commercial and household) Motor vehicle theft Arson	Rape Robbery (personal) Assault (aggravated and simple) Household burglary Larceny (personal and household) Motor vehicle theft
Scope	Crimes reported to the police in most jurisdictions; considerable flexibility	Crimes both reported and not reported to police; all data are available for a few large geographic areas
Collection method	Police department reports to FBI or to centralized state agencies that then report to FBI	Survey interviews; periodically measures the total number of crimes committed by asking a national sample of 49,000 households encompassing 101,000 persons age 12 and over about their experiences as victims of crime during a specified period
Kinds of information	In addition to offense counts, provides information on crime clearances, persons arrested, persons charged, law enforcement officers killed and assaulted, and characteristics of homicide victims	Provides details about victims (such as age, race, sex, education, income, and whether the victim and offender were related to each other) and about crimes (such as time and place of occurrence, whether or not reported to police, use of weapons, occurrence of injury, and economic consequences)
Sponsor	Department of Justice Federal Bureau of Investigation	Department of Justice Bureau of Justice Statistics

Source: Bureau of Justice Statistics, *Report to the Nation on Crime and Justice*, 2nd ed. (Washington, D.C.: U.S. Department of Justice, 1988), p. 11.

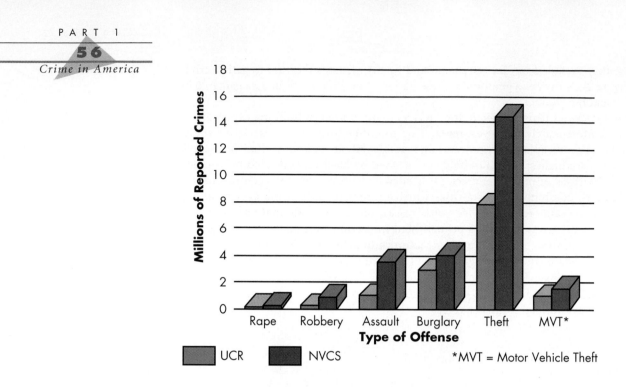

FIGURE 2–5   Comparison of UCR and NCVS data, 1992. *Sources:* U.S. Department of Justice, *Crime in the Nation's Households 1992* (Washington, D.C.: Bureau of Justice Statistics, 1993), and Federal Bureau of Investigation, *Crime in the United States 1992* (Washington, D.C.: U.S. Government Printing Office, 1993).

E MERGING PATTERNS

Planned revisions in both the National Crime Victimization Survey and the Uniform Crime Reports reflect the fact that patterns of criminal activity in the United States are changing. Georgette Bennett has termed the shift in crime patterns crimewarps.[46] Crimewarps, says Bennett, represent major changes in both what society considers criminal and in who future criminal offenders will be. Some areas of coming change that she predicts are:[47]

- The decline of street crime
- The growth of white-collar crime
- Increasing female involvement in crime
- Increased crime commission among the elderly
- A shift in high crime rates from the "Frost Belt" to the "Sun Belt"
- Safer cities, with increasing criminal activity in rural areas
- The growth of high-technology crimes

T HE   FEAR   OF   CRIME

The decline in traditional violent street crimes predicted by Bennett, should it materialize, will not automatically lead to a reduction in the fear of crime felt by many. As Bennett

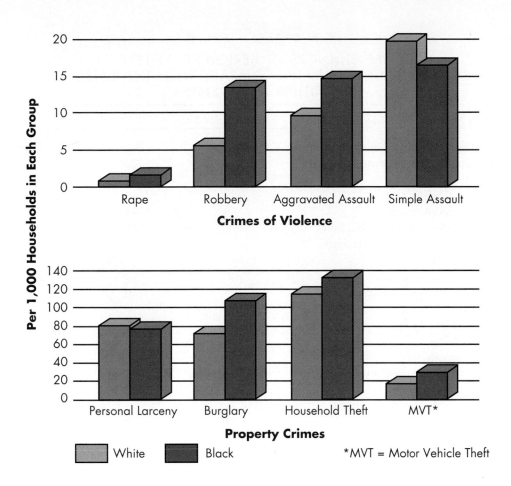

FIGURE 2–6   Annual victimization rates by race of victim and types of offense. *Source:* Bureau of Justice Statistics, *Black Victims* (Washington, D.C.: U.S. Department of Justice, 1990), p. 2.

recognizes[48] the fear of crime is often out of proportion to the likelihood of criminal victimization. Table 2–5 shows the chance of violent victimization compared to life chances of other serious events. For most people, the chance of accidental injury at work or at home is far greater than the chance of being criminally attacked.

The Bureau of Justice Statistics points out that "the fear of crime affects many people, including some who have never been victims of crime."[49] Sources of fear are diverse. Some flow from personal experience with victimization, but most people fear crime because of dramatizations of criminal activity on television and in movies, and because of frequent newspaper and media reports of crime. Feelings of vulnerability may result from learning that a friend has been victimized, or from hearing that a neighbor's home has been burglarized.

A recent survey of American voters, *The 1994 Battleground Survey,*[50] found that crime topped the list of citizens' concerns. In the words of the pollsters, "Americans say crime is the No. 1 problem facing the country today…" Crime was reported to be the respondents "top concern" by 26% of all those participating in the survey—easily outdistancing reported concerns over the economy (9%), jobs (7%), unemployment (7%), and drugs (6%). Interestingly, respondents to *The 1994 Battleground Survey,* which

TABLE 2 - 5

LIFE CHANCES OF SERIOUS EVENTS[1]
HOW DO CRIME RATES COMPARE WITH THE RATES
OF OTHER LIFE EVENTS?

Events	Rate per 1,000 Adults Per Year[2]
Accidental injury, all circumstances	242
Accidental injury at home	79
Personal theft	72
Accidental injury at work	58
Violent victimization	31
Assault (aggravated and simple)	24
Injury in motor vehicle accident	17
Death, all causes	11
Victimization with injury	10
Serious (aggravated) assault	9
Robbery	6
Heart disease death	4
Cancer death	2
Rape (women only)	2
Accidental death, all circumstances	0.5
Pneumonia/influenza death	0.3
Motor vehicle accidental death	0.2
Suicide	0.2
Injury from fire	0.1
Homicide/legal intervention death	0.1
Death from fire	0.03

[1] These rates approximate your chances of becoming a victim of these events. More precise estimates can be derived by taking account of such factors as your age, sex, race, place of residence, and life-style. Findings are based on 1982–1984 data, but there is little variation in rates from year to year.

[2] These rates exclude children from the calculations (those under age 12–17, depending on the series). Fire injury/death data are based on the total population, because no age-specific data are available in this series.

From: *Current Estimates from the National Health Interview Survey: United States, 1982*, National Center for Health Statistics; "Advance Report of Final Mortality Statistics, 1983." *Monthly Vital Statistics Report*, National Center for Health Statistics; *Estimates of the Population of the United States, by Age, Sex, and Race: 1980 to 1984*. U.S. Bureau of the Census; *The 1984 Fire Almanac*, National Fire Protection Association; and "Criminal Victimization 1984," *BJS Bulletin*, October 1985.

Source: Bureau of Justice Statistics, *Report to the Nation on Crime and Justice*, 2nd ed. (Washington, D.C.: U.S. Department of Justice, 1988), p. 24.

attempts to identify "hot" political issues, appeared to separate drug-related crimes from the threat of more personal crimes such as murder, rape and robbery. An independent *Washington Post* poll, conducted shortly after the Battleground Survey confirmed the survey's findings, showing that 21% of Americans were more concerned about crime than about any other issue.[51]

Interestingly, the groups at highest risk of becoming crime victims are not the ones who experience the greatest fear of crime. The elderly and women report the greatest fear of victimization, even though they are among the lowest risk groups for violent crimes. Young males, on the other hand, who stand the greatest statistical risk of victimization, often report feeling the least fear.[52] Similarly, although most people most fear violent victimization by a stranger, many such crimes are committed by non-strangers or by people known to victims by sight.

WOMEN AND CRIME

Women Victims

Women are victimized far less frequently than are men in every major crime category other than rape.[53] When women are victimized, however, they are more likely than men to be injured.[54] Even though experiencing lower rates of victimization, it is realistic to acknowledge that a larger proportion of women than men make modifications in the way they live because of the threat of crime.[55] Women, especially those living in cities, are increasingly careful about where they travel and the time of day they leave their homes—particularly if unaccompanied—and are wary of unfamiliar males in a diversity of settings.

The popular media, special interest groups, and even the government have contributed to a certain degree of confusion about women's victimization. Very real concerns reflected in movies, television programs, and newspaper editorial pages have properly identified date rape, familial incest, spouse abuse, and the exploitation of women through social order offenses such as prostitution and pornography, as major issues facing American society today. Testimony before Congress[56] has tagged domestic violence as the largest cause of injury to American women, and former Surgeon General Everett Koop identified violence against women by their partners as the number one health problem facing women in America today.

When the data on women's victimization are examined closely, however, a slightly different pattern emerges. The Bureau of Justice Statistics,[57] in a detailed analysis of female victims of violent crime, found that about twice as many women who are victims of violent crimes are likely to be victimized by strangers than by people whom they know. However, when women do fall victim to violent crime, they are far more likely to be victimized by individuals with whom they are (or have been) in intimate relationships than are men. When the perpetrators are known to them, women are most likely to be violently victimized by ex-spouses, boyfriends, and spouses, respectively. The BJS study also found that separated or divorced women are 6 times more likely to be victims of violent crime than widows, 4-1/2 times more likely than married women, and 3 times more likely than widowers and married men. Other findings indicated that (1) women living in central-city areas are considerably more likely to be victimized than women residing in the suburbs; (2) suburban women, in turn, are more likely to be victimized than women living in rural areas; (3) women from low-income families experience the highest amount of violent crime; (4) the victimization of women falls as family income rises; (5) unemployed women, female students, and those in the armed forces, are the most likely of all women to experience violent victimization; (6) black women are victims of violent crimes more frequently than are women of any other race; (7) Hispanic women find themselves victimized more frequently than white women; and (8) women in the age range 20–24 are most at risk for violent victimization, while those aged 16–19 comprise the second most likely group of victims.

These findings show that greater emphasis needs to be placed on alleviating the social conditions that victimize women. Suggestions already under consideration call for expansion in the number of federal and state laws designed to control domestic violence, a broadening of the federal Family Violence Prevention and Services Act, federal help in setting up state advocacy offices for battered women, increased funding for bat-

tered women's shelters, and additional moneys for prosecutors and courts to develop spouse abuse units. In an insightful article built around issues in criminal justice education, Nanci Koser Wilson[58] suggests a multifaceted role for women who are interested in improving the position of like-gender individuals in the criminal justice system. Aspects of the role include:

1. *Women lobbying for change in the criminal justice system.* Wilson points to the success which has met women who have worked to change rape laws, police procedure in domestic violence cases, and the recognition of the plight of battered women in cases of spousal homicide.
2. *Women creating help for women outside the system.* The creation of rape crisis centers, centers for battered women, and the like, all point to the possibility of women helping individuals of like-gender through noncriminal justice channels.
3. *Women working in movements outside traditional crime areas.* Ecofeminism, peace work, and other social movements have done much to enhance the status of women in general and may work in the long run to reduce some of the factors which result in the criminal victimization of women.
4. *Women producing research from a women's perspective.* Wilson points out that the tendency to dismiss the criminality of women because it is less frequent than that of males misses the opportunity to learn about crime in general via the model provided by women's criminality. Dismissing the criminality of women implies that the criminality of men is somehow "normal" and that other behavior patterns are less worthy of study. A gender-balanced approach to the study of crime, should have something to teach us all.

A domestic violence victim examines her bruises. According to sociologists, violence against women is perpetuated by social conditions which devalue females. *Photo: Donna Ferrato/Black Star.*

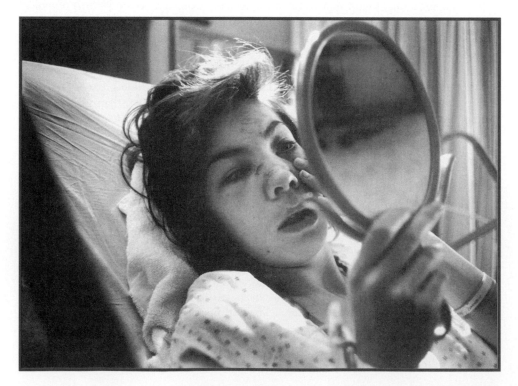

5. *Women working within the traditional criminal justice system in woman-defined ways.*
    Women who choose police work, or who work within correctional environments,
    have something to contribute to both professions by virtue of the unique perspec-
    tive they bring to their jobs. Because of potential benefits to the system and to them-
    selves, women should not be expected to automatically accept traditional masculin-
    ized understandings of criminal justice roles.

Women Offenders

On January 8, 1991, Aileen Carol Wuornos was arrested in Ocala, Florida, and charged
with the murder of a man who had apparently offered her a ride as she hitchhiked through
Florida.[59] The would-be Samaritan was shot, stripped of his clothing, and dumped on a
roadside, while Aileen and a female companion allegedly drove off in his car. Prosecutors
indicated that she would soon be indicted in as many as six other similar killings. Property
belonging to the seven victims—most of whom were robbed, killed, and left naked—was
found in a storage unit rented by Ms. Wuornos. One victim was a former police chief,
another a security guard. All were white, middle-aged men with blue-collar jobs who were
traveling alone. Each was killed with a small-caliber handgun.[60] If found guilty of all the
charges that are pending, Ms. Wuornos would become the first documented female serial
killer in decades.

Ms. Wuornos's alleged crimes, gruesome as they are, fall outside what we know of as
the pattern for female criminality. Although the popular media has sometimes portrayed
female criminals as similar to their male counterparts in motivation and behavior that
image is misleading. Similarly, the academic study of women's criminality has been fraught
with misconceptions.

One of the first writers to attempt a definitive explanation of the criminality of women
was Otto Pollak. Pollak's book, *The Criminality of Women,*[61] written in 1950, suggested
that women commit the same number of offenses as men—but that most of their criminality is hidden. Pollak claimed that women's roles (at the time, primarily those of home-
maker and mother) served to disguise the criminal undertakings of women. He also proposed that chivalrous treatment by a male-dominated justice system acted to bias every
stage of criminal justice processing in favor of women. Hence, according to Pollak,
although women are just as criminal as men, they are rarely arrested, tried, or imprisoned.
In fact, while the criminality of women may approach or exceed that of men in selected
offense categories, it is safe to say today that Pollak was incorrect in his assessment of the
degree of female criminality.

Contemporary statistics tell us that, although females comprise 51% of the population
of the United States, they are arrested for only 11% of all violent crimes and 24% of property crimes. The relatively small amount of reported female involvement in the FBI's eight
major crimes can be seen in Table 2–6. The number of women committing crime appears
to be increasing faster than the number of male offenders, however. Between 1980 and
1992 crimes committed by men grew by 90%, while crimes reported to have been committed by women increased 127%. Violent crimes by males increased 103% during the
period; by women 158%.[62] Property crimes perpetrated by men grew by 47%; by women
83%. Nonetheless, as the table shows, female offenders still account for only a small proportion of all reported crimes.

Statistics on the FBI's Part II offenses tell a somewhat different story. Arrests of women
for embezzlement, for example, increased by more than 200% between 1980 and 1992,
arrests of females for drug abuse grew by 221%, and liquor law violations by women
increased 123% (versus 71% for men).[63] Such statistics are difficult to interpret, however,
since reports of female involvement in crime may reflect more the growing equality

T A B L E   2 - 6

MALE/FEMALE INVOLVEMENT IN CRIME:
OFFENSE PATTERNS DIFFER

UCR Index Crimes	Percentage of All Arrests		Gender Differences
	Males	Females	
Murder and nonnegligent manslaughter	90.3%	9.7%	Men are more likely than women to be arrested for more serious crimes, such as murder, rape, robbery, or burglary
Rape	98.7	1.3	
Robbery	91.5	8.5	
Aggravated assault	85.2	14.8	
Burglary	90.8	9.2	Arrest, jail, and prison data all suggest that a higher proportion of women than of men who commit crimes are involved in property crimes, such as larceny, forgery, fraud, and embezzlement, and in drug offenses.
Larceny-theft	67.9	32.1	
Motor vehicle theft	89.2	10.8	
Arson	86.6	13.4	

Source: Federal Bureau of Investigation, *Crime in the United States, 1992* (Washington, D.C.: U.S. Government Printing Office, 1993).

accorded women in contemporary society than they do actual increases in criminal activity. In the past, when women committed crimes, they have been dealt with less officiously than is likely to be the case today. In only two officially reported categories—prostitution and runaways—do women outnumber men in the volume of offenses committed.[64] Other crimes in which significant numbers of women (relative to men) are involved include larceny-theft (where 32% of reported crimes are committed by women), forgery and counterfeiting (35%), fraud (42%), and embezzlement (42%).

These statistics dispel the myth that the female criminal has taken her place alongside male offenders—at least in terms of the absolute number of crimes committed. During the 1970s a number of writers had, in fact, suggested that as women achieve social equality, female criminality would emulate what had previously been male crime patterns. Two influential thinkers of the period were Rita Simon, who wrote *Women and Crime*,[65] and Freda Adler, author of *Sisters in Crime*.[66] Both books were published in 1975. Adler's work, subtitled *The Rise of the New Female Criminal*, suggested that, as women entered "nontraditional occupations," there "would be a movement toward parity with men in the commission of crime in terms of both incidence and type."[67] However, Darrell Steffensmeir[68] who studied changes in women's criminality over a 12-year period following the publication of Simon's and Adler's works, found almost no evidence to support the belief that gender differences in criminality are disappearing. Hence, although the criminality of women is changing, as evidenced by growing female involvement in a variety of offenses, "there is little to support the theory of a new female criminal."[69]

One reason why the changes foreseen by Adler and Simon have not occurred may be that the majority of women involved in the commission of crimes have not benefited substantially from women's movements, which have tended to increase opportunities primarily for middle-class women. Most incarcerated women, and many women who are charged

Crimes by women appear to be on the increase. Pamela Smart, dubbed the Ice Princess by the press, is shown here offering testimony in her 1991 murder trial. She was later convicted of plotting to have her husband killed by her teenage lover. *Photo: Evan Richman/Reuters/Bettmann.*

with male-dominated violent and property crimes come from the lower social classes. If equal rates of crime commission are to occur, based upon the predictive formula of Simon and Adler, they would most likely be seen first among women who stand most to benefit immediately from the women's movement of recent years—those of the upper middle class.

THE ECONOMIC COST OF CRIME

The Bureau of Justice Statistics estimates the personal cost of crime (direct dollar losses to individuals) at around $13 billion per year.[70] Robberies, burglaries, and larceny-thefts account for approximately $6 billion in losses per year. Not included in the Bureau's figures are the costs to crime victims of lost work, needed medical care, and the expense of new security measures they may implement. Lost work time was reported in 12% of aggravated assaults and 17% of rapes in 1991. A significant shortcoming of the BJS estimates is that they involve only dollar amounts and give no real picture of personal trauma, psychological disabilities resulting from victimization, and individual suffering caused by crime.

A more encompassing estimate is offered by the journal *Health Affairs*, which, in 1994, placed the economic cost of violent crime at $202 billion annually. This huge figure includes the costs of medical and psychological treatment services, as well as health costs associated with the lost quality of life suffered by crime victims.

The economic impact of crime is different for different groups. In 1991, for example, households reporting an annual family income of less than $7,500 suffered from twice the rate of burglary as did households reporting incomes over $50,000. In fact, as family income rose, the rate of reported burglaries steadily declined. The opposite was true of auto theft, where rates of auto vehicle theft rose in direct proportion to household income—and were three times greater for families in the highest income categories than for those in the lowest.[71]

The commercial costs of crime are substantial as well. Losses from commercial robberies (including bank robberies) and business burglaries have been put at $1.2 billion per year.[72] Frauds perpetrated against financial institutions in 1991 numbered 8,678 discovered cases with an associated dollar loss of nearly $2.3 billion.[73] The cost to businesses of white-collar crime are not known, but are thought to be substantial. To guard against crimes by employees and members of the public, private businesses spend in excess of $21 billion per year for alarms, surveillance, and private security operations.[74]

Costs to the government for the apprehension, prosecution, and disposition of offenders, including crime prevention efforts by the police, far outstrip the known dollar losses to all criminal enterprises other than drugs. Federal criminal justice expenditures in 1990 were estimated to be in excess of $10 billion,[75] while federal, state, and local expenditures totaled over $74 billion.[76] Nonetheless, government spending on criminal justice services amounts to only about 5% of all governmental expenditures. State and local governments absorb most of the costs of criminal justice–related activity.

DRUGS AND CRIME

Drugs and crime are often found together. Drug law violations are themselves criminal, but more and more studies are linking drug abuse to other serious crimes. A study by the Rand Corporation found that most of the "violent predators" among prisoners had extensive histories of heroin abuse, often in combination with alcohol and other drugs.[77] Some cities report that a large percentage of their homicides are drug related.[78] Many property crimes are committed to sustain "habits," and the numbers of both violent and property crimes committed by drug users have been shown to be directly related to the level at which they use drugs.[79] Substance abuse may well be the most expensive of all crimes. The social cost of drug abuse has been estimated at nearly $60 billion per year, with half of that amount being in lost job productivity.[80] Drunk driving alone is thought to cost over $13 billion in property losses and medical expenses yearly.[81] Chapter 15 will examine the drug–crime link in considerable detail. Suffice it to say here that the link appears strong and shows few signs of abating.

THE ELDERLY AND CRIME

UCR statistics define "older offenders" as those over 55 years of age. Relative to other age groups, older offenders rarely appear in the crime statistics. Criminality seems to decline with age, suggesting that a burn out factor applies to criminal behavior as it does to many other areas of life. In 1992 persons aged 65 and over accounted for less than 1% of all arrests.[82]

The type and number of crimes committed by older people, however, appear to be changing. According to the UCR, arrests of the elderly for serious crimes nearly doubled between 1975 and 1992, while arrests in the same age category for minor crimes tended to remain about the same.[83] Overall, arrests of persons 65 and older declined by about 10% during the period, while fraud arrests jumped nearly 400%.[84] When elderly people are sent to prison it is usually for violent crimes, while violent crimes account for far less than 50% of prison admissions among younger people. The population of prisoners aged 55 and over has steadily increased, having risen from 13,800 inmates nationally in mid-1988 to 20,500 by mid-1992, an increase of more than 48%.[85]

THE HIGH COST OF CRIME:
MURDER *v.* TOURISM IN FLORIDA

In fall 1993 Florida state officials struggled to deal with a growing problem: Tourists to the "Sunshine State" were canceling their reservations and staying home in droves following the robbery-related killings of a number of foreign visitors. Most of the murders occurred in the Miami area.

Although the killings of foreigners began early in the year (47-year-old Venezuelan diplomat Jesus Alberto Delgardo was shot outside a friend's home while being robbed in Miami on January 26, 1993), in September media attention focused on a spate of violence which left at least nine foreign tourists dead in less than a year. The media's precipitating event was the killing of Barbara Meller-Jensen, 39, of Berlin, Germany, who was robbed, run over, and beaten to death in front of her mother and two young children when she took a wrong turn on a Miami expressway and ended up in a city slum. After that, the killings seemed to come in a rush. Uwe-Wilhelm Rakebrand, another German tourist, was driving a rental car in Miami on September 8, when it was rammed from behind by a van. Rakebrand, with his pregnant wife in the car, followed safety instructions given to him by the rental car company, and wouldn't stop. The van pulled alongside and one of its passengers pointed a gun, and fired once, killing the 33-year-old Rakebrand instantly. A few days later Gary Colley, 34, of Wilsden, England, was shot and killed when he tried to back away from robbers at a Tallahassee-area rest stop. His girlfriend, a passenger in the car, was wounded.

Following the killings, Florida Governor Lawton Chiles held a hasty meeting with reporters. "I'm so distressed," he said, "I don't know what to do." In response to the violence Miami-area rental car companies stripped vehicles of company identifiers and asked that the give-away "Y" and "Z" prefixes on rental cars license plates be removed. New multilingual road signs were erected, tourists were handed safety pamphlets at airports, car rental agencies and hotels, and police stepped up patrols and arrests at highway rest stops. Five hundred and forty auxiliary officers from Florida's Game and Fresh Water Fish Commission and Marine Patrol were called into service to secure the state's 48 interstate highway rest areas.

Even so, fearful tourists began staying home. European tabloids labeled the "Sunshine State" the "State of Terror," and the British newspaper *Independent* called Florida "the main danger area" in the United States. Indicative of media sentiment across Europe, the London *Times* ran a cartoon picturing a revolver with a trigger shaped like the state of Florida, and Britain's largest newspaper, the *Sun*, ran a headline advising Florida tourists to "Get Your Butts Outta Here." The image portrayed by the media was one of a state and a nation where crime, and guns, are out of control. In response, Governor Chiles canceled foreign advertising, fearing that it would provoke only further cynicism.

Even so, some questioned the flurry of activity surrounding the tourist killings. Carl Hiaasen, writing in *The Miami Herald*, claimed, "[r]obbers kill innocent people every day in Florida. A former high school classmate of mine was shot to death in an ATM and nobody mobilized the state police. Oprah didn't show up. *Nightline* didn't call. The governor didn't hold a single news conference." Why, he asked, make such a fuss about a handful of tourists?

But to the world and to the people of the state of Florida the reason was clear: tourism is Florida's number one industry. In 1992 40-1/2 million tourists visited the state, including 7 million foreigners. All told, they spent $31 billion on their Florida vacations. If even a small proportion of would-be future tourists avoid Florida, the state, already deeply hurt by recession, faces economic ruin.

While it remains to be seen whether Florida's tourism industry will ever fully recover, there can be little doubt but that the state is currently reeling from the still-deepening sense of fear associated with highly visible crimes there. Florida Network Tours, which caters to German tourists, used to schedule 60 to 80 tour groups a day. "Now," says Suely Auerbach of the tour agency, "we're down to almost nothing. Florida is completely, completely dead." State Commerce Secretary Greg Farmer agreed. "It's going to be just catastrophic," he said, "It could be in the billions." In the words of Karohs Reinhard of Seigburg, Germany, who was returning his car to the Alamo counter in Miami when he learned of Rakebrand's murder, "Such things are terrible. One crime destroys the impressions of this wonderful country."

Sources: "Violence Shoots Holes in USA's Tourist Image," *USA Today*, September 9, 1993, p. 2A; "Killing Casts Shadow over Sunshine State," *USA Today*, September 9, 1993, p. 1A; "Tourists Taking a Nap Wake in a Nightmare," *Fayetteville Observer-Times* (North Carolina), September 15, 1993, p. 1A; "Fear of Florida," *USA Today*, September 17–19, 1993, p. 1A; "Florida Image Takes a Beating," *USA Today*, September 15, 1993, p. 3A.

Some authors have interpreted these statistics to presage the growth of a "geriatric delinquent" population, freed by age and retirement from jobs and responsibilities. Such people, say these authors, may turn to crime as one way of averting boredom and adding a little spice to life.[86] Statistics on geriatric offenders, however, probably require a more cautious interpretation. They are based upon relatively small numbers, and to say that "serious crime among the elderly doubled" does not mean that a geriatric crime wave is upon us. The apparent increase in criminal activity among the elderly may be due to the fact that the older population in this country is growing substantially, with even greater increases expected over the next three decades. Advances in health care have increased life expectancy and have made the added years more productive than ever before. World War II "baby boomers" will be reaching their late middle years by the year 2000, and present trends in criminal involvement among the elderly can be expected to continue. Hence, it may not be that elderly individuals in this country are committing crimes more frequently than before, but rather that the greater number of elderly in the population make for a greater prevalence of crimes committed by the elderly in the official statistics.

The elderly are also victims of crime. Although persons aged 65 and older generally experience the lowest rate of victimization of any age group[87] some aspects of serious crime against older people are worth noting. Elderly violent crime victims are more likely than younger victims to face offenders armed with guns. They are more likely to be victimized by total strangers. They are more likely than younger victims to be victimized in or near their homes. The older the victim, the greater the likelihood of physical injury.[88] When victimized by violent crime elderly people are less likely to attempt to protect themselves and more apt to report their victimization to the police than are younger people.[89]

Elderly people are victimized disproportionately if they fall into certain categories. Relative to their numbers in the elderly population, black men are overrepresented as victims. Similarly, separated or divorced persons and urban residents have higher rates of victimization than do other elderly persons.[90] As observed earlier, older people live in greater fear of crime than do younger people, even though their risk of victimization is considerably less. Elderly people, however, are less likely to take crime preventive measures than are any other age group.[91] Only 6% of households headed by persons over the age of 65 have a burglar alarm and only 16% engrave their valuables (versus a 25% national average).[92]

HATE CRIMES

The American criminal justice system of the twenty-first century will be buffeted by the expanding power of politically-oriented endemic groups with radical agendas. Domestic terrorism in the 1960s and early 1970s required the expenditure of considerable criminal justice resources. The Weathermen, Students for a Democratic Society, the Symbionize Liberation Army, the Black Panthers, and other radical groups challenged the authority of federal and local governments. Bombings, kidnapings and shootouts peppered the national scene.

A number of signs tell us that domestic terrorism will soon be on the increase again. Overseas terrorists are making continued efforts to invade American population centers, and there are indicators that "sleeper agents" residing within the United States are poised to act on the command of distant authorities. The terrorist bombing attack on the World Trade Centers in 1993, which left four dead and a 100-foot hole through four subfloors of concrete, demonstrated just how vulnerable the United States is to such attacks.

Mark Kohut (adjusting his collar), and 18-year-old Jeffrey Pellett, shown here in a Palm Beach, Florida, courtroom, were convicted along with a third man (Charles Rourk) in 1993 of setting fire to Chris Wilson (bottom photo) in a racially-motivated hate crime. Kohut received a short one-year sentence after cooperating with authorities. Pellett and Rourk were both sentenced to life in prison. *Photos: Scott Wiseman/The Palm Beach Post and Sam Mircovich/SIPA.*

More worrisome still are underground survivalist groups with their own vision of a future America. Among them are the White Patriot Party; the Order; Aryan Nations; Posse Comitatus; the Covenant, the Sword, and the Arm of the Lord; the Ku Klux Klan; and umbrella organizations such as the Christian Conservative Church. Described variously as the "radical right," "neo-Nazis," "skinheads," "white supremacists," and "racial hate groups," indications are that these groups are organized, well financed, and extremely well armed. John R. Harrell, leader of the Christian Conservative Church, preaches that the nation is on the eve of destruction. According to some authorities, Christian patriots are exhorted to stand ready to seize control of the nation before leadership can fall into the "wrong hands."[93] Such extremist groups adhere to identity theology, a religion which claims that members of the white race are God's chosen people. Identity theology envisions an America ruled exclusively by white people under "God's law."[94]

Supremacist groups are already committing acts of terrorism. Members of the Order were convicted in the machine-gun slaying of Denver radio talkshow host Allen Berg who they claimed was a puppet of ZOG—the "Zionist Occupational Government."[95] Later testimony revealed that many others were targeted for murder, including Henry Kissinger, Norman Lear, David Rockefeller, and Morris Dees, director of the Southern Poverty Law Center.[96] Other Order members have been found guilty of the murder of highway patrol troopers, while one of the groups' leaders was killed in a shootout with the FBI.[97]

Just as Hitler's biography *Mein Kampf* served as a call to arms for Nazis in Europe during the 1930s, a novel called *The Turner Diaries* is now used by extremist groups to map their rise to power.[98] *The Turner Diaries* describes an Aryan revolution set in the 1990s in which Jews, blacks, and other minorities are removed from positions of influence in government and society.

In 1993, 8 men and women were arrested by the FBI and accused of plotting to start a race war in Los Angeles. The plot allegedly involved bombing the prominent 8,500-member First African Methodist Episcopal Church in South Central Los Angeles, spraying its members with machine-gun fire, and assassinating Rodney King. Other targets may have included the Reverend Al Sharpton in New York, Nation of Islam Minister Louis Farrakhan, officials of the NAACP, and members of the black rap group Public Enemy. News reports linked groups known as the Fourth Reich Skinheads, the Florida Church of the Creator, and the White Aryan Resistance.[99] Figure 2–7 shows the location of various white supremacist groups throughout the United States.

The American justice system of today is ill prepared to deal with the threat represented by supremacist and radical groups. Intelligence gathering efforts focused on such groups have largely failed. Military-style organization and training are characteristic of the groups that are known. The armaments at their disposal include weapons of mass destruction which the firepower and tactical mobility that law enforcement agencies could not hope to match.

In any event, certain activities of supremacist groups may be constitutionally protected. Recent authors[100] suggest that statutes intended to control hate crimes may run afoul of constitutional considerations insofar as they (1) are vague, (2) criminalize thought, (3) attempt to control free speech, and (4) deny equal protection of the laws to those who wish to express their biases. In fact, in the 1992 case of *R.A.V. v. City of St. Paul*,[101] which involved a burning cross on the front lawn of a black family, the U.S. Supreme Court struck down a city ordinance designed to prevent the bias-motivated display of symbols or objects, such as Nazi swastikas or burning crosses. In the same year, in the case of *Forsyth County, Ga. v. Nationalist Movement*,[102] the Court held that a county requirement regulating parades was unconstitutional because it regulated freedom of speech—in this case a

THEORY INTO PRACTICE

HATE CRIMES

In 1987 Glenn Miller, then-leader of the White Patriot Party in North Carolina, declared war on ZOG—the "Zionist Occupational Government"—a conspiratorial coalition that Miller and his followers believed held the true reins of power in the United States. What follows is a portion of that strongly worded original document—authentically reproduced here to include the misspellings and typographical errors found in the original. Not long after the declaration was issued, Miller was arrested and sent to prison for his part in various crimes against the government.

DECLARATION OF WAR

Dear White Patriots: *April 6, 1987*

All 5,000 White Patriots are now honor bound and duty bound to pick up the sword and do battle against the forces of evil. In the name of our Aryan God, thru His beloved son, I Glenn Miller now this 6th day of April 1987 do hereby declare total war. I ask for no quarter. I will give none. I declare war against Niggers, Jews, Queers, assorted Mongrels, White Race traitors and despicable informants. We White Patriots will now begin the Race War and it will spread gloriously thru-out the nation. We will cleanse the land of evil, corruption, and mongrels. And, we will build a glorious future and a nation in which all our People can scream proudly, and honestly, "This is our Land. This is our People. This is our God, and this we will defend." War is the only way now, brothers and sisters. ZOG has pointed the way for us. He has left us no other choice. And, so fellow Aryan Warriors strike now. Strike for your home land. Strike for your Southern honor. Strike for the little children. Strike for your wives and loved ones. Strike for sweet Mother Dixie. Strike for the 16 million innocent White babies murdered by Jew-legalized abortion and who cry out from their graves for vengeance. Strike for the millions of your People who have been raped, assaulted, and murdered by niggers and other mongrels. Strike in vengence against the Jews for all the millions of our Race slaughtered in Jew-Wars. Strike my brothers and sisters, strike, for all the outrages committed against our People...

For God, Race, Nation and Southern Honor

Glenn Miller, Leader White Patriot Party and Loyal member of "The Order"

"THE ORDER WILL LIVE SO LONG AS ONE OF US BREATHES"

plan by an affiliate of the Klu Klux Klan to parade in opposition to a Martin Luther King birthday celebration. However, in 1993, in the case of *Wisconsin* v. *Mitchell*,[103] the Court held that Mitchell, a black man who's severe beating of a white boy was racially motivated, could be punished with additional severity as permitted by Wisconsin law because he acted out of race hatred. The Court called the assault "conduct unprotected by the First Amendment" and upheld the Wisconsin statute saying, "[since] the statute has no 'chilling effect' on free speech, it is not unconstitutionally overbroad."

ORGANIZED CRIME

While hate groups are often internally well coordinated, criminal organizations have existed in America since before the turn of the twentieth century. Contemporary organized crime groups are involved to some degree in just about every aspect of American life, but the manufacture, transportation, and sale of controlled substances has provided an especially lucrative form of illegal enterprise for many of them. A few such groups are thought to be among the largest business-like enterprises in the world.

The Mafia, perhaps the best known criminal organization in the United States, rose to power in this country largely through its exploitation of the widespread demand for consumable alcohol during prohibition years. The Mafia, now called the Cosa Nostra, came into existence when a group of small-time hoods, largely of Italian descent, began selling "protection" and other services such as gambling and prostitution in turn-of-the-century

FIGURE 2–7   White Supremacist Groups in the United States in 1992. *Source:* Klanwatch Project, reprinted with permission.

New York city. With the advent of prohibition, financial opportunities became enormous for those willing to circumvent the law, and organized gang activity spread. Soon Chicago, Detroit, Miami, San Francisco, and other major cities became gang havens. It was during this period that infamous gangsters such as Lucky Luciano and Al Capone were catapulted to the forefront of popular attention.

Today, the Cosa Nostra consists of 24 families based in various cities across the country. Their illegal take is estimated at around $60 billion per year.[104] Families are involved in a variety of illegal activities including drug trafficking, loan sharking, gambling, shakedowns of drug dealers, killings-for-hire, and the infiltration of various labor unions. Many run legitimate businesses as fronts for money laundering and other financial activities. Such businesses are often rife with "ghost workers," paid at high rates, but who actually do no work at all. Organized crime families will stop at little to increase their influence. Nicholas Caramandi, a former member of the Philadelphia mob led by Nicodemo Scarfo, responded to a question about how high the mob reaches into American society this way: "If politicians, doctors, lawyers, entertainment people all come to us for favors, there's got to be a reason. It's because we're the best. There are no favors we can't do."[105]

The Cosa Nostra requires new members to undergo an initiation ritual which has changed little since the days it was brought to American shores by Sicilian immigrants more than a hundred years ago. During a secretly recorded candle-lit Cosa Nostra induction ceremony recently held in Medford, Massachusetts, for example, new members were required to hold a burning picture of a Catholic saint in their cupped palms and made to swear to uphold the code of *omerta* (silence). *"Come si brucia questa santa, cosi si brucera la mia anima,"* the men repeated, which means "As burns this saint, so will burn my soul." Anyone violating the Cosa Nostra's code of silence recognizes that death is the penalty.

Crime families are hierarchically organized under a boss, and consist of a number of levels, each with varying authority. Bosses exercise their power through underbosses and lieutenants. Lieutenants pass orders along to soldiers. Soldiers, the lowest level of mob operatives, are charged with directly carrying out the activities of their families. In doing so they often make use of local community members, allowing organized crime to seamlessly integrate itself into almost any locale. Hierarchical organization has frequently allowed many Cosa Nostra higher-ups to avoid arrest and prosecution. Recently, however, federal agents armed with new statutes have been able to make inroads into many such operations. For example, John Gotti, leader of New York city's infamous Gambino crime family, was recently sent to federal prison, and 1,170 Cosa Nostra bosses, soldiers, and associates across the nation have been convicted and sentenced during the last few years.[106] Peter Milano, once boss of Los Angeles, is in prison. So, too, are leaders of Kansas City's Civella family, and a few years ago 13 members of New England's Patriarca family were convicted of murdering one of their underbosses.

Even as the power of the Cosa Nostra wanes, other groups stand ready to take its place. There is historical precedent for such a transition. Italian-led gangs were preceded in New York city and other places by Jewish criminal organizations. One infamous Jewish gang, for example, was headed at the start of the century by Arnold Rothstein, who dreamed of becoming kingpin of all organized criminal activity in America. Ethnic succession has typified organized criminal activity. Today gangs of Hispanics, Chinese, Japanese, Vietnamese, Puerto Ricans, Mexicans, Colombians, and African-Americans have usurped power traditionally held by the Cosa Nostra in many parts of the country. Similarly, some evidence indicates that Russian-led and Arabic-speaking gangs have begun to move into New York and other cities.

SUMMARY

Crime statistics provide a useful but conceptually limited approach to the social reality of crime. Statistics delineate the extent of crime according to the categories they are designed to measure, and they give a picture of victim characteristics through both self-reports and reports to the police. Today's comprehensive program of data gathering allows for a tabulation of the dollar costs of crime and permits a degree of predictability as to trends in crime.

Lacking in most crime statistics, however, are any realistic appraisals of the human costs of crime. The trauma suffered by victims and survivors, the lowered sense of security experienced after victimization, and the loss of human productivity and quality of life caused by crime are difficult to gauge.

On the other side of the balance sheet, statistics fail to identify social costs suffered by offenders and their families. The social deprivation which may lead to crime, the fragmentation of private lives following conviction, and the loss of individuality which comes with confinement are all costs to society, just as they are the culturally imposed consequences of crime and failure. Except for numbers on crimes committed, arrests, and figures on persons incarcerated, today's data gathering strategies fall far short of gauging the human suffering and wasted human potential which both causes and follows from crime.

Even where reports do provide quantitative measures, they may still fail to assess some of the objective costs of crime, including lowered property values in high-crime areas and inflated prices for consumer goods caused by the underground economy in stolen goods. White-collar crimes in particular are often well hidden and difficult to measure, yet many produce the largest direct dollar losses of any type of criminal activity.

Modern crime statistics are useful, but they do not provide the whole picture. Students of criminal justice need to be continually aware of aspects of the crime picture that fall outside of official data.

DISCUSSION QUESTIONS

1. What are the two major sources of crime statistics for the United States? How do they differ?

2. What can crime statistics tell us about the crime "picture" in America? How has that "picture" changed over time?

3. What are the potential sources of error in the major reports on crime? Can you image some popular usage of those statistics that might be especially misleading?

4. Why are many crime statistics expressed as a *rate?* How does the use of crime rates improve the reporting of crime data (over a simple numerical tabulation)?

5. What is the crime index? Why is it difficult to add offenses to (or remove them from) the index and still have it retain its value as a comparative tool?

6. What are the two major offense categories in Part I crimes? Are there some property crimes which might have a violent aspect? Are there any personal crimes which could be nonviolent?

7. What is the hierarchy rule in crime reporting programs? What purpose does it serve? What do you think of the proposed modifications in the hierarchy rule?

8. What does it mean to say that a crime has been "cleared"? Can you imagine a better way of reporting clearances?

ENDNOTES

1. "Point of View," *The Chronicle of Higher Education*, June 10, 1992, p. A40.
2. "Overheard," *Newsweek*, March 8, 1993, p. 17.
3. "Police Scour Denver for Killer," *USA Today*, June 19, 1991, p. 3A
4. As quoted in Frank Hagan, *Research Methods in Criminal Justice* (New York: Macmillan, 1982), from Eugene Webb et al., *Nonreactive Measures in the Social Sciences*, 2nd ed. (Boston: Houghton Mifflin, 1981), p. 89.
5. U.S. Bureau of Justice Statistics, *Criminal Victimization in the United States, 1985* (Washington, D.C.: U.S. Government Printing Office, 1987), p. 1.
6. Federal Bureau of Investigation, *Uniform Crime Reports for the United States, 1987* (Washington, D.C.: U.S. Government Printing Office, 1988), p. 1.
7. Hagan, *Research Methods in Criminal Justice and Criminology*.
8. Federal Bureau of Investigation, *Uniform Crime Reports for the United States, 1992* (Washington, D.C.: U.S. Government Printing Office, 1993), p. 16.
9. Federal Bureau of Investigation, *Uniform Crime Reports for the United States, 1975* (Washington, D.C.: U.S. Government Printing Office, 1976), p. 22.
10. FBI, *Uniform Crime Reports, 1992.*
11. All offense definitions in this chapter are derived from those used by the UCR reporting program and are taken from the *Uniform Crime Reports for the United States, 1990* or from *Criminal Justice Data Terminology*, 2nd ed. (Washington, D.C.: Bureau of Justice Statistics, 1981).
12. These and other statistics in this chapter are derived primarily from the *Uniform Crime Reports for the United States, 1992.*
13. Bureau of Justice Statistics, *Report to the Nation on Crime and Justice*, 2nd ed. (Washington, D.C.: U.S. Government Printing Office, 1988), p. 4.
14. Ibid.
15. Ibid.
16. "Study: Rape Vastly Underreported," *The Fayetteville Observer-Times* (North Carolina), April 26, 1992, p. 16A.
17. Ronald Barri Flowers, *Women and Criminality: The Woman as Victim, Offender and Practitioner* (Westport, CT: Greenwood Press, 1987), pp. 33–36.
18. A. Nichols Groth, *Men Who Rape: The Psychology of the Offender* (New York: Plenum Press, 1979).
19. Flowers, *Women and Criminality*, p. 36.

20. "Swim Coach Guilty of Statutory Rape," *USA Today*, August 13, 1993, p. 3A.

21. *Report to the Nation on Crime and Justice*, 2nd ed., p. 5.

22. Ibid.

23. *Uniform Crime Reports, 1992*. For UCR reporting purposes, "minorities" are defined as blacks, American Indians, Asians, Pacific Islanders, and Alaskan Natives.

24. Sometimes called assault with a deadly weapon with intent to kill, or AWDWWIK.

25. *Report to the Nation on Crime and Justice*, 2nd ed., p. 6.

26. Ibid., p. 6.

27. Ibid.

28. "Carjacking Case Goes to Trial," *USA Today*, April 13, 1993, p. 2A.

29. *Uniform Crime Reports, 1992*.

30. *Ibid., p. 5.*

31. As indicated in the UCR definition of arson, *Uniform Crime Reports, 1987*, p. 36.

32. *Uniform Crime Reports, 1992*.

33. While the old rule would have counted only one murder where a woman was raped and her husband murdered in the same criminal incident, the new rule would report both a murder and a rape.

34. FBI, *Crime in the United States, 1990* (Washington, D.C.: U.S. Government Printing Office, 1991), p. 5.

35. "12 Hate Crime Murders Reported to FBI in 1991," *Criminal Justice Newsletter*, December 15, 1992, p. 2.

36. For additional information, see: U.S. Department of Justice, Bureau of Justice Statistics, *Criminal Victimization in the United States, 1992* (Washington, D.C.: BJS, 1992).

37. Bureau of Justice Statistics, *Criminal Victimization in the United States, 1991* (Washington, D.C.: BJS, 1992).

38. Ibid.

39. *Report to the Nation on Crime and Justice*, 2nd ed., p. 26.

40. U.S. Department of Justice, "The Risk of Violent Crime," *BJS Special Report* (Washington, D.C.: Bureau of Justice Statistics, May 1985), p. 2

41. Catherine J. Whitaker, "The Redesigned National Crime Survey: Selected New Data," *BJS Special Report* (Washington, D.C.: U.S. Government Printing Office, 1989).

42. Ibid.

43. Bruce M. Taylor, "New Direction of the National Crime Survey," *BJS Technical Report* (Washington, D.C.: U.S. Government Printing Office, 1989).

44. Ibid.

45. *Report to the Nation on Crime and Justice*, 2nd ed., p. 27.

46. Georgette Bennett, *Crimewarps: The Future of Crime in America* (Garden City, N.Y.: Anchor/Doubleday, 1987).

47. Ibid.

48. Ibid., p. xiv.

49. *Report to the Nation on Crime and Justice*, 2nd ed., p. 24.

50. "Job Worries Persist, Poll Shows," *USA Today*, December 15, 1993, p. 4A, reporting on the 1994 *Battleground Survey* by the Tarrance Group and Mellman-Lazarus-Lake.

51. Washington Post wire services, December 20, 1993.

52. *Report to the Nation on Crime and Justice*, 2nd ed., p. 32.

53. The definition of rape employed by the UCR, however, automatically excludes crimes of homosexual rape such as might occur in prisons and jails. As a consequence, the rape of males is excluded from the official count for crimes of rape.

54. *Report to the Nation on Crime and Justice*, 2nd ed., p. 25.

55. See, for example, Elizabeth Stanko, "When Precaution Is Normal: A Feminist Critique of Crime Prevention," in Loraine Gelsthorpe and Allison Morris, *Feminist Perspectives in Criminology* (Philadelphia: Open University Press, 1990).

56. "Battered Women Tell Their Stories to the Senate," *The Charlotte Observer* (North Carolina), July 10, 1991, p. 3A.

57. Caroline Wolf Harlow, *Female Victims of Violent Crime* (Washington, D.C.: Bureau of Justice Statistics, 1991).

58. Nanci Koser Wilson, "Feminist Pedagogy in Criminology," *Journal of Criminal Justice Education*, Vol. 2, no. 2 (Spring 1991), pp. 81–93.

59. "Suspect Is Charged in 1 of 7 Murders," *Fayetteville Observer-Times* (North Carolina), January 19, 1991, p. 12A.

60. "Fla. Slayings: Men Beware," *USA Today*, December 17, 1990, p. 3A.

61. Otto Pollak, *The Criminality of Women* (Philadelphia: University of Pennsylvania Press, 1950).

62. *Uniform Crime Reports, 1980* and *1992.*

63. Ibid.

64. *Uniform Crime Reports, 1992.*

65. Rita Simon, *Women and Crime* (Lexington, MA: D.C. Heath, 1975).

66. Freda Adler, *Sisters in Crime: The Rise of the New Female Criminal* (New York: McGraw-Hill, 1975).

67. Jane Roberts Chapman, *Economic Realities and the Female Offender* (Lexington, MA: Lexington Books, 1980), p. 51, as cited in Flowers, *Women and Criminality*, p. 86.

68. Darrell J. Steffensmeir, "Sex Differences in Patterns of Adult Crime, 1965–1977: A Review and Assessment," *Social Forces*, Vol. 58 (1980), pp. 1098–99.

69. Flowers, *Women and Criminality*, p. 87.

70. *Report to the Nation on Crime and Justice*, 2nd ed.

71. Bureau of Justice Statistics, *Criminal Victimization in the United States, 1991* (Washington, D.C.: BJS, 1992).

72. *Report to the Nation on Crime and Justice*, 2nd ed.

73. Timothy J. Flanagan and Kathleen Maguire, eds. *Sourcebook of Criminal Justice Statistics, 1991* (Washington, D.C.: Bureau of Justice Statistics, 1992).

74. *Report to the Nation on Crime and Justice*, 2nd ed., p. 114.

75. Bureau of Justice Statistics, *Justice Expenditure and Employment, 1990* (Washington, D.C.: BJS, 1992).

76. Ibid.

77. J. M. Chaiken and M. R. Chaiken, *Varieties of Criminal Behavior* (Santa Monica, CA: The Rand Corporation, 1982).

78. D. McBride, "Trends in Drugs and Death," paper presented at American Society of Criminology annual meeting, Denver, Colorado, 1983.

79. B. Johnson et al., *Taking Care of Business: The Economics of Crime by Heroin Abusers* (Lexington, MA: Lexington Books, 1985). See also Bernard A. Grooper, *Research in Brief: Probing the Links Between Drugs and Crime* (Washington, D.C.: National Institute of Justice, February 1985).

80. *Report to the Nation on Crime and Justice*, 2nd ed., p. 114.

81. Ibid.

82. *Uniform Crime Reports, 1992.*

83. *Uniform Crime Reports, 1975* and *1992.*

84. Ibid.

85. American Correctional Association, *1993 Directory of Juvenile and Adult Correctional Departments, Institutions, Agencies and Paroling Authorities* (Laurel, MD: ACA, 1993).

86. Bennett, *Crimewarps*, p. 61.

87. Catherine J. Whitaker, *BJS Special Report: Elderly Victims* (Rockville, MD: Bureau of Justice Statistics, November 1987).

88. Ibid.

89. Ibid., p. 5.

90. Ibid.

91. Bureau of Justice Statistics, *Criminal Victimization in the United States, 1991.*

92. Ibid.

93. Michael E. Wiggins, "Societal Changes and Right Wing Membership," paper presented at the Academy of Criminal Justice Sciences Annual Meeting, San Francisco, California, April 1988.

94. Richard Holden, "God's Law: Criminal Process and Right Wing Extremism in America," paper presented at the annual meeting of the Academy of Criminal Justice Sciences, San Francisco, California, April 1988.

95. For additional details on supremacist groups see Michael E. Wiggins, "A Descriptive Profile of Criminal Activities of a Right-Wing Extremist Group," paper presented at the annual meeting of The Society of Police and Criminal Psychology, Little Rock, Arkansas, October 1985.

96. "Order Member: Group considered Killing TV Producer Norman Lear," *The Daily News* (Springfield, Missouri) September 16, 1985, p. 3, as cited by Michael E. Wiggins in "A Descriptive Profile of Criminal Activities of a Right-Wing Extremist Group."

97. Michael E. Wiggins, "An Extremist Right-Wing Group and Domestic Terrorism," unpublished manuscript, Center for Criminal Justice Research, Central Missouri State University, March 1986.

98. Michael E.Wiggins, "Rationale and Justification for Right-Wing Terrorism: A Politico-Social Analysis of the Turner Diaries," paper presented at the annual meeting of the American Society of Criminology, Atlanta, Georgia, October 1986.

99. "8 Accused of Plotting Los Angeles Race War," *The Austin American-Statesman*, July 16, 1993, p. A1, and "FBI: L.A. Race War Plot 'Despicable,'" *USA Today*, July 16–18, 1993, p. 1A.

100. John Kleinig, "Penalty Enhancements for Hate Crimes," *Criminal Justice Ethics* (Summer/Fall 1992), pp. 3–6.

101. *R.A.V.* v. *City of St. Paul, Minn.*, 112 S.Ct. 2538 (1992).

102. *Forsyth County, Ga.* v. *Nationalist Movement*, 112 S.Ct. 2395 (1992).

103. *Wisconsin* v. *Mitchell*, No. 92–515. Decided June 11, 1993.

104. Bonnie Angelo, "Wanted: A New Godfather," *Time*, April 13, 1992, Vol. 139, no. 15, p. 30.

105. Richard Behar, "In the Grip of Treachery," *Playboy*, November 1991, Vol. 38, no. 11, p. 92.

106. William Sherman, "Kingpins of the Underworld," *Cosmopolitan*, March 1992, Vol. 212, no. 3, p. 158.

CHAPTER 3

THE

SEARCH

FOR

CAUSES

I could kill everyone without blinking an eye![1]
—CHARLIE MANSON

An honest and fully professional police community would acknowledge in its police education the root causes of crime—poverty, unemployment, underemployment, racism, poor health care, bad housing, weak schools, mental illness, alcoholism, addiction, single-parent families, teenage pregnancy, and a society of selfishness and greed.
—PATRICK V. MURPHY, FORMER COMMISSIONER OF THE NYC POLICE DEPARTMENT

There was nothing to do.
—TERRANCE WADE, AGE 15 ON WHY HE AND HIS FRIENDS ALLEGEDLY RAPED, STOMPED, STABBED, AND ULTIMATELY MURDERED A BOSTON WOMAN

KEY CONCEPTS

atavism	radical criminology	criminal personality
reaction formation	somatotypes	differential association
supermale	social learning theory	Chicago School
phrenology	subculture	anomie
containment	Positivist School	Classical School
social disorganization	psychoanalysis	labeling

KEY NAMES

Jeremy Bentham	Sarnoff Mednick	Cesare Lombroso
Cesare Beccaria	Franz Joseph Gall	Sigmund Freud
William Sheldon	Clifford Shaw	Howard Becker
Ernest Burgess	Walter Reckless	Richard Quinney
Richard Herrnstein	Robert Merton	Albert Cohen
Walter Miller	Marvin Wolfgang	Edwin Sutherland

WHY IS THERE CRIME?

On April 26, 1991 Charles Russ of La Jolla, California, was sentenced to life in prison without possibility of parole for the 1987 murder of Pamela Russ—his young and beautiful wife.[2] With a spectacular home overlooking the ocean, luxury cars, trips around the world, and frequent lavish parties, the Russes had been considered the perfect couple by their friends. Pamela was an accomplished artist, whose work was recognized by patrons in the community where the couple lived. Unknown to friends, however, Charles Russ's telemarketing business had gone bankrupt and he had turned to heavy borrowing and fraudulent business activities to try and maintain the couple's public image. Late one night Russ lured Pamela to the quiet tip of the Del Mar peninsula. After she parked her Mercedes he bludgeoned her to the asphalt, then ran over her several times with her own car. Her body was so badly torn that the casket could not be opened at her funeral. Pamela was 33 years old when she died; Charles was 36 at the time.

Hours after the murder Russ filed a claim for $600,000 in life insurance monies on a policy he had taken out on his wife's life just months before the killing.[3] Failing to collect on the policy, Russ disappeared and lived under an assumed name for two years. He was finally captured in Florida, after his landlady recognized him while viewing the TV program "America's Most Wanted."

At his trial Russ claimed that his wife had been carrying a large amount of cash at the time of her death, and that she likely had been robbed and murdered by an acquaintance who must have known about the money. The trial lasted 12 weeks. At its conclusion, Russ was convicted of murder. Following the conviction both the prosecutor and Pamela's brother called upon Russ to admit his guilt and express remorse. Russ responded with a cold stare, and later turned down the opportunity to address the court prior to sentencing.

At sentencing, Judge Michael Wellington, said, "[t]he defendant is a man of good intelligence with charm and good looks.… He married a beautiful, talented, devoted woman. If there ever was an American dream, it seems to me he had his hands on it."[4] After the courtroom proceedings were over, according to newspaper reports, Russ quickly stalked out of the courtroom, "not looking at anyone, his head held high, his shoulders squared, his hands cuffed behind his back."[5] Today, Charles Russ is still appealing his conviction.

A crime like the one that Charles Russ committed might be explained in terms of individual circumstances or upbringing. Criminological theory, however, has often sought broader answers. Over the past two centuries criminologists have focused upon the following three questions:[6]

1. Why does the crime rate vary?
2. Why do individuals differ as to criminality?
3. Why is there variation in reactions to alleged criminality?

The first question deals with large groups of people—even entire societies—over time. Chapter 2 described American crime rates and provided some clues as to seasonal and long-term variations in such rates. The third question is political in nature and asks why certain behaviors are at times (or by certain groups) severely condemned while at other times (or by other groups) they may be condoned. This chapter spotlights the second question, which squarely focuses not on trends or social groups, but on the behavior of individuals. The second question can be stated in another way: Why do some people turn to crime while others do not?

Even on the level of the individual there is no single cause of crime. Crime is rooted in a diversity of causal factors and takes a variety of forms, depending upon the situation in which it occurs. Some theories of crime, however, help us to understand why certain people engage in behavior which society defines as criminal. Ideally, **theories** are composed of clearly stated propositions which posit relationships, often of a causal sort, between events and things under study. An old Roman theory, for example, proposed that insanity was caused by the influence of the moon—hence the term "lunacy."

When we consider the wide range of behaviors regarded as criminal—from murder, through drug use, to white-collar crime—it seems difficult to imagine a theory which can explain them all. Yet many past theoretical approaches to crime causation were unicausal and all inclusive. That is, they posited a single, identifiable, source for all serious deviant and criminal behavior. Some of the earliest of these theories have only recently been rediscovered through the work of archaeologists.

Early skeletal remains provide evidence that some human societies believed outlandish behavior was produced by spirit possession. Skulls, dated by various techniques to approximately 30,000 years ago, show signs of early surgery, apparently designed to release evil spirits residing within the heads of offenders. Surgical techniques were undoubtedly crude, and probably involved some fermented anesthesia along with flint or obsidian surgical implements. Any theory, however, gains credence if activity based on it produces results in keeping with what that theory would predict. Spirit possession, as an explanation for deviance, probably appeared well validated by positive behavioral changes in those "patients" who submitted to the surgery called for by the theory. The cause of reformation may have been brain infections resulting from unsanitary conditions, "slips" of the stone knife, or the pain endured by those undergoing the procedure. To the uncritical observer, however, the theory of spirit possession as a cause of deviance, and cranial surgery as a treatment technique, would have appeared to be supported by the "evidence."

Criminological theory over the intervening years has become increasingly scientific.[7] Generally accepted research designs, coupled with careful data gathering strategies and statistical techniques for data analysis, have yielded considerable confidence in certain explanations for crime, while at the same time tending to disprove others. Most modern theories of criminal behavior, however, remain nearly unicausal, often because modern research permits only a testing of narrowly defined causal propositions.

Theory A series of interrelated propositions that attempt to describe, explain, predict, and ultimately control some class of events. A theory gains explanatory power from inherent logical consistency and is "tested" by how well it describes and predicts reality.

While we will use the word "theory" in describing various explanations for crime throughout this chapter, it should be recognized that the word is only loosely applicable to some of the perspectives we will discuss. Many social scientists insist that to be considered "theories," explanations must consist of sets of clearly stated, logically interrelated, and measurable propositions. The fact that few of the "theories" which follow rise above the level of organized conjecture is one of the greatest failures of social science today.

Types of Theories

Explanations of criminal behavior fall into seven categories:

- Classical
- Biological
- Psychological
- Sociological
- Social–psychological
- Conflict
- Phenomenological

The differences between these approaches are summarized in Table 3–1.

The Classical School

Cesare Beccaria

In 1764 Cesare Beccaria (1738–1794) published his *Essays on Crimes and Punishment*. The book was an immediate success and stirred a hornet's nest of controversy over the treatment of criminal offenders. Beccaria proposed basic changes in the criminal laws of his day which would make them more "humanitarian." He called for abolition of physical punishments and an end to the death penalty. Beccaria believed in the thoughtful exercise of free will and is best remembered for his suggestion that punishments should be just strong enough to offset the tendency toward crime. Punishment, he said, should be sufficient to deter, but never excessive. Because Beccaria's writings stimulated many other thinkers throughout the 1700s and early 1800s, he is referred to today as the founder of the **Classical School** of criminology.

Classical School An eighteenth-century approach to crime causation and criminal responsibility which resulted from the Enlightenment and which emphasized the role of free will and reasonable punishments.

Jeremy Bentham

Among those influenced by Beccaria was the Englishman Jeremy Bentham. Bentham devised a "hedonistic calculus"[8] in keeping with the idea that the individual exercise of free will would lead people to avoid crime where the benefit to be derived from committing crime was outweighed by the pain of punishment. Bentham termed his philosophy of social control "utilitarianism." Both Bentham and Beccaria agreed that punishment had to be "swift and certain," as well as just, in order to be effective.

The Classical School of criminology represented a noteworthy advance over previous thinking about crime because it moved beyond superstition and mysticism as explanations for deviance. A product of the Enlightenment then sweeping Europe, the Classical School

T A B L E   3 - 1

TYPES OF CRIMINOLOGICAL THEORY

Type	Theorists	Characteristics
Classical		
Free will theories Hedonistic calculus	Beccaria Bentham	Crime is caused by the individual exercise of free will. Prevention is possible through swift and certain punishment which offsets any gains to be had through criminal behavior.
Biological		
Phrenology Atavism Somatotypes Chromosome theory Nutritional theory	Gall Lombroso Sheldon Jacobs	"Criminal genes" cause deviant behavior. Criminals are identifiable through physical characteristics or genetic composition. Treatment is generally ineffective, but aggression may be usefully redirected.
Psychological		
Psychoanalysis Behavioral theories Classification schemes	Freud Skinner	Crime is the result of negative early childhood experiences or the product of a desire to be caught Treatment necessitates extensive therapy.
Sociological		
Subcultures Anomie Labeling	Cohen Merton Becker	Aspects of social life produce crime through association with others already committed to criminal behavior or via the established social structure as it reacts to deviance and attempts to maintain existing power relationships. Therapy may require basic changes in socialization and pathways to opportunity.
Social–Psychological		
Differential association Restraint Containment Social control	Sutherland Burgess Reckless Hirschi	Crime results from the failure of self-direction or inadequate social roles. Treatment requires strengthened self-concepts.
Conflict		
Radical criminology The new criminology	Turk Vold Chambliss Quinney	Crime is a natural consequence of social, political, and economic inequities.

TABLE 3-1 (CONTINUED)

Type	Theorists	Characteristics
Phenomenological		
Criminal personality Career criminality	Yochelson Samenow	The source of criminal behavior is unknown, but an understanding of deviant behavior is available through case studies and detailed descriptions of deviant life-styles. Therapy requires a total reorientation of the offender.

demanded recognition of rationality and made possible the exercise of informed choice in human social life. Thinkers who were to follow, however, wasted little time in subjugating free will to a secondary role in the search for causal factors in crime commission. As Stephen Schafer puts it, "In the eighteenth-century individualistic orientation of criminal law the act was judged and the man made responsible. In the next scene in the historic drama of crime, the man is judged and the search is on for finding the responsible factor."[9]

BIOLOGICAL THEORIES

Biological School A perspective on criminological thought which holds that criminal behavior has a physiological basis. Genes, foods and food additives, hormones, and inheritance are all thought to play a role in determining individual behavior. Biological thinkers highlight the underlying animalistic aspect of being human as a major determinate of behavior.

Franz Joseph Gall

The idea that the quality of a person could be judged by a study of the person's face is as old as antiquity. Even today we often judge people on their looks, saying, "He has an honest face" or "She has tender eyes." Horror movies have played upon unspoken cultural themes as to how a "maniac" might look. Jack Nicholson's portrayal of crazed killers in *The Shining*, for example, turned that look into a fortune at the box office.

Franz Joseph Gall (1758–1828) was one of the first thinkers to present systematically the idea that bodily constitution might reflect personality. Gall was writing at a time when notions of the personality allowed for the belief that organs throughout the body determined one's mental state and behavior. People were said to be "hard hearted" or to have a "bad spleen" which filled them with bile. Gall focused instead on the head and the brain and called his approach "cranioscopy." It can be summarized in four propositions:

- The brain is the organ of the mind.
- The brain consists of localized faculties or functions.
- The shape of the skull reveals the underlying development (or corresponding lack of it) of areas within the brain.
- The personality can be revealed by a study of the skull.

Gall never systematically "tested" his theory in a way which would meet contemporary scientific standards. Even so, his approach to predicting behavior, which came to be known as phrenology, quickly spread through Europe. Gall's student Johann Gaspar Spurzheim (1776–1853) brought phrenology to America in a series of lectures and publications on the subject. By 1825, 29 phrenological journals were being produced in the United States and

Britain.[10] Phrenology remained viable in America in some circles until the turn of the twentieth century, where it could be found in some prison diagnostic schemes used to classify new prisoners.

Phrenology remains a part of popular culture today. Movies of the fictional Sherlock Holmes depict the great investigator making use of skulls inked with phrenological maps, and personality readings based upon liberal interpretations of Gall's theory are available at some county fairs, church socials, and fortune-telling booths.[11]

Cesare Lombroso's "Atavism"

Gall's theory was "deterministic" in the sense that it left little room for choice. What a person did depended more upon the shape of the skull than upon any exercise of choice. Other biological theories were soon to build upon that premise. One of the best known is that created by the Italian psychologist Cesare Lombroso (1835–1909).

Lombroso began his criminal anthropology with a postmortem evaluation of famous criminals, including one by the name of Vilella. Lombroso had the opportunity to interview Vilella on a number of occasions. After the man's death he correlated earlier observations of personality traits with measurable physical abnormalities. As a result of this and other studies, Lombroso reached the conclusion that criminals were atavistic human beings—throwbacks to earlier stages of evolution who were not sufficiently advanced mentally for successful life in the modern world. Atavism was identifiable in suspicious individuals, Lombroso suggested, through measures designed to reveal "primitive" physical characteristics.

In the late 1800s Darwin's theory of evolution was rapidly being applied to a diversity of fields. It was not surprising, therefore, that Lombroso would make the link between evolution and criminality. What separated Lombroso from his predecessors however, was the continual refinement of his theory through ongoing observation. Based upon studies of known offenders, whom he compared to conformists, Lombroso identified a large number of atavistic traits, which, he claimed, could lead to crime. Among them were long arms, large lips, crooked noses, an abnormally large amount of body hair, prominent cheekbones, eyes of different colors, and ears which lacked clearly defined lobes.

Atavism implies the notion of born criminals. Throughout his life Lombroso grappled with the task of identifying the proportion of born criminals from among the total population of offenders. His estimates ranged at different times between 70% and 90%. Career criminals and criminals of opportunity without atavistic features he termed criminaloids and recognized the potential causative roles of greed, passion, and circumstance in their behavior.

Today Lombroso is known as the founder of the Positivist School of criminology because of the role observation played in the formulation of his theories. Stephen Schafer calls Lombroso the "father of modern criminology,"[12] since most contemporary criminologists follow in the tradition that Lombroso began—of scientific observation and a comparison of theory with fact.

Atavism: The Evidence For and Against   After Lombroso died two English physicians, Charles Goring and Karl Pearson, decided to conduct a test of atavism. Goring and Pearson studied more than 3,000 prisoners and compared them along physiological criteria to an army detachment known as the Royal Engineers. No significant differences were found between the two groups, and Lombroso's ideas began to fall rapidly into disrepute.

Atavism A condition characterized by the existence of features thought to be common in earlier stages of human evolution

In a rare surviving photograph, Cesare Lombroso (left), who has been dubbed the "father of modern criminology," is shown sitting with friend Louis Lombard in 1909. *Photo: Culver Pictures.*

A further study of atavism was published in 1939 by Ernest A. Hooton, a distinguished Harvard University anthropologist. Hooton had spent 12 years constructing anthropometric profiles of 13,873 male convicts in ten different American states. He measured each inmate in 107 different ways and compared them to 3,203 volunteers from National Guard units, firehouses, beaches, and hospitals. Surprisingly, Hooton did find some basis for Lombroso's beliefs and concluded that the inmate population in his study demonstrated a decided physical "inferiority."

Hooton never did recognize the fact, however, that the prisoners he studied were only a subgroup of the population of all offenders throughout the country. They were, in fact, the least successful offenders—the ones who had been caught and imprisoned. Other criminals may have unknowingly been measured by Hooton among his "conformist" population, since they were the ones who had avoided capture. Hence the "inferiority" Hooton observed may have been an "artificial" product of a process of selection (arrest) by the justice system.

William Sheldon

The last of the famous constitutional[13] theorists was William Sheldon (1893–1977). Sheldon studied 200 juvenile delinquents between the ages of 15 and 21 at the Hayden Goodwill Institute in Boston, Massachusetts, and decided that the young men possessed one of three somatotypes (or body types). The types of bodies described by Sheldon were (in his words)

- *Mesomorphs:* with a relative predominance of muscle, bone, and connective tissue.
- *Endomorphs:* having a soft roundness throughout the various regions of the body; short tapering limbs; small bones; and soft, smooth, velvety skin.
- *Ectomorphs:* characterized by thinness, fragility, and delicacy of body.

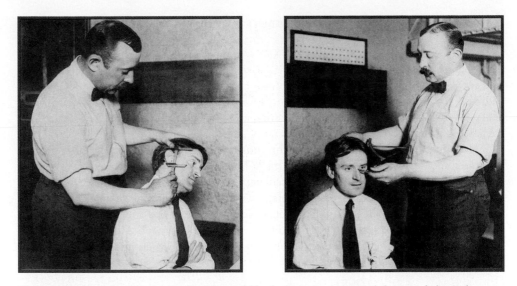

The theory of atavism, based upon the ideas of Charles Darwin, supported the use of physical anthropology in the identification of offenders. Here the Bertillion system of identification is applied to a suspect in the years prior to the development of fingerprinting. *Courtesy of the Library of Congress.*

Sheldon developed a system of measurements by which an individual's physique could be expressed as a combination of three numbers, such as 4.0–4.0–3.5 (the representation of an average male). The numbers represented the degree of endormorphy, mesomorphy, and ectomorphy present in the individual on a scale of 0 to 7, where 0 indicates a complete lack of features of one category. American females were said to average 5.0–3.0–3.5 on the scale. Although he wrote that each somatotype was possessed of a characteristic personality, Sheldon believed predominately mesomorphic individuals were most prone to aggression, violence, and delinquency.[14]

CONTEMPORARY BIOCHEMICAL THEORIES

Chromosome Theory

The ongoing mapping of human DNA and recent advances in the field of recombinant DNA have rekindled interest in genetic correlates of deviant behavior. More sophisticated than their historical counterparts, biological theories of today often draw upon the latest medical advances or build upon popular health concerns.

Chromosome theory became an explanation for criminal behavior in the 1960s. A normal female has a chromosome structure often diagrammed as "XX" because of how the sex-determining gene pair looks in an electron microscope. A male has a "Y" chromosome in place of the second "X," for a typical male "XY" pattern. Although it had been known for some time that a few people had abnormal patterns which included "extra" chromosomes (such as XXX females, or XXYY "double males"), it wasn't until the early 1960s that linkages between chromosome patterns and crime were explored. In 1965 the respected English journal *Nature* reported on the work of Patricia Jacobs who had discovered supermales—men with an extra "Y" chromosome. Jacobs found that supermales were more common in prisons than in the general population.[15]

Other early studies claimed that the XYY male was more aggressive than other males and that he possessed a number of specific physical and psychological traits, such as height (over 6'1"), thinness, acne, a tendency toward homosexuality, a somewhat low IQ, and "a marked tendency to commit a succession of apparently motiveless property crimes."[16] Later studies disputed many of these findings, and the significance of the XYY pattern for behavioral prediction is today in doubt.

It is interesting to consider what chromosome theories could lead to if validated. Would males be tested at birth for an extra "Y" chromosome? If they were determined to have the extra "Y," would they be immediately institutionalized or sterilized, or worse? Would someone, perhaps, suggest that males with chromosomes for enhanced aggression could be gainfully fitted into useful societal roles, whether in the military, sports, or elsewhere? Such considerations apply not only to imaginable scenarios involving chromosomes, but to all biological theories of one kind or another which imply that people are hostage to their biology.

Chemical Imbalance

Recent research in the area of nutrition has produced some limited evidence that the old maximum "You are what you eat!" may contain more than a grain of truth. Biocriminology is a field of study which has made some strides in linking violent or

Criminologists have yet to adequately explain the behavior of serial killers, such as Ted Bundy. *Photo: Bettmann.*

disruptive behavior to eating habits, vitamin deficiencies, genetics, inheritance, and other conditions which impact body tissues.

One of the first studies to focus on chemical imbalances in the body as a cause of crime was reported in the British medical journal *Lancet* in 1943.[17] Authors of the study linked murder to hypoglycemia, or low blood sugar. Low blood sugar, produced by too much insulin in the blood or by near-starvation diets, was said to reduce the mind's capacity to reason effectively or judge the long-term consequences of behavior.

Allergic reactions to common foods have been reported as the cause of violence and homicide in a number of studies.[18] Foods said to produce allergic reactions in sensitive individuals, leading to a swelling of the brain and brain stem, include milk, citrus fruit, chocolate, corn, wheat, and eggs. Involvement of the central nervous system in such allergies, it has been suggested, reduces the amount of learning which occurs during childhood and may contribute to delinquency as well as adult criminal behavior. Some studies have implicated food additives, such as monosodium glutamate, dyes, and artificial flavorings in producing criminal violence.[19]

Other research has found that the amount of coffee and sugar consumed by inmates is considerably greater than in the outside population.[20] Theorists have suggested that high blood levels of caffeine and sugar produce antisocial behavior.[21] It is unclear whether inmates consume more coffee through boredom, or whether "excitable" personalities feel a need for the kind of stimulation available through coffee drinking. On the other hand, habitual coffee drinkers in nonprison populations have not been linked to crime, and other studies, such as that conducted by Mortimer Gross of the University of Illinois, show no link between the amount of sugar consumed and hyperactivity.[22] Nonetheless, some prison programs have been designed to limit intake of dietary stimulants through nutritional management and the substitution of artificial sweeteners for refined sugar.

Vitamins have also been examined for their impact on delinquency. Hoffer found that disruptive children consumed far less than the optimum levels of vitamins B_3 and B_6 than did nonproblem youths.[23] He claimed that the addition of these vitamins to the diets of children who were deficient in them could control unruly behavior and improve school performance.

The role of food and diet in producing criminal behavior, however, has not been well established. The American Dietetic Association and the National Council Against Health Fraud have concluded that no convincing scientific relationship between crime and diet has yet been demonstrated.[24] Both groups are becoming concerned that poor nutrition may result from programs intended to have behavioral impacts and that reduce or modify diets in prisons or elsewhere.

Hormones have also come under scrutiny as potential behavioral determinants. The male sex hormone testosterone has been linked to aggressiveness in males. Some studies of blood levels of testosterone have shown a direct relationship between the amount of chemical present and the degree of violence used by sex offenders,[25] and steroid abuse among body builders has been linked to destructive urges and psychosis.[26]

Biology and Environment

Some contemporary biological theorists admit an environmental linkage. Sarnoff Mednick, for example, has found some basis for the claim that the autonomic nervous system (ANS) predisposes certain individuals toward criminality by limiting their ability to learn quickly.[27] Those with a slow ANS are thought to be unable to inhibit antisocial behavior quickly enough to avoid punishment and stigmatization.[28]

Studies of children adopted at birth have shown a tendency for the criminality of biological parents to be reflected in the behavior of their children, independent of the environment in which the children were raised.[29] Identical twins seem to exhibit a greater similarity in behavior than do nonidentical (or "fraternal") twins, and a number of studies have shown that identical twins are more alike in patterns and degree of criminal involvement than are fraternal twins.[30]

Perhaps the best known of modern-day biological perspectives on crime was proposed by James Q. Wilson and Richard Herrnstein in their book *Crime and Human Nature*, published in 1985.[31] Wilson and Herrnstein argue that inherited traits such as maleness, aggressiveness, mesomorphic body type, and low intelligence combine with environmental influences, including poor schools and strained family life, to produce crime. Although a firm determinism is rejected by the authors, who say that it is the interaction between environment and genetics that determines behavior, they do claim that children who will eventually grow up to be criminals can sometimes be identified early in their lives. The most important factor in the diversion of potential offenders from lives of crime, according to Wilson and Herrnstein, is a healthy family life in which affection for others and conscience can develop.[32] Wilson and Herrnstein also use cross-cultural data from Japan, where crime rates are very low, to suggest that inherited tendencies toward introversion among the Japanese result in fewer serious crimes than in the United States.

The Wilson–Herrnstein thesis has been criticized for its failure to explain "crime" that extends beyond "traditional lower-class street crime" and for its lack of recognition of the political nature of criminal definitions.[33]

Psychological School A perspective on criminological thought which views offensive and deviant behavior as the products of dysfunctional personalities. The conscious, and especially the subconscious, contents of the human psyche are identified by psychological thinkers as major determinants of behavior.

PSYCHOLOGICAL THEORIES

Criminal Families

Early psychological theories built upon existing biological perspectives. Mental degeneration as an inherited contributor to crime was first explored by Richard Dugdale.[34] Dugdale used the family tree method to study a family he called the Jukes, publishing his findings in 1877. The Juke lineage had its beginning in America with "Max" (whose last name is unknown), a descendant of Dutch immigrants to New Amsterdam in the early 1700s. Two of Max's sons married into the notorious "Juke family of girls," six sisters, all of whom were illegitimate. Male Jukes were reputed to have been "vicious," while one of the women, named Ada, had an especially bad reputation and eventually came to be known as "the mother of criminals."

Dugdale found that over the next 75 years Ada's heirs included 1,200 persons, most of whom were "social degenerates." Only a handful of socially productive progeny could be identified. In 1915 Dugdale's study of the Jukes was continued by Arthur A. Estabrook, who extended the line to include 2,094 descendants and found just as few conformists.

A similar study was published by Henry Goddard in 1912.[35] Goddard examined the Kallikak family, which contained two clear lines of descent. One emanated from an affair which Martin Kallikak, a Revolutionary War soldier, had with a feeble-minded bar maid. She bore a son, and the line eventually produced 480 identifiable descendants. After the war, Kallikak returned home and married a "virtuous" Quaker girl in Philadelphia. This legitimate line produced 496 offspring by 1912, of whom only 3 were abnormal; none was criminal. The illegitimate group, however, contained over half "feeble-minded" or deviant progeny.

The theme which runs through these studies is that crime is an outlet for degenerate urges, produced and propagated through the social group by bad genetic material. Lacking is any recognition of the roles socialization and life circumstances play in the development of criminal behavior.

Freudian Psychoanalysis

The name most widely associated with the field of psychology is that of Sigmund Freud (1856–1939). Freud wrote very little about crime, but his followers, who developed the school of Freudian **psychoanalysis**, believed that crime could result from at least three conditions.[36]

Freudian theory posits the existence of an id, ego, and superego within the personality. The id is the source of drives which are seen as primarily sexual. The ego is a rational mental entity, which outlines paths through which the desires of the id can be fulfilled. It has often been called the "reality principle," because of the belief that it relates desires to practical behavioral alternatives. The superego is a guiding principle, often compared to conscience, which judges the quality of the alternatives presented by the ego according to the standards of right and wrong acquired by the personality of which it is a part.

The first possible source of criminal behavior is a weak superego which cannot responsibly control the drives which emanate form the id. Sex crimes, crimes of passion, murder, and other violent crimes are thought to follow inadequate superego development. People who lack fully developed superegos are often called psychopaths or sociopaths to indicate that they cannot see beyond their own interests. Freudian psychologists would probably agree with Gwynn Nettler who has observed that "[c]ivilization is paid for through development of a sense of guilt."[37]

Freud also created the concept of sublimation to explain the process by which one thing is symbolically substituted for another. He believed that sublimation was necessary when the direct pursuit of one's desires was not possible. Freud suggested, for example, that many children learned to sublimate negative feelings about their mothers. In the society where Freud developed his theories, mothers closely controlled the lives of their

Psychoanalysis A theory of human behavior, based upon the writings of Sigmund Freud, which sees personality as a complex composite of interacting mental entities.

Sigmund Freud (1856–1939), founder of psychoanalysis, shown here as a young man in 1891. *Photo: The Granger Collection.*

children, and Freud saw the developing child as continually frustrated in seeking freedom to act on his or her own. The strain produced by this conflict could not be directly expressed by the child because the mother also controlled rewards and punishments. Hence, dislike for one's mother (which Freud thought was especially strong in boys) might show itself symbolically later in life. Crimes against women could then be explained as committed by men expressing such a symbolic hatred.

A final Freudian explanation for criminality is based upon the death wish, or Thanatos, which Freud believed each of us carries. Thanatos is the desire, often unrecognized, of animate matter to return to the inanimate. Potentially self-destructive activities, including smoking, speeding, sky diving, bad diets, "picking fights," and so on, can be explained by Thanatos. The self-destructive wish may also motivate offenders to commit crimes which are themselves dangerous or self-destructive—such as burglary, assault, murder, prostitution, and drug use—or it may result in unconscious efforts to be caught. Criminals who leave evidence behind, sometimes even items of personal identification like driver's licenses and wallets, may be responding to some basic need for apprehension and punishment.

Profiling

Psychological profiling began during World War II as an effort by William Langer (1896–1977), a government psychiatrist hired by the Office of Strategic Services to predict Adolph Hitler's actions.[38] Profiling in the area of criminal investigations is based upon the belief that criminality, because it is a form of behavior, can be viewed as symptomatic of the offender's personality. Psychological evaluations of crime scenes, including the analysis of remaining evidence, are used to re-create the offender's frame of mind during the commission of the crime. A profile of the offender is then constructed to help in the investigation of suspects.

During the 1980s the FBI led the movement toward psychological profiling[39] through its focus on violent sex offenses[40] and arson.[41] FBI studies provided descriptions of what they termed "lust murderers" and serial arsonists. Depicted often as loners with an aversion to casual social contact, lust murderers were shown rarely to arouse suspicions in neighbors or employers. Other personality characteristics became the focus of police efforts to arrest such offenders through a prediction of what they might do next.

New areas for psychological profiling include hostage negotiation[42] and international terrorism.[43] Right-wing terrorist groups in the United States have also been the subject of profiling efforts. Table 3–2 provides an example of typical social and psychological characteristics of Middle East terrorists—for both leaders and group members.

SOCIOLOGICAL THEORIES

Sociological theories are largely an American contribution to the study of crime causation. The famous Chicago School of sociology in the 1920s and 1930s explained criminality as a product of society's impact upon the individual. The structure of prevailing social arrangements, the interaction between individuals and groups, and the social environment were seen as major determinants of criminal behavior.

Social Ecology

The University of Chicago brought together such thinkers as Robert Park,[44] Clifford Shaw, Henry McKay,[45] and Ernest Burgess. Park and Burgess recognized that Chicago, like

TABLE 3-2

DEMOGRAPHIC PROFILE OF MIDDLE EAST LEFTIST GROUPS

Leader	*Follower*
Male	Male
College education or attendance	Poorly educated/illiterate
30–45 years old	17–25 years old
Middle class	Lower class, from a large family of 9–15 children
Urban/sophisticated	Refugee/not comfortable outside of Middle East
Multilingual	Poor verbal skills
High verbal skills	Unskilled worker
Well-trained perfectionist	Training poor to none
Dedicated	Limited dedication
Strong personality	Criminally active in street gang
Politically active prior to terrorist/ criminal activity	Politically naive

Source: FBI Law Enforcement Bulletin (April 1988), p. 18.

most cities, could be mapped according to its social characteristics. Their map resembled a target with a bull's-eye in the center. These concentric zones were adapted by Shaw and McKay to the study of crime when they realized that zones nearest the center of the city had the highest crime rates. In particular, zone two (one removed from the center) demonstrated the consistently highest crime rate over time, regardless of the groups or nationalities inhabiting it. This "zone of transition" (so called because new immigrant groups moved into it as earlier ones became integrated into American culture) demonstrated that crime was dependent to a considerable extent upon aspects of the social structure of the city itself. Structural elements identified by Shaw and McKay included poverty, illiteracy, lack of schooling, unemployment, and illegitimacy. In combination, these elements were seen to lead to social disorganization, which, in turn, produced crime.

Anomie Theory

The French word **anomie** has been loosely translated as a condition of "normlessness." Anomie entered the literature as a sociological concept with the writings of Emile Durkheim (1858—1917) in the late 1800s.[46] Robert Merton (1910—) applied anomie to criminology in 1938 when he used the term to describe a disjuncture between socially acceptable goals and means in American society.[47]

Merton believed that while the same goals and means were held out by society as desirable for everyone to participate in, they were not equally available to all. Socially approved goals in American society, for example, include wealth, status, and political power. The acceptable means to achieve these goals lie in education, wise investment, and hard work. Unfortunately, however, opportunities are not equally distributed throughout society, and some people will turn to illegitimate means to achieve the goals they are pressured to reach. Still others will reject both the acceptable goals and the legitimate means to reach them.

Merton represented his theory with a diagram, shown in Table 3–3, in which conformists were seen to accept both the goals and means which society held out as legitimate,

Anomie A socially pervasive condition of normlessness. A disjuncture between approved goals and means.

T A B L E   3 - 3

ROBERT MERTON'S ANOMIE THEORY AND IMPLIED TYPES OF CRIMINALITY

Category	Goals	Means	Examples
Conformist	+	+	Law-abiding behavior
Innovator	+	−	Property offenses White-collar crimes
Retreatist	−	−	Drug use/addiction, vagrancy, some "victimless" crimes
Ritualist	−	+	
Rebel	±	±	Political crime (ex: environmental activists who violate the law, violence-prone antiabortionists)

Source: From *Social Theory and Social Structure*, 1968 enlarged edition, by Robert K. Merton. Copyright 1967, 1968 by Robert K. Merton. Adapted with permission of The Free Press, a division of Macmillan, Inc.

while innovators accepted the goals, but rejected the means. It was innovators who Merton identified as criminal. They were not *inventors*, as invention is a legitimate path to success, but rather *innovators* in the use of illegal means to gain money, power, and success. The inherent logic of the table led Merton to posit other social types. Ritualists were said to be those who rejected success goals, but still performed their daily tasks in conformity with social expectations. They might hold regular jobs, but without the desire to advance in life. Retreatists rejected both the goals and means, and usually dropped out of society by becoming derelicts, drug users, or the like. Rebels constituted a special category—one in which the existence of both "pluses" and "minuses" indicated their desire to replace the existing system of socially approved goals and means with some other system more to their liking. They were the revolutionaries of the theory.

Merton believed that categories were not intentionally selected by the individuals who occupied them, but were imposed on people by structural aspects of society. Such factors as where they lived, how wealthy their families were, and what ethnic background they came from were all thought to be significant determinants of the "box" into which a person would be placed.

Modern writers on anomie have come to recognize that normlessness is not likely to be expressed as criminality, unless people who experience such a condition also feel that they are capable of doing something to change their lives. As Ross and Mirowsky put it, "A person who has high levels of normlessness and powerlessness is less likely to get in trouble with the law than a person who has a high level of normlessness and a high level of instrumentalism."[48]

Merton's anomie theory drew attention to the lack of equality of opportunity which existed in society at the time he was writing. An honest appraisal would probably recognize that while considerable efforts have been made to eradicate it, some of that same inequality continues today.

Subcultural Theory

Another sociological contribution to criminological theory is the idea of a subculture. A subculture is composed of a group of people who participate in a shared system of values

Answering the door in a Chicago neighborhood. Some theorists argue that neighborhood lifestyles contribute to crime. *Photo: Leonard Freed/Magnum.*

and norms which are at variance with those in the larger culture. Subcultural explanations of crime posit the existence of group values supportive of criminal behavior. Subcultures were first recognized in the enclaves formed by immigrants who came to America during the early part of the twentieth century. Statistics have shown that certain immigrant groups had low crime rates.[49] Among them were the Scandinavians, Chinese, Dutch, Germans, and Japanese. Other immigrant groups, including Italians, Mexicans, Puerto Ricans, and Africans, demonstrated a significantly greater propensity for involvement in crime.[50]

Albert Cohen (1918–) coined the term reaction formation to encompass the rejection of middle-class values by status-seeking lower-class youths who find they are not permitted access to approved opportunities for success.[51] In Cohen's eyes, it was such a reaction which led to the development of gangs and perpetuated the existence of subcultures. Walter Miller[52] described the focal concerns of subcultural participants in terms of "trouble," "toughness," "excitement," "smartness," "fate," and "autonomy." It was a focus on such concerns, Miller suggested, that led members of criminal subcultures into violations of the law. Richard Cloward and Lloyd Ohlin proposed the existence of an illegitimate opportunity structure that permitted delinquent youths to achieve in ways which were outside of legitimate avenues to success.[53]

Subcultures of Violence More recently Marvin Wolfgang and Franco Ferracuti examined homicide rates in Philadelphia and found that murder was a way of life among certain groups.[54] They discovered a "wholesale" and a "retail" price for murder—which depended upon who was killed and who did the killing. Killings which occurred within violent subgroups were more likely to be partially excused than were those that happened elsewhere. The term **subculture of violence** has come to be associated with their work and has since been applied to other locations across the country.

Critiques of subcultural theory have been numerous. A major difficulty for these theories lies in the fact that studies involving self-reports of crime commission have shown that much violence and crime occur outside of "criminal" subcultures. It appears that

Subculture of Violence A cultural setting in which violence is a traditional method of dispute resolution.

many middle- and upper-class law breakers are able to avoid handling by the justice system and therefore, do not enter the "official" crime statistics.

Hence, criminal subcultures may be those in which crime is more visible rather than more prevalent. Another criticism sees subcultures as tautological. Nettler suggests that the idea of subcultures is like saying, "(t)hose people fight because they are hostile."[55] The explanatory powers of subcultural theories would be greatly enhanced were they able to shed more light on the origins of criminal values and tendencies within the groups they describe.

SOCIAL-PSYCHOLOGICAL THEORIES

Social–Psychological School A perspective on criminological thought which highlights the role played in crime causation by weakened self-esteem and meaningless social roles. Social–psychological thinkers stress the relationship of the individual to the social group as the underlying cause of behavior.

While biological theories seem to strive for a unity of body and soul, psychological approaches uncover aspects of the personality hidden even from the mind in which they reside. Social–psychological approaches to crime causation, on the other hand, attempt to explain behavior by relating it to the cultural environment in which the individual matures and acts.

Many social–psychological theories highlight the role of social learning. They build upon the premise that behavior is learned and suggest that "bad" behavior can be unlearned. Social–psychological theories are probably the most in vogue today because they demand that responsibility be placed upon the offender for actively participating in rehabilitation efforts and because they are consistent with popular cultural and religious values centered upon teaching right from wrong.

Differential Association

In 1939 Edwin Sutherland (1883–1950) published the third edition of his *Principles of Criminology*. It contained, for the first time, a formalized statement of his theory of differential association, a perspective which Sutherland based upon the "laws of imitation" described by Gabriel Tarde.

Differential association viewed crime as the product of socialization and saw it as acquired by criminals according to the same principles that guided the learning of law-abiding behavior in conformists. Differential association removed criminality from the framework of the abnormal, and placed it squarely within a general perspective applicable to all behavior. In the 1947 edition of his text Sutherland wrote, "Criminal behavior is a part of human behavior, has much in common with non-criminal behavior, and must be explained within the same general framework as any other human behavior."[56] A study of the tenets of differential association (listed in Table 3–4) shows that Sutherland believed that even the sources of behavioral motivation were much the same for conformists as they were for criminals; that is, both groups strive for money and success, but choose different paths to the same goal.

The theory of differential association explained crime as a natural consequence of the interaction with criminal life-styles. Sutherland suggested that children raised in crime-prone environments were often isolated and unable to experience the values which would otherwise lead to conformity. Some modern writers refer to this lack of socialization in conformity as a failure to train.[57]

Differential association has considerable explanative applicability even today and still provides the basis for much research in modern criminology.[58] Even popular stories of young drug pushers, for instance, often refer to the fact that inner-city youth imitate what

TABLE 3 - 4

SUTHERLAND'S PRINCIPLES OF DIFFERENTIAL ASSOCIATION

1. Criminal behavior is learned.
2. Criminal behavior is learned in interaction with other persons in a process of communication.
3. The principal part of the learning of criminal behavior occurs within intimate personal groups.
4. When criminal behavior is learned, the learning includes (a) techniques of committing the crime, which are sometimes very complicated, sometimes very simple; (b) the specific direction of motives, drives, rationalizations, and attitudes.
5. The specific direction of motives and drives is learned from definitions of the legal codes as favorable or unfavorable.
6. A person becomes delinquent because of an excess of definitions favorable to violations of law over definitions unfavorable to violations of law.
7. Differential associations may vary in frequency, duration, priority, and intensity.
8. The process of learning criminal behavior by association with criminal and anti-criminal patterns involves all the mechanisms that are involved in any other learning.
9. While criminal behavior is an expression of general needs and values, it is not explained by those general needs and values since noncriminal behavior is an expression of the same needs and values.

Source: Edwin Sutherland, *Principles of Criminology*, 4th ed. (Chicago: J. B. Lippincott, 1947), pp. 6–7.

they see. Some residents of poverty-ridden ghettos learn quickly that fast money can be had in the illicit drug trade, and they tend to follow those examples of success with which they have experience.

Differential association theory fails, however, to explain why people have the associations they do, and why some associations seem to affect certain individuals more than others. Why, for example, are most prison guards unaffected by their constant association with offenders, while a few are brought over to the inmate side and take advantage of their position to smuggle contraband and the like? The theory has also been criticized for being so general and imprecise as to allow for little testing.[59] Complete testing of the theory would require that all the associations a person has ever had be recorded and analyzed from the standpoint of the individual—a clearly impossible task.

Other theorists continue to build on Sutherland's early work. Robert L. Burgess and Ronald L. Akers, for example, have constructed a differential association–reinforcement theory which seeks to integrate Sutherland's original propositions with B. F. Skinner's work on conditioning.[60] Burgess and Akers suggest that although values and behavior patterns are learned in association with others, the primary mechanism through which such learning occurs is operant conditioning. Reinforcement is the key, they say, to understanding any social learning as it takes place. The name social learning theory has been widely applied to the work of Burgess and Akers. It is somewhat a misnomer, however, since the term can easily encompass a wide range of approaches and should not be limited to one specific combination of the ideas found in differential association and reinforcement theory.

Restraint Theory

Containment and Social Control   Most criminological theories posit a cause of crime.[61] Some theories, however, focus less on causes than on constraints. Walter Reckless's (1899–1988) containment theory, for example, assumes that all of us are subject to inducements to crime.[62] Some of us resist these "pushes" toward criminal behavior, while others do not. The difference, according to Reckless, can be found in forces which contain behavior.

Reckless described two types of containment—inner and outer. Outer containment depends upon social roles and the norms and expectations which apply to them. People who occupy significant roles in society find themselves insulated from deviant tendencies. A corporate executive, for example, is probably less apt to hold up a liquor store than is a drifter. The difference, according to Reckless, is not due solely to income, but to the pressure to conform that the "successful" role exerts upon its occupant.

Inner containment involves a number of factors, including conscience, a positive self-image, a tolerance for frustration, and aspirations which are in line with reality. Reckless saw inner containment as more powerful than outer containment. Inner containment functions even in secret. An inner-directed person, for example, may come across a lost purse and feel compelled to locate its rightful owner and return it. If theft or greed cross the mind of the inner directed, they will say to themselves, "I'm not that kind of person. That would be wrong."

Reckless studied small, close-knit societies—including the Hutterites, Mennonites, and Amish—in developing his theory. He realized that the "containment of behavior…is…maximized under conditions of isolation and homogeneity of culture, class and population."[63] Hence, its applicability to modern American society, with its considerable heterogeneity of values and perspectives, is questionable.

Travis Hirschi emphasizes the bond of the individual to society as the primary operative mechanism in his social control theory.[64] Hirschi identifies four components of that bond: (1) emotional attachments to significant others, (2) a commitment to appropriate life-styles, (3) involvement or immersion in conventional values, and (4) a belief in the "correctness" of social obligations and the rules of the larger society. As any one of these components weakens, social control suffers and the likelihood of crime and deviance increases. Using self-reports of delinquency from high school students in California, Hirschi concluded that youngsters who were less attached to teachers and parents, and who had few positive attitudes toward their own accomplishments, were more likely to engage in crime and deviance than were others.[65]

Restraint theories provide only one-half of the causal picture. Since they focus primarily on why people do *not* break the law, they are especially weak in identifying the social–structural sources of motivations to commit crimes.[66] Similarly, the way in which bonds with different institutions interact with one another, and with personal attributes, as well as the variety of bonds operative throughout the life cycle have yet to be clarified.[67]

Neutralization Techniques   Complementing restraint theory is the neutralization approach of Gresham Sykes and David Matza.[68] Sykes and Matza believed that most people drift into and out of criminal behavior, but would not commit crime unless they had available to them techniques of neutralization. Such techniques are actually rationalizations which allow offenders to shed feelings of guilt and any sense of responsibility for their behavior. Sykes and Matza's study primarily concerned juveniles in whom, they suggested, neutralization techniques provided only a temporary respite from guilt. That respite, however, lasted long enough to avoid the twinges of conscience while a crime was being committed. Neutralization techniques include:

- Denial of responsibility ("I'm a product of my background.")
- Denial of injury ("No one was really hurt.")
- Denial of the victim ("They deserved it.")
- Condemnation of the condemners ("The cops are corrupt.")
- Appeal to higher loyalties ("I did it for my friends.")

Restraint theories suffer from a number of difficulties. They tend, as in the case of containment theory, to depend upon a general agreement as to values, or they assume that offenders are simply conformists who suffer temporary lapses. Neutralization techniques, by definition, are only needed when the delinquent has been socialized into middle-class values or where conscience is well developed. Even so, neutralization techniques do not in themselves explain crime. Such techniques are available to us all, if we make only a slight effort to conjure them up. The real question is why some people readily allow proffered neutralizations to impact their behavior, while others discount them seemingly out of hand.

Labeling

The worth of any theory of behavior is proven by how well it reflects the reality of the social world. In practice, however, theoretical perspectives find acceptance in the academic environment via a number of considerations. Labeling theory, for example, became fashionable in the 1960s. Its popularity, however, may have been due more to the cultural environment into which it was introduced rather than to any inherent quality of the theory itself.

In fact, labeling theory had been introduced by Frank Tannenbaum[69] (1893–1969) in 1938 under the rubric of "tagging." He wrote: "The young delinquent becomes bad because he is defined as bad and because he is not believed if he is good." He went on to say: "The process of making the criminal, therefore, is a process of tagging,… it becomes a way of stimulating…and evolving the very traits that are complained of.… The person becomes the thing he is described as being."[70] Tannenbaum focused on society's power to *define* an act or individual as bad and drew attention to the group need for a "scapegoat" in explaining crime. The search for causes inherent in individuals was not yet exhausted, however, and Tannenbaum's theory fell mostly on deaf ears.

Charles Manson, perhaps the most photographed criminal offender of all time, is shown here 20 years after he and his "family" shocked the world with their gruesome crimes. *Photo: Grey Villet/Black Star.*

Moral Enterprise The process undertaken by an advocacy group in order to have its values legitimated and embodied in law.

By the 1960s the social and academic environments in America had changed, and the issue of "responsibility" was seen more in terms of the group than the individual. In 1963 Howard Becker, in his book *Outsiders*, pointed out that "criminality" is not a quality inherent in an act or in a person. Crime, said Becker, results from a social definition, through law, of unacceptable behavior. That definition arises through **moral enterprise**, by which groups on both sides of an issue debate and, eventually, legislate their notion of what is moral and what is not. Becker wrote, "the central fact about deviance (is that) it is created by society.... [S]ocial groups," he said, "create deviance by making the rules whose infraction constitutes deviance."[71]

The criminal label, however, produces consequences for labeled individuals which may necessitate continued criminality. In describing the "criminal career," Becker wrote: "To be labeled a criminal one need only commit a single criminal offense.... Yet the word carries a number of connotations specifying auxiliary traits characteristic of anyone bearing the label."[72] The first time a person commits a crime, the behavior is called primary deviance, and may be a merely transitory form of behavior.

However, in the popular mind, a "known" criminal is not to be trusted, should not be hired because of the potential for crimes on the job, and would not be a good candidate for the military, marriage, or any position requiring responsibility. Society's tendency toward such thinking, Becker suggested, closed legitimate opportunities, ensuring that the only new behavioral alternatives available to the labeled criminal would be deviant ones. Succeeding episodes of criminal behavior were seen as a form of secondary deviance, which eventually became stabilized in the behavioral repertoire and self-concept of the labeled person.[73]

Labeling theory can be critiqued along a number of dimensions. First, it is not really a "theory" in that labeling does not uncover the genesis of criminal behavior. It is more powerful in its description of how such behavior continues than in explaining how it originates. Second, labeling theory does not recognize the possibility that the labeled individual may make successful attempts at reform and shed the negative label. Finally, the theory does not provide an effective way of dealing with offenders. Should people who commit crimes not be arrested and tried, so as to avoid the consequences of negative labels? It would be exceedingly naive to suggest that all repeat criminal behavior would cease, as labeling theory might predict, if people who commit crimes are not officially "handled" by the system.

CONFLICT THEORIES

Radical Criminology

Radical Criminology A conflict perspective which sees crime as engendered by the unequal distribution of wealth, power, and other resources—which it believes is especially characteristic of capitalist societies. Also called "critical criminology."

Criminological theory took a new direction during the 1960s and 1970s, brought about in part by the turmoil which characterized American society during that period. **Radical criminology** was born and, like so many other perspectives of the time, placed the blame for criminality and deviant behavior squarely upon officially sanctioned cultural and economic arrangements. The distribution of wealth and power in society was held to be the primary cause of criminal behavior, especially among those who were disenfranchised—or left out of the "American dream." Poverty and discrimination were seen to lead to frustration and pent-up hostilities that expressed themselves in murder, rape, theft, and other crimes.

Radical criminology had its roots in earlier conflict theories and in the thought of Dutch criminologist Willem A. Bonger. Some authors have distinguished between conflict theory and radical criminology by naming them "radical conflict theory" and "conservative conflict theory."[74] The difference, however, is mostly to be found in the rhetoric of the times. Early theories saw conflict as a natural part of any society and believed that struggles for power and control would always occur. "Losers" would tend to be defined as "criminal," and constraints on their behavior would be legislated. Characteristic of this perspective are the approaches of Austin Turk (1934–) and George Vold[75] (1896–1967). An even earlier **conflict perspective** can be found in the culture conflict notions of Thorsten Sellin, who was concerned with the clash of immigrant values and traditions with those of established American culture.[76]

Radical criminology went a step farther. It recognized that the struggle to control resources is central to society, and it encompassed the notion that the law itself is a tool of the powerful. The focus of radical criminology, however, was capitalism and the evils which capitalism was believed to entail. The ideas of Karl Marx (1818–1883) decisively entered the field of criminology through the writings of William Chambliss[77] (1933–) and Richard Quinney[78] (1934–). Marxist thought assumed that the lower classes were always exploited by the "owners" in society. According to Marx, the labor of the lower classes provides the basis for the accumulated wealth of the upper classes. Marx saw the working classes as suffering under the consequences of a "false class consciousness," perpetrated by the powerful. The poor were trained to believe that capitalism was in their best interests, and, according to Marx, only when the exploited workers realized their exploitation would they rebel and change society for the better.

American radical criminology built upon the ideals of the 1960s, and charged that the "establishment," controlled by the upper classes, perverted justice through the unequal application of judicial sanctions. As David Greenberg has observed, "many researchers attributed the overrepresentation of blacks and persons from impoverished family backgrounds in arrest and conviction statistics to the discriminatory practices of the enforcement agencies. It was not that the poor stole more, but rather that when they did, the police were more likely to arrest them."[79]

Conflict Perspective A theoretical approach which holds that crime is the natural consequence of economic and other social inequities. Conflict theorists highlight the stresses which arise between and within social groups as they compete with one another for resources and survival. The social forces which result are viewed as major determinants of group and individual behavior, including crime.

The New Criminology

While American criminologists were applying such structural interpretations to criminal justice data, some European theorists were developing a similar school of thought termed new criminology. New criminology evolved first in the social welfare societies of Scandinavia, where it focused on the needs of the poor.[80] Both radical criminology and the new criminology represented attempts to resolve the crime problem through social change. Criminologists were asked to become active agents of social change and to work for the elimination of injustice.

Gwynn Nettler, in an attack on radical criminology, has identified "epistemological, factual, sociological, moral, and promissory"[81] difficulties in the approach. Epistemological shortcomings, says Nettler, derive from the fact that radical criminologists are more political than objective and, he claims, interested in making the "world other than it is."[82] Nettler also suggests that conflict perspectives on criminology lack the evidence needed to support their most basic premises; worse still, he says, they have not "submitted their major thesis to empirical test."[83] Finally, according to Nettler, radical criminology suffers a moral debility because it reverses "the true order of affairs, as best we know them."[84] Governments are *not* the evildoers that radical criminology would make them out to be, nor are individual offenders innocent victims.

All conflict theories of criminality face the difficulty of realistic implementation. Radical criminology in particular is flawed by its narrow-sighted emphasis on capitalist societies. It fails to recognize adequately the role of human nature in the creation of social classes and in the perpetuation of the struggle for control of resources. Radical criminology seems to imply that some sort of utopian social arrangements—perhaps communism—would eliminate most crime. Such a belief is contrary to historical experience, as a close look at any contemporary communistic society will reveal both social conflict and crime.

THE PHENOMENOLOGICAL SCHOOL

The Criminal Personality

Phenomenological Criminology A perspective on crime causation which holds that the significance of criminal behavior is ultimately knowable only to those who participate in it. Central to this school of thought is the belief that social actors endow their behavior with meaning and purpose. Hence, a crime might mean one thing to the person who commits it, quite another to the victim, and something far different still to professional participants in the justice system.

Some recent attempts at understanding criminality have been more descriptive than explanatory. These attempts hold to the belief that an adequate description of any phenomenon allows for the accumulation of useful scientific knowledge through a familiarity with the thing under study. The old dictum, "It takes a thief to catch a thief," has meaning for this school of thought. Approaches such as these are referred to as phenomenological and depend upon detailed study of the criminal personality.

Phenomenological criminology built upon the ideas of George Herbert Mead[85] (1863–1931), W. I. Thomas[86] (1863–1947), and the German philosopher Alfred Schutz[87] (1899–1959). Mead propounded a theory called symbolic interaction, in which he demonstrated how people give meaning to the things around them and to their lives. Thomas explained that the significance of any human behavior is relative to the intentions behind it and to the situation in which it is interpreted. Hence behavior which, in one place or at one time, is taken for granted, may, in another place or time, be perceived as deviant or even criminal.

In the 1970s Samuel Yochelson (1906–1976) and Stanton E. Samenow (1941–) published their multivolume work *The Criminal Personality.*[88] Yochelson had been the director of the Program for the Investigation of Criminal Behavior at St. Elizabeth's Hospital in Washington, D.C., since 1961. Samenow joined Yochelson in 1970, and the pair eventually collected detailed data on 255 criminals. Many of the offenders were hospitalized, but others were on parole; some were never arrested, but were self-admitted offenders. Yochelson and Samenow identified 53 patterns of thought and action which they said were present in all 255 offenders. They described criminals as untrustworthy, demanding, and exploitive of others, with little capacity for love. Habitual offenders were said to harbor a persistent anger which could boil over at any time. Pride, another aspect of the criminal personality, was seen as based upon notions of what it takes to "be a man." Similarly, "superoptimism," or the belief that they could do no wrong, characterized many offenders immediately prior to the commission of crimes. This combination of pride, anger, and extreme optimism made the criminal, in the eyes of Yochelson and Samenow, dangerous indeed.[89]

Yochelson and Samenow also argued that the meaning criminal behavior had in the eyes of offenders themselves was at considerable variance with the way in which society interpreted that behavior. They found little use for the "causative" theories of criminal behavior, seeing them as further ammunition which the offender could use in defense of deviant behavior. To think of oneself, for example, as a "victim" of a bad family background provides a justification for a life of crime, with little responsibility being placed squarely on the offender to reform.

About the same time, Frank Schmalleger (1947–) described career criminals as living in a world quite different from that occupied by the nonoffending "conformist."[90] Schmalleger's thesis was that hardened offenders spurn conventionality as dull and choose criminality as a career because of its inherent excitement.

Phenomenologists, because of their avoidance of causality, provide little practical direction for treatment. Schmalleger says, "[y]ou cannot change a career criminal; you must convert him."[91] Total conversion—from a criminal to a conformist mode of thought—involves a dramatic change in life-style and self-concept. It is, unfortunately, unachievable except possibly through an intense commitment, which must begin with the offender.

OTHER EXPLANATIONS

Theories of crime continue to develop. Some new theories fall squarely into the mainstream of existing thought. Others, of varying scientific worth, are more innovative. Spiritual accounts, in which offenders are depicted as sinful, born evil, or demon possessed, are popular among some groups with transcendent world views. Unfortunately, such theories are difficult to test, and the evidence for or against them will always be more intuitive than scientific.

Occasionally novel approaches surface within the field of criminology. Recent debate among criminologists, for example, has highlighted the possible impact of climatological conditions upon crime rates.[92] At least one study has claimed that changes in the weather can have as much explanatory power as sociological explanations of deviant behavior.[93] Such studies attempt to use sociobiological concepts to provide an explanatory bridge between climate and behavior. Climatological explanations of crime have been criticized for failing to recognize the complexity of weather conditions and for conceptualizing of climatological variables as though they were social scientific entities.[94] Climatological approaches to crime and deviance are in their infancy. They represent, however, what may

The crimes of some law violators seem to defy explanation. Here Jeffrey Dahmer, accused in the dismemberment slayings of more than a dozen young men, listens as the charges against him are read. *Photo: Allan Fredrickson/Reuters/Bettmann.*

be a coming wave of fresh suggestions in a field which has grown somewhat rigid in its inability to transcend established explanations, even when the power of those explanations is clearly limited.

SUMMARY

Most of the theoretical explanations for crime which have been offered in this chapter are grounded in biology, psychology, or sociology. Biologically based theories posit a genetic basis for deviant and criminal behavior. The notion of a "weak" gene has recently been expanded to include the impact of environmental contaminants, poor nutrition, and food additives on behavior. Studies of fraternal twins and chromosome structure have led biological theories into the modern day.

Psychological explanations of crime are of two types: psychoanalytical and behavioral. Psychoanalytical theories are heard less frequently today than in the past. Some behavioral approaches depend considerably upon testing techniques which categorize offenders into "types," but whose explanatory power is limited. The stimulus–response model depicts behavior as the consequence of a conditioning process which extends over the entire life span of an individual.

Sociological theories, which hold that the individual is a product of the environment, constitute today's perspective of choice. These theories emphasize the role of social structure, inequality, and socialization in generating criminality. The danger, however, of most sociological approaches is that they tend to deny the significance of any differences beyond those which are acquired through group interaction. That the human being is a conglomeration of biology, mental processes, and acquired behavior is a more realistic perspective.

Criminology seems headed toward the day when a "unified theory" of conduct will draw upon all explanatory dimensions in order to interpret the whole range of human behavior. The circle begun with classical theorists will be complete when the role of individual choice takes its place alongside the more mechanistic determinants of behavior.

DISCUSSION QUESTIONS

1. What is a theory? Can you name or describe any theories that you use in making decisions in your daily life?

2. What is the purpose of criminological theory? Do any of the theories described in this chapter fill that purpose especially well?

3. What do we mean when we say that most theories are unicausal? What would a multicausal theory be like?

4. Describe the three major groups of theories in criminology? What are the shortcomings of each group? Which group do you think has the most explanatory power? Why?

5. Which of the major types of theories is probably the most accepted today? What dangers do you see in accepting any one type of theory over another type?

6. How do restraint theories differ from other kinds of explanations of crime causation? What do restraint theories assume is true about most of us?

7. Why are treatment modalities often based upon specific criminological theories? What form of treatment might be predicated upon phenomenological theories of crime?

8. How do radical criminologists explain crime? What form of "treatment" might be predicated upon radical theories of crime?

ENDNOTES

1. Cited in Gwynn Nettler, *Killing One Another* (Cincinnati, OH: Anderson, 1982), p. 194.
2. "Russ Sentenced to Life Without Parole," *The San Diego Union*, April 27, 1991, pp. B-1, 4.
3. "Russ Receives Life Sentence in Wife Killing," *The Los Angeles Times*, April 27, 1991, pp. B1, 10.
4. "Russ Sentenced to Life Without Parole."
5. "Russ Receives Life Sentence in Wife Killing."
6. Jack Gibbs, "The State of Criminological Theory," *Criminology*, Vol. 25, no. 4 (1987), pp. 821–827.
7. The word "scientific" is used here to refer to the application of generally accepted research strategies designed to reject explanations which rival the one under study.
8. The term "hedonistic calculus" is taken from Stephen Schafer's *Theories in Criminology* (New York: Random House, 1969), p. 106.
9. Ibid., p. 109.
10. *Cosmopolitan* (date unknown), p. 133.
11. For a modern reprint of a widely read nineteenth-century work on phrenology, see Orson Squire Fowler and Lorenzo Niles Fowler, *Phrenology: A Practical Guide to Your Head* (New York: Chelsea House, 1980).
12. Schafer, *Theories in Criminology*.
13. "Constitutional" theories of crime causation refer to the *physical constitution*, or bodily characteristics, of the offenders and have nothing to do with the Constitution of the United States.
14. For more information, see Richard Herrnstein, "Crime File: Biology and Crime," a study guide (Washington, D.C.: National Institute of Justice, no date).
15. Patricia Jacobs, et al., "Aggressive Behavior, Mental Subnormality and the XYY Male," *Nature*, Vol. 208 (1965), pp. 1351–1352.
16. Schafer, *Theories in Criminology*, p. 193.
17. D. Hill and W. Sargent, "A Case of Matricide," *Lancet*, Vol. 244 (1943), pp. 526–527.
18. See, for example, A. R. Mawson and K. J. Jacobs, "Corn Consumption, Tryptophan, and Cross-national Homicide Rates," *Journal of Orthomolecular Psychiatry*, Vol. 7 (1978), pp. 227–230, and A. Hoffer, "The Relation of Crime to Nutrition," *Humanist in Canada*, Vol. 8 (1975), p. 8.

19. See, for example, C. Hawley and R. E. Buckley, "Food Dyes and Hyperkinetic Children," *Academy Therapy*, Vol. 10 (1974), pp. 27–32, and Alexander Schauss, *Diet, Crime & Delinquency* (Berkeley, CA: Parker House, 1980).

20. "Special Report: Measuring Your Life with Coffee Spoons," *Tufts University Diet & Nutrition Letter*, Vol. 2, no. 2 (April 1984), pp. 3–6.

21. See, for example, "Special Report: Does What You Eat Affect Your Mood and Actions?" *Tufts University Diet & Nutrition Letter*, Vol. 2, no. 12 (February 1985), pp. 4–6.

22. See *Tufts University Diet & Nutrition Letter*, Vol. 2, no. 11 (January 1985), p. 2, and "Special Report: Why Sugar Continues to Concern Nutritionists," *Tufts University Diet & Nutrition Letter*, Vol. 3, no. 3 (May 1985), pp. 3–6.

23. A. Hoffer, "Children with Learning and Behavioral Disorders," *Journal of Orthomolecular Psychiatry*, Vol. 5 (1976), p. 229.

24. "Special Report: Does What You Eat Affect Your Mood and Actions?" *Tufts University Diet & Nutrition Letter*, Vol. 2, no. 12 (February 1985), p. 4.

25. See, for example, R. T. Rada, D. R. Laws, and R. Kellner, "Plasma Testosterone Levels in the Rapist," *Psychomatic Medicine*, Vol. 38 (1976), pp. 257–268.

26. "The Insanity of Steroid Abuse," *Newsweek*, May 23, 1988, p. 75.

27. Sarnoff Mednick and Jan Volavka, "Biology and Crime," in Norval Morris and Michael Tonry, eds., *Crime and Justice* (Chicago: University of Chicago Press, 1980), pp. 85–159.

28. Sarnoff Mednick and S. Gloria Shaham, eds., *New Paths in Criminology* (Lexington, MA: D. C. Heath, 1979).

29. R. B. Cattell, *The Inheritance of Personality and Ability: Research Methods and Findings* (New York: Academic Press, 1982).

30. Karl Christiansen, "A Preliminary Study of Criminality Among Twins," in Sarnoff Mednick and Karl O. Christiansen, eds., *Biosocial Bases of Criminal Behavior* (New York: Gardner Press, 1977).

31. James Q. Wilson and Richard J. Herrnstein, *Crime and Human Nature* (New York: Simon & Schuster, 1985).

32. "Criminals Born and Bred," *Newsweek*, September 16, 1985, p. 69.

33. William J. Chambliss, *Exploring Criminology* (New York: Macmillan, 1988), p. 202.

34. Richard Louis Dugdale, *The Jukes: A Study in Crime, Pauperism, Disease, and Heredity*, 3rd ed. (New York: G. P. Putnam's Sons, 1895).

35. Henry Herbert Goddard, *The Kallikak Family: A Study in the Heredity of Feeblemindedness* (New York: Macmillan, 1912).

36. Sigmund Freud, *A General Introduction to Psychoanalysis* (New York: Boni & Liveright, 1920).

37. Nettler, *Killing One Another*, p. 79.

38. Richard L. Ault and James T. Reese, "A Psychological Assessment of Crime Profiling," *FBI Law Enforcement Bulletin* (March 1980), pp. 22–25.

39. John E. Douglas and Alan E. Burgess, "Criminal Profiling: A Viable Investigative Tool Against Violent Crime," *FBI Law Enforcement Bulletin* (December 1986), pp. 9–13.

40. Robert R. Hazelwood and John E. Douglass, "The Lust Murderer," *FBI Law Enforcement Bulletin* (April 1980), pp. 18–22.

41. A. O. Rider, "The Firesetter—A Psychological Profile," *FBI Law Enforcement Bulletin*, Vol. 49, no. 6 (June 1980), pp. 4–11.

42. M. Reiser, "Crime-Specific Psychological Consultation," *The Police Chief* (March 1982), pp. 53–56.

43. Thomas Strentz, "A Terrorist Psychosocial Profile: Past and Present," *FBI Law Enforcement Bulletin* (April 1988), pp. 13–19.

44. Robert E. Park and Ernest Burgess, *Introduction to the Science of Sociology*, 2nd ed. (Chicago: University of Chicago Press, 1924), and Robert E. Park, ed. *The City* (Chicago: University of Chicago Press, 1925).

45. Clifford R. Shaw and Henry D. McKay, "Social Factors in Juvenile Delinquency," in Vol. II of the *Report of the Causes of Crime*, National Commission on Law Observance and Enforcement Report No. 13 (Washington, D.C.: U.S. Government Printing Office, 1931), and Clifford R. Shaw, *Juvenile Delinquency in Urban Areas* (Chicago: University of Chicago Press, 1942).

46. Emile Durkheim, *Suicide* (New York: The Free Press, 1951).

47. Robert K. Merton, "Social Structure and Anomie," *American Sociological Review*, Vol. 3 (1938), pp. 672–682.

48. Catherine E. Ross and John Mirowsky, "Normlessness, Powerlessness, and Trouble with the Law," *Criminology*, Vol. 25, no. 2 (May 1987), p. 257.

49. See Nettler, *Killing One Another*, p. 58.

50. This is not to say that all members of these groups engaged in criminal behavior, but rather that statistics indicated higher average crime rates for these groups than for certain others during the period of time immediately after they immigrated to the United States.

51. Albert K. Cohen, *Delinquent Boys: The Culture of the Gang* (Glencoe, IL: The Free Press, 1958).

52. Walter B. Miller, "Lower Class Culture as a Generating Milieu of Gang Delinquency," *Journal of Social Issues*, Vol. 14 (1958), pp. 5–19.

53. Richard Cloward and Lloyd Ohlin, *Delinquency and Opportunity: A Theory of Delinquent Gangs* (New York: The Free Press, 1960).

54. Marvin Wolfgang, *Patterns in Criminal Homicide* (Philadelphia: University of Pennsylvania Press, 1958). See also Marvin Wolfgang and Franco Ferracuti, *The Subculture of Violence: Toward an Integrated Theory in Criminology* (London: Tavistock, 1967).

55. Nettler, *Killing One Another*, p. 67.

56. Edwin Sutherland, *Principles of Criminology*, 4th ed. (Chicago: J. B. Lippincott, 1947), p. 4.

57. Nettler, *Killing One Another*.

58. See, for example, James D. Orcutt, "Differential Association and Marijuana Use: A Closer Look at Sutherland (with a Little Help from Becker)," *Criminology*, Vol. 25, no. 2 (1987), pp. 341–358.

59. John E. Conklin, *Criminology*, 3rd ed. (New York: Macmillan 1989), p. 278.

60. Robert L. Burgess and Ronald L. Akers, "A Differential Association-Reinforcement Theory of Criminal Behavior," *Social Problems*, Vol. 14 (Fall 1966), pp. 128–147.

61. Some theories are multicausal and provide explanations for criminal behavior which include a diversity of "causes."

62. Walter C. Reckless, *The Crime Problem*, 4th ed. (New York: Appleton-Century-Crofts, 1961).

63. Ibid., p. 472.

64. Travis Hirschi, *Causes of Delinquency* (Berkeley: University of California Press, 1969).

65. Ibid., p. 472.

66. For a more elaborate criticism of this sort, see John E. Conklin, *Criminology*, 3rd ed. (New York: Macmillan, 1989), p. 260.

67. Ibid., p. 260.

68. Gresham Sykes and David Matza, "Techniques of Neutralization: A Theory of Delinquency," *American Sociological Review*, Vol. 22 (1957), pp. 664–670.

69. Many of the concepts used by Howard Becker in explicating his theory of labeling, were, in fact, used previously not only by Frank Tannenbaum, but also appeared in the work of Edwin M. Lemert. Lemert wrote of "societal reaction," "primary" and "secondary deviance," and even used the word "labeling" in his book *Social Pathology* (New York: McGraw-Hill, 1951).

70. Frank Tannenbaum, *Crime and the Community* (Boston: Ginn and Co., 1938), pp. 19–20.

71. Howard Becker, *Outsiders: Studies in the Sociology of Deviance* (New York: The Free Press, 1963), pp. 8–9.

72. Ibid.

73. Ibid., p. 33.

74. See George B. Vold, *Theoretical Criminology* (New York: Oxford University Press, 1986).

75. Austin T. Turk, *Criminality and the Legal Order* (Chicago: Rand McNally, 1969).

76. Thorsten Sellin, *Culture Conflict and Crime* (New York: Social Science Research Council, 1938).

77. William B. Chambliss and Robert B. Seidman, *Law, Order, and Power* (Reading, MA: Addison-Wesley, 1971).

78. Richard Quinney, *The Social Reality of Crime* (Boston: Little, Brown, 1970).

79. David F. Greenberg, *Crime and Capitalism* (Palo Alto, CA: Mayfield, 1981), p. 3.

80. See Ivan Taylor, Paul Walton, and Jock Young, *The New Criminology* (New York: Harper & Row, 1973).

81. Gwynn Nettler, *Explaining Crime*, 2nd ed. (New York: McGraw-Hill, 1978), p. 230.

82. Ibid., p. 214.

83. Ibid., p. 215.

84. Ibid., p. 221.

85. George Herbert Mead, in *Mind, Self, and Society*, Charles W. Morris, ed. (Chicago: University of Chicago Press, 1934).

86. William I. Thomas and Florian Znaneicki, *The Polish Peasant in Europe and America* (Chicago: University of Chicago Press, 1918).

87. Alfred Schutz, *The Phenomenology of the Social World* (Evanston, IL: Northwestern University Press, 1967).

88. Samuel Yochelson and Stanton E. Samenow, *The Criminal Personality*, 3 vols. (New York: Jason Aronson, 1976).

89. For a good summary of Yochelson and Samenow's work, see Vergil L. Williams, *Dictionary of American Penology: An Introductory Guide* (Westport, CT: Greenwood Press, 1979).

90. Frank Schmalleger, "The World of the Career Criminal," *Human Nature* (March 1979).

91. Ibid.

92. Steven P. Lab and J. David Hirschel, "Climatological Conditions and Crime: The Forecast Is...?" *Justice Quarterly*, Vol. 5, no. 2 (June 1988), pp. 281–299.

93. Ibid., p. 297.

94. James L. LeBeau, "Comment— Weather and Crime: Trying to Make Social Sense of A Physical Process," *Justice Quarterly*, Vol. 5, no. 2 (June 1988), pp. 302–309.

CRIMINAL

LAW

Law is the art of the good and the fair.
—ULPIAN, ROMAN JUDGE (CIRCA 200 A.D.)

Every law is an infraction of liberty.
—JEREMY BENTHAM (1748-1832)

Law should be like death, which spares no one.
—MONTESQUIEU (1689-1755)

…No State shall make or enforce any law which shall abridge the privileges or immunities of citizens of the United States; nor shall any State deprive any person of life, liberty, or property, without due process of law; nor deny to any person within its jurisdiction the equal protection of the laws.
—FOURTEENTH AMENDMENT TO THE U.S. CONSTITUTION

KEY CONCEPTS

jural postulates	procedural law	precedent
misdemeanor	felony	Code of Hammurabi
civil law	criminal law	tort
McNaughten rule	substantial capacity	*stare decisis*
codification	entrapment	

KEY NAMES

John Stuart Mill	Daniel McNaughten	Nigel Walker
Roscoe Pound	Oliver Wendell Holmes	Karl Marx

KEY CASES

Jacobson v. *U.S.*	*U.S.* v. *Felix*

SOURCES OF MODERN CRIMINAL LAW

Twenty years ago, as South American jungles were being cleared to make way for farmers and other settlers, a group of mercenaries brutally attacked and wiped out a small tribe of local Indians. About 20 Indian men, women, and children were hacked to death with machetes or shot. The Indians had refused to give up their land, and would not move. At their arrest the killers uttered something that, to our ears, sounds frightening: "How can you arrest us?" they said. "We didn't know it was illegal to kill Indians!"

These men killed many people. But, they claimed, they were ignorant of the fact that the law forbade such a thing in this case. Their ignorance of the law was rejected as a defense at their trial, and they were convicted of murder. All received lengthy prison sentences.

The men in this story were hardly literate, with almost no formal education. They knew very little about the law, and, apparently, even less about basic moral principles. We, on the other hand, living in a modern society with highly developed means of communications, much formal schooling, and a large work force of professionals skilled in interpreting the law, usually know what the law *says*. But do we really know what the law *is*?

Most of us would probably agree that the law is whatever legislators, through the exercise of their politically sanctioned wisdom, tell us it is. If we hold to that belief, we would expect to be able to find the law unambiguously specified, in a set of books or codes.

Practically speaking, the laws of a nation or of a state are found in statutory provisions and constitutional enactments, as well as in the rulings of courts. According to the authoritative *Black's Law Dictionary*, the word *law* "generally contemplates both statutory and case law." If the law could be found entirely ensconced in written legal codes, we would need far fewer lawyers than we find practicing today. Some laws (in the sense of precedents established by the courts) do not exist "on the books," but even those that

The Code of Hammurabi, one of the oldest judicial codes known, was discovered inscribed on this stone obelisk which dates from 1950 B.C. Figures at the top of the stone depict King Hammurabi receiving the law from the Babylonian sun god. *Photo: The Granger Collection.*

do are open to interpretation. A complete and accurate understanding of modern American criminal law, can only be had by someone who is informed as to both its history and philosophical foundation.

THE CODE OF HAMMURABI

Modern **law** is the result of a long evolution of legal principles (see Table 4–1). The Code of Hammurabi is one of the first known bodies of law to survive and be available for study today. King Hammurabi ruled the ancient city of Babylon around the year 2000 B.C. The Code of Hammurabi is a set of laws engraved on stone tablets which were intended to establish property and other rights. Babylon was a commercial center, and the right of private property formed a crucial basis for prosperous growth. Hammurabi's laws spoke to issues of theft, ownership, sexual relationships, and interpersonal violence. As Marvin

Law A rule of conduct, generally found enacted in the form of a statute, which proscribes and/or mandates certain forms of behavior. Statutory law is often the result of moral enterprise by interest groups which, through the exercise of political power, are successful in seeing their valuative perspectives enacted into law.

TABLE 4 - 1

SOURCES OF THE LAW

Historical Sources of the Law	*Modern Sources of American Law*
Arguments from nature	The U.S. Constitution
Roman law	The Declaration of Independence
The Old and New Testaments	Statutes
The Magna Carta	Case law
Common law	
Religious belief and practice	

Wolfgang has observed, "In its day, 1700 B.C., the Hammurabi Code, with its emphasis on retribution, amounted to a brilliant advance in penal philosophy mainly because it represented an attempt to keep cruelty within bounds."[1] Prior to the Code, captured offenders often faced the most barbarous of punishments, frequently at the hands of revenge-seeking victims, no matter how minor their offenses had been.

> If a married woman shall be caught lying with another man, both shall be bound and thrown into the river.
>
> —*Code of Hammurabi*

EARLY ROMAN LAW

Of considerable significance for our own legal tradition is early Roman Law. Roman legions under the Emperor Claudius conquered England in the mid-first century. Roman authority over "Britannia" was consolidated by later rulers who built walls and fortifications to keep out the still-hostile Scots. Roman customs, law, and language were forced upon the English population during the succeeding three centuries under the Pax Romana—a peace imposed by the military of Rome.[2]

Roman law derived from the Twelve Tables, written about 450 B.C. The Twelve Tables were a collection of basic rules related to family, religious, and economic life. The Tables appear to have been based upon common and fair practices generally accepted among early tribes which existed prior to the establishment of the Roman Republic. Unfortunately, only fragments of the Tables survive today.

The best known legal period of Roman history occurred under the rule of the Emperor Justinian I, who ruled between 527 and 565 A.D. By the sixth century, the Roman Empire had declined substantially in size and influence and was near the end of its life. In what may have been an effort to preserve Roman values and traditions, Justinian undertook the laborious process of distilling Roman laws into a set of writings. The Justinian Code actually consisted of three lengthy legal documents: (1) the Institutes, (2) the Digest, and (3) the Code itself. Justinian's code distinguished between two major legal categories: public and private laws. Public laws dealt with the organization of the Roman state, its Senate, and governmental offices. Private law concerned itself with contracts, personal possessions, the legal status of various types of persons (citizens, free persons, slaves, freedmen, guardians, husbands and wives, etc.) and injuries to citizens. It contained elements of both our modern civil and criminal law, and, no doubt, influenced Western legal thought through the Middle Ages.

COMMON LAW

Common law forms the basis of much of our modern statutory and case law. It has often been called *the* major source of modern criminal law.

Common law refers to a traditional body of unwritten legal precedents created through everyday practice and supported by court decisions during the Middle Ages in English society. As novel situations arose and were dealt with by British justices, their declarations became the start for any similar future deliberation. These decisions generally incorporated the customs of society as it operated at the time.

Common law was given considerable legitimacy upon the official declaration that it was the law of the land by the English King Edward the Confessor in the eleventh century. The authority of common law was further reinforced by the decision of William the Conqueror to use popular customs as the basis for judicial action following his subjugation of Britain in 1066 A.D.

Eventually, court decisions were recorded and made available to barristers (the English word for trial lawyers) and judges. As Howard Abadinsky says, "Common law involved the transformation of community rules into a national legal system. The controlling element (was) precedent."[3]

Common Law A body of unwritten judicial opinion which was based upon customary social practices of Anglo-Saxon society during the Middle Ages.

THE MAGNA CARTA

The Magna Carta (literally, "great charter") is another important source of modern laws and legal procedure. The Magna Carta was signed on June 15, 1215 by King John of England at Runnymede, under pressure from British barons who took advantage of John's military defeats at the hands of Pope Innocent III and King Philip Augustus of France. The barons demanded a pledge from the king to respect their traditional rights and forced the king to agree to be bound by law.

At the time of its signing, the Magna Carta, although 63 chapters in length, was little more than a feudal document[4] listing specific royal concessions. Its wording, however, was later interpreted during a judicial revolt in 1613 to support individual rights. Sir Edward Coke, chief justice under James I, held that the Magna Carta guaranteed basic liberties for all British citizens and ruled that any acts of Parliament which contravened common law would be void. There is some evidence that this famous ruling became the basis for the rise of the U.S. Supreme Court, with its power to nullify laws enacted by Congress.[5] Similarly, one specific provision of the Magna Carta, designed originally to prohibit the king from prosecuting the barons without just cause, was expanded into the concept of "due process of law," a fundamental cornerstone of modern legal procedure. Because of these later interpretations the Magna Carta has been called "the foundation stone of our present liberties...."[6]

THE CONSTITUTION

The U.S. Constitution is one of the most significant and enduring well-springs of our modern criminal law. The Constitution was created through a long process of debate by the federal Constitutional Convention meeting in Philadelphia in 1787. The Constitution is the final authority in all questions pertaining to the rights of individuals, the power of the federal government and the states to create laws and prosecute offenders, and the limits of punishments which can be imposed for law violations.

EQUAL JUSTICE UNDER LAW

—Words inscribed above the entrance to the U.S. Supreme Court

Although the Constitution does not itself contain many prohibitions on behavior, it is the final authority in deciding whether existing laws are acceptable according to the principles upon which our country is founded. Historically, it has served to guide justices in gauging the merits of citizen's claims concerning the handling of their cases by the agencies of justice.

NATURAL LAW

Some people believe that the basis for many of our criminal laws can be found in immutable moral principles or some identifiable aspect of the natural order. The Ten Commandments, "inborn tendencies," the idea of sin, and perceptions of various forms of order in the universe and in the social world have all provided a basis for the assertion that a "natural law" exists. Natural law comes from outside the social group and is thought to be knowable through some form of revelation, intuition, or prophecy.

Natural law was used by the early Christian church as a powerful argument in support of its interests. Secular rulers were pressed to reinforce Church doctrine in any laws they decreed. Thomas Aquinas (1225–1274) wrote in his *Summa Theologica* that any man-made law which contradicts natural law is corrupt in the eyes of God.[7] Religious practice, which strongly reflected natural law conceptions, was central to the life of early British society. Hence, natural law, as it was understood at the time, was incorporated into English common law throughout the Middle Ages.

Natural law became an issue in the confirmation hearings conducted for U.S. Supreme Court judicial nominee Clarence Thomas. Here Senate Judiciary Committee members prepare to question Thomas, who was later confirmed. *Photo: Dennis Brack/Black Star.*

The Constitution of the United States is built around an understanding of the natural law as held by Thomas Jefferson and other framers of that important document. When the framers wrote of inalienable rights to "life, liberty, property,...," they referred to the natural due of all men and women. Truths which are held to be "self-evident" can only be such if they are somehow available to us all through reasoning or the promptings of conscience.

Students of natural law have set for themselves the task of uncovering just what that law encompasses. The modern debate over abortion is an example of the use of natural law arguments to support both sides in the dispute. Antiabortion forces, frequently called "pro lifers," claim that the unborn fetus is a person and that he or she is entitled to all the protections that we would give to any other living human being. Such protection, they suggest, is basic and humane, and lies in the natural relationship of one human being to another. They are striving for passage of a law or a reinterpretation of past Supreme Court precedent that would support their position.

Supporters of the present law (which allows abortion upon request under certain conditions) maintain that abortion is a "right" of any pregnant woman because she is the one in control of her body. Such "pro choice" groups also claim that the legal system must address the abortion question, but only by way of offering protection to this "natural right" of women. Keep in mind, however, that what we refer to as "the present law" is not so much a law "on the books," but rather a consequence of a decision rendered by the U.S. Supreme Court in the case of *Roe* v. *Wade.*[8]

Mala in Se/Mala Prohibita

Natural law lends credence to the belief that certain actions are wrong in themselves. These behaviors are called *mala in se*, a Latin term which generally includes murder, rape, theft, arson, and other crimes of violence. Some states have legislated a special offense category called crime against nature. Crimes against nature, as specified in modern law, mostly encompass sexual deviance which is regarded as "contrary to the order of nature." Homosexuality, lesbianism, bestiality, and oral copulation are often prosecuted under these statutes and may carry with them quite severe punishments.

Crimes which fall outside of this "natural" category are called *mala prohibita*, meaning that they are wrong only because they are prohibited by the law. Poaching on the king's land is an example of what was a *mala prohibita* crime under English common law.

It is easy to imagine that primitive societies, without a system of codified statutes, would still understand that some forms of behavior are wrong. This intuitive recognition of deviance forms the basis of both natural law and the classification of certain offenses as *mala in se*.

The terminology which distinguished *mala in se* from *mala prohibita* offenses derives from common law and was an important consideration in deciding sentences in early England. *Mala prohibita* crimes were tried by justices of the peace and carried penalties which were generally far less severe than those for *mala in se* crimes.

PURPOSES OF THE LAW

Max Weber (1864–1920), an eminent sociologist of the early twentieth century, said the primary purpose of law is to regulate the flow of human interaction.[9] By creating enforceable rules, laws make the behavior of others predictable. This first, and most significant, purpose of the law can be simply stated: laws support social order.

Laws also serve a variety of other purposes. They ensure that the philosophical, moral, and economic perspectives of their creators are protected and made credible. They maintain values and uphold established patterns of social privilege. They sustain existing power relationships, and, finally, they support a system for the punishment and rehabilitation of offenders. Modifications of the law, when gradually induced, promote orderly change in the rest of society.

The question of *what the law does* is quite different from the question of *what the law should do.* Writing in the mid-1800s, John Stuart Mill (1806–1873) questioned the liberal use of the criminal law as a tool for social reform.[10] Mill objected strongly to the use of law as a "way of compulsion and control" for any purpose other than to prevent harm to others. Behavior which might be thought morally "wrong" should not be contravened by law, said Mill, unless it was also harmful to others. In similar fashion, Nigel Walker, a British criminologist of this century, applied what he called "a sociological eye" to the criminal codes of Western nations and concluded that criminal statutes are not appropriate which seek to contravene behavior which lacks a clear and immediate harm to others; nor, he said, should laws be created for the purpose of compelling people to act in their own good.[11]

In reality, few legal codes live up to the Walker–Mill criteria. Most are influenced strongly by cultural conceptions of right and wrong and encompass many behaviors which are not immediately and directly harmful to anyone but those who choose to be involved with them. These illegal activities, often called victimless crimes, include drug abuse, certain forms of "deviant" sexuality, gambling, and various other legally proscribed consensual deeds. Advocates of legislation designed to curb these activities suggest that while such behavior is not always directly harmful to others, it may erode social cohesiveness and ruin the lives of those who engage in it.

Standing in strong opposition to the Walker–Mill perspective are legislators and theorists who purposefully use the law as a tool to facilitate social change. Modifications in the legal structure of a society can quickly and dramatically produce changes in the behavior of entire groups. A change in the tax laws, for example, typically sends people scrambling to their accountants to devise spending and investment strategies which can take advantage of the change.

Our legal system not only condemns interpersonal violence, but also supports the dominant economic order (capitalism) and protects the powerful and the wealthy (through an emphasis on private property and the rights which attach to property).

Throughout American criminal law Judeo-Christian principles hold considerable sway. Concepts such as sin and atonement provide for a view of men and women as willful actors in a world of personal and sensual temptations. Such ideas have made possible both the legal notion of guilt and the correctional ideal of individual reformation.

The realization that laws respond to the needs and interests of society at any given time was put into words by the popular jurist Oliver Wendell Holmes (1809–1894) in an address he gave at Harvard in 1881. Holmes said, "The life of the law has not been logic; it has been experience. The felt necessities of the time, the prevalent moral and political theories, institutions of public policy, avowed or unconscious, even the prejudices which judges share with their fellowmen have had a good deal more to do than the syllogism in determining the rules by which men should be governed."[12] The "syllogism," as Holmes used the term, referred to idealized theorizing as the basis for law. The importance of such "theorizing" he thoroughly discounted.

Once law has been created it is generally slow to change, because it is built upon years of tradition. The law can be thought of as a force which supports social order, but which is

THEORY INTO PRACTICE

WHAT DOES LAW DO?
THE FUNCTIONS OF LAW

Laws Maintain Order in Society
Laws Regulate Human Interaction
Laws Enforce Moral Beliefs
Laws Define the Economic Environment
Laws Support the Powerful
Laws Promote Orderly Social Change
Laws Sustain Individual Rights
Laws Redress Wrongs
Laws Identify Evildoers
Laws Mandate Punishment and Retribution

opposed to rapid social change. When law facilitates change, that change usually proceeds in an orderly and deliberate fashion. Revolutions, on the other hand, produce near-instantaneous legal changes, but bring with them massive social disorder.

JURAL POSTULATES

One of the greatest legal scholars of modern times was Roscoe Pound (1870–1964), dean of the Harvard Law School during the years 1916–1936. Pound saw the law as a type of social engineering.[13] The law is a tool, he said, which meets the demands of men and women living together in society. Pound strongly believed that the law must be able to change with the times and to reflect new needs as they arise.

Pound distilled his ideas into a set of jural postulates. Such postulates, claimed Pound, form the basis of all law because they reflect shared needs. In 1942 Pound published his postulates in the form of five propositions.[14]

Pound's postulates form a theory of "consensus" about the origins of law—both civil and criminal. They suggest that most laws are the product of shared social needs experienced by the majority of members in the society where they arise. However, a number of writers have criticized Pound for failing to recognize the diversity of society. How, they ask, can the law address common needs in society when society consists of many different groups—each with their own set of interests and needs? As a consequence of such criticism, Pound modified his theory to include a jurisprudence of interest. The concept of jurisprudence held that one of the basic purposes of law is to satisfy "as many claims or demands of as many people as possible."[15]

Jural Postulates:
Propositions developed by the famous jurist Roscoe Pound, which hold that the law reflects shared needs without which members of society could not coexist. Pound's jural postulates are often linked to the idea that the law can be used to engineer the structure of society in order to predetermine certain kinds of outcomes (such as property rights embodied in the law of theft do in capitalistic societies).

CONFLICT THEORY

Opposed to Pound's theory of consensus is William Chambliss's view of law as a tool of powerful individuals and groups acting in their own interests, and often in conflict with one another.[16] Conflict theory has its roots in the writings of Karl Marx, who explained all of social history as the result of an ongoing conflict between the "haves" and the "have-nots."

Chambliss believes we should not see the agencies of criminal justice as "neutral." Rather, he says, government is "a weapon of the dominant classes or interest groups in society."[17]

Putting it more mildly, Chambliss also writes, "…in one way or another, the laws which are passed, implemented, and incorporated into the legal system reflect the interests of those groups capable of having their views incorporated into the official (that is legal) views of the society."[18]

TYPES OF LAW

"Criminal" and "civil" law are the best known types of modern law. However, scholars and philosophers have drawn numerous distinctions between categories of the law which rest upon their source, intent, and application. Laws in modern societies can be usefully described in terms of the following groups:

- Criminal law
- Case law
- Procedural law
- Civil law
- Constitutional law
- Administrative law

CRIMINAL LAW

Criminal Law That branch of modern law which concerns itself with offenses committed against society, members thereof, their property, and the social order.

Criminal law is theoretically distinguishable from civil law primarily by the assertion that criminal acts injure not just individuals, but society as a whole. Social order, as reflected in the values supported by statute, is reduced to some degree whenever a criminal act occurs. In olden times offenders were said to violate the "King's Peace" when they committed a crime. They offended not just the victims, but contravened the order established under the rule of the monarch.

In criminal cases, the state, as the injured party, begins the process of bringing the offender to justice. Even if the victim is dead and has no one to speak on their behalf, the agencies of justice will investigate the crime and file charges against the offender.

Violations of the criminal law result in the imposition of punishment. Punishment is philosophically justified by the fact that the criminal *intended* the harm and is responsible for it. Punishment serves a variety of purposes, which we will discuss later in the chapter on sentencing. When punishment is imposed in a criminal case, however, it is for one basic reason: to express society's fundamental displeasure with the offensive behavior.

T H E O R Y   I N T O   P R A C T I C E

WHAT IS CRIME:
THE EXAMPLE OF CRIMES AGAINST
THE ENVIRONMENT

Crime can be defined best as a violation of the criminal law. Looking behind most criminal statutes, however, we can generally catch a glimpse of the concept of harm. Criminal activity, such as theft and assault, most of us would agree, is harmful to others. Some crimes, however, such as drug abuse, prostitution, gambling, and pornography, are sometimes referred to as "victimless crimes" (or social order offenses) because the harm they cause is not readily identifiable at the individual level. Statutes outlawing social order offenses are rooted in the notion of social harm—that is, although no one who participates in prostitution, say, runs to the police to file a complaint (unless they are robbed, or in some other way directly victimized) lawmakers recognize that the act somehow lessens the quality of social life. Prostitution, many lawmakers argue, is harmful to the family and (in the case of heterosexual prostitution) demeans the status of women in society.

Today, a whole new class of criminal offenses is emerging based upon the notion of environmental damage. In what may be the best known environmental catastrophe to date, the Exxon *Valdez*, a 1,000-foot supertanker, ran aground in Alaska in 1989 and spilled 11 million gallons of crude oil over 1,700 miles of pristine coastline. Animal life in the area was devastated. The U.S. Fish and Wildlife Service reported decimation to salmon spawning grounds, the death of 580,000 birds (including 144 bald eagles), and the demise of an unknown, but presumably vast amount of sea life (22 whales were known dead, along with 5,500 sea otters). The initial cleanup involved over 10,000 people and cost more than $1 billion. Damages were estimated as high as $5 billion, and Exxon, in an agreement which was later rejected by a federal court, agreed to pay $1 billion in restoration fees. Criminal penalties could add as much as another $700 million to that figure.

While the *Valdez* incident is still near the forefront of national consciousness, environmental crimes of all proportions are a common occurrence. Such crimes range from ecological terrorism, like that waged against Kuwait by Saddam Hussein, to small-scale recycling offenses which are frequently committed (sometimes unknowingly) by individual citizens. As ecological awareness continues to expand, new prohibitions are legislated and previously unheard-of offenses created. Today, a highly concerned society stands increasingly ready to define abuse of the environment in criminal terms. As a consequence, words like "curbside criminals," "recycling police," and "garbage crime" are becoming commonplace. The state of Pennsylvania, for example, recently enacted a recycling law which mandates stiff sanctions, including fines and jail sentences for violators. Under the law, what had formerly been routine daily activities (throwing out the trash) become criminal offenses unless properly conducted (plastics and glass separated from paper products, and lawn clippings and yard trash appropriately bagged).

While human beings have insulted the environment since before the dawn of history, it has only been in this century, as our dependence on the planet has become progressively obvious, that such activities have been ascribed criminal status. Hence, the question: What taken-for-granted aspects of our contemporary everyday lives will become subject to criminal sanctions in the twenty-first century?

Sources: "*Valdez* Spill Damage, Toll Much Worse," *USA Today*, April 10, 1991, p. 1A; Nanci Koser Wilson, "Recycling Offenses, the Routine Ground of Everyday Activities, and Durkheimian Functionality in Crime," paper presented at the annual meeting of the Academy of Criminal Justice Sciences, Nashville, TN, 1991; and the *FBI Law Enforcement Bulletin*, special issue on environmental crimes, April 1991.

Crime An act committed or omitted in violation of a law forbidding or commanding it for which the possible penalties for an adult upon conviction include incarceration, for which a corporation can be penalized by fine or forfeit, or for which a juvenile can be adjudged delinquent or transferred to criminal court for prosecution.

Criminal law functions to define offenses against the state. Because crimes injure the fabric of society, it is the state which becomes the plaintiff in criminal proceedings. Court cases reflect this fact by being cited as follows: *State of New York* v. *Smith* (where state law has been violated) or *U.S.* v. *Smith* (where the federal government is the injured party).

Criminal law is composed of statutory and case law. It is built upon constitutional principles and operates within the system established by procedural laws.

Some crimes against the environment occur on a massive scale. Here firefighters prepare to move in on one of the hundreds of oil well fires intentionally set in Kuwait by Iraqi troops during the Gulf war. *Photo: S. Compoint/Sygma.*

CAREERS IN JUSTICE

WORKING FOR THE U.S. PARK POLICE

TYPICAL POSITIONS. U.S. Park Police provide enforcement services in the nation's national parks. They also serve the nation's capital and grounds, including federal areas within the District of Columbia. Branches include the Horse-mounted Unit, the Criminal Investigations Branch, the Traffic Safety Unit, the Special Equipment and Tactics Team, the Motor Unit (which employs motorcycles), the Canine Unit, the Marine Unit, and the Aviation Unit.

EMPLOYMENT REQUIREMENTS.   Applicant must (1) be at least 21 years of age and have not reached his or her 31st birthday by the time of appointment, (2) be a U.S. citizen, (3) possess a high school diploma or equivalent, (4) have 20/60 vision or better that is correctable to 20/20, (5) have had two years of progressively responsible experience.

OTHER REQUIREMENTS.   Applicants must (1) successfully complete 18 weeks of intensive training at the Federal Law Enforcement Training Center (Glynco, Georgia) and (2) perform satisfactorily on periodic written tests.

SALARY.   Starting salary in mid-1993 was $29,647.

BENEFITS.   Benefits include (1) participation in the Federal Employee's Retirement System, (2) paid annual leave, (3) paid sick leave, (4) overtime that is compensated at the rate of time and one-half of regular pay, and (5) all uniforms and equipment, which are provided.

DIRECT INQUIRIES TO: U.S. Park Police, Personnel Office, 1100 Ohio Drive, S.W., Washington, D.C. 20242. Phone: (202) 619-7056.

Statutory law is the "law on the books." It is the result of legislative action and is often thought of as the "law of the land." Written laws exist in both criminal and civil areas, and are called codes. Federal statutes are compiled in the United States Code (U.S.C.). State codes and municipal ordinances are also readily available in written, or statutory, form. The written form of the criminal law is called the penal code.

Written criminal law in this country is of two types: substantive and procedural. Substantive law deals directly with specifying the nature of, and appropriate punishment for, particular offenses. For example, every state in our country has laws against murder, rape, robbery, and assault. Differences in the law among these various jurisdictions can be studied in detail because each offense and the punishment associated with it are available in the substantive law in written form.

The greatest happiness of the greatest number is the foundation of morals and legislation.

—*Jeremy Bentham*

Precedent A legal principle which operates to insure that previous judicial decisions are authoritatively considered and incorporated into future cases.

CASE LAW

Case law is also referred to as the law of **precedent**. It represents the accumulated wisdom of trial and appellate courts over the years. Once a court decision is rendered it is written down. At the appellate level, the reasoning behind the decision is recorded as well. Under the rule of precedent, this reasoning should then be taken into consideration by other courts in settling future cases.

Appellate courts have considerable power to influence new court decisions at the trial level. The court with the greatest influence, of course, is the U.S. Supreme Court. The precedents it establishes are incorporated as guidelines into the process of legal reasoning by which lower courts reach conclusions.

The principle of recognizing previous decisions as precedents to guide future deliberations is called *stare decisis*, and forms the basis for our modern "law of precedent." Lief H. Carter has pointed out how precedent operates along two dimensions.[19] He calls them the vertical and the horizontal. The vertical rules requires that decisions made by a higher court be taken into consideration by lower courts in their deliberations. Under this rule, state appellate courts, for example, should be expected to follow the spirit of decision rendered by their state supreme courts.

The horizontal dimension means that courts on the same level should be consistent in their interpretation of the law. The U.S. Supreme Court, operating under the horizontal rule, for example, should not be expected to change its ruling in cases similar to those it has already decided.

Stare decisis makes for predictability in the law. Defendants walking into a modern courtroom will have the opportunity to be represented by lawyers who are trained in legal precedents as well as procedure. As a consequence, they will have a good idea of what to expect about the manner in which their trial will proceed.

PROCEDURAL LAW

Procedural law is another kind of statutory law. It is a body of rules which regulates the processing of an offender by the criminal justice system. Procedural law, for example, specifies in most jurisdictions that the testimony of one party to certain "victimless crimes" cannot be used as the sole evidence against the other party. General rules of evidence, search and seizure, procedures to be followed in an arrest, and other specified processes by which the justice system operates are contained in procedural law.

As a great jurist once said, however, the law is like a living thing. It changes and evolves over time. Legislatures enact new statutory laws, and justices set new precedents, sometimes overruling established ones. Many jurisdictions today, for example, are beginning to allow wives to bring charges of rape against their husbands. Similarly, wives may testify against their husbands in certain cases, even though both actions are contrary to years of previously created precedents.

Civil Law That portion of the modern law which regulates contracts and other obligations involving primarily personal interests.

CIVIL LAW

Civil law provides a formal means for regulating noncriminal relationships between persons. The body of civil law contains rules for divorce, child support and custody, the creation of wills, property transfers, negligence, libel, and many other contractual and social obligations. When the civil law is violated, a civil suit may follow.

Civil suits seek not punishment, but compensation, usually in the form of property or monetary damages. They may also be filed in order to achieve an injunction or a kind of judicial cease-and-desist order. A violation of the civil law may be a tort (a breach of duty), or a contract violation, but it is not a crime. Because a tort is an injury to an individual, it is left to that individual to set the machinery of the court in motion.

Civil law is more concerned with assigning "blame" than it is with intent. Civil suits arising from automobile crashes, for example, do not allege that either driver intended to inflict bodily harm. Nor do they claim that it was the intent of the driver to damage either vehicle. However, when someone is injured, or property damage occurs, even in an accident, civil procedures make it possible to gauge responsibility and assign blame to one party or the other. The parties to a civil suit are referred to as the plaintiff and the defendant.

In a newsworthy 1993 case, which provides a good example of a civil suit, a Georgia court awarded $105 million in damages to the parents of a teenager killed in the crash of a General Motors pickup truck.[20] The court found that fuel tanks mounted externally on each side of the truck were a design flaw which contributed to the teenager's death. Later that year, a St. Louis jury ordered Domino's Pizza to pay 49-year-old Jean Kinder $79 million after she was struck and seriously injured by a delivery person attempting to honor the company's 30-minute guarantee. The guarantee has since been canceled.

Civil law pertains to injuries suffered by individuals which are unfair or unjust according to the standards operative in the social group. Breeches of contract, unfair practices in hiring, the manufacture and sale of consumer goods with hidden hazards for the user, and slanderous comments made about others have all been common grounds for civil suits. Suits may, on occasion, arise as extensions of criminal action. Monetary compensation, for example, may be sought through our system of civil laws by a victim of a criminal assault after a criminal conviction has been obtained.

Following the murder a few years ago of Sandra Black, for example, her son and mother successfully sued *Soldier of Fortune* magazine, winning damages of $9.4 million.[21] *Soldier of Fortune* had printed a classified advertisement by a "mercenary" who, as a result of the ad, eventually contracted with Mrs. Black's husband to commit the murder. In a quite different type of civil suit, Robert McLaughlin was awarded $1.9 million by a New York State Court of Claims in October 1989, after having spent six and one-half years in prison for a murder and robbery he did not commit.[22]

In a 1993 civil case, which may hold considerable significance for the criminal justice system, a Florida jury held K-mart stores liable for selling a gun to a drunken man. The buyer, Thomas W. Knapp, later used the weapon to shoot his girlfriend, Deborah Kitchen, in the neck—leaving her permanently paralyzed. K-mart was ordered to pay Kitchen $11 million, sending a message to gun retailers across the nation.

Even criminal action, not otherwise excusable, may be grounds for a civil suit by the offender. In 1992, for example, a civil jury awarded $2.15 million to convicted murderer William Freeman and his family. Freeman, a former assistant chief of police from Fort Stockton, Texas, is serving a life term in prison for killing his friend, Donnie Hazelwood. The jury agreed with Freeman's claim that the sleeping pill Halcion altered his personality and caused him to kill Hazelwood.[23]

ADMINISTRATIVE LAW

Administrative law refers to the body of regulations which have been created by governments to control the activities of industry, business, and individuals. Tax laws, health codes, restrictions on pollution and waste disposal, vehicle registration, building codes, and the like are examples of administrative law.

Other administrative laws cover practices in the areas of customs (imports/exports), immigration, agriculture, product safety, and most areas of manufacturing. Modern individualists claim that overregulation characterizes the American way of life, although they are in turn criticized for failing to adequately recognize the complexity of modern society. Overregulation has also been used on occasion as a rallying cry for political hopefuls who believe that many Americans wish to return to an earlier and simpler form of free enterprise.

Although the criminal law is, for the most part, separate from administrative regulations, the two may overlap. For instance, the rise in organized criminal activity in the area of toxic waste disposal has led to criminal prosecutions in several states. Denial of civil rights is another area which may lead to criminal sanctions through the federal system of laws.

Administrative agencies will sometimes arrange settlements which fall short of court action, but which are considered binding on individuals or groups who have not lived up to the intent of federal regulations. Education, environmental protection, and discriminatory hiring practices are all areas in which settlements have been employed.

Elements of Criminal Offenses

Statutory law specifies exactly what constitutes a crime. The crime of first-degree murder, for example, in almost every jurisdiction in the United States involves four elements:

1. An unlawful killing
2. Of a human being
3. Intentionally
4. With malice

The elements of a crime are the *statutory minimum* without which a crime cannot be said to have occurred. In any case that goes to trial, the task of the prosecution is to prove that all the elements were indeed present and that the accused was ultimately responsible for producing them.

Every element in a crime serves some purpose and is necessary. The crime of first-degree murder, for example, includes *an unlawful killing.* Even if all the other elements of first-degree murder are present, the act may still not be first-degree murder if the first element is not met. In a wartime situation, for instance, killings of human beings occur. They are committed with planning and sometimes with "malice." They are certainly intentional. Yet killing in war is not unlawful, so long as the belligerents wage war according to international conventions.

The second element of first-degree murder specifies that the killing must be of a "human being." People kill all the time. They kill animals for meat, they hunt, and they practice euthanasia upon aged and injured pets. Even if the killing of an animal is planned and involves malice (perhaps a vendetta against a neighborhood dog that wrecks trash cans), it does not constitute first-degree murder. Such a killing, however, may violate statutes pertaining to cruelty to animals.

The third element of first-degree murder, "intentionality," is the basis for the defense of accident. An unintentional killing is not first-degree murder, although it may violate some other statute.

Finally, murder has not been committed unless "malice" is involved. There are different kinds of malice. Second-degree murder involves malice in the sense of hatred or spite. A more extreme form of malice is necessary for a finding of first-degree murder. Sometimes the phrase used to describe this type of feeling is "malice aforethought." This extreme kind of malice can be demonstrated by showing that planning was involved in the commission of the murder. Often, first-degree murder is described as "lying in wait," a practice which shows that thought and planning went into the illegal killing.

Whether any particular behavior meets the statutory minimum to qualify as a crime may be open to debate. In November 1992, for example, Adam Brown, 30, of Roseburg, Oregon was charged with attempted murder for having knowingly exposed five children to the AIDS virus when he allegedly had unprotected sex with them. Mr. Brown, a lay minister, was informed that he had tested positive for the AIDS virus more than a year prior to the incidents. Brown was also charged with sodomy, rape, sexual penetration with a foreign object, and reckless endangerment.[24]

GENERAL CATEGORIES OF CRIME

Misdemeanors

Violations of the criminal law can be more or less serious. Misdemeanors are relatively minor crimes. They are usually thought of as any crime punishable by a year or less in prison. In fact, most misdemeanants receive suspended sentences involving a fine and supervised probation. If an "active sentence" is received for a misdemeanor violation of the law, it probably will involve time in a local jail, perhaps on weekends, rather than imprisonment in a long-term facility. Some misdemeanants have recently been sentenced to community service activities, requiring them to do such things as wash school buses, paint local government buildings, or clean parks and other public areas.

Normally, a police officer cannot arrest a person for a misdemeanor, unless the crime was committed in the officer's presence. If the in-presence requirement is missing, the officer will need to seek an arrest warrant from a magistrate or other judicial officer. Once a warrant has been issued, the officer may proceed with the arrest.

Misdemeanor An offense punishable by incarceration, usually in a local confinement facility, for a period of which the upper limit is prescribed by statute in a given jurisdiction, typically limited to a year or less.

Felonies

Felonies are serious crimes. Under common law, felons could be sentenced to death and/or have their property confiscated. Many felons receive prison sentences, although the potential range of penalties can include anything from probation and a fine to capital punishment in many jurisdictions. The federal government and many states have moved to a scheme of classifying felonies, from most to least serious, using a number or letter designation. The federal system,[25] for example, for purposes of criminal sentencing, assigns a score of 43 to first-degree murder, while the crime of theft is only rated a "base offense level" of 4. Attendant circumstances and the criminal history of the offender are also taken into consideration in sentencing decisions.

Felony A criminal offense punishable by death, or by incarceration in a prison facility for at least a year.

Because of differences between the states, a crime classified as a felony in one part of the country may be a misdemeanor in another. This is especially true of drug law violations and certain other social order crimes such as homosexuality, prostitution, and gambling.

People who have been convicted of felonies usually lose certain privileges. Some states make conviction of a felony and incarceration grounds for uncontested divorce. Others prohibit offenders from running for public office or owning a firearm, and exclude them from some professions such as medicine, law, and police work.

Offenses

A third category of crime is the offense. Offenses are minor violations of the law such as jaywalking, spitting on the sidewalk, littering, and certain traffic violations, including the failure to wear a seat belt. Another word used to describe offenses is infraction. People committing infractions are typically ticketed and released, usually upon a promise to later appear in court. Court appearances may often be waived through payment of a small fine, which is often mailed in.

SPECIAL CATEGORIES

Treason

Felonies, misdemeanors, offenses, and the people who commit them constitute the daily work of the justice system. Special categories of crime, however, exist and should be recognized. Treason is one of these. Treason has been defined as "the act of a U.S. citizen's helping a foreign government to overthrow, make war against, or seriously injure the United States."[26] Espionage, an offense akin to treason, refers to the "gathering, transmitting or losing"[27] of information related to the national defense in such a manner that the information becomes available to enemies of the United States and may be used to their advantage. In 1994, in what may be the last widely publicized incident of espionage of the cold war period, CIA agent Aldrich Hazen Ames and his wife, Rosario, were arrested and charged with conspiracy to commit espionage in a plot to sell U.S. government secrets to the Russian KGB. The Ames' allegedly told their Russian handlers of CIA operatives within the former Soviet Union and revealed the extent of American knowledge of KGB activities. Their activities had apparently gone undetected for nearly a decade.

Treason and espionage may be committed for personal gain or for ideological reasons, or both. They are crimes only under federal law and are often regarded as the most serious of felonies.

Inchoate Offenses

Inchoate Offense An offense which consists of an action or conduct which is a step toward the intended commission of another offense.

Another special category of crime is called inchoate. Inchoate offenses are those which have not been fully carried out. Conspiracies are an example. When a person conspires to commit a crime, any action undertaken in furtherance of the conspiracy is generally regarded as a sufficient basis for arrest and prosecution. For instance, a woman who intends to kill her husband may make a phone call in order to find a "hit man" to carry out her plan. The call itself is evidence of her intent and can result in her imprisonment for conspiring to murder.

Another type of inchoate offense is the attempt. Sometimes an offender is not able to complete the crime. Homeowners may arrive just as a burglar is beginning to enter their residence. The burglar may drop his tools and run. Even so, in most jurisdictions, this frustrated burglar can be arrested and charged with attempted burglary.

THE ELEMENTS OF A CRIME

Corpus Delicti

Traditionally, a crime can be said to have occurred only if certain necessary elements are present. *Corpus delicti* is a Latin term which refers to the "body of the crime." It does *not* mean the body of the victim, as is sometimes thought. For a criminal definition to be imposed upon a social situation, it is necessary that the "body of the crime," be established. In other words, the elements which constitute a crime must be present.

Each offense defined by law contains specific elements, as discussed earlier in the example of first-degree murder. All crimes, however, can be said to share certain general elements, which are described here.

The Criminal Act

A necessary first element is some act in violation of the law. Such an act is termed the *actus reus* of a crime. The term means a "guilty act." Generally, a person must commit some act before they are subject to criminal sanctions. Someone who admits (perhaps on a TV talk show) that they are a drug user, for example, cannot be arrested on that basis. To *be something* is not a crime—to *do something* is. In the case of the admitted drug user, police who heard the admission might begin gathering evidence to prove some specific law violation in that person's past, or perhaps they might watch that individual for future behavior in violation of the law. An arrest might then occur. If it did, it would be based upon a specific action in violation of the law pertaining to controlled substances.

Vagrancy laws, popular in the early part of the twentieth century, have generally been invalidated by the courts because they did not specify what act violated the law. In fact, the *less* a person did, the more vagrant they were.

An *omission to act*, however, may be criminal where the person in question is required by law to do something. Child-neglect laws, for example, focus on parents and child guardians who do not live up to their responsibilities for caring for their children.

Threatening to act can itself be a criminal offense. Telling someone, "I'm going to kill you," might result in an arrest based upon the offense of "communicating threats." Threatening the president of the United States is taken seriously by the Secret Service, and individuals are regularly arrested for boasting about planned violence to be directed at the president.

Attempted criminal activity is also illegal. An attempt to murder or rape, for example, is a serious crime, even though the planned act was not accomplished.

Conspiracy statutes were mentioned earlier in this chapter. When a conspiracy unfolds, the ultimate act that it aims to bring about does not have to occur for the parties to the conspiracy to be arrested. When people plan to bomb a public building, for example, they can be legally stopped before the bombing. As soon as they take steps to "further" their plan, they have met the requirement for an act. Buying explosives, telephoning one another, or drawing plans of the building may all be actions in "furtherance of the conspiracy."

All elements of a crime must be present in order for a defendant in a criminal case to be convicted and sentenced. Here Claus Von Bulow, accused of attempting to kill his wealthy wife via hypodermic injection, is shown after his acquittal on two counts of attempted murder. *Photo: AP/Wide World Photos.*

Similar to conspiracy statutes are many newly enacted antistalking laws. Antistalking statutes are intended to prevent harassment and intimidation, even when no physical harm occurs. According to the U.S. Senate's Judiciary Committee, "there are 200,000 people in the United States who are currently 'stalking' someone...."[28] It is estimated that half of those being stalked are celebrities. Stalkers often strike after their victims have unsuccessfully complained to authorities about stalking-related activities such as harassing phone calls and letters. Antistalking statutes, however, still face a constitutional hurdle of attempting to prevent people not otherwise involved in criminal activity from walking and standing where they wish, and from speaking freely. Ultimately, the U.S. Supreme Court will probably have to decide the legitimacy of such statutes.

Mens Rea

Mens rea The state of mind which accompanies a criminal act. Also, guilty mind.

Mens rea is the second element of a crime. It literally means "guilty mind" and recognizes a mental component to crime. The modern interpretation of *mens rea*, however, does not focus so much on whether a person feels guilty about his or her act—but rather looks to whether or not the act was intended. As the famous Supreme Court Justice Oliver Wendell Holmes once wrote, "even a dog distinguishes between being stumbled over and being kicked."[29]

The idea of *mens rea* has undergone a gradual evolution during recent centuries such that today the term can be generally described as signifying *blameworthiness*. The question asked, at least theoretically, in criminal prosecutions, is whether or not the person charged with an offense *should be blamed* and held accountable for their actions.

Mens rea is said to be present when a person *should have known better*, even if the person did not directly intend the consequences of his or her action. A person who acts recklessly, and thereby endangers others, may be found guilty of a crime when a harm occurs, even though no negative consequences were intended. For example, a mother who left her 15-month-old child alone in the tub can be later prosecuted for negligent homicide if the child drowns.

It should be recognized, however, that negligence in and of itself is not a crime. Negligent conduct can be evidence of a crime only when it falls below some acceptable standard of care. That standard is today applied in courts through the fictional creation of a *reasonable person*. The question to be asked in a given case is whether or not a reasonable person, in the same situation, would have known better, and acted differently, than the defendant. The reasonable person criterion provides a yardstick for juries faced with thorny issues of guilt or innocence.

Concurrence

The concurrence of act and intent is the third element of a crime. A person may intend to kill a rival, for example. As they drive to the intended victim's house, gun in hand, fantasizing about how they will commit the murder, the victim may be crossing the street on the way home from grocery shopping. If the two collide, and the intended victim dies, there has been no concurrence of act and intent.

The three elements of a crime we have just outlined are regarded by some legal scholars as sufficient to constitute the *corpus delicti* of a crime. When all three are present in a given situation, a crime has occurred. Other scholars, however, see modern Western law as more complex. They argue that four additional principles are necessary before the *corpus delicti* can be established. They are (1) a harm, (2) a causal relationship between the act and the harm, (3) the principle of legality, and (4) the principle of punishment.

Harm

A harm occurs in any crime, although not all harms are crimes. When a person is murdered or raped harm can clearly be identified. Some crimes, however, have come to be called "victimless." Perpetrators maintain that they are not harming anyone in committing such crimes. Rather, they say, the crime is pleasurable. Prostitution, gambling, homosexuality, "crimes against nature" (sexual deviance), and drug use are but a few crimes classified as "victimless." People involved in such crimes will argue that, if anyone is being hurt, it is only they. What these offenders fail to recognize is the social harm caused by their behavior. Areas afflicted with chronic prostitution, drug use, sexual deviance, and gambling usually will find property values falling, family life disintegrating, and other, more traditional crimes increasing as money is sought to support the "victimless" activities and law-abiding citizens flee the area.

Causation

Causation refers to the fact that a clear link needs to be identifiable between the act and the harm occasioned by the crime. A classic example of this principle involves assault with a deadly weapon with intent to kill. If a person shoots another, but the victim is seriously injured and not killed, the victim might survive for a long time in a hospital. Death may occur, perhaps a year later, because pneumonia sets in, or because blood clots form in the injured person from lack of activity. In such cases, defense attorneys will likely argue that the defendant did not cause the death, but rather the death occurred because of disease.

Legality

The principle of legality is concerned with the fact that a behavior cannot be criminal if no law exists which defines it as such. It is all right to drink beer, if you are of "drinking age," because there is no statute "on the books" prohibiting it. During prohibition times, of course, the situation was quite different. (In fact, some parts of the United States are still "dry," and the purchase or public consumption of alcohol can be a law violation regardless of age.) The principle of legality also includes the notion that a law cannot be created tomorrow which will hold a person legally responsible for something he or she does today. These are called *ex post facto* laws. Laws are binding only from the date of their creation, or from some future date at which they are specified as taking effect.

Punishment

Finally, the principle of punishment says that no crime can be said to occur where a punishment has not been specified in the law. Larceny, for example, would not be a crime in a jurisdiction where the law simply said, "It is illegal to steal." A punishment needs to be specified, so that if a person is found guilty of violating the law a sanction can be imposed.

DEFENSES

PERSONAL DEFENSES

Defenses (to a criminal charge) include claims based upon personal, special, and procedural considerations that the defendant should not be held accountable for their actions, even though they may have acted in violation of the criminal law.

When a person is charged with a crime, they will usually offer some defense. Our legal system has generally recognized two broad categories of defenses: personal and special. Table 4–2 lists most generally applicable defenses. Personal defenses are based upon some characteristic of the individual who is charged with the crime. They include the following.

Infancy

The defense of infancy has its roots in the ancient belief that children cannot reason logically until around the age of 7. Early doctrine in the Christian church sanctioned that belief by declaring that rationality develops around the age of 7. As a consequence, only children past that age could be held responsible for their "crimes."

The defense of infancy today has been expanded to include people well beyond the age of 7. Many states set the sixteenth birthday as the age at which a person becomes an adult for purposes of criminal prosecution. Others use the age of 14, and still others 18. When a person below the age required for adult prosecution commits a "crime," it is termed a *juvenile offense.* He or she is not guilty of a criminal violation of the law by virtue of youth. In most jurisdictions, children below the age of 7 cannot be charged even with juvenile offenses, no matter how serious their actions may appear to others.

T A B L E   4 - 2
TYPES OF DEFENSES

Personal	Special	Procedural
Infancy	Self-defense	Double jeopardy
Insanity	Defense of others	Collateral estoppel
Involuntary intoxication	Defense of home	Prosecutorial misconduct
Unconsciousness	Duress	Selective prosecution
Premenstrual stress syndrome	Entrapment	Denial of a speedy trial
Other biological defenses	Accident	
	Mistake	
	Necessity	
	Provocation	
	Consent	
	Alibi	

Insanity

Insanity is the second form of personal defense. It is important to realize that legal definitions of insanity often have very little to do with psychological or psychiatric understandings of mental illness. Legal insanity is a concept developed over time to meet the needs of the judicial system in assigning guilt or innocence to particular defendants. It is not primarily concerned with treatment, as is the idea of mental illness in psychiatry. Medical conceptions of mental illness do not always fit well into the legal categories created to deal with the phenomenon. This difference has led to a situation in which mental health professionals often appear to give contradictory testimony in criminal trials.

The McNaughten Rule   Prior to the nineteenth century the insanity defense was nonexistent. Insane people who committed crimes were punished in the same way as other law violators. It was Daniel McNaughten (also spelled M'Naghten), a woodworker from Glasgow, Scotland, who, in 1844, became the first person to be found not guilty of a crime by reason of insanity. McNaughten had tried to assassinate Sir Robert Peel, the British prime minister. He mistook Edward Drummond, Peel's secretary, for Peel himself, and killed Drummond instead. At his trial, defense attorneys argued that McNaughten suffered from vague delusions centered on the idea that the Tories, a British political party, were persecuting him. Medical testimony at the trial agreed with the assertion of McNaughten's lawyers that he didn't know what he was doing at the time of the shooting. The judge accepted McNaughten's claim, and the insanity defense was born. The McNaughten rule, as it has come to be called, was defined later by the courts and still plays a major role in determining insanity in criminal prosecutions in 15 states today.[30]

The McNaughten rule holds that *a person is not guilty of a crime if, at the time of the crime, they either didn't know what they were doing, or didn't know that what they were doing was wrong.* The inability to distinguish right from wrong must be the result of some mental defect or disability. The McNaughten case established a rule for the determination of

Insanity Defense A personal defense which claims that the person charged with a crime did not know what they were doing, or that they did not know that what they were doing was wrong. For purposes of the criminal law, insanity is a legal definition and not a psychiatric one. The differences between the psychiatric and legal conceptualizations of insanity lead often to disagreements among expert witnesses who, in criminal court, may provide conflicting testimony as to the sanity of a defendant.

Lorena Bobbitt, acquitted in 1994 of charges of malicious wounding, after she admittedly cut off her husband's penis with a kitchen knife as he slept. Ms. Bobbitt's attorneys successfully employed the irresistible impulse defense. *Photo: Stephen Jaffe/ Reuter/Bettmann.*

insanity which is still followed in many U.S. jurisdictions today. However, in most states, the burden of proving insanity falls upon the defendant. Just as defendants are assumed innocent, they are also assumed to be sane at the outset of any criminal trial.

Irresistible Impulse   The McNaughten rule worked well for a time. Eventually, however, some cases arose in which defendants clearly knew what they were doing, and they knew it was wrong. Even so, they argued in their defense, they couldn't help themselves. They couldn't stop doing that which was wrong. Such people are said to suffer from an irresistible impulse and may be found not guilty by reason of that particular brand of insanity in 18 of the United States. Some states which do not use the irresistible impulse test in determining insanity may still allow the successful demonstration of such an impulse to be considered in sentencing decisions.

In a spectacular 1994 Virginia trial, Lorena Bobbitt successfully employed the irresistible impulse defense against charges of malicious wounding stemming from an incident in which she cut off her husband's penis with a kitchen knife as he slept. The case, which made headlines around the world, found Bobbitt's defense attorney telling the jury, "what we have is Lorena Bobbitt's life juxtaposed against John Wayne Bobbitt's penis. The evidence will show that in her mind it was his penis from which she could not escape, that caused her the most pain, the most fear, the most humiliation."[31] The impulse to sever the organ, said the lawyer, became irresistible.

The irresistible impulse test has been criticized on a number of grounds. Primary among them is the belief that all of us suffer from compulsions. Most of us, however, learn to control them. Should we give in to a compulsion, the critique goes, then why not just say it was unavoidable so as to escape any legal consequences.

The Durham Rule

A third rule for gauging insanity is called the Durham rule. It was originally created in 1871 by a New Hampshire court and later adopted by Judge David Bazelon in 1954 as he decided the case of *Durham* v. *United States* for the Court of Appeals in the District of Columbia. The Durham rules states that *a person is not criminally responsible for their behavior if their illegal actions were the result of some mental disease or defect.*

Courts which follow the Durham rule will typically hear from an array of psychiatric specialists as to the mental state of the defendant. Their testimony will inevitably be clouded by the need to address the question of cause. A successful defense under the Durham rule necessitates that jurors be able to see the criminal activity in question as the *product* of mental deficiencies harbored by the defendant. And, yet, many people who suffer from mental diseases or defects never commit crimes. In fact, low IQ, mental retardation, or lack of general mental capacity are not allowable as excuses for criminal behavior. Because the Durham rule is especially vague, it provides fertile grounds for conflicting claims.

The Substantial Capacity Test

Nineteen states follow another guideline—the Substantial Capacity Test—as found in the Model Penal Code of the American Law Institute.[32] Also called the ALI rule or the MPC rule, it suggests that insanity should be defined as the lack of a substantial capacity to control one's behavior. This test requires a judgment to the effect that the defendant either had, or lacked, "the mental capacity needed to understand the wrongfulness of his act, or to conform his behavior to the requirements of the law."[33] The Substantial Capacity Test is a blending of the McNaughten rule with the irresistible impulse standard. "Substantial capacity" does not require total mental incompetence nor does the rule require the behavior in question to live up to the criterion of total irresistibility. The problem, however, of establishing just what constitutes "substantial mental capacity" has plagued this rule from its conception.

The Brawner Rule

Judge Bazelon, apparently dissatisfied with the application of the Durham rule, created a new criterion for gauging insanity in the 1972 case of *U.S.* v. *Brawner.* The Brawner rule, as it has come to be called, places responsibility for deciding insanity squarely with the jury. Bazelon suggested that the jury should be concerned with whether or not the defendant could be *justly* held responsible for the criminal act in the face of any claims of insanity. Under this proposal, juries are left with few rules to guide them other than their own sense of fairness.

Insanity and Social Reality

The insanity defense originated as a means of recognizing the social reality of mental disease. Unfortunately, the history of this defense has been rife with change, contradiction, and uncertainty. Psychiatric testimony is expensive, sometimes costing thousands of dollars per day for one medical specialist. Still worse is the fact that each "expert" is commonly contradicted by another.

Public dissatisfaction with the jumble of rules defining legal insanity peaked in 1982, when John Hinckley was acquitted of trying to assassinate then-President Reagan. At his trial, Hinckley's lawyers claimed that a series of delusions brought about by a history of schizophrenia left him unable to control his behavior. Government prosecutors were unable to counter defense contentions of insanity. The resulting acquittal shocked the nation and resulted in calls for a review of the insanity defense.

Guilty but Insane

A new finding of guilty but insane (in a few states the finding is guilty but mentally ill, or GBMI) is now possible in some jurisdictions. It is one form the response to public frustration with the insanity issue has taken. Guilty but insane means that a person can be held responsible for a specific criminal act, even though a degree of mental incompetence may be present in his or her personality. Upon return of this verdict, a judge may impose any sentence possible under the law for the crime in question. However, mandated psychiatric treatment will generally be part of the commitment order. The offender, once cured, will usually be placed in the general prison population to serve any remaining sentence. In 1975 Michigan became the first state to pass a "guilty but mentally ill" statute, permitting a GBMI finding.[34] At the time of this writing, 11 other states had also passed legislation making a verdict of "guilty but insane" possible.

As some authors have observed, the legal possibility of a guilty but mentally ill finding has three purposes: "[F]irst, to protect society; second, to hold some offenders who were mentally ill accountable for their criminal acts; (and) third, to make treatment available to convicted offenders suffering from some form of mental illness."[35]

The guilty but insane plea represents a conservative direction in criminal prosecution. The Supreme Court case of *Ford* v. *Wainwright*, however, recognized a problem of a different sort.[36] The 1986 decision specified that prisoners who become insane while

What is normal behavior? This note from John Hinckley, would-be presidential assassin, declaring his love for actress Jodie Foster, was used as evidence in the successful effort mounted by his defense team to prove him insane. *Photo: Roddey E. Mims/Sygma.*

incarcerated cannot be executed. Hence, although insanity may not be a successful defense to criminal prosecution, it can later become a block to the ultimate punishment.

Temporary Insanity   Temporary insanity is another possible defense against a criminal charge. Widely used in the 1940s and 1950s, temporary insanity meant that the offender claimed to be insane only at the time of the commission of the offense. If a jury agreed, the defendant virtually went free. The suspect was not guilty of the criminal action by virtue of having been insane and could not be ordered to undergo psychiatric counseling or treatment because the insanity was no longer present. This type of plea has become less popular as legislatures have regulated the circumstances under which it can be made.

The Insanity Defense Under Federal Law   In 1984 the U.S. Congress passed the federal Insanity Defense Reform Act. The act created major revisions in the federal insanity defense. Insanity under the law is now defined as a condition in which the defendant can be shown to have been suffering under a "severe mental disease or defect" and, as a result "was unable to appreciate the nature and quality or the wrongfulness of his acts."[37] This definition of insanity comes close to that set forth in the old McNaughten rule.

The act also places the burden of proving the insanity defense squarely on the defendant—a provision which has been challenged a number of times since the act was passed. Such a requirement was supported by the Supreme Court prior to the act's passage. In 1983, in the case of *Jones* v. *U.S.* (1983),[38] the Court ruled that defendants can be required to prove their insanity when it becomes an issue in their defense. Shortly after the act became law, the Court in *Ake* v. *Oklahoma* (1985),[39] held that the government must assure access to a competent psychiatrist whenever a defendant indicates that insanity will be an issue at trial.

Consequences of an Insanity Ruling   The insanity defense today is not an "easy way out" of criminal prosecution, as some have assumed. Once a verdict of "not guilty by reason of insanity" is returned, the judge may order the defendant to undergo psychiatric treatment until cured. Because psychiatrists are reluctant to declare any potential criminal "cured," such a sentence may result in more time spent in an institution than would have resulted from a prison sentence.

Involuntary Drunkenness

Another personal defense is involuntary intoxication. Either drugs or alcohol may produce intoxication. Intoxication itself is rarely a defense to a criminal charge because it is a self-induced state. An altered mental condition which is voluntary cannot be used to exonerate guilty actions which follow from it.

Involuntary intoxication, however, is different. On occasion a person may be tricked into consuming an intoxicating substance. Secretly "spiked" punch, popular aphrodisiacs, or drug-laced desserts all might be ingested unknowingly. Because the effects and taste of alcohol are so widely known in our society, the defense of involuntary drunkenness can be difficult to demonstrate, however. A more unusual situation results from a disease caused by the yeast *Candida albicans,* occasionally found living in human intestines. A Japanese physician was the first to identify this disease, in which a person's digestive processes ferment the food they eat. Fermentation turns a portion of the food into alcohol, and people with this condition become intoxicated whenever they eat. First recognized about ten years ago, the disease has not yet been used successfully in this country to support the defense of involuntary intoxication.

Unconsciousness

A very rarely used form of personal defense is that of unconsciousness. An individual who is unconscious cannot be held responsible for anything he or she does. Because unconscious people rarely do anything at all, this defense is almost never seen. However, cases of sleepwalking, epileptic seizure, and neurological dysfunction may result in injurious, although unintentional, actions by people so afflicted. Under such circumstances the defense of unconsciousness might be argued with success.

Premenstrual Stress Syndrome

The use of premenstrual stress syndrome (PMS) as a defense against criminal charges is very new and demonstrates how changing social conceptions and advancing technology may modify the way in which courts view illegal behavior. In 1980 British courts heard the case of Christine English, who killed her live-in lover when he threatened to leave her. An expert witness at the trial testified that English had been the victim of PMS for more than a decade. The witness, Dr. Katharina Dalton, advanced the claim that PMS had rendered Ms. English "irritable, aggressive,... and confused, with loss of self-control."[40] The jury, apparently accepting the claim, returned a verdict of "not guilty."

PMS is not an officially acceptable defense in American criminal courts. However, in 1991 a Fairfax, Virginia, judge dismissed drunk-driving charges against a woman who cited the role PMS played in her behavior.[41] The woman, an orthopedic surgeon named Dr. Geraldine Richter, admitted to drinking four glasses of wine and allegedly kicked and cursed a state trooper who stopped her car because it was weaving down the road. A Breathalyzer test showed a blood-alcohol level of 0.13 percent—higher than the 0.10 percent needed to meet the requirement for drunken driving under Virginia law. But a gynecologist who testified on Dr. Richter's behalf said that the behavior she exhibited is characteristic of PMS. "I guess this is a new trend," said the state's attorney in commenting on the judge's ruling.

Other Biological Considerations

Modern nutritional science appears to be on the verge of establishing a new category of personal defense related to "chemical imbalances" in the human body produced by eating habits. Vitamins, food allergies, the consumption of stimulants (including coffee and nicotine), and the excessive ingestion of sugar all will probably soon be advanced by attorneys in defense of their clients.

The case of Dan White provides an example of this new direction in the development of personal defenses.[42] In 1978 White, a former San Francisco policeman, walked into the office of Mayor Moscone and shot both the mayor and City Councilman Harvey Milk to death. It was established at the trial that White had spent the night before the murders drinking Coca-Cola and eating Twinkies, a packaged pastry. Expert witnesses testified that the huge amounts of sugar consumed by White prior to the crime substantially altered his judgment and ability to control his behavior. The jury, influenced by the expert testimony, convicted White of a lesser charge, and he served a short prison sentence.

The strategy used by White's lawyers has come to be known as the "Twinkie defense." It may well be characteristic of future defense strategies now being developed in cases across the nation.

The "Twinkie Defense," used by former San Francisco policeman Dan White during his trial on charges of murdering the city's mayor and a councilman, appears to have opened a whole new arena for criminal defense strategists. A smiling Dan White is shown here in happier times as owner of San Francisco's Hot Potato fast food stand. *Photo: Janet Fries/Black Star.*

SPECIAL DEFENSES

A defense against criminal charges can be based upon circumstances as well as personal attributes. Special defenses relate to circumstances surrounding the crime. They take into consideration external pressures, operating at the time the crime was committed, which might have lessened the responsibility or the resolve of the defendant in a way with which the rest of us could sympathize. *Special defenses based upon circumstance are nine in number.*

Self-defense

Self-defense is probably the best know of the special defenses. This defense strategy makes the claim that harm was committed in order to ensure one's own safety in the face of certain injury. A person who harms an attacker can generally use this defense. However, the courts have held that where a "path of retreat" exists for a person being attacked, it should be taken. In other words, the safest use of self-defense is only when "cornered," with no path of escape.

The extent of the injury inflicted in self-defense must be reasonable with respect to the degree of the perceived threat. In other words, although it may be acceptable for a person to defensively kill someone who is shooting at them, it would be inappropriate to shoot and kill someone who is just verbally insulting. Deadly force generally cannot be used to repel nondeadly force.

Self-defense extends to defense of others and to the defense of one's home. A person whose loved ones are being attacked can claim self-defense if the person injures or kills the attacker. Similarly, a person can defend his or her home from invasion or forced entry,

Self-defense The protection of oneself or one's property from unlawful injury or the immediate risk of unlawful injury; the justification for an act which would otherwise constitute an offense, that the person who committed it reasonably believed that the act was necessary to protect self or property from immediate danger.

even to the point of using deadly force. However, the circumstances which surround the claim of self-defense are limited. The defense is useless where the person provoked an attack or where the attacker is justified. In cases of forcible arrest, for example, family members may not intervene to protect their relatives, providing the use of force by the police is legitimate.

Self-defense has been used recently in a spate of killings, by wives, of their abusive spouses. Killings which occur while the physical abuse is in process, especially where a history of such abuse can be shown, are likely to be excused by juries as self-defense. On the other hand, wives who suffer repeated abuse, but coldly plan the killing of their husbands, have not fared well in court. On the same day in 1988, for example, two women were adjudicated by state courts under similar circumstances, but with far different results. Caroline Decker of Broadalbin, New York, was acquitted of homicide charges in the shooting death of her abusive husband. Lana Anderson of Kirksville, Missouri, however, was found guilty of hiring two men to kill her husband.[43] Even though a history of abuse could be demonstrated in both cases, the jury recommended that Ms. Anderson be sentenced to life in prison with no chance for parole, apparently because of the "cold-blooded" and pre-planned nature of her actions.

Duress

Duress is another of the special defenses. A person may act under duress if, for example, he or she steals an employer's payroll in order to meet a ransom demand for kidnapers holding the person's children. Should the person later be arrested for larceny or embezzlement, the person can claim that he or she felt compelled to commit the crime to help ensure the safety of the children. The defense of duress is sometimes also called coercion. Duress is generally not a useful defense when the crime committed involves serious physical harm.

Entrapment

Entrapment is a special defense which has become relatively popular in the news media and in the courts. It is a special defense which regulates the enthusiasm with which police officers may enforce the law. Entrapment defenses argue that enforcement agents effectively create a crime where there would otherwise have been none. Entrapment was claimed in the famous case of automaker John DeLorean. DeLorean was arrested on October 19, 1982, by federal agents near the Los Angeles airport.[44] An FBI videotape, secretly made at the scene, showed him allegedly "dealing" with undercover agents and holding packets of cocaine which he said were "better than gold." DeLorean was charged with narcotics smuggling violations involving a large amount of drugs.

At his 1984 trial, DeLorean claimed that he had been "set up" by the police to commit a crime which he would not have been involved in were it not for their urging. DeLorean's auto company had fallen upon hard times, and he was facing heavy debts. Federal agents, acting undercover, proposed to DeLorean a plan whereby he could make a great deal of money through drugs. Because the idea originated with the police, not with DeLorean, and because DeLorean was able to demonstrate successfully that he was repeatedly threatened not to "pull out" of the deal by a police informant, the jury returned a "not guilty" verdict.

The concept of entrapment is well summarized in a statement made by DeLorean's defense attorney to *Time* before the trial: "This is a fictitious crime. Without the Government there would be no crime. This is one of the most insidious and misguided law-enforcement operations in history."[45]

Accident

The defense of accident claims that the action in question was not intended, but the result of some happenstance. Hunting accidents, for example, rarely result in criminal prosecution because the circumstances surrounding them clearly show the unintentional nature of the shootings. What appear as accidents, of course, may actually be disguised criminal behavior. A hunter in North Carolina, for example, was recently convicted of shooting at an airplane (in which a passenger was seriously injured) even though he claimed that his gun accidentally discharged into the air. His defense fell apart when his girlfriend told authorities that he had confided in her as to what really happened.

Mistake

Mistake is a special defense with two components. One is mistake of law, and the other is mistake of fact. Rarely is the defense of mistake of law acceptable. Most people realize that it is their responsibility to know the law as it applies to them. "Ignorance of the law is no excuse" is an old dictum still heard today. On occasion, however, humorous cases do arise in which such a defense is accepted by authorities—for example, the instance of the elderly woman who raised marijuana plants because they could be used to make a tea which relieved her arthritis. When her garden was discovered she was not arrested, but advised as to how the law applied to her.

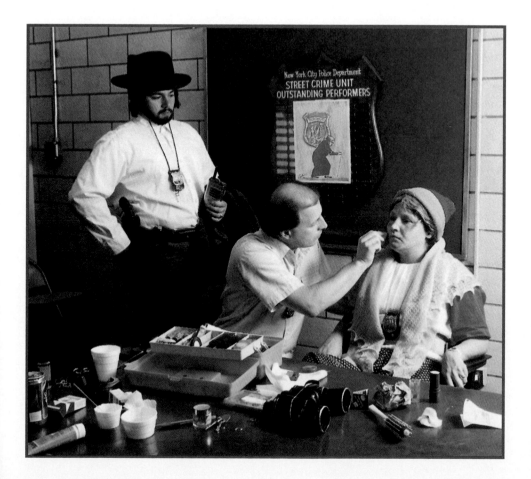

Members of the New York City Police Department's Street Crimes Unit prepare for a day's work. Entrapment will likely not be an effective defense for muggers who attack these decoys. *Courtesy of the New York City Police Department.*

Mistake of fact is a much more useful form of the "mistake" defense. In 1987, Jerry Hall, fashion model and girlfriend of Mick Jagger, a well-known rock star, was arrested in Barbados as she attempted to leave a public airport baggage claim area after picking up a suitcase.[46] The bag contained 20 pounds of marijuana and was under surveillance by officials who were waiting for just such a pickup. Ms. Hall defended herself by arguing that she had mistook the bag for her own, which looked similar. She was released after a night in jail.

Necessity

Necessity is a useful defense in cases which do not involve serious bodily harm. One of the most famous uses of this defense occurred in *Crown* v. *Dudly & Stephens* in the late 1800s.[47] The case involved a shipwreck in which three sailors and a cabin boy were set adrift in a lifeboat. After a number of days at sea without rations, two of them decided to kill and eat the cabin boy. At their trial, they argued that it was necessary to do so, or none of them would have survived. The court, however, reasoned that the cabin boy was not a direct threat to the survival of the men and rejected this defense. Convicted of murder, they were sentenced to death, although they were spared the gallows by royal intervention.

Although cannibalism is usually against the law, courts have sometimes recognized the necessity of consuming human flesh where survival was at issue. Those cases, however, involved only "victims" who had already died of natural causes.

Provocation

Provocation recognizes that a person can be emotionally enraged by another. Should they then strike out at their tormentor, some courts have held, they may not be guilty of any criminality. The defense of provocation is commonly used in barroom brawls where a person's parentage may have been called into question, although most states don't look favorably upon verbal provocation alone. It has also been used in some recent spectacular cases where wives have killed their husbands, or children their fathers, citing years of verbal and physical abuse. In these latter instances, perhaps because of the degree of physical harm inflicted, the defense of provocation has not been as readily accepted by the courts. As a rule, the defense of provocation is generally more acceptable in minor offenses than in serious violations of the law.

Consent

The defense of consent claims that whatever harm was done occurred only after the injured person gave their permission for the behavior in question. A 1980s trial saw Robert Chambers plead guilty to first-degree manslaughter in the killing of 18-year-old Jennifer Levin. In what was dubbed "the Preppy Murder Case,"[48] Chambers had claimed Levin died as a result of "rough sex" during which she had tied his hands behind his back and injured his testicles. Other cases, some involving sexual asphyxia (partial suffocation designed to heighten erotic pleasures) and bondage, culminated in a headline in *Time* heralding the era of "The Rough-Sex Defense."[49] The article suggested that such a defense works best with a good-looking defendant who appears remorseful; "[a] hardened type of character...,"[50] said the story, could not effectively use the defense.

In the "condom rapist" case, Joel Valdez was found guilty of rape in 1993 after a jury in Austin, Texas, rejected his claim that the act became consensual once he complied with his victim's request to use a condom. Valdez, who was drunk and armed with a knife at the time of the offense, claimed that his victim's request was a consent to sex. After that, he said, "we were making love."[51]

Alibi

A current reference book for criminal trial lawyers says, "Alibi is different from all of the other defenses…because…it is based upon the premise that the defendant is truly innocent…."[52] All the other defenses we have discussed are accepted ways to alleviate criminal responsibility. While they may produce findings of "Not Guilty," the defense of alibi, if believed, should support a ruling of "Innocent."

Alibi is best supported by witnesses and documentation. A person charged with a crime can use the defense of alibi to show that they were not present at the scene when the crime was alleged to have occurred. Hotel receipts, eyewitness identification, and participation in social events have all been used to prove alibis.

PROCEDURAL DEFENSES

Chapter 7 describes the legal environment in which the police must operate. When police officers violate constitutional guarantees of due process, they may create a situation in which guilty defendants can go free. Defenses based upon improper procedures may also occur as a consequence of actions by prosecutors and judges. Included among these procedural defenses are double jeopardy, collateral estoppel, prosecutorial misconduct, selective prosecution, and the denial of a speedy trial.

Double Jeopardy

The Fifth Amendment to the U.S. Constitution makes it clear that no person may be tried twice for the same offense. People who have been acquitted or found innocent may not be again put in "jeopardy of life or limb" for the same crime. Cases dismissed for a lack of evidence come under the double jeopardy rule, and cannot result in a new trial.

Double jeopardy, however, does not apply in cases of trial error. Hence, convictions which are set aside because of some error in proceedings at a lower court level will permit a retrial on the same charges. Similarly, when a defendant's motion for a mistrial is successful, a second trial may be held.

Defendants, however, may be tried in both federal and state courts without necessarily violating the principle of double jeopardy. For example, 33-year-old Rufina Canedo pleaded guilty to possession of 50 kilograms of cocaine in 1991 and received a six-year prison sentence in a California court.[53] Federal prosecutors, however, indicted her again—this time under a federal law—for the same offense. They offered her a deal—testify against her husband or face federal prosecution and the possibility of 20 years in a federal prison. Because state and federal statutes emanate from different jurisdictions, this kind of dual prosecution has been held constitutional by the U.S. Supreme Court. To prevent abuse, the U.S. Justice Department acted in 1960 to restrict federal prosecution in such cases to situations involving a "compelling federal interest"—such as civil rights violations. However, in recent years, in the face of soaring drug law violations, the restriction has been relaxed.

In 1992, in another drug case, the U.S. Supreme Court ruled that the double jeopardy clause of the U.S. Constitution "only prevents duplicative prosecution for the same offense," but that "a substantive offense and a conspiracy to commit that offense are not the same offense for double jeopardy purposes." In the case, *U.S.* v. *Felix* (1992),[54] a Missouri man was convicted in that state of manufacturing methamphetamine, and then convicted again in Oklahoma of conspiracy and manufacturing a controlled substance—in part based upon his activities in Missouri.

Collateral Estoppel

Collateral estoppel is similar to double jeopardy and applies to facts that have been determined by a "valid and final judgment."[55] Such facts cannot become the object of new litigation. Where a defendant, for example, has been acquitted of a multiple murder charge by virtue of an alibi, it would not be permissible to try that person again for the murder of a second person killed along with the first.

Selective Prosecution

The procedural defense of selective prosecution is based upon the Fourteenth Amendment's guarantee of equal protection of the laws. The defense may be available where two or more individuals are suspected of criminal involvement, but not all are actively prosecuted. Selective prosecution based fairly upon the strength of available evidence is not the object of this defense. But when prosecution proceeds unfairly on the basis of some arbitrary and discriminatory attribute, such as race, sex, friendship, age, or religious preference, protection may be feasible under it.

Denial of Speedy Trial

The Sixth Amendment to the Constitution guarantees a right to a speedy trial. The purpose of the guarantee is to prevent unconvicted and potentially innocent people from languishing in jail. The federal government[56] and most states have laws (generally referred to as "speedy trial acts") that define the time limit necessary for a trial to be "speedy" and generally set a reasonable period such as 90 or 120 days following arrest. Excluded from the counting procedure are delays which result from requests by the defense to prepare their case. If the limit set by law is exceeded, the defendant must be set free and no trial can occur.

Prosecutorial Misconduct

A final procedural defense may be found in prosecutorial misconduct. Prosecutors are expected to uphold the highest ethical standards in the performance of their roles. When they knowingly permit false testimony, when they hide information that would clearly help the defense, or when they make unduly biased statements to the jury in closing arguments, the defense of prosecutorial misconduct may be available to the defendant.

SUMMARY

Law serves many purposes. Primary among them is the maintenance of social order. Laws reflect the values held by society. The emphasis placed by law upon individual rights, personal property, and criminal reformation can tell us much about the cultural and philosophical basis of the society of which it is a part. Legal systems throughout the world reflect the experiences of the societies which created them. Islamic law, for example, has a strong religious component and requires judicial decisions in keeping with the Moslem Koran.

American law developed out of a long tradition of legal reasoning, extending back to the Code of Hammurabi, the earliest known codification of laws. The most recent historical source of modern law has been English "common law." Common law reflected the customs and daily practices of English citizens during the Middle Ages.

Western criminal law generally distinguishes between serious crimes (felonies) and those which are less grave (misdemeanors). Guilt can only be demonstrated if the *corpus delicti* of a crime can be proven in court.

Our judicial system has come to recognize a number of defenses to a criminal charge. Insanity and self-defense are two of the most important of the modern defenses. The insanity defense has met with considerable recent criticism. Efforts to reduce its blanket application are now underway in a number of states.

DISCUSSION QUESTIONS

1. Name some of the historical sources of modern law.

2. What kinds of concerns have influenced the development of the criminal law? How are social values and power arrangements in society represented in laws today?

3. Do you think there is a "natural" basis for laws? If so, what basis would you think it appropriate to build a system of laws upon? Do any of our modern laws appear to have a foundation in "natural law"?

4. What is "common law"? Is there a modern form of the common law? If so, what is it?

5. What is the *corpus delicti* of a crime? Are there any elements of a crime which you think are unnecessary? Why?

6. What is the difference between *mala in se* and *mala prohibita* offenses? Do you think this difference is real or only theoretical?

7. Does the insanity defense serve a useful function today? If you could create your own rule for determining insanity in criminal trials, what would it be? How would it differ from existing rules?

ENDNOTES

1. Marvin Wolfgang, *The Key Reporter* (Phi Beta Kappa), Vol. 52, no. 1.

2. Roman influence in England had ended by 442 A.D., according to Crane Brinton, John B. Christopher, and Robert L. Wolff, in *A History of Civilization*, 3rd ed., Vol. 1 (Englewood Cliffs, NJ: Prentice Hall, 1967), p. 180.

3. Howard Abadinsky, *Law and Justice* (Chicago: Nelson-Hall, 1988), p. 6.

4. Edward McNall Burns, *Western Civilization*, 7th ed. (New York: W. W. Norton, 1969), p. 339.

5. Ibid., p. 533.

6. Brinton, Christopher, and Wolf, *A History of Civilization*, p. 274.

7. Thomas Aquinas, *Summa Theologica* (Notre Dame, IN: University of Notre Dame Press, 1983).

8. *Roe* v. *Wade*, 410 U.S. 113 (1973).

9. Max Rheinstein, ed., *Max Weber on Law in Economy and Society* (Cambridge, MA: Harvard University Press, 1954).

10. John Stuart Mill, *On Liberty* (London: Parker, 1859).

11. Nigel Walker, *Punishment, Danger, and Stigma: The Morality of Criminal Justice* (Totowa, NJ: Barnes & Noble, 1980).

12. O. W. Holmes, *The Common Law* (Boston: Little, Brown, 1881).

13. Roscoe Pound, *Social Control Through the Law* (Hamden, CT: Archon, 1968), pp. 113–114.

14. As found in William Chambliss and Robert Seidman, *Law, Order, and Power* (Reading, MA: Addison-Wesley, 1971), pp. 154, 141–142.

15. Ibid., p. 140.

16. Ibid.

17. Ibid., p. 51.

18. Ibid.

19. Lief H. Carter, *Reason in Law*, 2nd ed. (Boston: Little, Brown, 1984).

20. "GM Appeals," *USA Today*, May 13, 1993, p. 1B.

21. *Facts on File, 1988* (New York: Facts on File, 1988), p. 175.

22. "Man Who Spent 6 1/2 Years in Jail Is Awarded $1.9 Million by Judge," *The Fayetteville Times* (North Carolina), October 20, 1989, p. 7A.

23. "Jury Says Halcion Led to Murder, Awards $2.15 million," *The Fayetteville Observer-Times* (North Carolina), November 13, 1992, p. 4A.

24. "Murder Attempt Charged in AIDS Exposure Case," *The Fayetteville Observer-Times* (North Carolina), November 16, 1992, p. 11A.

25. United States Sentencing Commission, *Federal Sentencing Guidelines Manual* (St. Paul, MN: West Publishing, 1987).

26. Daniel Oran, *Oran's Dictionary of the Law* (St. Paul, MN: West Publishing, 1983).

27. Henry Campbell Black, Joseph R. Nolan, and Jacqueline M. Nolan-Haley, *Black's Law Dictionary*, 6th ed. (St. Paul, MN: West Publishing, 1990), p. 24.

28. "Senate Begins to Consider Anti-Stalking Legislation," *Criminal Justice Newsletter*, March 2, 1993, p. 2.

29. Oliver Wendell Holmes, *The Common Law*, Vol. 3 (1881).

30. *American Jurisprudence*, 21/2 §§ 55–57.

31. "Mrs. Bobbitt's Defense 'Life Worth More Than Penis,'" *Reuter's* world wire services, January 10, 1994.

32. American Law Institute, *Model Penal Code: Official Draft and Explanatory Notes* (Philadelphia: The Institute, 1985).

33. Ibid.

34. John Klofas and Ralph Weischeit, "Guilty but Mentally Ill: Reform of the Insanity Defense in Illinois," *Justice Quarterly*, Vol. 4, no. 1 (March 1987), pp. 40–50.

35. Ibid.

36. *Ford* v. *Wainright*, 477 U.S. 106 S.Ct. 2595 (1986).

37. 18 United States Code, §401.

38. *Jones* v. *U.S.*, U.S. Sup. Ct. (1983), 33 CrL 3233.

39. *Ake* v. *Oklahoma*, U.S. Sup. Ct. (1985), 35 CrL 3159.

40. As reported in Arnold Binder, *Juvenile Delinquency: Historical, Cultural, Legal Perspectives* (New York: Macmillan, 1988), p. 494.

41. "Drunk Driving Charge Dismissed: PMS Cited," *The Fayetteville Observer-Times* (North Carolina), June 7, 1991, p. 3A.

42. *Facts on File, 1978* (New York: Facts on File, 1979).

43. *USA Today*, January 18, 1988, p. 3A.

44. *Time*, March 19, 1984, p. 26.

45. Ibid.

46. *Facts on File, 1987* (New York: Facts on File, 1988).

47. *The Queen* v. *Dudly & Stephens*, 14 Q.B.D. 273, 286, 15 Cox C. C. 624, 636 (1884).

48. "The Rough-Sex Defense," *Time*, May 23, 1988, p. 55.

49. Ibid., p. 55.

50. "The Preppie Killer Cops a Plea," *Time*, April 4, 1988, p. 22.

51. "Jury Convicts Condom Rapist," *USA Today*, May 14, 1993, p. 3A.

52. Patrick L. McCloskey and Ronald L. Schoenberg, *Criminal Law Deskbook* (New York: Matthew Bender, 1988), Section 20.03[13].

53. "Dual Prosecution Can Give One Crime Two Punishments," *USA Today*, March 29, 1993, p. 10A.

54. *U.S.* v. *Felix*, 112 S.Ct. 1377 (1992).

55. McCloskey and Schoenberg, *Criminal Law Deskbook*, Section 20.02[4].

56. Speedy Trial Act, 18 U.S.C. §3161. Significant cases involving the U.S. Speedy Trial Act are those of *U.S.* v. *Carter* (1986) and *Henderson* v. *U.S.* (1986).

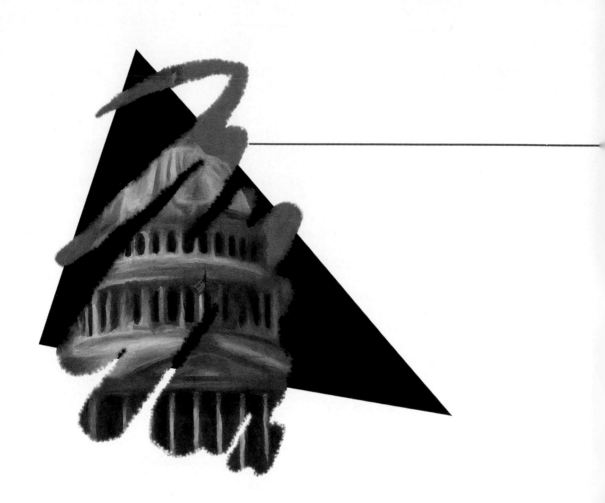

INDIVIDUAL RIGHTS VERSUS SOCIAL CONCERNS

THE RIGHTS OF THE ACCUSED UNDER INVESTIGATION

Common law, constitutional, and humanitarian rights of the accused:

A Right Against Unreasonable Searches
A Right Against Unreasonable Arrest
A Right Against Unreasonable Seizures of Property
A Right to Fair Questioning by Authorities
A Right to Protection from Personal Harm

The individual rights listed must be effectively balanced against these community concerns:

The Efficient Apprehension of Offenders
The Prevention of Crimes

How does our system of justice work toward balance?

THE PROCESS BEGINS

Laws are generally not understood by three sorts of persons: those that make them, those that execute them, and those that suffer if they break them.
　—HALIFAX (1633-1695)

If we are to keep our democracy, there must be one commandment: "Thou shalt not ration justice!"
　—JUSTICE LEARNED HAND (1872-1961)

There is no meaner tyranny than that which is perpetuated under the shield of law and in the name of justice.
　—MONTESQUIEU (1689-1755)

It is the spirit and not the form of law that keeps justice alive.
　—JUSTICE EARL WARREN (1891-1974)

CHAPTER 5

POLICING: HISTORY AND STRUCTURE

Unlike the soldier fighting a war on foreign soil, police officers, who provide for our safety at home, have never been given the honor that was their due.[1]
 —HUBERT WILLIAMS, PRESIDENT
  THE POLICE FOUNDATION

…[T]o introduce and implement new police ideas is not easy, but it is possible. More than that, it is essential if we are to achieve elementary public safety in American cities and confidence in the police by those who are being policed.[2]
 —JEROME H. SKOLNICK AND DAVID H. BAYLEY
  THE NEW BLUE LINE

If you want the present to be different from the past, study the past.
 —BARUCH SPINOZA (1632-1677)

The most fundamental weakness in crime control is the failure of federal and state governments to create a framework for local policing. Much of what is wrong with the police is the result of the absurd, fragmented, unworkable nonsystem of more than 17,000 local departments.
 —PATRICK V. MURPHY
  FORMER COMMISSIONER OF THE NYC POLICE
  DEPARTMENT

KEY CONCEPTS

KEY CONCEPTS

night watch

Statute of Winchester

Kansas City experiment

vigilantism

Bobbies

Bow Street Runners

Knapp Commission

witness protection program

LEAA

Exemplary projects

Wickersham Commission

KEY NAMES

Henry Fielding

Patrick Murphy

Charles Rowan

Robert Peel

Richard Mayne

DEVELOPMENT OF THE POLICE

THE ENGLISH EXPERIENCE

The rise of the police as an organized force in the Western world coincided with the evolution of strong centralized governments. While police forces have developed throughout the world, often in isolation from one another, the historical growth of the English police is of special significance to students of criminal justice in America, for it is upon the British model that much of early American policing was based.

Records indicate that efforts at law enforcement in early Britain, except for military intervention in the pursuit of bandits and habitual thieves, were not well organized until around the year 1200 A.D.[3] When a person committed an offense, and could be identified, he or she was usually pursued by an organized posse. All able-bodied men who were in a position to hear the hue and cry raised by the victim were obligated to join the posse in a common effort to apprehend the offender. The posse was led by the Shire Reeve—"leader of the county"—or by a mounted officer—the *comes stabuli*. Our modern words "sheriff" and "constable" are derived from these early terms. The *comes stabuli* were not uniformed, nor were they sufficient in number to perform all the tasks we associate today with law enforcement. This early system, employing a small number of mounted officers, depended for its effectiveness upon the ability to organize and direct the efforts of citizens toward criminal apprehension.

The offender, knowledgeable of a near-certain end at the hands of the posse, often sought protection from trusted friends and family. As a consequence, feuds developed between organized groups of citizens, some seeking revenge, and others siding with the offender. Suspects who lacked the shelter of a sympathetic group might flee into a church and invoke the time-honored custom of sanctuary. Sanctuary was rarely an ideal escape, however, as pursuers could surround the church and wait out the offender, while preventing food and water from being carried inside. The offender, once caught, became the victim. Guilt was usually assumed and trials were rare. Executions involving torture typified this early justice and served to provide a sense of communal solidarity and social retribution.

The development of law enforcement in English cities and towns grew out of an early reliance on bailiffs. Bailiffs were assigned the task of maintaining a night watch, primarily to detect fires and thieves. They were small in number, but served simply to rouse the sleeping population, which could then deal with whatever crisis was at hand. Larger cities expanded the idea of bailiffs by creating both a day ward and a night watch.

Comes Stabuli
Nonuniformed mounted early law enforcement officers in medieval England. Early police forces were small, and relatively unorganized, but made effective use of local resources in the formation of posse, the pursuit of offenders, and the like.

British police practices became codified in the Statute of Winchester, written in 1285. The statute specified (1) creation of the watch and the ward in cities and towns; (2) the draft of eligible males to serve either force; (3) institutionalized use of the "hue and cry," making citizens who disregarded this call for help subject to criminal penalties; and (4) that citizens must maintain weapons in their homes for answering the call to arms.

Some authors have attributed the growth of modern police forces to the gin riots which plagued London and other European cities in the 1700s and early 1800s. The invention of gin around 1720 provided, for the first time, a potent and inexpensive alcoholic drink readily available to the massed populations gathered in the early industrial ghettos of eighteenth-century cities. Seeking to drown their troubles, huge numbers of people, far beyond the ability of the bailiffs to control, began binges of drinking and rioting. These binges lasted for nearly a hundred years, and created an immense social problem for British authorities. The bailiff system by this time had evolved into a group of woefully inadequate substitutes, hired to perform their duties in place of the original—and far more capable—draftees. Staffed by incompetents, and unable to depend upon the citizenry for help in enforcing the laws, bailiffs became targets of mob violence, and were often attacked and beaten for sport.

The Bow Street Runners

The early 1700s saw the emergence in London of a large criminal organization led by Jonathan Wild. Wild ran a type of "fencing" operation built around a group of loosely organized robbers, thieves, and burglars, who would turn their plunder over to him. Wild would then negotiate with the legitimate owners for a ransom of their possessions.

The police response to Wild was limited by disinterest and corruption. However, when Henry Fielding, a well-known writer, became the magistrate of the Bow Street region of London, changes began to happen. Fielding attracted a force of dedicated officers, dubbed the Bow Street Runners, who soon stood out as the best and most disciplined enforcement agents that London had to offer. Fielding's personal inspiration, and his ability to communicate what he saw as the social needs of the period, may have accounted for his success.

In February 1725 Wild was arrested and arraigned on the following charges: "1.) that for many years past he had been a confederate with great numbers of highwaymen, pick-pockets, housebreakers, shop-lifters, and other thieves, 2.) that he had formed a kind of corporation of thieves, of which he was the head or director…, 3.) that he had divided the town and country into so many districts, and appointed distinct gangs for each, who regularly accounted with him for their robberies…, 4.) that the persons employed by him were for the most part felon convicts…, 5.) that he had, under his care and direction, several warehouses for receiving and concealing stolen goods, and also a ship for carrying off jewels, watches, and other valuable goods, to Holland, where he had a superannuated thief for his benefactor, and 6.) that he kept in his pay several artists to make alterations, and transform watches, seals, snuff-boxes, rings, and other valuable things, that they might not be known…."[4] Convicted of these and other crimes, Wild attempted suicide by drinking a large amount of laudanum—an opium compound. The drug merely rendered him senseless, and he was hanged the following morning, having only partially recovered from its effects.

In 1754 Henry Fielding died. His brother John took over his work and occupied the position of Bow Street magistrate for another 25 years. The Bow Street Runners remain famous for quality police work to this day.

The New Police

In 1829 Sir Robert Peel, who was later to become prime minister of England, formed what many have hailed as the world's first modern police force. Passage of the

New Police Also known as the Metropolitan Police of London, were formed in 1829 under the command of Sir Robert Peel. Peel's police became the model for modern-day police forces throughout the Western world.

Metropolitan Police Act that same year allocated the resources for Peel's force of 1,000 uniformed hand-picked men. The London Metropolitan Police, also known simply as the "new police," soon became a model for police forces around the world.

The Metropolitan Police were quickly dubbed "Bobbies," after their founder. London's Bobbies were organized around two principles: the belief that it was possible to discourage crime, and the practice of preventive patrol. Peel's police patrolled the streets, walking beats. Their predecessors, the watchmen, had previously occupied fixed posts throughout the city awaiting a public outcry. The new police were uniformed, resembling a military organization, and adopted a military administrative style.

London's first two police commissioners were Colonel Charles Rowan, a career military officer, and Richard Mayne, a lawyer. Rowan brought to law enforcement the belief that mutual respect between the police and citizenry would be crucial to the success of the new force. As a consequence, early Bobbies were chosen for their ability to reflect and inspire the highest personal ideals among young men in early nineteenth-century Britain.

Unfortunately, the new police were not immediately well received. Some elements of the population saw them as an occupying army, and open battles between the police and the citizenry ensued. The tide of sentiment turned, however, when an officer was viciously killed in the Cold Bath Fields riot of 1833. A jury, examining a murder charge against the killer, returned a verdict of not guilty, inspiring a groundswell of public support for the much-maligned force.

THE EARLY AMERICAN EXPERIENCE

Innovations in early American law enforcement were based to some degree upon the British experience. Towns and cities in colonial America depended upon Americanized versions of the night watch and day ward, and citizens evasive of the duty dramatically reduced the quality of police service.

The unique experience of the American colonies, however, quickly differentiated the needs of colonists from the masses remaining in Europe. Huge expanses of uncharted territory, vast wealth, a widely dispersed population involved mostly with agriculture, and a sometimes ferocious frontier, all combined to mold American law enforcement in a distinctive way. Recent writers on the history of the American police have observed that policing in America was originally "decentralized," "geographically dispersed," "idiosyncratic," and "highly personalized."[5]

The Frontier

Early colonial settlements, to those who lived in them, often seemed surrounded by wild and hostile environs. The backwoods areas provided a natural "haven" for outlaws and bandits. Henry Berry Lowery (the "popular outlaw" of the Carolinas), the James Gang, and many lesser known desperados felt at home in the unclaimed swamps and forests.

Efforts to police the frontier were undertaken by only the boldest of settlers. Among them was Charles Lynch, a Virginia farmer of the late 1700s. Lynch and his associates tracked and punished offenders, often according to the dictates of the still well-known "Lynch law," which they originated. Citizen posses and vigilante groups were often the only law available to settlers on the Western frontier. Judge Roy Bean ("the Law West of the Pecos"), "Wild Bill" Hickock, Bat Masterson, Wyatt Earp, and Pat Garrett were other popular figures of the time who took it upon themselves, sometimes in semiofficial capacities, to enforce the law on the books, along with standards of common decency.

Although vigilantism has today taken on a negative connotation, most of the original vigilantes of the American West were honest men and women trying to forge an organized and predictable life-style out of the challenging situations which they encountered. Often faced with unscrupulous, money-hungry desperados, they did what they could to bring the standards of civilization, as they understood them, to bear in their communities.

Policing America's Early Cities

Small-scale, organized law enforcement came into being quite early in America's larger cities. In 1658 paid watchmen were hired by the city of New York to replace drafted citizens.[6] By 1693 the earliest uniformed officer was employed by the city, and in 1731 the first precinct station was constructed. Boston, Cincinnati, and New Orleans were among American communities which followed the New York model and hired a force of watchmen in the early 1800s.

Peel's new police were closely studied by American leaders, and one year after their creation, Stephen Girard, a wealthy manufacturer, donated a considerable amount of money to the city of Philadelphia to create a capable police force. The city hired 120 men to staff a night watch and 24 to perform similar duties during the day.

In 1844 New York's separate day and night forces were combined into the New York City Police Department. Boston followed suit in 1855 with a similar merging of forces. Further advances in American policing, however, were precluded by the Civil War. Southern cities captured in the war found themselves under martial law and subject to policing by the military.

The turn of the century, coinciding as it did with numerous technological advances and significant social changes, brought a flood of reform. The International Association of Chiefs of Police (IACP) was formed in 1902 and immediately moved to create a nationwide clearinghouse for criminal identification. In 1915, the Fraternal Order of Police (FOP) initiated operations, patterning itself after labor unions, but prohibiting striking and accepting personnel of all ranks—from patrol officer to chief. In 1910 Alice Stebbins

Wyatt Earp, famous lawman
of the early American west.
Photo: Brown Brothers.

Wells became the first policewoman in the world, serving with the Los Angeles Police Department. Women had previously served as jail matrons, but had not been fully "sworn" with carrying out the duties of a police officer. In 1915, coinciding with the creation of the FOP, the International Association of Policewomen formed in the city of Baltimore. In 1918 Ellen O'Grady became the first woman to hold a high administrative post in a major police organization, when she was promoted to the rank of deputy police commissioner for the city of New York.

Automobiles, telephones, and radios all had their impact on the American police. Teddy Roosevelt, twenty-sixth president of the United States, pioneered his career by serving as a police commissioner in New York City from 1895 to 1897. While there, he promoted use of a call box system of telephones which allowed citizens to report crimes rapidly and made it possible for officers to call quickly for assistance. As president, Roosevelt later helped to organize the FBI, which was then called the Bureau of Investigation. Federal law enforcement already existed in the form of U.S. marshals, created by an act of Congress in 1789, and as postal inspectors, authorized by the U.S. Postal Act of 1829, but the FBI became a national investigative service designed to quickly identify and apprehend offenders charged with a growing list of federal offenses.

Automobiles, with the affordable era of rapid transportation they created, necessitated police forces with far-reaching powers, high mobility, and the ability to maintain constant communication with enforcement authorities. State police agencies arose to counter the threat of the mobile offender, with Massachusetts and Pennsylvania leading the way to statewide forces.

Prohibition and Police Corruption

A dark period began for American law enforcement agencies in 1920 with passage of a constitutional prohibition against all forms of alcoholic beverages. Until prohibition was repealed in 1933, the potential for corruption among police officials was considerable. In 1931 the Wickersham Commission, officially called the National Commission on Law Observance and Enforcement, recognized that prohibition was unenforceable, and reported that it carried a great potential for police corruption.[7] The Commission also established guidelines for enforcement agencies which guided many aspects of American law enforcement until the 1970s.

Law enforcement is a tool of power.

—*Alvin Toffler*

▌HE LAST HALF-CENTURY

Later in the text we will discuss the impact of the movement toward the increasing recognition of civil rights on law enforcement agencies. Suffice it to say here that the 1960s and 1970s were times of cultural reflection in America which forever altered the legal and valuative environment in which the police must work. During that period the Supreme Court frequently enumerated constitutionally based personal rights in the face of criminal prosecution. Although some "chipping away" at those rights occurred throughout the 1980s, the fundamental principles established in American criminal justice in the 1960s and 1970s will have a substantial impact on law enforcement for many years to come.

The 1960s and 1970s were also a period which saw intense examination of police activity, from day-to-day enforcement decisions, to administrative organization and police community relations. In 1967 the President's Commission on Law Enforcement and the Administration of Justice issued its report, *The Challenge of Crime in a Free Society,*[8] which found that the police were often interpersonally isolated from the communities they served. In 1969 the Law Enforcement Assistance Administration (LEAA) was formed to assist police forces across the nation in acquiring the latest in technology and enforcement methods. In 1973 the National Advisory Commission on Criminal Justice Standards and Goals[9] issued a comprehensive report detailing strategies for attacking and preventing crime, and for increasing the quality of law enforcement efforts at all levels. Included in the report was a call for greater participation in police work by women and ethnic minorities, and the recommendation that a college degree should become a basic prerequisite for police employment by the 1980s.

Scientific Police Management

In 1969, with passage of the Omnibus Crime Control and Safe Streets Act, the U.S. Congress created the Law Enforcement Assistance Administration. LEAA was charged with combating crime via the expenditure of huge amounts of money. Some have compared the philosophy establishing LEAA to that which supported the American space program's goal of landing people on the moon: "Put enough money into whatever problem there is, and it will be solved!" Unfortunately, the crime problem was more difficult to address than the challenge of a moon landing; even after the expenditure of nearly $8 billion, LEAA had not come close to its goal. In 1982 LEAA expired when Congress refused it further funding.

The legacy of LEAA is an important one for police managers, however. The research-rich years of 1969–1982, supported largely through LEAA funding, have left a plethora of scientific findings of relevance to police administration, and, more importantly, have established a tradition of evaluation within police management circles. This tradition is a natural outgrowth of LEAA's insistence that any funded program had to contain a plan for its evaluation.

Scientific Police Management The application of social scientific techniques to the study of police administration for the purpose of increasing effectiveness, reducing the frequency of citizen complaints, and enhancing the efficient use of available resources. The heyday of scientific police management probably occurred in the 1970s, when federal monies were far more readily available to support such studies than they are today.

Judge Roy Bean (seated on barrel), holding court in Langtry, Texas, circa 1900. *Photo: Culver Pictures.*

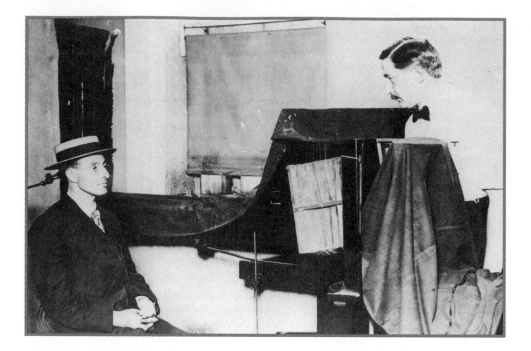

A New York City police officer "mugging" a prisoner in the early days of police photography. *Courtesy of the Library of Congress.*

Federal support for criminal justice research and evaluation continues today under the National Institute of Justice (NIJ) and the Bureau of Justice Statistics (BJS), both a part of the Office of Justice Assistance, Research, and Statistics (OJARS). OJARS was created by Congress in 1980 and functions primarily as a clearinghouse for criminal justice statistics and information. The National Criminal Justice Reference Service (NCJRS), a part of NIJ, is available to assist researchers nationwide in locating information applicable to their research projects. "Custom searches" of the NCJRS computer data base can be arranged at a small charge and yield voluminous information in most criminal justice subject areas. NIJ also publishes a series of informative reports, on a monthly basis (*NIJ Reports*), which serve to keep criminal justice practitioners and researchers informed about recent findings.

Exemplary Projects

Beginning in 1973 LEAA established the Exemplary Projects Program designed to recognize outstanding innovative efforts to combat crime and provide assistance to crime victims. One project which won exemplary status early in the program was the Street Crimes Unit of the New York City Police Department. The SCU used officers disguised as potential mugging victims and put them in areas where they were most likely to be attacked. In its first year, the SCU made nearly 4,000 arrests and averaged a successful conviction rate of around 80%. Perhaps the most telling statistic was the "average officer days per arrest." The SCU invested only 8.2 days in each arrest, whereas the department average for all uniformed officers was 167 days.[10]

Many other programs were supported and evaluated. The Hidden Cameras Project in Seattle, Washington, was one of those. The project utilized cameras hidden in convenience stores which were triggered when a "trip" bill located in the cash register drawer was removed. Clearance rates for robberies of businesses with hidden cameras were twice that of other similar businesses. Conviction rates for photographed robbers were shown to be over twice those of suspects arrested for robbing noncamera-equipped stores. Commercial robbery in Seattle decreased by 38% in the year following the start of the project.

LEAA was not alone in funding police research during the 1970s. On July 1, 1970, the Ford Foundation announced the start of a Police Development Fund totaling $30 million, to be spent over the next five years on police departments to support major crime-fighting strategies. This funding led to the establishment of the Police Foundation, which continues to exist today with the mission of "foster(ing) improvement and innovation in American policing."[11] Police Foundation–sponsored studies over the past 20 years have added to the growing body of scientific knowledge which concerns itself with policing.

The Kansas City Experiment

By far the most famous application of social research principles to police management was the Kansas City Preventive Patrol Experiment.[12] Sponsored by The Police Foundation, the results of this year-long study were published in 1974. The study divided the southern part of Kansas City into 15 areas. Five of these "beats" were patrolled in the usual fashion. Another 5 beats experienced a doubling of patrol activities and had twice the normal number of patrol officers assigned to them. The final third of the beats received a novel "treatment" indeed—no patrols were assigned to them, and no uniformed officers entered that part of the city unless they were called. The program was kept something of a secret, and citizens were unaware of the difference between the patrolled and "unpatrolled" parts of the city.

The results of the Kansas City experiment were surprising. Records of "preventable crimes," those toward which the activities of patrol were oriented—like burglary, robbery, auto theft, larceny, and vandalism—showed no significant differences in rate of occurrence among the three experimental beats. Similarly, citizens didn't seem to notice the change in patrol patterns in the two areas where patrol frequency was changed. Surveys conducted at the conclusion of the experiment showed no difference among citizens in the three areas as to their fear of crime before and after the study.

The 1974 study can be summed up in the words of the author of the final report: "…the whole idea of riding around in cars to create a feeling of omnipresence just hasn't worked.…Good people with good intentions tried something that logically should have worked, but didn't."[13]

A second Kansas City study focused on "response time."[14] It found that even consistently fast police response to citizen reports of crime had little effect on either citizen satisfaction with the police, or on the arrest of suspects. The study uncovered the fact that most reports made to the police came only after a considerable amount of time had passed. Hence, the police were initially handicapped by the timing of the report, and even the fastest police response was not especially effective.

The Kansas City study has been credited with beginning the now established tradition of scientific police evaluation. Patrick Murphy, former police commissioner in New York City and past president of the Police Foundation, said the Kansas City study "ranks among the very few major social experiments ever to be completed."[15] It, and other studies of special significance to law enforcement are summarized in Table 5–1.

Effects of the Kansas City Study on Patrol The Kansas City studies greatly impacted managerial assumptions about the role of preventive patrol and traditional strategies for responding to citizen calls for assistance. As Joseph Lewis, then director of evaluation at the Police Foundation said, "I think that now almost everyone would agree that almost anything you do is better than random patrol, and the so-called 'ten-cent' dispatch."[16]

While some basic assumptions about patrol were called into question by the Kansas City studies, patrol remains the backbone of police work. New patrol strategies for the

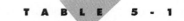

T A B L E   5 - 1

SCIENTIFIC STUDIES IN LAW ENFORCEMENT

Year	Study Name	Focus
1992	The New York City Police Department's Cadet Corps Study	Level of education among officers and hiring of minority officers
1992	Metro–Dade Spouse Abuse Experiment Replication	Replication of the 1984 Minneapolis study
1991	Quality Policing in Madison	Community policing and participatory police management
1990	Minneapolis "Hot Spot" Patrolling	Intensive patrol of problem areas
1987	Newport News Problem-Oriented Policing	Police solutions to community crime problems
1986	Citizen-Oriented Police Activities	Reducing citizen's fear of crime
1986	Crime Stoppers: A National Evaluation	Media crime reduction programs
1986	Reducing Fear of Crime in Houston and Newark	Strategies for fear reduction among urban populations
1984	Minneapolis Domestic Violence Experiment	Effective police action in domestic violence situations
1981	Newark Foot Patrol Experiment	Cots versus benefits of foot patrol
1977	Cincinnati Team Policing Experiment	Team versus traditional policing
1977	Patrol Staffing in San Diego	One- versus two-officer units
1976	Police Response Time	Citizen satisfaction
1976	The Police and Interpersonal Conflict	Police intervention in domestic and other disputes
1976	Managing Investigations	Detective/patrol officer teams
1976	Kansas City Peer Review Panel	Improving police behavior
1974	Kansas City Patrol Study	Effectiveness of police patrol

Directed Patrol A police management strategy designed to increase the productivity of patrol officers through the application of scientific analysis and evaluation to patrol techniques.

effective utilization of human resources have led to various kinds of **directed patrol** activities. One form of directed patrol varies the number of officers involved in patrolling according to time of day or on the basis of frequency of reported crimes within areas. The idea is to put the most officers where and when crime is most prevalent.

Following the preventive patrol experiments, Kansas City continued with patrol experiments and evaluated the use of "location-oriented patrol" (LOP) and "perpetrator-oriented patrol" (POP). Both were forms of "apprehension-oriented" directed patrol.[17] POP focused on individuals who were thought to be high-crime risks, while LOP concentrated police resources in areas where crimes were frequently reported. Both LOP and POP embodied low-visibility and high-visibility patrol in combination with each other. Low-visibility patrol made use of unmarked vehicles and nonuniformed personnel. The study demonstrated that focused approaches to crime prevention, such as those represented by POP and LOP, were considerably more effective than was routine patrol in reducing crime, producing arrests, and ensuring successful prosecution of suspects.

Other cities have prioritized calls for service,[18] ordering a quick police response only when crimes are in progress or where serious crimes have occurred. Less significant offense, such as minor larcenies or certain citizen complaints, are handled through the mail or by having citizens come to the police station to make a report. Wilmington, Delaware, was one of the first cities to make use of split-force patrol, in which only a part of the patrol force performed routine patrol.[19] The remainder were assigned the duty of responding to calls for service, taking reports, and conducting investigations.

Recent Studies

Recent studies of the police have been designed to identify and probe some of the basic, and often "taken for granted," assumptions which have guided police work throughout this century. The initial response to many of these studies was, "Why should we study that? Everybody knows the answer already!" The value of applying evaluative techniques to police work, however, can be seen in the following examples:

- The 1984 Minneapolis domestic violence experiment was the first scientifically engineered social experiment to test the impact of the use of arrest (versus alternative forms of disposition) upon crime.[20] In this case, the crime in focus was violence in the home environment. Investigators found that offenders who were arrested were less likely to commit repeat offenses than those who were handled in some other fashion. A Police Foundation–sponsored 1992 study of domestic violence in the Metro–Dade (Florida) area reinforced the Minneapolis findings, but found that the positive effect of arrest applied almost solely to those who were employed.
- A second example of modern scientific police management comes from Newport News, Virginia.[21] In the late 1980s, the police in Newport News decided to test traditional incident-driven policing against a new approach called problem-oriented policing. Incident-driven policing mobilizes police forces to respond to citizen complaints and offenses reported by citizens. It is what the Newport News police called "the standard method for delivering police services." Problem-oriented policing, on the other hand, was developed in Newport News to identify critical crime problems in the community and to address effectively the underlying causes of crime. For example, one identified problem involved thefts from vehicles parked in the Newport News ship-building yard. As many as 36,000 cars were parked in those lots during the day. Applying the principles of problem-oriented policing, Newport News officers sought to explore the dimensions of the problem. After identifying theft-prone lots and a small group of frequent offenders, officers arrested one suspect in the act of breaking into a vehicle. That suspect provided the information police were seeking: it turned out that drugs were the real target of the car thieves. "Muscle cars," rock music bumper stickers, and other indicators were used by the thieves as clues to which cars had the highest potential for yielding drugs. The police learned that what seemed to be a simple problem of thefts from automobiles was really a search for drugs by a small group of "hard-core" offenders. Strategies to address the problem were developed, including wider efforts to reduce illicit drug use throughout the city.

These and other studies have established a new basis for the use of scientific evaluation in police work today. The accumulated wisdom of police management studies can be summed up in the words of Patrick Murphy who, near retirement as director of the Police Foundation, stated five tenets for guiding American policing into the next century:[22]

1. Neighborhood policing programs of all kinds need to be developed, improved, and expanded.
2. More police officers need college and graduate-level education.

Evaluating the Police

In October of 1993 the Bureau of Justice Statistics published *Performance Measures for the Criminal Justice System*, a collection of discussion papers produced by the BJS–Princeton Project group. The papers represent the best official effort to date to identify performance goals and associated measures useful in assessing the day-to-day operations of criminal justice agencies.

Historically, according to Project authors, the effectiveness of policing has been measured via reported rates of crime, overall rates of arrests, clearance rates, and agency response times. However, the Project also identified the following emerging goals and performance indicators in the area of policing:

Goals	Performance Indicators
Doing justice, or "treating citizens in an appropriate manner based upon their conduct."	Nature and type of patrolling strategy, number of traffic tickets issued, crimes cleared, analysis of who calls the police, quality of investigations, cases released because of police misconduct, citizen complaints, lawsuits filed, and results of dispositions and officer-initiated encounters.
Promoting secure communities, or "enabling citizens to enjoy a life without fear of crime or victimization."	The existence of programs and resources allocated to crime prevention programs, time and money dedicated to problem-solving, rewards, monitoring of police, degree of public trust in the police, fear of crime, and home and business security checks by the police.
Restoring crime victims, by "restoring victims' lives and welfare as much as possible."	Number of contacts with victims after initial call for assistance, types of assistance provided to victims, including information, comfort, transportation, and referrals to other agencies.
Promoting noncriminal options, by "developing strong relationships with individuals in the community."	The existence of programs and resources allocated to strengthening relationships between the police and the community, including traditional community relations programs, school programs, storefront operations and officer contacts with citizens.

Project authors also concluded that performance criteria which measure the degree of police agency orientation toward the community are becoming appropriate. Such criteria would measure: "police-related and inter-governmental activities that improve the social fabric of the community, projects with the assistance of private industry that improve informal and formal social control in the community, fear of crime, [and] victimization and police service programs that help promote community spirit in those neighborhoods where none existed."

Source: Geoffrey Alpert and Mark H. Moore, "Measuring Police Performance in the New Paradigm of Policing," in John J. DiLulio, Jr., et al., *Performance Measures for the Criminal Justice System: Discussion Papers from the BJS–Princeton Project* (Washington, D.C.: Bureau of Justice Statistics, October 1993).

3. There should be more civilianization of police departments. Civilian specialists can add to department operations and release sworn officers for police duties.
4. Departments must continue to become more representative of the communities they serve by recruiting more women and minorities.
5. Restraint in the use of force, especially deadly force, must be increased.

AMERICAN LAW ENFORCEMENT TODAY: FROM THE FEDERAL TO THE LOCAL LEVEL

The organization of American law enforcement has been called the most complex in the world. Three major legislative and judicial jurisdictions exist in the United States—federal, state, and local—and each has created a variety of police agencies to enforce its laws. Unfortunately, there has been little uniformity among jurisdictions as to the naming, function, or authority of enforcement agencies. The matter is complicated still more by the rapid growth of private security firms which operate on a profit basis and provide services which have traditionally been regarded as law enforcement activities.

FEDERAL LAW ENFORCEMENT AGENCIES

There are 19 separate federal law enforcement agencies distributed among seven U.S. government departments. Table 5–2 lists these agencies and departments. In addition to the enforcement agencies listed here, dozens of other federal government offices are involved in enforcement activities through inspections, regulation, and control activities. Three of the best known federal law enforcement agencies are described in the paragraphs that follow.

Federal Bureau of Investigation

The Federal Bureau of Investigation (FBI) may be the most famous law enforcement agency in the country. It is held in high regard by many citizens, who think of it as an example of what a law enforcement organization should be and who believe that FBI agents are exemplary police officers. William Webster, former director of the FBI, reflected this sentiment when he said: "Over the years the American people have come to expect the most professional law enforcement from the FBI. Although we use the most modern forms of management and technology in the fight against crime, our strength is in our people—in the character of the men and women of the FBI. For that reason we seek only those who have demonstrated that they can perform as professional people who can, and will, carry on our tradition of fidelity, bravery, and integrity."[23]

History of the FBI The FBI has a history which spans nearly all this century. It began in 1908 as the Bureau of Investigation, when it was designed to serve as the investigative arm of the U.S. Department of Justice. Creation of the FBI was motivated, at least in part, by the inability of other agencies to stem the rising tide of American political and business corruption.

T A B L E   5 - 2

AMERICAN POLICING: FEDERAL LAW ENFORCEMENT AGENCIES

Department of the Treasury
Bureau of Alcohol, Tobacco, and Firearms
Internal Revenue Service
U.S. Customs Service
U.S. Secret Service
Federal Law Enforcement Training Center

Department of Justice
Bureau of Prisons
Drug Enforcement Administration
Federal Bureau of Investigation
U.S. Marshals Service
Immigration and Naturalization Service

Department of the Interior
Fish and Wildlife Service
National Park Service
U.S. Park Police

Department of Defense
Criminal Investigation Division
Office of Special Investigations
Naval Investigative Service
Defense Criminal Investigator Service

General Services Administration
Federal Protective Services

U.S. Postal Service
Postal Inspections Service

Washington, D.C.
Metropolitan Police Department

The Bureau began as a small organization. Thirty-five agents were hired to investigate crimes of limited jurisdiction, including antitrust violations by businesses and bankruptcy fraud, and to pursue some federal fugitives. However, the Bureau grew quickly as passage of the White Slave Traffic Act in 1910 necessitated a coordinated interstate law enforcement effort to fight organized prostitution. Incidents of sabotage and espionage on American soil during World War I also contributed to the rapid growth of the FBI, and the Espionage Act of 1917 provided a legal basis for many Bureau investigations into subversive activities.

In 1924 J. Edgar Hoover was appointed to direct the FBI. He immediately initiated a plan to increase professionalism among agents. New agents were hired only from among college graduates, with lawyers and accountants especially sought. Training was thorough, and assignments were made on a national basis. On July 1, 1924, the Bureau opened its Identification Division to serve as a national clearinghouse for information on criminals who, with the popular availability of the automobile, were becoming increasingly mobile.

The Division began operations with 810,188 fingerprint cards, received from the Federal Penitentiary at Leavenworth, Kansas, and from the International Association of Chiefs of Police.

In 1932 the Bureau opened its fledgling Crime Laboratory with a borrowed microscope. Before the laboratory had completed its first year of operations, 963 analyses had been performed—most focusing on homicide-related ballistics testing and handwriting examinations in fraud cases.

During the late 1920s and early 1930s, prohibition combined with organized criminal cartels to propel the Bureau into a "war" with well-armed and violent groups. Famous gangsters of the period who made the FBI's "Ten Most Wanted" list included "Baby Face" Nelson, Clyde Barrow, Bonnie Parker, "Ma" Barker, John Dillinger, "Pretty Boy" Floyd, "Machine Gun" Kelly, and Alvin Karpis. It was during this period of its development that the Bureau's trustworthy image and the popular conception of tough "G-Men" entranced the nation.

In 1935 the Bureau of Investigation officially changed its name to the Federal Bureau of Investigation and opened its first class at the FBI National Academy. The National Academy still provides training to FBI special agents as well as to selected police officers from around the country. In 1940 the National Academy moved from Washington, D.C., to the U.S. Marine Amphibious Base at Quantico, Virginia, where it remains today.

In 1936 President Franklin Roosevelt directed the FBI to collect information on radical groups within American borders, including communist and extremist organizations. During World War II the FBI proved highly effective in combating the efforts of Nazi and Japanese saboteurs. Following the war, FBI attention focused on Soviet spy rings which were designed to steal defense secrets, including techniques for the manufacture of atomic bombs.

During the 1960s, at the direction of Attorney General Robert F. Kennedy, the FBI became increasingly involved in investigations of civil rights violations. Some critics have charged that this era of burgeoning civil rights tarnished the image of the FBI, since FBI-sponsored investigations of rights activists were as common as those of antirights groups.[24]

The FBI Today Today the FBI operates 59 field offices and employs more than 21,000 people, including 10,400 special agents. Nearly 1,200 special agents are women, and in 1992 Burdena "Birdie" Pasenelli became the first woman to head an FBI field office. With a budget of over $1 billion per year, FBI jurisdiction extends to more than 200 specific crimes and certain broad areas of criminal activity.[25] The Identification Division maintains fingerprint records numbering slightly over 200 million and receives thousands of additional records each day. A modern FBI laboratory conducts nearly 1 million scientific analyses each year. The FBI National Academy now occupies 334 acres and trains over 1,000 local and state law enforcement officers every 12 months.

FBI activities are concentrated on white-collar crime, gambling law violations, drug offenses, arson, racketeering, foreign espionage, civil rights violations, violent serial offenders, and offenses involving high technology. The Uniform Crime Reporting Program of the FBI gathers statistics on reported crime throughout the United States and publishes yearly summary reports. The FBI Laboratory provides significant assistance to many local and state police agencies, and the Bureau's National Crime Information Center (NCIC) maintains millions of records on a variety of offenses in support of investigative efforts across the country.

Drug Enforcement Administration

History of the DEA The U.S. Drug Enforcement Administration (DEA) had its beginnings with passage of the Harrison Narcotic Act, which was signed into law on December 17, 1914, by President Woodrow Wilson. The Harrison Act was primarily a tax

CAREERS IN JUSTICE

WORKING FOR THE FBI

TYPICAL POSITIONS.   Special agent, crime laboratory technician, ballistics technician, computer operator, fingerprint specialist, explosives examiner, document
expert, and other nonagent technical positions.

EMPLOYMENT REQUIREMENTS.   General employment requirements include (1)
an age of between 23 and 37; (2) excellent physical health; (3) uncorrected vision of
not less than 20/200, correctable to 20/20 in one eye, and at least 20/40 in the other
eye; (4) good hearing; (5) U.S. citizenship; (6) a valid driver's license; (7) successful
completion of a background investigation; (8) a law degree or a Bachelor's degree
from an accredited college or university; (9) successful completion of an initial written examination; (10) an intensive formal interview; and (11) urinalysis. A polygraph examination may also be required.

OTHER REQUIREMENTS.   Five special agent entry programs exist in the areas of
law, accounting, languages, engineering/science, and a general "diversified" area
which requires a minimum of three years of full-time work experience, preferably
with a law enforcement agency. The FBI emphasizes education, and especially values degrees in law, graduate studies, and business and accounting. Most nonagent technical career paths also require Bachelor's or advanced degrees and U.S.
citizenship.

SALARY.   Special agents enter the bureau in Government Service (GS) grade 10 and
can advance to grade GS-13 in field assignments and GS-15 or higher in supervisory and management positions. Entry-level salary in 1993 was $31,623. A high-cost
area supplement ranging from 4% to 16% is paid in specified geographic areas.

BENEFITS.   Benefits include (1) 13 days of sick leave annually, (2) 2-1/2 to 5 weeks
of annual paid vacation and 10 paid federal holidays each year, (3) federal health and
life insurance, and (4) a comprehensive retirement program.

DIRECT INQUIRIES TO: Federal Bureau of Investigation, U.S. Department of
Justice, 9th Street and Pennsylvania Ave., N.W., Washington, D.C. 20535. Phone:
(202) 324-4991, or check your local telephone book.

law. However, Section 8 of the act made it unlawful for any "nonregistered" personnel to
possess heroin, cocaine, opium, morphine, or any of their products. Enforcement began in
1915 with agents of the "Miscellaneous Division" of the Bureau of Internal Revenue finding themselves charged with precedent-setting responsibilities under the new law. During
their first year of activity, agents of the Miscellaneous Division seized 44 pounds of heroin
and saw 106 convictions returned (mostly of errant physicians).[26]

The 1920s saw federal narcotics enforcement activities focus on organized gangs of
Chinese immigrants suspected of running much of the imported opium trade. San
Francisco's Chinatown became the scene of frequent raids, and hundreds of Chinese faced

deportation hearings for their alleged roles in drug running. Chief narcotics agent Joseph A. Manning identified the On Leong Tong as an organized criminal organization which employed murder-for-hire to retain control over its opium sales.

In 1919 the Volstead Act, designed to ensure enforcement of the Eighteenth Amendment on prohibition, was passed. The huge Prohibition Unit of the Revenue Bureau contained a smaller subelement called the Narcotic Division, headed by Levi G. Nutt, a former pharmacist. The Narcotic Division consisted of 170 agents working out of 13 offices around the country. The division was given new teeth by the Narcotic Drugs Import and Export Act of 1922, which brought into being the Federal Narcotics Control Board and strictly prohibited the importation of narcotic drugs for anything other than medical purposes.

On July 1, 1930, the Narcotics Division became the Federal Bureau of Narcotics, headed by Harry J. Anslinger, an appointee of President Herbert Hoover. Under Anslinger's leadership, the Bureau grew quickly. Marijuana abuse was identified as a serious drug problem during the 1930s, and the Marijuana Tax Act of 1937 created fines of $100 per ounce for possession of nontax-paid marijuana. The Mafia also became involved in drug trafficking. Famous criminal personalities of the times included Louis "Lepke" Buchalter, dubbed "Public Enemy Number One," whose organization allegedly smuggled 649 kilograms of pure heroin into the country from Shanghai before being broken up. His distribution network was headed by Lucky Luciano, and its investigation led to the discovery of the Mafia's enforcement arm known as "Murder Incorporated."

Following World War II the Bureau received legislative authority to control synthetic drugs and narcotics derivatives. The Boggs Act of 1956 made any use of heroin illegal and removed it from the shelves of pharmacies across the nation. In 1963 the President's Advisory Commission on Narcotic and Drug Abuse recommended numerous revisions in federal drug enforcement efforts. The 1960s also saw an explosion in the quantity of drugs seized in this country and overseas. The Bureau's Overseas Division, working with international police organizations, confiscated over 6 million tons of opium and its derivatives in 1964. Reorganization resulted in creation of the Bureau of Narcotics and Dangerous Drugs in 1968.

By 1970 LSD and other "designer drugs" had begun to appear, and Congress responded with passage of the Comprehensive Drug Abuse Prevention and Control Act. The act provided a firm legal basis for drug enforcement activities and established five schedules which classified controlled substances according to their abuse potential. Finally, in 1973 a separate agency, the Drug Enforcement Administration, was created and charged with enforcement of federal drug laws.

The DEA Today Today the DEA is rapidly becoming the largest federal law enforcement agency. The widespread sale, transportation, and use of illicit drugs throughout the country, and the associated potential for social disruption envisioned by many, has made enforcement of drug laws a top government priority.

Official DEA policy concentrates investigative resources on the "most significant individuals and organizations involved in drug trafficking both domestically and internationally."[27] Investigations often cross international borders, and indictments may name dozens of suspects.

During fiscal year 1993 DEA employed 3,547 special agents and another 200 intelligence specialists. Agents effected 24,186 arrests during 1992 and confiscated 467 kilograms of heroin, 78,416 kilograms of cocaine, and 201,373 kilograms of cannabis. Property worth nearly $1 billion was seized in connection with the arrests.[28]

The DEA maintains 19 field divisions and 113 resident offices within the United States, and has 286 agents and 108 support personal assigned to 72 offices in foreign countries.

The work of a DEA agent can be dangerous, but rewarding. Here agents tag 4,000 pounds of cocaine seized in Key West, Florida.
Photo: Chris Brown/Stock Boston.

The agency is especially responsive to changes in the pattern of drug flow and routinely reorients its enforcement activities to deal with perceived threats. In the mid-1970s for example, 200 new agents were added to areas along the Mexican border to stem the traffic in drugs entering the country through Mexico. Around 1980, that border traffic quieted down, while Florida's airports and harbors experienced increased illegal drug activity. The number of DEA agents in Florida rose to 300 to meet this increased threat. A shift is once again occurring in the pattern of drug flow, and the U.S.–Mexican border has become a renewed focal point of enforcement activity.

U.S. Marshals Service

History of the Marshals Service

The U.S. Marshals Service (USMS) began over 200 years ago when President George Washington appointed the first 13 marshals. The offices of U.S. Marshal and Deputy Marshal had been created by the Judiciary Act of 1789, which also established the Supreme Court. Marshals hired their own deputies who served at their pleasure and who had little job security. The Marshals Service performed most federal law enforcement functions until the formation of the U.S. Department of Justice. The Service also did much more, however, since (by what may have been historical oversight) no agency was provided for in the U.S. Constitution to represent the interests of the federal government within the states. Hence, many administrative roles fell to the Service, and marshals conducted the national census, registered

CAREERS IN JUSTICE

WORKING FOR THE DRUG ENFORCEMENT ADMINISTRATION

TYPICAL POSITIONS. Criminal investigator, diversion investigator, and intelligence research specialist.

EMPLOYMENT REQUIREMENTS. Applicants for GS-5 levels must (1) be U.S. citizens, (2) hold a four-year college degree, (3) be in good health, (4) pass a comprehensive background investigation, (5) possess effective oral and written communications skills, and (6) have three years of general job experience. Applicants for GS-7 levels must also demonstrate *one* of the following: (1) a 2.9 overall college average, (2) a 3.5 grade point average in the applicant's major field of study, (3) a standing in the upper one-third of the applicant's graduating class, (4) membership in a national honorary scholastic society, (5) one year of successful graduate study, or (6) one year of specialized experience (defined as "progressively responsible investigative experience").

OTHER REQUIREMENTS. Applicants must (1) be willing to travel frequently, (2) submit to a urinalysis test designed to detect the presence of controlled substances, and (3) successfully complete a two-month formal training program at the FBI's Training Center in Quantico, Virginia.

SALARY. Starting salary in 1993 for individuals with four-year college degrees was $30,603. Appointments are made at higher pay grades for individuals possessing additional education and experience.

BENEFITS. Benefits include (1) 13 days of sick leave annually, (2) 2-1/2 to 5 weeks of annual paid vacation and 10 paid federal holidays each year, (3) federal health and life insurance, and (4) a comprehensive retirement program.

DIRECT INQUIRIES TO: Drug Enforcement Administration, Office of Personnel, Recruitment, and Placement, 400 6th Street, S.W. Room 2558, N.W., Washington, D.C. 20024. Phone: (202) 401-7487.

aliens, exchanged fugitives, and rented space from local authorities for federal courtrooms. As Frederick S. Calhoun, historian of the U.S. Marshals Service writes, "For the American people, the marshals personified the authority of the federal government within their communities.…The marshal, in effect, was the point of contact in the friction between the national government and local communities."[29]

The infamous Whiskey Rebellion of 1794, civil rights violations during post–Civil War Reconstruction, settling of the "Wild West," and desegregation efforts during the 1950s and 1960s all precipitated intensive investigations led by U.S. marshals. Labor unrest in the early part of the twentieth century was often resolved through court injunctions served by marshals. Deputy marshals provided personal protection to outstanding figures in the civil

THEORY INTO PRACTICE

WHAT WENT WRONG IN WACO?

In the spring of 1993 the country stood enthralled by a standoff between members of the Treasury Department's Bureau of Alcohol, Tobacco, and Firearms (ATF) and David Koresh and his "Branch Davidian" followers, nearly 100 of whom were holed up in a 77-acre armed compound near Waco, Texas. ATF involvement began when agents heard reports of an illegal arms horde inside the compound. An initial raid on February 19 led to the shooting deaths of 4 ATF agents and 6 sect members. Following 51 days of negotiations, federal agents stormed the building. Koresh and 85 of his followers, 17 of them children, died in a fire that ensued. The fire appeared to have been set by those inside the compound.

Koresh had been alerted to the presence of ATF agents when a local TV cameraman asked postman David Jones for directions to the Koresh compound. The cameraman had been tipped off by an ambulance driver hired by the ATF. He was on the scene to cover what he thought would soon become a newsworthy confrontation. The postman turned out to be David Koresh's brother-in-law, and Koresh was alerted to ATF plans for what had been dubbed "Operation Trojan Horse." Such prior knowledge gave Koresh time to prepare for the initial raid, and to have armed followers in place to effectively repel advancing ATF agents.

An undercover ATF agent, Robert Rodriguez, who had infiltrated Koresh's compound reported Koresh's knowledge of the raid to his superiors. Even so, the raid proceeded—in a hurry and with little advance preparation after supervisors learned of Koresh's suspicions. After the initial raid proved a disaster, FBI personnel were called in to provide assistance. Psychological profiling teams attempted to predict the steps Koresh would take. Familiar mostly with serial killers and career offenders, none of these specialists foresaw his ordering a mass suicide—the apparent cause of the climactic fire which ended the siege. Similarly Koresh's pronouncements that he would soon surrender after he finished working on a series of revelational writings came to be disregarded after a number of deadlines passed. Authorities doubted that the writings even existed, although a computer disk later taken from a cult member who survived by leaping from the roof of the burning building contained portions of the manuscript.

A 220-page Treasury Department Report critical of the February raid was released in late 1993. It concluded that "[t]he decision to proceed (with the raid) was tragically wrong, not just in retrospect, but because of what the decision makers knew at the time." The Bureau, the report said, "not only handled a sensitive situation ineptly but tried to cover up its bumbling with lies and obfuscations." Agents should have called off the initial confrontation, according to the report's authors, when Koresh learned of their plan. Following release of the critical report, Treasury Secretary Lloyd Bentsen, whose department is in charge of ATF, announced replacement of the agency's entire top management. Dan Hartnett, 53, associate ATF director, and Dan Conroy, 50, deputy associate ATF director, left their positions immediately following release of the report, which also accused them of "lying and misleading the public after the raid." Stephen Higgins, ATF director at the time of raid, reacting to advance knowledge of the report's contents, had announced his retirement three days earlier.

A Justice Department report, released a week after the Treasury Department paper, rebuked lower- and midlevel FBI agents for the final stage of the disastrous operation—a tear-gas assault on Koresh's compound which ended in the fatal fire. Attorney General Janet Reno and then-FBI director William Sessions had ordered the assault. Sessions was replaced as director of the FBI by President Clinton in the summer of 1993.

Sources: Howard Chua-Eoan, "Waco: A Tragedy of Errors," *Time* on-line version, October 12, 1993. "Two Officials Named in Waco Report Resign," *Fayetteville Observer-Times* (North Carolina), October 4, 1993.

rights movement of the mid-1900s. James Meredith, the first Black student at the University of Mississippi at Oxford, was shielded by marshals from hostile crowds as he registered at the school. Dr. Martin Luther King was accompanied by deputy U.S. marshals on many of his marches and speeches.

The Marshals Service has sometimes fallen victim to differences between local and federal laws and policies. After the Civil War, for example, marshals attempting to enforce the civil rights of newly freed blacks throughout the South were often arrested and jailed by local authorities. As late as 1962 Chief Marshal James McShane was indicted in Mississippi for inciting a riot at the University of Mississippi where James Meredith was registering.[30]

The USMS has often played a quasi-military role, sometimes acting in public disorders to protect life and property. In 1973, for example, the Marshals Service was at the Sioux Indian occupation of Wounded Knee, South Dakota, and during the 1970s antiwar demonstrations were policed by Marshals Service agents.

David Koresh's Branch Davidian complex at Waco, Texas, burns after being attacked by agents of the FBI and ATF. *Photo: Dallas Morning News/Gamma Liaison.*

CAREERS IN JUSTICE

WORKING AS A U.S. MARSHAL

TYPICAL POSITIONS.   U.S. marshals are involved in the following activities: (1) court security, (2) fugitive investigations, (3) personal and witness security, (4) asset seizure, (5) special operations, and (6) transportation and custody of federal prisoners.

EMPLOYMENT REQUIREMENTS.   General employment requirements with the Marshals Service include (1) a comprehensive written exam, (2) a complete background investigation, (3) an oral interview, (4) excellent physical condition, and (5) a Bachelor's degree or three years of "responsible experience." Applicants must be between 21 and 35 years of age and be U.S. citizens with a valid driver's license.

OTHER REQUIREMENTS.   Successful applicants must complete 13 weeks of training.

SALARY.   At midyear 1993, starting salary was $22,600 per year (for individuals hired at GS-5 level position), $25,700 per year (for individuals hired at GS-7 level).

BENEFITS.   Benefits include (1) 13 days of sick leave annually, (2) 2-1/2 to 5 weeks of annual paid vacation and 10 paid federal holidays each year, (3) federal health and life insurance, and (4) a comprehensive retirement program.

DIRECT INQUIRIES TO: U.S. Marshals Service, 600 Army-Navy Drive, Arlington, Virginia 22202. Phone: (202) 307-9400.

The U.S. Marshals Service received agency status in 1969. Up until that time marshals had considerable independence in their functioning, but came under close centralized administrative supervision with the change in status. While U.S. marshals are still appointed by the president, deputy marshals are now hired through the Marshals Service and are federal employees, with all the privileges and job security characteristic of such positions.

The Marshals Service Today   Today the USMS is an enforcement arm of the office of the attorney general of the United States and is headquartered in McLean, Virginia. Ninety-four U.S. marshals direct the activities of over 2,400 deputy marshals throughout the United States and its territories. More than 1,000 other ("nonsworn") employees provide support for the activities of the Marshals Service. The USMS budget is substantial, with more than $333 million allocated for basic enforcement operations, and another $219 million earmarked in support of prisoner-related duties during fiscal year 1993.[31]

Typical tasks performed by the Marshals Service today include prisoner transportation and custody, the pursuit and arrest of fugitives, security in federal courts, personal protection for judges, and the guarding of federal witnesses. The Marshals Service Court Security Program provides protection at nearly 500 federal courtrooms and is responsible for the personal security of 960 federal judges and more than 200 full-time and 300 part-time U.S. magistrates.

The Marshals Service executes arrest warrants issued by federal courts and—through the use of numerous confiscated aircraft and other vehicles[32]—transports over 180,000 federal prisoners a year, some of whom, like John Hinckley, have high public profiles. The USMS receives approximately 76,500 federal warrants each year, of which about half are for fugitive felons. Unsentenced federal prisoners are supervised by the Marshals Service throughout the country. For that purpose the Service rents 3,200 detention "spaces" in jails and other prison facilities nationwide and shepherds nearly 300,000 individuals each year who must make appearances in federal courts. The service also provides prisoner transportation for other federal agencies, including the U.S. Bureau of Prisons and the Immigration and Naturalization Service. Marshals Service investigations extend to the international extradition of fugitives wanted for prosecution in the United States, and the Service works with foreign governments through its Fugitive Investigative Strike Team (FIST).

The Marshals Service is responsible for the handling, inventorying, and safekeeping of all assets seized under federal law for all Department of Justice agencies. In addition to cars, cash, jewelry, and other "routine" items, the Marshals Service has taken possession of banks, resorts, ranches, condominiums, golf courses, restaurants, and many businesses. In 1987 the Service became responsible for the safekeeping of the "Pearl of Allah," a 14-pound pearl with a 2,000-year history, worth over $42 million, which was seized under order of the federal district of Colorado.[33] On a typical day the Service manages seized property worth about $500 million. The effective operation, and possible resale, of businesses and properties requires expertise in operational areas outside of the traditional role of most law enforcement agencies.

The Witness Security Division of the Marshals Service provides physical protection for federal witnesses in cases of organized crime, major criminal activity, or where significant threats to witness safety are thought to exist. The Federal Witness Relocation Program, run by the Marshals Service since 1971, has afforded protection to over 6,000 primary witnesses, and more than 13,000 family members of witnesses since its inception.[34]

Changes Coming in Federal Agencies?

In addition to the 19 federal agencies whose primary duty is law enforcement, 121 other federal agencies have secondary law enforcement or quasi-enforcement responsibilities. All told, these 140 agencies are charged with enforcing 4,100 federal criminal laws. Recently, in what had been billed as an effort to achieve economies of scale, the Clinton Administration proposed merging the DEA, the ATF, and the FBI into one federal agency. Impetus for the proposal came from the National Performance Review, also known as the "task force for reinventing government" which was headed by Vice President Gore. The task force concluded that consolidating agencies would end duplication and fragmentation of law enforcement efforts as well as save $187 million over a five-year period.

Other recommendations included in the report of relevance to criminal justice were proposals to

- Enhance drug interdiction efforts.
- Improve law enforcement computer security.
- Reduce duplication in drug law enforcement intelligence systems.
- Develop low-cost alternatives for housing federal prisoners.

Months after recommendations for merger were made, however, Attorney General Janet Reno, whose office oversees Justice Department law enforcement agencies, gave FBI

TABLE 5-3

AMERICAN POLICING: STATE-LEVEL AGENCIES

Highway patrol	State police	State bureaus of investigation
Fish and wildlife agencies	State park services	Weigh station operations
Alcohol law enforcement agencies	State university police	Port authorities

Director Louis Freeh authority to resolve operational disputes between agencies. Mr. Freeh was also charged with ending duplication of efforts among and between agencies. Reno's action ended, at least for the time being, any possibility that FBI, DEA, ATF, and other federal agencies might merge. It can be anticipated, however, that continuing federal budget deficits will make similar moves in the future all the more likely.

STATE-LEVEL AGENCIES

A variety of policing agencies exist at state level. Table 5–3 provides a typical listing of these agencies.

State law enforcement agencies are usually organized after one of two models. The first, a centralized model, is well represented by agencies such as the Pennsylvania State Police, which combines the tasks of major criminal investigations with the patrol of state highways. Centralized state police agencies generally do the following:

- Assist local law enforcement departments in criminal investigations when requested to do so.
- Operate identification bureaus.
- Maintain a centralized records repository.
- Patrol the state's highways.
- Provide select training for municipal and county officers.

The Pennsylvania State Police was the first modern force to combine these duties and has served as a model to many states emulating the centralized model. Michigan, New Jersey, New York, Vermont, and Delaware are a few of the states which patterned their state-level enforcement activities after the Pennsylvania model.

The second state model is the decentralized model of police organization. The decentralized model tends to characterize operations in the southern United States, but is found as well in the Midwest and some western states. The model draws a clear distinction between traffic enforcement on state highways and other state-level law enforcement functions by creating at least two separate agencies. North Carolina, which is used here as an example of such a model, is one of the many states which employ both a highway patrol and a state bureau of investigation.

States which use the decentralized model usually have a number of other adjunct state-level law enforcement agencies. North Carolina, for example, has created a State Wildlife Commission with enforcement powers, a board of Alcohol Beverage Control with additional agents, and a separate Enforcement and Theft Bureau for enforcement of motor vehicle and theft laws.

North Carolina: An Example of the Decentralized Model

The Highway Patrol   The North Carolina Highway Patrol began operations on July 1, 1929. Authorized by an act of the state General Assembly, the Patrol was charged with enforcing the state's motor vehicle laws and with assisting the motoring public.[35]

Training of Patrol officers was initiated in May 1929, with the return of 10 men from the Pennsylvania State Training School. Of 400 original applicants, the Patrol accepted 67, but only 42 men successfully completed the initial training. In 1935 the North Carolina Highway Patrol was placed under the administrative auspices of the Department of Revenue and 80 new officers were hired. Silver roadsters, equipped with bulletproof windshields, became the agency's trademark. Running battles with bootleggers and gangsters soon ensued. A statewide radio communications system became operational in 1937, and by 1946 the Patrol Training School was established within the Institute of Government on the campus of the University of North Carolina at Chapel Hill. By legislative action the Patrol became a division of the Department of Crime Control and Public Safety in 1977.

The duties of the North Carolina Highway Patrol have not changed substantially since it was created. Headed by a colonel, it is administratively divided into six divisions—most under the direction of a major.

The Operations Division is the largest and is further subdivided into two "zones," each with four "troops." The tasks assigned to the Operations Division are succinctly described by Directive Number Two of the North Carolina State Highway Patrol. That directive states that the division must "Provide for an effective police traffic supervision program encompassing impartial traffic law enforcement, traffic collision investigation, traffic direction and control, and related services to highway users." These duties extend to enforcement of laws against driving while impaired, breath alcohol analysis, the maintenance of needed statistics on traffic flow, violations and accidents, and the ability to respond effectively in emergency situations.

The five other major functional divisions of the Patrol are (1) Administrative Services, (2) Training, (3) Communications and Logistics, (4) Inspection and Internal Affairs, and (5) Research and Planning. Administrative Services concerns itself with hiring, promotions, time keeping, and the preparation of budgets. The Communications and Logistics Section of the Patrol coordinates the purchase and maintenance of equipment, including vehicles, and sets standards for the equipment and devices used by the patrol—including radar, VASCAR, and radiological and breathalyzer machines. Internal Affairs develops Patrol policies and procedures, conducts investigations of charges of misconduct, and protects Patrol members against unjust accusations. The Research and Planning Section maintains a library and data base to support Patrol operations. The Planning Section analyzes existing data to ensure the most effective utilization of Patrol resources.

The State Bureau of Investigation   The North Carolina State Bureau of Investigation (SBI) is an agency of the North Carolina Department of Justice. The SBI was created by legislative action in 1937 for the purpose of providing law enforcement agencies across the state with investigative and laboratory assistance upon request.

The SBI also has original jurisdiction in certain drug and arson offenses, the misuse of state funds and equipment, election fraud, and mob violence within the state of North Carolina. Investigations of local government officials who misuse public funds can be conducted by the SBI at the request of a regional official, such as a district attorney. Protection for visiting dignitaries is another new area of responsibility for the SBI, as is the protection of public officials who request it.

TABLE 5 - 4

AMERICAN POLICING: LOCAL LEVEL AGENCIES

Municipal police departments	Housing authority agents	Marine patrol agencies
Campus police	City/county agencies	Sheriff's departments
		Transit police

The SBI today is charged with maintaining crime statistics for the state, and with the operation of a crime laboratory for the identification of offenders. Mobile crime laboratories, operated by the SBI, assist local agencies in the investigation of many offenses. An air operations wing provides the capability for airborne tracking of drug smugglers and the spotting of illegal crops.

LOCAL AGENCIES

The term "local police" encompasses agencies of wide variety. Municipal departments, rural sheriff's departments, and specialized groups such as campus police and transit police can all be grouped under the "local" rubric. A listing of conventional police agencies normally found at the local level is shown in Table 5–4.

Large municipal departments are highly visible because of their huge size, vast budgetary allotments, and innovative programs. Far greater in number, however, are local small-town and county sheriff's departments. Every incorporated municipality in the country has the authority to create its own police force. Some very small communities hire only one officer, who fills all the roles of chief, investigator, and night watch—as well as everything in between. A few communities have decided to contract with private security firms for police services, and a handful have no active police force at all, depending instead upon local sheriff's departments to deal with law violators.

City police chiefs are typically appointed by the mayor or selected by the city council. Their department's jurisdiction is limited by convention to the geographical boundaries of their communities. Sheriffs, on the other hand, are elected public officials whose agencies are responsible for law enforcement throughout the counties in which they function. Sheriff's deputies mostly patrol the "unincorporated" areas of the county, or those which lie between municipalities. They do, however, have jurisdiction throughout the county, and in some areas routinely work alongside municipal police to enforce laws within towns and cities.

Sheriff's departments are generally responsible for serving court papers, including civil summonses, and for maintaining security within state courtrooms. Sheriffs also run county jails and are responsible for more detainees awaiting trial than any other type of law enforcement department in the country. For example, the Los Angeles (L.A.) County Jail System, operated by the L.A. County Sheriff's Department, is the largest in the world.[36] In 1990, with eight separate facilities, it had an average daily population of 20,779 inmates—considerably larger than the number of inmates held in many state prison systems. Over 2,500 people work in the Custody Division of the L.A. County Sheriff's Department, and that division alone operates with a yearly budget in excess of $180 million.

Numbering approximately 3,100 nationwide, sheriffs' departments remain strong across most of the country, although in parts of New England, deputies mostly function as court agents with limited law enforcement duties. A 1992 report found that most sheriffs'

Sheriff The elected chief officer of a county law enforcement agency, usually responsible for law enforcement in unincorporated areas and for the operation of the county jail.

departments are small—with nearly two-thirds of them employing fewer than 25 sworn officers.[37] Only 12 departments were found to employ more than 1,000 officers. Even so, southern and western sheriffs are still considered the "chief law enforcement officers" in their counties.

The New York City Police Department

The New York City Police Department serves as a good example of a modern, progressive large-city police agency. New York has been described as a "World City,"[38] signifying that it is a gathering place for people of all races and nationalities from around the globe. The New York City metropolitan area is home to more than 18 million people.[39] Twenty-five percent of New York City residents were born outside the United States. In contrast to the "melting pot" image which the city earned in the early part of the twentieth century, ethnic neighborhoods are the rule today throughout the boroughs which comprise New York. Preferences in food, style of dress, customs, habits, and even language vary from block to block and street to street.

The New York City Police Department (NYPD) was formed in the mid-1800s and was modeled after the London Metropolitan Police. In 1845 the force had approximately 800 sworn officers policing about a half-million city inhabitants. The Department faced its first large-scale social disorder in July 1863, with the beginning of the "Draft Riots" fueled by the Civil War. On January 1, 1898, the City of Greater New York came into being with the merger of 24 towns and villages. What had been separate municipal agencies merged into a force of 7,457 officers called the Police Department of Greater New York.[40]

By 1975 the NYPD fielded a uniformed force of 30,600 sworn officers—the largest municipal police department in the world. Financial problems forced the city of New York to reduce personnel levels in many departments over the next seven years through a phased program of financial retrenchment. In January 1982, a "low" point of 21,809 uniformed officers was reached. Since then the number of sworn NYPD officers has grown and is again approaching preretrenchment levels. At the beginning of 1994 the number of sworn officers in all ranks stood at 29,474.[41]

Nearly 7,000 civilian employees work for the NYPD. They perform administrative and support tasks in the areas of records, crime analysis, computer operations, communications, auto mechanics, law, personnel, crime laboratory, jail operations, and custodial services. Increased effectiveness in the use of civilian employees in recent years has allowed the NYPD to field more officers on an average day than at any time in its history, and to answer more calls for assistance than ever before. In 1992 the volume of calls responded to by 911 operators exceeded 8.5 million.[42] Figure 5–1 provides a look at the organizational structure of the NYPD today.

NYPD Innovations   The NYPD has been a leader in innovative programs. The establishment a few years ago of the Bias Incident Investigating Unit to enforce laws among those who discriminate on the basis of race, ethnicity, religion, and sexual preference against city residents and workers was the first such action by a metropolitan police department. A few years later, the NYPD New Immigrants Unit was organized to provide helpful information to immigrants in their native language. The unit's activities were designed to dispel negative images of the police, which immigrants and their children were often found to have carried with them from their homelands. Within a few years of its inception, the New Immigrants Unit was providing information to nearly 100,000 new arrivals each year.

ORGANIZATION CHART
NEW YORK CITY
POLICE DEPARTMENT

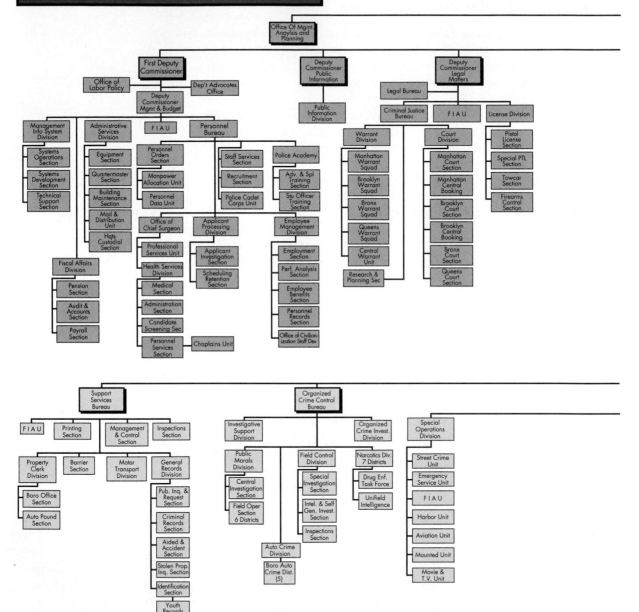

New York City Police Department
Communications Division
Cartography & Drafting Unit
for Office of Management Analysis
and Planning

FIGURE 5–1   NYPD Organizational Chart. *Courtesy of the New York City Police Department.*

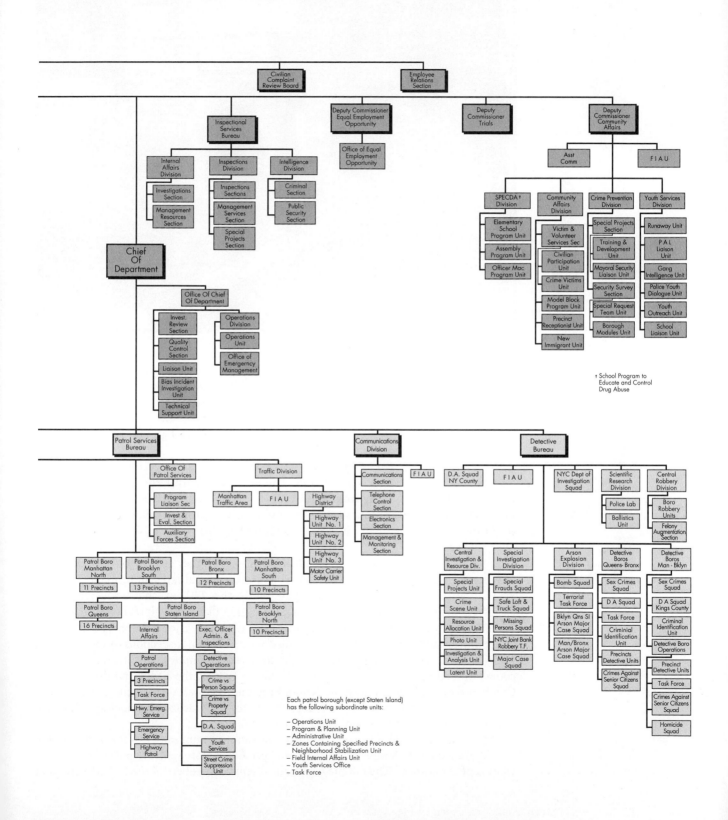

Civilian Complaint Review Board

Employee Relations Section

Deputy Commissioner Equal Employment Opportunity

Deputy Commissioner Trials

Deputy Commissioner Community Affairs

Inspectional Services Bureau

Internal Affairs Division
- Investigations Section
- Management Resources Section

Inspections Division
- Inspections Sections
- Management Services Section
- Special Projects Section

Intelligence Division
- Criminal Section
- Public Security Section

Office of Equal Employment Opportunity

Asst Comm

F I A U

SPECDA† Division
- Elementary School Program Unit
- Assembly Program Unit
- Officer Mac Program Unit

Community Affairs Division
- Victim & Volunteer Services Sec
- Civilian Participation Unit
- Crime Victims Unit
- Model Block Program Unit
- Precinct Receptionist Unit
- New Immigrant Unit

Crime Prevention Division
- Special Projects Section
- Training & Development Unit
- Mayoral Security Liaison Unit
- Security Survey Section
- Special Request Team Unit
- Borough Modules Unit

Youth Services Division
- Runaway Unit
- P A L Liaison Unit
- Gang Intelligence Unit
- Police Youth Dialogue Unit
- Youth Outreach Unit
- School Liaison Section

Chief Of Department

Office Of Chief Of Department
- Invest. Review Section
- Quality Control Section
- Liaison Unit
- Bias Incident Investigation Unit
- Technical Support Unit

Operations Division
- Operations Unit
- Office of Emergency Management

† School Program to Educate and Control Drug Abuse

Patrol Services Bureau

Communications Division
- Communications Section
- Telephone Control Section
- Electronics Section
- Management & Monitoring Section

F I A U

Detective Bureau

Office Of Patrol Services
- Program Liaison Sec
- Invest & Eval. Section
- Auxiliary Forces Section

Traffic Division

Manhattan Traffic Area

F I A U

Highway District
- Highway Unit No. 1
- Highway Unit No. 2
- Highway Unit No. 3
- Motor Carrier Safety Unit

D.A. Squad NY County

F I A U

NYC Dept of Investigation Squad

Scientific Research Division
- Police Lab
- Ballistics Unit

Central Robbery Division
- Boro Robbery Units
- Felony Augmentation Section

Patrol Boro Manhattan North — 11 Precincts

Patrol Boro Brooklyn South — 13 Precincts

Patrol Boro Bronx — 12 Precincts

Patrol Boro Manhattan South — 10 Precincts

Patrol Boro Queens — 16 Precincts

Patrol Boro Staten Island

Patrol Boro Brooklyn North — 10 Precincts

Internal Affairs

Exec. Officer Admin. & Inspections

Patrol Operations
- 3 Precincts
- Task Force
- Hwy. Emerg. Service
- Emergency Service
- Highway Patrol

Detective Operations
- Crime vs Person Squad
- Crime vs Property Squad
- D.A. Squad
- Youth Services
- Street Crime Suppression Unit

Central Investigation & Resource Div.
- Special Projects Unit
- Crime Scene Unit
- Resource Allocation Unit
- Photo Unit
- Investigation & Analysis Unit
- Latent Unit

Special Investigation Division
- Special Frauds Squad
- Safe Loft & Truck Squad
- Missing Persons Squad
- NYC Joint Bank Robbery T.F.
- Major Case Squad

Arson Explosion Division
- Bomb Squad
- Terrorist Task Force
- Bklyn Qns SI Arson Major Case Squad
- Man/Bronx Arson Major Case Squad

Detective Boros Queens- Bronx
- Sex Crimes Squad
- D A Squad
- Task Force
- Criminial Identification Unit
- Precincts Detective Units
- Crimes Against Senior Citizens Squad

Detective Boros Man - Bklyn
- Sex Crimes Squad
- D A Squad Kings County
- Criminal Identification Unit
- Detective Boro Operations
- Precinct Detective Units
- Task Force
- Crimes Against Senior Citizens Squad
- Homicide Squad

Each patrol borough (except Staten Island) has the following subordinate units:

– Operations Unit
– Program & Planning Unit
– Administrative Unit
– Zones Containing Specified Precincts & Neighborhood Stabilization Unit
– Field Internal Affairs Unit
– Youth Services Office
– Task Force

City police enforce municipal regulations as well as state laws. Here members of the New York City Police Department escort recent arrestees to jail. *Courtesy of the New York City Police Department.*

In May 1986, 101 handpicked narcotics investigators from the Department's Narcotics Division were assigned to the Special Anti-Crack Unit (SACU). By August the unit was expanded to include 223 officers. In just seven months, the SACU arrested 5,026 drug suspects and seized 28,420 vials of crack and 4,009 packets of cocaine. More than 3,000 bags of marijuana were also confiscated by the unit, along with 3,279 glassine packets of heroin, 278 vehicles, and over $300,000 in cash.[43]

A "crack hotline" (212-374-KRAK) was begun in the same year as the SACU and answered nearly 10,000 calls per month. The joint New York Drug Enforcement Task Force, composed of officers from the NYPD, the New York State Police, and the Drug Enforcement Administration, works with SACU investigators in following up tips from the hotline. The department's Narcotics Division has also grown in size, and now totals over 1,000 officers.[44]

Task forces differ from "units" and "divisions" in that they are assembled from existing organizational components in order to address a special law enforcement problem. NYPD officers, for example, participate with the FBI in the Joint Organized Crime/Narcotics Task Force, which is designed to interdict drug shipments controlled by organized crime. In a similar program, Operation Glass Eye, a joint action by NYPD narcotics officers and U.S. Coast Guard investigators, resulted in inspections of vessels entering New York harbor in a combined effort to deter the importation of drugs. Another cooperative effort to fight drug abuse was begun in 1986 by the NYPD and the New York City Board of Education. Called the School Program to Educate and Control Drug Abuse (SPECDA), the program strives to reduce the use of illicit drugs by school-age children, and to prevent sales of drugs on school property.

In other areas the NYPD has continued innovations begun earlier. A few years ago the NYPD opened a rape hotline (267-RAPE) to "provide a more sensitive police response to victims of sex crimes." The hotline uses trained female members of the Department, and

JUSTICE IN AMERICAN CONTEXT...
The Los Angeles Police Department
After Rodney King.

With 3,485,398 people, and covering 465 square miles, Los Angeles, California, is the nation's second largest city. Its police force numbers 8,295 sworn officers and 2,670 civilian employees. A total of 8,863,164 people live in the metropolitan area surrounding the city. The Los Angeles Police Department (LAPD) has more employees per resident (24 employees per every 10,000 citizens) than any other city or county department[1] in California except Beverly Hills (39 per 10,000) and San Francisco (25 per 10,000).

In 1993, following the highly publicized state and federal trials of officers charged in the beating of Black motorist Rodney King, the LAPD announced sweeping plans for reform. Newly appointed Chief Willie Williams announced that the department would fully implement principles of community policing in a massive and ongoing reorganization. In the words of Chief Williams, planning now being done will "begin the process of transforming the LAPD from a department which reacts to crime, disorder and neighborhood social problems, to a department which proactively seeks opportunities for community collaboration toward solving neighborhood problems." The department is spending $228,000 of its own money on planning and has received an additional $379,000 in grants from the National Institute of Justice to assist in the planning process.

The reform plan will focus on three basic issues: (1) the creation of police–community councils throughout the city to help set goals and priorities as a basis for law enforcement activities in culturally diverse sections of Los Angeles, (2) the initialization of a department-wide strategic planning process, and (3) a redesign of patrol activities to restore an effective bond between police officers and citizens.

Chief Williams, stressing the new emphasis on community policing, said "[p]olicing is an activity that occurs in the streets, and the quality of any department's police service is directly proportional to the quality of its street-level police service." Williams indicated that additional training, especially in the areas of problem-solving skills, will be needed to make LAPD officers effective providers of law enforcement services.

Since Los Angeles is huge and populated by a wide diversity of ethnic groups, plans call for 18 citizen councils, disseminated throughout the city, which will provide guidance to officers serving different geographic areas. Citizen councils will provide feedback to officers and issue yearly "State of the Community" reports outlining what are thought to be necessary future changes. One consultant working on design of the strategic plan said, "The only way to serve the needs of each community is to engage in a meaningful and active partnership with community representatives so that you can determine what the needs of that particular community are. Otherwise you have a sort of one-size-fits-all style of policing. And I think what we are recognizing is that one size doesn't fit everybody. In fact it often misses everybody because it produces a style of policing somewhere in the middle."

[1]Includes departments with 100 or more officers, only.
Sources: Brian A. Reaves, *Law Enforcement Management and Administrative Statistics, 1990: Data for Individual State and Local Agencies with More than 100 Officers* (Washington, D.C.: U.S. Department of Justice, September 1992), and "Los Angeles Police Chief Unveils Sweeping Reform Plan," *Criminal Justice Newsletter,* May 3, 1993, pp. 3–4.

focuses on providing medical attention for callers, calming the victim, and gathering information about the crime. The Under-age Drinking Task Force within the Department's Public Morals Division recently began intensive checks on possible under-age drinkers in the city's nightspots. The Task Force is using Protex Security Devices, which assist in identifying altered driver's licenses. Other operations have since targeted illegal massage parlors in Queens and gambling activities throughout the city. Successful ongoing programs include Crime Stoppers, which makes use of televised dramatizations of unsolved crimes, and the SCOFFLAW Plate Removal Program, under which automobiles with expired license plates or whose registration stickers do not match plate numbers are subject to plate removal and towing.

It is a privilege to be a police officer in a democratic society.

—*Patrick V. Murphy*
Former commissioner of the NYC Police Department

In recognition of the growing role of private security, the NYPD began a pilot program in 1986 called the "Midtown Area Police-Private Security Liaison." The program centered on midtown Manhattan and involved more than 4,500 officers from 100 private security organizations. Central to the program was the exchange of information on suspects, crime patterns, and stolen property. It is anticipated that the Liaison Program will soon be expanded to involve many other areas of the city.[45]

NYPD Training   Police training in the NYPD dates back to 1853, when a riot at the Astor Theatre resulted in crowd control classes being held for officers. During World War II the New York Police Academy helped train members of the Navy's Shore Patrol and the Army's Military Police. By 1955 the department was working with Baruch College in a cooperative venture leading toward credits in the school's Associate in Applied Science degree program for candidates who successfully completed the department's Recruit School. Other colleges became involved in training, and recognition of the quality of training at the NYPD was granted when the Board of Regents of the State University of New York accredited the Police Academy's Student Officer curriculum in 1974. Accreditation made possible the receipt of higher education credits for student officers.[46]

Under the leadership of Police Commissioner Benjamin Ward, who held office from 1984 to 1989, the Police Academy instituted additional changes. Today under a new commissioner, Dr. Lee Brown, the Academy requires all its academic instructors to hold at least a bachelor's degree from an accredited college or university. A graduate program has been established at the New York Institute of Technology to allow for expanded educational opportunities for instructors, and a Police Cadet Corps (created in 1985), similar in purpose to military ROTC programs, is available to college students in the New York area who wish to enter police work following graduation. Financial incentives attach to the PCC program, including summer internships which pay nearly $4,000 per year and interest-free loans of $1,500 per academic year during the cadet's last two years in college. Cadets who work with the department for two years following graduation have their loans forgiven.

Private Protective Services Independent or proprietary commercial organizations which provide protective services to employers on a contractual basis. Private security agencies, which already employ about half again as many people as public law enforcement, are expected to experience substantial growth over the next few decades.

PRIVATE PROTECTIVE SERVICES

Private police constitute a fourth level of enforcement activity in the United States today. Private security has been defined as "those self-employed individuals and privately funded business entities and organizations providing security-related services to specific clientele for a fee, for the individual or entity that retains or employs them, or for themselves, in

CAREERS IN JUSTICE

WORKING FOR THE U.S. SECRET SERVICE

TYPICAL POSITIONS.   Special agent, Uniformed Division police officers, and special officer. Clerical and administrative positions are also available.

EMPLOYMENT REQUIREMENTS.   Requirements for appointment at GS-5 level include (1) successful completion of the Treasury Enforcement Agent examination; (2) a Bachelor's degree from an accredited college or university; (3) excellent physical condition, including at least 20/40 vision in each eye, correctable to 20/20; and (4) successful completion of a thorough background investigation. Appointment at the GS-7 level also requires (1) one additional year of specialized experience, (2) a Bachelor's degree with Superior Academic Achievement, or (3) one year of graduate study in a related field (police science, police administration, criminology, law, law enforcement, business administration, accounting, economics, finance, or other directly related fields).

Superior academic achievement is defined as meeting one or more of the following criteria: (1) a "B" average (3.0 on a 4.0 scale) for all courses completed at time of application or for all courses during the last two years of the undergraduate curriculum, (2) a "B+" average (3.5 on a 4.0 scale) for all courses in the major field of study or all courses in the major during the last two years of the undergraduate curriculum, (3) rank in the upper third of the undergraduate class or major subdivision (i.e., school of liberal arts), and (4) membership in an honorary scholastic society which meets the requirements of the Association of College Honor Societies.

Specialized experience is defined as responsible criminal investigative or comparable experience which required (1) the exercise of tact, resourcefulness and judgment in collecting, assembling and developing facts, evidence and other pertinent data through investigative techniques which include personal interviews; (2) the ability to make oral and written reports and presentations of personally conducted or personally directed investigations; and (3) the ability to analyze and evaluate evidence and arrive at sound conclusions.

OTHER REQUIREMENTS.   Valid driver's license, urinalysis test for the presence of illegal drugs prior to appointment, and the ability to qualify for top secret security clearance.

SALARY.   Special Agent: GS-5 $22,600, GS-7 $25,700; Uniformed Division Police: $29,652; Special Officer: GS-5 $22,715, as of mid-1993. A high-cost area supplement ranging from 4% to 16% is paid in specified geographic areas.

BENEFITS.   Benefits include (1) 13 days of sick leave annually, (2) 2-1/2 to 5 weeks of annual paid vacation and 10 paid federal holidays each year, (3) federal health and life insurance, and (4) a comprehensive retirement program.

DIRECT INQUIRIES TO: Chief of Staffing, U.S. Secret Service, 1800 G. Street, N.W., Room 912, Washington, D.C. 20223. Phone: (202) 435-5800. Application are not accepted earlier than nine months prior to graduation.

Source: U.S. Office of Personnel Management.

order to protect their persons, private property, or interests from various hazards."[47] Public police are employed by the government and enforce public laws. Private security personnel work for corporate employers and secure private interests.

According to the *Hallcrest Report II*,[48] a major government-sponsored analysis of the private security industry, nearly 1.5 million people are employed in private security today—more than in all local, state, and federal police agencies combined. Employment in the field of private security is anticipated to expand by around 4% per year through the end of the century (see Figure 5–2), while public police agencies are expected to grow by only 2.8% per year during the same period. By the year 2000, 1.9 million people will be working in private security if projections hold, while only 700,000 persons will be engaged in public law enforcement. Still faster growth is predicted in private security industry revenues—anticipated to increase at around 7% per year through the year 2000, a growth rate almost three times greater than that projected for the nation's GNP. Table 5–5 lists the ten largest private security agencies in business today. It also lists some of the types of services they offer.

Private agencies provide tailored policing funded by the guarded organization rather than through the expenditure of public monies. Experts estimate that private security services cost American industries an astounding $52 billion in 1990, while monies spent on public policing totaled only $30 billion.[49] Contributing to this vast expenditure is the federal government, which is itself a major employer of private security personnel, contracting for services which range from guards to highly specialized electronic snooping and countermeasures at military installations and embassies throughout the world.

FIGURE 5–2   Private security and law enforcement employment; projected growth to 2000 A.D. *Source*: William C. Cunningham, John J. Struchs, and Clifford W. Van Meter, "Private Security: Patterns and Trends," *National Institute of Justice—Research in Brief* (Washington, D.C.: U.S. Department of Justice, 1991).

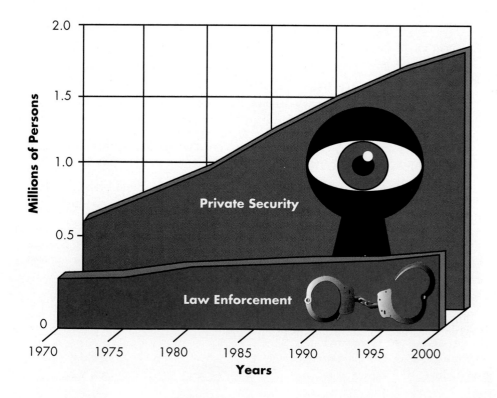

T A B L E   5 - 5

AMERICAN POLICING: PRIVATE POLICE AGENCIES

Private Security Services

Company guards	Store/mall security	ATM services
Airport security	School security	Railroad detectives
Bank guards	Nuclear facility security	Loss prevention specialists
Executive protection agencies	Hospital security	Computer/information security

The Largest Private Security Agencies in the United States[1]

Security Bureau, Inc.	Globe Security	Pinkerton's, Inc.
The Wackenhut Corp.	Wells Fargo Guard Services	Stanley Smith Security, Inc.
Allied Security, Inc.	Guardsmark, Inc.	Advance Security, Inc.
Burns International Security Services	American Protective Services	

[1]From *The Hallcrest Report II* (McLean, VA: Hallcrest Systems, 1990).

Major reasons for the quick growth of the American proprietary security sector include "(1) an increase in crimes in the workplace, (2) an increase in fear (real or perceived) of crime, (3) the fiscal crises of the states, [which] has limited public protection, and (4) an increased public and business awareness and use of…more cost-effective private security products and services."[50] In 1990, the influential yearly "Forecast Survey"[51] of private security operations identified substance abuse as the number one worry of security managers throughout American industry—the first time in the survey's 25-year history that property crime was replaced as the industry's front-running concern.

The Development of Private Policing

Private policing in America has a long and rich history. The first security firms began operation in the mid-1800s, hired mostly by the railroad companies which were laying tracks to support the burgeoning westward expansion of our nation. Company shipments of supplies, guns and money, as well as engineers and company officials, all needed protection from Indians, outlaws, and assorted desperados.

Allan Pinkerton opened his Pinkerton National Detective Agency in 1851 with the motto "We Never Sleep."[52] Pinkerton's agency specialized in railroad security and would protect shipments as well as hunt down thieves who had made a getaway. The Pinkerton service emblazoned an open eye, to signify constant vigilance, on its office doors and stationery. The term "private eye" is thought to have developed out of the use of this logo. Henry Wells and William Fargo built their still-famous Wells Fargo Company in 1852 and supplied detective and protective services to areas west of Missouri. Anyone willing to pay their fee could have a force of private guards and investigators working for them.

The early days of private security services led quickly to abuses by untrained and poorly disciplined agents. No licensing standards applied to the private security field, and security personnel sometimes became private "goons," catering only to the wishes of their employers. To cope with the situation, Pinkerton developed an elaborate code of ethics for his employees. Pinkerton's code prohibited his men and women from accepting rewards, from working for one political party against another, or from handling divorce cases (which are a primary source of revenue for private detectives today).

Another firm, the Brink's Company, began as a general package delivery service in 1859 and grew to a fleet of 85 armored wagons by 1900. The year 1859 was a busy one for private security, for in that year Edwin Holmes began the first electronic burglar alarm firm in Boston, Massachusetts. Former law enforcement administrators began to get into the private security field in 1909 when a former director of the Bureau of Investigation formed the William J. Burns International Detective Agency. In 1954 George R. Wackenhut formed the Wackenhut Security Corporation, which has become one of the largest private security firms today.

Much has changed since the early days of private policing. Security firms today provide services for hospitals, manufacturing plants, communications industries, retirement homes, hotels, casinos, exclusive communities and clubs, nuclear storage facilities and reactors, and many other types of businesses. Physical security, loss prevention, information security, and the protection of personnel are all service areas for private security organizations.

Private security agencies have been praised for their ability to adapt to new situations and technology. While most security personnel are poorly paid and perform typical "watchmen" roles, the security industry is able to contract with experts in almost any area. Specially assembled teams, hired on a subcontractual basis, have allowed some firms to move successfully into information and technology security. As financial opportunities continue to build in high-tech security, the industry is seeing the creation of a well-educated and highly specialized cadre of workers able to meet the most exacting needs of today's large and multinational corporations. The ability of private agents to work across state lines, and even international boundaries, is an added benefit of private security to many employers.

Private security personnel today outnumber public police officers by a ratio of 5 to 3. Here an early contingent of Pinkerton Guards is shown outside of the Kenilworth Park Race Track in Buffalo, New York, in 1907. *Photo: Culver Pictures.*

Security personnel sometimes work undercover, blending with company employees to learn who is pilfering inventories or selling business secrets to competitors. According to the Society of Competitor Intelligence Professionals, over 80% of the *Fortune* 1000 companies have regular in-house "snoops" on the payroll.[53] Interestingly, a corporate backlash is now occurring which has led to the hiring of even more security specialists by private industry—companies everywhere are becoming concerned with "spookproofing" their files and corporate secrets.[54]

Bodyguards, another area of private security activity, are commonplace among wealthy business executives, media stars, and successful musicians. One of the most respected executive protection programs in the world is offered by Executive Security International (ESI) in Aspen, Colorado. ESI was incorporated in 1981, and its founder, Bob Duggan, built terrorist simulation exercises into most course sequences.[55] A few years ago another firm, the Richard W. Kobetz Company, began an executive protection training program at its North Mountain Pines Training Center in Berryville, Virginia.[56] Training at Kobetz includes "offensive and escort driving techniques," threat assessment education, searches, alarms, weapons, communications, protocol, legal issues, and firearms and defensive techniques. Activities focus on "low-profile" protection utilizing limited personnel and resources, in contrast to the use of very expensive "high-profile" security as a deterrent technique which agencies like the Secret Service are able to use.[57] The Kobetz company offers "certification" as a personal protection specialist (PPS) following successful completion of its training.

The Private System of Justice

Security agencies work for paying clients, while law enforcement agencies are government entities. Differences between the role of private and public agencies were recently revealed in a National Institute of Justice–sponsored survey,[58] which showed that security executives order their managerial priorities as follows: (1) the protection of lives and property, (2) crime prevention, (3) loss prevention, (4) fire prevention, and (5) access control. In contrast, public law enforcement officials list a somewhat different set of priorities: (1) the protection of lives and property, (2) the arrest and prosecution of suspects, (3) the investigation of criminal incidents, (4) the maintenance of public order, and (5) crime prevention.

This difference in priorities, combined with the fact that hired security operatives serve the interest of corporate employers rather than the public, has led to charges that a private justice system operates next to the official government-sponsored system of criminal justice in America. The private system may see behavior, which public police agencies would interpret as a violation of the criminal law, as merely misguided employee activity. Within the private justice system conflict resolution, economic sanctions, and retraining can supplant criminal prosecution as the most efficacious system for dealing with offending parties. According to a survey[59] published by the National Institute of Justice, "security managers in all sectors…report that the most frequently investigated crime is employee theft, and nearly half of them resolve such incidents within their own organizations."

One reason why white-collar and business crimes may be substantially underreported in official crime statistics is that unofficial resolutions, based upon investigations by proprietary security forces, may be the most frequent method of handling such offenses. As some writers have observed, the public justice system may find itself increasingly bypassed by proprietary security operations who generally find in the courts "an unsympathetic attitude…concerning business losses due to crime."[60] The *Hallcrest* report points out that not only has a "fundamental shift in protection resources…occurred from public policing to the private sector," but "this shift has also been accompanied by a shift in the character of social control.[61] According to the report, "private security defines deviance in instrumental rather than moral terms:

protecting corporate interests becomes more important than fighting crime, and sanctions are applied more often against those who *create* opportunities for loss rather than those who *capitalize* on the opportunity—the traditional offenders."[62]

Hallcrest II identifies the growth of the private justice system as a major source of friction between private security and public law enforcement. According to the report, "(l)aw enforcement agencies have enjoyed a dominant position in providing protective services to their communities but now foresee an erosion of their 'turf' to private security."[63] Other sources of friction between the two include (1) "moonlighting" for private agencies by public officers, (2) the fact that "(c)ases brought by private security are usually well developed, putting the law enforcement agency in the thankless position of being an information processor for the prosecutor's office,"[64] and (3) the fact that many cases developed by private security agencies are disposed of through "plea bargaining, which police officers may not understand or support, but which may suit the purposes of a company interested in (deterrence)."[65] Moonlighting by public officers is a source of conflict because, under such circumstances, (1) police authority may be seen as used for personal gain, (2) officers who moonlight long hours may not be seen as fit for their official duties due to exhaustion, and (3) public police departments may be legally liable for the actions of their uniformed officers even though they are temporarily working for private employers.

The Professionalization of Private Security

An issue facing lawmakers across the country today is the extent of authority and the degree of force that can be legitimately used by security guards. Courts have generally held that private security personnel derive their legitimacy from the same basic authority that an employer would have in protecting his or her own property. In other words, if I have the legal right to use force to protect my home or business, then so do guards whom I have hired to act in my place. According to some courts, private security personnel, because their authority is simply an extension of private rights, are not directly bound by the legal strictures which govern the use of force, the gathering of evidence, and so on by sworn police officers.

Other courts, however, have ruled that private security personnel should be bound by the same procedural rules as sworn officers, because they are *perceived* by the public as wielding the authority of public law enforcement officers.[66] The situation is complicated by the fact that, as previously discussed, many police officers "moonlight" as private guards when they are off duty.

In order to ensure at least a minimal degree of competence among private security personnel, a number of states have moved to a licensing process for officers, although a few still require little other than an application and a small fee.[67] Twenty-three states mandate training if the security officers is to be armed, but only 14 require any training for unarmed guards.[68] Most training which does occur is relatively simplistic. Topics typically covered include (1) fire prevention, (2) first aid, (3) building safety, (4) equipment use, (5) report writing, and (6) the legal powers of private security personnel.[69] Reflecting on training and licensing requirements one specialist has warned, "We have a vast private police force largely untrained, with few restraints, with the power to use force to take liberty and life."[70]

Most private security firms today depend upon their own training programs to prevent actionable mistakes by employees. Training in private security operations is also available from a number of schools and agencies. One is the International Foundation for Protection Officers, with offices in Cochrane, Alberta (Canada), and Midvale, Utah. Following a home study course, successful students are accorded the status of certified protection officer (CPO). In an effort to increase the professional status of the private security industry, the 20,000-member American Society for Industrial Security (ASIS), established

CAREERS IN JUSTICE

WORKING IN PROPRIETARY NUCLEAR SECURITY

TYPICAL POSITIONS.   Armed guard, threat-response team member, midlevel management.

EMPLOYMENT REQUIREMENTS.   Basic requirements for armed private security personnel in the nuclear area are specified by Part 73 of the Code of Federal Regulations, which mandates (1) a high school education or equivalent, (2) an age of 21 years or older, (3) successful completion of comprehensive psychological and physical examinations, (4) corrected vision of 20/40, (5) good hearing, (6) no history of drug addiction or potentially disabling diabetes or epilepsy, and, (7) a thorough background investigation. A Bachelor's degree is preferred by companies hiring armed personnel in the nuclear security sector. Lateral-entry midlevel managers may be exempted from a number of the specified physical requirements, but are expected to have a substantially higher level of education (B.A. or M.A. degree) and/or experience in private security, law enforcement, or a related field.

OTHER REQUIREMENTS.   New officers undergo intensive training in as many as 78 subject matter areas specified by the federal Code.

SALARY: Armed guards earned $8 per hour in mid-1994, with incomes ranging to $27,000. Threat-response team (also called reactionary force teams) members earned $11.50 to $14.50 per hour, depending upon employer. Midlevel managers typically earned salaries in the $30,000 to $40,000 range, although contractual commissions paid to such personnel can push salaries to six figures.

DIRECT INQUIRIES TO: Proprietary nuclear security providers, including Burns International Security Services, 2 Campus Drive, Parsippany, New Jersey 07054. Phone: (201) 397-2000.

in 1955, administers a comprehensive examination periodically in various locations across the country. Applicants who pass the examination win the coveted title of certified protection professional (CPP). CPP examinations are thorough and usually require a combination of experience and study to earn a passing grade. Examination subject areas include[71] (1) security management, (2) physical security, (3) loss prevention, (4) investigations, (5) internal/external relations, (6) protection of sensitive information, (7) personnel security, (8) emergency planning, (9) legal aspects of security, and (10) substance abuse. In addition, candidates are allowed to select from a group of specialized topic areas (such as nuclear power security, public utility security, retail security, computer security, etc.) which pertain to the fields in which they plan to work.

ASIS also functions as a professional association, with yearly meetings held to address the latest in security techniques and equipment. ASISNET, an on-line computer bulletin board system sponsored by ASIS, provides subscribers with daily security news, up-to-date international travel briefings, and a searchable security news data base. In its efforts to heighten professionalism throughout the industry, ASIS has developed a private security code of ethics for its members which is reproduced in the "Theory Into Practice" box on page 187.

An additional sign of the increasing professionalization of private security is the ever-growing number of publications offered in the area. The *Journal of Security Administration*, published in Miami, Florida, ASIS's *Security Management* magazine, and the *Security Management* newsletter published semimonthly by the National Foremen's Institute in Waterford, Connecticut, along with the older journal *Security World*, serve the field as major sources of up-to-date information.

Integrating Public and Private Security

As the private security field grows, its relationship to public law enforcement continues to evolve. Although competition among the sectors remains, many experts now recognize that each can help the other. A government-sponsored report[72] makes the following policy recommendations designed to maximize the cooperative crime-fighting potential of existing private and public security resources:

1. The resources of proprietary and contract security should be brought to bear in cooperative, community-based crime prevention and security awareness programs.
2. An assessment should be made of (a) the basic police services the public is willing to support financially, (b) the types of police services most acceptable to police administrators and the public for transfer to the private sector, and (c) which services might be performed for a lower unit cost by the private sector with the same level of community satisfaction.

The link between public and private police agencies has a long history. Here Allan Pinkerton (seated, right), founder of the Pinkerton Detective Agency, is shown with Secret Service men at U.S. Army Headquarters on the Potomac river in 1862. *Photo: The Bettmann Archives.*

THEORY INTO PRACTICE

ETHICS IN PRIVATE SECURITY

American Society for Industrial Security Code of Ethics

I. A member shall perform professional duties in accordance with the law and the highest moral principles.
II. A member shall observe the precepts of truthfulness, honesty, and integrity.
III. A member shall be faithful and diligent in discharging professional responsibilities.
IV. A member shall be competent in discharging professional responsibilities.
V. A member shall safeguard confidential information and exercise due care to prevent its improper disclosure.
VI. A member shall not maliciously injure the professional reputation or practice of colleagues, clients, or employers.

Source: Courtesy of the American Society for Industrial Security.

3. With special-police powers, security personnel could resolve many or most minor criminal incidents prior to police involvement. State statutes providing such powers could also provide for standardized training and certification requirements, thus assuring uniformity and precluding abuses....Ideally, licensing and regulatory requirements would be the same for all states, with reciprocity for firms licensed elsewhere.
4. Law enforcement agencies should be included in the crisis-management planning of private organizations.... Similarly, private security should be consulted when law enforcement agencies are developing SWAT and hostage-negotiation teams. The federal government should provide channels of communication with private security with respect to terrorist activities and threats.
5. States should enact legislation permitting private security firms access to criminal history records, in order to improve the selection process for security personnel and also to enable businesses to assess the integrity of key employees.
6. Research should...attempt to delineate the characteristics of the private justice system; identify the crimes most frequently resolved; assess the types and amount of unreported crime in organizations; quantify the redirection of [the] public criminal justice workload...and examine [the]...relationships between private security and...components of the criminal justice system.
7. A federal tax credit for security expenditures, similar to the energy tax credit, might be a cost-effective way to reduce police workloads.

Law enforcement can ill afford to continue its traditional policy of isolating and even ignoring the activities of private security.

—*National Institute of Justice*
Crime and Protection in America

SUMMARY

Today's police departments owe a considerable historical legacy to Sir Robert Peel and the London Metropolitan Police. The "Met," begun in 1829, was the world's first "modern" police force and based its practices upon preventive patrol by uniformed officers. Patrol continues to be the hallmark of police work today, with investigative work and numerous support roles rounding out an increasingly specialized profession. Studies sponsored by the Police Foundation and the Law Enforcement Assistance Administration during the 1970s and 1980s, however, have brought many of the guiding assumptions of police work under scientific scrutiny.

American policing presents a complex picture, structured as it is along federal, state, and local lines. Police agencies function to enforce the statues of lawmaking bodies, and legislative authority is naturally reflected in the diversity of police forces which we have in our country today. All federal agencies, empowered by Congress to enforce specific statutes, have their enforcement arm, and tasks deemed especially significant by state legislatures, such as patrol of the highways, have resulted in the creation of specialized state law enforcement agencies. Private policing, represented by the recent tremendous growth of for-hire security agencies, adds another dimension to American policing.

Private security is now undergoing many of the changes which have already occurred in other law enforcement areas. Heightened training requirements, legislative regulation, court-mandated changes, and college-level educational programs in private security are all leading to increased professionalism. Municipal departments have begun concerted efforts to involve private security organizations in their crime detection and prevention efforts, and indications are that private security will soon take a legitimate place alongside other police agencies in the eyes of the public.

DISCUSSION QUESTIONS

1. What assumptions about police work did the Police Foundation and LEAA call into question with studies they supported? What other assumptions are made about police work today which might be similarly studied?

2. What are the four levels of law enforcement described in this chapter? Why do we have so many different types of enforcement agencies in the United States?

3. What do you think will be the role of private police services in the United States in the future? How can the quality of such services be insured?

ENDNOTES

1. The Police Foundation, *Annual Report 1991* (Washington, D.C.: The Foundation, 1992).

2. Jerome H. Skolnick and David H. Bayley, *The New Blue Line: Police Innovation in Six American Cities* (New York: The Free Press, 1986), p. 229.

3. For a good discussion of the development of the modern police, see Sue Titus Reid, *Criminal Justice: Procedures and Issues* (St. Paul, MN: West Publishing, 1987) pp. 110–115.

4. Camdem Pelham, *Chronicles of Crime*, Vol. 1 (London: T. Miles, 1887), p. 59.

5. Gary Sykes, "Street Justice: A Moral Defense of Order Maintenance Policing," *Justice Quarterly*, Vol. 3, no. 4 (December 1986), p. 504.

6. Law Enforcement Assistance Administration, *Two Hundred Years of American Criminal Justice: An LEAA Bicentennial Study* (Washington, D.C.: U.S. Government Printing Office, 1976), p. 15.

7. National Commission on Law Observance and Enforcement, *Wickersham Commission Reports*, 14 vols. (Washington, D.C.: U.S. Government Printing Office, 1931).

8. President's Commission on Law Enforcement and Administration of Justice, *The Challenge of Crime in a Free Society* (Washington, D.C.: U.S. Government Printing Office, 1967).

9. The National Advisory Commission on Criminal Justice Standards and Goals, *A National Strategy to Reduce Crime* (Washington, D.C.: U.S. Government Printing Office, 1973).

10. National Institute of Justice, *The Exemplary Projects Program* (Washington, D.C.: U.S. Government Printing Office, 1982), p. 11.

11. Thomas J. Deaken, "The Police Foundation: A Special Report," *FBI Law Enforcement Bulletin* (November 1986), p. 2.

12. George L. Kelling et al., *The Kansas City Patrol Experiment* (Washington, D.C.: The Police Foundation, 1974).

13. Kevin Krajick, "Does Patrol Prevent Crime?" *Police Magazine* (September 1978), quoting Dr. George Kelling.

14. William Bieck and David Kessler, *Response Time Analysis* (Kansas City, MO: Board of Police Commissioners, 1977). See, also, J. Thomas McEwen et al., *Evaluation of the Differential Police Response Field Test: Executive Summary* (Alexandria, VA: Research Management Associates, 1984), and Lawrence Sherman, "Policing Communities: What Works?" in Michael Tonry and Norval Morris, eds., *Crime and Justice: An Annual Review of Research*, Vol. 8 (Chicago: University of Chicago Press, 1986).

15. Ibid., p. 8.

16. "Does Patrol Prevent Crime?"

17. Ibid.

18. Ibid.

19. Ibid.

20. Lawrence W. Sherman and Richard A. Berk, *Minneapolis Domestic Violence Experiment*, Police Foundation Report #1 (Washington, D.C.: Police Foundation, April 1984).

21. National Institute of Justice, *Newport News Tests Problem-Oriented Policing*, National Institute of Justice Reports (Washington, D.C.: U.S. Government Printing Office, January–February 1987).

22. Adapted from Deakin, "The Police Foundation."

23. U.S. Department of Justice, *"A Proud History…a Bright Future: Careers with the FBI,"* FBI pamphlet (October 1986), p. 1.

24. Howard Abadinsky, *Crime and Justice: An Introduction* (Chicago: Nelson-Hall, 1987), p. 262.

25. Much of the information in this section comes from U.S. Department of Justice, *The FBI: The First 75 Years* (Washington, D.C.: U.S. Government Printing Office, 1986).

26. Drug Enforcement Administration recruitment pamphlets, 1988.

27. DEA memorandum, "Important Information for Special Agent Applicants" (Washington, D.C.: U.S. Department of Justice, DEA, no date).

28. Telephone conversation with DEA personnel, Offices of Intelligence and Public Information, August 30, 1993.

29. Frederick S. Calhoun, *The Lawmen: United States Marshals and Their Deputies, 1789 to the Present*, U.S. Marshals Service (no date), p. 3.

30. This section owes much to *The Lawmen*.

31. Telephone conversation with Marshals Service personnel, Public Information Office, August 30, 1993.

32. Aircraft and vehicles are typically acquired through the Asset Seizure and Forfeiture Program. Statistics on the Marshals Service from the pamphlet "Outline of the U.S. Marshals Service Activities," U.S. Marshals Service (no date).

33. U.S. Marshals Service, *The Pentacle*, January 1987.

34. Telephone conversation, August 30, 1993.

35. Arnold W. Rector, "Creation and History of the N.C. State Highway Patrol" (Raleigh, N.C.: Department of Crime Control and Public Safety, no date).

36. Timothy J. Flanagan and Kathleen Maguire, eds. *Sourcebook of Criminal Justice Statistics 1991* (Washington, D.C.: Bureau of Justice Statistics, 1992).

37. Brian A. Reaves, "Sheriffs' Departments 1990," *Bureau of Justice Statistics Bulletin* (Washington, D.C.: U.S. Department of Justice, 1992).

38. New York City Police Department, *New York City Police Department Annual Report, 1986* (New York: NYPD, 1987).

39. "Top Metro Areas," *USA Today*, September 30, 1988, p. 4B.

40. This section owes much to the New York City Police Department, *Annual Reports, 1985* and *1986*, and to Jess Maghan, former NYPD director of training (unpublished dissertation).

41. Telephone conversation with the Office of Public Information, New York City Police Department, January 10, 1994.

42. Ibid.

43. Ibid.

44. Ibid.

45. Maghan, unpublished dissertation, 1989.

46. Ibid.

47. *Private Security: Report of the Task Force on Private Security* (Washington, D.C.: U.S. Government Printing Office, 1976), p. 4.

48. William C. Cunningham, John J. Strauchs, and Clifford W. Van Meter, *The Hallcrest Report II: Private Security Trends 1970–2000* (McLean, VA: Hallcrest Systems, 1990).

49. Ibid., p. 229.

50. Ibid., p. 236.

51. "Forecast Survey: Executive Summary," *Security*, January 1990.

52. Dae H. Chang and James A. Fagin, eds., *Introduction to Criminal Justice: Theory and Application*, 2nd ed. (Geneva, IL: Paladin House, 1985), pp. 275–277.

53. "George Smiley Joins the Firm," *Newsweek*, May 2, 1988, pp. 46–47.

54. Ibid.

55. For more information on ESI, see E. Duane Davis, "Executive Protection: An Emerging Trend in Criminal Justice Education and Training," *The Justice Professional*, Vol. 3, no. 2 (Fall 1988).

56. "More than a Bodyguard," *Security Management*, February 10, 1986.

57. "A School for Guards of Rich, Powerful," *The Akron Beacon Journal* (Ohio), April 21, 1986.

58. National Institute of Justice, *Crime and Protection in America: A Study of Private Security and Law Enforcement Resources and Relationships*, Executive Summary (Washington, D.C.: U.S. Department of Justice, 1985), p. 42.

59. Ibid., p. 60.

60. Cunninghum, Strauch, and Van Meter, *Hallcrest II*, p. 299.

61. Ibid., p. 301.

62. Ibid. (italics added).

63. Ibid., p. 117.

64. National Institute of Justice, *Crime and Protection in America*, p. 12.

65. Ibid., p. 12.

66. *People* v. *Zelinski*, 594 P.2d 1000 (1979).

67. For additional information see Jospeh G. Deegan, "Mandated Training for Private Security," *FBI Law Enforcement Bulletin*, March 1987, pp. 6–8.

68. Cunninghum, Strauchs, and Van Meter, *Hallcrest II*, p. 147.

69. National Institute of Justice, *Crime and Protection in America*, p. 37.

70. Richter Moore, "Private Police: The Use of Force and State Regulation," unpublished manuscript.

71. "The Mark of Professionalism," *Security Management*, 35th Anniversary Supplement, 1990, pp. 97–104.

72. National Institute of Justice, *Crime and Protection in America*, pp. 59–72.

CHAPTER 6

POLICE

MANAGEMENT

I liken the Los Angeles police to a business. We have 3-1/2 million customers ...[1]
— **WILLIE WILLIAMS**
LOS ANGELES CHIEF OF POLICE

Pressures—from the community, from peers, from the circumstances in which police find themselves—are intense.[2]
— **JAMES Q. WILSON, FORMER CHAIRMAN OF THE BOARD**
THE POLICE FOUNDATION

The single most striking fact about the attitudes of citizens, black and white, toward the police is that in general these attitudes are positive, not negative.[3]
— **JAMES Q. WILSON**

Crime is a community problem and stands today as one of the most serious challenges of our generation. Our citizens must...recognize their responsibilities in its suppression.[4]
— **O. W. WILSON**

KEY CONCEPTS

discretion	working personality	internal affairs
police culture	police ethics	POST
Knapp Commission	Wickersham Commission	professionalism

KEY CASES

City of Canton, Ohio v. *Harris*   *Malley* v. *Briggs*   *Hunter* v. *Bryant*

CONTEMPORARY POLICING: THE ADMINISTRATIVE PERSPECTIVE

In November 1992 a Stanislaus County police SWAT team wearing ski masks, and acting on a tip that an illegal methamphetamine lab was in operation, kicked down the doors of the Oakdale, California, home of Marian and William Hauselmann.[5] Once inside they handcuffed Mrs. Hauselmann, put a pillowcase over her head, and wrestled her to the floor. Her 64-year-old husband, who suffers from a heart condition, was shouted into silence. His face was cut and officers stepped on his back after throwing him down. No illegal drugs were found. Police soon realized that they had been misled by their informant and apologized to the Hauselmanns. Then they borrowed a knife from the couple's kitchen to cut the plastic handcuffs from their wrists. The county sheriff offered to pay for the broken doors. Following the incident the Hauselmanns reported being unable to sleep.

A few months prior to the Hauselmann's ordeal, multimillionaire rancher Donald Scott was fatally shot during a drug raid gone wrong. His Malibu, California, property, the target of a police attack, yielded no drugs, and Scott appears to have been trying to protect himself from what he thought were intruders when he was shot.

Both these cases highlight the potentially disastrous consequences of police action gone astray. Effective police management may be the single most important emerging issue facing the criminal system in the twenty-first century. As Dorothy Ehrlich of northern California's ACLU says, efficient enforcement of the laws is necessary, "[b]ut terrorizing innocent people is a price no one should have to pay."[6]

STYLES OF POLICING

In a recent symposium, members of Harvard University's Kennedy School of Government divided the history of American policing into three different eras.[7] Each era was distinguished from the others by the apparent dominance of a particular administrative approach to police operations. The first period, the political era, was characterized by close ties between police and public officials. It began in the 1840s and ended around 1930. Throughout the period American police agencies tended to serve the interests of powerful politicians and their cronies, while providing community order maintenance services almost as an afterthought. The second period, the reform era, began in the 1930s and lasted until the 1970s. The reform era was characterized by pride in professional crime fighting. Police departments during this period focused most of their resources on solving "traditional" crimes such as murder, rape, and burglary and on capturing offenders. The final era—one which is just beginning—is the era of community problem solving. The problem-solving approach to police work stresses the service role of police officers and envisions a partnership between police agencies and their communities.

The influence of each historical phase identified by the Harvard team survives today in what James Q. Wilson calls policing styles.[8] Wilson's three types of policing—which he did not identify with a particular historical era—are (1) the watchman style (characteristic of the political era), (2) the legalistic style (professional crime fighting), and (3) the service style (which is becoming more commonplace today). These three styles, taken together, characterize nearly all municipal law enforcement agencies today—although some departments are a mixture of two or more styles.

The Watchman Style

Police departments marked by the watchman style of policing are primarily concerned with achieving a goal that Wilson calls "order maintenance." They see their job as one of controlling illegal and disruptive behavior. The watchman style, however, as opposed to the legalistic, makes considerable use of discretion. Order in watchman-style communities may be arrived at through informal police intervention, including persuasion and threats, or even by "roughing up" a few disruptive people from time to time. Some authors have condemned this style of policing, suggesting that it is unfairly found in lower-class, or lower-middle-class communities, especially where interpersonal relations may include a fair amount of violence or physical abuse.

The watchman style of policing appears to have been operative in Los Angeles, California, at the time of the well-known Rodney King beating (see Chapter 7 for details). Following the riots that ensued, the Independent Commission on the Los Angeles Police Department (The Christopher Commission) determined that the Los Angeles "[p]olice placed greater emphasis on crime control over crime prevention, a policy that distanced cops from the people they serve."

The Legalistic Style

Departments operating under the legalistic model are committed to enforcing the "letter of the law." Years ago, for example, when the speed limit on I-95 running north and south through North Carolina was 55 MPH, a state highway patrol official was quoted by newspapers as saying that troopers would issue tickets at 56 MPH. The law was the law, he said, and it would be enforced.

Conversely, legalistically oriented departments can be expected routinely to avoid involvement in community disputes arising from normative violations which do not break the law. Gary Sykes calls this enforcement style "laissez-faire policing," in recognition of its "hands-off" approach to behaviors which are simply bothersome or inconsiderate of community principles.

The Service Style

Departments which stress the goal of service reflect the felt needs of the community. In service-oriented departments, the police see themselves more as helpers than as embattled participants in a war against crime. Such departments work hand in hand with social service and other agencies to provide counseling for minor offenders and to assist community groups in preventing crimes and solving problems. Prosecutors may support the service

Watchman Style A style of policing which is marked by a concern for order maintenance. This style of policing is characteristic of lower-class communities where informal police intervention into the lives of residents is employed in the service of keeping the peace.

Legalistic Style A style of policing which is marked by a strict concern with enforcing the precise letter of the law. Legalistic departments, however, may take a "hands-off" approach to otherwise disruptive or problematic forms of behavior which are not violations of the criminal law.

Service Style A style of policing which is marked by a concern with helping rather than strict enforcement. Service-oriented agencies are more likely to take advantage of community resources, such as drug treatment programs, than are other types of departments.

style of policing by agreeing not to prosecute law violators who seek psychiatric help, or who voluntarily participate in programs like Alcoholics Anonymous, family counseling, drug treatment, and the like. The service style of policing is commonly found in wealthy neighborhoods, where the police are well paid and well educated. The service style is supported in part by citizen attitudes which seek to avoid the personal embarrassment which might result from a public airing of personal problems. Such attitudes reduce the number of criminal complaints filed, especially in the case of minor disputes.

Changing Styles

Historically, American police work has involved a fair amount of order maintenance activity. The United States a few decades ago consisted of a large number of immigrant communities, socially separated from one another by custom and language. Immigrant workers were often poorly educated, and some were prone toward displays of "manhood," which challenged police authority in the cities. Reports of police in "pitched battles" with bar-hopping laborers out for Saturday night "good times" were not uncommon. Arrests were infrequent but "street justice" was often imposed through the use of the "billy stick" and blackjack. In these historical settings, the watchman style of policing must have seemed especially appropriate to both the police and many members of the citizenry.

As times have changed, so too have American communities. Even today, however, it is probably fair to say that the style of policing which characterizes a community tends to flow, at least to some degree, from the life-styles of those who live there. Rough-and-tumble life-styles encourage an oppressive form of policing; refined styles produce a service emphasis with stress on working together.

JUSTICE IN AMERICAN CONTEXT...
The National Center for the Study of Police and Civil Disorder

In 1993, following the riots that swept Los Angeles and other American cities in the wake of the California acquittal of officers charged in the beating of black motorist Rodney King, The Police Foundation established the National Center for the Study of Police and Civil Disorder.

Hubert Williams, director of the Foundation, observed that police departments generally "possess little information on the underlying causes of civil unrest and lack standing policies and procedures detailing appropriate responses to incidents with the potential to escalate into disorder and destruction." "Moreover," said Williams, "the paramilitary crime-fighting style of many departments is based not on mutual trust and respect of police and community, but on an inbred suspicion and hostility that have served as tinder for civil disturbance." Finally, he said, "the police lack the capacity to resolve the deep-seated societal problems that form the basis for the anger and disenfranchisement felt by many in our inner cities."

Recognizing that the police cannot directly effect the fundamental social changes needed to "defuse much of this anger," Williams suggested that the police can:

- "[C]ontribute to the community's sense of well being through the use of police strategies designed to build cooperative, mutually beneficial relationships between police and citizens;
- "[M]onitor indicators of community tension and take action to relieve it before it reaches explosive levels;

- "[R]espond to potentially troublesome situations in ways that defuse rather than inflame citizen hostility; and
- "[F]ace the challenge of full-scale disorder with a timely, appropriate, and effective level of force."

The National Center for the Study of Police and Civil Disorders, funded by a grant from the Ford Foundation, will develop new information on civil disorders for use by practitioners, planners, researchers, and policymakers; provide fellowships for practitioners and scholars; maintain a national information clearinghouse; convene conferences and workshops on changing aspects of the police role in contemporary society; and publish materials contributing to the body of knowledge on civil disorders. The Center will also assist police departments across the nation in developing Emergency Response Teams designed to be first-on-the-scene officers trained in diffusing potentially dangerous situations.

Source: The Police Foundation, *Annual Report 1992* (Washington, D.C.: The Foundation, 1992).

POLICE-COMMUNITY RELATIONS

Police–Community Relations (PCR) An area of emerging police activity which stresses the need for the community and the police to work together effectively and emphasizes the notion that the police derive their legitimacy from the community they serve. PCR began to be of concern to many police agencies in the 1960s and 1970s.

In the 1960s, the legalistic style of policing, so common in America until then, began to yield to the newer service-oriented style of policing. The decade of the 1960s was one of unrest, fraught with riots and student activism. The war in Vietnam, civil rights concerns, and other burgeoning social movements produced large demonstrations and marches. The police, who were generally inexperienced in crowd control, all too often found themselves embroiled in tumultuous encounters with citizen groups. The police came to be seen by many as agents of "the establishment," and pitched battles between the police and the citizenry sometimes occurred.

As social disorganization increased, police departments across the nation sought ways to understand and deal better with the problems they faced. Significant outgrowths of this effort were the police–community relations (PCR) programs, which many departments created. Some authors have traced the development of the police–community relations concept to an annual conference begun in 1955.[9] Entitled, the "National Institute of Police and Community Relations," the meetings were sponsored jointly by the National Conference of Christians and Jews and the Michigan State University Department of Police Administration and Public Safety. PCR represented a movement away from an exclusive police emphasis on the apprehension of law violators and meant increasing the level of positive police–citizen interaction. At the height of the PCR movement city police departments across the country opened storefront centers where citizens could air complaints and easily interact with police representatives. As Egon Bittner recognized,[10] for PCR programs to be truly effective, they need to reach to "the grassroots of discontent," where citizen dissatisfaction with the police exists.

> I think I know what's wrong with the police—We're the only ticket in town. If you call the police, you get us!
>
> —*Superintendent Christopher R. Braiden*
> *Edmonton Police Service*
> *Alberta, Canada*

The maintenance of social order is a police function closely akin to strict law enforcement. Here Austin, Texas, police officers remove protesters at an anti-abortion sit-in. *Photo: Bob Daemmrich /Stock Boston.*

Many contemporary PCR programs involve public relations officers, appointed to provide an array of services to the community. "Neighborhood Watch" programs, drug awareness workshops, "Project ID"—which uses police equipment and expertise to mark valuables for identification in the event of theft—and police-sponsored victim's assistance programs are all examples of services embodying the spirit of PCR. Modern PCR programs, however, often fail to achieve their goal of increased community satisfaction with police services because they focus on providing services to groups who already are well satisfied with the police. PCR programs which reach disaffected community groups are difficult to manage and may even alienate participating officers. Thus, as Bittner says, "while the first approach fails because it leaves out those groups to which the program is primarily directed, the second fails because it leaves out the police department."[11]

Team Policing

During the 1960s and 1970s a number of communities began to experiment with the concept of team policing. An idea thought to have originated in Aberdeen, Scotland,[12] team policing rapidly became an extension of the PCR movement. Some authors have called team policing a "technique to deliver total police services to a neighborhood."[13] Others, however, have dismissed it as "little more than an attempt to return to the style of policing that was prevalent in the United States over a century ago."[14] Team policing assigned officers on a semipermanent basis to particular neighborhoods, where it was expected they would become familiar with the inhabitants and with their problems and concerns. Patrol officers were given considerable authority in processing complaints from receipt through to resolution. Crimes were investigated and solved at the local level, with specialists called in only if the needed resources to continue an investigation were not locally available.

THEORY INTO PRACTICE

COMMUNITY POLICING IN RENO, NEVADA

Reno, Nevada, is a city of 120,000 with a police department of 313 sworn officers. The department also serves the needs of as many as 60,000 visitors who frequent the city's gambling districts weekly. Community policing began in Reno following a 1987 survey of public opinion that revealed that the police department suffered from a serious image problem. Public opinion described policing in Reno as "uncaring and heavy handed." At the time of the survey, the Reno police department was run via a "management by objectives" (MBO) administrative philosophy that equated high arrest rates with successful policing. The first community policing efforts began under then-Chief R. V. Bradshaw, following the defeat of two public referendums to increase funding levels for the department.

In 1992 Richard Kirkland was appointed Reno's chief of police and immediately initiated a new program called "Community Oriented Policing and Problem Solving" (COPPS). COPPS was implemented as a department-wide philosophy under the motto "Your police, our community." A new 40-hour training program was required of every police employee, and administrative decentralization brought about a major change in the department's organizational structure. Neighborhood advisory groups (NAGs) were developed and a Quality Assurance Bureau was created to conduct both internal and external surveys with an eye toward improving police–community relations. NAGs encouraged the sharing of ideas between police officials and community groups. Patrol officers were encouraged to identify community groups that could host NAG meetings, and NAG sessions began in earnest.

As a result of NAG meetings and community surveys the Reno Police Department initiated a number of new police efforts. Among them were (1) an eviction program in the North/Stead area to remove drug traffickers from HUD-sponsored apartments; (2) an effort to take back control of Pat Baker Park from an army of drug dealers and users who had been using the park as a storefront for illicit transactions; (3) the use of a number of out-of-state undercover officers to eliminate "crack houses" in the Trainer Way portion of the city; (4) department-initiated towing of abandoned vehicles from Stead, an abandoned Air Force Base within the city limits; (5) establishment of a foodbeat program in the Patton Drive area, where drive-by shootings and gang-related activities had been identified as problems; (6) development of the Comprehensive Mental Health Assessment Program (COMPAS) to deal effectively with the city's mentally ill and homeless populations; (7) changes in traffic enforcement procedures to use a greater number of warning tickets, and the department's acquisition of a radar trailer displaying the speed of oncoming vehicles; (8) initiation of foot, bicycle, and dirtbike patrols in downtown areas to meet the needs of Reno's many visitors; and (9) the establishment of a new communications network to better link downtown casino security operations to the police department.

Following these and other well-publicized efforts to improve the department's image, community surveys reported a considerable degree of success. While the initial 1987 survey found only 31.6% of residents feeling good about the police department, a similar 1992 survey revealed 68.7% of the populace reporting such feelings. Similarly, the percentage of respondents reporting that officers "did not convey a feeling of concern" was cut by two-thirds between surveys. Eventually, renewed citizen satisfaction with the Reno Police Department resulted in the success of a local tax referendum that provided the department with 88 additional officers—a 39 percent increase in sworn personnel.

Sources: Richard Kirkland, *Community Oriented Police and Problem Solving: COPPS* (Reno, NV: Reno Police Department, 1992); Jim Weston, "Community Oriented Policing: An Approach to Traffic Management," *Law and Order*, May 1991; Robert V. Bradshaw, Ken Peak, and Ronald W. Glensor, "Community Policing Enhances Reno's Image," *The Police Chief*, October 1990; David M. Kennedy, "The Strategic Management of Police Resources," *Perspectives on Policing* (Washington, D.C.: National Institute of Justice, January 1993); and Ronald W. Glensor and Ken Peak, "Improving Perceptions of the Police with Community Policing: The Reno Experience," paper presented at the annual meeting of the Academy of Criminal Justice Sciences, March 1993.

Community Policing
An extension of the police-community relations concept which envisions an effective working partnership between the police and members of the community in order to solve problems which concern both.

Community Policing

In recent years the police–community relations concept has undergone a substantial shift in emphasis. The old PCR model was built around the unfortunate self-image held by many police administrators of themselves as enforcers of the law who were isolated from, and often in opposition to, the communities they policed. Under such jaded administrators, PCR easily became a shallowly disguised and insecure effort to overcome public suspicion and community hostility.

In contrast, an increasing number of law enforcement administrators today are embracing the role of service provider. Modern police departments are frequently called upon to help citizens resolve a vast array of personal problems—many of which involve no direct law enforcement activity. Such requests may involve help for a sick child or the need to calm a distraught person, open a car with the keys locked inside, organize a community crime prevention effort, investigate a domestic dispute, regulate traffic, or give a talk to a class of young people on the dangers of drug abuse. Calls for service today far exceed the number of calls received by the police which directly relate to law violations. As a consequence, the referral function of the police is crucial in producing effective law enforcement. Officers may make referrals, rather than arrests, for interpersonal problems to agencies as diverse as Alcoholics Anonymous, departments of social service, domestic violence centers, drug rehabilitation programs, and psychiatric clinics.

> The police in the United States are not separate from the people. They draw their authority from the will and consent of the people, and they recruit their officers from them. The police are the instrument of the people to achieve and maintain order; their efforts are founded on principles of public service and ultimate responsibility to the public.
>
> —*The National Advisory Commission on Criminal Justice Standards and Goals*

In contemporary America, according to Harvard University's Executive Session on Policing, three "corporate strategies" guide American policing.[15] They are (1) strategic policing, (2) problem-solving policing, and (3) community policing.

Contemporary police work involves a lot more than strict enforcement of the law. *Courtesy of the New York City Police Department.*

The first, strategic policing, is something of a holdover from the reform era of the mid-1900s. Strategic policing "emphasizes an increased capacity to deal with crimes that are not well controlled by traditional methods."[16] Strategic policing retains the traditional police goal of professional crime fighting, but enlarges the enforcement target to include non-traditional kinds of criminals such as serial offenders, gangs and criminal associations, drug distribution networks, and sophisticated white-collar and computer criminals. To meet its goals, strategic policing generally makes use of innovative enforcement techniques, including intelligence operations, undercover stings, electronic surveillance, and sophisticated forensic methods.

The other two strategies give greater cognizance to the service style described by Wilson. Problem solving (or problem-oriented policing) takes the view that many crimes are caused by existing social conditions in the communities served by the police. To control crime, problem-oriented police managers attempt to uncover and effectively address underlying social problems. Problem-solving policing makes thorough use of other community resources such as counseling centers, welfare programs, and job training facilities. It also attempts to involve citizens in the job of crime prevention through education, negotiation, and conflict management. Residents of poorly maintained housing areas, for example, might be asked to clean up litter, install better lighting, and provide security devices for their homes and apartments, in the belief that clean, secure, and well-lighted areas are a deterrent to criminal activity. According to Herman Goldstein, five concerns have "strongly influenced the development of problem-oriented policing."[17] They are (1) an historical preoccupation, among police managers, with internal procedures and efficiency, "to the exclusion of appropriate concern for effectiveness in dealing with substantive problems"; (2) the fact that police, in the past, have developed too little initiative on their own—instead responding mostly to public calls for service; (3) a growing recognition that the "community is a major resource with an enormous potential, largely untapped, for reducing the number and magnitude of problems that otherwise become the problems of the police"; (4) a new willingness to utilize the time and talent of the large numbers of rank-and-file officers, which, up until now, has not been effectively utilized; and (5) an increasing consciousness that internal police policies and organizational structures must change if policing is to be improved.

The third, and newest, police strategy goes a step beyond the other two. Community policing attempts to involve the community actively with the police in the task of crime control by creating an effective working partnership between the community and the police.[18] In the words of Jerome Skolnick, community policing is "grounded on the notion that, together, police and public are more effective and more humane coproducers of safety and public order than are the police alone."[19] Skolnick says that, under the community policing model, the police and the public are jointly responsible for social order.[20] According to Skolnick, community policing involves at least one of four elements: (1) community-based crime prevention, (2) the reorientation of patrol activities to emphasize the importance of nonemergency services, (3) increased police accountability to the public, and (4) a decentralization of command, including a greater use of civilians at all levels of police decision making.[21] Supporting Skolnick's view, Wesley Skogan[22] points out that "Community Policing is not an operational shopping list of specific policing programs. Neither is it a particular tactical *product* to be adopted. Rather, it involves reforming organizational decision-making *processes*.... A key to Community Policing is a shift in orientation from crime fighting to problem solving." A few years ago, for example, the Los Angeles County Sheriff's Department instituted a new program called "service-oriented policing," built around a better understanding of citizens' expectations, rights, and needs, and the Los Angeles Police Department recently developed a "Community Enhancement Request" form that "enables an officer to request specific services from city agencies to handle conditions that may result in crime or community decay."[23]

Innovative approaches to policing have produced a number of other innovative programs in recent years. In the early 1980s, for example, Houston's DART Program (Directed Area Responsibility Teams) emphasized problem-oriented policing; the Baltimore County, Maryland, police department began project COPE (Citizen Oriented Police Enforcement) in 1982; and Denver, Colorado, initiated its Community Service Bureau—one of the first major community policing programs. By the late 1980s, Jerome H. Skolnick and David Bayley's study at six American cities, entitled *The New Blue Line: Police Innovation in Six American Cities*,[24] documented the growing strength of community–police cooperation throughout the nation, giving further credence to the continuing evolution of service-oriented styles of policing.

Unfortunately, many problems remain.[25] There is some evidence that not all police officers are ready to accept new images of police work. Some authors have warned that police subculture is so committed to a traditional view of police work, that efforts at change can demoralize an entire department, rendering it ineffective at its basic tasks.[26] As the Independent Commission on the Los Angeles Police Department (The Christopher Commission) found following the "Rodney King riots," "[t]oo many ... patrol officers view citizens with resentment and hostility; too many treat the public with rudeness and disrespect."[27] Some analysts warn that only when the formal values espoused by today's innovative police administrators begin to match those of rank-and-file officers can any police organization begin to be high performing.[28]

Nor are all citizens ready to accept a greater involvement of the police in their personal lives. Although the turbulent protest-prone years of the 1960s and early 1970s are temporarily gone, some groups remain suspicious of the police. No matter how inclusive community policing programs become, it is doubtful that the gap between the police and the public will ever be entirely bridged. The police role of restraining behavior which violates the law will always produce friction between police departments and some segments of the community.

Table 6–1 highlights the differences between traditional and community policing.

T A B L E   6 - 1

TRADITIONAL VERSUS COMMUNITY POLICING

Question	Traditional	Community Policing
Who are the police?	A government agency principally responsible for law enforcement	Police are the public and the public are the police: the police officers are those who are paid to give full-time attention to the duties of every citizen.
What is the relationship of the police force to other public service departments?	Priorities often conflict.	The police are one department among many responsible for improving the quality of life.
What is the role of the police?	Focusing on solving crimes.	A broader problem-solving approach.
How is police efficiency measured?	By detection and arrest rates.	By the absence of crime and disorder.
What are the highest priorities?	Crimes that are high value (for example, bank robberies) and those involving violence.	Whatever problems disturb the community most.
What, specifically, do police deal with?	Incidents	Citizens' problems and concerns
What determines the effectiveness of police?	Response times	Public cooperation.
What view do police take of service calls?	Deal with them only if there is no real police work to do.	Vital function and great opportunity.
What is police professionalism?	Swift effective response to serious crime.	Keeping close to the community.
What kind of intelligence is most important?	Crime intelligence (study of particular crimes or series of crimes).	Criminal intelligence (information about the activities of individuals or groups).
What is the essential nature of police accountability?	Highly centralized; governed by rules, regulations, and policy directives; accountable to the law.	Emphasis on local accountability to community needs.
What is the role of headquarters?	To provide the necessary rules and policy directives	To preach organizational values.
What is the role of the press liaison department	To keep the "heat" off operational officers so they can get on with the job.	To coordinate an essential channel of communication with the community.
How do the police regard prosecutions?	As an important goal.	As one tool among many.

Source: Malcolm K. Sparrow, *Implementing Community Policing,* National Institute of Justice (Washington, D.C.: U.S. Department of Justice, 1988), pp. 8–9.

CONTEMPORARY POLICING: THE INDIVIDUAL OFFICER

Discretion The exercise of choice, by enforcement agents, in the disposition of suspects, in the carrying out of official duties, and in the application of sanctions.

Regardless of the "official" policing style espoused by a department, individual officers retain considerable **discretion** in what they do. As one author has observed, "police authority can be, at once, highly specific and exceedingly vague.[29] The determination to stop and question suspects, the choice to arrest, and many other police practices are undertaken solely by individual officers acting in a decision-making capacity. Kenneth Culp Davis says, "The police make policy about what law to enforce, how much to enforce it, against whom, and on what occasions."[30] The discretionary authority exercised by individual law enforcement officers is of potentially greater significance to the individual who has contact with the police than are all department manuals and official policy statements combined.

Patrolling officers will often decide against a strict enforcement of the law, preferring instead to handle situations informally. Minor law violations, crimes committed out of the officer's presence where the victim refuses to file a complaint, and certain violations of the criminal law where the officer suspects sufficient evidence to guarantee a conviction is lacking, may all lead to discretionary action short of arrest. Although the widest exercise of discretion is more likely in routine situations involving relatively less serious violations of the law, serious and clear-cut criminal behavior may occasionally result in discretionary decisions to avoid an arrest. Drunk driving, possession of controlled substances, and assault are but a few examples of crimes in which on-the-scene officers may decide warnings or referrals are more appropriate than arrest.

A summation of various studies of police discretion tells us that a number of factors influence the discretionary decisions of individual officers. Some of these factors are:

- *Background of the officer.* Law enforcement officers bring to their job all of life's previous experiences. Values shaped through early socialization in family environments, as well as attitudes acquired from ongoing socialization, impact the decisions an officer will make. If the officer has learned prejudice against certain ethnic groups, it is likely that such prejudices will manifest themselves in enforcement decisions. Officers who place a high value on the nuclear family may handle spouse abuse, child abuse, and other forms of domestic disputes in predetermined ways.

- *Characteristics of the suspect.* Some officers may treat men and women differently. A police friend of the author's has voiced the belief that women "are not generally bad … but when they do go bad, they go *very* bad." His official treatment of women has been tempered by this belief. Very rarely will this officer arrest a woman, but when he does, he spares no effort to see her incarcerated. Other characteristics of the suspect which may influence police decisions include demeanor, style of dress, and grooming. Belligerent suspects are often seen as "asking for it" and as challenging police authority. Well-dressed suspects are likely to be treated with deference, but poorly groomed suspects can expect less exacting treatment. Suspects sporting personal styles with a "message"—biker's attire, unkempt beards, outlandish haircuts, and other nonconformist styles—are more likely to be arrested than are others.

- *Department policy.* Discretion, while not entirely subject to control by official policy, can be influenced by it. If a department has targeted certain kinds of offenses, or if especially close control of dispatches and communications is held by supervisors who adhere to strict enforcement guidelines, discretionary release of suspects will be quite rare.

- *Community interest.* Public attitudes toward certain crimes will increase the likelihood of arrest for suspected offenders. Contemporary attitudes toward crimes involving children, including child sex abuse, the sale of drugs to minors, domestic violence involving children and child pornography, have all led to increased and strict enforcement of laws governing such offenses across the nation. Communities may identify particular problems affecting them and ask law enforcement to respond. Fayetteville, North Carolina, adjacent to a major military base, was plagued a few years ago by a downtown area notorious for prostitution and "massage" parlors. Once the community voiced its concern over the problem, and clarified the economic impact on the city, the police responded with a series of highly effective arrests which eliminated massage parlors within the city limits. Departments which require officers to live in the areas they police are operating in recognition of the fact that community interests impact citizens and officers alike.

• *Pressures from victims.* Victims who refuse to file a complaint are commonly associated with certain crimes such as spouse abuse, the "robbery" of drug merchants, and assault on customers of prostitutes. When victims refuse to cooperate with the police, there is often little that can be done. On the other hand, some victims are very vocal in insisting that their victimization be recognized and dealt with. Modern victim's assistance groups, including People Assisting Victims, the Victim's Assistance Network, and others, have sought to keep pressure on police departments and individual investigators to ensure the arrest and prosecution of suspects.

• *Disagreement with the law.* Some laws lack a popular consensus. Among them are many "victimless" offenses such as homosexuality, lesbianism, drug use, gambling, pornography, and some crimes involving alcohol. Not all of these behaviors are even crimes in certain jurisdictions. Gambling is legal in Atlantic City, New Jersey, on board cruise ships, and in Las Vegas, Nevada. Many states have now legalized homosexuality and lesbianism and most forms of sexual behavior between consenting adults. Prostitution is officially sanctioned in portions of Nevada, and some drug offenses have been "decriminalized," with offenders being ticketed rather than

Preparing for an IRS-sponsored public auction of the contents of the Mustang Ranch—previously one of Nevada's most famous bordellos. The conflict of popular morality, community interests, and the law can make for strange bedfellows. *Photo: Eric Risberg/AP Wide World Photos.*

arrested. Unpopular laws are not likely to bring much attention from law enforcement officers. Sometimes such crimes are regarded as just "part of the landscape" or as the consequence of laws which have not kept pace with a changing society. When arrests do occur, it may be because individuals investigated for more serious offenses were caught in the act of violating an unpopular statute. Drug offenders, for example, arrested in the middle of the night, may be "caught in the act" of an illegal sexual performance when the police break in. Charges may include "crime against nature," as well as possession or sale of drugs.

On the other hand, certain behaviors which are not law violations, and which may even be protected by guarantees of free speech, may be annoying, offensive, or disruptive according to the normative standards of a community or the personal standards of an officer. Where the law has been violated, and the guilty party is known to the officer, the evidence necessary for a conviction in court may be "tainted" or in other ways not usable. Sykes, in recognizing these possibilities, says, "One of the major ambiguities of the police task is that officers are caught between two profoundly compelling moral systems: justice as due process … and conversely, justice as righting a wrong as part of defining and maintaining community norms."[31] In such cases, discretionary police activity may take the form of "street justice" and approach vigilantism.

- *Available alternatives.* Police discretion can be impacted by the officer's awareness of alternatives to arrest. Community treatment programs, including outpatient drug and alcohol counseling, psychiatric, or psychological services, domestic dispute resolution centers, and other options may all be kept in mind by officers looking for a "way out" of official action.
- *Personal practices of the officer.* Some officers, because of actions undertaken in their personal lives, view potential law violations more or less seriously than other officers. The police officer who has an occasional marijuana cigarette with friends at a party may be inclined to deal less harshly with minor drug offenders than nonuser officers. The officer who routinely exceeds speed limits while driving the family car may be prone toward lenient action toward speeders encountered while on duty.

CONTEMPORARY POLICING: ISSUES

A number of issues hold special interest for today's police administrators and officers. Some concerns, such as police stress, danger, and the use of deadly force, derive from the very nature of police work. Others have arisen over the years due to commonplace practice, characteristic police values, and public expectations surrounding the enforcement of laws. Included here are such negatives as the potential for corruption, as well as positive efforts which focus on ethics and recruitment strategies to increase professionalism.

POLICE CULTURE

Police Culture (also subculture) A particular set of values, beliefs, and acceptable forms of behavior characteristic of American police, and with which the police profession strives to imbue new recruits. Socialization into the police subculture commences with recruit training and is ongoing thereafter.

A few years ago Jerome Skolnick described what he called the "working personality" of police officers.[32] Skolnick's description was consistent with William Westley's classic study[33] of the Gary, Indiana, police department, in which he found a police culture with its own "customs, laws, and morality," and with Niederhoffer's observation that cynicism was pervasive among officers in New York City.[34] More recent authors[35] have claimed that the "big curtain of secrecy" surrounding much of police work shields knowledge of the nature of the police personality from outsiders.

Skolnick found that a process of informal socialization, occurring when new officers begin to work with seasoned veterans, is often far more important than formal police academy training in determining how rookies will see police work. In everyday life, formal socialization occurs through schooling, church activities, job training, and so on. Informal socialization is acquired primarily from one's peers in less institutionalized settings and provides an introduction to value-laden subcultures. The information that passes between officers in the locker room, in a squad car, over a cup of coffee, or in many other relatively private moments produces a shared view of the world that can be best described as streetwise. The streetwise cop may know what official department policy is, but he or she also knows the most efficient way to get a job done. By the time they become streetwise, the officers will know just how acceptable various informal means of accomplishing the job will be to other officers. The police subculture creates few real "mavericks," but it also produces few officers who view their job exclusively in terms of public mandates and official dictums.

Skolnick says that the **police working personality** has at least six recognizable characteristics. Additional writers[36] have identified others. Taken in concert, they create the picture of the police personality shown in Table 6–2.

Some components of the police working personality are essential for survival and effectiveness. Officers are exposed daily to situations which are charged with emotions and potentially threatening. The need to gain control quickly over belligerent people leads to the development of authoritarian strategies for handling people. Eventually such strategies become "second nature," and the cornerstone of the police personality is firmly set. Cynicism evolves from a constant flow of experiences which demonstrate that people and events are not always what they seem to be. The natural tendency of most suspects, even when they are clearly guilty in the eyes of the police, is denial. Repeated attempts to mislead the police in the performance of their duty creates an air of suspicion and cynicism in the minds of most officers.

The origin of the police personality is at least bidimensional. On the one hand, some aspects of the world view which comprise that personality can be attributed to the socialization which occurs when rookie officers are inducted into police ranks. On the other, it may be that some of the components of the police personality already exist in some individuals and lead them into police work.[37] Supporting such a view are studies which indicate that police officers who come from conservative backgrounds continue to view themselves as defenders of middle-class morality.[38]

Police Working Personality All aspects of the traditional values and patterns of behavior evidenced by police officers who have been effectively socialized into the police subculture. Characteristics of the police personality often extend to the personal lives of law enforcement personnel.

T A B L E   6 - 2

THE POLICE PERSONALITY

Authoritarian
Cynical
Conservative
Suspicious
Hostile
Individualistic
Insecure
Loyal
Efficient
Honorable
Secret
Prejudiced

Police methods and the police culture are not static, however. Lawrence Sherman, for example, has reported on the modification of police tactics surrounding the use of weapons which characterized the period from 1970 to the 1980s.[39] Firearms, Sherman tells us, were routinely brought into play 25 years ago. Although not often fired, they would be frequently drawn and pointed at suspects. Few departmental restrictions were placed on the use of weapons, and officers employed them almost as they would their badge in the performance of duties. Today the situation has changed. It is a rare officer who will unholster a weapon during police work, and those who do know that only the gravist of situations can justify the public display of firearms.

Some authors attribute this shift in thinking about firearms to increased training and the growth of restrictive policies.[40] Changes in training, however, are probably more a response to a revolution in social understandings about the kind of respect due citizens. For example, the widespread change in social consciousness regarding the worth of individuals, which has taken place over the past few decades, appears to have had considerable impact upon police subculture itself.

CORRUPTION

Corruption Behavioral deviation from an accepted ethical standard.

The police role carries considerable authority, and officers are expected to exercise a well-informed discretion in all of their activities. The combination of authority and discretion, however, produces great potential for abuse.

Police deviance has been a problem in American society since the early days of policing. It is probably an ancient and natural tendency of human beings to attempt to placate or "win over" those in positions of authority over them. This tendency is complicated in today's materialistic society by greed and by the personal and financial benefits to be derived from evading the law. Hence, the temptations toward illegality offered to police

Detective Frank Serpico testifying before the Knapp Commission. *Photo: UPI/Bettmann.*

range all the way from a free cup of coffee given by a small restaurant owner in the thought that one day it may be necessary to call upon the goodwill of the officer, perhaps for something as simple as a traffic ticket, to huge monetary bribes arranged by drug dealers to guarantee the police will look the other way as an important shipment of contraband arrives.

Police corruption ranges from minor "offenses" to those which are themselves serious violations of the law. Barker and Carter distinguish between occupational deviance and abuse of authority in describing police deviance.[41] Occupational deviance, they say, is motivated by the desire for personal benefit. Abuse of authority, however, occurs most often in order to further the organizational goals of law enforcement—including arrest, ticketing, and the successful conviction of suspects. Examples of police deviance, ranked in what the author judges to be an increasing level of severity, are shown in Table 6–3.

Years ago, Frank Serpico made headlines as he testified before the Knapp Commission on police corruption in New York City.[42] Serpico, an undercover operative within the police department, revealed a complex web of corruption in which money and services routinely changed hands in "protection rackets" created by unethical officers. The Knapp Commission report distinguished between two types of corrupt officers which they termed grass eaters and meat eaters.[43] "Grass eating," the most common form of police deviance, was described as illegitimate activity which occurs from time to time in the normal course of police work. It involves mostly small bribes or relatively minor services offered by citizens seeking to avoid arrest and prosecution. "Meat eating" is a much more serious form of corruption, involving as it does the active *seeking* of illicit money-making opportunities by officers. Meat eaters solicit bribes through threat or intimidation, whereas grass eaters make the simpler mistake of not refusing those which are offered.

Popular books often tell the story of police misbehavior. A few years ago, Robert Daley's best-seller *Prince of the City*[44] detailed the adventures of New York City detective Robert

T A B L E   6 · 3

TYPES OF POLICE DEVIANCE BY CATEGORY AND EXAMPLE

High-Level
Corruption

Violent Crimes: The physical abuse of suspects, including torture and
    nonjustifiable homicide
Denying Civil Rights: Routinzed schemes to circumvent constitutional
    guarantees
Criminal Enterprise: The resale of confiscated drugs, stolen property, etc.
Property Crimes: Burglary, theft, etc., committed by police
Major Bribes: Accepting $1,000 to "overlook" contraband shipments, and
    other law violations.
Role Malfeasance: Destroying evidence, offering biased testimony, and
    protecting "crooked" cops
Being "Above" Inconvenient Laws: Speeding, smoking marijuana
Minor Bribes: Twenty dollars to "look the other way" on a ticket
Playing Favorites: Not ticketing friends, etc.
Gratuities: Accepting free coffee, meals, etc.

Low-Level
Corruption

Leuci who walked among corrupt cops with a tape recorder hidden on his body. The more recent best-seller *Buddy Boys,*[45] by Mike McAlary, is subtitled *When Good Cops Turn Bad.* McAlary, an investigative reporter with New York *Newsday,* began his efforts to uncover police corruption with a list of 13 names of officers who had been suspended in New York's 77th precinct. His book describes organized criminal activity among police in the "Big Apple," involving holdups of drug dealers, organized burglaries, fencing operations, and numerous other illegal activities conducted from behind the shield. McAlary says New York's criminal officers saw themselves as a kind of "elite" within the department and applied the name "Buddy Boys" to their gang.[46]

In 1993, during 11 days of corruption hearings reminiscent of the Knapp Commission era, a parade of crooked New York police officers testified before the Mollen Commission, headed by former judge and deputy mayor Milton Mollen. Among the many revelations, officers spoke of dealing drugs, stealing confiscated drug funds, stifling investigations, and beating innocent people. Officer Michael Dowd, for example, told the commission that he had run a cocaine ring out of his station house in Brooklyn and bought three homes on Long Island and a Corvette with the money he made. Most shocking of all, however, were allegations that high-level police officials attempted to hide embarrassing incidents in a "phantom file," and that many such officials may have condoned unprofessional and even criminal practices by law enforcement officers under their command. Honest officers, including internal affairs investigators, reported on how their efforts to end corruption among their fellows had been defused and resisted.

Spectacular as they were, however, many doubt that the Mollen hearings will have much impact on policing in New York City. "The Knapp Commission exposed a form of corruption that was systemic and pervasive," said Daniel Guido, a professor at John Jay College of Criminal Justice in New York. "It involved not only the working levels of the force and plain-clothes men but their supervisors. It was part of the culture of the force.... What we're seeing now is not systemic, and it involves only police officers in the main. It's all been sensational and revolting, but it's important not to overgeneralize the extent to which this is going on."

Some experts say that the New York Police Department actually has corruption under better control than most other large-city departments, and that the few cases of corruption identified by the Mollen Commission were trivial relative to the size of the department. Even so, the hearings do seem to show that corruption is nearly impossible to completely stamp out and that it reemerges with each new generation of officers.

Corruption, of course, is not unique to New York. In 1992 Detroit Police Chief William Hart was sentenced to a maximum of ten years in federal prison for embezzling $2.6 million from a secret police department fund and for tax evasion.[47] The fund, which was to be used for undercover drug buys and to pay informants, had secretly paid out nearly $10 million since its creation in 1980. Hart, who was 68 years old at the time of sentencing, had been police chief in Detroit since 1976. He resigned from office the day after his conviction, following a pension board ruling that he is entitled to receive a $53,000 annual pension despite the conviction. Hart's arrest had come on the heels of other problems for Detroit police. Two years earlier a city police officer was arrested for allegedly committing five robberies in one evening, and eight other officers were arrested for breaking and entering and assault. The *Detroit News,* a major newspaper in the city, conducted a study in which it found that Detroit police are "accused of committing crimes more often than officers in any other major U.S. city."[48]

The newspaper's claims appeared supported by the 1993 conviction of two former Detroit police officers in the beating death of Malice Green. Green, a black man who appeared to be clutching crack cocaine in his hand, died November 5, 1992, after white officers bludgeoned him with flashlights.

Even small cities are not immune to corruption. In 1992 former Rochester, New York, chief of police Gordon F. Urlacher was sentenced to four years in federal prison and fined $150,000 for embezzling about $300,000 from the city. Urlacher denied guilt, claiming that he was simply a bad accountant.

The police personality provides fertile ground for the growth of corrupt practices. Police "cynicism" develops out of continued association with criminals and problem-laden people. The cop who is "streetwise" is also ripe for corrupt influences to take root. Edwin Sutherland years ago applied the concept of differential association to deviant behavior.[49] Sutherland suggested that continued association with one type of person, more frequently than with any other, would make the associates similar.

Sutherland was talking about criminals, not police officers. Consider, however, the dilemma of the average officer: a typical day is spent running down petty thieves, issuing traffic citations to citizens who try to talk their way out of the situation, dealing with prostitutes who feel "hassled" by the police presence, and arresting drug users who think it should be their right to do what they want as long as it "doesn't hurt anyone." The officer encounters personal hostility and experiences a constant, and often quite vocal, rejection of society's formalized norms. Bring into this environment low pay and the resulting sense that police work is not really valued, and it is easy to understand how an officer might develop a jaded attitude about the double standards of the civilization he or she is sworn to protect.

Corruption is not unique to American police. During the 1960s and 1970s the formerly prestigious London Metropolitan Police force was beset by a series of scandals. In 1969 the London *Times* pictured the "Met" as protecting a "firm within a firm," from which payoffs and corrupt practices emanated. The Royal Commission on Criminal Procedures was formed in 1977 to investigate allegations of routine and intentional mistreatment of suspects, and public opinion polls following 1985 saw the level of citizen satisfaction with the London police decline substantially.[50]

Money—The Root of Police Evil?

Salaries paid to police officers in this country have been notoriously low when compared to other professions involving personal dedication, extensive training, high stress, and the risk of bodily harm. As police professionalism increases, salaries will rise. No matter how much police pay grows, however, it will never be able to compete with the staggering amounts of money to be made though dealing in contraband. In *The Underground Empire: Where Crime and Governments Embrace*, James Mills[51] tells the story of a man he calls a "young American entrepreneur," whom, he writes, has "criminal operations on four continents and a daily income greater than U.S. Steel's."[52] Mill's book is about "Centac," a semisecret arm of the Drug Enforcement Administration, which coordinates the operations of various agencies in the ongoing battle against illicit drugs. Although international drug trafficking is the focus of *The Underground Empire*, the book contains details of international police corruption purchased with the vast resources available to the trade.

Working hand in hand with monetary pressures toward corruption are the moral dilemmas produced by unenforceable laws which provide the basis for criminal profit. The Wickersham Commission warned during the Prohibition Era of the potential for official corruption inherent in the legislative taboos on alcohol. The demand for drink, immerse as it was, called into question the wisdom of the law, while simultaneously providing vast resources designed to circumvent the law. Today's drug scene bears some similarities to the Prohibition Era. As long as substantial segments of the population are willing to make large financial and other sacrifices to feed the drug trade, the pressures on the police to embrace corruption will remain substantial.

Combating Corruption

High moral standards, embedded into the principles of the police profession, and effectively communicated to individual officers through formal training and peer group socialization, would undoubtedly be the most effective way to combat corruption in police work. There are, of course, many officers of great personal integrity who hold to the highest of professional ideals, and there is evidence that law enforcement training programs are becoming increasingly concerned with instruction designed to reinforce the high ideals many recruits bring to police work. Practical efforts to combat corruption are also being brought to bear in many police organizations.

Most large law enforcement agencies have their own Internal Affairs Divisions which are empowered to investigate charges of wrong-doing made against officers. Where necessary, state police agencies may be called upon to examine reported incidents. Federal agencies, including the FBI and the DEA, involve themselves when corruption goes far enough to violate federal statutes. The U.S. Department of Justice, through various investigative offices, has the authority to examine possible violations of civil rights which may result from the misuse of police authority, and is often supported by the American Civil Liberties Union, the NAACP, and other "watchdog" groups in such endeavors.

A little over a decade ago a U.S. Department of Justice-sponsored report studied scandals involving police corruption in New York City; Oakland, California; Newburgh, New York; and an anonymous area termed "Central City" (somewhere in the Midwest).[53] A new police chief had been appointed in each city, and each arrived armed with a mandate to reform their departments. Three major strategies for controlling corruption evolved in the reorganized departments. The first of these, termed "managerial strategies" by the report, involved a four-pronged attack on corruption: (1) New officers were hired and personnel were "turned over," on the theory that corruption cannot survive where the people perpetrating it are removed. (Personnel turnover can also be accomplished by simply shifting agents from one division to another or from one geographical area to another.) (2) "Accountability" was clearly expected of supervisors. Those who wouldn't accept responsibility for combating corruption were asked to retire early or were removed from their command positions. (3) Closer supervision was required of commanders, especially sergeants, and other "first-line" supervisors. Sergeants were expected to spend more time with their officers, and to create procedures for making any work performed more visible within the context of the department. (4) "Corrupting practices" were ended. Quotas for vice arrests and reimbursements for out-of-pocket, job-related expenses (such as lunches, office supplies, etc.) were eliminated. Drug arrests through "buys" were well financed, ending the pressure to hold back money from other drug arrests to effect new ones.

A second strategy for reducing corruption was termed "changing the task environment." City officials made public pleas asking that citizens refrain from offering "gifts" to law enforcement officers. The chief of the Newburgh force asked for the repeal of a local ordinance allowing officers to accept gifts of under $25.00 in value. Special teams of officers concentrated on making highly visible arrests of citizens who attempted to bribe the police.

The last strategy identified in the report was called "changing the political environment." One police chief clearly communicated a new policy of enforcing "all the laws against all the people, including City Council Members." The Newburgh, New York, police executive tried to organize a federal investigation of political officials in the county. Corrupt politicians were either forced out of office or encouraged to retire.

The ability of the police to fulfill their sacred trust will improve as a lucid sense of ethical standards is developed.

—*Patrick V. Murphy*
Former commissioner of the NYC Police Department

A final technique to combat corruption, which was used by all the departments in the study, relied upon "internal policing strategies." Each department either created an Internal Affairs Division (IAD) or increased the numbers of officers participating in internal investigations. The New York Police Department, for example, originally had only 1 officer assigned to internal affairs for every 533 officers. Following reorganization, Internal Affairs increased in size almost ten times. One officer was assigned to IAD for every 64 enforcement officers. Each department also encouraged the Internal Affairs Division to become more active in seeking out information about corruption. Complaints were taken from numerous sources, including citizens who wished to remain anonymous, and former "reactive" strategies were turned into "proactive" efforts to gather information on corruption. The report revealed that Internal Affairs Divisions found especially useful wiretaps of known offenders (which sometimes implicated police "on the take"), "corruption patrolling" (in which IAD agents patrolled areas where the potential for police corruption was high), and "integrity tests" (which provided officers with an easy opportunity to commit criminal or corrupt acts).

Drug Testing of Police Employees

The widespread potential for corruption created by illicit drugs has led to focused efforts to combat drug use by officers. Drug testing programs at the department level are an example of such efforts. In 1986 the National Institute of Justice conducted a telephone survey of 33 large police departments across the nation to determine what measures were being taken to identify officers and civilian employees who were using drugs.[54] NIJ learned that almost all departments had written procedures to test employees who were reasonably suspected of drug abuse. Applicants for police positions were being tested by 73% of the departments surveyed, and 21% of the departments were actively considering testing all officers. In what some people found a surprisingly low figure, 21% reported that they might offer treatment to identified violators rather than dismiss them, depending upon their personal circumstances.

The International Association of Chiefs of Police has made available to today's police managers a "Model Drug Testing Policy." It is directed toward the needs of local departments and suggests:[55]

- Testing all applicants and recruits for drug or narcotics use
- Testing current employees when performance difficulties or documentation indicate a potential drug problem
- Testing current employees when they are involved in the use of excessive force or suffer or cause on-duty injury
- Routine testing of all employees assigned to special "high-risk" areas such as narcotics and vice

Drug testing based upon a reasonable suspicion that drug abuse has been or is occurring has been supported by the courts (*Maurice Turner* v. *Fraternal Order of Police, 1985*),[56] although random testing of officers was banned by the New York State Supreme Court in the case of *Philip Caruso, President of P.B.A.* v. *Benjamin Ward, Police Commissioner* (1986).[57] Citing overriding public interests, a 1989 decision by the U.S. Supreme Court upheld the testing of U.S. Customs personnel applying for transfer into positions involving drug law enforcement or carrying a firearm.[58] Many legal issues surrounding employee drug testing, however, remain to be resolved in court.

Complicating the situation is the fact that drug and alcohol addiction are "handicaps" protected by the Federal Rehabilitation Act of 1973. As such, federal law enforcement employees, as well as those working for agencies with federal contracts, are entitled to counseling and treatment before action toward termination can be taken.

The issue of employee drug testing in police departments, as in many other agencies, is a sensitive one. Some claim that existing tests for drug use are inaccurate, yielding a significant number of "false positives." Repeated testing and high "threshold" levels for narcotic substances in the blood may eliminate many of these concerns. Less easy to address, however, is the belief that drug testing intrudes upon the personal rights and professional dignity of individual employees.

THE DANGERS OF POLICE WORK

On October 15, 1991, the National Law Enforcement Memorial was unveiled in Washington, D.C. Initially, the memorial contained the names of 12,561 law enforcement officers killed in the line of duty. Other names have since been added.

Police work is, by its very nature, dangerous. While it is true that most officers throughout their careers never draw their weapons in the line of duty, it is also plain that some officers meet death while in the performance of their duties. On-the-job police deaths occur from stress, training accidents, and auto crashes. However, it is violent death at the hands of criminal offenders that police officers and their families fear most.

At 3:25 on a Friday morning in March 1988, New York City Police Officer Edward Byrne was gunned down while he sat in his patrol car protecting the home of a witness in a major narcotics case. Officer Byrne, who was 22-years-old, had decided to make policing his career. The cold-blooded killing motivated then-Mayor Ed Koch to place a large advertisement in *The New York Times* condemning the world of drug peddling and American policies which support countries where drugs are produced.[59] The ad, accompanied by a large picture of Officer Byrne in uniform, called for New Yorkers to exert political pressures to end economic and other forms of U. S. aid to countries from which drugs are smuggled.

Execution-style killings like those of Officer Byrne are rare. More common are line of duty deaths in battles with fleeing felons, in domestic disturbances, and while apprehending criminal suspects. Deputy Sheriff Douglas Hartman, for example, was killed when he attempted to serve a warrant on Larry Parker in Allentown, Pennsylvania, in July 1992. Hartman, who was not wearing his bulletproof vest, was shot once, with the bullet severing his aorta and spinal cord. Unknown to Hartman, the unemployed Parker, with a record of arrests for petty theft, had told friends that he intended to use his new .45-caliber handgun to "kill a police officer."[60]

Figure 6–1 shows the number of law enforcement officers killed during 1992 by circumstances and type of assignment. A recent study by the FBI found that slain officers appeared to be good natured and conservative in the use of physical force, "as compared to other law enforcement officers in similar situations. They were also perceived as being well-liked by the community and the department, friendly to everyone, laid back, and easy going."[61] Finally, the study also found, officers who were killed failed to wear protective vests.

For statistics on police killings to have meaning beyond the personal tragedy they entail, however, it is necessary to place them within a larger framework. Official statistics show that in 1992 there were 748,821 state and local police employees in this country,[62] and approximately 70,000 federal agents employed nationwide. Such numbers demonstrate that the rate of violent death among law enforcement officers in the line of duty is small indeed.

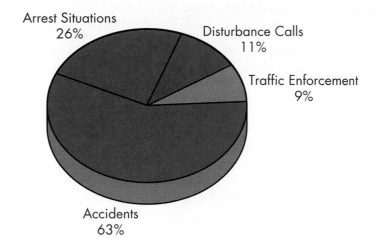

FIGURE 6–1   U.S. law enforcement officers killed—by type of incident, 1992. *Source:* Federal Bureau of Investigation, *Uniform Crime Reports 1992* (Washington, D.C.: U.S. Government Printing Office, 1993).

Infected Evidence

Not all the dangers facing law enforcement officers are as direct as out-right violence and assault. The increasing incidence of serious diseases capable of being transmitted by blood and other bodily fluids, combined with the fact that crime and accident scenes are inherently dangerous, has made "caution" a necessary byword among investigators and "first on the scene" officers. Potential for minor cuts and abrasions abound in the broken glass and torn metal of a wrecked car, in the sharp edges of weapons remaining at the scene of an assault or murder, and in drug implements such as razor blades and hypodermic needles secreted in vehicles, apartments, and in pockets. Such minor injuries, previously shrugged off by many police personnel, have become a focal point for warnings about the dangers of AIDS (Acquired Immune Deficiency Syndrome), hepatitis B, tuberculosis, and other diseases spread through contact with infected blood.

In 1988 Sonoma County, California, Sheriff Dick Michaelson became the first law enforcement supervisor to announce a clear-cut case of AIDS infection in an officer caused by interaction with a suspect. A deputy in Michaelson's department apparently contracted AIDS a few years earlier when he was pricked by a hypodermic needle during a "pat down" search.[63]

In 1992 a 46-year-old gay San Francisco police officer won $50,547 in disability pay and AIDS medical treatment expenses[64] and a possible $25,000-per-year permanent retirement benefit. Inspector Thomas Cady became infected with the HIV virus after being bitten and splashed with blood during an arrest a few years earlier.

Understandably, there is much concern among officers as to how to deal with the threat of AIDS and other bloodborne diseases. However, as a manual of the New York City Police Department reminds its officers, "Police officers have a professional responsibility to render assistance to those who are in need of our services. We cannot refuse to help. Persons with infectious diseases must be treated with the care and dignity we show all citizens.[65]

The FBI has also become concerned with the use of breath alcohol instruments on infected persons, the handling of evidence of all types, seemingly innocuous implements

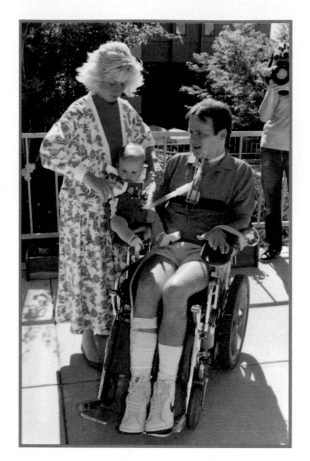

Police work can be dangerous. Steven McDonald, paralyzed and wheelchair-bound after being shot in the neck while working as a New York city police officer, is shown here with his wife and young son. *Photo: J. David Ake/UPI/Bettmann.*

such as staples, the emergency delivery of babies in squad cars, and with the risk of attack (especially bites) by infected individuals who are being questioned or who are in custody. The following are among the 16 recommendations made by the FBI as "defenses against exposure" to infectious substances (others are listed in Table 6–4):[66]

1. The first line of defense against infection at the crime scene is protecting the hands and keeping them away from the eyes, mouth, and nose.
2. Any person with a cut, abrasion, or any other break in the skin on the hands should never handle blood or other body fluids without protection.
3. Use gloves, and replace them whenever you leave the crime scene. Wash hands thoroughly.
4. No one at the crime scene should be allowed to smoke, eat, drink, or apply makeup.
5. Use the utmost care when handling knives, razors, broken glass, nails, and the like to prevent a puncture of the skin.
6. If a puncture of the skin does occur cleanse it thoroughly with rubbing alcohol and wash with soap and water. Then seek immediate medical assistance.
7. When possible, use disposable items at the crime scene, such as pencils, gloves, and throw-away masks. These items should be incinerated after use.
8. Nondisposable items such as cameras, notebooks, and so on, should be decontaminated using bleach mixed with water.

T A B L E 6 - 4

RESPONSES TO AIDS-RELATED LAW ENFORCEMENT CONCERNS

Issue/Concern	Educational and Action Messages
Human bites	Person who bites usually receives the victim's blood; viral transmission through saliva is highly unlikely. If bitten by anyone, milk wound to make it bleed; wash the area thoroughly, and seek medical attention.
Spitting	Viral transmission through saliva is highly unlikely.
Urine/feces	Virus isolated in only very low concentrations in urine; not at all in feces; no cases of AIDS or AIDS virus infection associated with either urine or feces.
Cuts/puncture wounds	Use caution in handling sharp objects and searching areas hidden from view; needle stick studies show risk of infection is very low.
CPR/first aid	To eliminate the already minimal risk associated with CPR, use masks/airways; avoid blood-to-blood contact by keeping open wounds covered and wearing gloves when in contact with bleeding wounds.
Body removal	Observe crime scene rules: do not touch anything. Those who must come into contact with blood or other bodily fluids should wear gloves.
Casual contact	No cases of AIDS or AIDS virus infection attributed to casual contact.
Any contact with blood or body fluids	Wear gloves if contact with blood or body fluids is considered likely. If contact occurs, wash thoroughly with soap and water; clean up spills with one part water to nine parts household bleach.
Contact with dried blood	No cases of infection have been traced to exposure to dried blood. The drying process itself appears to inactivate the virus. Despite low risk, however, caution dictates wearing gloves, a mask, and protective shoe coverings if exposure to dried blood particles is likely (e.g., crime scene investigation).

Source: National Institute of Justice, Report No. 206 (November/December 1987), p. 6.

The National Institute of Justice adds to this list the recommendations that suspects should be asked to empty their own pockets, where possible, and that puncture wounds should be "milked" as in the case of snakebites in order to help flush infectious agents from the wound.[67]

It is sometimes necessary for local police agencies to send evidence out for analysis by well-equipped laboratories. When using the U.S. Mail, Part 72 of the Code of Federal Regulations requires that packages containing potentially contaminated bodily fluids be labeled with warnings and that they be tightly sealed and wrapped. The National Bureau of Standards is working on a process to sterilize evidence using gamma radiation. If the process is perfected, blood proteins and other substances crucial in forensic analysis will be preserved. In the meantime, the FBI laboratory will accept evidence from AIDS cases for analysis only if

1. The contributor knows that the evidence will be "autoclaved," destroying its worth in serological analysis.
2. Letters from the prosecuting and defense attorneys accompany the evidence, acknowledging that it will be autoclaved.
3. The evidence is securely packaged and warning labels have been applied.

Police departments will face an increasing number of legal challenges in the years to come in cases involving infectious diseases such as AIDS. Some predictable areas of concern will involve (1) the need to educate officers and other police employees relative to AIDS and other serious infectious diseases, (2) the responsibility of police departments to prevent the spread of AIDS in police lockups, and (3) the necessity of effective and nondiscriminatory enforcement activities and life-saving measures by police officers in AIDS environments. With regard to nondiscriminatory activities, the National Institute of Justice has suggested that legal claims in support of an officer's refusal to render assistance to people with AIDS would probably not be effective in court.[68] The reason is twofold: The officer has a basic duty to render assistance to individuals in need of it, and the possibility of AIDS transmission by casual contact has been scientifically established as extremely remote. A final issue of growing concern involves activities by police officers infected with the AIDS virus. A recent issue of *Law Enforcement News* reports, "Faced with one of the nation's largest populations of AIDS sufferers—and perhaps one of the largest cadres of AIDS-infected officers—the New York City Police Department has debuted its own AIDS awareness effort.[69] Few statistics are currently available on the number of officers with AIDS, but public reaction to those officers may be a developing problem area which police managers will soon need to address.

Police Stress

Perhaps the most insidious and least visible of all threats facing law enforcement personnel today is debilitating stress. While some degree of stress can be a positive motivator, serious stress, over long periods of time, is generally regarded as destructive, even life threatening.

Stress is a natural component of police work. The American Institute of Stress, based in Yonkers, New York, ranks policing among the top ten stress-producing jobs in the country.[70] Danger, frustration, paperwork, the daily demands of the job, and a lack of understanding from family members and friends contribute to the negative stresses officers experience.

Joseph Victor has identified four sources of police stress:[71] (1) external stress, which results from "real dangers," such as responding to calls involving armed suspects; (2) organizational stress, generated by the demands of police organizations themselves, such as scheduling, paperwork, training requirements, and so on; (3) personal stress, produced by interpersonal relationships among officers themselves; and (4) operational stress, which Victor defines as "the total effect of the need to combat daily the tragedies of urban life."

Some of the stressors in police work are particularly destructive. One is frustration brought on by the inability to be effective, regardless of the amount of personal effort expended. From the point of view of the individual officer, the police mandate is to bring about some change in society for the better. The crux of police work involves making arrests based upon thorough investigations which lead to convictions and the removal of individuals who are damaging to the social fabric of the community—all under the umbrella of the criminal law. Unfortunately, reality is often far from the ideal. Arrests may not lead to convictions. Evidence which is available to the officer may not be allowed in court. Sentences which are imposed may seem too "light" to the arresting officer. The feelings of powerlessness and frustration which come from seeing repeat offenders back on the streets, and from experiencing numerous injustices worked upon seemingly innocent victims, may greatly stress police officers and cause them to question the purpose of their professional lives.

Another source of stress—that of living with constant danger—is incomprehensible to most of us, even to the family members of many officers. As James Mills says, "I kick in a door and I've gotta talk some guy into putting a gun down.... And I go home, and my wife's upset because the lawn isn't cut and the kids have been bad. Now, to *her* that's a real problem."[72]

Stress is not unique to the police profession, but because of the "macho" attitude that has traditionally been associated with police work, denial of the stress experience may be found more often among police officers than in other occupational groups. Certain types of individuals are probably more susceptible to the negative effects of stress than are others. The Type A personality was popularized a few years ago as the category of person more likely to perceive life in terms of pressure and performance. Type B personalities were said to be more "laid back" and less likely to suffer from the negative effects of stress. Police ranks, drawn as they are from the general population, are filled with both stress-sensitive and stress-resistant personalities.

Stress Reduction　Natural reactions to stress include attempts at its control. Health care professionals, for example, have long been noted for their ability to joke around patients who may be seriously ill or even dying, and humor is a well-recognized technique for stress management. Maintaining an emotional distance from stressful events is another way of coping with them, although such distance is not always easy to maintain. Police officers who have had to deal with serious cases of physical child abuse have often reported on the emotional turmoil they experienced as a consequence of what they saw.

The support of family and friends can be crucial in developing other strategies to handle stress. Exercise, meditation, abdominal breathing, biofeedback, self-hypnosis, guided imaging, induced relaxation, subliminal conditioning, music, prayer, and diet have all been cited as techniques which can be useful in stress reduction. Devices to measure stress levels are available in the form of hand-held heart rate monitors, blood pressure devices, "biodots" (which change color according to the amount of blood flow in the extremities), and psychological inventories.

POLICE CIVIL LIABILITY

An area of growing concern among police managers today is that of civil liability for official misconduct. Police officers may become involved in a variety of situations which create the potential for civil suits against the officers, their superiors and their departments. Major sources of police civil liability are listed in Table 6–5. Swanson says that the most common source of lawsuits against the police involve "assault, battery, false imprisonment, and malicious prosecution."[73]

Of all complaints brought against the police, assault charges are the best known, being, as they are, subject to high media visibility. Less visible, but not uncommon, are civil suits charging the police with false arrest or false imprisonment. In the 1986 case of *Malley* v. *Briggs*,[74] the U.S. Supreme Court held that a police officer who effects an arrest or conducts

T A B L E   6 - 5

MAJOR SOURCES OF POLICE CIVIL LIABILITY

Failure to protect property in police custody
Negligence in the care of persons in police custody
Failure to render proper emergency medical assistance
Failure to prevent a foreseeable crime
Failure to aid private citizens
Lack of due regard for the safety of others
False arrest
False imprisonment
Inappropriate use of deadly force
Unnecessary assault or battery
Malicious prosecution
Violations of constitutional rights

a search on the basis of an improperly issued warrant may be liable for monetary damages when a reasonably well-trained officer, under the same circumstances, "would have known that his affidavit failed to establish probable cause and that he should not have applied for the warrant." Significantly, the Court, in *Malley*, also ruled that an officer "cannot excuse his own default by pointing to the greater incompetence of the magistrate."[75]

When an officer makes an arrest without probable cause, or simply impedes an individual's right to leave the scene without good reason, he or she may also be liable for the charge of false arrest. Officers who enjoy "throwing their weight around" are especially subject to this type of suit, grounded at it is on the abuse of police authority. Because employers may generally be sued for the negligent or malicious actions of their employees, many police departments are finding themselves named as codefendants in lawsuits today.

Negligent actions by officers may also provide the basis for suits. High-speed chases are especially dangerous because of the potential they entail for injury to innocent bystanders. Flashing blue or red lights (the color of police vehicle lights varies by state) legally only *request* the right-of-way on a highway, they do not demand it. Officers who drive in such a way as to place others in danger may find themselves the subject of suits. In the case of *Biscoe* v. *Arlington* (1984),[76] for example, Alvin Biscoe was awarded $5 million after he lost both legs as a consequence of a high-speed chase while he was waiting to cross the street. Biscoe was an innocent bystander and was struck by a police car which had gone out of control. The fact that the police department in *Biscoe* had sanctioned high-speed chases as a part of official policy made the department especially liable. Departments may protect themselves to some degree through regulations limiting the authority of their personnel. In a 1985 case, for example, a Louisiana police department was exonerated in an accident which occurred during a high-speed chase because of its policy limiting emergency driving to no more than 20 miles over the posted speed limit. The officer, however, who drove 75 MPH in a 40-MPH zone was found to be negligent and held liable for damages.[77]

Law enforcement supervisors may find themselves the object of lawsuits by virtue of the fact that they are responsible for the actions of their officers. Where it can be shown that supervisors were negligent in hiring (as when someone with a history of alcoholism, mental problems, sexual deviance, or drug abuse is employed), or if supervisors failed in their responsibility to properly train officers before they armed and deployed them, findings of supervisory liability may result.

THEORY INTO PRACTICE

AN EXAMPLE OF POLICE CIVIL LIABILITY: THE CASE OF BERNARD MCCUMMINGS

A 1993 U.S. Supreme Court decision in a civil suit which drew wide outrage, saw convicted subway mugger Bernard McCummings awarded $4.3 million in a suit he had brought against the city of New York. McCummings was shot twice in the back in 1984 by Transit Authority officer Manuel Rodriguez as he attempted to flee a subway platform after beating and robbing a 71-year-old man. At the time of the crime McCummings had just gotten out of prison for robbery. Since the shooting McCummings, who was 23-years-old when he was injured, has remained paralyzed from the chest down. After pleading guilty to the mugging he was sentenced to prison, where he served two years. When McCummings brought suit against the city, however, a jury and appeals court found that officers had used excessive force. Before paying the award the city appealed to the Supreme Court. In upholding the cash award to McCummings, the Supreme Court reiterated earlier rulings that police officers cannot use deadly force against unarmed fleeing suspects who pose no apparent threat to officers or to the public.

McCummings's victim, Jerome Sandusky, who was carrying less than $30 at the time he was attacked, decried the ruling, saying "[i]t's justice turned upside down… and it sends a terrible message… that crime *does* pay." "Ordinarily I would be sorry for anyone that was made a cripple. But he was made a cripple because of his own action," Sandusky said. Gerald Arenberg of the National Association of Chiefs of Police sided with Sandusky. "The criminal is very well protected by the Supreme Court," Arenberg said in a national interview. Lawyers for the city were disappointed. "The message is," said one, when faced with a fleeing suspect, "it's probably wiser for a police officer to do nothing, in terms of civil liability."

Opinions on the case were, however, varied. "It was the right decision," said David Breibart, McCummings's lawyer. "It gives me great faith in the system." A Washington Post editorial, on the other hand, suggested that police should not be bound by the rules of fairplay, when criminals are not. "What if felons knew that cops could shoot them if they fled?" the editorial asked. "More of them would likely freeze and put up their hands … [C]riminal behavior should not be treated as if it were some sort of quasi-legitimate enterprise, governed by the laws of negligence." "McCummings" said the writer, "was as much a victim of his own criminality as he was of a violation of the rules regarding the use of deadly force. Once he chose to break the law he wasn't entitled to be compensated by it." McCummings's victim agreed. In December of 1993 Sandusky filed suit against McCummings seeking to get the $4.3 million award. Sandusky brought suit under New York's modified "Son of Sam" law, which is intended to prevent criminals from profiting from their crimes.

Sources: "Mugger Shot by Cop to Keep $4.3 million," *USA Today*, November 30, 1993, 1A. "Mugging Lawsuit," Associated Press wire services, December 15, 1993. "Compensation for a Criminal." *Washington Post* wire services, December 2, 1993. "Scouts-Excessive Force," Associated Press wire services, November 30, 1993.

Adequate training can offset claims of liability. Here a female police recruit is taught how to restrain a suspect without injuring him. *Photo: Bonnie Kamin /Comstock.*

In the 1989 case of the *City of Canton, Ohio* v. *Harris,*[78] the U.S. Supreme Court ruled that a "failure to train" can become the basis for legal liability on the part of a municipality where the "failure to train amounts to deliberate indifference to the rights of persons with whom the police come in contact."[79] In that case, Geraldine Harris was arrested and taken to the Canton, Ohio, police station. While at the station she slumped to the floor several times. Officers finally decided to leave her on the floor and never called for qualified medical assistance. Upon release, Ms. Harris was taken by family members to a local hospital. She was hospitalized for a week and received follow-up outpatient treatment for the next year. The Court ruled that although municipalities could not justifiably be held liable for limited instances of unsatisfactory training, they could be held accountable where the failure to train results from a deliberate or conscious choice.

Civil suits brought against law enforcement personnel are of two types: state or federal. Suits brought in state courts have generally been the most common form of civil litigation involving police officers. In recent years, however, an increasing number of suits are being brought in federal courts on the basis of the legal rationale that the civil rights of the plaintiff, as guaranteed by federal law, have been denied.

Federal suits are often called 1983 lawsuits because they are based upon Section 1983 of Title 42 of the United States Code—an act passed by Congress in 1871 to ensure the civil rights of men and women of all races. That act requires due process of law before any person can be deprived of life, liberty, or property and specifically provides redress for the denial of these constitutional rights by officials acting under color of *state* law. For example, a 1983 suit may be brought against officers who shoot suspects under questionable circumstances—thereby denying them of their right to life without due process. The 1981 case of *Prior* v. *Woods*[80] resulted in a $5.7 million judgment against the Detroit Police Department after David Prior—who was mistaken for a burglar—was shot and killed in front of his home.

THEORY INTO PRACTICE

TITLE 42, UNITED STATES CODE, SECTION 1983

Every person who, under color of any statute, ordinance regulation, custom, or usage, of any State or Territory, subjects, or causes to be subjected, any citizen of the United States or other person within the jurisdiction thereof to the deprivation of any rights, privileges, or immunities secured by the Constitution and laws, shall be liable to the party injured in an action at law, suit in equity, or other proper proceeding for redress.

Another type of liability action, this one directed specifically at federal officials or enforcement agents, is called a Bivens suit. The case of *Bivens* v. *Six Unknown Federal Agents* (1971)[81] established a path for legal action against agents enforcing federal laws which is similar to that found in a 1983 suit. Bivens actions may be addressed against individuals, but not the United States. Federal officers have generally been granted a court-created qualified immunity and have been protected from suits where they were found to have acted in the belief that their action was consistent with federal law.[82]

In times past, the doctrine of sovereign immunity barred legal actions against state and local governments. Sovereign immunity was a legal theory which held that a governing body could not be sued because it made the law and therefore could not be bound by it. Immunity is a much more complex issue today. Some states have officially abandoned any pretext of immunity through legislative action. New York State, for example, has declared that public agencies are equally as liable as private agencies for violations of constitutional rights. Other states, like California, have enacted statutory provisions which define and place limits on governmental liability.[83] A number of state immunity statutes have been struck down by court decision. In general, states are moving in the direction of setting dollar limits on liability and adopting federal immunity principles to protect individual officers, including "good faith" and "reasonable belief" rules.

For its part, the U.S. Supreme Court has supported a type of "qualified immunity" which "shields law enforcement officers from constitutional lawsuits if reasonable officers believe their actions to be lawful in light of clearly established law and the information the officers possess. In the context of a warrantless arrest," the Court stated, in *Hunter* v. *Bryant* (1991),[84] "even law enforcement officials who reasonably but mistakenly conclude that probable cause is present are entitled to immunity."[85]

Most departments carry liability insurance to protect them against the severe financial damage which can result from the loss of a large suit. Some officers make it a point to acquire private policies which provide coverage in the event they are named as individuals in such suits. Both types of insurance policies generally provide for a certain amount of legal fees to be paid by the police for defense against the suit, regardless of the outcome of the case. Police departments who face civil prosecution because of the actions of an officer, however, may find that legal and financial liability extend to supervisors, city managers, and the community itself. Where insurance coverage does not exist, or is inadequate, city coffers may be nearly drained to meet the damages awarded.[86]

In a recent five-year period, for example, the city of Los Angeles, California, paid out $23 million to people who brought suits against the LAPD for civil rights violations.[87] Former Los Angeles Chief of Police Daryl Gates, in commenting on the prevalence of law-suits against police officers today, has observed that although California cities are allowed to pay damage awards for individual officers, they do not have to. Gates continued:

> Think about the chilling factor in that. [It says] "Hey, Chief, you're on your own. We're not gonna pay anything." Think what that does. It says, "Hey Chief, don't open your mouth— Don't tell the public anything. Don't let them know what the real facts are in this case. Don't tell the truth." And what does it tell the police officers? Don't do your work, because you're liable to wind up in court, being sued. That, to me, is probably the most frightening thing that's happening in the United States today.[88]

Deadly Force

The use of deadly force by police officers is one area of potential civil liability which has received considerable attention in recent years. Historically, the fleeing felon rule applied to most U.S. jurisdictions. It held that officers could use deadly force to prevent the escape of a suspected felon, even when that person represented no immediate threat to the officer or to the public. The fleeing felon rule probably stemmed from early common law punishments which specified death for a large number of crimes. Today, however, the death penalty is far less frequent in application, and the fleeing felon rule has been called into question in a number of courts.

The 1985 Supreme Court case of *Tennessee* v. *Garner*[89] specified the conditions under which deadly force could be used in the apprehension of suspected felons. Edward Garner, a 15-year-old suspected burglar, was shot to death by Memphis police after he refused their order to halt and attempted to climb over a chain-link fence. In an action initiated by Garner's father, who claimed that his son's constitutional rights had been violated, the Court held that the use of deadly force by the police to prevent the escape of a fleeing felon might be justified only where the suspect could reasonably be thought to represent a significant threat of serious injury or death to the public or to the officer. In reaching its decision, the Court declared that "The use of deadly force to prevent the escape of all felony suspects, whatever the circumstances, is constitutionally unreasonable."[90]

Studies of killings by the police have often focused on claims of discrimination, that is, that black and minority suspects are more likely to be shot than whites. Research in the area, however, has not provided solid support for such claims. While individuals shot by police are more likely to be minorities, James Fyfe[91] found that police officers will generally respond with deadly force when mortally threatened and that minorities are considerably more likely to use weapons in assaults on officers than are whites. Complicating the picture further were Fyfe's data showing that minority officers are involved in the shooting of suspects more often than other officers, a finding that may be due to the assignment of such officers to inner-city and ghetto areas. However, a more recent study by Fyfe[92] which analyzed police shootings in Memphis, Tennessee, found that black property offenders were twice as likely as whites to be shot by police.

Although relatively few police officers will ever feel the need to draw their weapons during the course of their careers, those who do may find themselves embroiled in a web of social, legal, and personal complications. It is estimated that an average year sees 600 suspects killed by gunfire from public police in America, while another 1,200 are shot and wounded, and 1,800 individuals are shot at and missed.[93]

The personal side of police shootings is well summarized in the title of an article which appeared in *Police Magazine*. The article, "I've Killed That Man Ten Thousand Times,"[94] demonstrated how police officers who have to use their weapon may be haunted by years of depression and despair. Not long ago, according to Anne Cohen, author of the article, all departments did to help officers who had shot someone was to "give him enough bullets to reload him gun." The stress and trauma which result from shootings by officers in defense of themselves or others is only now beginning to be realized, and most departments have yet to develop mechanisms for adequately dealing with it.[95]

In 1993 the National Institute of Justice reported on efforts begun in 1987 to develop "less than lethal weapons" for use by law enforcement officers.[96] Questions to be answered include (1) "Can an officer stop a fleeing felon without use of deadly force?" (2) "Are there devices and substances that would rapidly subdue assailants before they could open fire or otherwise harm their hostages?" (3) "Can technology provide devices to incapacitate assailants without also harming nearby innocent hostages and bystanders?" Chemical agents, knockout gases, stunning explosives, tranquilizing darts, and remote-delivery electronic shocks are all being studied by the agency. NIJ says it is "moving forward with research development, and evaluation of devices for use by line patrol officers under a wide variety of circumstances. ... [T]he goal is to give line officers effective and safe alternatives to lethal force."[97]

PROFESSIONALISM AND ETHICS

Police administrators have responded in a variety of ways to issues of danger, liability, and the potential for corruption. Among the most significant responses have been calls for increased professionalism at all levels of policing. A profession is characterized by a body of specialized knowledge, acquired through extensive education,[98] and by a well-considered set of internal standards and ethical guidelines which hold members of the profession accountable to one another and to society. Associations of likeminded practitioners generally serve to create and disseminate standards for the profession as a whole.

Contemporary policing evidences many of the attributes of a profession. Specialized knowledge in policing includes a close familiarity with criminal law, laws of procedure, constitutional guarantees, and relevant Supreme Court decisions, a working knowledge of weapons and hand-to-hand tactics, driving skills and vehicle maintenance, a knowledge of radio communications, report-writing abilities, interviewing techniques, and media and human relations skills. Other specialized knowledge may include breathalyzer operation, special weapons firing, polygraph operation, conflict resolution, and hostage negotiation skills. Supervisory personnel require an even wider range of skills, including administrative knowledge, management techniques, personnel administration, and department strategies for optimum utilization of officers and physical resources.

Basic law enforcement training requirements were begun in the 1950s by the state of New York and through a voluntary system of Peace Officer Standards and Training (POST) in California. Today, such requirements are mandated by law in every state in the nation, although they vary considerably from region to region. Modern police education involves, at a minimum, more than 100 classroom contact hours (Missouri), and in some places nearly 1,000 hours of intensive training (Hawaii),[99] in subject areas which include human relations, firearms and weapons, communications, legal aspects of policing, patrol, criminal investigations, administration, report writing, and criminal justice systems. Contemporary POST standards are shown in a Theory into Practice box in this chapter.

Police Professionalism The increasing formalization of police work and the rise in public acceptance of the police which accompanies it. Any profession is characterized by a specialized body of knowledge and a set of internal guidelines which hold members of the profession accountable for their actions. A well-focused code of ethics, equitable recruitment and selection practices, and informed promotional strategies among many agencies contribute to the growing level of professionalism among American police agencies today.

THEORY INTO PRACTICE

POLICE TRAINING

The California Peace Officer Standards and Training program was one of this country's first selection and training standards-setting program for law enforcement officers. Today an updated POST program serves as a model for other similar programs in many parts of the United States. Shown here are POST training requirements for law enforcement officers at various levels of career development.

Basic POST Training (560 minimum required hours)

Professional orientation	11 hours	Criminal investigation	50 hours
Police–community relations	16 hours	Custody	4 hours
Law	52 hours	Physical fitness and	
Laws of evidence	20 hours	defense techniques	87 hours
Communications	32 hours		
Vehicle operations	24 hours	Practical exercise and	
Force and weaponry	54 hours	scenario testing	24 hours
Patrol procedures	125 hours		
Traffic	30 hours	Written examinations	31 hours

Successful curriculum completion also requires that "the Law Enforcement Code of Ethics shall be administered to peace officer trainees during the basic course."

Continuing Professional Training Requirement (24 hours every 2 years)

New laws
Recent court decisions and/or search and seizure refresher
Officer survival techniques
New concepts, procedures, technology
Discretionary decision making (practical field problems)
Civil liability–causing subjects

Supervisory Course (80 minimum required hours)

Introduction: Role identification	Discipline
Values, principles, ethics	Employee relations
Leadership styles	Administrative support
Liability issues	Planning and organizing
Assertive leadership	Communications
Employee performance appraisal	Training
Counseling	Report review
Investigations	Stress management
The transition (to supervisory level)	

Management Course (80 minimum required hours)

Management roles and responsibility
Leadership styles and decision making
Organization and manager development

Personnel management skills
Legal responsibilities

Executive Development Course (80 minimum required hours)

Leadership and management
Organization development
Contemporary issues

Legal responsibilities
Communications

Note: Every peace officer below the first middle-management level must satisfactorily complete the advanced officer course of 24 or more hours at least once every two years after completion of the basic course. This requirement may also be met by satisfactory completion of an accumulation of certified technical courses totaling 24 or more hours, or satisfactory completion of an alternative method of compliance as determined by the Commission. Supervisors may also satisfy the requirement by completing supervisory or management training courses.

Source: Commission on Peace Officer Standards and Training, *POST Administrative Manual* (Sacramento, CA: CPOST, 1990). Reprinted with permission.

Federal law enforcement agents receive schooling at the Federal Law Enforcement Training Center (FLETC) at Glynco, Georgia. The Center provides training for about 60 federal law enforcement agencies (excluding the FBI, which has its own training center at Quantico, Virginia) and has begun offering advanced training to state and local police organizations, where such training is not available under other auspices. Specialized schools, such as Northwestern University's Traffic Institute, have also been credited with raising the level of police practice from purely operational concerns to a more professional level.[100]

Police work is guided by an ethical code originated in 1956 by the Peace Officer's Research Association of California (PORAC), in conjunction with Dr. Douglas M. Kelley of Berkeley's School of Criminology.[101] *The Law Enforcement Code of Ethics* is reproduced in a box in this chapter. Ethics training is still not well integrated into most basic law enforcement training programs, but a movement in that direction has begun and calls for expanded training in ethics are on the increase.

Police Ethics The special responsibility for adherence to moral duty and obligation inherent in police work.

Professional associations abound in police work. The Fraternal Order of Police (FOP) is one of the best known organizations of public service workers in the United States. The International Association of Chiefs of Police (IACP) has done much to raise professional standards in policing and continually strives for improvements in law enforcement nationwide.

Accreditation provides another channel toward police professionalism. The Commission on Accreditation for Law Enforcement Agencies was formed in 1979. Police departments wishing to apply for accreditation through the Commission must meet hundreds of standards relating to areas as diverse as day-to-day operations, administration, review of incidents involving the use of a weapon by officers, and evaluation and promotion of personnel. To date, few police agencies are accredited, although a number have applied to begin the process. Those agencies are now conducting self-evaluations as part of the application process. Although accreditation makes possible the identification of high-quality police departments, it is often undervalued because it carries few incentives. Accreditation is still only "icing on the cake" and does not guarantee a department any rewards beyond the recognition of peers.

EDUCATION

As the concern for quality policing builds, increasing emphasis is being placed on the education of police officers. As early as 1931, the National Commission of Law Observance and Enforcement (the Wickersham Commission) highlighted the importance of a well-educated police force by calling for "educationally sound" officers.[102] In 1967 the President's Commission on Law Enforcement and the Administration of Justice voiced the belief that "(t)he ultimate aim of all police departments should be that all personnel with general enforcement powers have baccalaureate degrees." At the time, the average educational level of police officers in the United States was 12.4 years—slightly beyond a high school degree. In 1973 the National Advisory Commission on Criminal Justice Standards and Goals made the following rather specific recommendation:[103] Every police agency should, no later than 1982, require as a condition of initial employment the completion of at least 4 years of education ... at an accredited college or university."[104]

Recommendations, of course, do not always translate into practice. Today, the average level of educational achievement among law enforcement officers stands at almost 14 years, nearly the equivalent of an associate's degree from a "two-year" or community college.[105] Female officers (with an average level of educational achievement of 14.6 years) tend to be better educated than their male counterparts (who report an average attainment level of 13.6 years). Only 3.3% of male officers hold graduate degrees, while almost one-third (30.2%) of women officers hold such degrees. On the down side, 34.8% of male officers have no college experience, and 24.1% of female officers have none.

A report by the Police Executive Research Forum (PERF) explains the difference between male and female educational achievement by saying that "[w]omen tend to rely on higher education more than men as a springboard for a law enforcement career ... [and] [p]olice departments may utilize higher standards—consciously or unconsciously—for selecting women officers."[106]

The PERF report stresses the need for educated police officers, citing the following benefits which accrue to police agencies from the hiring of educated officers:[107] (1) better written reports, (2) enhanced communications with the public, (3) more effective job performance, (4) fewer citizens' complaints, (5) greater initiative, (6) a wiser use of discretion, (7) a heightened sensitivity to racial and ethnic issues, and (8) fewer disciplinary problems. On the other hand, a greater likelihood that educated officers will leave police work, and their tendency to question orders and request reassignment with relative frequency, are some of the education-induced drawbacks with the report lists.[108]

To meet the growing needs of police officers for college-level training, the International Association of Police Professors (IAPP) was formed in 1963. The IAPP later changed its name to the Academy of Criminal Justice Sciences (ACJS) and widened its focus to include criminal justice education.

A number of agencies now require the completion of at least some college-level work for officers seeking promotion. The San Diego Police Department, for example, requires two years of college work for promotion to the rank of sergeant.[109] In 1988 the Sacramento, California, police department set completion of a four-year college degree as a requirement for promotion to lieutenant, and, in the same year, the New York City Police Department announced a requirement of at least 64 college credits for promotion to supervisory ranks. At the state level, a variety of plans exist for integrating college work into police careers. Minnesota now requires a college degree for new candidates taking the state's Peace Office Standards and Training Board's licensing examination. Successful completion of all POST requirements permits employment as a fully certified law enforcement officer in the state of Minnesota. Beginning in 1991, the state of New York set 60 semester hours of college-level work as a mandated minimum for hiring into

THEORY INTO PRACTICE

THE LAW ENFORCEMENT CODE OF ETHICS

As a Law Enforcement Officer, my fundamental duty is to serve mankind; to safeguard lives and property; to protect the innocent against deception, the weak against oppression or intimidation, and the peaceful against violence or disorder; and to respect the Constitutional rights of all men to liberty, equality and justice.

I will keep my private life unsullied as an example to all; maintain courageous calm in the face of danger, scorn, or ridicule; develop self-restraint; and be constantly mindful of the welfare of others. Honest in thought and deed in both my personal and official life, I will be exemplary in obeying the laws of the land and the regulations of my department. Whatever I see or hear of a confidential nature or that is confided to me in my official capacity will be kept secret unless revelation is necessary in the performance of my duty.

I will never act officiously or permit personal feelings, prejudices, animosities or friendships to influence my decisions. With no compromise for crime and with relentless prosecution of criminals, I will enforce the law courteously and appropriately without fear or favor, malice or ill will, never employing unnecessary force or violence and never accepting gratuities.

I recognize the badge of my office as a symbol of public faith, and I accept it as a public trust to be held so long as I am true to the ethics of the police service. I will constantly strive to achieve these objectives and ideals, dedicating myself before God to my chosen profession … law enforcement.

Source: International Association of Chiefs of Police. Reprinted with Permission.

the New York State Police. Finally, as the boxes on employment found in Chapter 5 show, many federal agencies require college degrees for entry-level positions. Among them are the FBI, DEA, ATF, Secret Service, the U.S. Customs Service, and the Immigration and Naturalization Service.

> Effective police work in the emerging society will depend less on the holster and more on the head.
>
> —*Alvin Toffler*

RECRUITMENT AND SELECTION

Any profession needs informed, dedicated, and competent personnel. When the National Advisory Commission on Criminal Justice Standards and Goals issued its report on the "Police," it bemoaned the fact that "many college students are unaware of the varied, interesting, and challenging assignments and career opportunities that exist within the police service.[110] In the intervening years the efforts made by police departments to correct such misconceptions have had a considerable effect. Today police organizations actively recruit new officers from college campuses, professional organizations, and two-year junior colleges and technical institutes. Education is an important criterion in selecting today's police recruits.[111] Some departments require a minimum number of college credits for entry-level work. A policy of the Dallas, Texas, Police Department requiring a minimum of 45 semester hours of successful college-level study for new recruits was upheld in 1986 by the U.S. Supreme Court in the case of *Davis* v. *Dallas*.[112]

The National Commission report stressed the setting of high standards for police recruits and recommended a strong emphasis on minority recruitment, an elimination of residence requirements for new officers, a decentralized application and testing procedure, and various recruiting incentives. The Commission also suggested that a 4-year college degree should soon become a reasonable expectation for police recruits. A 1988 survey of 699 police departments by the Police Executive Research Forum found that the average level of education among both black and white officers was 14 years of schooling. Hispanic officers averaged 13 years spent in school. The survey also found that 62% of responding agencies had at least one formal policy in support of officers pursuing higher education.[113]

Effective policing, however, may depend more upon personal qualities than it does upon educational attainment. O. W. Wilson once enumerated some of the "desirable personal qualities of patrol officers."[114] They include (1) initiative; (2) the capacity for responsibility; (3) the ability to deal alone with emergencies; (4) the capacity to communicate effectively with persons of diverse social, cultural, and ethnic backgrounds; (5) the ability to learn a variety of tasks quickly; (6) the attitude and ability necessary to adapt to technological changes; (7) the desire to help people in need; (8) an understanding of others; (9) emotional maturity; and (10) sufficient physical strength and endurance.

Standard procedures employed by modern departments in selecting trainees usually include basic skill tests, physical agility measurements, interviews, physical examinations, eye tests, psychological evaluations, and background investigations into the personal character of applicants. After training, successful applicants are typically placed on a period of probation approximately one year in length. The probationary period in police work has been called the "first true job-related test … in the selection procedure,"[115] providing as it does the opportunity for supervisors to gauge the new officer's response to real-life situations.

Ethnic Minorities and Women

In 1967 the National Advisory Commission on Civil Disorders conducted a survey of supervisory personnel in police departments.[116] They found a marked disparity between the number of black and white officers in leadership positions. One of every 26 black police officers had been promoted to the rank of sergeant, while the ratio among whites was 1 in 12. Only 1 of every 114 black officers had become a lieutenant, while among whites the ratio was 1 out of 26. At the level of captain the disparity was even greater—1 out of every 235 black officers had achieved the rank of captain, while 1 of every 53 whites had climbed to that rank.

Since then, the emphasis placed upon minority recruitment by task forces, civil rights groups, courts, and society in general, has done much to rectify the situation. In 1979, for example, one of the first affirmative action disputes involving a police department was settled out of court. The settlement required the San Francisco Police Department to ensure that over the next ten years minorities would receive 50% of all promotions and that 20% of all new officers hired would be women.[117]

Today the situation is changing. Many departments, through dedicated recruitment efforts, have dramatically increased their complement of officers from underrepresented groups. The Metropolitan Detroit Police Department, for example, now has a force that is more than 50% black.

Unfortunately, although ethnic minorities have moved into policing in substantial numbers (see Figure 6–2), females are still substantially underrepresented (see Figure 6–3). A recent study by the Police Foundation[118] found that women accounted for nearly 9% of all officers in municipal departments serving populations of 50,000 or more but that they comprised only 3% of all supervisors in city agencies, and 1% of supervisors in state police agencies. Female officers made up 10.1% of the total number of officers in departments which were functioning under court order to increase their proportion of women officers, while women constituted 8.3% of officers in agencies with voluntary affirmative action programs, and only 6.1% of officers in departments without such programs.

A 1991 report[119] on women police officers in Massachusetts found that female officers (1) are "extremely devoted to their work," (2) "see themselves as women first, and then police officers," and (3) were more satisfied when working in nonuniformed capacities. Two groups of women officers were identified: (1) those who felt themselves to be well integrated into their departments and were confident in their jobs and (2) those who experienced strain and on-the-job isolation. The officers' children were cited as a significant influence on their self-perceptions, and on the way in which they viewed their jobs. The demands which attend child rearing in contemporary society were found to be major factors contributing to the resignation of female officers. The study also found that the longer women officers stayed on the job, the greater stress and frustration they tended to experience—primarily as a consequence of the non-cooperative attitudes of male officers. Some of the female officers interviewed identified networking as a potential solution to the stresses encountered by female officers, but also said that when women get together to solve problems they are seen as "crybabies" rather than professionals. Said one of the women in

FIGURE 6–2 Minorities in law enforcement and as a proportion of U.S. population. *Source:* Adapted from David L. Carter et al., *The State of Police Education* (Washington, D.C.: Police Executive Research Forum, 1989).

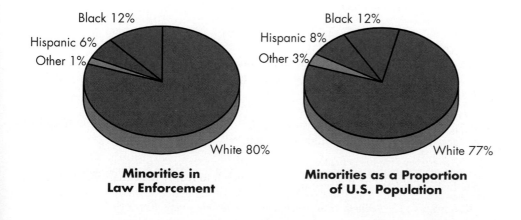

Black 12%
Hispanic 6%
Other 1%
White 80%

**Minorities in
Law Enforcement**

Black 12%
Hispanic 8%
Other 3%
White 77%

**Minorities as a Proportion
of U.S. Population**

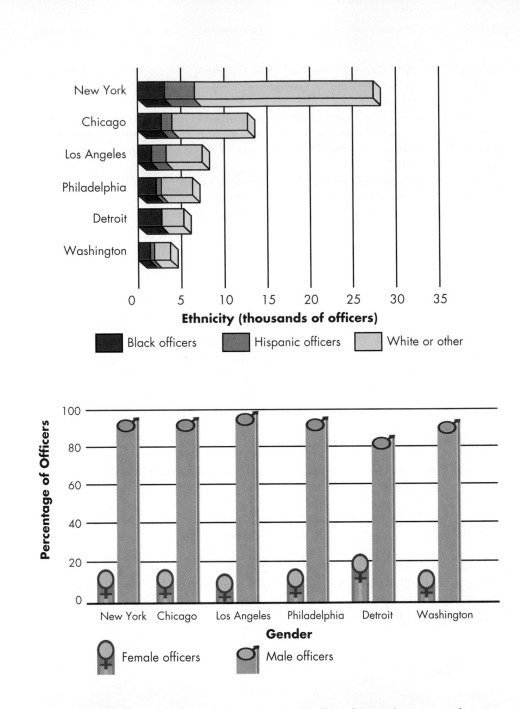

FIGURE 6–3   Municipal police departments: proportion of officers from underrepresented groups. *Source:* Bureau of Justice Statistics, *Sourcebook of Criminal Justice Statistics, 1989* (Washington, D.C.: BJS, 1990).

the study, "[w]e've lost a lot of good women who never should have left the job. If we had helped each other maybe they wouldn't have left."[120]

> When a woman makes a mistake, the men can't wait to jump on the band-wagon, but if a man makes a mistake it is covered up.
>
> —*Police Sgt. C. Lee Bennett, citing interviews with female police officers*

Networking is a concept which is quickly taking root among the nation's women police officers, as attested to by the growth of organizations like the International Association of Women Police, based in New York City. Mentoring, another method for introducing women to police work, has been suggested by some authors.[121] Mentoring would create semiformal relationships between experienced women officers and rookies entering the profession. Through such relationships, problems could be addressed as they arose, and the experienced officer could serve to guide her junior partner through the maze of formal and informal expectations which surround the job of policing.

Other studies, like those already discussed, have found that female officers are often underutilized and that many departments are hesitant to assign women to patrol and other potentially dangerous field activities. As a consequence, some women in police work experience frustrations and a lack of satisfaction with their jobs.[122] Other women are hesitant to consider a police career, and a few departments complain that it is difficult to find significant numbers of well-qualified minority recruits interested in police work. Also, harassment on the job continues to be a reality for some minority officers. For example, in the late 1980s a black FBI agent complained to his superiors and to the Justice Department's Office of Professional Responsibility about death threats, obscene mail, and threats against his family, apparently generated by fellow agents because he is black. An Equal Employment Opportunity Commission decision in the case concluded that the agent had indeed been the victim of a series of discriminatory activities, and the officer filed suit against the FBI alleging violation of his civil rights.[123] In 1993, settlement of a racial discrimination suit brought against the FBI by black agents required the FBI to provide increased training for blacks and placed supervision of the FBI's employment practices in the hands of a federal judge for a period of five years.[124] Only about 5% of the Bureau's agents are black.

Women in uniform have become a common sight throughout our nation's cities and towns. Here a female officer lectures a man who ran a red light. *Photo: Sepp Seitz/Contact Stock.*

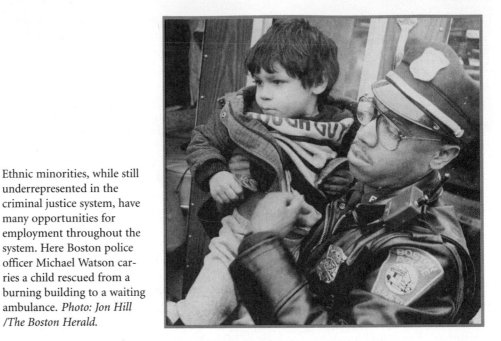

Ethnic minorities, while still underrepresented in the criminal justice system, have many opportunities for employment throughout the system. Here Boston police officer Michael Watson carries a child rescued from a burning building to a waiting ambulance. *Photo: Jon Hill /The Boston Herald.*

Barriers continue to fall. In 1979, for example, San Francisco became the first city in the world to actively recruit homosexuals for its police force. That action resulted in a reduced fear of reporting crimes among many city homosexuals, who for years had been victims of organized assaults by bikers and street gangs. Recently, Attorney General Janet Reno ordered all Justice Department agencies to end hiring discrimination based on sexual orientation.

In a continuing effort to increase the representation of women and ethnic minorities in police work, the Police Foundation recommends (1) involving underrepresented groups in affirmative action and long-term planning programs which are undertaken by police departments, (2) encouraging the development of an open system of promotions whereby women can feel free to apply for promotion, and in which qualified individuals of any race or gender will face equity in the promotion process, and (3) the use of periodic audits to ensure that women officers are not being underutilized by being ineffectively tracked into clerical and support positions.[125]

THE FUTURE OF POLICING

What does the future hold for policing in America? In a recent "Delphi" exercise[126] held at the FBI Academy in Quantico, Virginia, a panel of law enforcement managment experts, scholars, and executives constructed the scenario in Table 6–6 for future developments.

T A B L E   6 - 6

POSSIBLE FUTURE DEVELOPMENTS FOR POLICING IN AMERICA, 1995–2050

Year	Occurrence
1995	Community involvement and self-help (e.g., community-oriented policing) in local policing will become common practice in more than 70% of the nation.
	University and professionally conducted research will have a direct and positive influence on the development of crime reduction strategies.
	Acts of political terrorism in the United States will increase in number more than 50% over the 1984 rate.
1997	State-of-the-art high technology will be routinely used in crime reduction.
1999	Urban unrest and civil disorder (of the 1960–1970s variety) will take place throughout America.
2000	Computer-based instruction will become the standard for training in over 70% of police agencies.
	More than 70% of all "invasion of privacy" lawsuits will successfully demonstrate inadequacies of, and inaccuracies in, police computerized files.
	Crime committed using high technology will become so complex that the police will be unable to do more than take initial reports.
2005	Disparity between the haves and the have-nots will be identified as the major causative factors for traditional crime.
2025	Formal education will become the standard for entry and advancement in more than 70% of police agencies.
	More than 70% of police executives will adopt a nontraditional (proactive/goal-oriented) leadership style.
2035	Private security agencies will assume more than 50% of all law enforcement responsibilities.
2050	Law enforcement will achieve professional status.
	More than 50% of police agencies will have personnel competent to conduct rigorous empirical research.
	Medical (biochemical, genetic, nutritional, and brain) research will discover the means of identifying and treating violence.

Source: William L. Tafoya, "The Future of Law Enforcement? A Chronology of Events," *Criminal Justice International* (May/June 1991), p. 4.

SUMMARY

Police work today is characterized by the opportunity for individual officers to exercise considerable discretion, by a powerful subculture which communicates select values in support of a "police personality," and by the very real possibility of corruption and deviance. Opposed to the illegitimate use of police authority, however, are increased calls for an ethical awareness in police work and continuing growth of the professionalism ideal. Professionalism, with its emphasis on education, training, high ethical values, and personal accountability, should soon lead to greater public recognition of the significance of police work and to higher salaries for career police personnel. Increased salaries and clear public appreciation of the police should do much to decrease corruption and deviance in law enforcement ranks.

DISCUSSION QUESTIONS

1. What are the central features of the police "working personality"? How does the police working personality develop? What programs might be initiated to "shape" the police personality in a more desirable way?

2. Do you think police officers exercise too much discretion in the performance of their duties? Why or why not? If it is desirable to limit discretion, how would you do it?

3. What themes run through the findings of the Knapp Commission and the Wickersham Commission? What innovative steps might police departments take to reduce or eliminate corruption among their officers?

4. Is police work a profession? Why do you think it is, or why do you think it is not? What advantages are there to viewing policing as a profession? How do you think most police officers today see their work—as a "profession" or as just a "job"?

5. Reread the Law Enforcement Code of Ethics found in this chapter. Do you think most police officers make conscious efforts to apply the code in the performance of their duties? How might ethics training in police departments be improved.

ENDNOTES

1. "L.A. Police Chief: Treat People Like Customers," *USA Today*, March 29, 1993, p. 13A.
2. The Police Foundation, *Annual Report 1991* (Washington, D.C.: The Foundation, 1992).
3. James Q. Wilson, *Thinking About Crime* (New York: Basic Books, 1975), p. 99.
4. O. W. Wilson, "Reorganization in Chicago," in *The Police Yearbook* (Washington, D.C.: The International Association of Chiefs of Police, 1962), pp. 56–64.
5. "Bust 180 Degrees Wrong," *USA Today*, December 1, 1992, p. 3A.
6. Ibid.

7. Francis X. Hartmann, "Debating the Evolution of American Policing," *Perspectives on Policing*, No. 5 (Washington, D.C.: National Institute of Justice, November 1988).

8. James Q. Wilson, *Varieties of Police Behavior: The Management of Law and Order in Eight Communities* (Cambridge, MA: Harvard University Press, 1968).

9. Louis A. Radelet, *The Police and the Community* (Encino, CA: Glencoe, 1980).

10. Egon Bittner, "Community Relations," in Alvin W. Cohn and Emilio C. Viano, eds., *Police Community Relations: Images, Roles, Realities* (Philadelphia: J. B. Lippincott, 1976), pp. 77–82.

11. Ibid.

12. Charles Hale, *Police Patrol: Operations and Management* (New York: John Wiley, 1981), p. 112.

13. Paul B. Weston, *Police Organization and Management* (Pacific Palisades, CA: Goodyear, 1976), p. 159.

14. Hale, *Police Patrol.*

15. Mark H. Moore and Robert C. Trojanowicz, "Corporate Strategies for Policing," *Perspectives on Policing,* No. 6 (Washington, D.C.: National Institute of Justice, November 1988).

16. Ibid., p. 6.

17. Herman Goldstein, *Problem-Oriented Policing* (Philadelphia: Temple University Press, 1990), p. 14.

18. *Perspectives on Policing*, p. 8.

19. See Jerome H. Skolnick and David H. Bayley, *Community Policing: Issues and Practices Around the World* (Washington, D.C.: National Institute of Justice, 1988), and Jerome H. Skolnick and David H. Bayley, "Theme and Variation in Community Policing," in Norval Morris and Michael Tonry, eds., *Crime and Justice: An Annual Review of Research,* Vol. 10 (Chicago: University of Chicago Press, 1988), pp. 1–37.

20. Ibid.

21. Ibid.

22. Wesley G. Skogan, *Disorder and Decline: Crime and the Spiral of Decay in American Neighborhoods* (New York: The Free Press, 1990), pp. 90–91.

23. Edwin Meese III, "Community Policing and the Police Officer," *Perspectives on Policing* (Washington, D.C.: National Institute of Justice, January 1993), p. 8.

24. Jerome H. Skolnick and David H. Bayley, *The New Blue Line: Police Innovation in Six American Cities* (New York: The Free Press, 1986).

25. For a good critique of community policing, and of the current state of American policing in general, see Malcolm K. Sparrow, Mark H. Moore, and David M. Kennedy, *Beyond 911: A New Era for Policing* (New York: Basic Books, 1990).

26. Malcolm K. Sparrow, "Implementing Community Policing," *Perspectives on Policing*, No. 9 (Washington, D.C.: National Institute of Justice, 1988).

27. "L.A. Police Chief: Treat People Like Customers," *USA Today*, March 29, 1993, p. 13A.

28. Robert Wasserman and Mark H. Moore, "Values in Policing," *Perspectives in Policing*, No. 8 (Washington, D.C.: National Institute of Justice, November 1988), p. 7.

29. Howard Cohen, "Overstepping Police Authority," *Criminal Justice Ethics* (Summer/Fall 1987), pp. 52–60.

30. Kenneth Culp Davis, *Police Discretion* (St. Paul, MN: West Publishing, 1975).

31. Sykes, "Street Justice," p. 505.

32. Jerome H. Skolnick, *Justice Without Trial: Law Enforcement in a Democratic Society* (New York: John Wiley, 1966).

33. William A. Westley, *Violence and the Police: A Sociological Study of Law, Custom, and Morality* (Cambridge, MA: MIT Press, 1970), and William A. Westley "Violence and the Police," *American Journal of Sociology*, Vol. 49 (1953), pp. 34–41.

34. Arthur Niederhoffer, *Behind the Shield: The Police in Urban Society* (Garden City, NY: Anchor Press, 1967).

35. Thomas Baker and David L. Carter, *Police Deviance* (Cincinnati, OH: Anderson, 1986).

36. See, for example, Michael Brown, *Working the Street: Police Discretion and the Dilemmas of Reform* (New York: Russell Sage Foundation, 1981).

37. Richard Bennett and Theodore Greenstein, "The Police Personality: A Test of the Predispositional Model," *Journal of Police Science and Administration*, Vol 3. (1975), pp. 439–445.

38. James Teevan and Bernard Dolnick, "The Values of the Police: A Reconsideration and Interpretation," *Journal of Police Science and Administration* (1973) pp. 366–369.

39. Lawrence Sherman and Robert Langworthy, "Measuring Homicide by Police Officers," *Journal of Criminal Law and Criminology*, Vol. 4 (1979), pp. 546–560, and Lawrence W. Sherman et al., *Citizens Killed by Big City Police, 1970–1984* (Washington, D.C.: Crime Control Institute, 1986).

40. Joel Samaha, *Criminal Justice* (St. Paul, MN: West, 1988), p. 235.

41. Barker and Carter, *Police Deviance.*

42. *Knapp Commission Report on Police Corruption* (New York: George Braziller, 1973).

43. Ibid.

44. Robert Daley, *Prince of the City: The Story of a Cop Who Knew Too Much* (Boston: Houghton Mifflin, 1978).

45. Mike McAlary, *Buddy Boys: When Good Cops Turn Bad* (New York: G. P. Putnam's Sons, 1987).

46. Ibid.

47. "Ex-Detroit Police Chief Sentenced," *Fayetteville Observer-Times* (North Carolina), August 28, 1992, p. 6A.

48. Ibid., p. 5A.

49. Edwin H. Sutherland and Donald Cressey, *Principles of Criminology*, 8th ed. (Philadelphia: J. B. Lippincott, 1970).

50. See Robert Reiner, "Where Does the Met Go Now?" in *Criminal Justice International*, Vol. 4, no. 2 (March–April 1988), p. 23.

51. James Mills, *The Underground Empire: Where Crime and Governments Embrace* (New York: Dell, 1986), p. 15.

52. Ibid.

53. National Institute of Law Enforcement and Criminal Justice, *Controlling Police Corruption: The Effects of Reform Policies*, Summary Report (Washington, D.C.: U.S. Department of Justice, 1978).

54. See National Institute of Justice, "Employee Drug Testing Policies in Police Departments," National Institute of Justice Research in Brief (Washington, D.C.: U.S. Department of Justice, 1986).

55. Ibid.

56. *Maurice Turner* v. *Fraternal Order of Police*, no. 83–1213, D.C. Court of Appeals, November 13, 1985.

57. *Philip Caruso, President of P.B.A.* v. *Benjamin Ward, Police Commissioner*, New York State Supreme Court, Pat. 37, Index no. 12632–86, 1986.

58. *National Treasury Employees Union* v. *Von Raab*, 44 CRL 3192 (1989).

59. *The New York Times*, February 29, 1988, p. B7.

60. "Suspect Had Wanted to Kill Officer," *The Morning Call*, July 9, 1992, p. A1.

61. Anthony J. Pinizzotto and Edward F. Davis, "Cop Killers and Their Victims," *FBI Law Enforcement Bulletin*, December 1992, p. 10.

62. Federal Bureau of Investigation, *Crime in the United States 1992* (Washington, D.C.: U.S. Government Printing Office, 1993), p. 289.

63. As reported by The Headline News Network, April 26, 1988.

64. "Homosexual Officer Wins AIDS Ruling," *Fayetteville Observer-Times* (North Carolina), June 8, 1992, p. 5A.

65. New York City Police Department pamphlet, "AIDS and Our Workplace" (November 1987).

66. "Collecting and Handling Evidence Infected with Human Disease-Causing Organisms," *FBI Law Enforcement Bulletin* (July 1987).

67. Theodore M. Hammett, "Precautionary Measures and Protective Equipment: Developing a Reasonable Response," National Institute of Justice Bulletin (Washington, D.C.: U.S. Government Printing Office, 1988).

68. *National Institute of Justice Reports*, No. 206 (November/December 1987).

69. "Taking Aim at a Virus: NYPD Tackles AIDS on the Job and in the Ranks," *Law Enforcement News*, March 15, 1988, p. 1.

70. "Stress on the Job," *Newsweek*, April 25, 1988, p. 43.

71. Joseph Victor, "Police Stress: Is Anybody Out There Listening?" *New York Law Enforcement Journal* (June 1986), pp. 19–20.

72. Ibid.

73. Charles R. Swanson, Leonard Territo, and Robert W. Taylor, *Police Administration: Structures, Processes, and Behavior*, 2nd ed. (New York: Macmillan, 1988).

74. *Malley* v. *Briggs*, 475 U.S. 335, 106 S.Ct. 1092 (1986).

75. Ibid., *Malley* at 4246.

76. *Biscoe* v. *Arlington* (1984), 80–0766, *National Law Journal*, May 13, 1985.

77. *Kaplan* v. *Lloyd's Insurance Co.*, 479 So. 2d 961 (La. App. 1985).

78. *City of Canton, Ohio* v. *Harris*, U.S. 109 S.Ct. 1197 (1989).

79. Ibid., at 1204.

80. *Prior* v. *Woods* (1981), *National Law Journal*, November 2, 1981.

81. *Bivens* v. *Six Unknown Federal Agents*, 403 U.S. 388 (1971).

82. *Wyler* v. *U.S.*, 725 F. 2d 157 (2d Cir. 1983).

83. California Government Code, §818.

84. *Hunter* v. *Bryant*, 112 S.Ct. 534 (1991).

85. William U. McCormack, "Supreme Court Cases: 1991–1992 Term," *FBI Law Enforcement Bulletin*, November, 1992, p. 30.

86. For more information on police liability, see Daniel L. Schofield, "Legal Issues of Pursuit Driving," *FBI Law Enforcement Bulletin* (May 1988), pp. 23–29.

87. "Playboy Interview: Daryl Gates," *Playboy*, August 1991, p. 60.

88. Ibid., p. 63.

89. *Tennessee* v. *Garner*, 471 U.S. 1 (1985).

90. Ibid.

91. James Fyfe, *Shots Fired: An Examination of New York City Police Firearms Discharges* (Ann Arbor, MI: University Microfilms, 1978).

92. James Fyfe, "Blind Justice? Police Shootings in Memphis," paper presented at the annual meeting of the Academy of Criminal Justice Sciences, Philadelphia, March 1981.

93. It is estimated that American police shoot at approximately 3,600 people every year. See William Geller, "Deadly Force" study guide Crime File Series (Washington, D.C.: National Institute of Justice, no date).

94. Anne Cohen: "I've Killed That Man Ten Thousand Times," *Police Magazine* (July 1980).

95. For more information, see Joe Auten, "When Police Shoot," *North Carolina Criminal Justice Today*, Vol. 4, no. 4 (Summer 1986), pp. 9–14.

96. David W. Hayeslip and Alan Preszler, "NIJ Initiative on Less-than-Lethal Weapons," *NIJ Research in Brief* (Washington, D.C.: National Institute of Justice, 1993).

97. Ibid.

98. As quoted by Michael Siegfried, "Notes on the Professionalization of Private Security," *The Justice Professional* (Spring 1989).

99. Timothy J. Flanagan and Kathleen Maguire, *Sourcebook of Criminal Justice Statistics—1989* (Washington, D.C.: U.S. Government Printing Office, 1990), p. 16.

100. See Edward A. Farris, "Five Decades of American Policing, 1932–1982: The Path to Professionalism," *The Police Chief* (November 1982), p. 31.

101. Ibid., p. 34.

102. National Commission on Law Observance and Enforcement, *Report on Police* (Washington, D.C.: U.S. Government Printing Office, 1931).

103. National Advisory Commission on Criminal Justice Standards and Goals, *Report on the Police* (Washington, D.C.: U.S. Government Printing Office, 1973).

104. Ibid.

105. David L. Carter, Allen D. Sapp, and Darrel W. Stephens, *The State of Police Education: Policy Direction for the 21st Century* (Washington, D.C.: Police Executive Research Forum 1989).

106. Ibid., p. xiv.

107. Ibid, pp. xxii–xxiii.

108. Ibid, p. xxiii.

109. Carter, Sapp, and Stephens, *The State of Police Education*, p. 84.

110. National Advisory Commission on Criminal Justice Standards and Goals, *Police* (Washington, D.C.: U.S. Government Printing Office, 1973), p. 238.

111. "Dallas PD College Rule Gets Final OK," *Law Enforcement News*, July 7, 1986, pp. 1, 13.

112. *Davis* v. *Dallas*, 1986.

113. David L. Carter and Allen Sapp, *The State of Police Education: Critical Findings* (Washington, D.C.: Police Executive Research Forum, no date).

114. O. W. Wilson and Roy Clinton McLaren, *Police Administration*, 4th ed. (New York: McGraw-Hill, 1977), p. 259.

115. Ibid., p. 270.

116. Report of the National Advisory Commission on Civil Disorders, p. 332.

117. As reported in Charles Swanson and Leonard Territo, *Police Administration: Structures, Processes, and Behavior* (New York: Macmillan, 1983), p. 203, from *Affirmative Action Monthly* (February 1979), p. 22.

118. The Police Foundation, *On the Move: The Status of Women in Policing* (Washington, D.C.: The Foundation, 1990).

119. C. Lee Bennett, *Interviews with Female Police Officers in Western Massachusetts*, paper presented at the annual meeting of the Academy of Criminal Justice Sciences, Nashville, Tennessee, March 1991.

120. Ibid., p. 9.

121. See, for example, Pearl Jacobs, "Suggestions for the Greater Integration of Women into Policing," paper presented at the annual meeting of the Academy of Criminal Justice Sciences, Nashville, TN, March 1991, and Cynthia Fuchs Epstein, *Deceptive Distinctions: Sex, Gender, and the Social Order* (New Haven, CT: Yale University Press, 1988).

122. Carole G. Garrison, Nancy K. Grant, and Kenneth L. J. McCormick, "Utilization of Police Women," unpublished manuscript.

123. "Foot-Dragging Charged in FBI Racism Probe," *Fayetteville Times* (North Carolina), March 27, 1988.

124. "FBI Settles Bias Suit: Judge to Oversee Efforts," *USA Today*, January 27, 1993, p. 1A.

125. The Police Foundation, *On the Move*.

126. William L. Tafoya, "The Future of Law Enforcement? A Chronology of Events," *Criminal Justice International* (May/June 1991), p. 4.

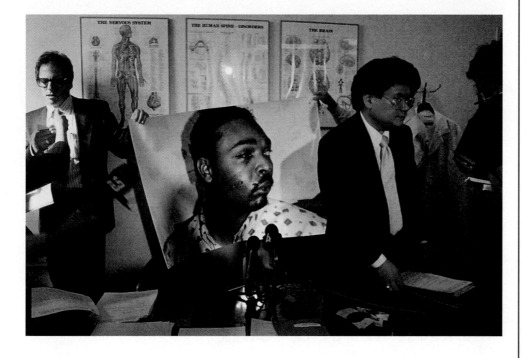

CHAPTER 7

POLICING: LEGAL ASPECTS

"Yeah," the detective mumbled. "Fifteen guys. You might want to think about that. Only two of us."…"On the other hand…". He shook his head. "Sneaking a bunch of cops into a neighborhood like this is going to be like trying to sneak the sun past a rooster."…As he started up the stairs, Angelo reached not for his gun but for his wallet. He took out a Chase Manhattan calendar printed on a supple but firm slip of plastic. He flicked the card at Rand. "I'll open the door with this. You step in and freeze them."

"Jesus Christ, Angelo," the agent almost gasped. "We can't do that. We haven't got a warrant."

"Don't worry about it, kid," Angelo said, drawing up to the second door on the right on the second floor. "It ain't a perfect world."[1]
**—LARRY COLLINS AND DOMINIQUE LAPIERRE
THE FIFTH HORSEMAN**

The right of the people to be secure in their persons, houses, papers, and effects, against unreasonable searches and seizures, shall not be violated, and no warrants shall issue but upon probable cause, supported by oath or affirmation, and particularly describing the place to be searched, and the persons or things to be seized.
—FOURTH AMENDMENT TO THE U.S. CONSTITUTION

KEY WORDS

Bill of Rights	landmark cases	*Miranda* rights
due process	Warren court	Burger court
search and seizure	exclusionary rule	good faith
probable cause	plain view	Rehnquist court

KEY CASES

Weeks v. *U.S.*	*Chimel* v. *California*	*California* v. *Hodari D.*
Mapp v. *Ohio*	*Terry* v. *Ohio*	*Arizona* v. *Fulminante*
Robinson v. *U.S.*	*Brown* v. *Mississippi*	*Minnick* v. *Mississippi*
Carroll v. *U.S.*	*Escobedo* v. *Illinois*	*Illinois* v. *Perkins*
Gideon v. *Wainwright*	*Nix* v. *Williams*	*Alabama* v. *White*
Miranda v. *Arizona*	*Florida* v. *Bostick*	*California* v. *Horton*
Silverthorne Lumber Co. v. *U.S.*	*California* v. *Acevedo*	*Smith* v. *Ohio*
U.S. Dept. of Justice v. *Landano*	*Illinois* v. *Condon*	*Brecht* v. *Abrahamson*

THE ABUSE OF POLICE POWER

In the spring of 1991 Rodney King, an unemployed 25-year-old black man, was stopped by Los Angeles police for an alleged violation of motor vehicle laws. Police said King had been speeding and refused to stop for a pursuing patrol car. Officers claimed to have clocked

The beating of Rodney King by Los Angeles police officers, captured here by a man trying out a new video camera. The incident raised many questions about police integrity, while simultaneously highlighting the power of new technology to uncover police abuses. *Photo: Rob Crandall/Picture Group.*

Police officers under arrest. Following the widely televised police beating of black motorist Rodney King, two of these four Los Angeles police officers were convicted in federal court of denying King his civil rights. Former officers Koon and Powell are now serving 30-month sentences at the federal prison camp in Dublin, California. All had been earlier acquitted in state court. *Photos: AP/Wide World Photos.*

King's 1988 Hyundai at 115 MPH on suburban Los Angeles' Foothill Freeway—even though the car's manufacturer later said the vehicle was not capable of speeds over 100 MPH and recordings of police radio communications surrounding the incident never mentioned excessive speed.

Eventually King did stop, but then officers of the Los Angeles Police Department attacked him—shocking him twice with electronic stun guns and striking him with nightsticks and fists. Kicked in the stomach, face, and back, he was left with 11 skull fractures, missing teeth, a crushed cheekbone, and a broken ankle. A witness told reporters she heard King begging officers to stop the beating, but that they "were all laughing, like they just had a party."[2] King eventually underwent surgery for brain injuries.

Twenty-five police officers—21 from the LAPD, 2 California Highway Patrol officers, and 2 school district officers—were involved in the incident. Four of them, who were later indicted, beat King, as the other 21 watched. Los Angeles County District Attorney Ira Reiner called the behavior of the officers who watched, "irresponsible and offensive," but not criminal.[3]

There are two important differences between this incident and the other crime stories related in this textbook: (1) this time the criminals wore police uniforms, and (2) the entire incident was captured on videotape by an amateur photographer from a nearby balcony, who was trying out his new night-sensitive video camera. The 2-minute videotape was repeatedly broadcast over national television and picked up by hundreds of local TV stations. The furor that erupted over the tape led to the ouster of LAPD Chief Daryl Gates and eventually initiated a Justice Department review of law enforcement practices across the country.[4] The immediate goal of the review, announced by then–U.S. Attorney General Richard Thornburg, was "to determine whether there is a pattern of abuse to a high degree in any particular region or police department."[5] Some defended the police, citing the "war zone" mentality of today's inner-city crime fighters as fostering a violent mind-set. Officers involved in the beating claimed that King, at 6 feet 3 inches and 225 pounds, appeared strung out on PCP and that he and his two companions made officers feel threatened.[6] In 1992 a jury found the police defendants not guilty—a verdict that resulted in days of rioting across Los Angeles. A year later, however, in the spring of 1993 two of the officers, Sergeant Stacey Koon and Officer Laurence Powell, were found guilty by a jury in federal court of denying King his constitutional right "not to be deprived of liberty without due process of law, including the right to be…free from the intentional use of unreasonable force."[7] Later that year both were sentenced to 2-1/2 years in prison, far less than might have been expected under federal sentencing guidelines. Officers Theodore Briseno and Timothy Wind were found not guilty of the same charge.

In 1994 King rejected the city's offer of $1 million, and filed a civil suit seeking $9.5 million in damages. Although King himself may not have been a model citizen (he was on parole at the time of the beating, after having served time for robbery, came under investigation for another robbery after the beating, and was arrested again three months after his release from the hospital—for allegedly picking up a male prostitute dressed as a woman and for trying to run over police who confronted him[8]), investigative reporters began to highlight a history of police abuse in Los Angeles. The month before the videotaped beating took place, Baseball Hall of Famer Joe Morgan won $540,000 in damages against the city of Los Angeles for mistreatment at the hands of the police who mistook him for a drug runner,[9] and the Southern California branch of the American Civil Liberties Union reported receiving 55 complaints each week about police brutality from black and Hispanic citizens.

A CHANGING CLIMATE

The Constitution of the United States is designed—especially in the Bill of Rights—to protect citizens against abuses of police power. Long after it occurred, the King incident served as a rallying point for individual rights activists concerned with ensuring that citizens would remain protected from such abuses in an increasingly conservative society. However, the legal environment surrounding the police in modern America is much more complex than it was just 30 years ago. In the interim the U.S. Supreme Court, under the direction of Chief Justice Earl Warren, forcefully guaranteed individual rights in the face of criminal prosecution. Most Supreme Court decisions of the past three decades in the area of criminal justice derive from the first ten amendments to the U.S. Constitution—otherwise known as the Bill of Rights. Warren court rulings bound the police to strict procedural requirements in the areas of investigation, arrest, and interrogation. Later rulings scrutinized trial court procedure and enforced humanitarian standards in sentencing and punishment. The Fourteenth Amendment provided a basis for requiring that state criminal justice agencies adhere to the interpretations of the Constitution rendered by the U.S. Supreme Court. The apex of the individual rights emphasis in Supreme Court decisions was reached in the 1965 case of *Miranda* v. *Arizona*, which established the famous requirement of a police "rights advisement" of suspects. In wielding its brand of idealism, the Warren court recognized the fact that a few guilty people would go free in order that the rights of the majority of Americans, as it understood them, would be protected.

Court decisions of the last few years, however, the product of a new and still emerging Court philosophy, have begun what some call a "reversal" of previous advances in the area of individual rights. By creating exceptions to the exclusionary rule such as the "plain view doctrine" and "stop and frisk authority" and in allowing for the "emergency questioning" of suspects prior to rights advisement, the Court has recognized the realities attending day-to-day police work and the need to ensure public safety. This practical approach to justice, characteristic of the Reagan–Bush political era, is all the more interesting for the fact that it must struggle within the confines of earlier Court decisions. Constitutional amendments of special significance to the justice system are summarized in Table 7–1.

CONSTRAINTS ON POLICE ACTION

The Constitution of the United States provides for a system of checks and balances. By this we mean that one branch of government is always held accountable to other branches. The system is designed to ensure that no one individual or agency can become powerful enough to usurp the rights and freedoms guaranteed under the Constitution. Without accountability, it is possible to imagine a police state in which the power of law enforcement is absolute and related to political considerations and personal vendettas more than to any objective considerations of guilt or innocence.

Under our system of government, courts become the arena for dispute resolution, not just between individuals, but between citizens and the agencies of government itself. After handling by the justice system, people who feel they have not received the respect and dignity due them under law can appeal to the courts for redress. Such appeals are usually based upon procedural issues and are independent of more narrow considerations of guilt or innocence.

TABLE 7 - 1

CONSTITUTIONAL AMENDMENTS OF SPECIAL SIGNIFICANCE TO THE AMERICAN SYSTEM OF JUSTICE, FROM THE BILL OF RIGHTS

This Right Is Guaranteed	*By This Amendment*
The Right Against Unreasonable Searches and Seizures	Fourth
No Arrest Without Probable Cause	Fourth
The Right Against Self-incrimination	Fifth
The Right Against "Double Jeopardy"	Fifth
The Right to Due Process of Law	Fifth, Fourteenth
The Right to a Speedy Trial	Sixth
The Right to a Jury Trial	Sixth
The Right to Know the Charges	Sixth
The Right to Cross-examine Witnesses	Sixth
The Right to a Lawyer	Sixth
The Right to Compel Witnesses on One's Behalf	Sixth
The Right to Reasonable Bail	Eighth
The Right Against Excessive Fines	Eighth
The Right Against Cruel and Unusual Punishments	Eighth
The Applicability of Constitutional Rights to All Citizens, Regardless of State Law or Procedure (not part of the Bill of Rights)	Fourteenth

The legal environment surrounding the police acts to help insure proper official conduct. In a traffic stop such as this, inappropriate behavior on the part of the officer can later become the basis for civil or criminal action against the officer and the police department. *Courtesy of the New York City Police Department.*

The cases discussed in this chapter are famous for having clarified constitutional guarantees related to individual liberties within the criminal justice arena. They involve issues which have come to be called "rights" by most of us. It is common to hear arrestees today say: "You can't do that! I know my rights!" Rights, because they are embodied in procedure, provide the "rules of the game," as far as agencies of justice are concerned. Rights violations have often become the basis for the dismissal of charges, acquittal of defendants, or the release on appeal of convicted offenders.

THE DUE PROCESS ENVIRONMENT

The police environment is infused with due process requirements. Most pertain to three major areas of activity: (1) evidence and investigation (often called "search and seizure"), (2) arrest, and (3) interrogation. Each of these areas has been addressed by a plethora of landmark U.S. Supreme Court decisions. Landmark cases are recognizable by the fact that they produce substantial changes in both the understanding of the requirements of due process and in the practical day-to-day operations of the justice system.

Another way to think of landmark decisions is that they help significantly in clarifying the "rules of the game"—the procedural guidelines by which the police and the rest of the justice system must abide.

The three areas we will discuss have been well defined by decades of court precedent. Keep in mind, however, that judicial interpretations of the constitutional requirement of due process are constantly evolving. As new decisions are rendered, and as the composition of the Court itself changes, additional refinements will occur.

SEARCH AND SEIZURE

The U.S. Constitution declares that people must be secure in their homes and in their persons against unreasonable searches and seizures. This right is asserted by the Fourth Amendment, which reads: "The right of the people to be secure in their persons, houses, papers, and effects, against unreasonable searches and seizures shall not be violated, and no warrants shall issue but upon probable cause, supported by oath or affirmation, and particularly describing the place to be searched, and the persons or things to be seized." This amendment, a part of the Bill of Rights, was adopted by Congress and became effective on December 15, 1791.

The language of the Fourth Amendment is familiar to all of us. "Warrants," "probable cause," and other phrases from the amendment are frequently cited in editorials, TV news shows, and daily conversation. It is the interpretation of these phrases over time by the U.S. Supreme Court, however, which has given them the impact they have on the justice system today.

Illegally Seized Evidence Evidence seized in opposition to the principles of due process as described by the Bill of Rights. Most illegally seized evidence is the result of police searches conducted without a proper warrant or of improperly conducted interrogations.

THE WARREN COURT

Prior to the decade of the 1960s, the U.S. Supreme Court intruded only infrequently upon the overall operation of the criminal justice system. As some authors have observed, however, the 1960s provided a time of youthful idealism, and "without the distraction of a depression or world war, individual liberties were examined at all levels of society."[10]

The Bill of Rights was given lip service in proceedings around the country, but in practice, law enforcement, especially on the state and local level, revolved around tried and true methods of search, arrest, and interrogation, which left little room for the practical recognition of individual rights.

The Warren court, led by Chief Justice Earl Warren, an Eisenhower nominee, permanently changed the day-to-day practice of American policing. The Court, in *Mapp* v. *Ohio* (1961),[11] quickly let it be known that past and future Supreme Court decisions were to be binding upon state law enforcement agents and state courts. Beginning with the now famous *Mapp* case, the Court set out to chart a course which would guarantee nationwide recognition of individual rights, as it understood them, by agencies at all levels of the justice system.

The Exclusionary Rule

The first landmark case in the area of search and seizure was that of *Weeks* v. *U.S.* (1914).[12] Freemont Weeks was suspected of using the U.S. mail to sell lottery tickets, a federal crime. Weeks was arrested and federal agents went to his home to conduct a search. They had no search warrant; at the time warrants were not routinely used by investigators. They confiscated many incriminating items of evidence, as well as personal possessions of the defendant, including clothes, papers, books, and even candy.

Prior to the trial, Weeks' attorney asked that the personal items be returned, claiming that they had been illegally seized. A judge agreed and ordered the materials returned. On the basis of the evidence which was retained, however, Weeks was convicted in federal court and sentenced to prison. His appeal eventually reached the Supreme Court. There his lawyer reasoned that if some of his client's belongings had been illegally seized, then the remainder of them were also taken improperly. The Supreme Court agreed, and overturned Weeks' earlier conviction.

Exclusionary Rule The understanding, operative in contemporary American criminal justice as a result of Supreme Court precedent, that incriminating information must be seized according to Constitutional specifications of due process, or it will not be allowable as evidence in criminal trials.

The *Weeks* case forms the basis of what is now called the **exclusionary rule**. The exclusionary rule means that evidence illegally seized by the police cannot be used in a trial. Contrary to much popular belief, Freemont Weeks could have been retried on the original charges following the Supreme Court decision in his case. He would not have faced double jeopardy because he was in fact not *finally convicted* on the earlier charges. His conviction was nullified on appeal, resulting in neither a conviction nor an acquittal. Double jeopardy becomes an issue only when a defendant faces retrial on the same charges following acquittal at his or her original trial or when the defendant is retried after having been convicted.

It is important to recognize that the decision of the Supreme Court in the *Weeks* case was binding, at the time, only upon federal officers, because it was federal agents who were involved in the illegal seizure.

Problems with Precedent

The *Weeks* case demonstrates the power of the Supreme Court in *enforcing* what we have called the "rules of the game." It also lays bare the much more significant role of rule creation by the Court. Until the *Weeks* case was decided, federal law enforcement officers had little reason to think they were acting in violation of due process. Common practice had not required that they obtain a warrant before conducting searches. The rule which resulted from *Weeks* was new, and it would forever alter the enforcement activities of federal officers. Yet the *Weeks* case was also retroactive, in the sense that it was applied to Weeks himself.

There is a problem in the way in which our system generates and applies principles of due process which may be obvious from our discussion of the *Weeks* case. The problem is that the present appeals system, focusing as it does upon the "rules of the game," presents a ready-made channel for the guilty to go free. There can be little doubt but that Freemont Weeks had violated federal law. A jury had convicted him. Yet he escaped punishment because of the illegal behavior of the police—behavior which, until the Court ruled, had not been regarded as anything but legitimate.

> [The police] are not perfect; we don't sign them up on some far-off planet and bring them into police service. They are products of society, and let me tell you, the human product today often is pretty weak.
>
> —*Former LAPD Chief Daryl Gates*

Even if the police knowingly violate the principles of due process, which they sometimes do, our sense of justice is compromised when the guilty go free. Famed Supreme Court Justice Benjamin Cardozo (1870–1938) once complained, "The criminal is to go free because the constable has blundered."

Students of criminal justice have long considered three possible solutions to this problem. The first solution suggests that rules of due process, especially when newly articulated by the courts, should be applied only to future cases, but not to the initial case in which they are stated. In other words, the justices in the *Weeks* case, for example, might have said, "We are creating the 'exclusionary rule,' based upon our realization in this case. Law enforcement officers are obligated to use it as a guide in all future searches. However, insofar as the guilt of Mr. Weeks was decided by a jury under rules of evidence existing at the time, we will let that decision stand."

A second solution would punish police officers or other actors in the criminal justice system who act illegally, but would not allow the guilty defendant to escape punishment. This solution would be useful in applying established precedent where officers and officials had the benefit of clearly articulated rules and should have known better. Under this arrangement, any officer today who intentionally violates due process guarantees might be suspended, reduced in rank, lose pay, or be fired. Some authors have suggested that "decertification" might serve as "an alternative to traditional remedies for police misconduct."[13] Departments which employed the decertification process would punish violators by removing their certification as police officers. Because officers in every state except Hawaii must meet the certification requirements of state boards (usually called Training and Standards Commissions or Peace Officer Standards and Training Boards) in order to hold employment, some authors[14] argue that decertification would have a much more personal (and therefore more effective) impact on individual officers than the exclusionary rule ever could.

A third possibility would allow for theoretical questions involving issues of due process to be addressed by the Supreme Court. Concerned supervisors and officials could put questions to the Court, inquiring as to what the Court would rule "if...." As things now work, the Court can only address real cases and does so on a writ of *certiorari*, in which the Court orders the record of a lower court case to be prepared for review.

The obvious difficulty with these solutions, however, is that they would substantially reduce the potential benefits available to defendants through the appeals process and, hence, would effectively eliminate the process itself.

Writ of *Certiorari* An order, by an appellate court, specifying whether or not that court will review the judgment of a lower court.

The Poisoned Tree Doctrine

In 1926 Frederick Silverthorne and his sons operated a lumber company and were accused of avoiding payment of federal taxes. When asked to turn over the company's books to federal investigators, the Silverthornes refused, citing their privilege against self-incrimination.

Shortly thereafter, federal agents, without a search warrant, descended on the lumber company and seized the wanted books. The Silverthornes' lawyer appeared in court and asked that the materials be returned, citing the need for a search warrant as had been established in the *Weeks* case. The prosecutor agreed to defense requests, and the books were returned to the Silverthornes.

The Silverthornes came to trial thinking they would be acquitted because the evidence against them was no longer in the hands of prosecutors. In a surprise move, however, the prosecution introduced photocopies of incriminating evidence which they had made from the returned books. The Silverthornes were convicted in federal court. Their appeal eventually reached the Supreme Court of the United States. The Court ruled that just as illegally seized evidence cannot be used in a trial, neither can evidence be used which *derives* from an illegal seizure.[15] The conviction of the Silverthornes was overturned, and they were set free.

The *Silverthorne* case articulated a new principle of due process which we today call the **fruit of the poisoned tree doctrine**. This doctrine is potentially far reaching. Complex cases developed after years of police investigative effort may be ruined if defense attorneys are able to demonstrate that the prosecution's case, no matter how complex, was originally based upon a search or seizure which violated due process. It such cases, it is likely that all evidence will be declared "tainted" and become useless.

Fruit of the Poisoned Tree Doctrine A legal principle which excludes from introduction at trial any evidence eventually developed as a result of an originally illegal search or seizure.

The Exclusionary Rule and the States

While the exclusionary rule became an overriding consideration in federal law enforcement from the time that it was first defined by the Supreme Court, it was not until 1961 that it became applicable to criminal prosecutions at the state level.[16] In that year, the case of Dolree Mapp was reviewed by the Supreme Court, and her conviction on charges of possessing obscene material was overturned.

Mapp was suspected of harboring a fugitive wanted in a bombing. When officers arrived at her house she refused to admit them. Eventually, they forced their way in. During the search which ensued, pornographic materials including photographs were uncovered. Mapp was arrested, and eventually convicted, under an Ohio law which made possession of such materials illegal.

Prior decisions by the U.S. Supreme Court, including *Wolf* v. *Colorado*,[17] had led officers to expect that the exclusionary rule did not apply to agents of state and local law enforcement. The precedent established in *Mapp* v. *Ohio*, however, firmly applied the principles developed in *Weeks* and *Silverthorne* to trials in state courts.

The case of *Chimel* v. *California* (1969)[18] involved both arrest and search activities by local law enforcement officers. Ted Chimel was convicted of the burglary of a coin shop, based upon evidence gathered at the scene of his arrest—his home. Officers, armed with a warrant, arrested Chimel at his residence and proceeded with a search of his entire three-bedroom house, including the attic, a small workshop, and the garage. The justification later provided for the search was that it was conducted incidental to arrest and that the officers involved believed that such a search, conducted for their own protection, was lawful.

A California police officers spot checks a seized substance suspected of being cocaine. The exclusionary rule means that illegally gathered evidence cannot be used later in court. *Photo: Mark Richards.*

Coins taken from the burglarized coin shop were found at various places in Chimel's residence, including the garage, and provided the evidence used against him.

Chimel's appeal eventually reached the U.S. Supreme Court, which ruled that the search conducted by officers, without a warrant, and incidental to arrest, became invalid when it went beyond the person arrested and the area subject to that person's "immediate control." The thrust of the Court's decision was that searches during arrest can be made to protect the arresting officers, but that, without a search warrant, their scope must be strongly circumscribed. Legal implications of *Chimel* v. *California* are summarized in Table 7–2.

The decision in the case of Ted Chimel followed earlier reasoning by the Court in the case of *U.S.* v. *Rabinowitz* (1950).[19] Rabinowitz, a stamp collector, had been arrested and charged by federal agents with selling altered postage stamps in order to defraud other collectors. Employing a valid arrest warrant, officers arrested Rabinowitz at his place of employment, then proceeded to search his desk, file cabinets, and safe. They did not have a search warrant, but his office was small—only one room—and the officers conducted the search with a specific object in mind, the illegal stamps. Eventually, 573 altered postage stamps were seized in the search, and Rabinowitz was convicted in federal court of charges related to selling altered stamps.

Rabinowitz's appeal to the U.S. Supreme Court, based upon the claim that the warrantless search of his business was illegal, was denied. The Court ruled that the Fourth Amendment provides protection against *unreasonable* searches, but that the search, in this case, followed legally from the arrest of the suspect. In the language used by the Court, "It is not disputed that there may be reasonable searches, incident to arrest, without a search warrant. Upon acceptance of this established rule that some authority to search follows from lawfully taking the person into custody, it becomes apparent that such searches turn upon the reasonableness under all the circumstances and not upon the practicability of procuring a search warrant, for the warrant is not required."

TABLE 7 - 2

IMPLICATIONS OF *CHIMEL* v. *CALIFORNIA*

What Arresting Officers May Search
- The defendant
- The physical area within easy reach of the defendant

Valid Reasons for Conducting a Search
- To protect the arresting officers
- To prevent evidence from being destroyed
- To keep the defendant from escaping

When a Search Becomes Illegal
- When it goes beyond the defendant and the area within the defendant's immediate control
- When it is conducted for other than a valid reason

Since the early days of the exclusionary rule, other court decisions have highlighted the fact that "the Fourth Amendment protects people, not places."[20] In other words, although the commonly heard claim that "a person's home is his or her castle" has a great deal of validity within the context of constitutional law, persons can have a reasonable expectation to privacy in "homes" of many descriptions. Apartments, duplex dwellings, motel rooms—even the cardboard boxes or makeshift tents of the "homeless"—can all become protected places under the Fourth Amendment. In *Minnesota* v. *Olson*[21] (1990), the U.S. Supreme Court extended the protection against warrantless searches to overnight guests residing in the home of another. The capacity to claim the protection of the Fourth Amendment, said the Court, depends upon whether the *person* who makes that claim has a legitimate expectation of privacy in the place searched.

THE BURGER AND REHNQUIST COURTS

The swing toward conservatism which our country experienced during the late 1970s and the 1980s gave rise to the "yuppie generation," designer jeans, and a renewed concern with protecting the financial and other interests of the well-to-do. The Reagan years and the popularity of a president in whom many saw the embodiment of "old-fashioned" values reflected the tenor of a nation seeking a return to simpler times.

The U.S. Supreme Court mirrored the conservative decade of the 1980s by distancing itself from certain earlier decisions of the Warren court. The underlying theme of the new Court, the Burger court, was its apparent adherence to the principle that criminal defendants need to bear the bulk of the responsibility in showing that the police went beyond the law in the performance of their duties.

Good Faith Exceptions to the Exclusionary Rule

The Burger court began what some have called a "chipping away" at the strict application of the exclusionary rule originally set forth in the *Weeks* and *Silverthorne* cases. In the case of *Illinois* v. *Gates* (1983),[22] the Court was asked to modify the exclusionary rule to permit the use of evidence in court which had been seized in "reasonable good faith" by officers, even though the search was later ruled illegal. The Court, however, chose not to address the issue at that time.

Good Faith A possible legal basis for an exception to the exclusionary rule. Law enforcement officers who conduct a search, or seize evidence, on the basis of good faith (that is, where they believe they are operating according to the dictates of the law) and who later discover that a mistake was made (perhaps in the format of the application for a search warrant) may still use, in court, evidence seized as the result of such activities.

Our police officers are high school graduates; they are not lawyers; they are not judges.

—*U.S. Representative Chuck Douglas (R, N.H.)*

The 1984 case of *U.S. v. Leon*[23] marked the first time the Court recognized what has now come to be called the good faith exception to the exclusionary rule. The *Leon* case involved the Burbank, California, Police Department and its investigation of a drug trafficking suspect. The suspect, Leon, was placed under surveillance following a tip from a confidential informant. Investigators applied for a search warrant based upon information gleaned through the surveillance. The affidavit in support of the warrant was reviewed by numerous deputy district attorneys, and a warrant was issued by a state judge. A search of Leon's three residences yielded a large amount of drugs and other evidence. A later ruling, in a federal district court, resulted in the suppression of the evidence gathered, on the basis that the original affidavit had not been adequate to establish probable cause.

The government petitioned the U.S. Supreme Court to consider whether evidence gathered by officers acting in good faith as to the validity of a warrant, should fairly be excluded at trial. The impending modification of the exclusionary rule was intoned in the first sentence of that court's written decision: "This case presents the question whether the Fourth Amendment exclusionary rule should be modified so as not to bar the use in the prosecution's case-in-chief of evidence obtained by officers acting in reasonable reliance on a search warrant issued by a detached and neutral magistrate but ultimately found to be unsupported by probable cause." The Court continued: "when law enforcement officers have acted in objective good faith or their transgressions have been minor, the magnitude of the benefit conferred on such guilty defendants offends basic concepts of the criminal justice system." The Court found for the government and reinstated the conviction of Leon.

In the same year the Supreme Court case of *Massachusetts v. Sheppard*[24] (1984) further reinforced the concept of "good faith." In the *Sheppard* case officers executed a search warrant which failed to describe accurately the property to be seized. Although they were aware of the error, they had been assured by a magistrate that the warrant was valid. After the seizure was complete and a conviction had been obtained, the Massachusetts Supreme Judicial Court reversed the finding of the trial court. Upon appeal the U.S. Supreme Court reiterated the good faith exception and let the original conviction stand.

Some people have cited the cases of *Leon* and *Sheppard* as beginning an erosion of personal rights guaranteed under the Constitution, and in particular as a reversal of U.S. Supreme Court philosophy in the face of growing conservative tendencies.

There is mounting evidence of such a tendency in the Court. A series of recent decisions appears to continue the trend begun in *Leon* and *Sheppard*. In the 1987 case of *Illinois v. Krull*,[25] for example, the Court found that the good faith exception applied to a warrantless search supported by state law even where the statute was later found to violate the Fourth Amendment.

Another 1987 Supreme Court case, *Maryland v. Garrison*,[26] supported the use of evidence obtained with a search warrant which was inaccurate in its specifics. Officers had procured a warrant to search an apartment believing it was the only one on a third floor. After searching the entire floor, they discovered that it housed more than one apartment. Evidence acquired in the search was held to be admissible based upon the reasonable mistake of the officers.

In the 1990 case of *Illinois v. Rodriguez*,[27] the Supreme Court further diminished the scope of the exclusionary rule. In *Rodriguez*, a badly beaten woman named Gail Fischer complained to police that she had been assaulted in a Chicago apartment. Fischer led police to the apartment—which she indicated she shared with the defendant—produced a key, and opened the door to the dwelling. Inside, investigators found the defendant, Edward Rodriguez, asleep on a bed, with drug paraphernalia and cocaine spread around him. Rodriguez was arrested and charged with assault and possession of a controlled substance.

Upon appeal, Rodriguez demonstrated that Fischer had not lived with him for at least a month—and argued that she could no longer be said to have legal control over the apartment. Hence, the defense claimed, Fischer had no authority to provide investigators with access to the dwelling. According to arguments made by the defense, the evidence, which had been obtained without a warrant, had not been properly seized. The Supreme Court disagreed, ruling that "even if Fischer did not possess common authority over the premises, there was no Fourth Amendment violation if the police *reasonably believed* at the time of their entry that Fischer possessed the authority to consent."

Legal scholars have suggested that the exclusionary rule may undergo even further modification in the near future. Erickson, for example, points to the fact that "the Court's majority is clearly committed to the idea that the exclusionary rule is not directly part of the Fourth Amendment (and Fourteenth Amendment due process), but instead is an evidentiary device instituted by the Court to effectuate it."[28] In other words, if the Court should be persuaded that the rule is no longer effective, or that some other strategy could better achieve the aim of protecting individual rights, the rule could be abandoned.

The Plain View Doctrine

Plain View A legal term describing the ready visibility of objects which might be seized as evidence during a search by police in the absence of a search warrant specifying the seizure of those objects. In order for evidence in plain view to be lawfully seized, officers must have a legal right to be in the viewing area and must have cause to believe that the evidence is somehow associated with criminal activity.

Police officers have the opportunity to begin investigations or confiscate evidence, without the need for a warrant, based upon what they find in plain view and open to public inspection. The plain view doctrine was first stated in the Supreme Court case of *Harris v. U.S.*,[29] in which a police officer inventorying an impounded vehicle discovered evidence of a robbery. In the *Harris* case the Court ruled that "objects falling in the plain view of an officer who has a right to be in the position to have that view are subject to seizure and may be introduced in evidence."[30]

The plain view doctrine applies only to sightings by the police under legal circumstances—that is, in places where the police have a legitimate right to be, and typically only if the sighting was coincidental. Similarly, the incriminating nature of the evidence seized must have been "immediately apparent" to the officers making the seizure.[31] If officers conspired to avoid the necessity for a search warrant by helping to create a plain view situation through surveillance, duplicity, or other means, the doctrine likely would not apply.

Common situations in which the plain view doctrine is applicable include emergencies such as crimes in progress, fires, and accidents. A police officer responding to a call for assistance, for example, might enter a residence intending to provide aid to an injured person and find drugs or other contraband in plain view. If so, he or she would be within his or her legitimate authority to confiscate the materials and effect an arrest if the owner of the substance could be identified.

The plain view doctrine, however, has recently been restricted by federal court decisions. In the 1982 cases of *U.S.* v. *Irizarry*[32] the First Circuit Court of Appeals held that officers could not move objects to gain a view of evidence otherwise hidden from view. Agents had arrested a number of men in a motel room in Isla Verde, Puerto Rico. A valid arrest warrant formed the legal basis for the arrest, and some quantities of plainly visible drugs were seized from the room. An agent, looking through a window into the room prior to the arrest, had seen one of the defendants with a gun. After the arrest was complete, and no gun had been found on the suspects, another officer noticed a bathroom ceiling panel out of place. The logical conclusion was that a weapon had been secreted there. Upon inspection, a substantial quantity of cocaine and various firearms were found hidden in the ceiling. The Court, however, refused to allow these weapons and drugs to be used as evidence because, it said, "the items of evidence found above the ceiling panel were not plainly visible to the agents standing in the room."[33]

In the Supreme Court case of *Arizona* v. *Hicks*[34] (1987), the requirement that evidence be in plain view, without the need for officers to move or dislodge evidence, was reiterated. In the *Hicks* case, officers responded to a shooting in an apartment. A bullet had been fired in a second floor apartment and had gone through the floor, injuring a man in the apartment below.

The quarters of James Hicks were found to be in considerable disarray when entered by investigating officers. As officers looked for the person who might have fired the weapon, they discovered and confiscated a number of guns and a stocking mask such as might be used in robberies. In one corner, however, officers noticed two expensive stereo sets. One of the officers, suspecting that the sets were stolen, went over to the equipment and was able to read the serial numbers of one of the components from where it rested. Some of the serial numbers, however, were not clearly visible, and the investigating officer moved some of the components in order to read the numbers. When he called the numbers into headquarters he was told that the equipment indeed had been stolen. The stereo components were seized and James Hicks was arrested. Hicks was eventually convicted on a charge of armed robbery, based upon the evidence seized.

Upon appeal, the *Hicks* case reached the U.S. Supreme Court, which ruled that the officer's behavior had become illegal when he moved the stereo equipment to record serial numbers. The Court held that persons have a "reasonable expectation to privacy,"[35] which means that officers, lacking a search warrant, even when invited into a residence, must act more like guests than inquisitors.

Most evidence seized under the plain view doctrine is discovered "inadvertently"— that is, by accident.[36] However, in 1990, the U.S. Supreme Court, in the case of *Horton* v. *California*, ruled that "even though inadvertence *is* a characteristic of most legitimate 'plain view' seizures, it *is not* a necessary condition."[37] In the *Horton* case, a warrant was issued authorizing the search of a defendant's home for stolen jewelry. The affidavit, completed by the officer who requested the warrant, alluded to an Uzi submachine gun and a stun gun—weapons purportedly used in the jewel robbery. It did not request that those weapons be listed on the search warrant. Officers searched the defendant's home, but did not find the stolen jewelry. They did, however, seize a number of weapons—among them the Uzi, two stun guns, and a .38-caliber revolver. Horton was convicted of robbery in a trial where the seized weapons were introduced into evidence. He appealed his conviction, claiming that officers had reason to believe that the weapons were in his home at the time of the search, and were therefore not seized inadvertently. His appeal was rejected by the Court.

As a result of the *Horton* case, "inadvertence" is no longer considered a condition necessary to ensure the legitimacy of a seizure which results when evidence other than that listed in a search warrant is discovered.

Emergency Searches

Certain emergencies may justify a police officer in searching a premises, even without a warrant. Recent decisions by U.S. Appeals Courts have resulted in such activities being termed exigent circumstances searches. According to the Legal Counsel Division of the FBI, there are three threats which "provide justification for emergency warrantless action."[38] They are clear dangers: (1) to life, (2) of escape, and (3) of the removal or destruction of evidence. Any one of these situations may create an exception to the Fourth Amendment's requirement of a search warrant. Where emergencies necessitate a quick search of premises, however, it will be the responsibility of law enforcement

Emergency Searches
Those searches conducted by the police without a warrant, which are justified on the basis of some immediate and overriding need—such as public safety, the likely escape of a dangerous suspect, or the removal or destruction of evidence.

officers to demonstrate that a dire situation did exist which justified their actions. Failure to do so successfully in court, will, of course, taint any seized evidence and make it unusable.

The need for emergency searches was first recognized by the U.S. Supreme Court in 1967 in the case of *Warden* v. *Hayden*.[39] There, the Court approved the search of a residence which was conducted without a warrant, but which followed reports that an armed robber had fled into the building. In *Mincey* v. *Arizona* (1978),[40] the Supreme Court held that "the Fourth Amendment does not require police officers to delay in the course of an investigation if to do so would gravely endanger their lives or the lives of others."[41]

A 1990 decision, rendered in the case of *Maryland* v. *Buie*,[42] extended the authority of police to search locations in a house where a potentially dangerous person could hide, while an arrest warrant is being served. The *Buie* decision was meant primarily to protect investigators from potential danger, and can apply even when officers lack a warrant, probable cause, or even reasonable suspicion. A general listing of established exceptions to the exclusionary rule is provided in Table 7–3.

Under certain circumstances, officers armed with a warrant need not knock and identify themselves before entering a dwelling or other premises. In 1993 the case of *Illinois* v. *Condon*[43] reiterated earlier decisions[44] which held that exigent circumstances, including the presence of narcotics on the premises which could be quickly destroyed and the ready availability to suspects of guns, justify an unannounced entry. The Court noted, without addressing the issue, that "state courts are particularly divided over whether the presence of illegal drugs *alone* will justify unannounced police entry...."

Suspicionless Searches
Those searches conducted by law enforcement personnel without a warrant and without suspicion. Suspicionless searches are only permissible if based upon an overriding concern for public safety.

A R R E S T

Most people think of arrest in terms of what they see on popular television crime shows. The suspect is chased, subdued, and "cuffed" after committing some loathsome act in view of the camera. Some arrests do occur that way. In reality, however, most instances of arrest are far more mundane.

In technical terms, an arrest occurs whenever a law enforcement officer restricts a person's freedom to leave. There may be no yelling *"You're under arrest!"* no *Miranda* warnings may be offered, and, in fact, the suspect may not even consider himself or herself to be in custody. Such arrests, and the decision to enforce them, evolve as the situation between the officer and suspect develops. They usually begin with polite conversation, and a request by the officer for information. Only when the suspect tries to leave, and tests the limits of the police response, may he or she discover that he or she is really in custody.

Arrests which follow the questioning of a suspect are probably the most common type of arrest. When the decision to arrest is reached, the officer has come to the conclusion that a crime has been committed and that the suspect is probably the one who committed it. The presence of these mental elements constitutes the **probable cause** needed for an arrest. Probable cause is the basic minimum necessary for an arrest under any circumstance.

Arrests may also occur when the officer comes upon a crime in progress. Such situations often require apprehension of the offender to ensure the safety of the public. Most arrests made during crimes in progress, however, are for misdemeanors. In fact, many states do not allow arrest for a misdemeanor unless it is committed in the presence of an officer. In any event, crimes in progress clearly provide the probable cause necessary for an arrest.

Probable Cause (Also discussed in Chapter 1) refers to that necessary level of belief which would allow for police seizures (arrests) of individuals and searches of dwellings, vehicles, and possessions. Probable cause can generally be found in a set of facts and circumstances which would cause a reasonable person to believe that a particular individual has committed a specific crime. Upon a demonstration of probable cause, magistrates will issue warrants authorizing law enforcement officers to effect arrests and conduct searches.

T A B L E   7 - 3

ESTABLISHED EXCEPTIONS TO THE EXCLUSIONARY RULE

Police Powers	*Supported by*
Stop and frisk	*Terry* v. *Ohio* (1968)
Warrantless searches incident to a lawful arrest	*U.S.* v. *Rabinowitz* (1950)
Seizure of evidence in "good faith," even in the	*U.S.* v. *Leon* (1984)
face of some exclusionary rule violations	*Illinois* v. *Krull* (1987)
Warrantless vehicle searches where probable	*Carroll* v. *U.S.* (1925)
cause exists to believe that the vehicle contains	*New York* v. *Belton* (1981)
contraband and/or the occupants have been	*U.S.* v. *Ross* (1982)
lawfully arrested	*California* v. *Carney* (1985)
	California v. *Acevedo* (1991)
Gathering of incriminating evidence during	*Beckwith* v. *United States* (1976)
interrogation in noncustodial circumstances	
Authority to search incidental to arrest and/or to	*Chimel* v. *California* (1969)
conduct a protective sweep in conjunction with	*U.S.* v. *Edwards* (1974)
an in-home arrest	*Maryland* v. *Buie* (1990)
Authority to enter and/or search an "open field"	*Hester* v. *U.S.* (1924)
without a warrant	*Oliver* v. *U.S.* (1984)
	U.S. v. *Dunn* (1987)
Permissibility of warrantless naked-eye aerial	*California* v. *Ciraolo* (1986)
observation of open areas and/or greenhouses	*Florida* v. *Riley* (1989)
Warrantless seizure of abandoned materials	*California* v. *Greenwood* (1988)
and refuse	
Prompt action in the face of threats to	*Warren* v. *Hayden* (1967)
public safety	*Borchardt* v. *U.S.* (1987)
	New York v. *Quarles* (1984)
Evidence in "plain view" may be seized	*Harris* v. *New York* (1968)
	Coolidge v. *New Hampshire* (1971)
	Horton v. *California* (1990)
Use of police informants in jail cells	*Kuhlman* v. *Wilson* (1986)
	Illinois v. *Perkins* (1990)
	Arizona v. *Fulminante* (1991)

Most jurisdictions allow arrest for a felony without a warrant when a crime is not in progress, as long as probable cause can be established. Some, however, require a warrant. Arrest warrants are issued by magistrates upon a demonstration of probable cause by police officials. Magistrates[45] are low-level judges and, under our system of checks and balances, act to ensure that the police have established the probable cause needed for an arrest. Magistrates will usually require that the officers seeking an arrest warrant submit a written affidavit outlining their reason for seeking an arrest.

Searches Incident to Arrest

The U.S. Supreme Court has established a clear rule that police officers have the right to conduct a search of a person being arrested, and to search the area under the immediate control of that person, to protect themselves from attack. This is true even if the officer and the arrestee are of different sexes.

Searches Incident to an Arrest Those warrantless searches of arrested individuals which are conducted in order to ensure the safety of the arresting officer(s). Because individuals placed under arrest may be in the possession of weapons, courts have recognized the need for arresting officers to protect themselves by conducting an immediate and warrantless search of arrested individuals without the need for a warrant.

This "rule of the game" was created in the *Rabinowitz* and *Chimel* cases cited earlier. It became firmly established in other cases involving personal searches, such as the 1973 case of *Robinson* v. *U.S.*[46] Robinson was stopped for a traffic violation, when it was learned that his driver's license was expired. He was arrested for operating a vehicle without a valid license. Officers subsequently searched the defendant thoroughly and discovered a substance which later proved to be heroin. When Robinson's appeal reached the U.S. Supreme Court, the Court upheld the officer's right to conduct a search for purposes of personal protection. In the words of the Court, "A custodial arrest of a suspect based upon probable cause is a reasonable intrusion under the Fourth Amendment; that intrusion being lawful, a search incident to the arrest requires no additional jurisdiction."[47]

The Court's decision in *Robinson* provided reinforcement for an earlier ruling involving a seasoned officer who conducted a "pat down" of two men whom he suspected were "casing" a store, about to commit a robbery.[48] The officer in the case was a 39-year veteran of police work, who testified that the men "did not look right." When he approached them, he suspected they might be armed. Fearing for his life, he quickly spun the men around, put them up against a wall, patted down their clothing, and found a gun on one of the men. The man, Terry, was later convicted in Ohio courts of carrying a concealed weapon.

Terry's appeal was based upon the argument that the suspicious officer had no probable cause to arrest him, and therefore no cause to search him. The search, he argued, was ille-

The courts have generally held that, in order to protect themselves and the public, officers have the authority to search persons being arrested. Here arresting officers pat down a drug suspect. *Photo: Craig Filipacchi/ Gamma Liaison.*

gal, and the evidence obtained should not have been used against him. The Supreme Court disagreed. Chief Justice Earl Warren wrote: "In view of these facts, we cannot blind ourselves to the need for law enforcement officers to protect themselves and other prospective victims of violence in situations where they may lack probable cause for an arrest."[49]

The *Terry* case has become the basis for what we today refer to as field interrogation. A popular name for on-the-street interrogation is "stop and frisk." The *Terry* case, for all the authority it conferred on officers, also made it clear that officers must have reasonable grounds for any stop or frisk that they conduct.

In 1989, the Supreme Court, in the case of *U.S. v. Sokolow,*[50] clarified the basis upon which law enforcement officers, lacking probable cause to believe that a crime has occurred, may stop and briefly detain a person for investigative purposes. In *Sokolow* the Court ruled that the legitimacy of such a stop must be evaluated according to a "totality of circumstances" criteria—in which all aspects of the defendant's behavior, taken in concert, may provide the basis for a legitimate stop. In this case, the defendant, Sokolow, appeared suspicious to police because, while traveling under an alias from Honolulu, he had paid $2,100 in $20 bills (from a large roll of money) for two airplane tickets after spending a surprisingly small amount of time in Miami. In addition, the defendant was obviously nervous and checked no luggage. A warrantless airport investigation by DEA agents uncovered more than 1,000 grams of cocaine in the defendant's belongings. The Court, in upholding Sokolow's conviction, ruled that, although no single activity was proof of illegal activity, taken together they created circumstances under which suspicion of illegal activity was justified.

Just as arrest must be based upon probable cause, officers may not stop and question an unwilling citizen whom they have no reason to suspect of a crime. In the case of *Brown* v. *Texas*[51] (1979), two Texas law enforcement officers stopped the defendant and asked for identification. Brown, they later testified, had not been acting suspiciously, nor did they think he might have a weapon. The stop was made simply because officers wanted to know who he was. Brown was arrested under a Texas statute which required a person to identify himself properly and accurately when requested to do so by peace officers. Eventually his appeal reached the U.S. Supreme Court, which ruled that, under circumstances found in the *Brown* case, a person "may not be punished for refusing to identify himself."

In *Smith* v. *Ohio*[52] (1990), the Court held that an individual has the right to protect his or her belongings from unwarranted police inspection. In *Smith,* the defendant was approached by two officers in plain clothes who observed that he was carrying a brown paper bag. The officers asked him to "come here a minute" and, when he kept walking, identified themselves as police officers. The defendant threw the bag onto the hood of his car and attempted to protect it from the officers' intrusion. Marijuana was found inside the bag, and the defendant was arrested. Since there was little reason to stop the suspect in this case, and because control over the bag was not thought necessary for the officer's protection, the Court found that the Fourth Amendment protects both "the traveler who carries a toothbrush and a few articles of clothing in a paper bag" and "the sophisticated executive with the locked attache case."[53]

The following year, however, in what some Court observers saw as a turnabout, the U.S. Supreme Court ruled in *California* v. *Hodari D.*[54] (1991) that suspects who flee from the police and throw away evidence as they retreat may later be arrested based upon the incriminating nature of the abandoned evidence. The case, which began in Oakland, California, centered on the behavior of a group of juveniles who had been standing around a parked car. Two city police officers, driving an unmarked car, but with the word "Police" emblazoned in large letters on their jackets, approached the youths. As they came close, the juveniles apparently panicked and fled. One of them tossed away a "rock" of crack

JUSTICE IN AMERICAN CONTEXT...

What are the limits to a "patdown" search?

In 1993 the U.S. Supreme Court placed new limits on an officer's ability to seize evidence discovered during a patdown search conducted for protective reasons. The opinion of the Court, in summarized form, follows:

> *Minnesota* v. *Dickerson*
> Supreme Court of the United States
> *certiorari* to the Supreme Court of Minnesota
> No. 91–2019 on-line syllabus
> Argued March 3, 1993–Decided June 7, 1993

Based upon respondent's seemingly evasive actions when approached by police officers and the fact that he had just left a building known for cocaine trafficking, the officers decided to investigate further and ordered respondent to submit to a patdown search. The search revealed no weapons, but the officer conducting it testified that he felt a small lump in respondent's jacket pocket, believed it to be a lump of crack cocaine upon examining it with his fingers, and then reached into the pocket and retrieved a small bag of cocaine. The state trial court denied respondent's motion to suppress the cocaine, and he was found guilty of possession of a controlled substance. The Minnesota Court of Appeals reversed. In affirming, the State Supreme Court held that both the stop and the frisk of respondent were valid under *Terry* v. *Ohio*, 392 U.S. 1, but found the seizure of the cocaine to be unconstitutional. Refusing to enlarge the "plain view" exception to the Fourth Amendment's warrant requirement, the court appeared to adopt a categorical rule barring the seizure of any contraband detected by an officer through the sense of touch during a patdown search. The court further noted that, even if it recognized such a "plain feel" exception, the search in this case would not qualify because it went far beyond what is permissible under *Terry*.

Held:

1. The police may seize nonthreatening contraband detected through the sense of touch during a protective patdown search of the sort permitted by *Terry*, so long as the search stays within the bounds marked by *Terry*.

    (a) *Terry* permits a brief stop of a person whose suspicious conduct leads an officer to conclude in light of his experience that criminal activity may be afoot, and a patdown search of the person for weapons when the officer is justified in believing that the person may be armed and presently dangerous. This protective search—permitted without a warrant and on the basis of reasonable suspicion less than probable cause—is not meant to discover evidence of crime, but must be strictly limited to that which is necessary for the discovery of weapons which might be used to harm the officer or others. If the protective search goes beyond what is necessary to determine if the suspect is armed, it is no longer valid under *Terry* and its fruits will be suppressed.

    (b) In *Michigan* v. *Long*, 463 U.S. 1032, the seizure of contraband other than weapons during a lawful *Terry* search was justified by reference to the Court's cases under the "plain-view" doctrine. That doctrine—which permits police to seize an object without a warrant if they are lawfully in a position to view it, if its incriminating character is immediately apparent, and if they have a lawful right of access to it—has an obvious application by analogy to cases in which an officer discovers contraband through the sense of touch during an otherwise lawful search. Thus, if an officer lawfully pats down a suspect's outer clothing and feels an object whose contour or mass makes its identity immediately apparent, there has been no invasion of the suspect's privacy beyond that already authorized by the officer's search for weapons. If the object is contraband, its warrantless seizure would be justified by the realization that resort to a neutral magistrate under such circumstances would be impracticable and would do little to promote the Fourth Amendment's objectives.

2. Application of the foregoing principles to the facts of this case demonstrates that the officer who conducted the search was not acting within the lawful bounds marked by *Terry* at the time he gained probable cause to believe that the lump in respondent's jacket was contraband. Under the state supreme court's interpretation of the record, the officer never thought that the lump was a weapon, but did not immediately recognize it as cocaine. Rather, he determined that it was contraband only after he squeezed, slid, and otherwise manipulated the pocket's contents. While *Terry* entitled him to place his hands on respondent's jacket and to feel the lump in his pocket, his continued exploration of the pocket after he concluded that it contained no weapon was unrelated to the sole justification for the search under *Terry*. Because this further search was constitutionally invalid, the seizure of the cocaine that followed is likewise unconstitutional.
481 N.W. 2d 840, affirmed.

---

cocaine, which was retrieved by the officers. The juvenile was later arrested and convicted of the possession of a controlled substance, but the California Court of Appeals reversed his conviction, reasoning that the officers did not have sufficient reasonable suspicion to make a "Terry-type stop." The Supreme Court, in reversing the finding of the California court, found that reasonable suspicion was not needed, since no "stop" was made. The suspects had not been "seized" by the police, the Court ruled. Therefore, the evidence taken was not the result of an illegal seizure within the meaning of the Fourth Amendment. The significance of *Hodari* for future police action was highlighted by California prosecutors who pointed out that cases like *Hodari* occur "almost everyday in this nation's urban areas."[55]

In a sharply worded dissenting opinion, Justices John Paul Stevens and Thurgood Marshall wrote: "It is too early to know the consequences of the court's holding. If carried to its logical conclusion, it will encourage unlawful displays of force that will frighten countless innocent citizens into surrendering whatever privacy rights they may still have."[56]

Emergency Searches of Persons

It is possible to imagine emergency situations in which officers may have to search people based upon quick decisions: a person who matches the description of an armed robber, a woman who is found lying unconscious, a man who has what appears to be blood on his shoes. Such searches can save lives by disarming fleeing felons, or by uncovering a medical reason for an emergency situation. They may also prevent the escape of criminals or the destruction of evidence.

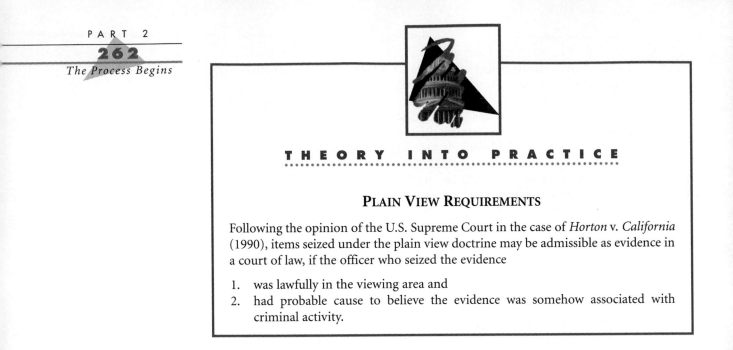

THEORY INTO PRACTICE

PLAIN VIEW REQUIREMENTS

Following the opinion of the U.S. Supreme Court in the case of *Horton* v. *California* (1990), items seized under the plain view doctrine may be admissible as evidence in a court of law, if the officer who seized the evidence

1. was lawfully in the viewing area and
2. had probable cause to believe the evidence was somehow associated with criminal activity.

Searches performed on an emergency basis fall under the exigent circumstances exception to the warrant requirement of the Fourth Amendment. The Supreme Court, in the 1979 case of *Arkansas* v. *Sanders*,[57] recognized the need for exigent searches of persons. The Court indicated such searches would be approved, "where the societal costs of obtaining a warrant, such as danger to law officers or the risk of loss or destruction of evidence, outweigh the reasons for prior recourse to a neutral magistrate."[58]

The 1987 case of *Borchardt* v. *U.S.*, [59] decided by the Fifth Circuit Court of Appeal, held that Borchardt could be prosecuted for heroin uncovered during medical treatment, even over the defendant's objections. Borchardt was a federal inmate at the time he was discovered unconscious in his cell. He was taken to a hospital where tests revealed heroin in his blood. His heart stopped and he was revived using CPR. Borchardt was given three doses of Narcan, a drug used to counteract the effects of heroin, and he improved, regaining consciousness. The patient refused requests to pump his stomach, but began to become lethargic, indicating the need for additional Narcan. Eventually he vomited nine plastic bags full of heroin, along with two bags which had burst. The heroin was turned over to federal officers, and Borchardt was eventually convicted of heroin possession. Attempts to exclude the heroin from evidence were unsuccessful, and the appeals court ruled that the necessity of the emergency situation overruled the defendant's objections to search his person.

The Legal Counsel Division of the FBI provides the following guidelines in conducting emergency warrantless searches of individuals, where the possible destruction of evidence is at issue (keep in mind that there may be no probable cause to *arrest* the individual being searched). All four conditions must apply:[60]

1. There was probable cause to believe at the time of the search that there was evidence concealed on the person searched.
2. There was probable cause to believe an emergency threat of destruction of evidence existed at the time of the search.
3. The officer had no prior opportunity to obtain a warrant authorizing the search.
4. The action was no greater than necessary to eliminate the threat of destruction of evidence.

Vehicle Searches

Vehicles present a special law enforcement problem. They are highly movable, and, when an arrest of a driver or an occupant occurs, the need to search them may be immediate.

The first significant Supreme Court case involving an automobile was that of *Carroll* v. *U.S.*,[61] in 1925. In the *Carroll* case a divided Court ruled that a warrantless search of an automobile or other vehicle is valid if it is based upon a reasonable belief that contraband is present.

In 1964, however, in the case of *Preston* v. *U.S.*[62] the limits of warrantless vehicle searches were defined. Preston was arrested for vagrancy and taken to jail. His vehicle was impounded, towed to the police garage, and later searched. Two revolvers were uncovered in the glove compartment, and more incriminating evidence was found in the trunk. Preston was convicted on weapons possession and other charges and eventually appealed to the U.S. Supreme Court. The Court held that the warrantless search of Preston's vehicle had occurred while the automobile was in secure custody and had been, therefore, illegal. Time and circumstances would have permitted, the Court reasoned, acquisition of a warrant to conduct the search.

When the search of a vehicle occurs after it has been impounded, however, that search may be legitimate if it is undertaken for routine and reasonable purposes. In the case of *South Dakota* v. *Opperman*[63] (1976), for example, the Court held that a warrantless search undertaken for purposes of the inventorying and safekeeping of personal possessions of the car's owner was not illegal, even though it turned up marijuana. The intent of the search had not been to discover contraband, but to secure the owner's belongings from possible theft. Again, in *Colorado* v. *Bertine* (1987), the Court reinforced the idea that officers may open closed containers found in a vehicle while conducting a routine search for inventorying purposes. In the words of the Court, such searches are "now a well-defined exception in the warrant requirement…".[64] In 1990, however, in the precedent-setting case of *Florida* v. *Wells*,[65] the Court agreed with a lower court's suppression of marijuana discovered in a locked suitcase in the trunk of a defendant's impounded vehicle. In *Wells* the Court held that standardized criteria authorizing the search of a vehicle for inventorying purposes were necessary before such a discovery could be legitimate. Standardized criteria, said the Court, might take the form of department policies, written general orders, or established routines.

Warrantless vehicle searches may extend to any area of the vehicle, and may include sealed containers, the trunk area, and the glove compartment if officers have probable cause to conduct a purposeful search, or if officers have been given permission to search the vehicle. In the 1991 case of *Florida* v. *Jimeno*,[66] arresting officers stopped a motorist who gave them permission to search his car. The defendant was later convicted on a drug charge, when a bag on the floor of the car was found to contain cocaine. Upon appeal to the Supreme Court, however, he argued that the permission given to search his car did not extend to bags and other items within the car. In a decision which may have implications beyond vehicle searches, the Court held that "[a] criminal suspect's Fourth Amendment right to be free from unreasonable searches is not violated when, after he gives police permission to search his car, they open a closed container found within the car that might reasonably hold the object of the search. The Amendment is satisfied when, under the circumstances, it is objectively reasonable for the police to believe that the scope of the suspect's consent permitted them to open the particular container."[67]

In *United States* v. *Ross*[68] (1982), the Court found that officers had not exceeded their authority in opening a bag in the trunk which was found to contain heroin. The search was

Warrantless vehicle searches such as this one, where the driver is suspected of a crime, have generally been justified by the fact that vehicles are highly mobile and can quickly leave police jurisdiction. *Photo: Curtis Ackerman/The Boston Herald.*

held to be justifiable on the basis of information developed from a search of the passenger compartment. The Court said, "if probable cause justifies the search of a lawfully stopped vehicle, it justifies the search of every part of the vehicle and its contents that may conceal the object of the search."[69]

The 1983 case of *U.S.* v. *Villamonte-Marquez*[70] widened the Carroll doctrine to include water craft. The case involved an anchored sailboat occupied by Villamonte-Marquez which was searched by a U.S. Customs officer after one of the crew members appeared unresponsive to being hailed. The officer thought he smelled burning marijuana after boarding the vessel and saw burlap bales through an open hatch which he suspected might be contraband. A search proved him correct, and the ship's occupants were arrested. Their conviction was overturned upon appeal, but the U.S. Supreme Court reversed the appeals court. The Court reasoned that a vehicle on the water can easily leave the jurisdiction of enforcement officials, just as a car or truck can.

In *California* v. *Carney* (1985),[71] the Court extended police authority to conduct warrantless searches of vehicles to include motor homes. Earlier arguments had been advanced that a motor home, because it is more like a permanent residence, should not be considered a vehicle in the same sense of an automobile for purposes of search and seizure. The Court, in a 6-to-3 decision, rejected those arguments, reasoning that a vehicle's appointments and size do not alter its basic function of providing transportation.

Houseboats were brought under the automobile exception to the Fourth Amendment warrant requirement in the 1988 Tenth Circuit Court case of *U.S.* v. *Hill*.[72] In the *Hill* case, DEA agents developed evidence which led them to believe that methamphetamine was being manufactured on board a houseboat traversing Lake Texoma in Oklahoma. Because a storm warning had been issued for the area, agents decided to board and search the boat prior to obtaining a warrant. During the search, an operating amphetamine laboratory was discovered, and the boat was seized. In an appeal, the defendants argued that the houseboat search had been illegal because agents lacked a warrant to search their home. The appellate court, however, in rejecting the claims of the defendants, ruled that a houseboat, because it is readily mobile, may be searched without a warrant where probable cause exists to believe that a crime has been or is being committed.

The 1991 Supreme Court case of *Florida* v. *Bostick*,[73] which permitted warrantless "sweeps" of intercity buses, moved the Court deeply into conservative territory. The *Bostick* case came to the attention of the Court as a result of the Broward County (Florida) Sheriff Department's routine practice of boarding buses at scheduled stops and asking passengers for permission to search their luggage. Terrance Bostick, a passenger on one of the buses, gave police permission to search his luggage, which was found to contain cocaine. Bostick was arrested and eventually pleaded guilty to charges of drug trafficking. The Florida Supreme Court, however, found merit in Bostick's appeal, which was based upon a Fourth Amendment claim that the search of his luggage had been unreasonable. The Florida court held that "a reasonable passenger in [Bostick's] situation would not have felt free to leave the bus to avoid questioning by the police" and overturned the conviction.

The state appealed to the U.S. Supreme Court, which held that the Florida Supreme Court erred in interpreting Bostick's *feelings* that he was not free to leave the bus. In the words of the Court, "Bostick was a passenger on a bus that was scheduled to depart. He would not have felt free to leave the bus even if the police had not been present. Bostick's movements were 'confined' in a sense, but this was the natural result of his decision to take the bus." In other words, Bostick was constrained not so much by police action as by his own feelings that he might miss the bus were he to get off. Following this line of reasoning, the Court concluded that police warrantless, suspicionless "sweeps" of buses, "trains, planes, and city streets" are permissible so long as officers (1) ask individual passengers for permission before searching their possessions, (2) do not coerce passengers to consent to a search, and (3) do not convey the message that citizen compliance with the search request is mandatory. Passenger compliance with police searches must be voluntary for the searches to be legal.

In contrast to the tone of Court decisions a decade earlier, the justices did not require officers to inform passengers that they were free to leave nor that they had the right to deny officers the opportunity to search (although Bostick himself was so advised by Florida officers). Any reasonable person, the Court ruled, should feel free to deny the police request. In the words of the Court, "[t]he appropriate test is whether, taking into account all of the circumstances surrounding the encounter, a reasonable passenger would feel free to decline the officers' requests or otherwise terminate the encounter." The Court continued: "[r]ejected, however, is Bostick's argument that he must have been seized because no reasonable person would freely consent to a search of luggage containing drugs, since the 'reasonable person' test presumes an innocent person."

Critics of the decision saw it as creating new "Gestapo-like" police powers in the face of which citizens on public transportation will feel compelled to comply with police requests for search authority. Dissenting Justices Blackmun, Stevens, and Marshall held that "the bus sweep at issue in this case violates the core values of the Fourth Amendment." However, in words which may presage a significant change of direction for other Fourth Amendment issues, the Court defended its ruling by intoning: "[t]he Fourth Amendment proscribes unreasonable searches and seizures; it does not proscribe voluntary cooperation."

◤HE INTELLIGENCE FUNCTION

The police role includes the need to gather information through the questioning of both suspects and informants. Even more often, the need for information leads police investigators to question potentially knowledgeable citizens who may have been witnesses or victims. Data gathering is a crucial form of intelligence, without which enforcement agencies would be virtually powerless to plan and effect arrests.

The importance of gathering information in police work cannot be overstressed. Studies have found that the one factor most likely to lead to arrest in serious crimes is the presence of a witness who can provide information to the police. Undercover operations, neighborhood watch programs, "crime stoppers" groups, and organized detective work—all contribute information to the police.

Many ethical questions have been raised about the techniques employed by police to gather information. Police use of paid informants, for example, is an area of concern to ethicists who believe that informants are often paid to get away with crimes. The police practice (endorsed by some prosecutors) of agreeing not to charge one offender out of a group if he or she will "talk," and testify against others, is another concern of students of justice ethics.

The Fourth Amendment specifies, "No warrants shall issue, but upon probable cause." As a consequence, the successful use of informants in supporting requests for a warrant depends upon the demonstrable reliability of their information. The use of informants was clarified by the case of *Aguilar* v. *Texas*[74] in 1964. That case established a two-pronged test to the effect that informant information could establish probable cause if *both* of the following criteria are met:

- The source of the informant's information is made clear.
- The police officer has a reasonable belief that the informant is reliable.

The two-pronged test of *Aguilar* v. *Texas* was intended to prevent the issuance of warrants on the basis of false or fabricated information. Two later cases provided exceptions to the two-pronged test. *Harris* v. *United States*[75] (1971) recognized the fact that information which was damaging to the informant probably had to be true when provided by the informant. In *Harris* an informant told police that he had purchased nontax-paid whiskey from another person. Since the information also implicated the informant in a crime, it was held to be accurate, even though it could not meet the second prong of the *Aguilar* test. The 1969 Supreme Court case of *Spinelli* v. *United States*[76] created an exception to the requirements of the first prong. In *Spinelli*, the Court held that some information can be so highly specific that it must be accurate, even if its source is not revealed. In 1983, in the case of *Illinois* v. *Gates*,[77] the Court adopted a totality of circumstances approach, which held that sufficient probable cause for issuing a warrant exists where an informer can be reasonably believed on the basis of everything that is known by the police. The *Gates* case involved an anonymous informant who provided incriminating information about another person through a letter to the police. Although the source of the information was not stated, and the police were unable to say whether or not the informant was reliable, the overall *sense* of things, given what was already known to police, was that the information supplied was probably valid.

In the 1990 case of *Alabama* v. *White*,[78] the Supreme Court ruled that an anonymous tip, even in the absence of other, corroborating information about a suspect, could form the basis for an investigatory stop where the informant accurately predicts the *future*

THEORY INTO PRACTICE

PUBLIC INTEREST AND THE RIGHT TO PRIVACY: SUSPICIONLESS SEARCHES

The right to privacy is a fundamental guarantee of the U.S. Constitution.[1] Most of us would probably agree that privacy is also a basic human need. Our legal system, on the other hand, has long recognized that the right to privacy must be limited in cases where individuals are reasonably suspected of having committed crimes. Arrest warrants, search warrants, and orders permitting electronic surveillance may be issued by courts upon a showing of probable cause by law enforcement officers that a crime has been committed.

In two 1989 decisions, however, the U.S. Supreme Court ruled for the first time in its history that there may be instances when the need to ensure public safety provides a "**compelling interest**" which negates the rights of any individual to privacy. In the case of *National Treasury Employees Union* v. *Von Rabb*[2] (1989), the Court, by a 5-to-4 vote, upheld a program of the U.S. Customs Service which required mandatory drug testing for all workers seeking promotions or job transfers involving drug interdiction and the carrying of firearms. The Court's majority opinion read: "We think the government's need to conduct the suspicionless searches required by the Customs program outweighs the privacy interest of employees engaged directly in drug interdiction, and of those who otherwise are required to carry firearms."

The second case, *Skinner* v. *Railway Labor Executives' Association*[3] (1989), was decided on the same day. In *Skinner*, the Justices voted 7 to 2 to permit the mandatory testing of railway crews for the presence of drugs or alcohol following serious train accidents. The *Skinner* case involved evidence of drugs in a 1987 train wreck outside of Baltimore, Maryland, in which 16 people were killed and hundreds injured.

Both decisions were decried by civil libertarians as indicating a dangerous change in high court direction. The Court's new willingness to permit "suspicionless searches" was condemned as infringing the rights of innocent citizens. Justices William J. Brennan, Jr., and Thurgood Marshall summed up the concerns of many when they warned in a dissenting opinion in *Skinner* that, "the first, and worst, casualty of the war on drugs will be the precious liberties of our citizens."

[1] The word used in the Fourth Amendment of the U.S. Constitution is "secure," not "private." Courts have generally equated the two terms.
[2] No. 86–1879 (upon appeal from the Fifth Circuit, 41 CrL. 2097, 5th Cir. May 6, 1987).
[3] No. 87–1555.
Sources: *All Things Considered*, National Public Radio, March 21, 1989; *Criminal Justice Newsletter*, April 3, 1989, p. 4; *Drug Enforcement Report*, March 23, 1989, p. 4; and "The High Court Weighs Drug Tests," *Newsweek*, April 3, 1989, p. 8.

Compelling Interest
A legal concept which provides a basis for suspicionless searches (urinalysis tests of train engineers, for example) when public safety is at issue. It is the concept upon which the Supreme Court cases of *Skinner* v. *Railway Labor Executives' Association* (1989) and *National Treasury Employees Union* v. *Von Rabb* (1989) turned. In those cases the Court held that public safety may provide a sufficiently compelling interest such that an individual's right to privacy can be limited under certain circumstances.

behavior of the suspect. The ability to predict a suspect's behavior demonstrates, the Court reasoned, a significant degree of familiarity with the suspect's affairs. In the words of the Court, "Because only a small number of people are generally privy to an individual's itinerary, it is reasonable for the police to believe that a person with access to such information is likely to also have access to reliable information about that individual's illegal activities."[79]

The identity of informants may be kept secret if sources have been explicitly assured of confidentiality by investigating officers, or if a reasonably implied assurance of confidentiality has been made. In *U.S. Department of Justice* v. *Landano* (1993),[80] the U.S. Supreme Court required that an informant's identity be revealed through a request made under the federal Freedom of Information Act. In that case, the FBI had not specifically assured an informant of confidentiality, and the Court ruled that "the government is not entitled to a presumption that all sources supplying information to the FBI in the course of a criminal investigation are confidential sources...."

POLICE INTERROGATION

Physical Abuse

Interrogation The information gathering activities of police officers which involve the direct questioning of suspects. The actions of officers during suspect interrogation are constrained by a number of significant Supreme Court decisions, the first of which was *Brown* v. *Mississippi* (1936).

Landmark decisions by the U.S. Supreme Court have clearly focused on issues of police interrogation. The first in a series of significant cases was that of *Brown* v. *Mississippi*,[81] decided in 1936. The *Brown* case began with the robbery of a white store owner in Mississippi in 1934. During the robbery, the victim was killed.

A posse formed spontaneously and went to the home of a local black man rumored to have been one of the perpetrators. They dragged the suspect from his home, put a rope around his neck, and hoisted him into a tree. They repeated this process a number of times, hoping to get a confession from the man, but failing. The posse was joined by a deputy sheriff who led them to the home of other suspects, where they repeated their "interrogation" technique. Finally, they were able to get a confession from one of the men. The remaining defendants were laid over chairs in the jail and whipped with belts and buckles until they also "confessed." These confessions were used in the trial which followed, and the three defendants were convicted of murder. Their convictions were upheld by the Mississippi Supreme Court. One of the defendants, named Brown, made further appeals. In 1936 his case was reviewed by the U.S. Supreme Court, which overturned Brown's conviction, saying that it was difficult to imagine techniques of interrogation more "revolting" to the sense of justice than those used in this case.

Inherent Coercion

Inherent Coercion Those tactics used by police interviewers which fall short of physical abuse, but which, nonetheless, pressure subjects to divulge information.

Interrogation need not involve physical abuse for it to be contrary to constitutional principles. In the case of *Ashcraft* v. *Tennessee*,[82] the Court found that inherently coercive interrogation was not acceptable. Ashcraft had been charged with the murder of his brother-in-law. He was arrested on a Friday night and interrogated by relays of skilled interrogators until Monday morning, when he finally confessed to the murder. During questioning he had been faced by a blinding light, but not physically mistreated. Investigators later testified that when the suspect requested cigarettes, food, or water, they "kindly" provided them. The Supreme Court's ruling in this case made it plain that the Fifth Amendment guarantee against self-incrimination excludes *any* form of official coercion or pressure during interrogation.

T H E O R Y   I N T O   P R A C T I C E

INDIVIDUAL RIGHTS VERSUS GROUP INTERESTS: THE FOURTH AMENDMENT AND SOBRIETY CHECKPOINTS

The Fourth and Fourteenth Amendments to the U.S. Constitution guarantee liberty and personal security to all persons residing within the United States. Lacking probable cause to believe that a crime has been committed, the courts have generally held that police officers have no legitimate authority to detain or arrest people who are going about their business in a peaceful manner. The U.S. Supreme Court has, however, in a number of cases, decided that community interests may necessitate a temporary suspension of personal liberty, even where probable cause is lacking. One such recent case is that of *Michigan Department of State Police* v. *Sitz* (1990),[1] which involved the legality of highway sobriety checkpoints—even those at which nonsuspicious drivers are subjected to scrutiny.

The Court had previously established that traffic stops, including those at checkpoints along a highway, are "seizures" within the meaning of the Fourth Amendment.[2] In *Michigan Department of State Police* v. *Sitz,* however, an increasingly conservative Court ruled that such seizures are reasonable insofar as they are essential to the welfare of the community as a whole. That the Court reached its conclusion based upon pragmatic social interests is clear from the words used by Chief Justice Rehnquist:

> No one can seriously dispute the magnitude of the drunken driving problem or the States' interest in eradicating it. Media reports of alcohol-related death and mutilation on the Nation's roads are legion. Drunk drivers cause an annual death toll of over 25,000 and in the same time span cause nearly one million personal injuries and more than five billion dollars in property damage…[t]he balance of the State's interest in preventing drunken driving, the extent to which this system can reasonably be said to advance that interest, and the degree of intrusion upon individual motorists who are briefly stopped, weighs in favor of the state program.

But, critics say, how far should the Court go in allowing officers to act without probable cause? Figures on domestic violence (child and spouse abuse, murder, incest, and other forms of victimization in the home), if compared to traffic statistics, are probably far more shocking. Using the same kind of reasoning as in *Michigan Department of State Police* v. *Sitz,* one could imagine the chief justice writing, "the balance of the State's interest in preventing domestic violence, the extent to which preventive programs briefly inconvenience individual citizens, and the relatively small degree of intrusion upon law-abiding citizens which such a program represents, weighs in favor of random home incursions by well-intentioned police officers."

[1] *Michigan Department of State Police* v. *Sitz,* 110 S.Ct. 2481 (1990)
[2] *U.S.* v. *Martinea-Fuerte,* 428 U.S. 543, 96 S.Ct. 3074 (1976), and *Brower* v. *County of Inyo,* 109 S.Ct. 1378 (1989).

A similar case, involving four black defendants, occurred in Florida in 1940.[83] The four men, including one whose name was Chambers, were arrested without warrants as suspects in a robbery and murder of an aged white man. After several days of questioning in a hostile atmosphere, the men confessed to the murder. The confessions were used as the primary evidence against them at a trial which ensued, and all four were sentenced to die. Upon appeal to the Supreme Court, the Court held that "the very circumstances surrounding their confinement and their questioning without any formal charges having been brought, were such as to fill petitioners with terror and frightful misgivings."[84]

Psychological Manipulation

Psychological Manipulation Manipulative actions by police interviewers, designed to pressure suspects to divulge information, which are based upon subtle forms of intimidation and control.

Interrogation must not only be free of coercion and hostility, but it also cannot involve sophisticated trickery designed to ferret out a confession. While interrogators do not necessarily have to be scrupulously honest in confronting suspects, and while the expert opinions of medical and psychiatric practitioners may be sought in investigations, the use of professionals skilled in psychological manipulation to gain confessions was banned by the Court in the case of *Leyra* v. *Denno*[85] in 1954.

The early 1950s were the "heyday" of psychiatric perspectives on criminal behavior. In the *Leyra* case, detectives employed a psychiatrist to question Leyra, who had been charged with the hammer slayings of his parents. Leyra had been led to believe that the medical doctor to whom he was introduced in an interrogation room had actually been sent to help him with a sinus problem. Following a period of questioning, including subtle suggestions by the psychiatrist that he would feel better if he confessed to the murders, Leyra did indeed confess.

The Supreme Court, on appeal, ruled that the defendant had been effectively, and improperly, duped by the police. In the words of the Court, "Instead of giving petitioner the medical advice and treatment he expected, the psychiatrist by subtle and suggestive questions simply continued the police effort of the past days and nights to induce petitioner to admit his guilt. For an hour and a half or more the techniques of a highly trained psychiatrist were used to break petitioner's will in order to get him to say he had murdered his parents."[86] After a series of three trials, each with less and less evidence permitted into the courtroom by appeals courts, and following convictions in each, Leyra was finally set free by a state appeals court which found insufficient evidence for the final conviction.

During the 1991 Supreme Court term, the case of *Arizona* v. *Fulminante*[87] threw a blanket of uncertainty over the use of sophisticated techniques to gain a confession. Oreste Fulminante was an inmate in a federal prison when he was approached secretly by a fellow inmate who was an FBI informant. The informant told Fulminante that other inmates were plotting to kill him because of a rumor that he had killed a child. He offered to protect Fulminante if he was told the details of the crime. Fulminante then described his role in the murder of his 11-year-old step-daughter. Fulminante was arrested for that murder, tried, and convicted. Upon appeal to the U.S. Supreme Court, his lawyers argued that Fulminante's confession had been coerced because of the threat of violence communicated by the informant. The Court agreed that the confession had been coerced and ordered a new trial at which the confession could not be admitted into evidence. Simultaneously, however, the Court found that the admission of a coerced confession should be considered a harmless "trial error" which need not necessarily result in reversal of a conviction, if other evidence still proves guilt. The decision was especially significant because it partially reversed the Court's earlier ruling, in *Chapman* v. *California*,[88] where it was held that forced confessions were such a basic form of constitutional error that they could never be used, and automatically invalidated any conviction to which they related.

THE RIGHT TO A LAWYER AT INTERROGATION

In 1964, in the case of *Escobedo* v. *Illinois*,[89] the right to have legal counsel present during police interrogation was recognized. Danny Escobedo was arrested without a warrant for the murder of his brother-in-law and was interrogated. He made no statement and was released the same day. A few weeks later another person identified Escobedo as the killer. Escobedo was rearrested and taken back to the police station. During the interrogation which followed, officers told him that they "had him cold" and that he should confess. Escobedo asked to see his lawyer, but was told that an interrogation was in progress, and that he couldn't just go out and see his lawyer. Soon the lawyer arrived and asked to see Escobedo. Police told him that his client was being questioned and could be seen after questioning concluded. Escobedo later claimed that while he repeatedly asked for his lawyer, he was told, "Your lawyer doesn't want to see you."

Eventually Escobedo confessed and was convicted at trial on the basis of his confession. Upon appeal to the U.S. Supreme Court, the Court overturned Escobedo's conviction, ruling that counsel is necessary at police interrogations to protect the rights of the defendant and should be provided when the defendant desires.

In 1981, the case of *Edwards* v. *Arizona*[90] established a "bright-line rule" for investigators to use in interpreting a suspect's right to counsel. In *Edwards*, the Supreme Court reiterated its *Miranda* concern that once a suspect, who is in custody and who is being questioned, has requested the assistance of counsel, all questioning must cease until an attorney is present. In 1990 the Court refined the rule in *Minnick* v. *Mississippi*, when it held that interrogation may *not* resume after the suspect has had an opportunity to consult his or her lawyer, when the lawyer is no longer present. Similarly, according to *Arizona* v. *Roberson*[91] (1988), the police may not avoid the defendant's request for a lawyer by beginning a new line of questioning, even if it is about an unrelated offense.

> While every person is entitled to stand silent, it is more virtuous for the wrongdoer to admit his offense and accept the punishment he deserves.... it is wrong, and subtly corrosive of our criminal justice system to regard an honest confession as a mistake.
>
> —*Justice Antonin Scalia, dissenting in* Minnick *v.* Mississippi

THE MIRANDA DECISION

In the area of suspect rights, no case is as famous as that of *Miranda* v. *Arizona*,[92] which was decided in 1965. Ernesto Miranda was arrested in Phoenix, Arizona, and accused of having kidnapped and raped a young woman. At police headquarters he was identified by the victim. After being interrogated for two hours, Miranda signed a confession which formed the basis of his later conviction on the charges.

Upon eventual appeal to the U.S. Supreme Court, the Court rendered what some regard as the most far-reaching opinion to have impacted criminal justice in the last few decades. The Court ruled that Miranda's conviction was unconstitutional because "The entire aura and atmosphere of police interrogation without notification of rights and an offer of assistance of counsel tends to subjugate the individual to the will of his examiner."

The Court continued, saying that the defendant, "must be warned prior to any questioning that he has the right to remain silent, that anything he says can be used against him in a court of law, that he has the right to the presence of an attorney, and that if he cannot afford an attorney one will be appointed for him prior to any questioning if he so desires.

Miranda Warnings The advisement of rights due criminal suspects by the police prior to the beginning of questioning. *Miranda* warnings were first set forth by the Court in the 1965 case of *Miranda* v. *Arizona*.

Opportunity to exercise these rights must be afforded to him throughout the interrogation. After such warnings have been given, and such opportunity afforded him, the individual may knowingly and intelligently waive these rights and agree to answer the questions or make a statement. But unless and until such warnings and waiver are demonstrated by the prosecution at the trial, no evidence obtained as a result of interrogation can be used against him."[93]

To ensure that proper advice is given to suspects at the time of their arrest, the now-famous *Miranda* rights are read before any questioning begins. These rights, as they appear on a *Miranda* warning card commonly used by police agencies, appear in the box on the next page.

Once suspects have had a *Miranda* rights advisement, they are commonly asked to sign a paper which lists each right, in order to confirm that they were advised of their rights, and that they understand each right. Questioning may then begin, but only if suspects waive their rights not to talk or to have a lawyer present during interrogation.

Some hailed the *Miranda* case as one which ensured the protection of individual rights guaranteed under the Constitution. To guarantee those rights, they suggested, what better agency is available than the police themselves, since the police are present at the initial stages of the criminal justice process.

Critics of the *Miranda* decision have argued that *Miranda* puts police agencies in the uncomfortable and contradictory position of not only enforcing the law, but also of having to offer defendants advice on how potentially to circumvent conviction and punishment. Under *Miranda* the police partially assume the role of legal advisor to the accused. During the last years of the Reagan administration, then–Attorney General Edwin Meese focused on the *Miranda* decision as the antithesis of "law and order." He pledged the resources of his office to an assault upon the *Miranda* rules to eliminate what he saw as the frequent release of guilty parties on the basis of "technicalities."

A Waiver of Rights

Suspects in police custody may waive their *Miranda* rights. The legal standard for the waiver of rights has been held to be a *voluntary* "knowing and intelligent" waiver. A *knowing waiver* can only be made if a suspect has had the benefit of a rights advisement, and if he or she was in a condition to understand the advisement. A rights advisement made in English, for example, to a Spanish-speaking defendant, cannot produce a knowing waiver. Likewise, an *intelligent waiver* of rights requires that the defendant be able to understand the consequences of not invoking the *Miranda* rights. In the case of *Moran* v. *Burbine* (1986),[94] the Supreme Court defined an intelligent and knowing waiver as one "made with a full awareness both of the nature of the right being abandoned and the consequences of the decision to abandon it."[95] Similarly, in *Colorado* v. *Spring* (1987),[96] the court held that an intelligent and knowing waiver can be made even though a suspect has not been informed of all the alleged offenses about which he or she is about to be questioned.

In 1992 *Miranda* rights were effectively extended to illegal immigrants living in the United States. In a settlement of a class-action lawsuit reached in Los Angeles with the Immigration and Naturalization Service, U.S. District Court Judge William Byrne, Jr., approved the printing of millions of notices in several languages to be given to those arrested. The approximately 1.5 million illegal aliens arrested each year will now be told they may (1) talk with a lawyer, (2) make a phone call, (3) request a list of available legal services,

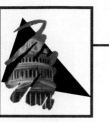

THEORY INTO PRACTICE

ADULT RIGHTS WARNING

Persons 18 years old or older who are in custody must be given this advice of rights before any questioning.

1. You have the right to remain silent.
2. Anything you say can be used against you in a court of law.
3. You have the right to talk to a lawyer and to have a lawyer present while you are being questioned.
4. If you want a lawyer before or during questioning but cannot afford to hire a lawyer, one will be appointed to represent you at no cost before any questioning.
5. If you answer questions now without a lawyer here, you still have the right to stop answering questions at any time.

WAIVER OF RIGHTS

After reading and explaining the rights of a person in custody, an officer must also ask for a waiver of those rights before any questioning. The following waiver questions must be answered affirmatively, either by express answer or by clear implication. Silence alone is not a waiver.

1. Do you understand each of these rights I have explained to you? (Answer must be YES.)
2. Having these rights in mind, do you now wish to answer questions? (Answer must be YES.)
3. Do you now wish to answer questions without a lawyer present? (Answer must be YES.)

For juveniles age 14, 15, 16, and 17, the following question must be asked:

4. Do you now wish to answer questions without your parents, guardians, or custodians present? (Answer must be YES.)

Source: N.C. Justice Academy. Reprinted with permission.

(4) seek a hearing before an immigration judge, (5) possibly obtain release on bond, and (6) contact a diplomatic officer representing their country. This kind of thing is "long overdue," says Roberto Martinez of the American Friends Service Committee's Mexico-U.S. border program. "Up to now, we've had total mistreatment of civil rights of undocumented people."[97]

Ernesto Miranda, whose conviction on rape and kidnapping charges after arresting officers failed to advise him of his rights led to the now famous "Miranda warnings." Miranda is shown here after a jury convicted him for a second time. *Photo: AP/Wide World Photos.*

Exceptions to *Miranda*

A good example of the change in Supreme Court philosophy, alluded to earlier in this chapter as a movement from "Warren" to "Rehnquist" court doctrine, can be had in the case of *Nix* v. *Williams* (1984).[98] The *Nix* case epitomizes what some have called a "nibbling away" at the advances in defendant rights which reached their apex in *Miranda*. The case had its beginnings in 1969 when Robert Anthony Williams was convicted of murdering a 10-year-old girl, Pamela Powers, around Christmas time. Although Williams had been advised of his rights, detectives searching for the girl's body were riding in a car with the defendant, when one of them made what has since come to be known as the "Christian burial speech." The detective told Williams that, since Christmas was almost upon them, it would be "the Christian thing to do" to see to it that Pamela could have a decent burial, rather than having to lay in a field somewhere. Williams relented and led detectives to the body. However, because Williams had not been reminded of his right to have a lawyer present during his conversation with the detective, the Supreme Court overturned Williams's conviction, saying that the detective's remarks were "a deliberate eliciting of incriminating evidence from an accused in the absence of his lawyer."[99]

That was in 1975. In 1977, Williams was retried for the murder, but his remarks in leading detectives to the body were not entered into evidence. The discovery of the body was itself used, however, prompting another appeal to the Supreme Court based upon the argument that the body should not have been used as evidence since it was discovered due to the illegally gathered statements. This time the Supreme Court affirmed Williams's conviction, holding that the body would have been found anyway, since detectives were searching in the direction where it lay. That ruling came in 1984 and clearly demonstrates a tilt by the Court away from suspect's rights, and an accommodation with the imperfect world of police procedure. The *Nix* case, as it was finally resolved, is said to have created the inevitable discovery exception to the *Miranda* requirements.

Public Safety Exceptions to *Miranda*

In 1984 the U.S. Supreme Court also established what has come to be known as the public safety exception to the *Miranda* rule. The case, *New York* v. *Quarles,*[100] centered upon an alleged rape in which the victim told police her assailant had fled, with a gun, into a nearby A&P supermarket. Two police officers entered the store and apprehended the suspect. One officer immediately noticed that the man was wearing an empty shoulder holster and, apparently fearing that a child might find the discarded weapon, quickly asked, "Where's the gun?"

Quarles was convicted of rape, but appealed his conviction, requesting that the weapon be suppressed as evidence because officers had not advised him of his *Miranda* rights prior to asking a question about the gun. The Supreme Court disagreed, stating that considerations of public safety were overriding and negated the need for rights advisement prior to limited questioning which focused on the need to prevent further harm.

Where coercive conduct on the part of the police is lacking, and *Miranda* warnings have been issued, the Supreme Court has held that even a later demonstration that a person may have been suffering from mental problems will not necessarily negate a confession. *Colorado* v. *Connelly* (1986)[101] involved a man who approached a Denver police officer and said he wanted to confess to the murder of a young girl. The officer immediately informed him of his *Miranda* rights, but the man waived them and continued to talk. When a detective arrived, the man was again advised of his rights, and again waived them. After being taken to the local jail the man began to hear "voices" and later claimed that it was these voices which had made him confess. At the trial the defense moved to have the earlier confession negated on the basis that it was not voluntarily or freely given, because of the defendant's mental condition. Upon appeal, the Supreme Court disagreed, saying that "no coercive government conduct occurred in this case."[102] Hence, "self-coercion," be it through the agency of a guilty conscience or faulty thought processes, does not appear to bar prosecution based on information revealed willingly by the defendant.

In a final refinement of *Miranda*, the lawful ability of a police informant, placed in a jail cell along with a defendant to gather information for later use at trial, was upheld in the 1986 case of *Kuhlmann* v. *Wilson*.[103] The passive gathering of information was judged to be acceptable, provided that the informant did not make attempts to elicit information.

In the case of *Illinois* v. *Perkins* (1990), the Court expanded its position to say that, under appropriate circumstances, even the active questioning of a suspect by an undercover officer posing as a fellow inmate does not require *Miranda* warnings. In *Perkins*, the Court found that, lacking other forms of coercion, the fact that the suspect was not aware of the questioner's identity as a law enforcement officer ensured that his statements were freely given. In the words of the Court, "[t]he essential ingredients of a 'police-dominated atmosphere' and compulsion are not present when an incarcerated person speaks freely to someone that he believes to be a fellow inmate."[104]

Miranda and the Meaning of Interrogation

Modern interpretations of the applicability of *"Miranda* warnings" turn upon an understanding of *interrogation*. The *Miranda* decision, as originally rendered, specifically recognized the necessity for police investigators to make inquiries at crime scenes in order to determine facts or establish identities. So long as the individual questioned is not yet in custody, and as long as probable cause to arrest is lacking in the investigator's mind, such questioning can proceed unencumbered by the need for *Miranda* warnings. In such cases, interrogation, within the meaning of *Miranda,* has not yet begun.

The case of *Rock* v. *Zimmerman* (1982)[105] provides a different sort of example—one in which a suspect willingly made statements to the police before interrogation began. The suspect had burned his own house and shot and killed a neighbor. When the fire department arrived, he began shooting again and killed the fire chief. Cornered later in a field, the defendant, gun in hand, spontaneously shouted at police, "How many people did I kill, how many people are dead?"[106] This spontaneous statement was held to be admissible evidence at the suspect's trial.

It is also important to recognize that the Supreme Court in the *Miranda* decision required that officers provide warnings only in those situations involving *both* arrest and custodial interrogation. In other words, it is generally permissible for officers to take a suspect into custody, and listen, without asking questions, while he or she tells a story. Similarly, they may ask questions without providing a *Miranda* warning, even within the confines of a police station house, as long as the person questioned is not a suspect and is not under arrest.[107] Warnings are required only when officers begin actively to solicit responses from the defendant. Recognizing this fact, the FBI, in some of its training literature, has referred to interrogation as the *Miranda* trigger.

Interrogation was itself the subject of definition by the Court in 1980 in the case of *Rhode Island* v. *Innis*.[108] Interrogation was defined to include any behaviors by the police "that the police should know are reasonably likely to elicit an incriminating response from the suspect." In the *Innis* case, the Court held that interrogation included "staged lineups, reverse lineups, positing guilt, minimizing the moral seriousness of crime, and casting blame on the victim or society."

It is noteworthy that the Court has held that "police words or actions normally attendant to arrest and custody do not constitute interrogation."[109] Officers were found to have acted properly in the case of *South Dakota* v. *Neville,* (1983)[110] in informing a DWI suspect, without reading him his rights, that he would stand to lose his driver's license if he did not submit to a breathalyzer test. When the driver responded, "I'm too drunk. I won't pass the test," his answer became evidence of his condition and was not subject to exclusion at trial.

A third-party conversation recorded by the police after a suspect has invoked the Miranda right to remain silent may be used as evidence, according to a 1987 ruling in *Arizona* v. *Mauro*.[111] In *Mauro,* a man who willingly conversed with his wife in the presence of a police tape recorder, even after invoking his right to keep silent, was held to have effectively abandoned that right.

When a waiver is not made, however, in-court references to a defendant's silence following the issuing of *Miranda* warnings is unconstitutional. In 1976 (*Doyle* v. *Ohio*),[112] the U.S. Supreme Court definitively ruled that "a suspect's [post-*Miranda*] silence will not be used against him." Even so, according to the Court in *Brecht* v. *Abrahamson* (1993),[113] prosecution efforts to use such silence against a defendant may not invalidate a finding of guilt by a jury unless such "error had substantial and injurious effect or influence in determining the jury's verdict."[114]

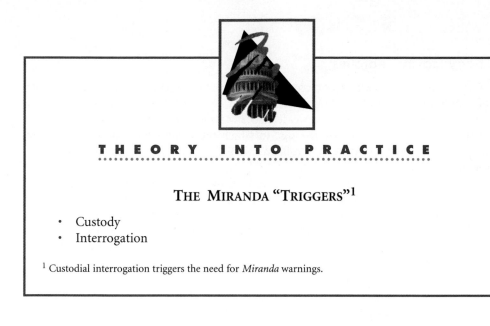

Miranda **Triggers** The
dual principles of custody
and interrogation, both
of which are necessary
before an advisement of
rights is necessitated.

THEORY INTO PRACTICE

THE MIRANDA "TRIGGERS"[1]

· Custody
· Interrogation

[1] Custodial interrogation triggers the need for *Miranda* warnings.

GATHERING NONTESTIMONIAL EVIDENCE

Right to Privacy

The police environment is complicated by the fact that suspects are often privy to evidence of a nontestimonial sort. The gathering of nontestimonial evidence from suspects is an area rich in precedent. The Fourth Amendment guarantee that persons should be secure in their homes and in their persons has been interpreted by the courts to mean generally that the involuntary seizure of physical evidence is illegal and will result in exclusion of that evidence at trial.

Two cases, *Hayes* v. *Florida*[115] and *Winston* v. *Lee*,[116] are examples of limits placed by the courts upon the seizure of nontestimonial evidence. The *Hayes* case established the right of suspects to refuse to be fingerprinted when probable cause necessary to effect an arrest does not exist. *Winston* demonstrated the inviolability of the body against surgical and other substantially invasive techniques which might be ordered by authorities against a suspect's will.

In the *Winston* case, Rudolph Lee, Jr., was found a few blocks from a store robbery with a gunshot wound in his chest. The robbery had involved an exchange of gunshots by the store owner and the robber, with the owner noting that the robber had apparently been hit by a bullet. At the hospital, the store owner identified Lee as the robber. The prosecution sought to have Lee submit to surgery to remove the bullet in his chest, arguing that the bullet would provide physical evidence linking him to the crime. Lee refused the surgery, and the Supreme Court in *Winson* v. *Lee* (1985) ruled that Lee could not be ordered to undergo surgery because such a magnitude of intrusion into his body was unacceptable under the right to privacy guaranteed by the Fourth Amendment. The *Winston* case was based upon precedent established in *Schmerber* v. *California* (1966).[117] The *Schmerber* case turned upon the extraction of a blood sample to be measured for alcohol content against the defendant's will. In *Schmerber* the Court ruled that warrants must be obtained for bodily intrusions unless fast action is necessary to prevent the destruction of evidence by natural physiological processes.

Body Cavity Searches

Body cavity searches are among the most problematic for police today. "Strip" searches of convicts in prisons, including the search of body cavities, have generally been held permissible. The 1985 Supreme Court case of *U.S.* v. *Montoya de Hernandez*[118] focused on the issue of "alimentary canal smuggling," in which the suspect typically swallows male prophylactics filled with cocaine or heroin and waits for nature to take its course to recover the substance.

In the *Montoya* case, a woman known to be a "balloon swallower" arrived in the United States on a flight from Colombia. She was detained by customs officials and given a "pat down" search by a female agent. The agent reported that the woman's abdomen was firm and suggested that X rays be taken. The suspect refused and was given the choice of submitting to further tests or taking the next flight back to Colombia. No flight was immediately available, however, and the suspect was placed in a room for 16 hours, where she refused all food and drink. Finally, a court order for an X ray was obtained. The procedure revealed "balloons," and the woman was detained another four days, during which time she passed numerous cocaine-filled plastic condoms. The Court ruled that the woman's confinement was not unreasonable, based as it was upon the supportable suspicion that she was "body-packing" cocaine. Any discomfort she experienced, the court ruled, "resulted solely from the method that she chose to smuggle illicit drugs."[119]

ELECTRONIC EAVESDROPPING

Historical Background

Modern technology makes possible increasingly complex forms of communication. From fiber optic phone lines, microwave transmissions, and fax machines, to computer communications involving modems and databases, today's global village is a close-knit weave of flowing information.

One of the first and best known of the Supreme Court decisions in the area of electronic communications was the case of *Olmstead* v. *U.S.*[120] in 1928. In the *Olmstead* case, bootleggers used their personal telephones to discuss and transact business. Agents had tapped the lines and based their investigation and ensuing arrests upon conversations they had overheard. The defendants were convicted and eventually appealed to the High Court, arguing that a seizure of information had in effect occurred and that, since agents had lacked a search warrant, it was an illegal seizure based upon their Fourth Amendment right to be secure in their homes. The Court ruled, however, that telephone lines were not an extension of the defendant's homes, and therefore were not protected by the constitutional guarantee of security. Subsequent federal statutes (discussed shortly) have substantially modified the significance of *Olmstead*.

Recording devices carried on the body of an undercover agent or an informant were ruled to produce admissible evidence in *On Lee* v. *U.S.* (1952)[121] and *Lopez* v. *U.S.* (1963).[122] The 1967 case of *Berger* v. *New York*[123] permitted wiretaps and "bugs" in instances where state law provided for the use of such devices, and where officers obtained a warrant based upon probable cause.

The Court appeared to undertake a significant change of direction in the area of electronic eavesdropping when, in 1967, it decided the case of *Katz* v. *U.S.*[124] Federal agents had monitored a number of telephone calls made by Katz from a public phone. They had used a device separate from the phone lines, and attached to the glass of the phone booth. The Court, in this case, stated that what a person makes an effort to keep private, even in a public place, requires a judicial decision, in the form of a warrant issued upon probable cause, to unveil. In the words of the Court, "The government's activities in electronically listening to and recording the petitioner's words violated the privacy upon which he justifiably relied while using the telephone booth and thus constituted a 'search and seizure' within the meaning of the Fourth Amendment."

The Court's reversal of direction was complete by 1968, with the case of *Lee* v. *Florida*.[125] In *Lee* the Court applied the Federal Communications Act[126] and held that evidence obtained without a warrant could not be used in state proceedings if it resulted from a wiretap. The only person who has the authority to permit eavesdropping, according to that act, is the sender of the message.

The Federal Communications Act was originally passed in 1934, but did not specifically mention the potential interest of law enforcement agencies in monitoring communications. Title III of the Omnibus Crime Control and Safe Streets Act of 1968, however, mostly prohibits wiretaps, but does allow officers to listen to electronic communications where (1) the officer is one of the parties involved in the communication, or (2) where one of the parties is not the officer, but willingly decides to share the communication with the officer, or (3) officers obtain a warrant based upon probable cause. In the 1971 case of *U.S.* v. *White*,[127] the Court held that law enforcement officers may intercept electronic information when one of the parties involved in the communication gives his or her consent, even without a warrant.

In 1984 the Supreme Court decided the case of *U.S.* v. *Karo*,[128] in which DEA agents had arrested James Karo for cocaine importation. Officers had placed a radio transmitter inside a 50-gallon drum of ether purchased by Karo for use in processing the cocaine. The transmitter was placed inside the drum with the consent of the seller of the ether, but without a search warrant. The shipment of ether was followed to the Karo house and later moved to a warehouse. Eventually, Karo and others were arrested and convicted of cocaine trafficking charges. Karo appealed to the Supreme Court, claiming that the radio beeper had violated his reasonable expectation of privacy inside his premises and that, without a warrant, the evidence it produced was tainted. The Court agreed and overturned his conviction.

Minimization Requirements

The Supreme Court established a minimization requirement pertinent to electronic surveillance in the case of *United States* v. *Scott*.[129] Minimization means that officers must make every reasonable effort to monitor only those conversations, through the use of phone taps, body bugs, and the like, which are specifically related to criminal activity under investigation. As soon as it becomes obvious that a conversation is innocent, then the monitoring personnel are required to cease their invasion of privacy. Problems arise if the conversation occurs in a foreign language, if it is "coded," or if it is ambiguous. It has been suggested that investigators involved in electronic surveillance maintain log books of their activities which specifically show monitored conversations, as well as efforts made at "minimization."[130]

The Electronic Communications Privacy Act

Passed by Congress in 1986, the Electronic Communications Privacy Act (ECPA)[131] has brought major changes in the requirements law enforcement officers must meet in the use of wiretaps. The ECPA deals specifically with three areas of communication: (1) wiretaps and bugs, (2) pen registers (which record the numbers dialed from a telephone), and (3) tracing devices which determine the number from which a call emanates. The act also addresses the procedures to be followed by officers in obtaining records relating to communications services, and it establishes requirements for gaining access to stored electronic communications and records of those communications.

The effective date of the ECPA was January 20, 1987, for federal law enforcement officers. State and local officers came under the provisions of the bill on October 2, 1988. In some jurisdictions, however, state law is more stringent than the ECPA, and local officers must, of course, follow those laws.

The ECPA basically requires that investigating officers must obtain wiretap-type court orders to eavesdrop on *ongoing communications*. The use of pen registers and recording devices, however, are specifically excluded by the law from court order requirements. *Stored communications*, such as computer files made from telephonic sources, fax reproductions, digitally stored information, electronic bulletin boards, and other physical and electronic records of communications which have already occurred are categorized by the act according to the length of time they have been stored. Messages stored less than 180 days are protected in the same manner as the contents of U.S. mail, and a search warrant issued upon probable cause is required to access them.[132] Information which has been on file in excess of 180 days, however, can be accessed with a court order based upon a simple showing that the information sought is relevant to an ongoing criminal investigation. Such a "showing" is less demanding than a demonstration of probable cause, which includes the claim that the information in question will provide evidence of a law violation.

Some provisions of the ECPA require that "service providers" give notification to users that stored information belonging to them has become the subject of a police request. Subjects so notified might be tempted to remove or erase the stored information, and investigating officers should, under such circumstances, immediately request that backup copies of any important information be made.

SUMMARY

The principles of individual liberty and social justice are the cornerstones upon which the American way of life rests. Ideally, the work of the criminal justice system is to ensure justice while guarding liberty. The liberty/justice issue is the dual thread which weaves the tapestry of the justice system together—from the simplest daily activities of police on the beat, to the often complex and lengthy renderings of the U.S. Supreme Court.

For the criminal justice system, the question becomes "How can individual liberties be maintained in the face of the need for official action, including arrest, interrogation, incarceration, and the like?" The answer is far from simple, but it begins with a recognition of the fact that "liberty" is a double-edged sword, entailing obligations as well as rights. For police action to be "just," it must recognize the rights of individuals while simultaneously holding them accountable to the social obligations defined by law.

DISCUSSION QUESTIONS

1. Which Supreme Court decisions discussed in this chapter do you see as most significant? Why?

2. Are there any Supreme Court decisions discussed in this chapter with which you disagree? Which ones? Why do you disagree?

3. Do you agree with the theme of this chapter's summary, that "for police action to be just, it must recognize the rights of individuals, while holding citizens to the social obligations defined by law?" What is the basis for your agreement or disagreement?

4. In your opinion, should the Supreme Court have created exceptions to the exclusionary rule? To *Miranda*? Why or why not?

5. What does the *due process environment* mean to you? How do you think we should try to ensure due process in our legal system?

6. Justice Benjamin Cardozo once complained, "The criminal is to go free because the constable has blundered." Can we afford to let some guilty people go free in order to ensure that the rights of the rest of us are protected? Is there some other (better) way to achieve the same goal?

ENDNOTES

1. Larry Collins and Dominique Lapierre, *The Fifth Horseman* (New York: Simon & Schuster, 1980).
2. "Police Brutality!" *Time*, March 25, 1991, p. 18.
3. "L.A. Officers Not Indicted," *The Fayetteville Observer-Times* (North Carolina), May 11, 1991, p. 10C.
4. "Police Brutality!" pp. 16–19.
5. Ibid., p. 16.
6. "Police Charged in Beating Case Say They Feared for Their Lives," *The Boston Globe*, May 22, 1991, p. 22.
7. "Cries of Relief," *Time*, April 26, 1993, p. 18.
8. "Rodney King's Run-ins," *USA Today*, May 30, 1991, 2A.
9. "Morgan Awarded $540,000 by Jurors," *Los Angeles Times*, February 15, 1991, p. B1.
10. Clemmens Bartollas, *American Criminal Justice* (New York: Macmillan, 1988), p. 186.
11. *Mapp* v. *Ohio*, 367 U.S. 643 (1961).
12. *Weeks* v. *U.S.*, 232 U.S. 383 (1914).
13. Roger Goldman and Steven Puro, "Decertification of Police: An Alternative to Traditional Remedies for Police Misconduct," *Hastings Constitutional Law Quarterly*, Vol. 15 (1988), pp. 45–80.
14. Ibid.
15. *Silverthorne Lumber Co.* v. *U.S.*, 251 U.S. 385 (1920).
16. *Mapp* v. *Ohio*.
17. *Wolf* v. *Colorado*, 338 U.S. 25 (1949).
18. *Chimel* v. *California*, 395 U.S. 752 (1969).

19. *U.S.* v. *Rabinowitz,* 339 U.S. 56 (1950).

20. *Katz* v. *U.S.,* 389 U.S. 347, 88 S.Ct. 507 (1967).

21. *Minnesota* v. *Olson,* 110 S.Ct. 1684 (1990).

22. *Illinois* v. *Gates,* 426 U.S. 318 (1982).

23. *U.S.* v. *Leon,* 468 U.S. (1984), 104 S.Ct. 3405.

24. *Massachusetts* v. *Sheppard,* 104 S.Ct. 3424 (1984).

25. *Illinois* v. *Krull,* 107 S.Ct. 1160 (1987).

26. *Maryland* v. *Garrison,* 107 S.Ct. 1013 (1987).

27. *Illinois* v. *Rodriguez,* 110 S.Ct. 2793 (1990).

28. William H. Erickson, William D. Neighbors, and B. J. George, Jr., *United States Supreme Court Cases and Comments* (New York: Matthew Bender, 1987), Section 1.13 [7].

29. *Harris* v. *U.S.,* 390 U.S. 234 (1968).

30. As cited in Kimberly A. Kingston, "Look But Don't Touch: The Plain View Doctrine," *FBI Law Enforcement Bulletin* (December 1987), p. 18.

31. *Horton* v. *California,* 110 S.Ct. 2301, 47 CrL. 2135 (#88-7164, 1990).

32. *U.S.* v. *Irizarry* (1982).

33. *FBI Law Enforcement Bulletin* (December 1987), p. 20.

34. *Arizona* v. *Hicks,* 107 S.Ct. 1149 (1987).

35. See *Criminal Justice Today,* North Carolina Justice Academy (Fall 1987), p. 24.

36. "Inadvertency" as a requirement of legitimate plain view seizures was first cited in the U.S. Supreme Court case of *Coolidge* v. *New Hampshire,* 403 U.S. 443, 91 S.Ct. 2022 (1971).

37. *Horton* v. *California.*

38. John Gales Sauls, "Emergency Searches of Premises," Part 1, *FBI Law Enforcement Bulletin* (March 1987), p. 23.

39. *Warden* v. *Hayden,* 387 U.S. 294 (1967).

40. *Mincey* v. *Arizona,* 437 U.S. 385, 392 (1978).

41. Sauls, "Emergency Searches of Premises," p. 25.

42. *Maryland* v. *Buie,* 110 S.Ct. 1093 (1990).

43. *Illinois* v. *Condon,* No. 92–379. Decided February 22, 1993.

44. For example, *U.S.* v. *Keene* 915 F.2d 1164, 1990, and *U.S.* v. *Moore,* 956 F.2d 843, 1992.

45. Judicial titles vary between jurisdictions. Many lower-level state judicial officers are referred to as "magistrates." Federal magistrates, however, are generally regarded as functioning at a significantly higher level of judicial authority.

46. *Robinson* v. *U.S.,* 414 U.S. 218 (1973).

47. Ibid.

48. *Terry* v. *Ohio,* 392 U.S. 1 (1968).

49. Ibid.

50. *U.S.* v. *Sokolow,* 109 S.Ct. 1581 (1989).

51. *Brown* v. *Texas,* 443 U.S. 47 (1979).

52. *Smith* v. *Ohio,* 110 S.Ct. 1288 (1990).

53. Ibid., at 1289.

54. *California* v. *Hodari D.,* 111 S.Ct. 1547 (1991).

55. *Criminal Justice Newsletter,* May 1, 1991, p. 2.

56. Dissenting opinion in *California* v. *Hodari D.*

57. *Arkansas* v. *Sanders,* 442 U.S. 753 (1979).

58. Ibid.

59. *Borchardt* v. *U.S.,* 809 F.2d 1115 (5th Cir. 1987).

60. *FBI Law Enforcement Bulletin,* January 1988, p. 28.

61. *Carroll* v. *U.S.,* 267 U.S. 132 (1925).

62. *Preston* v. *U.S.,* 376 U.S. 364 (1964).

63. *South Dakota* v. *Opperman,* 428 U.S. 364 (1976).

64. *Colorado* v. *Bertine,* 479 U.S. 367, 107 S.Ct. 741 (1987).

65. *Florida* v. *Wells,* 110 S.Ct. 1632 (1990).

66. *Florida* v. *Jimeno,* 111 S.Ct. 1801 (1991).

67. *Jimeno,* on-line syllabus.

68. *United States* v. *Ross,* 456 U.S. 798 (1982).

69. Ibid.

70. *U.S.* v. *Vilamonte-Marquez,* 462 U.S. 579 (1983).

71. *California* v. *Carney,* 471 U.S. (1985).

72. *U.S.* v. *Hill* 855 F.2d 664 (10th Cir. 1988).

73. *Florida* v. *Bostick,* 111 S.Ct. 2382 (1991).

74. *Aguilar* v. *Texas*, 378 U.S. 108 (1964).
75. *Harris* v. *United States*, 403 U.S. 573 (1971).
76. *Spinelli* v. *United States*, 393 U.S. 410 (1969).
77. *Illinois* v. *Gates*, 426 U.S. 318 (1982).
78. *Alabama* v. *White*, 110 S.Ct. 2412 (1990).
79. Ibid., at 2417.
80. *U.S. Department of Justice* v. *Landano*, No. 91–2054. Decided May 24, 1993.
81. *Brown* v. *Mississippi*, 297 U.S. 278 (1936).
82. *Ashcraft* v. *Tennessee*, 322 U.S. 143 (1944).
83. *Chambers* v. *Florida*, 309 U.S. 227 (1940).
84. Ibid.
85. *Leyra* v. *Denno*, 347 U.S. 556 (1954).
86. Ibid.
87. *Arizona* v. *Fulminante*, 111 S.Ct. 1246 (1991).
88. *Chapman* v. *California*, 386 U.S. 18 (1967).
89. *Escobedo* v. *Illinois*, 378 U.S. 478 (1964).
90. *Edwards* v. *Arizona*, U.S. 477, 101 S.Ct. 1880 (1981).
91. *Arizona* v. *Roberson*, 486 U.S. 675, 108 S.Ct. 2093 (1988).
92. *Miranda* v. *Arizona*, 384 U.S. 436 (1966).
93. Ibid.
94. *Moran* v. *Burbine*, 475 U.S., 106 S.Ct. 1135 (1986).
95. Ibid.
96. *Colorado* v. *Spring*, 479 U.S. 564, 107 S.Ct. 851 (1987).
97. "Immigrants Get Civil Rights," *USA Today*, June 11, 1992, p. 1A.
98. *Nix* v. *Williams*, 104 S.Ct. 2501 (1984).
99. Ibid.
100. *New York* v. *Quarles*, 104 S.Ct. 2626, 81 L.Ed. 2d 550 (1984).
101. *Colorado* v. *Connelly*, 107 S.Ct. 515, 93 L.Ed. 2d 473 (1986).
102. Ibid.
103. *Kuhlmann* v. *Wilson*, 477 U.S., 106 S.Ct. 2616 (1986).
104. *Perkins*, at 2397.
105. *Rock* v. *Zimmerman*, 543 F.Supp. 179 (M.D. Penna. 1982).
106. Ibid.
107. See *Oregon* v. *Mathiason*, 429 U.S. 492, 97 S.Ct. 711 (1977).
108. *Rhode Island* v. *Innis*, 446 U.S. 291 (1980).
109. *South Dakota* v. *Neville*, 103 S.Ct. 916 (1983).
110. Ibid.
111. *Arizona* v. *Mauro*, 107 S.Ct. 1931, 95 L.Ed. 2d 458 (1987).
112. *Doyle* v. *Ohio*, 426 U.S. 610 (1976).
113. *Brecht* v. *Abrahamson*, No. 91–7358. Decided April 21, 1993.
114. Citing *Kotteakos* v. *United States*, 328 U.S. 750 (1946).
115. *Hayes* v. *Florida*, 470 U.S., 105 S.Ct. 1643 (1985).
116. *Winston* v. *Lee*, 470 U.S., 105 S.Ct. 1611 (1985).
117. *Schmerber* v. *California*, 384 U.S. 757 (1966).
118. *U.S.* v. *Montoya de Hernandez*, 473 U.S., 105 S.Ct. 3304 (1985).
119. Ibid.
120. *Olmstead* v. *U.S.*, 277 U.S. 438 (1928).
121. *On Lee* v. *U.S.*, 343 U.S. 747 (1952).
122. *Lopez* v. *U.S.*, 373 U.S. 427 (1963).
123. *Berger* v. *New York*, 388 U.S. 41 (1967).
124. *Katz* v. *U.S.*, 389 U.S. 347 (1967).
125. *Lee* v. *Florida*, 392 U.S. 378 (1968).
126. Federal Communications Act, 1934.
127. *U.S.* v. *White*, 401 U.S. 745 (1971).
128. *U.S.* v. *Karo*, 104 S.Ct. 3296, 3301 (1984).
129. *United States* v. *Scott*, 436 U.S. 128 (1978).
130. For more information, see *FBI Law Enforcement Bulletin* (June 1987), p. 25.
131. The Electronic Communications Privacy Act, 1986.
132. For more information on the ECPA, see Robert A. Fiatal, "The Electronic Communications Privacy Act: Addressing Today's Technology," *FBI Law Enforcement Bulletin* (April 1988), pp. 24–30.

INDIVIDUAL RIGHTS VERSUS SOCIAL CONCERNS

THE RIGHTS OF THE ACCUSED BEFORE THE COURT

Common law, constitutional, and humanitarian rights of the accused:

The Right to a Speedy Trial
The Right to Legal Counsel
The Right Against Self-incrimination
The Right Not to Be Tried Twice for the Same Offense
The Right to Know the Charges
The Right to Cross-examine Witnesses
The Right to Speak and Present Witnesses
The Right Against Excessive Bail

The individual rights listed must be effectively balanced against these community concerns:

Conviction of the Guilty
Exoneration of the Innocent
The Imposition of Appropriate Punishment
Protection of Society
Efficient and Cost-effective Procedures

How does our system of justice work toward balance?

ADJUDICATION AND PUNISHMENT

When a man wants to murder a tiger, he calls it sport; when the tiger wants to murder him, he calls it ferocity. The distinction between crime and justice is no greater.
   —G.B. SHAW (1856–1950)

The love of justice in most men is only the fear of suffering injustice.
   —LA ROCHEFOUCAULD (1613–1680)

The concept of desert is the only connecting link between punishment and justice. It is only as deserved or undeserved that a sentence can be just or unjust.
   —C.S. LEWIS (1898–1963)

The story is told of the elderly judge who, looking back over a long career, observes with satisfaction that "when I was young, I probably let stand some convictions that should have been overturned, and when I was old I probably set aside some that should have stood; so overall, justice was done." I sometimes think that is an appropriate analog to this Court's constitutional jurisprudence, which alternately creates rights that the Constitution does not contain and denies rights that it does.
   —JUSTICE ANTONIN SCALIA, COMMENTING ON THE POWER OF THE U.S. SUPREME COURT

CHAPTER 8

THE

COURTS

There is no such thing as justice—in or out of court.
—CLARENCE DARROW (1857–1938)

No person shall be held to answer for a capital or otherwise infamous crime, unless on a presentment or indictment of a grand jury,…nor shall any person be subject for the same offense to be twice put in jeopardy of life or limb; nor shall be compelled in any criminal case to be a witness against himself, nor be deprived of life, liberty, or property, without due process of law…
—FIFTH AMENDMENT TO THE U.S. CONSTITUTION

After years of twisting the Constitution into a pretzel, handcuffing cops and drooling over the rights of killers and rapists, America's federal judges have suddenly discovered violent crime, and they're fretting that it might come to their neighborhood soon.
—WASHINGTON TIMES EDITORIAL

KEY CONCEPTS

judicial review
circuit courts
writ of *certiorari*
court of last resort
court administrator

dual court system
impeachment
trial court
plea bargaining
release on recognizance

jurisdiction
pretrial release
lower court
bond

KEY CASES

U.S. v. *Montalvo-Murillo*
Herrera v. *Collins*

County of Riverside (CA)
v. *McLaughlin*

Keeney v. *Tamayo-Reyes*
United States v.
Alvarez-Machain

INTRODUCTION

Federal Court System
The three-tiered structure of federal courts, involving U.S. district courts, U.S. courts of appeal, and the U.S. Supreme Court.

Between the often-enthralling police quest for suspects and the sometimes hopeless incarceration of offenders stands **the system of federal and state courts**. Courts dispense justice on a daily basis and work to ensure that all official actors in the justice arena carry out their duties in recognition of the rule of law.

At many points in this volume, and in three specific chapters (Chapter 7, Policing: Legal Aspects; Chapter 12, Prisons; and Chapter 11, Probation and Parole), we take a close look at court precedents which have defined the "legality" of enforcement efforts and correctional action. Another chapter (Criminal Law) explores the lawmaking function of courts. This chapter is primarily descriptive of the American court system at both the state and federal levels. The roles of official courtroom actors—from jurors to judges—and steps in a criminal trial are described in the chapter which follows. Figure 8–1 outlines the structure of contemporary federal and state courts.

State Court Systems State judicial structures. Most states have at least three court levels, generally referred to as trial courts, appellate courts, and a state supreme court.

AMERICAN COURT HISTORY

Two criminal court systems coexist in America today: (1) state courts and (2) federal courts. Today's dual court system is the result of general agreement among the nation's founders about the need for individual states to retain significant legislative authority and autonomy seperate from federal control. Under this concept, the United States developed as a relatively loose federation of semi-independent provinces. New states joining the union were assured of limited federal intervention into local affairs. Under this arrangement, state legislatures were free to create laws, and state court systems were needed to hear cases in which violations of those laws occurred. The last 200 years have seen a slow ebbing of states' rights relative to the power of the federal government. Even today, however, state courts do not hear cases involving alleged violations of federal law, nor do federal courts involve themselves in deciding issues of state law, unless there is a conflict between local statute and federal constitutional guarantees.

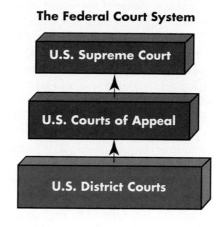

Typical State Court System

State Supreme Court

↑

Intermediate Appellate Court(s)

↑

Trial Courts of General Jurisdiction

Trial Courts of Limited Jurisdiction

The Federal Court System

U.S. Supreme Court

↑

U.S. Courts of Appeal

↑

U.S. District Courts

Note: Not all states have intermediate appellate courts. In those states appeals are made directly to the state supreme court.

FIGURE 8–1   The structure of state and federal courts.

In this chapter we will describe both federal and state court systems in terms of their historical development and current structure. It is to state courts that we first turn our attention.

STATE COURT DEVELOPMENT

Each of the original American colonies had its own system for resolving disputes, both civil and criminal. As early as 1629 the Massachusetts Bay Colony had created a "General Court," composed of the governor, his deputy, 18 assistants, and 118 elected officials. The General Court was a combined legislature/court, which made laws, held trials and imposed sentences.[1] By 1639, as the colony grew, county courts were created and the General Court took on as its primary job the hearing of appeals, retaining original jurisdiction only in cases involving "tryalls of life, limm, or banishment…" (and divorce).[2]

Pennsylvania began its colonial existence with the belief that "every man could serve as his own lawyer."[3] The Pennsylvania system utilized "common peacemakers" who served as referees. Parties to a dispute, including criminal suspects, could choose one person who would then hear the case pled by the aggrieved and the accused. The decision of the peacemaker was binding upon the suspect and the colony. Although the Pennsylvania referee system ended in 1766, lower-level judges, called magistrates in many other jurisdictions, are still referred to as "justices of the peace" in Pennsylvania and a few other states.

Prior to 1776 all American colonies had established fully functioning court systems. The practice of law, however, was substantially inhibited by a lack of trained lawyers. A number of the early colonies even displayed a strong reluctance to recognize the practice of law as a profession. A Virginia statute, for example, enacted in 1645, provided for the removal of "mercenary attorneys" from office and prohibited the practice of law for a fee. Most other colonies retained strict control over the number of authorized barristers by requiring formal training in English law schools and gubernatorial appointments. New York, which provided for the appointment of "counselors at law," permitted a total of only 41 lawyers to practice law between 1695 and 1769.[4]

Jurisdiction The territory,
subject matter, or persons
over which lawful author-
ity may be exercised by a
court or other justice
agency, as determined by
statute or constitution.

Appellate Jurisdiction
The lawful authority of a
court to review a decision
made by a lower court.

The tenuous status of lawyers in the colonies was highlighted by the 1735 New York
trial of John Zenger. Zenger was editor of the *New York Journal*, a newspaper, and was
accused of slandering then-governor Cosby. Cosby blatantly threatened to disbar any
lawyer who defended Zenger, prompting Zenger to hire Pennsylvania lawyer Andrew
Hamilton. Hamilton, by virtue of his out-of-state residence, was immune to the governor's
threats. Zenger's acquittal resulted in the country's first landmark decision supporting freedom of the press.[5]

Following the American Revolution, colonial courts provided the organizational basis
for the growth of fledgling state court systems. As there had been considerable diversity in
the structure of colonial courts, state courts were anything but uniform.

Initially, most states made no distinction between original and **appellate jurisdiction**,
and many had no provisions for appeal. Delaware, for example, did not allow for appeals
in criminal cases until 1897. States which did permit appeals often lacked any established
appellate courts and sometimes used state legislatures for that purpose.

By the late 1800s a dramatic increase in population and far-reaching changes in the
American way of life had led to a tremendous increase in civil litigation and criminal
arrests. Lawmaking bodies tried to keep pace with the rising tide of suits. They created a
multiplicity of courts at the trial, appellate, and supreme court levels, calling them by a
diversity of names and assigning functions which sometimes bore little resemblance
to like-sounding courts in neighboring states. City courts arose to handle the special problems of urban life and were limited in their jurisdiction by community boundaries. Other
tribunals, such as juvenile courts, developed to handle special kinds of problems or special
clients. Some, like magistrates' or small claims courts, handled only petty disputes and
minor law violations. Others, like traffic courts, were very narrow in focus. The result was
a patchwork quilt of hearing bodies, some very vaguely resembling modern notions of a
trial court.

State court systems did, however, have several models to follow during their development. One was the New York state Field Code of 1848, which was eventually copied by
most other states. The Field Code clarified jurisdictional claims and specified matters of
court procedure, but was later amended so extensively that its usefulness as a model dis-
solved. Another court systems model was provided by the federal Judiciary Act of 1789 and
the later federal Reorganization Act of 1801. States which followed the federal model developed a three-tiered structure of (1) trial courts of limited jurisdiction, (2) trial courts of
general jurisdiction, and (3) appellate courts.

STATE COURT SYSTEMS TODAY

The federal model was far from a panacea, however. Within the three-tiered structure it
provided, many local and specialized courts proliferated. Traffic courts, magistrates' courts,
municipal courts, recorders' courts, probate courts, and courts held by justices of the peace
were but a few which functioned at the lower levels. A movement toward simplification of
state court structures, led primarily by the American Bar Association and the American
Judicature Society, began in the early 1900s. Proponents of state court reform sought the
unification of redundant courts which held overlapping jurisdiction. Most reform-minded
thinkers suggested a uniform model for states everywhere which would build upon (1) a
centralized court structure composed of a clear hierarchy of trial and appellate courts, (2)
the consolidation of numerous lower-level courts holding overlapping jurisdiction, and (3)
a centralized state court authority which would be responsible for budgeting, financing,
and management of all courts within a state.

The court reform movement is still operative today. It has made a substantial number of inroads in many states. However, a large number of differences continue to exist between and among state court systems. Reform states, which early on embraced the reform movement, are now characterized by streamlined judicial systems consisting of precisely conceived trial courts of limited and general jurisdiction, supplemented by one or two appellate court levels. Nonreform, or traditional, states retain judicial systems which are a conglomeration of multilevel and sometimes redundant courts with poorly defined jurisdiction. Even in nonreform states, however, most criminal courts can be classified within the three-story structure of two trial court echelons and an appellate tier.

Trial Courts

Trial courts are where criminal cases begin. The trial court conducts arraignments, sets bail, takes pleas, and conducts trials. If the defendant is found guilty (or pleads guilty) the trial court imposes sentence. Trial courts of limited or special jurisdiction are also called lower courts. Lower courts are authorized to hear only less serious criminal cases, usually involving misdemeanors, or to hear special types of cases such as traffic violations, family disputes, small claims, and so on. Courts of limited jurisdiction rarely hold jury trials, depending instead on the hearing judge to make determinations of both fact and law. At the lower court level a detailed record of the proceedings is not maintained. Case files will only include information on the charge, the plea, the finding of the court, and the sentence.

Lower courts are much less given to formality than are courts of general jurisdiction. In an intriguing analysis of court characteristics, Thomas Henderson[6] found that misdemeanor courts process cases according to a decisional model. The decisional model is informal, personal, and decisive. It depends upon the quick resolution of relatively uncomplicated issues of law and fact.

Courts of general jurisdiction, called variously, high courts, circuit courts, or superior courts, are authorized to hear any criminal case. In many states they also provide the first appellate level for courts of limited jurisdiction. In most cases, superior courts offer defendants whose cases originated in lower courts the chance for a new trial instead of a review of the record of the earlier hearing. When a new trial is held it is referred to as **trial *de novo***.

Henderson[7] describes courts of general jurisdiction according to a procedural model. Such courts make full use of juries, prosecutors, defense attorneys, witnesses, and all the other actors we usually associate with American courtrooms. The procedural model is fraught with numerous court appearances to ensure that all of a defendant's due process rights are protected. The procedural model makes for a long, expensive, relatively impersonal, and highly formal series of legal maneuvers involving many professional participants.

Trial courts of general jurisdiction operate within a fact-finding framework called the adversarial process. That process pits the interests of the state, represented by prosecutorial resources, against the professional skills and abilities of defense attorneys. The adversarial process is not a free-for-all, but is, rather, constrained by procedural rules specified in law and sustained through tradition.

Appellate Courts

Most states today have an appellate division, consisting of an intermediate appellate court (often called the Court of Appeals) and a high-level appellate court (generally termed the state supreme court). High-level appellate courts are referred to as courts of last resort, to indicate that no other appellate route remains to a defendant within the state court

Trial *de Novo* Literally, a new trial. The term is applied to cases which are retried on appeal, as opposed to those which are simply reviewed on the record.

A courtroom in Travis County, Texas. Courts have often been called "the fulcrum of the criminal justice system." *Photo: Bob Daemmrich/Stock Boston.*

Appeal Generally, the request that a court with appellate jurisdiction review the judgment, decision, or order of a lower court and set it aside (reverse it) or modify it.

system once the high court rules on a case. All states have supreme courts, although only 36 have intermediate appellate courts.[8]

An **appeal** by a convicted defendant asks that a higher court review the actions of a lower one. Courts within the appellate division, once they accept an appeal, do not conduct a new trial. Instead they provide a review of the case on the record. In other words, appellate courts examine the written transcript of lower court hearings to ensure that those proceedings were carried out fairly and in accordance with proper procedure and state law. They may also allow brief oral arguments to be made by attorneys for both sides and will generally consider other briefs or information filed by the appellant (the party initiating the appeal) or appellee (the side opposed to the appeal). State statutes generally require that sentences of death or life imprisonments be automatically reviewed by the state supreme court.

Most convictions are affirmed upon appeal. Occasionally, however, an appellate court will determine that the trial court erred in allowing certain kinds of evidence to be heard, or that it failed to interpret properly the significance of a relevant statute. When that happens the verdict of the trial court will be reversed, and the case may be remanded, or sent back for a new trial. Where a conviction is overturned by an appellate court because of constitutional issues, or where a statute is determined to be invalid, the state usually has recourse to the state supreme court, or the U.S. Supreme Court (when an issue of federal law is involved, as when a state court has ruled a federal law unconstitutional).

Defendants who are not satisfied with the resolution of their case within a state court system may attempt an appeal to the U.S. Supreme Court. For such an appeal to have any chance of being heard, it must be based upon claimed violations of the defendant's rights as guaranteed under federal law or the U.S. Constitution. Under certain circumstances federal district courts may also provide a path of relief for state defendants who can show that their federal constitutional rights have been violated. However, in the 1992 case of *Keeney* v.

Tamayo-Reyes,[9] the U.S. Supreme Court ruled that a "respondent is entitled to a federal evidentiary hearing [only] if he can show cause for his failure to develop the facts in the state-court proceedings and actual prejudice resulting from that failure, or if he can show that a fundamental miscarriage of justice would result from failure to hold such a hearing." Justice Byron White, writing for the Court, said "[i]t is hardly a good use of scarce judicial resources to duplicate fact-finding in federal court merely because a petitioner has negligently failed to take advantage of opportunities in state court proceedings." Likewise, in *Herrera* v. *Collins* (1993),[10] the Court ruled that new evidence of innocence is no reason for a federal court to order a new state trial if constitutional grounds are lacking. In *Herrera,* where the defendant was under a Texas death sentence for the murder of two police officers, the Court said: "[w]here a defendant has been afforded a fair trial and convicted of the offense for which he was charged, the constitutional presumption of innocence disappears.... Thus, claims of actual innocence based on newly discovered evidence have never been held [to be] grounds for...relief absent an independent constitutional violation occurring in the course of the underlying state criminal proceedings. To allow a federal court to grant relief...would in effect require a new trial 10 years after the first trial, not because of any constitutional violation at the first trial, but simply because of a belief that in light of his new found evidence a jury might find him not guilty at a second trial." The *Keeney* and *Herrera* decisions had the effect of severely limiting routine access by state defendants to federal courts.

State Court Administration

To function efficiently, courts require uninterrupted funding, adequate staffing, trained support personnel, a well-managed case flow, and coordination between levels and among jurisdictions. To oversee these and other aspects of judicial management, every state today has its own mechanism for court administration. Most make use of **state court administrators.**

The first state court administrator was appointed in New Jersey in 1948.[11] Although other states were initially slow to follow the New Jersey lead, increased federal funding for criminal justice administration during the 1970s, and a growing realization that some form of coordinated management was necessary for effective court operation, eventually led most states to create similar administrative offices. The following tasks are typical of state court administrators today:[12]

1. The preparation, presentation, and monitoring of a budget for the state court system
2. The analysis of case flows and backlogs to determine where additional resources such as judges, prosecutors, and other court personnel are needed
3. The collection and publication of statistics describing the operation of state courts
4. Efforts to streamline the flow of cases through individual courts and the system as a whole
5. Service as a liaison between state legislatures and the court system
6. The development and/or coordination of requests for federal and other outside funding
7. The management of state court personnel, including promotions for support staff and the handling of retirement and other benefits packages for court employees
8. The creation and the coordination of plans for the training of judges and other court personnel (in conjunction with local chief judges and supreme court justices)
9. The assignment of judges to judicial districts (especially in states that use rotating judgeships)
10. The administrative review of payments to legal counsel for indigent defendants

State Court Administrators Coordinating personnel who function to assist with case flow management, budgeting of operating funds, and court docket administration.

Evaluating Courts

In October 1993 the Bureau of Justice Statistics published *Performance Measures for the Criminal Justice System*, a collection of discussion papers produced by the BJS–Princeton Project group. The papers represent the best official effort to date to identify performance goals and associated measures useful in assessing the day-to-day operations of criminal justice agencies.

Following the lead of the National Center for State Courts, the Project identified, among others, the following goals and performance indicators applicable to trial courts:

Goals	*Performance Indicators*
Standard 1. Access to justice 1.1 Public proceedings 1.2 Safety, accessibility, and convenience 1.3 Effective participation 1.4 Courtesy, responsiveness, and respect	Proceedings and other business are openly conducted. Court facilities are safe, convenient, and accessible. All who appear before the court are given the opportunity to participate effectively, without undue hardship or inconvenience.
Standard 2. Expeditiousness and timeliness 2.1 Case processing 2.2 Compliance with schedules 2.3 Prompt implementation of law and procedure	The court processes cases in a timely manner. The court provides reports and information according to schedules and responds to requests for information in a way which assures their effective use.
Standard 3. Equity, fairness, and integrity 3.1 Fair and reliable judicial process 3.2 Juries 3.3 Court decisions and actions 3.4 Clarity 3.5 Responsibility for enforcement 3.6 Production and preservation of records	Procedures adhere to law, procedural rules, and established policies. Jury lists are representative of the jurisdiction from which they are drawn. Trial courts take responsibility for the enforcement of their orders. Records of all court decisions and actions are accurate and properly preserved.
Standard 4. Independence and accountability 4.1 Independence and comity 4.2 Accountability for public resources 4.3 Personnel practices and decisions 4.4 Public education 4.5 Response to change	The court maintains institutional integrity. The court responsibly accounts for its resources. The court uses fair employment practices. The court informs the community of its programs. The court anticipates new conditions and adjusts its operations accordingly.

Standard 5. Public trust and confidence	The trial court and the justice it delivers are perceived by the public as accessible.
5.1 Accessibility	The public has trust and confidence in the court.
5.2 Expeditious, fair, and reliable court functions	The trial court is not perceived to be unduly influenced by other components of government.
5.3 Judicial independence and accountability	

Source: George F. Cole, "Performance Measures for Trial Courts, Prosecution, and Public Defense," in John J. DiLulio, Jr., et al., *Performance Measures for the Criminal Justice System: Discussion Papers from the BJS–Princeton Project* (Washington, D.C.: Bureau of Justice Statistics, October 1993).

Dispute Resolution Centers

Some communities have begun to recognize that it is possible to resolve at least minor disputes without the need for a formalized process of adjudication. Dispute resolution centers, which function to hear victim's claims of minor wrongs, such as bad checks, trespass, shoplifting, and petty theft, function today in over 200 locations throughout the country.[13] Frequently staffed by volunteer mediators, such programs work to resolve disagreements without the need to assign blame. Dispute resolution programs began in the early 1970s, with the earliest being the Community Assistance Project in Chester, Pennsylvania; the Columbus, Ohio, Night Prosecutor Program; and the Arbitration as an Alternative Program in Rochester, New York. Following the lead of these programs, the U.S. Department of Justice helped promote the development of three experimental "Neighborhood Justice Centers" in Los Angeles, Kansas City, and Atlanta. Each center accepted both minor civil and criminal cases.

Mediation centers are often closely integrated with the formal criminal justice process and may substantially reduce the caseload of lower-level courts. Some centers are, in fact, run by the courts in various jurisdictions and work only with court-ordered referrals. Others are semiautonomous, but may be dependent upon courts for endorsement of their decisions, while others function with complete autonomy. Rarely, however, do dispute resolution programs entirely supplant the formal criminal justice mechanism, and defendants who appear before a community mediator may also later be charged with a crime.

Mediation centers have been criticized for the fact that they typically work only with minor offenses, thereby denying the opportunity for mediation to victims and offenders in more serious cases, and for the fact that they may be seen by defendants as just another form of criminal sanction.[14] Other critiques claim that community dispute resolution centers do little other than provide a forum for shouting matches between the parties involved.

Dispute Resolution Centers Informal hearing infrastructures designed to mediate interpersonal disputes without need for the more formal arrangements of criminal trial courts.

THE RISE OF THE FEDERAL COURTS

State courts had their origins in early colonial arrangements. Federal courts, however, were created by the U.S. Constitution. Section 1 of Article III of the Constitution provides for the establishment of "one supreme Court, and…such inferior Courts as the Congress may

from time to time ordain and establish." Article III, Section 2, specifies that such courts are to have jurisdiction over cases arising under the Constitution, federal laws, and treaties. Federal courts are also to settle disputes between states and to have jurisdiction in cases where one of the parties is a state.

The federal court system of today represents the culmination of a series of congressional mandates which have expanded the federal judicial infrastructure so that it can continue to carry out the duties envisioned by the Constitution. Notable federal statutes which have contributed to the present structure of the federal court system include the Judiciary Act of 1789, the Judiciary Act of 1925, and the Magistrate's Act of 1968.

The Judiciary Act of 1789 created, in addition to the U.S. Supreme Court, 13 federal court districts, grouped into three circuits (see Figure 8–2). Under those early arrangements, judges would ride the circuit, a practice especially useful in dispensing justice to the widely scattered populations of the American West. In each circuit, federal appeals courts composed of two Supreme Court justices and one federal district judge were designated to hear appeals from district courts. The act also required states to enforce the Constitution and federal laws.

FIGURE 8–2   The 13 federal judicial circuits. Courtesy of West Publishing Company. Reprinted with permission.

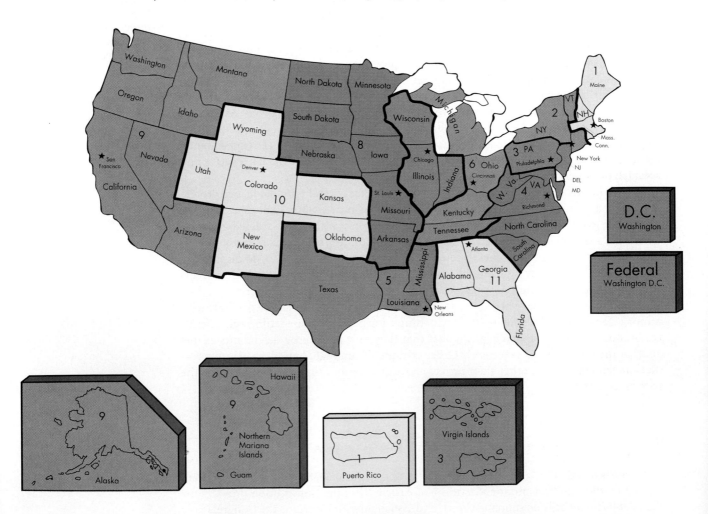

Note in the figure that only 11 of the 13 circuit courts are officially numbered. Those courts, plus the District of Columbia judicial circuit, are jurisdictionally organized according to the territory they serve. The jurisdiction of the U.S. Court of Appeals for the Federal Circuit (in effect, the "Thirteenth Circuit"), however, is defined by the nature of the cases heard.

By the mid-1800s Supreme Court justices had been relieved of circuit duties, and in 1891 Congress established nine intermediate federal appellate courts to reduce the number of appeals deluging the Supreme Court. The 1891 act also gave the Supreme Court the authority to choose only those cases for hearing which represented a significant legal principle.

Today's federal judiciary consists of three levels: (1) U.S. district courts, (2) U.S. courts of appeals, and (3) the U.S. Supreme Court. Each is described in turn.

Federal District Courts

The lowest level of the federal court system consists of 94 district courts located in the 50 states (except for the District of Wyoming, which includes the Montana and Idaho portions of Yellowstone National Park), Puerto Rico, the District of Columbia, and the U.S. territories of Guam, the Virgin Islands, and the Northern Mariana Islands. Each state has at least one U.S. district court, and some, like New York and California, have as many as four. District courts were first authorized by Congress through the 1789 Judiciary Act, which allocated one federal court to each state. Population increases over the years have necessitated the addition of new courts in a number of states. District courts are the trial courts of the federal judicial system. They have **original jurisdiction** over all cases involving alleged violations of federal statutes.

Nearly 600 district court judges staff federal district courts. District court judges are appointed by the president, confirmed by the Senate, and serve for life. An additional 460 U.S. magistrates serve the district court system and assist federal judges. Magistrates have the power to conduct assignments and may set bail, issue warrants, and try petty offenders and some misdemeanors.[15]

U.S. district courts handle thousands of criminal cases per year. Some courts are much busier than others. As a consequence, the number of district court judges varies from a low of 2 in some jurisdictions to a high of 27 in others. The Southern District of California adjudicated 174 criminal cases per judgeship in 1992, the highest number of any district.[16] During the past 20 years the number of cases handled by the entire federal district court system has grown exponentially. The hiring of new judges has not kept pace with the increase in caseload, and questions persist as to the quality of justice that can be delivered by overworked judges.

One of the most pressing issues facing district court judges is the fact that their pay, which at $133,600 in mid-1993[17] placed them in the top 1% of incoming-earning Americans, is small compared to what most could earn in private practice. Many federal judges, however, made substantial amounts of money from private practice before assuming the bench, while others had income from investments or held family fortunes.

U.S. Courts of Appeals

The 12 U.S. Courts of Appeals are the intermediate-level appellate courts of the federal system. Federal appellate courts are also called circuit courts because the federal system is geographically divided into 11 circuits. A twelfth circuit court of appeals serves the District of Columbia. More than 150 judges staff the various federal appeals courts.

Original Jurisdiction The lawful authority of a court to hear or act upon a case from its beginning and to pass judgment on the law and the facts.

Supreme Court justice Ruth Bader
Ginsburg, shown here with President
Clinton at her 1993 swearing-in ceremony, became the second woman to
serve on the nation's highest court,
and the first Democratic nominee to
assume the bench in 26 years.
Photo: Robert Trippett/Sipa Press.

Federal appellate courts have mandatory jurisdiction over the decisions of district courts within their circuits. Mandatory jurisdiction means that U.S. courts of appeals are required to hear the cases brought to them. Criminal appeals from federal district courts are usually heard by panels of three judges sitting on a court of appeals rather than by all the judges of each circuit.

Federal appellate courts operate under the *Federal Rules of Appellate Procedure*, although each has also created its own separate Local Rules. Local Rules may mean that one circuit, such as the Second, will depend heavily upon oral arguments, while others may substitute written summary dispositions in their place. Appeals generally fall into one of three categories:[18] (1) frivolous appeals, which have little substance, raise no significant new issues, and are generally quickly disposed of; (2) ritualistic appeals, which are brought primarily because of the demands of litigants, even though the probability of reversal is negligible; and (3) nonconsensual appeals, which entail major questions of law and policy, and on which there is considerable professional disagreement among the courts and within the legal profession. The probability of reversal is, of course, highest in the case of non-consensual appeals.

Because the Constitution guarantees a right to an appeal, federal circuit courts have found themselves facing an ever-increasing work load. Almost all appeals from federal district courts go to the court of appeals serving the circuit in which the case was first heard. A defendant's right to appeal, however, has been interpreted to mean the right to one appeal. Hence, the U.S. Supreme Court need not necessarily hear the appeals of defendants who are dissatisfied with the decision of a federal appeals court.

TABLE 8-1

JUSTICES OF THE U.S. SUPREME COURT

Justice	Sworn In	Views
Chief Justice		
William H. Rehnquist	January 1972	Very conservative
Associate Justices		
John Paul Stevens	December 1975	Moderate to liberal
Sandra Day O'Connor	September 1981	Moderate to conservative
Antonin Scalia	September 1986	Very conservative
Anthony M. Kennedy	February 1988	Conservative
David H. Souter	July 1990	Conservative
Clarence Thomas	October 1991	Conservative
Ruth Bader Ginsburg	August 1993	Moderate
One vacancy at time of writing		

The Supreme Court of the United States

At the apex of the federal court system stands the U.S. Supreme Court. The Supreme Court consists of nine justices, eight of whom are referred to as associate justices. Presiding over the Court is the chief justice of the United States. (See Table 8–1.) Supreme Court justices are nominated by the president, confirmed by the Senate, and serve for life. Lengthy terms of service are a tradition among justices. One of the earliest chief justices, John Marshall, served the Court for 34 years, from 1801 to 1835. The same was true of Justice Stephen J. Field who sat on the bench for 34 years, between 1863 and 1897. Justice Hugo Black passed the 34-year milestone, serving an additional month, before he retired in 1971. Justice William O. Douglas set a record for longevity on the bench, retiring in 1975, after 36 years and 6 months of service.

The Supreme Court of the United States wields immense power. The Court's greatest authority lies in its capacity for **judicial review** of lower court decisions and state and federal statute. By exercising its power of judicial review, the Court decides what laws and lower court decisions are in keeping with the intent of the U.S. Constitution. The power of judicial review is not explicit in the Constitution, but was anticipated by its framers. In the *Federalist Papers*, which urged adoption of the Constitution, Alexander Hamilton wrote that, through the practice of judicial review, the Court would ensure that "the will of the whole people," as grounded in the Constitution, would be supreme over the "will of the legislature…," which might be subject to temporary whims.[19]

It was not until 1803, however, that the Court forcefully asserted its power of judicial review. In an opinion written for the case of *Marbury* v. *Madison* (1803),[20] Chief Justice John Marshall established the Court's authority as final interpreter of the U.S. Constitution, declaring that "It is emphatically the province of the judicial department to say what the law is…."

Increasing Complexity and the Supreme Court The evolution of the U.S. Supreme Court provides one of the most dramatic examples of institutional development in American history. Sparsely described in the Constitution, the Court has grown from a handful of circuit riding justices into a modern organization that wields

Judicial Review The power of a court to review actions and decisions made by other agencies of government.

tremendous legal power over all aspects of American life. Much of the Court's growth has been due to its increasing willingness to mediate fundamental issues of law and to act as a resort from arbitrary and capricious processing by the justice systems of the states and national government.

The *Marbury* decision, described earlier, established the Court as a mighty force in federal government by virtue of the power of judicial review. It was the Court's willingness to apply that power during the 1960s to issues of crime and justice at the state and local levels, however, which has created a burdensome workload for the Court, which even today shows few signs of abatement. The Court's change in orientation was signaled in 1961 by the case of *Mapp* v. *Ohio*.[21] The *Mapp* case, described in detail in an earlier chapter, extended the exclusionary rule to the states. Such extension, combined with the near-simultaneous end of the hands-off doctrine which had previously exempted state prison systems from Court scrutiny, placed the authority of the Court squarely over the activities of state criminal justice systems.

In 1992, in what proved to be a controversial decision affecting international law enforcement, the Court ruled: "The fact of respondent's forcible abduction does not prohibit his trial in a United States court for violations of this country's criminal laws." In the case, *United States* v. *Alvarez-Machain*,[22] Alvarez Machain, a Mexican citizen, was forcibly kidnapped from his home in Mexico and flown by private plane to Texas, where he was arrested for his participation in the kidnapping and torture-murder of a Drug Enforcement Administration (DEA) agent and the agent's pilot. A federal district court ordered him returned to Mexico, reasoning that his kidnapping had violated the extradition treaty between the United States and Mexico. The Court of Appeals affirmed the district court's finding. The Supreme Court, however, disagreed, reasoning that "[n]either the Treaty's language nor the history of negotiations and practice under it supports the proposition that it prohibits abductions....The Treaty says nothing about either country refraining from forcibly abducting people from the other's territory or the consequences if an abduction occurs." Justices Stevens, Blackmun, and O'Connor dissented from the majority opinion, saying, "[a] State must not perform acts of sovereignty in the territory of another State. It is...a breach of International Law for a State to send its agents to the territory of another State to apprehend persons accused of having committed a crime."

The Supreme Court Today The Supreme Court has limited original jurisdiction and does not conduct trials, except in disputes between states and some cases of attorney disbarment. The Court, rather, reviews the decisions of lower courts and may accept cases from both U.S. courts of appeals and state supreme courts. The decision to review a case depends upon a vote of at least four justices who must be in favor of a hearing. When at least four justices agree that a case should be heard, the Court will issue a writ of *certiorari* to a lower court, ordering it to send the records of the case forward for review. Once having granted *certiorari*, the justices can revoke the decision. In such cases a writ is dismissed by ruling it improvidently granted.

The U.S. Supreme Court may review any decision appealed to it which it decides is worthy of review. In fact, however, the Court elects to review only cases which involve a substantial federal question. Of approximately 5,000 requests for review received by the Court yearly, only about 200 are actually heard.

A term of the Supreme Court begins, by statute, on the first Monday in October and lasts until early July. The term is divided between sittings, when cases will be heard, and time for the writing and delivering of opinions. Between 22 and 24 cases will be heard at each sitting, with each side allocated 30 minutes for arguments before the justices. Intervening recesses allow justices time to study arguments and supporting documentation and to work on their opinions.

The first permanent chamber of the U.S. Supreme Court, on the ground floor of the U.S. Capitol building. *Photo: AP/Wide World Photos.*

Rarely are the decisions rendered by the Supreme Court unanimous. Opinions agreed upon by a majority of the Court's justices make for the judgment of the Court. Concurring opinions are written by justices who agree with the Court's judgment, but for a different reason, or who feel that they have some new light to shed on a particular legal issue involved in the case. Dissenting opinions are provided by justices who do not agree with the decision of the Court. Dissenting opinions may offer new possibilities for successful appeals made at a later date.

Ideas for Change   Increasing caseloads at the federal appellate court level, combined with the many requests for Supreme Court review, have led to proposals to restructure the federal appellate court system. In 1973, a study group appointed by Chief Justice Burger suggested the creation of a National Court of Appeals, which would serve as a kind of "mini–Supreme Court."[23] Under the proposal, the National Court of Appeals would be staffed on a rotating basis by judges who now serve the various circuit courts of appeal. The purpose of the new court was suggested to include a review of cases awaiting hearings before the Supreme Court, so that the High Court's work load might be reduced.

A similar National Court of Appeals was proposed in 1975 by the Congressional Commission on Revision of the Federal Court Appellate System. The National Court proposed by the Commission would have heard cases sent to it via transfer jurisdiction, from lower appellate courts, and through reference jurisdiction—when the Supreme Court decided to forward cases to it. The most recent version of a mini–Supreme Court was proposed by the Senate Judiciary Committee in 1986, when it called for the creation of an Intercircuit Tribunal of the U.S. courts of appeals. To date, however, no legislation to establish such a court has passed both houses of Congress.

Thurgood Marshall (1909–1993), the
nation's first black Supreme Court justice. *Photo: Lynne Johnson/Black Star.*

PRETRIAL ACTIVITIES

The stages in criminal processing, from investigation and arrest through sentencing and
punishment, are described in overview fashion in Chapter 1. Because magistrates and other
judges issue search and arrest warrants, court involvement may be present at a very early
stage in the justice process. Most defendants, however, will not come into contact with an
officer of the court until their first appearance before a magistrate.[24]

THE MAGISTRATE'S REVIEW

Following an arrest in the absence of a warrant, many states require a magistrate's review
to determine whether or not there is cause to detain the suspect. The magistrate's review
of the arrest proceeds in a relatively informal fashion, with the judge seeking to decide
whether, at the time of apprehension, the arresting officer had reason to believe both (1)
that a crime had been or was being committed and (2) that the defendant was the person who committed it. Most of the evidence presented to the magistrate comes either
from the arresting officer or the victim. At this stage in the criminal justice process, the
suspect generally is not afforded an opportunity to present evidence. In cases where the
suspect is unruly, intoxicated, or uncooperative, the magistrate's review may occur in
their absence.

THEORY INTO PRACTICE

THE U.S. SUPREME COURT: A SHIFT TO THE RIGHT?

The U.S. Supreme Court is the final interpreter of the U.S. Constitution and of laws passed by Congress. It is supposed to be above politics. Given the power of the Court, however, a number of observers have called it a "second legislature"—one which, with increasing frequency, steps into the middle of social issues and makes its own laws through the powerful process of judicial decree. Even the justices themselves are occasionally surprised by the Court's unchallenged ability to impose its unique interpretations upon the law. Justices Scalia and Rehnquist recently bemoaned what they saw as the Court's virtual and misguided independence from constitutional principles. In a growing number of instances, the Court, they claimed, has freely used its wide power to create ideologically driven and self-serving rules which bear little relationship to the Constitution. In a dissenting opinion in the 1990 case of *Minnick* v. *Mississippi*[1] Scalia and Rehnquist wrote: "Today's [ruling] is the latest stage of [prohibition] built upon [prohibition], producing a veritable fairyland castle of imagined constitutional restriction upon law enforcement. This newest tower, according to the Court, is needed to avoid "inconsistency with [a previous]rule,…which was needed to protect Miranda's…right to have counsel present, which was needed to protect the right against compelled self-incrimination found—at last—in the Constitution."

If the Court does have an agenda, what kind of law is it making? During the 1970s and for part of the 1980s, the Court appeared to lean heavily in favor of the rights of criminal defendants and jealously guarded the concept of due process. By 1994, however, it had become clear that the Court had moved toward a much more conservative position. Some now charge that a conservative juggernaut is running the Court and that the Court's new emphasis on victim's rights and community interests will soon replace its historical concern with the rights of defendant's and supplant its efforts to ensure due process for all. The sentiments of many individual rights advocates were captured in a *USA Today* editorial which intoned, "The trend is worrisome. An innocent person is now far more vulnerable to harassment by police."[2]

At the end of the Court's term in 1991, amid a landslide of conservative decisions, which upheld mandatory life sentences without parole for certain drug offenders and which vindicated victims' rights advocates who claimed a right to be heard during the sentencing phase of death penalty trials, Justice Thurgood Marshall, perhaps the last liberal bastion on the Supreme Court bench, announced his retirement at the age of 82. Marshall, the Court's first black justice, had been a member of the Court for 24 years and had previously vowed to serve out his life term. Although Justice Marshall cited advancing age and declining health as his reasons for leaving, his resignation was seen by Court watchers as another sign that the conservative majority had taken full control of the Court.

Marshall seemed to agrees. In tersely worded dissent during his last day on the bench, Marshall penned: "Power, not reason, is the new currency of this court's decision-making."[3]

Individual rights advocates worried that the American legal environment would quickly change. *USA Today* carried a story that warned: "[f]ixtures on the USA's legal landscape—abortion rights, *Miranda* warnings, affirmative action, school busing, the ban on school prayer—may all be swept away…".[4] Public order advocates responded that whatever past Court decisions were not firmly rooted in the Constitution and law needed sweeping. Their position was given voice by Kent Scheidegger, of the Criminal Justice Legal Foundation, who observed, "[v]ictims of crime and their families have a right to a fair and speedy trial, too. The Supreme Court recognizes that. It is high time."[5]

[1] *Minnick* v. *Mississippi*, 111 S.Ct. 486 (1990).
[2] "Debate," *USA Today*, June 28, 1991, p. 14A.
[3] Ibid., p. 2A.
[4] "About Leaving, Justice Always Said 'Not Yet,'" *USA Today*, June 28, 1991, p. 1A.
[5] Kent S. Scheidegger, "Stop All the Fretting; Our Liberties Are Safe," *USA Today*, June 28, 1991, p. 14A.

Some states waive a magistrate's review and proceed directly to arraignment, especially when the defendant has been arrested on a warrant. In those states the procedures undertaken to obtain a warrant are regarded as sufficient to demonstrate a basis for detention.

Initial Appearance An appearance before a magistrate which entails the process whereby the legality of a defendant's arrest is initially assessed, and he or she is informed of the charges on which he or she is being held. At this stage in the criminal process, bail may be set or pretrial release arranged.

FIRST APPEARANCE

According to the procedural rules of all jurisdictions, defendants must be offered an in-court appearance before a magistrate "without unnecessary delay." The 1943 Supreme Court case of *McNabb* v. *U.S.*[25] established that any unreasonable delay in an initial court appearance would render inadmissible confessions obtained by interrogating officers during the delay. Based upon the *McNabb* decision, 48 hours following arrest became the rule of thumb for reckoning the maximum time by which a first appearance should have been held.

The 48-hour rule was formalized by the U.S. Supreme Court in a 1991 class action suit, entitled the *County of Riverside (California)* v. *McLaughlin*.[26] In *McLaughlin*, the Court held that "a jurisdiction that provides judicial determinations of probable cause within 48 hours of arrest will, as a general matter, comply with the promptness requirement…". The Court specified, however, that weekends and holidays could not be excluded from the 48-hour requirement (as they had been in Riverside County) and that, depending upon the specifics of the case, delays of less than two days may still be unreasonable. In a dissenting opinion, Justice Thurgood Marshall spurned the idea that an appropriate time limit of any kind could be usefully specified. He wrote, a "probable cause hearing is sufficiently 'prompt'…only when provided immediately upon completion of the 'administrative steps incident to arrest.' …"[27]

At the first appearance, the accused is brought before a magistrate and apprised of the charges on which he or she is being held. The U.S. Supreme Court has held that defendants are entitled to representation by counsel at their first appearance.[28] Indigent defendants may have counsel appointed to represent them, and proceedings may be adjourned until counsel can be obtained.

Bail

A highly significant aspect of the first appearance hearing is consideration of bail or pretrial release. Defendants charged with very serious crimes, or those thought likely to escape or injure others, will usually be held in jail until trial. Such a practice is called pretrial detention.

The majority of defendants, however, will be afforded the opportunity for release. The most commonly used means to ensure that released defendants will return for further court processing is bail. Bail serves two purposes: (1) it helps ensure reappearance of the accused, and (2) it prevents unconvicted persons from suffering imprisonment unnecessarily.

Bail involves the posting of a bond as a pledge that the accused will return for further hearings. **Bail bonds** are usually cash deposits, but may consist of property or other valuables. A fully secured bond requires the defendant to post the full amount of bail set by the court. The usual practice, however, is for a defendant to seek privately secured bail through the services of a professional bail bondsman. The bondsman will assess a percentage (usually 15%) of the required bond as a fee which the defendant will have to pay up front. Those who "skip bail" by hiding or fleeing will sometimes find their bond ordered forfeit by the court. Forfeiture hearings must be held before a bond can be taken, and most courts will not order bail forfeit unless it appears that the defendant intends permanently to avoid prosecution. Bail forfeiture will often be reversed where the defendant later willingly appears to stand trial.

In many states bondsmen are empowered to hunt down and bring back defendants who have fled. In some jurisdictions bondsmen hold virtually unlimited powers and have been permitted by courts to pursue, arrest, and forcibly extradite their charges from foreign jurisdiction without concern for the due process considerations or statutory limitations which apply to law enforcement officers.[29] Recently, however, a number of states have enacted laws which eliminate for-profit bail bond businesses, replacing them instead with state-operated pretrial service agencies.

Bail Bond A document guaranteeing the appearance of the defendant in court as required and recording the pledge of money or property to be paid to the court if he or she does not appear, which is signed by the person to be released and any other persons acting in his or her behalf.

Alternatives to Bail

The Eighth Amendment to the U.S. Constitution, while it does not guarantee the opportunity for bail, does state that "Excessive bail shall not be required...." Some studies, however, have found that many defendants who are offered the opportunity for bail are unable to raise the needed money. A report by the National Advisory Commission on Criminal Justice Standards and Goals found that as many as 93% of felony defendants in some jurisdictions were unable to make bail.[30]

To extend the opportunity for pretrial release to a greater proportion of nondangerous arrestees, a number of states and the federal government now make available various alternatives to the cash bond system. Alternatives include (1) release on recognizance, (2) conditional release, (3) third-party custody, (4) attorney affidavit, (5) unsecured or signature bond, (6) property bond, and (7) deposit bail.

Release on recognizance (ROR) involves no cash bond, requiring as a guarantee only that the defendant agree in writing to return for further hearings as specified by the court. As an alternative to cash bond, release on recognizance was tested during the 1960s in a social experiment called the Manhattan Bail Project.[31] In the experiment not all defendants were eligible for release on their own recognizance. Those arrested for serious crimes including murder, rape, robbery, and defendants with extensive prior criminal records were excluded from project participation. Remaining defendants were scored and categorized according to a number of "ideal" criteria used as indicators of both dangerousness and the likelihood of pretrial flight. Criteria included (1) no previous convictions, (2) residential stability, and (3) a good employment record. Those with too high a score were not released.

Release on Recognizance (**ROR**) Refers to the pretrial release of a criminal defendant on his or her-written promise to appear. No cash or property bond is required.

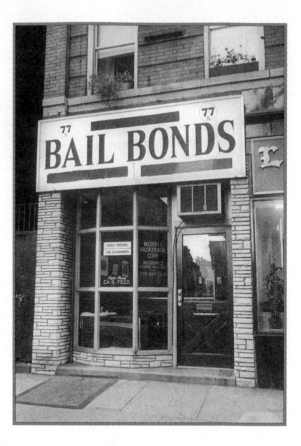

A typical bail bond office. Such offices can usually be found next to county and municipal jails—which provide a ready supply of clients. *Photo: Charles Gatewood.*

Studies of the bail project revealed that it released four times as many defendants prior to trial as had been freed under the traditional cash bond system.[32] Even more surprising was the finding that only 1% of those released fled from prosecution—a figure which was the same as for those set free on cash bond.[33] Later studies, however, were unclear as to the effectiveness of release on recognizance, with some finding a no-show rate as high as 12%.[34]

Property Bond The setting of bail in the form of land, houses, stocks, or other tangible property. In the event the defendant absconds prior to trial, the bond becomes the property of the court.

Property bonds also avoid the use of cash in order to secure release. Property bonds, however, substitute other items of value in place of cash. Land, houses, automobiles, stocks, and so on may be consigned to the court as collateral against pretrial flight.

An alternative form of cash bond available in some jurisdictions is deposit bail. Deposit bail places the court in the role of the bondsman, allowing the defendant to post a percentage of the full bail with the court. Unlike private bail operatives, court-run deposit bail programs usually return the amount of the deposit except for a small (perhaps 1%) administrative fee. If the defendant fails to appear for court the entire amount of court-ordered bail is forfeit.

Conditional release imposes a set of requirements upon the defendant. Requirements might include attendance at drug treatment programs, staying away from specified others such as potential witnesses, and regular job attendance. Release under supervision is similar to conditional release, but adds the stipulation that defendants report to an officer of the court or a police officer at designated times.

Third-party custody is a bail bond alternative that assigns custody of the defendant to an individual or agency which promises to assure his or her later appearance in court.[35] Some pretrial release programs allow attorneys to assume responsibility for their clients in this fashion. If clients fail to appear, however, the attorney's privilege to participate in the program may be ended.[36]

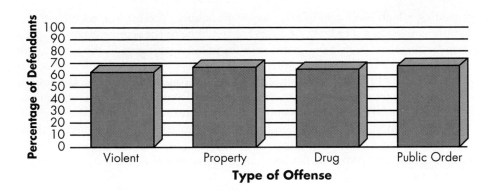

FIGURE 8–3   Proportion of state felony defendants released prior to trial in 1990. *Source:* Brian A. Reaves, *Pretrial Release of Felony Defendants, 1990* (Washington, D.C.: Bureau of Justice Statistics, November 1992).

An unsecured bond is based upon a court-determined dollar amount of bail. Like a credit contract, it requires no monetary deposit with the court. The defendant agrees in writing that failure to appear will result in forfeiture of the entire amount of the bond, which might then be taken in seizures of land, personal property, bank accounts, and so on.

A signature bond allows release based upon the defendant's written promise to appear. Signature bonds involve no particular assessment of the defendant's dangerousness or likelihood of later appearance in court. They are used only in cases of minor offenses such as traffic law violations and some petty drug law violations. Signature bonds may be issued by the arresting officer acting on behalf of the court.

Pretrial release is common practice. Approximately 85% of all state-level criminal defendants[37] and 82% of all federal criminal defendants[38] are released prior to trial. Sixty-five percent of all state-level felony defendants are similarly released (see Figure 8–3). A growing movement, however, stresses the fact that defendants released prior to trial may be dangerous to themselves or others and seeks to reduce the number of defendants released under any conditions. This conservative policy has been promoted by an increasing concern for public safety in the face of a number of studies documenting crimes committed by defendants released on bond. One such study found that 16% of defendants released before trial were rearrested, and, of those, 30% were arrested more than once.[39] Another determined that as many as 41% of those released prior to trial for serious crimes, such as rape and robbery, were rearrested before their trial date.[40] Not surprisingly, such studies generally find that the longer the time spent on bail prior to trial, the greater the likelihood of misconduct.

In response to claims like these, some states have enacted danger laws, which limit the right to bail for certain kinds of offenders.[41] Others, including Arizona, California, Colorado, Florida, and Illinois, have approved constitutional amendments restricting the use of bail.[42] Most such provisions exclude persons charged with certain crimes from bail eligibility and demand that other defendants being considered for bail meet stringent conditions. Some states combine these strictures with tough release conditions designed to keep close control over defendants prior to trial.

The 1984 federal Bail Reform Act allows judges to assess the danger represented by an accused to the community and to deny bail to persons who are thought dangerous. In the words of the act, a suspect held in pretrial custody on federal criminal charges is required to be detained if, "after a hearing…he is found to pose a risk of flight and a danger to others or the community and if no condition of release can give reasonable assurances against these contingencies."[43] Defendants seeking bail are faced with the necessity of demonstrating a high likelihood of later court appearance. The act also requires that a defendant is entitled to a speedy first appearance and, if he or she is to be detained, that a detention hearing must be held in consort with the initial appearance. In the 1990 case of *U.S. v. Montalvo-Murillo*,[44] however, a defendant who was not provided with a detention hearing at the time of his first appearance, and was subsequently released, was found to have no "right" to freedom because of this "minor" statutory violation. The Supreme Court held that "unless it has a substantial influence on the outcome of the proceedings...failure to comply with the Act's prompt hearing provision does not require release of a person who should otherwise be detained" because, "[a]utomatic release contravenes the statutory purpose of providing fair bail procedures while protecting the public's safety and assuring a defendant's appearance at trial."[45]

Court challenges to the constitutionality of pretrial detention legislation have not met with much success. The U.S. Supreme Court case of *U.S. v. Hazzard*[46] (1984), decided only a few months after enactment of federal bail reform, held that Congress was justified in providing for denial of bail to offenders who represent a danger to the community. Later cases have supported the presumption of flight which federal law presupposes for certain types of defendants.[47]

THE PRELIMINARY HEARING

Although the preliminary hearing is not nearly as elaborate as a criminal trial, it has many of the same characteristics. The defendant is taken before a lower court judge who will summarize the charges and review the rights to which all criminal defendants are entitled. The prosecution may present witnesses and will offer evidence in support of the complaint. The defendant will be afforded the right to testify and may also call witnesses. The purpose of the preliminary hearing is to afford the defendant an opportunity to challenge the legal basis for his or her detention. The hearing will turn on a determination of whether there is probable cause to believe that a crime has been committed and that the defendant committed it.

At this stage of the criminal justice process the defendant's guilt need not be proved beyond a reasonable doubt. All that is required for the wheels of justice to grind forward is a demonstration "sufficient to justify a prudent man's belief that the suspect has committed or was committing an offense."[48] If the magistrate finds enough evidence to justify a trial, the defendant is bound over to the grand jury—or sent directly to the trial court in those states which do not require grand jury review. If the complaint against the defendant cannot be substantiated the defendant is released. A release is not a bar to further prosecution, and the defendant may be rearrested if further evidence comes to light.

THE GRAND JURY

The federal government and about half of the states use grand juries as part of the pretrial process. Grand juries are composed of private citizens (often 23 in number) who hear evidence presented by the prosecution. Grand juries serve primarily as filters to eliminate from further processing cases for which there is not sufficient evidence.

In early times grand juries served a far different purpose. The grand jury system was begun in England in 1166 as a way of identifying law violators. Lacking a law enforcement agency with investigative authority, the government looked to the grand jury as a source of information on criminal activity in the community. Even today, grand juries in most jurisdictions may initiate prosecution independently of the prosecutor, although they rarely do.

A grand jury in action. Grand jury proceedings are generally very informal, as this picture shows.
Photo: Frank Fournier/Woodfin Camp & Associates.

Grand jury hearings are held in secret, and the defendant is not afforded the opportunity to appear before the grand jury.[49] Similarly, the opportunity to cross-examine prosecution witnesses is absent. Grand juries have the power to subpoena witnesses and to mandate a review of books, records, and other documents crucial to their investigations.

After hearing the evidence, the grand jury votes on the indictment presented to it by the prosecution. The indictment is a formal listing of proposed charges. If the majority of grand jury constituents agree to forward the indictment to the trial court, it becomes a true bill upon which further prosecution will turn. Jurisdictions which do not make use of the grand jury system depend instead upon an information, or complaint, filed by the prosecutor with the trial court.

ARRAIGNMENT

Once an indictment has been returned, or an information filed, the accused will be formally arraigned before the trial court. The arraignment is generally a brief process which serves two purposes: (1) it informs the defendant of the specific charges against him or her, and (2) it allows the defendant to enter a **plea**. The Federal Rules of Criminal Procedure allow for one of three types of pleas to be entered: (1) guilty, (2) not guilty, and (3) *nolo contendere* (no contest). Some defendants refuse to enter any plea and are said to "stand mute."

The Plea

Plea Bargaining Guilty pleas often are not as straightforward as they might seem, typically being arrived at only after complex negotiations referred to as plea bargaining. Plea bargaining is a process of negotiation which usually involves the defendant,

Plea In criminal proceedings, a defendant's formal answer in court to the charge contained in a complaint, information, or indictment that he or she is guilty or not guilty of the offense charged, or does not contest the charge.

Plea Bargaining The negotiated agreement between defendant, prosecutor, and the court as to what an appropriate plea and associated sentence should be in a given case. Plea bargaining circumvents the trial process and dramatically reduces the time required for the resolution of a criminal case.

prosecutor, and defense counsel. It is founded upon the mutual interests of all involved. Defense attorneys and their clients will agree to a plea of guilty when they are unsure of their ability to win acquittal at trial. Prosecutors may be willing to bargain because the evidence they have against the defendant is weaker than they would like it to be. From the prosecutorial perspective, plea bargaining results in a quick conviction, without the need to commit the time and resources necessary for trial. Benefits to the accused include the possibility of reduced or combined charges, lessened defense costs, and a lower sentence than might have otherwise been anticipated.

The U.S. Supreme Court has held that a guilty plea constitutes conviction.[50] In order to validate the conviction, negotiated pleas require judicial consent. Judges are often likely to accept pleas which are the result of a bargaining process because such pleas reduce the workload of the court. Although few judges are willing to guarantee a sentence before a plea is entered, most prosecutors and criminal trial lawyers know what sentences to expect from typical pleas.

In the past, plea bargaining, though apparently common, had often been veiled in secrecy. Judicial thinking held that, for pleas to be valid, they had to be freely given. Pleas struck as the result of bargains seemed to depend upon the state's coercive power to encourage the defendant's cooperation. The 1973 National Advisory Commission on Criminal Justice Standards and Goals recommended abolishing the practice of plea negotiation.[51] That recommendation came in the midst of a national debate over the virtues of trading pleas for reductions in sentences. However, in 1970, even before the Commission's recommendation, the U.S. Supreme Court had given its consent to the informal decision-making processes of bargained pleas. In the case of *Brady* v. *U.S.*,[52] the court reasoned that such pleas were voluntarily and knowingly made. A year later, in *Santobello* v. *New York* (1971),[53] the High Court forcefully ruled that plea bargaining is an important and necessary component of the American system of justice. In the words of the Court, "The disposition of criminal charges by agreement between the prosecutor and the accused, sometimes loosely called 'plea bargaining' is an essential component of the administration of justice. Properly administered, it is to be encouraged. If every criminal charge were subjected to a full-scale trial, the States and the Federal Government would need to multiply by many times the number of judges and court facilities."[54]

Today, bargained pleas are commonplace. Some surveys have found that 90% of all criminal cases prepared for trial are eventually resolved through a negotiated plea.[55] In a study of 37 big-city prosecutors,[56] the Bureau of Justice Statistics found that for every 100 adults arrested on a felony charge, half were eventually convicted of either a felony or a misdemeanor. Of all convictions, fully 94% were the result of a plea. Only 6% of convictions were the result of a criminal trial.

After a guilty plea has been entered, it may be withdrawn with the consent of the court. In the case of *Henderson* v. *Morgan* (1976),[57] for example, the U.S. Supreme Court permitted a defendant to withdraw a plea of guilty nine years after it had been given. In *Henderson* the defendant had originally entered a plea of guilty to second-degree murder, but attempted to withdraw it before trial. Reasons for wanting to withdraw the plea included the defendant's belief that he had not been completely advised as to the nature of the charge or the sentence he might receive as a result of the plea.

Recent Supreme Court decisions, however, have enhanced the prosecutor's authority in the bargaining process by declaring that negotiated pleas cannot be capriciously withdrawn by defendants.[58] Other rulings have supported discretionary actions by prosecutors in which sentencing recommendations were retracted even after bargains had been struck.[59] Some lower court cases have upheld the government's authority to withdraw from a negotiated plea where the defendant fails to live up to certain conditions.[60] Conditions may include requiring the defendant to provide information on other criminal involvement, criminal cartels, the activities of smugglers, and so on.

Because it is a process of negotiation involving many interests, plea bargaining may have unintended consequences. For example, while it is generally agreed that bargained pleas should relate in some way to the original charge, actual practice may not adhere to such expectations. Many plea negotiations turn on the acceptability of the anticipated sentence rather than on a close relationship between the charge and the plea. Entered pleas may be chosen for the punishments likely to be associated with them rather than for their accuracy in describing the criminal offense in which the defendant was involved.[61] This is especially true where the defendant is concerned with minimizing the socially stigmatizing impact of the offense. A charge of "indecent liberties," for example, in which the defendant is accused of sexual misconduct, may be pled out as assault. Such a plea, which takes advantage of the fact that "indecent liberties" can be thought of as a form of sexual assault, would effectively disguise the true nature of the offense.

Even though plea bargaining has been endorsed by the Supreme Court, the public continues to view it suspiciously. "Law and order" advocates, who generally favor harsh punishments and long jail terms, claim that plea bargaining results in unjustifiably light sentences. As a consequence, prosecutors who regularly engage in the practice rarely advertise it. Often unrealized is the fact that plea bargaining can be a powerful prosecutorial tool.

Power carries with it, however, the potential for misuse. Plea bargains, because they circumvent the trial process, hold the possibility of abuse by prosecutors and defense attorneys who are more interested in a speedy resolution of cases than they are in seeing justice done. Carried to the extreme, plea bargaining may result in defendants being convicted of crimes they did not commit. Although it probably happens only rarely, it is conceivable that innocent defendants (especially those with prior criminal records) who—for whatever reason—think a jury will convict them, may plead guilty to lessened charges in order to avoid a trial. In an effort to protect defendants against hastily arranged pleas, the new Federal Rules of Criminal Procedure require judges to (1) inform the defendant of the various rights he or she is surrendering by pleading guilty, (2) determine that the plea is voluntary, (3) require disclosure of any plea agreements, and (4) make sufficient inquiry to ensure there is a factual basis for the plea.[62]

Bargained pleas can take many forms and be quite inventive. The case of Steven Allen Butler is illustrative of an unusual bargained plea. In 1992 Butler, a 28-year-old Houston man, voluntarily agreed to surgical castration and a 10-year probationary sentence for repeatedly raping a 13-year-old girl while already on probation for molesting a 7-year-old. His alternative was to stand trial, facing a potential life sentence. However, after considerable public outcry over the arranged sentence, Judge Michael McSpadden withdrew the offer, saying no physician could be found to perform the surgery.[63]

Other Types of Pleas

A no contest (*nolo contendere*) plea is much the same as a plea of guilty. A defendant who pleads no contest is immediately convicted and may be sentenced just as though he or she had entered a plea of guilty. A no contest plea, however, is no admission of guilt and provides one major advantage to defendants: it may not be used as a later basis for civil proceedings which seek monetary or other damages against the defendant.

Standing mute is a defense strategy rarely employed by an accused. Defendants who choose this alternative simply do not answer the request for a plea. However, for procedural purposes, a defendant who stands mute is considered to have entered a plea of not guilty.

Another plea, acceptable in some jurisdictions, is that of once in jeopardy. The plea of once in jeopardy is based upon the constitutional right against double jeopardy. Double jeopardy is a guarantee against more than one trial for the same charge. Where a defendant has previously been acquitted of criminal charges, those same charges may not be used as the basis for renewed prosecution. However, hung juries and appellate reversals of conviction are not generally allowable as a basis for a claim of double jeopardy.

Nolo Contendere A plea of "no contest." A no contest plea may be used where the defendant does not wish to contest conviction. Because the plea does not admit guilt, however, it cannot provide the basis for later civil suits which might follow upon the heels of a criminal conviction.

SUMMARY

American criminal courts present an intriguing contrast. One the one hand, they exude an aura of highly formalized judicial procedure, while on the other, they demonstrate a surprising lack of organizational uniformity. Courts in one jurisdiction may bear little resemblance to those of another, especially when different states are compared. The separate systems of federal and state courts can lead to further confusion. Court reform, because it has not equally impacted all areas of the country, has in some instances exacerbated the differences between court systems.

This chapter has concerned itself mainly with pretrial practices. Prior to trial, courts often act to shield the accused from the punitive power of the state through the use of pretrial release. In doing so, they must balance the rights of the unconvicted defendant against the potential for future harm which that person may represent. A significant issue facing pretrial decision makers is how to ensure that all defendants, rich and poor, are afforded the same degree of protection.

DISCUSSION QUESTIONS

1. What is the "dual court system"? Why do we have a dual court system in America? Could the drive toward court unification eventually lead to a monolithic court system? Would such a system be effective?

2. This chapter says that 90% of all criminal cases carried beyond the initial stages are finally resolved through bargained pleas. What are some of the problems associated with plea bargaining? Given those problems, do you believe that plea bargaining is an acceptable practice in today's criminal justice system? Give reasons for your answer.

3. People who are accused of crimes are often granted pretrial release. Do you think all defendants accused of crimes should be so released? If not, what types of defendants might you keep in jail? Why?

4. What inequities exist in today's system of pretrial release? How might the system be improved?

ENDNOTES

1. Law Enforcement Assistance Administration, *Two Hundred Years of American Criminal Justice* (Washington, D.C.: U.S. Government Printing Office, 1976), p. 31.
2. Ibid., p. 31.
3. Ibid.
4. Ibid., p. 32.
5. Ibid.
6. Thomas A. Henderson, Cornelium M. Kerwin, Randall Guynes, Carl Baar, Neal Miller, Hildy Saizow, and

Robert Grieser, *The Significance of Judicial Structure: The Effects of Unification on Trial Court Operations* (Washington, D.C.: National Institute of Justice, 1984).

7. Ibid.

8. Bureau of Justice Statistics, *Report to the Nation on Crime and Justice*, 2nd ed. (Washington, D.C.: U.S. Department of Justice, 1988), p. 82.

9. *Keeney, Superintendent, Oregon State Penitentiary* v. *Tamayo-Reyes* No. 90–1859, syllabus. Decided May 4, 1992.

10. *Herrera* v. *Collins*, No. 91–7328. Decided January 25, 1993.

11. H. Ted Rubin, *The Courts: Fulcrum of the Justice System* (Pacific Palisades, CA: Goodyear, 1976), p. 200.

12. Ibid., p. 198.

13. Martin Wright, *Justice for Victims and Offenders* (Bristol, PA: Open University Press, 1991), p. 56.

14. Ibid., pp. 104 and 106.

15. Administrative Office of the U.S. Courts, *The United States Courts: A Pictoral Summary for the Twelve Month Period Ended June 30, 1985* (Washington, D.C.: U.S. Government Printing Office, 1985), p. 16.

16. Administrative Office of the United States Courts, *Annual Report 1992* (Washington, D.C.: U.S. Government Printing Office, 1993).

17. Telephone conversation, Administrative Office of the United States Courts, May 20, 1993.

18. Stephen L. Wasby, *The Supreme Court in the Federal Judicial System*, 3rd ed. (Chicago: Nelson-Hall, 1988), p. 58.

19. *The Supreme Court of the United States* (Washington, D.C.: U.S. Government Printing Office, no date), p. 4.

20. 1 Cranch 137 (1803).

21. *Mapp* v. *Ohio*, 367 U.S. 643 (1961).

22. *United States* v. *Alvarez-Machain*, 112 S.Ct. 2188 (1992).

23. Wasby, *The Supreme Court*, pp. 58–59.

24. "Arraignment" is also a term used to describe an initial appearance, although we will reserve use of that word to describe a later court appearance following the defendant's indictment by a grand jury or the filing of an information by the prosecutor.

25. *McNabb* v. *United States*, 318 U.S. 332 (1943).

26. *County of Riverside* v. *McLaughlin*, 111 S.Ct. 1661 (1991).

27. *McLaughlin*, dissenting opinion.

28. *White* v. *Maryland*, 373 U.S. 59 (1963).

29. *Taylor* v. *Taintor*, 83 U.S. 66 (1873).

30. National Advisory Commission on Criminal Justice Standards and Goals, *The Courts* (Washington, D.C.: U.S. Government Printing Office, 1973), p. 37.

31. C. Ares, A. Rankin, and H. Sturz, "The Manhattan Bail Project: An Interim Report on the Use of Pre-Trial Parole," *New York University Law Review*, Vol. 38 (January 1963), pp. 68–95.

32. H. Zeisel, "Bail Revisited," *American Bar Foundation Research Journal*, Vol. 4 (1979), pp. 769–789.

33. Ibid.

34. "12% of Those Freed on Low Bail Fail to Appear," *The New York Times*, December 2, 1983, p. 1.

35. Bureau of Justice Statistics, *Report to the Nation on Crime and Justice*, 2nd ed., p. 76.

36. Joseph B. Vaughn and Victor E. Kappeler, "The Denial of Bail: Pre-Trial Preventive Detention," *Criminal Justice Research Bulletin*, Vol. 3, no. 6 (Huntsville, TX: Sam Houston State University, 1987), p. 1.

37. M. A. Toborg, *Pretrial Release: A National Evaluation of Practice and Outcomes* (McLean, VA: Lazar Institute, 1981).

38. Bureau of Justice Statistics, *Report to the Nation on Crime and Justice*, 2nd ed., p. 77.

39. Donald E. Pryor and Walter F. Smith, "Significant Research Findings Concerning Pretrial Release," *Pretrial Issues*, Vol. 4, no. 1 (Washington, D.C.: Pretrial Services Resource Center, February 1982).

40. Bureau of Justice Statistics, *Report to the Nation on Crime and Justice*, 2nd ed., p. 77.

41. According to Vaughn and Kappeler, "The Denial of Bail," the first such legislation was the 1970 District of Columbia Court Reform and Criminal Procedure Act.

42. Ibid.

43. Bail Reform Act of 1984, 18 U.S.C. 3142(e).

44. *U.S.* v. *Montalvo-Murillo*, No. 89-163 (1990).

45. *U.S.* v. *Montalvo-Murillo* (1990), online syllabus.

46. *U.S.* v. *Hazzard*, 35 CrL 2217 (1984).

47. See, for example, *U.S.* v. *Motamedi*, 37 CrL 2394, CA 9 (1985).

48. Federal Rules of Criminal Procedure 5.1(a).

49. A few states now have laws that permit the defendant to appear before the grand jury.

50. *Kercheval* v. *U.S.*, 274 U.S. 220, 223, 47 S.Ct. 582, 583 (1927); *Boykin* v. *Alabama*, 395 U.S. 238 (1969); and *Dickerson* v. *New Banner Institute, Inc.*, 460 U.S. 103 (1983).

51. The National Advisory Commission on Criminal Justice Standards and Goals, *Courts* (Washington, D.C.: U.S. Government Printing Office, 1973), p. 46.

52. *Brady* v. *United States*, 397 U.S. 742 (1970).

53. *Santobello* v. *New York*, 404 U.S. 257 (1971).

54. Ibid.

55. U.S. Department of Justice, Bureau of Justice Statistics, *The Prosecution of Felony Arrests* (Washington, D.C.: U.S. Government Printing Office, 1983).

56. Barbara Boland, Wayne Logan, Ronald Sones, and William Martin, *The Prosecution of Felony Arrests, 1982* (Washington, D.C.: U.S. Government Printing Office, May 1988).

57. *Henderson* v. *Morgan*, 426 U.S. 637 (1976).

58. *Santobello* v. *New York*.

59. *Mabry* v. *Johnson*, 467 U.S. 504 (1984).

60. *U.S.* v. *Baldacchino*, 762 F.2d 170 (1st Cir. 1985); *U.S.* v. *Reardon*, 787 F.2d 512 (10th Cir. 1986); and *U.S.* v. *Donahey*, 529 F.2d 831 (11th Cir. 1976).

61. For a now classic discussion of such considerations, see David Sudnow, "Normal Crimes: Sociological Features of the Penal Code in a Public Defender Office," *Social Problems*, Vol. 12 (1965), p. 255.

62. *Federal Rules of Criminal Procedure*, No. 11.

63. "Nationline," *USA Today*, March 17, 1992, p. 3A, and "Man Volunteers Castration over Prison for Raping Child," *Fayetteville Observer-Times* (North Carolina), March 7, 1992, p. 1A.

CHAPTER 9

To hear patiently, to weigh deliberately and dispassionately, and to decide impartially; these are the chief duties of a Judge.
—ALBERT PIKE (1809-1891)

In civil jurisprudence it too often happens that there is so much law, there is no room for justice, and that the claimant expires of wrong, in the midst of right, as mariners die of thirst in the midst of water.
—COLTON (1780-1832)

In all criminal prosecutions the accused shall enjoy the right to a speedy and public trial, by an impartial jury…and to be informed of the nature and cause of the accusation; to be confronted with the witnesses against him; to have compulsory process for obtaining witnesses in his favor; and to have the assistance of counsel for his defense.
—SIXTH AMENDMENT TO THE U.S. CONSTITUTION

THE COURTROOM WORK GROUP AND THE CRIMINAL TRIAL

KEY CONCEPTS

prosecutor	impeachment	bailiff
confidentiality	public defender	subpoena
judge	advocacy model	Speedy Trial Act
expert witness	lay witness	victim compensation
hearsay	perjury	criminal trial

KEY CASES

Edmonson v. *Leesville Concrete Co., Inc.*	*Michigan* v. *Lucas*	*Idaho* v. *Wright*
Burns v. *Reed*	*Ohio* v. *Powers*	*Coy* v. *Iowa*
Mu'Min v. *Virginia*	*Demarest* v. *Manspeaker*	*Imbler* v. *Pachtman*
Crosby v. *U.S.*	*Maryland* v. *Craig*	*White* v. *Illinois*
Doggett v. *U.S.*	*Zafiro* v. *U.S.*	*Fex* v. *Michigan*
	Georgia v. *McCollum*	

COURTROOM ACTORS

"Every day, as he ambles through the cobwebbed halls of the New Orleans criminal court building, public defender Richard Teisser feels he violates his clients' constitutional rights"[1] to legal counsel. Teisser, an attorney who is paid just $18,500 per year by the state of Louisiana, has so many clients and so few resources he believes that he can't possibly do them all justice. To bring his plight before the public Teisser, in the spring of 1993, filed suit against his own office. A local judge agreed, finding Louisiana's system of indigent defense unconstitutional. Louisiana Governor Edwin Edwards, commenting on the ruling, said that underfunding is not limited to New Orleans, but is "a state problem and a national problem."[2]

Were it not for cases like Teisser's, few would be aware of the problems facing our nation's courts. To the public eye, criminal trials generally appear to be well managed and even dramatic events. Like plays on a stage, they involve many participants. Parties to the event can be divided into two categories: "professionals" and "outsiders." The "professional" category includes official courtroom actors, well versed in criminal trial practice, who set the stage for and conduct the business of the court. Judges, prosecutors, defense attorneys, public defenders, and others who earn a living serving the court fall into this category. Professional courtroom actors are also called the courtroom work group. Some writers have pointed out that, aside from statutory requirements and ethical considerations, courtroom interaction between professionals involves an implicit recognition of informal rules of civility, cooperation, and shared goals. Hence, even within the adversarial framework of a criminal trial, the courtroom work group is dedicated to bringing the procedure to a successful close.[3]

In contrast, "outsiders" are generally unfamiliar with courtroom organization and trial procedure. Most outsiders visit the court temporarily to provide information or to serve as members of the jury. Similarly, because of their temporary involvement with the court, defendant and victim are also outsiders, even though they may have more of a personal investment in the outcome of the trial than anyone else.

PROFESSIONAL COURTROOM ACTORS

The Judge

Role of the Judge

The trial judge is probably the figure most closely associated with a criminal trial. The judge has the primary duty of ensuring justice. In the courtroom the judge holds ultimate authority, ruling on matters of law, weighing objections, deciding on the admissibility of evidence, and disciplining anyone who challenges the order of the court. In most jurisdictions judges also sentence offenders after a verdict has been returned, and in some states judges serve to decide guilt or innocence for defendants who waive a jury trial.

Each state jurisdiction normally has a chief judge who, besides serving on the bench as a trial judge, must also manage the court system. Management includes hiring staff personnel, scheduling sessions of court, ensuring the adequate training of subordinate judges, and coordinating activities with other courtroom actors. Chief judges usually assume their positions by virtue of seniority and rarely have any formal training in management. Hence, the managerial effectiveness of a chief judge is often a matter of personality and dedication more than anything else.

Judicial Selection

At the federal level, judges are nominated by the president of the United States and take their place on the bench only after confirmation by the Senate. At the state level, things work somewhat differently. Depending upon the jurisdiction involved, state judgeships are won either through popular election or political (usually gubernatorial) appointment. The processes involved in judicial selection at the state level are set by law.

Both judicial election and appointment have been criticized for the fact that each system allows politics to enter the judicial arena—although in somewhat different ways. Under the appointment system, judicial hopefuls must be in favor with incumbent politicians in order to receive appointments. Under the elective system, judicial candidates must receive the endorsement of their parties, generate campaign contributions, and manage an effective campaign. Because partisan politics plays a role in both systems, critics have claimed that sitting judges can rarely be as neutral as they should be. They carry to the bench with them campaign promises, personal indebtedness, and possible political agendas.

To counter some of these problems, a number of states have adopted what has come to be called the Missouri Plan[4] (or the "Missouri Bar Plan") for judicial selection. The Missouri Plan combines elements of both election and appointment. It requires judicial vacancies to undergo screening by a nonpartisan state judicial nominating committee. Candidates selected by the committee are reviewed by an arm of the governor's office which selects a final list of names for appointment. Incumbent judges must face the electorate after a specified term in office. They then run unopposed, in nonpartisan elections, in which only their records may be considered. Voters have the choice of allowing a judge to continue in office or asking that another be appointed to take his or her place. Because the Missouri Plan provides for periodic public review of judicial performance, it is also called the merit plan of judicial selection.

THEORY INTO PRACTICE

THE FUNCTIONS OF THE TRIAL JUDGE

The American Bar Association Standards for Criminal Justice set forth the following duties of the trial judge:

1. General responsibility of the trial judge.

(a) The trial judge has the responsibility for safeguarding both the rights of the accused and the interests of the public in the administration of criminal justice. The adversary nature of the proceedings does not relieve the trial judge of the obligations of raising on his own initiative, at all appropriate times and in an appropriate manner, matters which may significantly promote a just determination of the trial. The only purpose of a criminal trial is to determine whether the prosecution has established the guilt of the accused as required by law, and the trial judge should not allow the proceedings to be used for any other purpose.

Source: ABA Standards for Criminal Justice, approved draft, 1972.

Qualifications of Judges   Only two decades ago many states did not require any special training, education, or other qualifications for judges. Anyone who won election or was appointed could assume a judgeship. Today, however, almost all states require that judges in appellate and general jurisdiction courts hold a law degree, be licensed attorneys, and be members of their state bar associations. Many states also require newly elected judges to attend state-sponsored training sessions dealing with subjects such as courtroom procedure, evidence, dispute resolution, judicial writing, administrative record keeping, and ethics.

While most states provide instruction to meet needs of trial judges, other organizations exist to provide specialized training. The National Judicial College, located on the campus of the University of Nevada at Reno, is one such institution. The National Judicial College was established in 1963 by the Joint Committee for the Effective Administration of Justice chaired by Justice Tom C. Clark of the U.S. Supreme Court.[5] Courses offered by the college attract over 1,500 judges every year.

Lower court judges such as justices of the peace, local magistrates, and "district" court judges in some parts of the United States may still be elected under the old system and are exempt from educational and other professional requirements. Today, in 43 states some 1,300 nonlawyer judges are serving in mostly rural courts of limited jurisdiction.[6] In New York, for example, lay judges hear around 3 million cases each year and collect $45 million in fines.[7] The majority of cases which come before New York lay judges involve alleged traffic violations, although they may also include misdemeanors, small claims actions, and some civil cases (of up to $3,000). Some authors have defended lay judges as being closer

The modern courtroom is often a complex cacophony of interests and participants. Here, a New York State Traffic Violations Court judge examines a defendant's record on a computer. *Photo: Eugene Gordon.*

to the citizenry in their understanding of justice.[8] Even so, a discernible tendency toward the elimination of lay judges is occurring in most areas. States which continue to use lay judges in lower courts do require that candidates for judgeships not have criminal records and that most attend special training sessions if elected.

   Judicial Misconduct   Occasionally, judges overstep the limits of their authority or commit social transgressions. Poor judgment may result from bad taste or archaic attitudes, as in the case of a lower court judge who kept telling a woman defense counselor that she was too pretty to be a lawyer and should be at home having children. Other sexist comments resulted in calls for that judge's dismissal. Many states have judicial conduct commissions to investigate allegations of impropriety against judges.

   Federal law provides a mechanism for administratively deciding complaints over judicial conduct. The Judicial Councils Reform and Judicial Conduct and Disability Act, passed by Congress in 1980, specifies the precise mechanisms which can be employed to register complaints against federal judges and, in serious cases, to begin the process of impeachment—or forced removal from the bench.

   In 1987, for example, Walter L. Nixon, Jr. a chief judge of the U.S. District Court for the Southern District of Mississippi was convicted by a jury of two counts of making false statements before a federal grand jury and sentenced to prison.[9] In 1993 his appeal to the U.S. Supreme Court was denied.[10] In the appeal, Nixon had claimed that his impeachment by the U.S. Senate, through the aegis of a Senate committee, violated the Impeachment Trial Clause (Article I, Section 3, Clause 6) of the U.S. Constitution.

The Prosecuting Attorney

The prosecuting attorney, called variously the "solicitor," "district attorney," "state's attorney," and so on, is the primary representative of the people by virtue of the belief that violations of the criminal law are an affront to the public. Except for U.S. attorneys and solicitors in five states, prosecutors are elected and generally serve four-year terms with the possibility of continuing re-election.[11] Widespread criminal conspiracies, whether they involve government officials or private citizens, may require the services of a special prosecutor whose office can spend the time and resources needed for efficient prosecution.[12]

In many jurisdictions the job of prosecutor entails too many duties for one person to handle. As a consequence, most prosecutors supervise a staff of assistant district attorneys. The burden of most in-court work is borne by assistants. Assistants are trained attorneys, usually hired directly by the chief prosecutor, and licensed to practice law in the states where they work. Approximately 2,300 chief prosecutors, assisted by 20,000 deputy attorneys, serve the nation's counties and independent cities.[13]

Prosecutorial Discretion
The decision-making power of prosecutors based upon the wide range of choices available to them in the handling of criminal defendants, the scheduling of cases for trial, the acceptance of bargained pleas, and so on. The most important form of prosecutorial discretion lies in the power to charge, or not to charge, a person with an offense.

Prosecutorial Discretion   Prosecutors occupy a unique position in the criminal justice system by virtue of the considerable discretion they exercise. As Justice Jackson noted in 1940, "the prosecutor has more control over life, liberty, and reputation than any other person in America."[14] Before a case comes to trial prosecutors may decide to accept a plea bargain, divert suspects to a public or private social service agency, or dismiss the case entirely for lack of evidence or for a variety for other reasons. Various studies have found that from one-third to one-half of all felony cases are dismissed by the prosecution prior to trial or before a plea bargain is made.[15] Prosecutors also play a significant role before grand juries. States which use the grand jury system depend upon prosecutors to bring evidence before the grand jury, and to be effective in seeing indictments returned against suspects.

Another prosecutorial role has traditionally been that of quasi-legal advisor to local police departments. Because prosecutors are sensitive to the kinds of information needed for conviction, they may help guide police investigations and will exhort detectives to identify usable

Criminal trial judges exercise nearly complete authority in the courtroom, and can draw upon the many resources of the justice system to insure compliance with their rulings. *Copyright 1989, USA Today. Reprinted with permission.*

THEORY INTO PRACTICE

SHOULD JUDGES BE HELD ACCOUNTABLE
FOR MISAPPLICATIONS OF THE LAW?

It is a generally accepted maxim that judges cannot be held liable for their official actions, although they can be sued for the untoward consequences of their "non-judicial" acts.[1] On the other hand, police officers, prosecutors, defense attorneys, and probation, parole, and correctional officials have not been blessed by the Court with a similar degree of immunity. The 1991 case of *Burns* v. *Reed,*[2] for example, held that prosecutors could be held liable "for giving (inaccurate) legal advice to the police," because in doing so they were stepping outside of their role as court officials. Similarly, police officers can be sued for exerting an unwarranted amount of force to effect an arrest or for detaining an individual or conducting a search without sufficient cause. In the 1993 case of *Buckley* v. *Fitzsimmons,*[3] the Court held that overzealous prosecutors who had concocted evidence during the preliminary investigation of a highly publicized rape and murder and who had made demonstrably false statements concerning the defendant at a press conference were not immune from civil liability.

Over time, the Supreme Court has held that every official actor in the justice system can be held responsible for mistakes in judgments—especially where it can be shown that the person in question should have known better. Judges and grand jurors are the exceptions.

Consider, however, the potentially serious consequences of judicial mistakes. On June 1, 1991, North Carolina District Court Judge Albert Kwasikpui issued an order declaring Orlander Roosevelt Bynum an "outlaw."[4] Bynum had escaped from jail by cutting his way through three metal bars while he was being held on six counts of drug trafficking. Under North Carolina's outlawry statute, Bynum could have been shot on sight by any citizen or law enforcement officer who encountered him. The problem was that, years before, North Carolina's outlawry statute had been held unconstitutional and could not legitimately be applied by any court in the state. The judge in this case should have known that, although clearly he did not.

Although this story has a relatively pleasant ending (Bynum was not shot after the state attorney general called the problem to the judge's attention), it could have ended differently. If the defendant had been killed by a citizen who came across him, should the judge then have been held liable for this mistake? Under the doctrine of unlimited judicial immunity, continually reinforced by Supreme Court precedent, he could not have been.

[1] *Forrester* v. *White,* 484 U.S. 219, 229 (1988).
[2] *Burns* v. *Reed,* No. 89–1715, 1991.
[3] *Buckley* v. *Fitzsimmons,* No. 91–7849. Decided June 24, 1993.
[4] "Outlaw Order Invalid," *The Fayetteville Observer-Times* (North Carolina), June 3, 1991, p. B1.

witnesses, uncover additional evidence, and the like. This role is limited, however. Police departments are independent of the administrative authority of the prosecutor and cooperation between them, although based on the common goal of conviction, is purely voluntary.[16]

Until relatively recently it has generally been held that prosecutors enjoyed much the same kind of immunity against liability in the exercise of their official duties that judges do. The 1976 Supreme Court case of *Imbler* v. *Pachtman*[17] provided the basis for such thinking wherein the Court ruled that "state prosecutors are absolutely immune from liability...for their conduct in initiating a prosecution and in presenting the State's case." However, the Court, in the 1991 case of *Burns* v. *Reed*,[18] held that "[a] state prosecuting attorney is absolutely immune from liability for damages...for participating in a probable cause hearing, but not for giving legal advice to the police." The *Burns* case involved Cathy Burns of Muncie, Indiana, who allegedly shot her sleeping sons while laboring under a multiple personality defect. In order to explore the possibility of multiple personality further, the police asked the prosecuting attorney if it would be appropriate for them to hypnotize the defendant. The prosecutor agreed that hypnosis would be a permissible avenue for investigation, and the suspect confessed while hypnotized. She later alleged in her complaint to the Supreme Court "that [the prosecuting attorney] knew or should have known that hypnotically induced testimony was inadmissible"[19] at trial.

In preparation for trial the prosecutor decides what charges are to be brought against the defendant, examines the strength of incriminating evidence, and decides what witnesses to call. Two important Supreme Court decisions have held that it is the duty of prosecutors to, in effect, assist the defense in building its case, by making available any evidence in their possession. The first case, that of *Brady* v. *Maryland*,[20] was decided in 1963. In *Brady*, the Court held that the prosecution is required to disclose to the defense exculpatory evidence that directly relates to claims of either guilt or innocence. A second, and more recent, case is that of *U.S.* v. *Bagley*,[21] decided in 1985. In *Bagley* the Court ruled that the prosecution must disclose any evidence that the defense requests. The Court reasoned that to withhold evidence, even when it does not relate directly to issues of guilt or innocence, may mislead the defense into thinking that such evidence does not exist.

One special decision made by the prosecutor concerns the filing of separate or multiple charges. The decision to try a defendant simultaneously on multiple charges can allow for the presentation of a considerable amount of evidence and permit an in-court demonstration of a complete sequence of criminal events. Such a strategy has a practical side as well; it saves time and money by substituting one trial for what might otherwise be any number of trials if each charge were to be brought separately before the court. From the prosecutor's point of view, however, trying the charges one at a time carries the advantage of allowing for another trial on a new charge if a "not guilty" verdict is returned the first time.

Once trial begins, the job of the prosecutor is to present the state's case against the defendant vigorously. Prosecutors introduce evidence against the accused, steer the testimony of witnesses "for the people," and argue in favor of conviction. Since defendants are presumed innocent until proven guilty, the burden of demonstrating guilt beyond a reasonable doubt rests with the prosecutor.

The activities of the prosecutor do not end with a finding of guilt or innocence. Following conviction prosecutors usually are allowed to make sentencing recommendations to the judge. They can be expected to argue that aggravating factors (see the next chapter), prior record, or especially heinous qualities of the offense in question call for strict punishment. When convicted defendants appeal, prosecutors may need to defend their own actions, and to argue, in briefs filed with appellate courts, that convictions were properly obtained. Most jurisdictions also allow prosecutors to make recommendations when defendants they have convicted are being considered for parole or early release from prison.

The Abuse of Discretion   The large amount of discretion wielded by prosecutors creates considerable abuse potential. Discretionary decisions not to prosecute friends or political cronies, or to accept guilty pleas to drastically reduced charges for personal considerations, are always dangerous possibilities. On the other hand, overzealous prosecution by district attorneys seeking heightened visibility in order to support grand political ambitions can be another source of difficulty. Administrative decisions, such as case scheduling, can also be used by prosecutors to harass defendants into pleading guilty.

Some forms of abuse may be unconscious. At least one study suggests that some prosecutors may have a built-in tendency toward leniency where female defendants are concerned, but tend to discriminate against minorities in deciding whether or not to prosecute.[22]

Although the electorate are the final authority to which prosecutors must answer, gross misconduct by prosecutors may be addressed by the state supreme court or by the state attorney general's office. Short of criminal misconduct, however, most of the options available to either the court or the attorney general are limited.

The Prosecutor's Professional Responsibility   As members of the legal profession, prosecutors are subject to the American Bar Association's (ABA) Code of Professional Responsibility. Serious violations of the code may result in their being disbarred from the practice of law. The ABA Standard for Criminal Justice 3–1.1 describes the prosecutor's duty this way: "The duty of the prosecutor is to seek justice, not merely to convict." Hence, a prosecutor is barred by the standards of the legal profession from advocating any fact or position which he or she knows is untrue.

Defense Counsel

The defense counsel is a trained lawyer, who may specialize in the practice of criminal law. The task of the defense attorney is to represent the accused as soon as possible after arrest and to ensure that the civil rights of the defendant are not violated through processing by the criminal justice system. Other duties of the defense counsel include testing the strength of the prosecution's case, possible involvement in plea negotiations, and the preparation of an adequate defense to be used at trial. In the preparation of a defense, criminal lawyers may enlist private detectives, experts, witnesses to the crime, and character witnesses. Some will perform aspects of the role of private detective or of investigator themselves. They will also review relevant court precedents in order to determine what the best defense strategy might be.

Defense preparation may involve intense communications between lawyer and defendant. Such discussions are recognized as privileged communications which are protected under the umbrella of lawyer-client confidentiality. In other words, lawyers cannot be compelled in court to reveal information which their client has confided in them.

If their client is found guilty, defense attorneys will be involved in arguments at sentencing, may be asked to file an appeal, and will probably counsel the defendant and the defendant's family as to what civil matters (payment of debts, release from contractual obligations, etc.) may need to be arranged after sentence is imposed. Hence, the role of defense attorney encompasses many aspects, including (1) attorney, (2) negotiator, (3) confidant, (4) family and personal counselor, (5) social worker, (6) investigator, and, as we shall see, (7) bill collector.

The Criminal Lawyer   Three major categories of defense attorneys assist defendants in the United States: (1) private attorneys, usually referred to as "criminal lawyers"; (2) court-appointed counsel; and (3) public defenders.

Private attorneys (also called "retained counsel") either have their own legal practices or work for law firms in which they may be partners or employees. As those who have had to hire defense attorneys know, the fees of private attorneys can be high. Most privately retained criminal lawyers charge in the range of $100 to $200 per hour. Included in their bill is the time it takes to prepare for a case as well as time spent in the courtroom. "High-powered" criminal defense attorneys who have established a regional or national reputation for successfully defending their clients can be far more expensive still.

Although the job of a criminal lawyer may appear glamorous, few law students actually choose to specialize in the study of criminal law. Monetary incentives attract most to contract law or civil law, where the litigation of major suits can result in healthy financial rewards. Some criminal defense attorneys begin their careers immediately following law school, while others seek to gain experience working as assistant district attorneys or assistant public defenders for a number of years before going into private practice. As one can imagine, the collection of fees can be a significant source of difficulty for criminal lawyers. Many defendants are poor. Those who aren't are often reluctant to pay what may seem to them to be an exorbitant fee, and woe be it to the defense attorney whose client is convicted before the fee has been paid!

Public Defender An attorney employed by a government agency or subagency, or by a private organization under contract to a unit of government, for the purpose of providing defense services to indigents.

Criminal Defense of the Poor In 1990 state and local governments spent $1.3 billion to provide legal representation for criminal defendants unable to afford their own—and over 80% of all defendants in felony cases depend upon court-appointed attorneys or public defenders to represent them.[23] A series of U.S. Supreme Court decisions have guaranteed that defendants unable to pay for private criminal defense attorneys will receive adequate representation at all stages of criminal justice processing.

In *Powell* v. *Alabama* (1932),[24] the Court held that the Fourteenth Amendment required state courts to appoint counsel for defendants in capital cases who were unable to afford their own. In 1938, in *Johnson* v. *Zerbst*,[25] the Court established the right of indigent defendants to receive the assistance of appointed counsel in all criminal proceedings in federal courts. The 1963 case of *Gideon* v. *Wainwright*[26] extended the right to appointed counsel in state courts to all indigent defendants charged with a felony. *Argersinger* v. *Hamlin* (1972)[27] saw the Court require adequate legal representation for anyone facing a potential sentence of imprisonment. Juveniles charged with delinquent acts were granted the right to appointed counsel in the case of *In re Gault* (1967),[28] which is discussed in detail in the chapter on juvenile justice.

States have responded to the federal mandate for indigent defense in a number of ways. Most now use one of three systems to deliver legal services to criminal defendants who are unable to afford their own: (1) court-assigned counsel, (2) public defenders, and (3) contract arrangements. Most such systems are administered at the county level, although funding arrangements may involve state, county, and municipal monies.

Court-appointed defense attorneys, whose fees are paid at a rate set by the state or local government, comprise the most widely used system of indigent defense. Assigned counsel is usually drawn from a roster of all practicing criminal attorneys within the jurisdiction of the trial court.

One problem with assigned counsel concerns degree of effort. Although most attorneys assigned by the court to indigent defense probably take their jobs seriously, some feel only a loose commitment to their clients. Paying clients, in their eyes, deserve better service and are apt to get it. The nationwide average cost per case for indigent defense in a recent year was $223, although the figure varied from a low of $63 in Arkansas to a high of $540 in New Jersey.[29]

Public defender programs employ a full-time salaried staff. Staff members include defense attorneys, defense investigators, and office personnel. Defense investigators gather information in support of the defense effort. They may interview friends, family members, and employers of the accused, with an eye toward effective defense. Public defender programs have shown some increase in popularity in recent years, with approximately 37% of counties nationwide now funding them. Critics charge that public defenders, because they are government employees, are not sufficiently independent from prosecutors and judges. For the same reason, clients may be suspicious of public defenders, viewing them as state functionaries. Finally, huge caseloads are typical of public defender's offices, and create pressures toward an excessive use of plea bargaining.

Contract attorney programs are those which arrange with local criminal lawyers to provide for indigent defense on a contractual basis. Individual attorneys, local bar associations, and multipartner law firms may all be used to provide for such arranged services. Contract defense programs are the least widely used at present, although their numbers are growing.

Critics of the current system of indigent defense point out that the system is woefully underfunded. "In 1990," for example, "states spent $1.3 billion to prosecute individuals, but only $548 on indigent defense; local governments spent $2.7 billion versus only $788 million; and the federal government $1.6 billion versus $408 million."[30] Overall, only 2.3% of monies spent on criminal justice activities goes to pay for indigent defense—an amount many consider too small.[31] As a consequence of such limited funding, many public defender's offices employ what critics call a "plead-'em-and-speed-'em through" strategy, often involving a heavy use of plea-bargaining and initial meetings with clients in courtrooms as trials are about to begin. Mary Broderick of the National Legal Aid and Defender Association says, "We aren't being given the same weapons.... It's like trying to deal with smart bombs when all you've got is a couple of cap pistols."[32]

Of course, defendants need not accept assigned counsel. Defendants who elect to do so may waive their right to an attorney and undertake their own defense—a right held to be inherent in the Sixth Amendment to the U.S. Constitution by the U.S. Supreme Court in the 1975 case of *Faretta* v. *California*.[33]

Defendants who are not pleased with the lawyer appointed to defend them are in a somewhat different situation. They may request, through the court, that a new lawyer be assigned to them. However, unless there is clear reason for reassignment, such as an obvious personality conflict between defendant and attorney, few judges are likely to honor a request of this sort. Short of obvious difficulties, most judges will trust in the professionalism of appointed counselors.

The Ethics of Defense
At trial, the job of defense counsel is to prepare and offer a vigorous defense on behalf of the accused. A proper defense often involves the presentation of evidence and the examination of witnesses, all of which requires careful thought and planning. Good attorneys, like quality craftspeople everywhere, may find themselves emotionally committed to the outcome of trials in which they are involved. Beyond the immediacy of a given trial, attorneys also realize that their reputation can be influenced by lay perceptions of their performance, and that their careers and personal financial success depend upon consistently "winning" in the courtroom.

The nature of the adversarial process, fed by the emotions of the participants, conspires with the often privileged and extensive knowledge that defense attorneys have about a case, to tempt the professional ethics of some counselors. Because the defense counsel may often know more about the guilt or innocence of the defendant than anyone else prior to trial, the defense role is one which is carefully prescribed by ethical and procedural considerations. Attorneys violate both law and the standards of their own profession if they knowingly misrepresent themselves or their clients.

Adversarial System The two-sided structure under which American criminal trial courts operate and which pits the prosecution against the defense. In theory, justice is done when the most effective adversary is able to convince the judge or jury that his or her perspective on the case is the correct one.

Portland (Oregon) public defender Will Smith in action. Here, Smith questions prospective jurors who are about to try a defendant on a charge of auto theft. *Photo: Frank Fournier/Contact Stock.*

> O Lord, look down upon these the multitudes,
> and spread strife and dissension, so that this,
> Thy servant, might prosper.
>
> —*The Lawyer's Prayer (anonymous)*

To help attorneys know what is expected of them, ethical standards abound. Four main groups of standards, each drafted by the American Bar Association, are especially applicable to defense attorneys:

1. Canons of Professional Ethics (1908)
2. Model Code of Professional Responsibility (revised, 1980)
3. Model Rules of Professional Conduct (1983)
4. ABA Project on Standards for Criminal Justice: The Prosecution Function and the Defense Function (2nd ed., 1980)

The ABA Standard for Criminal Justice, Number 4–1.1, reads in part:

(c) The defense lawyer, in common with all members of the bar, is subject to standards of conduct stated in statutes, rules, decisions of courts, and codes, canons, or other standards of professional conduct. The defense lawyer has no duty to execute any directive of the accused which does not comport with law or such standards. The defense lawyer is the professional representative of the accused, not the accused's alter ego.

(d) It is unprofessional conduct for a lawyer intentionally to misrepresent matters of fact or law to the court.

(e) It is the duty of every lawyer to know the standards of professional conduct as defined in codes and canons of the legal profession and in this chapter. The functions and duties of defense counsel are governed by such standards whether defense counsel is assigned or privately retained.

THEORY INTO PRACTICE

GIDEON V. *WAINWRIGHT*
372 U.S. 335, 83 S.CT. 792, 9 L.ED. 2D 799 (1963)

In the 1963 case of *Gideon* v. *Wainwright*, the U.S. Supreme Court extended the right to legal counsel to indigent defendants charged with a criminal offense. The reasoning of the Court is well summarized in this excerpt from the majority opinion written by Justice Black:

> …*Governments, both state and federal, quite properly spend vast sums of money to establish machinery to try defendants accused of crime. Lawyers to prosecute are everywhere deemed essential to protect the public's interest in an orderly society. Similarly, there are few defendants charged with crime, few indeed, who fail to hire the best lawyers they can get to prepare and present their defenses. That government hires lawyers to prosecute and defendants who have the money hire lawyers to defend are the strongest indications of the widespread belief that lawyers in criminal courts are necessities, not luxuries. The right of one charged with crime to counsel may not be deemed fundamental and essential to fair trials in some countries, but it is in ours. From the very beginning, our state and national constitutions and laws have laid great emphasis on procedural and substantive safeguards designed to assure fair trials before impartial tribunals in which every defendant stands equal before the law. This noble ideal cannot be realized if the poor man charged with crime has to face his accusers without a lawyer to assist him.*

Even so, defense attorneys are under no obligation to reveal information obtained from a client without the client's permission. In 1992, Minneapolis multimillionaire Russell Lund, Jr., was arrested and charged with the murder of his estranged wife and her boyfriend—a former Iowa state senator. Following the murder, attention shifted to the activities of Lund's attorneys who, police claim, waited until the day after the killings before reporting the shooting, hired a private detective who may have destroyed some evidence, and checked Mr. Lund into a private psychiatric facility under a different name without telling police where he was.[34]

In 1986, the supreme Court case of *Nix* v. *Whiteside*[35] clarified the duty of lawyers to reveal known instances of client perjury. The *Nix* case came to the Court upon the complaint of the defendant, Whiteside, who claimed that he was deprived of the assistance of effective counsel during a murder trial because his lawyer would not allow him to testify untruthfully. Whiteside wanted to testify that he had seen a gun or something metallic in his victim's hand before killing him. Before trial, however, Whiteside admitted to his lawyer that he had actually seen no weapon, but he believed that to testify to the truth would result in his conviction. The lawyer told Whiteside that, as

THEORY INTO PRACTICE

THE WORLD'S DEADLIEST DISTRICT ATTORNEY

In 1976 Joe Freeman Britt, district attorney for North Carolina's rural 16th judicial district, entered the *Guiness Book of World Records* as the "world's deadliest district attorney"—a record which stands to this day. During his career as D.A., Britt, a cigar-smoking, 6-foot 6-inch mountain of a man, achieved the grim distinction of winning 46 death penalty convictions and sending 33 men and women to North Carolina's death row. One of those convicted, Velma Barfield, became the first woman executed in the United States in more than 22 years. Of all the defendants tried by Britt in death penalty cases, none have ever been acquitted, although 5 received life sentences rather than death.

As Britt's fame spread, press interest in the "world's deadliest district attorney" grew. Britt was soon featured in dozens of interviews and profiles. *The* (London) *Times*, *Newsweek*, the *New York Times*, the *Los Angeles Times*, *People* magazine, the German magazine *Stern*, and the television show *60 Minutes* all portrayed Britt as a prosecutor who gives no quarter. A "masterful orator with a deep booming voice," the *Atlanta Journal* depicted Britt this way: "He prowls the courtroom like an outraged Minotaur. He storms, scowls, gesticulates wildly and quotes the Old Testament with authority." But he doesn't shoot from the hip. Britt prepares months for each capital case. His greatest battle, he says, is with the jury. "In every prospective juror's breast there beats the flame that whispers, 'Preserve human life.' It's my job to extinguish that flame. I'll tell you, it destroys my faith in humanity the way a prospective juror will say he believes in the death penalty and then turn around and say, 'But I ain't gonna be no part of it.' "

Surprisingly, Britt has not always favored capital punishment. As an undergraduate student at Wake Forest University he led a campaign against the death penalty. Today he describes himself as a "true believer." "The changeover was gradual," he says. "I had no blinding revelation." Imagine yourself "walking down a muddy ditch in the fog at daybreak…and the fog begins to lift and you find a 13-year-old girl with her dress up over her head and a bloody grin from ear to ear where someone slit her throat. Multiply that by a lot of sights and sounds and smells and see that enough times and it affects your perspective."

Britt describes himself as subscribing to a "classic" understanding of crime. "I think punishment must have some meaning for there to be any justice," he says. "The victim's lawyer is the prosecutor.… That poor victim lying 6 feet underground has nobody to speak for him but me." Asked whether he considers himself merciless, Britt responds, "it depends on your point of view, whether you're holding a sobbing sister of the killer or (of) the victim."

What motivates Joe Freeman Britt? His closing arguments to juries can be revealing. Once he described a murder victim as someone who had been "a living, breathing human being…just like you and me…and now he's gone.… My God, it's good to be alive!" he exclaimed. "Did you watch the sun come up this morning?"

Sources: "Joe Freeman Britt, 'Deadliest Prosecutor,' " *The Fayetteville Observer-Times* (North Carolina), January 20, 1985, p. 1F; "N. Carolina Prosecutor Called World's 'Deadliest,' " *The Atlanta Journal*, March 9, 1986, p. 33A; "Controversial Britt Known as Tough," *The Charlotte Observer* (North Carolina), April 3, 1988, p. 12A; "World's Deadliest Prosecutor," *Greensboro News and Record* (North Carolina), March 29, 1987, p. 1B.

Joe Freeman Britt, the world's deadliest district attorney. *Photo: Terry Parke/Time, Inc.*

a professional counselor, he would be forced to challenge Whiteside's false testimony if it occurred and to explain to the court the facts as he knew them. On the stand Whiteside said only that he thought the victim was reaching for a gun, but did not claim to have seen one. He was found guilty of second-degree murder and appealed to the Supreme Court, on the claim of inadequate representation.

The Court, recounting the development of ethical codes in the legal profession, held that a lawyer's duty to a client "is limited to legitimate, lawful conduct compatible with the very nature of a trial as a search for truth.... counsel is precluded from taking steps or in any way assisting the client in presenting false evidence or otherwise violating the law."[36]

The Bailiff

Also called a "court officer," the bailiff is usually an armed law enforcement officer. The job of the bailiff is to ensure order in the courtroom, announce the judge's entry into the courtroom, call witnesses, and prevent the escape of the accused (if the accused has not been released on bond). The bailiff also supervises the jury when it is sequestered and controls public and media access to the jury. Bailiffs in federal courtrooms are deputy U.S. marshals.

Courtrooms can be dangerous places. In 1993, George Lott was sentenced to die for a courtroom shooting in Tarrant County, Texas, which left two lawyers dead and three other people injured.[37] Lott said he had been frustrated by the court's handling of his divorce and by child molesting charges filed against him by his ex-wife. In a similar case, on May 5, 1992, a man opened fire with two pistols in a St. Louis courtroom during divorce proceedings, killing his wife and wounding her two lawyers and a security officer. The same day a presiding judge in Grand Forks, North Dakota, was shot to death by a man accused of failing to pay child support.[38]

Bailiff The court officer whose duties are to keep order in the courtroom and to maintain physical custody of the jury.

THEORY INTO PRACTICE

AMERICAN BAR ASSOCIATION STANDARDS
OF PROFESSIONAL RESPONSIBILITY

The intense effort of defense advocacy results, for most criminal trial lawyers, in an emotional and personal investment in the outcome of a case. To strike a balance between zealous and effective advocacy, on the one hand, and just professional conduct within the bounds of the law on the other, the American Bar Association has developed a Code of Professional Responsibility which reads in part:

In his representation of a client, a lawyer shall not:

File a suit, assert a position, conduct a defense, delay a trial, or take other action on behalf of his client when he knows or when it is obvious that such action would serve merely to harass or maliciously injure another.

Knowingly advance a claim or defense that is unwarranted under existing law...

Conceal or knowingly fail to disclose that which he is required by law to reveal.

Knowingly use perjured testimony or false evidence.

Knowingly make a false statement of law or fact.

Participate in the creation or preservation of evidence when he knows or it is obvious that the evidence is false.

Counsel or assist his client in conduct that the lawyer knows to be illegal or fraudulent.

Source: Excerpted from American Bar Association, *Code of Professional Responsibility*, Disciplinary Rule 7–102. All rights reserved. Reprinted with permission.

Local Court Administrators

Many states now employ trial court administrators whose job it is to facilitate the smooth functioning of courts in particular judicial districts or areas. A major impetus toward the hiring of local court administrators came from the 1967 President's Commission on Law Enforcement and Administration of Justice. Examining state courts, the report found: "A system that treats defendants who are charged with minor offenses with less dignity and consideration than it treats those who are charged with serious crimes."[39] A few years later, the National Advisory Commission on Criminal Justice Standards and Goals recommended that all courts with five or more judges should create the position of trial court administrator.[40]

Court administrators provide uniform court management, assuming many of the duties previously performed by chief judges, prosecutors, and court clerks. Where court administrators operate, the ultimate authority for running the court still rests with the chief judge. Administrators, however, are able to relieve the judge of many routine and repetitive tasks such as record keeping, scheduling, case flow analysis, personnel administration, space utilization, facilities planning, and budget management. They may also serve to take minutes at meetings of judges and their committees.

Juror management is another area in which trial court administrators are becoming increasingly involved. Juror utilization studies can identify such problems as the overselection of citizens for the jury pool and the reasons for what may be excessive requests to be excluded from jury service. They can also reduce the amount of wasted time jurors spend waiting to be called or empaneled.

Effective court administrators are able to track lengthy cases and identify bottlenecks in court processing. They then suggest strategies to make the administration of justice increasingly efficient for courtroom professionals and more humane for lay participants.

The Court Recorder

Also called the "court stenographer" and "court reporter," the role of the recorder is to create a record of all that occurs during trial. Especially significant are all verbal comments made in the courtroom, including testimony, objections, the rulings of the judge, the charge to the jury, arguments made by the attorneys, and the results of conferences between the attorneys and the judge. Occasionally, the judge will rule that a statement should be "stricken from the record" because it is inappropriate or unfounded. The official trial record, often taken on a stenotype machine or audio recorder, may later be transcribed in manuscript form and will become the basis for any appellate review of the trial.

Clerk of Court

The duties of the clerk of court (also known as the "county clerk") extend beyond the courtroom. The clerk maintains all records of criminal cases, including all pleas and motions made before and after the actual trial. The clerk also prepares a jury pool and issues jury summonses and subpoenas witnesses for both the prosecution and defense. During the trial the clerk (or an assistant) marks physical evidence for identification as instructed by the judge and maintains custody of such evidence. The clerk also swears in witnesses and performs other functions as the judge directs.

Some states allow the clerk limited judicial duties. The clerk may have the power to issue warrants and can also serve as judge of probate—overseeing wills and the administration of estates and handling certain matters relating to persons declared mentally incompetent.[41]

The Expert Witness

Expert witnesses provide a highly effective technique for the introduction of scientific evidence at criminal trials. An expert witness, like the other courtroom "actors" described in this chapter, is generally a paid professional. A witness is recognized as an expert by virtue of having specialized skills in a recognized profession or technical area. Experts may provide the court with scientific information in areas such as medicine, psychology, ballistics, crime scene analysis, photography, and many other disciplines. Unlike other ("lay") witnesses, they are allowed to express opinions and draw conclusions, but only within their areas of expertise. Expert witnesses may be veterans of many trials. Some well-known expert witnesses traverse the country and earn very high fees by testifying at one trial after another.

Expert Witness A person who has special knowledge recognized by the court as relevant to the determination of guilt or innocence. Expert witnesses may express opinions or draw conclusions in their testimony—unlike lay witnesses.

A ballistics expert demonstrates a bullet's path during a Los Angeles murder trial. Expert witnesses often provide compelling testimony. *Photo: Sygma Photo.*

Expert witnesses are usually called upon to demonstrate their expertise before being allowed to testify. Education, work experience, publications, and awards may all support the expertise of a witness. Expert witnesses may testify only in their particular area of expertise. Like all other witnesses, they are subject to cross-examination.

Expert witnesses have played significant roles in many well-known cases. The trial of John Hinckley, for example, saw the testimony of psychiatric experts result in a finding of "not guilty by reason of insanity" for the man accused of shooting then-President Reagan. The highly publicized trial of Wayne Williams, arrested a number of years ago for the murder of many black children in Atlanta, concluded in a conviction based largely upon the testimony of witnesses expert in the field of fiber analysis and textiles.

One of the difficulties with expert testimony is that it can be confusing. Sometimes the trouble is due to the nature of the subject matter, and sometimes to disagreements between the experts themselves. Often, however, it arises from the strict interpretation given to expert testimony by procedural requirements. The difference between medical and legal definitions of insanity, for example, points to a divergence in both history and purpose between the law and science. Courts which attempt to apply criteria such as the McNaughten rule (discussed earlier) in deciding claims of "insanity," often find themselves faced with the testimony of psychiatric experts who refuse even to recognize the word. Such experts may prefer, instead, to speak in terms of psychosis and neurosis—words which have no place in judicial jargon. Such legal requirements, because of the uncertainties they create, may pit experts against one another and result in considerable confusion for the jury.

Even so, most authorities agree that expert testimony is usually interpreted by jurors as more trustworthy than other forms of evidence. In a study of scientific evidence, one prosecutor commented that if he had to choose between presenting a fingerprint or an eyewitness at trial, he would always go with the fingerprint.[42] As a consequence of the effectiveness of scientific evidence, the National Institute of Justice recommends that "prosecutors consider the potential utility of such information in all cases where such evidence is available."[43] Some authors have called attention to the difficulties surrounding expert testimony. Legal interpretations often severely limit the kind of information which experts can provide.

NONPROFESSIONAL PARTICIPANTS

A number of people find themselves either unwilling or unwitting participants in criminal trials. Into this category fall defendants, victims, and most witnesses. Even though they lack the status of paid, professional, participants, these are precisely the people who provide the "grist" for the judicial mill. Without them, trials could not occur, and the professional roles described earlier would be rendered meaningless.

Lay Witnesses

Nonexpert witnesses, otherwise known as lay witnesses, may be called by either the prosecution or defense. Lay witnesses may be eye witnesses, who saw the crime in question being committed or who came upon the crime scene shortly after the crime had occurred. Another type of lay witness is the character witness, who provides information about the personality, family life, business acumen, and so on of the defendant in an effort to show that he or she is not the kind of person who would commit the crime of which they stand charged. Of course, the victim may also be a witness, providing detailed and sometimes lengthy testimony about the defendant and the event in question.

Witnesses are officially notified that they are to appear in court to testify by a written document called a subpoena. Subpoenas are generally "served" by an officer of the court or by a police officer. Both sides in a criminal case may subpoena witnesses and might ask that persons called to testify bring with them books, papers, photographs, videotapes, or other forms of physical evidence. Witnesses who fail to appear when summoned may face contempt of court charges.

The job of a witness is to provide accurate testimony concerning only those things of which he or she has direct knowledge. Normally witnesses will not be allowed to repeat things told to them by others, unless it is necessary to do so in order to account for certain actions of their own. Since few witnesses have much familiarity with courtroom procedure, the task of testifying is fraught with uncertainty and can be traumatizing.

Anyone who testifies in a criminal trial must do so under oath, in which some reference to God is made, or after affirmation,[44] where a pledge to tell the truth is used by those who find either "swearing" or a reference to God objectionable. All witnesses are subject to cross-examination, discussed in detail elsewhere in this chapter. Lay witnesses may be surprised to find that cross-examination can force them to defend their personal and moral integrity. A cross-examiner may question a witness about past vicious, criminal, or immoral acts, even where such matters have never been the subject of a criminal proceeding.[45] As long as the intent of such questions is to demonstrate to the jury that the witness may not be a person who is worthy of belief, they will normally be permitted by the judge.

Witnesses have traditionally been shortchanged by the judicial process. Subpoenaed to attend court, they have often suffered from frequent and unannounced changes in trial dates. A witness who promptly responds to a summons to appear may find that legal maneuvering has resulted in unanticipated delays. Strategic changes by either side may make the testimony of some witnesses entirely unnecessary, and people who have prepared themselves for the psychological rigors of testifying often experience an emotional let down.

Lay Witness An eyewitness, character witness, or any other person called upon to testify who is not considered an expert. Lay witnesses must testify to facts alone and may not draw conclusions or express opinions.

In order to compensate witnesses for their time, and to make up for lost income, many states pay witnesses for each day that they spend in court. Payments range from $5 to $30 per day,[46] although some states pay nothing at all. In the case of *Demarest* v. *Manspeaker* (1991),[47] the U.S. Supreme Court held that federal prisoners, subpoenaed to testify, are entitled to witness fees just as nonincarcerated witnesses would be.

In another move to make the job of witnesses less onerous, 39 states and the federal government have laws or guidelines requiring that witnesses be notified of scheduling changes and cancellations in criminal proceedings.[48] In 1982 Congress passed the Victim and Witness Protection Act, which required the U.S. attorney general to develop guidelines to assist victims and witnesses in meeting the demands placed upon them by the justice system. A number of victim assistance programs (also called victim/witness assistance programs), described shortly, have also taken up a call for the rights of witnesses and are working to make the courtroom experience more manageable.

Jurors

Article III of the U.S. Constitution requires that "[t]he trial of all crimes…shall be by jury…". States have the authority to determine the size of criminal trial juries. Most states use juries composed of 12 persons and 1 or 2 alternates designated to fill in for jurors who are unable to continue due to accident, illness, or personal emergency. Some states allow for juries smaller than 12, and juries with as few as 6 members have survived Supreme Court scrutiny.[49]

Jury duty is regarded as a responsibility of citizenship. Other than juveniles and certain job occupants such as police personnel, physicians, members of the armed services on active duty, and emergency services workers, persons called for jury duty must serve unless they can convince a judge that they should be excused for overriding reasons. Aliens, those convicted of a felony, and citizens who have served on a jury within the past two years are excluded from jury service in most jurisdictions.

The names of prospective jurors are often gathered from the tax records or voter registration rolls of a county or municipality. Minimum qualifications for jury service include adulthood, a basic command of spoken English, citizenship, "ordinary intelligence," and local residency. Jurors are also expected to possess their "natural faculties," meaning that they should be able to hear, speak, see, move, and so forth. Some jurisdictions have recently allowed handicapped persons to serve as jurors, although the nature of the evidence to be presented in a case may preclude persons with certain kinds of handicaps from serving.

Ideally the jury is to be a microcosm of society, reflecting the values, rationality, and common sense of the average person. The idea of a peer jury stems from the Magna Carta's original guarantee of jury trials for "freemen." "Freemen" in England during the thirteenth century, however, were more likely to be of similar mind than is a cross section of Americans today. Hence, although the duty of the jury is to deliberate upon the evidence and, ultimately, determine guilt or innocence, social dynamics may play just as great a role in jury verdicts as do the facts of a case.

The U.S. Supreme Court has held that criminal defendants have a right to have their cases heard before a jury of their peers.[50] Ideally, peer juries are those composed of a representative cross section of the community in which the alleged crime has occurred and where the trial is to be held. In a 1945 case, *Thiel* v. *Southern Pacific Company*,[51] the Supreme Court clarified the concept of a "jury of one's peers" by noting that while it is not necessary for every jury to contain representatives of every conceivable racial, ethnic, religious, gender, and economic group in the community, court officials may not systematically and intentionally exclude any juror solely because of his or her social characteristics.

THEORY INTO PRACTICE
....

REPLACING JURORS DURING THE DELIBERATION PROCESS... THE CASE OF REGINALD DENNY

In a 1993 case with close parallels to the "Rodney King trial" discussed earlier, two men, Damian Monroe Williams, 20, and Henry Keith Watson, 29, were convicted of assault charges in the videotaped beating of truck driver Reginald Denny. Denny was caught driving his rig in a riot-torn section of inner-city Los Angeles immediately following the pronouncement of not-guilty verdicts in the initial 1992 California trial of police officers accused of beating King. Watson and Williams were also charged with attempted murder in the attack on Denny and with robbing and beating 7 other people in the riot-torn city. The riots which followed the King verdict left 53 people dead and resulted in more than $1 billion in damages in Los Angeles alone.

Like the "King case," the "Denny case" was captured on videotape—this time by a news crew operating a helicopter in the area. Other similarities between the cases were seen in the fact that the officers who beat King are white, while King is black. Denny is white, his attackers, black. Both Denny and King suffered serious injuries; either might have died, and both were hospitalized for extended periods of time as a result of the injuries they suffered. Both incidents were fortuitously videotaped and broadcast nationwide. Even today, images of both beatings continue to haunt the American conscience.

The Denny case, however, holds special significance for the role of juries in future criminal trials where the events leading up to them have become media events. In the opinion of many experts, the videotaped beating and other evidence against the defendants supported verdicts of guilt on much more serious charges than those which were actually returned—including attempted murder, malicious assault, and aggravated mayhem (felonies under California law). The jury, however, opted to convict the defendants on far less serious charges. Some analysts suggested that the jury in the Denny case interpreted its role as one of meting out justice according to criteria previously established in the King case. The two officers convicted in the King case were sentenced to 30 months in prison. The verdicts returned in the Denny case held the potential for almost exactly the same kind of sentence to be imposed on Watson and Williams. If, in fact, the Denny jury was guided more by its knowledge of the King case than by an objective interpretation of the facts before it, then the judicial process has demonstrated the potential to be determined, at least in highly publicized cases in which popular precedents exist, far more by an informal communal sense of justice rather than by the strict applicability of specific criminal statutes.

Unfortunately for the veracity of the Denny verdict, a second significant issue arose when the jury deliberation stage of the trial came to be marked by seemingly unusual activity. Within days after the presentation of evidence was completed and deliberations began, Superior Court Judge John Ouderkirk removed 2 jurors from active deliberation and replaced them with alternates. One of the removed jurors, a black woman, was described by all 11 fellow jurors as unable to "comprehend anything that we've been trying to accomplish." The other dismissed juror, a white man, asked to be sent home after telling the judge that he was suffering from severe personal problems.

Although California law permits the removal of a juror who, after deliberations have begun, dies or becomes ill "or upon other good cause shown to the court is found to be unable to perform his duty," defense attorneys were quick to charge that jurors were being intimidated by the threat of additional dismissals. Edi M. O. Faal, William's lawyer, called for the removal of two other jurors who he said were "incompetent and have engaged in worse misconduct than the black woman" who was dismissed. His motion, however, was denied.

Complicating the trial process still further, Judge Ouderkirk invalidated two earlier verdicts which the jury had reached without announcing them after dismissing the second of the two released jurors. The verdicts had applied to 2 of the 12 charges against Watson and Williams. The judge also ordered jurors to "set aside the earlier deliberations as if they had not taken place." Early on in the trial two other jurors were replaced because of illness, and another was removed for misconduct.

Even if the judge's decisions are upheld upon appeal (as analysts think they will be should appeals take place), the removal of jurors at the deliberation phase of the trial process only led to heightened concerns in the black community that Watson and Williams could not get a fair trial, and that they were being made into scapegoats for the Los Angeles riots which followed the King verdict. The trial itself was declared "tainted" by John Mack, president of the Los Angeles Urban League because of the "bizarre events" surrounding the removal of the jurors.

In the words of Peter Arenella, a professor of law at UCLA, "[w]e used to trust juries at trials to resolve guilt or innocence. But in our Court TV media age…the public believes it's in the same position as the jurors and can reach its own conclusion of guilt or innocence."

Sources: William Hamilton, "Replacement of 2 Jurors Brings Out Critics in L.A.; Judge in Denny Case to Rule on 3rd Panelist Today," *The Washington Post* wire service, October 14, 1993; Reuters Wire Services, "Judge Again Removes Juror in Riot Beating Case," October 12, 1993; Court TV, "Focus on Justice," October 19, 1993, 11 P.M. EST; and Haya El Nasser, "Jury Trouble Puts Denny Trial in Doubt," *USA Today*, October 14, 1993, p. 1A.

The Role of the Victim in a Criminal Trial

Not all crimes have clearly identifiable victims. Some, like murder, do not have victims who survive. Where there is an identifiable surviving victim, however, he or she (actually the proper term is "alleged victim," unless the guilt of the defendant is established) is often one of the most forgotten people in the courtroom. Although the victim may have been profoundly affected by the crime itself, and is often emotionally committed to the proceedings and trial outcome, they may not even be permitted to participate directly in the trial process. It is not unusual for crime victims to be totally unaware of the final outcome of a case which intimately concerns them.[52]

Hundreds of years ago the situation surrounding victims was far different. During the early Middle Ages in much of Europe, for example, victims, or their survivors, routinely played a central role in trial proceedings and in sentencing decisions. They testified, examined witnesses, challenged defense contentions, and pleaded with the judge or jury for justice, honor, and often revenge. Sometimes they were even expected to carry out the sentence of the court, by flogging the offender or by releasing the trapdoor used for hangings. This "golden age" of the victim ended with the consolidation of power into the hands of monarchs who declared that vengeance was theirs.

Today, victims, like witnesses, experience many hardships as they participate in the criminal court process. Some of the rigors they endure are

1. Uncertainties as to their role in the criminal justice process, as well as to what is expected of them
2. A general lack of knowledge about the criminal justice system, courtroom procedure, and legal issues
3. Trial delays which result in frequent travel, missed work, and wasted time
4. Fear of the defendant or retaliation from the defendant's associates
5. The trauma of testifying and of cross-examination

The trial process itself can make for a bitter experience. If victims take the stand, defense attorneys may test their memory, challenge their veracity, or even suggest that they were somehow responsible for their own victimization. After enduring cross-examination, some victims report feeling as though they, and not the offender, have been portrayed as the criminal to the jury. The difficulties encountered by victims have been compared to a second victimization at the hands of the criminal justice system.

A grass-roots resurgence of concern for the plight of victims began in the early 1970s and continues to grow. In 1982 the President's Task Force on Victims of Crime[53] gave focus to the movement and urged the widespread expansion of victim's assistance programs which were just beginning. Victim assistance programs today tend to offer services in the areas of crisis intervention, follow-up counseling, and helping victims secure their rights.[54] Following successful prosecution, some victim assistance programs also advise victims in the filing of civil suits in order to recoup financial losses directly from the offender.

The Alameda County (California) Victim/Witness Assistance Program is characteristic of others like it. A few years ago the Alameda program discovered that victims were having difficulty learning the outcome of their cases and additional difficulties in recovering property used as evidence. The program promptly set up property return and information services as a way of helping victims.[55]

Victim advocates argue that a victim's bill of rights is needed to provide the same kind of fairness to victims that is routinely accorded to defendants. In 1982 two significant steps were taken toward the development of a comprehensive victim's rights bill. In that year the President's Task Force on Victims of Crime[56] recommended 68 programmatic and legislative incentives for states and concerned citizens to pursue on behalf of victims. Also in 1982, voters in California approved "Proposition 8," a resolution which called for changes in the state's constitution to reflect concern for crime victims.

In 1984 the Victims of Crime Act (VOCA) was enacted with substantial bipartisan support. It authorized federal funding to help states establish victim assistance and victim compensation programs. Under VOCA the U.S. Department of Justice's Office for Victims of Crime provides a significant source of funding for victim assistance programs. For fiscal years 1991–1994, Congress authorized the office to provide $150 million annually to states to aid victims of state and federal criminal offenses.[57] Funds come from bond forfeitures, penalties, and fines imposed in federal criminal court cases. By midyear 1993, 49 states, the District of Columbia, and the Virgin Islands all had crime victim compensation programs. Maine, the only state without such a program in place, had one pending in its legislature.

The contemporary thrust of victim advocacy groups is in the direction of an amendment to the U.S. Constitution. The Victim's Constitutional Amendment Network (Victim's CAN), affiliated with the National Organization for Victim Assistance, Mothers Against Drunk Driving, Parents of Murdered Children, Justice for Crime Victims, and other groups, is seeking to add the phrase—"likewise, the victim, in every criminal prosecution, shall have the right to be present and to be heard at all critical stages of judicial proceedings"—to the Sixth Amendment.

Victim compensation programs provide another means of recognizing the needs of crime victims. Today, all 50 states have passed legislation providing for monetary payments to victims of crime. Such payments are primarily designed to compensate victims for medical expenses and lost wages. All existing programs require that applicants meet certain eligibility criteria, and most set limits on the maximum amount of compensation that can be received. Generally disallowed are claims from victims who are significantly responsible for their own victimization.

The Role of the Defendant in a Criminal Trial

Generally, defendants must be present at their trials—at least in federal court. Federal rules of criminal procedure require that a defendant "must be present at every stage of a trial…[except that a defendant who] is initially present may…be voluntarily absent after the trial has commenced." The rule defines "voluntary absence." In *Crosby* v. *U.S.* (1993),[58] the U.S. Supreme Court held that a defendant may not be tried in absentia even if he or she was present at the beginning of a trial where his or her absence is due to escape or failure to appear. In a related issue, *Zafiro* v. *U.S.* (1993)[59] held that, at least in federal courts, defendants charged with similar or related offenses may be tried together—even when their defenses differ substantially.

The majority of criminal defendants are poor, uneducated, and often alienated from the philosophy which undergirds the American justice system. A common view of the defendant in a criminal trial is that of a relatively powerless person at the mercy of judicial mechanisms. Many defendants are just that. However, such an image is often far from the truth. Defendants, especially those who seek an active role in their own defense, choreograph many courtroom activities. Experienced defendants, notably those who are career offenders, may be well versed in courtroom demeanor.

Every defendant who chooses to do so can substantially influence events in the courtroom. Defendants exercise choice in (1) deciding whether or not to testify personally, (2) selecting and retaining counsel, (3) planning a defense strategy in coordination with their attorney, (4) deciding what information to provide to (or withhold from) the defense team, (5) deciding what plea to enter, and (6) deciding whether or not to file an appeal, if convicted.

Even the most active defendants suffer from a number of disadvantages, however. One is the tendency of others to assume that anyone on trial must be guilty. Although a person is "innocent until proven guilty," the very fact that he or she is accused of an offense casts a shadow of suspicion that may foster biases in the minds of jurors and other courtroom actors. Another disadvantage lies in the often-substantial social and cultural differences which separate the offender from the professional courtroom staff. While lawyers and judges tend to identify with upper-middle-class values and life-styles, few offenders do. The consequences of such a gap between defendant and courtroom staff may be insidious but far reaching.

The Press in the Courtroom

Often overlooked, because they do not have an "official" role in courtroom proceedings, are spectators and the press. At any given trial both spectators and media representatives may be present in large numbers. Spectators include members of the families of both victim and defendant, friends of either side, and curious onlookers—some of whom are avocational court watchers.

Newswriters are apt to be present at "spectacular" trials (those involving some especially gruesome aspect, or famous personality) and at those in which there is a great deal of community interest. The right of reporters and spectators to be present at a criminal trial is supported by the Sixth Amendment's insistence upon a public trial.

Press reports at all stages of a criminal investigation and trial often create problems for the justice system. Significant pretrial publicity about a case may make it difficult to find jurors who have not already formed an opinion as to the guilt or innocence of the defendant. News reports from the courtroom may influence nonsequestered jurors who hear them, especially when they contain information brought to the bench, but not heard by the jury.

In the 1976 case of *Nebraska Press Association* v. *Stuart*,[60] the U.S. Supreme Court ruled that trial court judges could not legitimately issue gag orders, preventing the pretrial publication of information about a criminal case, as long as the defendant's right to a fair trial and an impartial jury could be ensured by traditional means.[61] These means include (1) a change of venue, whereby the trial is moved to another jurisdiction less likely to have been exposed to the publicity; (2) trial postponement, which would allow for memories to fade and emotions to cool; and (3) jury selection and screening to eliminate biased persons from the jury pool. In 1986 the Court extended press access to preliminary hearings, which, according to state rules of criminal procedure, are "sufficiently like a trial to require public access."[62] In 1993, in the case of *Caribbean International News Corporation* v. *Puerto Rico*,[63] the Court effectively applied that requirement to territories under U.S. control.

An artist's depiction of a portion of the 1990 "Central Park Jogger" trial. Some jurisdictions still restrict the use of cameras in the courtroom. *Photo: AP/Wide World Photos.*

Some people say the verdicts in the Rodney King and Reginald Denny trials were unfair, while others claim that they represent a burgeoning social awareness among jurors involved in well-publicized trials. *Source: Seattle Post-Intelligencer. Reprinted with permission.*

Today members of the press as well as video, television, and still cameras are allowed into most courtrooms. Forty-seven states now allow courtroom cameras,[64] and organizations like Court TV have capitalized on the opportunity for live courtroom broadcasts.

The U.S. Supreme Court has been less favorably disposed to television coverage than have state courts. In 1981, a Florida defendant appealed his burglary conviction to the Supreme Court,[65] arguing that the presence of TV cameras at his trial had turned the court into a circus for attorneys and made the proceedings more a sideshow than a trial. The Supreme Court, recognizing that television cameras have an untoward effect upon many people, agreed. In the words of the Court, "Trial courts must be especially vigilant to guard against any impairment of the defendant's right to a verdict based solely upon the evidence and the relevant law."[66]

THE CRIMINAL TRIAL

From arrest through sentencing, the criminal justice process is carefully choreographed. Arresting officers must follow proper procedure in the gathering of evidence, and in the arrest and questioning of suspects. Magistrates, prosecutors, jailers, and prison officials are all subject to similar strictures. Nowhere, however, is the criminal justice process more closely circumscribed than at the stage of the criminal trial.

Procedures in a modern courtroom are highly formalized. Rules of evidence and other procedural guidelines determine the course of a criminal hearing and trial. Rules of evidence are partially based upon tradition. All U.S. jurisdictions, however, have formalized rules of evidence in written form. Criminal trials at the federal level generally adhere to the requirements of *Federal Rules of Evidence.*

Trials are also circumscribed by informal rules and professional expectations. An important component of law school education is the teaching of rules which structure and define appropriate courtroom demeanor. In addition to statutory rules, law students are thoroughly exposed to the ethical standards of their profession as found in the *American Bar Association Standards* and other writings.

In the next few pages we will describe the chronology of a criminal trial and comment on some of the widely accepted rules of criminal procedure. Before we begin the description, however, it is good to keep two points in mind. One is that the primary purpose of any criminal trial is the determination of the defendant's guilt or innocence. In this regard it is important to recognize the crucial distinction made by legal scholars between legal guilt and factual guilt. Factual guilt deals with the issue of whether or not the defendant is actually responsible for the crime of which he or she stands accused. If the defendant "did it," then he or she is, in fact, guilty. Legal guilt is not so clear. Legal guilt is established only when the prosecutor presents evidence which is sufficient to convince the judge (where the judge determines the verdict) or jury that the defendant is guilty as charged. Legal guilt necessitates the adequate presentation of proof by the prosecution that the defendant is the guilty party. The distinction between legal guilt and factual guilt is crucial, because it points to the fact that the burden of proof rests with the prosecution, and it indicates the possibility that guilty defendants may, nonetheless, be found "not guilty."

The second point to remember is that criminal trials under our system of justice are built around an adversary system, and that central to such a system is the advocacy model. Participating in the adversary system are advocates for the state (the prosecution or district attorney) and for the defendant (defense counsel, public defender, etc.). The philosophy behind the adversary system holds that the greatest number of just resolutions in all foreseeable criminal trials will occur when both sides are allowed to argue effectively and vociferously their cases before a fair and impartial jury. The system requires that advocates for both sides do their utmost, within the boundaries set by law and professional ethics, to protect and advance the interests of their client. The advocacy model makes clear that it is not the job of the defense attorney or the prosecution to judge the guilt of any defendant. Hence, even defense attorneys who are convinced that their client is guilty are still exhorted to offer the best possible defense and to counsel their client as effectively as possible.

The adversarial model has been criticized by some thinkers who point to fundamental differences between law and science in the way the search for truth is conducted.[67] While proponents of traditional legal procedure accept the belief that truth can best be uncovered through an adversarial process, scientists adhere to a painstaking process of research and replication to acquire knowledge. Most of us would agree that scientific advances in recent years may have made factual issues less difficult to ascertain. For example, some of the new scientific techniques in evidence gathering, such as DNA fingerprinting (discussed in detail in Chapter 17), are now able to unequivocally link suspects to criminal activity. Whether scientific findings should continue to serve a subservient role to the adversarial process itself is a question which is now being raised. The ultimate answer will probably be couched in terms of the results either process is able to produce. If the adversarial model results in the acquittal of too many demonstrably guilty people because of legal "technicalities," or the scientific approach inaccurately identifies too many suspects, either could be restricted.

We turn now to a discussion of the steps in a criminal trial. Trial chronology consists of 11 stages: (1) trial initiation, (2) jury selection, (3) opening statements, (4) presentation of the prosecution's case, (5) defense motions to dismiss, (6) presentation of the defense, (7) closing arguments, (8) the judge's charge to the jury, (9) jury deliberations, (10) the verdict, and (11) sentencing. For purposes of brevity, stages 3 and 5 will be discussed jointly. Sentencing is reviewed in detail in a separate chapter.

TRIAL INITIATION: THE SPEEDY TRIAL ACT

The Sixth Amendment to the U.S. Constitution guarantees that "In all criminal prosecutions, the accused shall enjoy the right to a speedy and public trial." Clogged court calendars, limited judicial resources, and general inefficiency, however, often combine to produce what appears to many to be unreasonable delays in trial initiation. The attention of the Supreme Court was brought to bear on trial delays in three precedent-setting cases: *Klopfer* v. *North Carolina* (1967),[68] *Baker* v. *Wingo* (1972),[69] and *Strunk* v. *United States* (1973).[70] The *Klopfer* case involved a Duke University professor and focused on civil disobedience in a protest against segregated facilities. In Klopfer's long-delayed trial, the Court asserted that the right to a speedy trial is a fundamental guarantee of the Constitution. In the *Baker* case, the Court held that Sixth Amendment guarantees to a quick trial could be illegally violated even in cases where the accused did not explicitly object to delays. In *Strunk*, it found that denial of a speedy trial should result in a dismissal of all charges.

In 1974, against the advice of the Justice Department, the U.S. Congress passed the federal Speedy Trial Act.[71] The act, which was phased in gradually, and became fully effective in 1980, allows for the dismissal of federal criminal charges in cases where the prosecution does not seek an indictment or information within 30 days of arrest (a 30-day extension is granted when the grand jury is not in session) or where a trial does not commence within 70 working days after indictment for defendants who plead not guilty. If a defendant is not available for trial, or witnesses cannot be called within the 70-day limit, the period may be extended to 180 days. Delays brought about by the defendant, through requests for a continuance, or because of escape, are not counted in the specified time periods. The Speedy Trial Act has been condemned by some as shortsighted. One federal trial court judge, for example, wrote: "The ability of the criminal justice system to operate effectively and efficiently has been severely impeded by the Speedy Trial Act. Resources are misdirected, unnecessary severances required, cases proceed to trial inadequately prepared, and in some indeterminate number of cases, indictments against guilty persons are dismissed."[72]

In an important 1988 decision, *U.S.* v. *Taylor*,[73] the U.S. Supreme Court applied the requirements of the Speedy Trial Act to the case of a drug defendant who had escaped following arrest. The Court made it clear that trial delays, when they derive from the willful actions of the defendant, do not apply to the 70-day period. The Court also held that trial delays, even when they result from government action, do not necessarily provide grounds for dismissal if they occur "without prejudice." Delays without prejudice are those which are due to circumstances beyond the control of criminal justice agencies.

In 1993, an Indiana prisoner, William Fex, appealed a Michigan conviction on armed robbery and attempted murder charges, claiming that he had to wait 196 days after submitting a request to Indiana prison authorities for his Michigan trial to commence. In *Fex* v. *Michigan* (1993),[74] the U.S. Supreme Court ruled that "common-sense compel[s] the conclusion that the 180-day period does not commence until the prisoner's disposition request has actually been delivered to the court and prosecutor of the jurisdiction that lodged the detainer against him." In Fex's case, Indiana authorities had taken 22 days to forward his request to Michigan.

However, in a 1992 case, *Doggett* v. *U.S.*,[75] the Court held that a delay of 8½ years violated speedy trial provisions because it resulted from government negligence. In Doggett, the defendant was indicted on a drug charge in 1980, but left the country for Panama, where he lived until 1982 when he reentered the United States. He lived openly in the United States until 1988 when a credit check revealed him to authorities. He was arrested, tried, and convicted of federal drug charges stemming from his 1980

T H E O R Y   I N T O   P R A C T I C E

PRE- AND POSTTRIAL MOTIONS

A motion is defined by the *Dictionary of Criminal Justice Data Terminology*[1] as "[a]n oral or written request made to a court at any time before, during, or after court proceedings, asking the court to make a specified finding, decision, or order." Written motions are called petitions. This box lists the typical kinds of motions that may be made by both sides in a criminal case before and after trial.

Motion for Discovery

A motion for discovery, filed by the defense, asks the court to allow the defendant's lawyers to view the evidence which the prosecution intends to present at trial. Physical evidence, lists of witnesses, documents, photographs, and so on which the prosecution plans to introduce in court will usually be made available to the defense as a result of such a motion.

Motion to Suppress Evidence

In the preliminary hearing, or through pretrial discovery, the defense may learn of evidence which the prosecution intends to introduce at the trial. If some of that evidence has been, in the opinion of the defense counsel, unlawfully acquired, a motion to suppress the evidence may be filed.

Motion to Dismiss Charges

A variety of circumstances may result in the filing of a motion to dismiss. They include (1) an opinion, by defense counsel, that the indictment or information is not sound; (2) violations of speedy trial legislation; (3) a plea bargain with the defendant (which may require testimony against codefendants); (4) the death of an important witness or the destruction or disappearance of necessary evidence; (5) the confession, by a supposed victim, that the facts in the case have been fabricated; and (6) the success of a motion to suppress evidence which effectively eliminates the prosecution's case.

Motion for Continuance

This motion seeks a delay in the start of the trial. Defense motions for continuance are often based upon the inability to locate important witnesses, the illness of the defendant, or a change in defense counsel immediately prior to trial.

Motion for Change of Venue

In well-known cases, pretrial publicity may lessen the opportunity for a case to be tried before an unbiased jury. A motion for a change in venue asks that the trial be moved to some other area where prejudice against the defendant is less likely to exist.

Motion for Severance of Offenses

Defendants charged with a number of crimes may ask to be tried separately on all or some of the charges. Although consolidating charges for trial saves time and money, some defendants may think that it is more likely to make them appear guilty.

Motion for Severance of Defendants

Similar to the preceding motion, this request asks the court to try the accused separately from any codefendants. Motions for severance are likely to be filed where the defendant believes that the jury may be prejudiced against him or her by evidence applicable only to other defendants.

Motion to Determine Present Sanity

"Present sanity," even though it may be no defense against the criminal charge, can delay trial. A person cannot be tried, sentenced, or punished while insane. If a defendant is insane at the time a trial is to begin, this motion may halt the proceedings until treatment can be arranged.

Motion for a Bill of Particulars

This motion asks the court to order the prosecutor to provide detailed information about the charges which the defendant will be facing in court. Defendants charged with a number of offenses, or with a number of counts of the same offense, may make such a motion. They may, for example, seek to learn which alleged instances of an offense will become the basis for prosecution, or which specific items of contraband allegedly found in their possession are held to violate the law.

Motion for a Mistrial

A mistrial may be declared at any time, and a motion for mistrial may be made by either side. Mistrials are likely to be declared where highly prejudicial comments are made by either attorney. Defense motions for a mistrial do not provide grounds for a later claim of double jeopardy.

Motion for Arrest of Judgment

After the verdict of the jury has been announced, but before sentencing, the defendant may make a motion for arrest of judgment. Such a motion means the defendant believes that some legally acceptable reason exists as to why sentencing should not occur. Defendants who are seriously ill, hospitalized, or who have gone insane prior to judgment being imposed may file such a motion.

Motion for a New Trial

After a jury has returned a guilty verdict a defense motion for a new trial may be entertained by the court. Acceptance of such a motion is most often based upon the discovery of new evidence which is of significant benefit to the defense, and will set aside the conviction.

[1]U.S. Department of Justice, *Dictionary of Criminal Justice Data Terminology*, 2nd ed (Washington, D.C.: U.S. Government Printing Office, 1982).

indictment. In overturning his conviction, the U.S. Supreme Court ruled: "…even delay occasioned by the Government's negligence creates prejudice that compounds over time, and at some point, as here, becomes intolerable."[76]

The Speedy Trial Act is applicable only to federal courts. However, the *Klopfer* case effectively made constitutional guarantees of a speedy trial applicable to state courts. In keeping with the trend toward reduced delays, many states have since enacted their own speedy trial legislation. Typical state legislation sets limits of 120 or 90 days as a reasonable period of time for a trial to commence.

JURY SELECTION

The Sixth Amendment also guarantees the right to an impartial jury. An impartial jury is not necessarily an ignorant one. In other words, jurors will not always be excused from service on a jury if they have some knowledge of the case which is before them.[77] Jurors, however, who have already formed an opinion as to the guilt or innocence of a defendant are likely to be excused.

A number of different types of juror challenges are available to both prosecution and defense attorneys. Challenges are intended to ensure the impartiality of the jury which is being empaneled. Three types of challenges are recognized in criminal courts:

1. Challenges to the array
2. Challenges for cause
3. Peremptory challenges

Challenges to the array signify the belief, generally by the defense attorney, that the pool from which potential jurors are to be selected is not representative of the community, or is biased in some significant way. A challenge to the array is argued before the hearing judge before jury selection begins. The jury selection process includes the questioning of potential jurors by both prosecution and defense attorneys. This questioning is known as *voir dire.*

Jurors are expected to be unbiased and free of preconceived notions of guilt or innocence. Challenges for cause, which may arise during *voir dire* examination make the claim that an individual juror cannot be fair or impartial. One special issue of juror objectivity has concerned the Supreme Court. It is whether jurors with philosophical opposition to the death penalty should be excluded from juries whose decisions might result in the imposition of capital punishment. In the case of *Witherspoon* v. *Illinois* (1968),[78] the Court ruled that a juror opposed to the death penalty could be excluded from such juries if it were shown that (1) the juror would automatically vote against conviction without regard to the evidence, or (2) the juror's philosophical orientation would prevent an objective consideration of the evidence. The *Witherspoon* case has left unresolved a number of issues, among them the concern that how a juror would automatically vote is difficult to demonstrate, and may not even be known to the juror before the trial begins.

> No citizen possessing all other qualifications which are or may be prescribed by law shall be disqualified for service as grand or petit juror in any court of the United States, or of any State on account of race, color, or previous condition of servitude…
>
> —*18 U.S.C. 243*

Another area of concern, which has been addressed by the Supreme Court, involves the potential bias which jurors may experience as a result of exposure to stories about a case which appear in the news media prior to the start of trial. One such case in which

Peremptory Challenge
A means of removing unwanted potential jurors without the need to show cause for their removal. Prosecutors and defense attorneys routinely use peremptory challenges in order to eliminate from juries individuals who, although they express no obvious bias, may be thought to hold the potential to sway the jury in an undesirable direction.

the Court addressed the issue is that of *Mu'Min* v. *Virginia* (1991).[79] Mu'Min was a Virginia inmate who was serving time for first-degree murder. While accompanying a work detail outside of the institution, he committed another murder. At the ensuing trial, 8 of the 12 jurors who were eventually seated admitted that they had heard or read something about the case, although none indicated that he or she had formed an opinion in advance as to Mu'Min's guilt or innocence. Following his conviction, Mu'Min appealed to the Supreme Court, claiming that his right to a fair trial had been denied due to pretrial publicity. The Court disagreed, however, citing the admittedly unbiased nature of the original jurors.

The third kind of challenge, the peremptory challenge, effectively removes potential jurors without need for a reason. Peremptory challenges are limited in number. Federal courts allow each side up to 20 peremptory challenges in capital cases and as few as 3 in minor criminal cases.[80]

A developing field, which seeks to take advantage of peremptory challenges, is that of scientific jury selection. Scientific jury selection uses correlational techniques from the social sciences to gauge the likelihood that potential jurors will vote for conviction or acquittal. It makes predictions based on the economic, ethnic, and other personal and social characteristics of each member of the juror pool. There have been some recent indications, however, that scientific jury selection may soon run afoul of the requirement established by the Supreme Court in *Thiel* v. *Southern Pacific Co.*[81] (discussed earlier).

Criticisms of jury selection techniques have focused on the end result of the process. Such techniques generally remove potential jurors who have any knowledge or opinions about the case to be tried. Also removed are persons trained in the law or in criminal justice. Anyone working for a criminal justice agency, or anyone who has a family member working for such an agency, or for a defense attorney will likely be dismissed through peremptory challenges, on the chance that they may be biased in favor of one side or the other. Scientific jury selection techniques may result in the additional dismissal of educated or professionally successful individuals, to eliminate the possibility of such individuals exercising undue control over jury deliberations. The end result of the jury selection process may be to produce a jury composed of people who are uneducated, uninformed, and generally inexperienced at making any type of well-considered decision. Such a jury may not understand the charges against the defendant or comprehend what is required for a finding of guilt or innocence. Some of the selected jurors may not even possess the span of attention needed to hear all the testimony that will be offered in the case. As a consequence, decisions rendered by such a jury may be based more upon emotion than upon findings of fact.

Intentional jury selection techniques appear to have played a significant role in the outcome of the trial of Larry Davis. Davis, who was black, was charged with the 1986 shooting of seven white New York City police officers as they attempted to arrest the heavily armed defendant for the alleged murder of four drug dealers.[82] None of the officers died and Davis was later apprehended. At the trial, defense attorney William Kunstler assembled a jury of ten blacks and two Hispanics. On two occasions Judge Bernard Fried had dismissed previous juries before the trial could begin, saying that Kunstler was packing the panel with blacks.[83] Although many of the wounded officers testified against Davis, and no one seriously disputed the contention that Davis was the triggerman in the shooting of the officers, the jury found him innocent. The finding prompted one of the injured policemen to claim, "It was a racist verdict."[84] Explaining the jury's decision another way, a spokesperson for the NAACP Legal Defense Fund said after the trial, "The experience of blacks in the criminal justice system may make them less prone to accept the word of a police officer."[85]

Juries intentionally selected so that they are racially imbalanced may soon be a thing of the past. As long ago as 1880, the U.S. Supreme Court held that "a statute barring blacks from service on grand or petit juries denied equal protection of the laws to a black man convicted of murder by an all-white jury."[86]

Even so, peremptory challenges continued to provide an avenue toward racial imbalance. In 1965, for example, a black defendant in Alabama was convicted of rape by an all-white jury. The local prosecutor had used his peremptory challenges to exclude blacks from the jury. The case eventually reached the Supreme Court, where the conviction was upheld.[87] At that time, the Court refused to limit the practice of peremptory challenges, reasoning that to do so would place them under the same judicial scrutiny as challenges for cause.

However, in 1986, following what many claimed were widespread abuses of peremptory challenges by prosecution and defense alike, the Supreme Court was forced to overrule its earlier decision. It did so in the case of *Batson* v. *Kentucky*.[88] Batson, a black man, had been convicted of second-degree burglary and other offenses by an all-white jury. The prosecutor had used his peremptory challenges to remove all blacks from jury service at the trial. The Court agreed that the use of peremptory challenges for apparently purposeful discrimination constitutes a violation of the defendant's right to an impartial jury.

> [N]inety-five percent of the time, the only black thing a black defendant sees in the courtroom is the judge's robe.
>
> —*Delano Stewart, Former chairman
>   of the Florida chapter
>   of the National Bar Association*

The *Batson* decision established requirements which defendants seeking to address the discriminatory use of peremptory challenges must establish. They include the need to prove that the defendant is a member of a recognized racial group which has been intentionally excluded from the jury and the need to raise a reasonable suspicion that the prosecutor used peremptory challenges in a discriminatory manner. Justice Thurgood Marshall, writing a concurring opinion in *Batson*, presaged what was to come: "The inherent potential of peremptory challenges to destroy the jury process," he wrote, "by permitting the exclusion of jurors on racial grounds should ideally lead the Court to ban them entirely from the criminal justice system."

A few years later, in *Ford* v. *Georgia* (1991),[89] the Court moved much closer to Justice Marshall's position when it remanded a case for a new trial, based upon the fact that the prosecutor had used peremptory challenges to remove potential minority jurors. Nine of the ten peremptory challenges available to the prosecutor under Georgia law had been used to eliminate prospective black jurors. Following his conviction, on charges of kidnapping, raping, and murdering a white woman, the black defendant, James Ford, argued that the prosecutor had demonstrated a systematic and historical racial bias in other cases as well as his own. Specifically, Ford argued that his Sixth Amendment right to an impartial jury had been violated by the prosecutor's racially based method of jury selection. His defense attorney's written appeal to the Supreme Court made the claim that "The exclusion of members of the black race in the jury when a black accused is being tried is done in order that the accused will receive excessive punishment if found guilty, or to inject racial prejudice into the fact finding process of the jury."[90] While the Court did not find a basis for such a Sixth Amendment claim, it did determine that the civil rights of the jurors were violated under the Fourteenth Amendment due to a pattern of discrimination based on race.

THEORY INTO PRACTICE

PEREMPTORY CHALLENGES AND RACE

"[A] peremptory challenge to a **juror** means that one side in a trial has been given the right to throw out a certain number of possible jurors before the trial without giving any reasons."[1]

Historically, as the definition—borrowed from a legal dictionary—indicates, attorneys had been able to remove unwanted potential jurors from a criminal case during jury selection procedures through the use of a limited number of peremptory challenges without having to provide any reason whatsoever for the choices they made. (Challenges for cause, on the other hand, although not limited in number, require an acceptable rationale for juror removal.) The understanding of peremptory challenges was changed forever by the 1991 landmark U.S. Supreme Court case of *Powers* v. *Ohio*.[2] The *Powers* case dealt with a white defendant's desire to ensure a racially balanced jury. In *Powers* the Supreme Court identified three reasons why peremptory challenges may not be issued if based on race. The Court provided the following rationale for its decision:[3]

First, the discriminatory use of peremptory challenges causes the defendant cognizable injury, and he or she has a concrete interest in challenging the practice, because racial discrimination in jury selection casts doubt on the integrity of the judicial process and places the fairness of the criminal proceeding in doubt.

Second, the relationship between the defendant and the excluded jurors is such that... both have a common interest in eliminating racial discrimination from the courtroom....

Third, it is unlikely that a juror dismissed because of race will possess sufficient incentive to set in motion the arduous process needed to vindicate his or her own rights.

The Court continued:

The very fact that [members of a particular race] are singled out and expressly denied...all right to participate in the administration of the law, as jurors, because of their color, though they are citizens, and may be in other respects fully qualified, is practically a brand upon them, affixed by the law, an assertion of their inferiority, and a stimulant to that race prejudice which is an impediment to securing to individuals of that race equal justice which the law aims to secure to all others.

In a move that surprised many court watchers, the Supreme Court, near the end of its 1991 term, extended its ban on racially motivated peremptory challenges to civil cases. In *Edmonson* v. *Leesville Concrete Co., Inc.*,[4] the Court ruled: "The harms we recognized in *Powers* are not limited to the criminal sphere. A civil proceeding often implicates significant rights and interests. Civil juries, no less than their criminal counterparts, must follow the law and act as impartial fact-finders. And, as we have observed, their verdicts, no less than those of their criminal counterparts, become binding judgments of the court. Racial discrimination has no place in the courtroom, whether the proceeding is civil or criminal."

Following *Powers* and *Edmonson* v. *Leesville Concrete Co., Inc.*, it is clear that neither prosecuting nor civil attorneys in the future will be able to exclude minority potential jurors consistently unless they are able to articulate clearly credible race-neutral rationales for their actions.

[1]Daniel Oran, *Oran's Dictionary of the Law* (St. Paul, MN: West Publishing, 1983), p. 312.
[2]*Powers* v. *Ohio*, No. 89–5011, 1991.
[3]Ibid., on-line syllabus of the majority opinion.
[4]*Edmonson* v. *Leesville Concrete Co., Inc.*, No. 89–7743, 1991.

In another 1991 case, *Powers* v. *Ohio*[91] (see box in this chapter), the Court found in favor of a white defendant who claimed that his constitutional rights were violated by the intentional exclusion of blacks from his jury through the use of peremptory challenges. In *Powers*, the Court held that "[a]lthough an individual juror does not have the right to sit on any particular petit jury, he or she does possess the right not to be excluded from one on account of race." In a civil case with significance for the criminal justice system, the Court held in *Edmonson* v. *Leesville Concrete Co., Inc.*[92] (1991), that peremptory challenges in *civil* suits were not acceptable if based upon race: "The importance of

This pen and ink drawing depicts one of the first jury trials on which blacks and whites served. Circa 1867. *Courtesy of the Library of Congress.*

(*Edmonson*) lies in the Court's significant expansion of the scope of state action—the traditionally held doctrine that private attorneys are immune to constitutional requirements because they do not represent the government." Justice Kennedy, writing for the majority, said that race-based juror exclusions are forbidden in civil lawsuits because jury selection is a "unique governmental function delegated to private litigants" in a public courtroom.

Finally, in the 1992 case of *Georgia* v. *McCollum*,[93] the Court barred defendants and their attorneys from using peremptory challenges to exclude potential jurors on the basis of race. In *McCollum*, Justice Harry Blackman writing for the majority said, "Be it at the hands of the state or defense, if a court allows jurors to be excluded because of group bias, it is a willing participant in a scheme that could only undermine the very foundation of our system of justice—our citizen's confidence in it." Soon thereafter, peremptory challenges based upon gender were similarly restricted (*J.E.B.* v. *Alabama*, 1994).

After wrangling over jury selection has run its course, the jury is sworn in and alternates are selected. At this point the judge will decide whether the jury is to be sequestered during the trial. Members of **sequestered juries** are not permitted to have contact with the public and are often housed in a motel or hotel until completion of the trial. Anyone who attempts to contact a sequestered jury or to influence members of a nonsequestered jury may be held accountable for jury tampering. Following jury selection, the stage is set for opening arguments[94] to begin.

Sequestered Jury One which is isolated from the public during the course of a trial and throughout the deliberation process.

Opening Statement

The presentation of information to the jury begins with opening statements made by the prosecution and defense. The purpose of opening statements is to advise the jury of what the attorneys intend to prove and to describe how such proof will be offered. In cases where a defendant maintains innocence, the jury will have to weigh the evidence and decide between the effectiveness of the arguments made by both sides. Where a defendant may in fact be guilty, it will be the job of the defense attorney to dispute the veracity of the prosecution's version of the facts. Under such circumstances defense attorneys may choose not to present any evidence, focusing instead on the burden of proof requirement facing the prosecution. During opening arguments the defense attorney is likely to stress the human qualities of the defendant and to remind jurors of the awesome significance of their task.

Evidence Anything useful to a judge or jury in deciding the facts of a case. Evidence may take the form of witness testimony, written documents, videotapes, magnetic media, photographs, physical objects, and so on.

Lawyers for both sides are bound by a "good faith" ethical requirement in their opening statements. That requirement limits the content of such statements to only that evidence which the attorneys actually believe can and will be presented as the trial progresses. Allusions to evidence which an attorney has no intention of offering are regarded as unprofessional and have been defined as "professional misconduct" by the Supreme Court.[95]

Direct Evidence Evidence which, if believed, directly proves a fact. Eyewitness testimony (and, more recently, videotaped documentation) account for the majority of all direct evidence heard in the criminal courtroom.

The Presentation of Evidence

Although procedural rules prescribe almost every routine activity within the courtroom, the area most closely scrutinized is the introduction of evidence at a criminal trial. **Evidence** is of two types: direct and circumstantial. **Direct evidence** is that which, if believed by the judge or jury, proves a fact without needing to draw inferences. Direct evidence may consist, for example, of the information contained on a photograph or videotape. It might also consist of testimonial evidence provided by a witness on the stand. A straightforward statement by a witness, such as "I saw him do it!" is a form of direct evidence.

Circumstantial evidence requires the judge or jury to make inferences and draw conclusions. At a murder trial, for example, a person who heard gunshots, and moments later saw someone run by with a smoking gun in their hand, might testify to those facts. Even though there may have been no eyewitness to the actual homicide, the jury might later conclude that the person seen with the gun was the one who pulled the trigger and committed homicide. Contrary to popular belief, circumstantial evidence is sufficient to produce a verdict and conviction in a criminal trial. In fact, some prosecuting attorneys claim to prefer working entirely with circumstantial evidence, weaving a tapestry of the criminal act in their arguments to the jury.

Real evidence consists of physical material or traces of physical activity. Weapons, tire tracks, ransom notes, and fingerprints all fall into the category of physical evidence. Physical evidence is introduced into the trial process by means of exhibits. Exhibits are objects or displays which, once formally accepted as evidence by the judge, may be shown to members of the jury. Documentary evidence includes writings such as business records, journals, written confessions, and letters. Documentary evidence can extend beyond the media of paper and pen to include magnetic and optical storage devices used in computer operations and video and voice recordings.

One of the most significant decisions made by a trial court judge is deciding what evidence can be presented to the jury. In making that decision, judges will examine the relevance of the information in question to the case at hand. Relevant evidence is that which has a bearing on the facts at issue. For example, a decade or two ago, it was not unusual for a woman's sexual history to be brought out in rape trials. Under "rape shield statutes," most states today will not allow such a practice, recognizing that these details often have no bearing on the case. Rape shield statutes have been strengthened by recent U.S. Supreme Court decisions, including the 1991 case of *Michigan* v. *Lucas.*[96] In this case, the defendant, Lucas, had been charged with criminal sexual conduct involving his ex-girlfriend. Lucas had forced the woman into his apartment at knifepoint, beat her, and forced her to engage in several nonconsensual sex acts. At his trial, Lucas asked to have evidence introduced demonstrating that a prior sexual relationship had existed between the two. At the time, however, Michigan law required that a written motion to use such information had to be made within 10 days following arraignment—a condition Lucas failed to meet. Lucas was convicted and sentenced to a term of from 44 to 180 months in prison, but appealed his conviction, claiming that the Sixth Amendment to the U.S. Constitution guaranteed him the right to confront witnesses against him. The U.S. Supreme Court disagreed, however, and ruled that the Sixth Amendment guarantee does not necessarily extend to evidence of a prior sexual relationship between a rape victim and a criminal defendant.

A second decision judges have to make is to weigh the probative value of an item of evidence against its potential inflammatory or prejudicial qualities. Evidence has probative value when it is useful and relevant. Even useful evidence, however, may unduly bias a jury if it is exceptionally gruesome or presented in such a way as to imply guilt. For example, gory photographs, especially in full color, may be withheld form the jury's eyes. In one recent case, a new trial was ordered when 35mm slides projected on a wall over the head of the defendant as he sat in the courtroom were found by an appellate court to have prejudiced the jury.

On occasion, some evidence will be found to have only limited admissibility. Limited admissibility means that the evidence can be used for a specific purpose, but that it might not be accurate in other details. Photographs, for example, may be admitted as evidence for the narrow purpose of showing spatial relationships between objects under discussion,

Circumstantial Evidence Evidence which requires interpretation, or which requires a judge or jury to reach a conclusion based upon what the evidence indicates. From the close proximity of a smoking gun to the defendant, for example, the jury might conclude that she pulled the trigger.

even though the photographs themselves may have been taken under conditions that did not exist (such as daylight) when the offense was committed.

When judges err in allowing the use of evidence that may have been unconstitutionally gathered, grounds may be created for a later appeal if the trial concludes with a "guilty" verdict. Even when evidence is improperly introduced at trial, however, a number of Supreme Court decisions[97] have held that there may be no grounds for an effective appeal unless such introduction "had substantial and injurious effect or influence in determining the jury's verdict."[98] Called the "harmless error" rule, this standard does place the burden upon the prosecution to show that the jury's decision would most likely have been the same even in the absence of such inappropriate evidence. The rule is not applicable when a defendant's constitutional guarantees are violated by "structural defects in the constitution of the trial mechanism"[99] itself—as when a judge gives constitutionally improper instructions to a jury.

THE TESTIMONY OF WITNESSES

Witness testimony is generally the chief means by which evidence is introduced at trial. Witnesses may include victims, police officers, the defendant, specialists in recognized fields, and others with useful information to provide. Some of these witnesses may have been present during the commission of the alleged offense, while most will have had only a later opportunity to investigate the situation or to analyze evidence.

Before a witness will be allowed to testify to any fact it is necessary that the questioning attorney establish the competence of the witness. Competency to testify requires that the witness have personal knowledge of the information about to be discussed and that he or she understands the duty of a witness to tell the truth.

One critical decision which has to be made by the defense, is whether or not to put the defendant on the stand. Defendants have a Fifth Amendment right to remain silent and to refuse to testify. In the precedent-setting case of *Griffin v. California* (1965),[100] the U.S. Supreme Court declared that if a defendant refuses to testify, prosecutors and judges are enjoined from even commenting on the fact, other than to instruct the jury that such a failure cannot be held to indicate guilt. Griffin was originally arrested for the beating death of a woman whose body was found in an alley. Charged with first-degree murder, he refused to take the stand when his case came to trial. At the time of the trial Article I, Section 13, of the California Constitution provided in part: "…in any criminal case, whether the defendant testifies or not, his failure to explain or to deny by his testimony any evidence or facts in the case against him may be commented upon by the court and by counsel, and may be considered by the court or the jury." The prosecutor, remarking on the evidence in closing arguments to the jury, declared: "These things he has not seen fit to take the stand and deny or explain…Essie Mae is dead, she can't tell you her side of the story. The defendant won't." The judge then instructed the jury that they might infer from the defendant's silence his inability to deny the evidence which had been presented against him. Griffin was convicted of first-degree murder and his appeal reached the Supreme Court. The Court ruled that the Fifth Amendment, made applicable by the Fourteenth Amendment to the states, protected the defendant from any inferences of guilt based upon a failure to testify. The verdict of the trial court was voided.

Direct examination of a witness takes place when a witness is first called to the stand. If the prosecutor calls the witness, the witness is referred to as a witness for the prosecution. Where the direct examiner is a defense attorney, witnesses are called witnesses for the defense.

THEORY INTO PRACTICE

"PLEADING THE FIFTH"

The Fifth Amendment to the U.S. Constitution is one of the best known entries in the Bill of Rights. Television shows and crime novels have popularized phrases such as "pleading the Fifth," or "taking the Fifth." As these media recognize, the Fifth Amendment is a powerful ally of any criminal defendant. When the accused, generally upon the advice of counsel, decides to invoke the Fifth Amendment right against self-incrimination, the state cannot require the defendant to testify. In the past, defendants who refused to take the stand were often denigrated by comments the prosecution made to the jury. In 1965 the U.S. Supreme Court, in the case of *Griffin* v. *California*,[1] ruled that the defendant's unwillingness to testify could not be interpreted as a sign of guilt. The Court reasoned that such interpretations forced the defendant to testify and effectively negated Fifth Amendment guarantees. Defendants who choose to testify, however, but who fail to adequately answer the questions put to them, may lawfully find themselves the target of a prosecutorial attack.

[1] *Griffin* v. *California*, 380 U.S. 609 (1965).

The direct examiner may ask questions which require a "yes" or "no" answer, but can also employ narrative questions which allow the witness to tell a story in his or her own words. During direct examination courts generally prohibit the use of leading questions, or those which suggest answers to the witness.[101] Many courts also consider questions which call for "yes" or "no" answers to be inappropriate since they are inherently suggestive.

Cross-examination refers to the examination of a witness by anyone other than the direct examiner. Anyone who offers testimony in a criminal court has the duty to submit to cross-examination.[102] The purpose of cross-examination is to test the credibility and memory of a witness.

Most states and the federal government restrict the scope of cross-examination to material covered during direct examination. Questions about other matters, even though they may relate to the case before the court, are not allowed. A small number of states allow the cross-examiner to raise any issue as long as it is deemed relevant by the court. Leading questions, generally disallowed in direct examination, are regarded as the mainstay of cross-examination. Such questions allow for a concise restatement of testimony which has already been offered and serve to focus efficiently on potential problems that the cross-examiner seeks to address.

Some witnesses offer perjured testimony, or statements which they know to be untrue. Reasons for perjured testimony vary, but most witnesses who lie on the stand probably do so in an effort to help friends accused of crimes. Witnesses who perjure themselves are subject to impeachment, in which either the defense counsel or prosecution demonstrates that they have intentionally offered false testimony. Such a demonstration may occur through the use of prior inconsistent statements, whereby previous statements made by the witness

Perjury The intentional making of a false statement as part of testimony by a sworn witness in a judicial proceeding on a matter material to the inquiry.

A witness demonstrates the
position assumed by an
accused murderer as he
fired. Eyewitnesses, if credible,
often offer the type of evidence most likely to convince
a jury. *Photo: Jim Davis/The
Boston Herald.*

are shown to be at odds with more recent declarations. Perjury is a serious offense in its
own right, and dishonest witnesses may face fines or jail time. When it can be demonstrated that a witness has offered inaccurate or false testimony, the witness has been effectively impeached.

At the conclusion of the cross-examination the direct examiner may again question the
witness. This procedure is called redirect examination and may be followed by a recross-
examination and so on, until both sides are satisfied that they have exhausted fruitful lines
of questioning.

Children as Witnesses

An area of special concern involves the use of children as witnesses in a criminal
trial, especially where the children may have been victims. Currently, in an effort to
avoid what may be traumatizing direct confrontations between child witnesses and the
accused, 37 states allow the use of videotaped testimony in their criminal courtrooms,
and 32 permit the use of closed-circuit television—which allows the child to testify out
of the presence of the defendant. In 1988, however, the U.S. Supreme Court, in the case
of *Coy* v. *Iowa*,[103] ruled that a courtroom screen, used to shield child witnesses from
visual confrontation with a defendant in a child sex abuse case, had violated the confrontation clause of the Constitution.

On the other hand, in the 1990 case of *Maryland* v. *Craig*,[104] the Court upheld the use
of closed-circuit television to shield children who testify in criminal courts. The Court's
decision was partially based upon the realization that "…a significant majority of States
have enacted statutes to protect child witnesses from the trauma of giving testimony in
child-abuse cases…[which]…attests to the widespread belief in the importance of such a
policy."

The case involved Sandra Craig, a former preschool owner and administrator in
Clarksville, Maryland, who had been found guilty by a trial court with 53 counts of child
abuse, assault, and perverted sexual practices which she had allegedly performed on the children under her care. During the trial, four young children, none past the age of 6, had

testified against Ms. Craig while separated from her in the judge's chambers. Questioned by the district attorney, the children related stories of torture, burying alive, and sexual assault with a screwdriver.[105] Sandra Craig watched the children reply over a television monitor which displayed the process to the jury seated in the courtroom. Following the trial, Craig appealed, arguing that her ability to communicate with her lawyer (who had been in the judge's chambers and not the courtroom during questioning of the children) had been impeded and that her right to a fair trial under the Sixth Amendment to the U.S. Constitution had been denied since she was not given the opportunity to be "confronted with the witnesses" against her. In finding against Craig, Justice Sandra Day O'Connor, writing for the Court's majority, stated, "…if the State makes an adequate showing of necessity, the State interest in protecting child witnesses from the trauma of testifying in a child-abuse case is sufficiently important to justify the use of a special procedure that permits a child witness in such cases to testify…in the absence of face-to-face confrontation with the defendant."[106]

Although a face-to-face confrontation with a child victim may not be necessary in the courtroom, until 1992 the Supreme Court had been reluctant to allow into evidence descriptions of abuse and other statements made by children, even to child care professionals, when those statements are made outside of the courtroom. The Court, in *Idaho* v. *Wright* (1990),[107] reasoned that such "statements [are] fraught with the dangers of unreliability which the Confrontation Clause is designed to highlight and obviate."

However, in *White* v. *Illinois* (1992),[108] the Court seemed to reverse its stance, ruling that in-court testimony provided by a medical provider and the child's baby-sitter, which repeated what the child had said to them concerning White's sexually abusive behavior, was permissible. The Court rejected White's claim that out-of-court statements should be admissible only when the witness is unavailable to testify at trial, saying instead: "a finding of unavailability of an out-of-court declarant is necessary only if the out-of-court statement was made at a prior judicial proceeding." Placing *White* within the context of generally established exceptions, the court intoned: "A statement that has been offered in a moment of excitement—without the opportunity to reflect on the consequences of one's exclamation—may justifiably carry more weight with a trier of fact than a similar statement offered in the relative calm of the courtroom. Similarly, a statement made in the course of procuring medical services, where the declarant knows that a false statement may cause misdiagnosis or mistreatment, carries special guarantees of credibility that a trier of fact may not think replicated by courtroom testimony."[109]

The Hearsay Rule

One aspect of witness testimony bears special mention. **Hearsay** is anything not based upon the personal knowledge of a witness. A witness may say, for example, "John told me that Fred did it!" Such a witness becomes a hearsay declarant, and, following a likely objection by counsel, the trial judge will have to decide whether the witness's statement will be allowed to stand as evidence. In most cases the judge will instruct the jury to disregard such comments from the witness, thereby enforcing the **hearsay rule**. The hearsay rule does not permit the use of "secondhand evidence."

There are some exceptions to the hearsay rule, however, that have been established by both precedent and tradition. One is the dying declaration. Dying declarations are statements made by a person who is about to die. When heard by a second party, they may usually be repeated in court, providing that certain conditions have been met. Dying declarations are generally valid exceptions to the hearsay rule when they are made by someone who knows that they are about to die, and when the statements made relate to the cause and circumstances of the impending death.

Hearsay Something which is not based upon the personal knowledge of a witness. Witnesses who testify, for example, about something they have heard, are offering hearsay by repeating information about a matter of which they have no direct knowledge.

Hearsay Rule The long-standing American courtroom precedent that hearsay cannot be used in court. Rather than accepting testimony based upon hearsay, the American trial process asks that the person who was the original source of the hearsay information be brought into court to be questioned and cross-examined. Exceptions to the hearsay rule may occur when the person with direct knowledge is dead or otherwise unable to testify.

Spontaneous statements provide another exception to the hearsay rule. Statements are considered spontaneous when they are made in the heat of excitement before time for fabrication exists. For example, a defendant who is just regaining consciousness following a crime may make an utterance which could later be repeated in court by those who heard it.

Out-of-court statements made by a witness, especially when they have been recorded in writing or by some other means, may also become exceptions to the hearsay rule. The use of such statements usually requires the witness to testify that at the time they were made, the statements were accurate. This past recollection recorded exception to the hearsay rule is especially useful in drawn-out court proceedings which occur long after the crime. Under such circumstances, witnesses may no longer remember the details of an event. Their earlier statements to authorities, however, can be introduced into evidence as past recollection recorded.

CLOSING ARGUMENTS

At the conclusion of a criminal trial both sides have the opportunity for a final narrative presentation to the jury. This summation provides a review and analysis of the evidence. Its purpose is to persuade the jury to draw a conclusion favorable to the presenter. Testimony can be quoted, exhibits referred to, and attention drawn to inconsistencies in the evidence which has been presented by the other side.

States vary as to the order of closing arguments. Nearly all allow the defense attorney to speak to the jury before the prosecution makes its final points. A few permit the prosecutor the first opportunity for summation. Some jurisdictions and the *Federal Rules of Criminal Procedure*[110] authorize a defense rebuttal. Rebuttals are responses to the closing arguments of the other side.

Some specific issues may need to be addressed during summation. If, for example, during the trial the defendant has not taken the stand, the defense attorney's closing argument will inevitably stress that the failure of the accused to testify can not be regarded as indicative of guilt. Where the prosecution's case rests entirely upon circumstantial evidence, the defense can be expected to stress the lack of any direct proof, while the prosecutor is likely to argue that circumstantial evidence can be stronger than direct evidence, since it is not as easily affected by human error or false testimony.

THE JUDGE'S CHARGE TO THE JURY

With the completion of closing arguments, the judge will charge the jury to "retire and select one of your number as a foreman…and deliberate upon the evidence which has been presented until you have reached a verdict." The words of the charge will vary somewhat between jurisdictions and among judges, but all judges will remind members of the jury of their duty to consider objectively only the evidence which has been presented, and of the need for impartiality. Most judges will also remind jury members of the statutory elements of the alleged offense, of the burden of proof which rests upon the prosecution, and of the need for the prosecution to have proven guilt beyond a reasonable doubt before a guilty verdict can be returned.

In their charge many judges will also provide a summary of the evidence presented, usually from notes they have taken during the trial, as a means of refreshing the juror's memories of events. About half of all the states allow judges the freedom to express their own views as to the credibility of witnesses and the significance of evidence. Other states only permit judges to summarize the evidence in an objective and impartial manner.

Following the charge the jury will be removed from the courtroom and permitted to begin its deliberations. In the absence of the jury, defense attorneys may choose to challenge portions of the judge's charge. If they feel that some oversight has occurred in the original charge, they may also request that the judge provide the jury with additional instructions or information. Such objections, if denied by the judge, often become the basis for appeals when a conviction is returned.

JURY DELIBERATIONS AND THE VERDICT

In cases where the evidence is either very clear or very weak, jury deliberations may be brief, lasting only a mater of hours or even minutes. Some juries, however, deliberate days or sometimes weeks, carefully weighing all the nuances of the evidence they have seen and heard. Many jurisdictions require that juries reach a unanimous verdict, although the U.S. Supreme Court has ruled that unanimous verdicts are not required in non-capital cases.[111] Even so, some juries are unable to agree upon any verdict. Such juries are referred to as deadlocked or hung. Where a unanimous decision is required, juries may be deadlocked by the strong opposition of only one member to a verdict agreed upon by all the others.

> In suits at common law…the right of trial by jury shall be preserved, and no fact tried by a jury shall be otherwise reexamined in any court of the United States, than according to the rules of the common law.
>
> —*Seventh Amendment to the U.S. Constitution*

Lyle and Erik Menendez. Their first trial, on charges of killing their parents after an alleged lifetime of sexual abuse, resulted in essentially "hung" juries. *Photo: AP/Wide World Photos.*

In some states, judges are allowed to add a boost to nearly hung juries by recharging them under a set of instructions agreed upon by the Supreme Court in the 1896 case of *Allen* v. *United States.*[112] The Allen Charge, as it is known in those jurisdictions, urges the jury to vigorous deliberations and suggests to obstinate jurors that their objections may be ill founded if they make no impression upon the minds of other jurors.

Problems with the Jury System

The jury system has received much criticism as an inefficient and outmoded method for determining guilt or innocence.[113] Jurors cannot be expected to understand modern legal complexities and to appreciate all the nuances of trial court practice. Many instructions to the jury are probably poorly understood and rarely observed by even the best-meaning jurors.[114] Emotions are difficult to separate from fact. During deliberations many juries are probably dominated by one or two forceful personalities. Jurors may also become confused over legal technicalities, suffer from inattention, or be unable to understand fully the testimony of expert witnesses or the significance of technical evidence.

Many such problems became evident in the trial of Raymond Buckey and his mother, Peggy McMartin Buckey, who were tried in Los Angeles for allegedly molesting dozens of children at their family-run preschool.[115] The trial, which involved 65 counts of child sexual molestation and conspiracy, and 61 witnesses, ran for more than three years. Many jurors were stressed to the breaking point by the length of time involved. Family relationships suffered as the trial droned on, and jurors were unable to accompany their spouses and children on vacation. Small-business owners, who were expected to continue paying salaries to employees serving as jurors, faced financial ruin and threatened their absent employees with termination. Careers were put on hold, and at least one juror had to be dismissed for becoming inattentive to testimony. The trial cost taxpayers more than $12 million, but was nearly negated as jury membership and the number of alternate jurors declined due to sickness and personal problems. Ultimately, the defendants were acquitted.

Another trial in which the defendants were similarly acquitted of the majority of charges against them involved state-level prosecution of the officers accused in the now-infamous Rodney King beating. Following the riots in Los Angeles and elsewhere which came on the heels of their verdict, jurors in the "Rodney King trial" reported being afraid for their lives. Some slept with weapons by their side, and others sent their children away to safe locales.[116] Because of the potential for harm jurors faced in the 1993 federal trial of the same officers, U.S. District Judge John G. Davies ruled that the names of jurors be forever kept secret. The secrecy order was called "an unprecedented infringement of the public's right of access to the justice system"[117] by members of the press. Similarly, in the 1993 trial of three black men charged with the beating of white truck driver Reginald Denny during the Los Angeles riots, Los Angeles Superior Court Judge John Ouderkirk ordered that the identities of jurors not be released.

Opponents of the jury system have argued that it should be replaced by a panel of judges who would both render a verdict and impose sentence. Regardless of how well considered such a suggestion may be, however, such a change could not occur without modification of the Constitution's Sixth Amendment right to trial by jury.

> I do not know whether the jury is useful to those who are in litigation; but I am certain it is highly beneficial to those who decide the litigation; and I look upon it as one of the most efficacious means for the education of the people which society can employ.
>
> —*Alexis de Tocqueville*

An alternative suggestion for improving the process of trial by jury has been the call for professional jurors. Professional jurors would be paid by the government, just as are judges, prosecutors, and public defenders. Sitting on any jury would be their job, and they would be expected to carry out that job with acquired expertise. Professional jurors would be trained to listen objectively and would be schooled with the kinds of decision-making skills necessary to function effectively within an adversarial context. They could be expected to hear one case after another, perhaps moving between jurisdictions in cases of highly publicized crimes.

The advantages a professional jury system offers are

1. *Dependability.* Professional jurors could be expected to report to the courtroom in a timely fashion and to be good listeners, since both would be required by the nature of the job.
2. *Knowledge.* Professional jurors would be trained in the law, would understand what a finding of guilt requires, and would know what to expect from other actors in the courtroom.
3. *Equity.* Professional jurors would understand the requirements of due process and would be less likely to be swayed by the emotional content of a case, having been schooled in the need to separate matters of fact from personal feelings.

A professional jury system would not be without difficulties. Jurors under such a system might become jaded, deciding cases out of hand as routines lead to boredom and suspects are categorized according to whether they "fit the type" for guilt or innocence developed on the basis of previous experiences. Job requirements for professional jurors would be difficult to establish without infringing on the jurors' freedom to decide cases as they understand

Virginia McMartin, one of the defendants in the infamous "McMartin Preschool Case," billed as the longest-running jury trial in American history. The case, which began with 109 charges of child sexual molestation in 1984, concluded with not guilty verdicts in 1990. *Photo: AP/Wide World Photos.*

them. For the same reason, any evaluation of the job performance of professional jurors would be a difficult call. Finally, professional jurors might not truly be peer jurors, since their social characteristics might be skewed by education, residence, and politics.

IMPROVING THE ADJUDICATION PROCESS

Courts today are coming under increasing scrutiny. Researchers and concerned citizens have identified a number of aspects of court activity which might benefit from reform. Court unification is one area which many consider to hold the promise of better justice and greater economy through the efficient handling of cases.

Today's multiplicity of jurisdictions frequently leads to what many believe are avoidable conflicts and overlaps in the handling of criminal defendants. Problems are exacerbated by the lack of any centralized judicial authority in some states which might resolve jurisdictional and procedural disputes.[118] Proponents of unification suggest the elimination of overlapping jurisdictions, the creation of special-purpose courts, and the formulation of administrative offices in order to achieve economies of scale.[119]

Court-watch citizens groups are rapidly growing in number. Such organizations focus on the trial court level, but they are part of a general trend toward seeking greater openness in government decision making at all levels.[120] Court-watch groups monitor court proceedings on a regular basis and attempt to document and often publicize inadequacies. They frequently focus on the handling of indigents, fairness in the scheduling of cases for trial, unnecessary court delays, the reduction of waiting time, the treatment of witnesses and jurors, and adequacy of rights advisements for defendants throughout judicial proceedings.

The statistical measurement of court performance is another area which is receiving increased attention. Research has looked at the efficiency with which prosecutors schedule cases for trial, the speed with which judges resolve issues, the amount of time judges spend on the bench, and the economic and other costs to defendants, witnesses, and communities involved in the judicial process.[121] Statistical studies of this type often attempt to measure elements of court performance as diverse as sentence variation, charging accuracy, fairness in plea bargaining, evenhandedness, delays, and attitudes toward the court by lay participants.[122]

SUMMARY

The criminal trial, which owes its legacy to the evolution of democratic principles, stands as a centerpiece of American criminal justice. It has long been seen as a peer-based fact-finding process intended to protect the rights of the accused while sifting out disputed issues of guilt or innocence. The adversarial environment, which has served American courts for over 200 years, however, is now itself being questioned. A plethora of far-reaching social and technological changes, many of them unanticipated by the framers of our judicial system, have recently transpired. In many cases new technologies, such as DNA fingerprinting (discussed in detail in Chapter 17), may soon unequivocally link suspects to criminal activity. Newspapers and the electronic media can rapidly and widely disseminate findings. This combination, of investigative technologies and readily available information, may eventually make courtroom debates about guilt or innocence obsolete. Whether the current adversarial system can continue to serve the interests of justice in an information-rich and technologically advanced society will be a central question for the future.

DISCUSSION QUESTIONS

1. We described participants in a criminal trial as working together to bring about a successful close to courtroom proceedings. What do you think a "successful close" might mean to a judge? To a defense attorney? To a prosecutor? To the jury? To the defendant?

2. What is a dying declaration? Under what circumstances might it be a valid exception to the hearsay rule? Why do most courts seem to believe that a person who is about to die is likely to tell the truth?

3. Do you think the present jury system is outmoded? Might "professional jurors" be more effective than the present system of "peer jurors?" On what do you base your opinion?

4. What is an expert witness? A lay witness? What different kinds of testimony may both provide? What are some of the difficulties in expert testimony?

5. What are the three forms of indigent defense used throughout various regions of the United States? Why might defendants prefer private attorneys over public counsel?

ENDNOTES

1. Jill Smolowe, "The Trials of the Public Defender," *Time*, February 8, 1993, p. 46.

2. "Louisiana's Public Defender System Found Unconstitutional," *Criminal Justice Newsletter*, Vol. 23, no. 5, March 3, 1992, p. 1.

3. See, for example, Edward J. Clynch and David W. Neubauer, "Trial Courts as Organizations," *Law and Policy Quarterly*, Vol. 3 (1981), pp. 69–94.

4. In 1940 Missouri became the first state to adopt a plan for the "merit selection" of judges based upon periodic public review.

5. The National Judicial College, *1988 Course Catalog* (Reno: University of Nevada Press, 1987), p. 3.

6. Doris Marie Provine, *Judging Credentials: Nonlawyer Judges and the Politics of Professionalism* (Chicago: University of Chicago Press, 1986).

7. Ibid.

8. Ibid.

9. *U.S.* v. *Nixon*, 816 F.2d 1022 (1987).

10. *Nixon* v. *U.S.*, No. 91–740. Decided January 13, 1993.

11. Bureau of Justice Statistics, *Report to the Nation on Crime and Justice: The Data* (Washington, D.C.: U.S. Department of Justice, 1983).

12. For a discussion of the resource limitations of district attorneys in combating corporate crime, see Michael L. Benson, William J. Maakestad, Francis T. Cullen, and Gilbert Geis, "District Attorneys and Corporate Crime: Surveying the Prosecutorial Gatekeepers," *Criminology*, Vol. 26, no. 3 (August 1988), pp. 505-517.

13. John M. Dawson, *Prosecutors in State Courts, 1990* (Washington, D.C.: Bureau of Justice Statistics, 1992).

14. Kenneth Culp Davis, *Discretionary Justice* (Baton Rouge: Louisiana State University Press, 1969), p. 190.

15. Barbara Borland, *The Prosecution of Felony Arrests* (Washington, D.C.: Bureau of Justice Statistics, 1983).

16. Many large police departments have their own legal counselors who provide advice on civil liability and who may also assist in weighing the quality of evidence which has been assembled.

17. *Imbler* v. *Pachtman*, 424 U.S. 409 (1976).

18. *Burns* v. *Reed*, No. 89–1715, 1991.

19. Ibid., complaint, p. 29.

20. *Brady* v. *Maryland*, 373 U.S. 83 (1963).

21. *U.S.* v. *Bagley*, 473 U.S. 667 (1985).

22. Cassia Spohn, John Gruhl, and Susan Welch, "The Impact of the Ethnicity and Gender of Defendants on the Decision to Reject or Dismiss Felony Charges," *Criminology*, Vol. 25, no. 1 (1987), pp. 175–191.

23. "Pay the Costs of Justice," *USA Today*, March 30, 1993, p. 8A.

24. *Powell* v. *Alabama*, 287 U.S. 45 (1932).

25. *Johnson* v. *Zerbst*, 304 U.S. 458 (1938).

26. *Gideon* v. *Wainwright*, 372 U.S. 335 (1963).

27. *Argersinger* v. *Hamlin*, 407 U.S. 25 (1972).

28. *In re Gault*, 387 U.S. 1 (1967).

29. Bureau of Justice Statistics, *Criminal Defense for the Poor, 1986.*

30. "Pay the Costs of Justice," *USA Today*, March 30, 1993, p. 8A.

31. Smolowe, "The Trials of the Public Defender," p. 46.

32. Ibid.

33. *Faretta* v. *California*, 422 U.S. 806 (1975).

34. "Killings Spotlight Lawyers' Ethics," *The Fayetteville Observer-Times* (North Carolina), September 13, 1992, p. 11A.

35. *Nix* v. *Whiteside*, 475 U.S. 157 (1986).

36. Ibid.

37. "Courtroom Killings Verdict," *USA Today*, February 15, 1993, p. 3A.

38. "How Crucial Is Courtroom Security?" *Security Management* (August 1992), p. 78.

39. President's Commission on Law Enforcement and Administration of Justice, *The Challenge of Crime in a Free Society* (Washington, D.C.: U.S. Government Printing Office, 1967), p. 129.

40. National Advisory Commission on Criminal Justice Standards and Goals, *Courts* (Washington, D.C.: U.S. Government Printing Office, 1973), Standard 9.3.

41. See, for example, Joan G. Brannon, *The Judicial System in North Carolina* (Raleigh, NC: The Administrative Office of the Courts, 1984), p. 14.

42. Joseph L. Peterson, "Use of Forensic Evidence by the Police and Courts," a National Institute of Justice, *Research in Brief* (Washington, D.C.: NIJ, 1987), p. 3.

43. Ibid., p. 6.

44. *California* v. *Green*, 399 U.S. 149 (1970).

45. Patrick L. McCloskey and Ronald L. Schoenberg, *Criminal Law Deskbook* (New York: Matthew Bender, 1988), Section 17, p. 123.

46. Bureau of Justice Statistics, *Report to the Nation on Crime and Justice*, 2nd ed., p. 82.

47. *Demarest* v. *Manspeaker et al.*, No. 89–5916 (1991).

48. Ibid., p. 82.

49. *Williams* v. *Florida*, 399 U.S. 78, 90 S.Ct. 1893, 26 L.Ed. 2d 446 (1970).

50. *Smith* v. *Texas*, 311 U.S. 128 (1940).

51. *Thiel* v. *Southern Pacific Co.*, 328 U.S. 217 (1945).

52. Speaking from a personal experience, the author was himself the victim of a felony in 1973. My car was stolen in Columbus, Ohio, and recovered a year later in Cleveland. I was informed that the person who had taken it was in custody, but I never heard what happened to him, nor could I learn where or whether a trial was to be held.

53. President's Task Force on Victims of Crime, *Final Report* (Washington, D.C.: U.S. Government Printing Office, 1982).

54. Peter Finn and Beverly N. W. Lee, *Establishing and Expanding Victim-Witness Assistance Programs* (Washington, D.C.: National Institute of Justice, August 1988).

55. Ibid.

56. President's Task Force on Victims of Crime, *Final Report*.

57. Dale G. Parent, Barbara Auerbach, and Kenneth E. Carlson, *Compensating Crime Victims: A Summary of Policies and Practices* (Washington, D.C.: National Institute of Justice, 1992), p. 39.

58. *Crosby* v. *U.S.*, No. 91–6194. Decided January 13, 1993.

59. *Zafiro* v. *U.S.*, No. 91–6824. Decided January 25, 1993.

60. *Nebraska Press Association* v. *Stuart*, 427 U.S. 539 (1976).

61. However, it is generally accepted that trial judges may issue limited gag orders aimed at trial participants.

62. *Press Enterprise Company* v. *Superior Court of California, Riverside County*, 478 U.S. 1 (1986).

63. *Caribbean International News Corporation* v. *Puerto Rico*, No. 92–949, May 17, 1993.

64. Dennis Cauchon, "Federal Courts Camera-Less," *USA Today*, March 10, 1993, p. 2A.

65. *Chandler* v. *Florida*, 499 U.S. 560 (1981).

66. Ibid.

67. Marc G. Gertz and Edmond J. True, "Social Scientists in the Courtroom: The Frustrations of Two Expert Witnesses," in Susette M. Talarico, ed., *Courts and Criminal Justice: Emerging Issues* (Beverly Hills, CA: Sage Publications, 1985), pp. 81–91.

68. *Klopfer* v. *North Carolina*, 386 U.S. 213 (1967).

69. *Barker* v. *Wingo*, 407 U.S. 514 (1972).

70. *Strunk* v. *U.S.*, 412 U.S. 434 (1973).

71. The Federal Speedy Trial Act, 18 U.S.C., Section 3161 (1974).

72. *U.S.* v. *Brainer*, 515 F. Supp. 627 (D.Md.1981).

73. *U.S.* v. *Taylor*, U.S. 108, S.Ct. 2413 (1988).

74. *Fex* v. *Michigan*, No. 91–7873. Decided February 23, 1993.

75. *Doggett* v. *U.S.*, 112 S.Ct. 2686 (1992).

76. William U. McCormack, "Supreme Court Cases: 1991–1992 Term," *FBI Law Enforcement Bulletin*, November, 1992, pp. 28–29.

77. See, for example, the U.S. Supreme Court's decision in the case of *Murphy* v. *Florida*, 410 U.S. 525 (1973).

78. *Witherspoon* v. *Illinois*, 391 U.S. 510 (1968).

79. *Mu'Min* v. *Virginia*, No. 90–5193 (1991).

80. Rule 24(6) of the *Federal Rules of Criminal Procedure*.

81. *Thiel* v. *Southern Pacific Co.*

82. "Are Juries Colorblind?" *Newsweek*, December 5, 1988, p. 94.

83. Ibid.

84. Ibid.

85. Ibid.

86. Supreme Court majority opinion in *Powers* v. *Ohio*, No. 89–5011 (1991), citing *Strauder* v. *West Virginia*, 100 U.S. 303 (1880).

87. *Swain* v. *Alabama*, 380 U.S. 202 (1965).

88. *Batson* v. *Kentucky*, 476 U.S. 79, 106 S.Ct. 1712 (1986).

89. *Ford* v. *Georgia*, No. 87–6796, 1991, footnote 2.

90. Ibid.

91. *Powers* v. *Ohio*.

92. *Edmonson* v. *Leesville Concrete Co., Inc.*, No. 89–7743 (1991).

93. *Georgia* v. *McCollum*, No. 91–372. Argued February 26, 1992; decided June 18, 1992.

94. Although the words "argument" and "statement" are sometimes used interchangeably in alluding to opening remarks, defense attorneys are enjoined from drawing conclusions or "arguing" to the jury at this stage in the trial. Their task, as described in the section which follows, is simply to provide information to the jury as to how the defense will be conducted.

95. *U.S.* v. *Dinitz*, 424 U.S. 600, 612 (1976).

96. *Michigan* v. *Lucas*, No. 90–149 (1991).

97. *Kotteakos* v. *United States*, 328 U.S. 750 (1946); *Becht* v. *Abrahamson*, No. 91–7358, decided April 21, 1993; and *Arizona* v. *Fulminante*, 111 S.Ct. 1246 (1991).

98. The Court, citing *Kotteakos* v. *United States*, 328 U.S. 750 (1946) in *Brecht* v. *Abrahamson*, No. 91–7358. Decided April 21, 1993.

99. *Sullivan* v. *Louisiana*, No. 92–5129. Decided June 1, 1993.

100. *Griffin* v. *California*, 380 U.S. 609 (1965).

101. Leading questions may, in fact, be permitted for certain purposes, including refreshing a witness's memory, impeaching a hostile witness, introducing nondisputed material, and helping a witness with impaired faculties.

102. *In re Oliver*, 333 U.S. 257 (1948).

103. *Coy* v. *Iowa*, 487 U.S. 1012, 108 S.Ct. 2798 (1988).

104. *Maryland* v. *Craig*, 1990.

105. "The Right to Confront Your Accuser," *The Boston Globe* magazine, April 7, 1991, pp. 19, 51.

106. *Maryland* v. *Craig*.

107. *Idaho* v. *Wright*, No. 89–260 (1990).

108. *White* v. *Illinois*, 112 S.Ct. 736 (1992).

109. *White* v. *Illinois*, Project Hermes on-line decision.

110. Rule 29.1 of the *Federal Rules of Criminal Procedure*.

111. See *Johnson* v. *Louisiana*, 406 U.S. 356 (1972), and *Apodaca* v. *Oregon*, 406 U.S. 404 (1972).

112. *Allen* v. *U.S.*, 164 U.S. 492 (1896).

113. See, for example, John Baldwin and Michael McConville, "Criminal Juries," in Norval Morris and Michael Tonry, eds., *Crime and Justice*, Vol. 2 (Chicago: University of Chicago Press, 1980).

114. Amiram Elwork, Bruce D. Sales, and James Alfini, *Making Jury Instructions Understandable* (Charlottesville, VA: Michie, 1982),.

115. "Juror Hardship Becomes Critical as McMartin Trial Enters Year 3," *Criminal Justice Newsletter*, Vol. 20 (May 15, 1989), pp. 6–7.

116. "King Jury Lives in Fear from Unpopular Verdict," *Fayetteville Observer-Times* (North Carolina), May 10, 1992, p. 7A.

117. "Los Angeles Trials Spark Debate over Anonymous Juries," *Criminal Justice Newsletter*, February 16, 1993, pp. 3–4.

118. Some states have centralized offices called "Administrative Offices of the Courts" or something similar. Such offices, however, are often primarily data-gathering agencies which have little or no authority over the day-to-day functioning of state or local courts.

119. See, for example, Larry Berkson and Susan Carbon, *Court Unification: Its History, Politics, and Implementation* (Washington, D.C.: U.S. Government Printing Office, 1978), and Thomas Henderson et al., *The Significance of Judicial Structure: The Effect of Unification on Trial Court Operators* (Alexandria, VA: Institute for Economic and Policy Studies, 1984).

120. See, for example, Kenneth Carlson, et al., *Citizen Court Watching: The Consumer's Perspectives* (Cambridge, MA: Abt Associates, 1977).

121. See, for example, Thomas J. Cook and Ronald W. Johnson, et al., *Basic Issues in Court Performance* (Washington, D.C.: National Institute of Justice, 1982).

122. See, for example, Sorrel Wildhorn et al., *Indicators of Justice:* Measuring the Performance of Prosecutors, Defense, and Court Agencies Involved in Felony Proceedings (Lexington, MA: Lexington Books, 1977).

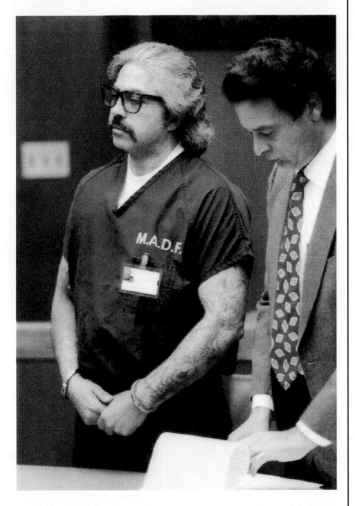

CHAPTER 10

SENTENCING

We will not punish a man because he hath offended, but that he may offend no more; nor does punishment ever look to the past, but to the future; for it is not the result of passion, but that the same thing be guarded against in time to come.
—SENECA (B.C. 3–65 A.D.)

The root of revenge is in the weakness of the Soul; the most abject and timorous are the most addicted to it.
—AKHENATON (CIRCA B.C. 1375)

Punishment, that is justice for the unjust.
—SAINT AUGUSTINE (345–430 A.D.)

To make punishments efficacious, two things are necessary. They must never be disproportioned to the offence, and they must be certain.
—WILLIAM SIMS (1806–1870)

KEY CONCEPTS

retribution
specific deterrence
presumptive
    sentencing
victim impact
    statements

general deterrence
incapacitation
aggravating factors
indeterminate sentence

presentence report
rehabilitation
mitigating factors
just deserts

KEY CASES

Wilkerson v. *Utah*
Furman v. *Georgia*
Mistretta v. *U.S.*
In re Kemmler
Smith v. *U.S.*

Coker v. *Georgia*
Woodson v. *North Carolina*
Gregg v. *Georgia*
Booth v. *Maryland*
Deal v. *U.S.*

Payne v. *Tennessee*
Coleman v. *Thompson*
McCleskey v. *Zandt*
Stinson v. *U.S.*

THE PHILOSOPHY OF CRIMINAL SENTENCING

A few years ago, John Angus Smith and a friend went from Tennessee to Florida to buy cocaine. They hoped to resell it at a profit. While in Florida, they met an acquaintance of Smith's, Deborah Hoag. Hoag purchased cocaine for Smith and then accompanied him and his friend to her motel room, where they were joined by a drug dealer. While Hoag listened, Smith and the dealer discussed Smith's MAC-10 firearm, which had been modified to operate as an automatic. The MAC-10, small, compact, and lightweight, can be equipped with a silencer, and is a favorite among criminals. A fully automatic MAC-10 can be devastating. It can fire more than 1,000 rounds per minute. The dealer expressed his interest in becoming the owner of a MAC-10, and Smith promised that he would discuss selling the gun if his arrangement with another potential buyer fell through.

Unfortunately for Smith, Hoag had contacts not only with narcotics traffickers but also with law enforcement officials. She was a confidential informant, and she informed the Broward County Sheriff's Office of Smith's activities. The Sheriff's Office responded quickly, sending an undercover officer to Hoag's motel room. Several other officers were assigned to keep the motel under surveillance. Upon arriving at Hoag's room, the undercover officer presented himself to Smith as a pawnshop dealer. Smith, in turn, presented the officer with a proposition: he had an automatic MAC-10 and silencer with which he might be willing to part, if a good price could be arranged. Smith then pulled the MAC-10 out of a black canvas bag and showed it to the officer. The officer examined the gun and asked petitioner what he wanted for it. Rather than asking for money, however, petitioner asked for drugs. He was willing to trade his MAC-10, he said, for two ounces of cocaine. The officer told petitioner that he was just a pawnshop dealer and did not distribute narcotics. Nonetheless, he indicated that he wanted the MAC-10 and would try to get the cocaine. The undercover officer then left, promising to return within an hour, and went to the Sheriff's Office to arrange for Smith's arrest. But Smith did not wait. The officers who were conducting surveillance saw him leave the motel room carrying a gun bag; he then climbed into his van and drove away. The officers reported Smith's departure and began following him. When law enforcement authorities tried to stop Smith, he led them on a high-speed chase, which ended in his apprehension. Smith, it turns out, was well armed. A search of his van revealed the MAC-10, a silencer, ammunition, and a "fast-feed" mechanism. In addition, police found a MAC-11 machine gun, a loaded .45-caliber pistol, and a .22-caliber pistol with a scope and homemade silencer. Smith also had a loaded 9-millimeter handgun in his waistband.

A grand jury for the Southern District of Florida returned an indictment charging Smith with, among other offenses, two drug trafficking crimes—conspiracy to possess cocaine with intent to distribute and attempt to possess cocaine with intent to distribute. More important, the indictment alleged that Smith knowingly used the MAC-10 and its silencer during and in relation to a drug trafficking crime. Under federal law, a defendant who so uses a firearm must be sentenced to 5 years' incarceration. And where, as here, the firearm is a "machine gun" or is fitted with a silencer, the sentence is 30 years. The jury convicted Smith on all counts.

The wording in this story is taken directly from the majority opinion in the 1993 U.S. Supreme Court case of *Smith* v. *U.S.*,[1] which held that "[a] criminal who trades his firearm for drugs 'uses' it within the meaning" of federal sentencing guidelines. The plain language of the statute, the high court explained, imposes no requirement that the firearm be used as a weapon. Smith's appeal of his 30-year sentence was denied.

Sentencing is the imposition of a penalty upon a person convicted of a crime. Most sentencing decisions are made by judges, although in some cases, especially where a death sentence is possible, juries may be involved in a special sentencing phase of courtroom proceedings. The sentencing decision is one of the most difficult made by any judge or jury. Not only does it involve the future, and perhaps the very life, of the defendant, but society looks to sentencing to achieve a diversity of goals.

Traditional sentencing options have included imprisonment, fines, probation, and—for very serious offenses—death. Limits on the range of options available to sentencing authorities are generally specified in law. Historically those limits have shifted as understandings of crime and the goals of sentencing have changed. Sentencing philosophies, or the justifications upon which various sentencing strategies are based, are manifestly intertwined with issues of religion, morals, values, and emotions.[2] Philosophies which gained ascendancy at a particular point in history were likely to be reflections of more deeply held social values.

The mentality of centuries ago, for example, held that crime was due to sin, and suffering was the culprit's due. Judges were expected to be harsh. Capital punishment, torture, and corporeal penalties served the ends of criminal sentencing.

An emphasis on rehabilitation became more prevalent around the time of the American and French revolutions, brought about, in part, by Enlightenment philosophies. Offenders came to be seen as highly rational beings who, more often than not, intentionally and somewhat carefully chose their course of action. Sentencing philosophies of the period stressed the need for sanctions which outweighed the benefits to be derived from making criminal choices. Severity of punishment became less important than quick and certain penalties.

Recent thinking has emphasized the need to limit the potential for future harm by separating offenders from society. Not unknown, however, is the belief that offenders are deserving of punishment; nor has the hope for rehabilitation been entirely abandoned. Modern sentencing practices are influenced by five goals which weave their way through widely disseminated professional and legal models, continuing public calls for sentencing reform, and everyday sentencing practice. The five goals of contemporary sentencing are (1) retribution, (2) incapacitation, (3) deterrence, (4) rehabilitation, and (5) victim restoration. Each goal represents a sentencing philosophy since it makes assumptions about human nature and holds implications for sentencing practice.

Sentencing The imposition of a criminal sanction by a judicial authority.

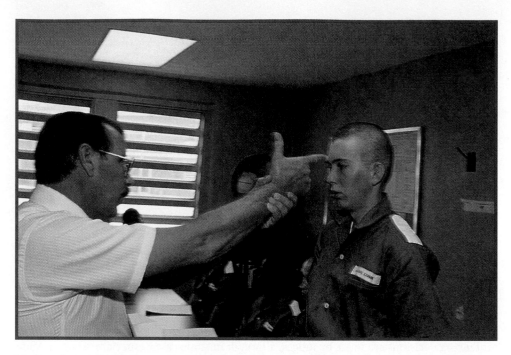

Modern-day retribution in practice: A counselor in a prison "boot camp" program shows a robber what it feels like to have a gun pointed at his head. *Photo: Starr/Stock Boston.*

RETRIBUTION

Retribution The act of taking revenge upon a criminal perpetrator.

Retribution is punishment based upon a felt, but often inarticulate, need. To those who seek retribution, crimes cry out for vengeance. Retribution is an ancient goal. Most early societies punished offenders whenever they could catch them. Punishment was swift and immediate—often without the benefit of a hearing—and it was generally extreme. Death and exile were commonly imposed. The Old Testament dictum of "An eye for an eye, a tooth for a tooth"—often cited as an ancient justification for retribution—was actually intended to reduce the severity of punishment for relatively minor crimes.

> Excessive bail shall not be required, nor excessive fines imposed, nor cruel and unusual punishments inflicted.
>
> —*Eighth Amendment to the U.S. Constitution*

In its modern guise, retribution corresponds to the just deserts model of sentencing. The just deserts philosophy holds that offenders are responsible for their crimes. It sees punishment as deserved, justified—and even required[3]—by the behavior of the offender. The primary sentencing tool of the just deserts model is imprisonment, although in extreme cases capital punishment may become the ultimate retribution.

INCAPACITATION

Incapacitation The use of imprisonment or other means to reduce the likelihood that an offender will be capable of committing future offenses.

The protection of innocent members of society is the primary goal of incapacitation. In olden times mutilation and amputation were sometimes used to prevent offenders from repeating their crimes. Modern incapacitation strategies separate offenders from the community in order to reduce opportunities for further criminality. Incapacitation is sometimes called the "lock 'em up approach" and forms the basis for the contemporary movement toward prison "warehousing" discussed later in this book.

Incapacitation is used as a justification for imprisonment, just as is retribution. A significant difference between the two perspectives, however, lies in the fact that incapacitation requires only restraint—and not punishment. Hence advocates of the incapacitation philosophy of sentencing are sometimes also active prison reformers, seeking to humanize correctional institutions. At the forefront of technology, confinement innovations are now offering ways to achieve the goal of incapacitation without the need for imprisonment. Electronic confinement (discussed shortly) and biomedical intervention (such as "chemical castration") may be able to prevent repeat offenses and bring society the protection it seeks through effective sentencing.

DETERRENCE

Deterrence A goal of criminal sentencing which seeks to prevent others from committing crimes similar to the one for which an offender is being sentenced.

Deterrence relies upon the use of punishment as an example to convince people that criminal activity is not worthwhile. Its overall goal is crime prevention. When efforts are made to reduce the likelihood of recidivism by convicted offenders we speak of specific deterrence. General deterrence, on the other hand, strives to influence the future behavior of people not yet arrested, who may be tempted to turn to crime.

Deterrence is one of the more "rational" goals of sentencing. It is rational because it is an easily articulated goal, and also because the amount of punishment required to deter is amenable to objective investigation. Jeremy Bentham's hedonistic calculus, discussed earlier in this text, laid the groundwork for many later calculations of just how harsh punishments need to be in order to deter effectively. It is generally agreed today that harsh punishments can virtually eliminate many minor forms of criminality.[4] Few traffic tickets would have to be written, for example, if minor driving offenses were punishable by death. A free society such as our own, of course, is not willing to impose extreme punishments on petty offenders, and even harsh punishments are not demonstrably effective in reducing the incidence of serious crimes such as murder and drug running.

Deterrence is compatible with the goal of incapacitation, since at least specific deterrence can be achieved through incapacitating offenders. Hugo Bedau,[5] however, points to significant differences between retribution and deterrence. Retribution is oriented toward the past, says Bedau. It seeks to redress wrongs already committed. Deterrence, in contrast, is a strategy for the future. It aims to prevent new crimes. But as H. L. A. Hart has observed,[6] retribution can be the means through which deterrence is achieved. By serving as an example of what might happen to others, punishment may have an inhibiting effect.

REHABILITATION

Rehabilitation The attempt to reform a criminal offender. Also, the state in which a reformed offender is said to be.

Rehabilitation seeks to bring about fundamental changes in offenders and their behavior. As in the case of deterrence, the ultimate goal of rehabilitation is a reduction in the number of criminal offenses. Whereas deterrence, however, depends upon a "fear of the law" and the consequences of violating it, rehabilitation generally works through education and psychological treatment to reduce the likelihood of future criminality.

The term "rehabilitation" however, may actually be a misnomer for the kinds of changes that its supporters seek. Rehabilitation literally means to return a person (or thing) to their previous condition. Hence, medical rehabilitation programs seek to restore

Rehabilitation is an important goal of
modern sentencing. Here inmates in a
Texas prison learn how to work with
computers. Skills acquired through
such prison programs might translate
into productive, non-criminal, careers.
Photo: Bob Daemmrich/Stock Boston.

functioning to atrophied limbs, rejuvenate injured organs, and mend shattered minds. In
the case of criminal offenders, however, it is unlikely that restoring many to their previous
state will result in anything other than a more youthful type of criminality.

> Nobody gets rehabilitated. Well, I shouldn't say no one; some of them die.

> —*Former LAPD Chief Daryl Gates*

In the past, rehabilitation as a sentencing strategy, if it existed at all, was primarily
applied to youths. One of the first serious efforts to reform adult offenders was begun by
the Pennsylvania Quakers, who initiated the development of the late–eighteenth-century
penitentiary. The penitentiary, which attempted to combine enforced penance with religious instruction, proved, however, to be something of an aberration. Within a few decades
it had been firmly supplanted by a retributive approach to corrections.

It was not until the 1930s that rehabilitation achieved a primary role in the sentencing
of adult offenders in the United States. At the time, the psychological world view of thera-
pists such as Sigmund Freud was entering popular culture. Psychology held out, as never
before, the possibility of a structured approach to rehabilitation through therapeutic intervention. The rehabilitative approach of the mid-1900s became known as the medical
model of corrections, since it was built around a perscriptive approach to the treatment of
offenders which provided at least the appearance of clinical predictability.

The primacy of the rehabilitative goal in sentencing fell victim to a "nothing works"
philosophy in the late 1970s. The nothing works doctrine was based upon studies of

recidivism rates which consistently showed that rehabilitation was more an ideal than a reality. With as many as 90% of former convicted offenders returning to lives of crime following release from prison-based treatment programs, public sentiments in favor of incapacitation grew. Although the rehabilitation ideal has clearly suffered in the public arena, however, some emerging evidence has begun to suggest that effective treatment programs do exist and may even be growing in number.[7]

RESTORATION

Victims or their survivors are frequently traumatized by the victimization experience. Some are killed and others receive lasting physical injuries. For many the world is never the same. The victimized may live in constant fear, reduced in personal vigor, and unable to form trusting relationships. Restoration is a sentencing goal which seeks to make the victim and the community "whole again."

The "healing" of victims involves many facets, arrayed throughout the criminal justice system, ranging from victim assistance programs to legislation supporting victim compensation. Sentencing options which seek to restore the victim have focused primarily on restitution payments which offenders are ordered to make either to their victims or to a general fund which may then go to reimburse victims for suffering, lost wages, and medical expenses. In support of these goals, the 1984 Federal Comprehensive Crime Control Act specifically requires: "If sentenced to probation, the defendant must also be ordered to pay a fine, make restitution, and/or work in community service."[8]

Texas provides an example of a statewide strategy to utilize restitution as an alternative to prison.[9] The Texas Residential Restitution Program operates community-based centers which house selected nonviolent felony offenders. Residents work at regular jobs in the community, pay for support of their families, make restitution to their victims, and pay for room and board. During nonworking hours they are required to perform community service work.

Some advocates of the restoration philosophy of sentencing point out that court-ordered restitution payments or work programs which benefit the victim, can also have the added benefit of rehabilitating the offender. The hope is that such sentences may teach the offender personal responsibility through structured financial obligations, work programs, regularly scheduled payments, and the like.

INDETERMINATE SENTENCING

During most of the twentieth century, the rehabilitative goal held primacy. Rehabilitation required a close consideration of the personal characteristics of individual offenders to define effective treatment strategies. Hence, judges were permitted wide discretion in choosing from among sentencing options. Although incapacitation is increasingly becoming the sentencing strategy of choice, many state criminal codes still allow judges to impose fines, probation, or widely varying prison terms, all for the same offense. These sentencing practices, characterized primarily by vast judicial choice, constitute an indeterminate sentencing model.

Indeterminate sentencing relies heavily upon the discretionary decisions of judges who not only choose among types of sanctions, but also set upper and lower limits on the length of prison stays. Indeterminate sentences are typically imposed with wording such as

Restoration A goal of criminal sentencing which attempts to make the victim "whole again."

Indeterminate Sentencing A model of criminal punishment which encourages rehabilitation via the use of general and relatively unspecific sentences (such as a term of imprisonment of "from one to ten years").

Good Time The amount of time deducted from time to be served in prison on a given sentence(s) and/or under correctional agency jurisdiction, at some point after a prisoner's admission to prison, contingent upon good behavior and/or awarded automatically by application of a statute or regulation.

"The defendant shall serve not less than five, not more than twenty-five years in the state's prison, under the supervision of the state department of correction…" Judicial discretion under the indeterminate model also extends to the imposition of concurrent or consecutive sentences, where the offender is convicted on more than one charge. Consecutive sentences are served one after the other, while concurrent sentences expire simultaneously.

Under the indeterminate sentencing model, the inmate's behavior while incarcerated is the primary determinant of the actual amount of time served. State parole boards wield great discretion under the model, acting as the final arbiters of the actual sentence served.

Indeterminate sentencing has both an historical and a philosophical basis in the belief that convicted offenders are more likely to participate in their own rehabilitation if they can reduce the amount of time they have to spend in prison. Inmates on good behavior will be released early, while recalcitrant inmates will remain in prison until the end of their terms. For that reason, parole generally plays a significant role in states which employ the indeterminate sentencing model.

The indeterminate model was also created to take into consideration detailed differences in culpability. Under the model judges could weigh minute differences between cases, situations and offenders. All of the following could be considered before sentence was passed: (1) whether the offender committed the crime out of a need for money, for the thrill it afforded, out of a desire for revenge, or for the "hell of it"; (2) the harm the offender intended; (3) the contribution of the victim to his or her own victimization; (4) the extent of the damages inflicted; (5) the mental state of the offender; (6) the likelihood of successful rehabilitation; (7) the degree of the offender's cooperation with authorities; and (8) a near infinity of other individual factors.

A few states employ a partially indeterminate sentencing model. Partially indeterminate sentencing systems allow judges who are imposing prison sentences to specify only the maximum amount of time to be served. Some minimum is generally implied by law, but is not under the control of the sentencing authority. General practice is to set one year as a minimum for all felonies, while a few jurisdictions assume no minimum time at all—making persons sentenced to imprisonment eligible for immediate parole.

PROBLEMS WITH THE INDETERMINATE MODEL

Indeterminate sentencing is still the rule in many jurisdictions. The model, however, has come under increasing fire in recent years for contributing to inequality in sentencing. Critics claim that the indeterminate model allows divergent judicial personalities, and the often too-personal philosophies of judges, to produce an unwarranted gamut of sentencing practices ranging from very lenient to very strict. The "hanging judge," who still exists in some jurisdictions, was one who, more often than not, tended to impose the maximum sentence allowable under law. Worse still, the indeterminate model allows for the possibility that offenders might be sentenced, at least by some judges, more on the basis of social characteristics rather than culpability.

Offenders who face sentencing under the indeterminate model often depend upon the counsel of their attorneys to appear before a judge predicted to be a good sentencing risk. Requests for delays became a commonly used defense strategy in attempts to manipulate the selection of personalities involved in sentencing decisions.

Another charge leveled against indeterminate sentencing was that it tended to produce dishonesty in sentencing. Because of sentence cutbacks for good behavior, and other reductions available to inmates through involvement in work and study programs, punishments

TABLE 10-1

ESTIMATED TIME TO BE SERVED IN STATE PRISON VERSUS MEAN PRISON SENTENCE

Offense	Mean Prison Sentence	Estimated Time to Be Served in Prison
Murder	221 months	86 months
Rape	151	66
Robbery	139	57
Aggravated assault	97	41
Burglary	75	31
Larceny	46	20
Drug trafficking	69	22
Other felonies	56	24
Average for all felonies	**81 months**	**33 months**

Source: Bureau of Justice Statistics, "Felony Sentences in State Courts, 1986," *Bureau of Justice Statistics Bulletin*, February 1989.

rarely meant what they said. A sentence of five to ten years, for example, might actually see an inmate released in a matter of months after all "gain time" had been calculated. Even today, time served in prison is generally far less than sentences would seem to indicate. Table 10–1 shows recent estimates of time to be served in prison versus actual sentences of felons convicted under state jurisdiction. Figure 10–1 provides a graphical representation of the data.

Indeterminate sentencing came under increasing fire as studies identified widely disparate sentencing practices. An early New Jersey study[10] of six judges handling similar

FIGURE 10–1 Time served in state prisons versus court sentence for violent offenses. *Source:* Bureau of Justice Statistics, *National Judicial Reporting Program 1988* (Washington, D.C.: U.S. Department of Justice, 1992).

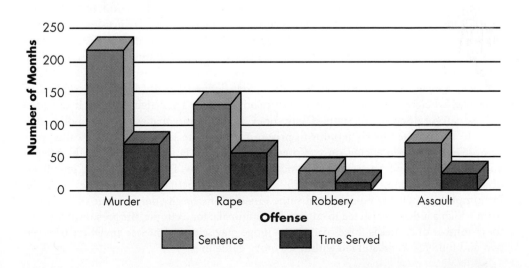

cases found, for example, that the strictest judge imposed prison sentences on 57.7% of convicted criminal defendants who came before him for sentencing, while another, more lenient judge, ordered such sentences only 33.6% of the time. Sentencing practices of the other four judges fell somewhere between these two extremes. A later experiment,[11] which presented 43 active federal trial judges with 20 criminal case scenarios, resulted in enormously varied decisions. One judge chose a sanction of 3 to 20 years; another, probation to 7½ years. "The norm," concluded commentators, "was the absence of a norm."[12]

THE RISE OF DETERMINATE SENTENCING

Determinate Sentencing A model for criminal punishment which sets one particular punishment, or length of sentence, for each specific type of crime. Under the model, for example, all offenders convicted of the same degree of burglary would be sentenced to the same length of time behind bars.

Until the 1970s some form of indeterminate (or partially indeterminate) sentencing was the model employed by all 50 states. Soon, however, calls for equity and proportionality in sentencing, heightened by claims of racial disparity in the sentencing practices[13] of some judges, led many states to move toward closer control over their sentencing systems.

Critics of the indeterminate model called for the recognition of three fundamental sentencing principles: proportionality, equity, and social debt. Proportionality refers to the belief that the severity of sanctions should bear a direct relationship to the seriousness of the crime committed. Equity is based upon a concern with social equality. Equality in sentencing means that similar crimes should be punished with the same degree of severity, regardless of the general social or personal characteristics of offenders. According to the principle of equity, for example, two bank robbers in different parts of the country, who use the same techniques and weapons, with the same degree of implied threat, even though they are tried under separate circumstances, should receive roughly the same kind of sentence. The equity principle needs to be balanced, however, against the notion of social debt. In the case of the bank robbers, the offender who has a prior criminal record can be said to have a higher level of social debt than the one-time robber, where all else is equal. Greater social debt, of course, would suggest a heightened severity of punishment or a greater need for treatment, and so on.

In 1976 Maine became the first state to eliminate old sentencing practices and adopt determinate sentencing. It was quickly followed by other states, including Colorado, California, Connecticut, Florida, Illinois, Indiana, Minnesota, New Mexico, North Carolina, and Washington.[14] Colorado, while opting for determinate sentencing in 1979, returned to the use of an indeterminate model in 1985. Determinate sentencing states observe a pattern of abolishing parole, eliminating parole boards, and establishing sentencing commissions with the authority to develop and modify sentencing guidelines.

Aggravating Circumstances Those elements of an offense or of an offender's background which could result in a harsher sentence under the determinate model than would otherwise be called for by sentencing guidelines.

Determinate sentencing depends upon a well-defined penalty hierarchy codified in state law, whereby specified terms of imprisonment are associated with each criminal offense category. Sentencing statutes may, for example, require that assault on a police officer is to be punished by six months in prison. Determinate sentencing is also called presumptive or fixed sentencing since it presumes a direct relationship between the offense and the sentence and sets sentences which are fixed by law. Even presumptive sentences, however, often allow judges a certain leeway in the actual sentences they impose. Presumptive sentencing guidelines in some jurisdictions specify only a range of sentences from which a judge is expected to choose. In California, for example, the presumptive term for a number of crimes is three years, but a judge may select a sentence anywhere between two and four years and still fall within statutory guidelines.

Even states which use a single presumptive sentence for a given offense generally allow for "aggravating" or "mitigating" factors, indicating greater or lesser degrees of culpability, which judges can take into consideration in imposing a sentence somewhat at variance from the presumptive term. Aggravating factors are those which appear to call for a tougher sentence and may include especially heinous behavior, cruelty, injury to more than one person, and so on. In death penalty cases, however, the U.S. Supreme Court has held that aggravating factors must "provide specific and detailed guidance and make rationally reviewable the death sentencing process.... In order to decide whether a particular aggravating circumstance meets these requirements, a federal court must determine whether the statutory language defining the circumstance is itself too vague to guide the sentencer...."[15]

Mitigating factors, or those which indicate that a lesser sentence is called for, are generally similar to legal defenses, although in this case they only reduce criminal responsibility, not eliminate it. Mitigating factors include such things as cooperation with the investigating authority, surrender, good character, and so on. Common aggravating and mitigating factors are listed in the accompanying "Theory Into Practice" box.

Mitigating Circumstances Those elements of an offense or of an offender's background which could result in a lesser sentence under the determinate model than would otherwise be called for by sentencing guidelines.

A CRITIQUE OF THE DETERMINATE MODEL

Determinate sentencing models, which have sought to address the shortcomings of their predecessors through legislative curtailment of judicial discretion in the sentencing realm, are not without their critics. Detractors charge that determinate sentencing is overly simplistic, based upon a primitive concept of culpability, and incapable of offering hope for rehabilitation and change. For one thing, they say, determinate sentencing has built-in limitations which render it far less capable of judging the blameworthiness of individual offenders. Legislatures simply cannot anticipate all the differences that individual cases can present. Aggravating and mitigating circumstances, while intended to cover most circumstances, will inevitably shortchange some defendants who don't fall neatly into the categories they provide.

A second critique of determinate sentencing is that such a strategy, while it may reduce the discretion of judges substantially, may do nothing to hamper the huge discretionary decision-making power of prosecutors.[16] In fact, federal sentencing reformers, who have adopted the determinate sentencing model, have specifically decided not to modify the discretionary power of prosecutors, citing the large number of cases which are resolved through plea bargaining. Such a shift in discretionary authority, away from judges and into the hands of prosecutors, may be misplaced.

Another criticism of determinate sentencing questions its fundamental purpose. Advocates of determinate sentencing inevitably cite greater equity in sentencing as the primary benefits of such a model. Reduced to its essence, this means that "those who commit the same crime get the same time." Sentencing reformers have thus couched the drive toward determinate sentencing in progressive terms. Others, however, have pointed out that the philosophical underpinnings of the movement may be quite different. Albert Alschuler,[17] for example, suggests that determinate sentencing is a regressive social policy which derives from a weariness among Americans for considering offenders as individuals. Describing this kind of thinking, Alschuler writes: "Don't tell us that a robber was retarded. We don't care about his problems. We don't know what to *do* about his problems, and we are no longer interested in listening to a criminal's sob stories. The most important thing about this robber is simply that he *is* a robber."[18]

THEORY INTO PRACTICE

AGGRAVATING AND MITIGATING FACTORS

Listed here are some typical aggravating and mitigating factors which judges may take into consideration in arriving at sentencing decisions in determinate sentencing states.

Aggravating Factors

- The defendant induced others to participate in the commission of the offense.
- The offense was especially heinous, atrocious, or cruel.
- The defendant was armed with or used a deadly weapon at the time of the crime.
- The offense was committed for the purpose of avoiding or preventing a lawful arrest or effecting an escape from custody.
- The offense was committed for hire.
- The offense was committed against a present or former law enforcement officer, correctional officer, while engaged in the performance of official duties, or because of the past exercise of official duties.
- The defendant took advantage of a position of trust or confidence to commit the offense.

Mitigating Factors

- The defendant has no record of criminal convictions punishable by more than 60 days of imprisonment.
- The defendant has made substantial or full restitution.
- The defendant has been a person of good character or has had a good reputation in the community.
- The defendant aided in the apprehension of another felon or testified truthfully on behalf of the prosecution.
- The defendant acted under strong provocation, or the victim was a voluntary participant in the criminal activity, or otherwise consented to it.
- The offense was committed under duress, coercion, threat, or compulsion which was insufficient to constitute a defense but significantly reduced the defendant's culpability.
- The defendant was suffering from a mental or physical condition that was insufficient to constitute a defense but significantly reduced culpability for the offense.

A different line of thought is proposed by Christopher Link and Neal Shover[19] who found in a study of state-level economic, political, and demographic data that determinate sentencing may ultimately be the result of declining economic conditions and increasing fiscal strain on state governments rather than any particular set of ideals.

A fourth critique of determinate sentencing centers on its alleged inability to promote effective rehabilitation. Under indeterminate sentencing schemes, offenders have the opportunity to act responsibly and thus to participate in their own rehabilitation.[20] Lack of responsible behavior results in denial of parole and extension of the sentence. Determinate sentencing schemes, by virtue of dramatic reductions in good-time allowances and parole opportunities, leave little incentive for offenders to participate in educational programs, to take advantage of opportunities for work inside of correctional institutions, to seek treatment, or to contribute in any positive way to their own change.

While these critiques may be valid, they will probably do little to stem the tide toward presumptive sentencing. The rise of determinate sentencing represents the ascendancy of the "just deserts" perspective over other sentencing goals. In a growing number of jurisdictions, punishment, deterrence, and incapacitation have replaced rehabilitation and restitution as the goals which society seeks to achieve through sentencing practices.

FEDERAL SENTENCING GUIDELINES

In 1984, with passage of The Comprehensive Crime Control Act, the federal government adopted determinate sentencing for nearly all federal offenders.[21] The act established the seven-member U.S. Sentencing Commission, composed of presidential appointees, including three federal judges. Heading the Commission was William W. Wilkins, Jr., U.S. circuit judge for the Fourth Circuit. The Commission was given the task of creating federal determinate sentencing guidelines. To guide the Commission, Congress specified the purposes of sentencing to include deterring criminals, incapacitating and/or rehabilitating offenders, and providing "just deserts" in punishing criminals. Congress charged the Commission with eliminating sentencing disparities, with reducing confusion in sentencing, and asked for a system which would permit flexibility in the face of mitigating or aggravating elements. Under the act, perjury at trial is punishable by an enhanced sentence, a feature upheld in *U.S. v. Dunnigan* (1993).[22]

The 1984 Crime Control Act also addressed the issue of honesty in sentencing. Under the old federal system, a sentence of ten years in prison might actually have meant only a few years spent behind bars before the offender was released. On average, good-time credits and parole reduced time served to about one-third of actual sentences.[23] While such a reduction in time may have benefited the offender, it often outraged victims who felt betrayed by the sentencing process. The act nearly eliminated good-time credits,[24] and targeted 1992 (which was later extended to 1997) as the date for phasing out parole and eliminating the U.S. Parole Commission. The emphasis on honesty in sentencing, created, in effect, a sentencing environment of "what you get is what you serve."

FEDERAL GUIDELINE PROVISIONS

Guidelines established by the Commission took effect in November 1987. They immediately became embroiled in appellate battles, many of which focused on the constitutionality of the membership of the Sentencing Commission.[25] The U.S. Supreme Court considered the constitutionality question in 1989. By the time it did, 158 federal district courts had ruled the guidelines unconstitutional, while 116 others had upheld them.[26] The Ninth

U.S. Circuit Court of Appeals had struck the guidelines down, while the Third Circuit Court had found them acceptable. On January 18, 1989, in deciding the case of *Mistretta* v. *U.S.*,[27] the Supreme Court, by a vote of 8 to 1, held that Congress had acted appropriately and that the guidelines developed by the Commission could be applied nationwide.

The federal guidelines specify a sentencing range for each criminal offense, from which judges must choose. If a particular case represents "atypical features," judges are allowed to depart from the guidelines. Departures are generally expected to be made only in the presence of mitigating or aggravating factors—a number of which are specified in the guidelines. Any departure may, however, become the basis for appellate review concerning the reasonableness of the sentence imposed.

Federal sentencing guidelines are built around a table containing 43 rows, each corresponding to one offense level. Penalties associated with each level overlap those of levels above or below in order to discourage unnecessary litigation. A person charged with a crime involving $11,000, for example, upon conviction is unlikely to receive a penalty substantially greater than if the amount involved had been somewhat less than $10,000—a sharp contrast to the old system. A change of six levels roughly doubles the sentence imposed under the guidelines, regardless of the level at which one starts. The sentencing table is reproduced in Table 10–2.

To determine what sentences would be most appropriate for each range, the Commission began by computing the actual sentences being served, on average, under the old system for each type of offense.[28] The Commission also considered relevant federal law, parole guidelines, and the anticipated impact of changes upon federal prison populations. One boundary was set by statute: in creating the Sentencing Commission, Congress had also specified that the degree of discretion available in any one sentencing category could not exceed 25% of the basic penalty for that category or six months, whichever might be greater.

The sentencing table also contains six rows, corresponding to the criminal history category into which an offender falls. Criminal history categories are determined on a point basis. Offenders earn points through previous convictions. Each prior sentence of imprisonment for more than one year and one month counts as three points. Two points are assigned for each prior prison sentence over six months, or if the defendant committed the offense while on probation, parole, or work release. The system also assigns points for other types of previous convictions, and for offenses committed less than two years after release from imprisonment. Points are added together to determine the criminal history category into which an offender falls. Thirteen points or more are required for the highest category. At each offense level, sentences in the highest criminal history category are generally two to three times as severe as for the lowest category.

Defendants may also move into the highest criminal history category (number VI) by virtue of being designated career offenders. Under the sentencing guidelines, a defendant is a career offender if "(1) the defendant was at least 18 years old at the time of the...offense, (2) the...offense is a crime of violence or trafficking in a controlled substance, and (3) the defendant has at least two prior felony convictions of either a crime of violence or a controlled substance offense."[29]

According to the U.S. Supreme Court, an offender may be adjudged a career offender in a single hearing—even when previous convictions are lacking. In *Deal* v. *U.S.* (1993),[30] the defendant, Thomas Lee Deal, was convicted in a single proceeding of six counts of carrying and using a firearm during a series of bank robberies which occurred in the Houston, Texas, area. A federal district court sentenced him to 105 years in prison as a career offender—5 years for the first count and 20 years each on the five other counts, with sentences to run consecutively. In the words of the Court, "[w]e see no reason why [the defendant should not receive such a sentence], simply because he managed to evade detection, prosecution, and conviction for the first five offenses and was ultimately tried on all six in a single proceeding."

TABLE 10-2

THE FEDERAL SENTENCING TABLE (MONTHS)

| Offense Level | Criminal History Category | | | | | |
	I 0 or 1	II 2 or 3	III 4, 5, 6	IV 7, 8, 9	V 10, 11, 12	VI 13 or more
1	0– 1	0– 2	0– 3	0– 4	0– 5	0– 6
2	0– 2	0– 3	0– 4	0– 5	0– 6	0– 7
3	0– 3	0– 4	0– 5	0– 6	2– 8	3– 9
4	0– 4	0– 5	0– 6	2– 8	4– 10	6– 12
5	0– 5	0– 6	1– 7	4– 10	6– 12	9– 15
6	0– 6	1– 7	2– 8	6– 12	9– 15	12– 18
7	1– 7	2– 8	4– 10	8– 14	12– 18	15– 21
8	2– 8	4– 10	6– 12	10– 16	15– 21	18– 24
9	4– 10	6– 12	8– 14	12– 18	18– 24	21– 27
10	6– 12	8– 14	10– 16	15– 21	21– 27	24– 30
11	8– 14	10– 16	12– 18	18– 24	24– 30	27– 33
12	10– 16	12– 18	15– 21	21– 27	27– 33	30– 37
13	12– 18	15– 21	18– 24	24– 30	30– 37	33– 41
14	15– 21	18– 24	21– 27	27– 33	33– 41	37– 46
15	18– 24	21– 27	24– 30	30– 37	37– 46	41– 51
16	21– 27	24– 30	27– 33	33– 41	41– 51	46– 57
17	24– 30	27– 33	30– 37	37– 46	46– 57	51– 63
18	27– 33	30– 37	33– 41	41– 51	51– 63	57– 71
19	30– 37	33– 41	37– 46	46– 57	57– 71	63– 78
20	33– 41	37– 46	41– 51	51– 63	63– 78	70– 87
21	37– 46	41– 51	46– 57	57– 71	70– 87	77– 96
22	41– 51	46– 57	51– 63	63– 78	77– 96	84–105
23	46– 57	51– 63	57– 71	70– 87	84–105	92–115
24	51– 63	57– 71	63– 78	77– 96	92–115	100–125
25	57– 71	63– 78	70– 87	84–105	100–125	110–137
26	63– 78	70– 87	78– 97	92–115	110–137	120–150
27	70– 87	78– 97	87–108	100–125	120–150	130–162
28	78– 97	87–108	97–121	110–137	130–162	140–175
29	87–108	97–121	108–135	121–151	140–175	151–188
30	97–121	108–135	121–151	135–168	151–188	168–210
31	108–135	121–151	135–168	151–188	168–210	188–235
32	121–151	135–168	151–188	168–210	188–235	210–262
33	135–168	151–188	168–210	188–235	210–262	235–293
34	151–188	168–210	188–235	210–262	235–293	262–327
35	168–210	188–235	210–262	235–293	262–327	292–365
36	188–235	210–262	235–293	262–327	292–365	324–405
37	210–262	235–293	262–327	292–365	324–405	360–life
38	235–293	262–327	292–365	324–405	360–life	360–life
39	262–327	292–365	324–405	360–life	360–life	360–life
40	292–365	324–405	360–life	360–life	360–life	360–life
41	324–405	360–life	360–life	360–life	360–life	360–life
42	360–life	360–life	360–life	360–life	360–life	360–life
43	life	life	life	life	life	life

Source: U.S. Sentencing Commission, *Federal Sentencing Guideline Manual* (Washington, D.C.: U.S. Government Printing Office, 1987), p. 210.

PLEA BARGAINING UNDER THE GUIDELINES

Plea bargaining plays a major role in the federal judicial system. Approximately 90% of all federal sentences are the result of guilty pleas,[31] and the large majority of those are the result of plea negotiations. In the words of Commission Chairman Wilkins, "With respect to plea bargaining, the Commission has proceeded cautiously...the Commission did not believe it wise to stand the federal criminal justice system on its head by making too drastic and too sudden a change in these practices."[32]

Although the Commission allowed for the continuation of plea bargaining, it did require that the agreement (1) be fully disclosed in the record of the court (unless there is an overriding and demonstrable reason why it should not) and (2) detail the actual conduct of the offense. Under these requirements defendants will no longer be able to "hide" the actual nature of their offense behind a substitute plea.

The thrust of the new rules concerning plea bargaining is to reduce the veil of secrecy which had heretofore surrounded the process. Information on the decision-making process itself will be available to victims, the media, and the public. Although for now the Commission has assumed a "hands-off" approach to the actual negotiations involved in plea bargaining, it is planning a future review of the process.[33]

EFFECTS OF THE GUIDELINES

The new guidelines are predicted to alter dramatically sentencing practices in the federal criminal justice system. The following changes are likely to occur:[34]

- Probationary sentences that require no confinement (i.e., excluding split sentences) will decline dramatically.
- Drug crimes and violent crimes will see the greatest decrease in the use of probation and the largest increase in active prison time.
- For most property crimes, time served will stay about the same. Exceptions will include burglary, and income tax fraud, where time served will increase.
- Federal prison populations will grow dramatically by the start of the twenty-first century.

Prior to implementation of the new guidelines, 41.4% of all persons convicted of federal crimes received some form of probation.[35] Under the new guidelines, it is predicted that only 18.5% of federal offenders will be able to avoid prison. Similar estimates project that only 13.3% of federal drug offenders will receive probation. More than 33% of such offenders were released on probation under the old system.

Stiffer penalties under the new sentencing guidelines, combined with the elimination of good time and parole will inevitably contribute to an increase in the number of federal prisoners. In 1987 federal prisons held about 42,000 inmates. By 1997 the federal prison population is expected to increase to as many as 118,000 prisoners.[36] By 2002 the figure may reach 156,000—an increase of 300% in 15 years.[37]

Analyses of the impact of various factors on the growth of federal prison populations, however, attribute only 4% to 7% of the overall increment to the new guidelines. Career criminal provisions of the 1984 Comprehensive Crime Control Act, considered separately from the guidelines themselves, are expected to add substantially to the increase in federal inmates. The largest addition will most likely be due, however, to the Anti-Drug Abuse Act of 1986, which substantially ups the penalty for many federal drug offenses.

Early implementation studies[38] during the first year the guidelines were operational showed that 82% of sentences handed down by federal judges were within the sentencing parameters established by the guidelines. Nine percent of sentences were less than the guidelines called for, and 3% were greater. During the first year, 5% of sentences imposed by federal judges were reduced because the offender cooperated with authorities.[39]

In mid-1993, however, a kind of minirevolt began among the federal judiciary over some provisions of both the federal sentencing guidelines and the Anti-Drug Abuse Act. In April of that year two senior judges, Whitman Knapp and Jack B. Weinstein, both of New York City, declared that they would no longer hear drug cases calling federally specified minimum sentences "repressive criminal statutes with huge minimum penalties."[40] The judges criticized federally mandated sentences as "an angry and ineffective response to the drug problem." Independent research confirmed that federal drug offenders were being sentenced to an average of 84.2 months in prison, whereas 23.1 months had been the average sentence for such offenders in 1987.[41] Shortly after the Weinstein and Knapp rebellion, U.S. District Court Judge Harold H. Greene ruled that "a mandatory 30-year sentence required by a sentencing guideline for a career criminal convicted of a new drug crime would be cruel and unusual punishment."[42] In that case, the defendant, Cordell Spencer of Washington, D.C., possessed only 7½ grams of cocaine base and heroin at the time of his arrest. His two prior drug convictions had also involved only small amounts of drugs. Greene sentenced Spencer to 10 years in prison, calling anything greater "unjust."

A few days after the Greene decision, the U.S. Supreme Court, in *Stinson* v. *U.S.* (1993),[43] ruled that federal judges are obligated to follow not only federal sentencing guidelines, but the comments that the Sentencing Commission has offered to interpret the guidelines. Amidst the turmoil over the sentencing guidelines, Attorney General Janet Reno ordered a Justice Department review of the impact of the guidelines on the justice system. She said she was concerned because "I am receiving information…from the United States Attorneys around the country saying that their hands are tied by the approach of the minimum mandatory sentence, and that money is being wasted because [low-level, nonviolent drug offenders] could be reintegrated into the community without further concern about crime."[44]

THE SENTENCING ENVIRONMENT

A number of studies have attempted to investigate the decision-making process that leads to imposition of a particular sentence. Early studies[45] found a strong relationship between the informal influence of members of the courtroom work group and the severity, or lack thereof, of sentences imposed. A number suggested that minorities ran a much greater risk of imprisonment.[46] Other studies have found that sentencing variations are responsive to extralegal conditions[47] and that public opinion can play a role in the type of sentence handed down.[48] If these findings about public opinion are true, they might explain some of the increase in prison populations. A 1987 public opinion study conducted by Bowling Green State University, for example, found that 71% of respondents selected incarceration as the preferred punishment for serious offenses.[49]

JUSTICE IN AMERICAN CONTEXT...

Proposed caps on drug sentences.

A judicial panel recently proposed restructuring federal sentencing guidelines as they relate to drug offenses. In 1987 federally sentenced drug offenders received an average of two years in prison. Today the average is over seven years. The federal prison population in 1987 totaled approximately 44,000 persons. Today it is more than double that figure, and growing—with the largest increase coming from drug-sentenced offenders.

The panel is working to ensure that minor offenders receive appropriate penalties. Under current law, minor drug offenders often receive sentences similar to those handed out to drug kingpins. The problems stem from peculiarities in the law. Among the proposals:

- Punish crack cocaine offenders the same as powdered cocaine offenders. The way the sentencing act was originally written means that crack offenders can receive 100 times the amount of prison time as those caught with powdered cocaine. Many consider the original law racist since, when arrested for drug offenses, minorities are more likely to be found with crack than with other forms of cocaine. In fact, statistics show that 92.6% of those arrested for crack-related offenses are black, while 70.3% of powdered cocaine defendants are white.
- Bring sentences for LSD into line with other drug sentences. Under the original law offenders could be sentenced according to the weight of the controlled substance in their possession. Since a typical dose of LSD is practically weightless, authorities were allowed to count the weight of the substance on which the LSD was transported or stored—in many cases pieces of paper. When the weight of the paper was included, offenders in possession of $1,000 of LSD received sentences similar to those handed out to offenders holding $120,000 worth of heroin at the time of their arrest.
- Stop sentencing defendants to prison for crimes of which they are acquitted. Under current law, defendants facing multiple charges can be sentenced for the total amount of drugs found in their possession, even when they are found actually guilty of possessing only a fraction of that amount.
- Increase judicial discretion in deciding which defendants get lessened sentences for cooperating with authorities. In practice, federal prosecutors now make such decisions with the result that higher-ranking drug defendants who are likely to have more information to barter with receive lower sentences than less serious offenders who have little or no information to exchange.

Each of these proposals, the panel feels, will result in greater equity and fairness, as well as reduce the strain on overcrowded federal prisons.

Source: "Judicial Panel Proposes Cap on Drug Sentences," *USA Today*, March 22, 1993, p. 2A.

More recent analyses, especially in determinate sentencing jurisdictions, however, have begun to show that sentences in a number of jurisdictions are becoming more objective and, hence, predictable. A California study[50] of racial equity in sentencing, for example, found that the likelihood of going to prison was increased by:

- Having multiple current conviction counts, prior prison terms, and juvenile incarcerations.
- Being on adult and/or juvenile probation or parole at the time of the offense.
- Having been released from prison within 12 months of the current offense.
- Having a history of drug and/or alcohol abuse.
- Being over 21 years of age.
- Going to trial.
- Not being released prior to trial.
- Not being represented by a private attorney.

The same study found that, perhaps partly because of the 1977 California Determinate Sentencing Act, "California courts are making racially equitable sentencing decisions."[51] Findings applied only to the crimes of assault, robbery, burglary, theft, forgery, and drug abuse, but held for sentences involving both prison and probation. Similarly, no disparities were noted in the lengths of sentences imposed.[52] Other recent studies have found that female felons are not treated substantially differently by sentencing authorities than are their male counterparts.[53]

One of the most comprehensive studies of sentencing to date was published in 1987 by Martha Myers and Susette Talarico.[54] Myers and Talarico studied sentencing practices in Georgia and found an "absence of system-wide bias or discrimination"[55] and a reliance by judges on the seriousness of offenses and statutory guidelines in arriving at sentencing decisions. Myers and Talarico also reported that the social background of judges had little direct influence on sentencing outcomes. However, older judges, and those who were Baptists and religious fundamentalists, were found to be generally stricter than were younger judges. One interesting result of the study was the finding that Baptist and fundamentalist judges, while they did not appear to discriminate against minority defendants, seemed to hold white defendants to a higher standard of behavior.[56]

THE PRESENTENCE INVESTIGATION REPORT

Prior to imposing sentence a judge may request information on the background of a convicted defendant. This is especially true in nondeterminate sentencing jurisdictions, where judges retain considerable discretion in selecting sanctions. Traditional wisdom has held that the presence of certain factors in the lives of less serious offenders increase the likelihood of rehabilitation and reduce the need for lengthy prison terms. These indicators include a good job record, satisfactory educational attainment, strong family ties, church attendance, an arrest history of only nonviolent offenses, and psychological stability.

Information about a defendant's background often comes to the judge in the form of a presentence report. The task of preparing presentence reports usually falls to the probation/parole office. Presentence reports take one of three forms: (1) a detailed written report on the defendant's personal and criminal history, including an assessment of present conditions in the defendant's life (often called the "long form"); (2) an abbreviated written report summarizing the type of information most likely to be useful in a sentencing decision (the "short form"); and (3) a verbal report to the court made by the investigating

Presentence Investigation The examination of a convicted offender's background prior to sentencing. Presentence examinations are generally conducted by probation/parole officers and submitted to sentencing authorities.

officer based on field notes, but structured according to categories established for the purpose. A presentence report is much like a resume or *vitae* except that it focuses on what might be regarded as negative as well as positive life experiences.

Jurisdictions vary in their use of presentence reports and in the form they take. Federal law mandates presentence reports in federal criminal courts and specifies 15 topical areas which each report is to contain. The 1984 federal Determinate Sentencing Act directs report writers to include information on the classification of the offense and of the defendant under the categories established by the statute.

Some states require presentence reports only in felony cases, and others in cases where defendants face the possibility of incarceration for six months. Still others may have no requirement for presentence reports beyond those ordered by a judge. Even so, report writing, rarely anyone's favorite, may seriously tax the limited resources of probation agencies. According to Andrew Klein,[57] during a recent year New York state probation officers wrote 108,408 presentence investigation reports. Most (63,902) were for misdemeanors, but 44,506 reports described the backgrounds of newly convicted felons. In the same year in New York City alone, more than 37,000 presentence investigation reports were completed, averaging 25 reports per probation officer per month.

The length of the completed form is subject to great variation. One survey[58] found that Texas used one of the shortest forms of all—a one-page summary supplemented by other materials which the report writer thought might provide meaningful additional details. Orange County, California, provides an example of the opposite kind and may use the most detailed form of any jurisdiction in the country. The instructions for completing the form consist of a dozen single-spaced pages.[59]

A typical "long form" is divided into ten major informational sections as follows: (1) personal information and identifying data describing the defendant, (2) a chronology of the current offense and circumstances surrounding it, (3) a record of the defendant's previous convictions, if any, (4) home life and family data, (5) educational background, (6) health history and current state of health, (7) military service, (8) religious preference, (9) financial condition, and (10) sentencing recommendations made by the probation/parole officer completing the report.

The data on which a presentence report is based come from a variety of sources. Since the 1960s modern computer-based criminal information clearinghouses, such as the FBI's National Crime Information Center (NCIC), have simplified at least a part of the data gathering process. The NCIC began in 1967 and contains information on wanted persons throughout the United States. Individual jurisdictions also maintain criminal records repositories which are able to provide comprehensive files on the criminal history of persons processed by the justice system. In the late 1970s the federal government encouraged states to develop criminal records repositories utilizing computer technology.[60] The 15 years that followed have been described as "the focus of a data gathering effort more massive and more coordinated than any other in criminal justice."[61]

Almost any third-party data are subject to ethical and legal considerations. The official records of almost any agency or organization, while they may prove to be an ideal source of information, are often protected by state and federal privacy requirements. In particular, the Federal Privacy Act of 1974[62] may limit records access. Investigators should first check on the legal availability of all records before requesting them and should receive in writing the defendant's permission to access records. Other public laws, among them the federal Freedom of Information Act,[63] may make the presentence report itself available to the defendant, although courts and court officers have generally been held to be exempt from the provision of such statutes.

Sometimes the defendant is a significant source of much of the information which appears in the presentence report. When such is the case, efforts should be made to corroborate the information provided by the defendant. Unconfirmed data will generally be marked on the report as "defendant supplied data" or simply "unconfirmed."

The final section of a presentence report is usually devoted to recommendations made by the investigating officer. A recommendation may be made in favor of probation, split sentencing, a term of imprisonment, or any other sentencing options available in the jurisdiction. Participation in community service programs may be recommended for probationers, and drug or substance abuse programs may be suggested as well. Some authors have observed that a "judge accepts an officer's recommendation in an extremely high percentage of cases."[64] Most judges are willing to accept the report writer's recommendation because they recognize the professionalism of presentence investigators and because they know that the investigator may well be the supervising officer assigned to the defendant should a community alternative be the sentencing decision.

Presentence reports may be useful sentencing tools. Many officers who prepare them take their responsibility seriously. A recent study,[65] however, shows a tendency among presentence investigators to satisfy judicial expectations about defendants by tailoring reports to fit the image the defendant projects. Prior criminal record and present offense may provide a kind of shorthand used by investigators to interpret all the other data they gather.[66]

VICTIM IMPACT STATEMENTS

Victim Impact Statement The in-court use of victim- or survivor-supplied information by sentencing authorities wishing to make an informed sentencing decision.

The growth of a national victim-witness rights movement has been described earlier in this book. One consequence of the movement has been a call for the use of victim impact statements prior to sentencing. A victim impact statement generally takes the form of a written document which describes the losses, suffering, and trauma experienced by the crime victim or the victim's survivors. Judges are expected to consider it in arriving at an appropriate sanction for the offender.

Although the drive to mandate inclusion of victim impact statements in sentencing decisions has gathered much momentum, their final role has yet to be decided. The Victim Task Force, commissioned by then-President Reagan shortly after he took office, recommended adoption of a change to the Sixth Amendment of the U.S. Constitution. The Commission specifically recommended adding the words "Likewise, the victim, in every criminal prosecution shall have the right to be present and to be heard at all critical stages of judical proceedings."[67] Although such an amendment may be a long way off, significant federal legislation has already occurred. The 1982 Victim and Witness Protection Act[68] requires victim impact statements to be considered at sentencing, and places responsibility for their creation on federal probation officers.

Some states have gone the federal government one better. In 1984 the state of California, for example, passed legislation[69] to allow victims a right to attend and participate in sentencing and parole hearings. Approximately 20 states now have laws mandating citizen involvement in sentencing. Where written victim impact statements are not available, courts may invite the victim to testify directly at sentencing.

The case of actress Theresa Saldana is representative of the many victims who feel they need more say in sentencing and parole decisions. Saldana, featured in such movies as *Raging Bull* and *I Want to Hold Your Hand*, was attacked outsider her apartment by a crazed drifter in 1982. She was stabbed ten times, and may have been saved only by the fact that the knife her attacker was wielding bent from the force of the blows. Although seriously injured, she recovered. The man who attacked her, Arthur Jackson, had a long history of psychiatric problems and claimed to be on a divine mission to unite with Ms. Saldana in heaven. Although imprisoned for the attack, Jackson continued to write his victim, promising that when he got out he would finish the job. California prison authorities claimed they were powerless to stop his letters.

In 1984, under California's new victim's right statute, Ms. Saldana testified before a resentencing body considering Jackson's case. "I will never forget the searing, ghastly pain, the grotesque and devastating experience of this person nearly butchering me to death, or the bone-chilling sight of my own blood splattered everywhere,"[70] she told the examiners. Her testimony resulted in Jackson's release being delayed until June 1989. As Jackson's release date arrived, Ms. Saldana told reporters: "It is just unbelievable that he is getting out. I feel like I am in a nightmare. I really feel my rights are being overlooked. Why is it life, liberty and the pursuit of happiness (are) being taken from me?"[71]

There is little information to date on what changes, if any, the appearance of victims at sentencing is having on the criminal justice system. At least one study, however, found that very few victims are taking advantage of their new-found opportunities. Fewer than 3% of California victims chose to appear or testify at sentencing hearings after that state's new victim rights law was enacted.[72]

In 1987 the constitutionality of victim impact statements was called into question by the U.S. Supreme Court in the case of *Booth* v. *Maryland.*[73] The case involved Irvin Bronstein, age 78, and his wife Rose, age 75, who were robbed and brutally murdered in their home in Baltimore, Maryland, in 1983. The killers were John Booth and Willie Reid, acquaintances of the Bronstein's, caught stealing to support heroin habits. The bodies were discovered two days later by a son. The murder had occurred at the time a family wedding was scheduled.

The rights of victims are still emerging. Here, actress Theresa Saldana, who survived a gruesome knife attack by a crazed drifter, speaks out in support of victim's rights. *Photo: AP/Wide World Photos.*

After being convicted of murder, Booth decided to allow the jury (rather than the judge) to set his sentence. The jury considered a victim impact statement which was part of a presentence report prepared by probation officers—as required by state law. The victim impact statement used in the case was a powerful one, describing the wholesome personal qualities of the Bronsteins and the emotional suffering experienced by their children as a result of the murder.

After receiving a death sentence, Booth appealed to the U.S. Supreme Court. The Court overturned his sentence, reasoning that victim impact statements, at least in capital cases, violate the Eighth Amendment ban on cruel and unusual punishments. In a close (5-to-4) decision, the majority held that information in victim impact statements leads to the risk that the death penalty might be imposed in an arbitrary and capricious manner.

In a complete about face, affected in no small part by the gathering conservative majority among its justices, the Supreme Court held in the 1991 case of *Payne* v. *Tennessee*[74] that the *Booth* ruling had been based upon "a misreading of precedent."[75] The *Payne* case began with a 1987 double murder, in which a 28-year-old mother and 2-year-old daughter were stabbed to death in Millington, Tennessee.[76] A second child, 3-year-old Nicholas Christopher, himself severely wounded in the incident, witnessed the deaths of his mother and young sister. In a trial following the killings, the prosecution claimed that Pervis Tyrone Payne, a 20-year-old retarded man, had killed the mother and child after the woman resisted his sexual advances. Payne was convicted of both murders. At the sentencing phase of the trial Mary Zvolanek, Nicholas's grandmother, testified that the boy continued to cry out daily for his dead sister. Following *Booth*, Payne's conviction was upheld by the Tennessee supreme court in an opinion which then-Justice Thurgood Marshall said did little to disguise the Tennessee court's contempt for the precedent set by *Booth*.

> There can be no doubt that the taking of the life of the President creates much more societal harm than the taking of the life of a homeless person.
>
> —*Tennessee Attorney General Charles Burson
> arguing before the U.S. Supreme Court in*
> Payne *v.* Tennessee (*1991*)

This time, however, the Supreme Court agreed with the Tennessee justices, holding that "[v]ictim impact evidence is simply another form or method of informing the sentencing authority about the specific harm caused by the crime in question, evidence of a general type long considered by sentencing authorities." As Chief Justice Rehnquist wrote for the majority, "[c]ourts have always taken into consideration the harm done by the defendant in imposing sentence." In a concurring opinion, Justice Antonin Scalia held that "*Booth* significantly harms our criminal justice system…" and had been decided with "plainly inadequate rational support." Given the seemingly firm authority with which the Court's conservative majority now speaks, it is likely that the *Payne* decision will remain in place for a long time to come.

TRADITIONAL SENTENCING OPTIONS

Sentencing is fundamentally a risk management strategy designed to protect the public while serving the ends of rehabilitation, deterrence, retribution, and restoration. Because the goals of sentencing are difficult to agree upon, so are sanctions. Lengthy prison terms do little for rehabilitation, while community release programs can hardly protect the innocent from offenders bent on continuing criminality.

Assorted sentencing philosophies continue to permeate state-level judicial systems. Each state has its own sentencing laws, and frequent revisions of those statutes are not uncommon. Because of huge variation from one state to another in the laws and procedures which control the imposition of criminal sanctions, sentencing has been called "the most diversified part of the Nation's criminal justice process."[77]

There is at least one common ground, however. It can be found in the four traditional sanctions which continue to dominate the thinking of most legislators and judges. The four traditional sanctions are

- Incarceration
- Probation
- Fines
- Death

In the case of indeterminate sentencing, the first three options are widely available to judges. The option selected generally depends upon the severity of the offense and the judge's best guess as to the likelihood of future criminal involvement on the part of the defendant. Sometimes two or more options are combined, as when an offender might be fined and sentenced to prison or placed on probation and fined in support of restitution payments.

Jurisdictions which operate under presumptive sentencing guidelines generally limit the judge's choice to only one option and often specify the extent to which that option can be applied. Dollar amounts of fines, for example, are rigidly set, and prison terms are specified for each type of offense. The death penalty remains an option in a fair number of jurisdictions, but only for a highly select group of offenders.

Recently, the Bureau of Justice Statistics reported on the sentencing practices of state felony courts.[78] Highlights of the study, using data gathered by the National Judicial Reporting Program, showed that state courts annually convict about 677,000 persons of felonies. Of these,

- 43% are sentenced to active prison terms.
- 26% receive jail sentences, usually involving less than a year's confinement.
- 30% are sentenced to straight probation.
- 1% receive other sentences not involving incarceration.
- the average prison sentence is six years and three months.
- the average amount of time served in confinement for felons receiving active sentences will average about two years before release, due to considerations for good time and other credits.

Figure 10–2 shows these data graphically.

The same survey revealed that 41% of those convicted in state courts of drug trafficking were sentenced to prison. Twenty-eight percent of drug trafficking convictions, however, resulted in probation, while 30% of convicted traffickers were sent to local jails for brief terms of imprisonment. Although the number of active sentences handed out may seem low to some, the number of criminal defendants receiving such sentences is increasing. Figure 10–3 shows that court-ordered prison commitments have increased approximately fourfold in the past 30 years.

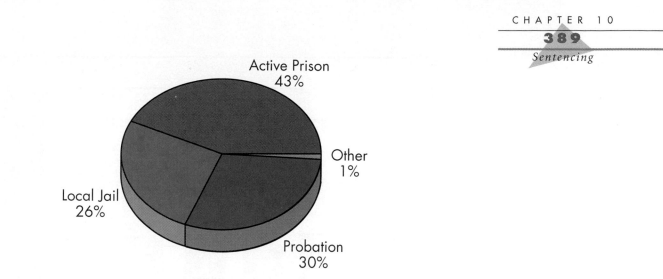

FIGURE 10–2   The sentencing of convicted felons in state courts by type of sentence. *Source:* Richard Solari, *National Judicial Reporting Program 1988* (Washington, D.C.: Bureau of Justice Statistics, 1992).

FINES

The fine is one of the oldest forms of punishment, predating even the Code of Hammurabi.[79] Until recently, however, the use of fines as criminal sanctions suffered from built-in inequities and a widespread failure to collect them. Inequities arose when offenders with vastly different financial resources were fined similar amounts. A fine of $100, for example, can place a painful economic burden upon a poor defendant, but is only laughable when imposed on a wealthy offender.

Today fines are once again receiving attention as serious sentencing alternatives. One reason for the renewed interest is the stress placed upon state resources by burgeoning prison populations. The extensive imposition of fines not only results in less crowded prisons but can contribute to state and local coffers and lower the tax burden of law-abiding citizens. Other advantages of the use of fines as criminal sanctions include the following:

- Fines can deprive offenders of the proceeds of criminal activity.
- Fines can promote rehabilitation by enforcing economic responsibility.
- Fines can be collected by existing criminal justice agencies, and are relatively inexpensive to administer.
- Fines can be made proportionate to both the severity of the offense and the ability of the offender to pay.

A recent National Institute of Justice survey found that an average of 86% of convicted defendants in courts of limited jurisdiction receive fines as sentences, some in combination with another penalty.[80] Fines are also experiencing widespread use in courts of general jurisdiction, where the National Institute of Justice study found judges imposing fines in 42% of all cases which came before them for sentencing. Some studies estimate that over $1 billion in fines are collected nationwide each year.[81]

Fines are often imposed for relatively minor law violations such as driving while intoxicated, reckless driving, disturbing the peace, disorderly conduct, public drunkenness, and

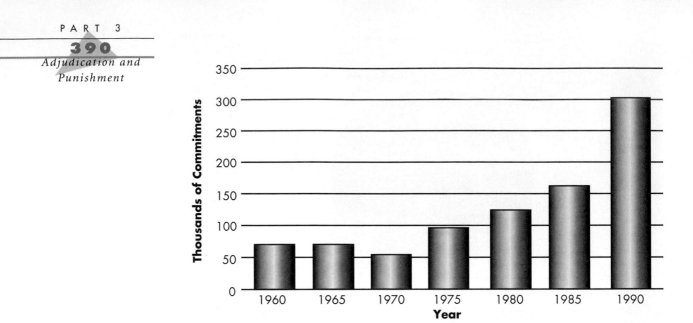

FIGURE 10–3 Court-ordered prison commitments, 1960–1990. *Source:* Bureau of Justice Statistics, telephone conference June 11, 1993, and BJS, *Prisoners in 1992* (Washington, D.C.: BJS, 1993).

vandalism. Judges in many courts, however, report the use of fines for relatively serious violations of the law, including assault, auto theft, embezzlement, fraud, and the sale and possession of various controlled substances. Fines are much more likely to be imposed, however, where the offender has both a clean record and the ability to pay.[82]

Opposition to the use of fines is based upon the following arguments:

- Fines may result in the release of convicted offenders into the community, but do not impose stringent controls on their behavior.
- Fines are a relatively mild form of punishment, and are not consistent with "just deserts" philosophy.
- Fines discriminate against the poor and favor the wealthy.
- Indigent offenders are especially subject to discrimination since they entirely lack the financial resources with which to pay fines.
- Fines are difficult to collect.

A number of these objections can be answered by procedures which make available to judges complete financial information on defendants. Studies have found, however, that courts of limited jurisdiction, which are the most likely to impose fines, are also the least likely to have adequate information on offenders' economic status.[83] Perhaps as a consequence, judges themselves are often reluctant to impose fines. Two of the most widely cited objections by judges to the use of fines are (1) fines allow more affluent offenders to "buy their way out" and (2) poor offenders cannot pay fines.[84]

A solution to both objections can be found in the Scandinavian system of day fines. The day-fine system is based upon the idea that fines should be proportionate to the severity of the offense, but also need to take into account the financial resources of the offender. Day fines are computed by first assessing the seriousness of the offense, the defendant's degree of culpability, and his or her prior record as measured in "days." The use of days as a benchmark of seriousness is related to the fact that, without fines, the offender could be sentenced to a number of days (or months or years) in jail or prison. The number of days

Fines are a widely used sentencing option in today's criminal justice system. Here a Phoenix Municipal court clerk works out a payment schedule for a court-imposed fine. The computer in the background alerts personnel when offenders fall behind in scheduled payments. *Courtesy of the Phoenix Municipal Court.*

an offender is assessed is then multiplied by the daily wages that person earns. Hence, if two persons were sentenced to a five-day fine, but one earned only $20 per day, and the other $200 per day, the first would pay a $100 fine, and the second $1,000.

In 1992 the National Institute of Justice reported on an experimental program conducted by the Richmond County Criminal Court in Staten Island, New York, which was designed to introduce and assess the use of day fines in the United States.[85] The Institute also reported on a similar 12-week experimental program involving the use of day fines by the Milwaukee Municipal Court. Both studies concluded that "the day fine can play a major...role as an intermediate sanction"[86] and that "the day-fine concept could be implemented in a typical American limited-jurisdiction court."[87]

DEATH: THE ULTIMATE SANCTION

Capital punishment has a long and gruesome history. As times changed, so did accepted methods of execution. Under the Davidic monarchy, biblical Israel institutionalized the practice of stoning convicts to death.[88] The entire community where the crime occurred had the opportunity to participate in dispatching the offender. As an apparent aid to deterrence, the convict's deceased body could be impaled on a post at the gates of the city or otherwise exposed to the elements for a period of time.[89]

Capital Punishment
Another term for the death penalty. Capital punishment is the most extreme of all sentencing options.

Athenian society, around 200 B.C., was progressive by the standards of its day. The ancient Greeks restricted the use of capital punishment and limited the suffering of the condemned through the use of poison derived from the hemlock tree. Socrates, the famous Greek orator, accused of being a political subversive, died this way.

The Romans were far less sensitive. Beheading was the form capital punishment most often took in ancient Rome, although the law provided that arsonists should be burned and false witnesses thrown from a high rock.[90] Suspected witches were clubbed to death, and slaves were ignominiously strangled. Even more brutal sanctions, including drawing and quartering, and throwing to the lions were used on rabble rousers, Christians, and other social outcasts.

After the fall of the Roman Empire, Europe was plunged into the Dark Ages, a period of superstition marked by widespread illiteracy and political turmoil. The Dark Ages lasted from 426 A.D. until the early thirteenth century. During the Dark Ages, executions were institutionalized through the use of ordeals designed to both judge and punish. Suspects were submerged in cold water, dumped in boiling oil, crushed under huge stones, forced to do battle with professional soldiers, or thrown into bonfires. Theological arguments prevalent at the time held that innocents, protected by God and heavenly forces, would emerge from any ordeal unscathed, while guilty parties would perish. Trial by ordeal was eliminated through a decree of the Fourth Lateran Council of 1215, under the direction of Pope Innocent III, after later evidence proved that many who died in ordeals could not have committed the crimes of which they were accused.[91]

Capital Offense A criminal offense punishable by death.

> ...the evolving standards of human decency will finally lead to the abolition of the death penalty in this country
>
> —*William Brennan*
> *Former U.S. Supreme Court Justice*

Following the Fourth Lateran Council, trials, much as we know them today, became the basis for judging guilt or innocence. The death penalty remained in widespread use. As recently as a century and a half ago, 160 crimes were punishable in England by death.[92] The young received no special privilege. In 1801 a child of 13 was hanged in Tyburn, England, for stealing a spoon.[93]

Sophisticated techniques of execution were in use by the nineteenth century. One engine of death was the guillotine, invented in France around the time of the French Revolution. The guillotine was described by its creator, Dr. Joseph-Ignace Guillotin, as "a cool breath on the back of the neck"[94] and found widespread use in eliminating opponents of the Revolution.

In America hanging became the preferred mode of execution. It was especially popular on the frontier, since it required little by way of special materials, and was a relatively efficient means of dispatch. By the early 1890s electrocution had replaced hanging as the preferred form of capital punishment in America. The appeal of electrocution was that it stopped the heart without visible signs of gross bodily trauma.

Executions: The Grim Facts

The twentieth century has seen a constant decline in the number of persons legally executed in the United States. Accurate statistics on the number of persons legally executed began to be collected around 1930. Between 1930 and 1967, when the U.S. Supreme Court ordered a stay of pending executions, nearly 3,800 persons were put to death. The years 1935 and 1936 were peak years, with nearly 200 legal killings each year. Executions declined substantially

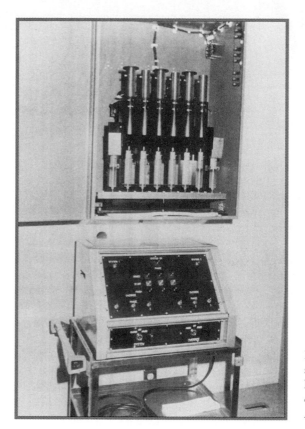

Lethal injection apparatus. Most states still retain capital punishment and the large majority of those authorize execution through lethal injection. *Photo: AP/Wide World Photos.*

every year thereafter. Between 1967 and 1977 a de facto moratorium existed, with no executions carried out in any U.S. jurisdiction. Following the lifting of the moratorium executions increased. In 1992, 31 offenders were put to death, the highest since the lifting of the ban.

Today, 36 of the 50 states and the federal government retain capital punishment laws. All 36 permit execution for first-degree murder, while treason, kidnaping, the murder of a police or correctional officer, and murder while under a life sentence are punishable by death in selected jurisdictions.[95] Of the 2,623 persons under sentence of death throughout the United States at midyear 1992, 98% were male, 53% were white, 40% were black, and 5% were Hispanic (Native Americans, Pacific Islanders, and "others" made up the remainder of groups reported in statistical tabulations).[96]

Methods of imposing death vary by state. The majority of death penalty states authorize execution through lethal injection. Electrocution is the second most common means of dispatch, while hanging, the gas chamber, and firing squads have survived, at least as options available to the condemned, in a few states.

Opposition to Death

Capital punishment is not without recognized problems. One serious difficulty centers on the fact that automatic review of all death sentences by appellate courts and constant legal maneuvering by defense counsel often lead to a dramatic delay between the time sentence is passed and the time it is carried out. Such lengthy delays, compounded with uncertainty over whether a sentence will ever be finally imposed, directly contravene the generally accepted notion that punishment should be swift and certain.

THEORY INTO PRACTICE

IS IT CRUEL AND UNUSUAL PUNISHMENT TO EXECUTE JUVENILES AND THE RETARDED?

The death penalty has undergone considerable legal scrutiny. Following the 1972 Supreme Court decision of *Furman* v. *Georgia*, which effectively struck down the capital punishment statutes of 37 states, many predicted the end of executions in the United States. The *Furman* decision was quickly and effectively laid aside two years later, however, when the Court, in *Gregg* v. *Georgia*, accepted modified state statutes which reduced discretion in the application of the death penalty and which required a two-stage trial procedure: one for determinations of guilt or innocence and the other for sentencing considerations.

In 1989 an increasingly conservative Supreme Court, led by Chief Justice William Rehnquist, returned two historic decisions. In one, the Court ruled that the Eighth Amendment ban on cruel and unusual punishment does not forbid the execution of youths who commit crimes at 16 or 17 years of age. In the other, the Court held that mentally retarded defendants who commit capital offenses cannot be automatically excluded from facing the same sanctions as others. At the time of the decision, 24 of the 2,189 inmates awaiting execution had committed their crimes at age 16 or 17. As many as 300 might have been considered retarded.

Public opinion polls conducted by *Time* magazine and Cable News Network at the time of the decisions showed that 75% of Americans polled favored the death penalty for persons convicted of serious crimes, while 17% were opposed. A smaller majority, 57%, favored the death penalty for 16- and 17-year-olds convicted of such crimes. In its majority opinion, the Court, as it had done in *Gregg*, cited the role public support for capital punishment had in its decision. Justice Scalia, in counting the relatively small number of states which prohibit the execution of persons under 18, wrote, "This does not establish the degree of national consensus…" needed to overrule such a practice.

Reaction to the decisions included support from a wide range of groups. Daniel Popeo, head of the conservative Washington Legal Foundation, declared that "the days of criminals' getting off on technicalities are over." Similar sentiments were echoed by Phil Caruso, president of the New York Patrolmen's Benevolent Association. Caruso saw the decisions as reasonable: "These are sound decisions," he said, "in keeping with what's happening on our streets today." On the other side of the issue, American Civil Liberties Union spokesperson Henry Schwarzchild berated the justices for listening too closely to public opinion. Said Schwarzchild, "For the court to act as though it were a political instrumentality, which merely reacts to the wishes of the general society, is an abdication of the responsibility to make constitutional judgments." Richard Burr of the NAACP's Legal Defense and Educational Fund summed up the problems with the Court's strategy: "If all the Justices can do is survey…and declare a winner, you don't need a court," Burr said. "All you need is someone who can count."

Sources: "Bad News for Death Row," *Time*, July 10, 1989, pp. 48–49, and Tony Mauro, "Court called 'Barbaric' on Death Penalty." *USA Today*, June 27, 1989, p. 1A.

Delays in the imposition of capital sanctions have been the source of much anguish for condemned prisoners as well as for the victims and the family members of both. In a recent speech before the American Bar Association, Chief Justice William H. Rehnquist called for reforms of the current federal habeas corpus system, which allows condemned prisoners constant opportunities for appeal. In the words of Rehnquist, "The capital defendant does not need to prevail on the merits in order to accomplish his purpose; he wins temporary victories by postponing a final adjudication."[97]

The first recorded attempt to abolish the death penalty in the United States occurred at the home of Benjamin Franklin in 1787.[98] At a meeting on March 9 of that year, Dr. Benjamin Rush, a signer of the Declaration of Independence and leading medical pioneer, read a paper against capital punishment to a small but influential audience. Although his immediate efforts came to naught, his arguments laid the groundwork for many debates which followed. Michigan, widely regarded as the first abolitionist state, joined the Union in 1847 without a death penalty. A number of other states, including New York, Massachusetts, West Virginia, Wisconsin, Minnesota, Alaska, and Hawaii, have since spurned death as a possible sanction for criminal acts. Many Western European countries have also rejected the death penalty. As noted earlier, it remains a viable sentencing option in 36 of the states and all federal jurisdictions. As a consequence, arguments continue to rage over its value.

Today, four main abolitionist rationales are heard:

1. The death penalty can and has been inflicted on innocent people.
2. Evidence has shown that the death penalty is not an effective deterrent.
3. The imposition of the death penalty is, by the nature of our legal system, completely arbitrary and even discriminatory.
4. Human life is sacred, and killing at the hands of the state is not a righteous act, but rather one which is on the same moral level as the crimes committed by the condemned.

The first three abolitionist claims are pragmatic; that is, they are subject to at least limited measurability and therefore some degree of verifiability. The last claim is primarily philosophical and therefore not amenable to scientific investigation.

While some evidence does exist that a few innocent people have been executed, most research by far has centered on examining the deterrent effect of the death penalty. During the 1970s and 1980s[99] the deterrent effect of the death penalty became a favorite subject for debate in academic circles. Studies[100] of states which had eliminated the death penalty failed to show any increase in homicide rates. Similar studies[101] of neighboring states, in which jurisdictions retaining capital punishment were compared with those which had abandoned it, also failed to demonstrate any significant differences. Although death penalty advocates remain numerous, few any longer argue for the penalty based on its deterrent effects. Deterrent studies continue, however. In 1988, for example, a comprehensive review[102] of capital punishment in Texas, which correlated executions since 1930 with homicide rates, failed again to find any support for the use of death as a deterrent. The study was especially significant because Texas had been very active in the capital punishment arena, executing 317 persons between 1930 and 1986.[103]

The abolitionist claim that the death penalty is discriminatory is harder to investigate. While there may be past evidence that blacks and other minorities in the United States have been disproportionately sentenced to death,[104] the present evidence is not so clear. At first glance, disproportionality seems apparent: 45 of the 98 prisoners executed between January 1977 and May 1988 were black or Hispanic; 84 of the 98 had been convicted of killing whites.[105] For an accurate appraisal to be made, however, any claims of disproportionality must go beyond simple comparisons with racial representation in the larger population and must somehow measure both frequency and seriousness of capital crimes between and within racial groups. Following that line of reasoning, the Supreme Court, in the 1987 case of *McCleskey* v. *Kemp*[106] held that a simple showing of racial discrepancies in the application of the death penalty does not constitute a constitutional violation.

Justifications for Death

Justifications for the death penalty are collectively referred to as the retentionist position. Retentionist arguments are three in number. They are (1) revenge, (2) just deserts, and (3) protection. Those who justify capital punishment as revenge, attempt to appeal to the visceral feeling that survivors, victims, and the state are entitled to "closure." Only after execution of the criminal perpetrator, they say, can the psychological and social wounds engendered by the offense begin to heal.

The just deserts argument is slightly different. It makes the simple and straightforward claim that some people deserve to die for what they have done. Death is justly deserved; anything less cannot suffice as a sanction for the most heinous crimes. As Justice Potter Stewart once wrote, "the decision that capital punishment may be the appropriate sanction in extreme cases is an expression of the community's belief that certain crimes are themselves so grievous an affront to humanity that the only adequate response may be the penalty of death."[107]

The third retentionist claim, that of protection, asserts that offenders, once executed, can commit no further crimes. Clearly the least emotional of the retentionist claims, the protectionist argument may also be the weakest, since societal interests in protection can also be met in other ways such as incarceration. In addition, various studies have shown that there is little likelihood of repeat offenses among people convicted of murder and later released.[108] One reason for such observations, however, may be that murderers generally serve lengthy prison sentences prior to release and may have lost whatever youthful propensity for criminality they previously possessed.

The Future of the Death Penalty

Because of the nature of the positions both advocate, there is little common ground even for discussion between retentionists and abolitionists. Foes of the death penalty hope that its demonstrated lack of deterrent capacity will convince others that capital punishment should be abandoned. Their approach, based as it is upon statistical evidence, appears on the surface to be quite rational. However, it is doubtful that many capital punishment opponents could be persuaded to support the death penalty even if statistics showed it to be a deterrent. Likewise, the tactics of death penalty supporters are equally instinctive. Retentionists could probably not be swayed by statistical studies of deterrence, no matter what they show, since their support is bound up with emotional calls for retribution.

The future of the death penalty rests primarily on legislative authority. Short of renewed Supreme Court intervention, the future of capital punishment may depend more upon popular opinion than it does on arguments pro or con. Elected legislatures, because the careers of their members lie in the hands of their constituency, are likely to follow the public mandate. Hence, it may be that studies of public attitudes toward the death penalty may have the greatest utility in predicting the sanction's future.

National opinion polls conducted by the Gallup and Harris organizations detail massive support for capital punishment as far back as 1936, but show a gradual decline in backing until 1966, when a resurgence in support began.[109] The proportion of the American public which today endorses the death penalty in national polls is at an all-time high since record keeping began, surpassing even the support of 1936.[110] When asked if they would still favor the death penalty if evidence showed conclusively that it did not deter criminals, a slim majority of Americans still say "yes."[111]

Demographic differences account for a considerable degree of variation in public opinion polls. Robert Bohm, for example, analyzing differences among respondents in nearly two dozen polls reports that[112] (1) "[i]n all 21 polls, the percentage of whites who favor the death penalty is greater than the percentage of blacks, while the percentage of blacks opposed and undecided is greater than the percentage of whites"; (2) "[i]n every year for which there are data, people in the top income or socioeconomic category have been more likely to support the death penalty and less likely to oppose it than people in the bottom category"; (3) "[i]n all 21 polls, the percentage of males who favor the death penalty exceeds the percentage of females, and the percentage of females opposed to the death penalty exceeds the percentage of males"; (4) "Democrats have shown the greatest opposition and the least support for the death penalty, Independents are less opposed and more supportive, and Republicans are least opposed and most supportive"; and (5) "...the South, surprisingly, has been the region least likely to support and most likely to oppose the death penalty." Other variables, such as age, religion, occupation, and city size, show less clear-cut relationships to self-avowed attitudes toward the death penalty.[113]

Some contemporary studies[114] have purported to show that support for capital punishment may be a relatively abstract form of endorsement. According to Frank P. Williams and Dennis Longmire, "A majority of citizens assert support for the general concept of the death penalty but their willingness to advocate execution as an acceptable sanction decreases as they are asked about its use in specific instances.[115] Even so, few legislators are apt to examine closely the results of polls which show such strong public leanings.

Changes in public opinion could conceivably come quickly, however. Citing the First Amendment to the U.S. Constitution, California TV station KQED filed suit in 1990 in U.S. District Court in San Francisco asking that it be allowed to provide broadcast coverage of executions. The lawsuit claimed that the current state policy, of barring cameras at executions, "impedes effective reporting of executions which are events of major public and political significance."[116] Although the station's claims were denied by the court in a 1991 opinion, the station is considering an appeal.

The Courts and Death

The U.S. Supreme Court has served as a constant sounding board for issues surrounding the death penalty. One of the court's earliest cases in this area was *Wilkerson* v. *Utah* (1878),[117] which questioned shooting as a method of execution and raised Eighth Amendment claims that firing squads constituted a form of cruel and unusual punishment. The Court disagreed, however, contrasting the relatively civilized nature of firing squads with the various forms of torture often associated with capital punishment around the time the Bill of Rights was written.

In similar fashion, electrocution was supported as a permissible form of execution in *In re Kemmler* (1890).[118] In *Kemmler*, the Court defined cruel and unusual methods of execution as follows: "Punishments are cruel when they involve torture or a lingering death; but the punishment of death is not cruel, within the meaning of that word as used in the Constitution. It implies there something inhuman and barbarous, something more than the mere extinguishing of life."[119] Almost 60 years later, the Court ruled that a second attempt at the electrocution of a convicted person did not violate the Eighth Amendment.[120] The Court reasoned that the initial failure was the consequence of accident or unforeseen circumstances, and not the result of an effort on the part of executioners to be intentionally cruel.

It was not until 1972, however, in the landmark case of *Furman* v. *Georgia*,[121] that the Court recognized "evolving standards of decency"[122] which might necessitate a reconsideration of Eighth Amendment guarantees. In a 5-to-4 ruling the *Furman* decision invalidated Georgia's death penalty statute on the basis that it allowed a jury unguided discretion in the imposition of a capital sentence. The majority of justices concluded that the Georgia statute, which permitted a jury to decide simultaneously issues of guilt or innocence while it weighed sentencing options, allowed for an arbitrary and capricious application of the death penalty.

Many other states with statutes similar to Georgia's were affected by the *Furman* ruling, but moved quickly to modify their procedures. What evolved was a two-step procedure to be used in capital cases. During the first, or trial phase, the guilt or innocence of the defendant was decided. If conviction resulted, then a second, or sentencing, stage was initiated during which separate arguments were made as to the appropriateness of death or other sanctions.

The two-step trial procedure was specifically approved by the Court in *Gregg* v. *Georgia* (1976).[123] In *Gregg* the Court upheld the two-stage procedural requirements of Georgia's new capital punishment law as necessary for ensuring the separation of the highly personal information needed in a sentencing decision, from the kinds of information reasonably permissible in a jury trial where issues of guilt or innocence alone are being decided. In the opinion written for the majority, the Court for the first time recognized the significance of public opinion in deciding upon the legitimacy of questionable sanctions.[124] Its opinion cited the strong showing of public support for the death penalty following *Furman* to mean that death was still a socially and culturally acceptable penalty.

Post-*Gregg* decisions set limits upon the use of death as a penalty for all but the most severe crimes. In 1977, in the case of *Coker* v. *Georgia*,[125] the Court struck down a Georgia law imposing the death penalty for the rape of an adult woman. The Court concluded that capital punishment under such circumstances would be "grossly disproportionate" to the crime. Somewhat later, in *Woodson* v. *North Carolina*[126] a law requiring mandatory application of the death penalty for specific crimes was overturned.

In two 1990 rulings, *Blystone* v. *Pennsylvania*, and *Boyde* v. *California*, the Court upheld state statutes which had been interpreted to dictate that death penalties must be imposed where juries find a lack of mitigating factors capable of offsetting obvious aggravating circumstances. Similarly, in the 1990 case of R. Gene Simmons, an Arkansas mass murderer convicted of killing 16 relatives during a 1987 shooting rampage, the Court granted inmates under sentence of death the right to waive appeals. Prior to the *Simmons* case, any interested party could file a brief on behalf of condemned persons—with or without their consent.

Today, an average of 7 years and 11 months[127] passes between the time a sentence of death is imposed and it is carried out. In a strong move to reduce delays in the conduct of executions, the U.S. Supreme Court, in the case of *McCleskey* v. *Zandt* (1991),[128] limited the numbers of appeals a condemned person may lodge with the courts. Saying that repeated filings for the sole purpose of delay promotes "disrespect for the finality of convictions" and "disparages the entire criminal justice system," the Court established a two-pronged criterion for future appeals. According to *McCleskey*, in any petition beyond the first, filed with the federal court, capital defendants must demonstrate (1) good cause why the claim now being made was not included in the first filing and (2) how the absence of that claim may have harmed the petitioner's ability to mount an effective defense. Two months later, the Court reinforced *McCleskey*, when it ruled, in *Coleman* v. *Thompson*,[129] that state prisoners could not cite "procedural default," such as a defense attorney's failure to meet a state's filing deadline for appeals, as the basis for an appeal to federal court.

Observers noted that the Court's spate of decisions limiting the opportunity of convicted offenders to appeal would swiftly and dramatically increase the rate of executions across the nation. Shortly thereafter, Florida death row inmate Bobby Marion Francis became the first person put to death in the post-*McCleskey* period. Francis had been convicted of the 1975 torture death of a drug informant, Titus R. Walters. In an attempt to kill Walters, Francis injected him with Drano and battery acid, then shot him twice in the head.

Still conscious, Walters was finally shot through the heart. Francis died in Florida's electric chair on June 25, 1991 at 7:07 A.M., 16 years after torturing and killing Walters.

Finally, in a 1993 hearing, *Poyner* v. *Murray*,[130] the U.S. Supreme Court hinted at the possibility of reopening questions first raised in *Kemmler*. The case challenged Virginia's use of the electric chair as a form of cruel and unusual punishment. Syvasky Lafayette Poyner, who originally brought the case before the Court, lost his bid for a stay of execution and was electrocuted in March 1993. Nonetheless, in *Poyner*, Justices Souter, Blackmun, and Stevens wrote: "The Court has not spoken squarely on the underlying issue since *In re Kemmler*…and the holding of that case does not constitute a dispositive response to litigation of the issue in light of modern knowledge about the method of execution in question."

SUMMARY

The just deserts model, with its emphasis on retribution and revenge, is today the ascendant sentencing philosophy in the United States. Many citizens, however, still expect sentencing practices to provide for the general goals of deterrence, rehabilitation, incapacitation, and restitution. This ambivalence toward the purpose of sentencing reflects a more basic cultural uncertainty regarding the root causes of crime and the goals of the criminal justice system.

Determinate sentencing is the child of the just deserts philosophy. The determinate sentencing model, while apparently associated with a reduction in biased and inequitable sentencing practices, may not be the panacea it once seemed. Inequitable practices under the indeterminate model may never have been as widespread as opponents of the model claimed them to be. Worse still, the determinate sentencing model may not reduce sentencing discretion, but simply move it out of the hands of judges and into the ever-widening sphere of plea bargaining. Doubly unfortunate, determinate sentencing, by its deemphasis of parole, weakens incentives among the correctional population for positive change and tends to swell prison populations until they're overflowing.

DISCUSSION QUESTIONS

1. Outline the various sentencing rationales discussed in this chapter. Which of these rationales do you find most acceptable as the goal of sentencing? How might the acceptability of the choice you make vary with type of offense? Can you envision any other circumstances which might make your choice less acceptable?

2. In your opinion, is the return to "just deserts" consistent with the determinate sentencing model?

3. Trace the differences between determinate and indeterminate sentencing. Which model holds the best long-term promise for crime reduction? Why?

4. What is a victim impact statement? Do you think victim impact statements should be admissible at the sentencing stage of criminal trials? If so, what material should they contain? What material should not be permitted in such reports? How could the information in victim impact statements be best verified?

ENDNOTES

1. *Smith* v. *U.S.*, No. 91–8674. Decided June 1, 1993.

2. For a thorough discussion of the philosophy of punishment and sentencing, see David Garland, *Punishment and Modern Society: A Study in Social Theory* (Chicago: University of Chicago Press, 1990); Ralph D. Ellis and Carol S. Ellis, *Theories of Criminal Justice: A Critical Reappraisal* (Wolfeboro, NH: Longwood Academic, 1989); and Colin Summer, *Censure, Politics and Criminal Justice* (Bristol, PA: Open University Press, 1990).

3. The requirement for punishment is supported by the belief that social order (and the laws which represent it) could not exist for long if transgressions went unsanctioned.

4. For a thorough review of the literature on deterrence, see Raymond Paternoster, "The Deterrent Effect of the Perceived Certainty and Severity of Punishment: A Review of the Evidence and Issues." *Justice Quarterly*, Vol. 4, no. 2 (June 1987), pp. 174–217.

5. Hugo Adam Bedau, "Retributivism and the Theory of Punishment," *Journal of Philosophy*, Vol. 75 (November 1978), pp. 601–620.

6. H. L. A. Hart, *Punishment and Responsibility: Essays in the Philosophy of Law* (Oxford: Clarendon Press, 1968).

7. Paul Gendreau and Robert R. Ross, "Revivification of Rehabilitation: Evidence from the 1980s." *Justice Quarterly*, Vol. 4, no. 3 (September 1987), pp. 349–408.

8. 18 U.S.C. 3563 (a) (2).

9. See Joan Petersilia, *Expanding Options for Criminal Sentencing* (Santa Monica, CA: The Rand Corporation, 1987).

10. Federick J. Gaudet, "Individual Differences in the Sentencing Tendencies of Judges," No. 230, *Archives of Psychology* (New York: Columbia University Press, 1933).

11. Patridge and Eldridge, *The Second Circuit Sentencing Study: A Report to the Judges of the Second Circuit* (1974).

12. Michael H. Tonry and Norval Morris, "Sentencing Reform in America," in Gordon Hawkins and Franklin E. Zimring, eds., *The Pursuit of Criminal Justice* (Chicago: University of Chicago Press, 1984), pp. 249–266.

13. For a thorough consideration of alleged disparities, see G. Kleck, "Racial Discrimination in Criminal Sentencing: A Critical Evaluation of the Evidence with Additional Evidence on the Death Penalty," *American Sociological Review*, no. 46 (1981), pp. 783–805, and G. Kleck, "Life Support for Ailing Hypotheses: Modes of Summarizing the Evidence for Racial Discrimination in Sentencing," *Law and Human Behavior*, no. 9 (1985), pp. 271–285.

14. Bureau of Justice Statistics, *Report to the Nation on Crime and Justice*, 2nd ed. (Washington, D.C.: U.S. Department of Justice, 1988), p. 91.

15. *Arave* v. *Creech*, No. 91–1160. Decided March 30, 1993. See also *Richmond* v. *Lewis*, No. 91–7094, 1992.

16. For an early statement of this problem, see Franklin E. Zimring, "Making the Punishment Fit the Crime: A Consumer's Guide to Sentencing Reform," In Hawkins and Zimring, eds., *The Pursuit of Criminal Justice*, pp. 267–275.

17. Albert W. Alschuler, "Sentencing Reform and Prosecutorial Power: A Critique of Recent Proposals for 'Fixed' and 'Presumptive' Sentencing," in Sheldon L. Messinger and Egon Bittner, *Criminology Review*

Yearbook, Vol. 1 (Beverly Hills, CA: Sage Publications, 1979), pp. 416–445.

18. Ibid., p. 422.

19. Christopher T. Link and Neal Shover, "The Origins of Criminal Sentencing Reforms," *Justice Quarterly*, Vol. 3, no. 3 (September 1986), pp. 329–342.

20. For a good discussion of such issues, see Hans Toch, "Rewarding Convicted Offenders," *Federal Probation* (June 1988), pp. 42–48.

21. As discussed later in this chapter, federal sentencing guidelines did not become effective until 1987 and still had to meet many court challenges.

22. *U.S.* v. *Dunnigan*, No. 91–1300. Decided February 23, 1993.

23. U.S. Sentencing Commission, *Federal Sentencing Guidelines Manual* (Washington, D.C.: U.S. Government Printing Office, 1987), p. 2.

24. A maximum of 54 days per year of good-time credit can still be earned.

25. Litigants claimed that Congress had violated constitutional guarantees of a separation of powers by including three judges on the Commission.

26. "Supreme Court Upholds Federal Sentencing Reforms," *Criminal Justice Newsletter*, Vol. 20, no. 3 (February 1, 1989), p. 1.

27. *Mistretta* v. *U.S.*, No. 87–7028, 1989.

28. U.S. Sentencing Commission, *Guidelines*, p. 10.

29. Ibid., p. 207.

30. *Deal* v. *U.S.*, No. 91–8199. Decided May 17, 1993.

31. U.S. Sentencing Commission, *Guidelines*, p. 8.

32. "Sentencing Commission Chairman Wilkins Answers Questions on the Guidelines," National Institute of Justice, *Research in Action Report* (September 1987), p. 7.

33. U.S. Sentencing Commission, *Guidelines*, p. 8.

34. Michael K. Block and William M. Rhodes, "The Impact of the Federal Sentencing Guidelines," National Institute of Justice, *Research in Action Report* (1987), p. 1.

35. Ibid.

36. Block and Rhodes, "The Impact of the Federal Sentencing Guidelines."

37. These figures represent a "high-growth scenario." Low-growth scenarios place the 1997 figure at 92,000 and the 2002 population at 105,000 inmates (Block and Rhodes), still a very substantial increase.

38. "Sentencing Rules," *USA Today*, June 28, 1989, p. 3A.

39. Ibid.

40. "2 Judges Decline Drug Cases, Spark Mandatory Minimum Debate," *Criminal Justice Newsletter*, Vol. 24, no. 9, May 3, 1993, p. 2.

41. "Judicial Revolt over Sentencing Picks up Steam," *USA Today*, May 3, 1993, p. 9A.

42. "U.S. District Judge Rejects Sentencing Guideline Minimum," *Criminal Justice Newsletter*, Vol. 24, no. 9, May 3, 1993, p. 2.

43. *Stinson* v. *U.S.*, No. 91–8685, April 1993.

44. "2 Judges Decline Drug Cases."

45. James Eisentein and Herbert Jacob, *Felony Justice* (Boston: Little, Brown, 1977).

46. Joan Petersilia, *Racial Disparities in the Criminal Justice System* (Santa Monica, CA: The Rand Corporation, 1983).

47. Anthony J. Ragona and John P. Ryan, *Beyond the Courtroom: A Comparative Analysis of Misdemeanor Sentencing—Executive Summary* (Chicago: American Judicature Society, 1983).

48. James H. Kuklinski and John E. Stanga, "Political Participation and Government Responsiveness: The Behavior of California Superior Courts," *American Political Science Review*, Vol. 73 (1979), pp. 1090–1099.

49. See Joseph Jacoby and Christopher Dunn, *National Survey on Punishment for Criminal Offenses—Executive Summary* (Washington, D.C.: Bureau of Justice Statistics, 1987). For a critique of this survey,

see Barry Krisberg, "Public Attitudes About Criminal Sanctions," *The Criminologist*, Vol. 13, no. 2 (March/April 1988), pp. 12, 16.

50. Stephen P. Klein, Susan Turner, and Joan Petersilia, *Racial Equity in Sentencing* (Santa Monica, CA: The Rand Corporation, 1988).

51. Ibid., p. 11.

52. Ibid.

53. William Wilbanks, "Are Female Felons Treated More Leniently by the Criminal Justice System?" *Justice Quarterly*, Vol. 3, no. 4 (December 1986), pp. 517–529.

54. Martha A. Myers and Susette M. Talarico, *The Social Contexts of Criminal Sentencing* (New York: Springer-Verlag, 1987).

55. Ibid., p. 170.

56. Martha A. Myers, "Sentencing Background and the Sentencing Behavior of Judges," *Criminology*, Vol. 26, no. 4 (1988), pp. 649–675.

57. Andrew Klein, *Alternative Sentencing: A Practitioner's Guide* (Cincinnati, OH: Anderson, 1988).

58. Ibid., p. 23.

59. Ibid.

60. National Criminal Justice Information and Statistics Service, *Privacy and Security Planning Instructions* (Washington, D.C.: U.S. Government Printing Office, 1976).

61. U.S. Department of Justice, "State Criminal Records Repositories," Bureau of Justice Statistics, *Technical Report* (1985).

62. Privacy Act of 1974, 5, U.S.C.A. Section 522a, 88 Statute 1897, Public Law 93–579 (December 31, 1974).

63. Freedom of Information Act, 5 U.S.C. 522, and amendments. The status of presentence investigative reports has not yet been clarified under this act to the satisfaction of all legal scholars, although generally state and federal courts are thought to be exempt from the provisions of the act.

64. Alexander B. Smith and Louis Berlin,

Introduction to Probation and Parole (St. Paul, MN: West Publishing, 1976), p. 75.

65. John Rosecrance, "Maintaining the Myth of Individualized Justice: Probation Presentence Reports," *Justice Quarterly*, Vol. 5, no. 2 (June 1988), pp. 237–256.

66. Ibid.

67. President's Task Force on Victim's of Crime, *Final Report* (Washington, D.C.: U.S. Government Printing Office, 1982).

68. Public Law 97–291.

69. Proposition 8, California's Victim's Bill of Rights.

70. "Crazed Fan's Deadly 'Mission' Threat Terrified Actress." *The Fayetteville Observer-Times* (North Carolina), June 8, 1989, p. 11D.

71. Ibid.

72. Edwin Villmoare and Virginia V. Neto, "Victim Appearances at Sentencing Under California's Victim's Bill of Rights," National Institute of Justice, *Research in Brief* (August 1987).

73. *Booth* v. *Maryland*, 107 S.Ct. 2529 (1987).

74. *Payne* v. *Tennessee*, No. 90–5721 (1991).

75. "Supreme Court Closes Term with Major Criminal Justice Rulings," *Criminal Justice Newsletter* (July 1, 1991), Vol. 22, no. 13, p. 2.

76. See "What Say Should Victims Have?" *Time*, May 27, 1991, p. 61.

77. *Report to the Nation on Crime and Justice*, 2nd ed. (Washington, D.C.: U.S. Department of Justice, 1988), p. 90.

78. Richard Solari, *National Judicial Reporting Program, 1988* (Washington, D.C.: Bureau of Justice Statistics, 1992).

79. Sally T. Hillsman, Barry Mahoney, George F. Cole, and Bernard Auchter, "Fines as Criminal Sanctions," National Institute of Justice, *Research in Brief* (September 1987), p. 1.

80. Ibid., p. 2.

81. Sally T. Hillsman, Joyce L. Sichel, and Barry Mahoney, *Fines in Sentencing* (New York: Vera Institute of Justice, 1983).

82. Ibid., p. 2.

83. Ibid., p. 4.

84. Ibid.

85. Douglas C. McDonald, Judith Greene, and Charles Worzella, *Day Fines in American Courts: The Staten Island and Milwaukee Experiments* (Washington, D.C.: National Institute of Justice, 1992).

86. Ibid., p. 56.

87. Laura A. Winterfield and Sally T. Hillsman, *The Staten Island Day-Fine Project* (Washington, D.C.: National Institute of Justice, 1993), p. 1.

88. Johnson, *History of Criminal Justice*, pp. 30–31.

89. Ibid., p. 31.

90. Ibid., p. 36.

91. Ibid., p. 51.

92. Arthur Koestler, *Reflections on Hanging* (New York: Macmillan, 1957), p. xi.

93. Ibid., p. 15.

94. Merle Severy, "The Great Revolution," *National Geographic* (July 1989), p. 20.

95. U.S. Department of Justice, *Capital Punishment, 1990.* (Washington, D.C.: U.S. Government Printing Office, 1991).

96. American Correctional Association, *1993 Directory of Juvenile and Adult Correctional Departments, Institutions, Agencies and Paroling Authorities* (Laurel, MD: ACA, 1993).

97. "Chief Justice Calls for Limits on Death Row Habeas Appeals," *Criminal Justice Newsletter*, February 15, 1989, pp. 6–7.

98. Koestler, *Reflections on Hanging*, p. xii.

99. Some recent studies include S. Decker and C. Kohfeld, "A Deterrence Study of the Death Penalty in Illinois: 1933–1980," *Journal of Criminal Justice*, Vol. 12, no. 4 (1984), pp. 367–379, and S. Decker and C.

Kohfeld, "An Empirical Analysis of the Effect of the Death Penalty in Missouri," *Journal of Crime and Justice*, Vol. 10, no. 1 (1987), pp. 23–46.

100. See, especially, the work of W. C. Bailey, "Deterrence and the Death Penalty for Murders in Utah: A Time Series Analysis," *Journal of Contemporary Law*, Vol. 5, no. 1 (1978), pp. 1–20, and "An Analysis of the Deterrent Effect of the Death Penalty for Murder in California," *Southern California Law Review*, Vol. 52, no. 3 (1979), pp. 743–764.

101. B. E. Forst, "The Deterrent Effect of Capital Punishment: A Cross-State Analysis of the 1960's," *Minnesota Law Review*, Vol. 61 (1977), pp. 743–767.

102. Scott H. Decker and Carol W. Kohfeld, "Capital Punishment and Executions in the Lone Star State: A Deterrence Study," *Criminal Justice Research Bulletin*, Criminal Justice Center, Sam Houston State University, Vol. 3, no. 12 (1988).

103. Ibid.

104. As some of the evidence presented before the Supreme Court in *Furman v. Georgia* (408 U.S. 238, 1972) suggested.

105. *USA Today*, April 27, 1989, p. 12A.

106. *McCleskey* v. *Kemp*, 1987.

107. Justice Stewart, as quoted in *USA Today*, April 27, 1989, p. 12A.

108. Koestler, *Reflections on Hanging*, pp. 147–148, and Gennaro F. Vito and Deborah G. Wilson, "Back from the Dead: Tracking the Progress of Kentucky's Furman-Commuted Death Row Population," *Justice Quarterly*, Vol. 5, no. 1 (1988), pp. 101–111.

109. P. Harris, "Over-Simplification and Error in Public Opinion Surveys on Capital Punishment," *Justice Quarterly* (1986), pp. 429–455.

110. Ibid.

111. James O. Finckenauer, "Public Support for the Death Penalty: Retribution as Just Deserts or Retribution

as Revenge?" *Justice Quarterly,* Vol. 5, no. 1 (March 1988), p. 83.

112. Robert M. Bohm, *The Death Penalty in America: Current Research* (Cincinnati, OH: Anderson, 1991), pp. 119–127.

113. Ibid., p. 135.

114. Frank P. Williams III, Dennis R. Longmire, and David B. Gulick, "The Public and the Death Penalty: Opinion as an Artifact of Question Type," a Sam Houston State University *Criminal Justice Research Bulletin,* Vol. 3, no. 8 (1988).

115. Ibid., p. 4.

116. *Criminal Justice Newsletter,* Vol. 21, no. 23 (December 3, 1990), p. 1.

117. *Wilkerson* v. *Utah,* 99 U.S. 130 (1878).

118. *In re Kemmler,* 136 U.S. 436 (1890).

119. Ibid., 447.

120. *Louisiana ex rel. Francis* v. *Resweber,* 329 U.S. 459 (1947).

121. *Furman* v. *Georgia,* 408 U.S. 238 (1972).

122. A position first ascribed to in *Trop* v. *Dulles,* 356 U.S. 86 (1958).

123. *Gregg* v. *Georgia,* 428 U.S. 153 (1976).

124. Ibid., 173.

125. *Coker* v. *Georgia,* 433 U.S. 584 (1977).

126. *Woodson* v. *North Carolina,* 428 U.S. 280 (1976).

127. Lawrence A. Greenfeld, *Capital Punishment, 1989* (Washington, D.C.: Bureau of Justice Statistics, 1990), p. 1.

128. *McCleskey* v. *Zandt,* No. 89–7024 (1991).

129. *Coleman* v. *Thompson,* No. 89–7662 (1991).

130. *Syvasky Lafayette Poyner* v. *Edward W. Murray, Ellis B. Wright, Jr., and John Doe,* No. 92–7944. Decided May 17, 1993.

CHAPTER 11

PROBATION

AND

PAROLE

[C]ommunity corrections is an integral part of the criminal justice system and should be fully implemented and promoted in order to save expensive and scarce jail and prison space for violent and serious offenders.[1]
    –NATIONAL ASSOCIATION OF COUNTIES'
    JUSTICE AND PUBLIC SAFETY STEERING
    COMMITTEE

Despite the "get tough" image of recent legislative initiatives, the United States relies primarily on a community-based system of sentencing.[2]
    –JAMES M. BYRNE
    UNIVERSITY OF LOWELL

...probation and parole services are characteristically poorly staffed and often poorly administered.[3]
    –PRESIDENT'S COMMISSION ON LAW ENFORCEMENT
    AND ADMINISTRATION OF JUSTICE

K E Y   C O N C E P T S

probation	parole	general conditions
special conditions	parole board	caseloads
mixed sentencing	community service	intensive supervision
revocation hearing	shock probation	home confinement

K E Y   C A S E S

Morrissey v. *Brewer*	*Gagnon* v. *Scarpelli*	*Bearden* v. *Georgia*
Greenholtz v. *Nebraska*	*Kelly* v. *Robinson*	*Black* v. *Ramano*
Minnesota v. *Murphy*	*Mempa* v. *Rhay*	

NTRODUCTION

Fifteen years ago Michael Kelley was convicted of raping two Massachusetts women. He was paroled in June 1991 after having spent 13 years in the Bridgewater Treatment Center for Sexually Dangerous Persons. His review board, three specialists, and a judge all declared him "not sexually dangerous." One year later Kelley was back in custody, charged with the rape-murders of Colleen Coughlin, 21, and Debra Levangie, 24, both of Plymouth, Massachusetts.[4]

In 1992 Nathaniel White of Middletown, New York, was charged with the killings of six women after he told officers where to find the bodies of three victims. White had spent two years in state prisons for robbing three convenience stores. Still free since his parole in 1989, White had been arrested in 1991 for assault and kidnapping—charges that involved the knifepoint abduction of a woman. Around the time of White's arrest, William Lester Suff, a Texas parolee, was "indicted in the serial slayings of 14 prostitutes whose strangled and stabbed bodies were found dumped throughout Riverside County,"[5] California. Suff had been paroled from a Texas prison in 1984, after having served 10 years for the beating death of his 2-month-old daughter.

In 1992 39-year-old Leslie Allen Williams, a parolee with a 20-year history of attacks on women, confessed to killing four teen-age girls in Pontiac, Michigan. Williams confessed to the murders while jailed on charges he had abducted a young woman from a cemetery after she placed a wreath on her mother's grave. Before his latest arrest, Williams was paroled in 1990, having been in and out of prison for abducting and attacking women since 1971. Patrick Urbin, the father of 16- and 14-year-old sisters Michelle and Melissa Urbin—two of Williams' latest victims—said "[t]he system has failed us by letting this person out early...[w]e don't personally believe in the death penalty, but he should be behind bars for the rest of his life...[w]hy did they let him get so far and do so much in 20 years?"[6]

Stories like these, appearing daily in papers across the country, have cast a harsh light on the early release of criminal offenders. This chapter takes a close look at the realities behind the practice of probation and parole.

WHAT IS PROBATION?

Probation is "a sentence served while under supervision in the community."[7] Like other sentencing options, probation is a court-ordered sanction. Its goal is to allow for some degree of control over criminal offenders while employing available community programs in the service of rehabilitation. Although probation can be directly imposed, most probationers are technically sentenced to confinement, but have their sentence suspended and are remanded into the custody of an officer of the court—the probation officer.

Probation has a diversity of historical roots. By the 1300s English courts had established the practice of "binding over for good behavior,"[8] in which offenders could be entrusted into the custody of willing citizens. John Augustus (1784–1859), however, is generally recognized as the world's first probation officer. Augustus, a Boston shoemaker, attended sessions of criminal court in the 1850s and would offer to take carefully selected offenders into his home as an alternative to imprisonment.[9] At first he supervised only drunkards, but by 1857 Augustus was accepting many kinds of offenders and devoting all his time to the service of the court.[10] Augustus died in 1859, having bailed out more than 2,000 convicts in his lifetime. In 1878 the Massachusetts legislature enacted a statute which authorized the city of Boston to hire a salaried probation officer. Missouri (1897) followed suit, along with Vermont (1898) and Rhode Island (1899).[11] Before the end of the nineteenth century, probation had become an accepted and widely used form of community-based supervision. By 1925 all 48 states had adopted probation legislation. In the same year the National Probation Act enabled federal district court judges to appoint paid probation officers and impose probationary terms.[12]

Today, probation is the most common form of criminal sentencing used in the United States. Figure 11–1 shows that 53% of all persons under correctional supervision in the United States during 1992 were on probation. Not shown is the fact that the number of persons supervised yearly on probation is increasing at almost twice the rate of imprisonment.[13] This observation has caused some writers to call "probation crowding" an "immediate threat to the criminal justice process and to community protection."[14]

Probation The conditional freedom granted by a judicial officer to an adjudicated adult or juvenile offender, as long as the person meets certain conditions of behavior.

Judgment Suspending Sentence A court-ordered sentencing alternative which results in the convicted offender being placed on probation.

PROBATION CONDITIONS

Those sentenced to probation must agree to abide by court-mandated conditions of probation. Such conditions are of two types: general and specific. General conditions apply to all probationers in a given jurisdiction and usually include requirements that the probationer "obey all laws," "maintain employment," "remain within the jurisdiction of the court," "possess no firearm," "allow the probation officer to visit at home or at work," and so forth. General conditions of probation are shown in Figure 11–2, which depicts a sample form commonly used by judges to impose probation. Many probationers are also required to pay a fine to the court, usually in a series of installments. Monthly payments are designed to reimburse victims for damages and to pay lawyers' fees and other costs of court.

Special conditions may be mandated by a judge who feels that the probationary client is in need of particular guidance or control. A number of special conditions are shown in Figure 11–2 and are routinely imposed upon sizable subcategories of probationers. Special condition number 11, for example, is applicable in cases of driving

Conditions of Probation and Parole The general (state-ordered) and special (court- or board-ordered) limits imposed upon an offender who is released on either probation or parole. General conditions tend to be fixed by state statute, while special conditions are mandated by the sentencing authority and take into consideration the background of the offender and circumstances surrounding the offense.

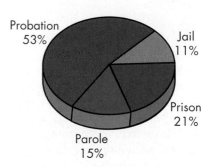

FIGURE 11–1   Persons under correctional supervision
in the United States by type of supervision, 1992.
Sources: Bureau of Justice Statistics, *Jail Inmates 1992*
(Washington, D.C.: BJS, 1993); American
Correctional Association, *1993 Directory of Juvenile
and Adult Correctional Departments, Institutions,
Agencies and Paroling Authorities* (Laurel, MD: ACA,
1993); and Criminal Justice Institute, *The Corrections
Yearbook 1993* (South Salem, NY: The Institute, 1993).

under the influence, while number 12 is useful in dealing with thieves, burglars, and other property offenders. Special conditions may be tailored specifically to individual probationers. Such conditions, when added by the judge, can be typed onto the form. In Figure 11–2 they would be indicated under number 18—"Other." Individualized conditions may prohibit a person from associating with named others (a co-defendant, for example); they may require that the probationer be at home during the hours of darkness, or they may demand that a particular treatment program be completed within a set time period.

WHAT IS PAROLE?

Parole The status of an
offender conditionally
released from a prison by
discretion of a paroling
authority prior to expiration of sentence, required
to observe conditions of
parole, and placed under
the supervision of a parole
agency.

Parole is the supervised early release of inmates from correctional confinement. Parolees have already served a part of their sentence in prison, being released upon a determination by a paroling authority (usually called a parole board or parole commission) that they are ready for a safe return to community life. While probation is a sentencing strategy, parole is a correctional strategy whose primary purpose is to return offenders gradually to productive lives. Parole, by making early release possible, can also act as a stimulus for positive behavioral change.

The use of parole in this country began with the Elmira Reformatory in 1876. The indeterminate sentence, upon which the reformatory philosophy depended, was made possible by an innovative New York law following the call of leading correctional innovators. Parole was a much-heralded tool of nineteenth-century corrections, whose advocates had been looking for a behavioral incentive to induce reformation among youthful offenders. Parole, through its promise of earned early release, seemed the ideal innovation.

Parolees comprise the smallest of the correctional categories shown in Figure 11–1 (other than "jail"). At the beginning of 1993, only 573,844 people were on parole in the United States out of a total correctional population of almost 4 million adults.[15] A growing reluctance to use parole seems due to the expanding realization that today's correctional routines have been generally ineffective at producing any substantial reformation among many offenders prior to their release back into the community. The abandonment of the rehabilitation goal, combined with a return to determinate sentencing in many jurisdictions, including the federal judicial system, has substantially reduced the amount of time the average correctional client spends on parole. Where parole supervision might have involved a 5-year period only a decade ago, modern parole is often quite brief, and may extend for 90 days or less. Similarly, the power of

Parole and probation are both forms of supervised release. Parole officers are shown here visiting a parolee (right) at his home. *Photo: Warren Jorgensen/AP Wide World Photos.*

parole boards is declining. The percentage of release decisions made by parole boards fell from 72% of all releases in 1977 to 43% today.[16]

PAROLE CONDITIONS

In those jurisdictions which retain parole, the conditions of parole remain very similar to the conditions agreed to by probationers. Figure 11–3 shows both sides of a typical parole agreement form, which parolees must sign before their release. The general conditions of parole are listed on the front of the form and include agreements not to leave the state as well as a waiver of extradition from other jurisdictions.

The successful and continued employment of parolees is one of the major concerns of parole boards and their officers, and studies have found that successful employment is a major factor in reducing the likelihood of repeat offenses.[17] The importance of employment is stressed on the form in Figure 11–3, with the stricture that failure to find employment within 30 days may result in revocation of parole. Working offenders can pay fines and penalties. A provision for making restitution payments is included at the bottom of the first page with the names and addresses of recipients clearly specified.

Special parole conditions have been added to the form in Figure 11–3. One of them requires the parolee to pay a "parole supervisory fee of $15" every month, a requirement now being routinely imposed in some jurisdictions (although monetary amounts may vary). A relatively new innovation, parole supervision fees, shifts some of the expenses of community corrections to the offender.

STATE OF NORTH CAROLINA

File No. _____

_____ County _____ Seat Of Court

In The General Court Of Justice
☐ District ☐ Superior Court Division

NOTE:
(This form is not to be used for multiple offenses unless they are consolidated for judgment.)

STATE VERSUS	**JUDGMENT SUSPENDING SENTENCE**
Defendant	**AND**

COMMITMENT ON SPECIAL PROBATION

G.S. 15A-1341, 15A-1342, 15A-1343, 15A-1346

Race	Sex	DOB

Attorney For State	Def. Found ☐ Not Indigent	Def. Waived ☐ Attorney	Attorney For Defendant ☐ Appointed ☐ Retained

The defendant ☐ pled guilty to: ☐ was found guilty by the Court of: ☐ was found guilty by a jury of: ☐ pled no contest to:

File No.(s) And Offense(s)	Date Of Offense	G.S. No.	Fel./M.	Class	Max. Term	Presumptive

The Court has considered the aggravating and mitigating factors in G.S. 15A-1340.4(a) and
☐ makes no written findings because the prison term imposed does not require such findings.
☐ makes no written findings because the prison term imposed is pursuant to a plea arrangement as to sentence.
☐ makes the Findings Of Factors In Aggravation And Mitigation Of Punishment set forth on the attached AOC-CR-303.

The Court, having considered evidence, arguments of counsel and statement of defendant, finds that the defendant's plea was freely, voluntarily, and understandingly entered, and Orders the above offenses be consolidated for judgment and the defendant be imprisoned.

for a term of	in the custody of the	☐ N.C. Dept. of Correction
		☐ Sheriff of _____ County

The defendant shall be given credit for _____ days spent in confinement prior to the date of this Judgment as a result of this charge, to be applied toward the ☐ sentence imposed above. ☐ imprisonment required for special probation below.

SUSPENSION OF SENTENCE

With the consent of the defendant and subject to the conditions set out below, the execution of this sentence is suspended and the defendant is placed on ☐ supervised probation for _____ years. ☐ unsupervised probation for _____ years.

☐ The above period of probation shall begin: ☐ when the defendant is paroled or otherwise released from incarceration in the case referred to below. ☐ at the expiration of the sentence in the case referred to below.
(**NOTE:** *List Case number, Date, County And Court In Which Prior Sentence Imposed.*)

SPECIAL PROBATION – G.S. 15A-1351

☐ As a condition of special probation, the defendant shall ☐ serve an active term of _____ ☐ days ☐ months in the custody of the ☐ N.C. DOC. ☐ Sheriff of this County. ☐ submit to IMPACT imprisonment per attached CR-302, Page Two. ☐ pay jail fees.
(**NOTE:** *This term shall NOT be reduced by good time, gain time or parole, or, unless provided above, by time in jail awaiting trial.*)

The defendant shall report in a sober condition to begin serving his term on:	Day	Date	Hour	☐ AM ☐ PM	and shall remain in custody until:	Day	Date	Hour	☐ AM ☐ PM

☐ The defendant shall again report in a sober condition to continue serving this term on the same day of the week for the next _____ consecutive weeks, and shall remain in custody during the same hours each week.

MONETARY CONDITIONS

The defendant shall pay to the Clerk of Superior Court the "Total Amount Due" shown below, plus the probation supervision fee set by law ☐ pursuant to a schedule determined by the probation officer. ☐ at the rate of $_____ per _____ , beginning on _____ and continuing on the same day of each _____ thereafter until paid in full. ☐ Other:

Fine	Costs	Restitution*	Attorney's Fee	Community Service Fee	Total Amount Due
$	$	$	$	$	$

*The name(s) and address(es) and amount(s) due the person(s) to receive this restitution are:

☐ All payments received by the Clerk shall first be disbursed pro rata among the persons entitled to restitution.
☐ Upon payment of the "Total Amount Due", the probation officer may transfer the defendant to unsupervised probation.

AOC-CR-302, Rev. 7/91   Material opposite unmarked squares is to be disregarded as surplusage.

FIGURE 11–2   Probation agreement form. Courtesy North Carolina Department of Correction, Division of Adult Probation and Parole. Reprinted with permission.

REGULAR CONDITIONS OF PROBATION – G.S. 15A-1343(b)

The defendant shall: 1. Commit no criminal offense in any jurisdiction. 2. Possess no firearm, explosive device or other deadly weapon list ed in G.S. 14-269. 3. Remain gainfully and suitably employed or faithfully pursue a course of study or of vocational training that will equip him for suitable employment. 4. Satisfy child support and family obligations, as required by the Court. If the defendant is on supervised pro bation, he shall also: 5. Remain within the jurisdiction of the Court unless granted written permission to leave by the Court or his probation officer. 6. Report as directed by the Court or his probation officer to the officer at reasonable times and places and in a reasonable manner, permit the officer to visit him at reasonable times, answer all reasonable inquiries by the officer and obtain prior approval from the officer for, and notify the officer of, any change in address or employment. 7. Notify the probation officer if he fails to obtain or retain satisfactory employment. 8. At a time to be designated by his probation officer, visit with his probation officer at a facility maintained by the Division of Prisons.

If the defendant is to serve an active sentence as a condition of special probation, he shall also: 9. Obey the rules and regulations of the Department of Correction governing the conduct of inmates while imprisoned. 10. Report to a probation officer in the State of North Carolina within 72 hours of his discharge from the active term of imprisonment.

SPECIAL CONDITIONS OF PROBATION – G.S. 15A-1343(b1), 143B-262(c)

The defendant shall also comply with the following special conditions which the Court finds are reasonably related to his rehabilitation:

☐ 11. Surrender his driver's license to the Clerk of Superior Court for transmittal to the division of Motor Vehicles and not operate a motor vehicle for a period of _____ or until relicensed by the Division of Motor Vehicles, whichever is later.

☐ 12. Submit at reasonable times to warrantless searches by a probation officer of his person, and of his vehicle and premises while he is present, for the following purposes which are reasonably related to his probation supervision: ☐ stolen goods ☐ controlled substances ☐ contraband ☐ _____

☐ 13. Not use, possess or control any illegal drug or controlled substance unless it has been prescribed for him by a licensed physician and is in the original container with the prescription number affixed on it; not knowingly associate with any known or previously convicted users, possessors or sellers of any illegal drugs or controlled substances; and not knowingly be present at or frequent any place where illegal drugs or controlled substances are sold, kept or used.

☐ 14. Supply a breath, urine and/or blood specimen for analysis of the possible presence of a prohibited drug or alcohol, when instructed by his probation officer.

☐ 15. Successfully pass the General Education Development Test (G.E.D.) during the first _____ months of the period of probation.

☐ 16. Complete _____ hours of community or reparation service suring the first _____ days of the period of probation, as directed by the community service coordinator and pay the fee prescribed by G.S. 143B-475. 1(b) ☐ pursuant to the schedule set out under monetary conditions above. ☐ within _____ days of this Judgment and before begin- ning service.

☐ 17. Report for initial evaluation by _____, participate in all further evaluation, counseling, treatment or education programs recommended as a result of that evaluation, and comply with all other therapeutic requirements of those programs until discharged.

☐ 18. Other:

☐ 19. Comply with the Additional Conditions Of Probation which are set forth on AOC-CR-302, Page Two.

☐ A hearing was held in open court in the presence of the defendant at which time a fee, including expenses, was awarded the defendant' appointed counsel or assigned public defender.

ORDER OF COMMITMENT/APPEAL ENTRIES

☐ It is ORDERED that the Clerk deliver three certified copies of this Judgment and Commitment to the Sheriff or other qualified officer and that the officer cause the defendant to be delivered with these copies to the custody of the agency named on the reverse to serve the sentence imposed or until he shall have complied with the conditions of release pending appeal.

☐ The defendant gives notice of appeal from the judgment of the District Court to the Superior Court. The current pretrial release order shall remain in effect. ☐ except that:

☐ The defendant gives notice of appeal from the judgment of the Superior Court to the Appellate Division. Appeal entries and any conditions of post conviction release are set forth on Form AOC-CR-350.

SIGNATURE OF JUDGE

Date	Name Of Presiding Judge (Type Or Print)	Signature Of Presiding Judge

CERTIFICATION

I certify that this Judgment and the attachment(s) marked below are true copies of the originals.

☐ Judgment Suspending Sentence, Page Two [Additional Conditions Of Probation (AOC-CR-302, Page Two)]

☐ Findings Of Factors In Aggravation And Mitigation Of Punishment (AOC-CR-303)

Date of Certification	Date Certified Copies Delivered To Sheriff	Signature And Seal
		☐ Deputy CSC ☐ Assistant CSC ☐ Clerk Of Superior Court

NOTE: Defendant signs the following statement in all cases except unsupervised probation without community or reparation service. I have received a copy of this Judgment which contains all of the conditions of my probation and I agree to them. I understand that no person who supervises me or for whom I work while performing community or reparation service is liable to me for any loss or damage which I may sustain unless my injury is caused by that person's gross negligence or intentional wrongdoing.

Date Signed	Signature Of Defendant	Witnessed By:

AOC-CR-302, Side Two, Rev. 7/91   Material opposite unmarked squares is to be disregarded as surplusage.

FIGURE 11-2 (continued.)

PC-104a
7/81

STATE OF NORTH CAROLINA
PAROLE AGREEMENT BETWEEN THE NORTH CAROLINA PAROLE COMMISSION
AND

_____ , PAROLEE

In accepting this parole I understand that the North Carolina Parole Commission may modify its terms. I also understand that I am under the legal custody of the Parole Commission until duly discharged by the Commission. I understand that should I violate parole the Commission may cause me to be returned to custody for further action as provided by law. I understand that my term of parole shall be for no less than either (1) the remainder of the maximum term if the maximum term is less than one year or (2) one year if the remainder of the maximum term is one year or more. I understand that I shall receive no credit for time spent on parole against the remainder of my sentence and that in the event my parole is revoked I will be reimprisoned for the unserved portion of the maximum term of imprisonment imposed by the court. I understand that in the event of an alleged violation of parole, my parole time may be frozen at the time of the alleged violation. If my parole time is frozen, it may remain frozen until such time as the alleged violations are disposed of even if it becomes necessary to extend my release date beyond its normal period. I further understand that if I abide by the terms and conditions of this parole, the Parole Commission will unconditionally discharge me no later than my maximum release date. In accepting this parole, I agree to abide by the following rules:

1. I will report promptly to my Probation/Parole Officer when instructed to do so and in the manner prescribed by my Probation/Parole Officer and the Parole Commission.
2. I will work steadily at an approved job and not change my job or my residence without permission from my Probation/Parole Officer. If I am discharged from my job or evicted from my home, I will notify my Probation/Parole Officer. I will also support any persons dependent on me to the best of my ability.
3. I will obey all municipal, county, and state and federal laws, ordinances and orders. If I am arrested or receive a citation to appear in court while on parole, I will report this fact to my Probation/Parole Officer within 24 hours of such arrest or citation.
4. I will not leave my county of residence without obtaining permission from my Probation/Parole Officer. I will not leave the State of North Carolina without permission from the Parole Commission or my Probation/Parole Officer.
5. I will not consume alcoholic beverages to excess or use or possess drugs in violation of state and federal laws.
6. I will not own or possess any firearms or deadly weapon without written permission from the Parole Commission.
7. I will notify my Probation/Parole Officer in writing three weeks in advance of any plans to alter my marital status (marriage, separation, divorce).
8. I will allow my Probation/Parole Officer to visit my home or place of employment at any time.
9. I do hereby waive extradition to the State of North Carolina from any state of the United States and also agree that I will not contest any effort by any state to return me to the State of North Carolina.
10. I will not enter into any agreement to act as an "informer" or special agent for any law enforcement agency without permission from the Parole Commission.
11. I will not assault, or harm, or threaten to assault or harm, any person.
12. I will comply with the following Special Conditions which have been imposed by the Parole Commission:

☐ In the event (1) I do not have a plan of employment at this time, or (2) my employment plan has been found to be only temporarily suitable, I understand and agree that I must diligently seek employment which is satisfactory to the Parole Commission, and I will use my best efforts to secure the same, and will report the progress of my efforts to my Probation/Parole Officer twice weekly until satisfactory employment is obtained. I further understand and agree that if I have not obtained satisfactory employment within 30 days from today, I may be returned to prison and my parole or conditional release may be revoked, in the discretion of the Commission.

☐ I, _____ , will pay to the Department of Correction the sum

of _____ per week/month to be used to make restitution to the following named payee(s) in the following amounts:

Name of Payee	Address	Amount to be Paid
_____	_____	_____
_____	_____	_____
_____	_____	_____

It shall be my responsibility to send my weekly/monthly payments to the Department of Correction at the following address: WORK RELEASE ACCOUNTING OFFICE, 831 West Morgan St., Raleigh, N.C. 27603.

PAYMENTS SHALL BE MADE EITHER BY CASHIER CHECK, CERTIFIED CHECK OR POSTAL MONEY ORDER (NO PERSONAL CHECKS ACCEPTED). CHECKS SHALL BE MADE PAYABLE TO THE DEPARTMENT OF CORRECTION AND INCLUDE THE NAME AND ADDRESS OF THE PAROLEE LISTED ABOVE.

FIGURE 11–3 Parole agreement form. Courtesy North Carolina Department of Correction, Division of Adult Probation and Parole. Reprinted with permission.

I will accept counseling and/or treatment for drug and/or alcohol abuse at the discretion of the supervising officer.

I will not associate with known drug offenders, users and/or pushers.

I will consent to a warrantless search of my person, premises or any vehicle under my control by my supervising officer for any purpose reasonably related to parole supervision.

I will stay away from places where the selling and/or serving of alcohol is the primary business.

I will submit to any physical, chemical or breathalyzer test when requested to do so by the Parole Commission or by supervising PPO for detection of alcohol and/or controlled substances and pay costs thereof.

I will abide by curfew at discretion of PPO.

I will pay a parole supervision fee of $15 within 30 days after my release on parole and each month thereafter until my parole is terminated unless the Parole Commission relieves me of this obligation because of undue economic burden. I will send my parole supervision fee to the Clerk of Superior Court, Wake County, Raleigh, N.C.

I agree to:

1. Be under the Intensive Parole Supervision Program for a minimum of 6 months.

2. Obey any curfew imposed by the Parole Commission or by my Supervising Officer.

3. Submit to request for blood and urine samples for possible presence of drugs.

4, Attend and participate in counseling, treatment or educational programs as directed by the Parole Commission or the Intensive/Parole Officer as approved by the Parole Commission and abide by all rules, regulations and directives of such programs.

5. Submit at reasonable times to warrantless searches by a Parole Officer of my person, vehicle or premises while I am present for purposes which are reasonably related to parole supervision.

    I will remain at   School until completion of course.

    I will have no contact with   (co-defendant).

If I violate any of the conditions or Special Conditions of parole, I may be arrested and held as a parole violator. In this event I will be given a hearing at which time I may be represented by counsel and, if the Commission decides that I am in violation of one or more of the conditions of my parole, I may be returned to prison.

I have read or have had read to me the foregoing conditions of my parole. I fully understand them and will strictly follow them and I understand and know what I am doing. No promises or threats have been made to me, and no pressure of any kind has been used against me at the time of signing this Parole Agreement.

DATE _____   SIGNED _____

DATE _____   SIGNED _____

DATE _____   SIGNED _____

NOTE TO CONVICTED FELONS: *The possession of a firearm by a convicted felon is a violation of both federal and state law. Also, the act of registering or voting is punishable by law until such time as these rights are restored.

FIGURE 11–3 (continued.)

THE EXTENT OF PROBATION AND PAROLE

Probation is the most commonly used alternative to imprisonment. Between 60% and 80% of all persons found guilty of crimes are sentenced to some form of probation.[18] Even serious offenders stand about a 1-in-4 chance of receiving a probationary term, as Figure 11–4 shows. A Rand Corporation study[19] of 28 jurisdictions found that 8% of people convicted of homicide were placed on probation, as were 16% of convicted rapists. Thirteen percent of convicted robbers and 25% of burglars were similarly sentenced to probation rather than active prison time. In a 1992 example,[20] 47-year-old Carrie Mote of Vernon, Connecticut, was sentenced to probation for shooting her fiancé in the chest with a .38-caliber handgun after he called off their wedding. Ms. Mote, who faced a maximum of 20 years in prison, claimed to be suffering from diminished psychological capacity because of the emotional stress brought on by the canceled wedding.

Table 11–1 summarizes the extent of parole supervision in the United States. It shows that over 573,000 people were on parole throughout the United States at the beginning of 1993. States vary considerably in the use they make of parole, influenced as they are by the legislative requirements of sentencing schemes. For example, in 1993 Maine, a state which is phasing out parole, reported only 50 people under supervision, and North Dakota only 106, while Texas had a parole population in excess of 74,790, and California officials were busy supervising more than 86,000 persons.[21] Maine's reported parole population of only 50 individuals was the lowest of all the states.

Most inmates who are freed from prison are paroled (about 75%) or are granted some other form of conditional release (about 5.5%).[22] Discretionary parole refers to release decisions made by a parole board. Mandatory release describes discharge from prison at a time fixed by sentencing statutes. Some states operating under determinate sentencing guidelines require that inmates serve a short period of time, such as 90 days, on reentry parole—a form of mandatory release. Mandatory releases have increased fivefold—from 6% of all releases in 1977 to over 31% today.[23] Mandatory sentencing schemes have changed the face of parole in America, resulting in a dramatic reduction of the average time spent under post-prison supervision, while having little impact upon the number of released inmates who experience some form of parole.

FIGURE 11–4   Percentage of convicted offenders receiving probation by type of crime. *Source:* Adapted from J. Petersilia et al., *Granting Felons Probation* (Santa Monica, CA: The Rand Corporation, 1985).

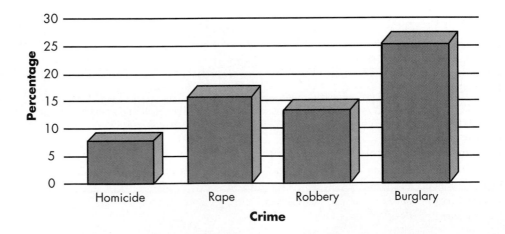

TABLE 11-1

ADULTS ON PROBATION AND PAROLE IN THE UNITED STATES, JANUARY 1, 1993

Jurisdiction	Parolees	Probationers	Jurisdiction	Parolees	Probationers
U.S. total	**573,844**	**2,079,881**			
Federal	39,912	46,485	Montana	802	5,013
Alabama	6,807	27,047	Nebraska	758	19,499
Alaska	600[2]	3,744	Nevada	2,852	7,803
Arizona	4,570	25,600	New Hampshire	618	4,104
Arkansas	3,779	16,448	New Jersey	34,190	103,254
California	86,389	300,000	New Mexico	1,200[2]	8,190
Colorado	2,010	22,105	New York	47,093	152,165
Connecticut	640	48,567	North Carolina	13,544	88,871
Delaware	1,120	14,887	North Dakota	106	1,937
Florida	2,582	95,565	Ohio	7,407	10,772
Georgia	23,470	154,750	Oklahoma	3,354	25,636
Hawaii	1,427	4,260	Oregon	8,262	21,185
Idaho	445	4,051	Pennsylvania	19,539	4,851
Illinois	23,304	75,262	Rhode Island	520	12,175
Indiana	2,892	75,909	South Carolina	4,825	31,401
Iowa	2,140	14,143	South Dakota	701	3,497
Kansas	4,812	16,421	Tennessee	11,819	21,100
Kentucky	3,684	8,796	Texas	74,794	234,141
Louisiana	12,864	30,948	Utah	1,998	6,671
Maine[1]	50	7,584	Vermont	416	4,746
Maryland	10,000[2]	47,242	Virginia	12,393	23,530
Massachusetts	4,645	57,263	Washington	2,500	37,900
Michigan	13,950	52,958	West Virginia	869	4,413
Minnesota	285	8,354	Wisconsin	4,549	36,071
Mississippi	2,402	8,686	Wyoming	379	3,039
Missouri	11,940	32,841			

[1]Maine eliminated parole in 1976.
[2]Author estimates.

Source: George M. and Camille Graham Camp, *The Corrections Yearbook 1993: Probation and Parole* (South Salem, NY: Criminal Justice Institute, 1993).

Statistics from the National Corrections Reporting Program show that the average time served in prison for individuals who are later paroled is about 17 months.[24] As measured by the program, average time served included jail time credited toward the offender's prison sentence. The study found that time served in confinement was about 45% of the original court-ordered sentence. The more serious the offense, the longer the time served in prison prior to parole. Murderers, for example, served an average of 78 months behind bars; rapists, 44 months; robbers, 30 months; burglars, 17 months; and drug traffickers, 16 months.[25]

Females under parole supervision, although far fewer in number than males, are more likely to be successful than male parolees. Studies have found about 22% of men were returned to custody for a parole violation versus 14% of women.[26] However, men released from custody have generally served longer periods in confinement than women for the same types of offenses.[27]

At the beginning of 1993, a total of 2,079,881 adults were reportedly[28] on probation across the nation—making probation the correctional choice for the majority of offenders. As with parole, individual states made greater or lesser use of probation. North Dakota authorities, with the smallest probationary population, supervised only 1,937 people, while California reported 300,000 persons on probation (see Table 11–1). Over the decade 1980–1990, the probation population increased by 126%, while the number of individuals on parole increased by 107%.

Correctional personnel involved in probation/parole supervision totaled 43,198 (including approximately 2,500 federal officers) throughout the United States in 1990 according to the American Correctional Association (ACA).[29] Some 15,352 of these officers supervised probationers only, while 13,833 supervised both probationers and parolees. Salaries for entry-level parole officers were reported to be as low as $15,300 in 1993, although some states began officers at $35,600.[30] Chief parole officers in some jurisdictions were earning as much as $107,700. Probation officer salaries were within the same range.

PROBATION AND PAROLE: THE PLUSES AND MINUSES

Advantages of Probation and Parole

Probation is used to meet the needs of offenders who require some correctional supervision short of imprisonment, while at the same time providing a reasonable degree of security to the community. Parole fulfills a similar purpose following release from confinement. As sentencing strategies, probation and parole provide a number of advantages over imprisonment:

1. *Lower Cost.* Imprisonment is expensive. One study found that incarcerating a single offender in Georgia consumes approximately $7,760 per year while the cost of intensive probation is as little as $985 per probationer.[31] The expense of imprisonment in some other states may be nearly three times as high as it is in Georgia. Not only do probation and parole save money, they may even help fill the public coffers. Some jurisdictions require that offenders pay a portion of the costs associated with their own supervision. Georgia, for example, charges clients between $10 and $50 per month while they are being supervised,[32] while Texas, in an innovative program which uses market-type incentives encouraging probation officers to collect fees,[33] has been able to annually recoup monies totaling more than half of the total that the state spends on probation services.

2. *Increased Employment.* Few people in prison have the opportunity to work. Work-release programs, correctional industries, and inmate labor programs operate in most states, but they usually provide only low-paying jobs and require few skills. At best, such programs include only a small portion of the inmates in any given facility. Probation and parole, on the other hand, make it possible for offenders under correctional supervision to work full time at jobs in the "free" economy. As such, they can contribute to their own support and the support of their families, stimulate the local economy through the expenditure of their wages, and support government through the taxes they pay.

3. *Restitution.* Offenders who are able to work are candidates for court-ordered restitution. Society's interest in "making the victim whole again" may be better served by a

Historians generally credit the Elmira Reformatory in New York as being the birthplace of parole in the United States. In this scene from the 1950s, a hopeful Elmira inmate is about to meet the state's parole board. *Photo: AP/Wide World Photos.*

probationary sentence or parole than it is by imprisonment. Restitution payments to victims may help restore their standard of living and personal confidence while teaching the offender responsibility.

4. *Community Support.* The decision to release a prisoner on parole, or to sentence a convicted offender to a probationary term, is often partially based upon considerations of family and other social ties. Such decisions are made in the belief that offenders will be more malleable and subject to control in the community if they participate in a web of positive social relationships. An advantage of both probation and parole is that each allows for the continuation of such ties. Family fragmentation is avoided by probationary sentences and parole may reunite family members split by criminal sanctions.

5. *Reduced Risk of Criminal Socialization.* Prison has been charged with being a "school in crime." Probation insulates adjudicated offenders, at least to some degree, from the kinds of criminal values which permeate prison. Parole, by virtue of the fact that it follows time served in prison, is less successful than probation in reducing the risk of criminal socialization.

6. *Increased Use of Community Services.* Probationers and parolees are able to take advantage of services offered through the community. These services include psychological therapy, substance abuse counseling, financial services, support groups, church outreach programs, and social services. While a few similar opportunities may be available in prison, the community environment itself can enhance the effectiveness of treatment programs by reducing the stigmatization of the offender and allowing for program participation within the context of a more "normal" environment.

7. *Increased Opportunity for Rehabilitation.* Probation and parole can both be useful behavioral management tools. They reward cooperative offenders with freedom and allow for the opportunity to shape the behavior of offenders who may be difficult to reach through other programs.

Disadvantages of Probation and Parole

Any honest appraisal of probation and parole must recognize that they share a number of strategic drawbacks:

1. *A Relative Lack of Punishment.* The "just deserts" model of criminal sentencing insists that punishment should be a central theme of the justice process. While rehabilitation and treatment are recognized as worthwhile goals, the model highlights punishment as serving both society's need for protection and the victim's need for revenge. Probation, however, is seen as practically no punishment at all and is coming under increasing criticism as a sentencing strategy. Parole is likewise accused of unhinging the scales of justice because (1) it releases some offenders early, even when they have been convicted of serious crimes, while other, relatively minor offenders, may remain in prison and (2) it is dishonest because it does not require completion of the offender's entire sentence behind bars.

2. *Increased Risk to the Community.* Probation and parole are strategies designed to deal with convicted *criminal* offenders. The release into the community of such offenders increases the risk that they will commit additional offenses. Community supervision can never be so complete as to eliminate such a possibility entirely, and recent studies on parole have pointed to the fact that an accurate assessment of offender dangerousness is beyond our present capability.[34]

    A 1992 Bureau of Justice Statistics study[35]—the nation's largest ever follow-up survey of felons on probation—found that 43% of probationers were rearrested for a felony within three years of receiving a probationary sentence, and while still on probation. Half of the arrests were for a violent crime or a drug offense. An even greater percentage, 46%, were either sent to prison or jail or had absconded.

3. *Increased Social Costs.* Some offenders placed on probation and parole will effectively and responsibly discharge their obligations. Others, however, will become social liabilities. In addition to the increased risk of new crimes, probation and parole increase the chance that added expenses will accrue to the community in the form of child support, welfare costs, housing expenses, legal aid, indigent health care, and the like.

PAROLE ADMINISTRATION

Parole Board A state paroling authority. Most states have parole boards (also called "commissions") which decide when an incarcerated offender is ready for conditional release and which may also function as revocation hearing panels.

While probation is a sentencing option available to a judge, who determines the form probation will take, parole results from an administrative decision made by a legally designated paroling authority. States differ as to the type of parole decision-making mechanism they utilize, as well as the level at which it operates. Two major models prevail: (1) **parole boards**, which "grant" parole according to judgmental assessments undertaken by their members or representatives, and (2) statutory decrees, which establish a mandatory parole release date, usually near the completion of the inmate's sentence, minus good time and gain time. Parole boards (sometimes called parole commissions) can be further classified[36] into four administrative models: (1) the institutional model, (2) the independent authority, (3) the consolidation model, and (4) the transitional model.

The Institutional Model

The institutional model places parole decisions in the hands of staff members in individual correctional facilities. Under the institutional model, parole boards are constituted from among supervisory personnel, program directors, guards, psychologists, and

CAREERS IN JUSTICE

WORKING FOR THE ADMINISTRATIVE OFFICE OF THE U.S. COURTS

TYPICAL POSITIONS.   U.S. probation officer, pretrial services officer, statistician, defender services officer, and defense investigator.

EMPLOYMENT REQUIREMENTS.   To qualify for the position of probation officer at the GS-5 level, an applicant must possess a Bachelor's degree from an accredited college or university and have a minimum of 2 years of general work experience. General experience must have been acquired after obtaining the Bachelor's degree, and cannot include experience as a police, custodial, or security officer unless work in such positions involved criminal investigative experience. In lieu of general experience a Bachelor's degree from an accredited college or university in an accepted field of study (including criminology, criminal justice, penology, correctional administration, social work, sociology, public administration, and psychology) will qualify an applicant for immediate employment at the GS-5 level providing that at least 32 semester hours or 48 quarter hours were taken in one or more of the accepted fields of study. One year of study qualifies applicants for appointment at the GS-7 level, while a Master's degree in an appropriate field or a law degree may qualify the applicant for advanced placement.

OTHER REQUIREMENTS.   Applicants must be less than 37 years of age at the time of hiring and be in excellent physical health.

SALARY.   Appointees at the GS-5 level were earning $18,340 or more in mid-1993, and GS-7 appointees earned $22,717 or more. Experienced statisticians with Bachelor's degrees earned between $33,000 and $60,000.

BENEFITS.   U.S. probation and pretrial services officers are included in the federal hazardous-duty law enforcement classification and are covered by liberal federal health and life insurance programs. A comprehensive retirement program is available to all federal employees.

DIRECT INQUIRIES TO: Administrative Office of the U.S. Courts, Personnel Office, Washington, D.C. 20544. Phone: (202) 273-1297.

Source: Administrative Office of the United States Courts.

administrators whose primary job responsibilities relate to the running of the institution housing the offender. Although many detention centers (especially those for juveniles) have used this form of organization in the past, it is less common today.

The institutional model has been criticized for its almost unavoidable emphasis on facility exigencies at the expense of both the rehabilitative ideal and the needs of offenders. Some writers have observed that the pressures of overcrowding might lead to early parole under the model.[37] The institutional model has been mostly abandoned, with no adult parole system today leaving release decisions exclusively in the hands of institutional authorities.

The Independent Model

Independent parole agencies have been the rule in adult corrections over the past few decades. The independent model looks to a parole authority outside of the prison system, usually at the level of state government. Members of the parole board or commission may be appointees of the governor or the governor's designee. They may or may not be experienced in the corrections field. Parole boards of this sort typically make use of investigators, sometimes called "case analysts," who serve to provide the board with information needed to make a parole decision. The number of board members varies by state and is usually in the range of 3 to 12.

The Consolidated Model

The consolidated model has been described as "a central decision-making authority organizationally situated in an overall department of corrections, but possessing independent powers."[38] The consolidated approach has attributes of both the institutional and independent models, with some of the benefits of both. It is said to provide for a fair appraisal of individual cases, while at the same time recognizing the needs of the correctional system. Some authors believe that, in jurisdictions where parole remains a viable alternative, the trend today is toward the consolidated model.[39]

The Transitional Model

A fourth kind of administrative approach to parole is the transitional model. As discussed in Chapter 10, a number of states today are undergoing a move from indeterminate back to fixed or determinate sentencing. Transitional boards oversee this legislatively mandated change. They have little or no control over inmates sentenced under "new" determinate sentencing laws, since those laws usually mandate a set, but minimal, period of parole designed solely to facilitate practical aspects of the inmate's reentry into the community. Some states, by statute, require a 90-day period of reentry parole for offenders who have served their fixed term (minus considerations for good time, gain time, etc). Parole boards in determinate-sentencing states generally cannot mandate a longer period of supervision nor can they vote for early release. On the other hand, transitional states may still have a substantial number of imprisoned offenders who have been sentenced under "old" indeterminate-sentencing laws. These offenders are routinely subject to the authority of the board, and parole decisions must be made when their parole eligibility dates are reached. With the passage of time, transitional parole boards will find themselves with decreasing authority.

Federal parole decisions are made by the U.S. Parole Commission, which uses hearing examiners to visit federal prisons. Examiners typically ask inmates to describe why, in their opinion, they are ready for parole. The inmate's job readiness, home plans, past record, accomplishments while in prison, good behavior, and previous experiences on probation or parole form the basis for a report made by the examiners to the **parole commission**. The 1984 Comprehensive Crime Control Act, which mandated federal fixed sentencing and abolished parole for offenses committed after November 1, 1978, began a planned phase-out of the U.S. Parole Commission. Under the act, the Commission was to be abolished by 1992. However, action taken by Congress in late 1990 extended the life of the Commission until at least 1997.

THE LEGAL ENVIRONMENT

Nine Supreme Court decisions provide a legal framework for probation and parole supervision. Among recent cases, that of *Griffin* v. *Wisconsin* (1987)[40] may be the most significant. In *Griffin* the U.S. Supreme Court ruled that probation officers may conduct searches of a probationer's residence without need for either a search warrant or probable cause. According to the Court, "[a] probationer's home, like anyone else's, is protected by the Fourth Amendment's requirement that searches be 'reasonable.'" However, "[a] State's operation of a probation system…presents 'special needs' beyond normal law enforcement that may justify departures from the usual warrant and probable cause requirements." Probation, the Court concluded, is similar to imprisonment because it is a "form of criminal sanction imposed upon an offender after a" determination of guilt.

Other cases focus on the conduct of **revocation** hearings. Revocation of probation or parole may be requested by the supervising officer if a client has allegedly violated the conditions of community release or has committed a new crime. Revocation hearings may result in an order that a probationer's suspended sentence be made "active" or that a parolee return to prison to complete his or her sentence in confinement. In a 1935 decision (*Escoe* v. *Zerbst*)[41] which has since been greatly modified, the Supreme Court held that probation "comes as an act of grace to one convicted of a crime…" and that the revocation of probation without hearing or notice to the probationer was acceptable practice.

By 1967, however, the case of *Mempa* v. *Rhay*[42] found the Court changing direction as it declared that both notice and a hearing were required, along with the opportunity for representation by counsel before a prison sentence, which had been deferred[43] pending probation, could be imposed. Jerry Mempa had been convicted of riding in a stolen car at age 17 in 1959 and sentenced to prison, but his sentence was deferred and he was placed on probation. A few months later he was accused of burglary. A hearing was held, and Mempa admitted his involvement in the burglary. An active prison sentence was then imposed.

At the hearing Mempa had not been offered the chance to have a lawyer represent him, nor was he given the chance to present any evidence or testimony in his own defense. In response to a writ of *habeas corpus* filed by Mempa's attorneys, the Supreme Court ruled that probationers are entitled to the representation of counsel in a revocation hearing.

Two of the most widely cited cases affecting parolees and probationers are *Morrissey* v. *Brewer* (1972)[44] and *Gagnon* v. *Scarpelli* (1973).[45] The Supreme Court decided *Morrissey* in 1972, declaring the need for procedural safeguards in revocation hearings involving *parolees*. The *Morrissey* case began with John J. Morrissey and G. Donald Booher, two Iowa convicts. Morrissey had pled guilty in 1967 to a bad-check charge and was sentenced to not more than seven years in prison. He was paroled a year later, but was rearrested within seven months for obtaining credit and buying a car under an assumed name, for failing to inform his parole officer of changes in his address, and for giving false information to the police. Booher had also been convicted of forgery in 1966, was sentenced to a maximum of ten years, and was paroled in 1968. In 1969 a report alleging violation of the conditions of parole was filed by Booher's parole officer, claiming that Booher had obtained a driver's license using a fictitious identity, operated a motor vehicle without permission, and had improperly left the jurisdiction of the parole authority. Both Morrissey and Booher had their parole revoked after an administrative review of violation reports written by parole officers. In ruling for the petitioners, the Court established procedural requirements pertaining to parole revocation proceedings.

Probation (or Parole) Violation An act or a failure to act by a probationer (or parolee) which does not conform to the conditions of probation (or parole).

Probation (or Parole) Revocation The administrative action of a probation (or paroling) authority removing a person from probationary (or parole) status in response to a violation of lawfully required conditions of probation (or parole), including the prohibition against commission of a new offense, and usually resulting in a return to prison.

After Morrissey, revocation proceedings would require that (1) written notice specifying the alleged violation be given to the parolee; (2) evidence of the violation be disclosed; (3) a neutral and detached body constitute the hearing authority; (4) the parolee should have the chance to appear and offer a defense, including testimony, documents, and witnesses; (5) the parolee has the right to cross-examine witnesses; and (6) a written statement be provided to the parolee at the conclusion of the hearing which includes the decision of the hearing body, the testimony considered, and reasons for revoking parole if such occurs.[46]

In 1973 the Court extended the procedural safeguards of *Morrissey* to *probationers* in *Gagnon* v. *Scarpelli* (1973). John Gagnon had pleaded guilty to armed robbery in Wisconsin and was sentenced to 15 years in prison. His sentence was suspended, and the judge ordered him to serve a 7-year probationary term. One month later, and only a day after having been transferred to the supervision of the Cook County, Illinois, Adult Probation Department, Gagnon was arrested by police in the course of a burglary. He was advised of his rights, but confessed to officers that he was in the process of stealing money and property when discovered. His probation was revoked without a hearing. Citing its own decision a year earlier in *Morrissey* v. *Brewer*, the Supreme Court ruled that probationers, because they face a substantial loss of liberty, were entitled to two hearings—the first, a preliminary hearing, to determine whether there is "probable cause to believe that he has committed a violation of his parole," and the second, "a somewhat more comprehensive hearing prior to the making of the final revocation decision." The Court also ruled that probation revocation hearings were to be held "under the conditions specified in *Morrissey* v. *Brewer*."

A separate question dealt with by the Court centered on the indigent status of petitioner Gagnon. While being careful to emphasize the narrowness of the particulars in this case, the Court added to the protections granted under *Morrissey* v. *Brewer*, ruling that probationers have the right to a lawyer, even if indigent, provided they claimed that either (1) they had not committed the alleged violation or (2) they had substantial mitigating evidence to explain their violation. In *Gagnon* and later cases, however, the Court reasserted that probation and parole revocation hearings were not a stage in the criminal prosecution process, but a simple adjunct to it, even though they might result in substantial loss of liberty. The difference is a crucial one, for it permits hearing boards and judicial review officers to function, at least to some degree, outside of the adversarial context of the trial court and with lessened attention to the rights of the criminally accused guaranteed by the Bill of Rights.

A more recent case, *Greenholtz* v. *Nebraska* (1979),[47] established that parole boards do not have to specify the evidence used in deciding to deny parole. The *Greenholtz* case focused on a Nebraska statute which required that inmates denied parole be provided with reasons for the denial. The Court held that reasons for parole denial might be provided in the interest of helping inmates prepare themselves for future review, but that to require the disclosure of evidence used in the review hearing would turn the process into an adversarial proceeding.

The 1983 Supreme Court case of *Bearden* v. *Georgia*[48] established that a defendant's probation could not be revoked for failure to pay a fine and make restitution if it could not be shown that the defendant was responsible for the failure. The Court also held that alternative forms of punishment must be considered by the hearing authority and be shown to be inadequate before the defendant can be incarcerated. Bearden had pleaded guilty to burglary and had been sentenced to three years' probation. One of the conditions of his probation required that he pay a fine of $250 and make restitution payments totaling $500. Bearden successfully made the first two payments, but then lost his job. His probation was

Restitution A court requirement that an alleged or convicted offender pay money or provide services to the victim of the crime or provide services to the community.

POLICY ISSUES

Evaluating Probation and Parole

In October 1993 the Bureau of Justice Statistics published *Performance Measures for the Criminal Justice System*, a collection of discussion papers produced by the BJS–Princeton Project group. The papers represent the best official effort to date to identify performance goals and associated measures useful in assessing the day-to-day operations of criminal justice agencies.

The Project identified, among others, the following goals and performance indicators in the area of community corrections:

Goals	Performance Indicators
1. Assess offender's suitability for placement	Accuracy and completeness of presentence investigation
	Timeliness of revocation and termination hearings
	Percentage of offenders recommended for probation and parole who violate their conditions or repeat offenses
2. Enforce court-ordered sanctions	Number of arrests and technical violations during supervision
	Percentage of ordered payments collected.
	Number of hours/days of community service performed
	Number of favorable discharges
3. Protect the community	Number and type of supervision contacts
	Number and type of technical violations during supervision
4. Assist offenders to change	Number of times clients attend treatment or work programs
	Employment during supervision
	Number of arrests and/or other violations during supervision
	Number of drug-free and/or alcohol-free days during supervision
	Attitude change
5. Restore crime victims	Degree of payment of restitution
	Extent of victim satisfaction with services and department

Source: Joan Petersilia, "Measuring the Performance of Community Corrections," in John J. DiIulio, Jr., et al., *Performance Measures for the Criminal Justice System: Discussion Papers from the BJS–Princeton Project* (Washington, D.C.: Bureau of Justice Statistics, October 1993).

revoked and he was imprisoned. The Supreme Court decision stated that "if the State determines a fine or restitution to be the appropriate and adequate penalty for the crime, it may not thereafter imprison a person solely because he lacked the resources to pay it."[49] The Court held that if a defendant lacks the capacity to pay a fine or make restitution, then the hearing authority must consider any viable alternatives to incarceration prior to imposing a term of imprisonment.

In another ruling affecting restitution, *Kelly* v. *Robinson* (1986),[50] the Court held that a restitution order cannot be vacated by a filing of bankruptcy. In the *Kelly* case, a woman convicted of illegally receiving welfare benefits was ordered to make restitution in the amount of $100 per month. Immediately following the sentence, the defendant filed for bankruptcy and listed the court-ordered restitution payment as a debt from which she sought relief. The bankruptcy court discharged the debt, and a series of appeals resulted in the U.S. Supreme Court granting *certiorari* and eventually holding that fines and other financial penalties ordered by criminal courts are not capable of being voided by bankruptcy proceedings.

Incriminating statements made by a probationer to a probation officer may be used as evidence if the probationer did not specifically claim a right against self-incrimination, according to *Minnesota* v. *Murphy* (1984).[51] Marshall Murphy was sentenced to three years' probation in 1980 on a charge of "false imprisonment" (kidnapping) stemming from an alleged attempted sexual attack. One condition of his probation required him to be entirely truthful with his probation officer "in all matters." Some time later Murphy admitted to his probation officer that he had confessed to a rape and murder in conversations with a counselor. He was later convicted of first-degree murder, partially on the basis of the statements made to his probation officer. Upon appeal, Murphy's lawyers claimed that their client should have been advised of his right against self-incrimination during his conversation with the parole officer. Although the Minnesota supreme court agreed, the U.S. Supreme Court found for the state, saying that the burden of invoking the Fifth Amendment privilege against self-incrimination in this case lay with the probationer.

An emerging legal issue today surrounds the potential liability of probation officers and parole boards and their representatives for the criminal actions of offenders under their supervision, or who they have released. Some courts have held that officers are generally immune from suit because they are performing a judicial function on behalf of the state.[52] Other courts, however, have indicated that parole board members who did not carefully consider mandated criteria for judging parole eligibility could be liable for injurious actions committed by parolees.[53] In general, however, most experts agree that parole board members cannot be successfully sued unless release decisions are made in a grossly negligent or wantonly reckless manner.[54] Discretionary decisions of individual probation and parole officers which result in harm to members of the public, however, may be more actionable under civil law, especially where their decisions were not reviewed by judicial authority.[55]

In a case that is unresolved as of this writing, a 15-year-old Oakland, California, girl brought suit in July 1991 against the California Department of Corrections, the California Parole Board, and Alameda County claiming negligence in the release of a man who raped her when she was 9 years old. The man, released from prison after serving 6 years of a 12-year sentence for the original rape, allegedly kidnaped and attacked the same girl again almost immediately after he was set free. In commenting on the case, the girl's attorney, Melvin Belli, said[56] "It's utterly inexcusable and intolerable in a civilized society that a Department of... Corrections could have been so negligent to have let this dangerous man out.... Their failure to protect that young girl and notify her or her family of his impending release, after he had violated her before, displays utter incompetence on their part." Parole officials said the family had never made a request to be notified of the offender's release.

THE FEDERAL PROBATION SYSTEM

The Federal Probation System is seventy years old.[57] In 1916 the U.S. Supreme Court in the *Killets* case[58] ruled that federal judges did not have the authority to suspend sentences and order probation. After a vigorous campaign by the National Probation Association, Congress finally passed the National Probation Act in 1925, authorizing the use of probation in federal courts. The bill came just in time to save a burgeoning federal prison system from serious overcrowding. The Mann Act, prohibition legislation, and the growth of organized crime had all led to increased arrests and a dramatic growth in the number of federal probationers in the early years of the system.

Although the 1925 act authorized one probation officer per federal judge, it allocated only $25,000 for officers' salaries. As a consequence, only 8 officers were hired to serve 132 judges, and the system came to rely heavily upon voluntary probation officers. Some sources indicate that as many as 40,000 probationers were under the supervision of volunteers at the peak of the system.[59] By 1930, however, Congress provided adequate funding, and a corps of salaried professionals began to provide probation services to the U.S. courts.

In recent years the work of federal probation officers has been dramatically affected by new rules of federal procedure. Presentence investigations have been especially affected. Revised Rule 32 of the *Federal Criminal Rules of Procedure*, for example, now mandates that federal probation officers who prepare presentence reports must:[60]

- Evaluate the evidence in support of facts.
- Resolve certain disputes between the prosecutor and defense attorney.
- Testify when needed to provide evidence in support of the administrative application of sentencing guidelines.
- Utilize an addendum to the report which, among other things, demonstrates that the report has been disclosed to the defense attorney, defendant, and government counsel.

Some authors have argued that these new requirements demand previously unprecedented skills from probation officers. Officers must now be capable of drawing objective conclusions based upon the facts they observe, and they must be able to make "independent judgments in the body of the report regarding which sets of facts by various observers the court should rely upon in imposing sentence."[61] They must also be effective witnesses in court during the trial phase of criminal proceedings. While in the past officers have often been called upon to provide testimony during revocation hearings, the informational role now mandated throughout the trial itself is new.

THE JOB OF A PROBATION/PAROLE OFFICER

The tasks performed by probation and parole officers are often quite similar. Some jurisdictions combine the roles of both into one job. This section describes the duties of probation and parole officers, whether they function separately from one another or whether they are performed by the same individual wearing the proverbial different hats. Probation/parole work consists primarily of four functions: (1) presentence investigations, (2) intake procedures, (3) needs assessment and diagnosis, and (4) the supervision of clients.

Both presentence investigations and intake procedures are applicable only where probation is a possibility. Presentence investigations were described in the last chapter. Intake procedures involve a dispute settlement process during which the probation officer works with the defendant and victim to resolve the complaint. Intake duties tend to be more common among juvenile probation officers than they are in adult criminal court, but all officers may find themselves in the position of having to recommend to the judge what sentencing alternative would best answer the needs of the case.

Diagnosis refers to the psychological inventorying of the probation/parole client, and may be done on either a formal basis involving the use of written tests administered by certified psychologists or through informal arrangements which typically depend upon the observational skills of the officer. Needs assessment extends beyond the psychological needs of the client to a cataloging of the services necessary for a successful experience on probation or parole.

Supervision is potentially the most active stage of the probation/parole process, involving months (and sometimes years) of periodic meetings between the officer and client and an ongoing assessment of the success of the probation/parole endeavor.

One special consideration affecting the work of all probation/parole officers is the need for confidentiality. The details of the presentence investigation, psychological tests, needs assessment, conversations between the officer and client, and so on, should not be public knowledge. On the other hand, courts have generally held that communications between the officer and client are not privileged, as they might be between a doctor and patient.[62] Hence, incriminating evidence related by a client can be shared by officers with appropriate authorities.

Difficulties with the Job

Probation and parole officers walk a fine line between the provision of quasi–social work services and custodial responsibilities. In effect, two conflicting images of the officer's role coexist. One is the social work model, which stresses a service role for officers and views probationers and parolees as "clients." Under the social work model, officers are seen as "caregivers," who attempt to assess accurately the needs of their clients and, through an intimate familiarity with available community services—from job placement, indigent medical care, and family therapy, to psychological and substance abuse counseling—match clients and community resources. The social work model depicts probation/parole as a "helping profession," wherein officers assist their clients in meeting the conditions imposed upon them by their sentence.

The other model is a correctional one. Under the correctional model, probation/parole clients are seen as "wards" whom officers are expected to control. This model emphasizes community protection, which officers are supposed to achieve through careful and close supervision. Custodial supervision means that officers will periodically visit their charges at work and at home, often arriving unannounced. It also means that they will be ready and willing to report clients for new offenses and for violations of the conditions of their release.

Most officers, by virtue of their personality and experiences, probably identify selectively with one of the two models we have described. They think of themselves either primarily as care givers or as correctional officers. Regardless of the emphasis which appeals most to individual officers, however, demands of the job are bound to generate role conflict at one time or another.

A second problem in probation/parole work is high caseloads. The President's Commission on Law Enforcement and the Administration of Justice recommended that probation/parole caseloads should average around 35 clients per officer.[63] However, caseloads of 250 clients are common in some jurisdictions. Various authors have found that high caseloads, combined with limited training, and time constraints forced by administrative and other demands, culminate in stopgap supervisory measures.[64] "Postcard probation," in which clients mail in a letter or card once a month to report on their whereabouts and circumstances, is an example of one stopgap measure used by harried agencies facing large caseloads, to keep track of their wards.[65]

Another difficulty with probation/parole work is the lack of opportunity for career mobility.[66] Probation and parole officers are generally assigned to small agencies, serving limited geographical areas, with one or two lead officers (usually called chief probation officers). Unless retirement or death claims the supervisors, there will be little chance for other officers to advance.

THE MOVE TOWARD INNOVATIVE OPTIONS IN SENTENCING

Alternative Sanctions
The use of split sentencing, shock probation and parole, home confinement, shock incarceration, and community service in lieu of other, more traditional, sanctions such as imprisonment and fines. Alternative sanctions are becoming increasingly popular as prison crowding grows.

Significant new options in sentencing have become available to judges in innovative jurisdictions over the past few decades. Impetus toward the widening of sentencing alternatives is being provided by a number of citizen groups and special interest organizations. One organization of special note is the Washington, D.C.–based Sentencing Project. The Sentencing Project was formed in 1986[67] through support from foundation grants.[68] It is dedicated to promoting a greater use of alternatives to incarceration and provides technical assistance to public defenders, court officials, and other community organizations.

The Sentencing Project and associated groups have contributed to the development of over 100 alternative sentencing service organizations. Most alternative sentencing services work in conjunction with defense attorneys to develop written sentencing plans. Such plans are basically well-considered citizen suggestions as to what appropriate sentencing should entail. Plans are often quite detailed, and may include letters of agreement from employers, family members, the defendant, and even victims. Sentencing plans may be used in plea bargaining sessions or presented to judges following trial and conviction. The basic philosophy behind defense-based alternative sentencing programs is quite simple: Where well-planned alternatives to imprisonment can be offered to judges, the likelihood of a prison sentence can be reduced. An early analysis of alternative sentencing plans such as those sponsored by the Sentencing Project show that they are accepted by judges in up to 80% of the cases in which they are recommended and that as many as two-thirds of offenders who receive alternative sentences successfully complete them.[69]

THE NEW OPTIONS

Innovative sentencing alternatives are also called intermediate sanctions. They include shock probation, split sentencing, shock parole, intensive supervision, shock incarceration, and home confinement. Intermediate sanctions have three distinct advantages:[70] (1) They are less expensive to operate on a per offender basis than imprisonment; (2) they are "socially cost effective," because they keep the offender in the community, thus avoiding

Split Sentence A sentence explicitly requiring the convicted person to serve a period of confinement in a local, state, or federal facility followed by a period of probation.

Shock Probation The practice of sentencing offenders to prison, allowing them to apply for probationary release, and enacting such release in surprise fashion. Offenders who receive shock probation may not be aware of the fact that they will be released on probation and may expect to spend a much longer time behind bars.

Shock Incarceration A sentencing option which makes use of "boot camp"-type prisons in order to impress upon convicted offenders the realities of prison life.

both the breakup of the family and the stigmatization which accompanies imprisonment; and (3) they provide flexibility in terms of resources, time of involvement, and place of service. Some of these new options are described in the paragraphs that follow.

Split Sentencing

In jurisdictions where split sentencing is an option, judges may impose a combination of a brief period of imprisonment and probation. Defendants sentenced under split sentencing are often ordered to serve time in a local jail rather than in a long-term confinement facility. "Ninety days in jail, together with two years of supervised probation," would be a typical split sentence.

Shock Probation/Shock Parole

Shock probation bears a considerable resemblance to split sentencing. Again, the offender serves a relatively short period of time in custody (usually in a prison rather than jail) and is released on probation by court order. The difference is that shock probation clients must *apply* for probationary release from confinement and cannot be certain of the judge's decision. Shock probation is, in effect, a resentencing decision made by the court. Probation is only a statutory possibility, and often little more than a vague hope of the offender as imprisonment begins. If probationary release is ordered, it may well come as a "shock" to the offender who, facing a sudden reprieve, may forswear future criminal involvement. Shock probation was first begun in Ohio in 1965[71] and is used today in about half the United States.[72]

New Jersey runs a model modern shock probation program which is administered by a specially appointed Screening Board composed of correctional officials and members of the public. The New Jersey program has served as an example to many other states. It has a stringent set of selection criteria which allow only inmates serving sentences for nonviolent crimes to apply to the Screening Board for release.[73] Inmates must have served at least 30 days prior to making application. Those who have served over 60 days are ineligible. Offenders are required to submit a personal plan describing anticipated activities upon release. The plan must include descriptions of the offender's problems, future plans, community resources, and people who can be relied upon to provide assistance. Part of the plan involves a community sponsor with whom the inmate must reside for a fixed period of time (usually a few months) following release. The New Jersey program is especially strict because it does not grant outright release, but rather allows only a 90-day initial period of freedom. If the inmate successfully completes the 90-day period, continued release may be requested.

Shock probation lowers the cost of confinement, maintains community family ties, and may be an effective rehabilitative tool.[74] Similar to shock probation is shock parole. Whereas shock probation is ordered by judicial authority, shock parole is an administrative decision made by a paroling authority. Parole commissions or their representatives may order an inmate's early release, hoping that brief exposure to prison may have reoriented the offender's life in a positive direction.

Shock Incarceration

Shock incarceration is the newest of the alternative sanctions discussed here. Shock incarceration, designed primarily for young, first offenders, utilizes military-style "boot camp" prison settings to provide a highly regimented program involving strict discipline,

A boot camp correctional officer greets a new arrival. Shock incarceration programs—also called boot camp prisons—provide a sentencing alternative which is growing rapidly in popularity. *Photo: R. Maiman/Sygma.*

physical training, and hard labor. Shock incarceration programs are of short duration, lasting for only 90 to 180 days. Offenders who successfully complete these programs are generally placed under community supervision. Program "failures" may be moved into the general prison population for longer terms of confinement.

The first shock incarceration program began in Georgia in 1983.[75] Since then, other programs have opened in Alabama, Arkansas, Arizona, Florida, Louisiana, Maryland, Michigan, Mississippi, New Hampshire, New York, Oklahoma, South Carolina, Texas, Massachusetts,[76] and other states. New York's program is the largest, with a capacity for 1,602 participants, while Tennessee's program can handle only 102.[77] There are other substantial differences between the states. About half provide for voluntary entry into their shock incarceration programs. A few allow inmates to decide when and whether they want to quit. Although most states allow judges to place offenders in such programs, some delegate that authority to corrections officials. Two states, Louisiana and Texas, authorize judges and corrections personnel joint authority in the decision-making process.[78]

Some states, such as Massachusetts, have begun to accept classes of female inmates into boot camp settings. The Massachusetts program, which first accepted women in 1993, requires inmates to spend nearly four months undergoing the rigors of training.

The few studies of shock incarceration programs which have been done appear to indicate that the programs are having a rehabilitative effect.[79] Participating offenders tend to report positive feelings about the programs and about their ability to modify their law-violating behavior.[80]

Mixed Sentencing and Community Service

Mixed sentences require that offenders serve weekends in jail while undergoing probation supervision during the week. Other types of mixed sentencing require participation in treatment or community service programs while a person is on probation. Community service programs began in Minnesota in 1972 with the Minnesota Restitution Program,[81] which gave property offenders the opportunity to work and turn over part of their pay as restitution to their victims. Courts throughout the nation quickly adopted the idea and began to build restitution orders into suspended-sentence agreements.

Community Service
A sentencing alternative which requires offenders to spend at least part of their time working for a community agency.

Community service is more an adjunct to, rather than a type of, correctional sentence. Community service is compatible with most other forms of innovation in probation and parole, except, perhaps for home confinement. Even there, however, offenders could be sentenced to community service activities which might be performed in the home or at a job site during the hours they are permitted to be away from their homes. Washing police cars, cleaning school buses, refurbishing public facilities, and assisting in local government offices are typical forms of community service. Some authors have linked the development of community service sentences to the notion that work and service to others are good for the spirit.[82] Community service participants are usually minor criminals, drunk drivers, and youthful offenders.

One problem with community service sentences is that authorities rarely agree on what they are supposed to accomplish. Most people admit that offenders who work in the community are able to reduce the costs of their own supervision. There is little agreement, however, over whether such sentences reduce recidivism, provide a deterrent, or act to rehabilitate offenders.

Intensive Supervision

Intensive probation supervision (IPS) has been described as the "strictest form of probation for adults in the United States."[83] In 1982 Georgia became one of the first states to implement intensive probation supervision. The Georgia program involves a minimum of five face-to-face contacts between the probationer and supervising officer per week, mandatory curfew, required employment, a weekly check of local arrest records, routine and unannounced alcohol and drug testing, automatic notification of arrest via the State Crime Information Network, and 132 hours of community service.[84] Caseloads of probation officers involved in IPS are much lower than the national average. Georgia officers work as a team with 1 probation officer and 2 surveillance officers supervising around 40 probationers.[85] IPS is designed to achieve control in a community setting over offenders who would otherwise have gone to prison.

North Carolina's Intensive Supervision Program follows the model of the Georgia program and adds a mandatory "prison awareness visit" within the first three months of supervision. North Carolina selects candidates for the Intensive Supervision Program on the basis of six factors: (1) the level of risk the offender is deemed to represent to the community; (2) assessment of the candidate's potential to respond to the program; (3) existing community attitudes toward the offender; (4) the nature and extent of known substance abuse; (5) the presence or absence of favorable community conditions, such as positive family ties, the possibility of continuing meaningful employment, constructive leisure-time activities, and adequate residence; and (6) the availability of community resources relevant to the needs of the case (such as drug treatment services, mental health programs, vocational training facilities, and volunteer services).[86]

Some states have extended intensive supervision to parolees, allowing the early release of persons who would otherwise serve lengthy prison terms. The North Carolina program, for example, contained 1,522 probationers and 260 parolees under intensive supervision during 1987, and reported a failure (revocation) rate of 15.2%.[87]

Via an alternative sentencing program, juvenile offenders in Bellflower, California, work with children who are physically challenged. *Photo: Bart Barthalomew/Black Star.*

Home Confinement

Home confinement is also referred to as house arrest. It has been defined as "a sentence imposed by the court in which offenders are legally ordered to remain confined in their own residences."[88] They may leave only for medical emergencies, employment, and purchasing household essentials. House arrest has been cited as offering a valuable alternative to prison for offenders with special needs. Pregnant women, geriatric convicts, offenders with special handicaps, seriously or terminally ill offenders, and the mentally retarded might all be better supervised through home confinement than traditional incarceration.

Florida's Community Control Program, authorized by the state's Correctional Reform Act of 1983, is the most ambitious home confinement program in the country.[89] On any given day in Florida as many as 5,000 offenders are restricted to their homes and supervised by community control officers who visit unannounced. Candidates for the program are required to agree to specific conditions, including (1) restitution, (2) family support payments, and (3) supervisory fees (around $50 per month). They are also obligated to fill out daily logs about their activities. Community control officers are required to maintain a minimum of 20 contacts per month with each offender. Additional discussions are held with neighbors, spouses, friends, landlords, employers, and others in order to allow the earliest possible detection of program violations or renewed criminality.

Florida's most serious home confinement offenders are monitored via a computerized system of *electronic bracelets*. Random telephone calls require the offender to insert a computer chip worn in a wrist band into a specially installed modem in the home, verifying his or her presence. More modern units make it possible to record the time a supervised person enters or leaves the home and whether the phone line or equipment has been tampered with, and to send or receive messages.[90] Electronic monitoring of offenders has undergone dramatic growth both in Florida and across the nation. A survey by the National Institute of Justice[91] showed only 826 offenders being monitored electronically in mid-1987, while

Home Confinement
House arrest. Individuals ordered confined in their homes are sometimes monitored electronically to be sure they do not leave during the hours of confinement (absence from the home during working hours is often permitted).

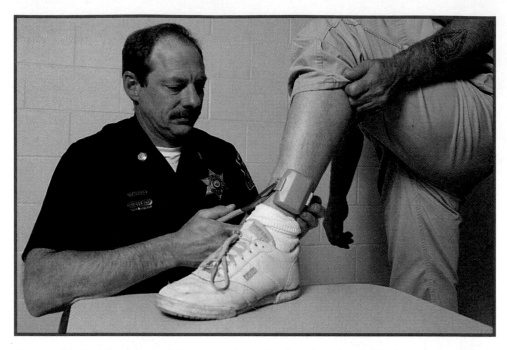

Commonly called "house arrest," the electronic monitoring of convicted offenders appears to have the capacity to dramatically reduce correctional costs for non-dangerous offenders. This photograph demonstrates the use of a electronic "ankle bracelet," capable of answering a computer's call to verify that the wearer is at home. *Photo: Larry Downing/Sygma.*

by 1989 the number had grown to around 6,500. By the start of 1990, industry sources reported having shipped over 15,000 monitoring devices.

House arrest is viewed by many states as a cost-effective response to the rising expense of imprisonment. Estimates show that traditional home confinement programs cost about $1,500 to $7,000 per offender per year, while electronic monitoring increases the costs by at least $1,000.[92] Advocates of house arrest argue that it is also socially cost-effective,[93] as it provides no opportunity for the kinds of negative socialization which occur in prison. Opponents have pointed out that house arrest may endanger the public, that it may be illegal,[94] and that it may be little or no punishment. In 1988 John Zaccaro, Jr., the son of former vice-presidential candidate Geraldine Ferraro, was sentenced to four months of house arrest for selling cocaine. His $1,500-a-month luxury apartment, with maid service, cable TV, and many other expensive amenities, was in a building designed for expense account businesspeople on short assignments to the Burlington, Vermont, area. Zaccaro's prosecutor observed, "This guy is a drug felon and he's living in conditions that 99.9 percent of the people of Vermont couldn't afford."[95]

QUESTIONS ABOUT ALTERNATIVE SANCTIONS

As prison populations continue to rise, alternative sentencing strategies will become increasingly attractive. Many questions remain to be answered, however, before most alternative sanctions can be employed with confidence. These questions have been succinctly stated in a Rand Corporation study authored by Joan Petersilia.[96] Unfortunately, while the questions can be listed, few answers are yet available. Some of the questions Petersilia identifies are

- Do alternative sentencing programs threaten public safety?
- How should program participants be selected?
- What are the long-term effects of community sanctions on people assigned to them?
- Are alternative sanctions cost-effective?
- Who should pay the bill for alternative sanctions?
- Who should manage stringent community-based sanctions?
- How should program outcomes be judged?
- What kind of offenders benefit most from alternative sanctions?

THE FUTURE OF PROBATION

AND PAROLE

Parole has been widely criticized in recent years. Citizen groups claim that it unfairly reduces prison sentences imposed on serious offenders. Officials say that parole gives a false impression of the realities of criminal punishment. Academicians allege that parole programs can provide no assurance against continued criminal victimization. Media attacks upon parole have centered on recidivism and have highlighted the so-called "revolving door" of prisons as representative of the failure of parole.

In the late 1980s the case of Larry Singleton came to represent all that is wrong with parole. Singleton was convicted of raping 15-year-old Mary Vincent, then hacking off her arms and leaving her for dead on a hillside.[97] When an apparently unrepentant[98] Singleton was paroled after eight years in prison, public outcry was tremendous. Communities banded together to deny him residence, and he had to be paroled to the grounds of San Quentin prison.

Official attacks upon parole have come from some powerful corners. Senator Edward Kennedy has called for the abolition of parole, as did former Attorney General Griffin Bell and former U.S. Bureau of Prisons Director Norman Carlson.[99] Prisoners have also challenged the fairness of parole, saying it is sometimes arbitrarily granted and creates an undue amount of uncertainty and frustration in the lives of inmates. Parolees have complained about the unpredictable nature of the parole experience, citing their powerlessness in the parole contract. Against the pressure of official attacks and cases like that of Singleton, parole advocates struggle to clarify and communicate the value of parole in the correctional process.

Probation, although it has generally fared better than parole, is not without its critics. The primary purpose of probation has always been rehabilitation. Probation is a powerful rehabilitative tool because, at least in theory, it allows the resources of a community to be brought to bear in a focused rehabilitative effort. Unfortunately for advocates of probation, however, the rehabilitative ideal holds far less significance today than it has in the past. The contemporary demand for "just deserts" has eclipsed the rehabilitative ideal and appears to have reduced the tolerance society as a whole feels for even relatively minor offenders. Added to that is the fact that the image of probation has not benefited from its all-too-frequent and inappropriate use with repeat or relatively serious offenders. Probation advocates themselves have been forced to admit that it is not a very powerful deterrent because it is far less punishing than a term of imprisonment.

Lawrence Singleton, shown here immediately prior to release, caused a national uproar when he was paroled. Singleton had been convicted of the rape and mutilation of a 15-year-old girl, whose arms he cut off. Singleton was later rearrested and convicted in Florida for the theft of a disposable camera. *Photo: AP/Wide World Photos.*

Other arguments in support of probation have been weakened because some of the positive contributions probation had to offer are now being made available from other sources. Victims' compensation programs, for example, have taken the place of direct restitution payments to victims by probationers.

Acknowledging the complexities of the present situation, Vincent O'Leary has identified six trends bound to affect the future of both probation and parole.[100]

1. Increasing pressure to ensure that community supervision reflects the goals society has established for the handling of offenders
2. The acknowledgment of risk control as an important function of the criminal justice system and the need to recognize that errors can be made in assessing risks
3. The increased use of a variety of supervisory methods and variation in the size of caseloads supervised by one officer
4. A clarification in the process by which offenders are moved from one level of supervision to another
5. A greater emphasis on the accountability of individual officers as to the specific behavioral objectives to be achieved in working with clients
6. The creation of information systems useful in judging effectiveness and in providing feedback on specific supervisory practices.

Probation will probably always remain a viable sentencing option if only because there will always be minor offenders for whom imprisonment is hard to justify. The return to determinate sentencing, however, cited earlier in this book, is a clear indication that parole, as it has existed for the last half century, is in for serious restructuring and may not survive in recognizable form. The overcrowded conditions of our nation's prisons, however, will probably work to continue at least a limited use of parole. Even states which have adopted determinate sentencing statutes still depend upon a brief parole experience to meet successfully the basic needs faced by ex-offenders of finding housing, employment, and social services.

The movement toward determinate sentencing, generally seen as the death knell of parole programs, may in fact eliminate two of the most often-cited shortcomings of parole, while allowing at least limited forms of parole to continue. Where determinate sentencing laws coexist with parole programs, release on parole is no longer the result of potentially arbitrary decisions made by parole boards staffed with nonexpert political appointees. Second, because determinate sentencing laws specify parole release dates and the precise period of parole supervision which an inmate can anticipate serving, they eliminate the unpredictability complained of by parolees themselves.

SUMMARY

Probation and parole are two of the most recent large-scale innovations in the long history of correctional supervision. They can be seen as either a blessing or a curse, depending upon which of their attributes are emphasized. Both probation and parole provide opportunities for the reintegration of offenders into the community through the use of resources not readily available in institutional settings. Unfortunately, however, increased freedom for criminal offenders also means some degree of increased risk for other members of society. Until and unless probation and parole solve the problems of accurate risk assessment, reduced recidivism, and adequate supervision, they will continue to be viewed with suspicion by clients and citizenry alike.

DISCUSSION QUESTIONS

1. Probation is a sentence served while under supervision in the community. Do you believe that a person who commits a crime should be allowed to serve all or part of his or her sentence in the community? If so, what conditions would you impose on the offender?

2. Can you think of any other "general conditions" of probation or parole that you might add to the list of those found in the sample probation and parole forms in this chapter? If so, what would they be? Why would you want to add them?

3. Do you believe that ordering an offender to make restitution to his or her victim will teach the offender to be a more responsible person? Offer support for your opinion.

4. Do you believe that "role conflict" is a real part of most probation and parole officer's jobs? If so, do you see any way to reduce the role conflict experienced by probation and parole officers? How might you do it?

5. Do you think home confinement is a good idea? What do you think is the future of home confinement? In your opinion, does it discriminate against certain kinds of offenders? How might it be improved?

ENDNOTES

1. As quoted in *Criminal Justice Newsletter*, January 19, 1993, p. 1.
2. James M. Byrne, "Probation," a National Institute of Justice Crime File Series Study Guide (Washington, D.C.: U.S. Department of Justice, 1988), p. 1.
3. President's Commission on Law Enforcement and Administration of Justice, *The Challenge of Crime in a Free Society* (Washington, D.C.: U.S. Government Printing Office, 1967), p. 166.
4. "Paroled Rapist, Called 'Cured,' Charged with Murder of 2," *Fayetteville-Observer Times* (North Carolina), June 16, 1992, p. 4A.
5. "2-Time Parolee Charged in Slayings of 6 Women," *Fayetteville Observer-Times* (North Carolina), August 5, 1992.
6. "Parolee Confesses to Killing 4 Girls," *The Robesonian*, May 29, 1992, p. 1A.
7. President's Commission.
8. Alexander B. Smith and Louis Berlin, *Introduction to Probation and Parole* (St. Paul, MN: West Publishing, 1976), p. 75.
9. John Augustus, *John Augustus, First Probation Officer: John Augustus' Original Report on His Labors—1852* (Montclair, NJ: Patterson-Smith, 1972).
10. Smith and Berlin, *Introduction to Probation and Parole*, p. 77.
11. Ibid., p. 80.
12. George C. Killinger, Hazel B. Kerper, and Paul F. Cromwell, Jr., *Probation and Parole in the Criminal Justice System* (St. Paul, MN: West Publishing, 1976), p. 25.
13. Byrne, "Probation," p. 1.
14. Ibid.
15. Criminal Justice Institute, *The Corrections Yearbook 1993* (South Salem, NY: The Institute, 1993).
16. Bureau of Justice Statistics, *Report to the Nation on Crime and Justice*, 2nd ed. (Washington, D.C.: U.S. Department of Justice, 1988), p. 105.
17. "The Effectiveness of Felony Probation: Results from an Eastern State," *Justice Quarterly* (December 1991), p. 525–543.
18. Joan Petersilia, Susan Turner, James Kahan, and Joyce Peterson, *Granting Felons Probation: Public Risks and Alternatives* (Santa Monica, CA: The Rand Corporation, 1985).
19. Ibid.
20. "Woman Gets Probation for Shooting Fiance," *Fayetteville Observer-Times* (North Carolina), April 16, 1992, p. 9A.
21. George M. and Camille Graham Camp, *The Corrections Yearbook: Probation and Parole 1993* (South Salem, NY: Criminal Justice Institute, 1993).
22. Stephanie Minor-Harper and Christopher A. Innes, "Time Served in Prison and on Parole, 1984," Bureau of Justice Statistics Special Report (1987).

23. Ibid.

24. Ibid.

25. Ibid.

26. Ibid., p. 6.

27. Ibid., p. 4.

28. George M. and Camille Graham Camp, *The Corrections Yearbook: Probation and Parole 1993* (South Salem, NY: Criminal Justice Institute, 1993).

29. American Correctional Association, *Vital Statistics in Corrections*, p. 55.

30. *The Corrections Yearbook: Probation and Parole 1993*.

31. Byrne, "Probation."

32. Ibid., p. 3.

33. Peter Finn and Dale Parent, *Making the Offender Foot the Bill: A Texas Program* (Washington, D.C.: National Institute of Justice, 1992), and "Benefits of Probation Fees Cited in Texas Program," *Criminal Justice Newsletter*, January 19, 1993, p. 5.

34. See Andrew von Hirsch and Kathleen J. Hanrahan, *Abolish Parole?* (Washington, D.C.: Law Enforcement Assistance Administration, 1978).

35. Patrick A. Langan and Mark A. Cunniff, *Recidivism of Felons on Probation 1986–1989* (Washington, D.C.: Bureau of Justice Statistics, 1992).

36. Paul F. Cromwell, Jr., George Killinger, Hazel B. Kerper, and Charles Walker, *Probation and Parole in the Criminal Justice System*, 2nd ed. (St. Paul, MN: West Publishing, 1985).

37. Ibid., p. 177.

38. Ibid.

39. Ibid., p. 178.

40. *Griffin* v. *Wisconsin*, 483 U.S. 868, 107 S.Ct. 3164 (1987).

41. *Escoe* v. *Zerbst*, 295 U.S. 490 (1935).

42. *Mempa* v. *Rhay*, 389 U.S. 128 (1967).

43. A deferred sentence involves postponement of the sentencing decision, which may be made at a later time, following an automatic review of the defendant's behavior in the interim. A suspended sentence requires no review unless the probationer violates the law or conditions of probation. Both may result in imprisonment.

44. *Morrissey* v. *Brewer*, 408 U.S. 471 (1972).

45. *Gagnon* v. *Scarpelli*, 411 U.S. 778 (1973).

46. Smith and Berlin, *Introduction to Probation and Parole*, p. 143.

47. *Greenholtz* v. *Inmate of Nebraska Penal and Correctional Complex*, 442 U.S. 1 (1979).

48. *Bearden* v. *Georgia*, 461 U.S. 660, 103 S.Ct. 2064, 76 L.Ed. 2d 221 (1983).

49. Ibid.

50. *Kelly* v. *Robinson*, U.S. 107, S.Ct. 353, 93 L.Ed. 2d 216 (1986).

51. *Minnesota* v. *Murphy*, U.S. 104, S.Ct. 1136, 79 L.Ed. 2d 409 (1984).

52. *Harlow* v. *Clatterbuick*, 30 CLr. 2364 (VA S.Ct. 1986); *Santangelo* v. *State*, 426 N.Y.S. 2d. 931 (1980); *Welch* v. *State*, 424 N.Y.S. 2d. 774 (1980); and *Thompson* v. *County of Alameda*, 614 P. 2d. 728 (1980).

53. *Tarter* v. *State of New York*, 38 CLr. 2364 (NY S.Ct. 1986); *Grimm* v. *Arizona Board of Pardons and Paroles*; 115 Arizona 260, 564 P. 2d. 1227 (1977); and *Payton* v. *United States*, 636 F. 2d. 132 (5th Cir.).

54. Rolando V. del Carmen, *Potential Liabilities of Probation and Parole Officers* (Cincinnati, OH: Anderson, 1986), p. 89.

55. See, for example, *Semler* v. *Psychiatric Institute*, 538 F. 2d 121 (4th Cir. 1976).

56. "Girl Sues County, State for Attack by Parolee," *Fayetteville Observer-Times* (North Carolina), July 7, 1991, p. 5A.

57. This section owes much to Sanford Bates, "The Establishment and Early Years of the Federal Probation System," *Federal Probation* (June 1987), pp. 4–9.

58. *Ex parte United States*, 242 U.S. 27.

59. Bates, "The Establishment and Early Years of the Federal Probation System," p. 6.

60. As summarized by Susan Krup

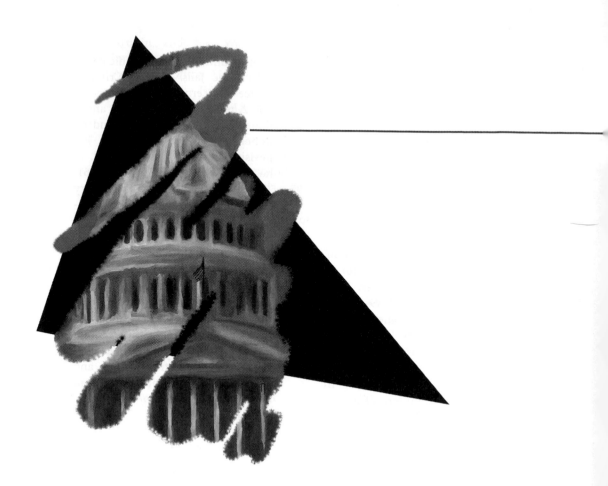

INDIVIDUAL RIGHTS VERSUS SOCIAL CONCERNS

THE RIGHTS OF THE IMPRISONED

Common law, constitutional, and humanitarian rights of the imprisoned:

A Right Against Cruel or Unusual Punishment
A Right to Religious Freedom While Imprisoned
A Right to Freedom of Speech
A Right to Legal Assistance
A Right to Sanitary and Healthy Conditions
A Right to Protection from Physical Harm
A Right Against Corporal Punishments
A Right to Due Process Prior to Denial of Privileges

The individual rights listed must be effectively balanced against these community concerns:

Secure Prisons
Control over Inmates
The Prevention of Escape
Punishment of the Guilty
The Reduction of Recidivism
Affordable Prisons
Rehabilitation

How does our system of justice work toward balance?

P A R T   F O U R

PRISONS

Eye for eye, tooth for tooth, hand for hand, foot for foot.
    —EXODUS 21:24 (B.C. CIRCA 1200)

The work of eradicating crimes is not by making punishment familiar, but formidable.
    —OLIVER GOLDSMITH (1728-1774)

Justice delayed is justice denied.
    —WILLIAM GLADSTONE (1809-1898)

Prisons and jails are still, as they have been for almost 200 years, the centerpiece around which other criminal sanctions revolve. But this is not because [they] have been found to be the most effective or cost-efficient way of punishing individuals or protecting the public's safety. The focus on, and some would say obsession with, incarceration rather stems from the unquestioning assumption that what we have done in the past should be done in the future.
    —REPORT OF THE AMERICAN BAR ASSOCIATION (1992)

PRISONS

To put people behind walls and bars and do little or nothing to change them is to win a battle but lose a war. It is wrong. It is expensive. It is stupid.[1]
    —FORMER CHIEF JUSTICE WARREN E. BURGER

The person of a prisoner sentenced to imprisonment in the State prison is under the protection of the law, and any injury to his person, not authorized by law, is punishable in the same manner as if he were not convicted or sentenced.
    —CALIFORNIA PENAL CODE, SECTION 2650

Years ago I began to recognize my kinship with all living beings....I said then, and I say now, that while there is a lower class I am in it; while there is a criminal element, I am of it; while there is a soul in prison, I am not free.
    —EUGENE V. DEBS
    AMERICAN SOCIALIST LEADER (1855–1926)

KEY WORDS

lex talionis

penitentiary

congregate but silent

Alexander Maconochie

industrial prison

community corrections

justice model

recidivism

design capacity

workhouse

Pennsylvania system

Alexis de Tocqueville

Sir Walter Crofton

state-use system

deinstitutionalization

warehousing

Robert Martinson

accreditation

brideswell

Auburn system

reformatory

work release

Ashurst-Sumners Act

medical model

incapacitation

privatization

EARLY PUNISHMENTS

Prison A state or federal confinement facility having custodial authority over adults sentenced to confinement.

To the popular mind, **prisons** stand as bastions of criminal punishment. Because they are so much with us, however, we tend to forget that prisons, as correctional institutions, are relatively new. Prior to the emergence of imprisonment, convicted offenders were subjected to fines, physical punishment, or death. Corporal punishments were the most common and generally fit the doctrine of *lex talionis* (the law of retaliation). Under *lex talionis* the convicted offender was sentenced to a punishment which most closely approximated the original injury. Also called "an eye for an eye, and a tooth for a tooth," this early rule of retaliation generally duplicated the offence, with the offender as the substitute victim. If a person blinded another, they were blinded in return. Murderers were themselves killed, with the form of execution sometimes being tailored to approximate the method they had used.

FLOGGING

Historically, the most widely used of physical punishments was flogging.[2] The Bible mentions instances of whipping, and Christ himself was scourged. Whipping was widely used in England throughout the Middle Ages, and some offenders were beaten as they ran. American colonists carried the practice of flogging with them to the new world. The Western frontier provided the novel opportunity, quickly seized upon by settlers, of whipping convicted criminals as they were run out of town and into the hinterlands. Banishment may have been little better than a death sentence, since it afforded little opportunity for the exiled offender to survive.

Whipping could be deadly. The Russian knot, for example, was fashioned out of leather thongs tipped with fishhooklike wires. A few stripes with the knot produced serious lacerations and blood loss. The cat-o'-nine tails used at least nine strands of leather or rope instead of the single strip of leather which makes up most whips.

The practice of whipping is still with us. Amnesty International has reported its use in various parts of the world for political and other prisoners. The last officially sanctioned flogging of a criminal offender in the United States happened in Delaware on June 16, 1952, when a burglar received 20 lashes.[3]

MUTILATION

Flogging was a painful punishment whose memory might deter repeat offenses. Mutilation, on the other hand, was primarily a strategy of specific deterrence which incapacitated individuals in the interest of preventing future crimes. Throughout history various societies have amputated the hands of thieves and robbers, blinded spies, and castrated rapists. Blasphemers have had their tongues ripped out, and pickpockets have suffered broken fingers. Extensive mutilation was instituted in eleventh-century Britain and imposed upon hunters who poached on royal lands.[4]

Some countries in the Arab world today still rely upon a limited use of mutilation as a penalty which incapacitates, among them Iran and Saudi Arabia. Mutilation also creates a general deterrent by providing potential offenders with walking examples of the consequences of crime.

BRANDING

In some societies branding has been used as a lesser form of mutilation. Prior to modern technology and the advent of mechanized record keeping, branding served to identify convicted offenders readily and to warn others with whom they might come into contact of their potential for deviance.

The Romans, Greeks, French, British, and many other societies have all used branding at one time or another. It was not until 1829 that the British Parliament officially eliminated branding as a punishment for crime, although the practice had probably ended somewhat earlier.

Barnes and Teeters report that branding in the American colonies was customary for certain crimes, with first offenders being branded on the hand and repeat offenders receiving an identifying mark on the forehead.[5] Women were rarely marked physically, although they were shamed and forced to wear marked clothing. Nathaniel Hawthorne's story of the

The whipping post and pillory at New Castle, Delaware, in the early 1800s. *Courtesy of the Library of Congress.*

Scarlet Letter is a report on that practice, where the central figure is required to wear a red letter "A," signifying adultery.

Public humiliation

A number of early punishments were designed to impose public humiliation and to allow members of the community an opportunity for vengeance. The stocks and the pillory were two such punishments. The pillory closed over the head and hands and held the offender in a standing position, while the stocks kept the person sitting with the head free. A few hundred years ago each town had its stocks or pillory usually located in some central square or alongside a major thoroughfare.

Offenders found themselves captive and on public display. They could expect to be heckled and spit upon by passers-by. Other citizens might gather to throw tomatoes or rotten eggs. On occasion, citizens who were particularly outraged by the magnitude or nature of the offense would substitute rocks for other less lethal missiles and end the offender's life. Retribution remained a community prerogative, and citizens wielded the power of final sentencing. Barnes and Teeters report that the pillory was still used in Delaware as late as 1905.[6]

The brank and ducking stool provided other forms of public humiliation. The brank was a bird cage–like device which fit over the offender's head. On it was a small door which, when closed, caused a razor-sharp blade to be inserted into the mouth. The ducking stool looked like a see-saw. The offender was tied to it, and when operated, it lowered the person into a river or lake, turning them nearly upside down like a duck searching for food underwater. Both devices were used in colonial times to punish gossips and were designed to fit that crime by teaching the offender to keep a shut mouth or a still tongue.

Workhouses

The sixteenth century was a time of economic upheaval in Europe, caused partly by wars and partly by the growing roots of the industrial revolution which was soon to sweep the continent. By midcentury thousands of unemployed and vagrant people were scouring towns and villages seeking food and shelter. It was not long before they depleted the economic reserves of churches, which were the primary social relief agencies of the time.

> Incarceration is a crash course in extortion and criminal behavior.
>
> —*Vincent Schiraldi*
> *National Center on Institutions and Alternatives*

In the belief that poverty was caused by laziness, governments were quick to create workhouses designed to instill "habits of industry" in the unemployed. The first workhouse in Europe opened in 1557 in a former British palace called Saint Bridget's Well. The name was shortened to "Brideswell," and brideswells became a synonym for workhouses. Brideswells taught work habits, not specific skills. Inmates were made to fashion their own furniture, build additions to the facility, and raise gardens. When the number of inmates exceeded the volume of useful work to be done, "make-over" projects, including treadmills and cranks, were invented to keep them busy.

Workhouses were judged successful, if only because they were constantly filled. By 1576 Parliament decreed that every county in England should build a workhouse.

Although workhouses are forerunners of our modern prisons, they did not incarcerate criminal offenders—only vagrants. Nor were they designed to punish convicts, but served instead to reinforce the value of hard work.

TRANSPORTATION

The ancient Hebrews periodically forced a sacrificial member of the tribe into the wilderness, a practice which has given us the modern word "scapegoating." In following suit, many societies have banished their outlaws. The French sent offenders to Devil's Island, and the Russians have used Siberia for centuries for the same purpose.

England sent convicts to the American colonies beginning in 1618. Transportation served the dual purpose of providing a captive labor force for development of the colonies while assuaging growing English sentiments opposing corporal punishments. In 1776, however, the Revolution forced the practice to end, and British penology fostered the use of aging ships, called hulks, as temporary prisons. Hulks were anchored in harbors throughout the country and served as floating confinement facilities even after transportation was resumed.

In 1787, only 17 years after Captain Cook had discovered the continent, Australia became the new port of call for English prisoners. The name of Captain William Bligh, governor of the New South Wales penal colony, survives down to the present day as a symbol of the difficult conditions and rough men and women of the times.

THE EMERGENCE OF PRISONS

The world's first true prison may never be known. John Howard, an early prison reformer, mentions prisons in Hamburg, Germany; Berne, Switzerland; and Florence, Italy, in his 1777 text, *State of Prisons.*[7]

Some early efforts at the imprisonment of offenders, in which serving time became a punishment for crime, can be found in the Hospice of San Michele, a papal prison which opened in 1704, and the Maison de Force, begun at Ghent, Belgium, in 1773. The Hospice was actually a residential school for delinquent boys and housed 60 youngsters at its opening. Both facilities stressed reformation over punishment and became early alternatives to the use of physical and public punishments. Figure 12–1 depicts the historical stages through which prisons progressed following introduction of the concept of incarceration as a punishment for crime.

THE PENETENTIARY ERA (1790-1825)

In 1790 Philadelphia's Walnut Street Jail was converted into a penitentiary by the Pennsylvania Quakers. The Quakers, following the legacy of William Penn, intended to introduce religious and humane principles into the handling of offenders. The strategy of imprisonment which they established carries over to the present day.[8]

Inmates of the Philadelphia Penitentiary were held in solitary confinement from which they were expected to wrestle with the evils they harbored. Penance was the vehicle through which rehabilitation was anticipated, and a study of the Bible was strongly encouraged.

Pennsylvania Style A form of imprisonment developed by the Pennsylvania Quakers around 1790 as an alternative to corporal punishments. The style made use of solitary confinement and resulted in the nation's first penitentiaries.

Era	Dates	Representative Institutions
Penitentiary	1790–1825	Pennsylvania System (Eastern and Western Institutions at Cherry Hill and Pittsburgh, PA)
Mass prison stage (congregate)	1825–1876	New York System (Auburn, NY)
Reformatory	1876–1890	Elmira Reformatory (Elmira, NY)
Industrial	1890–1935	Auburn, Sing Sing, Statesville, San Quentin, Attica and others
Punitive	1935–1945	Alcatraz and most former "industrial" institutions
Treatment	1945–1967	Federal penitentiary at Marion, Il, and many others
Community-based decarceration)	1967–1980	Massachusetts Youth services and others
Warehousing	1980–1990	Most major prisons
Overcrowding/Early release	1990–Present	Most state prison systems

Note: With the possible exception of the Industrial Era, dates shown are approximations. Ending dates are generally more indicative of a decline in emphasis than an actual ending of a particular orientation. For example, the Treatment Era, now in decline, is still very much a part of contemporary American corrections, although the primary concern in prisons today is on "overcrowding."

FIGURE 12–1   Stages of prison development in the United States.

Solitary confinement was the rule, and the penitentiary was designed to minimize contact between inmates and between inmates and staff. Exercise was allowed in small high-walled yards attached to each cell. Eventually handicrafts were introduced into the prison setting, permitting prisoners to work in their cells.

Following the Philadelphia model, the Eastern Penitentiary (1829) opened in Cherry Hill, Pennsylvania, and the Western Penitentiary (1826) in Pittsburgh. Solitary confinement and individual cells, supported by a massive physical structure with impenetrable walls became synonymous with the Pennsylvania system of imprisonment. Supporters of the Pennsylvania style included many well-known figures of the day, among them Benjamin Franklin and Benjamin Rush, both members of the influential Philadelphia Society for Alleviating the Miseries of Public Prisons.[9]

THE MASS PRISON STAGE (1825–1876)

Vermont, Massachusetts, Maryland, and New York all built institutions modeled after Pennsylvania's penitentiaries. As prison populations began to grow, however, solitary confinement became prohibitively expensive. One of the first large prisons to abandon the Pennsylvania model was the New York State Prison at Auburn. Auburn prison innovated the congregate but silent system, at which inmates lived, ate, and worked together in enforced

The Walnut Street Jail—America's first "true" prison, circa 1800. *Photo: Culver Pictures.*

silence. Congregate workshops were much more profitable than were the solitary handicrafts of the Pennsylvania system, and this style of imprisonment came to be known as the Auburn system. The Auburn system reintroduced corporal punishments into the handling of offenders. Whereas isolation and enforced idleness were inherent punishments under the Pennsylvania system, Auburn depended upon whipping and hard labor to maintain the rule of silence.[10]

An avowed test of the Pennsylvania style, an experiment in solitary confinement, was conducted at the Auburn prison. Eighty-three men were placed in small solitary cells on Christmas Day of 1821 and released in 1823 and 1824. Five of the 83 died, 1 went insane, another attempted suicide, and the others became "seriously demoralized."[11] Although the Auburn experiment did not accurately simulate the conditions in Pennsylvania (it allowed for no handicrafts or exercise and placed prisoners in tiny cells), it was widely used in condemnation of the Pennsylvania style. The Reverend Louis Dwight, an influential prison reformer of the time, became an advocate of the Auburn system, citing its lower cost[12] and humane conditions.[13] As a consequence, most American prisons built after 1825 followed the Auburn architectural style and system of prison discipline.

A number of European governments sent representatives to study the virtues of the two American systems. Interestingly, most concluded that the Pennsylvania style was more conducive to reformation than was Auburn, and many European prisons adopted the strict separation of inmates. Gustave de Beaumont and Alexis de Tocqueville, two French visitors, stressed the dangers of contamination, whereby prisoners housed in Auburn-like systems could negatively influence one another.[14]

THE REFORMATORY STAGE (1876-1890)

With the tension between the Auburn and Pennsylvania systems, American penology existed in an unsettled state for a half-century. That tension was resolved in 1876 by the emergence of a new institutional style—reformatory. The reformatory concept grew out of practices innovated by two outstanding correctional leaders of the mid-1880s: Captain Alexander Maconochie and Sir Walter Crofton.

Auburn Style A form of imprisonment developed in New York State around 1820 which depended upon mass prisons, where prisoners were held in congregate fashion. This style of imprisonment was a primary competitor with the Pennsylvania style.

Reformatory Concept A late–nineteenth-century correctional model based upon the use of the indeterminate sentence and belief in the possibility of rehabilitation, especially for youthful offenders. The reformatory concept faded with the emergence of industrial prisons around the turn of the century.

THEORY INTO PRACTICE

CHAPLAIN JAMES FINLEY'S LETTER
FROM THE OHIO PENITENTIARY 1850

It is true, there are yet two systems of prison discipline still in use, but both claim to have the two parties—the criminal and society—equally in view. The congregate system, going on the supposition that habits of labor and moral character are the chief desiderata among this class of men, set them to work at those trades for which their physical and mental powers, together with the consideration of their former occupations, may more especially adapt them; religious instruction is also given them by men appointed expressly for the purpose; and they are permitted to labor in large communities, where they can see but not converse with each other, as the friends of this system imagine that social intercourse, of some kind and to some extent, is almost as necessary to man as food. The separate system, on the other hand, looking upon all intercourse between criminals as only evil in its tendency, by which one rogue becomes the instructor or accomplice of another, secludes the convicts from each other but, to atone for this defect, it encourages the visits of good men to the cells of the prisoners; and the officers of these prisons make it a particular point of duty to visit the inmates very frequently themselves. The physical habits of the imprisoned are provided for by such trades as can be carried on by individual industry; a teacher is employed to lead them on in the study of useful branches of education; while the Gospel is regularly taught them, not only by sermons on the Sabbath, but by private efforts of the chaplain in his daily rounds.

Source: James Finley, *Memorials of Prison Life* (Cincinnati, OH: Swormstedt and Poe, 1855).

Captain Alexander Maconochie

During the 1840s Maconochie served as the warden of Norfolk Island, a prison off the coast of Australia for "doubly condemned" inmates. English prisoners sent to Australia, who committed other crimes while there, were taken to Norfolk to be segregated from less recalcitrant offenders. Prior to Maconochie's arrival, conditions at Norfolk had been atrocious. Disease on the island was rampant, fights between inmates left many dead and more injured, sanitary conditions were practically nonexistent, and physical facilities were unconductive to good supervision. Maconochie immediately set out to reform the island prison. He is still remembered for saying, "When a man keeps the key of his own prison, he is soon persuaded to fit it to the lock."[15] In that belief, he worked to create conditions which would provide incentives for prisoners to participate in their own reformation.

Maconochie developed a system of marks, through which prisoners could earn enough credits to buy their freedom. Bad behavior removed marks from the inmate's ledger, while acceptable behavior added to the number of marks earned. The mark system made possible early release and led to a recognition of the indeterminate sentence as a useful tool in

New York's Auburn Prison, shown here in the mid-1800s, began a congregate form of imprisonment which eventually overshadowed Pennsylvania's penitentiary style. *Photo: Culver Pictures.*

the reformation of offenders. Prior to Maconochie, inmates had been sentenced to determinate sentences specifying a fixed number of years they had to serve before release. The mark system squarely placed responsibility for winning an early release upon the inmate. Because of the system's similarity to the later practice of parole, it won for Maconochie the title "father of parole."

Maconochie's methods, however, were seen as too lenient by opinion leaders in England. Many pointed to the fact that the indeterminate sentence made possible new lives for criminals in a world of vast opportunity (the Australian content) at the expense of the British empire, while many good citizens had to live out lives of quiet desperation and poverty back home. Amid charges that he coddled inmates, Maconochie was relieved of his duties as warden in 1844.

Sir Walter Crofton

Maconochie's innovations had come to the attention of Sir Walter Crofton, head of the Irish Prison System. Crofton adapted the idea of early release to his program of progressive stages. Inmates who entered Irish prisons had to work their way through four stages. The first, or entry level, involved solitary confinement and dull work. Most prisoners in the first level were housed at Mountjoy Prison in Dublin. The second stage assigned prisoners to Spike Island where they worked on fortifications. The third stage placed prisoners in field units which worked directly in the community on public service projects. Unarmed guards supervised the prisoners. The fourth stage depended upon what Crofton called the "ticket of leave." The ticket allowed prisoners to live and work in the community under the occasional supervision of a "moral instructor." The leave ticket could be revoked at any time up until the expiration of the offender's original sentence.

Crofton was convinced that convicts could not be rehabilitated without successful reintegration into the community. His innovations were closely watched by reformers across Europe. Unfortunately a wave of violent robberies swept England in 1862 and led to pas-

T H E O R Y   I N T O   P R A C T I C E

AN EARLY TEXAS PRISON

In 1860, an unknown writer described conditions in the Texas Penitentiary at Huntsville as follows:

By a special enactment of the Legislature, the front of the cell of any prisoner sentenced to solitary confinement for life, is painted black, and his name and sentence distinctly marked thereon. The object would seem to be to infuse a salutary dread into the minds of the other prisoners. Upon the only black-painted cell in the prison was the following inscription, in distinct white letters: William Brown, aged twenty-four years, convicted for murder in Grimes County, spring term, 1858, for which he is now suffering solitary confinement for life. Brown himself, however, was in fact at work in the factory with the other convicts! He entered the Penitentiary in May, 1859, and had been kept in close confinement in his cell, without labor, never being permitted to leave it for any purpose, until about the first of October, when his health was found to have suffered so much that, to preserve his life, he was, under a discretionary power vested in the Directors, released from the rigor of his sentence, and subjected to only the ordinary confinement of the prison. His health had since greatly improved. It is not to be wondered at that his health should decline under the strict enforcement of such a sentence. The cell in which he was confined was the same as to size, ventilation, and light as the rest; and being one of the lower tier of cells, the top of the doorway was some feet below the lower edge of the window upon the opposite side of the corridor in the outside wall. He had even less chance for fresh air than if his cell had been in almost any other location. It is the sight and knowledge of such instances of solitary unemployed confinement as this, and a willful neglect or refusal to inform themselves upon, and recognize, the very wide distinction between the terms separate and solitary, that renders many persons so violently prejudiced against, and opposed to the "Separate System."

Source: *The Journal of Prison Discipline and Philanthropy*, Vol. 15, no. 1 (January 1860), pp. 7–17.

sage of the 1863 Garrotters Act, which mandated whipping for robberies involving violence and longer prison sentences for many other crimes.

The Elmira Reformatory

In 1865 Gaylord B. Hubbell, warden of Sing Sing prison, visited England and studied prisons there. He returned to the United States greatly impressed by the Irish system and

The New York State reformatory at Elmira, circa 1876. Under the innovative leadership of Warden Zebulon Brockway, the Elmira Reformatory began the practice of earned early release. *Photo: Culver Pictures.*

recommended implementation of indeterminate sentences in American prisons. The New York Prison Association supported Hubbell and called for the creation of a "reformatory" based upon the concept of an earned early release.

When the new National Prison Association held its first conference in 1870 in Cincinnati, Ohio, it brought together men and women of vision. Sir Walter Crofton addressed the group, and Enoch C. Wines, the meeting's organizer, called upon "all men of good will throughout the world (to) join in a plan for an ideal prison system."[16] A 37-paragraph Declaration of Principles was adopted and called for reformation to replace punishment as the goal of imprisonment. The most significant outgrowth of the conference, however, was the move to embody those principles in a reformatory built on American soil.

In 1876 the Elmira Reformatory opened in Elmira, New York, under the direction of Zebulon Brockway. The state of New York had passed an indeterminate sentencing bill which made possible early release for inmates who earned it. However, because reformation was thought most likely among youths, the Elmira Reformatory accepted only first offenders between the ages of 16 and 30. A system of graded stages required inmates to meet educational, behavioral, and other goals. Schooling was mandatory, and trade training was available in telegraphy, tailoring, plumbing, carpentry, and other areas.

Unfortunately the reformatory "proved a relative failure and disappointment,"[17] Many inmates reentered lives of crime following their release, and high rates of recidivism called the success of the reformatory ideal into question. Some authors attributed the failure of the reformatory to "the ever-present jailing psychosis"[18] of the prison staff, which made it difficult to implement many of the ideals upon which the reformatory had been based.

Even though the reformatory was not a success, the principles which it established remain important today. The indeterminate sentencing, parole, trade training, education, and primacy of reformation over punishment all serve as a foundation for ongoing debates about the purpose of punishment.

THE INDUSTRIAL PRISON ERA (1890-1935)

With the failure of the reformatory, concerns over security and discipline became dominant in American prisons. Inmate populations rose, costs soared, and states began to study practical alternatives to the reformatory model. An especially attractive option was found in the potential profitability of inmate labor, and the era of the industrial prison in America was born.

Industrial prisons in the northern United States were characterized by thick high walls, stone or brick buildings, guard towers, and smoke-stacks which rose from within the walls. These prisons smelted steel, manufactured cabinets, molded tires, and turned out many other goods for the open market. Prisons in the South, which had been devastated by the Civil War, tended more toward farm labor and public works projects. The South, with its labor-intensive agricultural practices used inmate labor to replace slaves who had been freed during the war.

Barnes and Teeters identified the following six systems of inmate labor in use in the early 1900s:[19]

- *Contract system.* Private businesses paid for the rent of inmate labor. They provided the raw materials and supervised the manufacturing process inside of prison facilities.
- *Piece-price system.* Goods were produced for private businesses under the supervision of prison authorities. Prisons were paid according to the number and quality of the goods manufactured.
- *Lease system.* Prisoners were taken to the work site under the supervision of armed guards. Once there they were turned over to the private contractor who employed them and maintained discipline.
- *Public account system.* Eliminated the use of private contractors. Industries were entirely prison owned, and prison authorities managed the manufacturing process from beginning to end.
- *State-use system.* Under this arrangement prisoners manufactured only goods which could be used by other state offices, or they provided labor to assist other state agencies.
- *Public works.* The maintenance of roads and highways, the cleaning of public parks and recreational facilities, and the maintenance and restoration of public buildings all come under the rubric of "public works."

State-Use System A form of inmate labor in which items produced by inmates are salable only by or to state offices. Items which only the state can sell include such things as license plates and hunting licenses, while items sold only to state offices include furniture and cleaning supplies.

Large industrial prisons that were built included San Quentin (California), Sing Sing (New York), Auburn, and the Illinois State Penitentiary at Statesville. Many prison industries were quite profitable and contributed significantly to state treasuries. Beginning as early as the 1830s, however, workers began to complain of being forced to compete with cheap prison labor. In 1834 mechanics in New York filed a petition with the state legislature asking that prison industries paying extremely low wages be eliminated. Labor unions became very well organized and powerful by the early part of the twentieth century, and the Great Depression of the 1930s brought with it a call for an end to prison industries.

In 1929 union influence led Congress to pass the Hawes–Cooper Act, which required prison made goods to conform to regulations of the states through which they were shipped. The end of prison industries came in 1935 with passage of the Ashurst–Sumners Act, which prohibited the interstate transportation of prison goods where state laws forbade them. Immediately following the Ashurst–Sumners legislation, most states passed statutes which curtailed prison manufacturing of most items.

Two aspects of prison industry survive into the present day. One is the state-use system, described earlier. Most states permit the prison manufacture of goods which will be used exclusively by the prison system itself, or other state agencies, or which only the state can legitimately sell on the open market. An example of the latter is license plates, whose sale is a state monopoly. The federal government also operates a kind of state-use system in its institutions through a government-owned corporation called Federal Prison Industries, Incorporated (also called UNICOR).[20] The corporation was established in 1934 as a prelude to the elimination of free market prison industries. Criticisms of UNICOR include charges that inmates are paid very low wages and are trained for jobs which do not exist in the free economy.[21]

North Carolina provides a good example of a modern state-use system. Its Correction Enterprises operates 24 inmate-run businesses, each of which is self-supporting. North Carolina inmates manufacture prison clothing (at the North Carolina Correctional Center for Women in Raleigh); raise vegetables and farm animals (at Caldonia–Odum Prison) to feed inmates throughout the state; operate an oil refinery, a forestry service, and a cannery; and manufacture soap, license plates, and some office furniture. All manufactured goods other than license plates are for use within the prison system or in other state agencies.[22]

Prison industries also survive in the public works area. Public works projects are undertaken by inmates in a number of states. North Carolina inmates collect trash along the state's highways, cut brush, and keep drainage ditches clear. Other Southern states follow a similar system, and it is not unusual to see guards armed with shotguns supervising prison work crews alongside highways throughout the South.

Money-making prison industries may soon be staging a comeback, funded by private sector investment. In 1981 Florida became the first state to experiment with the wholesale transfer of its correctional industry program from public to private control. Florida's Prison Rehabilitative Industries and Diversified Enterprises, Inc., legislation, commonly called the PRIDE Act, was signed into law by Governor Bob Graham on June 23, 1981.[23]

Church services in Sing Sing prison in 1906. Note the "ushers" with shotguns. *Photo: Underwood Photo Archives.*

Jack Eckerd, retired president and chairman of the Eckerd drugstore chain, was appointed chairman of PRIDE's board of directors. Eckerd brought with him the belief that government and business, acting as a team, could address social problems more effectively and economically than could either acting alone. PRIDE exempts prison employees from civil service and state purchasing regulations. PRIDE industries include sugar cane processing, construction, and automotive repair.

In other states, a number of private firms have contracted with correctional institutions to manufacture office furniture and computer equipment and to provide telephone answering services for motel and hotel reservations.

Indications are that we will soon see a burgeoning of privately supported prison industry. In 1986 the National Task Force on Prison Industries, headed by U.S. Supreme Court Chief Justice Warren E. Burger, issued a report stating five primary principles:[24]

- The private sector should be involved in prison industries.
- Practices and regulations that impede the progress of prison industries should be rescinded, changed, or otherwise streamlined.
- Prison industries should provide meaningful and relevant work opportunities for inmates.
- Prison industries should operate in a businesslike manner.
- Prison industries should reduce inmate idleness.

The Task Force sought enabling legislation from the Congress and state legislatures to permit prison industries to flourish under controlled conditions. Movements in that direction continue today.

THE PUNITIVE ERA (1935-1945)

The moratorium on free market prison industries initiated by the Ashurst–Sumners Act was to last for half a century. Prison administrators, caught with few ready alternatives, emphasized the custodial purpose of correctional facilities and ushered in an era of punitive custody. The punitive era was characterized by its emphasis on security and by the belief that prisoners owed a debt to society which only a rigorous period of custody could absolve. Writers of the period termed such beliefs the convict bogey and the lock psychosis.[25] Large maximum security institutions flourished, and a prisoner's daily routine was one of monotony and frustration. The term "stir crazy" grew out of the experience of many prisoners with the punitive era's lack of programs. In response inmates created their own diversions, frequently attempting to escape or inciting riots. One especially secure and still notorious facility of the punitive era, the federal penitentiary on Alcatraz Island, is described in a box in this chapter.

The punitive era was a lackluster time in American corrections. Innovations were rare, and an "out-of-sight, out-of-mind" philosophy characterized American attitudes toward inmates. Popular accounts of the times portrayed criminals as "mad dogs" and the rehabilitation-oriented officials as "sob sisters" and "cream puffs."[26] Writing from the midst of the punitive era Barnes and Teeters observed: "Even earnest administrators who sincerely believe in rehabilitation are afraid to introduce a whole-hearted program that might improve treatment procedures. Such rehabilitative treatment required flexibility and experimentation, but these increase escape risks and even the most enlightened warden realizes that his work will be judged by newspapers, politicians, and the public on the basis of how successful he is in preventing escapes."[27] Correctional officers were even more single-minded in their security consciousness. Barnes and Teeters wrote: "The mental habits

of the custodial staff revolve around the mania to keep prisoners either locked up or scrupulously accounted for. Considerations of reformation and humanity evaporate in the face of this inexorable and all-encompassing anxiety."[28]

THE ERA OF TREATMENT (1945-1967)

By the late 1940s, the mood of the nation was euphoric. World War II was a dimming memory, industries were productive beyond the best hopes of most economic forecasters, and America's position of world leadership was fundamentally unchallenged. Amid the bounty of a postwar boom economy, politicians and the public accorded themselves the additional luxury of restructuring the nation's prisons. A new interest in "corrections" combined with the latest in behavioral techniques to usher in an era of treatment built around what was then a prevailing psychiatric model. Inmates came to be seen more as "clients" or "patients" than as offenders, and terms like "resident" or "group member" replaced the "inmate" label. The treatment era was based upon a **medical model** of corrections—one which implied that the offender was sick and that rehabilitation was only a matter of finding the right treatment.

Therapy during the period took a number of forms, many of which are still used today. Most therapeutic models assumed that the inmate had to be brought to mature psychologically and taught to assume responsibility for his or her life. Therapeutic categories can be delineated in terms of the level at which they operate and the strategy for personal change which they employ. The two most common operative approaches have been individual treatment and group therapy.

Individual treatment depends upon a face-to-face relationship between the offender and the therapist. Most individual approaches depict the offender as someone who has not developed sufficiently to be an effective behavioral manager. Psychological development may have been thwarted by traumatic experiences in early life, which the therapist will try to uncover.

Group therapy relies upon members of the therapeutic group to facilitate the growth process, often by first revealing to the client the emotional basis of criminal behavior. What the inmate regards as personal strengths may be shown to be really nothing more than excuses for the inability to "own up" to responsibility. Some group strategies are attack therapies in which new group members are verbally pummeled to rid them of old self-conceptions and criminal values. While individual therapy may uncover past personal traumas, group therapy may itself be traumatic in its relentless destruction of all personal armor.

One of the most famous forms of group therapy was Synanon, developed in the 1950s as a treatment for drug addiction. The word "Synanon" derived from a group member's attempt to say "seminar" and developed into a privately owned foundation providing drug treatment for addicts in Santa Monica, California. In the 1960s Synanon-like programs became widespread and served as models for other attack therapies.

Guided group interaction (GGI) is an example of a treatment strategy which combines elements of individual treatment with group therapy. In guided group interaction, the therapist assists the group in uncovering individual fears, hidden experiences, and anxieties which act as barriers to conventional behavior. During the 1970s Florida and Georgia adopted GGI as their primary approach to the treatment of juvenile offenders, and many other states were reported to use it extensively.[29]

Other forms of therapy used in prisons have included behavior therapy, chemotherapy, aversion therapy, sensory deprivation, and neurosurgery. Prison environments based

The Medical Model A theoretical framework for the handling of prisoners which held that offenders were "sick" and could be "cured" through the application of behavioral and other appropriate forms of therapy.

THEORY INTO PRACTICE

ALCATRAZ FEDERAL PENITENTIARY

Alcatraz Island in San Francisco Bay is home to one of the best known prisons of all time. The prison had its beginnings as a fort for the U.S. Army in 1854 and was used to house the Bay Area's prisoners following the great earthquake of 1906. By the 1930s organized criminal elements were terrorizing the country, and Sanford Bates, the director of the federal prison system, began the call for one highly secure institution for the isolation of notorious offenders. Alcatraz Island was the obvious choice. The wide expanse of bay waters which separated the island from the coast were notorious for treacherous currents, making unaided escape a virtual impossibility.

During the early 1930s the island prison was built on the foundation of the old fort. Some of the first prison-used metal detectors were installed, and barbed wire perimeter fences and walls were built and reinforced with armed guards in towers at strategic points.

Alcatraz Federal Penitentiary opened in 1934 with James Johnson, former warden of San Quentin and Folsom prisons, as warden. One prisoner per cell was the rule. Cells measured $5' \times 9' \times 7'$ and were equipped with basic metal furniture. A rule of silence prevailed, and no newspapers or radios were permitted. Security was so strict that no original letters were delivered to inmates. Correspondence was heavily screened and retyped by the staff who then gave only a copy to the prisoner.

Alcatraz accepted inmates only from other institutions. No direct court commitments could be made. The most difficult, dangerous, and troublesome prisoners from other facilities in the federal system were sent to Alcatraz. One of the first was Al "Scarface" Capone. George "Machine Gun" Kelly, Robert Stroud (the "Birdman of Alcatraz"), "Doc" Barker, Alvin Karpis, and many others followed.

Fourteen known escapes, involving as many as 30 men, were attempted during the time Alcatraz served as a prison. Only one attempt, involving 2 men—Theodore Cole and Ralph Roe—may have been successful. Cole, serving a 50-year sentence for kidnaping while on the run from McAlester Penitentiary, and Roe, a career offender sentenced to 99 years for bank robbery, cut their way through the bars on a window of the prison shop. They had picked December 16, 1937, an especially foggy and damp day. Although an extensive sea and land search was underway within a half hour following the escape, Cole and Roe were never found. Official accounts point to the strong currents of the bay (which on the day of their escape were measured as swiftly flowing toward the open sea) and wintry temperatures to conclude that the attempt must have failed.

Although not successful, the most costly escape attempt came on May 2, 1946. It resulted in a three-day hostage situation which claimed the lives of two officers and three prisoners. It ended only when U.S. Marines provided demolition grenades used to flush prisoners out of occupied corridors. Seventeen guards and one prisoner were wounded. Two other inmates were sentenced to die for their role in the riot and were put to death on December 3, 1946.

By the 1950s Alcatraz Penitentiary was in a state of disrepair. The salt water of the bay had contributed to an early disintegration of the concrete used in building construction, and many of the steel rods and bars had been weakened by the corrosive air. Local residents grouped together to demand an upgrading of the environmental impact the prison was having on the bay. The final blow to Alcatraz, however, was the undermining of its purpose by a reformation-oriented society which had moved firmly into the treatment era and away from earlier concerns with "escapeproof" institutions. As described by one writer, "Alcatraz (was) a monument to the thesis that some criminals cannot be reformed and should be repressed and disciplined by absolute inflexibility."[1] On March 21, 1963, under the direction of Attorney General Robert Kennedy, Alcatraz Penitentiary closed its doors as a prison. Today the island institution survives as a tourist attraction and has spawned a number of shops selling prison memorobilia.

[1]Harry Barnes and Negley Teeters, *New Horizons in Criminology*, 3rd ed. (Englewood Cliffs, NJ: Prentice Hall, 1959), p. 383.
Source: James Fuller, *Alcatraz Federal Penitentiary, 1934–1963*. (San Francisco: Asteron Production, 1987); E. E. Kirkpatrick, *Voices from Alcatraz* (San Antonio, TX: Naylor, 1947); and James A. Johnston, *Alcatraz Island Prison* (New York: Scribners, 1949).

upon behavior therapy were structured so as to provide rewards for approved behavior, while punishing undesirable behavior. Rewards took the form of better housing conditions, canteen allotments, or TV privileges. Chemotherapy involved the use of drugs, especially tranquilizers, to modify behavior. Neurosurgery, including the now-notorious frontal lobotomy, was used on some highly aggressive inmates to control their destructive urges. Sensory deprivation sought to calm disruptive offenders by denying them the stimulation which might set off outbursts of destructive behavior. Sensory deprivation isolated inmates in a quiet, secluded environment. Aversion therapy used drugs or electric shocks in an attempt to teach the offender to associate pain and displeasure with stimuli which previously led to criminal behavior. Homosexual child abusers, for example, were shown pictures of nude children and simultaneously given shocks, often in especially sensitive parts of their anatomy.

Inmates have not always been happy with the treatment model. In 1972 a group of prisoners at the Marion, Illinois, federal prison joined together and demanded a right to no treatment. The group, calling itself the Federal Prisoner's Coalition, insisted that inmates have a basic right "to resist rehabilitation techniques designed to change their attitudes, values or personalities."[30] Supporting the inmate's claims to no treatment was the National Prison Project of the American Civil Liberties Union. Alvin J. Bronstein, executive director of the National Prison Project, argued that personality altering techniques constituted a violation of prisoners' civil rights.[31] Other suits followed. Worried about potential liability, Donald E. Santarelli, the head of the Law Enforcement Assistance Administration, banned the expenditure of LEAA funds to support any prison programs utilizing psychosurgery, medical research, chemotherapy, and behavioral modification. Santarelli's decision was based on an LEAA report of a year earlier, which had concluded that LEAA lacked the expertise to appropriately evaluate such programs.[32]

The treatment era also suffered from attacks upon the medical model on which it depended. Academics and legal scholars pointed to a lack of evidence in support of the model[33] and began to stress individual responsibility rather than treatment in the handling

Alcatraz Federal Penitentiary, shown here in its heyday—circa 1947. The island prison closed in 1963, a victim of changing attitudes toward corrections. It survives today as a San Francisco tourist attraction. *Photo: AP/Wide World Photos.*

of offenders. Indeterminate sentencing statutes, designed to reward inmates for improved behavior, fell before the swelling drive to replace treatment with punishment.

Any honest evaluation of the treatment era would conclude that in practice treatment was more an ideal than a reality. Many treatment programs existed, some of them quite intensive. Unfortunately, the correctional system in America was never capable of providing any consistent or widespread treatment because the majority of its guards and administrators were primarily custody oriented and not trained as treatment personnel. However, although we have identified 1970 as the end of the treatment era, many correctional rehabilitation programs continue to survive into the present day.

THE COMMUNITY-BASED FORMAT (1967-1980)

Community-Based Corrections A sentencing style which represents a movement away from traditional confinement options and an increased dependence upon correctional resources which are available in the community.

Beginning in the 1960s prison crowding, combined with a renewed faith in humanity, inspired a movement away from institutionalized corrections and toward the creation of opportunities for reformation within local communities. The transition to community-based corrections (also variously called "deinstitutionalization," "diversion," and "decarceration"[34]) was based upon the premise that rehabilitation cannot occur in isolation from the free social world to which inmates must eventually return. Advocates of community corrections portrayed prisons as dehumanizing, claiming they further victimized offenders who had already been negatively labeled by society. Some states strongly embraced the movement toward decarceration. In 1972, under the leadership of its new director of youth services, Jerome Miller, the state of Massachusetts drew national attention when it closed all its reform schools and replaced them with group homes.[35]

Decarceration utilized a variety of programs to keep offenders in contact with the community and out of prison. Among them were halfway houses, work-release programs, and open institutions. Halfway houses have sometimes been called "halfway in" or "halfway out" houses, depending upon whether offenders were being given a second chance prior to incarceration or were in the process of gradual release from prison. Some early halfway houses were begun in Boston in the 1920s, but operated for only a few years.[36] It was not until 1961, however, that the Federal Bureau of Prisons opened a few experimental residential centers in support of its new prerelease programs focusing on juveniles and youthful offenders. Called prerelease guidance centers, the first of these facilities were based in Los Angeles and Chicago.[37] In 1967 the President's Commission on Law Enforcement and the Administration of Justice strongly recommended use of community-based facilities to restore ties between offenders and their families, employers, training facilities, and other social agencies.

A typical residential treatment facility today houses 15 to 20 residents and operates under the supervision of a director supported by a handful of counselors. The environment is nonthreatening, and residents are generally free to come and go during the workday. The building looks more like a motel or a house than it does a prison. Fences and walls are nonexistent. Transportation is provided to and from work or educational sites, and a portion of the resident's wages are retained by the facility to pay the costs of room and board. Residents are expected to remain in the facility following work, and some group therapy may be provided.

Work-release programs house offenders in traditional correctional environments—unusually minimum security prisons—but permit them to work at jobs in the community during the day and return to the prison at night. Inmates are usually required to pay a token amount for their room and board in the institution. The first work-release law was passed by Wisconsin in 1913, but it was not until 1957 that a comprehensive program created by North Carolina spurred the development of work-release programs nationwide.[38] Work release for federal prisoners was authorized by the Federal Prisoner Rehabilitation Act of 1965.[39] As work-release programs grew, study release was initiated in most jurisdictions as an adjunct to them.

Work-release programs are still very much a part of modern corrections. Almost all states have them, and many inmates work in the community as they approach the end of their sentences. Unfortunately work-release programs are not without their social costs. Some inmates commit new crimes while in the community, and others use the opportunity to effect escapes. A number of departments have created more stringent eligibility requirements for inmates wishing to work outside of prison.

The community-based format led to innovations in the use of volunteers and to the extension of inmate privileges. Open institutions were those which routinely provided inmates with a number of opportunities for community involvement, and which encouraged the community to participate in the prison environment. Most open institutions, for example, made training available to citizens who wished to sponsor prisoners on day trips into the community for recreation, meals, and the like. Others allowed weekend passes or extended visits by family members and friends, while a few experimented with conjugal visiting and coeducational incarceration. Based on a merit system, conjugal visiting made possible intimate visits between male inmates and their spouses in motel-like environments constructed on the prison grounds. Some writers point to unofficial conjugal visits occurring as early as 1918 at the Mississippi State Penitentiary at Parchman.[40] It was not until 1963, however, that state funding for "red houses" authorized the practice. In 1968 the California Correctional Institute at Tehachapi initiated conjugal visits in which inmates who were about to begin parole were permitted to live with their families for three days per month in apartments on the prison grounds. The practice extended to inmates at Soledad, San Quentin, and the Rehabilitation Center at Corona. By the late 1960s conjugal visitation was under consideration in many other states, and the National Advisory Commission on Criminal Justice Standards and Goals recommended that correctional authorities should make "provisions for family visits in private surroundings conducive to maintaining and strengthening family ties."[41]

Coeducational prisons housed both men and women, allowing the sexes to join in educational programs, work tasks, and certain forms of recreation. Separate dormitories were maintained, and physical intimacy was disapproved. The Federal Bureau of Prisons began experimenting with coed facilities in 1971, and the Pleasanton Youth Center in California became one of the first institutions in the nation to house both men and women.

Warehousing (1980–1990)

Public disappointment, bred of high **recidivism**[42] rates coupled with highly visible news stories of inmates who committed gruesome crimes while on assignment in the community, led many legislatures to curtail the most liberal aspects of educational and work-release programs. Media descriptions of institutions where inmates lounged in supposed luxury with regular visits from wives and took frequent weekend passes infused the popular imagination with images of "prison country clubs." The failure of the rehabilitative ideal in community-based corrections, however, was due as much to changes in the individual sentencing decisions of judges as it was to citizen outrage and restrictive legislative action. Evidence points to the fact that many judges today view rehabilitation programs as failures and have decided to implement what we have called a justice model[43] in criminal sentencing. The justice model, as discussed in Chapter 10, depends upon a renewed belief in just deserts (that offenders should "get what's coming to them") and has led to a policy of warehousing serious offenders for the protection of society. Deterrence and punishment go hand and hand in the just deserts model.

Recidivism rates are widely quoted in support of the justice model. Nearly 70% of young adults paroled from prison in 22 states during 1978 were rearrested for serious crimes one or more times within six years of their release.[44] The 1978 study group was estimated to have committed 36,000 new felonies within the six years following their release, including 324 murders, 231 rapes, 2,291 robberies, and 3,053 violent assaults.[45] Worse still, was the fact that 46% of recidivists would have been in prison at the time of their readmission if they had fully served the maximum term to which they were originally sentenced.[46] Those with long prior arrest records (six or more previous adult arrests) were found rearrested 90% of the time following release, and the younger the parolee was at first arrest, the greater the chance of a new crime violation. Equally intriguing was the finding that "[t]he length of time that a parolee has served in prison had no consistent impact on recidivism rates."[47] The proportion of individuals rearrested and reconvicted for any offense within three years of release from prison is shown in Figure 12–2.

The failure of the rehabilitative model in corrections was proclaimed emphatically by Robert Martinson in 1974.[48] Martinson and his colleagues had surveyed 231 research studies conducted to evaluate correctional treatments between 1945 and 1967. They were unable to identify any treatment program which successfully reduced recidivism. Although Martinson argued for fixed sentences, a portion of which would be served in the community, his findings were often interpreted to mean that lengthy prison terms were necessary to incapacitate offenders incapable of reformation. The prestigious National Academy of Sciences released a report in support of Martinson, saying "we do not now know of any program or method of rehabilitation that could be guaranteed to reduce the criminal activity of released offenders."[49] This combined attack on the treatment model led to the nothing works doctrine which, beginning in the late 1970s, cast a pall of doubt over the American correctional enterprise.

Research on incapacitation suggests that warehousing does reduce the number of serious criminal offenses in society.[50] Not all offenders need to be imprisoned, however, and those who do are difficult to identify.[51] Repeat offenders, with records of serious and vio-

Warehousing An imprisonment strategy based upon the desire to prevent recurrent crime but which has abandoned any hope of rehabilitation.

Recidivism The repetition of criminal behavior. In statistical practice, a recidivism rate may be any of a number of possible counts or instances of arrest, conviction, correctional commitment, and correctional status changes, related to counts of repetitions of these events within a given period of time.

Nothing Works Doctrine The belief, popularized by Robert Martinson in the 1970s, that correctional treatment programs had little success in rehabilitating offenders.

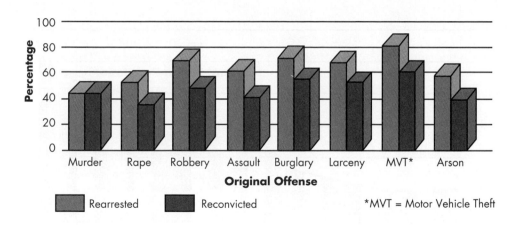

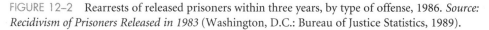

FIGURE 12–2   Rearrests of released prisoners within three years, by type of offense, 1986. *Source: Recidivism of Prisoners Released in 1983* (Washington, D.C.: Bureau of Justice Statistics, 1989).

lent crimes, are the most likely candidates for incapacitation—as are those who will probably commit such crimes in the future even though they have no record. But potentially violent offenders cannot be readily identified, and those thought likely to commit crimes cannot be sentenced to lengthy prison terms for things they have not done yet.

Some authors have identified the problem as one of selective versus collective incapacitation.[52] Collective incapacitation would warehouse almost all serious offenders and is found today in states which rely upon predetermined, or fixed, sentences for given offenses. Collective incapacitation is, however, prohibitively expensive as well as unnecessary. In most jurisdictions, warehousing now tends to operate on a selective basis and seeks to identify potentially dangerous inmates. In support of selective incapacitation, many states have enacted career offender statutes. The strategy of selective incapacitation, however, depends upon accurately identifying potentially dangerous offenders out of existing criminal populations. It has been criticized for yielding a rate of "false positives" of over 60%,[53] and some authors were quick to call incapacitation a "strategy of failure."[54] Warehousing has, to date, already produced record prison populations and has the potential to expand the number of people in prison even farther. Even so, advocates of incapacitation can still find support for their position. Recently the Justice Department reported that new crimes committed by released prisoners cost society about $430,000 per year per offender for police work, court costs, and losses to victims. The report argued that continued confinement, even in newly built prison cells, cost only around $25,000 per year per offender and was "not too expensive when weighed against the price of crimes that would otherwise be prevented by incapacitation."[55] A similar study,[56] reported by Wisconsin researchers in 1991, found that while imprisonment costs that state about $14,000 per inmate per year, the financial burden to the state of allowing the typical Wisconsin inmate "to freely roam the streets in search of victims" would be about $28,000 in new crimes per average offender each year. Researchers who conducted the study concluded that "prison pays" and suggested that "[i]mprisonment is a valuable corrections option from which the state cannot afford to shrink."

OVERCROWDING/EARLY RELEASE (1990–PRESENT)

Over the past 30 years the American prison population has grown dramatically (see Figure 12–3), and prisons everywhere have become notoriously overcrowded (see Figure 12–4). In

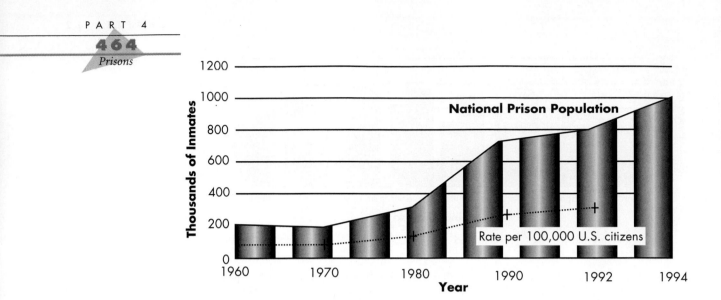

FIGURE 12–3   U.S. prison population and rates of imprisonment, historical and projected growth, 1960–1994. *Sources: American Correctional Association, Vital Statistics in Corrections (Laurel, MD: ACA, 1991), p. 44; American Correctional Association, 1993 Directory of Juvenile and Adult Correctional Departments, Institutions, Agencies and Paroling Authorities (Laurel, MD: ACA, 1993).*

February 1990, in a startling example of just how bad crowding is, Hampden County, Massachusetts, Sheriff Michael Ashe, supported by 30 deputies commandeered a National Guard Armory for use as a jail. Sheriff Ashe claimed that a seventeenth-century state law gave him the authority to seize public property "when there is imminent danger of a breach of peace." Ashe cited the "collapse of the criminal justice system" as having led to a loss of "the ability to implement sentences," especially those requiring imprisonment.[57] Although he quickly ran out of money to support operations at the armory-jail, Sheriff Ashe was rewarded in 1992 with a new jail—his state's largest and newest—and monies to operate it.[58]

A survey of 1,400 criminal justice officials across the country conducted in the 1980s by the National Institute of Justice identified crowding in prisons and jails as the most serious problem facing the criminal justice system.[59] Between 1980 and 1990 state and federal prison populations more than doubled.[60] In four states, California, New Hampshire, Alaska, and New Jersey, prison populations tripled, with California experiencing the largest increase (from 23,264 inmates in 1980 to 97,309 by 1990).[61] States experiencing the fastest growth in their prison populations over five years are identified in Figure 12–5. By 1990, federal prisons had become as much as 73% overcrowded,[62] and a major program of expansion had been implemented.

A 1992 report[63] by the American Bar Association attributes overcrowding to a systemwide overemphasis on drug-related offenses—an emphasis which tends to imprison mostly poor, undereducated black youths who are rarely dangerous. The report points out that while the per capita rate of *reported* crime dropped 2.2% across the nation during the 1980s, "the incarceration rate increased more than 110 percent."[64]

In any event, building programs in most jurisdictions have not been able to keep pace with burgeoning populations. During 1988 increased incarceration rates translated into a nationwide need for 800 additional prison beds per week.[65] During the first half of 1989, the fastest growth in U.S. incarceration ever recorded occurred—necessitating 1,800 additional prison beds per week.[66] The American Correctional Association estimates that prison populations will reach a total of more than 1 million persons under confinement throughout the country by 1995.[67]

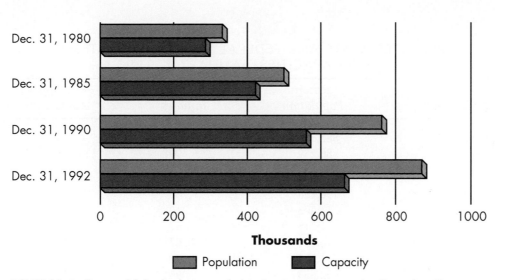

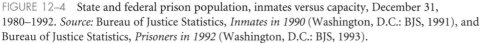

FIGURE 12–4   State and federal prison population, inmates versus capacity, December 31, 1980–1992. *Source:* Bureau of Justice Statistics, *Inmates in 1990* (Washington, D.C.: BJS, 1991), and Bureau of Justice Statistics, *Prisoners in 1992* (Washington, D.C.: BJS, 1993).

By 1992, institutions in 40 states and the District of Columbia were operating under court orders to alleviate crowded conditions.[68] Entire prison systems in nine jurisdictions had come under court control. These jurisdictions were Alaska, Florida, Kansas, Louisiana, Mississippi, Nevada, Rhode Island, South Carolina, and Texas.[69] Table 12–1 depicts overcrowding in state and federal prison systems through a comparison of present inmate populations with the original design capacity of existing facilities. Even so, incarceration rates vary dramatically from one state to another, as Figure 12–6 shows.

Some states have dealt with overcrowded facilities by constructing "temporary" tent cities within prison yards. Others have moved more beds into already packed dormitories, often stacking prisoners three high in triple bunk beds. A few states have declared a policy of early release for less dangerous inmates and instituted mandatory diversion programs

FIGURE 12–5   Prison population increase, fastest-growing states, 1985–1990. *Source:* Bureau of Justice Statistics, *Prisoners in 1990* (Washington, D.C.: BJS, May 1991).

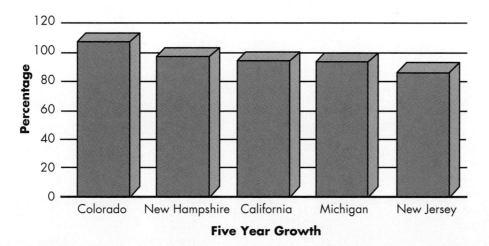

TABLE 12-1

REPORTED STATE AND FEDERAL PRISON POPULATIONS AND CAPACITIES, JANUARY 1, 1993

Jurisdiction	Prison Population	Female Inmates	Percentage of Capacity[1]
U.S. total	883,593	48,328	
Federal	80,259	6,399	137
State	803,334	41,929	
Northeast	138,156	7,200	
Connecticut	11,403	710	113
Maine	1,515	62	112
Massachusetts	10,056	567	144
New Hampshire	1,777	73	153
New Jersey	22,653	1,095	131
New York	61,736	3,499	125
Pennsylvania	24,974	1,106	149
Rhode Island	2,775	195	84
Vermont	1,267	37	193
Midwest	166,339	8,065	
Illinois	31,640	1,456	152
Indiana	13,166	720	110
Iowa	4,518	196	138
Kansas	6,028	293	91
Michigan	39,019	1,859	144
Minnesota	3,822	173	104
Missouri	16,198	858	104
Nebraska	2,565	138	150
North Dakota	464	31	81
Ohio	38,378	2,419	177
South Dakota	1,487	80	132
Wisconsin	9,054	343	139
South	324,454	16,740	
Alabama	17,453	1,101	111
Arkansas	8,433	437	104
Delaware	3,977	240	136
District of Col.	10,875	720	121
Florida	48,302	2,599	127
Georgia	25,290	1,455	100
Kentucky	10,364	545	110
Louisiana	20,810	1,020	95
Maryland	19,977	954	155
Mississippi	9,083	562	95
North Carolina	20,455	951	114
Oklahoma	14,821	1,400	162
South Carolina	18,643	1,127	145
Tennessee	11,849	459	99
Texas	61,178	2,487	112
Virginia	21,199	1,163	139
West Virginia	1,745	70	104

T A B L E   1 2 - 1   (C O N T I N U E D)

Jurisdiction	Prison Population	Female Inmates	Percentage of Capacity[1]
West	174,385	9,904	
Alaska	2,865	132	116
Arizona	16,477	1,001	106
California	109,496	6,747	191
Colorado	8,997	527	138
Hawaii	2,926	167	187
Idaho	2,475	121	113
Montana	1,553	73	134
Nevada	6,049	432	127
New Mexico	3,271	160	99
Oregon	6,596	409	101
Utah	2,699	120	89
Washington	9,959	618	161
Wyoming	1,022	57	105

[1]"Percent of capacity is shown as a percentage of "lowest capacity" and may be expressed in terms of design, operational, or rated capacity, depending upon availability of information. Information on women inmates is for 1991, except for those 27 states holding more than 500 inmates each, where year-end 1992 figures are shown.
Source: Adapted from Bureau of Justice Statistics, *Prisoners in 1992* (Washington, D.C.: Bureau of Justice Statistics, 1993), and *Correctional Populations in the United States, 1991* (Washington, D.C.: Bureau of Justice Statistics, 1993).

FIGURE 12–6   Variation in incarceration rates, highest and lowest states, 1992. *Source:* Bureau of Justice Statistics, *Prisoners in 1992* (Washington, D.C.: BJS, May 1993).

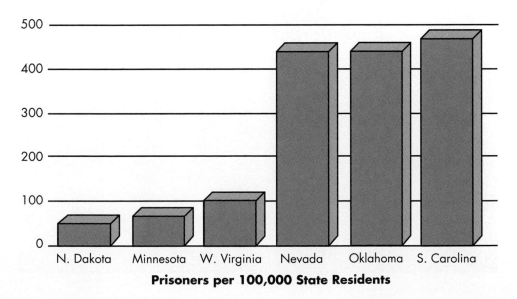

Prisoners per 100,000 State Residents

for first-time nonviolent offenders. Others use sentence rollbacks to reduce the sentences of selected inmates by a fixed amount, usually 90 days. Early parole is similarly employed by numerous states to reduce overcrowded conditions. Almost all states have shifted some of the correctional burden to local jails, with jails now housing over 18,000 sentenced inmates because of overcrowding at long-term institutions.[70]

Overcrowding is sometimes difficult to define. Most experts agree that crowding can be measured along a number of dimensions, which include[71]

- Space available per inmate (such as square feet of floor space)
- How long inmates are confined in cells or housing units (versus time spent on recreation, etc.)
- Living arrangements (i.e., single versus double bunking)
- Type of housing (use of segregation facilities, tents, etc., in place of general housing).

Complicating the crowding picture still further is the fact that prison officials have developed three definitions of prison capacity. **Rated capacity** refers to the size of the inmate population a facility can handle according to the judgment of experts. **Operational capacity** is the number of inmates that a facility can effectively accommodate based on an appraisal of the institution's staff, programs, and services. **Design capacity** refers to the inmate population the institution was originally built to handle. Rated capacity estimates usually yield the largest inmate capacities, while design capacity (upon which this chapter is based) typically shows the highest amount of overcrowding.

Crowding by itself is not cruel and unusual punishment according to the Supreme Court in *Rhodes* v. *Chapman* (1981),[72] which considered the issue of double bunking among other alleged forms of "deprivation" at the Southern Ohio correctional facility. The Ohio facility, built in 1971, was substantially overcrowded according to the original housing plans on which it was constructed. Designed to house one inmate per cell, the cells were small (only 63 square feet of floor space on the average). However, at the time the suit was filed the facility held 2,300 inmates, 1,400 of whom were doubled celled. Kelly Chapman,

An inmate tends plants around his quarters in a Texas tent city prison. Many prisons today are dramatically overcrowded. *Photo: Stock Boston.*

an inmate serving a sentence as an armed robber and prison escapee, claimed that his portion of a cell was too small—smaller even than the space recommended by Ohio State Veterinarian Services for a 5-week-old calf. Thirty-six states joined the case in support of the Ohio practice of double celling, while the American Medical Association and the American Public Health Association took Chapman's side.[73] The court, reasoning that overcrowding is not necessarily dangerous if other prison services are adequate, held that prison housing conditions may be "restrictive and even harsh," for they are part of the penalty that offenders pay for their crimes.

We are likely to see continued record overcrowding no matter how many prisons we build.

—*U.S. Representative Charles B. Rangel (D., N.Y)*

However, overcrowding combined with other negative conditions may lead to a finding against the prison system. The American Correctional Association believes that such a totality of conditions approach requires the court to judge the overall quality of prison life while viewing overcrowded conditions in combination with

- The prison's meeting of basic human needs
- The adequacy of the facility's staff
- The program opportunities available to inmates
- The quality and strength of the prison management

New Prison Construction

Diversion, early release, and a number of practices cited earlier provide techniques for alleviating overcrowding. Another approach is to increase prison populations via the construction of new prison facilities. Prison construction is very expensive, with costs averaging between $50,000 to $75,000 per bed.[74] To assist states in the efficient expansion of prison facilities the National Criminal Justice Reference Service began a Construction Information Exchange in the mid-1980s. The Exchange functions to disseminate information on innovative construction techniques to states throughout the nation. Since its implementation, the Exchange has issued a number of "construction bulletins" highlighting programs such as Florida's use of prefabricated modular concrete cells, California's precast and "tilt-up" construction innovations, and South Carolina's use of inmate labor in new prison construction.[75] To prevent escapes while saving money, many new prisons are built with fences reinforced with detection devices in place of the traditional high wall. Electronic perimeter detection devices include video motion sensors, infrared detectors, microwave sensors, and seismic sensors and are now being installed in new and existing prisons in record numbers. Some critics of the devices argue that they produce too many false alarms and have not been adequately tested under rigorous conditions.[76]

PRISONS TODAY

Today there are approximately 900 state and 70 federal prisons in operation across the country. As of January 1993, they held 883,593 inmates,[77] 97% of whom were housed in traditional confinement facilities, with the remaining 3% held in community-based institutions.[78] Six percent of those imprisoned were women.

The size of prison facilities varies greatly. One out of every four state institutions is a large, maximum security prison, with a population approaching 1,000 inmates. A few exceed that figure, but the typical state prison is small, with an inmate population of less than 500, while community-based facilities average around 50 residents.

Most people sentenced to state prisons have been convicted of burglary (21.2%), while robbery (13.3%) and drug crimes (13.2%) are the next most common offenses for which "active" sentences are imposed. Studies show that larceny (10.1%) accounts for the fourth largest group of imprisoned offenders, with only 6.2% of prison admissions occurring for the offense of murder and 2.7% for rape. Overall, one-third of prisoners entering correctional facilities are there for a violent crime.[79] The inmate population in general suffers from a low level of formal education, comes from a socially disadvantage background, and lacks significant vocational skills.[80] Most adult inmates have served some time in juvenile correctional facilities.[81]

In a recent year, approximately 352,000 staff members were employed in corrections,[82] with the majority performing direct custodial tasks in state institutions. Females accounted for 20% of all correctional officers in 1992, with the proportion of women officers increasing at around 19% per year.[83] In an effort to encourage the increased employment of women in corrections, the American Correctional Association has formally adopted a statement[84] to that effect. The statement reads: "Women have a right to equal employment. No person who is qualified for a particular position/assignment or for job-related opportunities should be denied such employment or opportunities because of gender." The official statement goes on to encourage correctional agencies to "ensure that recruitment, selection, and promotion opportunities are open to women."

According to a recent report by the American Correctional Association, 70% of correctional officers are white, 22% are black, and slightly over 5% are Hispanic.[85] The inmate/custody staff ratio in state prisons averages around 4.1 to 1. Incarceration costs the states an average of $11,302 per inmate per year, while the federal government spends about $13,162 to house one inmate for a year.[86] The ACA reports[87] that in 1991, entry-level correctional officers were paid between $13,520 and $33,996, depending upon the state in which they were hired. Salaries for systems administrators in adult correctional systems were as high as $131,731 (South Carolina), with institutional superintendents earning in the range of $26,436 to $93,693.

Carter, McGee, and Nelson[88] describe the typical state prison system (in relatively populous states) as consisting of

- One high-security prison for long-term, high-risk cases
- One or more medium-security institutions for the bulk of offenders who are not high risks
- One institution for adult women
- One or two institutions for young adults (generally under age 25)
- One or two specialized mental hospital–type security prisons for mentally ill prisoners
- One or more open-type institutions for low-risk nonviolent populations

JAILS

Jails are short-term confinement facilities which were originally intended to hold suspects following arrest and pending trial. Today, jails also house convicted misdemeanants serving relatively short sentences and felony offenders awaiting transportation to long-term confinement facilities. Numerically, 52% of jail inmates are pretrial detainees or are

Jail A confinement facility administered by an agency of local government, typically a law enforcement agency, intended for adults but sometimes also containing juveniles, which holds persons detained pending adjudication and/or persons committed after adjudication, usually those committed on sentences of a year or less.

defendants involved in some stage of the trial process.[89] Ten percent of all jail inmates are being held for drunken driving, and driving under the influence is the most common charge for jailed persons 45 years of age or older.[90] Bond has been set by the court, although not yet posted, for almost nine out of ten jail inmates.[91] Significantly, the fastest-growing sector of the jail population consists of sentenced offenders serving time in local jails because overcrowded prisons cannot accept them.

A total of 3,316 jails are in operation throughout the United States today, staffed by approximately 92,600 correctional workers. Overall, the jail budget is huge, and facilities overflowing. Some $3.5 billion is spent yearly to operate the nation's jails, with more than $1 billion in additional moneys earmarked for new jail construction and for renovations. Approximately 10 million people are admitted to the nation's jails each year.[92] Some stay for as little as one day, while others serve extended periods of jail time. Most jails are small. Two out of three were built to house 50 or fewer inmates. Most people who spend time in jail, however, do so in larger institutions.[93] In 1992, 81% of the nation's jail population was housed in the jails of 503 large jurisdictions.[94] Due to overcrowding 131 of these jurisdictions were laboring under court order to reduce populations or improve the conditions of confinement.[95]

Although there are many small and medium-sized jails across the country, a handful of "megajails" house thousands of inmates. The largest such facilities can be found in New York City's Riker's Island (with an average daily population of around 12,000 inmates), Los Angeles County's Men's Central Jail (7,679 inmates), the Cook County jail in Chicago (7,257 inmates), Houston's Harris County Downtown Central Jail (6,751 inmates),[96] the New Orleans Parish Prison System (3,677 inmates), and Los Angeles County's Pitchess Honor Ranch (3,254 inmates). The Custody Division of the Los Angeles Sheriff's Department found its jails swelled to over 26,500 inmates during the rioting in Los Angeles following the first of the verdicts in the "Rodney King case." The largest employer among these huge jails is the Cook County facility, with over 1,200 personnel on its payroll.

Jails are busy places. In 1992 there were approximately 20 million jail admissions and releases throughout the nation, while the daily jail population averaged around 445,000 persons, of whom 2,800 were juveniles.[97] Most people processed through the country's jails are members of minority groups (60%) and male (91%). On average, approximately $11,000 is spent yearly to house one jail inmate.

Women and Jail

Although women comprise only 9% of the country's jail population, they are "virtually the largest growth group in jails nationwide."[98] Jailed women face a number of special problems. Only 25.7% of the nation's jails report having a classification system specifically designed to evaluate female inmates,[99] and, although "a large proportion of jurisdictions" report plans "to build facilities geared to the female offender,"[100] not all jurisdictions today even provide separate housing areas for female inmates. Educational levels are very low among jailed women, and fewer than half are high school graduates.[101] Pregnancy is another problem. Nationally 4% of female inmates are pregnant at the time they come to jail,[102] but as much as 10% of the female population of urban jail is reported to be pregnant on any given day.[103] As a consequence, a few hundred children are born in jails each year. Jailed mothers are not only separated from their children, they may have to pay for their support. Twelve percent of all jails in one study group reported requiring employed female inmates to contribute to the support of their dependent children.

Drug abuse is another significant source of difficulty for jailed women. Over 30% of women who are admitted to jail have a substance abuse problem at the time of admission, and in some parts of the country, that figure may be as high as 70%.[104] Adding to the problem is the fact that substantive medical programs for female inmates, such as obstetrics and gynecological care, are often lacking. In planning medical services for female inmates into the next century, some writers have advised jail administrators to expect to see an increasingly common kind of inmate: "[a]n opiate-addicted female who is pregnant with no prior prenatal care having one or more sexually transmitted diseases, and fitting a high-risk category for AIDS (prostitution, IV drug use)."[105]

Female inmates are only half the story. Women working in corrections are the other. In a 1991 study[106] Linda Zupan, one of the new generation of outstanding jail scholars, found that women comprised 22% of the correctional officer force in jails across the nation. The deployment of female personnel, however, was disproportionately skewed toward jobs in the lower ranks. Although 60% of all support staff (secretaries, cooks, and janitors) were women, only one in every ten chief administrators was female. Zupan explains this pattern by pointing to the "token-status" of women staff members in some of the nation's jails.[107] Even so, Zupan did find that women correctional employees were significantly committed to their careers and that attitudes of male workers toward female coworkers in jails were generally positive. Zupan's study uncovered 626 jails in which over 50% of the correction officer force consisted of women. On the opposite side of the coin, 954 of the nation's 3,316 jails have no female officers.[108] As Zupan notes, "[a]n obvious problem associated with the lack of female officers in jails housing females concerns the potential for abuse and exploitation of women inmates by male staff."[109]

Jails which do hire women generally accord them equal footing with male staffers. Although cross-gender privacy is a potential area of legal liability, few jails limit the supervisory areas which may be visited by female officers working in male facilities. In three

Children whose mothers are behind bars in a Rhode Island facility await their turn to visit. Women in jail face special problems, many of which are associated with child care. *Photo: Gale Zucker/Stock Boston.*

quarters of the jails studied by Zupan, women officers were assigned to supervise male housing areas. Only one in four jails which employed women restricted their access to unscreened shower and toilet facilities used by men and/or to other areas such as sexual offender units.

Crowding in Jails

Jails have been called the "shame of the criminal justice system." Many are old, overcrowded, poorly funded, scantily staffed by underpaid and poorly trained employees, and given low priority in local budgets. Court-ordered caps on jail populations are increasingly common. Recently, for example, the Harris County Jail in Houston, Texas, was forced to release 250 inmates after missing a deadline for reducing its resident population of 6,100 people.[110] A nationwide survey, published by the Bureau of Justice Statistics in 1991, found that 46% of all jails were built more than 25 years ago and of that percentage, over half were more than 50 years old.[111]

Overcrowded jails have become a critical issue throughout the justice system.[112] A 1983 national census revealed that jails were operating at only 85% of their rated capacity.[113] By 1990, however, the nation's jails were running at 108% of capacity, and new jails could be found on drawing boards and under construction across the country. By 1993, new facilities had opened, and overall jail occupancy was reported at 99% of rated capacity. With square footage per inmate averaging only 58.3[114] in jails today, managers still cite crowding and staff shortages as the two most critical problems facing jails today.[115]

The root cause of jail overcrowding can be found in a growing crime rate combined with a punitive public attitude which has heavily influenced correctional practice. In addition, prison overcrowding in recent years has forced many states to begin using jails instead of prisons for the confinement of convicted felons, exacerbating the crowding of jails still further. In 1992, 18,191 inmates were being held in local jails because of crowding in state prisons. Another problem arises from the sentencing of individuals who are unable to make restitution, alimony, or child care payments to jail time—a practice which has made the local lockup at least partially a debtor's prison. Symptomatic of problems brought on by overcrowding, the National Center on Institutions and Alternatives reported 401 suicides in jails across the nation during a recent year.[116] Recently, however, other than deaths from natural causes, AIDS has replaced suicide as the leading cause of jail deaths in the nation, as shown in Figure 12–7.

Although the societal underpinnings of overcrowding are difficult to assess, some causes of jail crowding which can be immediately addressed include the following:[117]

- The inability of jail inmates to make bond due to bonds [wo]men practices and lack of funding sources for indigent defendants
- Unnecessary delays between arrest and final case disposition
- Unnecessarily limited access to vital information about defendants which could be useful in facilitating court-ordered pretrial release
- The limited ability of the criminal justice system to handle cases expeditiously due to a lack of needed resources (judges, assistant prosecuting attorneys, etc.)
- Inappropriate attorney delays in moving cases through court (motions to delay cases as part of an attorney's strategy, etc.)
- Unproductive statutes requiring that specified nonviolent offenders be jailed (including those requiring mandatory pretrial jailing of DWI's, minor drug offenders, second offense shoplifting, etc.)

Some innovative jurisdictions have already substantially reduced jail crowding. San Diego, California, for example, uses a privately operated detoxification reception program

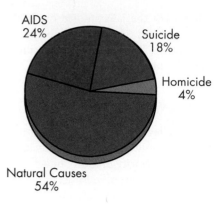

FIGURE 12–7   Causes of jail deaths, U.S. total, 1992. *Source:* Criminal Justice Institute, *The Corrections Yearbook 1993* (South Salem, NY: The Institute, 1993).

in order to divert many inebriates from the proverbial "drunk tank."[118] Officials in Galveston County, Texas, routinely divert mentally ill arrestees directly to a mental health facility.[119] Some areas use pretrial services and magistrates offices which are open 24 hours a day for the purpose of setting bail, making release possible.

Direct Supervision Jails   Temporary confinement facilities which eliminate many of the traditional barriers between inmates and correctional staff. Physical barriers in direct supervision jails are far less common than in traditional jails allowing staff members the opportunity for greater interaction with, and control over, residents.

Direct Supervision Jails

Some authors have suggested that the dilemmas found in many jails today stem from "mismanagement, lack of fiscal support, heterogeneous inmate populations, overuse and misuse of detention, overemphasis on custodial goals, and political and public apathy."[120] Others propose that environmental and organizational elements inherent in traditional jail architecture and staffing have given rise to today's difficulties.[121] Traditional jails, say these observers, were built upon the assumption that inmates are inherently violent and potentially destructive. Hence, most of today's jails were constructed in such a way as to maximize custodial control over inmates—via the use of thick walls, bars, and other architectural barriers to the free movement of inmates. Such institutions, however, have the adverse effect of limiting the visibility and access of correctional personnel to many confinement areas. As a consequence, they tend to encourage just the kinds of inmate behavior that jails were meant to control. Inefficient hallway patrols and expensive video technology have provided temporary patches, intended to overcome the limits that old jail architecture places on supervisory activities.

In an effort to solve many of the problems which have dogged jails in the past, a new jail management strategy emerged during the 1980s. Called direct supervision, this contemporary approach "joins podular/unit architecture with a participative, proactive management philosophy."[122] Often built in a system of "pods," or modular self-contained housing areas linked to one another, direct supervision jails eliminate the old physical barriers which separated staff and inmates. Gone are bars and isolated secure observation areas for officers. They are replaced by an open environment, in which inmates and correctional personnel mingle with relative freedom. In a growing number of such "new-generation" jails, large reinforced Plexiglas panels have supplanted walls and serve to separate activity areas, such as classrooms and dining halls, from one another. Soft furniture is often found throughout these institutions, and individual rooms take the place of cells, allowing inmates at least a modicum of personal privacy. In today's direct supervision jails, 16 to 46 inmates typically live in one pod, with correctional staffers present among the inmate population on an around-the-clock basis.

The first direct supervision jail opened in the 1970s in Contra Costa County, California. This 386-bed facility became a model for the nation, and other new-generation

Inside a direct supervision jail. Inmates and officers can mingle in this Hillsborough County (New Hampshire) jail. *Photo: Rick Friedman/ Black Star.*

jails soon commenced operations in Las Vegas; Portland; Reno; New York City; Bucks County, Pennsylvania; Vancouver, British Columbia; and Miami.

Direct supervision jails have been touted for their tendency to reduce inmate dissatisfaction, and for their ability to deter rape and violence among the inmate population. By eliminating architectural barriers to staff/inmate interaction, direct supervision facilities are said to place officers back in control of institutions. While these innovative facilities are still too new to assess fully, a number of studies have already demonstrated their success at reducing the likelihood of inmate victimization. One such study,[123] published in 1983, found that traditional facilities averaged nearly 15 times as many aggravated assaults (between inmates) as did direct supervision jails. Similarly homicide, sexual assault, jail rape, suicide, and escape have all been found to occur far less frequently in direct supervision facilities than in traditional institutions.[124] Staff members working in direct supervision jails report being happier and less stressed than in old-style facilities.[125] Significantly, new-generation jails appear to reduce substantially the number of lawsuits brought by inmates and lower the incidence of adverse court-ordered judgments against jail administrators.

A recent report[126] compared correctional officers working in direct supervision jails with those in more traditional settings and found that direct supervision officers "1.) were more satisfied with their jobs, 2.) reported slightly lower levels of overall stress and job-related stress, and 3.) reported fewer instances of on-the-job hassles and stress-inducing events...."

Direct supervision jails are not without their problems. Some authors[127] have recognized that new-generation jails are too frequently run by old-style managers and that correctional personnel sometimes lack the training needed to make the transition to the new style of supervision. Others[128] have suggested that managers of direct supervision jails, especially those at the mid-level, could benefit from clearer job descriptions and additional training. In the words of one Canadian advocate of direct supervision,[129] "training becomes particularly critical in direct supervision jails where relationships are more immediate and are more complex." Finally, recommendations have arisen from those tasked with hiring[130] that potential new staff members should be psychologically screened and that intensive use be made of preemployment interviews, in order to determine the suitability of applicants for correctional officer positions in direction supervision jails.

Jails and the Future

In contrast to more visible issues confronting the justice system, such as the death penalty, gun control, the war on drugs, and big-city gangs, jails have received relatively little attention from the media and have generally escaped close public scrutiny. National efforts, however, to improve the quality of jail life are under way. Some changes involve programmatic additions. A recent American Jail Association study of drug treatment programs in jails, for example, found that "a small fraction (perhaps fewer than 10%) of inmates needing drug treatment actually receive these services."[131] Follow-up efforts were aimed at developing standards to guide jails administrators in increasing the availability of drug treatment services to inmates.

Jail industries are another growing programmatic area. The best of them serve the community while training inmates in marketable skills.[132] In an exemplary effort to humanize its megajails,[133] for example, the Los Angeles County Sheriff's Department recently opened an inmate telephone answering service. Many calls are received by the Sheriff's Department daily, requesting information about a significant number of the county's 22,000 jail inmates. These requests for information were becoming increasingly difficult to handle due to the growing fiscal constraints facing local government. To handle the huge number of calls effectively without tying up sworn law enforcement personnel, the department began using inmates specially trained to handle incoming calls. Eighty inmates were assigned to the project, with groups of different sizes covering shifts throughout the day. Each inmate staffer went through a program designed to provide coaching in proper telephone procedures and to teach each operator how to run computer terminals containing routine data on the department's inmates. The new system is now fully in place and handles 4,000 telephone inquiries a day. The time needed to answer a call and provide information has dropped from 30 minutes under the old system to a remarkable 10 seconds today.

Another innovative program operates out of the Jackson County Detention Center (JCDC) in Kansas City, Missouri.[134] The JCDC initiated the use of citizen volunteers more than a decade ago. Today 123 volunteers work in the facility—many of them as tutors in the general education program. Others offer substance abuse counseling, marriage counseling, and chaplain's services. Citizen volunteers have contributed 50,000 hours of service time during the past six years, at a value of over half a million dollars.

One final element in the unfolding saga of jail development should be mentioned: the emergence of state jail standards. Thirty-two states have set standards for municipal and county jails.[135] In 25 states those standards are mandatory. The purpose of jail standards is to identify some basic minimum level of conditions necessary for inmate health and safety. On a national level, the Commission on Accreditation for Corrections, operated jointly by the American Correctional Association and the federal government, has developed its own set of jail standards,[136] as has the National Sheriff's Association. Both sets of standards are designed to ensure a minimal level of comfort and safety in local lockups. Increased standards, though, are costly. Local jurisdictions, already hard pressed to meet other budgetary demands, will probably be slow to upgrade their jails to meet such external guidelines, unless forced to. Ken Kerle, in a study[137] of 61 jails which was designed to test compliance with National Sheriff's Association guidelines, discovered that in many standards areas—especially those of tool control, armory plan-

THEORY INTO PRACTICE

American Jail Association Code of Ethics for Jail Officers

As an officer employed in a detention/correctional capacity, I swear (or affirm) to be a good citizen and a credit to my community, state, and nation at all times. I will abstain from all questionable behavior which might bring disrepute to the agency for which I work, my family, my community, and my associates. My lifestyle will be above and beyond reproach and I will constantly strive to set an example of a professional who performs his/her duties according to the laws of our country, state, and community and the policies, procedures, written and verbal orders, and regulations of the agency for which I work.

On the job I promise to:

Keep	The institution secure so as to safeguard my community and the lives of the staff, inmates, and visitors on the premises.
Work	With each individual firmly and fairly without regard to rank, status, or condition.
Maintain	A positive demeanor when confronted with stressful situations of scorn, ridicule, danger, and/or chaos.
Report	Either in writing or by word of mouth to the proper authorities those things which should be reported, and keep silent about matters which are to remain confidential according to the laws and rules of the agency and government.
Manage	And supervise the inmates in an evenhanded and courteous manner.
Refrain	At all times from becoming personally involved in the lives of the inmates and their families.
Treat	All visitors to the jail with politeness and respect and do my utmost to ensure that they observe the jail regulations.
Take	Advantage of all education and training opportunities designed to assist me to become a more competent officer.
Communicate	With people in or outside of the jail, whether by phone, written word, or word of mouth, in such a way so as not to reflect in a negative manner upon my agency.
Contribute	To a jail environment which will keep the inmate involved in activities designed to improve his/her attitude and character.
Support	All activities of a professional nature through membership and participation that will continue to elevate the status of those who operate our nation's jails.

Do my best through word and deed to present an image to the public at large of a jail professional, committed to progress for an improved and enlightened criminal justice system.

The American Jail Association's Board of Directors has approved the AJA Code of Ethics as part of an integral program to achieve a high standard of professional conduct among those officers employed in our nation's jails.

Adopted 1/10/91
by AJA Board of Directors

Source: The American Jail Association, *Code of Ethics for Jail Officers* as adopted January 10, 1991. (Hagerstown, MD, The Association, 1991). Reprinted with permission.

ning, community resources, release preparation, and riot planning—the majority of jails were sorely out of compliance. Lack of a written plan was the most commonly cited reason for failing to meet the standards.

In what may be one of the best set of recommendations designed to foster the development of jails which can serve into the next century, Joel A. Thompson and G. Larry Mays[138] suggest that (1) states should provide financial aid and/or incentives to local governments for jail construction and renovation, (2) mandatory jail standards must be developed by all states, (3) mandatory jail inspections should become commonplace in the enforcement of standards, (4) citizens should be educated as to the function and significance of jails in an effort to increase the public's willingness to fund new jail construction, (5) all jails need to have written policies and procedures to serve as training tools and as a basis for a defense against lawsuits, and (6) "[c]ommunities should explore alternatives to incarceration [because]…[m]any jail detainees are not threats to society and should not occupy scarce and expensive cell space."

Private Prisons
Correctional institutions operated by private firms on behalf of local and state governments.

PRIVATE PRISONS

Some states have begun to supplement their prison resources through contracts with private firms for the provision of custodial and other services. The aim is to reduce overcrowding, lower operating expenses, and avoid lawsuits targeted at state officials and employees. Corrections Corporation of America (CCA) was one of the first companies to offer privately operated correctional facilities to states. In 1985 CCA made an unsuccessful bid to assume operation of the entire Tennessee prison system and now operates a few dozen facilities across the country, including a halfway house for the Federal Bureau of Prisons.[139] In 1986 U.S. Corrections Corporation, another private firm, opened a 300-bed minimum security facility in Kentucky. By the late 1980s more than 1,900 prisoners were held in privately operated secure correctional facilities.[140] The movement toward privatization of prisons rests on sound historical ground. State-run prisons have contracted with private industry for food, psychological testing, training, recreational, and other services in the past, and it is estimated that today over three dozen states rely on private businesses to provide a variety of correctional needs.[141]

Many hurdles remain before the privatization movement can effectively provide large-scale custodial supervision. Some of the questions being raised today about the movement toward private prisons are shown in a box in this chapter. One of the most significant barriers to privatization lies in the fact that some states have old laws which prohibit private involvement in correctional management. Other practical hurdles exist. States which do contract with private firms may face the specter of strikes by guards, who do not come under state laws restricting the ability of employees to strike. Responsibility for the protection of inmate rights still lies with the state, and liability will not transfer to private corrections.[142] In today's legal climate, it is unclear whether a state can shield itself or its employees through private prison contracting, but it would appear that such shielding is unlikely to be recognized by the courts. To limit liability, states will probably have to oversee private operations as well as set standards for training and custody. Opponents of the movement toward privatization claim that cost reductions can only be achieved through lowered standards for the treatment of prisoners. They fear a return to the inhumane conditions of early jails, as private firms seek to turn prisons into profit-making operations. For states which do choose to contract with private firms, the National Institute of Justice recommends a "regular and systematic sampling" of former inmates to appraise prison conditions, as well as "on-site inspections at least every year" of each privately run institution. State personnel serving as monitors should be stationed in large facilities, and a "meticulous review" of all services should be conducted prior to the contract renewal date.[143]

SECURITY LEVELS

Maximum custody prisons are the institutions most often portrayed in movies and on television. They tend to be massive old prisons with large inmate populations. Some, like Central Prison in Raleigh, North Carolina, are much newer and incorporate advances in prison architecture to provide tight security without sacrificing building aesthetics. Maximum custody prisons tend to locate cells and other inmate living facilities at the center of the institution and place a variety of barriers between the living area and the institution's outer perimeter. Maximum custody is actually a level of security characterized by high fences, thick walls, secure cells, gun towers, and armed prison guards. Technological innovations such as electric perimeters, laser motion detectors, electronic and pneumatic locking systems, metal detectors, X-ray machines, television surveillance, radio communications, and computer information systems are frequently used today to reinforce the more traditional maximum security strategies. These new technologies have helped to lower the cost of new prison construction, although some argue that prison electronic detection devices may be relied upon too heavily and have not yet been adequately tested.[144] Death row inmates are all maximum security prisoners, although the level of security on death row exceeds even that experienced by most prisoners held in maximum custody. Prisoners on death row must spend much of the day in single cells and are often permitted a brief shower only once a week under close supervision.

Most states today have one large centrally located maximum security institution. Some of these prisons combine more than one custody level and may be both maximum and medium security facilities. Medium security is a custody level which bears many resemblances to maximum security. Medium security prisoners are generally permitted more freedom to associate with one another and are able to frequent the prison yard, exercise room, library, and shower and bathroom facilities under less intense supervision than their maximum security counterparts. An important security tool in medium security prisons is the count, which is literally a headcount of inmates taken at regular intervals. Counts may be taken four times a day and usually require inmates to report to designated areas to be counted. Until the count has been "cleared," all other inmate activity must cease. Medium security prisons tend to be smaller than maximum security institutions and often have barbed-wire–topped chain-link fences in place of the more secure stone or concrete block walls found in many of the older maximum security facilities. Cells and living quarters tend to have more windows and are often located closer to the perimeter of the institution than is the case in maximum security. Dormitory-style housing, where prisoners live together in "ward"-like arrangements, may be

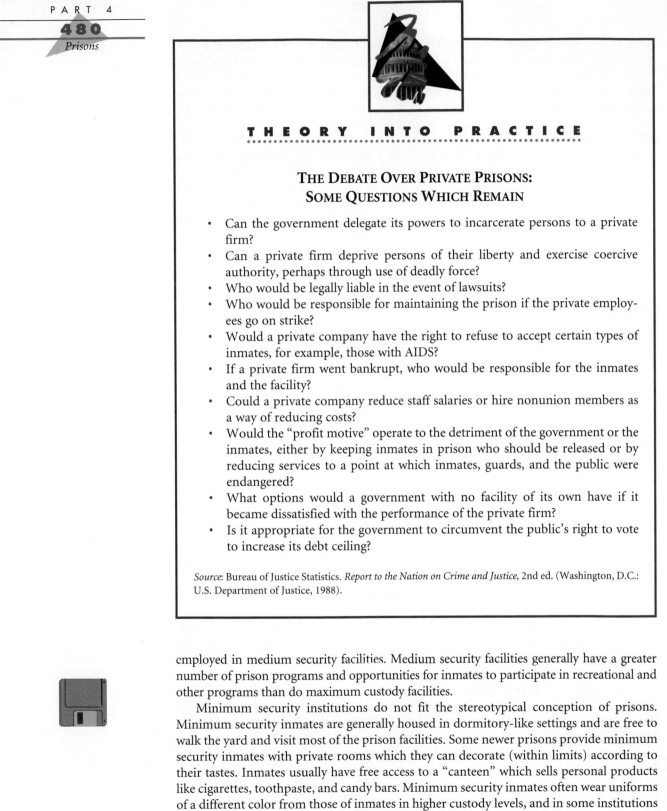

THEORY INTO PRACTICE

THE DEBATE OVER PRIVATE PRISONS: SOME QUESTIONS WHICH REMAIN

- Can the government delegate its powers to incarcerate persons to a private firm?
- Can a private firm deprive persons of their liberty and exercise coercive authority, perhaps through use of deadly force?
- Who would be legally liable in the event of lawsuits?
- Who would be responsible for maintaining the prison if the private employees go on strike?
- Would a private company have the right to refuse to accept certain types of inmates, for example, those with AIDS?
- If a private firm went bankrupt, who would be responsible for the inmates and the facility?
- Could a private company reduce staff salaries or hire nonunion members as a way of reducing costs?
- Would the "profit motive" operate to the detriment of the government or the inmates, either by keeping inmates in prison who should be released or by reducing services to a point at which inmates, guards, and the public were endangered?
- What options would a government with no facility of its own have if it became dissatisfied with the performance of the private firm?
- Is it appropriate for the government to circumvent the public's right to vote to increase its debt ceiling?

Source: Bureau of Justice Statistics. *Report to the Nation on Crime and Justice*, 2nd ed. (Washington, D.C.: U.S. Department of Justice, 1988).

employed in medium security facilities. Medium security facilities generally have a greater number of prison programs and opportunities for inmates to participate in recreational and other programs than do maximum custody facilities.

Minimum security institutions do not fit the stereotypical conception of prisons. Minimum security inmates are generally housed in dormitory-like settings and are free to walk the yard and visit most of the prison facilities. Some newer prisons provide minimum security inmates with private rooms which they can decorate (within limits) according to their tastes. Inmates usually have free access to a "canteen" which sells personal products like cigarettes, toothpaste, and candy bars. Minimum security inmates often wear uniforms of a different color from those of inmates in higher custody levels, and in some institutions may wear civilian clothes. They work under only general supervision and usually have access to recreational, educational, and skills training programs on the prison grounds. Guards are unarmed, gun towers do not exist, and fences, if they are present at all, are

Prison contraband on display in a supervisor's office. Note the handmade quality and concealability of most of the weapons. *Photo: Laimute E. Druskis.*

usually low and sometimes even unlocked. Many minimum security prisoners participate in some sort of work- or study-release program, and some have extensive visitation and furlough privileges. Counts may still be taken, although most minimum security institutions keep track of inmates through daily administrative work schedules. The primary "force" holding inmates in minimum security institutions is their own restraint. Inmates live with the knowledge that minimum security institutions are one step removed from close correctional supervision and that any failure on their part to meet the expectations of administrators will result in their being transferred into more secure institutions and will probably delay their release. Inmates returning from assignments in the community may be frisked for contraband, but body cavity searches are rare in minimum custody, being reserved primarily for inmates suspected of smuggling.

Upon entry into the prison system most states assign prisoners to initial custody levels based upon their perceived dangerousness, escape risk, and type of offense. Some inmates may enter the system at the medium (or even minimum) custody level. Inmates move through custody levels according to the progress they are judged to have made in self-control and demonstrated responsibility. Serious, violent criminals who begin their prison careers with lengthy sentences in maximum custody have the opportunity in most states to work their way up to minimum security, although the process usually takes a number of years. Those who "mess up" and represent continuous disciplinary problems are returned to closer custody levels. Minimum security prisons, as a result, house inmates convicted of all types of criminal offenses.

The typical American prison today is medium or minimum custody. Some states have as many as 80 or 90 small institutions, which may originally have been located in every county to serve the needs of public works and highway maintenance. Medium and minimum security institutions house the bulk of the country's prison population and offer a number of programs and services designed to assist with the rehabilitation of offenders and to create the conditions necessary for a successful reentry of the inmate into society.

Most prisons offer programs in the following areas:[145]

- Psychiatric services
- Academic education
- Vocational education
- Substance abuse treatment
- Health care

- Counseling
- Recreation
- Library services
- Religious programs
- Industrial and agricultural services

THE FEDERAL PRISON SYSTEM

In 1895 the federal government opened a prison at Leavenworth, Kansas, for civilians convicted of violating federal law. Leavenworth had been a military prison and control over the facility was transferred from the Department of the Army to the Department of Justice. By 1906 the Leavenworth facility had been expanded to a 1,200-inmate capacity, and another prison—in Atlanta, Georgia—had been built. McNeil Island Prison in Washington State was functioning by the early 1900s. The first federal prison for women opened in 1927 in Alderson, West Virginia. With increasing complexity in the federal criminal code, the number of federal prisoners grew.[146]

On May 14, 1930, the Federal Bureau of Prisons was created under the direction of Sanford Bates. The Bureau inherited a system which was dramatically overcrowded. Many federal prisoners were among the most notorious criminals in the nation, and ideals of humane treatment and rehabilitation were all but lacking in the facilities of the 1930s. Director Bates began a program of improvements to relieve overcrowding and to increase the treatment capacity of the system. In 1933 the Medical Center for Federal Prisoners opened in Springfield, Missouri, with a capacity of around 1,000 inmates. Alcatraz Island began operations in 1934.

By the 1960s the federal prison system classified its institutions according to six security levels. The most severe security risks were housed in maximum custody facilities called U.S. penitentiaries. All such penitentiaries were designed to house adult male offenders. Among those functioning today, those in Atlanta, Georgia; Lewisburg, Pennsylvania; Terre Haute, Indiana; and Leavenworth, Kansas, are probably the best known maximum security federal institutions. Medium security prisons were called "federal correctional institutions" and generally housed inmates with shorter sentences and those who were judged to represent small security risks. Terminal Island, California; Lompoc, California; and Seagoville, Texas, are well-known homes of a few such prisons. Minimum custody prisoners were held at the Allenwood facility in Montgomery, Pennsylvania; Eglin Air Force Base, Florida; and Maxwell Air Force Base, Alabama. Other minimum custody facilities held juveniles, such as those at Pleasanton, California; Englewood, Colorado; and Ashland, Kentucky. A number of community treatment centers, operated in large cities across the nation, complemented the Bureau's prisons.

The federal system today is substantially unchanged. Approximately 70 federal prisons are in operation (see Figure 12–8), with one of the most recent additions to the system—the Federal Correctional Institution at Butner, North Carolina—designed to house suicidal and acutely psychotic offenders. A new grading system classifies facilities according to six security levels, and custodial terms such as "maximum" and "minimum" are avoided. Crowding in federal prisons is pervasive. The number of inmates held in federal prisons has risen from 24,000 in 1980 to more than 80,000 today. Estimates are that, without changes, the federal prison population will exceed 116,000 inmates by 1999, with most of the increase due to lengthy sentences for drug offenders.

In an effort to combat rising expenses, the U.S. Congress recently passed legislation that imposes a "user fee" on federal inmates able to pay the costs associated with their incarceration.[147] Under the law, inmates may be assessed a dollar amount up to the cost of a year's incarceration—currently around $20,000. The statue, which was designed so as not to impose hardships on poor defendants or their dependents, directs that collected funds, estimated to soon total $48 million per year, are to be used to improve alcohol and drug abuse programs within federal prisons.

RECENT IMPROVEMENTS

In the midst of frequent lawsuits, court-ordered changes in prison administration, and overcrowded conditions, outstanding prison facilities are being recognized through the American Correctional Association's program of accreditation. The ACA Commission on Accreditation has developed a set of standards which correctional institutions can use in self-evaluation. Those which meet the standards can apply for accreditation under the program. Unfortunately, accreditation of prisons has few "teeth." Although unaccredited universities would not long be in business, few prisoners can choose the institution they want to be housed in.

Another avenue toward improvement of the nation's prisons can be found in the National Academy of Corrections, the training arm of the National Institute of Corrections. The Academy, located in Boulder, Colorado, offers seminars and training sessions for state and local correctional managers, trainers, personnel directors, sheriffs, and state legislators.[148] Issues covered include strategies to control overcrowding, community corrections program management, prison programs, gangs and disturbances, security, and public and media relations, as well as many other topics.[149]

FIGURE 12–8 The federal correctional system. *Source:* Federal Bureau of Prisons, *Facilities 1992* (Washington, D.C.: U.S. Department of Justice, 1993).

CAREERS IN JUSTICE

WORKING WITH THE FEDERAL BUREAU OF PRISONS

TYPICAL POSITIONS. Psychologists, physicians, nurses, chaplains, correctional treatment specialists, safety specialists, teachers, program officers, vocational instructors, correctional officers, and others.

EMPLOYMENT REQUIREMENTS. Applicants must (1) be U.S. citizens, (2) be less than 35 years of age (although for some hard-to-fill positions an age waiver may be granted), (3) successfully complete an employee interview, (4) pass a physical examination, and (5) pass a field security investigation.

OTHER REQUIREMENTS. Successful completion of in-service training at the Federal Law Enforcement Training Academy at Glynco, Georgia.

SALARY. Correctional officers are appointed at the GS-5 level, with entry-level salaries set at $22,617 in mid-1993. GS-6 level appointees start at $23,484. A correctional officer may be advanced to the next higher grade level after six months of satisfactory service.

BENEFITS. Benefits include (1) participation in the Federal Employees' Retirement System, (2) paid annual leave, (3) paid sick leave, (4) low-cost health and life insurance, and (5) paid holidays. Other benefits naturally accrue from what the Bureau describes as "strong internal merit promotion practices" and "unlimited opportunities for advancement in one of the fastest-growing government agencies."

DIRECT INQUIRIES TO: Federal Bureau of Prisons, Room 400, 320 First Street, N.W., Washington, D.C. 20534. Phone: (202) 317-5250.

SUMMARY

Modern prisons are the result of historical efforts to humanize the treatment of offenders. "Doing time for crime" has become society's answer to the corporal punishments of centuries past. Even so, questions remain about the conditions of imprisonment in contemporary prisons and jails, and modern corrections is far from a panacea. The security orientation of correctional staff and administration leaves little room for capable treatment programs. Existing prisons are overcrowded, and new ones are expensive. An end to crowding is nowhere in sight. Studies demonstrating the likelihood of recidivism among prior correctional clients have called the whole correctional process into question, and the modern practice of "warehousing" seems more a strategy of frustration than one of hope.

Prisons today exist in a kind of limbo. Emphasis is on reducing the costs and the pains of incarceration. Uncertainties about the usefulness of treatment have left few officials confident of their ability to rehabilitate offenders. The return of prison industries, the interest in efficient technologies of effective imprisonment, and court-mandated reforms are all signs that society has given up any hope of large-scale reformation among inmate populations.

DISCUSSION QUESTIONS

1. Trace the historical development of imprisonment, beginning with the Pennsylvania system. Why has the style of imprisonment changed as it has over time?

2. In your opinion, would a return to physical punishments and public humiliation be effective deterrents of crime in today's world? Why?

3. What future do you believe the move toward new prison industries will face? Why?

4. What do you see as the role of private prisons? What will be the state of private prisons two decades from now?

5. Explain the pros and cons of the present warehousing model of corrections. Do you believe that new rehabilitative models will be developed which will make warehousing a thing of the past?

6. What solutions do you see to the present overcrowded conditions of many prison systems?

ENDNOTES

1. As cited in the National Conference on Prison Industries, *Discussions and Recommendations* (Washington, D.C.: U.S. Government Printing Office, 1986), p. 23.

2. This section owes much to Harry Elmer Barnes and Negley K. Teeters, *New Horizons in Criminology*, 3rd ed. (Englewood Cliffs, NJ: Prentice Hall, 1959).

3. Ibid., p. 290.

4. Ibid., p. 292.

5. Ibid.

6. Ibid., p. 293.

7. John Howard, *State of Prisons* (London, 1777), reprinted by E. P. Dutton, New York, 1929.

8. Although some writers hold that the Quakers originated the concept of solitary confinement for prisoners, there is evidence that the practice already existed in England prior to 1789. John Howard describes solitary confinement in use at Reading Brideswell in the 1780s.

9. Vergil L. Williams, *Dictionary of American Penology: An Introduction* (Westport, CT: Greenwood, 1979), p. 200.

10. Barnes and Teeters, *New Horizons in Criminology*, p. 348.

11. Williams, *Dictionary of American Penology*, p. 29.

12. With regard to cost, supporters of the Pennsylvania system argued that it was less expensive than the Auburn style of imprisonment because it led to reformation much faster than did the New York style.

13. Williams, *Dictionary of American Penology*, p. 30.

14. Gustave de Beaumont and Alexis de Tocqueville, *On the Penitentiary System in the United States, and its Application in France* (Philadelphia, PA: Carey, Lea and Blanchard, 1833).

15. As cited in Barnes and Teeters, *New Horizons in Criminology*, p. 418.

16. Frank Schmalleger, *A History of Corrections: Emerging Ideologies and Practices* (Bristol, IN: Wyndham Hall, 1986), p. 44.

17. Barnes and Teeters, *New Horizons in Criminology*, p. 428.

18. Ibid.

19. Ibid.

20. Williams, *Dictionary of American Penology*, pp. 68–70.

21. Robert Mintz, "Federal Prison Industry—The Green Monster. Part One: History and Background," *Crime and Social Justice*, Vol. 6 (Fall/Winter 1976), pp. 41–48.

22. Patty McQuillan, *North Carolina Department of Correction, 1986* (Raleigh, NC: Correctional Enterprises Print Shop, 1986).

23. Criminal Justice Associates, *Private Sector Involvement in Prison-Based Businesses: A National Assessment* (Washington, D.C.: U.S. Government Printing Office, 1985). See also National Institute of Justice (Reports), *Corrections and the Private Sector* (Washington, D.C.: U.S. Government Printing Office, 1985).

24. Gail S. Funke, *National Conference on Prison Industries: Discussions and Recommendations* (Washington, D.C.: U.S. Government Printing Office, 1986).

25. Barnes and Teeters, *New Horizons in Criminology*, p. 355.

26. Ibid., p. 381.

27. Ibid., p. 357.

28. Ibid., p. 359.

29. Williams, *Dictionary of American Penology*, p. 90.

30. Ibid., p. 225.

31. Ibid., p. 64.

32. Ibid., p. 227.

33. Donal E. J. MacNamara, "Medical Model in Corrections: Requiescat in Pace," in Fred Montanino, ed., *Incarceration: The Sociology of Imprisonment* (Beverly Hills, CA: Sage Publications, 1978).

34. For a description of the community based format in its heyday, see Andrew T. Scull, *Decarceration: Community Treatment and the Deviant—A Radical View* (Englewood Cliffs, NJ: Prentice Hall, 1977).

35. Ibid., p. 51.

36. Williams, *Dictionary of American Penology*, p. 45.

37. Ibid.

38. Clemens Bartollas, *Introduction to Corrections* (New York: Harper & Row, 1981), pp. 166–167.

39. Harry Allen, *Corrections in America: An Introduction* (Beverly Hills, CA: Glencoe, 1975), p. 468.

40. Williams, *Dictionary of American Penology*, p. 48.

41. National Advisory Commission on Criminal Justice Standards and Goals, Std. 2.17, part 2 c.

42. Recidivism can be defined in various ways according to the purpose it is intended to serve in a particular study or report. Recidivism is usually defined as rearrest (versus reconviction) and generally includes a time span of five years, although some Bureau of Justice Statistics studies have used six years and other studies one or two years as definitional criteria.

43. Various advocates of the "justice model" can be identified. For a detailed description of the two models, see Michael A. Pizzi, Jr., "The Medical Model and the 100 Years War," *Law Enforcement News*, July 7,

1986, pp. 8, 13; and MacNamara, "Medical Model in Corrections."

44. Bureau of Justice Statistics, *Annual Report, 1987* (Washington, D.C.: BJS, 1988), p. 70.

45. Ibid.

46. Ibid.

47. Lawrence Greenfeld, "Examining Recidivism," *BJS Special Report* (Washington, D.C.: U.S. Government Printing Office, 1985).

48. R. Martinson, "What Works: Questions and Answers About Prison Reform" *Public Interest*, No. 35 (1974), pp. 22–54. See also Douglas Lipton, Robert M. Martinson, and Judith Wilkes, *The Effectiveness of Correctional Treatment: A Survey of Treatment Evaluation Studies* (New York: Praeger, 1975).

49. L. Sechrest, S. White, and E. Brown, eds., *The Rehabilitation of Criminal Offenders: Problems and Prospects* (Washington, D.C.: The National Academy of Sciences, 1979).

50. Christy A. Visher, "Incapacitation and Crime Control: Does a 'Lock 'Em 'Up' Strategy Reduce Crime?" *Justice Quarterly*, Vol. 4, no. 4 (December 1987), pp. 513–543.

51. For information on identifying dangerous repeat offenders, see M. Chaiken and J. Chaiken "Selecting Career Criminals for Priority Prosecution," final report (Cambridge, MA: Abt Associates, 1987).

52. D. Greenberg, "The Incapacitative Effect of Imprisonment, Some Estimates," *Law and Society Review*, Vol. 9 (1975), pp. 541–580. See also Jacqueline Cohen, "Incapacitating Criminals: Recent Research Findings," National Institute of Justice, *Research in Brief* (December 1983).

53. J. Monahan, *Predicting Violent Behavior: An Assessment of Clinical Techniques* (Beverly Hills, CA: Sage Publications, 1981).

54. S. Van Dine, J. P. Conrad, and S. Dinitz, *Restraining the Wicked: The Incapacitation of the Dangerous Offender* (Lexington, MA: Lexington Books, 1979).

55. *Fayetteville Observer-Times* (North Carolina), July 4, 1988, p. 2A, citing James K. Stewart, director of the National Institute of Justice.

56. Wisconsin Policy Research Institute, *Crime and Punishment in Wisconsin* (Milwaukee: Wisconsin Policy Research Institute, 1990).

57. "A Sheriff Takes Over an Armory to Ease Jail Crowding Crisis," *Criminal Justice Newsletter*, Vol. 21, no. 5 (March 1, 1990), p. 5.

58. "Sheriff Who Seized Armory Gets Jail," *Fayetteville Observer-Times* (North Carolina), September 20, 1992, p. 9A.

59. Bureau of Justice Statistics, *Prisoners in 1987*, (Washington, D.C.: U.S. Government Printing Office, 1988).

60. Bureau of Justice Statistics, *Prisoners in 1990* (Washington, D.C.: BJS, 1991).

61. Ibid.

62. Wade B. Houck, "Acquiring New Prison Sites: The Federal Experience," *NIJ Construction Bulletin* (Washington, D.C.: NIJ, 1987).

63. Lynn S. Branham, *The Use of Incarceration in the United States: A Look at the Present and the Future* (Washington, D.C.: American Bar Association, 1992).

64. "Reliance on Prisons Is Costly but Ineffective, ABA Panel Says," *Criminal Justice Newsletter*, April 15, 1992, p. 7.

65. Bureau of Justice Statistics, *Prisoners in 1988* (Washington, D.C.: BJS, 1989).

66. Ibid.

67. American Correctional Association, *Vital Statistics in Corrections* (Laurel, MD: ACA, 1991), p. 44.

68. *Criminal Justice Newsletter*, Vol. 23, no. 3 (February 3, 1992), p. 8.

69. American Correctional Association, *Vital Statistics in Corrections*, p. 52.

70. Bureau of Justice Statistics, *Prisoners in 1992* (Washington, D.C.: BJS, May, 1993).

71. Adapted from U.S. Department of Justice, *Report to the Nation on Crime and Justice*, 2nd ed., p. 108.

72. *Rhodes* v. *Chapman*, 452 U.S. 337 (1981).

73. James Lieber, "The American Prison: A Tinderbox," *The New York Times* Magazine, March 8, 1981.

74. Alfred Blumstein, "Prison Crowding," National Institute of Justice, *Crime File Study Guide* (date unknown), p. 2.

75. Stephen Carter and Ann C. Humphries, "Inmates Build Prisons in South Carolina," National Institute of Justice, *Construction Bulletin* (December 1987).

76. George and Camille Camp, "Stopping Escapes: Perimeter Security," National Institute of Justice, *Construction Bulletin* (August 1987).

77. Bureau of Justice Statistics, *Prisoners in 1992* (Washington, D.C.: BJS, May 1993).

78. American Correctional Association, *1993 Directory of Juvenile and Adult Correctional Departments, Institutions, Agencies and Paroling Authorities* (Laurel, MD: ACA, 1993).

79. Bureau of Justice Statistics, *National Corrections Reporting Program, 1985* (Washington, D.C.: BJS, December 1990), p. 14.

80. Ibid., p. 54.

81. Ibid.

82. American Correctional Association, *1993 Directory of Juvenile and Adult Correctional Departments, Institutions, Agencies and Paroling Authorities* (Laurel, MD: ACA, 1993).

83. American Correctional Association, "Correctional Officers in Adult Systems," *Vital Statistics in Corrections* (Laurel, MD: ACA, 1991), p. 30.

84. Ibid., p. 73.

85. Ibid, p. 30. Note: "Other" minorities round out the percentages to a total of 100%.

86. U.S. Department of Justice, *Report to the Nation on Crime and Justice*, 2nd ed. (Washington, D.C.: U.S. Government Printing Office, 1988), p. 123.

87. Ibid., p. 11.

88. Robert M. Carter, Richard A. McGee, and E. Kim Nelson, *Corrections in America* (Philadelphia: J. B. Lippincott, 1975), pp. 122–123.

89. U.S. Department of Justice, Bureau of Justice Statistics, *BJS Data Report, 1988* (Washington, D.C.: U.S. Government Printing Office, April 1989), p. 62.

90. Ibid., p. 19.

91. Ibid., p. 63.

92. U.S. Department of Justice, Bureau of Justice Statistics, *Jail Inmates, 1992* (Washington, D.C.: U.S. Department of Justice, 1993), p. 2.

93. U.S. Department of Justice, *Report to the Nation on Crime and Justice*, 2nd ed., p. 106.

94. U.S. Department of Justice, *Jail Inmates, 1992*, p. 2.

95. Ibid.

96. Statistics from: Louis W. Jankowski, *Jail Inmates 1991* (Washington, D.C.: Bureau of Justice Statistics, 1992); Robert J. Ciulik, "Population Management Efforts," *American Jails*, (November/December 1992); and "Jail Overcrowding in Houston Results in Release of Inmates," *Criminal Justice Newsletter*, October 15, 1990, p. 5.

97. U.S. Department of Justice, *Jail Inmates, 1992*.

98. William Reginald Mills and Heather Barrett, "Meeting the Special Challenge of Providing Health Care to Women Inmates in the '90's," *American Jails*, Vol. 4, no. 3. (September/October, 1990), p. 55.

99. American Correctional Association, *The Female Offender: What Does the Future Hold?* (Washington, D.C.: St. Mary's Press, 1990), p. 14.

CHAPTER 12

489

Prisons

100. Ibid., p. 21.

101. Ibid.

102. American Correctional Association, *Vital Statistics in Corrections.*

103. Mills and Barrett, "Meeting the Special Challenge," p. 55.

104. Ibid.

105. Ibid.

106. Linda L. Zupan "Women Corrections Officers in the Nation's Largest Jails," *American Jails* (January–February 1991), pp. 59–62.

107. Ibid., p. 11.

108. Linda L. Zupan, "Women Corrections Officers in Local Jails," paper presented at the annual meeting of the Academy of Criminal Justice Sciences, Nashville, Tennessee, March 1991.

109. Ibid., p. 6.

110. "Jail Overcrowding in Houston Results in Release of Inmates," *Criminal Justice Newsletter*, October 15, 1990, p. 5.

111. Bureau of Justice Statistics, *Census of Local Jails, 1988*, (Washington, D.C.: BJS, 1991), p. 31.

112. Jamieson and Flanagan, *Sourcebook of Criminal Justice Statistics, 1988.*

113. Ibid.

114. Bureau of Justice Statistics, *Census of Local Jails, 1988*, (Washington, D.C.: BJS, 1991), p. 15.

115. Randall Guynes, *Nation's Jail Managers Assess Their Problems* (Washington, D.C.: National Institute of Justice, 1988).

116. Lindsay M. Hayes and Joseph R. Rowan, *National Study of Jail Suicides: Seven Years Later* (Alexandria, VA: National Center on Institutions and Alternatives, 1988), p. 11.

117. As identified in George P. Wilson and Harvey L. McMurray, *System Assessment of Jail Overcrowding Assumptions*, paper presented at the annual meeting of the Academy of Criminal Justice Sciences, Nashville, Tennessee, March 1991.

118. Andy Hall, *Systemwide Strategies to Alleviate Jail Crowding* (Washington, D.C.: National Institute of Justice, 1987).

119. Ibid.

120. Linda L. Zupan and Ben A. Menke, "The New Generation Jail: An Overview," in Joel A. Thompson and G. Larry Mays, eds., *American Jails: Public Policy Issues* (Chicago: Nelson-Hall, 1991), p. 180.

121. Ibid.

122. Herbert R. Sigurdson, Billy Wayson, and Gail Funke, "Empowering Middle Managers of Direct Supervision Jails," *American Jails* (Winter 1990), p. 52.

123. National Institute of Corrections, *New Generation Jails* (Boulder, CO: NIC, 1983).

124. H. Sigurdson, *The Manhattan House of Detention: A Study of Podular Direct Supervision* (Washington, D.C.: National Institute of Corrections, 1985).

125. See, for example, Linda L. Zupan, *Jails: Reform and the New Generation Philosophy* (Cincinnati, OH: Anderson, 1991), pp. 133–150.

126. Robert Conroy, Wantland J. Smith, Linda L. Zupan, "Officer Stress in the Direct Supervision Jail: A Preliminary Case Study," *American Jails* (November/December 1991), p. 36.

127. Jerry W. Fuqua, "New Generation Jails: Old Generation Management," *American Jails* (March/April 1991), pp. 80–83.

128. Sigurdson, Wayson, and Funke, "Empowering Middle Managers."

129. Duncan J. McCulloch and Time Stiles, "Technology and the Direct Supervision Jail," *American Jails* (Winter 1990), pp. 97–102.

130. Susan W. McCampbell, "Direct Supervision: Looking for the Right People," *American Jails* (November /December 1990), pp. 68–69.

131. Robert L. May II, Roger H. Peters, and William D. Kearns "The Extent of Drug Treatment Programs in Jails:

A Summary Report," *American Jails* (September/October 1990), pp. 32–34.

132. See, for example, John W. Dietler, "Jail Industries: The Best Thing That Can Happen to a Sheriff," *American Jails* (July/August 1990), pp. 80–83.

133. Robert Osborne, "Los Angeles County Sheriff Opens New Inmate Answering Service," *American Jails* (July/August 1990), pp. 61–62.

134. Nancy E. Bond and Dave Smith, "The Challenge: Community Involvement in Corrections," *American Jails* (November/December 1992), p. 19–20.

135. Tom Rosazza, "Jail Standards: Focus on Change," *American Jails* (November/December 1990), pp. 84–87.

136. American Correctional Association, *Manual of Standards for Adult Local Detention Facilities*, 3rd ed. (College Park, MD: ACA, 1991).

137. Ken Kerle, "National Sheriff's Association Jail Audit Review," *American Jails* (Spring 1987), pp. 13–21.

138. Joel A. Thompson and G. Larry Mays, "Paying the Piper but Changing the Tune: Policy Changes and Initiatives for the American Jail," in Joel A. Thompson and G. Larry Mays, eds. *American Jails: Public Policy Issues* (Chicago: Nelson-Hall, 1991), pp. 240–246.

139. John J. Di Iulio, Jr., "Private Prisons," National Institute of Justice *Crime File Study Guide* (no date).

140. Ibid., p. 1.

141. Bureau of Justice Statistics, *Report to the Nation on Crime and Justice*, p. 119. See also Judith C. Hackett et al., "Contracting for the Operation of Prisons and Jails," National Institute of Justice *Research in Brief* (June 1987), p. 2.

142. For a more detailed discussion of this issue, see Ira Robbins, *The Legal Dimensions of Private Incarceration* (Chicago: American Bar Foundation, 1988).

143. Hackett et al., "Contracting for the Operation of Prisons and Jails," p. 6.

144. Camp and Camp, "Stopping Escapes: Perimeter Security."

145. Adopted from Grizzle et al., "Measuring Corrections Performance," p. 31.

146. Ibid.

147. "Congress OKs Inmates Fees to Offset Costs of Prison," *Criminal Justice Newsletter*, October 15, 1992, p. 6.

148. National Institute of Corrections, "National Academy of Corrections: Outreach Training Programs" (July 1987).

149. National Institute of Corrections, "Correctional Training Programs" (July 1987).

CHAPTER 13

PRISON LIFE

Our policy of confining large numbers of offenders seems to have been ineffective in reducing the violent crime rate.
> —JOHN H. KRAMER, EXECUTIVE DIRECTOR
> PENNSYLVANIA COMMISSION ON SENTENCING

We must remember always that the "doors of prisons swing both ways."[1]
> —MARY BELLE HARRIS
> FIRST FEDERAL WOMAN WARDEN

…infinite are the nine steps of a prison cell, and endless is the march of him who walks between the yellow brick wall and the red iron gate, thinking things that cannot be chained and cannot be locked…
> —ARTURO GIOVANNITTI (1884–1959)

KEY CONCEPTS

total institutions	prison subculture	prisonization
argot	prisoner unions	grievance
hands-off doctrine	civil death	balancing test

KEY CASES

Pell v. *Procunier*	*Houchins* v. *KQED*	*Wolff* v. *McDonnell*
Block v. *Rutherford*	*Johnson* v. *Avery*	*Estelle* v. *Gamble*
Bounds v. *Smith*	*Newman* v. *Alabama*	*Katz* v. *U.S.*
Ruiz v. *Estelle*	*Hudson* v. *Palmer*	*Jones* v. *North Carolina*
Cruz v. *Beto*	*Helling* v. *McKinney*	*Prisoner's Union*
Hudson v. *McMillian*		

THE REALITIES OF PRISON LIFE

For the first 150 years of their existence, prisons and prison life could be described by the phrase "out of sight, out of mind." Very few citizens cared about prison conditions, and those unfortunate enough to be locked away were regarded as lost to the world. By the mid-1900s such attitudes had begun to change. Concerned citizens began to offer their services to prison administrations, neighborhoods began accepting work-release prisoners and halfway houses, and social scientists initiated a serious study of prison life.

Hans Reimer, then chairman of the Department of Sociology at Indiana University, set the tone for studies of prison life in 1935 when he voluntarily served three months in prison as an incognito participant observer.[2] Reimer reported the results of his studies to the American Prison Association, stimulating many other, albeit less spectacular, efforts to examine prison life. Other early studies include Donald Clemmer's *The Prison Community* (1940),[3] Gresham M. Sykes's *The Society of Captives: A Study of a Maximum Security Prison* (1958),[4] Richard A. Cloward and Donald R. Cressey's *Theoretical Studies in Social Organization of the Prison* (1960), and Donald R. Cressey's *The Prison: Studies in Institutional Organization and Change* (1961).[5]

These studies and others focused primarily on maximum security prisons for men. They treated correctional institutions as formal or complex organizations and employed the analytical techniques of organizational sociology, industrial psychology, and administrative science.[6] As modern writers on prisons have observed: "[t]he prison was compared to a primitive society, isolated from the outside world, functionally integrated by a delicate system of mechanisms, which kept it precariously balanced between anarchy and accommodation."[7]

Total Institutions Enclosed facilities, generally separated from society both physically and socially, where the inhabitants share all aspects of their lives on a daily basis.

TOTAL INSTITUTIONS

Another approach to the study of prison life was developed by Erving Goffman who coined the term **total institutions** in a 1961 study of prisons and mental hospitals.[8] Goffman described total institutions as places where the same people work, play, eat, sleep, and recreate together on a daily basis. Such places include prisons, concentration camps, mental hospitals, seminaries, and other facilities in which residents are cut off from the

Custody and security remain the primary concern of prison staffers throughout the country—a fact seemingly belied by the apparent disregard of this posted notice. *Photo: Laimute E. Druskis.*

larger society either forcibly or willingly. Total institutions are small societies. They evolve their own distinctive styles of life and place pressures on residents to fulfill rigidly proscribed behavioral roles.

PRISON SUBCULTURES

Two social realities coexist in prison settings. One is the official structure of rules and procedures put in place by the wider society and enforced by prison staff. The other is the far less formal, but decidedly more powerful inmate world. The inmate world, best described by its pervasive immediacy in the lives of inmates, is also called the prison subculture. The realities of prison life—a large and often densely packed inmate population which must look to the prison environment for all its needs—mean that such subcultures are not easily subject to the control of prison authorities.

Prison subcultures develop independently of the plans of prison administrators, and inmates entering prison discover a social world not mentioned in the handbooks prepared by the staff. Inmate concerns, values, roles, and even language weave a web of social reality in which new inmates must participate. Those who try to remain aloof soon find themselves subjected to dangerous ostracism and may even be suspected of being in league with the prison administration.

The socialization of new inmates into the prison subculture has been described as a process of prisonization.[9] Prisonization refers to the learning of convict values and attitudes. When the process is complete inmates have become "cons." The values of the inmate social system are embodied in a code whose violations can produce sanctions ranging from ostracism and avoidance to physical violence and homicide.[10] Sykes and Messinger[11] recognize five elements of the prison code:

Prison Subculture The values and behavioral patterns characteristic of prison inmates. Prison subculture has been found to have surprising consistencies across the country.

1. Don't interfere with the interests of other inmates. Never rat on a con.
2. Don't lose your head. Play it cool and do your own time.
3. Don't exploit inmates. Don't steal. Don't break your word. Be right.
4. Don't whine. Be a man.
5. Don't be a sucker. Don't trust the guards or staff.

Prison Argot The slang characteristic of prison subcultures and prison life.

Distant prisons share aspects of a common inmate culture,[12] and prisonwise inmates entering a facility far from their home will already know the ropes. **Prison argot**, or language, provides one example of how widespread prison subculture can be. The terms used to describe inmate roles in one institution are generally understood in others. The word "rat," for example, is prison slang for an informer. Popularized by crime movies of the 1950s, the term "rat" is understood today by members of the wider society. Other words common to prison argot are shown in the accompanying box.

Prisonization The process whereby institutionalized individuals come to accept prison lifestyles and criminal values. While many inmates begin their prison experience with only a modicum of values supportive of criminal behavior, the socialization experience they undergo while incarcerated leads to a much wider acceptance of such values.

The concept of **prisonization** was closely examined by Stanton Wheeler in a study of the Washington State Reformatory.[13] Wheeler found that the degree of prisonization experienced by inmates tends to vary over time. He described changing levels of inmate commitment to prison norms and values by way of a "U-shaped" curve. When an inmate first enters prison, Wheeler said, the conventional values of outside society are of paramount importance. As time passes the life-style of the prison is adopted. However, within the half-year prior to release, most inmates begin to demonstrate a renewed appreciation for conventional values.

Some criminologists have suggested that inmate codes are simply a reflection of general criminal values. If so, they are brought to the institution rather than created there. Either way, the power and pervasiveness of the inmate code require convicts to conform to the world view held by the majority of prisoners.

The Functions of Prison Society

Why do prison societies exist? Human beings are by nature social beings. All around the world people live in groups and create a culture suited to their needs. Rarely, however, does the intensity of human interaction approach the level found in prisons. The prisons of today are crowded places where inmates can find no retreat from the constant demands of staff and the pressures brought by fellow prisoners. Even solitary confinement occurs within the context of prison rules and inmate expectations. In *The Society of Captives*, Gresham Sykes described the "pains of imprisonment."[14] The pains of imprisonment—the result of deprivations and frustrations forced upon inmates by the rigors of confinement—form the nexus of a deprivation model of prison culture. Sykes grouped them into five areas: (1) liberty, (2) goods and services, (3) heterosexual relationships, (4) autonomy, and (5) personal security. Prison subculture, according to Sykes, is an adaptation to such deprivations.

In contrast to the deprivation model, the importation model of prison culture suggests that inmates bring with them values, roles, and behavior patterns from the outside world. Such external values, second nature as they are to career offenders, depend substantially upon the criminal world view. Upon confinement, these external elements shape the inmate social world.

Social structure is a term that refers to accepted social arrangements. Donald Clemmer's early study of the prison recognized nine structural dimensions in inmate society. He said that prison society could be described in terms of:[15]

THEORY INTO PRACTICE

PRISON ARGOT: THE LANGUAGE OF CONFINEMENT

Writers who have studied prison life often comment on the use by prisoners of a special language or *argot*. This language generally refers to the roles assigned by prison culture to types of inmates as well as to prison activities. This box lists words identified in past studies by various authors. The first group of words are characteristic of male prisons; the last few have been used in prisons for women.

Rat: An inmate who squeals (provides information about other inmates to the prison administration).

Gorilla: The inmate who uses force to take what he wants from others.

Merchant (or pedlar): One who sells when he should give.

Fish: The newly arrived inmate.

Wolf: The male inmate who assumes the aggressive masculine role during homosexual relations.

Punk: The male inmate who is forced into a submissive or feminine role during homosexual relations.

Fag: The male inmate who is believed to be a "natural" or "born" homosexual.

Lemon Squeezer: The inmate who has an unattractive "girlfriend."

Screw: Guard.

Stud Broad (or Daddy): The female inmate who assumes the role of a male during lesbian relations.

Femme (or Mommy): The female inmate who plays the female role during lesbian relations.

Cherry (or Cherrie): The female inmate who has not yet been introduced to lesbian activities.

Fay Broad: A white female inmate.

Sources: Gresham Sykes, *The Society of Captives* (Princeton, NJ: Princeton University Press, 1958); Rose Giallombardo, *Society of Women: A Study of A Woman's Prison* (New York: John Wiley, 1966); and Richard A. Cloward et al., *Theoretical Studies in Social Organization of the Prison* (New York: Social Science Research Council, 1960).

1. The prisoner/staff dichotomy
2. The three general classes of prisoners
3. Work gangs and cellhouse groups
4. Racial groups
5. Type of offense
6. The power of inmate "politicians"
7. Degree of sexual abnormality
8. The record of repeat offenses
9. Personality differences due to preprison socialization

Clemmer's nine structural dimensions are probably still descriptive of prison life today. When applied in individual situations, they designate an inmate's position in the prison "pecking order" and create expectations of the appropriate role for that person. Prison roles serve to satisfy the needs of inmates for power, sexual performance, material possessions, individuality, and personal pleasure. For example, inmate leaders, sometimes referred to as "real men" or "toughs" by prisoners in early studies, offer protection to those who live by the rules. They also provide for a redistribution of wealth inside of prison and see to it that the rules of the complex prison-derived economic system—based on barter, gambling, and sexual favors—are observed.

The Evolution of Subcultures

By the time John Irwin was about to complete his now-famous study of *The Felon* (1970), he expressed the worry that his book was already obsolete.[16] *The Felon*, for all of its insights into prison subculture, follows in the descriptive tradition of works by Clemmer and Reimer. Irwin recognized that by 1970 prison subcultures had begun to reflect cultural changes sweeping America. A decade later some authors were able to write: "It was no longer meaningful to speak of a single inmate culture or even subculture. By the time we began our field research…it was clear that the unified, oppositional convict culture, found in the sociological literature on prisons, no longer existed."[17]

Stastny and Tyrnauer, describing prison life at Washington State Penitentiary in 1982, discovered four clearly distinguishable subcultures: (1) official, (2) traditional, (3) reform, and (4) revolutionary. Official culture was promoted by the staff and by administrative rules of the institution. Enthusiastic participants in official culture were mostly correctional officers and other staff members, although inmates were also well aware of the normative expectations official culture imposed on them. Official culture impacted the lives of inmates primarily through the creation of a prisoner hierarchy based upon sentence length, prison jobs, and the "perks" which cooperation with the dictates of official culture could produce. Traditional prison culture, as described by Clemmer and Sykes, still existed, but its participants spent much of their time lamenting the decline of the convict code among younger prisoners. Reform culture was unique at Washington State Penitentiary. It was the result of a brief experiment with inmate self-government during the early 1970s. Elements of prison life which evolved during the experimental period sometimes survived the termination of self-government and were eventually institutionalized in what Stastny and Tyrnauer call reform culture. Such elements included inmate participation in civic-style clubs, citizen involvement in the daily activities of the prison, banquets, and inmate speaking tours. Revolutionary culture built upon the radical political rhetoric of the disenfranchised and found a ready audience among minority prisoners who saw themselves as victims of society's basic unfairness. Although they did not participate in it, revolutionary inmates understood traditional prison culture and generally avoided running afoul of its rules.

Homosexuality in Prison

Sykes's early study of prison argot found many words describing homosexual activity. Among them were the terms "wolf," "punk," and "fag." Wolves were aggressive men who assumed the masculine role in homosexual relations. Punks were forced into submitting to the female role, often by wolves. Fags described a special category of men who had a natural proclivity toward homosexual activity. While both wolves and punks were fiercely committed to their heterosexual identity and participated in homosexuality only because of prison conditions, fags generally engaged in homosexual life-styles before their entry into prison.

A group of male inmates dressed as women in a California institution. Homosexuality is common in both men's and women's prisons. *Photo: Rasmussen/Sipa Press.*

Prison homosexuality depends to a considerable degree upon the naivete of young inmates experiencing prison for the first time. Older prisoners looking for homosexual liaisons may ingratiate themselves with new arrivals by offering cigarettes, money, drugs, food, or protection. At some future time these "loans" will be "called in," with payoffs demanded in sexual favors. Because the inmate code requires the repayment of favors, the "fish" who tries to resist may quickly find himself face to face with the brute force of inmate society.

Prison rape represents a special category of homosexual behavior behind bars. Estimates of the incidence of rape in prison vary. One study found 4.7% of inmates in the Philadelphia prison system willing to report sexual assaults.[18] Most studies find that black inmates are far more likely to commit rape in prison than are whites.[19] Victims of rape, on the other hand, are more likely to be white. This difference seems to hold even in prisons where there is considerable variation in the proportion of black and white inmates.[20]

Lee Bowker, summarizing studies of sexual violence in prison,[21] provides the following observations:

1. Most sexual aggressors do not consider themselves to be homosexuals.
2. Sexual release is not the primary motivation for sexual attack.
3. Many aggressors must continue to participate in gang rapes in order to avoid becoming victims themselves.
4. The aggressors have themselves suffered much damage to their masculinity in the past.

As in cases of heterosexual rape, sexual assaults in prison are likely to leave psychological scars long after the physical event is over.[22] The victims of prison rape live in fear, may feel constantly threatened, and can turn to self-destructive activities.[23] At the very least victims question their masculinity and undergo a personal devaluation. In some cases victims of prison sexual attacks turn to violence. Frustrations, long bottled up through abuse and fear, may explode and turn the would-be rapist into a victim of prison homicide.

Prison Life-styles

Prison society is strict and often unforgiving. Even so, inmates are able to express some individuality through the choice of a prison life-style. John Irwin was the first well-known author to describe prison life-styles, viewing them as adaptations to the prison environment.[24] Other writers have since elaborated on these coping mechanisms. Listed in the pages that follow are some of the types of prisoners described by commentators.

Inmate Types

1. *The Mean Dude.* Some inmates adjust to prison by being mean. They are quick to fight, and when they fight, they fight like wild men (or women). They give no quarter and seem to expect none in return. Other inmates know that such prisoners are best left alone. The mean dude receives frequent write-ups and spends much time in solitary confinement.

    The mean dude role is supported by the fact that some prisoners occupy it naturally, having filled it in free society. Similarly, certain personality types, such as the psychopathic, may feel a natural attraction to this role. On the other hand, prison culture supports the role of the mean dude in two ways: (a) by expecting inmates to be tough and (b) through the prevalence of a type of wisdom which says that "only the strong survive" inside prison.

    A psychologist might say that the mean dude is acting out against the fact of captivity, striking out at anyone he (or she) can. This type of role performance is more common in male institutions and in maximum security prisons. It tends to become less common as inmates progress to lower security levels.

2. *The Hedonist.* Some inmates build their lives around the limited pleasures which can be had within the confines of prison. The smuggling of contraband, homosexuality, gambling, drug running, and other officially condemned activities provide the center of interest for prison hedonists. Hedonists generally have an abbreviated view of the future, living only for the "now." Such a temporal orientation is probably characteristic of the personality type of all hedonists and exists in many persons, incarcerated or not.

3. *The Opportunist.* The opportunist takes advantage of the positive experiences prison has to offer. Schooling, trade-training, counseling, and other self-improvement activities are the focal points of the opportunist's life in prison. Opportunists are the "do-gooders" of the prison subculture. They are generally well liked by prison staff, but shunned and mistrusted by other prisoners because they come closest to accepting the role which the staff defines as "model prisoner." Opportunists may also be religious, a role adaptation worthy of a separate description (given shortly).

4. *The Retreatist.* Prison life is rigorous and demanding. Badgering by the staff and actual or feared assaults by other inmates may cause some prisoners to attempt psychological retreat from the realities of imprisonment. Such inmates may experience neurotic or psychotic episodes, become heavily involved in drug and alcohol abuse, or even attempt suicide. Depression and mental illness are the hallmarks of the retreatist personality in prison. The best hope for the retreatist, short of release, is protective custody combined with therapeutic counseling.

5. *The Legalist.* The legalist is the "jail house lawyer." Just like the mean dude, the legalist fights confinement. The weapons in this fight are not fists or clubs, however, but the legal "writ." Convicts facing long sentences, with little possibility for early release through the correctional system, are most likely to turn to the courts in their battle against confinement.

6. *The Radical.* Radical inmates picture themselves as political prisoners. Society, and the successful conformists who populate it, are seen as oppressors who have forced criminality upon many "good people" through the creation of a system which distributes wealth and power inequitably. The radical inmate speaks a language of revolution and may be versed in the writings of the "great" revolutionaries of the past.

   The inmate who takes on the radical role is unlikely to receive much sympathy from prison staff. Radical rhetoric tends to be diametrically opposed to staff insistence on accepting responsibility for problematic behavior.

7. *The Colonist.* Some inmates think of prison as their home. They "know the ropes," have many "friends" inside, and may feel more comfortable institutionalized than on the streets. They typically hold either positions of power or respect (or both) among the inmate population. These are the prisoners who don't look forward to leaving prison. Most colonizers grow into the role gradually, and only after already having spent years behind bars. Once released, some colonizers have been known to attempt new crimes in order to return to prison.

8. *The Religious.* Some prisoners profess a strong religious faith. They may be "born again" Christians, committed Muslims, or even Hare Krishnas. Religious inmates frequently attend services, may form prayer groups, and sometimes ask the prison administration to allocate meeting facilities or create special diets to accommodate their claimed spiritual needs.

   While it is certainly true that some inmates have a strong religious faith, staff members are apt to be suspicious of the overly religious prisoner. The tendency is to

A San Diego (California) inmate shows off his physique. Some inmates attempt to adapt to prison life by acting tough. *Photo: Armineh Johannes/Sipa Press.*

Prison inmates adapt diverse coping strategies. Here convicted murderer Henry Lee Lucas claims to have found God. *Photo: Bob Daemmrich/Stock Boston.*

view such prisoners as "faking it" in order to demonstrate a fictitious rehabilitation and thereby gain sympathy for an early release.

9. *The Realist.* The realist is a prisoner who sees confinement as a natural consequence of criminal activity. Time spent in prison is an unfortunate "cost of doing business." This stoic attitude toward incarceration generally leads the realist to "pull his (or her) own time" and to make the best of it. Realists tend to know the inmate code, are able to avoid trouble, and continue in lives of crime once released.

It is better to prevent crimes than to punish them.

—*Cesare Bonesana, Marchese Di Beccaria*

THE STAFF WORLD

The flip side of inmate society can be found in the world of the correctional officer. Prison staff members bring diverse values and a variety of personality types to the institution. Staff roles encompass those of warden, psychologist, counselor, area supervisor, program director, instructor, and guard, and in some large prisons, physician, and therapist. Officers, generally seen as at the bottom of the staff hierarchy, may be divided into cellbock and tower guards, while some are regularly assigned to administrative offices where they perform clerical tasks.

Lucien Lombardo has described the process by which officers are socialized into the prison work world.[25] Lombardo interviewed 359 correctional personnel at New York's Auburn prison and found that rookie officers had to quickly abandon preconceptions of both inmates and other staff members. According to Lombardo, new officers learn that inmates are not the "monsters" much of the public makes them out to be. On the other hand, the disappointment the rookie finds in the experienced worker comes from the realization that ideals of professionalism, often stressed during early training, are rarely translated into reality. The pressures of the institutional work environment, however, soon force most correctional personnel to adopt a united front in relating to inmates.

One of the leading formative influences on staff culture is the potential threat posed by inmates. Inmates far outnumber correctional personnel in any institution, and the hostility they feel for guards is only barely hidden even at the best of times. Correctional personnel know that however friendly inmates may appear, a sudden change in institutional climate—as can happen in anything from simple disturbances on the yard to full-blown riots—can quickly and violently unmask deep-rooted feelings of mistrust and hatred.

CUSTODY AND CONTROL—STILL PRIMARY TODAY

As in years past, custody and control are still the paramount concerns of prison staffers today. Custody is what society expects of correctional staff. It is the basic prerequisite of successful job performance. Custody is necessary before any other correctional activities, such as instruction or counseling, can be undertaken.

Control, the other major staff concern, ensures order, and an orderly prison is thought to be safe and secure. In routine daily activities, control over almost all aspects of inmate behavior becomes paramount in the minds of most correctional officers. It is the twin interests of custody and control that lead to institutionalized procedures for ensuring security in most facilities. The use of strict rules, body and cell searches, counts, unannounced shakedowns, the control of dangerous items, materials, and contraband, and the extensive use of bars, locks, fencing, cameras, and alarms all support the human vigilance of the staff in maintaining security.

TYPES OF CORRECTIONAL OFFICERS

Staff culture, in combination with naturally occurring personality types, gives rise to a diversity of officer "types." Like the inmate typology described earlier, correctional staff can be classified according to certain distinguishing characteristics. Among the most prevalent types are:

1. *The Dictator.* Some officers go by the book. Others go beyond it, using prison rules to enforce their own brand of discipline. The guard who demands signs of inmate subservience, from constant use of the word "sir" or "ma'am" to frequent free shoeshines, is one type of dictator. Another goes beyond legality, beating or "macing" inmates even for minor infractions or perceived insults. Dictator guards are bullies. They find their counterpart in the mean inmate described earlier.

   Dictator guards may have sadistic personalities and gain ego satisfaction through the feelings of near omnipotence which come from the total control of others. Some may be fundamentally insecure and employ a false bravado to hide their fear of inmates. Officers which fit the dictator category are the most likely to be targeted for vengeance should control of the institution temporarily revert to the inmates.

2. *The Friend.* Friendly officers try to fraternize with inmates. They approach the issue of control by trying to be "one of the guys." They seem to believe that they can win inmate cooperation by being nice. Unfortunately, such guards do not recognize that fraternization quickly leads to unending requests for special favors—from delivering mail to bending "minor" prison rules. Once a few rules have been "bent," the officer may find that inmates have the upper hand through the potential for blackmail.

   Many officers have amiable relationships with inmates. In most cases, however, affability is only a convenience which both sides recognize can quickly evaporate. Friendly officers, as the term is being used here, are *overly* friendly. They may be young and inexperienced. On the other hand, they may simply be possessed of kind and idealistic personalities built on successful friendships in free society.

3. *The Merchant.* The presence of contraband in any correctional facility is testimony to the prevalence of the merchant officer. The merchant participates in the inmate economy, supplying drugs, pornography, alcohol, and sometimes even weapons to inmates who can afford to pay for them.

   Probably only a very few officers consistently perform the role of merchant, although a far larger proportion may occasionally turn a few dollars by smuggling some item through the gate. Low salaries create the potential for mercantile corruption among many otherwise "straight arrow" officers. Until salaries rise substantially, the merchant will remain an institutionalized feature of most prisons.

4. *The Indifferent.* The indifferent type of officer cares little for what goes on in the prison setting. Officers who fit this category may be close to retirement, or they may be alienated from their jobs for various reasons. Low pay, the view that inmates are basically "worthless" and incapable of changing, and the monotonous ethic of "doing time" all combine to numb the professional consciousness of even young officers.

   The indifferent officer is not seen as a threat by inmates, nor is such an officer likely to challenge the status quo in institutions where merchant guards operate.

5. *The Climber.* The climber is apt to be a young officer with an eye for promotion. Nothing seems impossible to the climber, who probably hopes eventually to be warden or program director or to hold some high-status position within the institutional hierarchy. Climbers are likely to be involved in schooling, correspondence courses, and professional organizations. They may lead a movement toward unionization for correctional personnel and tend to see the guard's role as a "profession" which should receive greater social recognition.

   Climbers have many ideas. They may be heavily involved in reading about the latest confinement or administrative technology. If so, they will suggest many ways to improve prison routine, often to the consternation of other complacent staff members.

   Like the indifferent officers, climbers turn a blind eye toward inmates and their problems. They are more concerned with improving institutional procedures and with their own careers than they are with the treatment or day-to-day control of inmates.

6. *The Reformer.* The reformer is the "do-gooder" among officers. This is the person who believes that prison should offer opportunities for personal change. The reformer tends to lend a sympathetic ear to the personal needs of inmates and is apt to offer "arm-chair" counseling and suggestions. Many reformers are motivated by personal ideals, and some of them are highly religious. Inmates tend to see the reformer guard as naive, but harmless. Because the reformer actually tries to help, even when help is unsolicited, he or she is the most likely of all the guard types to be accepted by prisoners.

Security is the primary concern of correctional staff. *Photo: Laimute E. Druskis.*

Testing and Training of Correctional Officers

Expectations of correctional officers have never been high. Prison staffers are generally accorded low status in occupational surveys. Guard jobs require minimal formal education and hold few opportunities for professional growth and advancement. They are low-paying, frustrating, and often boring. Growing problems in our nation's prisons, including emerging issues of legal liability, however, require a well-trained and adequately equipped professional guard force. As correctional personnel become more and more proficient, the old concept of *guard* is becoming supplanted by that of a professional *correctional officer*.

A few states and some large-city correctional systems make efforts to eliminate individuals with potentially harmful personalities from correctional officer applicant pools. New York, New Jersey, Ohio, Pennsylvania, and Rhode Island all use some form of psychological screening in assessing candidates for prison jobs.[26]

Although only a few states utilize psychological screening, all make use of training programs intended to prepare successful applicants for prison work. New York, for example, requires trainees to complete six weeks of classroom-based instruction, followed by another six weeks of on-the-job training. New York's 244-hour correctional officer curriculum is supplemented with 40 hours of rifle range practice. Training days begin around 5 A.M. with a mile run and conclude after dark with study halls for students who need extra help. To keep pace with rising inmate populations, the state has often had to run a number of simultaneous training academies.[27]

On the federal level a new model for correctional careers confronts many of the problems of correctional staffing head on. The Federal Bureau of Prisons' Career Development

THEORY INTO PRACTICE

CODE OF ETHICS: AMERICAN CORRECTIONAL ASSOCIATION PREAMBLE

The American Correctional Association expects of its members unfailing honesty, respect for the dignity and individuality of human beings, and a commitment to professional and compassionate service. To this end we subscribe to the following principles:

- Members will respect and protect the civil and legal rights of all individuals.
- Members will treat every professional situation with concern for the person's welfare and with no intent of personal gain.
- Relationships with colleagues will be such that they promote mutual respect within the profession and improve the quality of service.
- Public criticisms of colleagues or their agencies will be made only when warranted, verifiable and constructive in purpose.
- Members will respect the importance of all disciplines within the criminal justice system and work to improve cooperation with each segment.
- Subject to the individual's rights to privacy, members will honor the public's right to know, and will share information with the public to the extent permitted by law.
- Members will respect and protect the right of the public to be safeguarded from criminal activity.
- Members will not use their positions to secure personal privileges or advantages.
- Members will not, while acting in an official capacity, allow personal interest to impair objectivity in the performance of duty.
- No member will enter into any activity or agreement, formal or informal, which presents a conflict of interest or is inconsistent with the conscientious performance of his or her duties.
- No member will accept any gift, service or favor that is or appears to be improper or implies an obligation inconsistent with the free and objective exercise of his or her professional duties.
- In any public statement, members will clearly distinguish between personal views and those statements or positions made on behalf of an agency or the Association.
- Each member will report to the appropriate authority any corrupt or unethical behavior where there is sufficient cause to initiate a review.
- Members will not discriminate against any individual because of race, gender, creed, national origin, religious affiliation, age or any other type of prohibited discrimination.

- Members will preserve the integrity of private information; they will neither seek data on individuals beyond that needed to perform their responsibilities, nor reveal nonpublic data unless expressly authorized to do so.
- Any member who is responsible for agency personnel actions will make all appointments, promotions, or dismissals in accordance with established civil service rules, applicable contract agreements and individual merit, and not in furtherance of partisan interests.

Adopted August 1975 at the 105th Congress of Correction
Revised August 1990 at the 120th Congress of Correction

Source: American Correctional Association, *Code of Ethics* (Laurel, Maryland: American Correctional Association, 1990). Reprinted with permission.

Model stands as an example of what state departments of correction can do in the area of staff training and development. The model establishes five sequential phases for the development of career correctional officers:[28] (1) Phase I, Career Assessment; (2) Phase II, Career Path Development; (3) Phase III, Career Enhancement and Management Development; (4) Phase IV, Advanced Management Development; and (5) Phase V, Senior Executive Service Development. Using a psychological personality inventory, the model seeks to identify the skills, abilities, and interests of officers and matches them with career opportunities in the federal correctional system.

The new federal model builds upon the large number and diverse types of federal institutions which allow personnel a wide choice in the conditions of employment. Such a situation may not be possible to duplicate in state correctional systems. Small institutions often have few opportunities for added responsibility, and state systems offer neither the geographical nor the programmatic diversity of the Federal Bureau of Prisons.

Whilst we have prisons it matters little which of us occupies the cells.

—*George Bernard Shaw*

PRISON RIOTS

The ten years between 1970 and 1980 have been called the "explosive decade" of prison riots.[29] The decade began with a massive uprising at Attica prison in New York State in September 1971. The Attica riot resulted in 43 deaths. More than 80 men were wounded. The "explosive decade" ended in 1980 at Santa Fe, New Mexico. There, in a riot at the New Mexico penitentiary, 33 inmates died, the victims of revengeful prisoners out to eliminate rats and informants. Many of the deaths involved mutilation and torture. More than 200 other inmates were beaten and sexually assaulted, and the prison was virtually destroyed.

Prison riots did not stop with the end of the explosive 1970s. For 11 days in 1987 the Atlanta (Georgia) Federal Penitentiary fell into the hands of inmates. The institution was "trashed," and inmates had to be temporarily relocated while it was rebuilt. The Atlanta riot followed closely on the heels of a similar, but less intense, disturbance at the federal detention center at Oakdale, Louisiana. Both outbreaks were attributed to the dissatisfaction of Cuban inmates, most of whom had arrived on the Mariel boat lift.[30] More recently, a two-night rampage in October 1989 left more than 100 people injured and the Pennsylvania prison at Camp Hill in shambles. At the time of the riot, the State Correctional Institution at Camp Hill was 45% over its capacity of 2,600 inmates.[31] Easter Sunday 1993 saw the beginning of an 11-day rebellion at the 1,800-inmate Southern Ohio Correctional facility in Lucasville, Ohio—one of the country's toughest maximum security prisons. The riot ended with nine inmates and one correctional officer dead. The officer had been hung. Paul W. Goldberg, executive director of the Ohio Civil Service Employees Association, told an Ohio senate panel that "[t]hose of us who deal with our prisons every day—the men and women on the front lines—know that overcrowding and understaffing are at the heart of Ohio's prison crisis...." "Lucasville is not an aberration," said Goldberg. "Every prison in Ohio is a powder keg."[32] The close of the riot—involving a parade of 450 inmates—was televised as prisoners had demanded. Among other demands were: 1.) no retaliation by officials, 2.) review of medical staffing and care, 3.) review of mail and visitation rules, 4.) review of commissary prices, and 5.) better enforcement against what the inmates called "inappropriate supervision."[33]

CAUSES OF RIOTS

A satisfactory explanation of why prisoners riot is difficult to achieve. Riots are routinely followed by study groups which attempt to piece together the "facts" leading up to the incident under scrutiny. After the riot at Attica, the New York State Special Commission of Inquiry filed a report which recommended the creation of inmate advisory councils, changes in staff titles and uniforms, and other institutional improvements. Emphasis was placed on "enhancing (the) dignity, worth, and self-confidence" of inmates. The New Mexico attorney general, in a final report on the violence at Santa Fe, placed blame upon a breakdown in informal controls and the subsequent emergence of a new group of violent inmates among the general prison population.[34]

A number of authorities[35] have suggested a variety of causes for prison riots. Among the suggested causes are the following:

1. Riots result from an insensitive prison administration and neglected inmates' demands. Calls for "fairness" in disciplinary hearings, better food, more recreational opportunities, and the like may lead to riots when ignored.
2. Riots are a direct consequence of the life-styles most inmates are familiar with on the streets. It should be no surprise that prisoners use organized violence when many of them are violent people anyway.
3. Riots are the result of dehumanizing prison conditions. Overcrowded facilities, the lack of opportunity for individual expression, and other aspects of total institutions culminate in explosive situations of which riots are but one form.
4. Riots serve to regulate inmate society and to redistribute power balances among inmate groups. Riots provide the opportunity to "cleanse" the prison population of informers and rats and to resolve struggles between power brokers and ethnic groups within the institution.
5. Riots result from "power vacuums" created by changes in prison administration, the transfer of influential inmates, or court-ordered injunctions which significantly alter the informal social control mechanisms of the institution.

Prison riots can have disastrous consequences. Here, the federal prison in Atlanta burns after inmates set it afire in 1989. *Photo: Federal Bureau of Investigation.*

Although riots are difficult to predict in specific institutions, some state prison systems appear ripe for disorder. Texas, for example, has a system which meets a number of the causal criteria listed. Overcrowding and poor conditions have been endemic in the Texas system. Making matters worse, Texas prisons house a number of rapidly expanding gangs among whom turf violations can easily lead to widespread disorder. Gang membership among inmates in the Texas prison system, practically nonexistent in 1983, is now estimated at over 1,400.[36] The Texas Syndicate, the Aryan Brotherhood of Texas, and the Mexican Mafia are probably the largest gangs now functioning in the Texas prison system. Each has around 300 members.[37] Table 13–1 summarizes what is known about functioning gangs in the Texas prison system.

Gangs in Texas were given a green light by the "power vacuum" created via a recent court ruling which brought an end to the "building tender" system.[38] Building tenders were tough inmates who were given an almost free reign by prison administrators in keeping other inmates in line. The Texas prison system depended upon building tenders to keep order in many of the state's worst prisons. The end of the building tender system brought powerful new demands on the Texas Department of Corrections for increased abilities and professionalism among its guards and other prison staff.

The "real" reasons for any riot are probably institution specific and may not allow for easy generalization. However, it is no simple coincidence that the "explosive decade" of prison riots coincided with the growth of revolutionary prisoner subcultures referred to earlier. As the old convict code began to give way to an emerging perception of social victimization among inmates, it was probably only a matter of time until those perceptions turned to militancy. Seen from this perspective, riots are more a revolutionary activity undertaken by politically motivated cliques rather than spontaneous and disorganized expressions of the frustrations of prison life.

S TAGES IN RIOTS

The time and place of individual riots cannot be predicted.[39] Riots are generally unplanned and tend to occur spontaneously, the result of some relatively minor precipitating event. Once the stage has been set, prison riots tend to evolve through five phases:[40] (1) explosion, (2) organization (into inmate-led groups), (3) confrontation (with authority),

T A B L E   1 3 - 1

PRISON GANGS AND GANG MEMBERSHIP IN THE TEXAS PRISON SYSTEM, 1990

Name of Gang	Racial Composition	Membership	Year Formed
Texas Syndicate	Predominantly Hispanic	289	1975
Texas Mafia	Predominantly White	80	1982
Aryan Brotherhood of Texas	All white	170	1983
Mexican Mafia	All Hispanic	417	1984
Nuestro Carneles	All Hispanic	31	1984
Mandingo Warriors	All Black	36	1985
Self-defense Family	Predominantly Black	76	1985
Hermanos De Pistolero	All Hispanic	75	1985
Total		1,174	

Source: Robert S. Fong, Ronald E. Vogel and S. Buentello "Prison Gang Dynamics: A Look Inside the Texas Department of Corrections," in A. V. Merlo and P. Menekos, eds., *Dilemmas and Directions in Corrections* (Cincinnati, OH: Anderson, 1992).

(4) termination (through negotiation or physical confrontation), and (5) reaction and explanation (usually by investigative commissions). Donald Cressey[41] points out that the early stages of a riot tend to involve "binges" during which inmates exult in their new-found freedom with virtual orgies of alcohol and drug use or sexual activity. Buildings are burned, facilities are wrecked, and old grudges between individual inmates and inmate groups are settled, often through violence. After this initial explosive stage, leadership changes tend to occur. New leaders emerge who, at least for a time, may effectively organize inmates into a force able to resist attempts by officials to regain control of the institution. Bargaining strategies then develop and the process of negotiation begins.

WOMEN IN PRISON

Nearly 50,000 women were imprisoned in state and federal correctional institutions throughout the United States at the start of 1993.[42] California had the largest number of female prisoners (6,747), exceeding even the federal government (6,399).[43] Figure 13–1 provides a breakdown of the total American prison population by gender and ethnicity. Most women inmates were housed in centralized state facilities known as "women's prisons," which are dedicated exclusively to the holding of female felons. Many states, however, particularly those with small populations, continue to keep women prisoners in special wings of what are otherwise institutions for men.

While there are still far more men imprisoned across the nation than women (approximately 17 men for every woman), the number of female inmates is rising quickly—faster, in fact, than the proportion of male inmates.[44] The number of female inmates nearly tripled during the 1980s, and women now account for 6% of all imprisoned persons (see Figure 13–1). A little over a decade ago—in 1981—women comprised only 4.2% of the nation's overall prison population.

Women's prisons are overcrowded, which individual cases demonstrate. The California Institution for Women at Frontera, for example, was originally designed to hold 1,011 inmates. As of this writing, it holds more than 2,500 women. At Bedford Hills Correctional Facility in Westchester County, New York, double bunking is the rule, and conditions there are so crowded that inmates barely have the room necessary to turn around in their living quarters. Even well-managed prisons with nice facades, however, can have problems. One study of a pleasant-appearing women's prison in New York concluded that it was a place of "intense hostility, frustrations and anger."[45]

Professionals working with imprisoned women attribute the rise in female prison populations largely to drugs. Figure 13–2 shows, in relative graphics, the proportion of men and women imprisoned for various kinds of offenses. While the figure shows that approximately 33% of all women in prison are there explicitly for drug offenses, other estimates say that the impact of drugs on the imprisonment of women is far greater than a simple reading of the figure indicates. Warden Robert Brennan, of New York City's Rose M. Singer jail for women, estimates that drugs—either directly or indirectly—account for the imprisonment of around 95% of the inmates there. In fact, incarcerated women most frequently list (1) trying to pay for drugs, (2) attempts to relieve economic pressures, and (3) poor judgment as the reasons for their arrest.[46] Drug-related offenses committed by women include larceny, burglary, fraud, prostitution, embezzlement, and robbery, as well as other crimes stimulated by the desire for drugs.

Another reason for the rapid growth in the number of women behind bars may be the demise, over the last decade or two, of the "Chivalry Factor." The Chivalry Factor, so called because it was based upon an archaic cultural perspective which depicted women as helpless or childlike in their social roles relative to men, allegedly lessened the responsibility of female offenders in the eyes of some male judges and prosecutors—resulting in fewer active prison sentences for women involved in criminal activity. Recent studies show that the Chivalry Factor is now primarily of historical interest. In jurisdictions examined, the gender of convicted offenders no longer affects sentencing practices except insofar as it may be tied to other social variables. B. Keith Crew,[47] for example, in a comprehensive study of gender differences in sentencing observes, "[a] woman does not

FIGURE 13–1   Prison inmates by gender and ethnicity, state prisons only, 1992. *Source:* Adapted from Bureau of Justice Statistics, *National Corrections Reporting Program* (Washington, D.C.: U.S. Government Printing Office, 1993), and Bureau of Justice Statistics, *Prisoners in 1992* (Washington, D.C.: U.S. Government Printing Office, 1993).

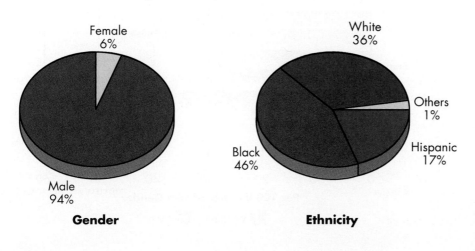

Gender   **Ethnicity**

automatically receive leniency because of her status of wife or mother, but she may receive leniency if those statuses become part of the official explanation of her criminal behavior (e.g., she was stealing to feed her children, an abusive husband forced her to commit a crime)."

Although there may be no one "typical" prison for women, and no perfectly "average" female inmate, the American Correctional Association's 1990 report by the Task Force on the Female Offender found that women inmates and the institutions which house them could be generally described as follows:[48]

1. "Most prisons for women are located in towns of less than 25,000 inhabitants."
2. "A significant number of facilities were not designed for the housing of females."
3. "The number of female offenders being sent to prison is on the rise."
4. "Most facilities housing female inmates also house males."
5. "Not many facilities for women have classification programs designed for the female offender."
6. "Very few major disturbances or escapes are reported among female inmates."
7. "Substance abuse among female inmates is very high."
8. "Very few work assignments are available to female inmates."
9. "The number of female inmates without a high school education is very high."

Statistics[49] show that the average age of female inmates is 29–30, most are black or Hispanic (57%), most come from single-parent or broken homes, and 50% have other family members who are incarcerated. The typical female inmate is a high school dropout (50%), who left school either because she was bored or because of pregnancy (34%). She has been arrested an average of two to nine times (55%) and has run away from home between one and three times (65%). Thirty-nine percent report using drugs to make them feel better emotionally, while 28% have attempted suicide at least once. Sixty-two percent were single parents with one to three children prior to incarceration, and many have been physically and/or sexually abused.[50]

Eighty percent of women entering prison are mothers, and 85% of those women retain custody of their children at the time of prison admission. One out of four women

FIGURE 13–2   Men and women in prison by type of offense, 1991. *Source:* Bureau of Justice Statistics, *Survey of State Prison Inmates 1991* (Washington, D.C.: U.S. Government Prining Office, 1993).

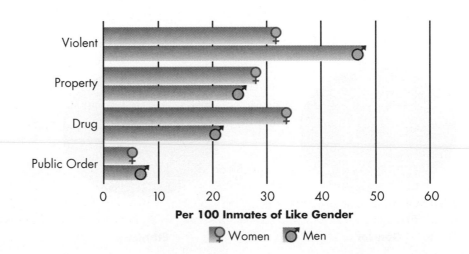

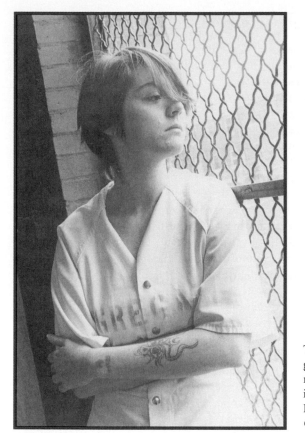

The number of women in prison is growing steadily. Because of disciplinary problems, this woman is housed in the segregation unit of a Rhode Island correctional facility. *Photo: Gal Zucker/Stock Boston.*

entering prison has either recently given birth or is pregnant. Critics charge that women inmates face a prison system designed for male inmates and run by men. Hence, pregnant inmates, many of whom are drug users, malnourished, or sick, often receive little prenatal care—a situation that risks additional complications. Separation from their children is a significant deprivation facing incarcerated mothers. Although husbands and/or boyfriends may assume responsibility for the children of imprisoned spouses/girlfriends, such an outcome is the exception to the rule. Eventually, a large proportion of children are released by their imprisoned mothers into foster care or put up for adoption.

Some states do offer parenting classes for women inmates with children. In a national survey[51] of prisons for women, 36 states responded with information about parenting programs which deal with caretaking, reducing violence toward children, visitation problems, and related issues. Some offer facilities as diverse as play areas complete with toys, while others attempt to alleviate difficulties attending mother/child visits. The typical program studied lasts from four to nine weeks, and provides for a meeting time of two hours per week. Twenty-five inmates participate in an average parenting program at any given time.

Other meaningful prison programs for women are often lacking—perhaps because the ones which are in place were originally based upon traditional models of female roles which left little room for substantive employment opportunities. Many trade-training programs still emphasize low-paying jobs such as cook, beautician, or laundry machine operator. Classes in homemaking are not uncommon.

Social structure

Most studies of women's prisons have revealed a unique feature of such institutions: the existence of organized families artificially constructed by the inmates. Typical of such studies are Ward and Kassebaum's *Women's Prison: Sex and Social Structure,*[52] E. Heffernan's *Making It in Prison: The Square, The Cool, and the Life,*[53] and Rose Giallombardo's *Society of Women: A Study of Women's Prisons.*[54]

Giallombardo, for example, examined the Federal Reformatory for Women at Alderson, West Virginia, spending a year in gathering data (1962–1963). Focusing closely on the formation of families, she entitled one of her chapters, "The Homosexual Alliance as a Marriage Unit." In it she describes in great detail the sexual identities assumed by women at Alderson and the symbols they chose to communicate those roles. Hair style, dress, language, and mannerisms were all used to signify "maleness" or "femaleness." Giallombardo details "the anatomy of the marriage relationship from courtship to 'fall out,' that is, from inception to the parting of the ways, or divorce."[55] Romantic love at Alderson was seen as of central importance to any relationship between inmates, and all homosexual relationships were described as voluntary. Through marriage the "stud broad" became the husband and the "femme" the wife.

Studies attempting to document the extent of inmate involvement in prison "families" produce varying results. Some have found as many as 71% of women prisoners involved in the phenomenon, while others have found none.[56] The kinship systems described by Giallombardo and others, however, extend beyond simple "family" ties to the formation of large, intricately related, groups. In these groups the roles of "children," "in-laws," "grandparents," and so on may be explicitly recognized. Even "birth order" within a family can be become an issue for kinship groups.[57] Kinship groups sometimes occupy a common household—usually a prison cottage or dormitory area. The description of women's prisons provided by authors like Giallombardo show a closed society in which social interaction—including expectations, normative forms of behavior, and emotional ties—is regulated by an inventive system of artificial relationships which mirror the outside world.

Some authors have suggested that this emphasis on describing family structures and sexual relationships in women's prisons is unfortunate because it tends to deny other structural features of those institutions.[58] The family emphasis may, in fact, be due to traditional explanations of female criminality which were intertwined with narrow understandings of the role of women in society.

Types of women inmates

As in institutions for men, the subculture of women's prisons is multidimensional. Esther Heffernan, for example, found that three terms used by women prisoners she studied—the "square," the "cool," and the "life"—were indicative of three styles of adaptation to prison life.[59] Square inmates had few early experiences with criminal life-styles and tended to sympathize with the values and attitudes of conventional society. Cool prisoners were more likely to be career offenders. They tended to keep to themselves and were generally supportive of inmate values. Women who participated in the "life" subculture were well familiar with lives of crime. Many had been arrested repeatedly for prostitution, drug use, theft, and so on. "Life" group members were full participants in the economic, social, and familial arrangements of the prison. Heffernan believed that "the life" offered an alternative life-style to women who had experienced early and constant rejection by conventional society. Within "the life" women could establish relationships, achieve status, and find meaning in their lives. The "square," the "life," and the "cool" represented subcultures to Heffernan, because individuals with similar adaptive choices tended to closely relate to one another and to support the life-style characteristic of that type.

"Square" inmates are definitely in the minority in prisons for both men and women. Perhaps for that reason they have rarely been studied. In an insightful self-examination, however, one such inmate, Jean Harris, published her impressions of prison life after more than seven years in the maximum security Bedford Hills (New York) Correctional Facility. Harris was convicted of killing the "Scarsdale Diet Doctor," Herman Tarnower, over a romance gone sour. A successful socialite in her early fifties at the time of the crime, Harris had an eye-opening experience in prison. Her book, *They Always Call Us Ladies*,[60] argues hard for prison reform. Sounding like the "square" she was, Harris says other inmates are "hard for you and me to relate to"[61] and describes them as "childlike women without social skills."[62] Speaking to a reporter Harris related, "There's really nobody for me to talk to here."[63] Harris was granted clemency by New York Governor Mario Cuomo on December 29, 1992—after having served 12 years in prison.[64]

Recently, the social structure of women's prison has become dichotomized by the advent of "crack kids," as they are called in prison argot. "Crack kids" are streetwise young women with little respect for traditional prison values, for their elders, or even for their own children. Known for frequent fights, and for their lack of even simple domestic skills, these young women quickly estrange many older inmates, some of whom call them "animalescents."

VIOLENCE IN WOMEN'S PRISONS

Some authors have suggested that violence in women's prisons is less frequent than it is in institutions for men. Bowker observes that "[e]xcept for the behavior of a few "guerrillas," it appears that violence is only used in women's prisons to settle questions of dominance and subordination when other manipulative strategies fail to achieve the desired effect."[65] It appears that few homosexual liaisons are forced, perhaps representing a general aversion among women to such victimization in wider society. At least one study, however, has shown the use of sexual violence in women's prisons as a form of revenge against inmates who are overly vocal in their condemnation of such practices among other prisoners.[66]

Not all abuse occurs at the hands of inmates. On November 15, 1992, 14 correctional officers, 10 men and 4 women, were indicted for the alleged abuse of female inmates at the 900-bed Women's Correctional Institute in Hardwick, Georgia. The charges resulted from affidavits filed by 90 female inmates charging "rape, sexual abuse, prostitution, coerced abortions, sex for favors and retaliation for refusal to participate"[67] in such activities. One inmate, who was forced to have an abortion after becoming pregnant by a male staff member, said "[a]s an inmate, I simply felt powerless to avoid the sexual advances of staff and to refuse to have an abortion."[68]

The Task Force on the Female Offender[69] recommends a number of changes in the administration of prisons for women. Among them are

1. Substance abuse programs are absolutely necessary in the treatment of today's female offender.
2. Women inmates need to acquire greater literacy skills, and literacy programs should form the basis upon which other programs are built.
3. "Female offenders should be housed in buildings independent of male inmates."
4. Institutions for women should develop programs for keeping children in the facility in order to "fortify the bond between mother and child."
5. "To ensure equal access to programming, institutions should be built to accommodate programs for female offenders."

PRISONER RIGHTS

THE HANDS-OFF DOCTRINE

Until the 1960s American courts took a neutral approach—commonly called the hands-off doctrine—toward the running of prisons. Judges assumed that prison administrators were sufficiently professional in the performance of their duties to balance institutional needs with humane considerations. The hands-off doctrine rested upon the belief that defendants lost most of their rights upon conviction, suffering a kind of civil death. Many states defined the concept of civil death through legislation which denied inmates the right to vote, hold public office, or even marry. Some states made incarceration for a felony a basis for uncontested divorce at the request of the noncriminal spouse.

The hands-off doctrine ended in 1969 when a federal court declared the entire Arkansas prison system unconstitutional after hearing arguments that it constituted a form of cruel and unusual punishment.[70] The court's decision resulted from what it judged to be pervasive overcrowding and primitive living conditions. Stories about the system by longtime inmates claimed that a number of other inmates had been beaten or shot to death by guards and buried over the years in unmarked graves on prison property. An investigation did unearth some skeletons in old graves, but their origin was never resolved.

Detailed media coverage of the Arkansas prison system gave rise to suspicions about correctional institutions everywhere. Within a few years federal courts intervened in the running of prisons in Florida, Louisiana, Mississippi, New York City, and Virginia.[71] In 1975, in a precedent-setting decision, U.S. District Court Judge Frank M. Johnson issued an order which banned the Alabama Board of Corrections from accepting any more inmates. Citing a population which was more than double the capacity of the state's system, Judge Johnson enumerated 44 standards to be met before additional inmates could be admitted to prison. Included in the requirements were specific guidelines on living space, staff/inmate ratios, visiting privileges, the racial makeup of staff, and food service modifications.

THE LEGAL BASIS OF PRISONERS' RIGHTS

The past two decades have seen many lawsuits brought by prisoners challenging the constitutionality of some aspect of confinement. The American Correctional Association says that most suits have been based upon: "1. the Eighth Amendment prohibition against cruel and unusual punishment; 2. the Fourteenth Amendment prohibition against the taking of life, liberty, or property without due process of law; and 3. the Fourteenth Amendment provision requiring equal protection of the laws."[72] Aside from appeals by inmates which question the propriety of their convictions and sentences, such constitutional challenges represent the bulk of legal action initiated by those imprisoned. State statutes and federal legislation, however, including Section 1983 of the Civil Rights Act of 1871, provide other bases for challenges to the legality of specific prison conditions and procedures.

The Balancing Test

In the 1974 case of *Pell* v. *Procunier*,[73] the Supreme Court established a balancing test which, although it was at the time addressed only to First Amendment rights, served to define a guideline generally applicable to all prison operations. In *Pell* the Court ruled that the "prison inmate retains those First Amendment rights that are not inconsistent with his status as a prisoner or with the legitimate penological objectives of the corrections system."[74] In other words, inmates have rights much the same as people who are not incarcerated, provided that the legitimate needs of the prison are not compromised. Other decisions have declared that order maintenance, security, and rehabilitation are all legitimate concerns of prison administration, but that financial exigency and convenience are not. As the balancing test makes clear, we see reflected in prisoner rights a microcosm of the due process versus social order dilemma found in wider society.

Prisoner rights, because they exist within the context of the legitimate needs of imprisonment, are more conditional rights than they are absolute rights. The Second Amendment to the U.S. Constitution, for example, grants citizens the right to bear arms. The right to arms is, however, necessarily compromised by the need for order and security in prison. Conditional rights, because they are subject to the exigencies of imprisonment, bear a strong resemblance to privileges, which should not be surprising since "privileges" were all that inmates officially had until the modern era. The practical difference between a privilege and a right stems from the fact that privileges exist only at the convenience of granting institutions and can be revoked at any time for any reason. The rights of prisoners, on the other hand, have a basis in the Constitution and in law external to the institution. Although they may be modified by the legitimate correctional needs of the institution, they may not be infringed without good cause demonstrable in a court of law.

To date, the Supreme Court has not spoken with finality on many questions of inmate rights, and there is some evidence of a trend back to a modified "hands-off doctrine."[75] However, high court decisions of the last few decades can be interpreted along with a number of lower court findings to enumerate the conditional rights of prisoners shown in Table 13–2.

Precedents in Inmate Rights

Communications   As previously discussed, the rights listed in Table 13–2 are not absolute. They need to be balanced against the security, order maintenance, and treatment needs of the institution. The Supreme Court has indicated that institutional exigency can abbreviate any right. In the case of *Procunier* v. *Martinez* (1974),[76] for example, the Court ruled that a prisoner's mail may be censored if it is necessary to do so for security purposes. On the other hand, institutional convenience does not provide a sufficient basis for the denial of rights. In *McNamara* v. *Moody* (1979),[77] a federal court upheld the right of an inmate to write vulgar letters to his girlfriend in which he made disparaging comments about the prison staff. The court reasoned that the letters may have been embarrassing to prison officials but that they did not affect the security or order of the institution. However, libelous materials have generally not been accorded First Amendment protection in or out of institutional contexts.

Concerning inmate publications, legal precedent has held that prisoners have no inherent right to publish newspapers or newsletters for use by other prisoners, although many

TABLE 13-2

THE CONDITIONAL RIGHTS OF INMATES

Religious Freedom
The Right of Assembly for Religious Services and Groups
The Right to Attend Services of Other Religious Groups
The Right to Receive Visits from Ministers
The Right to Correspond with Religious Leaders
A Right to Observe Religious Dietary Laws
The Right to Wear Beards and Religious Insignia

Freedom of Speech
The Right to Meet with Members of the Press[1]
The Right to Receive Publications Directly from the Publisher
The Right to Communicate with Nonprisoners

Access to Legal Assistance
A Right of Access to the Courts
A Right to Visits from Attorneys
A Right to Mail Communications with Lawyers[2]
A Right to Communicate with Legal Assistance Organizations
A Right to Consult "Jail House Lawyers"[3]
A Right to Assistance in Filing Legal Papers, which should include *one* of the following:
    Access to an Adequate Law Library
    Paid Attorneys
    Paralegal Personnel or Law Students

Medical Treatment
A Right to Sanitary and Healthy Conditions
A Right to Medical Attention for Serious Physical Problems
A Right to Needed Medications
A Right to Treatment in Accordance with "Doctor's Orders"

Protection
A Right to Food, Water, and Shelter
A Right to Protection from Foreseeable Attack
A Right to Protection from Predictable Sexual Abuse
A Right to Protection Against Suicide

Institutional Punishment and Discipline
An Absolute Right Against Corporal Punishments
A Right to Due Process Prior to Punishment, including
    Notice of Charges
    A Fair and Impartial Hearing
    An Opportunity for Defense
    A Right to Present Witnesses
    A Written Decision

---

[1]But not beyond the opportunities afforded for inmates to meet with members of the general public.
[2]Mail communications are generally designated as privileged or nonprivileged. Privileged communications include those between inmates and their lawyers or court officials, and cannot legitimately be read by prison officials. Nonprivileged communications include most other written communications.
[3]Jail house lawyers are inmates with experience in the law, usually gained from filing legal briefs on their own behalf or on the behalf of others. Consultation with jail house lawyers was ruled permissible in the Supreme Court case of *Johnson* v. *Avery*, 393 U.S. 483 (1968), unless inmates are provided with paid legal assistance.

institutions do permit and finance such periodicals.[78] Publications originating from outside of prison, such as newspapers, magazines, and special interest tracts, have generally been protected when mailed directly from the publisher, although magazines which depict deviant sexual behavior can be banned according to *Mallery* v. *Lewis* (1983)[79] and other precedents. Nudity by itself is not necessarily obscene, and federal courts have held that prisons cannot ban nude pictures of inmate's wives and girlfriends.[80]

Religious Practice   The early Supreme Court case of *Cruz* v. *Beto* (1972)[81] established that inmates must be given a "reasonable opportunity" to pursue their faith, even if it differs from traditional forms of worship. Meeting facilities must be provided for religious use when those same facilities are made available to other groups of prisoners for other purposes,[82] but no group can claim exclusive use of a prison area for religious reasons.[83] Although prisoners cannot be made to attend religious services,[84] records of religious activity can be maintained in order to administratively determine dietary needs and eligibility for passes to religious services outside of the institution.[85] In *Dettmer* v. *Landon* (1985),[86] a federal court held that an inmate who claimed to practice witchcraft must be provided with the artifacts necessary in his worship services. Included were items such as sea salt, sulfur, a quartz clock, incense, candles, and a white robe without a hood. However, drugs and dangerous substances have not been considered permissible even when inmates claimed they were a necessary part of their religious services.[87] Prison regulations prohibiting the wearing of beards, even those grown for religious reasons, were held acceptable for security considerations in the 1985 federal court case of *Hill* v. *Blackwell*.[88]

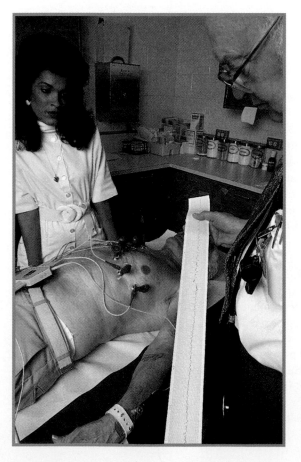

Court decisions over the years have established a firm set of inmate rights. Among them is a right to health care. Here an elderly inmate undergoes an EKG test in New Jersey's Riverfront Prison. *Photo: J. Griffin/The Image Works.*

The right to assemble for religious purposes, however, can be denied to inmates who use such meetings to plan escapes or who take the opportunity to dispense contraband. Similarly, prisoners in segregation do not have to be permitted the opportunity to attend group religious services.[89]

Visitation   Visitation and access to the news media are other areas which have come under court scrutiny. Maximum security institutions rarely permit "contact" visits, and some have on occasion suspended all visitation privileges. In the case of *Block* v. *Rutherford* (1984),[90] the Supreme Court upheld the policy of the Los Angeles County Central Jail which prohibited all visits from friends and relatives. The Court agreed that the large jail population and the conditions under which visits might take place could combine to threaten the security of the jail.

In *Pell* v. *Procunier* (1974),[91] the Court found in favor of a California law which denied prisoners the opportunity to hold special meetings with members of the press. The Court reasoned that media interviews could be conducted through regular visitation arrangements and that most of the information desired by the media could be conveyed through correspondence. In *Pell*, the Court also held that any reasonable policy of media access was acceptable so long as it was administered fairly and without bias.

In a later case, the Court ruled that news personnel cannot be denied correspondence with inmates, but also ruled that they have no constitutional right to interview inmates or to inspect correctional facilities beyond the visitation opportunities available to others.[92] This equal access policy was set forth in *Houchins* v. *KQED, Inc.* (1978) by Justice Stewart who wrote that "The Constitution does no more than assure the public and the press equal access once government has opened its doors."[93]

Legal Access to the Courts   A well-established right of prisoners is access to the courts[94] and to legal assistance. The right of prisoners to petition the court was recognized in *Bounds* v. *Smith* (1977),[95] a far-reaching Supreme Court decision. While attempting to define "access," the Court imposed upon the states the duty of assisting inmates in the preparation and filing of legal papers. Assistance could be provided through trained personnel knowledgeable in the law or via law libraries in each institution, which many states have since built.

In the earlier case of *Johnson* v. *Avery* (1968),[96] the Court had ruled that persons under correctional supervision have a right to consult "jail house lawyers," for advice when assistance from trained professionals is not available. Other court decisions have established that inmates have a right to correspond with their attorneys,[97] and with legal assistance organizations. Such letters, however, can be opened and inspected for contraband[98] (but not read) by prison authorities in the presence of the inmate. The right to meet with hired counsel for reasonable lengths of time has also been upheld.[99]

On the other side of the coin, inmates do not have the right to an appointed lawyer, even when indigent, if no judicial proceedings against them have been initiated.[100] Indigent defendants must be provided with stamps for the purpose of legal correspondence,[101] and inmates cannot be disciplined for communicating with lawyers or requesting legal help. Conversations between inmates and their lawyers can be monitored, although any evidence obtained through such a process cannot be used in court.[102]

Medical Care   The duty of prison officials to provide for the medical care of inmates was specified in the historic Supreme Court case of *Estelle* v. *Gamble* (1976).[103] In *Estelle*, however, the Court concerned itself only with "deliberate indifference" on the part of the staff toward a prisoner's need for serious medical attention. "Deliberate indifference" means a wanton disregard for the health of inmates. While poor treatment, misdiagnosis,

RELIGIOUS ASSEMBLY

The following statements, excerpted from prison "rule books" of two different states, capture the essence of the court-created balancing test as it weighs prison administrative and security concerns against the right to freedom of religion which is guaranteed by the U.S. Constitution:

Religious Services. Religious services, speeches, or addresses by inmates other than those approved by the Superintendent or designee are prohibited.

Source: Standards of Inmate Behavior, All Institutions, State of New York, Department of Correctional Services (1988).

Freedom of Religion. Inmates will be able to practice their religion in keeping with the security needs of each unit. Ministers and other religious counselors will be allowed to visit inmates. The time, place, and method of such visits are controlled by the custody and security needs of each unit.

Source: Rules and Procedures Governing the Management and Conduct of Inmates Under the Control of the Division of Prisons, North Carolina Division of Prisons (1983).

and the like may constitute medical malpractice, they do not necessarily constitute deliberate indifference.[104] Taking the *Estelle* decision a step farther, the Supreme Court ruled in 1988 that inmates may sue prison doctors for malpractice in federal courts.[105]

Two other cases, *Ruiz* v. *Estelle* (1982)[106] and *Newman* v. *Alabama* (1972)[107] have had substantial impacts concerning the rights of prisoners to medical attention. In *Ruiz* the Texas Department of Corrections was found lacking in its medical treatment programs. The court ordered an improvement in record keeping, physical facilities, and general medical care, while it continued to monitor the progress of the department. In *Newman*, Alabama's prison medical services were found so inadequate as to be "shocking to the conscience." Problems with the Alabama program included:[108]

- A lack of sufficient medical personnel
- Poor physical facilities for medical treatment
- Poor administrative techniques for dispersal of medications
- Poor medical records
- A lack of medical supplies
- Poorly trained or untrained inmates who provided some medical services and performed minor surgery
- Medically untrained personnel who determined the need for treatment

Concerning the issue of forced medication, a 1984 federal court case held that inmates could be medicated in emergency situations against their wills.[109] The court did recognize that unwanted medications designed to produce only psychological effects might be refused more readily than life-sustaining drugs.[110] Similarly, other courts have held that inmates do not have a right to starve themselves to death.

In 1993, the Court gave indication that environmental conditions of prison life which pose a threat to inmate health may have to be corrected. In *Helling* v. *McKinney*,[111] Nevada inmate William McKinney claimed that exposure to secondary cigarette smoke circulating in his cell was threatening his health in violation of the Eighth Amendment's prohibition on cruel and unusual punishment. The Court, in ordering that a federal district court provide McKinney with the opportunity to prove his allegations, held that "[a]n injunction cannot be denied to inmates who plainly prove an unsafe, life-threatening condition on the ground that nothing yet has happened to them." In effect, the *Helling* case gave notice to prison officials that they are responsible not only for "inmates' current serious health problems," but also for maintaining environmental conditions under which health problems might be prevented from developing.

Privacy   Many court decisions, including the Tenth Circuit case of *U.S.* v. *Ready* (1978)[112] and the U.S. Supreme Court decisions of *Katz* v. *U.S.* (1967)[113] and *Hudson* v. *Palmer* (1984)[114] have held that inmates cannot have a reasonable expectation to privacy while incarcerated. Palmer, an inmate in Virginia, claimed that Hudson, a prison guard, had unreasonably destroyed some of his personal (noncontraband) property following a cell search. Palmer's complaint centered on the lack of due process which accompanied the destruction. The Court disagreed, saying that the need for prison officials to conduct thorough and unannounced searches precludes inmate privacy in personal possessions.

In *Block* v. *Rutherford* (1984)[115] the Court established that prisoners do not have a right to be present during a search of their cells. Some lower courts, however, have begun to indicate that body cavity searches may be unreasonable unless based upon a demonstrable suspicion or conducted after prior warning has been given to the inmate.[116] They have also indicated that searches conducted simply to "harass or humiliate" inmates are illegitimate.[117] These cases may be an indication that the Supreme Court will soon recognize a limited degree of privacy in prison cells searches, especially those which uncover legal documents and personal papers prepared by the prisoner.[118]

A RETURN TO THE HANDS-OFF DOCTRINE? MIXED SIGNALS

In June 1991, an increasingly conservative U.S. Supreme Court signaled what may be at least a partial return to the "hands-off" doctrine of earlier times. The case, *Wilson* v. *Seiter*,[119] involved a 1983 suit brought against Richard P. Seiter, director of the Ohio Department of Rehabilitation and Correction, and Carl Humphreys, warden of the Hocking Correctional Facility (HCF) in Nelsonville, Ohio. In the suit, Pearly L. Wilson, a felon incarcerated at HCF, alleged that a number of the conditions of his confinement—specifically, overcrowding, excessive noise, insufficient locker storage space, inadequate heating and cooling, improper ventilation, unclean and inadequate restrooms, unsanitary dining facilities and food preparation, and housing with mentally and physically ill inmates—constituted cruel and unusual punishment in violation of the Eighth and Fourteenth Amendments to the U.S. Constitution. Wilson asked for a change in prison conditions and sought $900,000 from prison officials in compensatory and punitive damages.

Both the federal district court in which Wilson first filed affidavits and the Sixth Circuit Court of Appeals held that no constitutional violations existed because the conditions cited by Wilson were not the result of malicious intent on the part of officials. The U.S. Supreme Court agreed, noting that the "deliberate indifference" standard applied in *Estelle* v. *Gamble*[120] to claims involving medical care is similarly applicable to other cases in which prisoners challenge the conditions of their confinement. In effect, the Court created a standard which effectively means that all future challenges to prison conditions by inmates, which are brought under the Eighth Amendment, must show "deliberate indifference" by the officials responsible for the existence of those conditions before the Court will hear the complaint.

The written opinion of the Court in *Wilson* v. *Seiter* is telling. Writing for the majority, Justice Scalia observed that "if a prison boiler malfunctions accidentally during a cold winter, an inmate would have no basis for an Eighth Amendment claim, even if he suffers objectively significant harm. If a guard accidentally stepped on a prisoner's toe and broke it, this would not be punishment in anything remotely like the accepted meaning of the word."

Although the criterion of deliberate indifference is still evolving, it is likely that such indifference could be demonstrated by petitioners able to show that prison admistrators have done nothing to alleviate life-threatening prison conditions after those conditions had been called to their attention. Even so, critics of *Wilson* are concerned that the decision may excuse prison authorities from the need to improve living conditions within institutions on the basis of simple budgetary constraints. Four of the justices themselves recognized the potential held by *Wilson* for a near-return to the days of the "hands-off doctrine." Although concurring with the Court's majority, Justices White, Marshall, Blackmun, and Stevens noted their fear that "[t]he ultimate result of today's decision, [may be] that 'serious deprivations of basic human needs'…will go unredressed due to an unnecessary and meaningless search for 'deliberate indifference.' "

In the 1992 case of *Hudson* v. *McMillian*,[121] however, the Court seemed to send a different signal. *Hudson* began in 1983 when Keith Hudson, an inmate at the Louisiana State Penitentiary at Angola, was beaten by correctional officers following an argument. Hudson suffered loosened teeth, a cracked dental plate, and minor facial bruises—injuries not judged "serious" by the Court, since they did not require medical attention. Even so, the Court ruled, such a use of force by correctional officers contravenes the Eighth Amendment's prohibition against cruel and unusual punishment since it is an "unnecessary and wanton infliction of pain."

In an analysis[122] of the Rehnquist court's changing perspective on prisoner rights, Michael A. Fitzgerald and Richard G. Frey conclude, "[t]he years ahead will probably see the Court increasingly exercising its supervisory function over the federal courts…in a hodgepodge of cases…. The prisoner litigant will rarely be successful, and no new expansive rights doctrines will be announced."

Writ of *Habeas Corpus* The writ which directs the person detaining a prisoner to bring him or her before a judicial officer to determine the lawfulness of the imprisonment.

DISCIPLINARY AND GRIEVANCE PROCEDURES

A major area of concern to inmates is the hearing of grievances. Complaints may arise in ares as diverse as food service (quality of food or special diets for religious purposes or health regimens), interpersonal relations between inmates and staff, denial of privileges, and accusations of misconduct levied against an inmate. By the early 1970s prisoners quickly recognized abandonment of the "hands-off doctrine," and there is some evidence that formal grievance plans were established in many prisons in an attempt to divert

**Grievance
Procedure** Formalized
arrangements, usually
involving a neutral hear-
ing board, whereby insti-
tutionalized individuals
have the opportunity to
register complaints about
the conditions of their
confinement.

potential inmate-originated lawsuits. While only about 2,000 petitions per year concerning inmate problems were being filed with the courts in 1961, by 1975 the number of filings had increased to around 17,000.

In an effort to reduce the court's burden, Chief Justice Warren E. Burger urged the creation of formal grievance procedures in correctional institutions.[123] Even earlier, in 1972, the National Council on Crime and Delinquency had developed a Model Act for the Protection of Rights of Prisoners, and the 1973 National Advisory Commission on Criminal Justice Standards and Goals called for the establishment of responsible practices for the hearing of inmate grievances.

Today most prisons have an established **grievance procedure** which usually involves the filing of a complaint by an inmate with local authorities and a mandated response to the grievance. The number of grievances filed by inmates has increased substantially in most states since Chief Justice Burger's recommendation was made. In the state of New York, for example, the inmate population between 1981 and 1987 rose from 25,921 to 40,850—while the number of inmate grievances increased from 8,426 to 26,900 during the same period.[124] In New York correctional facilities during 1987, the largest number of filed grievances concerned staff conduct (4,227).[125] Another 2,241 focused on medical services, and 2,363 dealt with housing conditions.[126] The accompanying box outlines the procedures to be followed in the filing of grievances in the New York state correctional system.

Modern grievance procedures range from the use of a hearing board composed of staff members and inmates to a single staff appointee charged with the resolution of complaints. Inmates who are dissatisfied with the handling of their grievance can generally appeal beyond the level of the local prison unit.

Some states have experimented with the use of an ombudsman, a neutral party with investigative powers who mediates conflict between inmates and staff. The first correctional ombudsman in America was Theatrice Williams who was appointed to that post in Minnesota in 1972. That an opportunity of some sort must exist for the airing of inmate grievances was supported by the Supreme Court in *Jones* v. *North Carolina Prisoners' Labor Union, Inc.*,[127] which found that existing prison grievance procedures were adequate.

Disciplinary actions by prison authorities are another area requiring a formalized hearing process. Staff members may bring charges of rule violations against inmates which might result in some form of punishment being imposed on them. In a precedent-setting decision, the Supreme Court decided, in the case of *Wolff* v. *McDonnell* (1974),[128] that sanctions could not be levied against inmates without appropriate due process. The *Wolff* case involved an inmate who had been deprived of previously earned "good-time" credits because of misbehavior. The Court established that "good-time" credits were a form of "state-created right(s)," which, once created, could not be "arbitrarily abrogated."[129] Such state-created rights and privileges have come to be called protected liberties in later court decisions and include any significant change in a prisoner's status. *Wolff* also mandated a hearing prior to a prisoner's being confined in segregation and suggested that hearings were generally required whenever a significant change in the inmate's status was possible through disciplinary action. A balancing strategy was recognized by the *Wolff* court when it said that the rights of prisoners to hearings were subject to "the penological need to provide swift discipline" and could be denied if they were "unduly hazardous to institutional safety or correctional goals."

In the interest of due process, courts have generally held that inmates are entitled to (1) notice of the charges brought against them, (2) the chance to organize a defense, (3) an impartial hearing, and (4) the opportunity to present witnesses and evidence on their behalf. A written statement of the hearing board's conclusions should be provided to the inmate.[130] More recently, in the case of *Ponte* v. *Real* (1985),[131] the Supreme Court held that prison officials must provide an explanation to inmates who are denied

T H E O R Y   I N T O   P R A C T I C E

PROCEDURES FOR THE FILING OF INMATE GRIEVANCES IN THE STATE OF NEW YORK

1. Inmate grievance forms shall be made available to any inmate through the facility's duty office within 24 hours of a request. The grievance complaint form shall be filled out by the inmate with the assistance of any other inmate or staff member of the inmate's choice.
2. The completed grievance form shall be transmitted to the designated staff person who shall attempt to help resolve the grievance informally.
3. If the grievance cannot be resolved informally within four working days, the designated staff shall convene an IGRC (Inmate Grievance Review Committee) hearing within seven working days from the date the grievance was received by that staff person. The IGRC shall be composed of two staff representatives appointed by the superintendent, two inmates selected by the grievant, and the nonvoting chairperson designated by the superintendent or his or her designee.
4. At the IGRC hearing, the inmate, the advisor, and the other parties shall hear the grievance and the IGRC shall render a recommendation (to the superintendent).

Source: State of New York, Department of Correctional Services, Directive 4041, *Inmate Grievance Program Modification Plan.*

the opportunity to have a desired witness at their hearing. The case of *Vitek* v. *Jones* (1980) extended the requirement of due process to inmates about to be transferred from prisons to mental hospitals.[132]

So that inmates can know what is expected of them as they enter prison, the American Correctional Association recommends: "A rulebook that contains all chargeable offenses, ranges of penalties and disciplinary procedures [be] posted in a conspicuous and accessible area; [and] a copy...given to each inmate and staff member"[133] A list of "major" and "minor" rule violations, typical of many prisons, are shown in the box on the next page.

PRISONER UNIONS

In 1970 prisoners at California's Folsom Prison began a work strike which lasted 19 days. Following the strike inmates submitted 29 written demands to the prison administration. Among them was a demand for permission to form a prisoner's union. The resulting California Prisoners Union eventually established 14 locals in institutions across the state. As first organized, the union was run by former prisoners, not those

THEORY INTO PRACTICE

TYPICAL RULES GOVERNING THE CONDUCT OF PRISONERS' MAJOR AND MINOR OFFENSES

1.00	All Penal Law offenses are prohibited and may be referred to law enforcement agencies for prosecution through the courts.
100.10	Inmates shall not assault, inflict or attempt to inflict bodily harm upon any other inmate.
100.11	Inmates shall not assault, inflict or attempt to inflict bodily harm upon any staff member.
100.13	Inmates shall not engage in fighting.
101.10	Inmates shall not engage in, encourage, solicit or attempt to force others to engage in sexual acts.
101.21	Physical contact between inmates, including but not limited to kissing, embracing or hand holding, is prohibited.
104.11	Inmates shall not engage in any violent conduct or conduct involving the threat of violence.
105.10	The unauthorized assembly of inmates in groups is prohibited.
105.11	Religious services, speeches or addresses by inmates other than those approved by the superintendent or designee are prohibited.
106.10	All orders of facility personnel will be obeyed promptly and without argument.
108.10	Inmates shall not escape, attempt to escape, conspire to, or be an accessory to an escape.
113.10	Inmates shall not make, possess, sell or exchange any item of contraband that may be classified as a weapon by description, use or appearance.
113.12	Inmates shall not make, possess, use, sell or exchange any narcotic, narcotic paraphernalia, or controlled substance.

Source: Excerpted from State of New York, Department of Correctional Services, *Standards of Inmate Behavior, All Institutions,* revised June 1988.

then incarcerated. The right to bargain with correctional administrators was an inherent part of the union's charter, and inmates could carry out work strikes in support of union goals.[134]

The prisoner union movement developed quickly. By 1972 a union was in place at New York's Greenhaven Prison, and inmates at Walpole Prison in Massachusetts formed the National Prisoners' Reform Association (NPRA). NPRA established chapters in other major institutions in Massachusetts including Framingham, Concord, and Norfolk. The New England Prison Coalition, a group with ties to NPRA, coordinated the efforts of prisoners to establish unions throughout the Northeast.

Prisoner unions have espoused a variety of goals. Chief among them have been:[135]

- The right to organize
- The right to bargain collectively
- The right to earn a minimum wage
- The right to safe working conditions
- The right to workers' compensation insurance

Some prisoner unions quickly moved toward political agendas, and many states made efforts to counter unionization. In a bid to limit their effectiveness, union leaders were transferred to other institutions, and court battles over inmate rights to collectively organize began.

The best known Supreme Court case to address the issue of prisoner unions is that of *Jones* v. *North Carolina Prisoners' Labor Union, Inc.* (1977).[136] In the *Jones* case, the Court ruled against one aspect of the union movement, holding that restrictions against union grievance procedures were permissible in the presence of alternative organized and effective grievance procedures established by the prison administration. Also upheld were institutional prohibitions against union meetings and against the solicitation of new members. In *Jones*, "The court recognized the 'sincerely held' beliefs of the prison officials that the union, if recognized and allowed to develop, would be detrimental to the order and security of the institution."[137]

ISSUES FACING PRISONS TODAY

Prisons are society's answer to a number of social problems. They house outcasts and misfits. While prisons provide a part of the answer to the question of crime control, they also face problems of their own. A few of those special problems are discussed in what follows.

AIDS

An earlier chapter discussed the steps being taken by police agencies to deal with health threats represented by AIDS. As early as October 1, 1987 the Centers for Disease Control reported confirming 1,964 cases of AIDS among inmates of the nation's prisons.[138] Sixty-two percent of reported AIDS cases among correctional inmates were found in the Mid-Atlantic states.

Some prisons covered by the CDC survey counted no cases of AIDS among their inmates. More than 70% of state and federal systems had fewer than 10 cases. However, at the other extreme, six states and one city/county system reported over 50 cases each.

Recent surveys[139] have placed the number of HIV-infected inmates at much higher levels. Positive seroprevalence rates have been found to vary from region to region—falling between 2.1% and 7.6% of all men entering prison and between 2.5% and 14.7% of women. Some states have especially high rates. New York, for example, recently reported that 20% of all inmates it houses are HIV positive, with slightly less than 10% of those exhibiting symptoms of AIDS.

Men account for 95% of all inmates affected by AIDS. Blacks, at 58%, comprise the largest racial/ethnic category; 32% of those infected are white, and 10% are Hispanic.

The incidence of HIV infection among the general population stood at 8.6 cases per 100,000 at the time of the Centers for Disease Control's report. Among inmates, the incidence rate of AIDS was 54 cases per 100,000—more than six times as great. The fact that inmates tend to have histories of high-risk behavior, especially intravenous drug use, probably explains the difference.

Contrary to popular opinion, AIDS transmission inside of prisons appears minimal. In a test of inmates at a U.S. Army military prison, 542 prisoners who, upon admission had tested negative for exposure to the AIDS virus, were retested two years later. None showed any signs of exposure to the virus.[140] On the other hand, some authorities suggest that it is only a matter of time before intravenous drug abuse and homosexual activity inside of prisons begin to make a visible contribution to the spread of AIDS.[141] Similarly, prison staffers fear infection from AIDS through routine activities, such as cell searches, responding to fights, performing body searches, administering CPR, and confiscating needles or weapons.

A recent report by the National Institute of Justice[142] suggests that there are two types of strategies available to correctional systems to reduce the transmission of AIDS. One strategy relies upon medical technology to identify seropositive inmates and segregate them from the rest of the prison population. Mass screening and inmate segregation, however, may be prohibitively expensive. They may also be illegal. Some states specifically prohibit HIV antibody testing without the informed consent of the person tested.[143] The related issue of confidentiality may be difficult to manage, especially where the purpose of testing is to segregate infected inmates from others. In addition, civil liability may result where inmates are falsely labeled as infected or where inmates known to be infected are not prevented from spreading the disease.

The second strategy is one of prevention through education. Educational programs teach inmates about the dangers of continued high-risk behavior. An NIJ model program[144] recommends the use of simple straightforward messages presented by knowledgeable and approachable trainers. Alarmism, says NIJ, is to be avoided. In anticipation of court rulings which will likely prohibit the mass testing of inmates for the AIDS virus, the second strategy seems best. A third, but controversial strategy—not suggested by the report—involves issuing condoms to prisoners. This last alternative is sometimes rejected because it implicitly condones sexual behavior among inmates.

GERIATRIC OFFENDERS

Some prisoners grow old behind bars. Others are old before they get there. American prisons, serving an aging population, are seeing more geriatric prisoners than ever before. Authorities estimate that while 10% of today's prisoners are over 50 years old, around 40% will fall into that category by the year 2000.[145]

The "graying" of America's prison population is due to a number of causes: (1) increasing crime among those over 50, (2) the gradual aging of the society from which prisoners come, (3) a trend toward longer sentences, especially for violent offenders, and (4) the gradual accumulation of older habitual offenders in prison.[146]

Crimes of violence are what bring most older inmates into the correctional system. According to one study, 52% of inmates who were over the age of 50 at the time they entered prison had committed violent crimes, compared with 41% of younger inmates.[147] Ronald Wikberg and Burk Foster provide a snapshot of long-termers in their recent study

Evaluating Prisons

In October 1993 the Bureau of Justice Statistics published *Performance Measures for the Criminal Justice System*, a collection of discussion papers produced by the BJS–Princeton Project group. The papers represent the best official effort to date to identify performance goals and associated measures useful in assessing the day-to-day operations of criminal justice agencies.

The Project identified, among others, the following goals and performance indicators in the area of corrections:

Goals	Performance Indicators
1. Security: "keep them in"	Ratings of how building design affects surveillance, frequency of shakedowns and body searches, inmate security violations, drug-related incidents, the number of escapes, and the ratio of resident population to security staff.
2. Safety: "keep them safe"	Likelihood of an inmate being assaulted in the living area, rate of armed assaults involving inmates, rate of sexual assaults upon inmates, proportion of inmates unjustly assaulted by staff, perceived danger of staff members, proportion of staff assaulted, dangerousness rating of inmate population, and frequency of accidents.
3. Order: "keep them in line"	Perceived security of inmate personal property, number of inmates "written up," number of disturbances, number of significant incidents in which restraint was used, average number of good time days taken away, and proportion of major report sanctions imposed.
4. Care: "keep them healthy"	Average number of days inmates were ill or injured, number of significant incidents involving suicide attempts, clinical contacts, medical appointments, lab appointments, physicals and TB tests, dental visits, number of counseling sessions, type and rated effectiveness of counseling, and the proportion of inmates involved in counseling, substance abuse, and employment counseling.
5. Activity: "keep them busy"	Number and type of inmate jobs, proportion of population eligible, proportion working, vocational training courses provided, grievances related to work, religious and recreational services available, and the extent of adult basic education and secondary educational opportunities available.

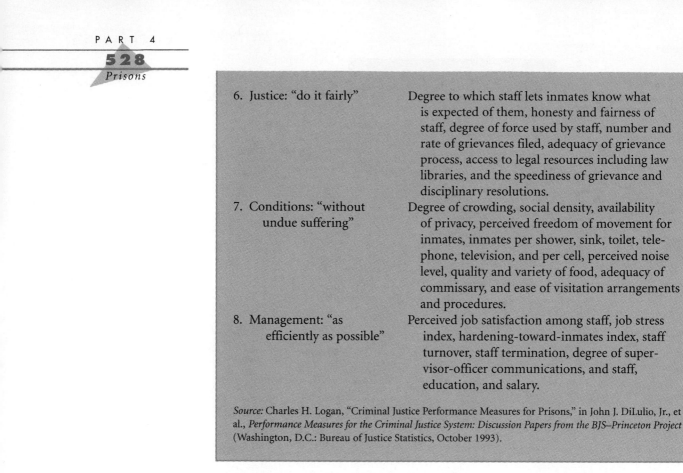

6. Justice: "do it fairly"	Degree to which staff lets inmates know what is expected of them, honesty and fairness of staff, degree of force used by staff, number and rate of grievances filed, adequacy of grievance process, access to legal resources including law libraries, and the speediness of grievance and disciplinary resolutions.
7. Conditions: "without undue suffering"	Degree of crowding, social density, availability of privacy, perceived freedom of movement for inmates, inmates per shower, sink, toilet, telephone, television, and per cell, perceived noise level, quality and variety of food, adequacy of commissary, and ease of visitation arrangements and procedures.
8. Management: "as efficiently as possible"	Perceived job satisfaction among staff, job stress index, hardening-toward-inmates index, staff turnover, staff termination, degree of supervisor-officer communications, and staff, education, and salary.

Source: Charles H. Logan, "Criminal Justice Performance Measures for Prisons," in John J. DiIulio, Jr., et al., *Performance Measures for the Criminal Justice System: Discussion Papers from the BJS–Princeton Project* (Washington, D.C.: Bureau of Justice Statistics, October 1993).

of Angola prison.[148] Wikberg and Foster described 31 inmates at the Louisiana State Penitentiary at Angola who had served a continuous sentence of 25 years or longer, as of early 1988. They found the typical long-termer to be black (27 out of 31), with many of them sentenced for raping or killing a white. Inmate ages ranged from 42 to 71. A common thread linking most of these inmates was that their release was opposed by victims' families and friends. Some had a record as prison troublemakers, but a few had been near-model prisoners.

Long-termers and geriatric inmates have special needs. They tend to suffer from handicaps, physical impairments, and illnesses not generally encountered among their more youthful counterparts. Unfortunately, few prisons are equipped to deal adequately with the medical needs of aging offenders. Some large facilities have begun to set aside special sections to care for elderly inmates with "typical" disorders such as Alzheimer's disease, cancer, or heart disease. Unfortunately, such efforts have barely kept pace with problems. The number of inmates requiring round-the-clock care is expected to increase dramatically over the next two decades.[149]

Even the idea of rehabilitation takes on a new meaning where geriatric offenders are concerned. What kinds of programs are most likely to be useful in providing the older inmate with the needed tools for success on the outside? Which counseling strategies hold the greatest promise for introducing socially acceptable behavior patterns into the long-established life-styles of elderly offenders about to be released? There are few answers to these questions. To date, no federal studies have been done to prepare the nation's prison system for handling the needs of older inmates.[150]

Mentally ill inmates

The mentally ill are another inmate category with special needs. Some inmates are neurotic or have personality problems which increase tension in prison. Others have serious psychological disorders which may have escaped earlier diagnosis (at trial) or which did not provide a legal basis for the reduction of criminal responsibility. A fair number of offenders develop psychiatric symptoms while in prison. Some news accounts of modern prisons have focused squarely on the problem: "raging mental illness is so common it's ignored," wrote a *Newsweek* staffer visiting a women's prison.[151]

Unfortunately, few states have any substantial capacity for the psychiatric treatment of mentally disturbed inmates. In 1982 Hans Toch described the largely ineffective practice of bus therapy, whereby disturbed inmates are shuttled back and forth between mental health centers and correctional facilities.[152] In February 1990, the U.S. Supreme Court, in the case of *Washington State* v. *Harper*, ruled that mentally ill inmates could be required to take antipsychotic drugs, even against their wishes. The ruling stipulated that such a requirement would apply where "the inmate is dangerous to himself or others, and the treatment is in the inmate's medical interest."

Mentally deficient inmates constitute still another group with special needs. Some studies estimate the proportion of mentally deficient inmates at about 10%.[153] Retarded inmates are less likely to complete training and rehabilitative programs successfully than are other inmates. They also evidence difficulty in adjusting to the routines of prison life. As a consequence they are likely to exceed the averages in proportion of sentence served.[154] Only seven states report special facilities or programs for the mentally retarded inmate.[155] Other state systems "mainstream" such inmates, making them participate in regular activities with other inmates.

Texas, one state which does provide special services for retarded inmates, began a Mentally Retarded Offender Program (MROP) in 1984. Inmates in Texas are given a battery of tests that measure intellectual and social adaptability skills, and prisoners who are identified as retarded are housed in special satellite correctional units. The Texas MROP program provides individual and group counseling, along with training in adult life skills.

SUMMARY

Prisons are small societies with their own rules, values, norms, and social roles. Complicating life behind bars are the numerous conflicts of interest between inmates and staff. Lawsuits, prisoner unions, and frequent grievances are symptoms of these differences.

The problems which exist in conventional society are mirrored and often magnified inside of prison. Crime does not stop at the prison door, nor does rehabilitation automatically begin. If we are to expect prisons to meet the demands of rehabilitation and reformation, we must be willing to solve the problems of prison first.

DISCUSSION QUESTIONS

1. Explain the concept of prison subcultures. What purpose do you think such subcultures serve? Why do they develop?

2. What does "prisonization" mean? Describe the U-shaped curve developed by Wheeler as it relates to prisonization. Why do you think the curve is U-shaped?

3. What is prison argot? What purpose does it serve?

4. What are the primary concerns of prison staff? Do you agree that those concerns are important? What other goals might staff focus on?

5. Explain the "balancing test" established by the Supreme Court in deciding issues of prisoners' rights. How might such a test apply to the emerging area of inmate privacy?

6. What are some of the special problems facing prisons today which are discussed in this chapter? What new problems do you think the future might bring?

ENDNOTES

1. Joseph W. Rogers, "Mary Belle Harris: Warden and Rehabilitation Pioneer," *Criminal Justice Research Bulletin*, Vol. 3, no. 9 (Huntsville, TX: Sam Houston State University, 1988), p. 8.

2. Hans Reimer, "Socialization in the Prison Community," *Proceedings of the American Prison Association, 1937*, (New York: American Prison Association, 1937), pp. 151–155.

3. Donald Clemmer, *The Prison Community* (Boston: Christopher, 1940).

4. Gresham M. Sykes, *The Society of Captives: A Study of a Maximum Security Prison* (Princeton, NJ: Princeton University Press, 1958).

5. Donald R. Cressey, ed., *The Prison: Studies in Institutional Organization and Change* (New York: Holt, Rinehart and Winston, 1961).

6. Lawrence Hazelrigg, ed., *Prison Within Society: A Reader in Penology* (Garden City, NY: Anchor Books, 1969), preface.

7. Charles Stastny and Gabrielle Tyrnauer, *Who Rules the Joint? The Changing Political Culture of Maximum-Security Prisons in America* (Lexington, MA: Lexington Books, 1982), p. 131.

8. Erving Goffman, *Asylums: Essays on the Social Situation of Mental Patients and Other Inmates* (Garden City, NY: Anchor Books, 1961).

9. The concept of prisonization is generally attributed to Clemmer, *The Prison Community*, although Quaker penologists of the late 1700s were actively concerned with preventing "contamination" (the spread of criminal values) among prisoners.

10. Gresham M. Sykes and Sheldon L. Messinger, "The Inmate Social System," in Richard A. Cloward et al., *Theoretical Studies in Social Organization of the Prison* (New York: Social Science Research Council, 1960), pp. 5–19.

11. Ibid., p. 5.

12. Sykes, *The Society of Captives*, p. xiii.

13. Stanton Wheeler, "Socialization in Correctional Communities," *American Sociological Review*, Vol. 26 (October 1961), pp. 697–712.

14. Sykes, *The Society of Captives*.

15. Donald Clemmer, *The Prison Community* (New York: Holt, Rinehart and Winston, 1940), pp. 294–296.

16. Stastny and Tyrnauer, *Who Rules the Joint?* p. 135.

17. Ibid.

18. Alan J. Davis, "Sexual Assaults in the Philadelphia Prison System and Sheriff's Vans," *Trans-Action*, Vol. 6 (December 1968), pp. 8–16.

19. Lee H. Bowker, *Prison Victimization* (New York: Elsevier-North Holland, 1980), p. 8, and Lee H. Bowker, *Prisoner Subcultures* (Lexington Books, 1977), p. 42.

20. Bowker, *Prison Victimization*, p. 9.

21. Ibid., p. 42.

22. Ibid., p. 1.

23. Hans Toch, *Living in Prison: The Ecology of Survival* (New York: The Free Press, 1977), p. 151.

24. John Irwin, *The Felon* (Englewood Cliffs, NJ: Prentice Hall, 1970).

25. Lucien X. Lombardo, *Guards Imprisoned: Correctional Officers at Work* (New York: Elsevier, 1981), pp. 22–36.

26. Leonard Morgenbesser, "NY State Law Prescribes Psychological Screening for CO Job Applicants," *Correctional Training* (Newsletter of the American Association of Correctional Training Personnel, Winter 1983), p. 1.

27. "A Sophisticated Approach to Training Prison Guards," *Newsday*, August 12, 1982.

28. Rosalie Rosetti, "Charting Your Course: Federal Model Encourages Career Choices," *Corrections Today* (August 1988), pp. 34–38.

29. Stastny and Tyrnauer, *Who Rules the Joint?* p. 1.

30. See Frederick Talbott, "Reporting from Behind the Walls: Do It Before the Siren Wails," *The Quill* (February 1988), pp. 16–21.

31. "Prison Riot Leaves Injuries," *The Fayetteville Observer-Times* (North Carolina), October 28, 1989, p. 1A.

32. Lee Leonard, "Lucasville Guards Were Outnumbered 50–1 Before Riot," *Columbus Dispatch*, May 12, 1993.

33. "Ohio Prison Rebellion Is Ended," *USA Today*, April 22, 1993, p. 2A.

34. *Report of the Attorney General on the February 2 and 3, 1980 Riot at the Penitentiary of New Mexico* (two parts), June and September 1980.

35. See, for example, American Correctional Association, *Riots and Disturbances in Correctional Institutions* (College Park, MD: ACA, 1981); Michael Braswell et al., *Prison Violence in America* (Cincinnati, OH: Anderson, 1985); and R. Conant, "Rioting, Insurrectional and Civil Disorderliness," *American Scholar*, Vol. 37 (Summer 1968), pp. 420–433.

36. Robert S. Fong, "A Comparative Study of the Organizational Aspects of Two Texas Prison Gangs: Texas Syndicate and Mexican Mafia," paper presented at the annual meeting of the Academy of Criminal Justice Sciences, (Washington, D.C., 1989).

37. Ibid.

38. *Ruiz* v. *Estelle*, 503 F.Supp. 1265 (S.D. Texas, 1980).

39. S. Dillingham and R. Montgomery, J., "Prison Riots: A Corrections Nightmare Since 1774," in Braswell et al., *Prison Violence in America*, pp. 19–36.

40. Vernon Fox, "Prison Riots in a Democratic Society," *Police*, Vol. 26, no. 12 (December 1982), pp. 35–41.

41. Donald R. Cressey, "Adult Felons in Prison," in Lloyd E. Ohlin, ed., *Prisoners in America* (Englewood Cliffs, NJ: Prentice Hall, 1972), pp. 117–150.

42. Bureau of Justice Statistics, *Prisoners in 1992* (Washington, D.C.: BJS, 1993).

43. Ibid.

44. This section owes much to the American Correctional Association, Task Force on the Female Offender, *The Female Offender: What Does the Future Hold?* (Washington, D.C.: St. Mary's Press, 1990), and "The View from Behind Bars," *Time*, Fall 1990 (special issue), pp. 20–22.

45. James C. Fox, "Women's Prison Policy, Prisoner Activism, and the Impact of the Contemporary Feminist Movement: A Case Study," *The Prison Journal*, Vol. 64, no. 1 (Spring–Summer 1984), pp. 15–36.

46. American Correctional Association, *The Female Offender*.

47. B. Keith Crew, "Sex Differences in Criminal Sentencing: Chivalry or Patriarchy?" *Justice Quarterly*, Vol. 8, no. 1 (March 1991), pp. 59–83.

48. American Correctional Association, *The Female Offender*.

49. Ibid.

50. Mary Jeanette Clement, "National Survey of Programs for Incarcerated Women," paper presented at the Academy of Criminal Justice Sciences annual meting, Nashville, Tennessee, March 1991.

51. Ibid., pp. 8–9.

52. D. Ward and G. Kannebaum, *Women's Prison: Sex and Social Structure* (London: Weidenfeld and Nicolson, 1966).

53. Esther Heffernan, *Making It in Prison: The Square, the Cool and the Life* (London: Wiley-Interscience, 1972).

54. Rose Giallombardo, *Society of Women: A Study of Women's Prisons* (New York: John Wiley, 1966).

55. Ibid., p. 136.

56. For a summary of such studies (including some previously unpublished), see Bowker, *Prisoner Subcultures*, p. 86.

57. Giallombardo, *Society of Women*, p. 162.

58. Russell P. Dobash, P. Emerson Dobash, and Sue Gutteridge, *The Imprisonment of Women* (Oxford: Basil Blackwell, 1986), p. 6.

59. Heffernan, *Making It in Prison*.

60. Jean Harris, *They Always Call Us Ladies* (new York: Scribners, 1988).

61. "The Lady on Cell Block 112A," *Newsweek*, September 5, 1988, p. 60.

62. Ibid.

63. Ibid.

64. "Scarsdale Diet Doctor's Killer Given Clemency," *USA Today*, December 30, 1992, p. 3A.

65. Bowker, *Prison Victimization*, p. 53.

66. Giallombardo, *Society of Women*.

67. "Georgia Indictments Charge Abuse of Female Inmates," *USA Today*, November 16, 1992, p. 3A.

68. Ibid.

69. American Correctional Association, *The Female Offender*, p. 39.

70. *Holt* v. *Sarver*, 309 F.Supp. 362 (E.D. Ark 1970).

71. Vergil L. Williams, *Dictionary of American Penology: An Introduction* (Westport, CT: Greenwood, 1979), pp. 6–7.

72. American Correctional Association, *Legal Responsibility and Authority of*

Correctional Officers: A Handbook on Courts, Judicial Decisions and Constitutional Requirements (College Park, MD: ACA, 1987), p. 8.

73. *Pell* v. *Procunier*, 417 U.S. 817, 822 (1974).

74. Ibid.

75. According to the ACA, *Legal Responsibility*, p. 57, "A trend may be developing in favor of less intrusive remedial orders in conditions cases in favor of allowing institutional official an opportunity to develop and implement relief with as little court involvement as possible." For further information on this and other issues in the area of prisoners' rights, see Barbara B. Knight and Stephen T. Early, Jr., *Prisoner's Rights in America* (Chicago: Nelson-Hall, 1986).

76. *Procunier* v. *Martinez*, 416 U.S. 396 (1974).

77. *McNamara* v. *Moody*, 606 F.2d 621 (5th Cir. 1979).

78. *The Luparar* v. *Stoneman*, 382 F.Supp. 495 (D. Vt. 1974).

79. *Mallery* v. *Lewis*, 106 Idaho 227 (1983).

80. See for example, *Pepperling* v. *Crist*, 678 F. 2d 787 (9th Cir. 1981).

81. *Cruz* v. *Beto*, 405 U.S. 319 (1972).

82. *Aziz* v. *LeFevre*, 642 F.2d 1109 (2nd Cir. 1981).

83. *Glasshofer* v. *Thornburg*, 514 F.Supp. 1242 (E.D. Pa. 1981).

84. *Campbell* v. *Cauthron*, 623 F.2d 503 (8th Cir. 1980).

85. *Smith* v. *Blackledge*, 451 F.2d 1201 (4th Cir. 1971).

86. *Dettmer* v. *Landon*, 617 F.Supp. 592, 594 (D.C. Va. 1985).

87. *Lewellyn (L'Aquarius)* v. *State*, 592 P.2d 538 (Okla. Crim. App. 1979).

88. *Hill* v. *Blackwell*, 774 F.2d 338, 347 (8th Cir. 1985).

89. See, for example, *Smith* v. *Coughlin*, 748 F.2d 783 (2d Cir. 1984).

90. *Block* v. *Rutherford*, 486 U.S. 576 (1984).

91. *Pell* v. *Procunier*, 417 U.S. 817, 822 (1974).

92. *Houchins* v. *KQED, Inc.*, 438 U.S. at 11 (1978).

93. Ibid.

94. For a Supreme Court review of the First Amendment right to petition the courts, see *McDonald* v. *Smith*, 105 S.Ct. 2787 (1985).

95. *Bounds* v. *Smith*, 430 U.S. 817, 821 (1977).

96. *Johnson* v. *Avery*, 393 U.S. 483 (1968).

97. *Bounds* v. *Smith*.

98. *Taylor* v. *Sterrett*, 532 F.2d 462 (5th Cir. 1976).

99. *In re Harrell*, 87 Cal. Rptr. 504, 470 P.2d 640 (1970).

100. *U.S.* v. *Gouveia*, 104 S.Ct. 2292, 81 L.Ed. 2d 146 (1984).

101. *Guajardo* v. *Estelle*, 432 F.Supp. 1373 (S.D. Texas, 1977).

102. *O'Brien* v. *United States*, 386 U.S. 345 (1967); and *Weatherford* v. *Bursey*, 429 U.S. 545 (1977).

103. *Estelle* v. *Gamble*, 429 U.S. 97 (1976).

104. Ibid., pp. 105–106.

105. *USA Today*, "U.S. Supreme Court," June 21, 1988, p. 8A.

106. *Ruiz* v. *Estelle*, 679 F.2d 1115 (5th Cir. 1982).

107. *Newman* v. *Alabama*, 349 F.Supp. 278 (M.D. Ala. 1972).

108. Adapted from American Correctional Association, *Legal Responsibility and Authority of Correctional Officers*, pp. 25–26.

109. *In re Caulk*, 35 CrL 2532 (New Hampshire S.Ct. 1984).

110. Ibid.

111. *Helling* v. *McKinney*, No. 91–1958. Decided June 18, 1993.

112. *U.S.* v. *Ready*, 574 F.2d 1009 (10th Cir. 1978).

113. *Katz* v. *U.S.*, 389 U.S. 347, 88 S.Ct. 507, 19 L.Ed. 2ed 576 (1967).

114. *Hudson* v. *Palmer*, 468 U.S. 517 (1984).

115. *Block* v. *Rutherford*, 104 S.Ct. 3227, 3234–35 (1984).

116. *U.S.* v. *Lilly*, 576 F.2d 1240 (5th Cir. 1978).

117. *Palmer* v. *Hudson*, 697 F.2d 1220 (4th Cir. 1983).

118. William H. Erickson et al., *United States Supreme Court Cases and Comments* (New York: Matthew Bender, 1987), Section 10.02 2 (c), pp. 10–38.

119. *Wilson* v. *Seiter et al.*, No. 89–7376 (1991).

120. *Estelle* v. *Gamble*, 429 U.S. 97, 106 (1976).

121. *Hudson* v. *McMillian*, 60 U.S.L.W. 4151 (1992).

122. Michael A. Fitzgerald, Sr., and Richard G. Frey, "Prisoners' Rights on the Rehnquist Court," paper presented at the annual meeting of the Academy of Criminal Justice Sciences, Nashville, Tennessee, March 1991.

123. Williams, *Dictionary of American Penology*, p. 89.

124. New York State Department of Correctional Services, "Inmate Grievance Program Year End Report, 1987," memorandum (Albany: NYSDCS, 1988), p. 1.

125. Ibid.

126. Ibid.

127. *Jones* v. *North Carolina Prisoners' Labor Union, Inc.*, 433 U.S. 119, 53 L.Ed. 2d 629, 641 (1977).

128. *Wolff* v. *McDonnell*, 94 S.Ct. 2963 (1974).

129. Ibid.

130. Ibid.

131. *Ponte* v. *Real*, U.S. 105 S.Ct. 2192 L.Ed. 2d (1985).

132. *Vitek* v. *Jones*, 445 U.S. 480 (1980).

133. American Correctional Association, Standard 2–4346. See ACA, *Legal Responsibility and Authority of Correctional Officers*, p. 49.

134. J. E. Baker, *The Right to Participate: Inmate Involvement in Prison Administration* (Metuchen, NJ: Scarecrow Press, 1974).

135. See C. Ron Huff, "Unionization Behind the Walls," *Criminology*, Vol. 12, no. 2 (August 1974), pp. 175–194.

136. *Jones* v. *North Carolina Prisoners' Labor Union, Inc.*, 433 U.S. 119, 53 L.Ed. 2d 629, 641 (1977).

137. American Correctional Association, *Legal Responsibility and Authority of Correctional Officers*, p. 20.

138. Theodore M. Hammett, *AIDS in Correctional Facilities: Issues and Options*, 3rd ed. (Washington, D.C.: National Institute of Justice, 1988), p. 23.

139. National Research Council, *The Social Impact of AIDS in the United States* (Washington, D.C.: National Academy Press, 1993), p. 180.

140. Hammett, *AIDS in Correctional Facilities*, p. 29.

141. M. A. R. Kleiman and R. W. Mockler, "AIDS, the Criminal Justice System, and Civil Liberties," *Governance: Harvard Journal of Public Policy* (Summer/Fall 1987), pp. 48–54.

142. Hammett, *AIDS in Correctional Facilities*, p. 37.

143. At the time of this writing, California, Wisconsin, Massachusetts, New York, and the District of Columbia were among such jurisdictions.

144. Hammett, *AIDS in Correctional Facilities*, pp. 47–49.

145. Sol Chaneles, "Growing Old Behind Bars," *Psychology Today* (October 1987), pp. 47–51.

146. Ronald Wikbert and Burk Foster, "The Longtermers: Louisiana's Longest Serving Inmates and Why They've Stayed So Long," paper presented at the annual meeting of the Academy of Criminal Justice

Sciences, Washington, D.C., 1989.

147. Lincoln J. Fry, "The Older Prison Inmate: A Profile," *The Justice Professional*, Vol. 2, no. 1 (Spring 1987), pp. 1–12.

148. Wikberg and Foster, "The Longtermers."

149. Ibid., p. 51.

150. Chaneles, "Growing Old Behind Bars," p. 51.

151. "The Lady in Cell Block 112A," *Newsweek*, September, 5, 1988, p. 60.

152. Hans Toch, "The Disturbed Disruptive Inmate: Where Does the Bus Stop?" *The Journal of Psychiatry and Law*, Vol. 10 (1982), pp. 327–349.

153. Robert O. Lampert, "The Mentally Retarded Offender in Prison," *The Justice Professional*, Vol. 2, no. 1 (Spring 1987), p. 61.

154. Ibid., p. 64.

155. George C. Denkowski and Kathryn M. Denkowski, "The Mentally Retarded Offender in the State Prison System: Identification, Prevalence, Adjustment, and Rehabilitation," *Criminal Justice and Behavior*, Vol. 12 (1985), pp. 55–75.

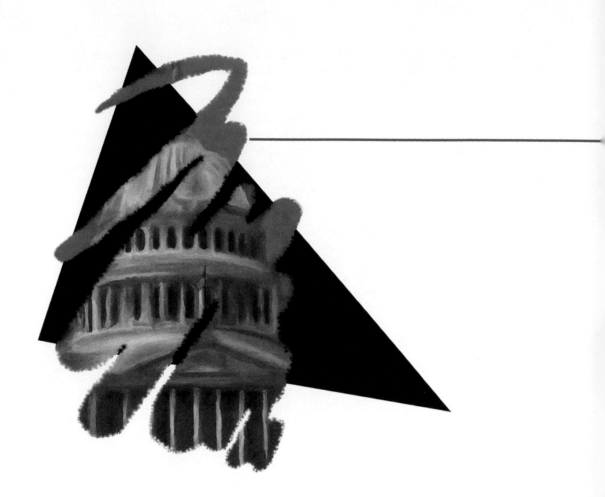

INDIVIDUAL RIGHTS VERSUS SOCIAL CONCERNS

ISSUES FOR THE FUTURE

Common law, constitutional, and humanitarian rights of the accused which may soon be threatened by technological advances and other developments:

A Right to Privacy
A Right to Be Assumed Innocent
A Right Against Self-incrimination
A Right to Equal Protection of the Laws
A Right Against Cruel and Unusual Punishment

The individual rights listed must be effectively balanced against these present and emerging community concerns:

Widespread Drug Abuse Among Youth
The Threat of Juvenile Crime
Urban Gang Violence
High-Technology and Computer Crimes
Terrorism and Narcoterrorism
Occupational and White-Collar Crime

How does our system of justice work toward balance?

SPECIAL ISSUES

The future influences the present just as much as the past.
—**FRIEDRICH WILHELM NIETZSCHE (1844-1900)**

The farther backward you can look, the farther forward you are likely to see.
—**WINSTON CHURCHILL (1874-1965)**

Our nation spends untold billions of dollars every year on adult correctional programs in the interest of protecting the public. Substantially fewer dollars are provided for prevention programs that are desperately needed for juvenile offenders. By preventing delinquency among those who would otherwise be the future occupants of the adult system, we can save the nation much time and expense in future generations.
—**NATIONAL JUVENILE CORRECTIONS AND DETENTION FORUM (1993)**

JUVENILE DELINQUENCY

America's best hope for reducing crime is to reduce juvenile delinquency and youth crime.
—PRESIDENT'S COMMISSION (1967)

Under our Constitution, the condition of being a boy does not justify a kangaroo court.
—IN RE GAULT, 387 U.S. 1 (1967)

We know that many [youths] who are on the streets are there as a result of sound rational choices they have made for their own safety and welfare, such as avoiding physical abuse, sexual abuse, or extreme neglect at home.
—NATIONAL COUNCIL OF JUVENILE
AND FAMILY COURT JUDGES

Each year, tens of thousands of youngsters unnecessarily suffer the negative consequences of costly incarceration in overcrowded, unsafe juvenile detention facilities.
—DOUGLAS W. NELSON, EXECUTIVE DIRECTOR
ANNIE E. CASEY FOUNDATION

INTRODUCTION

In what can only be described as a very sad case, 11-year-old Alejandro Vargas was shot to death in a Compton, California, schoolyard on April 24, 1991. Alejandro was struck in the face, just below the left eye, by a bullet from a small-caliber handgun as he waited with friends after school for a ride home. Witnesses said a single shot came from a gang of four youths standing in an alley across from the school. They had been chased from the school grounds minutes earlier by a campus security officer. Alejandro, who was known for self-lessly helping older residents near his home with their chores, was described by neighbors as "the sweetest thing this side of heaven."[1] In the words of Benjamin Vann, also 11, who had vacationed with Alejandro that spring,"[h]e was wonderful. He was my best friend."[2] Ironically, Alejandro was still on campus at the time of the shooting waiting for a ride, because he was afraid to walk home through the tough, gang-ridden, neighborhoods surrounding the school. Following the shooting, two local gang members, ages 14 and 17, were arrested and charged with murder. They had not known Alejandro personally.

Alejandro Vargas's story is only one of many tragic tales involving American youth today. In the same part of California, during the year preceding Vargas's shooting, a Compton High School student was shot in the face, an elementary school janitor killed, and one Centennial High School student was wounded and another killed.[3] During that school year 726 crimes, including 1 homicide, were reported at Compton, California, schools. As school trustee John Stewart said after Vargas's death,"…the shooting is related to an overall increase in gang activity in the community. Social forces beyond the control of school administrators were to blame for the tragedy."[4]

Contrast the case of Alejandro Vargas, a young victim, with that of Craig Price, a youthful offender.[5] Price, known as the Iron Man to his friends because of his muscular build (at 5 feet 10 inches tall, he weighs 240 pounds), pled guilty recently to the murder of two Rhode Island women and two girls. The girls were 10 and 8 years old at the time they were killed. All the victims had been beaten and stabbed—one as many as 58 times. At the time of the killings, Price was already on probation for assault and burglary. And he was only 14 years old (13 at the time of the first murder). Rhode Island law has no provision which would allow anyone under the age of 16 to be tried as an adult, and it requires that juveniles sentenced to incarceration be released on or before their 21st birthdays. Hence, following his plea of guilty to four murders and two burglaries, Craig Price was sentenced to the maximum the law allows—incarceration in the Rhode Island Training School until he reaches the age of 21. His 21st birthday, on October 11, 1994, is a date preset by law for Craig's release.

Another young victim. The mother of 13-year-old Bayron Alvarado-Martinez holds her son's picture. Bayron, an eighth-grader, was shot to death by San Francisco street gangs. *Photo: Mark Costantini/San Francisco Examiner.*

Both of these cases are tragedies, albeit in different ways. Both are also, to some degree, the result of a juvenile justice system that has failed.

A significant proportion of all illegal activity today is committed by juveniles. Although states vary as to the age at which a person enters adulthood, statistics on crime make it clear that young people are involved disproportionately in certain offenses. A recent report, for example, found that persons aged 15 to 19 account for over 15% of all violent crimes and 32% of property crimes, while comprising only 9% of the population of the United States.[6] On the average, over 30% of all arrests in any year are of juveniles.[7] Juveniles under the age of 18 have a higher likelihood of being arrested for robbery and UCR index property crimes than any other age group.[8] One estimate placed the number of males who would be arrested at least once before their eighteenth birthday at 27%.[9] Figure 14–1 shows *Uniform Crime Report* statistics on juvenile arrests for selected offense categories.

Another reason for studying juvenile delinquency comes from reports which indicate that many adults involved in criminal acts began their illegal activities while young. The case of 12-year-old Fort Lauderdale, Florida's "Crime Boy" is illustrative. Crime Boy, so dubbed by the local media who cannot legally release his name, committed his first crime—a burglary—at the age of 8. Since then he has been arrested for a variety of offenses—57 in all—and chances are that he has committed many other crimes which will never come to light.[10] Crime Boy lives with his 41-year-old grandmother. His mother is serving time in prison for murder and his father's whereabouts are unknown. A brief review of records in Crime Boy's hometown revealed that he is not the only juvenile with a long string of offenses. Another 12-year-old has accumulated 58 charges, and a 13-year-old living there has been arrested 78 times.

This chapter has three purposes. First, we will describe the **juvenile justice system** from its historical beginnings to the present. The juvenile justice system has its roots in the adult system. In the juvenile system, however, we find a more uniform philosophical base, and a

Juvenile Justice System Government agencies which function to investigate, supervise, adjudicate, care for, or confine youthful offenders and other children subject to the jurisdiction of the juvenile court.

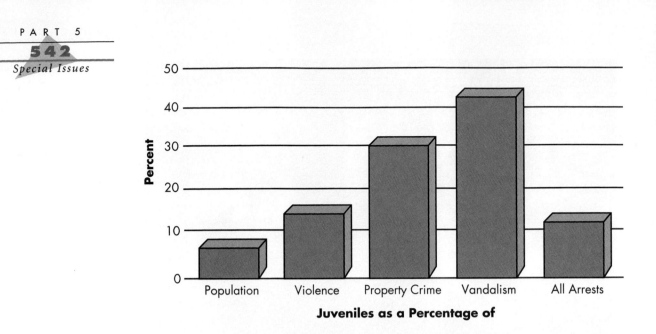

FIGURE 14–1   Juvenile involvement in crime versus system totals, 1992. *Source:* Federal Bureau of Investigation, *Crime in the United States, 1992* (Washington, D.C.: U.S. Department of Justice, 1993).

generally clear agreement as to the system's purpose. Both may be due to the system's relative youth and to the fact that society generally agrees that young people who have gone wrong are worthwhile salvaging.

Delinquency   Juvenile actions or conduct in violation of criminal law, juvenile status offenses, and other juvenile misbehavior.

Our second purpose will be to compare the juvenile and adult systems as they currently operate. The philosophy behind the juvenile justice system has led to administrative and other procedures not found in the adult system. For example, the juvenile justice process is not as open as the adult system. Hearings may be held in secret, the names of offenders are not published, and records of juvenile proceedings may be later destroyed.

Our third focus will be to describe in detail the agencies, processes, and problems of the juvenile justice system itself. Although each state may have variations, a common system structure is shared by all. And, of course, the juvenile justice system is not without its critics. Just as the adult criminal justice system has not been able to eliminate adult criminality, the juvenile system has been unable to entirely curb youth crime.

DEALING WITH CHILDREN THROUGH HISTORY

THE EARLY YEARS

The history of the Western world reveals that children who committed crimes in past centuries could expect no preferential treatment by virtue of their youth. For purposes of adjudication and punishment they were processed alongside of adults. The laws of King Aethelbert, the earliest legal document written in the English language (circa 600 A.D.), made no special allowances for the age of the offender, and a number of recorded cases have come down through history of children as young as six or eight being hanged or burned at the stake. Short of execution, children were imprisoned along with adults. No segregated juvenile facilities existed. Neither the development of gaols (jails) in the thirteenth century nor the early English prisons provided any leniency on the basis of age.[11] In like fashion, little distinction was made between criminal and **delinquent acts** or other kinds of undesirable behavior. Problems such as epilepsy, insanity, retardation, or poverty were seen in the same light as crime,[12] and people suffering from these conditions were shut away in facilities shared by juveniles and adult offenders.

By the Middle Ages, social conceptions of children had become strongly influenced by the Church of Rome. Church doctrine held that children under the age of 7 had not yet reached the age of reason and could not be held liable for spiritual transgressions. In adopting the perspective of the Church, English law of the period excepted children under the age of 7 from criminal responsibility. Juveniles aged 7 to 14 were accorded a special status, being tried as adults only if it could be demonstrated that they fully understood the nature of their criminal acts.[13] Adulthood was considered to begin at age 14, and it was at that age that marriage was allowed.[14]

Court philosophy in dealing with juveniles derived from another early Roman principle called *patria postestas*. Under Roman law (circa 753 B.C.) children had membership in their family, but the father had absolute control over children and they in turn had an absolute responsibility to obey his wishes. The power of the father extended to issues of life and death for all members of the family, including slaves, spouses, and children.[15] Roman understanding of the social role of children strongly influenced English culture, and eventually led to development of the legal principle of *parens patriae*. *Parens patriae* allowed the king, or the English state, to take the place of parents in dealing with children who broke the law.

Early English institutions placed a large burden of responsibility on the family, and especially the father, who, as head of the household, was held accountable for the behavior of all family members. Children, and even wives, were almost totally dependent upon the father and had a status only slightly above that of personal property. When the father failed in his responsibility to control family members, the king, through the concept of *parens patriae*, could intervene. *Parens patriae* held that the king was father of the country and thus had parental rights over all his citizens.

The inexorable power of the king, often influenced by unpredictable whims, combined with a widespread fear of dismal conditions in English institutions to make many families hide their problem kin. The retarded, insane, and epileptic were kept in attics or basements, sometimes for their entire lives. Delinquent children were confined to the home or, if the family from which they came was wealthy enough, sent overseas to escape the conditions of asylums and gaols (an old word for jails).

JUVENILES IN EARLY AMERICA

Early American solutions to the problems of delinquency were much like those of the English. Puritan influence in the colonies, with its heavy emphasis upon obedience and discipline, led to a frequent use of jails and prisons for both juveniles and adults. Legislation reflected the biblical Ten Commandments and often provided harsh punishments for transgressors of almost any age. For example, one Massachusetts law in the seventeenth century provided in part that

> If a man have a stubborn or rebellious son of sufficient years of understanding, viz. sixteen, which will not obey the voice of his father or the voice of his mother, and that when they have chastened him will not harken to them, then shall his father and mother, being his natural parents, lay hold on him and bring him to the magistrate assembled in Court, and testify to them by sufficient evidence that this their son is stubborn and rebellious and will not obey their voice and chastisement, but lives in sundry notorious crime. Such a son shall be put to death.[16]

Delinquent Act An act committed by a juvenile for which an adult could be prosecuted in a criminal court, but for which a juvenile can be adjudicated in a juvenile court.

Parens Patriae A common law principle which allows the state to assume a parental role and to take custody of a child when he or she becomes delinquent, is abandoned, or is in need of care which the natural parents are unable or unwilling to provide.

Severe punishment was consistent with Puritan beliefs that unacknowledged social evils might bring the wrath of God down upon the entire colony. In short, disobedient children had no place in a social group whose life was committed to a spiritual salvation understood as strict obedience to the wishes of the Divine.

By the end of the eighteenth century, social conditions in Europe and America began to change. The Enlightenment, a highly significant social movement, focused on human potential, and generally rejected supernatural explanations in favor of scientific ones. It was accompanied by the growth of an industrialized economy, with a corresponding move away from agrarianism. Poor laws, lower infant death rates, and other social innovations born of the Enlightenment led to a reassessment of the place of children in society. In this new age children were recognized as the only true heirs to the future, and society became increasingly concerned about their well-being.

THE INSTITUTIONAL ERA

The nineteenth century was a time of rapid social change in the United States. The population was growing dramatically, cities were burgeoning, and the industrial era was in full swing. Industrial tycoons, the new rich, and frontier-bound settlers lived elbow-to-elbow with immigrants eking out a living in the sweat shops of the new mercantile centers. In this environment children took on new value as a source of cheap labor. They fueled assembly lines and proved invaluable to shop owners whose businesses needed frequent but inexpensive attention. Parents were gratified by the income-producing opportunities available to their offspring. On the frontier, settlers and farm families put their children to work clearing land and seeding crops.

Unfortunately, economic opportunities and the luck of the draw were not equally favorable to all. Some immigrant families became victims of the cities which drew them, settling in squalor in hastily formed ghettos. Many families, seeing only the economic opportunities represented by their children, neglected to provide them with anything but a rudimentary education. Children who did work labored for long hours, and had little time for family closeness. Other children, abandoned by families unable to support them, were forced into lives on the streets where they formed tattered gangs—surviving off the refuse of the glittering cities.

The House of Refuge

An 1823 report by the Society for the Prevention of Pauperism in the City of New York called for the development of "houses of refuge" to save children from lives of crime and poverty. The Society also cited the problems caused by locking up children with mature criminals. Houses of refuge were to be places of care and education where children could learn positive values toward work.

In 1824 the first house of refuge opened in New York City.[17] The New York House of Refuge was intended only for those children who could still be "rescued" and sheltered mostly young thieves, vagrants, and runaways.[18] Other children, especially those with more severe delinquency problems, were placed in adult prisons and jails. Houses of refuge became popular in New York and were quickly copied by other cities. It was not long before overcrowding developed, and living conditions in them deteriorated.

The 1838 case of *Ex parte Crouse* clarified the power states had in committing children to institutions.[19] The case involved Mary Ann Crouse, who had been committed to the Philadelphia House of Refuge by a lower court over the objections of her father. The commitment was based upon allegations made by the girl's mother that she was incorrigible, or beyond the control of her parents. Mary Ann's father petitioned the court to release his daughter on the grounds that she had been denied the right to trial by jury.

The decision by the appeals court upheld the legality of Mary Ann's commitment. It pointed to the state's interest in assisting children and denied that punishment or retribution played any part in her treatment. The court also focused on parental responsibilities in general and stressed the need for state intervention to provide for the moral development of children whose parents fail them. Most important of all, the court built its decision around the doctrine of *parens patriae*, taking what had previously been an English judicial concept and making it applicable to the American scene. The court wrote:

> The object of the charity is reformation, by training its inmates to industry; by imbuing their minds with principles of morality and religion; by furnishing them with means to earn a living; and above all, by separating them from the corrupting influence of improper associates. To this end, may not the natural parents, when unequal to the task of education, or unworthy of it, be superseded by the *parens patriae*, or common guardianship of the community?[20]

The Chicago Reform School

Around the middle of the 1800s the child savers movement began. Child savers espoused a philosophy of productivity and eschewed idleness and unprincipled behavior. Anthony Platt,[21] a modern writer who is credited with recognizing the significance of the child savers movement, suggests that the mid-1800s provided an ideological framework combining Christian principles with a strong emphasis on the worth of the individual. It was a social perspective which held that children were to be guided and protected.

One product of the child savers movement was the reform school—a place for delinquent juveniles which embodied the atmosphere of a Christian home. By the middle of the nineteenth century, the reform school approach to handling juveniles was well under way. The Chicago Reform School, which opened in the 1860s, provided an early model for the reform school movement. The movement focused primarily on predelinquent youth who showed tendencies toward more serious criminal involvement. Reform schools attempted to emulate wholesome family environments in order to provide the security and affection thought necessary in building moral character.

The reform school movement also emphasized traditional values and the worth of hard work. The movement tended to idealize country living, apparently in the belief that the frantic pace of city life made the transition from child to adult difficult. Some early reform schools were built in rural settings and many were farms. A few programs even developed which tried to relocate problem children to the vast open expanses of the Western states.

The reform school movement was not without its critics. As one modern-day observer writes, "if institutions sought to replicate families, would it not have been better to place the predelinquents directly in real families?"[22] As with houses of refuge, reform schools soon became overcrowded. What began as a meaningful attempt to help children ended in routinized procedures devoid of the reformer's original zeal.

In the 1870s the Illinois Supreme Court handed down a decision that practically put the reform school movement out of business. The case of *People ex rel. O'Connell* v. *Turner*[23] centered on Daniel O'Connell who had been committed to the Chicago Reform School under an Illinois law which permitted confinement for "misfortune." Youngsters classified as "misfortunate" had not necessarily committed any criminal offense. They were, rather, ordered to reform school because their families were unable to care for them or because they were seen as social misfits.

O'Connell had not been convicted of a crime, however, and the Illinois Supreme Court ordered him released. The court reasoned that the power of the state under *parens patriae* could not exceed the power of the natural parents except in punishing crime. The *O'Connell* case is still remembered today for the lasting distinction it made between criminal and noncriminal acts committed by juveniles.

Early Juvenile Reform in Europe

While the house of refuge, the reform school movement, and the reformatory concept (discussed in Chapter 12) were developing in the United States, similar alternatives for the treatment of juveniles were evolving in Europe. One of the first European facilities for youthful delinquents was the Hospice of San Michele. Conceived by Pope Clement XI, the hospice opened in 1704 as a facility for wayward boys. An exhortation inscribed in the large central hallway where the boys worked embodied the rehabilitative philosophy of the Hospice. It read: "It is of little advance to restrain the bad by punishment, unless you render them good by discipline."[24]

The hospice sheltered not only juveniles. It also served as a home for orphans, a Catholic school, and a rest home for more than 500 aged and needy people. More than 100 years later Johann Pestalozzi opened a home exclusively for delinquents on the Hofwyl estate in Argau, Switzerland.[25] Known as the Wehrli institution, it emphasized a homelike environment centered on education. Wehrli began with 20 juveniles but eventually expanded to accommodate more than 60. Its success led to the development of similar institutions across Europe.[26]

One of the most widely studied European institutions for juveniles was the English facility at Borstal. The Borstal System was the direct result of an 1897 visit by Sir Evelyn Ruggles-Brise, then director of the English prison system, to the Elmira Reformatory in New York. Impressed with what he saw at Elmira, Ruggles-Brise opened a specialized institution in England for boys between the ages of 16 and 21. Other facilities followed, and the Borstal System was in full swing by the early 1900s.[27] Borstal philosophy emphasized education, trade training, and individualized treatment both during and after institutionalization.

THE JUVENILE COURT ERA

The Juvenile Court

An expanding recognition of the needs of children led the state of Massachusetts to enact legislation in 1870 which required separate hearings for juveniles.[28] New York followed with a similar law in 1877.[29] The New York law also prohibited contact between juvenile and adult offenders. Rhode Island enacted juvenile court legislation in 1898, and in 1899 the Colorado School Law became the first comprehensive piece of legislation designed to adjudicate problem children.[30]

It was, however, the 1899 codification of Illinois juvenile law which became the model for juvenile court statutes throughout the nation.

The Illinois Juvenile Court Act created a juvenile court, separate in form and function from adult criminal courts. In order to avoid the lasting stigma of criminality, the law applied the term "delinquent" rather than "criminal" to adjudicated offenders. The act specified that juvenile court judges were to be guided in their deliberations by what they determined to be in the best interests of the child. In effect, the judge was to serve as an advocate for the juvenile, seeking to guide the development of the child in socially desirable directions. Concerns with guilt or innocence took second place to the betterment of the child. A strict adherence to the due process requirements of adult prosecutions was sacrificed, allowing for the use of informal procedures designed to scrutinize the child's situation. By sheltering the juvenile from the punishment philosophy of the adult system, the Illinois juvenile court emphasized reformation in place of retribution.[31]

In 1938 the federal government passed the Juvenile Court Act which embodied many of the features of the Illinois statute. By 1945 every state had enacted special legislation focusing on the handling of juveniles and the juvenile court movement had become well established.[32]

The juvenile court movement was based upon five identifiable philosophical principles which can be summarized as follows:

1. The belief that the state is the "higher or ultimate parent" of all the children within its borders.
2. The belief that children are worth saving, and the concomitant belief in the worth of nonpunitive procedures designed to save the child.
3. The belief that children should be nurtured. While the nurturing process is underway they should be protected from the stigmatizing impact of formal adjudicatory procedures.
4. The belief that justice, to accomplish the goal of reformation, needs to be individualized; that is, each child is different, and the needs, aspirations, living conditions, and so on, of each child must be known in their individual particulars if the court is to be helpful.
5. The belief that the use of noncriminal procedures are necessary in order to give primary consideration to the needs of the child. The denial of due process could be justified in the face of constitutional challenges because the court acted not to punish, but to help.[33]

Categories of Children

By the time of the Great Depression most states had expanded juvenile statutes to include six categories of children, as follows: (1) delinquent, (2) undisciplined, (3) dependent, (4) neglected, (5) abused, and (6) status offenders.

Delinquent children were those who violated the criminal law. If they were adults the word "criminal" would have been applied to them. Undisciplined children were said to be beyond parental control, as evidenced by their refusal to obey legitimate authorities such as school officials and teachers. The dependent category encompassed children in need of state protection. **Dependent children** typically had no parents or guardians to care for them, or had been abandoned, or placed for adoption in violation of the law. **Neglected children** were defined as those who did not receive proper care from their parents or guardians. They may have suffered from malnutrition, not been provided with adequate shelter, or did not receive a proper upbringing. **Abused children** included those who suffered physical abuse at the hands of their custodians—a category which was later expanded to include emotional and sexual abuse, as well. Status offenders, a special category which was to lead to many later disputes, embraced children who violated laws written only for children. These terms are still used today in describing the variety of children subject to juvenile court jurisdiction.

Delinquent Child A child who has engaged in activity which would be considered a crime if the child were an adult. The term "delinquent" is applied to such a child in order to avoid the social stigma which comes from application of the term "criminal."

Dependent Child A child who has no parents or whose parents are unable to care for him or her.

Neglected Child A child who is not receiving the proper level of physical or psychological care from his or her parent(s) or guardian(s) or who has been placed for adoption in violation of the law.

Abused Child A child who has been physically, sexually, or mentally abused. Most states also consider a child abused who is forced into delinquent activity by a parent or guardian.

Status Offense An act or conduct which is declared by statute to be an offense, but only when committed or engaged in by a juvenile and which can be adjudicated only by a juvenile court.

Status Offender A child who commits an act which is contrary to the law by virtue of the juvenile's status as a child. Purchasing cigarettes, buying alcohol, and truancy are examples of such behavior.

Status Offenses

Status offenses are illegal forms of behavior which apply only to juveniles. They include offenses such as truancy, vagrancy, running away from home, and incorrigibility. The youthful "status" of juveniles is a necessary element in such offenses. Adults, for example, may decide to run away from home and not violate any law. Runaway children, however, are subject to apprehension and juvenile court processing because state laws require that they be subject to parental control.

Status offenses were a natural outgrowth of juvenile court philosophy. However, critics of the juvenile court movement quickly focused on the abandonment of due process rights, especially in the case of **status offenders**, as a major source of problems. Detention and incarceration, they argued, became viable but inappropriate options where children had not committed crimes. Juveniles in need of help often faced procedural dispositions which treated them the same as if they were delinquent. As a result, rather than lowering the rate of juvenile incarceration, the juvenile court movement led to its increase.

EXPLANATIONS

OF DELINQUENCY

One of the first comprehensive social scientific explanations for delinquency was advanced by Clifford Shaw and Henry McKay.[34] Their theory, known as social ecology, influenced policymakers of the early 1930s. The social ecology approach saw delinquency as the result of social disorganization. Geographic areas characterized by economic deprivation were said to have high rates of population turnover and cultural heterogeneity, both of which were seen as contributors to social disorganization. Social disorganization weakened otherwise traditional societal controls, such as family life, church, jobs, and schools, making delinquency more likely in such areas.

The first large-scale delinquency prevention program grew out of the work of Shaw and McKay. Known as the Chicago Area Project, the program developed self-help neighborhood centers staffed by community volunteers. Each center offered a variety of counseling services, education programs, camps, recreational activities, and discussion groups.

The approach of Shaw and McKay was replaced in the 1960s by a perspective known as opportunity theory. Opportunity theorists saw delinquency as the result of the limited legitimate opportunities for success available to most lower-class youth. Richard A. Cloward and Lloyd E. Ohlin[35] described the most serious delinquents as facing limited opportunities due to their inherent alienation from middle-class institutions. Others have claimed that delinquency is a natural consequence of participation in lower-class culture. Even stable lower-class communities, these authors suggest,[36] produce delinquency as a matter of course. A combination of both approaches is found in the work of Albert K. Cohen,[37] who held that delinquency, especially gang-related activity, is a response to the status frustration experienced by lower-class youth, who find themselves unable to share in the rewards of a middle-class life-style. According to Cohen, vengeance and protest are major motivators among deprived youth and may account for vandalism and other seemingly senseless acts.

Opportunity theory gave rise to treatment models designed to increase chances for legitimate success among lower-class youth. Programs such as New York City's Mobilization for Youth provided education, skills training, and job placement services to young men and women. Mobilization for Youth, through the federal funds it received, hired hundreds of unemployed neighborhood youths to work on community projects such as parks conservation and building renovation.

At least partial recognition was given to the role of individual choice in delinquent behavior by Gresham M. Sykes and David Matza,[38] who described the neutralization of responsibility as a first step toward law violation. The delinquent, according to Sykes and Matza,[39] typically drifts between conformity and law violation and will choose the latter when social norms can be denied or explained away.

Cohort analysis is a useful technique for identifying the determinants of delinquency. Cohort analysis usually begins at birth and traces the development of a population which shares common characteristics until they reach a certain age. One well-known analysis of a birth cohort, undertaken by Marvin Wolfgang during the 1960s, found that a small nucleus of chronic juvenile offenders accounted for a disproportionately large share of all juvenile arrests.[40] Wolfgang studied males born in Philadelphia in 1945 until they reached age 18. He concluded that a relatively small number of violent offenders were responsible for most of the crimes committed by the cohort. Eighteen percent of cohort members accounted for 52% of all arrests. A follow-up study found that seriousness of offenses among the cohort increased in adulthood, but that the actual number of offenses decreased as the cohort aged.[41] Wolfgang's analysis has since been criticized for its lack of a second cohort, or "control group," against which the experiences of the cohort under study could be compared.[42]

Cohort A group of individuals sharing similarities of age, place of birth, and residence. Cohort analysis is a social scientific technique by which such groups are tracked over time in order to identify unique and observable behavioral traits which characterize them.

THE PROBLEMS OF CHILDREN TODAY

While the categories of children are set firmly in legislation and court precedent, many of the problems facing children today are quite different from those that existed when the juvenile court was formed. One general problem facing children today is lack of purpose. In April 1989, New York citizens were outraged by the actions of a group of East Harlem teenagers who attacked joggers and cyclists in near-desolate sections of Central Park.[43] Before their spree of intimidation and violence ended the gang, which at one point numbered as many as 30 kids between the ages of 14 and 17, had attacked, raped, and viciously beaten a 28-year-old investment banker jogging through the area. The victim, who was working her way through Yale business school with a job at Salomon Brothers, suffered two skull fractures and serious brain damage. Following police questioning the youngsters—who remained largely unrepentant—described how evenings spent "wilding" (the pack's slang term for violent mischief) had given vent to the frustrations which exist among some urban juveniles today. Said one psychologist attempting to explain the event, "Feelings of frustration and alienation are widespread, particularly among lower classes."[44] Today's "angry adolescents" have been described as sharing these traits: (1) aggressiveness, (2) immaturity, (3) susceptibility to peer pressure, and (4) a lack of accountability.[45]

How did the angry adolescent come to be a problem in America? Over half a century ago many of the problems encountered by juveniles grew out of their value as inexpensive laborers in the "sweat shops" and factories of the awakening industrial giant that was America. The economic prosperity which followed World War II, however, was based on a less labor-intensive form of production. Complicating matters still farther was the need for the national economy to absorb millions of women who were entering the labor force. Juveniles, no longer needed for their labor, were thrown into a cultural limbo. Some, unable to meaningfully participate in the long educational process that was becoming increasingly necessary for future success, turned to delinquency and vandalism. For these disenfranchised youth criminal activity became an alternative avenue to excitement and some limited sense of purpose.

By the 1960s a self-indulgent ethic had replaced the sense of personal responsibility among a goodly proportion of American youth. For lower-class youth the ethic led to violence, theft, and increased participation in gangs. Middle-class youth, because they were more affluent, focused on what some authors at the time called the "automobile-alcohol-sex combination,"[46] rejecting middle-class values of social duty and personal restraint.

While much of the literature of delinquency focuses on the criminality of lower-class youth, there is evidence that middle- and upper-class youths today commit a fair number of delinquent acts. A recent study of the "lifetime delinquency" of Ivy League college students, for example, found "substantial levels of involvement in a variety of serious offenses."[47] According to the study, 167 students admitted to 4,100 past offenses ranging from public intoxication to forcible rape.

Regardless of class background, there are a number of common problems facing juveniles today. Each is described in the sections that follow.

The values and experiences of many children today are far different from those of the past, as this photo of female gang members shows. *Photo: Curtis Ackerman/The Boston Herald.*

When young people are taken into custody, they are confined separately from adult offenders. Here a teenager is arrested following a disturbance at a concert. *Photo from AP/Wide World Photos.*

DRUG AND ALCOHOL ABUSE

Many of today's adolescents have experimented with illegal drugs. The trend, at least over the last few years, is encouraging, however. Latest statistics show a decline in cocaine abuse among high school seniors. A 1993 report[48] by the U.S. Department of Health and Human Services found that "[a]mong the graduating class of 1992, 40.7% said they had used an illicit drug at least once at some point in their lifetime, down from 44.1% in the class of 1991 and dramatically down from a peak of 65.6% reported by the class of 1981." Unfortunately, according to the study, eighth graders report higher rates of illicit drug use than did eighth graders a year earlier.

Other substances are also abused. The 1993 survey found that 17% of students at each grade level 8 through 12 had tried inhalants at least once in their lifetimes, while 4.7% of eighth graders reported currently using inhalants. Lifetime use of LSD among tenth through twelfth graders stood at 2%, but was almost twice that among eighth graders. Twenty-eight percent of seniors, 21% of tenth graders, and 13% of eighth graders reported binge drinking—consuming five or more alcoholic drinks in a row—within two weeks before the survey.

According to Richard A. Millstein, acting director of the National Institute on Drug Abuse, "These contrasting findings among eighth graders' use of a range of substances…are troubling [and] may represent a reversal of previously improving conditions among teenagers."[49]

As Figure 14–2 shows, drug-related arrests of juveniles have recently been on the rise—although they have not returned to pre-1980 levels. In 1985, for example 64,246 individuals under the age of 18 were arrested for drug offenses nationwide. By 1992 the figure had risen to 73,981.[50] Although a far cry from the number of arrests made in 1975 (122,857),

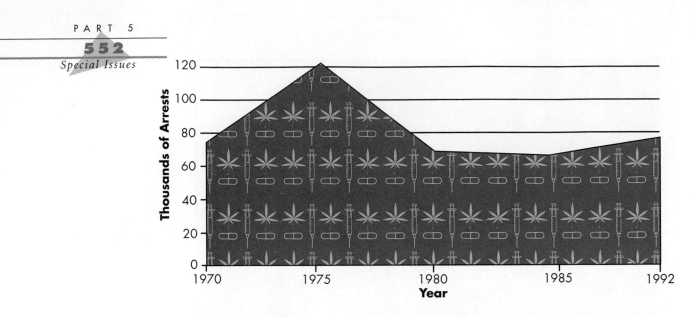

FIGURE 14–2   Drug-related arrests of juveniles, 1970–1992. *Source:* Federal Bureau of Investigation, *Crime in the United States* (Washington, D.C.: U.S. Government Printing Office, various years).

evidence indicates that a juvenile arrested today is far more likely to be using cocaine or crack cocaine than were juveniles in earlier periods. The most commonly abused drug in 1975 was marijuana.

Drug abuse may also lead to other types of crime. One recent study found that seriously delinquent youth were regular drug users.[51] The Bureau of Justice Statistics concludes: "The involvement of adolescent users in other destructive behavior is strongly associated with the number and types of harmful substances they use; the more substances they use, the greater their chance of being involved in serious destructive or assaultive behavior."[52]

INCREASING VIOLENCE

Observers of the national scene have recently reported an apparent epidemic of violence among the nation's teenagers. While the numbers are still too small (there are approximately 3,000 homicides committed by juveniles annually) to significantly impact tabular data such as the Uniform Crime Reports, there is little denying that childhood violence is on the increase. One year ago, for example, 12-year-old Shanda Renee Sharer was bludgeoned, sodomized, tortured, doused with gasoline, and set afire by four other teenage girls. The killing, which took place in the small town of Madison, Indiana, appears to have been motivated by lesbian jealousies.[53] In an unrelated case that happened about the same time, two teen-age Gulfport, Mississippi, girls were accused of choking their mother to death while the boyfriend of one of the girls stabbed the woman. The mother had punished the girls for sneaking away from the house at night.[54] In 1993 two Chicago girls, aged 12 and 13, were arrested for planning to kill their English teacher at the end of class—by stabbing her in the chest with a fillet knife brought from home. The girls had apparently taken a few hundred dollars in lunch money bets from fellow students over whether they would be able to follow through.[55] Cases such as these have led some observers to conclude that girls are beginning to catch up with boys in the area of violence.

The recent spate of violence among children seems to know no religious, age, or geographic boundaries. A bit more than a year ago, devout Christians and community stalwarts Harold Read and his wife Janet were killed in the small town of Madras, Oregon,

T H E O R Y   I N T O   P R A C T I C E

VANDALISM
DELINQUENCY WITHOUT PURPOSE

Vandalism is a delinquent act that is committed for the "hell of it." To many observers it appears to be a purposeless activity. Most vandalism is of property. The example below involves physical injury, although it bears the seemingly purposeless characteristic of vandalism.

> PHILADELPHIA (UPI)—Three teenagers unleashed two pitbull dogs into a crowded schoolyard during a noon recess Thursday, inflicting savage injuries on five children.
>
> There were about 150 children in the schoolyard when the teenagers walked in, unleashed the dogs and told them to attack the children, police said.
>
> The injured children—fourth, fifth, and sixth graders at St. Edward's School in the city's Northeast section—were bitten numerous times on their feet and ankles.

Source: United Press International, December 16, 1988. Reprinted with permission.

by blasts from a 12-gauge shotgun—apparently fired by 12-year-old Jacob Colman, whom they had befriended and taken into their home.[56] In late 1992 a 22-month-old Savannah, Georgia, girl apparently killed her 6-month-old baby brother by dragging him from bed and repeatedly biting him,[57] and in mid-1993 England was horrified by the kidnapping and killing of 2-year-old James Bolger—a crime committed by two 10-year-olds.[58]

GANGS

Juvenile gangs have been an inner-city phenomenon for decades. Detailed descriptions of gang activities in the United States date from the 1920s and 1930s.[59] Recent gang activities, however, differ substantially from those early reports. Whereas membership in early gangs served to provide some sense of personal identity in the cultural heterogeneity of the immigrant's world, many of today's juvenile gangs have developed into financial enterprises. Their activities may center on the acquisition and sale of stolen goods, and on drug running. They use ruthless violence to protect financial opportunities. One study of an East Coast gang of the 1930s found that weapons of choice included milk bottles, flower pots, and banana tree stalks.[60] In contrast, some members of large-city gangs today brandish semiautomatic weapons and Uzi submachine guns.

Gangs exist in many of our nation's major cities, and evidence shows that they are spreading to still others. Los Angeles is considered the "gang capital"[61] with more than 70,000 juveniles participating in over 600 different gangs. During 1992 Los Angeles

A teenage girl negotiates the price of crack in a run down North Philadelphia neighborhood. The problem of drug abuse has been exacerbated by the decline of inner-city areas. *Photo: Eugene Richards/Magnum.*

County saw more than 800 gang-related homicides, and over 12,000 injuries were caused by gang activity.[62]

Most Los Angeles gangs are loosely affiliated with two large groups—the Crips and the Bloods. Drugs form the centerpiece of gang activity, with large quantities of "crack"—a highly addictive form of cocaine—being produced and sold by many groups.

Los Angeles police have resorted to massive arrests in order to gain some control over the gang problem. The first LAPD sweep focused on city schools, where officers made 127 arrests, half of them for felonies.[63] However, few arrested juveniles remain in custody for long. In California, one report found gang culture flourishing inside of California Youth Authority (CYA) institutions, with members of rival gangs forming branches for protection.[64]

Local police efforts may not be enough to stem gang violence. Current evidence indicates that as many as 25 Los Angeles street gangs are expanding their drug activities into other cities across the United States. Authorities have been able to pinpoint L.A. gang involvement in drug transactions involving 45 American cities from Anchorage, Alaska, to Washington, D.C.[65]

Runaways

The U.S. Department of Health and Human Services puts the number of children reported missing each year at over 1.5 million.[66] A 1990 in-depth study[67] of missing children found that the largest subgroup (approximately 583,000) are runaways, while a sizable proportion (approximately 190,000) are "thrownaways"—children no longer wanted by their parents. Family abductions and children who are lost through accident, injury, or misadventure make up the remainder of all missing children. Although most runaway children eventually return home, there is evidence that runaway and thrownaway children are beginning to contribute to the increasing number of homeless on city streets.

Los Angeles gang members display signs of membership in front of a street mural. *Photo: A. Reininger/Woodfin Camp & Associates.*

Children run away for a variety of reasons. Some come from homes where there is little love and affection. Others clash with their parents over disputed activities within the home, problems in school, and because of difficulties with friends. Some are lured away from home by the promise of drugs or the money that drugs might bring. Official statistics show that one-third of runaways leave home because of sexual abuse,[68] while another half leave because of beatings.

Whatever the reason, the number of runaway children has become a problem of near-epidemic proportions. The Office for Juvenile Justice and Delinquency Prevention estimates that the vast majority of those children "who remain at large for a few weeks will resort to theft or prostitution as a method of self-support."[69] Of all children who do run away, only approximately 20% will ever come into official contact with police or social service agencies.[70]

The juvenile justice system is hampered by statute in its ability to deal effectively with runaways. Running away from home is not a criminal act. Under the 1974 Juvenile Justice and Delinquency Prevention Act runaways are designated status offenders. As a result, although many runaway children are placed in unguarded group homes by police officers and social service workers, neither shelter workers nor the police have any legal authority to force a child to stay in the facility.

There are no illegitimate children—only illegitimate parents.

—*U.S. District Court Judge Leon R. Yankwich*
  Zipkin *v.* Mozon (*1928*)

In recent years the number of runaway children has become a problem of near-epidemic proportions. This adolescent runaway lives under a highway overpass in Hollywood, California. *Photo: Dorothy Littell/Stock Boston.*

Short-term solutions to the runaway problem are being sought in clearinghouses for cataloging and disseminating information about missing and located children. The Missing Children Act of 1982 mandates that the parents, legal guardians, or the next of kin of missing children may have information about a missing child entered into the FBI's National Criminal Information Center (NCIC). The essence of these information strategies is speed. The fast dissemination of information, and the rapid reunion of family members with runaway children may provide the best hope that distraught children can be persuaded to return home.

Until the Juvenile Justice and Delinquency Prevention Act is amended to provide states and local jurisdictions with the needed authority to take runaway children into custody and safely control them, however, the problem of runaways will remain. The U.S. Attorney General's Advisory Board on Missing Children has called for just such a change,[71] and indications are that it won't be long in coming.

Sexual abuse

Some parents exploit their children for personal gain. In a famous case of a few years ago, a mother living in Ft. Lauderdale, Florida, was sentenced to a year in prison and two years of house arrest for forcing her 17-year-old daughter to work as a topless dancer.[72] The daughter committed suicide.

THEORY INTO PRACTICE

PARENTS ON TRIAL

Faced with a significant increase in crime among juveniles, a number of jurisdictions have responded with laws which place responsibility for children's behavior squarely on the parents. California's Street Terrorism Enforcement and Prevention Act, one of the first of its kind in the nation, subjects parents of wayward youths to arrest. Gloria Williams, the first person arrested[1] under the law, was charged with neglecting her parental duties after her 15-year-old son was charged with rape. Police said photo evidence proved she had known her son was a gang member. Charges against her were dropped when she was able to show that she had taken a parenting course in an effort to gain better control over her son.

A number of other states now have similar laws. In 1989 Florida legislators enacted a statute which imposes a five-year prison term and a $5,000 fine on the parents of children who find and use guns left around the house. In Indiana, based upon the testimony of a state psychiatrist that the parent's drug and alcohol abuse had contributed to their son's delinquency, a judge recently ordered the boy's mother, Judy Carnahan, to repay the state more than $30,000 for the treatment her son received while incarcerated. In Wisconsin, a 1985 law makes both sets of grandparents financially liable for a child born to unmarried minor children. The purpose of the Wisconsin law is to reduce abortion and prevent teenage pregnancy by making parents financially responsible for their children's sexual behavior. Wisconsin also has a law which can cause welfare parents to lose their benefits if their children are habitually truant from school.

Some cities are beginning to follow the trend of the states. After 25 youngsters were killed in two years of gang violence, Atlanta passed an 11 P.M. curfew for anyone under 17 enforceable by a $1,000 fine with which the parents of violators can be saddled.[2]

Supporters of the new laws say they are trying to force parents to be parents. Critics claim that the statutes go "well beyond the pale of traditional law."[3] The American Civil Liberties Union, for example, objects strenuously to the idea that now people can go to prison for a crime committed by someone else. "[T]he crime is having a kid who commits a crime…," says Jay Jacobson, director of the Arkansas section of the ACLU. In 1993 the California Supreme Court, in the case of *Williams* v. *Garcetti*, unanimously upheld California's statute. Whether or not the new laws ultimately survive challenges to their constitutionality—which are bound to continue—they represent, for the moment at least, society's interest in using the familial bond as a mechanism of social control.

[1]"Now, Parents on Trial," *Newsweek*, October 2, 1989, pp. 54–55.
[2]*ABC Nightly News*, December 17, 1990.
[3]"Now, Parents on Trial," p. 55.

Many parents, driven by a significant increase in crimes against children, make special efforts to assist in the identification of their offspring. Here a Concord, Massachusetts, policeman finger-prints a young girl. *Photo: Bruce M. Wellman/Stock Boston.*

All states have laws circumscribing the procuring of minor children for sexual performances. In recent years the sexual abuse of children has repeatedly made headlines. In some parts of the country, day care center operators have been charged with the sexual molestation of their charges, and many grade schools now routinely train young children to resist and report the inappropriate advances of adults.

Much of the concern is over pedophiles who seek sexual gratification through physical contact with children. One recent study of 561 child molesters found that the typical molester is male, molests children outside the home (is not generally an adoptive father or stepfather), is five times more likely to victimize boys than girls, and has committed 281 acts of molestation prior to coming to the attention of authorities.[73] Child pornography also victimizes young people by involving them in activities and situations beyond what their years have prepared them for.

OTHER FORMS OF ABUSE

Most forms of child abuse are crimes committed by adults against children. Because they are the crimes of adults they are not discussed in detail in this chapter. All forms of abuse, however, are damaging to children and should be prosecuted. Some forms of abuse, such as the instance of sexual procurement mentioned earlier, may lead to the child's involvement in delinquency. Parental encouragement of delinquency is a problem sometimes encountered by juveniles who come from families already engaged in criminal activities. Prostitutes, for example, sometimes encourage their daughters to learn the profession. In families where the theft and sale of stolen goods is a way of life, children may be recruited for shoplifting or for burglaries which require wiggling into tight spaces where an adult might not fit.

Research has shown that children who are encouraged in delinquency by adults tend to become criminals when they reach maturity. More surprising, however, is the finding that abused children have a similar tendency toward adult criminality.[74] A recent National Institute of Justice survey found that children "who had been abused or neglected...were more likely to be arrested as juveniles, as adults, and for a violent crime."[75] Although some recent studies[76] have questioned the strength of the relationship, maltreatment and delinquency appear to be intertwined. If so, early intervention into abusive environments may lead to an overall reduction in future criminality.

Unfortunately, however, some studies show that police officers called to the scene of child abuse situations are reluctant to make an arrest or even to report cases to social service agencies.[77] In an effort to support vigorous prosecution of child abuse cases, the National Center for the Prosecution of Child Abuse was formed in 1985.[78] The Center serves as a national clearinghouse for legal and other information on child abuse and publishes comprehensive training manuals and materials for prosecutors and police officers to use in attacking the child abuse problem. (See Figure 14–3.)

> Our vision is that every child experience success in caring families and nurturing communities that cherish children and teach them to value family and community.

—*Juvenile Executive Assembly (1992)*

A memorial to 12-year-old Polly Klaas, whose recent kidnapping and murder galvanized the nation. *Photo: Bettman.*

TEEN SUICIDE

Children today face many stressors unheard of years ago. Drugs, peer pressure, parents' insistence on success, sexual and other forms of abuse, and violent and broken homes lead some children to take their own lives. In mid-1993, with her mother terminally ill, 6-year-old Jackie Johnson of Dania, Florida, told friends she wanted to be with the angels—then calmly stepped in front of a speeding freight train.[79] Her brother, sister, and cousin watched. In late May 1991, Susan Zingales and Julie Pallach, two 14-year-old girls, sat on train tracks outside of Chicago[80] with their knees drawn up and their hands covering their ears as they waited for a commuter train to come around a curve in the tracks. Both died at the scene as the train ran over them. The girls' suicides shocked suburban Round Lake, Illinois, where both had been on the Magee Middle School basketball team. The two left behind a suicide note which said that life had become unbearably stressful.

Suicide among teenagers is a quickly growing phenomenon. Only 475 teenage suicides were recorded across the nation in 1960, but by 1988, the most recent year for which reliable data are available, 2,059 such deaths were reported—bringing the suicide rate for 15- to 19-year-old teenagers to 11.3 per 100,000. Although no one is certain why suicide rates are on the increase, some warning signals have been identified. The American Academy of Child and Adolescent Psychiatry,[81] for example, cites the following indicators that a teenager may be suicidal: (1) changes in eating habits; (2) changes in sleep patterns; (3) withdrawal from friends, family members, and school activities; (4) rebellious or violent behavior; (5) running away; (6) drug or alcohol abuse; (7) disregard for personal hygiene; (8) decline in the quality of school work and grades; (9) frequent headaches, fatigue, and stomachaches; (10) constant boredom; (11) giving away favorite personal possessions; and (12) verbal clues, such as "this is the last time we will be together."

FIGURE 14-3 Reports of child abuse and neglect, 1976–1992. *Sources:* The American Association for Protecting Children and the National Committee for Prevention of Child Abuse.

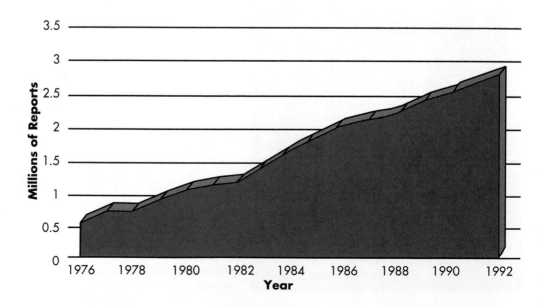

WHAT CAN BE DONE?

Although the problems facing children today are many and varied, there are those who believe that children in trouble share some characteristics in common. Broken homes, little parental contact, poor role models, lack of educational opportunity, and poverty are seen as factors contributing to delinquency and later criminality. In 1991, a bipartisan national commission[82] issued a comprehensive plan for improving the lives of the nation's children. Headed by Senator John D. Rockefeller (D., W.V.), the commission pointed to the added expense faced by those raising children and called for a $1,000 tax credit for each child, regardless of family income or size. To pay the bill for the plan, estimated at an additional $40 billion over current federal budgetary levels, the commission proposed higher taxes on industries and employers. The report also called for (1) a federal health insurance plan for children and pregnant women; (2) tougher enforcement of child support judgments, including a federally supported fund which would pay support when benefits could not be collected; (3) a broadening of the Head Start program; (4) additional family-oriented practices, such as day care opportunities and family leave policies, among private and government employers; and (5) major reforms to the welfare system designed to encourage the development of strong families.

Although the report was widely praised, critics cited the plan's potential to increase the American birth rate via cash payments to parents for their offspring. Other critics charged that many families who stood to receive the credits might decide to spend them on things unrelated to the welfare of children.

SIGNIFICANT COURT DECISIONS

AFFECTING JUVENILES

Throughout the first half of this century, the U.S. Supreme Court followed a "hands-off" approach to juvenile justice. The adjudication and further processing of juveniles by the system was left mostly to specialized juvenile courts or local appeals courts. Although one or two early Supreme Court decisions[83] dealt with issues of juvenile justice, it was not until the 1960s that the Court began close legal scrutiny of the principles which underlay the system itself.

KENT V. U.S., 383 U.S. 541 (1966)

The first U.S. Supreme Court case to have a significant impact on the juvenile justice system was *Kent* v. *U.S.*,[84] decided in 1966. The *Kent* case focused upon the long-accepted concept of *parens patriae* and signaled the beginning of a systematic review by the Court of all lower court practices involving delinquency hearings.

Morris Kent, Jr., age 14, was apprehended in the District of Columbia in 1959 and charged with several house burglaries and an attempted purse snatching. Kent was placed on juvenile probation and released into the custody of his mother. In September 1961, an intruder entered a woman's Washington apartment, took her wallet, and raped her. At the scene police found fingerprints which matched those on file belonging to Morris Kent. At the time Kent was 16 years old and, according to the laws of the District of Columbia, was still under the exclusive jurisdiction of the juvenile court.

Kent was taken into custody and interrogated. He volunteered information about the crime and spoke about other offenses involving burglary, robbery, and rape. Following interrogation his mother retained counsel on his behalf. Kent was kept in custody for another week, during which time psychological and psychiatric evaluations were conducted. Reports from professionals conducting the evaluations concluded that Kent was a "victim of severe psychopathology." The juvenile court judge hearing the case did not confer with Kent, his parents, or their lawyer. The judge, however, ruled that Kent should be remanded to the authority of the adult court system, and he was eventually tried in U.S. District Court for the District of Columbia. The judge gave no reasons for assigning Kent to the adult court.

Kent was indicted in criminal court on eight counts of burglary, robbery, and rape. Citing the psychological evaluations performed earlier, Kent's lawyers argued that his behavior was the product of mental disease or defect. Their defense proved fruitless, and Kent was found guilty on six counts of burglary and robbery. He was sentenced to 5 to 15 years in prison on each count.

Kent's lawyers appealed ultimately to the U.S. Supreme Court. They argued that Kent should have been entitled to an adequate hearing at the level of the juvenile court and that, lacking such a hearing, his transfer to adult jurisdiction was unfair.

The Supreme Court, agreeing with Kent's attorneys, reversed the decision of the district court and ordered adequate hearings for juveniles being considered for transfer to adult court. At such hearings, the Court ruled, juveniles are entitled to representation by attorneys who must have access to their records.

Although it focused only on a narrow issue, the *Kent* decision was especially important because, for the first time, the need for at least minimal due process in juvenile court hearings was recognized. The *Kent* decision set the stage for what was to come, but it was the *Gault* decision, to which we now turn our attention, that bent the juvenile justice system upside down.

IN RE GAULT, 387 U.S. 1 (1967)

On June 8, 1964 Gerald Gault and a friend, Ronald Lewis, were taken into custody by the Sheriff of Gila County, Arizona, on the basis of a complaint filed by a neighbor who alleged that the boys had telephoned her, making lewd remarks. At the time, Gault was on probation for having been in the company of another boy who had stolen a wallet.

When Gerald was apprehended, his parents were both at work. No notice was posted at their house to indicate that their son had been taken into custody, a fact which they later learned from Lewis's parents. Gault's parents could learn very little from authorities. Although they were notified when their son's initial hearing would be held, they were not told the nature of the complaint against him. Nor could they learn the identity of the complainant, who was not present at the hearing.

At the hearing the only evidence presented were statements made by young Gault and testimony given by the juvenile officer as to what the complainant had alleged. Gault was not represented by counsel. He admitted having made the phone call, but stated that after dialing the number he turned the phone over to his friend, Ronald. After hearing the testimony, Judge McGhee ordered a second hearing, to be held a week later.

At the second hearing Mrs. Gault requested that the complainant be present so that she could identify the voice of the person making the lewd call. Judge McGhee ruled against her request. Finally, young Gault was adjudicated delinquent and remanded to the State Industrial School until his twenty-first birthday.

On appeal, eventually to the U.S. Supreme Court, Gault's attorney argued that his constitutional rights were violated due to the denial of due process inherent in all juvenile proceedings. The appeal focused specifically on six areas:

1. *Notice of charges.* Gault was not given notice sufficiently in advance to prepare a reasonable defense to the charges against him.
2. *Right to counsel.* Gault was not notified of his right to an attorney or allowed to have one at his hearing.
3. *Right to confront and to cross-examine witnesses.* The court did not require the complainant to appear at the hearing.
4. *Protection against self-incrimination.* Gault was never advised that he had the right to remain silent, nor was he informed that his testimony could be used against him.
5. *Right to a transcript.* In preparing for the appeal, Gault's attorney was not provided a transcript of the adjudicatory hearing.
6. *Right to appeal.* At the time, the state of Arizona did not give juveniles the right to appeal.

The Supreme Court ruled in Gault's favor on four of the six issues raised by his attorneys. The majority opinion read, in part, as follows:

> In *Kent* v. *United States*, we stated that the Juvenile Court Judge's exercise of the power of the state as *parens patriae* was not unlimited.... Notice, to comply with due process requirements, must be given sufficiently in advance of scheduled court proceedings so that reasonable opportunity to prepare will be afforded.... The probation officer cannot act as counsel for the child. His role in the adjudicatory hearing, by statute and in fact, is as arresting officer and witness against the child. There is no material difference in this respect between adult and juvenile proceedings of the sort here involved.... A proceeding where the issue is whether the child will be found to be "delinquent" and subjected to the loss of his liberty for years is comparable in seriousness to a felony prosecution. The juvenile needs the assistance of counsel to cope with the problems of law, to make skilled inquiry into the facts, to insist upon regularity of the proceedings, and to ascertain whether he has a defense and to prepare and submit it.

The Court did not agree with the contention of Gault's lawyers relative to appeal, nor with their arguments in favor of transcripts. Right to appeal, where it exists, is usually granted by statute or by state constitution—not by the Constitution of the United States. Similarly, the Court did not require a transcript because (1) there is no constitutional right to a transcript, and (2) no transcripts are produced in the trials of most adult misdemeanants.

Today the impact of *Gault* is widely felt in the juvenile justice system. Juveniles are now guaranteed many of the same procedural rights as adults. Most precedent-setting Supreme Court decisions which followed *Gault* further clarified the rights of juveniles, focusing primarily on those few issues of due process not explicitly addressed by this precedent-setting case.

IN RE WINSHIP, 397 U.S. 358 (1970)

A New York Family Court judge found Winship, then a 12-year-old boy, delinquent on the basis of a petition which alleged that he had illegally entered a locker and stolen $112 from a pocketbook. The judge acknowledged to those present at the hearing that the evidence in the case might not be sufficient to establish Winship's guilt beyond a reasonable doubt. Statutory authority, however, in the form of the New York Family Court Act required a determination of facts based only on a *preponderance of the evidence*—the same standard required in civil suits. Winship was sent to a training school for 18 months, subject to extensions until his eighteenth birthday.

Winship's appeal to the U.S. Supreme Court centered on the evidentiary standard used by the lower court. His attorney argued that Winship's guilt should have been proven beyond a reasonable doubt—the evidentiary standard of adult criminal trials. The Court agreed, ruling that

> the constitutional safeguard of proof beyond a reasonable doubt is as much required during the adjudicatory stage of a delinquency proceeding as are those constitutional guards applied in *Gault*.... We therefore hold…that where a 12 year old child is charged with an act of stealing which renders him liable to confinement for as long as six years, then, as a matter of due process…the case against him must be proved beyond a reasonable doubt.

As a consequence of *Winship*, allegations of delinquency today must be established beyond a reasonable doubt. The court allowed, however, the continued use of the lower evidentiary standard in adjudicating juveniles charged with status offenses. Even though both standards continue to exist, most jurisdictions have chosen to use the stricter burden of proof requirement for all delinquency proceedings.

McKEIVER V. PENNSYLVANIA, 403 U.S. 528 (1971)

Cases like *Winship* and *Gault* have not extended all adult procedural rights to juveniles charged with delinquency. Juveniles, for example, do not have the constitutional right to trial by a jury of their peers. The case of *McKeiver* v. *Pennsylvania*[85] (1971) reiterated what earlier decisions had established and legitimized some generally accepted practices of juvenile courts.

Joseph McKeiver, age 16, was charged with robbery, larceny, and receiving stolen property, all felonies in the state of Pennsylvania. McKeiver had been involved with 20 to 30 other juveniles who chased three teenage boys and took 25 cents from them. He had no previous arrests and was able to demonstrate a record of gainful employment. McKeiver's attorney requested that his client be allowed a jury trial. The request was denied. McKeiver was adjudicated delinquent and committed to a youth development center. McKeiver's attorney pursued a series of appeals and was finally granted a hearing before the U.S. Supreme Court. There he argued that his client, even though a juvenile, should have had the opportunity for a jury trial as guaranteed by the Sixth and Fourteenth Amendments to the Constitution.

The Court, although recognizing existent difficulties in the administration of juvenile justice, held to the belief that jury trials for juveniles were not mandated by the Constitution. In the opinion of the Court:

> The imposition of the jury trial on the juvenile court system would not strengthen greatly, if at all, the fact-finding function, and would contrarily, provide an attrition of the juvenile court's assumed ability to function in a unique manner. It would not remedy the defects of the system.... If the jury trial were to be injected into the juvenile court system as a matter of right, it would bring with it into that system the traditional delay, the formality, and the clamor of the adversary system and, possibly, the public trial.... If the formalities of the criminal adjudicative process are to be superimposed upon the juvenile court system, there is little need for its separate existence.

CHAPTER 14

McKeiver v. *Pennsylvania* did not set any new standards. Rather, it reinforced the long-accepted practice of conducting juvenile adjudicatory hearings in the absence of certain due process considerations, particularly those pertaining to trial by jury. It is important to note, however, that the *McKeiver* decision did not specifically prohibit jury trials for juveniles. As a consequence, approximately 12 states today continue to provide for the option of jury trials for juveniles.

Breed v. Jones, 421 U.S. 519 (1975)

On February 2, 1971, a delinquency petition was filed against Jones, age 17, alleging that he committed robbery while armed with a deadly weapon. At the adjudicatory hearing, Jones was declared delinquent. A later dispositional hearing determined that Jones was "unfit for treatment as a juvenile," and he was transferred to Superior Court for trial as an adult. The Superior Court found Jones guilty of robbery in the first degree and committed him to the custody of the California Youth Authority.

In an appeal eventually heard by the Supreme Court, Jones alleged that his transfer to adult court, and the trial which ensued, placed him in double jeopardy because he had already been adjudicated in juvenile court. Double jeopardy is prohibited by Fifth and Fourteenth Amendments to the Constitution. The state of California argued that Superior Court trial was only a natural continuation of the juvenile justice process and, as a consequence, did not fall under the rubric of double jeopardy. The state further suggested that double jeopardy existed only where an individual ran the risk of being punished more than once. In the case of *Jones* no punishment had been imposed by the juvenile court.

The U.S. Supreme Court did not agree that the possibility of only one punishment negated double jeopardy. The Court pointed to the fact that the double jeopardy clause speaks in terms of "potential risk of trial and conviction—not punishment," and concluded that two separate adjudicatory processes were sufficient to warrant a finding of double jeopardy. Jones's conviction was vacated, clearing the way for him to be returned to juvenile court. However, by the time the litigation had been completed, Jones was beyond the age of juvenile court jurisdiction and he was released from custody.

The *Jones* case severely restricted the conditions under which transfers from juvenile to adult courts may occur. In effect the court mandated that such transfers as do occur must be made prior to an adjudicatory hearing in juvenile court.

Schall v. Martin, 104 467 U.S. 253 (1984)

Gregory Martin, age 14, was arrested in New York City and charged with robbery and weapons possession. He was detained for more than two weeks in a secure detention facility until his hearing. The detention order drew its authority from a New York preventive detention law which allowed for the jailing of juveniles thought to represent a high risk of continued delinquency.

Martin was adjudicated delinquent. His case eventually reached the U.S. Supreme Court, on the claim that the New York detention law had effectively denied Martin's freedom prior to conviction and that it was therefore in violation of the Fourteenth Amendment to the U.S. Constitution.

The U.S. Supreme Court upheld the constitutionality of the New York statute. The Court ruled that states have a legitimate interest in preventing future delinquency by juveniles thought to be dangerous. Preventive detention, the Court reasoned, is nonpunitive in its intent and is, therefore, not a "punishment."

While the *Schall* decision upheld the practice of preventive detention, it seized upon the opportunity provided by the case to impose procedural requirements upon the detaining authority. Consequently, preventive detention today cannot be imposed without (1) prior notice, (2) an equitable detention hearing, and (3) a statement by the judge setting forth the reason(s) for detention.

A SUMMARY OF DIFFERENCES IN ADULT AND JUVENILE JUSTICE

The cases we've discussed have two common characteristics. They all (1) turn on due process guarantees specified by the Bill of Rights and (2) make the claim that adult due process should serve as a model for juvenile proceedings. Due process guarantees, as interpreted by the court, are clearly designed to ensure that juvenile proceedings are fair and that the interests of juveniles are protected. Those interpretations do not, however, offer any pretense of providing juveniles with the same kinds of protections guaranteed to adult defendants. While the high court has tended to agree that juveniles are entitled to the protection of due process, it has refrained from declaring that juveniles have a right to all the aspects of due process afforded adult defendants.

Juvenile court philosophy brings with it other differences from the adult system. Among them are (1) an absence of legal guilt, (2) a primacy of treatment rather than punishment, (3) privacy and protection from public scrutiny, (4) an emphasis on the techniques of social science in dispositional decision making, (5) no long-term confinement,

Although the physical conditions surrounding the confinement of children may often be bleak, most jurisdictions no longer hold juveniles in adult facilities. *Photo: AP/Wide World Photos.*

(6) separate facilities for juveniles, and (7) broad discretionary alternatives at all points in the process.[86] This combination of court philosophy and due process requirements yields a unique justice system for juveniles which takes into consideration the special needs of young people while offering reasonable protection to society.

OTHER LEGAL ASPECTS OF THE JUVENILE JUSTICE PROCESS

Most jurisdictions today have statutes designed to extend the *Miranda* provisions to juveniles. Many police officers routinely offer *Miranda* warnings to juveniles in their custody prior to questioning. Less clear, however, is whether or not juveniles are able to legally waive their *Miranda* rights. A 1979 U.S. Supreme Court ruling held that juveniles should be accorded the opportunity to a knowing waiver where they were old enough and sufficiently educated to understand the consequences of a waiver.[87] A later high court ruling upheld the murder conviction of a juvenile who had been advised of his rights and waived them in the presence of his mother.[88]

An emerging area of juvenile rights centers on investigative procedures. In 1985, for example, the Supreme Court ruled in *New Jersey* v. *T.L.O.*[89] that schoolchildren have a reasonable expectation of privacy in personal property. The case involved a 14-year-old girl who was accused of violating school rules by smoking in a high school bathroom. A vice principal searched the girl's purse and found evidence of marijuana use. Juvenile officers were called, and the girl was eventually adjudicated in juvenile court and found delinquent.

Upon appeal to the New Jersey Supreme Court lawyers for Ms. T.L.O. were successful in having her conviction reversed on the grounds that the search of her purse, as an item of personal property, had been unreasonable. The state's appeal to the U.S. Supreme Court resulted in a ruling which prohibited school officials from engaging in *unreasonable* searches of students or their property. A reading of the Court's decision leads to the conclusion that a search could be considered reasonable if it: (1) is based upon a logical suspicion of rule-breaking actions; (2) is required to maintain order, discipline, and safety among students; and (3) does not exceed the scope of the original suspicion.

LEGISLATION

In response to the rapidly increasing crime rates of the late 1960s, Congress enacted the Omnibus Crime Control and Safe Streets Act (1968). The act was to provide money and technical assistance for states and municipalities seeking to modernize their justice systems. The Safe Streets Act, in combination with monies funneled through the Law Enforcement Assistance Administration, the Youth Development and Delinquency Prevention Administration of the Department of Health, Education, and Welfare, and the Model Cities Program of the Department of Housing and Urban Development, provided funding for youth services bureaus. Youth services bureaus had been recommended by the 1967 presidential commission report *The Challenge of Crime in a Free Society*. Such bureaus were to be available to police, juvenile courts, and probation departments in order to act as a centralized community resource in handling delinquents and status offenders. Youth services bureaus also handled juveniles referred to them by schools and self-referrals. Guidelines for setting up and running youth services bureaus were provided through the Youth Development and Delinquency Prevention Administration and the National Council on Crime and Delinquency. Unfortunately,

THEORY INTO PRACTICE

A COMPARISON OF ADULT AND JUVENILE JUSTICE SYSTEMS IN THE UNITED STATES

Adult Proceedings	*Juvenile Proceedings*
Focus on criminality	Focus on delinquency and a special category of "status offenses"
Comprehensive rights against unreasonable searches of person, home, and possessions	Limited rights against unreasonable searches
A right against self-incrimination; a knowing waiver is possible	A right against self-incrimination; waivers are questionable
Assumed innocent until proven guilty	Guilt and innocence are not primary issues; the system focuses on the interests of the child
Adversarial setting	Helping context
Arrest warrants form the basis for most arrests	Petitions or complaints legitimize apprehension
Right to an attorney	Right to an attorney
Public trial	Closed hearing; no right to a jury trial
System goals are punishment and reformation	System goals are protection and treatment
No right to treatment	Specific right to treatment
Possibility of bail or release on recognizance	Release into parental custody
Public record of trial and judgment	Sealed records; may be destroyed by specified age
Possible incarceration in adult correctional facility	Separate facilities at all levels.

within a decade after their establishment, most youth services bureaus had succumbed to a lack of continued federal funding.

In 1974, recognizing the special needs of juveniles, Congress passed the Juvenile Justice and Delinquency Prevention Act (JJDP). Employing much the same strategy as the 1968 bill, the Delinquency Prevention Act provided federal grants to states and cities seeking to improve their handling and disposition of delinquents and status offenders.

Nearly all states chose to accept federal monies through the JJDP Act. Two conditions attached to funding, however:

1. Participating states were required to agree to a "separation mandate," under which juveniles were not to be held in institutions where they might come into regular contact with adult prisoners.
2. Status offenders were to be deinstitutionalized. States receiving funding under the JJDP Act had five years to meet both conditions.

Within a few years institutional populations were cut by more than half and community alternatives to juvenile institutionalization were rapidly being developed. Jailed juveniles were housed in separate wings of adult facilities or removed from adult jails entirely. When the JJDP Act was reauthorized for funding in 1980, the separation mandate was expanded to include a new jail removal mandate requiring physically separate detention facilities exclusively for juveniles. Studies supporting reauthorization of the JJDP Act in 1984 and 1988, however, found that nearly half the states had failed to come into "substantial compliance" with the jail removal mandate. As a consequence, Congress modified the requirements of the act, continuing funding for states making "meaningful progress" toward removing juveniles from adult jails.[90] Recent reauthorizations of the Juvenile Justice and Delinquency Prevention Bill have found a significant new focus in combating gang delinquency and in addressing the issue of minority overrepresentation in the juvenile justice system.

THE JUVENILE JUSTICE PROCESS TODAY

Modern juvenile court jurisdiction rests upon the twin bases of age and conduct. The majority of states today define a child subject to juvenile court jurisdiction as a person who has not yet reached his or her eighteenth birthday. A few states set the age at 16, and several use 17 or 19. Table 14–1 lists the ages at which children in various states leave the purview of the juvenile court and become subject to the jurisdiction of adult criminal courts.

Depending upon the laws of the state and the behavior involved, the jurisdiction of the juvenile court may be exclusive. Exclusive jurisdiction applies when the juvenile court is the only court that has statutory authority to deal with children for specified infractions. For example, status offenses such as truancy normally fall within the exclusive jurisdiction of juvenile courts. Delinquency, however, which involves violations of the criminal law, is often not within the exclusive jurisdiction of juvenile court. All 50 states, the District of Columbia, and the federal government have judicial waiver provisions which allow for juveniles who commit serious crimes to be bound over to criminal court, although in practice few such transfers occur.[91] Juveniles who commit violent crimes or who have prior records are among the most likely to be transferred to adult courts.[92] In a hearing which made headlines in 1989, Cameron Kocher, a 10-year-old Pennsylvania youngster, was arraigned as an adult for the murder of 7-year-old Jessica Carr.[93] Cameron, 9 years old at the time of the crime, was alleged to have used his father's scope-sighted hunting rifle to shoot the girl from a bedroom window while she was riding on a snowmobile in a neighbor's yard. The two had argued earlier over who would get to ride on the vehicle. The case was resolved in 1992 when the Pennsylvania supreme court overruled Kocher's arraignment as an adult, and the boy was placed on probation.

Where juvenile court authority is not exclusive, the jurisdiction of the court may be original or concurrent. Original jurisdiction means that a particular offense must originate, or begin, with juvenile court authorities. Juvenile courts have original jurisdiction over most delinquency petitions, and all status offenses. Concurrent jurisdiction exists where other courts have equal statutory authority to originate proceedings. If a juvenile has committed a homicide, rape, or other serious crime, for example, an arrest warrant may be issued by the adult court.

T A B L E   1 4 - 1

AGES AT WHICH CRIMINAL COURTS GAIN JURISDICTION OVER YOUNG OFFENDERS

Age of Offender When Under Criminal Court Jurisdiction	States
16 years	Connecticut, New York, North Carolina
17	Georgia, Illinois, Louisiana, Massachusetts, Missouri, South Carolina, Texas
18	Alabama, Alaska, Arizona, Arkansas, California, Colorado, Delaware, District of Columbia, Florida, Hawaii, Idaho, Indiana, Iowa, Kansas, Kentucky, Maine, Maryland, Michigan, Minnesota, Mississippi, Montana, Nebraska, Nevada, New Hampshire, New Jersey, New Mexico, North Dakota, Ohio, Oklahoma, Oregon, Pennsylvania, Rhode Island, South Dakota, Tennessee, Utah, Vermont, Virginia, Washington, West Virginia, Wisconsin, federal districts
19	Wyoming

Source: Bureau of Justice Statistics, *Report to the Nation on Crime and Justice,* 2nd ed. (Washington, D.C.: U.S. Department of Justice, 1988), p. 79.

Some states specify that juvenile courts have no jurisdiction over certain excluded offenses. Delaware, Louisiana, and Nevada, for example, allow no juvenile court jurisdiction over children charged with first-degree murder.

THE   SYSTEM

The juvenile justice system can be viewed as a process which, when carried to completion, moves through four stages. They are intake, adjudication, disposition, and postadjudication review. Though organizationally similar to the adult criminal justice process, the juvenile system is far more likely to maximize the use of discretion and to employ diversion at every point in the process.

Intake

Delinquent juveniles may come to the attention of the police or juvenile court authorities either through arrest or via the filing of a **juvenile petition** by an aggrieved party. Juvenile petitions are much like criminal complaints in that they allege illegal behavior. Petitions are most often filed by teachers, school administrators, neighbors, store managers, or others who have frequent contact with juveniles. Parents, unable to control the

Juvenile Petition   A document filed in juvenile court alleging that a juvenile is delinquent, a status offender, or a dependent, and asking that the court assume jurisdiction over the juvenile, or asking that an alleged delinquent be transferred to a criminal court for prosecution as an adult.

THEORY INTO PRACTICE

JUVENILE REFORM IN MASSACHUSETTS: AN EXPERIMENT IN RADICAL DEINSTITUTIONALIZATION

An interesting social experiment in the deinstitutionalization of juvenile offenders took place in Massachusetts in the early 1970s. In 1969 the governor of Massachusetts named Dr. Jerome Miller state commissioner of youth services and appointed him to head the newly created Massachusetts Department of Youth Services.[1] Dr. Miller was firmly committed to the belief that institutionalization was a highly negative and criminalizing experience for most juveniles. With the full support of the governor, Miller quickly moved to close every juvenile institution in the state. Deinstitutionalization was accomplished by placing juveniles in foster care, group homes, mental health facilities, and other programs. Many were simply sent home. The problems caused by hard-core offenders among the released juveniles, however, soon convinced authorities that complete deinstitutionalization was not a workable solution to the problem of delinquency. The Massachusetts experiment ended as quickly as it began.

[1] See Yitzhak Baka, ed., *Closing Correctional Institutions* (Lexington, MA: D. C. Health, 1973). See also, Jerome G. Miller, *Last One over the Wall: The Massachusetts Experiment in Closing Reform Schools* (Columbus: The Ohio State University Press, 1991).

behavior of their teenage children, are the source of many other petitions. Crimes in progress result in other juveniles coming to the attention of the police. Three quarters of all referrals to juvenile court come directly from law enforcement authorities.[94]

Many police departments have juvenile officers, specially trained in dealing with juveniles. Because of the emphasis on rehabilitation which characterizes the juvenile justice process, juvenile officers usually have a number of discretionary alternatives available to them, especially in the handling of nonviolent offenses.

In Delaware County, Pennsylvania, for example, police departments participate in "Youth Aid Panels." Such panels are composed of private citizens who volunteer their services in order to provide an alternative to the formal juvenile court process. Youngsters who are referred to a panel, and agree to abide by the decision of the group, are diverted from additional handling by the juvenile court.

Even youth who are eventually diverted from the system may spend some time in custody. One juvenile case in five involves detention prior to adjudication.[95] Unlike the adult system, where jail is seen as the primary custodial alternative for persons awaiting an initial appearance, the use of secure detention for juveniles is acceptable only as a last resort. Detention hearings will investigate whether candidates for confinement represent a "clear and immediate danger to themselves and/or to others." Such a judgment, made through a detention hearing, is normally rendered within 24 hours of apprehension. Runaways, since they are often not dangerous, are especially difficult to confine. Juveniles who are not

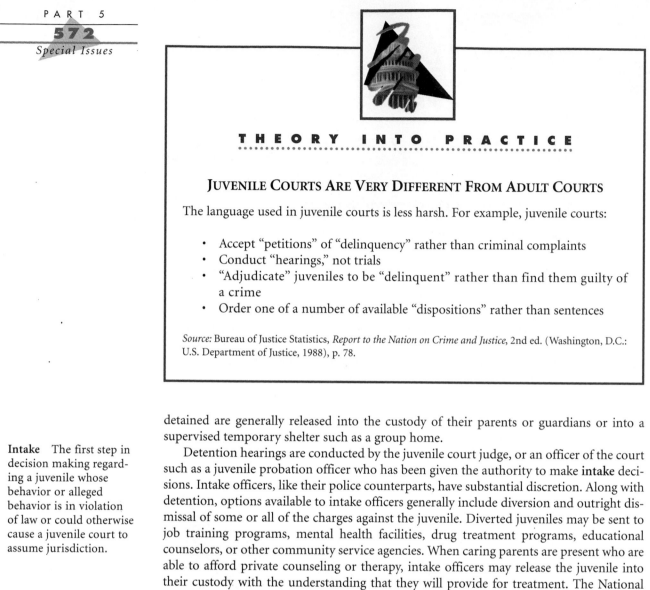

THEORY INTO PRACTICE

JUVENILE COURTS ARE VERY DIFFERENT FROM ADULT COURTS

The language used in juvenile courts is less harsh. For example, juvenile courts:

- Accept "petitions" of "delinquency" rather than criminal complaints
- Conduct "hearings," not trials
- "Adjudicate" juveniles to be "delinquent" rather than find them guilty of a crime
- Order one of a number of available "dispositions" rather than sentences

Source: Bureau of Justice Statistics, *Report to the Nation on Crime and Justice*, 2nd ed. (Washington, D.C.: U.S. Department of Justice, 1988), p. 78.

Intake The first step in decision making regarding a juvenile whose behavior or alleged behavior is in violation of law or could otherwise cause a juvenile court to assume jurisdiction.

detained are generally released into the custody of their parents or guardians or into a supervised temporary shelter such as a group home.

Detention hearings are conducted by the juvenile court judge, or an officer of the court such as a juvenile probation officer who has been given the authority to make **intake** decisions. Intake officers, like their police counterparts, have substantial discretion. Along with detention, options available to intake officers generally include diversion and outright dismissal of some or all of the charges against the juvenile. Diverted juveniles may be sent to job training programs, mental health facilities, drug treatment programs, educational counselors, or other community service agencies. When caring parents are present who are able to afford private counseling or therapy, intake officers may release the juvenile into their custody with the understanding that they will provide for treatment. The National Center for Juvenile Justice estimates that more than half of all juvenile cases disposed of at intake are handled informally without a petition and are dismissed or diverted to a social service agency.[96]

Preliminary Hearing

If a juvenile is in custody, a preliminary hearing may be held in conjunction with the detention hearing. The purpose of the preliminary hearing is to determine if there is probable cause to believe the juvenile committed the alleged act. At the hearing, the juvenile, along with his or her parents or guardian, will be advised of his or her rights as established by state legislation and court precedent. If probable cause is established, the juvenile may still be offered diversionary options, such as an "improvement period" or "probation with adjudication." Such diversionary alternatives usually provide a one-year period during which the juvenile must avoid legal difficulties, attend school, and obey his or her parents. Charges may be dropped at the end of this informal probationary period, provided the juvenile has met the conditions specified.

Where a serious offense is involved, statutory provisions may allow for transfer of the case to adult court. Transfer proceedings generally begin with a request from the prosecuting attorney. Transfer hearings are held in juvenile court and focus on (1) the applicability of transfer statutes to the case under consideration and (2) whether the juvenile is amenable to treatment through the resources available to the juvenile justice system. Exceptions exist where statutes mandate transfer.

Adjudication

Adjudicatory hearings for juveniles are similar to adult trials, with some notable exceptions. Similarities derive from the fact that the due process rights of children and adults are essentially the same. Differences include

1. *No Right to Trial.* As recognized by the U.S. Supreme Court in the case of *McKeiver* v. *Pennsylvania*,[97] juveniles do not have a constitutional right to trial by jury.[98] Nor do most states provide juveniles with a statutory opportunity for jury trial.

    Some jurisdictions, however, allow juveniles to be tried by their peers. The juvenile court in Columbus County, Georgia, for example, began experimenting with peer juries in 1980.[99] In Georgia peer juries are composed of youths under the age of 17 who receive special training by the court. Jurors are required to be successful in school and may not be under the supervision of the court or have juvenile petitions pending against them. Training consists of classroom-like exposure to the philosophy of the juvenile court system, Georgia's juvenile code, and Supreme Court decisions affecting juvenile justice.[100] The county's youthful jurors are used only in the dispositional (or sentencing) stage of the court process, and then only when adjudicated youths volunteer to go before the jury.

    Another early program, after which many have since been modeled, can be found in Odessa, Texas. The Odessa Teen Court was started by the local Junior League in 1983. Since then it has handled thousands of cases, with all major courtroom participants—other than the judge—coming from the ranks of local juveniles. Youngsters fill the role of prosecutor, defense attorney, and a four-person peer jury. As in Georgia, the court does not decide guilt, but imposes sentences only. Defendants are selected by the police from among youngsters who have already pled guilty to relatively minor offenses. The court has been amazingly successful in reducing recidivism. Only 2% of defendants in Odessa's Teen Court go on to commit another crime. As a spokesperson for the Odessa Police Department put it, "It's one peer saying to another, 'This is not acceptable behavior.'…[T]he defendant cannot come back on the grown-up and say, 'You adults don't understand what I am going through.' "[101]

2. *Emphasis on Privacy.* Another important distinction derives from the emphasis on privacy characteristic of the juvenile system. One purpose of privacy is to prevent juveniles from being negatively labeled by the community. In support of privacy, juvenile hearings are not open to the public. Witnesses are permitted to be present only to offer testimony, and not for the duration of the hearing. The media are not accorded direct access to delinquency proceedings, and no transcript of the proceedings is created.

3. *Informality.* While the adult criminal trial is highly structured, the juvenile hearing borders on informality. The courtroom atmosphere may give more the appearance of a friendly discussion than of adversarial battle. The juvenile court judge will take an active role in the fact-finding process rather than serving as arbitrator between prosecution and defense.

Adjudicatory Hearing
The courtroom stage of a juvenile hearing, which is similar in substance to a criminal hearing or trial.

Juvenile court in action. Theoretically, juvenile courts are expected to act in the best interests of the children who come before them. *Photo: Billy Barnes/Stock Boston.*

4. *Speed.* Informality, the lack of a jury, and the absence of an adversarial environment promote speed. While the adult trial may run into days, or even months, the juvenile hearing is normally completed in a matter of hours or days.
5. *Evidentiary Standard.* Upon completion of the hearing, the juvenile court judge must weigh the evidence. If the charge involves a status offense, the judge may adjudicate the juvenile upon a "preponderance of the evidence." If the charge involves a criminal-type offense, the evidentiary standard rises to the level of "reasonable doubt."
6. *Philosophy of the Court.* Even in the face of strong evidence pointing to the guilt of the juvenile, the judge may decide that it is not in the best interest of the child to be adjudicated delinquent. The judge also has the power, even after the evidence is presented, to divert the juvenile from the system.

    Juvenile court statistics indicate that only 64% of cases which reach the hearing stage result in a finding of delinquency. Of those adjudicated delinquent, 60% are placed on probation, and 29% are placed in an out-of-home environment.[102]

Disposition

Dispositionary Hearing
The final stage in the processing of adjudicated juveniles, in which a decision is made on the form of treatment or penalty which should be imposed upon the child.

Once a juvenile has been found delinquent the judge will set a time for a **dispositional hearing**. Dispositional hearings are similar to adult sentencing hearings. They are used to decide what action the court should take relative to the child. As in adult courts, the judge may order a presentence investigation before making a dispositional decision. Such investigations are conducted by special court personnel, sometimes called juvenile court counselors who are, in effect, juvenile probation officers. Attorneys on both sides of the issue will also have the opportunity to make recommendations concerning dispositional alternatives.

The juvenile justice system typically provides the judge a much wider range of sentencing alternatives than does the adult system. Two major classes of dispositional alternatives exist: to confine or not to confine. Because rehabilitation is the primary objective of the juvenile court, the judge is likely to select the "least restrictive alternative" available in meeting the needs of the juvenile while recognizing the legitimate concerns of society for protection.

Nonconfinement is the most frequently selected judicial alternative in juvenile disposition. Juvenile court statistics indicate that 70% of children adjudicated delinquent (for both criminal and status offenses) are placed on probation.[103] Probatory disposition usually means that juveniles will be released into the custody of a parent or guardian and ordered to undergo some form of training, education, or counseling. As in the adult system, juveniles placed on probation may be ordered to pay fines or make restitution. Because juveniles rarely have financial resources, most economic sanctions take the form of court-ordered work programs, as in the refurbishing of schools, cleaning of school busses, and so on.

Four percent of all dispositionary hearings result in outright release. Twelve percent of adjudicated delinquents are given some "other" (most likely nonsecure) type of sanction.[104] Nearly 30% of dispositionary hearings place the delinquent outside the home.[105] Many are domiciled in nonsecure residential facilities called group homes or halfway houses. Group homes, usually located in the community where the juvenile lives, are thought to be capable of providing a higher level of care than is available to the child's natural home. Children placed in group homes continue to attend school and live in a family-like environment in the company of other adjudicated children, shepherded by "house parents."

INSTITUTIONS FOR JUVENILES

Juveniles who evidence the potential for serious new offenses may be ordered to participate in rehabilitative programs within a secure environment such as a youth center or training school. Juvenile institutions generally have enough security and are sufficiently staffed to manage all but the most difficult delinquents. Some are much like adult prisons in appearance, while others are organized around farms, ranches, forestry camps, or wilderness programs.

The operative philosophy of custodial programs for juveniles focuses squarely on the rehabilitative ideal. Commitment to secure facilities is usually indeterminate, and the typical stay is less than one year, with release timed to coincide with the beginning or end of the school year.

Most juvenile facilities are small, with 80% designed to hold 40 residents or fewer.[106] Many institutionalized juveniles are held in the approximately 1,000 homelike facilities across the nation which are limited to 10 residents or fewer.[107] At the other end of the scale, are the nation's 70 large juvenile institutions, each designed to hold over 200 hard-core delinquents.[108] Residential facilities for juveniles are intensively staffed. One study found that staff members outnumber residents 10 to 9 on the average in state-run institutions, and by an even greater ratio in privately run facilities.[109]

Kids with Special Problems

Institutionalized juveniles are a small, but special category of young people with serious problems. A report on institutionalized youth by the Bureau of Justice Statistics found 12 striking characteristics: Of the total,

Juvenile Disposition
The decision of a juvenile court, concluding a disposition hearing, that an adjudicated juvenile be committed to a juvenile correctional facility, or placed in a juvenile residence, shelter, or care or treatment program, or required to meet certain standards of conduct, or released.

1. 93.1% were male.
2. 46.8% were ethnic minorities or black.
3. 12.7% had completed the sixth grade or less.
4. 2.9% had completed high school.
5. 70% did not live with both parents while growing up.
6. 43% had been arrested more than five times, with over 20% experiencing more than ten arrests in the past year.
7. 39.3% were being held for a violent offense.
8. more than 60% used drugs regularly, and almost 40% were under the influence of drugs at the time of the commission of their offense.
9. 82.2% had previously been on probation.
10. 58.5% had previously been incarcerated.
11. the average age was 15.7 years, with 12.8 years as the average age at first arrest.
12. on average, institutionalized juveniles had spent 8.3% of their lives incarcerated.[110]

Overcrowded Facilities

As in adult prisons, overcrowding exists in many juvenile institutions. A recent study by the Commonweal Research Institute, for example, found that California's juvenile detention facilities, while originally designed to handle a population of 5,840 juveniles, were holding nearly 9,000.[111] One cause of overcrowding is increased length of stay. Another California study found that nearly half of all delinquents in California Youth Authority (CYA) institutions (48.5%) could have been better placed in community-based programs.[112] The number of juveniles under correctional supervision on a state-by-state basis is shown in Table 14–2.

Another cause of overcrowding is the growing use of incarceration for juveniles. Office of Juvenile Justice and Delinquency Prevention (OJJDP) data show that between 1978 and 1989 the number of juveniles in custody increased nationally by 31%, while the *rate* of juvenile detention increased nearly 50% (from 251 per 100,000 juveniles in 1979 to 367 per 100,000 in 1989).[113] In 1989, males constituted the majority of detained juveniles (81%). Reflecting widespread socioeconomic disparities, the OJJDP report found that "a juvenile held in a public facility…was most likely to be black, male, between 14 and 17 years of age, and held for a delinquent offense such as a property crime or a crime against a person. On the other hand, a juvenile held in custody in a private facility…was most likely to be white, male, 14 to 17 years of age, and held for a nondelinquent offense such as running away, truancy, or incorrigibility."[114] The report also noted that "juvenile corrections has become increasingly privatized." Between 1978 and 1989, admission to private facilities (comprised primarily of halfway houses, group homes, shelters, and ranches, camps, or farms) increased by 104%, compared with only 9% for public facilities (mostly detention centers and training schools).[115] The fastest-growing category of detained juveniles involves drug and alcohol offenses. Approximately 12% of all juvenile detainees are being held because of alcohol and drug-related offenses.[116]

States vary widely in their use of secure detention for juveniles. Rates of incarceration range from a high of 1,211 (per 100,000 juveniles) in Washington, D.C., to a low of nearly 0 in some states, with a national average of 245.[117] Such rate differences reflect both economic realities and philosophical beliefs. Some jurisdictions, like California, expect rehabilitative costs to be born by the state rather than by families or local government agencies. Hence, California shows a higher rate of institutionalization than many other states. Similarly, some states have more securely embraced the reformation ideal and are more likely to use diversionary options where juveniles are concerned.

TABLE 14-2

JUVENILES UNDER CUSTODIAL SUPERVISION, MIDYEAR 1992

Jurisdiction	Juvenile Population	Jurisdiction	Juvenile Population
U.S. total	62,869	Montana	168
Alabama	599	Nebraska	518
Alaska	193	Nevada	335
Arizona	831	New Hampshire	246
Arkansas	264	New Jersey	1,353
California	8,741	New Mexico	446
Colorado	1,037	New York	2,925
Connecticut	687	North Carolina	6,982
Delaware	247	North Dakota	491
Florida	6,745	Ohio	2,307
Georgia	1,725	Oklahoma	155
Hawaii	51	Oregon	546
Idaho	349	Pennsylvania	1,281
Illinois	1,398	Rhode Island	213
Indiana	694	South Carolina	1,089
Iowa	225	South Dakota	177
Kansas	1,805	Tennessee	1,274
Kentucky	1,210	Texas	2,327
Louisiana	2,220	Utah	662
Maine	313	Vermont	193
Maryland	1,561	Virginia	2,264
Massachusetts	1,747	Washington	991
Michigan	836	West Virginia	490
Minnesota	211	Wisconsin	774
Mississippi	368	Wyoming	114
Missouri	527		

Source: American Correctional Association, *1993 Directory of Juvenile and Adult Correctional Departments, Institutions, Agencies and Paroling Authorities* (Laurel, MD: ACA, 1993).

POSTADJUDICATORY REVIEW

The detrimental effects of institutionalization may make the opportunity for appellate review more critical for juveniles than it is for adults. However, federal court precedents to date have not established a clear right to appeal from juvenile court. Even so, most states do have statutory provisions that make such appeals possible.[118]

From a practical point of view juvenile appeals may not be as consequential as are appeals of adult criminal convictions. About 66% of all juvenile complaints are handled informally. Further, only about 29% of adjudicated delinquents are placed outside the family.[119] Because sentence lengths are so short for most confined juveniles, appellate courts hardly have time to complete the review process before release occurs.

DISSATISFACTION WITH TODAY'S SYSTEM

The juvenile justice system is not without its critics. An emerging recognition of repetitive serious criminal activity by a small number of "hard-core" delinquents, combined with a concern for public safety has prompted efforts at reform which focus on three areas: (1) lessening the degree of privacy which surrounds juvenile proceedings; (2) increasing penalties associated with certain kinds of delinquent acts; and (3) reducing diversionary opportunities for habitual, violent, and serious offenders. Modern critics of the juvenile justice system argue that it is time to replace a court philosophy ostensibly based upon achieving the best interests of the child with one which gives primacy to justice.[120] The overall thrust of the juvenile justice reform movement is intended to bring about changes which would recognize the harm suffered by victims of delinquency and which would result in juveniles being treated more like adults.

While privacy may shield the juvenile from labeling, it does little to protect society from further victimization. In a recent situation, for example, a 27-year-old teacher, pregnant with her first child, was stabbed repeatedly by a 14-year-old transfer student with a past record of violence and disruption.[121] School officials, however, had not had access to the child's previous record. To protect the public, the National School Safety Center recommends modifying state and federal laws to allow for a sharing of information about dangerous juveniles on a need-to-know basis.[122] The movement to lessen privacy is consistent with the Bureau of Justice Statistics' belief that "the nation's information policy (is moving) in the direction of enhancing the public's access to criminal history record information."[123]

Stiffer penalties for some delinquents have been proposed by those who cite continued and frequent delinquent acts by a minority of adjudicated delinquents. The same critics argue that the present system is limited in its capacity to reform, often releasing dangerous juvenile offenders back to the streets. Evidence from the Habitual Serious and Violent Juvenile Offender Program, which targeted 13 cities for vigorous prosecution of violent and repeat offenders, tends to support such claims. The program combined careful case screening with victim/witness support to remove habitual juvenile offenders effectively from society.[124] Supporting the movement toward stiffer penalties for delinquent youth, sentencing guidelines for juveniles proposed by the Justice Department recommend that state legislatures adopt fixed penalties for certain law violations.[125] In a similar move, the Office of Juvenile Justice and Delinquency Prevention has developed a monetary and direct victim service restitution program for juvenile courts.[126] Called RESTTA (for Restitution Education, Specialized Training, and Technical Assistance Program) the program provides local juvenile courts with the information needed to make restitution a meaningful part of the dispositional process.

On the other side of the reform movement are those who argue for still greater protections on behalf of juveniles. Because they lack all the rights of adults, such critics say, juveniles are apt to be "railroaded" through a system which does not live up to its purpose of protecting children.[127] Others cite the criminalizing influence of juvenile institutions and suggest that juveniles should be kept from institutionalization wherever possible. The National Council on Crime and Delinquency has identified four continuing problems in juvenile justice today:[128]

1. Unreasonably high numbers of youth who are not dangerous are being kept in state training schools at high cost to taxpayers.
2. Many areas lack adequate individualized community treatment alternatives for nondangerous youth.

3. Black and Hispanic youth are confined at a rate three times that of white youth.
4. In some locales youth are being held in jail facilities intended for adults.

To address these and other issues the Council suggests the use of home confinement, court-ordered restitution, and a thorough examination of current juvenile justice policies.

In 1993 the National Juvenile Corrections and Detention Forum, a group of leading juvenile correctional administrators from all 50 states, developed a list of recommendations intended to guide the juvenile justice system into the next century. Among the recommendations were[129]

1. Develop, introduce, and pass congressional legislation that guarantees due process rights and humane treatment to juveniles in pre- and postdispositional confinement.
2. Prohibit the use of detention as a dispositional (pre-adjudicatory) placement.
3. Develop and implement a juvenile justice philosophy of using the least restrictive placement that is consistent with providing for public safety.
4. Develop and implement quality assurance programs to ensure continuous quality of life and services in juvenile justice facilities.

SUMMARY

Children are the future hope of each mature generation, and under today's laws they occupy a special status. That status is tied closely to cultural advances which occurred in the Western world during the past 200 years, resulting in a reevaluation of the child's role. Many children today lead privileged lives which would have been unimaginable a few scant decades ago.

Others are not so lucky, and the problems they face are as diverse as they are staggering. Some problems are a direct consequence of increased national wealth and the subsequent removal of children from the economic sphere, which have lessened expectations for responsible behavior during the childhood years. Others grow from the easy availability of illicit drugs—a fact which has dramatically altered the early life experiences of many children, especially in the nation's large cities. Finally, the decline of traditional institutions and the seeming plethora of broken homes have all combined with the moral excesses of adult predators interested in the acquisition of sexual services from children, to lead to a quick abandonment of innocence by many young people today. Gang involvement, child abuse and neglect, juvenile runaways and suicides, and serious incidents of delinquency have been the result.

In the face of these massive challenges, the juvenile justice system remains committed to a philosophy of protection and restoration. It differs substantially from the adult criminal justice system in the multitude of opportunities it provides for diversion, and in the emphasis it places on rehabilitation rather than punishment. The professionalization of delinquency, the hallmark of which is the intense and repetitive criminal involvement of juveniles in drug-related gang activity, represents a major new challenge to the idealism of the juvenile justice system. Addressing that challenge may well prove to be the most significant future determinate of system change.

DISCUSSION QUESTIONS

1. How does the philosophy and purpose of the juvenile justice system differ from that of the adult system of criminal justice?

2. What was the impact of the *Gault* decision on juvenile justice in America? What adult rights were *not* accorded to juveniles by *Gault*?

3. Describe the six categories of children found under the laws of most states. Do some of the problems faced by children today necessitate consideration of new categories? If so, what might such categories be? If not, how are existing categories able to handle illicit drug use by juveniles or the repetitive and apparently vicious delinquency of inner-city gang members?

4. In your opinion are status offenses still a useful concept in our system of juvenile justice? Should laws which circumscribe status offenses be retained or abandoned? Why?

5. One reason given in this chapter for delinquency is the lack of meaningful roles for juveniles in modern society. Do you agree with this explanation? Why or why not?

6. One problem with secrecy in juvenile hearings and records is that others in society are not protected from continued delinquency. Do you think that secrecy in the juvenile justice system is justified? Or do you think that those who stand to be injured by the future delinquency of adjudicated offenders should be warned? Why or why not?

ENDNOTES

1. "School Assaults Bring Tragedy to Compton," *The Los Angeles Times*, April 25, 1991, pp. A1, A3.

2. Ibid., p. A3.

3. Ibid.

4. Ibid.

5. As told by Charles Patrick Ewing in the book *Kids Who Kill* (Lexington, MA: Lexington Books, 1990), p. 1.

6. Bureau of Justice Statistics, *Report to the Nation on Crime and Justice*, 2nd ed. (Washington, D.C.: U.S. Department of Justice, 1988), p. 41.

7. Where "juvenile" refers to persons under 18 years of age. See ibid., p. 42.

8. Ibid., p. 43.

9. Alfred Blumstein, "Systems Analysis and the Criminal Justice System," *Annals of the American Academy of Political and Social Science*, Vol. 474 (1967).

10. "Young in Years, Old at Crime," *USA Today*, April 26, 1993, p. 2A.

11. For an excellent review of the handling of juveniles through history, see Wiley B. Sanders, ed., *Juvenile Offenders for a Thousand Years* (Chapel Hill: University of North Carolina Press, 1970).

12. Robert M. Mennel, *Thorns and Thistles: Juvenile Delinquents in the United States, 1925–1940* (Hanover, NH: University Press of New England, 1973).

13. Thomas A. Johnson, *Introduction to the Juvenile Justice System* (St. Paul, MN: West Publishing, 1975), p. 1.

14. Charles E. Springer, *Justice for Juveniles*, 2nd printing (Washington, D.C.: Office of Juvenile Justice and Delinquency Prevention, 1987), p. 18.

15. Arnold Binder et al., *Juvenile Delinquency: Historical, Cultural, Legal Perspectives* (New York: Macmillan, 1988), p. 45.

16. Ibid., p. 50.

17. See Sanford Fox, "Juvenile Justice Reform: An Historical Perspective," in Sanford Fox, *Modern Juvenile Justice: Cases and Materials* (St. Paul, MN: West Publishing, 1972), pp. 15–48.

18. Ibid., p. 19.

19. 4 Whart. 9 (Pa., 1839).

20. Fox, "Juvenile Justice Reform," p. 27.

21. Anthony Platt, *The Child Savers: The Invention of Delinquency*, 2nd ed. (Chicago: University of Chicago Press, 1977).

22. Ibid., p. 29.

23. 55 Ill. 280, 8 Am. Rep. 645.

24. Frank Schmalleger, *A History of Corrections: Emerging Ideologies and Practices* (Bristol, IN: Wyndham Hall, 1986), p. 29.

25. Torsten Eriksson, *The Reformers* (New York: Elsevier, 1976), p. 107.

26. Ibid., pp. 108–109.

27. Robert Caldwell, *Criminology* (New York: The Ronald Press, 1956), p. 480.

28. Johnson, *Introduction to the Juvenile Justice System*, p. 3.

29. Ibid., p. 3.

30. Ibid.

31. Fox, "Juvenile Justice Reform," p. 47.

32. Ibid., p. 5.

33. Principles adapted from Robert G. Caldwell, "The Juvenile Court: Its Development and Some Major Problems," in Rose Giallombardo, ed., *Juvenile Delinquency: A Book of Readings* (New York: John Wiley, 1966), p. 358.

34. Clifford Shaw, Frederick Zorbaugh, Henry McKay, and Leonard Cottrell, *Delinquency Areas* (Chicago: University of Chicago Press, 1929).

35. Richard A. Cloward and Lloyd E. Ohlin, *Delinquency and Opportunity: A Theory of Delinquent Gangs* (New York: The Free Press, 1960).

36. Walter B. Miller, "Lower Class Culture as a Generating Milieu of Gang Delinquency," *Journal of Social Issues*, Vol. 14, no. 3 (1958), pp. 5–19.

37. Albert K. Cohen, *Delinquent Boys, The Culture of the Gang* (New York: The Free Press of Glencoe, 1955).

38. David Matza, *Delinquency and Drift* (New York: John Wiley, 1964).

39. Gresham M. Sykes and David Matza, "Techniques of Neutralization: A Theory of Delinquency, *American Sociological Review*, Vol. 22 (December 1957), pp. 664–666.

40. Marvin Wolfgang, Robert Figlio, and Thorsten Sellin, *Delinquency in a Birth Cohort* (Chicago: University of Chicago Press, 1972).

41. Marvin Wolfgang, Terence Thornberry, and Robert Figlio, *From Boy to Man, From Delinquency to Crime* (Chicago: University of Chicago Press, 1987).

42. Steven P. Lab, "Analyzing Change in Crime and Delinquency Rates: The Case for Cohort Analysis," *Criminal Justice Research Bulletin*, Vol. 3, no. 10 (Huntsville, TX: Sam Houston State University, 1988), p. 2.

43. "Going 'Wilding': Terror in Central Park," *Newsweek*, May 1, 1989, p. 27.

44. "Angry Teens Explode in Violent Wilding Sprees," *USA Today*, April 27, 1989, p. 1D.

45. Marco R. della Cava, "The Societal Forces That Push Kids Out of Control," *USA Today*, April 27, 1989, p. 6D.

46. Ruth Shonle Cavan, *Juvenile Delinquency: Development, Treatment, Control*, 2nd ed. (Philadelphia: J. B. Lippincott, 1969), p. 152.

47. Alexis M. Durham III, "Ivy League Delinquency: A Self-report Analysis," *American Journal of Criminal Justice*, Vol. 12, no. 2 (Spring 1988), p. 188.

48. U.S. Department of Health and Human Services, *HHS News*, April 13, 1993.

49. Ibid.

50. *Uniform Crime Reports, 1992.*

51. Cheryl Carpenter, Barry Glassner, Bruce Johnson, and Julia Loughlin, *Kids, Drugs, and Crime* (Lexington, MA: Lexington Books, 1988).

52. Chaiken and Johnson, *Characteristics of Different Types of Drug-Involved Offenders*, p. 9, citing Delbert S. Elliott, David Huizinga, and Barbara Morse, "Self-reported Violent Offending: A Descriptive Analysis of Juvenile Violent Offenders and Their Offending Careers," *Journal of Interpersonal Violence*, Vol. 1, no. 4 (1986), pp. 472–514.

53. "Torture Killing," *USA Today*, January 29, 1993, p. 3A.

54. "Girls Just Catching Up to Boys," *USA Today*, July 9, 1992, p. 10A.

55. "The Knife in the Book Bag," *Time*, February 8, 1993, p. 37.

56. "Haunting Slayings in Oregon," *USA Today*, April 27, 1992, p. 3A.

57. "Child Kills Infant Brother," *The Robesonian*, September 8, 1992, p. 2A.

58. "Liverpool Boys Back in Court," *USA Today*, March 4, 1993, p. 4A.

59. See, for example, Frederick M. Thrasher, *The Gang* (Chicago: University of Chicago Press, 1927), and William Foote Whyte, *Street Corner Society, the Social Structure of an Italian Slum* (Chicago: University of Chicago Press, 1943).

60. "Young Urban Terrorists," *The Ohio State University Quest* (Fall 1988), p. 11.

61. *Criminal Justice Newsletter*, Vol. 19, no. 19 (October 3, 1988), p. 2.

62. "Gangs Put L.A. on Edge," *USA Today*, February 16, 1993, p. 1A.

63. Ibid., p. 2.

64. Paul Demuro, Anne Demuro, and Steven Lerner, *Reforming the California Youth Authority: How to End Crowding, Diversify Treatments, and Protect the Public—Without Spending More Money* (Bolinas, CA: Commonweal Research Institute, 1988).

65. "Los Angeles Drug Gangs Move into Other Cities, Police Told," *The Fayetteville Observer-Times* (North Carolina), July 16, 1988, p. 2A.

66. U.S. Attorney General's Advisory Board on Missing Children, *America's Missing and Exploited Children: Their Safety and Their Future* (Washington, D.C.: Office of Juvenile Justice and Delinquency Prevention, 1986), p. 11.

67. David Finkelhor, Gerald Hotaling, and Andrea Sedlak, *Missing Abducted, Runaway, and Thrownaway Children in America* (Washington, D.C.: Office of Juvenile Justice and Delinquency Prevention, 1990).

68. "Runaway Children and the Juvenile Justice and Delinquency Prevention Act: What Is Its Impact?" *Juvenile Justice Bulletin* (Washington, D.C.: Office of Juvenile Justice and Delinquency Prevention, no date).

69. Ibid., p. 1.

70. Ibid., p. 2.

71. U.S. Attorney General, *America's Missing and Exploited Children*, p. 19.

72. "Teen Stripper's Mom Gets Year in Jail," United Press International, January 22, 1988.

73. Gene G. Abel, et al., "Self-reported Sex Crimes of Nonincarcerated Paraphiliacs," *Journal of Interpersonal Violence*, Vol. 2, no. 1 (March 1987).

74. National Committee for Prevention of Child Abuse, *Child Abuse: Prelude to Delinquency?* (Washington, D.C.: Office of Juvenile Justice and Delinquency Prevention, 1986).

75. Charles B. DeWitt, *The Cycle of Violence*, National Institute of Justice (Washington, D.C.: NIJ, October 1992), p. 2.

76. Matthew T. Zingraff, Jeffrey Leiter, Kristen A. Myers, and Matthew C. Johnsen, "Child Maltreatment and Youthful Problem Behavior," *Criminology*, Vol. 31, no. 2 (May 1993), pp. 173–202.

77. Cecil L. Willis and Richard H. Wells, "The Police and Child Abuse: An Analysis of Police Decisions to Report Illegal Behavior," *Criminology*, Vol. 26, no. 4 (1988), pp. 695–715.

78. See "The Role of the National Center for the Prosecution of Child Abuse," in *Prosecutors Perspective*, Vol. 2, no. 1 (January 1988), p. 19.

79. "Kids Struggle with Horror of Girl's Suicide," *USA Today*, June 17, 1993, p. 3A.

80. "Girls' Suicides 'Like a Bombshell,'" *USA Today*, May 22, 1991, 3A.

81. Ibid., p. 3A.

82. "Child Tax Credit Urged," *The Fayetteville Observer-Times*, (North Carolina), June 25, 1991, pp. 1A–2.

83. See, for example, *Haley* v. *Ohio*, 332 U.S. 596 (1948).

84. *Kent* v. *U.S.*, 383 U.S. 541 (1966).

85. *McKeiver* v. *Pennsylvania*, 403 U.S. 528 (1971).

86. Adapted from Peter Greenwood, *Juvenile Offenders*, a Crime File Study Guide (Washington, D.C.: National Institute of Justice, no date).

87. *Fare* v. *Michael C.*, 442 U.S. 707 (1979).

88. *California* v. *Prysock*, 453 U.S. 355 (1981).

89. *New Jersey* v. *T.L.O.*, 105 S.Ct. 733 (1985).

90. "Drug Bill Includes Extension of OJJDP, with Many Changes," *Criminal Justice Newsletter*, Vol. 19, no. 22 (November 15, 1988), p. 4.

91. Bureau of Justice Statistics, *Report to the Nation on Crime and Justice*, 2nd ed., p. 79.

92. Ibid.

93. "Ten-Year-Old Faces Murder Trial as Adult," *The Fayetteville Observer-Times* (North Carolina), August 27, 1989, p. 5A.

94. Bureau of Justice Statistics, *Report to the Nation on Crime and Justice*, 2nd ed., p. 78.

95. Ibid.

96. Ibid.

97. *McKeiver* v. *Pennsylvania*.

98. Some states, such as West Virginia, do provide juveniles with a statutory right to trial.

99. Peer juries in juvenile court have been identified in Denver, Colorado; Duluth, Minnesota; Deerfield, Illinois; Thompkins County, New York; and Spanish Fork City, Utah. See Philip Reichel and Carole Seyfrit, "A Peer Jury in the Juvenile Court," *Crime and Delinquency*, Vol. 30, no. 3 (July 1984), pp. 423–438.

100. Ibid.

101. "In This Court, Teens Sit in Stern Judgment on Violators," *Fayetteville Observer-Times* (North Carolina), May 3, 1992, p. 22A.

102. Harold N. Snyder and Terrence A. Finnegan, *Delinquency in the United States, 1983* (Washington, D.C.: Office of Juvenile Justice and Delinquency Prevention, 1987), p. 3.

103. Bureau of Justice Statistics, *Report to the Nation on Crime and Justice*, 2nd ed., p. 95.

104. Ibid.

105. Ibid.

106. Ibid., p. 110.

107. Ibid.

108. Ibid.

109. Ibid.

110. Allen Beck, Susan Kline, and Lawrence Greenfeld, "Survey of Youth in Custody, 1987," (Washington, D.C.: Bureau of Justice Statistics, 1988).

111. "California Relies Too Much on Training Schools, Report Says," *Criminal Justice Newsletter*, Vol. 19, no. 19 (October 3, 1988), p. 3.

112. Ibid.

113. Office of Juvenile Justice and Delinquency Prevention, *National Juvenile Custody Trends, 1978–1989* (Washington, D.C.: U.S. Department of Justice, 1992).

114. Ibid., p. 2–3.

115. Ibid., p. 2.

116. Ibid., p. 22.

117. U.S. Census Bureau, *Children in Custody* (Washington, D.C.: U.S. Government Printing Office, 1985).

118. Section 59 of the Uniform Juvenile Court Act recommends the granting of a right to appeal for juveniles (National Conference of Commissioners on Uniform State Laws, Uniform Juvenile Court Act, 1968).

119. Snyder and Finnegan, *Delinquency in the United States, 1983*, p. 3.

120. Springer, *Justice for Juveniles.*

121. Bureau of Justice Statistics, *Open vs. Confidential Records: Proceedings of a BJS/SEARCH Conference* (Washington, D.C.: Bureau of Justice Statistics, November 1988), p. 42.

122. Ronald D. Stephens, "Access to Juvenile Justice Records," in *Open vs. Confidential Records* (Washington, D.C.: Bureau of Justice Statistics, 1988), p. 45.

123. Bureau of Justice Statistics, *Public Access to Criminal History Record Information* (Washington, D.C.: Bureau of Justice Statistics, 1988), p. 70.

124. American Institutes for Research, *Evaluation of the Habitual Serious and Violent Juvenile Offender Program: Executive Summary* (Washington, D.C.: Office of Juvenile Justice and Delinquency Prevention, 1988), and "Targeting Serious Juvenile Offenders for Prosecution Can Make a Difference," National Institute of Justice Reports (September/October 1988), p. 9.

125. "Federal Study on Youth Urges Fixed Sentences," *The New York Times,* August 29, 1987.

126. "Introducing RESTTA," *Juvenile Justice Bulletin* (Washington, D.C.: Office of Juvenile Justice and Delinquency Prevention, 1985).

127. Greenwood, *Juvenile Offenders*, p. 2.

128. Adapted from The National Council on Crime and Delinquency, *Progress Report, 1986–87* (annual report).

129. National Juvenile Corrections and Detention Forum, *Recommendations for Juvenile Corrections and Detention in Response to–Conditions of Confinement: A Study to Evaluate the Conditions in Juvenile Correctional and Detention Facilities* (Laurel, MD: American Correctional Association, 1993).

CHAPTER 15

DRUG

ABUSE

…drug trafficking is the number one crime problem facing our country and the world…[1]
—FORMER ATTORNEY GENERAL RICHARD THORNBURGH IN AN OPEN LETTER TO PRESIDENT BUSH

If we fail, it means that what we have been saying is true—that drugs may represent to our civilization, to many of our cities, a life-or-death situation. If we don't get control of this drug problem, we may not go into the 21st century intact.[2]
—THE FIRST "DRUG CZAR," WILLIAM BENNETT

I keep in my house a letter from Bill O'Dwyer, who once was the mayor of New York, and who wrote to me, 'There is no power on earth to match the power of the poor, who, just by sitting in their hopelessness, can bring the rest of us down.' It always sounded right, but I never saw it happen until crack came along.

And with it, there are no more rules in American crime. The implied agreements on which we were raised are gone. You now shoot women and children. A news reporter is safe as long as he is not there. A cop in his uniform means nothing.[3]
—JIMMY BRESLIN, "CRACK"

KEY CONCEPTS

victimless crimes

controlled substance

The Harrison Act

forfeiture

legalization

addiction

recreational user

schedules

RICO

decriminalization

narcoterrorism

abuse

money laundering

interdiction

KEY CASES

Florida v. *Riley*

California v. *Greenwood*

U.S. v. *A Parcel of Land
  in Rumson, N.J.*

Oliver v. *U.S.*

Austin v. *U.S.*

U.S. v. *Dunn*

Alexander v. *U.S.*

THE DRUG PROBLEM

Some years ago, the first half hour of the *Today* television show focused on the "war on drugs" being waged by this country.[4] Jane Pauley, the then–network anchor-woman for that program, interviewed three big-city police officials to learn their opinion on the progress of the "war."

Chief Fred Taylor of Florida's Metro–Dade Police Department told viewers that up to 60% of today's crime in Miami is drug related. Crack, according to Chief Taylor, is the "drug of choice" in the city. Lt. Bill Callaghan of the Chicago Police Department, who was also on the program, stated flatly that 80% of all crimes committed in the city of Chicago are in some way related to drugs. The difference between Chicago and Miami, according to Callaghan, is only that the powdered form of cocaine is still more common than crack. The third participant, Deputy Chief Glenn Levant of the Narcotics Division of the Los Angeles Police Department, concurred with the estimates of the panel. He reported that at least 70% of all police activity in Los Angeles today revolves around illegal drugs.

Following the law enforcement officers on the program was U.S. Representative Charles Rangel, of the House Select Committee on Narcotics Abuse and Control. Representative Rangel expressed his belief that the solution to the modern situation is to get serious about drugs. Law enforcement is hopelessly overwhelmed, said Rangel. He cited education and effective foreign policy as the best available tools to free American society from the grip of illegal drugs.

DRUG ABUSE AND SOCIAL ORDER CRIMES

Very few textbooks in criminal justice devote an entire chapter to drug law violations and drug-related crime. Most prefer, instead, to describe a general category of social order or victimless crimes. This book, however, directly addresses drug crime for the reasons cited on that early morning television program:

1. Drug abuse accounts for a large proportion of present-day law violations.

2. Drug abuse contributes to many other types of criminal activity including smuggling, theft, robbery, and murder.
3. Drug abuse has led to a large number of arrests, clogged courtrooms, and overcrowded prisons.
4. Drug crime may be the major challenge facing the nation's criminal justice system today.
5. The fight against drug abuse is rapidly becoming one of the most expensive activities ever undertaken by federal, state, and local governments.

Drug abuse is only one of a great number of social order crimes. As such it shares a number of characteristics in common with other victimless crimes like prostitution, gambling, and the diverse forms of sexual deviance which occur among consenting partners. A hallmark of such crimes is that they involve willing participants. In the case of **drug law violations**, buyers, sellers, and users willingly purchase, sell, and consume illegal drugs. They do not complain to the authorities of criminal injuries to themselves or others.

Few victimless crimes, however, are truly without an injured party. Even where the criminal participant does not perceive an immediate or personal injury, the legitimate interests of nonparticipants may be affected by the behavior involved. In many victimless crimes, it is society, defined as a set of well-ordered interpersonal arrangements, which is the ultimate victim. Prostitution, for example, may victimize the customer or his family through the spread of AIDS, other venereal diseases, and economic hardship. Prostitution has many other negative consequences, including (1) lowered property values in areas where it regularly occurs, (2) degradation of the status of women, (3) victimization of the prostitute, and (4) the seeming legitimacy it lends to interpersonal immorality of all kinds.

The negative consequences of drug abuse include lost productivity, an inequitable distribution of economic resources among the poorest members of society, disease, wasted human potential, fragmented families, violence, and other crimes. Some evidence has even linked the current drug crisis to international terrorism and efforts to overthrow the democratic governments of the Western Hemisphere. Each of these consequences will be discussed in some detail in this chapter.

WHAT IS A DRUG?

Drug abuse terminology has evolved over the years into an agreed-upon nomenclature which describes the chemical structure of drugs, their effect upon the body, psychological and physical addiction, and so forth.

Before we begin any comprehensive discussion of drugs, however, we must first grapple with the concept of what a drug is. Common usage holds that a drug may be any ingestible substance which has a noticeable effect upon the mind or body. Drugs may enter the body via injection, inhalation, swallowing, or even by direct absorption through the skin or mucous membranes. Some drugs, like penicillin and tranquilizers, are useful in medical treatment, while others, like heroin and cocaine, are attractive only to "recreational" users[5] or to those who are addicted to them.

Both the law and social convention, however, make strong distinctions between drugs which are socially acceptable and those which are not. Some ingestible substances with profound effects upon the body and mind are not even thought of as drugs. Gasoline fumes, chemical vapors of many kinds, perfumes, certain vitamins, sugar-rich foods, and toxic chemicals may all have profound effects upon the mind and body. Even so, most people do not think of such substances as drugs, and they are rarely regulated by the criminal law.

Controlled Substance A specifically defined bioactive or psychoactive chemical substance which is proscribed by law.

THEORY INTO PRACTICE

DRUG USE AND ABUSE—COMMONLY USED TERMS

Drug: Any chemical substance defined by social convention as bio- or psychoactive. Not all "drugs" are socially recognized as such, while those which are may not be well understood. Among recognized drugs some are "legal" and readily available, while others are closely controlled.

Controlled Substance: A specifically defined bioactive or psychoactive chemical substance which is proscribed by law.

Abuse: The frequent, overindulgent, or long-term use of a controlled substance in such a way so as to create problems in the user's life, or in the lives of those with whom the user associates.

Psychological Addiction: A craving for a specific drug which results from long-term substance abuse. People who are psychologically addicted use the drug in question as a "crutch" to deal with the events in their lives. Also referred to as psychological dependence.

Physical Addiction: A biologically based craving for a specific drug, which results from frequent use of the substance. Also referred to as physical dependence.

Addict: Generally, someone who abuses drugs and is psychologically dependent, physically dependent, or both.

Soft Drugs: Psychoactive drugs with relatively mild effects whose potential for abuse and addiction is substantially less than for the hard drugs described below. By social convention, soft drugs include marijuana, hashish, and some tranquilizers and mood elevators.

Hard Drugs: Psychoactive substances with serious potential for abuse and addiction. By social convention, hard drugs include heroin, quaaludes, sopors, LSD, mescaline, peyote, psilocybin, and MDA. Cocaine and its derivative, crack, are often placed in the hard drug category.

Recreational User: A person who uses drugs relatively infrequently, and whose use occurs primarily among friends and within social contexts which define drug use as pleasurable. Most addicts began as recreational users.—

Recent social awareness has reclassified substances like alcohol, caffeine, and nicotine as drugs. Prior to the 1960s it is doubtful that this threesome would have been recognized as drugs by the majority of Americans. Even today alcohol, caffeine, and nicotine are readily available throughout the country, with only minimal controls on their manufacture and distribution. As such, they are three drugs which continue to enjoy favored status in both our law and culture. Nonetheless, alcohol abuse and addiction are commonplace in American society, and anyone who has tried to quit smoking knows the power that nicotine can wield.

Occupying a middle ground of social awareness are substances which have medical applicability but are usually available only on a prescription basis. Antibiotics, diet pills,

ALL DOPE PUSHERS AND PEDDLERS AND WHATEVER! YOU BETTER MOVE YOUR OPERATION TO SOME OTHER LOCATION. NAMES AND LICENSE PLATE NUMBERS OF ANYONE MAKING SALES ON THIS PROPERTY WILL BE TURNED OVER TO THE POLICE!

Drug abuse has become one of the most significant problems facing the criminal justice system today. *Courtesy of the Fayetteville Publishing Co.*

and, in particular, tranquilizers and stimulants, are culturally and legally acceptable only upon the advice of a physician. These substances are clearly recognized as drugs, albeit useful ones, by the majority of Americans.

Powerful drugs, those with the ability to produce substantially altered states of consciousness, and with a high potential for addiction, occupy the "high ground" in social and legal condemnation. Among them are substances such as heroin, peyote, mescaline, LSD, and cocaine. Even here, however, legitimate uses for such drugs may exist. Cocaine is used in the treatment of certain medical conditions and can be applied as a topical anesthetic during medical interventions. LSD has been employed experimentally to investigate the nature of human consciousness, and peyote and mescaline may be used legally by members of the Native American Church in Indian religious services. Even heroin has been advocated by some as beneficial in relieving the suffering associated with some forms of terminal illnesses.

In determining what substances should be called "drugs," it is useful to recognize that any phenomenon is understood in a certain way by a majority of people only because it is socially defined. Hence, what Americans today consider to be drugs depends more upon social convention than it does upon any inherent property of the "drugs" themselves.

The history of marijuana provides a case in point. Prior to the early 1900s marijuana was freely available in the United States. Although alcohol was the recreational drug of choice at the time, marijuana found a following among some artists and musicians. Marijuana was also occasionally used for medicinal purposes to "calm the nerves" and to treat hysteria. Howard Becker, in a now-classic study of the early Federal Bureau of Narcotics, demonstrates how federal agencies worked to outlaw marijuana in order to increase their power.[6] Federally funded publications voiced calls for laws against the substance, and movies such as *Reefer Madness* led the drive toward classifying marijuana as a dangerous drug. The 1939 Marijuana Tax Act was the result, and marijuana has been thought of as a drug worthy of federal and local enforcement efforts ever since.

Hence, any answer to the question of "What is a drug?" can be had only by looking at the social definitions operative at the moment. Some of the clearest definitional statements relating to controlled substances can be found in the law.

Psychoactive Drug A chemical substance which affects cognition, feeling, and/or awareness.

ALCOHOL ABUSE

Although this chapter focuses primarily on controlled substances as defined by federal legislation, a word about alcohol abuse is in order. Alcohol abuse has been called "one of the Nation's gravest health and social problems."[7] It is a serious problem which shows no signs of abating. Although 30% of the American population are abstainers, evidence indicates that more Americans drink today than at any time since World War II, and those who drink, drink more excessively.[8] Surveys show that 93% of high school seniors have tried alcoholic beverages and that up to one-half of teenagers in the United States become intoxicated on the average once every two weeks.[9]

Per capita alcoholic beverage consumption in the United States now exceeds 27.6 gallons yearly.[10] Some perspective on consumption can be gained by realizing that the typical American drinks 25.9 gallons of coffee per year, 27.1 gallons of milk, and 45.6 gallons of soft drinks.[11] The average American adult consumes 34.5 gallons of beer, 3.5 gallons of wine, and 2.5 gallons of liquor per year.[12] Some individuals are especially heavy drinkers. It is estimated that one-half of all the alcohol consumed yearly in the United States is ingested by just 5% of the adult population.[13]

Alcohol, sometimes in combination with other drugs, is often a factor in the commission of crimes. One crime closely associated with the use of alcohol is drunk driving. Most states define a blood alcohol level of 0.10% or more as intoxication and hold that anyone who drives with that amount of alcohol in his or her blood is driving under the influence (DUI) of alcohol.[14] Drunk driving has become a major social concern. Groups such as Mothers Against Drunk Driving (MADD) and Remove Intoxicated Drivers (RID) have given impetus to enforcement efforts to curb drunk drivers. Between 1970 and 1992 arrests for DUI increased 200% across the nation, while the number of licensed drivers grew by only 42%.[15] Today there are nearly 2 million drunk driving arrests made annually—more than for any other offense on which statistics are maintained. The average driver arrested for DUI is substantially impaired. Studies show that he or she has consumed an average of 6 ounces of pure

Police test a drunk driving suspect. Alcohol abuse, especially in the form of drunken driving, has been getting considerable attention from law makers and enforcement agencies in recent years. *Photo: Bachmann/The Image Works.*

CAREERS IN JUSTICE

WORKING FOR THE BUREAU OF ALCOHOL, TOBACCO, AND FIREARMS

TYPICAL POSITIONS.   Explosives expert, firearms specialist, bomb scene investigator, and liquor law violations investigator.

EMPLOYMENT REQUIREMENTS.   ATF special agent applicants must meet the same employment requirements as most other federal agents, including (1) successful completion of the Treasury Enforcement Agent Examination, (2) a field interview, and (3) a thorough background investigation. See the box on employment with the U.S. Secret Service for additional details on Treasury agent general employment requirements.

OTHER REQUIREMENTS.   Other general requirements for employment as a federal officer apply. They include (1) U.S. citizenship, (2) an age between 21 and 35, (3) good physical health, and (4) eyesight of no less than 20/40 uncorrected. New agents undergo eight weeks of specialized training at the Federal Law Enforcement Training Center in Glynco, Georgia.

SALARY.   A Bachelor's degree qualifies applicants for appointment at the GS-5 level (earning $22,617 or more in mid-1993), although some appointments are made at the GS-7 level ($25,745 and higher in mid-1993). Depending on geographic area of assignment, this salary can be raised from 16% to 30% above the established base level.

BENEFITS.   Benefits include (1) 13 days of sick leave annually, (2) 2-1/2 to 5 weeks of annual paid vacation and 10 paid federal holidays each year, (3) federal health and life insurance, and (4) a comprehensive retirement program.

DIRECT INQUIRIES TO: Bureau of Alcohol, Tobacco, and Firearms, U.S. Treasury Department, 650 Massachusetts Ave., N.W., Room 4170, Washington, D.C. 20226. Phone: (202) 927-8610.

alcohol (the equivalent of a dozen bottles of beer) in the 4 hours preceding arrest.[16] Twenty-six percent of arrestees have consumed nearly twice that amount.

Driving under the influence is costly for both offenders and society. The National Highway Traffic Safety Administration estimates that as many as 250,000 people have been killed in alcohol-related motor vehicle accidents over the past decade. More than 650,000 persons are injured in such crashes yearly.[17]

Another offense directly related to alcohol consumption is public drunkenness. During the late 1960s and early 1970s, some groups fought to decriminalize drunkenness and treat it as a health problem. Although the number of arrests for public drunkenness reached 832,300[18] in 1992, the offense is one in which law enforcement officers retain a great deal of discretion. Many individuals who are drunk in public, if they are not assaultive or involved in other crimes, are likely to receive an "official escort" home rather than face arrest.

The use of alcohol may also lead to the commission of other, very serious, crimes. Some experts have suggested that use of alcohol lowers inhibitions and increases the likelihood of aggression.[19] Studies show that about half of all prison inmates report that they had been drinking just prior to the crime for which they are now serving time.[20] Alcohol use has been found most often among individuals imprisoned for assault (60%; see Figure 15–1), but tends to be less prevalent among property offenders (40%) and drug offenders (30%).[21] In self-reports, male prison inmates have revealed that prior to imprisonment they were three times as likely as other men to consume an ounce or more of alcohol each day.[22] Female inmates were five times more likely than women in general to consume that amount.[23]

The problems caused by alcohol abuse are many. Besides crime, alcohol abuse produces illnesses, on-the-job accidents, lost productivity, family problems, and a lowered quality of life. There are few reasons to think, however, that the legal environment surrounding alcohol consumption will change anytime soon. Cultural acceptance of alcoholic beverages remains high. Beer, wine, and mixed drinks are served at many parties, weddings, and funerals. They are present in numerous homes and restaurants.

Lawmakers appear willing to deal with the problems caused by alcohol only tangentially. The American experience with prohibition is not one that legislators are anxious to repeat. In all likelihood efforts to reduce the damaging effects of alcohol will take the form of educational programs, legislation to raise the drinking age, and enforcement efforts designed to deter the most visible forms of abuse. Struggles in other areas may also have some impact. For example, lawsuits claiming civil damages are now being brought against some liquor companies on behalf of accident victims, cirrhosis patients, and others. We can anticipate that the concern over alcohol abuse will continue but that few sweeping changes in either law or social custom will occur anytime soon.

FIGURE 15–1   Percentage of criminals who had been drinking prior to crime commission, 1988. *Source:* Bureau of Justice Statistics, *Report to the Nation on Crime and Justice,* 2ed (Washington, D.C.: U.S. Government Printing Office, 1988), p. 51.

A HISTORY OF DRUG ABUSE IN AMERICA

Alcohol is but one example of the many conflicting images of drug use to be found in contemporary American social consciousness. The modern "War on Drugs," initiated by the Reagan administration and given added impetus by President Bush, portrays an America fighting for its very existence against the scourge of drug abuse. While many of today's highly negative images may be correct, they have not always been a part of the American world view.

Opium and its derivatives, for example, were widely available in "patent" medicines of the 1800s and early 1900s. Corner drugstores stocked mixtures of opium and alcohol which were available for the asking. Traveling road shows extolled the virtues of these magical curatives which offered relief from almost any malady. Such "elixirs" were promoted as curealls, and did indeed bring about feelings of well-being in almost anyone who consumed them. Although no one is certain just how widespread opium use was in the United States a hundred years ago, some authors have observed that even baby formulas containing opium were in use for feeding infants born to mothers who were addicted.[24]

Opium was also in widespread use among Chinese immigrants who came to the West Coast in the 1800s, often to work on railroads. Opium dens, in which the drug was smoked, flourished, and the use of opium quickly spread to other ethnic groups throughout the West. Some of the more affluent denizens of West Coast cities ate the substance, and avant-garde poetry was written extolling the virtues of opium.

Morphine, an opium derivative, has a similar history. Although it was legally available in this country almost since its invention, battlefield injuries during the Civil War dramatically heightened public awareness of its pain-killing properties.[25] In the late 1800s morphine was being widely prescribed by physicians and dentists, many of whom abused the substance themselves. By 1896, when per capita morphine consumption peaked, addiction to the substance throughout the United States was apparently widespread.[26]

Heroin, the most potent derivative of opium ever created, was invented as a substitute for morphine by German chemists in 1898. When first introduced, its addictive properties were unknown and it was marketed as a nonaddictive cough suppressant, also useful in treating morphine addiction.[27]

Marijuana, a considerably less potent drug than heroin, has a relatively short history in this country. Imported by Mexican immigrants around the turn of the twentieth century, marijuana use quickly became associated with marginal groups. By 1930 most of the states in the Southwest had passed legislation outlawing marijuana, and some authors have suggested that anti-marijuana laws were primarily targeted at Spanish-speaking immigrants who were beginning to challenge whites in the economic sector.[28] As mentioned earlier, other writers have suggested that the rapidly growing use of marijuana throughout the 1920s and 1930s provided a rationale for the development of drug legislation and the concomitant expansion of drug enforcement agencies.[29] By the 1960s public attitudes regarding marijuana had begun to change. The Hippie generation popularized the drug, touting its "mellowing" effects upon people who smoked it. In a short time marijuana use became epidemic across the country, and books on marijuana cultivation and preparation flourished.

Another drug which found adherents among some youthful idealists of the 1960s and 1970s was LSD. LSD, whose chemical name is lysergic acid diethylamide, was first synthesized in Switzerland in 1938. LSD found limited use in this country in the 1950s for the treatment of psychiatric disorders.

By the mid-1960s LSD had come to the attention of two Harvard psychologists, Timothy Leary and Richard Alpert. Leary and Alpert first used the drug in an experimental treatment program for prisoners at Concord State Prison in Massachusetts. Later, very much impressed with LSD's ability to produce intense introspective states, Leary began to publicly advocate widespread use of the drug as a kind of social "cure-all." Leary's messianic vision implied that if America could be "turned on" to LSD, there would be no more war (the war in Vietnam was raging), racial harmony would emerge, and all social problems would be cured. Not surprisingly, Leary's contract for employment at Harvard University was not renewed, and he was arrested repeatedly for the possession of various controlled substances. Leary eventually escaped from confinement, made his way to Africa, and continued to promote the use of "acid," as LSD is still called today.

Many drugs when first "discovered" have been touted for their powerful analgesic or therapeutic effects. Cocaine was one of them. An early leading proponent of cocaine use, for example, was Sigmund Freud, who prescribed it for a variety of psychological disorders. Freud was himself a user and wrote a book, *The Cocaine Papers*, describing the many benefits cocaine offered. The cocaine bandwagon reached the United States in the late 1800s, and various medicines and beverages containing cocaine were offered to the American public. Prominent among them was Coca-Cola, which combined seltzer water, sugar and cocaine in a new soda advertised as providing a real "pick-me-up." Cocaine came out of Coca-Cola before 1910, but found continued adherents among jazz musicians and artists. Beginning in the 1970s cocaine became associated with exclusive parties, the well-to-do, and the "jet set." Television shows and movies often portrayed the drug as glamorous, and cocaine soon became the drug of choice among the young and upwardly mobile. In testimony to both the cost of the drug and the economic success of some of its users, sterling silver "coke spoons" and rolled $100 bills became preferred paraphernalia. Words like "snorting" and "free-basing" entered common usage, and it was not long before an extensive drug underworld developed, catering to the demands of the affluent users.

Some people argue that official public policy toward drugs has reached a near-hysterical level. *Copyright 1988, USA Today. Reprinted with permission.*

DRUG USE AND SOCIAL AWARENESS

As we have seen, drugs were not strangers to the American social scene of the late 1800s and early 1900s. While drug use still permeates American society, there have been dramatic alterations over the last 100 years in the form such use takes, and in the social consequences of involvement with drugs. Specifically, six elements have emerged which today cast drug use in a far different light than that of the past:

1. An understanding of addiction
2. A belief that drug use is associated with other kinds of criminal activity
3. Generally widespread social condemnation of drug use
4. Laws regulating the use and/or availability of drugs
5. A growing involvement with illicit drugs among the urban poor and the socially disenfranchised, both as an escape from the conditions of life and as a path to monetary gain
6. A shift from a definition of drug abuse as a medical problem to the view that such abuse is a law enforcement issue

In his classic study of the evolution of marijuana laws,[30] Howard S. Becker identified three American values which led to increased regulation of all drugs: (1) the belief "that the individual should exercise complete responsibility for what he does and what happens to him; he should never do anything that might cause loss of self-control," (2) "disapproval of action taken solely to achieve states of ecstasy," and (3) "humanitarianism."[31] Of humanitarianism, Becker says, "[r]eformers believed that people enslaved by the use of alcohol and opium would benefit from laws making it impossible for them to give in to their weaknesses."[32] Becker believes that these values rest upon the Protestant Ethic and a strong "cultural emphases on pragmatism and utilitarianism."[33] Together, these three values form the basis for all modern condemnation of drug use and legitimate legislative and other actions taken to combat drugs.

Drug Abuse Legislation

Antidrug abuse legislation in the Untied States dates back to around 1875 when the city of San Francisco enacted a statute prohibiting the smoking of opium.[34] Other western states were quick to follow San Francisco's lead. The San Francisco law, and others like it, however, clearly targeted Chinese immigrants and were rarely applied to other ethnic groups which may have been involved in the practice.

The first major piece of federal antidrug legislation came in 1914, with enactment of the Harrison Act. The Harrison Act required persons dealing in opium, morphine, heroin, cocaine, and specified derivatives of these drugs, to register with the federal government and to pay a tax of $1.00 per year. The only people permitted to register were physicians, pharmacists, and members of the medical profession. Nonregistered drug traffickers faced a maximum fine of $2,000 and up to five years in prison.

Because the Harrison Act allowed physicians to prescribe controlled drugs for the purpose of medical treatment, heroin addicts and other drug users could still legally purchase the drugs they needed. All the law required was a physician's prescription. By 1920, however, court rulings had established that drug "maintenance" only prolonged addiction and did not qualify as "treatment."[35] The era of legally available heroin had ended.

By the 1930s government attention was riveted on marijuana. At the urging of the Federal Bureau of Narcotics, Congress passed the Marijuana Tax Act in 1937. As the title of the law indicates, the Marijuana Tax Act simply placed a tax of $100 per ounce on cannabis. Individuals not paying the tax were subject to prosecution. With the passage of the Boggs Act in 1951, however, marijuana, along with a number of other drugs, entered the class of federally prohibited controlled substances. The Boggs Act also removed heroin from the list of medically useful substances and required the removal, within 120 days, of any medicines containing heroin from pharmacies across the country.[36]

The Narcotic Control Act of 1956 increased penalties for drug trafficking and possession and made the sale of heroin to anyone under age 18 a capital offense. However, on the eve of the massive explosion in drug use which was to begin in the mid-1960s, the Kennedy administration began a shift in emphasis from the strict punishment of drug traffickers and users to rehabilitation. A 1963 presidential commission[37] recommended elimination of the Federal Bureau of Narcotics, reduced prison terms for drugs offenders, and stressed the need for research and social programs in dealing with the drug problem.

By 1970 America's drug problem was clear to almost everyone, and legislators were anxious to return to a more punitive approach to controlling drug abuse. Under President Nixon, legislation designed to encompass all aspects of drug abuse and to permit federal intervention at all levels of use was enacted. Termed the Comprehensive Drug Abuse Prevention and Control Act of 1970, the bill still forms the basis of federal enforcement efforts today. Title II of the Comprehensive Drug Abuse Prevention and Control Act is the Controlled Substances Act (CSA). The CSA sets up five schedules which classify psychoactive drugs according to their degree of psychoactivity and abuse potential.[38] The discussion that follows is summarized in Table 15–1.

Schedule I controlled substances are those with great potential for abuse, without established medical usage, and which lack safety of use.[39] Federal law requires that any research employing Schedule I substances be fully documented and that the substances themselves be stored in secure vaults. Included under this category are heroin, LSD, mescaline, peyote, methaqualone (quaaludes), psilocybin, marijuana,[40] and hashish as well as other specified hallucinogens. Penalties for a first-offense possession and sale of Schedule I controlled substances under the federal Narcotic Penalties and Enforcement Act of 1986 range up to life imprisonment and a $10 million fine. Penalties increase for subsequent offenses.

Schedule II substances are defined as drugs with high abuse potential for which there is a currently accepted pharmacological or medical use. Most Schedule II substances are also considered to be addictive.[41] Drugs which fall into this category include opium, morphine, codeine, cocaine, phencyclidine (PCP), and their derivatives. Certain other stimulants such as methylphenidate (Ritalin®) and phenmetrazine (Preludin®) and a few barbiturates with high abuse potential also come under Schedule II. Legal access to Schedule II substances requires written nonrefillable prescriptions, vault storage, and thorough record keeping by vendors. Penalties for first-offense possession and sale of Schedule II controlled substances under the federal Narcotic Penalties and Enforcement Act range up to 20 years imprisonment and a $5 million fine. Penalties increase for subsequent offenses.

Schedule III substances involve lower abuse potential than do those in previous schedules. They are drugs with an accepted medical use, but which may lead to a high level of psychological dependence or to moderate or low physical dependence.[42] Schedule III substances include many of the drugs found in Schedule II, but in derivative or diluted form. Common low-dosage antidiarrheals, such as opium-containing paregoric, and cold medicines or pain relievers with low concentrations of codeine fall into this category. Anabolic steroids, whose abuse by professional athletes is coming under increased scrutiny, were

CATEGORIES OF CONTROLLED SUBSTANCES UNDER
THE FEDERAL CONTROLLED SUBSTANCES ACT

Drugs	Schedule	Names	Physical Dependency	Psychological Dependency	Cost	Primary Sources of Supply
NARCOTICS						
Opium	II, III, V	Dover's Powder, Paregoric, Parepectolin	High	High		Asia, Mexico
Morphine	II, III	Morphine, Pectoral syrup	High	High		Pharmaceutical diversion
Codeine	II, III, V	Codeine, Empirin Compound with Codeine, Robitussin A-C	Moderate	Moderate		
Heroin	I	Diacetylmorphine, horse, smack	High	High	$2.00 per milligram (or $100 per day for an average user)	Asia, Mexico, Afghanistan, Pakistan, Iran
Hydromorphone	II	Dilaudid	High	High		
Meperidine (pethidine)	II	Demerol, Pethadol	High	High		Pharmaceutical diversion
Methadone	II	Dolophine, Methadone, Methadose	High	High		
Other narcotics	I, II, III, IV, V	LAAM, Leritine, Levo-Dromoran, Percodan, Tussionex, Fentanyl, Darvon, Talwin, Lomotil	High-low	High-low		
DEPRESSANTS						
Cloral hydrate	IV	Noctec, Somnos	Moderate	Moderate		
Barbiturates	II, III, IV	Amobarbital, Phenobarbital, Butisol, Phenoxbarbital, Secobarbital, Tuinal	High-moderate	High-moderate		Domestic production
Glutethimide	III	Doriden	High	High		
Methaqualone	II	Optimil, Parest, Quaalude, Somnafac, Sopor	High	High	$3.00–10.00 (retail)	Pharmaceutical diversion

Drugs	Schedule	Names	Physical Dependency	Psychological Dependency	Cost	Primary Sources of Supply
Benzodiazepines	IV	Ativan, Azene, Clonopin, Dalmane, Diazepam, Librium, Serax, Tranxene, Valium, Verstran	Low	Low		
Other depressants	III, IV	Equanil, Miltown, Noludar, Placidyl, Valmid	Moderate	Moderate		
STEROIDS						
Anabolic steroids	III	Anabolin, Androlone, Durabolin, Kabolin, Winstrol	Low	High	$5–100 per day for an average user	Pharmaceutical diversion
STIMULANTS						
Cocaine	II	Coke, flake, snow	Possible	High	$800 to $2,100 per ounce (wholesale) $120 per gram (retail)	Peru, Bolivia, Colombia, Ecuador
Amphetamines	II, III	Biphetamine, Delcobese, Desoxyn, Dexedrine, Mediatric, Crank, Ice	Possible	High	$3.00 per dosage unit (retail)	Domestic production
Phenmetrazine	II	Preludin	Possible	High		
Methylphenidate	II	Ritalin	Possible	High		Pharmaceutical diversion
Other stimulants	III, IV	Adipex, Bacarate, Cylert, Didrex, Ionamin, Plegine, PreSate, Sanorex, Tenuate, Tepanil, Voranil	Possible	High		
HALLUCINOGENS						
LSD	I	Acid, microdot	None	Degree unknown	$2.00–8.00 per dose	Clandestine laboratories, American Southwest

Drugs	Schedule	Names	Physical Dependency	Psychological Dependency	Cost	Primary Sources of Supply
Mescaline and peyote	I	Mesc, buttons, cactus	None	Degree unknown		
Amphetamine variants	I	2, 5-DMA, PMA, STP MDA, MMDA, TMA, DOM DOB	Unknown	Degree unknown		Clandestine laboratories
Phencyclidine	II	PCP, angel dust, hog	Degree unknown	High		
Phencyclidine analogs	I	PCE, PCPy, TCP	Degree unknown	Degree unknown		
Other hallucinogens	I	Bufotenine, Ibogaine, DMT, DET Psilocybin, Psilocyn	None	Degree unknown		
CANNABIS						
Marijuana	I	Pot, Acapulco gold grass, reefer, sinsemilla, Thai sticks	Degree unknown	Moderate	Marijuana, $60–130 per ounce (retail)	Domestic production
Tetrahydro-cannabinol	I	THC	Degree unknown	Moderate	Sinsemilla, $165–210 per ounce (retail)	
Hashish	I	Hash	Degree unknown	Moderate		Southeast Asia
Hashish oil	I	Hash oil	Degree unknown	Moderate		

Source: Adapted from the National Narcotics Intelligence Consumer's Committee, *The NNICC Report: The Supply of Illicit Drugs to the United States* (Washington, D.C.: NNICC, 1988); Drug Enforcement Administration, *Drugs of Abuse* (Washington, D.C.: U.S. Department of Justice, 1990) and; United States Pharmacopeial Convention, *United States Pharmacopeial Formulary* Vol. II, 11th edition (Rockville, MD: USPC, 1991).

added to the list of Schedule III controlled substances by congressional action in 1991. Legitimate access to Schedule III drugs is through a doctor's prescription (written or oral) with refills authorized in the same manner. Maximum penalties associated with first-offense possession and sale of Schedule III controlled substances under federal law include five years imprisonment and fines of up to $1 million.

Schedule IV substances have a relatively low potential for abuse (when compared to higher schedules), are useful in established medical treatments, and involve only a limited risk of psychological or physical dependency.[43] Depressants and minor tranquilizers such as Valium, Librium, and Equanil fall into this category, as do some stimulants. Schedule IV substances are medically available in the same fashion as Schedule III drugs. Maximum penalties associated with first-offense possession and sale of Schedule IV substances under federal law include three years in prison and fines of up to $1 million.

Schedule V controlled substances are prescription drugs with a low potential for abuse, and with only a very limited possibility of psychological or physical dependence.[44] Cough medicines (antitussives) and antidiarrheals containing small amounts of opium, morphine, or codeine are found in Schedule V. A number of Schedule V medicines may be purchased through retail vendors with only minimal controls, or upon the signature of the buyer (with some form of identification required). Maximum federal penalties for first-offense possession and sale of Schedule V substances include one year in prison and a $250,000 fine.

The Controlled Substances Act also includes provisions for determining which new drugs should be controlled and into which schedule they should be placed. Pharmacologists, chemists, and botanists are constantly discovering and creating new drugs. Likewise, street-corner "chemists" in clandestine laboratories churn out inexpensive designer drugs—psychoactive substances with widely varying effects and abuse potential. Under the CSA, criteria for assigning a new drug to one of the existing schedules include[45] (1) the drug's actual or relative potential for abuse; (2) scientific evidence of the drug's pharmacological effects; (3) the state of current scientific knowledge regarding the substance; (4) its history and current pattern of abuse; (5) the scope, duration, and significance of abuse; (6) what, if any, risk there is to the public health; (7) the drug's psychic or physiological dependence liability; and (8) whether the substance is an immediate precursor of a substance already controlled. Proceedings to add a new chemical substance to the list of those controlled by law or to delete or change the schedule of an existing drug may be initiated by the chief administrator of the Drug Enforcement Administration, the Department of Health and Human Services, or a petition from any interested person—including manufacturers, medical societies, or public interest groups.[46]

The Anti–Drug Abuse Act of 1988

Recent federal efforts in the war on drugs are intended to be far reaching. In 1988 then-President Reagan created a new cabinet-level post for a "drug czar" who was to be in charge of federal drug-fighting initiatives. William Bennett, the former hard-nosed secretary of education, was named to fill the post. At about the same time, the 1988 Anti–Drug Abuse Act was passed by Congress. The intention of the new law is clear from its preamble, which reads: "It is the declared policy of the United States Government to create a Drug-Free America by 1995."[47]

Under the Anti–Drug Abuse Act, penalties for "recreational" drug users increased substantially,[48] and weapons purchases by suspected drug dealers became more difficult. The law also denies federal benefits, ranging from loans (including student loans) to contracts and licenses, to convicted drug offenders.[49] Earned benefits, such as social security, retirement, health and disability benefits are not affected by the legislation. Nor are welfare payments or existing public housing arrangements (although separate legislation does provide for termination of public housing tenancy for drug offenses). Under the law, civil penalties of up to $10,000 may be assessed against convicted "recreational" users for possession of even small amounts of drugs.

The legislation also includes the possibility of capital punishment for drug-related murders. The killing of a police officer by offenders seeking to avoid apprehension or prosecution is specifically cited as carrying a possible death sentence, although other murders by major drug dealers also fall under the capital punishment provision.[50]

On May 14, 1991, 37-year-old David Chandler, an Alabama marijuana kingpin, became the first person sentenced to die under the law.[51] Chandler had been convicted of ordering the murder of a police informant in 1990.

Ben Johnson, the Canadian super champion of track and field events, was suspended from competition for two years after testing positive for steroid use following his victory in the 100-meter race at the Seoul Olympic Games. Anabolic steroids were added to the list of Schedule III controlled substances by Congress in 1991. *Photo: Canada Wide/Sygma.*

Among other provisions of the law, about $2.8 billion in funding was made available over the 1989 and 1990 fiscal years to combat drug use. Most of the funding was intended to bolster agencies on the front line of the fight against drugs.[52]

One especially interesting aspect of the 1988 statute was its provision for designating selected urban areas as high-intensity drug trafficking zones, making them eligible for federal drug-fighting assistance. Criteria for "drug zone" designation include:[53]

1. The extent to which the area is a center of illegal drug production, manufacturing, importation, or distribution.
2. The extent to which state and local law enforcement agencies have committed resources to respond to the drug trafficking problem in the area.
3. The extent to which drug-related activities in the area are having a harmful impact in other areas of the country.
4. The extent to which a significant increase in allocation of federal resources is necessary to respond adequately to drug-related activities in the area.

Using the law, former **Drug Czar** William Bennett, in March 1989, declared Washington, D.C., a "drug zone." His designation was based in part upon the city's reputation as the murder capital of the country. At the time of the declaration over 60% of Washington's murders (372 in 1988) were said to be drug-related,[54] and legislators and tourists were clamoring for action. Bennett's plan called for more federal investigators, prosecutors, and

Drug Czar A cabinet-level position, originally created during the years of the Reagan presidency, which functions to organize federal drug-fighting efforts.

THEORY INTO PRACTICE

DRUGS: WHAT'S IN A NAME?

Drug names have been a source of confusion to many people attempting to grapple with the drug problem. A single drug may have a dozen or more names. Drugs may be identified according to:

Brand Name: The name given to a chemical substance by its manufacturer. Brand names are registered idioms and are often associated with trademarks. They are used to identify a drug in the pharmaceutical marketplace and may not be used by other manufacturers. Psychoactive substances with no known medical application or experimental use are not produced by legitimate companies and have no brand name.

Generic Name: The chemical or other identifying name of a drug. Generic names are often used by physicians in writing prescriptions which are less costly than when brand names are specified. Generic names are also used in most drug abuse legislation at the federal and state levels in order to specify controlled substances. Generic names are sometimes applicable only to the psychoactive chemical substances in drugs, and not the "drugs" themselves. In marijuana, for example, the chemical tetrahydrocannabinol, or THC, is the active substance.

Psychoactive Category: Psychoactive drugs are categorized according to the effects they produce on the human mind. Narcotics, stimulants, depressants, and hallucinogens are typical psychoactive categories.

Street Names: Street names are slang terms. Many of them originated with the pop culture of the 1960s, and others continue to be produced by modern-day drug subculture. Street names for cocaine include "coke," "flake," and "snow," while heroin is known as "horse," "smack," or "H."

"PCP," an Example: "PCP" and "angel dust" are the street names for a veterinary anesthetic marketed under the brand name Sernylan. Sernylan contains the psychoactive chemical phencyclidine. Phencyclidine is classified as a depressant under the Controlled Substances Act.

specially built prisons to handle accused drug dealers. The only immediate results of the secretary's action, however, were squabbles between federal and city officials over who should be responsible for drug enforcement efforts within the city.

The Investigation of Drug Abuse

The police investigation of drug manufacturing activities has given rise to an area of case law which supplements the *plain view* doctrine, alluded to in Chapter 7. Two legal concepts, "abandonment" and "curtilage," while generally applicable elsewhere, have taken on special significance in drug investigations. Abandonment refers to the fact that property, once it has been clearly thrown away, or discarded, ceases to fall under Fourth Amendment protections. Curtilage is a legal term which describes the area surrounding a residence which can reasonably be said to be a part of the residence for Fourth Amendment purposes.

In 1988 the U.S. Supreme Court decided the case of *California* v. *Greenwood*,[55] which began when Officer Jenny Stracner, of the Laguna Beach, California, Police Department arranged with a neighborhood trash collector for the delivery of garbage collected at a suspect's residence. The refuse was later found to include items "indicative of narcotics use."[56] Based upon this evidence, Stracner applied for a search warrant, which was used in a search of the defendant's home. The search uncovered controlled substances, including cocaine and hashish. The defendant, Greenwood, was arrested. Upon conviction, Greenwood appealed, arguing that he had a reasonable expectation of privacy with respect to his trash. The trash, he said, had been placed in opaque bags and could reasonably be expected to remain unopened until it was collected and disposed of.

The Supreme Court disagreed, saying that "[a]n expectation of privacy does not give rise to Fourth Amendment protection unless society is prepared to accept that expectation as objectively reasonable...[i]t is common knowledge that plastic garbage bags left on or at the side of a public street are readily accessible to animals, children, scavengers, snoops, and other members of the public." Hence, the Court concluded, the property in question had been abandoned, and no reasonable expectation of privacy can accrue to trash left for collection "in an area accessible to the public." The concept of abandonment extends beyond trash which is actively discarded. In *Abel* v. *U.S.* (1960),[57] for example, the Court found that the warrantless search of a motel room by an FBI agent immediately after it had been vacated was acceptable.

Curtilage, a concept which initially found clear recognition in the case of *Oliver* v. *U.S.* (1984),[58] refers to the fact that household activity generally extends beyond the walls of a residence. People living in a house, for example, spend some their time in their yard—an area which they probably think of as private and under the control of their household. Territory within the curtilage of a residence has generally been accorded the same Fourth Amendment guarantees against search and seizure as areas within the walls of a house or apartment. But just how far does the curtilage of a residence extend? Does it vary according to the type or location of the residence? Is it necessary for an area to be fenced in order for it to fall within residential curtilage?

A collateral area of concern is that of activity conducted in fields, out of doors. The open fields doctrine began with the case of *Hester* v. *U.S.* (1924),[59] in which the Supreme Court held that law enforcement officers could search an open field without need for a warrant. The *Oliver* case extended that authority to include secluded and fenced fields posted with no trespassing signs.

In *U.S.* v. *Dunn* (1987),[60] the U.S. Supreme Court considered a Houston-area defendant's claim that the space surrounding a barn, which was located approximately 50 yards from the edge of a fence surrounding a farmhouse, was protected against intrusion by the Fourth Amendment. The Court rejected the defendant's arguments and concluded that, even though an area may be fenced, it is not within the curtilage of a residence if it is sufficiently distant from the area of household activity which attends the residence.

Other, related decisions, have supported seizures based upon warrantless aerial observation of marijuana plants growing in the backyard of defendant's homes[61] and those based upon naked-eye sightings from helicopters of the contents of greenhouses.[62] The Court's reasoning in cases such as this, is that flights within navigable airspace are common, and do not lead to a reasonable expectation of privacy, where no comprehensive efforts to secure privacy are made, even within areas that might normally be considered curtilage. Were sophisticated surveillance techniques to be employed by law enforcement authorities, however—such as the use of drone aircraft, satellite, or infrared photography—the Court's decision would be in doubt.

SIZE OF THE DRUG PROBLEM

The sale of illegal drugs is a $50–100 billion annual industry in the United States.[63] Some perspective can be gained on this figure by recognizing that Americans spend approximately $44 billion on alcohol products and another $37 billion on tobacco products annually.[64] Cocaine, which has replaced marijuana as the drug of choice in some cities, appears to be the leading income producer for the illegal drug industry. The U.S. attorney general reports that, in frequency of use, cocaine has surpassed marijuana in New York City and the District of Columbia.[65] The retail (street) value of illegal drugs sold in the United States for 1990 is graphically represented in Figure 15–2.

According to a federal study released in 1993,[66] 11.4 million Americans were users of illegal drugs—defined as those "having used an illicit drug in the month before the survey." Cocaine use, which declined 31% over the previous year, involved 1.3 million Americans, but the number who used the drug weekly remained at 640,000—a figure that has stayed nearly constant for the past decade during which such surveys have been conducted. Weekly marijuana use was reported by 5.2 million people—a figure that also remained constant from the year before.

Another way to look at the size of the drug problem in the United States is to consider the amount of money spent to combat it. Figures from the federal Office of Management and Budget, for example, show that, for fiscal 1994, $4.7 billion was allocated for drug law enforcement and prosecution efforts, $4.3 billion for prevention and treatment programs, $1.8 billion for interdiction activities, $0.5 billion for international aid in the fight against drugs, another $0.5 billion for research to develop new antidrug technologies, and $1.2 billion in assistance to state and local governments for use in combating drug abuse. The total spent in 1994, $13 billion, shows a shifting emphasis—away from interdiction efforts characteristic of earlier years and toward prevention and treatment programs.

FIGURE 15–2   Retail value of illicit drugs in the United States, 1990. *Source:* Office of National Drug Control Policy, *What America's Users Spend on Illegal Drugs* (Washington, D.C.: ONDCP, 1991).

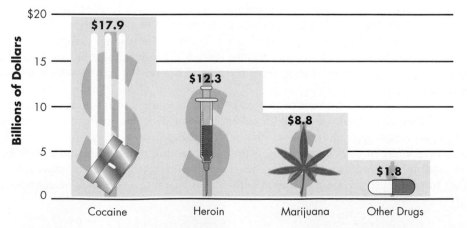

JUSTICE IN AMERICAN CONTEXT...
The Impact Of Drug Offenses on State Justice Systems.

ADVANCE FOR RELEASE AT 5 P.M. EDT
SUNDAY, MARCH 28, 1993
The Bureau of Justice Statistics

DRUG CRIMES ARE GROWING SHARE OF STATE FELONY CONVICTIONS

WASHINGTON, D.C.—Approximately 168,000 men and women were convicted of trafficking in illegal drugs in state felony courts during 1990—more than twice the number convicted in 1986, the Bureau of Justice Statistics (BJS) announced today.

The Bureau, a Department of Justice agency, said about 49% of the convicted drug-trafficking violators were sent to a state prison, compared to an estimated 37% in 1986. An additional 106,253 people were convicted of possessing illegal drugs during 1990. "BJS estimates that total state court convictions on all felony charges throughout the U.S. grew 42 percent in the four-year period, reaching 829,000 convictions in 1990," said BJS Acting Director Lawrence A. Greenfeld. "About 92,000 more people were convicted of felony drug trafficking during 1990 than during 1986. This accounted for 37 percent of the total increase in felony convictions nationwide. In 1990 drug trafficking convictions comprised 20 percent of all state felony convictions, compared to 13 percent in 1986."

The estimated percentages of 1990 state court felony convictions across the country by various crime types were as follows:

Violent crimes	17.8%
Murder and manslaughter	1.3
Rape	2.2
Robbery	5.7
Aggravated assault	6.5
Other violent crimes[1]	2.1
Property crimes	33.9
Burglary	13.2
Larceny	13.6
Fraud and forgery	7.0
Drug offenses	33.1
Possession	12.8
Trafficking	20.3
Weapons offenses	2.5
Other nonviolent crimes[1]	12.7

[1]Other violent crimes include negligent manslaughter, sexual assault, and kidnapping. Other nonviolent crimes include receiving stolen property and drunk driving.
Source: Bureau of Justice Statistics, National Criminal Justice Reference Service, Electronic Bulletin Board Service.

During 1990 state courts sentenced 46% of convicted felons to a state prison, 25% to a local jail (usually for a year or less), and the remaining 29% to straight probation without jail or prison time.

The survey included a special study of state court activity in large urban counties with populations exceeding 600,000 inhabitants. In such jurisdictions there was a 61% increase in felony convictions during the 1986–1990 period, averaging 15% a year, BJS noted. Convictions in all offense categories grew, but drug-trafficking convictions increased the most—by 128%, or 32% annually.

The survey was conducted in 300 counties (or about 10% of the nation's 3,109 counties) selected to be representative of the whole country. Included were the District of Columbia and at least one county from each state except, by chance, Vermont. The survey excluded federal courts and those state or local courts that do not handle felonies. Federal courts convicted 36,686 people of felonies during 1990, or 4% of the combined state and federal caseload.

Source: For additional information on how to contact the National Institute of Justice's electronic bulletin board call the Bureau of Justice Assistance Clearinghouse at 800-688-4252. The BBS number is 301-738-8895.

A number of agencies report on the amount of various types of drugs which enter the country or are produced here. One such group is the National Narcotics Intelligence Consumers Committee (NNICC). The NNICC was established in 1978 to coordinate the collection and analysis of foreign and domestic strategic drug-related intelligence.[67] Members of the NNICC include the DEA, FBI, CIA, IRS, INS, Coast Guard, and other federal agencies charged with drug law enforcement. NNICC data describe the availability and use of marijuana, cocaine, PCP, and heroin. Other dangerous drugs and the money laundering schemes of drug traffickers are also a focus of NNICC activity. NNICC data for each of the major drug categories are described in the paragraphs that follow.

Marijuana

Marijuana, whose botanical name is *cannabis sativa L.*, grows wild throughout most of the tropic and temperate regions of the world.[68] Marijuana has no established medical use, although experiments with the drug to help cancer patients deal with the nauseating effects of chemotherapy have proved promising. Marijuana commonly comes in loose form, as the ground leaves and seeds of the hemp plant. Also available to street-level users are stronger forms of the drug, such as sinsemilla (the flowers and the leaves of the female cannabis plant), hashish (the resinous secretions of the hemp plant), and hash oil (a chemically concentrated form of delta-9-tetrahydrocannabinol, or THC, the psychotropic agent in marijuana).

Marijuana is usually smoked, although it may be eaten or made into a "tea." Low doses of marijuana create restlessness and an increasing sense of well-being, followed by dreamy relaxation and a frequent craving for sweets.[69] Sensory perceptions may be heightened by the drug, while memory and rational thought are impaired (see Table 15–2). Marijuana's effects begin within a few minutes following use and may last for two to three hours.

In 1992, according to the NNICC, marijuana use among high school students hit its lowest level since the committee began gathering data in 1978. The proportion of seniors who used marijuana declined from 37% in 1978 to 32.6% in 1992.[70]

Intelligence shows that domestic production accounts for about 19% of all marijuana in the United States. During 1991 more than 5.2 million cultivated marijuana plants were destroyed by authorities across the country and 2,848 cannabis-growing greenhouses were seized.[71] Most marijuana brought into the United States comes from Mexico (70%), while only 9% comes into the country from Colombia—once the primary supplier of imported marijuana.[72] Of all the marijuana entering the country or produced domestically, approximately one quarter or 4,000 metric tons is seized or lost in transit.[73]

Cocaine

Cocaine (cocaine hydrochloride) is the most potent central nervous system stimulant of natural origin.[74] Cocaine is extracted from the leaves of the coca plant (whose botanical name is *Erythroxylon coca*). Since ancient times the drug has been used by native Indians throughout the highlands of Central and South America to overcome altitude sickness and to provide high energy levels for rigorous farming.

Cocaine has some medicinal value as a topical anesthetic for use on sensitive tissues such as the eyes and mucous membranes. Throughout the early 1900s cocaine was valued by physicians for its ability to anesthetize tissue while simultaneously constricting blood vessels and reducing bleeding. Recently, more effective products have replaced cocaine in many medical applications.

Street-level users of cocaine often "snort" the drug through the nose, although it may be injected, and some of its derivatives—like crack—are smoked. Cocaine generally reaches the United States in the form of a much-processed white crystalline powder. It is often diluted with a variety of other ingredients including sugar and anesthetics such as lidocaine. Dilution allows sellers to reap high profits from small amounts of the drug.

Cocaine produces intense psychological effects, including a sense of exhilaration, superabundant energy, hyperactivity, and extended wakefulness.[75] Irritability and apprehension may be unwanted side effects. Excessive doses may cause seizures and death from heart failure, cerebral hemorrhage, and respiratory collapse. Some studies show that repeated use of cocaine may heighten sensitivity to the toxic side effects of the drug.[76]

NNICC data indicate that cocaine has become the country's most dangerous commonly used drug. During a recent year, nearly 100,000 hospital emergencies involving cocaine abuse were reported across the country.[77] At the time of the NNICC report, cocaine was available in all major American metropolitan areas and most small communities. The cocaine derivative crack, manufactured by numerous street-level laboratories, was available primarily in large urban areas.

The sale and consumption of illicit drugs comprise a multibillion-dollar annual industry in the United States. Here a heroin addict shoots up. *Photo: Alan Mercer/Stock Boston.*

There is evidence that cocaine use among young people is declining. Until 1986 all statistics had either shown an increase or stability in cocaine use among high school students.[78] However, a 1987 survey of drug use among 16,000 high school seniors conducted by the Institute for Social Research found a decrease of about 33% (from 6.2% to 4.3% of all seniors) over the previous 12-month period in the proportion of students who had used cocaine at least once in the past month.[79] The decline continued through 1992.[80] On the other hand, recent DEA data show that individuals aged 35 and over are using various forms of cocaine with dramatically increasing frequency.[81]

Most cocaine enters the United States from Peru, Bolivia, Colombia, or Ecuador. Together, these four countries have an estimated annual production capability of around 1,290 tons of pure cocaine.[82] A single Los Angeles drug bust on September 28, 1989 amazed investigators with the size of their catch. In a warehouse in a quiet section of the city, police seized 20 tons of cocaine, valued at up to $20 billion if sold on the street.[83] Found along with the cocaine was $10 million in cash. Other large caches were quickly uncovered, including 9 more tons of cocaine in a house in Harlingen, Texas; 6 tons on a ship in the Gulf of Mexico; and more than 5 tons hidden in barrels of lye in New York City.[84] Fiscal year seizures of cocaine in the United States totaled 120 tons (with an estimated wholesale value of $40 billion) during 1992 alone—a 7.6-ton decrease from the previous year.[85] By 1993, apparently in response to decreased American demand, a small reduction in South American cocaine production was being noted.[86]

H E R O I N

Classified as a narcotic, heroin is a derivative of opium—itself the product of the milky fluid found in the flowering poppy plant (*Papaver somniferum*). Opium poppies have been grown in the Mediterranean region since 300 B.C.[87] and are now produced in many other parts of the world as well. Although heroin is not used medicinally in this country, many of the substances to which it is chemically related—such as morphine, codeine, hydrocodone, naloxone, and oxymorphone—do have important medical uses as pain relievers.

Heroin is a highly seductive and addictive drug which, when smoked, injected underneath the skin (skin popping), or "shot" directly into the bloodstream (mainlining), produces euphoria. Because tolerance for the drug increases with use, larger and larger doses of heroin must be injected to achieve the pleasurable effects desired by addicts. Heroin deprivation causes withdrawal symptoms which initially include watery eyes, runny nose, yawning, and perspiration. Further deprivation results in restlessness, irritability, insomnia, tremors, nausea, and vomiting. Stomach cramps, diarrhea, chills, and other flu-like symptoms are also common. Most withdrawal symptoms disappear within seven to ten days,[88] or when the drug is readministered.

Street-level heroin varies widely in purity. It is often cut with powdered milk, food coloring, cocoa, or brown sugar. Most heroin sold in the United States is only 5% pure.[89] Because of dosage uncertainties, overdosing is a common problem for addicts. Mild overdoses produce lethargy and stupor. Larger doses may cause convulsions, coma, and death. Other risks, including infectious hepatitis and AIDS, are associated with self-administered heroin through the use of dirty needles. The National Institute on Drug Abuse (NIDA) notes that the number of intravenous drug users with AIDS is doubling every 14 to 16 months.[90] The causes of such spread include (1) the sharing of "dirty" needles containing small amounts of contaminated blood left in the equipment by other users, (2) needle sharing at parties, and (3) the lax practices of "shooting galleries" where drug paraphernalia may be passed among many people.

Heroin abuse has remained fairly constant over the past few decades. Some indicators point to an increased availability of heroin in the last few years.[91] Street-level heroin prices have declined in recent years, while heroin-related emergency room admissions nation-wide have reached almost 40,000 per year.

Most heroin in the United States comes from Southwest Asia (Afghanistan, Pakistan, and Iran), Southeast Asia (Burma, Laos, and Thailand), and Mexico. According to data from the Heroin Signature Program (HSP), which uses chemical analysis of the trace elements in heroin supplies to identify source countries, 56% of all heroin entering the U.S. in 1992 came from Southeast Asia.[92]

Evidence indicates that the heroin abuse picture is changing. East Coast cities, including New York, Philadelphia, Boston, and Baltimore, continue to show an increase in heroin-related health problems, while Western cities such as Los Angeles and San Francisco show the opposite trend.[93] Hospital statistics give credence to the belief that heroin is being replaced by other drugs among younger users and that most heroin addicts are "old-timers."

SCOPE OF THE PROBLEM

The drug problem in the United States is not simply one of drug use. The manufacture, possession, sale, and use of controlled substances are related to a variety of criminal activities and produce other large-scale social problems. Some of these problems are examined over the next few pages.

DRUGS AND CRIME

The link between drugs and crime has at least three dimensions: (1) the possession, use, or sale of controlled substances which directly violates antidrug laws; (2) crimes committed by drug users in order to obtain more drugs, or crimes committed by persons whose judgment is altered by drugs; and (3) organized criminal activities in support of the drug trade and associated money laundering activities.

As Figure 15–3 shows, approximately 800,000 persons were arrested in 1992 for drug law violations (excluding alcohol) in the United States.[94] Sixty-eight percent of all arrests nationally were for possession of controlled substances; the remainder were for sale, possession, or manufacture.[95] Arrests for heroin or cocaine possession accounted for 32.4% of all arrests, while only 25.5% of all drug arrests were for marijuana possession.[96] Possession of PCP, LSD, amphetamines, and tranquilizers accounted for only a relatively small number of arrests.

A close examination of official statistics reveals considerable regional variation. Marijuana arrests in the Western states, for example, were less than half as frequent as arrests for cocaine or heroin possession. Midwestern states, on the other hand, reported 50 percent more arrests for marijuana than they did for possession of cocaine and heroin.[97] The rate of drug law violations also varies greatly from region to region. Arrest rates are highest in the Western part of the country (564 per 100,000) and lowest in the Midwest (256 per 100,000).[98]

The number of persons arrested for drug law violations is increasing. In a recent six-year period, 51% of the overall increases in federal convictions for all types of crimes were accounted for by drug offenses alone.[99] Much of the overcrowding in federal and state prisons today is due to an accompanying increase in convictions for drug law violations. In a recent year, 54% of all federal prisoners were charged with drug law violations.[100]

T A B L E   1 5 - 2

MAJOR CONTROLLED SUBSTANCES: THEIR USES AND EFFECTS

Substances	*Use/Effects*
Narcotics, including opium, morphine, heroin, codeine, dilaudid	*Legitimate:* pain relief, antidiarrheal, cough suppressant *Street Use:* pleasure, euphoria, lack of concern, general feelings of well-being
Stimulants, including amphetamines such as Dexedrine and Benzedrine and other drugs such as cocaine, crack, crank, and ice	*Legitimate:* increase alertness, reduce fatigue, control weight *Street Use:* produce excitability, feelings of competence and power
General depressants, including sedatives and tranquilizers such as Nembutal, Seconal, Phenobarbital, Quaalude, Sopor, Valium, Librium, Thorazine, and Equanil	*Legitimate:* release from anxiety, mood elevators; treatment of psychological problems *Street Use:* in high doses to produce intoxication, also used to counter the effects of other drugs or in the self-treatment of withdrawal
Marijuana including hashish, cannabis, sinsemilla, and hashish oil	*Legitimate:* none fully recognized; possible use in cancer chemotherapy *Street Use:* euphoria, relaxation, intoxication, time distortion, memory alterations, focused awareness
Hallucinogens, including LSD, mescaline, psilocybin, peyote, and MDA	*Legitimate:* none *Street Use:* to produce hallucinations and distortions of reality
Inhalants, including nitrous oxide, gasoline, toluene, amyl nitrite and butyl nitrite	*Legitimate:* some are used as medical sedatives *Street Use:* to produce a "rush" or sense of lightheadedness
Anabolic steroids, including nandrolene, oxandrolene, oxymetholone and stanozolol	*Legitimate:* weight gain, treatment of anemia, breast cancer, and angioedema *Street Use:* to build body bulk and increase strength (in weightlifters, professional athletes, others)

Note: Each drug may have a variety of effects or may produce different effects on individual users. Drugs used in combination with one another may have unpredictable effects.
Source: Adapted from Drug Enforcement Administration, *Drug of Abuse: 1989 Edition* (Washington, D.C.: U.S. Department of Justice, 1990), and U.S. Pharmacopeial Convention, *Drug Information*, 11th ed., Vol. II (1991).

The link between drugs and other types of crime came into clearer focus at the end of 1987 with the establishment of the federal Data Center and Clearinghouse for Drugs and Crime, a part of the National Institute of Justice. A recent NIJ study[101] of 201 heroin users in Central and East Harlem (New York City) found that daily users each committed on average about 1,400 crimes per year. Of these offenses, 1,116 were directly drug related, involving primarily drug sales and use. Another 75 were relatively minor crimes such as shoplifting, but the remaining 209 offenses committed by each user involved relatively serious violations of the law such as robbery, burglary, theft, forgery, fraud, and the fencing of stolen goods. A separate study which followed the daily activities of 354 Baltimore heroin addicts over a nine-year period found that they had committed a total of nearly 750,000 criminal offenses.[102]

A comprehensive effort designed to gauge the degree of drug use among criminal offenders is the NIJ's Drug Use Forecasting (DUF) program. DUF utilizes voluntary urine specimens and analyzes anonymous interview data from randomly selected male and female arrestees in 25 cities across the country. The percentage of sampled arrestees testing positive for any drug, including marijuana (but no alcohol) in selected cities during late 1992 is shown in Figure 15–4. The data range from a high of 80% of sampled arrestees in Philadelphia who had drugs present in their bodies at the time of arrest, to a low of 50% of arrested males in Houston who either tested positive for or admitted to recent drug use.[103] Cocaine was the most widely abused drug among arrestees in most cities, although there is evidence that its use may be declining. Eighty-three percent of sampled arrestees in New York City in mid-1988, for example, had cocaine present in their bodies at the time of arrest,[104] while by 1992 the figure had declined to 77%.

A number of cautions should be held in mind when interpreting Figure 15–4. First, although the tendency among some who view the statistics is to conclude that drug use *causes* crime, it could be that both crime and drug use are the result of some other factor such as poverty, socialization, and so on. Second, given the rising number of drug arrests, it is not entirely surprising that many arrestees have drugs in their systems. Many of those arrested were arrested for drug sales, possession, or use. Third, self-reports of state correctional facility inmates, while still indicating a high level of drug use prior to criminal activity, do not necessarily support the data available through the Drug Use Forecasting Program. A 1986 survey of state prison inmates showed, for example, that 43% had been involved in daily drug use in the month before their current offense, while "only" 19% were using a major drug (heroin, methadone, cocaine, PCP, or LSD) on a daily or near-daily basis.[105]

FIGURE 15–3   Adult arrests for drug law violations, 1985–1992. *Source:* Federal Bureau of Investigation, *Crime in the United States* (Washington, D.C.: U.S. Department of Justice, various years).

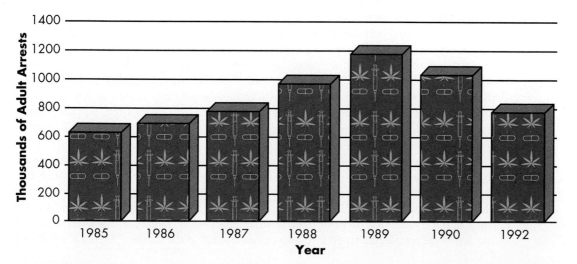

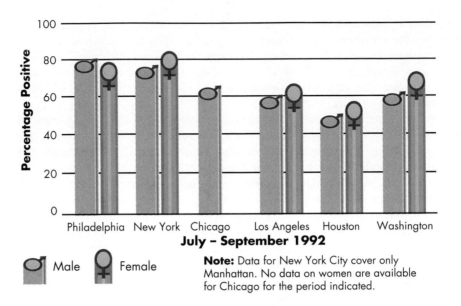

FIGURE 15–4   Percentage of arrestees testing positive for any drug in selected cities. *Source:* National Institute of Justice, *Drug Use Forecasting* (Washington, D.C.: NIJ, 1993).

Money Laundering The process of converting illegally earned assets, originating as cash, to one or more alternative forms to conceal such incriminating factors as illegal origin and true ownership. *Source:* Clifford Karchmer and Douglas Ruch, "State and Local Money Laundering Control Strategies," *NIJ Research in Brief* (Washington, D.C.: NIJ, 1992), p. 1.

MONEY LAUNDERING

Money laundering is the name given to the process used by drug dealers to disguise the source of their revenue.[106] Drug profits are laundered by converting them into other assets, such as real estate, stocks and bonds, racehorses, diamonds, gold, or other valuables. The NNICC says that millions of dollars in drug monies are laundered through commercial banks and other financial institutions each year, with major money laundering operations flourishing in South Florida and Los Angeles.[107] Other estimates put the laundered amount as high as $300 billion.[108] The Police Executive Research Forum (PERF) estimates that profits in excess of $100 billion a year are generated in the United States through narcotics trafficking and related underworld activities.[109] PERF also points out that successful money laundering can only be accomplished with the cooperation of lawyers, accountants, stockbrokers, and other investment advisers.[110]

In 1988 U.S. Customs agents in Tampa, Florida, arrested seven high-level banking executives who had been lured back into U.S. jurisdiction from other countries.[111] "The Cash Cleaners," as the men were dubbed, were arrested after allegedly laundering $14 million for narcotics agents in a "sting" operation. Estimates were that many times that amount had been laundered for real criminals.[112] Indictments named 80 individuals and the first banking company ever charged with money laundering under U.S. law. The company, Bank of Credit and Commerce International, based in Luxembourg, was the seventh largest privately owned financial institution in the world."[113] BCCI was closed in 1991 by International Banking Regulators.

In an effort to catch money launderers, U.S. banking law requires financial institutions to report deposits in excess of $10,000. Traffickers attempt to avoid the law through two techniques known as smurfing and structuring.[114] Smurfers repeatedly purchase bank checks in denominations of less than $10,000 which are then sent to accomplices in other parts of the country who deposit them in existing accounts. Once the checks have cleared the funds are transferred to other banks or moved out of the country. Structuring is very

Drugloot—confiscated money, weapons, and police scanners. The cash take from illegal drug sales must be laundered before it can enter the flow of legitimate assets. *Photo: New York City Police Department.*

similar and involves cash deposits to bank accounts in amounts of less than $10,000 at a time. After accounts are established the money is withdrawn and deposited in increments elsewhere, making it difficult to trace. Countries which have secrecy laws protecting depositors are favorites for drug traffickers. Among them are Switzerland, Panama, Hong Kong, the United Arab Emirates, and the Bahamas.[115]

Although federal law prohibits the laundering of money, only two states—California and Georgia—have similar laws.[116] As a consequence, many local enforcement agencies are reluctant to investigate money laundering activities in their states. To counteract this reluctance, the federal government is moving to facilitate interagency activities of its enforcement personnel. The new federal task force, the Financial Crimes Enforcement Network (FINCEN), formed to coordinate the fight against money laundering, is beginning to pay off. In December 1989, the Network successfully traced records contained on computer disks, which had been captured by the Colombian government, to bank accounts in the United States, Luxembourg, Switzerland, Austria, and Britain. As a result, over $60 million in assets belonging to Colombian drug lord Jose Gonzalo Rodriguez Gacha were frozen.[117]

NARCOTERRORISM

Some authors have identified a link between major drug traffickers and terrorist groups.[118] A number of South American traffickers appear especially willing to finance the activities of terrorist groups as a way of purchasing protection for themselves and their operations. The insurgents with whom they deal have their own political agendas, including the disruption of society, the overthrow of constitutional governments, and the spread of Marxist-Leninism. In 1989 the Colombian government became involved in what can only

Narcoterrorism A political alliance between terrorist organizations and drug-supplying cartels. The cartels provide financing for the terrorists, who in turn provide quasimilitary protection to the drug dealers.

be described as a civil war, involving the constitutionally elected government, on the one hand, and armed representatives of the Medellin, Cali, and Bogota drug cartels, on the other. While the government sought to close down drug laboratories and money laundering operations, the cartels threatened to topple the government and targeted opposing judges, newspaper editors, and government officials for assassination. By 1990, Colombian cartels had succeeded in murdering 11 Colombian Supreme Court justices, over 30 other judges, 2 powerful newspaper editors, the country's attorney general, and hundreds of Colombian national police officers, and in forcing the resignation of the minister of justice.[119] The battle continues. In 1993, in an attempt to hide criminal activities behind a political facade, Colombian narcotics kingpin Pablo Emilio Escobar-Gaviria created an antigovernment armed revolutionary group called the "Antioquian Rebellion." During the last six months of 1992 Escobar assassins killed more than 50 of the country's police officers. The drug kingpin was himself shot to death by government forces in December of 1993.

The link between drug traffickers and insurgents has been termed narcoterrorism.[120] Narcoterrorism, simply defined, is the involvement of terrorist organizations and insurgent groups in the trafficking of narcotics.[121] The first documented instance of an insurgent force financed, at least in part, with drug money, came to light during an investigation of the virulent anti-Castro Omega 7 group in the early 1980s.[122] Clear-cut evidence of modern narcoterrorism, however, is difficult to obtain. Contemporary insurgent organizations with links to drug dealers probably include (1) the 19th of April Movement (M-19) operating in Colombia, (2) Peru's *sendero luminoso* (shining path), (3) the Revolutionary Armed Forces of Colombia, and (4) the large Farabundo Marti National Liberation Front (FMLN), which has long sought to overthrow the elected government of El Salvador.[123]

The symbiotic relationship which exists between terrorist organizations and drug traffickers is mutually beneficial. Insurgents derive financial benefits from their support role in drug trafficking, while the traffickers themselves receive protection and benefit from the use of terrorist tactics against foes and competitors.

Narcoterrorism, because it is a relatively new phenomenon, raises a number of questions. James A. Inciardi summarizes them as follows:[124]

1. What is the full threat posed by narcoterrorism?
2. How should narcoterrorism be dealt with?
3. Is narcoterrorism a law enforcement problem or a military one?
4. How might narcoterrorism be affected by changes in official U.S. policy toward drugs and drug use?
5. Is the international drug trade being used as a tool by anti-U.S. and other interests to undermine Western democracies in a calculated way?

Lost Productivity

Drug abuse has many personal and social costs which extend beyond handling by the criminal justice system. Among them are lost productivity (estimated at as high as $60 billion annually[125]), poor job performance, medical claims, the corruption of public officials, the loss of human life, and disease.

Studies of Postal Service workers have shown that applicants who tested positive for drug use in preemployment screening, but were hired anyway, had 43% higher rates of absenteeism and were 40% more likely to be fired than were other workers.[126] The same study suggested that absenteeism and job turnover are only two of many areas potentially affected by drug use among workers.[127] Job quality and on-the-job safety, although not measured by the study, are probably also negatively impacted by employee drug abuse. A poll conducted by the Institute for a Drug Free Workplace found that one in four U.S. workers have personal knowledge of coworkers using illegal drugs on the job.[128] The Institute also found that 97% of workers agree that drug testing at work can be appropriate under some circumstances.

The potential for official corruption posed by widespread drug abuse is another area in which social costs may be substantial. Recently, the judge executive of Morgan County, Kentucky, and the Morgan County sheriff were found guilty of accepting $5,000 monthly payments to protect a large cocaine distribution ring.[129] Over the past few years, seven sheriffs and two former sheriffs in the Eastern Federal District of Tennessee have been convicted of accepting bribes from drug dealers.[130] Some analysts of police behavior have cited a new generation of police officers who have grown up in environments where drugs are generally accepted, and the huge amounts of money at the disposal of drug kingpins, as a potentially lethal mix in the fight to keep enforcement agents honest.[131]

A generation ago the Knapp Commission found wide-ranging corruption in the police department of New York City. Bribes were being paid to officers to overlook streetside gambling operations, prostitution activities, and the like. Today, however, the threat to police integrity is much greater. The daily Knapp era bribes of $10 to $20 have been replaced with monetary amounts that, in some cases, rival the yearly salary of many police personnel. Programs to promote police reporting of corruption within the ranks, internal investigation units, and undercover officers who keep watch on other officers have all been tried in order to halt the spread of corruption. In the long run, such efforts, because of the cynicism they engender, may be self-defeating. Experts[132] who have studied the problem cite the need for greater professionalism and a heightened sense of purpose as the only real long-term solutions to drug-based corruption. Better training, higher pay, more education, and increased individual responsibility, they say, are the most effective building blocks of police professionalism.[133]

SOLVING THE PROBLEM

Any problem as complex and as large as drug abuse is unlikely to yield to simple strategies. Many methods of attacking the problem have been proposed. Among them are the following:

STRICT ENFORCEMENT

Trafficking in controlled substances is, by definition, an illegal activity. Unfortunately, current legal prohibitions appear to be doing little to discourage widespread drug abuse. Those who look to strict law enforcement as a primary drug control strategy usually stress the need for secure borders, drug testing to identify users, and stiff penalties to discourage others from drug involvement. The U.S. Coast Guard policy of "zero tolerance," begun in the late 1980s, for example, led to the seizure of multimillion-dollar vessels when even small amounts of drugs (probably carried aboard by members of the crew) were found on board.

Calls for harsh punishments are being heard across the country. Even rural areas and traditional "liberal" enclaves have joined the bandwagon. Officials in the state of Minnesota, for example, have attributed at least 75% of major crimes in that state over the past few years to drug abuse and are now considering reinstatement of the death penalty to quell drug-related violence.[134] In other actions initiated by the concern over drugs,

Minnesota's legislators are planning to fund a major expansion of the state's prison system and are considering eliminating parole for certain crimes.[135]

But strict enforcement measures may be only a stop-gap strategy—and may lead to greater long-run problems. As James Q. Wilson observes, "…it is not clear that enforcing the laws against drug use would reduce crime. On the contrary, crime may be caused by such enforcement because it keeps drug prices higher than they would otherwise be."[136]

FORFEITURE

RICO Stands for "Racketeer Influenced Corrupt Organization" and refers to a federal statute which allows for the federal seizure of assets derived from illegal enterprise.

Forfeiture is an enforcement strategy supported by federal statutes and some state laws, which bears special mention. Antidrug forfeiture statutes authorize judges to seize "all moneys, negotiable instruments, securities, or other things of value furnished or intended to be furnished by any person in exchange for a controlled substance…(and) all proceeds traceable to such an exchange."[137] The first federal laws to authorize forfeiture as a criminal sanction were both passed in 1970. They were the Continuing Criminal Enterprise statute, commonly called the CCE, and the Organized Crime Control Act. A section of the Organized Crime Control Act, known as the **RICO** statute (for Racketeer Influenced Corrupt Organizations), was designed to prevent criminal infiltration of legitimate businesses and has since been extensively applied in federal drug smuggling cases. In 1978 Congress authorized civil forfeiture of any assets acquired through narcotics trafficking in violation of federal law. Many states modeled their own legislation after federal law, and now have similar statutes.

The newer civil statutes have the advantage of being relatively easy to enforce. Civil forfeiture requires proof only by a preponderance of the evidence rather than proof beyond a reasonable doubt as mandated by the standards of criminal prosecution. In civil proceedings based upon federal statutes, there is no need to trace the proceeds in question to a particular narcotics transaction. It is enough to link them to narcotics trafficking generally.[138]

Forfeiture amounts can be huge. In a recent 15-month period, for example, the South Florida–Caribbean Task Force, composed of police agencies from the federal, state, and local levels, seized $47 million in airplanes, vehicles, weapons, cash, and real estate.[139] In a single investigation involving two brothers convicted of heroin smuggling, the federal government seized a shopping center, three gasoline stations, and seven homes worth over $20 million in New York City.[140]

A 1991 Virginia forfeiture case may hold special interest for college and university students. In March of that year, federal agents seized three University of Virginia fraternity houses and indicted 12 students on charges of drug distribution. The 12 were allegedly involved in a series of small sales of illegal drugs to undercover agents over the months preceding the seizure. The action was part of an effort by law enforcement agencies to counter charges that enforcement activities had been focused only on inner-city areas. Following the arrests, E. Montgomery Tucker, U.S. attorney for the Western District of Virginia, said "[these arrests show] there are no safe havens, no safe places, to conduct illegal drug trafficking." Fraternity members were allowed to return to the houses, which are now owned by the federal government.

> In this crime-weary, drug-infested nation, it now appears that any tough-on-crime proposal goes, no matter how dangerous it may be to individual rights.
>
> —USA Today *editorial*

Forfeiture statutes find a legal basis in the relation-back doctrine. The relation-back doctrine assumes that because the government's right to illicit proceeds relate back to the

CAREERS IN JUSTICE

WORKING FOR THE U.S. CUSTOMS SERVICE

TYPICAL POSITIONS.   Criminal investigator, special agent, customs inspector, canine enforcement officer, and import specialist. Support positions include intelligence research specialist, computer operator, auditor, customs aide, investigative assistant, and clerk.

EMPLOYMENT REQUIREMENTS.   Applicants must (1) be U.S. citizens, (2) pass an appropriate physical examination, (3) pass a personal background investigation, (4) submit to urinalysis for the presence of controlled substances, (5) have at least three years of work experience, and (6) be under 35 years of age. Appointment at the GS-7 level also requires (1) one year of specialized experience (i.e., "responsible criminal investigative or comparable experience"), (2) a Bachelor's degree with demonstration of superior academic achievement (a 3.0 grade point average in all courses completed at time of application or a 3.5 grade point average for all courses in the applicant's major field of study, or rank in the upper third of the applicant's undergraduate class, or membership in a national honorary scholastic society), or (3) one year of successful graduate study in a related field.

OTHER REQUIREMENTS.   Applicants must (1) be willing to travel frequently, (2) be able to work overtime, (3) be capable of working under stressful conditions, and (4) be willing to carry weapons and be able to qualify regularly with firearms.

SALARY.   Mid-1993, Customs Inspector: GS-5 $18,340, GS-7 $22,717; Customs Investigator: GS-5 $22,627, GS-7 $25,745.

BENEFITS.   Benefits include (1) 13 days of sick leave annually, (2) 2-1/2 to 5 weeks of annual paid vacation and 10 paid federal holidays each year, (3) federal health and life insurance, and (4) a comprehensive retirement program.

DIRECT INQUIRIES TO: Office of Human Resources, U.S. Customs Service, 1301 Constitution Ave., N.W. Gelman Blvd., Room 220, Washington, D.C. 20229. Phone: (202) 634-2534.

time they are generated, anything acquired through the expenditure of those proceeds also belongs to the government.[141]

Although almost all states now have forfeiture statutes, prosecutions built upon them have met with less success than prosecutions based on federal law. The Police Executive Research Forum[142] attributes the difference to (1) the fact that federal law is more favorable to prosecutors than most state laws, (2) greater federal resources, and (3) the difficulties imposed by statutory requirements that illegal proceeds be traced to narcotics trafficking.

In 1993, in *U.S.* v. *A Parcel of Land in Rumson, N.J.*,[143] the U.S. Supreme Court established an "innocent owner defense" in forfeiture cases, whereby the government was forbidden from seizing assets associated with drug transactions which were later acquired by a new and innocent owner. In the same year, in the case of *Austin* v. *U.S.*,[144] the Court

U.S. Customs officers with seized cocaine. Lower Photo: Officer Rick Dallent shows how four tons of packaged cocaine were hidden in hardwood boards designed for picnic tables shipped from Honduras to Florida. *Photos: Bob Sherman/Time Magazine and UPI/Bettmann.*

placed limits on the government's authority to use forfeiture laws against drug criminals, finding that seizures of property must not be excessive when compared to the seriousness of the offense charged. Otherwise, the justices wrote, the Eighth Amendment's ban on excessive fines could be contravened. The justices, however, refused to establish a rule by which excessive fines could be judged, saying, "[t]he Court declines to establish a test for determining whether a forfeiture is constitutionally 'excessive,' since prudence dictates that the lower courts be allowed to consider that question." The *Austin* ruling was supported by two other 1993 cases, *Alexander* v. *U.S.*, and *U.S.* v. *Real*.[145] In *Alexander*, the Court found that forfeitures under the RICO statute must be limited according to the rules established in *Austin*, while in *Real*, the Court held that "[a]bsent exigent circumstances, the Due Process Clause requires the Government to afford notice and a meaningful opportunity to be heard before seizing real property subject to civil forfeiture."

INTERDICTION

Interdiction involves efforts aimed at stopping drugs from entering the United States. The Coast Guard, Border Patrol, and Customs agents have played the most visible roles in interdiction efforts over the last few decades. Interdiction strategies in the fight against drugs, however, are almost doomed to failure by the sheer size of the task. Although most enforcement efforts are focused on international airports and major harbors, the international boundary of the United States extends for over 12,000 miles. Rough coastline, sparsely populated desert, and dense forests provide natural barriers to easy observation and make detection of controlled substances entering the country very difficult. Add to this the fact that over 420 billion tons of goods and more than 270 million people cross over the American border annually and the job of interdiction becomes more complicated still.[146] Experts estimate that the total flow of illegal heroin and cocaine entering the country annually is less than 20 tons, much of it carried in small lots of only a few pounds or ounces.[147] Although the quantity of illegally shipped marijuana is considerably higher—a few hundred tons[148]—it is still tiny in comparison with the total tonnage crossing the border. Because even minute quantities of most drugs can be highly potent, the interdiction strategy suffers from the proverbial "needle in the haystack" predicament.

A number of suggestions have surfaced recently on expanding interdiction efforts. Some would supplement current border patrol efforts with Armed Forces personnel and equipment. Advanced AWACS radar surveillance airplanes, helicopter gunships, naval vessels, and infantry soldiers could be called upon to identify, track, and search all vessels bound for the United States. Such action met with considerable approval from both Houses of Congress prior to the 1988 elections. The House of Representatives, for example, tagged an amendment onto the $230 billion defense authorization bill calling for the military to seal off U.S. borders to drug runners. The Senate passed a similar, although less far-reaching bill.[149] Neither bill reached the status of law.

Opposition to the planned use of the military in the war against drugs came from many corners. One source of concern was the Posse Comitatus Act of 1878, which forbids the military from enforcing civilian law. The Pentagon and the Joint Chiefs of Staff were themselves strongly opposed to military involvement. Military estimates of the cost of such an operation included $14 billion for additional surveillance aircraft and $6.2 billion to physically patrol the border.[150]

Interdiction as a drug control policy has itself come under fire recently. In 1993 Attorney General Janet Reno questioned the effectiveness of federal interdiction efforts in Florida, pointing out that only approximately 15% of drugs entering Dade County, Florida, are interdicted.[151] About the same time U.S. Representative Charles E. Schumer, chairman of the House Judiciary's Committee's Subcommittee on Crime and Criminal Justice, said, "[t]he international eradication and interdiction effort has been a near-total failure," and added "[w]e should seriously consider eliminating almost all spending on foreign eradication and overseas interdiction."[152] Schumer advocated a change in govern-

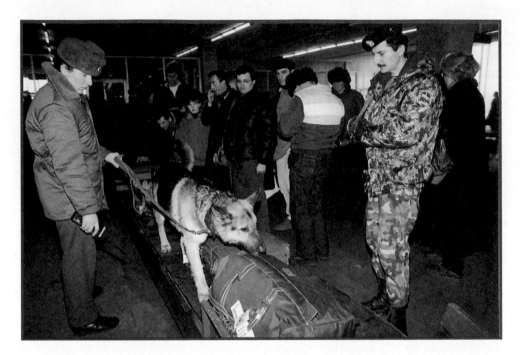

Drug interdiction, which involves efforts aimed at stopping drugs from entering the country, is an international strategy. Here a drug dog alerts on a bag at Moscow's international airport. *Photo: Reuters/Bettmann.*

ment expenditures, with the lion's share of the federal antidrug budget going to fund education, treatment, and prevention programs, rather than law enforcement or military interdiction efforts. In keeping with the prevailing sentiment, the Clinton administration drug strategy, unveiled in late-1993, deemphasizes interdiction and shifts resources toward democratic institution building in source countries.

CROP CONTROL

Crop control strategies attempt to limit the amount of drugs available for the illicit market by targeting foreign producers. Crop control in source countries generally takes one of two forms. In the first, government subsidies (often with U.S. support) are made available to farmers to induce them to grow other kinds of crops. Sometimes illegal crops are bought and burned. The second form of control depends upon aerial spraying or ground-level crop destruction.

Source country crop control suffers from two major drawbacks.[153] One is that the potentially large profits which can be made from illegal acreage encourage farmers in unaffected areas to take up the production of crops which might have been destroyed elsewhere. Another derives from the difficulties involved in trying to gain effective cooperation on eradication efforts by foreign governments. In some parts of the world, opium and coca are major cash crops, causing considerable reluctance on the part of local governments to undertake any action directed against them at all.

Some international efforts have been successful, however. Operation Snowcap, for example, a program operated by the DEA, involves efforts by 12 Latin American countries working in conjunction with U.S. agents to reduce the flow of cocaine into the United States. In 1991, in Peru alone, Operation Snowcap resulted in the seizure of the largest cocaine laboratory outside of Colombia as well as several metric tons of chemicals used in the processing of cocaine.[154]

CAREERS IN JUSTICE

WORKING WITH THE IMMIGRATION & NATURALIZATION SERVICE

TYPICAL POSITIONS.   Special agent, immigration examiner, border patrol agent, immigration inspector, deportation officer.

EMPLOYMENT REQUIREMENTS.   Applicants for the position of special agent must meet the general requirements for a federal law enforcement officer, and must (1) be a United States citizen, (2) hold a Bachelor's degree or have 3 years of responsible experience, or an equivalent combination of education and experience, (3) be in excellent physical condition, with good eyesight and hearing, (4) submit to urinalysis screening prior to employment, (5) possess emotional and mental stability, (6) be 21–34 years of age at the time of employment, (7) have no felony convictions or records of improper or criminal conduct.

OTHER REQUIREMENTS.   Border patrol agents are required to demonstrate proficiency in the Spanish language.

SALARY.   All positions provide for entry at GS-5 or GS-7 levels, depending upon qualifications. A Bachelor's degree qualifies applicants for appointment at the GS-5 level (earning $18,340 or more in mid-1993). Individuals with exceptional experience or education may be appointed at the GS-7 level ($22,717 and higher in mid-1993).

BENEFITS.   Paid annual vacation, sick leave, life and health insurance, and a liberal retirement plan.

DIRECT INQUIRIES TO: Immigration and Naturalization Service, U.S. Department of Justice, 425 I Street, N.W., Washington, D. C. 20536. Phone: (202) 514-2525.

EDUCATION

Although every proposed solution to the drug crisis has its difficulties, many people believe that education provides the best solution to the problem. As some writers have observed, "[s]ociety's readiness to seek educational solutions for social ills reflects the value it attaches to education per se, and its commitment to the notion of education based upon rational argument and experience."[155]

Michael S. Goodstadt, of the Addiction Research Foundation,[156] groups drug education programs into three categories: (1) those providing factual information about drugs; (2) those that are concerned with feelings, values, and attitudes; and (3) those that focus directly on behavior. Most modern programs contain elements of all three approaches.

Drug education programs can be found in schools, churches, and youth groups and may be provided by police departments, social service agencies, hospitals, and private citizens groups. Media advertisements against drugs also make use of educational principles.

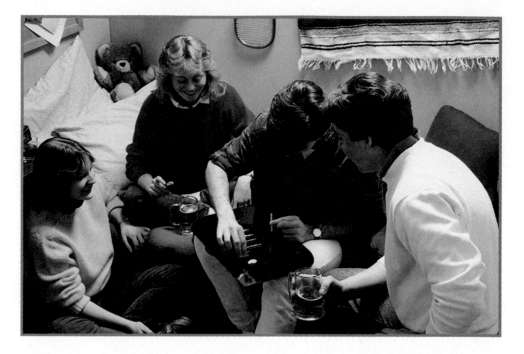

A dorm room drug party. Drug abuse extends to all social groups and can be found among all ages.
Photo: Lynn Eskenazi/ Comstock.

An example of a school-based program provided through the use of police resources is the School Program to Educate and Control Drug Abuse (SPECDA), which began in New York City in 1984.[157] SPECDA began with 50 officers selected to provide anti–drug abuse instruction to students in the city's fifth and sixth grades. The program, which elicits parental involvement, consists of Sixteen 45-minute classroom sessions dealing with such topics as the dangers of drug abuse, self-awareness, peer pressure, decision making, leadership, and drug-refusal strategies.[158]

In 1988 the Bureau of Justice Assistance, a part of the U.S. Department of Justice, initiated efforts to standardize and upgrade the quality of drug education efforts throughout the nation's schools[159] Project DARE, the Bureau's Drug Abuse Resistance Education Program, was widely publicized and has begun to serve as a model for school-based programs. DARE began as a cooperative effort between the Los Angeles Police Department and the Los Angeles Unified School District in 1983. It uses uniformed law enforcement officers to conduct classes in elementary schools and, like SPECDA, focuses on decision-making skills, peer pressure, and alternatives to drug use.[160]

A common thread running between almost all of today's educational efforts is an attempt by service providers to buttress general interpersonal coping skills among those exposed to drug use. The idea that it is OK to "say no to drugs" is being promoted through a variety of techniques. Some educational efforts, recognizing that the source of any message is itself important, use well-known movie and music superstars as spokespersons.

Regardless of the program used, there is little evidence to date to support the belief that education will produce the desired effect upon problem drug users or those at risk of beginning drug use.[161]Table 15–3, for example, which reports state-by-state spending on school-based drug education, shows little relationship between the amount of money spent on drug education and the number of hard-core cocaine users. To increase the impact of drug education efforts, experts have suggested that each program be evaluated fully as to its effectiveness and applicability to other situations. To be effective, programs will proba-

TABLE 15-3

STATE SPENDING ON DRUG EDUCATION AND NUMBER OF COCAINE ADDICTS, 1990

State/Region	Addicts per 1,000 Population	Total Addicts	Per Student Spending in 1990 on Drug Education
Alabama	7.2	29,000	$6.90
Alaska	6.6	3,500	12.87
Arizona	13.7	46,000	5.87
Arkansas	4.4	10,000	5.80
California	12.2	337,000	5.67
Colorado	10.5	34,000	6.08
Connecticut	5.7	18,000	27.53
Delaware	4.9	3,200	13.26
District of Columbia	40.5	25,000	NA
Florida	8.2	98,000	6.94
Georgia	8.7	54,000	6.29
Hawaii	10.5	11,000	7.02
Idaho	3.7	3,700	6.35
Illinois	13.8	160,000	8.82
Indiana	3.3	18,000	6.22
Iowa	3.1	9,000	6.14
Kansas	4.8	12,000	5.99
Kentucky	6.6	24,000	6.37
Louisiana	7.6	34,000	7.08
Maine	2.9	3,400	11.46
Maryland	6.4	29,000	5.99
Massachusetts	4.9	29,000	7.47
Michigan	7.3	67,000	7.66
Minnesota	6.9	29,000	8.55
Mississippi	2.6	6,900	6.48
Missouri	11.5	59,000	6.20
Montana	1.8	1,500	8.86
Nebraska	8.6	14,000	5.90
Nevada	24.9	25,000	7.26
New Hampshire	3.3	3,400	7.74
New Jersey	5.4	72,000	7.69
New Mexico	10.2	15,000	5.83
New York	24.5	436,000	17.67
North Carolina	7.0	45,000	9.18
North Dakota	2.0	1,300	11.09
Ohio	6.4	69,000	6.25
Oklahoma	7.7	25,000	6.46
Oregon	6.5	18,000	6.33
Pennsylvania	7.2	86,000	8.11
Rhode Island	4.7	4,600	9.42
South Carolina	4.0	14,000	6.22
South Dakota	1.8	1,300	10.07
Tennessee	7.4	36,000	6.10

T A B L E 1 5 - 3 (C O N T I N U E D)

State/Region	Addicts per 1,000 Population	Total Addicts	Per Student Spending in 1990 on Drug Education
Texas	10.3	173,000	6.37
Utah	7.7	13,000	6.36
Vermont	2.1	1,100	13.31
Virginia	9.4	55,000	6.39
Washington	4.5	21,000	5.70
West Virginia	2.2	4,200	6.55
Wisconsin	10.8	52,000	8.05
Wyoming	3.1	1,500	14.17

NA = Not available.
Source: USA Today, September 6, 1990, p. 8A, citing a report by the United States Senate Judiciary Committee.

bly also have to acknowledge the perceived positive aspects of the drug experience, as well as cultural messages that encourage drug use.[162] Until they do, many recipients of today's messages may discount them as conflicting with personal experience.

LEGALIZATION AND DECRIMINALIZATION

Decriminalization The redefinition of certain previously criminal behaviors into regulated activities, which become "ticketable" rather than "arrestable."

Often regarded as the most "radical" approach to solving the drug problem, decriminalization and legalization have been proposed repeatedly. Although the words decriminalization and legalization are often used interchangeably, there is a significant difference. Legalization refers to the removal of all legal strictures from the use or possession of the drug in question. Manufacture and distribution might still be regulated. Decriminalization, on the other hand, substantially reduces penalties associated with drug use, but may not eliminate them entirely. States, such as Oregon, which have decriminalized marijuana possession, for example, still consider simple possession of small amounts of the substance a ticketable offense similar to jay-walking or improper parking.[163]

Arguments in support of both legalization and decriminalization include:[164]

1. Legal drugs would be easy to track and control. The involvement of organized criminal cartels in the drug distribution network could be substantially curtailed.
2. Legal drug sales could be taxed, generating huge revenues.
3. Legal drugs would be cheap, significantly reducing the number of drug-related crimes committed in order to feed expensive drug habits.
4. Since some people are attracted to anything "taboo," legalization could, in fact, reduce the demand for drugs.
5. The current war on drugs is already a failure and will be remembered as one of history's follies.[165] Prohibiting drugs is too expensive in terms of tax dollars, sacrificed civil liberties, and political turmoil.
6. Drug dealers and users care little about criminal justice sanctions. They will continue their illegal activities no matter what the penalties.
7. Drug use should ultimately be a matter of personal choice.

Many suggest that any solution to the American drug problem must begin at home. In this photo young boys search through hundreds of crack vials dropped by a drug dealer as he fled from a competitor on a Philadelphia street. *Photo: Eugene Richards/Magnum.*

Modern advocates of legalization are primarily motivated by cost-benefit considerations, weighing the social costs of prohibition against its results.[166] The results, they say, have been meager at best, while the costs have been almost more than society can bear.

Whatever the arguments for legalization or decriminalization, however, the nation appears unready to hear them. Drugs are now the voting public's top crime-rated concern, and politicians everywhere are talking tough about strict laws and substantial punishments for law violators.[167] Opponents of legalization argue from both a moral and a practical stance. Some, like New York City mayor Rudolph Giuliani, believe that legalization would only condone a behavior that is fundamentally immoral.[168] Others argue that under legalization drug use would increase, causing more widespread drug-related social problems than exist today. Robert DuPont, former head of the National Institute on Drug Abuse, for example, estimates that up to ten times the number of people who now use cocaine would turn to the substance if it were legal.[169]

A compromise approach has been suggested in the two-market system.[170] The two-market approach would allow inexpensive and legitimate access to controlled substances for registered addicts. Only maintenance amounts of the needed drugs would be available. The two-market approach would purportedly reduce the massive profits available to criminal drug cartels while simultaneously discouraging new drug use among the nonaddicted population. Great Britain provides a modern example of the two-market system. During the 1960s and 1970s British heroin addicts who registered with the government were able to receive prescriptions for limited amounts of heroin dispensed through medical clinics. Because of concern about system abuses, clinics in the late 1970s began to dispense reduced amounts of heroin, hoping to "wean" addicts away from the drug.[171] By 1980 British policy replaced heroin with methadone,[172] a synthetic drug designed to prevent the physical symptoms of heroin withdrawal. Methadone, in amounts sufficient to prevent withdrawal, does not produce a heroin-like high.

It is doubtful that the two-market system will be adopted in the United States. American cultural condemnation of major mind-altering substances has created a reluctance to accept the legitimacy of drug treatment using controlled substances. In addition, cocaine is much more of a problem in the United States than is heroin. The large number of drug abusers in the country, combined with the difficulty of defining and measuring "addiction" to drugs such as cocaine, would make any maintenance program impractical.

SUMMARY

The widespread use of illegal drugs in America today carries with it a high social cost. Of direct concern to the criminal justice system are the crimes committed by those associated with the drug life-style. While the manufacture, importation, sale, and use of illegal drugs account for a substantial number of law violations, many other offenses may also be linked to drug use. Among them are thefts of all kinds, burglary, assault, and murder.

Drug-related crimes derive from the fact that drugs are both expensive for users and extremely profitable for suppliers. The cost of drugs forces many users, some of whom have little legitimate income, into the commission of property crimes to acquire the funds necessary to continue their drug lifestyles. Users of illicit drugs who have substantial legitimate incomes may indirectly shift the cost of drug use to society through lowered job productivity, psychological or family problems, and medical expenses.

Numerous criminal enterprises are supported by the street-level demand for drugs. Some of these illegitimate businesses are massive international cartels which will stop at nothing to protect their financial interests. Kidnapping, bribery, threats, torture, and murder are tools of the trade among drug kingpins in their battle to continue reaping vast profits.

Any realistic appraisal of the current situation must admit that the resources of the criminal justice system in dealing with it are strained to the limit. There are simply not enough agents, airplanes, equipment, or money to entirely remove illegal drugs from American communities. The justice system faces the added problem of corruption inherent in any social control situation where large amounts of money frequently change hands. Until attitudes supportive of drug use are modified or replaced by more sanguine values, law enforcement can only hope to keep the problem from becoming worse.

DISCUSSION QUESTIONS

1. Why have drugs become a large-scale problem in the United States today? In your opinion, are there identifiable elements of contemporary American culture which support drug use? If so, what might they be?

2. What commonly used legal substances might qualify as drugs, even though they are generally not recognized as such? Why do people use such substances?

3. Why does drug use tend to lead to other types of crime commission? What kinds of crimes might be involved?

4. How would you deal with the problem of illicit drug use facing American society today? Discuss the choices offered in this chapter, listing the "pros" and "cons" of each.

5. What characteristics does drug use share in common with other social order or "victimless" crimes? Should social order crimes be legalized and left to individual choice? Why or why not?

ENDNOTES

1. Office of the Attorney General, *Drug Trafficking: A Report to the President of the United States, August 3, 1989* (Washington, D.C.: U.S. Department of Justice, 1989).

2. Interview with William Bennett, *USA Today*, March 20, 1989, p. 11A.

3. Jimmy Breslin, "Crack," *Playboy*, December 1988, p. 110.

4. "Good Morning America," March 1, 1988 (broadcast at 7:20 A.M. EST).

5. The term "recreational user" is well established in the literature of drug abuse. Unfortunately, it tends to minimize the seriousness of drug abuse by according even hard drugs the status of a hobby.

6. Howard Becker, *Outsiders: Studies in the Sociology of Deviance* (New York: The Free Press, 1963).

7. James B. Jacobs, "Drinking and Crime," an NIJ *Crime File Study Guide* (Washington, D.C.: National Institute of Justice, no date), p.1.

8. Ibid.

9. Ibid.

10. *Statistical Abstracts of the United States, 1987* (Washington, D.C.: U.S. Government Printing Office, 1988), Table 181.

11. Ibid.

12. Steven Olson and Dean R. Gerstein, *Alcohol in America: Taking Action to Prevent Abuse* (Washington, D.C.: National Academy Press, 1985), p. 13.

13. Ibid.

14. In most states individuals may also be arrested for "driving under the influence" of other drugs and controlled substances, including prescription medicines.

15. Bureau of Justice Statistics, "Drunk Driving," a BJS *Special Report* (Washington, D.C.: U.S. Government Printing Office, 1988), p. 1, and Federal Bureau of Investigation, *Crime in the United States 1992* (Washington, D.C.: U.S. Government Printing Office, 1993).

16. Ibid.

17. Ibid.

18. U.S. Department of Justice, *Crime in the United States, 1992* (Washington, D.C.: U.S. Government Printing Office, 1993).

19. Bureau of Justice Statistics, *Report to the Nation on Crime and Justice*, 2nd ed. (Washington, D.C.: Department of Justice, 1988), p. 50.

20. Ibid., p. 51.

21. Ibid.

22. Ibid., p. 50.

23. Ibid.

24. Howard Abadinsky, *Drug Abuse: An Introduction* (Chicago: Nelson-Hall, 1989), p. 32.

25. Charles E. Terry and Mildred Pellens, *The Opium Problem* (New York: The Committee on Drug Addiction, 1928).

26. Ibid.

27. Ibid., p. 76.

28. David Musto, *The American Disease: Origins of Narcotic Control* (New Haven, CT: Yale University Press, 1973).

29. Becker, *Outsiders.*

30. Ibid.

31. Ibid., p. 136.

32. Ibid.

33. Ibid.

34. *The President's Commission on Organized Crime* (Washington, D.C.: U.S. Government Printing Office, 1986).

35. *Webb* v. *U.S.*, 249 U.S. 96.

36. Drug Enforcement Administration, *Drug Enforcement: The Early Years,* (Washington, D.C., DEA, December 1980) p. 41.

37. White House Conference on Drug Abuse, *Commission Report* (Washington, D.C.: U.S. Government Printing Office, 1963).

38. For a good summary of the law, see Drug Enforcement Administration, *Drugs of Abuse, 1988 Edition* (Washington, D.C.: U.S. Government Printing Office, 1988).

39. Drug Enforcement Administration, *Drug Enforcement Briefing Book* (Washington, D.C.: DEA, n.d.), p. 3.

40. A number of states have now recognized that marijuana may be useful in the treatment of nausea associated with cancer chemotherapy, glaucoma, and other medical conditions.

41. DEA, *Drug Enforcement Briefing Book,* p. 3.

42. Ibid.

43. Ibid., p. 4.

44. Ibid.

45. DEA, *Drugs of Abuse, 1988 Edition,* p. 5.

46. Ibid., p. 4.

47. Anti–Drug Abuse Act of 1988, P.L. 100–690, Sec. 5251.

48. This provision became effective on September 1, 1989.

49. "Congress Gives Final OK to Major Antidrug Bill," *Criminal Justice Newsletter,* Vol. 19, no. 21 (November 1, 1988), pp. 1–4.

50. Ibid., p. 2.

51. "Drug Lord Sentenced to Death," *USA Today,* May 15, 1991, p. 3A.

52. Ibid., p. 3.

53. *Drug Enforcement Report,* Vol. 5, no. 12 (New York: Pace Publications, March 23, 1989), p. 1.

54. Ibid.

55. *California* v. *Greenwood,* 486 U.S. 35, 108 S.Ct. 1625 (1988).

56. Ibid.

57. *Abel* v. *U.S.,* 363 U.S. 217 (1960).

58. *Oliver* v. *U.S.,* 466 U.S. 170 (1984).

59. *Hester* v. *U.S.,* 265 U.S. 57, 44 S.Ct. 445 (1924).

60. *U.S.* v. *Dunn,* 480 U.S. 294, 107 S.Ct. 1134 (1987).

61. *California* v. *Ciraolo,* 476 U.S. 207, 106 S.Ct. 1809 (1986).

62. *Florida* v. *Riley,* U.S. 109, S.Ct. 693 (1989).

63. The Attorney General of the United States, *Drug Trafficking: A Report to the President of the United States* (Washington, D.C.: U.S. Department of Justice, August 3, 1989).

64. Office of National Drug Control Policy, *What America's Users Spend on Illegal Drugs* (Washington, D.C.: ONDCP, 1991) p. 4.

65. "Attorney General Announces NIJ Drug Use Forecasting System," *NIJ Reports* (Washington, D.C.: National Institute of Justice, March/April 1988), p. 9.

66. "Use of Illegal Drugs Declines Again in 1992," *USA Today,* June 24, 1993, 1A.

67. National Narcotics Intelligence Consumers Committee, *The NNICC Report, 1987* (April 1988), preface.

68. DEA, *Drugs of Abuse,* p. 45.

69. Ibid.

70. National Narcotics Intelligence Consumers Committee, *The NNICC Report, 1992* (Washington, D.C.: Drug Enforcement Administration, 1993).

71. National Narcotics Intelligence Consumers Committee, *The NNICC Report, 1991* (Washington, D.C.: Drug Enforcement Administration, 1992).

72. Ibid.

73. Ibid.

74. Ibid., p. 37.

75. Ibid.

76. Ibid., p. 40.

77. Ibid.

78. Ibid.

79. "Survey Shows Declining Rate of Drug Use by High School Seniors," *Criminal Justice Newsletter,* Vol. 20, No. 6 (March 15, 1989), p. 7.

80. NNICC, *The NNICC Report, 1992.*
81. Ibid.
82. Ibid.
83. "Drug Raid Called Biggest Ever," *The Fayetteville Observer-Times* (North Carolina), September 30, 1989, p. 1A.
84. "Cocaine Found Packed in Toxic Chemical Drums," *The Fayetteville Observer-Times*, (North Carolina), November 5, 1989.
85. NNICC, *The NNICC Report, 1992.*
86. Ibid.
87. DEA, *Drugs of Abuse*, p. 14.
88. Ibid., p. 12.
89. Ibid., p. 15.
90. Ibid., p. 54.
91. Ibid.
92. NNICC, *The NNICC Report, 1992.*
93. Ibid.
94. Federal Bureau of Investigation, *Crime in the United States 1992* (Washington, D.C.: U.S. Government Printing Office, 1993).
95. Ibid.
96. Ibid. Unfortunately, UCR data combine arrests for heroin and cocaine possession into one category. They do the same for sale/manufacture arrests.
97. Ibid.
98. Ibid.
99. Bureau of Justice Statistics, "Drug Law Violators, 1980–1986," a BJS *Special Report* (Washington, D.C.: U.S. Government Printing Office, 1988), p.1.
100. Office of the Attorney General, *Drug Trafficking*, p. 3.
101. Bernard A. Gropper, "Probing the Links Between Drugs and Crime," a National Institute of Justice *Research in Brief*, February 1985, p. 4.
102. J. C. Ball, J. W. Shaffer, and D. N. Nurco, "Day to Day Criminality of Heroin Addicts in Baltimore: A Study in the Continuity of Offense Rates," *Drug and Alcohol Dependence*, 1983, p. 12.
103. National Institute of Justice, *Drug Use Forecasting: 1988* (Washington, D.C.: NIJ, December 1989).
104. National Institute of Justice, *Drug Use Forecasting: June–September 1992* (Washington, D.C.: NIJ, 1993).
105. Bureau of Justice Statistics, "Drug Use and Crime: State Prison Inmate Survey, 1986," a BJS *Special Report* (Washington, D.C.: BJS, 1988), p. 1.
106. For a true-life account of money laundering activities, see Nick Tosches, *Power on Earth: Michele Sindona's Explosive Story* (New York: Arbor House, 1986).
107. NNICC, *The NNICC Report, 1987*, p. 80.
108. Clifford Karchmer and Douglas Ruch, "State and Local Money Laundering Control Strategies," *NIJ Research in Brief* (Washington, D.C.: NIJ, 1992), p. 1.
109. Clifford L. Karchmer, *Illegal Money Laundering: A Strategy and Resource Guide for Law Enforcement Agencies* (Washington, D.C.: Police Executive Research Forum, 1988), p. iv.
110. Ibid.
111. "The Cash Cleaners," *Time*, October 24, 1988, p. 65.
112. Ibid.
113. Ibid.
114. NNICC, *The NNICC Report, 1987*, p. 82.
115. Ibid., p. 85.
116. Karchmer, *Illegal Money Laundering*, p. 5.
117. Beaty and Hornik, "A Torrent of Dirty Dollars."
118. Daniel Boyce, "Narco-Terrorism," *FBI Law Enforcement Bulletin* (October 1987), p. 24, and James A. Inciardi, "Narcoterrorism: A Perspective and Commentary," in Robert O. Slater and Grant Wardlaw, eds., *International Narcotics* (London: Macmillan/St. Martins, 1989).
119. Office of the Attorney General, *Drug Trafficking*, p. 19.
120. A term reportedly invented by former Peruvian President Fernando Belaunde Terry; see James A. Inciardi, "Narcoterrorism," a paper

presented at the 1988 annual meeting of the Academy of Criminal Justice Sciences, San Francisco, p. 8.

121. Boyce, "Narco-Terrorism," p. 24.

122. Ibid., p. 25.

123. U.S. Department of State, *Terrorist Group Profiles* (Washington, D.C.: U.S. Government Printing Office, 1989).

124. James A. Inciardi, "Narcoterrorism: A Perspective and Commentary," paper presented at the annual meeting of the Academy of Criminal Justice Sciences, San Francisco, CA, 1988, p. 20.

125. Jack Kelley, "Poll: On-Job Drug Use Is Significant," *USA Today*, December 13, 1989, p. 1A.

126. Associated Press (Washington), "High Firing, Absentee Rates Tied to Drug Use," preliminary report of a study conducted by the National Institute on Drug Abuse for the U.S. Postal Service, January 14, 1989.

127. Ibid.

128. Ibid.

129. Ibid., p. 4.

130. Ibid.

131. Todd S. Purdum, "Drugs Threatening Integrity of New York Police," *The New York Times*, November 12, 1988, p. 10Y.

132. Ibid.

133. Ibid.

134. "Hardening Their Hearts: Minnesota Gets Tough," *Newsweek*, April 3, 1989, p. 28.

135. Ibid.

136. James Q. Wilson, "Drugs and Crime," in Michael Tonry and James Q. Wilson, eds., *Drugs and Crime* (Chicago, University of Chicago Press, 1990), p. 522.

137. 21 U.S.C. § 881 (a) (6).

138. *U.S.* v. *$4,255,625.39 in Currency*, 762 F.2d 895, 904.

139. Bureau of Justice Assistance, *Asset Forfeiture Bulletin* (October 1988), p. 2.

140. Ibid.

141. Michael Goldsmith, *Civil Forfeiture:*

Tracing the Proceeds of Narcotics Trafficking (Washington, D.C.: Police Executive Research Forum, 1988), p. 3.

142. Ibid., p. 1.

143. *U.S.* v. *A Parcel of Land in Rumson, N.J.*, No. 91–781. Decided February 24, 1993.

144. *Austin* v. *U.S.*, No. 92–6073. Decided June 28, 1993.

145. *Alexander* v. *U.S.*, No. 91–1526 Decided June 28, 1993. *U.S.* v. *James Daniel Good Real*, No. 92–1180. Decided December 13, 1993.

146. Mark Moore, *Drug Trafficking*, a National Institute of Justice Crime File Study Guide (Washington, D.C.: U.S. Government Printing Office, 1988), p. 3.

147. Ibid.

148. Ibid.

149. "Military Can't Stop Drug Running, Study Says," *The Fayetteville Times* (North Carolina), May 19, 1988, p. 9A.

150. "Is the War on Drugs Another Vietnam?" *Newsweek*, May 30, 1988, p. 38.

151. "Officials Raise Doubts About Drug Interdiction Efforts," *Criminal Justice Newsletter*, May 17, 1993, pp. 1–3.

152. Ibid.

153. Moore, *Drug Trafficking*

154. NNICC, *The NNICC Report, 1991.*

155. Michael S. Goodstadt, *Drug Education*, National Institute of Justice Crime File Study Guide (Washington, D.C.: U.S. Government Printing Office, no date), p. 1.

156. Ibid.

157. See Wilhelmina E. Holliday, "Operation SPECDA: School Program to Educate and Control Drug Abuse," *FBI Law Enforcement Bulletin* (February 1986), pp. 1–4.

158. Ibid.

159. Bureau of Justice Assistance, "An Invitation to Project DARE: Drug Abuse Resistance Education," program brief (Washington, D.C.: U.S. Government Printing Office, 1988).

160. Ibid.
161. Goodstadt, *Drug Education*, p. 3.
162. Ibid.
163. Paul H. Blachy, "Effects of Decriminalization of Marijuana in Oregon," *Annals of the New York Academy of Sciences*, Vol. 282 (1976), pp. 405–415. For more information on the decriminalization of marijuana, see James A. Inciardi, "Marijuana Decriminalization Research: A Perspective and Commentary," *Criminology*, Vol. 19, no. 1 (May 1981), pp. 145–159.
164. For a more thorough discussion of some of these arguments, see Ronald Hamowy, ed., *Dealing with Drugs: Consequences of Government Control* (Lexington, MA: Lexington Books, 1987).

165. See Kurt Schmoke (*Washington Post* editorial author), "Considering Decriminalization: War on Drugs, Policy of Folly?" reprinted in *The Fayetteville Observer-Times* (North Carolina) May 16, 1988, p. 4A.
166. "Should Drugs Be Legal?" *Newsweek*, May 30, 1988, p. 36.
167. Ibid.
168. Ibid., p. 37.
169. Ibid., pp. 37–38.
170. For a more detailed discussion of the two market system, see John Kaplan, *Heroin, an NIJ Crime File Study Guide* (Washington, D.C.: National Institute of Justice, no date)
171. Ibid., p. 3.
172. Ibid., p. 4.

 CHAPTER 16

MULTI- NATIONAL CRIMINAL JUSTICE

…our indebtedness to American Criminology is immense and lasting, but non-American countries possess not only their own crime problems but also their own criminological literature.… [They] have to be interpreted more independently and without a wholesale take-over of American ideas.[1]
—HERMAN MANNHEIM
UNIVERSITY OF LONDON

KEY CONCEPTS

comparative
   criminology
political criminals
Hudud crimes
cultural revolution
Act of Settlement
New Scotland Yard

ethnocentrism
procuratorate
World Crime Surveys
Islamic law
Parliament
Standard Minimum
   Rules for the
   Treatment of
   Prisoners

Koran
INTERPOL
Crown Court

THE INTERNATIONAL PERSPECTIVE

On October 17, 1992, Yoshi Hattori, a Japanese exchange student living in Baton Rouge, Louisiana, was shot to death with a .44 Magnum handgun when he stopped at the home of Rodney Peairs to ask directions to a Halloween party. Hattori, who was wearing a tuxedo, did not understand Peairs' shouts of "freeze."[2] Peairs said he thought Hattori was a burglar. A half year later, in May 1993 Peairs, a meatcutter, was found innocent of manslaughter charges brought against him in the case. The jury deliberated only 3 1/2 hours, and there was applause in the courtroom as the verdict was read. The case had received widespread publicity in Japan, and the televised-live verdict shocked many in that country. Hattori's father called the verdict "unbelievable," and a groundswell of popular opinion throughout Japan—where citizens cannot legally own guns—depicted the United States as a violent nation. As one Japanese businessman put it, "People should not have guns in their homes…all over the world, society (sic) should not have to have guns."

Criminologists who study crime and criminal justice on a cross-national level are referred to as comparative criminologists, and their field is called comparative criminology. Comparative criminology is becoming increasingly valued for the insights it provides. By contrasting American institutions of justice with similar institutions in other countries, procedures and problems which have been taken for granted under the American system can be reevaluated in the light of world experience. As communications, rapid travel, and other technological advances effectively "shrink" the world, we find ourselves in a nearly ideal situation of being able to learn firsthand about the criminal justice systems of other countries.

ETHNOCENTRISM AND THE STUDY OF CRIMINAL JUSTICE

Ethnocentrism The phenomenon of culture-centeredness, by which one uses one's own culture as a benchmark against which to judge all other patterns of behavior.

We often assume that the way we do things is the best way in which they can possibly be done. Such belief is probably part of human nature. As a consequence of this attitude, however, the study of criminal justice in America has been largely ethnocentric. The word "ethnocentric" literally means centered on one's own culture. Only in recent years have American students of justice begun to examine other cultures and their justice systems.

Ethnocentrism is not a uniquely American phenomenon. In some societies, even the *study* of criminal justice is taboo. As a result, data gathering strategies taken for granted in a Western society may not be well received elsewhere. For example, speaking about China, one author has observed, "The seeking of criminal justice information through face-to-face questioning takes on a different meaning in Chinese officialdom than it does generally in the Western world. While we accept this method of inquiry because we prize thinking on our feet and quick answers, it is rather offensive in China because it shows lack of respect and appreciation for the information given through the preferred means of prepared questions and formal briefings."[3]

PROBLEMS WITH DATA

Similar difficulties arise in the comparison of crime rates from one country to another. The crime rates of different nations are difficult to compare[4] because of (1) definitional differences, (2) diverse crime reporting practices, and (3) political and other influences on the reporting of statistics to international agencies.

Definitional differences create what may be the biggest problem. For cross-national comparisons of crime data to have significance it is essential that the reported data share conceptual similarities. Unfortunately that is rarely the case. Nations report offenses according to the legal criteria by which arrests are made and under which prosecution can occur. Switzerland, for example, includes bicycle thefts in its reported data for "auto theft." The Netherlands have no crime category for "robberies," counting them as thefts. Japan classifies an assault that results in death as "assault," or "aggravated assault," not homicide. Greek rape statistics include crimes of sodomy, "lewdness," seduction of a child, incest, and prostitution. Some communist countries report only robberies and thefts which involve the property of citizens, since crimes against state-owned property fall into a separate category.[5]

Social, cultural, and economic differences between countries compound the difficulties we have identified. Auto theft statistics, for example, when compared between countries like the United States and China need to be placed in an economic context. While the United States has two automobiles for every three people, China has only one car per 100 citizens. For the Chinese auto theft rate to equal that of the United States, every automobile in the country would have to be stolen nearly twice each year!

Reporting practices vary substantially between nations. INTERPOL and the United Nations are the only international organizations which regularly collect crime statistics from a large number of countries.[6] Both agencies can only request data, and have no way of checking on the accuracy of the data reported to them. Many countries do not disclose the requested information, and those that do often make only partial reports. In general, small countries are more likely to report than are large ones, and nonsocialist countries are more likely to report than are socialist nations.[7]

Political biases are found in crime statistics reported by nations whose values will not allow an accurate admission of the number or frequency of certain kinds of culturally reprehensible crimes. Communist countries, for example, appear loathe to report property crimes such as theft, burglary, and robbery because the very existence of such offenses demonstrates felt inequities within the communist system.

A final problem with international reports of crime is that they are often delayed. Complete up-to-date data are rare, since the information made available to agencies like the United Nations and INTERPOL arrives over a wide period of time. In addition, official United Nations world crime surveys are conducted only infrequently. To date, four such surveys have been undertaken. Data from the most recent survey are reported in Table 16–1.

TABLE 16-1
CRIMES IN SELECTED COUNTRIES, 1990

Country	Homicide	Assault	Rape	Robbery	Theft	Burglary
Argentina	245	2,388	31	16,024	34,439	NA
Australia	329	NA	2,806	9,015	610,374	341,724
Austria	236	29,757	949	1,884	140,597	89,156
Bahamas	5	NA	18	3,372	NA	362
Barbados	30	1,736	71	339	3,937	214
Botswana	281	11,833	192	523	11,315	7,220
Canada	1,561	207,328	27,842	28,111	1,014,574	379,357
Chile	400	43,823	753	76,709	19,118	NA
Costa Rica	447	203	256	13,134	7,600	8,689
Denmark	242	7,690	486	2,127	307,525	122,371
Finland	429	20,654	381	2,627	110,467	71,405
Hong Kong	148	7,537	111	8,029	32,008	12,701
Hungary	347	9,066	751	2,864	154,369	77,077
India	66,421	NA	10,068	36,529	353,191	131,331
Israel	118	11,006	369	716	120,845	43,972
Italy	4,781	19,412	687	36,830	1,605,329	1,074,250
Jordan	102	498	28	4,348	1,956	2,905
Lithuania	252	2,051	196	334	23,572	5,215
Luxemborg	NA	1,552	28	23	18,812	NA
Malawi	313	2,583	638	5,817	40,503	18,634
Mauritius	26	11,680	38	347	8,483	527
Netherlands	2,206	22,079	1,321	11,946	463,648	390,451
Norway	128	7,949	376	1,047	175,165	4,934
Peru	1,289	5,738	NA	54,130	15,987	4,969
Philippines	8,986	25,389	1,814	15,545	27,977	NA
Poland	NA	14,350	1,840	16,217	216,626	431,056
Qatar	12	202	22	315	711	135
R. of Korea	633	172,095	4,247	4,760	78,431	NA
Romania	2,489	1,792	947	1,788	29,900	1,373
Rwanda	926	4,762	721	2,747	NA	NA
Singapore	48	923	111	1,577	28,211	3,790
Spain	636	61,112	1,790	586,366	574,017	NA
Sri Lanka	2,353	15,093	369	5,702	13,177	9,895
Swaziland	874	9,183	558	1,514	8,155	7,466
Sweden	676	40,690	1,410	5,967	580,379	154,030
Switzerland	NA	3,376	428	1,821	135,649	72,638
Syria	273	NA	107	13	NA	2,168
Thailand	5,586	21,752	2,514	3,396	33,698	38,301
Turkey	NA	1,026	177	816	38,411	NA
United States	23,440	1,054,860	102,560	639,270	7,945,700	3,073,900

NA = Not available.

Source: United Nations, *Fourth United Nations Survey of Crime Trends and Operations of Criminal Justice Systems,* preliminary data sets (Vienna, Austria: UN Crime Prevention and Criminal Justice Branch, 1993), as compiled by the author.

Fraud	Embezzlement	Drug Offenses	Total Crime	Population	Crime Rate
698	NA	1,952	55,777	32,800,000	170
99,180	NA	67,863	1,131,291	17,100,000	6,616
17,631	2,636	5,300	288,146	7,600,000	3,791
136	9	171	4,073	500,000	815
384	1	555	7,267	300,000	2,422
170	NA	780	32,314	1,300,000	2,486
130,621	NA	60,645	1,850,039	26,800,000	6,903
3,971	NA	29	144,803	13,400,000	1,081
1,396	281	311	32,317	3,100,000	1,042
11,156	1,435	13,926	466,967	5,100,000	9,156
86,608	2,465	2,546	297,582	5,000,000	5,952
1,489	NA	3,604	65,627	5,800,000	1,132
7,762	3,027	42	255,305	10,500,000	2,431
24,466	16,552	14,176	652,734	871,300,000	75
10,144	357	7,803	195,330	4,800,000	4,069
30,146	NA	30,691	2,802,126	57,600,000	4,865
475	152	135	10,599	4,300,000	246
460	444	76	32,600	3,600,000	906
NA	NA	751	21,166	400,000	5,292
1,991	983	10,961	82,423	9,300,000	1,917
681	362	943	23,087	1,100,000	2,099
5,455	5,906	5,897	980,909	15,000,000	6,059
7,114	1,676	9,091	207,480	4,200,000	4,940
5,332	5,262	NA	92,707	22,400,000	414
NA	NA	NA	79,711	68,600,000	116
7,935	4,300	1,105	693,429	38,600,000	1,796
33	NA	85	1,515	500,000	303
44,035	8,478	2,213	314,892	67,800,000	464
939	434	4	39,669	23,400,000	170
245	154	649	10,204	75,000,000	14
2,554	493	NA	37,707	2,700,000	1,397
7,456	4,903	25,418	1,261,698	39,500,000	3,194
2,803	NA	NA	49,392	17,400,000	284
366	260	495	28,871	800,000	3,610
96,161	11,167	26,517	916,997	8,500,000	10,788
9,238	NA	18,880	242,030	6,600,000	3,667
534	14	442	3,551	13,000,000	27
3,155	4,971	15,659	129,032	57,400,000	225
2,404	NA	940	43,774	57,800,000	76
291,600	15,300	1,089,500	14,236,130	252,500,000	5,638

THE CHINESE JUSTICE SYSTEM

In the spring of 1989, the world focused its attention on the People's Republic of China, where students and workers supported mass demonstrations favoring freedom and democracy. Tiananmen Square, in the center of Beijing, became the rallying point for protestors. The huge and famous portrait of Mao Zedong, China's revolutionary communist leader, which overlooks the square, was defaced with paint. Students even constructed a small replica of the Statue of Liberty on the bricks of the square. As the world looked on, the Chinese Red Army, acting on orders of party leader Deng Xiaoping and members of the Chinese Communist Party Central Committee, moved decisively to end the demonstrations. On June 4, 1989, at least 800 people died in a hail of rifle fire directed at the protestors. It is estimated that thousands more perished in the weeks that followed.[8] Some were victims of government action to suppress continuing demonstrations, while others were summarily tried and executed for inciting riots and for plotting against the government. While the Chinese democratic revolution of 1989 did not succeed, it gives evidence of the sense of single-minded purpose so characteristic of Chinese society. It is that shared sense of purpose which underlies the Chinese legal system today.

MAOIST JUSTICE

Under party Chairman Mao Zedong, criminal justice in the People's Republic of China was based upon informal societal control. Mao abhorred bureaucratic agencies and procedures and, during his reign, accused offenders found themselves turned over to the populace for a hearing and punishment.[9] The infamous Chinese Cultural Revolution, which began in 1966 and lasted until 1973,[10] was intended to integrate Maoist teaching and principles into Chinese society. During the revolutionary period Mao called upon his hordes of fanatical followers known as Red Guards to "smash the police and the courts." One of Mao's most popular sayings intoned: "Depend on the rule of man, not the rule of law."[11] Because of Maoist thinking the People's Republic of China had no criminal or procedural legal codes, no lawyers, and no officially designated prosecutors until after 1978. Under Mao, the police were replaced by military control with arrest powers residing in the People's Liberation Army.

According to the concept of "class justice," taught by the Cultural Revolution, the severity of punishment an offender received depended upon his or her social and political

China: A police officer lectures a young man.
Photo: Office of International Criminal Justice.

identity. Consistent with the tenor of the times, a Chinese textbook of the late 1960s proclaimed, "the point of our criminal law is chiefly directed toward the enemies of socialism."[12] Wealthy, successful, and educated people, because of their high status under previous regimes, were automatically suspected of crimes, and were often summarily tried and severely punished for the vaguest of allegations. Following Mao's death, the Cultural Revolution was denounced by the Central Committee of the Chinese Communist party as "responsible for the most severe setback and the heaviest losses suffered by the party, the state and the people since the founding of the People's Republic."[13]

CHINESE JUSTICE AFTER MAO

In 1978, two years after the death of Chairman Mao, another wave of reform swept China. This time a formalized legal system, based upon codified laws, was created and a radically revised Constitution was given life on December 4, 1982. Predictability and security, especially for the potentially most productive members of society, became the goal of the new National People's Congress. The Congress sought to ensure internal stability, international commerce, and modernization through legislation. The Chinese Constitution now contains 24 articles on the fundamental rights and duties of citizens[14] and guarantees equality before the law for everyone.

Modern Chinese Courts

The modern Chinese justice system is structured along jurisdictional lines similar to those in the United States. At the highest level, the Chinese justice system is built around four national offices: the Supreme People's Court, the Ministry of Public Security, the People's **Procuratorate**, and the Ministry of Justice. The Supreme People's Court is the highest court in China. It deals with cases which may have an impact on the entire country.[15] Most cases come before the Court on appeal. The Court is divided into three sections: criminal court, which deals with felony violations of the law, mostly on appeal, and death penalty reviews; civil affairs court; and economic court.

At the opposite judicial extreme, the Basic People's Court operates at the county level as the court with original jurisdiction over most criminal cases. Two judicial levels—the Intermediate People's Courts, and the Higher People's Courts—stand between the Basic Court and the Supreme Court. Both function as courts of appeal, although Intermediate Courts have original jurisdiction in criminal cases with the potential for sentences involving death or life imprisonment. They also hear criminal charges brought against foreigners.

Defendants may choose to be represented in Chinese courts by an attorney, a relative, or a friend, or may choose to represent themselves. If they desire, a lawyer will be appointed for them. Attorneys in China, however, have a far different role from that of their American counterparts. While they work to protect the rights of the defendant, attorneys have a responsibility to the court which transcends their duties to the accused. Defense lawyers are limited to helping the court render a just verdict.[17] The Chinese believe that vigorous defense strategies such as those found in the adversarial framework of Western justice can lead to criminals escaping responsibility.[18]

A visit by a delegation of the American Bar Association to Shanghai determined that 78% of the work load of Chinese attorneys consisted of defending accused criminals. The remaining 22% was divided about equally between family practice (wills, divorces, adoptions, inheritance, etc.) and civil suits.[19] The legal profession in China is not, on the whole, well trained. While most lawyers probably have some formal legal education, many simply meet the conditions of Article 8 of the Chinese constitution, which requires persons who

Procuratorate (also Procuracy) A term used in many countries to refer to agencies with powers and responsibilities similar to those of prosecutor's offices in the United States.[16]

THEORY INTO PRACTICE

INDIVIDUAL RIGHTS GUARANTEED
UNDER THE CONSTITUTION OF THE PEOPLE'S REPUBLIC OF CHINA
(ADAPTED DECEMBER 4, 1982 BY THE FIFTH NATIONAL
PEOPLE'S CONGRESS, BEIJING)

Right	*Guaranteed by*
1. *Equality Before the Law*	*Article 33*
2. *Freedom from Unlawful Detention*	*Article 37*
3. *Right Against Unlawful Personal Searches*	*Article 37*
4. *Protection from Unlawful Arrest*	*Article 37*
5. *Right Against Unlawful Searches of a Residence*	*Article 39*
6. *Right to a Public Trial*	*Article 126*
7. *Right of Defense in a Criminal Trial*	*Article 126*
8. *A Right to Use One's Native Spoken and Written Language in Court*	*Article 134*

wish to engage in the practice of law to "have the cultural level of graduates of institutions of higher learning, and be suitable to be lawyers."

The Chinese justice system has a built-in system of checks and balances which, in theory, operates to prevent abuses of power. Arrests made by public security agents, for example, must be approved by the local procurators office. If a decision is made to prosecute, the court may conduct its own investigation prior to the start of trial to determine whether prosecution is warranted.

The official Chinese crime rate is astoundingly low—only 49 crimes per every 100,000 citizens. In 1986, the latest year for which data are available, the Chinese government reported only 11,510 homicides, 18,364 assaults, 39,121 cases of rape, 12,124 robberies, and approximately 426,000 instances of theft to the United Nations.[20] In a country of 1.07 billion people the official prison population stands at only 500,000 (one-sixth the rate of imprisonment found in the United States).

Illegal drug use, however, which was said to have been virtually eliminated by the communist government in post–World War II China, is making a strong comeback. In 1993 more than 1,000 people were sentenced to death for drug trafficking,[21] although most of the sentences were later suspended and commuted to life in prison. Recently,[22] authorities in the central Chinese province of Shaanxi reportedly formed a special antidrug trafficking force to combat organized gangs who were importing heroin from the Golden Triangle area of Thailand, Laos, and Burma. Reports said that 20 people had been arrested and that education programs were being started to assist addicts and prevent others from becoming addicted.

Once arrested, suspects face a high likelihood of conviction. Records show only a 1% acquittal rate in Chinese criminal courts (versus 31% in the United States).[23] A crime problem of growing concern to the Chinese, however, is juvenile delinquency. Juvenile gang activity is on the increase, with gang members often coming from the families of high communist party functionaries.[24] Some officials have also suggested that international gang-related drug trafficking is on the rise in the People's Republic of China. However, although China has had a history of problems with opium abuse, actual consumption of illicit drugs by Chinese citizens probably occurs at a rate much below that of the Western world.[25]

Mediation Committees

One reason for the low official crime rate is the Chinese system of People's Mediation Committees. By virtue of the large number of cases they resolve, mediation committees may be the most important component of justice in modern China.

Such committees generally consist of from five to seven people, with judicial assistants assigned to them by the Bureau of Justice, the courts, and the procuratorates.[26] Committees function informally and are based upon the belief that minor disputes and misdemeanor offenses can be best handled at local levels without unnecessary protocol. Minor assaults, thefts, and vandalism, are typical of the kinds of cases dealt with by the mediation committees. Mediation committees are also believed to play a significant role in crime prevention by resolving disputes before they evolve into serious altercations. Hence, in addition to minor criminal cases, housing disputes, divorce cases, and land sharing problems commonly come before such committees. Committees are officially guided by law and government policy. Their power, however, comes from the force of public opinion.[27] Education and persuasion are their primary tools.

People's mediation committees are everywhere in China—in factories, on farms, in schools, and in businesses. According to some authorities, over 800,000 Chinese mediation committees functioning on a regular basis handle over 8 million cases per year.[28] In contrast, only 3,000 regular courts are in existence at all levels throughout the entire country.[29] Mediation committees serve to divert a large number of people from processing by county and provincial courts. They also serve to unintentionally, but dramatically, lower the number of officially reported offenses throughout China.

Chinese Criminal Punishments

The punishment of offenders in China can be severe in cases which go beyond mediation and enter the court system. Thirty-eight percent of convicted offenders in China are sentenced to more than five years in prison,[30] and repeat offenders are subject to harsh punishments. Habitual thieves may be ordered shot, and the annual number of executions in China is probably high. A survey of notices posted on Chinese courthouses and of announcements in Chinese newspapers determined that in one 12-month period approximately 200 persons were executed and more than 2,000 others were sentenced to death with a two-year reprieve.[31] Although death sentences must be reviewed by the Supreme People's Court, the court may rule on the legality of a case in advance of the actual sentence, clearing the way for speedy executions.

Chinese justice has a public dimension which harks back to the highly visible executions carried out by Western authorities in years past. In 1981, for example, 40,000 people gathered at Nanning Municipal Stadium to witness the sentencing and immediate dispatch of an

Mediation Committees
Chinese civilian dispute resolution groups found throughout the country. Mediation committees successfully divert many minor offenders from handling by the more formal mechanisms of justice.

infamous murderer and robber.[32] Such public gatherings are an innate feature of Chinese criminal justice and serve what some authorities see as a communal need for vengeance.

For all its seeming harshness in dealing with repeat offenders, the Chinese justice system is based upon a strong cultural belief in personal reformation. As one author has observed, "Repentance, which means reclaiming individuals for society, is at the heart of Chinese justice."[33] Confucius taught that "Man is at birth by nature good,"[34] and Chinese authorities seek to build opportunities into their criminal justice system which allow offenders to change for the better. Even persons sentenced to death are generally granted a two-year period during which they may repent and attempt to demonstrate that they have changed. If they can successfully convince the court that they have reformed, their sentence will be commuted.[35] Faith in repentance is apparently well placed. The official rate of recidivism in China is only 4.7% for serious offenders.[36]

Prison sentences in China allow for parole after completion of one-half of the time imposed (ten years for life sentences).[37] Violation of prison rules may result in extended incarceration, solitary confinement, or "group criticism." Inmates sleep on hard beds in ten-person cells averaging about 300 square feet per cell. The study of communist policy, according to official Chinese interpretation, is required of all inmates. Such study is the focal point of prison treatment programs.[38]

Political prisoners, by some estimates numbering as many as 10 million in over 1,000 camps[39] since the Tiananmen Square uprising, are subjected to *laogai*,[40] or "thought-reform-through-labor," and are required to work at prison farms, factories, and the like. Official Chinese estimates place the number of political prisoners at around 160,000,[41] making any realistic appraisal of the situation difficult.

Official parole eligibility comes only after the offender has shown repentance and performed "meritoriously" while in prison. In practice, parole may be granted routinely after half the sentence has been served. Chinese parole follows the institutional model, in which individual confinement facilities recommend parole to the court, which then makes the final decision. Parole officers are unknown in China, but parolees are supervised by local police agencies and by citizens groups.

In what may have been the most famous criminal hearing in Chinese history, the infamous "gang of four"—Mao's widow and three of her political cronies—are shown here during their trial in 1980. Each was convicted of various crimes against the state.

CRIMINAL JUSTICE IN IRAN

In April 1980, a popular revolution, supported by forces loyal to the Ayatollah Ruhollah Khomeini, who was then living in exile in France, forced the resignation of the shah of Iran. The shah and his family fled the country, and the Islamic Republic of Iran was born. Following the 1980 revolution Ayatollah Khomeini returned to Iran, where he quickly became the country's spiritual and political leader. At the urging of Khomeini and his followers, the Iranian Parliament adopted a new constitution, officially making it an Islamic state. Although Khomeini died in 1989, his vision of Islam continues to rule the country over which he presided. The Iranian criminal justice system today represents a classic reflection of traditional Islamic law.

THE HUDUD CRIMES

Modern Iran is especially interesting for students of criminal justice for two reasons: (1) it provides a contemporary example of a legal system based upon natural law, and (2) it is a nation in which social interests have distinct primacy over individual rights. Many civil rights which are accorded strong constitutional protections in the United States take second place to Iranian national concerns.

Islamic law (or *sharia* in Arabic, which means "path of God") is based upon four sources. In order of importance these sources are (1) the Koran or Holy Book of Islam, (2)

Hudud Crimes Serious violations of Islamic law regarded as offenses against God. Hudud crimes include such behavior as theft, adultery, sodomy, drinking alcohol, and robbery.

Islamic tradition and Muslim law strongly influence the style of dress worn by this Iranian woman. Criminal law in Iran is based upon the teachings of the Koran and the sayings of the Prophet Mohammed. *Photo: A. Johannes/Sygma.*

the teachings of the Prophet Mohammed, (3) a consensus of the clergy when in cases where neither the Koran nor the prophet directly address an issue, and (4) reason or logic which should be used when no solution can be found in the other three sources.[42]

The Iranian criminal justice system today recognizes seven "Hudud" (sometimes called Hodood), or serious crimes. Hudud crimes are essentially violations of "natural law" as interpreted by Persian culture. Divine displeasure is thought to be the basis of crimes defined as Hudud. Four Hudud crimes for which punishments are specified in the Koran are (1) making war upon Allah and His messengers, (2) theft, (3) adultery, and (4) false accusation of fornication or adultery. Three other offenses are specifically mentioned by the Koran, for which no punishment is specified—(1) sodomy, (2) drinking of alcohol, and (3) robbery—crimes for which punishments are determined by tradition.[43] The seven Hudud offenses, and associated typical punishments, are shown in Table 16–2.

The religious basis of Iranian law makes for strict punishment of moral failure. Sexual offenses, even those considered essentially victimless in many Western societies, are subject to especially harsh treatment. The Islamic penalty for fornication, for example, is 100 lashes. Men are stripped to the waist, women have their clothes bound tightly, and flogging is carried out with a leather whip. Adultery carries a much more severe penalty: flogging and stoning to death.

Under Islamic law even property crimes can be firmly punished. Theft is censured by amputation of the thief's right hand. In a reputedly humane move, Iranian officials recently began the use of an electric guillotine, specially made for the purpose, which can sever a hand at the wrist in one-tenth of a second.

For amputation to be imposed, the item stolen must have value in Islam. Pork and alcohol, for example, are regarded as being without value, and their theft is not subject to punishment. Iranian legal codes have established a minimum value of stolen items which could result in amputation being imposed upon the offender. Likewise, offenders who have stolen because they are hungry, or are in need, are exempt from the punishment of amputation and receive fines or prison terms.

Slander and the consumption of alcohol are both punished by 80 lashes. The Iranian legal code also specifies whipping for the crimes of pimping, lesbianism, kissing by an unmarried couple, cursing, and failure of a woman to wear a veil.

Robbers receive especially harsh sentences. Islamic law provides for the execution, usually through crucifixion, of robbers. The law stipulates that anyone who survives three days on the cross may be spared. Depending upon the circumstances of the robbery, however, the offender may suffer the amputation of opposite hands and feet, or simply exile.

Rebellion, or revolt against a legitimate political leader, is punishable by death. The offender may be killed outright in a military or police action or, later, by sentence of the court.

The last of the Hudud crimes is rejection of Islam. The penalty, once again, is death, and can be imposed for denying the existence of God or angels, denying any of the prophets of Islam, or rejecting any part of the Koran.

Tazirat Crimes Minor violations of Islamic law, which are regarded as offenses against society, not God.

All crimes other than Hudud fall into an offense category called **tazirat** (minor offenses). Tazir crimes are regarded as crimes against society, but not against God. They are not punishable by death, but may call for *Quesas* (retribution) or *Diyya* (compensation). Crimes requiring Quesas usually call for physical punishments, while Diyya crimes are punished through fines. Quesas offenses include murder, manslaughter, assault, and maiming. Such crimes require the victim or his representative to serve as prosecutor. The state plays a role only in providing the forum for a trial and in imposing punishment.

TABLE 16-2

CRIME AND PUNISHMENT
IN ISLAMIC LAW: THE IRANIAN EXAMPLE[1]

Islamic law looks to the Koran and the teachings of the Prophet Mohammed to determine which acts should be classified as crimes. The Koran and tradition specify punishments to be applied to designated offenses, as the following verse from the Koran demonstrates: "The only reward of those who make war upon Allah and His messenger and strive after corruption in the land will be that they will be killed or crucified, or have their hands and feet on alternate sides cut off, or will be expelled out of the land" (Surah V, Verse 33). Other crimes and punishments include the following:

Offense	*Punishment*
Theft	Amputation of the hand
Adultery	Stoning to death
Fornication	One hundred lashes
False accusation (of adultery or fornication)	Eighty lashes
Sodomy	Death by the sword or burning
Drinking alcohol	Eighty stripes; death if repeated three times
Robbery	Cutting off of hands and feet on alternate sides

[1]For more information, see Parviz Saney, "Iran," in Elmer H. Johnson, *International Handbook of Contemporary Developments in Criminology* (Westport, CT: Greenwood, 1983), pp. 356–369.

IRANIAN COURTS

Courts in Iran exist on three levels.[44] Criminal Court One hears cases involving the potential for serious punishments, including death, amputation, and exile. Criminal Court Two deals with relatively minor matters, such as traffic offenses, and violations of city ordinances. Islamic revolutionary courts, composed of revolutionary guards, hear cases involving crimes against the government, narcotics offenses, state security, and corruption.

Under Islamic law, men and women are treated very differently. Testimony, for example, provided by a man can be heard in court. The same evidence, however, can only be provided by two virtuous women—one female witness will not be sufficient to have the evidence heard.

Appeals in Iran are only possible under rare circumstances and are by no means routine. A decision rendered by Criminal Court Two will generally stand without intervention by higher judicial authorities.

The Iranian constitution specifies a number of individual rights, including notification of the reason for an arrest, legal representation, speedy appearance before a judicial officer, the presumption of innocence, the abolishment of torture, and a respect for the human dignity of the accused. In practice, however, few of these "rights" seem to be available to arrestees. Amnesty International recently reported that torture, solitary confinement, rape, and mock executions are the rule in Iranian jails. Defendants are, in practice, not presumed innocent, and judges' personal biases may be just as important in decisions as the evidence presented in court.

Executions in Sanandaj, Iran. Islamic law, as interpreted by Iranian courts, makes for strict and unforgiving punishments. *Photo: UPI/Bettmann Newsphotos.*

The central role played by the Koran in Iranian criminal justice makes the country a modern-day example of the use of natural law as the foundation for a complex legal system. Islamic law and the Iranian legal system in particular, however, seem barbaric to many Westerners. Islamic officials, on the other hand, defend their system by pointing to the low crime rates at home and alleging near anarchy in Western nations.

An early criticism of Islamic law was offered by Max Weber at the start of the twentieth century.[45] Weber said that Islamic justice is based more upon the moral conceptions of individual judges than it is upon any rational and predictable code of laws. He found that the personality of each judge, what he called "charisma," was more important in reaching a final legal result than was the written law. Weber's conclusion was that a modern society could not develop under Islamic law because enforcement of the law was too unpredictable. Complex social organizations, he argued, could only be based upon a rational law, which is relatively unchanging from place to place and over time.[46] Whether natural law could form the basis of a rational and predictable judicial system is a question which is still open to debate.

CRIMINAL JUSTICE IN ENGLAND

The country of England is quite small—only a little larger than the state of New Jersey, but with a population of nearly 40 million people. One of the original participants in the industrial revolution, it remains a highly industrialized nation. England is linked closely to its neighbors—Wales, Scotland, and Northern Ireland—an alliance which created the political entity of "Great Britain" and which today is officially known as the "United Kingdom of Great Britain."

Our American heritage, both legal and cultural, has been strongly influenced by Great Britain. Chapter 4 describes the way in which British common law formed the basis of our own legal traditions, and Chapter 5 shows how American police forces and other criminal justice agencies in their formative periods drew upon earlier English experience.

THE BRITISH POLITICAL SYSTEM

England is a country without a constitution in the strict sense of the word. The legal basis of English government, however, can be found in at least three significant documents: (1) the Magna Carta, (2) the Bill of Rights, and (3) the Act of Settlement. The Magna Carta, written in 1215, was forced upon the king by English nobility and the upper classes. It guarantees a number of legal rights to British citizens accused of crimes, including the right to due process of law and a hearing before one's peers. The English Bill of Rights, passed by Parliament in 1688, established the two houses of Parliament (the House of Lords and the House of Commons), guaranteed free elections, and placed Parliamentary authority in statutory matters over that of the Sovereign. As a consequence, although modern England still has a Royal family whose members perform ceremonial functions, the real power to make laws and run the nation lies in the hands of the two houses of Parliament and the prime minister. In 1700 the Act of Settlement reinforced the powers of Parliament and made clear the authority of judges and other officials.

As Richard Terrill points out,[47] at least three major differences can be found between the British and American systems of government, all of which bear significance for the administration of criminal justice:

1. The British system, unlike the American, makes no provision for judicial review of Parliamentary action. Acts of Parliament are the law of the land and cannot be overruled by any court.
2. In Britain a unity of powers, rather than a separation of branches, characterizes the government. Executive, legislative, and judicial authority all ultimately rest in Parliament.
3. England is a unified nation. No separate state legislatures or state governmental offices exist. Parliamentary law applies at both the national and local level.

MODERN CRIMINAL LAW IN ENGLAND

In 1967 Parliament passed the Criminal Act, a sweeping piece of legislation which substantially altered English criminal procedure. The old distinction between "felonies" and "misdemeanors" was eliminated in favor of two new offense categories: "arrestable" and "nonarrestable" offenses. Under English common law, the arrest powers of the police without a warrant were limited to treason, felonies, and breaches of the peace. The Criminal Law Act broadened arrest powers in the absence of a warrant to all offenses "for which (a) sentence is fixed by law," and to attempts to commit such offenses. The 1967 act also extended arrest powers to private citizens who caught offenders in criminal activity or who had reasonable suspicion to believe that someone had committed an arrestable offense.

Police in England

The historical development of police forces in nineteenth-century Britain is described in Chapter 5. By World War II 183 police departments—some large, some very small—existed throughout England and Wales.[48] Each was headed by a chief constable, and jurisdictional disputes between departments were common. Major efforts to consolidate police departments culminated in the Police Acts of 1946 and 1964, to which contemporary British policing owes its structure. The Local Government Act of 1972 further reduced the number of police forces throughout England and Wales until the combined forces numbered just 43. The smallest police agency in Britain today has over 600 officers—a good-sized department by American standards.

The police of Britain are subject to local civilian control through local commissions called police authorities. Two-thirds of each police authority is comprised of elected civilians, while one-third of the authority's members are judicial officers elected by fellow magistrates. Each police authority appoints a local chief constable, with overall authority for the daily operations of the police, and an assistant chief constable.

Beyond the local level, the British home secretary has statutory authority to intervene in police administration, police discipline, and suspected cases of corruption and mismanagement. The home secretary also provides for the coordination of police services throughout Britain, runs the Police College and local police training centers, maintains forensic laboratories, and is ultimately responsible for information management, including national data bases and telecommunications.

Britain does not have a national police force.[49] The Metropolitan Police District, one of the nation's 43 police agencies, however, falls under the exclusive control of the home secretary. The Metropolitan Police District encompasses 32 boroughs and portions of four counties surrounding London.[50] The Metropolitan Police, numbering over 26,000 sworn and civilian personnel,[51] are headquartered at *New Scotland Yard*, perhaps the most

British "Bobbies." Uniformed English police officers have a recognizable appearance rooted in the time of Sir Robert Peel. *Photo: Comstock.*

famous address of any police force in the world. Scotland Yard serves as a national repository for information on crime statistics, criminal activity, fingerprints, missing persons, and wayward and delinquent juveniles. It also maintains links with INTERPOL and handles requests for information from police agencies in other countries.

In 1992 the National Criminal Intelligence Service (NCIS), charged with intelligence-gathering and record-keeping, began operation[52] in England. Likened by some to the American FBI, few real similarities exist—primarily because NCIS agents do not have an operational role but function only as staff officers to exchange information on criminal activity with other police agencies throughout England.

In 1948 the Police College opened at Ryton-upon-Dunsmore. The Police College was designed to enhance professionalism among the nation's constables. The training it provided made possible professional advancement within police ranks. In 1960 the college relocated to Bramshill. Known today by its new name, the Police Staff College at Bramshill serves as an international model for police management training.[53]

Traditionally, British police officers have gone on patrol unarmed, except for a nightstick or billy club. Events in the 1980s, especially terrorist attacks on civilian targets including London's Heathrow airport, led to a reassessment of traditional policy. That reassessment continues today, although most beat constables remain unarmed. Weapons are kept on hand in local police stations and can be issued upon the order of senior police personnel. Officers who routinely patrol highly congested areas, including those with considerable international traffic such as major airports, are now armed with handguns and automatic weapons as a precaution against terrorist attack. In emergencies, local chief constables are authorized to call upon the military for armed assistance.

Evidentiary standards, such as the American exclusionary rule, do not apply to the British police. Unlike their American counterparts, British courts have not utilized precedent-setting decisions to carve out individual rights for citizens who face apprehension and criminal prosecution. What they have done, through judicial conferences, is draw up "directions" for acceptable police procedure. A key document to emerge from such conferences was the *Judges' Rules and Administrative Directions*, drawn up in 1964. Rules such as this have the weight of law even though they are technically only administrative regulations.

Even so, the police of Britain have not been immune to charges of corruption and brutality. A series of scandals shook Scotland Yard during the 1970s, and a Royal Commission report in 1981 found evidence of consistent maltreatment of suspects. Public criticism of the police resulted in the Police and Criminal Evidence Act of 1984 which placed procedural restrictions on police activity and mandated training in technical and human relations skills. Charges of police corruption emerged again in 1991, when a British appeals court freed six men who had been convicted in 1975 of an alleged Irish Republican Army bomb attack on two Birmingham pubs which killed 21 people and injured 162.[54] The men, who had served 16 years in prison, had their sentences reversed on the basis of inaccuracies in the police gathering of evidence. Even so, few offenders in contemporary England are released on "technicalities" such as illegal arrest, unfounded searches, and so on. Instead, police compliance with procedural requirements depends upon the threatened prosecution of arresting officers. Officers who are in violation of procedural laws can be held liable for false imprisonment and wrongful denial of liberty.

Courts in Britain

The dual court system which characterizes the United States is unknown in England. The British court system, although hierarchical, is monolithic. At its lowest level are the approximately 900 magistrates' courts. Magistrates' courts are staffed by underpaid lay justices who are not required to have formal training in the law. Magistrates sit as a body, usually in groups of three or more, and hear cases without a jury. While they generally try less

INTERPOL An acronym for the International Police Association. INTERPOL began operations in 1946 and today has 137 members.

In 1993 English attention was captivated by the trial of two 10-year-old boys who lured 2½-year-old James Bulger (shown here) away from his mother's side in a Liverpool shopping mall and brutally beat him to death. The boys, Robert Thompson and Jon Venables, were both sentenced to indefinite detention. *Photo: Mercury Press/Sipa.*

serious cases, criminal defendants charged with certain major crimes may waive the right to trial by jury and be tried in magistrates' court. It has been estimated that magistrates' courts[55] handle 98% of all criminal cases in Great Britain.

Although English common law originally provided for hearings before a grand jury, the grand jury system was abolished by parliamentary action in 1933. Magistrates' courts have taken over some of the functions of the grand jury, including that of binding over serious offenders for trial by higher courts. Magistrates are limited in their sentencing authority to a maximum of six months' imprisonment. In serious cases, however, they are able to refer convicted defendants to higher courts for sentencing.

Persons charged with major offenses may be bound over for trial in a crown court after an initial hearing (called a preliminary inquiry) by a magistrate. Crown courts are recent additions to the English system of criminal justice, having been created in 1971. They are headed by justices appointed by the monarch on the recommendation of the lord chancellor. Twelve-member juries hear crown court cases. Conviction requires only a majority consensus, not unanimous agreement among jurors.

Tradition dictates considerable formality at all court levels. Crown court judges and counsel both wear white powdered wigs and black flowing robes. Verbal give and take is highly structured and polite. Sharp exchanges between the bench and counsel almost never occur, and lawyers are expected to treat one another with respect.

Crown courts also hear appeals from magistrates' courts. Appeals are heard without a jury. Petitions from magistrates' courts which concern questions of law sometimes go directly to an appellate court called the high court. The high court is divided into three divisions: (1) the Queen's Bench, (2) Family Court, and (3) the Chancery. The Chancery Division deals with

THEORY INTO PRACTICE

BRITISH POLICE ARE UNARMED

In a tradition dating back to the days of the "Wild West," American law enforcement officers routinely carry guns. Expertise with a handgun or rifle has long been regarded as a sign of accomplishment among police ranks. The development of a well-financed and often brutal drug subculture within the country, however, has left many police officers feeling outgunned. In a tragic Florida shootout a few years ago, three FBI agents were killed by heavily armed bank robbers. The agents' traditional sidearms were no match for the robbers automatic pistols and machine guns. Since then, many federal law enforcement agencies have increased the "firepower" available to their agents by issuing 9mm semiautomatic pistols and Uzi-type machine guns. As a consequence, American law enforcement officers today, especially on the federal level, are routinely well armed.

In contrast to the American situation, the police of England (with the exception of those guarding international airports and a few highly sensitive locations) do not carry weapons beyond a simple "billy club." The typical British municipal police department, which may have as many as 380 officers, will probably maintain no more than six handguns under lock and key for use only in emergencies.[1] In fact, only a small percentage of British officers are authorized to use a weapon under any circumstances, and firearms practice is not a routine part of law enforcement training in England.

The 1993 opening of the newly completed "Chunnel," linking France and England for the purposes of train and vehicular travel under the English Channel, became another focus for the British aversion to armed police. Under an agreement between the two countries, French police, typically armed, may not carry weapons on tunnel trains and are permitted to have weapons only in a controlled zone at the tunnel mouth. They have to surrender their weapons if they leave the area.[2]

There are a number of significant reasons for the British reluctance to arm their police. Of greatest significance may be the fact that British citizens are themselves unarmed. The "right to bear arms" is foreign to English law, and very few guns are in private hands in any part of the country.

People Killed by Handguns in 1990[3]	
Australia	10
Sweden	13
Britain	22
Canada	68
Japan	87
Switzerland	91
United States	10,567

[1]"CBS Early Morning News," March 17, 1989
[2]"Chunnel Patrol," *Criminal Justice Europe* (March/April 1992), p. 3.
[3]Handgun Control, Inc., telephone conversation, January 10, 1994.

matters of inheritance, trusts, property, and so on, while the Family Division of the Court concerns itself with marriages, divorces, adoption, and the like. The section of the high court which focuses on criminal matters is the divisional court of the Queen's Branch. Like other divisions of the high court, the Queen's Branch sits without a jury when hearing criminal appeals.

Another intermediate appellate court occupies a level above the high court. Called the court of appeals, it has two branches: one civil and one criminal. The court of appeals consists of 16 lord justices of appeal and is headed by a judge called the master of the rolls. Criminal appeals not resolved by the high court may go to the court of appeals. Appeals involving the sentencing decisions made by magistrates' or crown courts can go directly to the criminal division of the court of appeals.

At the apex of the appellate process stands the House of Lords, one of the houses of Parliament. The House of Lords may hear appeals from both the Queen's Branch and the criminal division. An appeal to the House will be heard only by those members who specialize in the appeals process. Although the House of Lords is the highest appellate court in Britain, it has nothing like the power of the U.S. Supreme Court. Acts of Parliament are inviolate and cannot be "struck down" or significantly modified by judicial interpretation.

Corrections in England

The British correctional system is under the administrative control of the home secretary. The home secretary makes appointments to the national Prison Board which sets policy for the Prison Department. The Prison Department oversees the activities of the nation's prisons, the parole board, and probation and after care services. A separate agency, the Board of Visitors, permits lay volunteers to serve as hearing boards attached to individual prisons. Each Board of Visitors is empowered to hear alleged violations of prison regulations and is expected to prepare a yearly report on prison conditions.

In keeping with tradition, British judges still wear the obligatory "wig" when sitting on the bench. *Photo: Rick Smolan/Stock Boston.*

THEORY INTO PRACTICE

Judicial Officers in England

The court system in the United Kingdom is highly dependent upon tradition. Three principal judicial officers ensure the effective functioning of the courts. They are:

The Lord Chancellor. The lord chancellor is appointed by the monarch upon recommendation of the prime minister. Tradition calls for an appointee well versed in the law. The lord chancellor presides over the House of Lords, one of the two houses of the British Parliament. Because the House of Lords is the highest English court, the lord chancellor is also the highest judicial officer in the kingdom. The lord chancellor recommends for appointment all members of the judiciary.

The Attorney General. Appointed by the prime minister, the attorney general is legal advisor to the monarch and Parliament. The attorney general officially serves as "guardian of the public interest" and handles most controversial legal issues affecting the government—both criminal and civil.

The Director of Public Prosecutions. The director of public prosecutions is charged with advising police agencies involved in criminal investigations, and with coordinating the activities of prosecutors throughout the kingdom. Appointed by the home secretary, and supervised by the attorney general, the director is a lawyer in charge of a staff of professional "solicitors" who specialize in criminal law and procedure.

Source: Adapted from Richard J. Terrill, *World Criminal Justice Systems: A Survey* (Cincinnati, OH: Anderson, 1984).

Three kinds of prisons exist in England: short term, medium term, and long term. Short-term institutions house offenders serving less than 18 months, while medium-term institutions hold persons sentenced to between one-and-a-half and four years. Long-term prisons hold prisoners sentenced to more than four years. Inmates in all British prisons are expected to work, although meaningful work programs are not available for everyone.[56]

The death penalty was eliminated in England in 1969, and the rehabilitative ideal is very much at home in British prisons. The three-tiered structure based upon sentence length allows for a natural division of inmates according to rehabilitative potential. The rehabilitative ideal has led to an increased use of probation throughout England. As in the United States, courts look to the availability of community alternatives in imposing probationary terms. Official consideration is also given to the offender's record and to the threat the offender represents to the community. Beginning in the 1970s a new sentencing alternative, called the Community Service Order, which requires as much as 240 hours of unpaid community service, began to be used with youthful offenders. Hospital work, nursing home care, and environmental projects constitute the bulk of community service activities. In 1990 children under the age of 14 became exempt from possible incarceration.

In contrast to these developments, the British Parliament has recently come under pressure to require longer and more frequent prison sentences for many offenders. Growing crime rates, high levels of unemployment, increased drug use, and the development of poverty-ridden ghetto-like areas in many of the nation's large cities have all contributed to a public perception of unnecessary leniency in the criminal justice system.

As in the United States, which sports the highest incarceration rate among democratic nations (see Figure 16–1), the call for longer sentences has come up against the reality of prison crowding. The British prison population today is around 50,000 inmates[57]—more than three times what it was following World War II. A 1989 report by a prison reform group found that "[t]he United Kingdom has a higher proportion of its population in prison than any other European Economic Community country...[and], the proportion of offenders who are imprisoned has markedly increased over the last decade."[58] Reflecting growing incarceration rates, government spending on prisons tripled between 1978 and 1990—from £231.8 million to £870.3 million.[59] While an active prison reform movement exists in Britain, it faces many barriers. Many British prisons are antiquated, and some have been described as "...dilapidated to the point of hazardousness.[60] Unfortunately, the financial crisis which the country has experienced for the past two decades provides little hope for modernization in the near future.

INTERNATIONAL CRIMINAL JUSTICE ORGANIZATIONS

The first international conference on criminology and criminal justice met in London in 1872.[61] The London conference evolved out of emerging humanitarian concerns about the treatment of prisoners. Human rights, the elimination of corporal punishment, and debates over capital punishment occupied the conference participants.

Although other meetings were held from time to time, little agreement could be reached among the international community on criminal etiology, justice paradigms, or the philosophical and practical bases for criminal punishment and rehabilitation. Finally, in 1938 the International Society for Criminology (ISC) was formed to bring together people from diverse cultural backgrounds who shared an interest in social policies relating to crime and justice. In its early years membership in the ISC consisted mostly of national officials and academicians with close government ties.[62] As a consequence, many of the first conferences (called International Congresses) sponsored by the ISC strongly supported the status quo and were devoid of any significant recommendations for change or growth.

Throughout the 1960s and 1970s the ISC was strongly influenced by a growing worldwide awareness of human rights. About the same time, a number of international organizations began to press for an understanding of the political and legal processes through

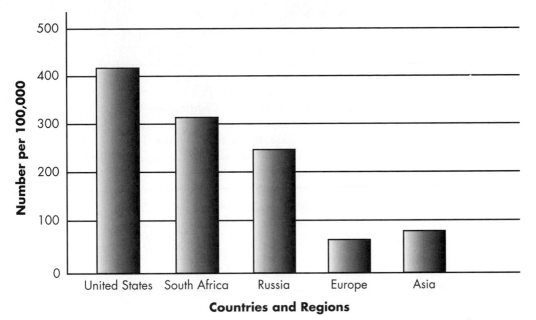

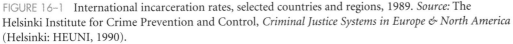

FIGURE 16-1 International incarceration rates, selected countries and regions, 1989. *Source:* The Helsinki Institute for Crime Prevention and Control, *Criminal Justice Systems in Europe & North America* (Helsinki: HEUNI, 1990).

which deviance and crime come to be defined. Among them were the Scandinavian Research Council for Criminology (formed in 1962), the Criminological Research Council (created in 1962 by the Council of Europe), and other regional associations concerned with justice issues.

A number of contemporary organizations and publications continue to focus world attention on criminal justice issues. Table 16–3 lists a number of the better known organizations. Perhaps the best known modern center for the academic study of cross-national criminal justice is the International Center of Comparative Criminology at the University of Montreal. Established in 1969, the center serves as a locus of study for criminal justice professionals from around the world and maintains an excellent library of international criminal justice information.

The University of Illinois at Chicago's Office of International Criminal Justice has also become a well-known contributor to the study of comparative criminal justice. In conjunction with the University's Center for Research in Law and Justice, the office publishes the newsletter *Criminal Justice International* and sponsors study tours of various nations.

Many sources of contemporary information on criminal justice agencies and activities around the world are now being published. They include (with their sponsor/publisher): *International Annals of Criminology* (ISC), *International Review of Criminal Policy* (United Nations), *International Journal of Criminal Policy* (United Nations), *International Journal of Penal Law* (International Association of Penal Law), *International Journal of Comparative and Applied Criminal Justice* (Wichita State University), *International Journal of Criminology and Penology* (Academic Press), *Victimology: An International Journal* (National Institute of Victimology), *Howard Journal of Criminal Justice* (the Howard League for Penal Reform), *International Review of Criminal Police* (INTERPOL), and *International Security* (Unisaf Publications Ltd.).

TABLE 16 - 3

HISTORICAL AND MODERN INTERNATIONAL CRIMINAL JUSTICE ORGANIZATIONS

The International Society of Criminology
The International Federation of Senior Police Officers
Scandinavian Research Council for Criminology
Criminological Research Council (Council of Europe)
International Association of Youth Magistrates
International Commission of Jurists
International Association of Penal Law
International Society of Social Defense
Amnesty International
International Chiefs of Police
International Criminal Police Organization (INTERPOL)
International Prisoners Aid Association
Howard League for Penal Reform

THE ROLE OF THE UNITED NATIONS IN CRIMINAL JUSTICE

The United Nations (UN), comprised of 184 member states and based in New York City, is the largest and most inclusive international body in the world. From its inception the UN has been very interested in international crime prevention and world criminal justice systems. A United Nations' resolution entitled the International Bill of Human Rights supports the rights and dignity of all persons who come into contact with the criminal justice system.

One of the best known specific United Nations' recommendations on criminal justice is its Standard Minimum Rules for the Treatment of Prisoners, adopted in 1967. The Rules call for the fair treatment of prisoners, to include recognition of the basic humanity of all inmates, and set specific standards for housing, nutrition, and medical care. Follow-up surveys conducted by the United Nations have shown that the Rules have had a considerable influence upon national legislation and prison regulations throughout the world.[63] A more recent, but potentially significant set of recommendations can be found in the UN Code of Conduct for Law Enforcement Officials. The Code calls upon law enforcement officers throughout the world to be cognizant of human rights in the performance of their duties and specifically proscribes the use of torture and other abuses.

The United Nations World Crime Surveys provide a global portrait of criminal activity. Seen historically, the Surveys have shown that crimes against property are most characteristic of nations with developed economies (where they constitute 82% of all reported crime), while crimes against the person occur much more frequently in developing countries (where they account for 43% of all crime).[64]

The United Nations continues to advance the cause of crime prevention and to disseminate useful criminal justice information. The Crime Prevention and Criminal Justice Program, the Program's 40 Member State Commission on Crime Prevention and Criminal Justice, and its secretariat, the Crime Prevention and Criminal Justice Branch of the United Nations Offices at Vienna, provide forums for ongoing discussions of justice practices around the world.

JUSTICE IN AMERICAN CONTEXT...
The Ninth United Nations Crime Congress.

The Ninth United Nations Crime Congress will be held in 1995 at a location which had yet to be determined at the time of this writing. Egypt and Iran have both offered to host the event. The meeting will be officially referred to as The Ninth United Nations Congress on the Prevention of Crime and the Treatment of Offenders. Similar congresses are held every five years. Eight have been held to date. Previous congresses have dealt with issues as diverse as the rights of prisoners, the human rights of suspects, increased international cooperation to eliminate government-protected safe havens for terrorists, hostage/terrorism negotiation, and the development of compensation programs for victims of terrorism. Items on the agenda for the upcoming congress include

- the use of international criminal justice information with special attention to providing technical assistance to developing countries
- collaborative action against economic, organized, and environmental crime
- the computerization of criminal justice operations
- urban planning and architectural design in relation to crime prevention and control
- the prevention of violent crime
- the mass media and crime prevention
- extradition and international cooperation

Organized crime, money-laundering, crime prevention in urban areas, violence, and juvenile crime are also of special interest to organizations planning for the Ninth Congress. Although the resolutions which will be passed by the Ninth Congress will not carry the weight of law, they hold considerable political and moral authority for member nations which are obliged to implement them as fully as possible.

Sources: United Nations Information Service (UNIS), "Omnibus Draft Resolution on Criminal Justice Issues Introduced in Crime Prevention Commission," April 22, 1993, and UNIS, "Crime Prevention Commission Takes Up Preparations for Ninth UN Crime Congress," April 15, 1993.

At its formation, the Crime Prevention and Criminal Justice Program announced as its goals: "1.) the prevention of crime within and among states; 2.) the control of crime both nationally and internationally; 3.) the strengthening of regional and international cooperation in crime prevention, criminal justice and the combating of transnational crime; 4.) the integration and consolidation of the efforts of Member States in preventing and combating transnational crime; 5.) more efficient and effective administration of justice, with due respect for the human rights of all those affected by crime and all those involved in the criminal justice system; and 6.) the promotion of the highest standards of fairness, humanity, justice and professional conduct."[65]

At its formation in 1992, the Commission on Crime Prevention and Criminal Justice recommended "1.) that developed countries...strengthen their aid programs and commit themselves to support technical assistance and advisory services in the field of crime prevention and criminal justice; 2.) the collection and dissemination of information, in particular, research results and academic and scientific literature, to both professionals and the general public in order to permit the development and evaluation of measures and strategies for crime prevention and criminal justice and the identification of viable policy options for States of different regions; and 3.) the analysis of information on the impact of organized criminal activities upon society at large…with special emphasis on economic crimes and the laundering of illicit funds."[66]

INTERPOL

The International Police Association (INTERPOL) traces its origins back to the first International Criminal Police Congress of 1914, which met in Monaco.[67] The theme of that meeting was international cooperation in the investigation of crimes and the apprehension of fugitives. INTERPOL, however, did not officially begin operations until 1946, when the end of World War II brought about a new spirit of international harmony.

Today, 137 nations belong to INTERPOL. The U.S. INTERPOL unit is the U.S. National Central Bureau (USNCB) and is a separate agency within the U.S. Department of Justice. USNCB (also called INTERPOL-USNCB) is staffed with personnel from 12 federal agencies. Among them are the DEA, Secret Service, FBI, Immigration and Naturalization Service, IRS, ATF, and the Federal Law Enforcement Training Center.

American support of and participation in INTERPOL has increased substantially since 1980.[68] USNCB handles an annual caseload of around 32,000 (with 12,000 new cases each year), consisting of requests for information, fugitive alerts, and the like. Through USNCB, INTERPOL is linked to all major U.S. computerized criminal records repositories, including the FBI's National Crime Information Index, the State Department's Advanced Visa Lookout System, and the Immigration Naturalization Service's Master Index.[69]

INTERPOL's primary purpose is to act as a clearinghouse for information on offenses and suspects who are believed to operate across national boundaries. The organization is committed to "promot(ing) the widest possible mutual assistance between all criminal police authorities within the limits of laws existing in…different countries and in the spirit of the Universal Declaration of Human Rights."[70] INTERPOL does not intervene in religious, political, military, or racial disagreements in participant nations. As a consequence, a number of bombings and hostage situations were not officially investigated until 1984, when INTERPOL pledged itself to the fight against international terrorism. More recently, the world traffic in illegal drugs has also become a major focus of INTERPOL's efforts.

INTERPOL does not have its own field investigators. It draws, instead, upon the willingness of local and national police forces to lend support to its activities. The headquarters staff of INTERPOL consists of around 250 individuals, many with prior police experience, who direct data gathering efforts around the world and who serve to alert law enforcement organizations to the movement of suspected offenders within their jurisdiction.

In 1985 more than 50,000 cases requiring information were handled by INTERPOL, and 635,000 radio messages were sent by its headquarters. Because it serves primarily as a source of information, INTERPOL files are large, with nearly 5 million records of various sorts maintained at its new headquarters[71] in Lyon, France.

SUMMARY

The international perspective has much to contribute to the study of American criminal justice. Law enforcement agencies, court personnel, and correctional officials in the United States can benefit from exposure to innovative crime prevention, investigative, and treatment techniques found in other parts of the world. Policymakers, through a study of foreign legal codes and the routine practice of criminal justice in other countries, can acquire a fresh perspective on upcoming decisions in the area of law and justice.

A number of barriers, however, continue to limit the applicability of cross-national studies. One is the continuing unavailability of sufficiently detailed, up-to-date and reliable international information on crime rates, victimization, and adjudication. Another, more difficult limit to counter, is imposed by ethnocentrism. Ethnocentrism, a culturally determined hesitancy on the part of some people to consider any personal or professional viewpoints other than their own, reduces the likelihood for serious analysis of even the limited international information which is available in the area of criminal justice.

Given enough time most barriers are overcome. Although political, economic, and ideological differences will remain dominant throughout the world for many years, the globe is shrinking. Advances in communications, travel, and the exchange of all types of information are combining with an exponential growth in technology to produce a worldwide interdependence among nations. As new international partnerships are sought and formed, barriers to understanding will fall.

DISCUSSION QUESTIONS

1. What benefits can be had from the study of criminal justice systems in other countries? Are there any potential negative consequences of such study?

2. If you were to study the criminal justice systems of other countries which nations would you select for analysis? Why?

3. What is "ethnocentrism"? Where does it come from? What purpose does it serve? How can it be overcome? Should it be?

4. What are some of the limitations facing the serious international study of criminal justice today? Do you see any way in which those limitations can be overcome?

5. Do you think the practice of criminal justice in England could benefit from the creation of a precedent-setting exclusionary rule by the courts? Why or why not? Could British courts effect the creation of such a rule?

ENDNOTES

1. Herman Mannheim, *Comparative Criminology* (Boston: Houghton Mifflin, 1967), pp. x–xi.
2. "Killer of Japan Teen Acquitted," *USA Today*, May 24, 1993, p. 1A.
3. Robert Lilly, "Forks and Chopsticks: Understanding Criminal Justice in the PRC," *Criminal Justice International*, Vol. 2, no. 2 (March/April 1986), p. 15.
4. Adapted from Carol B. Kalish, "International Crime Rates," a Bureau of Justice Statistics *Special Report* (Washington, D.C.: BJS, 1988).
5. Ibid.
6. Ibid.
7. Ibid.
8. "China: The Hope and the Horror," *Reader's Digest*, September 1989, p. 75.
9. This section draws heavily upon Shao-Chuan Leng and Hungdah Chiu, *Criminal Justice in Post-Mao China: Analysis and Documents* (Albany: SUNY at Albany Press, 1985).
10. Various authorities give different dates for the ending of the Cultural Revolution. We have chosen 1973 because it represents the date at which military control over law enforcement finally ended.
11. *China Mainland Magazine*, No. 625, September 3, 1968, p. 23.
12. Central Political-Judicial Cadre's School, *Lectures on the General Principles of Criminal Law in the People's Republic of China* (Peking, 1957), as cited by Leng and Chiu, *Criminal Justice in Post-Mao China*, p. 21.
13. "On Questions of Party History," *Beijing Review*, Vol. 24, no. 27 (July 6, 1981), p. 20, as quoted in Leng and Chiu, *Criminal Justice in Post-Mao China*.
14. Leng and Chiu, *Criminal Justice in Post-Mao China*, p. 42.
15. Zhenxiong (Joseph) Zhou, "An Introduction to the Present Legal System of the People's Republic of China," *North Carolina Criminal Justice Today*, Vol. IV, no. 6, pp. 8–15 (Salemburg: NC Justice Academy, 1987).
16. The 1979 Chinese constitution specifies that the procuratorate is directly responsible for supervising the administration of criminal justice throughout the country, including the investigation of crimes, the activities of the courts, the police and correctional institutions, and to initiate prosecution (Article 5).
17. Robert Lilly, "Forks and Chopsticks: Understanding Criminal Justice in the PRC," *Criminal Justice International*, Vol. 2, no. 2 (March/April 1986), pp. 14–15.
18. Ibid., p. 14.
19. Leng and Chiu, *Criminal Justice in Post-Mao China*, p. 75.
20. United Nations Asia and Far East Institute for the Prevention of Crime and Treatment of Offenders and the Australian Institute of Criminology, *Crime and Justice in Asia and the Pacific* (Tokyo: UNAFEI/AIC, 1990), p. 85.
21. Dick Ward, "Drug Crackdown Nets Citizens and Foreigners, But Punishments Differ," *Criminal Justice International* (November/December 1992), p. 3.
22. "Anti–Drug Unit Forms in Shaanxi," *Fayetteville Observer-Times* (North Carolina), December 28, 1990, p. 14B.
23. Statistics on arrest, conviction, and imprisonment in China are taken from Robert Elegant, "Everyone Can Be Reformed," *Parade*, October 30, 1988, pp. 4–7.
24. Leng and Chiu, *Criminal Justice in Post-Mao China*, p. 141–142.

25. Zhu Entao, "A Perspective on Drug Abuse," *Criminal Justice International*, Vol. 3, no. 1 (January/February 1987), pp. 5–6.

26. Zhou, "An Introduction to the Present Legal System of the People's Republic of China," p. 13.

27. Ibid.

28. Ibid.

29. Leng and Chiu, *Criminal Justice in Post-Mao China*, p. 64.

30. Elegant, "Everyone Can Be Reformed," p. 5.

31. Jay Mathews, "Plagued by Crime, Chinese Increase Use of Executions," *The Washington Post*, August 5, 1980, p. A13.

32. *Renmin Ribao*, June 20, 1981, p. 4, as cited by Leng and Chiu, *Criminal Justice in Post-Mao China*.

33. Elegant, "Everyone Can Be Reformed," p. 6.

34. Ibid.

35. Constitution, People's Republic of China, Article 13.

36. Elegant, "Everyone Can Be Reformed," p. 5.

37. E. Eugene Miller, "Corrections in the People's Republic of China," in *International Corrections: An Overview* (College Park, MD: American Correctional Association, 1987), pp. 65–71.

38. Ibid., p. 69.

39. "Challenging China: Ex-Prisoner—10 Million in Labor Camps," *USA Today*, July 27, 1992, p. 2A.

40. Harry Wu, "A Prisoner's Journey," *Newsweek*, September 23, 1991, p. 30.

41. "Challenging China."

42. Parviz Saney, "Iran," in Elmer H. Johnson, ed., *International Handbook of Contemporary Developments in Criminology* (Westport, CT: Greenwood, 1983), p. 359.

43. This section owes much to Matthew Lippman, "Iran: A Question of Justice?" *Criminal Justice International*, Vol. 3, no. 6 (1987), pp. 6–7.

44. For additional information on Islamic law, see Adel Mohammed el Fikey, "Crimes and Penalties in Islamic Criminal Legislation," *Criminal Justice International*, Vol. 2, no. 4 (1986), pp. 13–14, and Sam S. Souryal, "Shariah Law in Saudi Arabia," *Journal for the Scientific Study of Religion*, Vol. 26, no. 4 (1987), pp. 429–449.

45. Max Weber, in Max Rheinstein, ed., *On Law in Economy and Society* (New York: Simon & Schuster, 1967), translated from the 1925 German edition.

46. Ibid.

47. Richard Terrill, *World Criminal Justice Systems* (Cincinnati, OH: Anderson, 1984), p. 3.

48. Philip John Stead, *The Police of Britain* (New York: Macmillan, 1985), p. 94.

49. Exceptions might include the Transport Police who supervise the operation of the nation's ports and secretive intelligence gathering agencies such as "M.I. 5."

50. A locally run police force, the City of London Police, with around 800 sworn officers is a separate force. City of London Police patrol the one-square-mile center city area which is the financial heart of London.

51. "An Interview with Sir Kenneth Newman, Commissioner of the Metropolitan Police," *Criminal Justice International*, Vol. 2, no. 6 (November/December 1986), p. 17.

52. "New Intelligence Service Begins Operation," *Criminal Justice International* (July/August 1992), p. 3.

53. For a good discussion of the curriculum at Bramshill, see Dennis Rowe, "On Her Majesty's Service: Policing England and Wales," *Criminal Justice International*, Vol. 2, no. 6 (November/December 1986), pp. 9–16.

54. "Birmingham Six Free After 16 Years," *USA Today*, March 15, 1991, p. 4A.

55. Stead, *The Police of Britain*, p. 147.

56. Terrill, *World Criminal Justice Systems*, p. 71.

57. Philip Jenkins, "Prison Crowding: A Cross-national Study," in American Correctional Association, *International Corrections: An Overview* (College Park, MD: ACA, 1987), p. 23.

58. Apex Trust et al., *A Joint Manifesto for Penal Reform* (London, 1989), as cited in Mike Carlie, "Prison Reform in England: An Overview," paper presented at the annual meeting of the Academy of Criminal Justice Sciences, Nashville, Tennessee, March 1990, p. 11.

59. Ibid.

60. Sean McConville, "Some Observations on English Prison Management," in *International Corrections*, p. 37.

61. Paul Friday, "International Organization: An Introduction," in Johnson, *International Handbook of Contemporary Developments in Criminology*, p. 31.

62. Ibid., p. 32.

63. Gerhard O. W. Mueller, "The United Nations and Criminology," in Johnson, *International Handbook of Contemporary Development in Criminology*, pp. 74–75.

64. Ibid., pp. 71–72.

65. Resolutions adopted on the reports of the Third Committee at The Forty-sixth Session of the United Nations General Assembly.

66. United Nations, *Report of the Commission on Crime Prevention and Criminal Justice on its First Session* (Vienna, Austria: United Nations, 1992).

67. Michael Fooner, "INTERPOL: Global Help in Fight Against Drugs, Terrorists, and Counterfeiters," *NIJ Reports*, September 1985, p. 5.

68. Ibid., p. 4.

69. Ibid.

70. "INTERPOL at Forty," *Criminal Justice International*, Vol. 2, no. 6 (November/December 1986), pp. 1, 22.

71. Ibid., p. 22.

CHAPTER 17

THE

FUTURE

OF

CRIMINAL

JUSTICE

Terrorism is going to join the omnipresence of crime as one of the things we have to worry about in American cities.
   —BRUCE HOFFMAN
   RAND CORPORATION

…technological innovations offer social benefits that respond to the current pressures for reduction of crime, the just and equitable administration of justice, and relief of prison overcrowding. However, technology throughout history has been a double-edged sword, equally capable of enhancing or endangering democratic values.[1]
   —JOHN H. GIBBONS
   DIRECTOR, OFFICE OF TECHNOLOGY ASSESSMENT
   U.S. CONGRESS

The future comes one day at a time.
   —DEAN ACHESON (1893-1971)

The rise of a new kind of America requires a new kind of law enforcement system.
   —ALVIN TOFFLER

KEY CONCEPTS

white-collar crime
organizational crime
DNA profiling
Computer Fraud and
    Abuse Act

computer virus
data encryption
occupational crime
federal interest
    computer

DNA fingerprinting
expert systems
hackers
high-technology crime
forensic anthropology

KEY NAMES

Alphonse Bertillon
Sir Francis Galton

William J. Herschel
James Coleman

Henry Faulds

KEY CASES

U.S. v. *Jakobetz*

Holt v. *Sarver*

CRIMINAL JUSTICE IN THE TWENTY-FIRST CENTURY

On June 28, 1993 Kirk Bloodsworth walked out of a Jessup, Maryland, prison a free man[2]—after serving nine years for a murder he did not commit. Standing before media cameras, Bloodsworth sobbed for his mother, who had died before seeing him cleared. Bloodsworth had been convicted in 1984 of the rape-murder of 9-year-old Dawn Hamilton and sentenced to die. He had consistently claimed he'd never met the girl. Recently, an FBI DNA test of semen found on the girl's underwear showed that Bloodsworth could not have been the killer. Were it not for modern technology, Bloodsworth would doubtlessly have remained imprisoned.

Modern technology will change many of the practical aspects of the criminal justice system of the twenty-first century—from the way in which evidence is gathered to the development of innovative forms of sentencing. Even so, the criminal justice system of the next century will look much like the system we know today. It will rest upon constitutional mandates and will be responsive to court precedent. The system itself will remain recognizable through its backbone of subsystems: the police, courts, and corrections. Deterrence, apprehension, and reformation will continue to serve as the philosophical trilogy guiding the day-to-day operations of criminal justice agencies. New issues will arise, but most of them will be resolved within the context of the question which has guided American criminal justice since its inception: how to ensure public safety while guaranteeing justice in a free society.

Inevitable changes about to occur in the fabric of American society, however, will necessitate some predictable large-scale system responses. Many demographic, ideological, and behavioral transformations, such as widespread illegal drug use and a greater social acceptance of certain victimless crimes, have already occurred and are now firmly rooted in substantial segments of American society. In the area of drugs much is already known. Drug culture has been studied, the impact of drug abuse on society is becoming clear, and the economic and human cost of drugs has been charted. Because the battle lines in the "war on drugs" are firmly drawn, a picture of drug abuse and the system response to it can be provided, as we have done in an earlier chapter. Only the final outcome of the "war" is still unknown.

Less clear, however, are changes yet to come—where we can now only begin to discern some early signs. This chapter attempts to identify some of these coming changes, and to predict what impact they will have on American criminal justice. Two arenas of change are identified: the technological and the social. Because technology may be the more important harbinger of change in the modern world, it is upon the opportunities and threats that technology represents to the justice system that this chapter first focuses.

Throughout history the interplay between technology and culture has been weighted in favor of cultural norms and ideals. Scientific advances often came before society was ready for them. When they did, they were denied or suppressed. Today, however, the situation is reversed. Technology is now often the prime mover, unable to be denied, and forcing social change when it occurs.

TECHNOLOGY AND CRIMINAL JUSTICE

We live in a world governed by rapid change. Technology and science are the modern-day engines of change, and they continue to run relentlessly forward. The impact of change on all areas of human life has been dramatic. The automobile and the airplane have made the world a smaller place, and journeys that would have required months a century ago can now be made in a day. Radio and television have transformed the planet into a "global village," in which every human being can be in touch with events of importance as they happen anywhere around the globe. Computers have dramatically altered the rate at which information is being produced, so much so that precedence is given today to storing

Fingerprinting, which became widespread as a crime fighting technique in the late 1800s, provided one of the first nearly foolproof methods of identification available to investigators. The fingerprint shown here provides an example of a "tented arch"—a particularly distinguishable characteristic. *Photo: Courtesy of the FBI.*

information rather than using it. Future computers, it is hoped, will sort through the accumulated information, allowing us to distinguish the significant from the mundane and permitting us to make use of that which is of interest.

Advancing technology, along with legislation designed to control it, will create crimes never before imagined. The future will see a race between technologically sophisticated offenders and law enforcement authorities as to who can wield the most advanced skills on either side of the age-old battle between crime and justice.

Technological advances signal both threats and opportunities for the justice field. By the turn of the twentieth century police callboxes became standard features in many cities, utilizing the new technology of telephonic communications to pass along information on crimes in progress or to describe suspects and their activities. A few years later police departments across the nation adapted to the rapid growth in the number of private automobiles and the laws governing their use. Motorized patrol, VASCAR devices, radar, police helicopters, and aircraft were all called into service as solutions to the need for a rapid response to criminal activity. Today's citizen's-band radios, often monitored by local police and highway patrol agencies, and cellular car telephones with direct numbers to police dispatchers, are continuing the trend of adapting advances in communications technology to police purposes.

Technology impacts criminal justice in many areas. The Technology Assessment Program (TAP) of the National Institute of Justice performs yearly assessments of key technological needs and opportunities facing the justice system. TAP concentrates on four areas of advancing technology: (1) communications and electronics, (2) forensic science, (3) transportation and weapons, and (4) protective equipment.[3] Once opportunities for improvement are identified in any area, referrals are made to the Law Enforcement Standards Laboratory (LESL)—a part of the National Bureau of Standards—for the testing of available hardware.

While TAP concentrates primarily on suspect apprehension and the protection of enforcement personnel, other authors have pointed to the potential held by emerging technologies in the area of offender treatment. Simon Dinitz, for example, has suggested that novel forms of biomedical intervention, building upon the earlier practices of castration, psychosurgery, and drug treatment, will continue to be adapted from advances in the biological sciences and serve as innovative treatment modalities.[4] The possibilities are limited only by the imagination. Chemical substances to reform the offender, drugs to enhance the memories of witnesses and victims, and microchip extensions of the personality all appear to be on the horizon of applicability.[5]

Technology: Hope of the Future

The use of technology in the service of criminal investigation is a modern subfield of criminal justice referred to as criminalistics. Criminalistics had its beginnings with the need for the certain identification of individuals. Early methods of personal identification were notoriously inaccurate. In the 1800s, for instance, one day of the week was generally dedicated to a "parade" of newly arrested offenders during which experienced investigators from distant jurisdictions would scrutinize the convicts, looking for recognizable faces.[6] By the 1840s the Quetelet system[7] of anthropometry was making itself known. The Quetelet system depended upon precise measurements of various parts of the body to give an overall "picture" of a person for use in later identification.

The first "modern" system of personal identification was created by Alphonse Bertillon.[8] Bertillon was the director of the Bureau of Criminal Identification of the Paris Police Department during the late 1800s. The Bertillon system of identification made the assertion that certain bodily aspects, such as eye color, skeletal size and shape, and ear form, did not change substantially after physical maturity had been reached. It combined physical measurements with the emerging technology of photography. Although photography had been used previously in criminal identification, Bertillon standardized the technique by positioning measuring guides beside suspects so that their physical dimensions could be calculated from their photographs and by the use of both front views and profiles.

Fingerprints, produced by contact with the ridge patterns in the skin on the fingertips, became the subject of intense scientific study in the mid-1840s. While their importance in criminal investigation today seems obvious, it was not until the 1880s that scientists began to realize that fingerprints were both unique to individuals and unchangeable over a lifetime. Both discoveries appear to have come from the Englishmen William J. Herschel and Henry Faulds working in Asia.[9] Some writers have observed that Asiatic lore about finger ridges and their significance extends back to antiquity, and suggest that Herschel and Faulds must have been privy to such information.[10] As early as the Tang dynasty (618–906A.D.) inked fingerprints in China were being used as personal seals on important documents, and there is some evidence that the Chinese had classified patterns of the loops and whorls found in fingerprints, and were using them for the identification of criminals as much as 1,000 years ago.[11]

The use of fingerprints in the identification of offenders was popularized by Sir Francis Galton[12] and officially adopted by Scotland Yard in 1901. By the 1920s fingerprint identification was in use in police departments everywhere, having quickly replaced the anthropometric system of Bertillon.

Fingerprint comparisons typically required a great deal of time and a modicum of luck for examiners to produce a match. Suspects were fingerprinted and their prints compared with those lifted from a crime scene. In the meantime, fingerprint inventories in the United States grew huge, including those of all persons in the armed services and certain branches of federal employment. Researchers looked constantly for an efficient way to rapidly compare large numbers of prints. Until the 1980s most effective comparison schemes depended upon classification methods which automatically eliminated large numbers of prints from needed comparisons. As late as 1974 one author lamented: "Considering present levels of technology in other sciences…[the] classification of fingerprints has profited little by technological advancements, particularly in the computer sciences. [Fingerprint comparisons are] limited by the laborious inspection by skilled technicians required to accurately classify and interpret prints. Automation of the classification process and potentially comparison as well, would open up fingerprinting to its fullest potential."[13]

Within a decade, advances in computer hardware and software made possible CAL-ID, an automated fingerprint identification system (AFIS) belonging to the California State Department of Justice. Such computerized systems have grown rapidly in capability and linkages in the past few years. The new technology also employs proprietary electrooptical scanning systems which digitize live fingerprints, eliminating the need for traditional inking and rolling techniques.[14] The use of lasers in fingerprint lifting recently allowed the FBI to detect a 40-year-old fingerprint of a Nazi war criminal on a postcard.[15] Computerization and digitization improve accuracy and reduce the incidence of "false positives" in ongoing comparisons.[16] The Los Angeles Police Department, which also uses an automated fingerprint identification system, now estimates that fingerprint comparisons which in the past would have taken as long as 60 years can now be performed in a single day.[17]

Computerized fingerprint identification systems took another giant step forward in 1986 with the introduction of the American National Standard for Information Systems—Fingerprint Identification—Data Format for Information Interchange.[18] This electronic standard makes possible the on-line exchange of fingerprint data between different automated fingerprint identification systems. Prior to its invention, the comparison of fingerprint data between AFIS systems was often difficult or impossible. Using the standard, cities across the nation can share and compare fingerprint information over telephone lines linking their AFIS systems.[19]

Modern criminalistics also depends heavily upon ballistics, the analysis of weapons, ammunition, and projectiles; medical pathology, to determine the cause of injury or death; forensic anthropology, to reconstruct the likeness of a decomposed or dismembered body; the photography of crime scenes (now often done with video cameras); plaster and polymer casting of tire tracks, boot prints, and marks made by implements; polygraph and voice print identification; as well as a plethora of other techniques. Many criminal investigation practices have been thoroughly tested and are now accepted by most courts for the evidence they offer (polygraph and voiceprint identification techniques are still being refined and have not yet won the wide acceptance of the other techniques mentioned).

Emerging Technologies   The future will see criminalistics aided by a number of technologies now in their infancy. They include DNA profiling and new serological techniques, on-line clearinghouses for criminal justice information, computer-generated profiles and photographic enhancements, forensic animation (computer simulations of criminal activity), and chemical and microscopic examination of fibers and other materials. A brief description of these technologies, including their current state of development and the implications they hold for the future, is provided in the paragraphs that follow.

DNA Profiling The use of biological residue found at the scene of a crime for genetic comparisons in aiding the identification of criminal suspects.

DNA Profiling   DNA (deoxyribonucleic acid) profiling is also termed DNA fingerprinting[20] (see Figure 17–1) because of the fact that genetic material is unique to each individual and can serve as the basis for suspect identification. DNA profiling is a new investigative technology which began as a test for determining paternity. One of the first successful adaptations of the technique to criminal prosecution occurred in 1987 when 32-year-old Robert Melias was convicted of raping a 43-year-old disabled woman. The conviction came after genetic tests on the semen left on the woman's clothes positively identified him as the perpetrator.[21] To date, courts in 49 states have admitted DNA evidence in 417 trials and hearings.[22] Although, as of this writing, the U.S. Supreme Court has yet to address the acceptability of DNA profiling in criminal prosecutions, the U.S. Court of Appeals for the Second Circuit ruled, in *U.S.* v. *Jakobetz* (1992),[23] that DNA tests results are admissible in federal criminal trials.

DNA profiling requires only a few human cells for comparison purposes. One drop of blood, a few hairs, a small amount of skin, or a trace of semen usually provide sufficient genetic material for comparison purposes. Because the DNA molecule is very stable, genetic tests can be conducted on evidence taken from crime scenes long after latent fingerprints have disappeared. DNA fingerprinting, however, has not yet been universally accepted in American courts of law.[24] The process, diagrammed in Figure 17–1, involves the use of a highly technical process called electrophoresis, which has not found wide acceptance in criminal courts. Some authors have suggested that, at least over the next few years, DNA profiling will find its greatest use as an investigative tool rather than as a courtroom test of guilt or innocence.[25] A recent government report, for example, found reason to believe that DNA fingerprinting may contravene a suspect's reasonable expectation of privacy.[26]

The FBI opened its first DNA-typing laboratory on October 17, 1988,[27] and by mid-1991 had become "the principal provider of forensic DNA testing services in the nation."[28] In 1992 alone, the FBI laboratory conducted more than 2,900 cases of DNA testing.[29]

A number of private firms are moving into the area and offering DNA comparisons to law enforcement departments on a fee-paid basis. Such firms provide customized reports of DNA comparisons with a turnaround time of from four to eight weeks, and usually offer the services of expert witnesses. Experts on the cutting edge of the new technology already have plans to develop a computerized DNA data base, where a person's genetic structure could be digitized, stored, and searched for as fingerprints are today.[30]

JUSTICE IN AMERICAN CONTEXT...

The most pressing problems facing the criminal justice system today.

A recent National Assessment Program survey of more than 2,000 criminal justice personnel and administrators conducted by the National Institute of Justice revealed that heightened caseloads, overcrowded courts and prisons, funding and staff shortages, and information management needs constitute the most pressing issues facing the justice system today. The following chart illustrates these and other problems by type of respondent. The circles (•) in the chart highlight the top three problems facing administrators by category.

Most Pressing Problems Facing the Criminal Justice System Today

	Caseload Increases	Court Delay	Drugs	Funding Shortages	Inadequate Facilities	Inadequate Program Facilities	Information Management	Inmate Programs and Education	Jail/Prison Crowding	Lack of Coordination	Organizational Problems	Staff Shortages	Staff Training
Local-level respondents													
Police			•	•			•					•	
Sheriffs			•	•					•			•	
Prosecutors	•			•			•					•	
Superior court judges	•	•		•								•	
Trial court Administrators (TCAs)				•		•			•			•	
Probation/parole agencies	•			•			•					•	
Jail managers				•		•			•			•	
Public defenders	•			•			•					•	
Victim assistance agencies				•						•	•		
State-level respondents													
Wardens				•				•	•				
Commissioners of corrections				•					•	•			
State probation and parole agencies	•			•								•	•
State attorneys general		•		•								•	
State court officers	•			•							•	•	

Source: Adapted from Charles B. DeWitt, *Assessing Criminal Justice Needs* (Washington, D.C.: National Institute of Justice, 1992), p. 2.

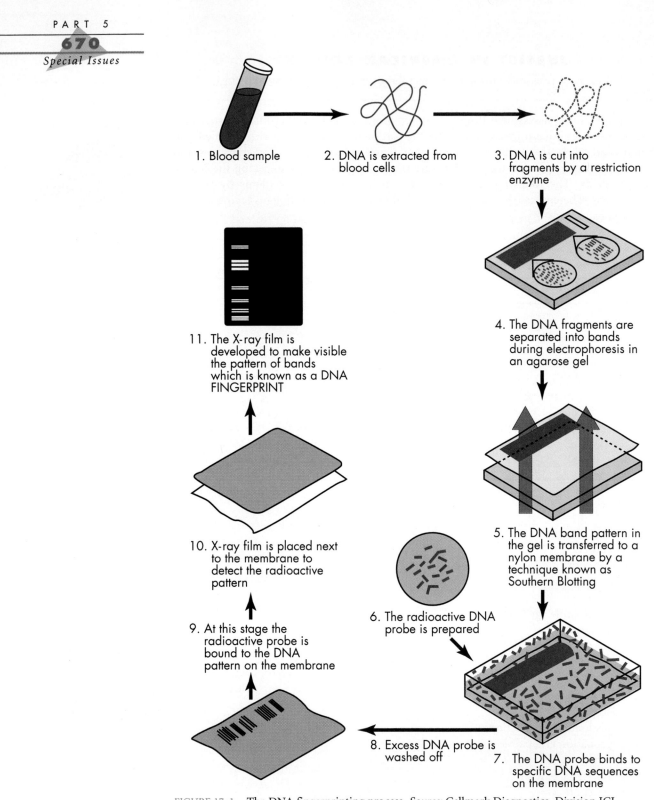

FIGURE 17–1   The DNA fingerprinting process. *Source:* Cellmark Diagnostics, Division ICI Americas, Inc. Reprinted with permission.

On-line Clearinghouses   Computers are already an integral part of most police departments. They perform such routine tasks as word processing, filing, record keeping, printing reports, and scheduling human resources and facilities. Computers which serve as investigative tools have, however, the greatest potential to impact criminal justice in the near future. The automated fingerprint technology discussed earlier is but one example of information-based systems designed to help in identifying offenders and solving crimes. Others include the nationwide National Crime Information Center (NCIC) and Violent Criminal Apprehension Program (VICAP) data bases, state-operated police identification networks, and specialized services like METAPOL, an information-sharing network run by the Police Executive Research Forum (PERF). Electronic facsimile systems (fax machines) now provide for easy hands-on distribution of on-line information. NCIC and PIN-type networks furnish a 24-hour channel to information on suspects, stolen vehicles, and other data, and can be accessed through computers installed in patrol cars. In 1993 William Sessions, then-director of the FBI, announced the creation of the Criminal Justice Information Services Division (CJIS) within the FBI. CJIS, Sessions said, "will provide state-of-the-art identification and information services...and will act as a focal point for the continual advancement of existing information systems and the development of new information services."[31]

Computer-Aided Investigations   Some police departments have begun to build and use large computer data bases with the ability to cross-reference specific information about crimes in order to determine patterns and identify suspects. One such program, HITMAN, developed by the Hollywood, California, Police Department in 1985, has since been adapted by the entire Los Angeles Police Department to help detectives solve violent crimes. In a similar use of computers, the LAPD keeps track of a target population of over 60,000 gang members.[32]

The developing field of artificial intelligence uses computers to make inferences based upon available information, and to draw conclusions or make recommendations to the system's operators. Expert systems, as these computer models are often called, depend upon three components: (1) a user interface or terminal, (2) a knowledge base containing information on what is already known in the area of investigation, and (3) a computer program known as an "inference engine" which makes comparisons between user input and stored information according to established decision-making rules.

A number of expert systems already exist. One is being used by the FBI's National Center for the Analysis of Violent Crime (NCAVC) in a project designed to profile serial violent criminals. The NCAVC system depends upon computer models of criminal profiling to provide a theoretical basis for the development of investigative strategies. A number of other systems are under development, including some which focus on serology analysis, narcotics interdiction, serial murder and rape, and counterterrorism.[33]

Similar to expert systems are relational data bases which permit fast and easy sorting of large records. Perhaps the best known criminal justice data base of this sort is called Big Floyd, which was developed by the FBI in conjunction with the Institute for Defense Analyses. Big Floyd was designed to access the more than 3 million records in the FBI's Organized Crime Information System and allow investigators to decide which federal statutes apply in a given situation and whether investigators have enough evidence for a successful prosecution.[34]

Computer-aged image of a missing child. The child, Autumn Jade Young, is shown at the time of her disappearance in the left photo when she was 3 years old. Computer imaging updated her appearance in the photo on the top right to what she might be expected to look like at age 9. Shortly after the image was released, Autumn (shown below) was returned to her family. *Photo: The National Center for Missing and Exploited Children.*

Some systems are problem specific. For example, ImAger, a product of Face Software, Inc., uses computer technology to artificially age photographs of missing children. The program has been used successfully to identify and recover a number of children. One of them was only 6 months old when he disappeared and was found after ImAger created a photo of what the child was predicted to look like at age 5. The photo was recognized by viewers who called police after it was broadcast on NBC television.[35] Another composite imaging program, Compusketch, by Visatex Corporation, is used by police artists to create simulated photographs of criminal suspects.[36]

NCAVC says that expert systems and relational data bases:[37] (1) help eliminate useless investigative paths, (2) store information that might otherwise be forgotten or not shared between investigators, (3) train beginning investigators to think like experienced profilers, and (4) are not subject to human failings such as the need for rest.

Computer-Based Training Computers provide an ideal training medium for criminal justice agencies. They have the advantage of allowing users to work at their own pace, and they can be made available around the clock to provide instruction on-site to personnel whose job requirements make other kinds of training difficult to implement. Computer-based training (CBT) is already well established as a management training tool. It is now under development by criminal justice education specialists for specific applicability in the field of law enforcement.[38] CBT has the added advantage of familiarizing personnel with computers so that they will be better able to use them in other tasks.

Some of the more widely used computer training programs include shoot/no shoot decision-based software and police pursuit driving simulators. The Atari Mobile Operations Simulator (AMOS), firearms training simulation (FATS), and ROBBEC'S JUST (Judgment Under Stress Training) are just a few of the contemporary products available to police training divisions. Other high-technology–based training is available via the Law Enforcement Satellite Training Network (LESTN), a privately owned company operating out of Carrollton, Texas.

Many other high-technology areas of opportunity stand ready for utilization by the criminal justice system. Laser fingerprint lifting devices, space-age photography, video camera-equipped patrol cars, satellite mapping, advanced chemical analysis techniques, and hair and fiber identification are all crime-fighting techniques of the future which are already being utilized to some extent by enforcement agencies. Refinements in technology, lower costs, and better training will see many of these technologies become common investigative tools. Field test kits for drug analysis, chemical sobriety checkers, and hand-held ticket-issuing computers, have already made the transition from high-technology to widespread use. As one expert has observed, "police agencies throughout the world are entering an era in which high technology is not only desirable but necessary in order to combat crime effectively."[39]

Problems in Implementation Technological innovations, however, do not represent all smooth sailing. Three areas of concern bear watching. First, the speed with which justice agencies successfully adapt to the opportunities brought by technology may be limited. Some writers have observed that "law enforcement has been slow to utilize new technology,"[40] and a study by the International Association of Chiefs of Police found that only 10% of police departments are innovative in their use of computers.[41] Factors which prevent criminal justice agencies from successfully adapting available high technology include (1) the rapid rate of change in most technologies, (2) a lack of personal experience and technological knowledge by decision makers, (3) uncertainty as to the future legal acceptability and social applicability of specific technologies, (4) the known or suspected inability of some high-technology vendors to deliver the products they advertise, and (5) the immobilizing plethora of too many options and choices.[42]

A second area of concern arises from the "supersleuth" capabilities of some high-technology items. As high-tech gadgetry becomes more commonplace in criminal justice agencies, we can be sure that the courts will keep an eye open to potential violations of individual rights. The use of photographic techniques developed for the space program, for example, which permit enlargement of details never before thought possible, or the use of superlistening devices, such as those now used to isolate and amplify the voices of referees and quarterbacks on weekend television, may extend investigative capabilities beyond previous understandings of limited search and seizure.

Finally, it must be recognized that the investigative and other opportunities created by technology for the agents of criminal justice have their flip side in the threats represented by the products of modern science in the hands of criminals.

The Bane of Technology: High-Tech Crimes

The flip side of high technology, as far as the justice system is concerned, is the potential it creates for committing old crimes in new ways, or for the commission of new crimes never before imagined. Sometimes in today's high-tech world it's even difficult to tell when a crime has occurred. As a security manager with the Boeing Corporation observed, "The main problem…with computer crime prosecution has been lack of clear legal definitions and the resultant difficulty in convincing a judge or jury of the crime."[43]

White-Collar Crime Because of the skill and knowledge required by their crimes, most, but not all, today's high-tech offenders can aptly be labeled white-collar criminals. The term **white-collar crime** was coined by Edwin Sutherland in his 1939 presidential address to the American Sociological Society.[44] Sutherland later defined the term to include crimes committed by persons in authority during the normal course of their business transactions. White-collar crimes include embezzlement, bribery, political corruption, price fixing, misuse and theft of company property, corporate tax evasion, fraud, and money laundering (which obscures the source of funds earned through illegal activities, allowing them to enter the legitimate financial arena). White-collar crimes tend to be committed by financially secure, well-educated, middle- or upper-class persons. Sutherland claimed that the prevalence of white-collar crimes shows that "The theories of criminologists that crime is due to poverty or to psychopathic and sociopathic conditions statistically associated with poverty are invalid."[45]

The insider-trading scam of stock market tycoon Ivan Boesky, which was estimated to have netted $250 million[47] for Boesky and his friends, and the $600 million fine levied against junk bond king Michael Milken in 1990 for securities fraud provide two recent examples of white-collar crime. Another can be found in the savings and loan fiasco of the late 1980s and early 1990s, which has been called "the biggest white-collar crime in history."[48] The S&L disaster was a long time in the making. While the boom days following World War II were lucrative for the savings and loan industry, hard times set in during the 1970s, when low-interest long-term housing loans made by member institutions were costing the industry more than it could earn. Then, falling interest rates and a surge in land development combined with decreased federal regulation to produce a climate in which savings and loan institutions could quickly turn big profits by signing increasingly risky loans. Following deregulation, made possible in part by Congress's passing of the Depository Institutions Deregulation and Monetary Control Act of 1980, organized criminal groups began working the S&L market. As Frank Hagan notes, "[t]he S&L scandal reflected increased criminal opportunity due to an economic crisis that was taken advantage of by greedy insiders who collectively looted financial institutions and left the bill to the U.S. taxpayers."[49]

As individual savings and loans closed, costs began to mount. The bankruptcy of Charles Keating's California-based Lincoln Savings and Loan Association cost taxpayers around $2.5 billion, while the collapse of Neil Bush's Silverado Banking S&L in Denver cost nearly $1 billion.[50] Once called the "granddaddy of all S&L crooks,"[51] Donald Dixon, the former chief of Vernon Savings and Loan (in Vernon, Texas) is typical of the fraudulent operators who enriched themselves via S&L mismanagement. Dixon, through the help of personally approved high-risk loans, spent tens of millions of dollars for jets, fast cars, prostitutes, and a 110-foot yacht. While paying himself a multimillion-dollar salary from

---

Computer Crime Any crime which takes advantage of computer-based technology in its commission. This definition highlights the manner in which a crime is committed, more than it does the target of the offense. Hence, the physical theft of a computer, or of a floppy disk, would not be a computer crime, while the use of computer software to analyze a company's security operations prior to committing a robbery might be.

White-Collar Crime Nonviolent crime for financial gain committed by means of deception by persons having professional status or specialized technical skills during the everyday pursuit of their business endeavors.[46]

1981 to 1987, Dixon bought Ferraris and million-dollar beach houses in Del Mar and Solana Beach, California. When the Vernon S&L was finally shut down in 1987, 96% of its loans were delinquent. Dixon was finally convicted on December 20, 1990 of 23 counts of misappropriation of funds—including $42 million spent on, among other things, a 5,500-square-foot beach house and a party where prostitutes were provided for guests.[52] Estimates are that the total S&L debacle will cost American taxpayers nearly $500 billion over the next 30 years—an amount far larger than that lost in all bank robberies throughout the course of American history.

> More money has been stolen at the point of a fountain pen than at the point of a gun.
>
> —*Woody Guthrie*

White-collar criminals tend to be punished less severely than other offenders. In the 1930s and 1940s Edwin Sutherland studied the 70 largest corporations of his time and found that 547 adverse court and regulatory agency decisions had been made against them—an average of 7.8 decisions per corporation.[53] Although this should have been evidence of routine corporate involvement in white-collar criminality, almost no corporate executives were sentenced to prison. More recent studies have shown that about 40% of convicted federal white-collar offenders are sentenced to prison versus 54% of nonwhite-collar criminals.[54] When prison sentences *are* imposed, white-collar offenders are sentenced to only 29 months on average, versus 50 months for other inmates.[55] As other authors have noted, "[f]or some reason our system has seen nothing unjust in slapping an 18-year-old inner-city kid with a 20-year prison sentence for robbing a bank of a couple of

Indicted junk bond king Michael Milken addresses a California forum shortly before his conviction for improper securities trading practices. Milken was eventually convicted and fined $600 million, although experts estimate that that figure is far less than the profit he reaped. Milken spent 22 months in prison and was released in 1993. *Photo: Paul Richard/ UPI Bettmann.*

Occupational Crime
Any act punishable by law which is committed through opportunity created in the course of an occupation that is legal.

thousand dollars while putting a white-collar criminal away for just two years in a "prison camp" for stealing $200 million through fraud."[56]

Occupational Crime   Criminologists were quick to realize that if persons of high socioeconomic status could commit crimes while handling normal business, then so could persons of lower social standing.[57] The term "occupational crime" was coined to describe the on-the-job illegal activities of employees. Thefts of company property, vandalism, the misuse of information, software piracy which occurs in the workplace, and many other activities come under the rubric of occupational crime. The employee who uses company phones for personal calls, the maintenance worker who steals cleaning supplies for home use, and the store clerk who lifts items of clothing or jewelry provide other examples of occupational criminality. The Council of Better Business Bureaus estimates that one-third of all plant and office workers steal from their employers.[58] Total losses are said to be in the range of $10 to $20 billion per year.[59] The Council believes that one-third of all business failures are directly attributable to employee crime.[60]

In a recent book on occupational crime,[61] Gary S. Green defines occupational crime as "any act punishable by law which is committed through opportunity created in the course of an occupation that is legal."[62] Green has developed the following typology which considerably broadens the classification of occupational criminality: "(a) crimes for the benefit of an employing organization (organizational occupational crime); (b) crimes by officials through the exercise of their state-based authority (state authority occupational crime); (c) crimes by professionals in their capacity as professionals (professional occupational crime); and (d) crimes by individuals as individuals (individual occupational crime)."[63]

James Coleman provides a further distinction between types of white-collar crime.[64] Coleman points out that some white-collar crimes affect only property while others endanger the safety and health of people. The knowing sale of tainted food products or medicine are examples of the latter type of crime. Coleman has also suggested that the term organizational crime is useful to distinguish those offenses which are designed to further the goals of corporate entities, from business-related crimes committed by individuals to further their own desires.[65] Organizational crimes are the "crimes of big business." Sometimes, however, it pays to remember that all crimes are committed by people and not by institutions.

Some authors maintain that occupational and corporate crime are a way of life in American businesses.[66] Examples abound.[67] Government investigations in the late 1950s revealed that the General Electric Company was heavily involved in price fixing.[68] In 1975 Allied Chemical Corporation was fined $5 million and agreed to donate another $8 million to a cleanup fund after it was revealed that former Allied employees had arranged to establish a small, seemingly independent business to supply Allied with the highly toxic chemical Kepone.[69] Workers in the Kepone manufacturing facility became seriously ill, and the St. James River near the plant was badly contaminated. Most readers of this volume will recognize the acronym "PCBs" and the role of such chemicals in cases of criminal contamination of the environment. A few may remember the infamous "Love Canal Incident" or the exploding gas tanks on Ford Pintos which were manufactured between 1971 and 1976. There is evidence that Ford executives may have known of the defects before the Pinto was even put into production.[70] The Ford Motor Company ultimately paid more than $100 million in recall fees and civil settlements directly related to the gas tank coverup.[71]

Corporate Crime   a violation of a criminal statute either by a corporate entity or by its executives, employees, or agents acting on behalf of and for the benefit of the corporation, partnership, or other form of business entity.

Recent examples of corporate crime come from the $10 billion 1985 mail and wire fraud scheme of E. F. Hutton[72] and the 1988 stock fraud case of Wall Street giant Drexel Burnham Lambert, Incorporated. In late 1988 Drexel agreed to pay $650 million in fines and restitution and pleaded guilty to six felony counts involving securities law violations.[73] Government prosecutors used the case to prove other wrongdoings on the part of some of the nation's best known corporate traders.[74]

THEORY INTO PRACTICE

THE TERMINOLOGY OF COMPUTER AND HIGH-TECHNOLOGY CRIME

Software

Computer programs or instructions to machines which control their operations. Software is generally found in magnetic storage media, but can be reproduced on paper or held in either machine or human memory.

Hardware

Computer machinery, to include, keyboards, disk or tape drives, optical scanners, "mice," video monitors, printers, central processing units, modems, terminals, add-on boards, peripherals, etc.

CPU

Central processing unit. That part of the computer which houses the microprocessor and performs data manipulations.

Modem

A telecommunications device used to link computers. A modem is generally used by hackers to gain illegal access to other computers.

Hackers

Computer hobbyists or professionals, generally with advanced programming skills. The term "hackers" is often used to describe computer operators involved in "computer trespass."

Copying

The duplication of software or the transfer of data from one storage media to another. One of the most prevalent problems in computer crime is the unauthorized duplication of copyrighted software.

Illegal Access

Unauthorized entrance into a computer's files or operating system. Entrance may be made through the use of private information (a password), physical trespass, or electronically via a modem and software. In legal terminology illegal access is often referred to as "computer trespass."

Theft by Computer

The illegal use of a computer to transfer money, valuables, software, data, or other property from one account or machine to another.

Theft of Computer Services

The illegal use of computer time or of information or other services available on-line or directly. Employees of computer-based industries may use machines for personal purposes (such as check-book balancing, games, etc.), while hackers may acquire on-line services illegally by circumventing security and fee systems.

Virus

A computer program which is designed to secretly invade systems and modify either the way in which they operate or alter the information they store. Viruses are destructive software which may effectively vandalize computers of all sizes. Other destructive programs include *logic bombs*, *worms*, and *Trojan horse* routines, which hide inside of seemingly innocent software or disks.

Federal Interest Computer

A computer owned by the federal government or a financial institution, or one which is accessed across state lines without prior authorization. Federal Interest Computers are defined by the Computer Fraud and Abuse Act, as amended in 1986.

Computer and High-Technology Crime During Sutherland's time, political corruption and corporate bribery were serious concerns. Although both offenses exist today, computer crimes are rapidly becoming the white-collar crime *par excellence* in the modern world. Computer crimes use the computer as a tool in crime commission. Thefts of computer equipment are not computer crimes, but are, rather, classified as larcenies. Computer criminals focus on the information stored in computer systems and generally manipulate it in some way.

Prosecution of Computer and High-Tech Crime Computer crimes bear some resemblance to other more traditional crimes such as burglary (illegal entry into a computer system), theft (the stealing of information), and embezzlement (the electronic transfer of funds). Some prosecutions of computer criminals occur under statutes originally designed for other purposes. For example, an employee of Texas Instruments Corporation who stole more than 50 written copies of software programs was convicted of theft under Texas law.[75] Had the software been stolen in electronic form, or through the use of random access computer memory, prosecution under the state larceny statute would have been much more difficult. In another case, Wisconsin authorities found themselves at a loss as to how to prosecute the "414 gang"—a teenage group of computer hackers based in Milwaukee who had infiltrated the computers of 60 businesses, including government computer systems, the Los Alamos National Laboratory, the Sloan-Kettering Cancer Center, and the Security Pacific National Bank in Los Angeles.[76] At the time of the offense (1983), neither Wisconsin nor the federal government had specific legislation applicable to the hackers' activity, and they had to be arraigned under a law pertaining to telephone mischief.

Because existing laws have often not been adequate in prosecution of computer criminals, most states and the federal government have moved rapidly to create computer and high-technology criminal statutes. In October 1984 the first federal computer crime law was enacted.[77] Called the Computer Fraud and Abuse Act, it made unauthorized access to government computers or to computers containing information protected under the Federal Privacy Act a crime.[78] It also defined unauthorized interstate entry into any

Federal Interest Computers Are those that (1) are the property of the federal government, (2) belong to financial institutions, or (3) are located in the state other than the one in which the criminal perpetrator is operating.

computer as illegal. In 1986 Congress expanded the penalty for illegal access to computers which represent a "unique federal interest." Federal interest computers are those that (1) are the property of the federal government, (2) belong to financial institutions, or (3) are located in a state other than the one in which the criminal perpetrator is operating. Under the law, convicted offenders face penalties of up to ten years imprisonment and fines which can extend to twice the amount of the "unlawful gain."

High-tech criminals may also be prosecuted under a variety of other federal legislation. One authority estimates that as many as 40 different sections of the federal criminal code may be applicable to thefts which occur through the use of a computer.[79] Applicable federal statutes include aspects of the Electronic Communications Privacy Act of 1986; the National Stolen Property Act;[80] the Federally Protected Property Act;[81] the Federal Trade Secrets Act;[82] the amended Copyright Act of 1980;[83] and federal wire, mail, and bank fraud statutes. All can support prosecutions of high-tech offenders.[84] Unfortunately, federal laws do not necessarily guard the interests of many small corporations, nor do they adequately protect the activities of the nation's millions of home computer users. Such laws are generally designed to thwart the "big-time" offender and require the violation of federal interests.

To fill the gap, most states have developed their own computer crime laws. The New York state Computer Crime Bill is an example of such legislation.[85] It was enacted in July 1986 and created six new crime categories involving software and computer misuse. The law specifically prohibits the duplication of copyrighted software and makes the possession of illegally duplicated software a felony. Other activities now defined as illegal include the "unauthorized use of a computer," "computer trespass," and "theft of computer services." The New York bill also created sweeping amendments to existing law. Theft laws were modified to specifically include "computer program" and "computer data" under the definition of "property," and computer terminology was incorporated into forgery laws. Most state computer crime laws impose punishments proportional to the damage done, although California bases penalties on the number of violations.

Reprinted by permission of NEA, Inc.

"That's funny. I could have sworn that computer hacker got five years and $50,000 in fines. But here it is — six months suspended and five bucks.

THEORY INTO PRACTICE

FEDERAL STATUTES APPLICABLE TO THE PROSECUTION OF COMPUTER AND HIGH-TECHNOLOGY CRIME

Computer Fraud and Abuse Act of 1984 (18 U.S.C., § 1030, Amended 1986)

Provides specifically for the protection of "government-interest computers." Covered are government-owned computers or computers which serve a government interest such as bank-operated machines.

Electronic Communications Privacy Act of 1986 (18 U.S.C., §§ 2510–21)

Especially relevant to the prosecution of crimes involving intercepted data communications.

Federal Wiretap Act (Title III of the 1968 Omnibus Crime Control and Safe Streets Act)

Recent modifications have made this act specifically applicable to on-line thefts of computer software.

Right to Financial Privacy Act (12 U.S.C., § 3401)

Protects the privacy of personal financial records. Hackers who gain access to bank records, credit bureaus, and so on, are in violation of this statute.

Copyright Act as Amended, 1980 (17 U.S.C., § 101,117)

Permits copyrighting authored computer software as a literary work. Allows for the creation of archival copies of software by legitimate purchasers, and provides for the prosecution of "software pirates."

National Stolen Property Act (18 U.S.C., § 2311)

Allows for federal prosecution when stolen property is taken across state or national boundaries. On-line thefts of computer time, software, data, and funds are generally subsumed under this statute.

Federally Protected Property Act (18 U.S.C., § 641)

Crimes involve stealing or embezzlement from federally protect agencies. Applicable to thefts, destruction, or vandalism of hardware and software.

Federal Trade Secrets Act (18 U.S.C., § 1905)

Protects confidential information provided by individuals and corporations to the federal government. Useful in the prosecution of thefts of data and software.

Federal Fraud Provisions (18 U.S.C., §§ 1343, 1344)

Covers the use of false or fraudulent pretenses to obtain money or property. Federal jurisdiction is clear when interstate wire services or financial instiutions are involved. May be applicable to the unauthorized invasion of computer data bases, including the use of illicit passwords or schemes to neutralize computer security systems.

Types of Computer Crime   One problem in the development of comprehensive laws is lack of appreciation for the potentially wide variety of crimes which can be perpetrated using a computer. While a comprehensive typology of computer-based crime has yet to be developed (see Figure 17–2 for one suggested grouping), the following categories probably encompass most such offenses today:

Robert Morris, creator of the infamous "internet worm." Morris, shown here with his mother leaving the Federal Courthouse in Syracuse, New York, was found guilty of the November 1988 attack on thousands of networked computers across the nation. *Photo: AP/Wide World.*

1. *Unauthorized Access to Data.* An old adage says that "knowledge is power." Information stored in today's magnetic and laser-read media is often sensitive (like personnel records) or necessarily secret (such as corporate marketing plans or the detailed technical description of a new product). Unauthorized access to data can lead to lawsuits over patent infringements, loss of a competitive edge, and the need to redo many hours or even months of work.

The frequent need for access to computer-based data, and the routine use of telephone lines for data transfer make such information particularly susceptible to snooping. Four techniques are used today to prevent the compromise of sensitive data. They are

a. *Physical security.* Locked disk files, key-operated hard disks, removable storage media, and limited access computer rooms are all physical security measures which can be taken to thwart the potential viewing or theft of information.

b. *Software which requires the user to properly enter a password or other form of identification.* Some advanced systems use optical imaging to recognize the unique vascular system on the retinas of users requesting access to highly secure computer networks. "Eyeball scanners," voice recognition units, hand geometry scanners, keyboard rhythm recognition units, and other high-technology gadgetry, known in the trade as biometric security devices, are not readily available to most businesses because of cost.

Data Encryption
Methods used to encode computerized information.

c. *Data encryption methods.* Data encryption uses either hardware or software to turn information into gibberish until it is uncoded by authorized users.[86] Two types of data encryption techniques exist today: unique operations developed by companies and peculiar to their products, and methods which make use of the Data Encryption Standard (DES) of the National Bureau of Standards. DES makes it possible for banks and other businesses freely to exchange and decrypt coded data even when the computer systems used in the exchange differ substantially.

d. *Screen blanking.* Screen blanking lacks the sophistication of some of the other methods we have described. It depends upon a relatively simple technology which causes video monitors to go blank after a set period of nonuse. Hence, data entry stations left unattended cannot be casually viewed by unauthorized personnel.

FIGURE 17–2   Types of computer crime. *Source:* National Center for Computer Crime Data, Los Angeles, California.

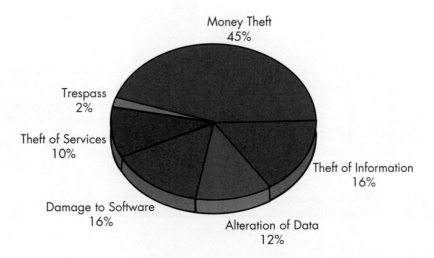

2. *Willful Destruction of Data.* As computer systems grow in complexity they challenge the inventiveness of sophisticated "hackers" or computer buffs. Some are tempted to try their skill at invading highly protected systems. Such top-level invaders typically leave some sign of their accomplishment. It may be something as simple as a message which appears in printed documents or on the screens of legitimate users. It may also take the form of a set of hidden instructions which cause the computer to destroy its data or alter its software instructions. The sophisticated but destructive computer programs involved in this modern kind of vandalism are called computer viruses. Viruses spread from one computer to another through disk swapping or over data lines which link one machine to another.

    As society becomes more dependent upon computers, the damage potential of viruses increases. In 1988 the "Pakistani" virus (also called the "Pakistani brain" virus) became widespread in personal and office computers across the United States.[87] The Pakistani virus had been created by Amjad Farooq Alvi and his brother Basit Farooq Alvi, two cut-rate computer software dealers in Lahore, Pakistan. The Alvi brothers made copies of costly software products and sold them at low prices to mostly Western shoppers looking for a bargain. Through a convoluted logic, the brothers hid a virus on each disk they sold in order to punish buyers for seeking to evade copyright laws.

    A more serious virus incident affected sensitive machines in NASA, nuclear weapons labs, federal research centers, and universities across the United States in late 1988.[88] The virus did not destroy data. Instead it made copies of itself and multiplied so rapidly that it clogged machines and effectively shut them down within hours after it invaded them. Robert Morris, creator of the virus, was finally sentenced in April 1990 to 400 hours of community service and 3 years probation and was fined $10,000.[89]

    The first criminal prosecution of a person accused of creating a virus involved 40-year-old Fort Worth, Texas, programmer Donald Gene Burleson. Prosecutors claimed Burleson infected a former employer's computer with a program that erased over 168,000 business records.[90] Burleson's alleged motive was revenge for office disagreements.

3. *Data Manipulation.* Data manipulation may be the most serious kind of computer crime. People who are able to effect an unauthorized entry into computer files are often able to modify the data they contain. Students who access university administrative computers in order to change records of their grades are one example of data manipulation. A few years ago a 17-year-old Chicago high school student broke into a computer system operated by AT&T and stole communications software valued at over $1 million.[91] Other skilled operators may transfer funds between private accounts, download trade secrets, hide the evidence of embezzlement, or steal customer lists. The hit movie *WarGames* depicted a scenario in which a teenage hacker nearly began a world war. More recently computer experts have warned of a very real potential for international terrorism through computer subterfuge.[92]

    What may be the largest computer crime in history (in dollar amounts) happened rather early in the computer age. In 1984 a ring of employees at Volkswagen's Wolfsburg, West Germany, headquarters modified files in the company's computers to hide the theft of $428 million.[93] Some experts say that banks around the world routinely transfer over $3 trillion a day through electronic media.[94] Such huge amounts represent potentially easy prey to technologically sophisticated criminals.

Combating Computer Crime   Computer criminals are generally young, well educated, aggressive, and technically sophisticated.[95] They commit their crimes for various reasons. Some seek personal riches, while others are attracted to the offense by the technical challenge it represents. A study of computer felons showed that they saw themselves as pitted against the computer.[96] The computer criminal is the type of person who would probably resist the temptation to commit most other types of crimes. Because the offense is against a machine, however, this otherwise conformist type of personality may deny that they are involved in crime commission.

Computer criminals are highly skilled, and the crimes they commit are often difficult for the technically uninitiated to detect. Many large corporations employ experts to detect unauthorized access to data processing equipment. A growing cadre of consultants serve the computer security needs of smaller companies. Police departments have been hard-pressed to keep pace with the growing sophistication of computer equipment and the criminals who prey upon it. Among law enforcement agencies, expertise in computer crime investigations is rare. Some agencies, such as the FBI, do maintain substantial investigative capabilities in the computer area. Others, however, must rely upon personnel minimally trained in computer crime investigation. Given the wide range of expertise demanded of today's law enforcement personnel, it is probably unrealistic to expect detectives to be experts in the investigation of computer crime. Some authorities have suggested that competent criminal investigators today should at least be able to recognize that a computer crime has occurred.[97] Once the offense has been recognized investigators can then call upon the services of persons skilled in combating it.

Terrorism   A violent act or an act dangerous to human life in violation of the criminal laws of the United States or of any state to intimidate or coerce a government, the civilian population, or any segment thereof, in furtherance of political or social objectives.

TERRORISM

The American criminal justice system of the twenty-first century will be buffeted by the expanding power of politically oriented endemic groups with radical agendas. Throughout the 1960s and 1970s, domestic terrorism in the United States required the expenditure of considerable criminal justice resources. The Weathermen, Students for a Democratic Society, the Symbionese Liberation Army, the Black Panthers, and other radical groups challenged the authority of federal and local governments. Bombings, kidnappings, and shootouts peppered the national scene. As overt acts of domestic terrorism declined in frequency in the 1980s international terrorism took their place. The war in Lebanon, terrorism in Israel, bombings in France, Italy, and Germany, and the many violent offshoots of the Iran-Iraq war occupied the attention of the media and of much of the rest of the world. Vigilance by the FBI, CIA, and other agencies largely prevented the spread of terrorism to the United States.

After incidents such as the terrorist attacks on Rome's Leonardo da Vinci airport in 1987 and the 1988 bombing of Pan American's London–to–New York flight, Americans began to realize that international terrorism was knocking on the domestic door. Pan American flight number 103 was destroyed over Scotland by a powerful two-stage bomb as it reached its cruising altitude of 30,000 feet, killing all the 259 passengers and crew aboard. Another 11 people on the ground were killed, and many others injured as flaming debris from the airplane crashed down on the Scottish town of Lockerbie.

In 1992 142 anti-U.S. attacks of terrorism were reported worldwide.[98] Most occurred in Latin America, with businesses being the most prevalent targets. Bombings were the most common form of attack, and two Americans were killed overseas by terrorists in 1992.

The 1993 bombing of the World Trade Center in New York city, and the arrest later that year of eight Muslim fundamentalists who were allegedly planning to bomb New York's Holland and Lincoln tunnels, as well as the 39-story United Nations complex and the Jacob Javits Federal Building in Manhattan,[99] indicate to many observers that the quietude of the last decade has ended. Senator Alfonse D'Amato (R., N.Y.), a staunch supporter of Israel and

Workmen repair damage done to the sub-basement area of the World Trade Center after a terrorist bomb detonated there on February 26, 1993, killing six and injuring more than 1,000 people. The powerful blast tore a six-story crater into the base of one of the 110-story twin towers and caused hundreds of millions of dollars in damage. *Photo: Reuters/Bettmann.*

advocate of the death penalty for terrorists, and other lawmakers were apparently targeted by the same fundamentalist group for assassination. Many of those arrested were Sudanese nationals who had gained U.S. residency in the late 1980s by marrying U.S. citizens. Sudan is a well-known breeding ground for Islamic holy warriors, often trained there under the tutelage of Iranian Revolutionary Guards. Many now suspect that sleeper agents, planted by nations as diverse as Libya, Syria, North Korea, Cuba, Iran and Iraq, have taken up residence throughout the United States and are awaiting the appropriate signal to attack.

According to some terrorism experts, the 1993 bombing of the World Trade Center ushered in an era of serious domestic terrorism. Robert Kupperman, of the Center for Strategic and International Studies, says,[100] "We're in for very deep trouble. The terrorism infrastructure operating in the United States is altogether deeper than what we've thought so far."[101] Confirming Kupperman's observations, Siddig Ibrahim Siddig Ali, one of the eight accused terrorists said, following his arrest, "We can get you anytime." The United States has lax security according to Philip Jenkins, a counterterrorism expert. "In Europe," says Jenkins, "if you leave a bag at a railroad station, it will be blown up when you come back 30 minutes later. Here, it will be taken to lost and found."[102]

The technological sophistication of state-sponsored terrorist organizations is rapidly increasing. Handguns and even larger weapons are now being manufactured out of plastic polymers and ceramics. Capable of firing Teflon-coated armor-piercing bullets, such weapons are extremely powerful and impossible to uncover with metal detectors. Evidence points to the black market availability of other sinister devices, including liquid metal embrittlement (LME). LME is a chemical which slowly weakens any metal it contacts. It could be applied easily with a Magic Marker® to fuselage components in domestic aircraft, causing delayed structural failure.[103] Backpack-type electromagnetic pulse generators may soon be available to terrorists. Such devices could be carried into major cities, set up next to important computer installations, and activated to wipe out billions of items of financial, military, or other information now stored on magnetic media. International terrorists, along with the general public, have easy access to maps and other information which could be easily used to cripple the nation. The approximately 500 extremely high-voltage (EHV) transformers on which the nation's electronic grid depends are entirely undefended, but specified with extreme accuracy on easily available power network maps.

Equally worrisome are endemic underground survivalist groups and potentially violent special interest groups with their own vision of a future America, such as David Koresh's Branch Davidians whose fiery end under federal siege in 1993 captured the nation's attention. Supremacist groups are already committing acts of terrorism, as the "hate crimes" section of Chapter 2 describes. A few years ago, for example, members of the Order were convicted in the machine gun slaying of Denver radio talk show host Allen Berg who they claimed was a puppet of ZOG, the "Zionist Occupational Government."[104] Later testimony revealed that many others were targeted for murder, including Henry Kissinger, Norman Lear, David Rockefeller, and Morris Dees, director of the Southern Poverty Law Center.[105] Other Order members have been found guilty of the murder of highway patrol troopers, while one of the group's leaders was killed in a shootout with the FBI.[106]

Special interests gained violent notoriety with the 1993 murder of a well-known Florida abortion clinic doctor, David Gunn. Gunn, 47, was shot three times in the back with a .38-caliber pistol as he walked from his car to the Pensacola Women's Medical Services building.[107] Harassment and arson have also characterized antiabortion groups. Besides antiabortionists, many other special interest groups with the potential for violence exist throughout the United States. As most experts would readily agree, the American justice system of today is ill prepared to deal with the threat represented by supremacist and radical groups. Intelligence-gathering efforts focused on such groups have largely failed, and military-style organization and training are characteristic of a number of the groups that are known—especially those with a survivalist bent. The armaments at the disposal of some domestic groups include weapons of mass destruction which the firepower and tactical mobility of law enforcement agencies could not hope to match.

Even more frightening is the prospect of cooperation between international terrorist organizations and disaffected domestic groups. Such joint activities have already occurred. In 1986, for example, around the time of the Libyan crisis which led to the American bombing of Tripoli, the FBI intercepted communications between a Chicago-based drug gang and the Libyan government. The gang, seeing the opportunity for fast profit, proposed to engage in acts of domestic terrorism for the Libyans. Gang leaders were sentenced to prison for the scheme.

Rules of Terrorism

According to criminologist Gwynn Nettler, any terrorism, domestic or international, has six characteristics.[108] They are:

- *No rules.* There are no moral limitations upon the type or degree of violence which terrorists can use.
- *No innocents.* No distinctions are made between soldiers and civilians. Children can be killed as easily as adults.
- *Economy.* Kill 1, frighten 10,000.
- *Publicity.* Terrorists seek publicity, and publicity encourages terrorism.
- *Meaning.* Terrorist acts give meaning and significance to the lives of terrorists.
- *No clarity.* Beyond the immediate aim of destructive acts, the long-term goals of terrorists are likely to be poorly conceived or impossible to implement.

Controlling Terrorism

Terrorism represents a difficult challenge to all societies. The open societies of the Western world, however, are potentially more vulnerable than are totalitarian regimes such as dictatorships. Democratic ideals in the West restrict police surveillance of likely terrorist groups and curtail luggage, vehicle, and airport searches. Press coverage of acts of terrorism encourage copycat activities by other fringe groups or communicate information on workable techniques. Laws designed to limit terrorist access to technology, information, and physical locations are stop-gap measures at best. The federal Terrorist Firearms Detection Act of 1988 is an example. Designed to prevent the development of plastic firearms by requiring handguns to contain at least 3.7 ounces of detectable metal,[109] it applies only to weapons manufactured within U.S. borders.

There are no signs that international terrorism will abate anytime soon. If diplomatic and other efforts fail to keep terrorism at bay, the criminal justice system may soon find itself embroiled in an undeclared war waged on American soil. The system, whose original purpose was to resolve disputes and to keep order among the citizenry, cannot be expected to adequately counter well-planned, heavily financed, covert paramilitary operations. As long as terrorists can find safe haven in countries antagonistic to the rule of international law their activities will continue. Until all nations of the world are willing to work together to ensure the safety of people everywhere, there can be little hope that the problem of terrorism will be solved. As Nettler has observed, "[t]errorism that succeeds escalates."[110]

TECHNOLOGY AND INDIVIDUAL RIGHTS

The Office for Technology Assessment of the U.S. Congress notes that, "What is judicially permissible and socially acceptable at one time has often been challenged when technology changes."[111] Cutting-edge technology, when used by agencies of the criminal justice system, inevitably brings up fears of an Orwellian future in which the rights of citizens are abrogated to advancing science. Individual rights, equal treatment under the law, and due process issues all require constant reinterpretation as technology improves. However, because some of the technology available today is so new, few court cases have yet directly addressed the issues involved. Even so, it is possible to identify areas which hold potential for future dispute.

TECHNOLOGY AND THE FOURTH AMENDMENT

The Fourth Amendment to the U.S. Constitution guarantees "[t]he right of the people to be secure in their persons, houses, papers, and effects, against unreasonable searches and seizures." Given the electronic network which permeates contemporary society, today's "houses" are far less secure from prying eyes than were those of the 1700s. Modern dwellings are linked to the outside world through phone lines, modems, fax machines, electronic mail, and even direct radio and television communications. One highly significant question centers on where the "security" of the home ends and the public realm begins.

Complicating matters still further are today's "supersnoop" technologies which provide investigators with the ability to literally hear through walls (using vibration detectors), listen into conversations over tremendous distances (with parabolic audio receivers), and record voices in distant rooms (via laser readings of windowpane vibrations).

Another question concerns the Fourth Amendment's guarantee of secure "papers and effects." The phrase "papers and effects" takes on a much wider meaning when we enter the world of modern technology. Although the framers of the Constitution could not envision electronic data bases, for example, their admonition would seem to apply to such records. Data bases may already be the repositories of more information than is routinely stored on paper. Tax listings, records of draft registrants, social security rolls, health reports, criminal histories, credit bureau ratings, and government and bank logs all contain billions of items of information on almost every man, woman, and child in the country. Most agree that official access to such information should be limited. A report to the U.S. Congress asks "whether the new technology is making everyone subject at all times to an electronic search even where traditional police searches would require a warrant issued on the basis of probable cause."[112]

A third question centers on the privacy of various kinds of information, the proper legal steps to be used in acquiring information for investigative purposes, and the types of information that can be appropriately stored in criminal justice data repositories. The kinds of information which can be appropriately stored in criminal justice data bases, along with considerations of who should have access to such data are both legal and ethical questions. In 1974 the Justice Department established the one-year rule, prohibiting the FBI from disseminating criminal records more than a year old. The department was concerned about the potential for inaccuracy in older files.

Even "official" records may be misleading or incomplete. A study of FBI criminal records data bases, for example, recently concluded that about 50% of arrest entries do not show the disposition of cases.[113] Inquiring agencies using such records could be falsely

High technology at work. Customs officer uses a night vision device to scan the border for illegal immigrants and drug traffickers. *Photo: J. P. Laffont/Sygma.*

misled into prejudging the "guilt" of an offender against whom earlier charges had been dropped. The same study also found that as many as 20% of the arrest-dispositional data contained in FBI records may be erroneous. Evidence seized as the result of an arrest based upon inaccurate NCIC information can be suppressed.[114] Half of all requests for criminal records made to the FBI, however, are from employers and licensing agencies. If an applicant is refused employment or rejected for licensing (or bonding) on the basis of criminal record inaccuracies he or she may needlessly suffer.

Data base management in criminal justice agencies is not an area which has been directly addressed by the U.S. Supreme Court. A number of lower courts, however, have held that criminal justice agencies have a duty to maintain accurate and reliable records.[115] In one important decision, the Federal Court of Appeals for the District of Columbia found, in *Menard* v. *Saxbe* (1974), that the FBI has a duty to be more than a "mere passive recipient" of records. The court held that it is the duty of the FBI to avoid unnecessary harm to people listed in its files.[116] In answer to its critics, the FBI has implemented NCIC-2000, a study designed to introduce more than 60 upgrades to the agency's computer operations.[117]

TECHNOLOGY AND THE FIFTH AMENDMENT

The Fifth and Fourteenth Amendments to the Constitution require that the accused be accorded the opportunity for "due process of law" prior to the imposition of any criminal sanction. Due process necessitates a presumption of innocence, and lawful prosecutions must proceed according to the standards of the Sixth Amendment.

What may be the greatest potential threat to the due process guarantee comes not from the physical sciences but from psychology, sociology, and other social scientific approaches to the study and prediction of human behavior. Social science research generally involves the observation of large numbers of individuals, often in quasi-experimental settings. Many studies produce results of questionable validity when applied to other settings. Even so, the tendency has been for social scientists to create predictive models of behavior with widely claimed applicability. Worse still, legislatures and criminal justice decision makers have often been quick to adopt them for their own purposes. Behavioral models, for example, are now used to tailor sophisticated law enforcement investigations, such as those based on the FBI's criminal profiling program. Statutory guidelines,[118] including the Federal Sentencing Guidelines,[119] are written with an eye to predictive frameworks which allegedly measure the danger potential of certain types of offenders. This growing use within the justice system of behavioral models, demonstrates a heightened faith in the reliability of the social sciences, but also holds the danger of punishment in anticipation of a crime.

The major threat from the social sciences to individual rights comes from the tendency they create to prejudge individuals based upon personal characteristics rather than facts. Persons who fit a conceptual profile defined as dangerous may be subject to investigation, arrest, conviction, and harsh sentences solely on the basis of scientifically identified characteristics. In effect, some social scientific models may produce a veiled form of discrimination. This is especially true when the predictive factors around which they are built are mere substitutions for race, ethnicity, and gender.

As an example, some early predictive models from studies of domestic violence tended to show that, among other things, the typical offender was male, unemployed or with a record of spotty employment, poorly educated, and was abused as a child and/or came from a broken home. Because many of these characteristics also describe a larger proportion of the nation's black population than they do whites, they created a hidden tendency to strongly accuse black males suspected of such offenses (and sometimes to suspect them even when they were not accused).

With these considerations in mind, social scientific models may nonetheless prove to be useful tools. The most acceptable solution would treat individuals on a case-by-case basis, looking to the general predictive models of social science only for guidance once all the facts became known.

The Fifth Amendment raises a second issue—this one outside the purview of social science. The amendment reads, "No person shall be held to answer for a capital, or otherwise infamous crime, unless on a presentment or indictment of a Grand Jury,…nor shall be compelled in any criminal case to be a witness against himself."

Statements made under hypnosis or during psychiatric examination are generally protected by court decision and are not available as evidence at trial.[120] However, modern technological procedures appear to make self-incrimination a possibility even in the absence of any verbal statements. The Supreme Court has held that suspects must submit to blood-alcohol tests under certain circumstances[121] and that samples of breath, semen, hair, and tissue may also be taken without consent when the procedures used do not "shock the conscience."[122] Technological advances over the next few decades are anticipated to increase the potential for incriminating forms of nontestimonial evidence.

TECHNOLOGY AND THE SIXTH AMENDMENT

The Sixth Amendment guarantees the right to a public trial by an impartial jury. The meaning of the words "public" and "impartial," however, have been rendered ambiguous by advancing technology. A famous author once coined the term "global village" to describe how advances in communications technology have increased the ready availability of information for us all. Are public trials ones in which TV cameras should be allowed? Would broadcasts of trials be permissible? Although courts in some jurisdictions now allow video recordings of trials with great public interest, courts at higher levels have yet to address the question.

Also at issue is the expanding use of scientific jury selection techniques, which are discussed briefly in Chapter 9. This new "technology" attempts to predict the outcome of jury deliberations based upon an assessment of the economic, social, cultural, and demographic characteristics of individual jurors.[123] Using jury selection techniques, some lawyers attempt to choose jurors likely to be predisposed to a finding in favor of their client.[124] The constitutional merits of scientific jury selection techniques have yet to be decided by the high court.

The Sixth Amendment allows an accused person to "be confronted with the witnesses against him." Some courts now permit only an indirect confrontation, through the use of television, videotapes, and the like. Abused juveniles, for example, appear to jurors in some jurisdictions only on television screens to spare them the trauma and embarrassment of the courtroom. Although such strategies may appear to be an "end run" around the Sixth Amendment, they are complicated by claims that justice is better served by an articulate witness rather than a frightened one and by the fact that most such testimonial strategies involve juveniles as witnesses.

> The principle all…moralists out there should remember, is that when you erode one individual's rights, it can come back to attack you and *your* family at a later time.
>
> —*Sandra Craig, following her conviction on 53 counts of assault, child abuse, and perverted sexual practices*

TECHNOLOGY AND THE FOURTEENTH AMENDMENT

Section One of the Fourteenth Amendment to the U.S. Constitution concludes with the phrase, "No state shall...deny to any person within its jurisdiction the equal protection of the laws." Modern technology, because it is expensive and often experimental, is not always equally available. Criminal justice programs which depend upon technology that is limited in its availability may contravene this Fourteenth Amendment provision. Court-ordered confinement, for example, which utilizes electronic monitoring and house arrest is an alternative much preferred by offenders. The technology supporting such confinement is, however, expensive, which dramatically limits its availability. Although the Court has yet to address this particular topic, it has ruled that programs which require the offender to bear a portion of the cost of confinement are unconstitutional when their availability is restricted to only those offenders who can afford them.[125]

TECHNOLOGY AND THE EIGHTH AMENDMENT

The Eighth Amendment is the most concise statement in the Bill of Rights. It reads, "Excessive bail shall not be required, nor excessive fines imposed, nor cruel and unusual punishments inflicted."

Modern technology brings with it the possibility of a host of new treatments for the criminal offender, most of which by virtue of their being court-imposed upon unwilling subjects, can also be construed as "punishments." Examples of unusual "punishments" today might include drug and hormone therapy and the use of electronic bracelets to monitor the public movements of convicted offenders. A few years ago authorities in Arapahoe County, Colorado,[126] decided to experiment with an electronic system that alerts the potential victim via an alarm when a convicted stalker approaches. Although similar bracelets have been used to monitor compliance with probationary sentences of home confinement, some claim that the public use of such devices lends credence to the "brave new world" form of authoritarianism feared by many as undue governmental intrusion on privacy. Drug therapy is another area under scrutiny.

Two innovative drugs already in use are Antabuse® and Depo-Provera.® Antabuse® is utilized in the treatment of alcoholics. It produces nausea and vomiting when alcohol is ingested. Depo-Provera® is the trade name given by the Upjohn Company to its brand of medroxyprogesterone acetate, a synthetic form of the female hormone progesterone. Depo-Provera® has been shown to reduce the male sex drive and is sometimes administered to sex offenders by court order. A recent survey found that 14% of rehabilitative programs across the nation specializing in the treatment of adult sex offenders had used Depo-Provera® on an experimental basis.[127]

Drugs such as Antabuse® and Depo-Provera®, and surgical procedures like castration and lobotomy, may run afoul of the Eighth Amendment's ban on cruel and unusual punishment. In most cases where these alternate treatments are contemplated by the court, criminal offenders are offered a choice between prison or a chemical or surgical remedy. The American Civil Liberties Union, however, has argued that the use of Depo-Provera® and other drugs in the treatment of criminal offenders is a form of coercion. The ACLU claims that the offered alternative, prison, is so dangerous as to force acceptance of any other choice.[128]

As with many emerging issues, drugs like Antabuse® and Depo-Provera® have not been subject to Supreme Court scrutiny. A few lower court cases have, however, begun to provide some general guidance in judging what treatments are permissible. For example, in the 1970 case of *Holt* v. *Sarver*,[129] the federal court for the Eastern District of Arkansas defined cruel and unusual punishment to be that which is "shocking to the conscience of reasonably civilized people." Whether "chemical castration" falls into such a category, and whether the U.S. Supreme Court will agree with the *Holt* standard are questions which remain unanswered.

> And say, finally, whether peace is best preserved by giving energy to the government, or information to the people—this last is the most certain, and the most legitimate engine of government. Educate and inform the whole mass of the people.
>
> —*Inscription on the atrium wall, Jefferson Hall, FBI National Academy, Quantico, Virginia*

SUMMARY

Old concepts of criminality, and of white-collar crime in particular, have undergone significant revision as a result of emerging technologies. Science fiction–like products, already widely available, have brought with them a plethora of possibilities for new high-stakes crimes. The well-equipped technologically advanced occupational offender in tomorrow's world will be capable of property crimes involving dollar amounts undreamed of only a few decades ago.

Barring global nuclear war or world catastrophe, advances in technology will continue to occur. Citizens of the future will regard as commonplace much of what is only fantasy today. Gradual life-style modifications will accompany changes in technology and result in taken-for-granted expectations foreign to today's world. Within that changed social context the "reasonableness" of technological intrusions into personal lives will be judged according to standards tempered by the new possibilities technology has to offer.

Coming social changes, combined with powerful technologies, threaten to produce a new world of challenges for criminal justice agencies. Domestic and international terrorism, widespread drug running, and changing social values, will evolve into a complex tangle of legal and technological issues which will confront the best law enforcement minds of the future.

On the other hand, the ability of law enforcement agencies to respond to everyday crimes will be enhanced by the advantage of "cutting-edge" technology. Only through a massive infusion of funds to support the purchase of new equipment and the hiring or training of technologically sophisticated personnel can tomorrow's law enforcement agencies hope to compete with high-technology criminals.

DISCUSSION QUESTIONS

1. How has technology affected the practice of criminal justice over the past 100 years?

2. What future benefits and threats to the practice of criminal justice can you imagine emanating from technological advances which are bound to occur over the next few decades?

3. What threats to civil liberties do you imagine advances in technology might create? Will our standards as to what constitute admissible evidence, what is reasonable privacy, and so on, undergo a reevaluation as a result of burgeoning technology?

4. What are the major differences between the concepts of white-collar crime and occupational crime? How have advances in technology created new opportunities for white-collar or occupational criminals? What is the best hope of the criminal justice system for coping with such criminal threats?

5. Has criminal law kept pace with the opportunities for dishonest behavior created by advancing technology? What modifications in current laws defining criminal activity might be necessary in order to meet the possibilities created by technological advances?

ENDNOTES

1. U.S. Congress, Office of Technology Assessment, *Criminal Justice, New Technologies, and the Constitution, A Special Report* (Washington, D.C.: U.S. Government Printing Office, May 1988), p. iii.

2. "DNA Evidence Spells Freedom," *USA Today*, June 19, 1993, 3A.

3. Lester D. Shubin, "Research, Testing, Upgrade Criminal Justice Technology," National Institute of Justice Reports (Washington, D.C.: U.S. Government Printing Office, 1984), pp. 2–5.

4. Simon Dinitz, "Coping with Deviant Behavior Through Technology," *Criminal Justice Research Bulletin*, Vol. 3, no. 2 (Huntsville, TX: Criminal Justice Center, 1987).

5. See, for example, L. R. Tancredi and D. N. Weistub, "Forensic Psychiatry and the Case of Chemical Castration," *International Journal of Law and Psychiatry*, Vol. 8 (1986), p. 259.

6. Harry Soderman and John J. O'Connell, *Modern Criminal Investigation* (New York: Funk and Wagnalls, 1945), p. 41.

7. Invented by Lambert Adolphe Jacques Quetelet (1796–1874), Belgian astronomer and statistician.

8. For a summation of Bertillon's system, see *Signaletic Instructions* (New York: Werner, 1896).

9. Robert D. Foote, "Fingerprint Identification: A Survey of Present Technology, Automated Applications and Potential for Future Development," Criminal Justice Monograph Series, Vol. 5, no. 2 (Huntsville, TX: Sam Houston State University, 1974), pp. 3–4.

10. Soderman and O'Connell, *Modern Criminal Investigation*, p. 57.

11. Ibid.

12. Francis Galton, *Finger Prints* (London: Macmillan, 1892).

13. Foote, "Fingerprint Identification," p. 1.

14. U.S. Congress, Office of Technology Assessment, *Criminal Justice: New Technologies and the Constitution: A Special Report* (Washington, D.C.: U.S. Government Printing Office, 1988), p. 18. Electrooptical systems for live fingerprint scanning were developed on a proprietary basis by Fingermatric, Inc., of White Plains, New York.

15. T. F. Wilson and P. L. Woodard, U.S. Department of Justice, Bureau of Justice Statistics, *Automated Fingerprint Identification Systems—Technology and Policy Issues* (Washington, D.C.: U.S. Department of Justice, 1987), p. 5.

16. *Los Angeles Police Department Annual Report, 1985–1986*, p. 26.

17. Ibid., p. 27.

18. American National Standards Institute, *American National Standard for Information Systems—Fingerprint Identification—Data Format for Information Interchange* (New York: ANSI, 1986). Originally proposed as the *Proposed American National Standard Data Format for the Interchange of Fingerprint Information* by the National Bureau of Standards (Washington, D.C.: National Bureau of Standards, April 7, 1986).

19. Dennis G. Kurre, "On-Line Exchange of Fingerprint Identification Data," *FBI Law Enforcement Bulletin* (December 1987), pp. 14–16.

20. As of this writing Cellmark Diagnostics has applied to register the phrase "DNA Fingerprinting" as a trademark.

21. "Genetic Fingerprinting Convicts Rapist in U.K.," *The Globe and Mail*, November 14, 1987, p. A3.

22. John T. Sylvester and John H. Stafford, "Judicial Acceptance of DNA Profiling," *FBI Law Enforcement Bulletin* (July 1991), p. 29.

23. *U.S.* v. *Jakobetz*, 955 F.2d 786 (2 Cir. 1992).

24. Some recent cases have allowed the admissability of evidence derived through the use of DNA profiling. Among them are *State of Maryland* v. *Yorke* (Case No. 84–CR-3828), *Commonwealth of Virginia* v. *Johnson* (Case No. K056096), and *State of Ohio* v. *Dascenzo* (Case No. 88–CR-1057).

25. "DNA Fingerprinting ID Method May Streamline Investigations," Current Reports, *BNA Criminal Practice Manual*, Vol. 1, no. 19 (September 23, 1987).

26. U.S. Congress, Office of Technology Assessment, *Criminal Justice: New Technologies and the Constitution, Special Report* (Washington, D.C.: U.S.

Government Printing Office, 1988).

27. "DNA, the Genetic Crime Fighter," *USA Today*, September 27, 1988, p. 1D.

28. Jay V. Miller, "The FBI's Forensic DNA Analysis Program," *FBI Law Enforcement Bulletin* (July 1991), p. 11.

29. "Fighting Crime, and Convictions, with DNA," *USA Today*, January 4, 1993, p. 8A.

30. Preston Gralla, "Hollywood Confidential: PC Crime Fighters," *PC Computing* (January 1989), p. 188.

31. William S. Sessions, "Criminal Justice Information Services: Gearing Up for the Future," *FBI Law Enforcement Bulletin* (February 1993), p. 2.

32. Ibid., pp. 181–188.

33. *Criminal Justice: New Technologies and the Constitution*, p. 29.

34. Ibid., p. 29.

35. "Saving Face," *PC Computing*, December 1988, p. 60.

36. *Omni Magazine*, February 1988, p. 12.

37. David J. Icove, "Automated Crime Profiling," *FBI Law Enforcement Bulletin* (December 1986) pp. 27–30.

38. John C. LeDoux and Henry H. McCaslin, "Computer-Based Training for the Law Enforcement Community," *FBI Law Enforcement Bulletin* (June 1988), pp. 8–13.

39. Matt L. Rodriguez, "The Acquisition of High Technology Systems by Law Enforcement," *FBI Law Enforcement Bulletin* (December 1988), p. 10.

40. William L. Tafoya, "Law Enforcement Beyond the Year 2000," *The Futurist* (September/October 1986), pp. 33–36.

41. Ibid.

42. Adapted from Rodriguez, "The Acquisition of High Technology Systems by Law Enforcement," pp. 11–12.

43. Charles B. Carkeek, "Ensuring Computer Security," *FBI Law Enforcement Journal* (October 1986), p. 5.

44. James William Coleman, *The Criminal Elite: The Sociology of White Collar Crime*, 2nd ed. (New York: St. Martin's Press, 1989), p. 2.

45. Edwin H. Sutherland, "White-Collar Criminality," *American Sociological Review* (February 1940), p. 12.

46. This definition combines elements of Sutherland's original terminology with the definition of "white-collar crime" as found in the *Dictionary of Criminal Justice Data Terminology*, 2nd ed. (Washington, D.C.: Bureau of Justice Statistics, 1981). It recognizes the fact that the socioeconomic status of today's "white-collar criminals" is not nearly so high as Sutherland imagined when he coined the term.

47. "Tennis, Anyone? Ivan Boesky Does Time," *Business Week*, April 25, 1988, p. 70.

48. Frank E. Hagan and Peter J. Benekos, "The Biggest White Collar Crime in History: The Great Savings and Loan Scandal," paper presented at the annual meeting of the American Society of Criminology, Baltimore, Maryland, 1990.

49. Ibid., p. 4.

50. "Silverado Suit Tentatively Settled for $49.5 Million," *Fayetteville Observer-Times* (North Carolina), May 30, 1991, p. 4A.

51. "Dixon Faces Sentence Today," *USA Today*, April 2, 1991, pp. B1–2.

52. Ibid.

53. Edwin H. Sutherland, "Is White Collar Crime Crime?" *American Sociological Review* (April 1945), pp. 132–139.

54. *White Collar Crime*, A Bureau of Justice Statistics *Special Report* (Washington, D.C.: BJS, 1987).

55. Ibid., p. 1.

56. Stephen Pizzo, Mary Fricker, and Paul Muolo, *Inside Job: The Looting of America's Savings and Loans* (New York: McGraw-Hill, 1989), p. 284.

57. See Gilbert Geis and Robert F. Meier, eds. *White Collar Crime*, 2nd ed. (New York: The Free Press, 1977).

58. "The Venture Survey: Crime and Your Business," *Venture Magazine*, February 1986, p. 26.

59. Ibid.

60. Ibid.

61. Gary S. Green, *Occupational Crime* (Chicago: Nelson-Hall, 1990).

62. Ibid., p. 16.

63. Ibid.

64. James William Coleman, *The Criminal Elite: The Sociology of White Collar Crime* (New York: St. Martin's Press, 1989), p. 9.

65. Ibid.

66. William J. Chambliss, *Exploring Criminology* (New York: Macmillan, 1988), p. 64.

67. See, for example, M. David Ermann and Richard J. Lundman, eds., *Corporate and Government Deviance: Problems of Organizational Behavior in Contemporary Society*, 3rd ed. (New York: Oxford University Press, 1987), and Stuart L. Hills, ed., *Corporate Violence: Injury and Death for Profit* (Totowa, NJ: Roman and Littlefield, 1987).

68. Gilbert Geis, "The Heavy Electrical Equipment Antitrust Cases of 1961," in Gilbert Geis and Robert Meier, eds., *White Collar Crime*, rev. ed. (New York: The Free Press, 1977), p. 123.

69. Coleman, *The Criminal Elite*, p. 34.

70. "Ford Pinto Scored in Coast Magazine on Peril from Fires," *The New York Times*, August 11, 1977.

71. Coleman, *The Criminal Elite*, p. 41.

72. As cited in Gwynne Nettler, *Criminology Lessons* (Cincinnati, OH: Anderson, 1989), p. 116.

73. "After Drexel: Are Raiders Next Target?" *USA Today*, December 23, 1988, p. B-1.

74. Ibid.

75. *Hancock v. State*, 402 S.W.2d 906 (Tex. Crim. Appl. 1966).

76. Stanley S. Arkin et al., *Prevention and Prosecution of Computer and High Technology Crime* (New York: Matthew Bender, 1988), 3.05.

77. Public Law no. 98–473, Title II, Section 2102 (a), October 12, 1984.

78. William J. Hughes, "Congress vs. Computer Crime," *Information*

Executive, Vol. 1, no. 1 (Fall 1988), pp. 30–32.

79. Arkin, *Prevention and Prosecution of Computer and High Technology Crime*, 3.05 [B].

80. 18 U.S.C., § 2311.

81. 18 U.S.C., § 641.

82. 18 U.S.C., § 1905.

83. 17 U.S.C., §§ 101, 117

84. 18 U.S.C., §§ 1341, 1343, and 1344.

85. N.Y. Penal Law, §§ 156.30 and 156.35.

86. For information on specific software programs used for data encryption, see Ted Chiang, "Data Encryption: Computer Security with Data Encryption Programs," in *Profiles* (December 1987), pp. 71–74.

87. "Invasion of the Data Snatchers!" *Time*, September 26, 1988, pp. 62–67.

88. "Virus Infects NASA, Defense, University Computer Systems," *The Fayetteville Observer-Times* (North Carolina), November 4, 1988, p. 19A.

89. *Raleigh News and Observer*, April 27, 1990.

90. "Invasion of the Data Snatchers!"

91. Hughes, "Congress vs. Computer Crime," p. 32.

92. "Crime in the Computer Age," *MacLean's Magazine*, Vol. 101, no. 5 (January 25, 1988), pp. 28–30.

93. Ibid.

94. Ibid., p. 29.

95. August Bequai, *Computer Crime* (Lexington, MA: Lexington Books, 1978), p. 4.

96. Ibid.

97. Bill D. Colvin, "Computer Crime Investigations: A New Training Field," *FBI Law Enforcement Bulletin* (July 1979).

98. U.S. Department of State, Bureau of Counterterrorism, as cited in "Anti-U.S. Attacks in 1992," *USA Today*, June 25, 1993, p. 2A.

99. "FBI Foils Terror Spree," *USA Today*, June 25–27, 1993, p. 1A.

100. "Wouldn't Be Hard to Hit U.S. Target," *USA Today*, June 25–27, 1993, p. 1A.

101. Ibid.

102. Ibid.

103. Technological devices described in this section depend upon G. Gordon Liddy, "Rules of the Game," *Omni Magazine* (January 1989), pp. 43–47, 78–80.

104. For additional details on supremacist groups, see Michael E. Wiggins, "A Descriptive Profile of Criminal Activities of a Right-Wing Extremist Group," paper presented at the annual meeting of The Society of Police and Criminal Psychology, Little Rock, Arkansas (October 1985).

105. "Order Member: Group Considered Killing TV Producer Norman Lear," *The Daily News* (Springfield, Missouri), September 16, 1985, p. 3, as cited by Michael E. Wiggins in "A Descriptive Profile of Criminal Activities of a Right-Wing Extremist Group," paper presented at the annual meeting of the Society of Police and Criminal Psychology, Little Rock, Arkansas (October 1985).

106. Michael E. Wiggins, "An Extremist Right-Wing Group and Domestic Terrorism," unpublished manuscript, Center for Criminal Justice Research, Central Missouri State University, March 1986.

107. "One Doctor Down, How Many More?" *Time*, March 22, 1993, pp. 46–47.

108. Gwynn Nettler, *Killing One Another* (Cincinnati, OH: Anderson, 1982).

109. The actual language of the bill sets a standard for metal detectors through the use of a "security exemplar" made of 3.7 ounces of stainless steel in the shape of a handgun. Weapons made of other substances might still pass the test provided that they could be detected by metal detectors adjusted to that level of sensitivity. See "Bill Is Signed Barring Sale or Manufacture of Plastic Guns," *Criminal Justice Newsletter*, Vol. 19, no. 23 (December 1, 1988), pp. 4–5.

110. *Killing One Another*, p. 253.

111. *Criminal Justice: New Technologies and the Constitution*, p. 51.

112. Ibid., p. 20.

113. Ibid., p. 47.

114. *United States* v. *Mackey,* 387 F.Sup 1121, 1125 (D. Nev. 1975).

115. See Louis F. Solimine, "Safeguarding the Accuracy of FBI Records: A Review of *Menard* v. *Saxbe* and *Tarlton* v. *Saxbe,*" *University of Cincinnati Law Review,* Vol. 44 (1975), pp. 325, 327.

116. *Criminal Justice: New Technologies and the Constitution,* p. 47.

117. William S. Sessions, "The FBI and the Challenge of the 21st Century," *FBI Law Enforcement Bulletin,* Vol. 58, no. 1 (January 1989), pp. 1–6.

118. The Bail Reform Act of 1996 allowed magistrates to consider elements of the offender's background, such as family ties and prior offenses, in setting bail. Factors cited by the act were based in part on social scientific findings at the time.

119. See U.S. Sentencing Commission, *Sentencing Guidelines and Policy Statements,* submitted to Congress April 13, 1987, with amendments submitted April 13, 1987.

120. *Estelle* v. *Smith,* 451 U.S. 454 (1981).

121. *Schmerber* v. *California,* 384 U.S. 757, 86 S.Ct. 1826 (1966).

122. *Rochin* v. *California,* 342 U.S. 165 (1952).

123. For a discussion of such techniques, see Patrick Moynihan, "Social Science and the Courts," *The Public Interest,* No. 54 (Winter 1979), pp. 12–31.

124. Arnold Urken and Stephen Traflet, "Optimal Jury Design," *Jurimetrics* (Journal of the American Bar Association), Vol. 24 (Spring 1984), p. 218.

125. *Bearden* v. *Georgia,* 461 U.S. 660 (1983).

126. "Stalkers Get Electronic Guard," *The Fayetteville Observer-Times* (North Carolina), September 20, 1992, p. 16A.

127. *Criminal Justice Newsletter,* (June 16, 1986), p. 6.

128. *Criminal Justice: New Technologies and the Constitution,* p. 43.

129. *Holt* v. *Sarver,* 309 F.Sup 362 (E.D. Ark. 1970).

THE

CONSTITUTION

OF THE

UNITED STATES

OF AMERICA

WE THE PEOPLE of the United States, in Order to form a more perfect Union, establish Justice, insure domestic Tranquility, provide for the common defence, promote the general Welfare, and secure the Blessings of Liberty to ourselves and our Posterity, do ordain and establish this CONSTITUTION for the United States of America.

ARTICLE I.

SECTION 1. All legislative Powers herein granted shall be vested in a Congress of the United States, which shall consist of a Senate and House of Representatives.

SECTION 2. The House of Representatives shall be composed of Members chosen every second Year by the People of the several States, and the Electors in each State shall have the Qualifications requisite for Electors of the most numerous Branch of the State Legislature.

No Person shall be a Representative who shall not have attained to the Age of twenty-five Years, and been seven Years a Citizen of the United States, and who shall not, when elected, be an Inhabitant of that State in which he shall be chosen.

Representatives and direct Taxes shall be apportioned among the several States which may be included within this Union, according to their respective Numbers, which shall be determined by adding to the whole Number of free Persons, including those bound to Service for a Term of Years, and excluding Indians not taxed, three fifths of all other Persons. The actual Enumeration shall be made within three Years after the first Meeting of the Congress of the United States, and within every subsequent Term of ten Years, in such Manner as they shall by Law direct. The Number of Representatives shall not exceed one for every thirty Thousand, but each State shall have at Least one Representative; and until such enumeration shall be made, the State of New Hampshire shall be entitled to chuse three, Massachusetts eight, Rhode-Island and Providence Plantations one, Connecticut five, New York six, New Jersey four Pennsylvania eight, Delaware one, Maryland six, Virginia ten, North Carolina five, South Carolina five, and Georgia three.

When vacancies happen in the representation from any State, the Executive Authority thereof shall issue Writs of Election to fill such Vacancies.

The House of Representatives shall chuse their Speaker and other Officers; and shall have the sole Power of Impeachment.

SECTION 3. The Senate of the United States shall be composed of two Senators from each State, chosen by the Legislature thereof for six Years; and each Senator shall have one Vote.

Immediately after they shall be assembled in Consequence of the first Election, they shall be divided as equally as may be into three Classes. The Seats of the Senators of the first Class shall be vacated at the Expiration of the second Year, of the second Class at the Expiration of the fourth Year, and of the third Class at the Expiration of the sixth Year, so that one third may be chosen every second Year; and if Vacancies happen by Resignation, or otherwise, during the recess of the Legislature of any State, the Executive thereof may make temporary Appointments until the next Meeting of the Legislature, which shall then fill such Vacancies.

No Person shall be Senator who shall not have attained to the Age of thirty Years, and been nine Years a Citizen of the United States, and who shall not, when elected, be an Inhabitant of that State for which he shall be chosen.

The Vice President of the United States shall be President of the Senate, but shall have no Vote, unless they be equally divided.

The Senate shall chuse their other Officers, and also a President pro tempore, in the absence of the Vice President, or when he shall exercise the Office of President of the United States.

The Senate shall have the sole Power to try all Impeachments. When sitting for that Purpose, they shall be on Oath or Affirmation. When the President of the United States is tried, the Chief Justice shall preside: And no Person shall be convicted without the Concurrence of two thirds of the Members present.

Judgment in Cases of Impeachment shall not extend further than to removal from Office, and disqualification to hold and enjoy any Office of honor, Trust, or Profit under the United States: but the Party convicted shall nevertheless be liable and subject to Indictment, Trial, Judgment and Punishment, according to Law.

SECTION 4. The Times, Places and Manner of holding Elections for Senators and Representatives, shall be prescribed in each State by the Legislature thereof; but the Congress may at any time by Law make or alter such Regulations, except as to the Place of chusing Senators.

The Congress shall assemble at least once in every Year, and such Meeting shall be on the first Monday in December, unless they shall by law appoint a different Day.

SECTION 5. Each House shall be the Judge of the Elections, Returns and Qualifications of its own Members, and a Majority of each shall constitute a Quorum to do Business; but a smaller Number may adjourn from day to day, and may be authorized to compel the Attendance of absent Members, in such Manner, and under such Penalties as each House may provide.

Each House may determine the Rules of its Proceedings, punish its Members for disorderly Behaviour, and, with the Concurrence of two thirds, expel a Member.

Each House shall keep a Journal of its Proceedings, and from time to time publish the same, excepting such Parts as may in their Judgment require Secrecy; and the Yeas and Nays of the Members of either House on any question shall, at the Desire of one fifth of those Present, be entered on the journal.

Neither House, during the Session of Congress, shall, without the Consent of the other, adjourn for more than three days, nor to any other Place than that in which the two Houses shall be sitting.

SECTION 6. The Senators and Representatives shall receive a Compensation for their Services, to be ascertained by Law, and paid out of the Treasury of the United States. They shall in all Cases, except Treason, Felony and Breach of the Peace, be privileged from Arrest during their Attendance at the Session of their respective Houses, and in going to and returning from the same; and for any Speech or Debate in either House, they shall not be questioned in any other Place.

No Senator or Representative shall, during the Time for which he was elected, be appointed to any civil Office under the Authority of the United States, which shall have been created, or the Emoluments whereof shall have been encreased during such time; and no Person holding any Office under the United States, shall be a Member of either House during his Continuance in Office.

SECTION 7. All Bills for raising Revenue shall originate in the House of Representatives; but the Senate may propose or concur with Amendments as on other Bills.

Every Bill which shall have passed the House of Representatives and the Senate, shall, before it become a Law, be presented to the President of the United States; If he approve he shall sign it, but if not he shall return it, with his Objections to that House in which it shall have originated, who shall enter the Objections at large on their Journal, and proceed to reconsider it. If after such Reconsideration two thirds of that House shall agree to pass the Bill, it shall be sent, together with the Objections, to the other House, by which it shall likewise be reconsidered, and if approved by two thirds of that House, it shall become a Law. But in all such Cases the Votes of both Houses shall be determined by Yeas and Nays, and the Names of the Persons voting for and against the Bill shall be entered on the Journal of each House respectively. If any Bill shall not be returned by the President within ten Days (Sundays excepted) after it shall have been presented to him, the Same shall be a Law, in like Manner as if he had signed it, unless the Congress by their Adjournment prevent its Return, in which Case it shall not be a Law.

Every Order, Resolution, or Vote to which the Concurrence of the Senate and House of Representatives may be necessary (except on a question of Adjournment) shall be presented to the President of the United States; and before the Same shall take Effect, shall be approved by him, or being disapproved by him, shall be repassed by two thirds of the Senate and House of Representatives, according to the Rules and Limitations prescribed in the Case of a Bill.

SECTION 8. The Congress shall have Power to lay and collect Taxes, Duties, Imposts and Excises, to pay the Debts and provide for the common Defence and general Welfare of the United States; but all Duties, Imposts and Excises shall be uniform throughout the United States;

To borrow Money on the credit of the United States;

To regulate Commerce with foreign Nations, and among the several States, and with the Indian Tribes;

To establish an uniform Rule of Naturalization, and uniform Laws on the subject of Bankruptcies throughout the United States;

To coin Money, regulate the Value thereof, and of foreign Coin, and fix the Standard of Weights and Measures;

To provide for the Punishment of counterfeiting the Securities and current Coin of the United States;

To establish Post Offices and post Roads;

To promote the Progress of Science and useful Arts, by securing for limited times to Authors and Inventors the exclusive Right to their respective Writings and Discoveries;

To constitute Tribunals inferior to the supreme Court;

To define and punish Piracies and Felonies committed on the high Seas, and Offences against the Law of Nations;

To declare War, grant Letters of Marque and Reprisal, and make Rules concerning Captures on Land and Water;

To raise and support Armies, but no Appropriation of Money to that Use shall be for a longer Term than two Years;

To provide and maintain a Navy;

To make Rules for the Government and Regulation of the land and naval Forces;

To provide for calling froth the Militia to execute the Laws of the Union, suppress Insurrections and repel Invasions;

To provide for organizing, arming, and disciplining the Militia, and for governing such Part of them as may be employed in the Service of the United States, reserving to the States respectively, the Appointment of the Officers, and the Authority of training the Militia according to the discipline prescribed by Congress;

To exercise exclusive Legislation in all Cases whatsoever, over such District (not exceeding ten Miles square) as may, by Cession of particular States, and the Acceptance of Congress, become the Seat of the Government of the United States, and to exercise like Authority over all Places purchased by the Consent of the Legislature of the State in which the Same shall be, for the Erection of Forts, Magazines, and Arsenals, dock-Yards, and other needful Buildings;—And

To make all Laws which shall be necessary and proper for carrying into Execution the foregoing Powers, and all other Powers vested by this Constitution in the Government of the United States, or in any Department or Officer thereof.

SECTION 9. The Migration or Importation of such Persons as any of the States now existing shall think proper to admit, shall not be prohibited by the Congress prior to the Year one thousand eight hundred and eight, but a Tax or duty may be imposed on such Importation, not exceeding ten dollars for each Person.

The privilege of the Writ of Habeas Corpus shall not be suspended, unless when in Cases of Rebellion or Invasion the public Safety may require it.

No Bill of Attainder or ex post facto Law shall be passed.

No Capitation, or other direct, Tax shall be laid, unless in Proportion to the Census or Enumeration herein before directed to be taken.

No Tax or Duty shall be laid on Articles exported from any State.

No Preference shall be given by any Regulation of Commerce or Revenue to the Ports of one State over those of another: nor shall Vessels bound to, or from, one State, be obliged to enter, clear, or pay Duties in another.

No Money shall be drawn from the Treasury, but in Consequence of Appropriations made by Law; and a regular Statement and Account of the Receipts and Expenditures of all public Money shall be published from time to time.

No Title of Nobility shall be granted by the United States: And no Person holding any Office of Profit or Trust under them, shall, without the Consent of the Congress, accept of any present, Emolument, Office, or Title, of any kind whatever, from any King, Prince, or foreign State.

SECTION 10. No State shall enter into any Treaty, Alliance, or Confederation; grant Letters of Marque and Reprisal; coin Money; emit Bills of Credit; make any Thing but gold and silver Coin a Tender in Payment of Debts; pass any Bill of Attainder, ex post facto Law, or Law impairing the Obligation of Contracts, or grant any Title of Nobility.

No State shall, without the consent of the Congress, lay any Imposts or Duties on Imports or Exports, except what may be absolutely necessary for executing it's inspection Laws: and the net Produce of all Duties and Imposts, laid by any State on Imports or Exports, shall be for the Use of the Treasury of the United States; and all such Laws shall be subject to the Revision and Control of the Congress.

No State shall, without the Consent of Congress, lay any Duty of Tonnage, keep Troops, or Ships of War in time of Peace, enter into any Agreement or Compact with another State, or with a foreign Power, or engage in War, unless actually invaded, or in such imminent Danger as will not admit of delay.

ARTICLE II.

SECTION 1. The executive Power shall be vested in a President of the United States of America. He shall hold his Office during the Term of four Years, and, together with the Vice President, chosen for the same Term, be elected, as follows

Each State shall appoint, in such Manner as the Legislature thereof may direct, a Number of Electors, equal to the whole Number of Senators and Representatives to which the State may be entitled in the Congress: but no Senator or Representative, or Person holding an Office of Trust or Profit under the United States, shall be appointed an Elector.

The Electors shall meet in their respective States, and vote by Ballot for two persons, of whom one at least shall not be an Inhabitant of the same State with themselves. And they shall make a List of all the Persons voted for, and of the Number of Votes for each; which List they shall sign and certify, and transmit sealed to the Seat of the Government of the United States, directed to the President of the Senate. The President of the Senate shall, in the Presence of the Senate and House of Representatives, open all the Certificates, and the Votes shall then be counted. The Person having the greatest Number of Votes shall be the President, if such Number be a Majority of the whole Number of Electors appointed; and if there be more than one who have such Majority, and have an equal Number of Votes, then the House of Representatives shall immediately chuse by Ballot one of them for President; and if no Person have a Majority, then from the five highest on the List the said House shall in like Manner chuse the President. But in choosing the President, the Votes shall be taken by States, the Representation from each State having one Vote; A quorum for this Purpose shall consist of a Member or Members from two thirds of the States, and a Majority of all the States shall be necessary to a Choice. In every Case, after the Choice of the President, the Person having the greatest Number of Votes of the Electors shall be the Vice President. But if there should remain two or more who have equal Votes, the Senate shall chuse from them by Ballot the Vice President.

The Congress may determine the Time of chusing the Electors, and the Day on which they shall give their Votes; which Day shall be the same throughout the United States.

No person except a natural born Citizen, or a Citizen of the United States, at the time of Adoption of this Constitution, shall be eligible to the Office of President; neither shall any Person be eligible to that Office who shall not have attained to the Age of thirty five Years, and been fourteen Years a Resident within the United States.

In Case of the Removal of the President from Office, or of his Death, Resignation, or Inability to discharge the Powers and Duties of the said Office, the same shall devolve on the Vice President, and the Congress may by Law provide for the Case of Removal, Death, Resignation or Inability, both of the President and Vice President, declaring what Officer shall then act as President, and such Officer shall act accordingly, until the Disability be removed, or a President shall be elected.

The President shall, at stated Times, receive for his Services, a Compensation, which shall neither be encreased nor diminished during the Period for which he shall have been elected, and he shall not receive within that Period any other Emolument from the United States, or any of them.

Before he enter on the Execution of his Office, he shall take the following Oath or Affirmation:—"I do solemnly swear (or affirm) that I will faithfully execute the Office of President of the United States, and will to the best of my Ability, preserve, protect and defend the Constitution of the United States."

SECTION 2. The President shall be Commander in Chief of the Army and Navy of the United States, and of the Militia of the several States, when called into the actual Service of the United States; he may require the Opinion in writing, of the principal Officer in each of the executive Departments, upon any subject relating to the Duties of their respective Offices, and he shall have Power to grant Reprieves and Pardons for Offenses against the United States, except in Cases of Impeachment.

He shall have Power, by and with the Advice and Consent of the Senate, to make Treaties, provided two thirds of the Senators present concur; and he shall nominate, and by and with the Advice and Consent of the Senate, shall appoint Ambassadors, other public Ministers and Consuls, Judges of the supreme Court, and all other Officers of the United States, whose Appointments are not herein otherwise provided for, and which shall be established by Law: but the Congress may by Law vest the Appointment of such inferior Officers, as they think proper, in the President alone, in the courts of Law, and in the Heads of Departments.

The President shall have Power to fill up all Vacancies that may happen during the Recess of the Senate, by granting Commissions which shall expire at the End of their next Session.

SECTION 3. He shall from time to time give to the Congress Information of the State of the Union, and recommend to their Consideration such Measures as he shall judge necessary and expedient; he may, on extraordinary Occasions, convene both Houses, or either of them, and in Case of Disagreement between them, with Respect to the Time of Adjournment, he may adjourn them to such Time as he shall think proper; he shall receive Ambassadors and other public Ministers; he shall take Care that the Laws be faithfully executed, and Shall Commission all the Officers of the United States.

SECTION 4. The President, Vice President and all civil Officers of the United States, shall be removed from Office on Impeachment for, and Conviction of, Treason, Bribery, or other high Crimes and Misdemeanors.

ARTICLE III.

SECTION 1. The judicial Power of the United States, shall be vested in one supreme Court, and in such inferior Courts as the Congress may from time to time ordain and establish. The Judges, both of the supreme and inferior Courts, shall hold their Offices during good Behavior, and shall, at stated Times, receive for their Services, a Compensation, which shall not be diminished during their Continuance in Office.

SECTION 2. The judicial Power shall extend to all Cases, in Law and Equity, arising under this Constitution, the Laws of the United States, and Treaties made, or which shall be made, under their Authority;—to all Cases affecting Ambassadors, other public Ministers and Consuls;—to all Cases of admiralty and maritime Jurisdiction;—to Controversies to which the United States shall be a Party;—to Controversies between two or more States;—between a State and Citizens of another State;—between citizens of different States;—between Citizens of the same State claiming Lands under Grants of different States, and between a State, or the Citizens thereof, and foreign States, Citizens or Subjects.

In all Cases affecting Ambassadors, other public Ministers and Consuls, and those in which a State shall be Party, the supreme Court shall have original Jurisdiction. In all the other Cases before mentioned, the supreme Court shall have appellate Jurisdiction, both as to Law and Fact, with such exceptions, and under such Regulations as the Congress shall make.

The Trial of all Crimes, except in Cases of Impeachment, shall be by Jury; and such Trial shall be held in the State where the said Crimes shall have been committed; but when not committed within any State, the Trial shall be at such Place or Places as the Congress may by Law have directed.

SECTION 3. Treason against the United States, shall consist only in levying War against them, or in adhering to their Enemies, giving them Aid and Comfort. No Person shall be convicted of Treason unless on the Testimony of two Witnesses to the same overt Act, or on Confession in open Court.

The Congress shall have Power to declare the Punishment of Treason, but no Attainder of Treason shall work Corruption of Blood, or Forfeiture except during the Life of the Person attainted.

ARTICLE IV.

SECTION 1. Full Faith and Credit shall be given in each State to the public Acts, Records, and judicial Proceedings of every other State. And the Congress may by general Laws prescribe the Manner in which such Acts, Records and Proceedings shall be proved, and the Effect thereof.

SECTION 2. The Citizens of each State shall be entitled to all Privileges and Immunities of Citizens in the several States.

A Person charged in any State with Treason, Felony, or other Crime, who shall flee from Justice, and be found in another State, shall on Demand of the executive Authority of the State from which he fled, be delivered up, to be removed to the State having Jurisdiction of the Crime.

No Person held to Service or Labour in one State, under the Laws thereof, escaping into another, shall, in Consequence of any Law or Regulation therein, be discharged from such Service or Labour, but shall be delivered up on Claim of the Party to whom such Service or Labour may be due.

SECTION 3. New States may be admitted by the Congress into this Union; but no new State shall be formed or erected within the Jurisdiction of any other State; nor any State be formed by the Junction of two or more States, or parts of States, without the Consent of the Legislatures of the States concerned as well as of the Congress.

The Congress shall have Power to dispose of and make all needful Rules and Regulations respecting the Territory or other Property belonging to the United States; and nothing in this Constitution shall be so construed as to Prejudice any Claims of the United States, or of any particular State.

SECTION 4. The United States shall guarantee to every State in this Union a Republican Form of Government, and shall protect each of them against Invasion; and on Application of the Legislature, or of the Executive (when the Legislature cannot be convened) against domestic Violence.

ARTICLE V.

The Congress, whenever two thirds of both Houses shall deem it necessary, shall propose Amendments to this Constitution, or, on the Application of the Legislatures of two thirds of the several States, shall call a Convention for proposing Amendments, which, in either Case, shall be valid to all Intents and Purposes, as Part of this Constitution, when ratified by the Legislatures of three fourths of the several States, or by Conventions in three fourths thereof, as the one or the other Mode of Ratification may be proposed by the Congress; Provided that no Amendment which may be made prior to the Year One thousand eight hundred and eight shall in any Manner affect the first and fourth Clauses in the Ninth Section of the first Article; and that no State, without its Consent, shall be deprived of its equal Suffrage in the Senate.

ARTICLE VI.

All Debts contracted and Engagements entered into, before the Adoption of this Constitution, shall be as valid against the United States under this Constitution, as under the Confederation.

This Constitution, and the Laws of the United States which shall be made in Pursuance thereof; and all Treaties made, or which shall be made, under the Authority of the United States, shall be the supreme Law of the Land; and the Judges in every State shall be bound thereby; any Thing in the Constitution or Laws of any State to the Contrary notwithstanding.

The Senators and Representatives before mentioned, and the Members of the several State Legislatures, and all executive and judicial Officers, both of the United States and of the several States, shall be bound by Oath or Affirmation, to support this Constitution; but no religious Test shall ever be required as a Qualification to any Office or pubic Trust under the United States.

ARTICLE VII.

The Ratification of the Conventions of nine States shall be sufficient for the Establishment of this Constitution between the States so ratifying the Same.

Articles in Addition to, and Amendment Of, the Constitution of the United States of America, Proposed by Congress, and Ratified by the Legislatures of the Several States, Pursuant to the Fifth Article of the Original Constitution.

AMENDMENT I. (1791)

Congress shall make no law respecting an establishment of religion, or prohibiting the free exercise thereof; or abridging the freedom of speech, or of the press; or the right of the people peaceably to assemble, and to petition the Government for a redress of grievances.

AMENDMENT II. (1791)

A well regulated Militia, being necessary to the security of a free State, the right of the people to keep and bear Arms, shall not be infringed.

AMENDMENT III. (1791)

No Soldier shall, in time of peace be quartered in any house, without the consent of the Owner, nor in time of war, but in a manner to be prescribed by law.

AMENDMENT IV. (1791)

The right of the people to be secure in their persons, houses, papers, and effects, against unreasonable searches and seizures, shall not be violated, and no Warrants shall issue, but upon probable cause, supported by Oath or affirmation, and particularly describing the place to be searched, and the persons or things to be seized.

AMENDMENT V. (1791)

No person shall be held to answer for a capital, or otherwise infamous crime, unless on a presentment or indictment of a Grand Jury, except in cases arising in the land or naval forces, or in the Militia, when in actual service in time of War or public danger; nor shall any person be subject for the same offence to be twice put in jeopardy of life or limb; nor shall be compelled in any criminal case to be a witness against himself, nor be deprived of life, liberty, or property, without due process of law; nor shall private property be taken for public use, without just compensation.

AMENDMENT VI. (1791)

In all criminal prosecutions, the accused shall enjoy the right to a speedy and public trial, by an impartial jury of the State and district wherein the crime shall have been committed, which district shall have been previously ascertained by law, and to be informed of the nature and cause of the accusation; to be confronted with the witnesses against him; to have compulsory process for obtaining Witnesses in his favor, and to have the Assistance of Counsel for his defence.

AMENDMENT VII. (1791)

In Suits at common law, where the value in controversy shall exceed twenty dollars, the right of trial by jury shall be preserved, and no fact tried by a jury, shall be otherwise reexamined in any Court of the United States, than according to the rules of the common law.

AMENDMENT VIII. (1791)

Excessive bail shall not be required, nor excessive fines imposed, nor cruel and unusual punishments inflicted.

AMENDMENT IX. (1791)

The enumeration of the Constitution, of certain rights, shall not be construed to deny or disparage others retained by the people.

AMENDMENT X. (1791)

The powers not delegated to the United States by the Constitution, nor prohibited by it to the States, are reserved to the States respectively, or to the people.

AMENDMENT XI. (1798)

The Judicial power of the United States shall not be construed to extend to any suit in law or equity, commenced or prosecuted against one of the United States by Citizens of another State, or by Citizens or Subjects of any Foreign State.

AMENDMENT XII. (1804)

The Electors shall meet in their respective states and vote by ballot for President and Vice-President, one of whom, at least, shall not be an inhabitant of the same state with themselves; they shall name in their ballots the person voted for as President, and in distinct ballots the person voted for as Vice-President, and they shall make distinct lists of all persons voted for as President, and of all persons voted for as Vice-President, and of the number of votes for each, which lists they shall sign and certify, and transmit sealed to the seat of the government of the Untied States, directed to the President of the Senate;—The President of the Senate shall, in the presence of the Senate and House of Representatives, open all the certificates and the votes shall then be counted;—The person having the greatest number of votes for President, shall be the President, if such number be a majority of the whole number of Electors appointed; and if no person have such majority, then from the persons having the highest numbers not exceeding three on the list of those voted for as President, the House of Representatives shall choose immediately, by ballot, the President. But in choosing the President, the votes shall be taken by states, the representation from each state having one vote; a quorum for this purpose shall consist of a member or members from two-thirds of the states, and a majority of all the states shall be necessary to a choice. And if the House of Representatives shall not choose a President whenever the right of choice shall devolve upon them, before the fourth day of March next following, then the Vice-President shall act as President, as in the case of the death or other constitutional disability of the President. The person having the greatest number of votes as Vice-President, shall be the Vice-President, if such number be a majority of the whole number of Electors appointed, and if no person have a majority, then from the two highest numbers on the list, the Senate shall choose the Vice-President; a quorum for the purpose shall consist of two-thirds of the whole number of Senators, and a majority of the whole number shall be necessary to a choice. But no person constitutionally ineligible to the office of President shall be eligible to that of Vice-President of the United States.

AMENDMENT XIII. (1865)

SECTION 1. Neither slavery nor involuntary servitude, except as a punishment for crime whereof the party shall have been duly convicted, shall exist within the United States, or any place subject to their jurisdiction.

SECTION 2. Congress shall have power to enforce this article by appropriate legislation.

AMENDMENT XIV. (1868)

SECTION 1. All persons born or naturalized in the United States, and subject to the jurisdiction thereof, are citizens of the United States and of the State wherein they reside. No State shall make or enforce any law which shall abridge the privileges or immunities of citizens of the United States; nor shall any State deprive any person of life, liberty, or property, without due process of law; nor deny to any person within its jurisdiction the equal protection of the law.

SECTION 2. Representatives shall be apportioned among the several States according to their respective numbers, counting the whole number of persons in each State, excluding Indians not taxed. But when the right to vote at any election for the choice of electors for President and Vice-President of the United States, Representatives in Congress, the Executive and Judicial officers of a State, or the members of the Legislature thereof, is denied to any of the male inhabitants of such State, being twenty-one years of age, and citizens of the United States, or in any way abridged, except for participation in rebellion, or other crime, the basis of representation therein shall be reduced in the proportion which the number of such male citizens shall bear to the whole number of male citizens twenty-one years of age in such State.

SECTION 3. No person shall be a Senator or Representative in Congress, or elector of President and Vice-President, or hold any office, civil or military, under the United States, or under any State, who, having previously taken an oath, as a member of Congress, or as an officer of the Untied States, or as a member of any State legislature, or as an executive or judicial officer of any State, to support the Constitution of the United States, shall have engaged in insurrection or rebellion against the same, or given aid or comfort to the enemies thereof. But Congress may by a vote of two-thirds of each House, remove such disability.

SECTION 4. The validity of the public debt of the United States, authorized by law, including debts incurred for payment of pensions and bounties for services in suppressing insurrection or rebellion, shall not be questioned. But neither the United States nor any State shall assume or pay any debt or obligation incurred in aid of insurrection or rebellion against the United States, or any claim for the loss or emancipation of any slave; but all such debts, obligations and claims shall be held illegal and void.

SECTION 5. The Congress shall have power to enforce, by appropriate legislation, the provisions of this article.

AMENDMENT XV. (1870)

SECTION 1. The right of citizens of the Untied States to vote shall not be denied or abridged by the United States or by any State on account of race, color, or previous condition of servitude.

SECTION 2. The Congress shall have power to enforce this article by appropriate legislation.

AMENDMENT XVI. (1913)

The Congress shall have power to lay and collect taxes on incomes, from whatever source derived, without apportionment among the several States, and without regard to any census or enumeration.

AMENDMENT XVII. (1913)

The Senate of the United States shall be composed of two Senators from each State, elected by the people thereof, for six years; and each Senator shall have one vote. The electors in each State shall have the qualifications requisite for electors of the most numerous branch of the State legislatures.

When vacancies happen in the representation of any State in the Senate, the executive authority of such State shall issue writs of election to fill such vacancies: *Provided*, That the legislature of any State may empower the executive thereof to make temporary appointments until the people fill the vacancies by election as the legislature may direct.

This amendment shall not be so construed as to affect the election or term of any Senator chosen before it becomes valid as part of the Constitution.

AMENDMENT XVIII. (1919)

SECTION 1. After one year from the ratification of this article the manufacture, sale, or transportation of intoxicating liquors within, the importation thereof into, or the exportation thereof from the Untied States and all territory subject to the jurisdiction thereof for beverage purposes is hereby prohibited.

SECTION 2. The Congress and the several States shall have concurrent power to enforce this article by appropriate legislation.

SECTION 3. This article shall be inoperative unless it shall have been ratified as an amendment to the Constitution by the legislatures of the several States, as provided in the Constitution, within seven years from the date of the submission hereof to the States by the Congress.

AMENDMENT XIX. (1920)

The right of citizens of the United States to vote shall not be denied or abridged by the United States or by any State on account of sex.

Congress shall have power to enforce this article by appropriate legislation.

AMENDMENT XX. (1933)

SECTION 1. The terms of the President and Vice President shall end at noon on the 20th day of January, and the terms of Senators and representatives at noon on the 3d day of January, of the years in which such terms would have ended if this article had not been ratified; and the terms of their successors shall then begin.

SECTION 2. The Congress shall assemble at least once in every year, and such meeting shall begin at noon on the 3d day of January, unless they shall by law appoint a different day.

SECTION 3. If, at the time fixed for the beginning of the term of the President, the President elect shall have died, the Vice President elect shall become President. If a President shall not have been chosen before the time fixed for the beginning of his term, or if the President elect shall have failed to qualify, then the Vice President elect shall act as President until a President shall have qualified; and the Congress may by law provide for the case wherein neither a President elect nor a Vice President elect shall have qualified, declaring who shall then act as President, or the manner in which one who is to act shall be selected, and such person shall act accordingly until a President or Vice President shall have qualified.

SECTION 4. The Congress may by law provide for the case of the death of any of the persons from whom the House of Representatives may choose a President whenever the right of choice shall have devolved upon them, and for the case of the death of any of the persons from whom the Senate may choose a Vice President whenever the right of choice shall have devolved upon them.

SECTION 5. Sections 1 and 2 shall take effect on the 15th day of October following the ratification of this article.

SECTION 6. This article shall be inoperative unless it shall have been ratified as an amendment to the Constitution by the legislatures of three-fourths of the several States within seven years from the date of submission.

AMENDMENT XXI. (1933)

SECTION 1. The eighteenth article of amendment to the Constitution of the United States is hereby repealed.

SECTION 2. The transportation or importation into any State, Territory, or possession of the United States for delivery or use therein of intoxicating liquors, in violation of the laws thereof, is hereby prohibited.

SECTION 3. This article shall be inoperative unless it shall have been ratified as an amendment to the Constitution by conventions in the several States, as provided in the Constitution, within seven years from the date of the submission hereof to the States by the Congress.

AMENDMENT XXII. (1951)

SECTION 1. No person shall be elected to the office of the President more than twice, and no person who has held the office of President, or acted as President, for more than two years of a term to which some other person was elected president shall be elected to the office of the President more than once. But this Article shall not apply to any person holding office of President when this Article was proposed by the Congress, and shall not prevent any person who may be holding the office of President, or acting as President, during the term within which this Article becomes operative from holding the office of President or acting as President during the remainder of such term.

SECTION 2. The article shall be inoperative unless it shall have been ratified as an amendment to the Constitution by the legislatures of three-fourths of the several States within seven years from the date of its submission to the States by the Congress.

AMENDMENT XXIII. (1961)

SECTION 1. The District constituting the seat of Government of the United States shall appoint in such manner as the Congress may direct:

A number of electors of President and Vice President equal to the whole number of Senators and Representatives in Congress to which the District would be entitled if it were a State, but in no event more than the least populous State; they shall be in addition to those appointed by the States, but they shall be considered, for the purposes of the election of President and Vice President, to be electors appointed by a State; and they shall meet in the District and perform such duties as provided by the twelfth article of amendment.

SECTION 2. The Congress shall have power to enforce this article by appropriate legislation.

AMENDMENT XXIV. (1964)

SECTION 1. The right of citizens of the United States to vote in any primary or other election for President or Vice President, for electors for President or Vice President, or for Senator or Representative in Congress, shall not be denied or abridged by the United States or any State by reason of failing to pay any poll tax or other tax.

SECTION 2. The Congress shall have power to enforce this article by appropriate legislation.

AMENDMENT XXV. (1967)

SECTION 1. In case of the removal of the President from office or of his death or resignation, the Vice President shall become President.

SECTION 2. Whenever there is a vacancy in the office of the Vice President, the President shall nominate a Vice President who shall take office upon confirmation by a majority vote of both Houses of Congress.

SECTION 3. Whenever the President transmits to the President pro tempore of the Senate and the Speaker of the House of Representatives his written declaration that he is unable to discharge the powers and duties of his office, and until he transmits to them a written declaration to the contrary, such powers and duties shall be discharged by the Vice President as Acting President.

SECTION 4. Whenever the Vice President and a majority of either the principal officers of the executive departments or of such other body as Congress may by law provide, transmit to the President pro tempore of the Senate and the Speaker of the House of Representatives their written declaration that the President is unable to discharge the powers and duties of his office, the Vice President shall immediately assume the powers and duties of the office as Acting President.

Thereafter, when the President transmits to the President pro tempore of the Senate and the Speaker of the House of Representatives his written declaration that no inability exists, he shall resume the powers and duties of his office unless the Vice President and a majority of either the principal officers of the executive department or of such other body as Congress may by law provide, transmit within four days to the President pro tempore of the Senate and the Speaker of the House of Representatives their written declaration that the President is unable to discharge the powers and duties of his office. Thereupon Congress shall decide the issue, assembling within forty-eight hours for that purpose if not in session. If the Congress, within twenty-one days after receipt of the latter written declaration, or, if Congress is not in session, within twenty-one days after Congress is required to assemble, determines by two-thirds vote of both Houses that the President is unable to discharge the powers and duties of his office, the Vice President shall continue to discharge the same as Acting President; otherwise, the President shall resume the powers and duties of his office.

AMENDMENT XXVI. (1971)

SECTION 1. The right of citizens of the United States, who are eighteen years of age or older, to vote shall not be denied or abridged by the United States or by any State on account of age.

SECTION 2. The Congress shall have power to enforce this article by appropriate legislation.

G L O S S A R Y

The 17 chapters of *Criminal Justice Today* contain over 100 terms commonly used in the field of criminal justice. This glossary contains many more. All concepts, wherever they appear, are explained, whenever possible, according to definitions provided by the Bureau of Justice Statistics under a 1979 mandate of the Justice System Improvement Act. That mandate was to create a consistent terminology set for use by criminal justice students, planners, and practitioners. It found its most complete expression in the *Dictionary of Criminal Justice Data Terminology*,[1] the second edition of which provides many of our definitions. Others (especially those in Chapter 2) are derived from the FBI's Uniform Crime Reporting Program.

Standardization is becoming increasingly important because of the fact that American criminal justice agencies, justice practitioners, and involved citizens now routinely communicate over vast distances, about the criminal justice system itself. For communications to be meaningful, a shared terminology is necessary. Standardization, however desirable, is not easy to achieve. In the words of the Bureau of Justice Statistics, "It is not possible to construct a single national standard criminal justice data terminology where every term always means the same thing in all of its appearances. However, it is possible and necessary to standardize the language that represents basic categorical distinctions."[2] Although this glossary should be especially valuable to the student who will one day work in the criminal justice system, it should also prove beneficial to anyone seeking a greater insight into that system.

abused child A child who has been physically, sexually, or mentally abused. Most states also consider a child abused who is forced into delinquent activity by a parent or guardian.

acquittal The judgment of a court, based on a verdict of a jury or a judicial officer, that the defendant is not guilty of the offense(s) for which he or she has been tried.

adjudication The process by which a court arrives at a decision regarding a case; also, the resultant decision.

adjudicatory hearing In juvenile justice usage, the fact-finding process wherein the juvenile court determines whether or not there is sufficient evidence to sustain the allegations in a petition.

admission (corrections) In correctional usage, the entry of an offender into the

---

[1]Bureau of Justice Statistics, *Dictionary of Criminal Justice Data Terminology*, 2nd ed. (Washington, D.C.: U.S. Government Printing Office, 1982).
[2]Ibid., p. 5.

legal jurisdiction of a corrections agency and/or physical custody of a correctional facility.

adult In criminal justice usage, a person who is within the original jurisdiction of a criminal, rather than a juvenile, court because his or her age at the time of an alleged criminal act was above a statutorily specified limit.

adversarial system The two-sided structure under which American criminal trial courts operate and that pits the prosecution against the defense. In theory, justice is done when the most effective adversary is able to convince the judge or jury that their perspective on the case is the correct one.

aftercare In juvenile justice usage, the status or program membership of a juvenile who has been committed to a treatment or confinement facility, conditionally released from the facility, and placed in a supervisory and/or treatment program.

aggravated assault Unlawful intentional causing of serious bodily injury with or without a deadly weapon, or unlawful intentional attempting or threatening of serious bodily injury or death with a deadly or dangerous weapon.

aggravating circumstances Circumstances relating to the commission of a crime which cause its gravity to be greater than that of the average instance of the given type of offense.

alias Any name used for an official purpose that is different from a person's legal name.

alternative sanctions The use of split sentencing, shock probation and parole, home confinement, shock incarceration, and community service in lieu of other, more traditional, sanctions such as imprisonment and fines. Alternative sanctions are becoming increasingly popular as prison crowding grows.

anomie A socially pervasive condition of normlessness.

appeal Generally, the request that a court with appellate jurisdiction review the judgment, decision, or order of a lower court and set it aside (reverse it) or modify it; also, the judicial proceedings or steps in judicial proceedings resulting from such a request.

appearance (court) The act of coming into a court and submitting to the authority of that court.

appellant The person who contests the correctness of a court order, judgment, or other decision and who seeks review and relief in a court having appellate jurisdiction, or the person in whose behalf this is done.

appellate court A court of which the primary function is to review the judgments of other courts and of administrative agencies.

appellate jurisdiction The lawful authority of a court to review a decision made by a lower court.

arraignment I. Strictly, the hearing before a court having jurisdiction in a criminal case, in which the identity of the defendant is established, the defendant is informed of the charge(s) and of his or her rights, and the defendant is required to enter a plea. II. In some usages, any appearance in court prior to trial in criminal proceedings.

arrest Taking an adult or juvenile into physical custody by authority of law, for the purpose of charging the person with a criminal offense or a delinquent act or status offense, terminating with the recording of a specific offense.

arrest (UCR) In Uniform Crime Reports terminology, all separate instances where a person is taken into physical custody or notified or cited by a law enforcement officer or agency, except those relating to minor traffic violations.

arrest rate The number of arrests reported for each unit of population.

arrest warrant A document issued by a judicial officer which directs a law enforcement officer to arrest an identified person who has been accused of a specific offense.

arson The intentional damaging or destruction or attempted damaging or destruction, by means of fire or explosion of the property of another without the consent of the owner, or of one's own property or that of another with intent to defraud.

arson (UCR) In Uniform Crime Reports terminology, the burning or attempted burning of property with or without intent to defraud.

assault Unlawful intentional inflicting, or attempted or threatened inflicting, of injury upon the person of another.

assault on a law enforcement officer A simple or aggravated assault, where the victim is a law enforcement officer engaged in the performance of his or her duties.

atavism A condition characterized by the existence of features thought to be common in earlier stages of human evolution.

attorney A person trained in the law, admitted to practice before the bar of a given jurisdiction, and authorized to advise, represent, and act for other persons in legal proceedings.

Auburn style A form of imprisonment developed in New York state around 1820 that depended upon mass prisons, where prisoners were held in congregate fashion. This style of imprisonment was a primary competitor with the Pennsylvania style.

backlog (court) The number of cases awaiting disposition in a court which exceed the court's capacity for disposing of them within the period of time considered appropriate.

bail I. To effect the release of an accused person from custody, in return for a promise that he or she will appear at a place and time specified and submit to the jurisdiction and judgment of the court, guaranteed by a pledge to pay to the court a specified sum of money or property if the person does not appear. II. The money or property pledged to the court or actually deposited with the court to effect the release of a person from legal custody.

bail bond A document guaranteeing the appearance of the defendant in court as required and recording the pledge of money or property to be paid to the court if he or she does not appear, which is signed by the person to be released and any other persons acting in his or her behalf.

bail bondsman A person, usually licensed, whose business it is to effect release on bail for persons charged with offenses and held in custody, by pledging to pay a sum of money if a defendant fails to appear in court as required.

bailiff The court officer whose duties are to keep order in the courtroom and to maintain physical custody of the jury.

bail revocation The court decision withdrawing the status of release on bail previously conferred upon a defendant.

bench warrant A document issued by a court directing that a law enforcement officer bring the person named therein before the court, usually one who has failed to obey a court order or a notice to appear.

bind over I. To require by judicial authority that a person promise to appear for trial, appear in court as a witness, or keep the peace. II. The decision by a court of limited jurisdiction requiring that a person charged with a felony appear for trial on that charge in a court of general jurisdiction, as the result of a finding of probable cause at a preliminary hearing held in the limited jurisdiction court.

biological school A perspective on criminological thought that holds that criminal behavior has a physiological basis. Genes, foods and food additives, hormones, and inheritance are all thought to play a role in determining individual behavior. Biological thinkers highlight the underlying animalistic aspect of being human as a major determinate of behavior.

booking A law enforcement or correctional administrative process officially recording an entry into detention after arrest, and identifying the person, the place, time, and reason for the arrest, and the arresting authority.

burglary I. By the narrowest and oldest definition, trespassory breaking and entering of the dwelling house of another in the nighttime with the intent to commit a felony. II. Unlawful entry of any fixed structure, vehicle, or vessel used for regular residence, industry or business, with or without force, with intent to commit a felony or larceny.

burglary (UCR) Unlawful entry of any fixed structure, vehicle, or vessel used for regular residence, industry, or business, with or without force, with intent to commit a felony, or larceny.

capacity In criminal justice usage, the legal ability of a person to commit a criminal act; the mental and physical ability to act with purpose and to be aware of the certain, probable, or possible results of one's conduct.

capacity (prison) See **prison capacity**.

capital offense I. A criminal offense punishable by death. II. In some penal codes, an offense which may be punishable by death or by imprisonment for life.

capital punishment Another term for the death penalty. Capital punishment is the most extreme of all sentencing options.

career criminal In prosecutorial and law enforcement usage, a person having a past record of multiple arrests or convictions for serious crimes, or an unusually large number of arrests or convictions for crimes of varying degrees of seriousness.

caseload (corrections) The total number of clients registered with a correctional agency or agent on a given date or during a specified time period, often divided into active supervisory cases and inactive cases, thus distinguishing between clients with whom contact is regular, and those with whom it is not.

caseload (court) The number of cases requiring judicial action at a certain time or the number of cases acted upon in a given court during a given time period.

certiorari See writ of *certiorari*.

change of venue The movement of a case from the jurisdiction of one court to that of another court which has the same subject matter jurisdictional authority but is in a different geographic location.

charge In criminal justice usage, an allegation that a specified person(s) has committed a specific offense, recorded in a functional document such as a record of an arrest, a complaint, information or indictment, or a judgment of conviction.

child abuse The illegal physical, emotional, or sexual mistreatment of a child by his or her parent(s) or guardian(s).

child neglect The illegal failure by a parent(s) or guardian(s) to provide proper nourishment or care to a child.

circumstantial evidence Evidence that requires interpretation, or that requires a judge or jury to reach a conclusion based upon what the evidence indicates. From the close proximity of a smoking gun to the defendant, for example, the jury might conclude that she pulled the trigger.

citation (to appear) A written order issued by a law enforcement officer directing an alleged offender to appear in a specific court at a specified time in order to answer a criminal charge, and not permitting forfeit of bail as an alternative to court appearance.

citizen's arrest The taking of a person into physical custody, by a witness to a crime other than a law enforcement officer, for the purpose of delivering him or her to the physical custody of a law enforcement officer or agency.

civil death The legal status of prisoners in some jurisdictions who are denied the opportunity to vote, hold public office, marry, or enter into contracts by virtue of their status as incarcerated felons. While civil death is primarily of historical interest, some jurisdictions still place limits on the contractual opportunities available to inmates.

civil law That portion of the modern law that regulates contracts and other obligations involving primarily personal interests.

classical school A perspective on criminological thought that centered on the idea of free will and held that punishment, if it was to be an effective deterrent, had to outweigh the potential pleasure to be derived from criminal behavior. Classical thinkers, who had their roots in the intellectual enlightenment which swept Europe a few centuries ago, highlighted the role that rationality and free choice play in determining human behavior.

clearance (UCR) The event where a known occurrence of a Part I offense is followed by an arrest or other decision which indicates a solved crime at the police level of reporting.

clearance rate A traditional measure of investigative effectiveness that compares the number of crimes reported and/or discovered to the number of crimes solved through arrest or other means (such as the death of a suspect).

clemency In criminal justice usage the name for the type of executive or legislative action where the severity of punishment of a single person or a group of persons is reduced or the punishment stopped, or a person is exempted from prosecution for certain actions.

cohort In statistics, the group of individuals having one or more statistical factors in common in a demographic study.

comes stabuli Nonuniformed mounted early law enforcement officers in medieval England. Early police forces were small, and relatively unorganized, but made effective use of local resources in the formation of possees, the pursuit of offender, and the like.

commitment The action of a judicial officer ordering that a person subject to judicial proceedings be placed in a particular kind of confinement or residential facility, for a specific reason authorized by law; also, the result of the action, the admission to the facility.

common law A body of unwritten judicial opinion that was based upon customary social practices of Anglo-Saxon society during the Middle Ages.

community-based corrections A sentencing style that represents a movement away from traditional confinement options and an increased dependence upon correctional resources which are available in the community.

community policing An extension of the police community relations concept that envisions an effective working partnership between the police and members of the community in order to solve problems which concern both.

community service A sentencing alternative that requires offenders to spend at least part of their time working for a community agency.

compelling interest A legal concept that provides a basis for suspicionless searches (urinalysis tests of train engineers, for example) when public safety is at issue. It is the concept upon which the Supreme Court cases of *Skinner* v. *Railway Labor Executives' Association* (1988) and *National Treasury Employees Union* v. *Von Rabb* (1989) turned. In those cases the Court held that public safety may provide a sufficiently compelling interest such that an individual's right to privacy can be limited under certain circumstances.

complaint I. In general criminal justice usage, any accusation that a person(s) has committed an offense(s), received by or originating from a law enforcement or prosecutorial agency, or received by a court. II. In judicial process usage, a formal document submitted to the court by a prosecutor, law enforcement officer, or other person, alleging that a specified person(s) has committed a specified offense(s) and requesting prosecution.

computer crime A popular name for crimes committed by use of a computer or crimes involving misuse or destruction of computer equipment or computerized information, sometimes specifically theft committed by means of manipulation of a computerized financial transaction system, or the use of computer services with intent to avoid payment.

concurrent sentence A sentence that is one of two or more sentences imposed at the same time after conviction for more than one offense and to be served at the same time, or a new sentence imposed upon a person already under sentence(s) for a previous offense(s), to be served at the same time as one or more of the previous sentences.

conditional release The release by executive decision from a federal or state correctional facility, of a prisoner who has not served his or her full sentence and whose freedom is contingent upon obeying specified rules of behavior.

conditions of probation and parole The general (state-ordered) and special (court- or board-ordered) limits imposed upon an offender who is released on either probation or parole. General conditions tend to be fixed by state statute, while special conditions are mandated by the sentencing authority and take into consideration the background of the offender and circumstances surrounding the offense.

confinement In correctional terminology, physical restriction of a person to a clearly defined area from which he or she is lawfully forbidden to depart and from which departure is usually constrained by architectural barriers and/or guards or other custodians.

conflict model A perspective on the study of criminal justice that assumes that the system's subcomponents function primarily to serve their own interests. According to this theoretical framework, "justice" is more a product of conflicts among agencies within the system, than it is the result of cooperation among component agencies.

consecutive sentence A sentence that is one of two or more sentences imposed at the same time, after conviction for more than one offense, and which is served in sequence with the other sentences, or a new sentence for a new conviction, imposed upon a person already under sentence(s) for previous offense(s), which is added to a previous sentence(s), thus increasing the maximum time the offender may be confined or under supervision.

contempt of court Intentionally obstructing a court in the administration of justice, or acting in a way calculated to lessen its authority or dignity, or failing to obey its lawful orders.

controlled substance A specifically defined bioactive or psychoactive chemical substance which is proscribed by law.

conviction The judgment of a court, based on the verdict of a jury or judicial officer, or on the guilty pleas or *nolo contendere* pleas of the defendant, that the defendant is guilty of the offense(s) with which he or she has been charged.

corporate crime a violation of a criminal statute either by a corporate entity or by its executives, employees or agents acting on behalf of and for the benefit of the corporation, partnership, or other form of business entity.[1]

correctional agency A federal, state, or local criminal or juvenile justice agency, under a single administrative authority of which the principal functions are the intake screening, supervision, custody, confinement, treatment, or presentencing or predisposition investigation of alleged or adjudicated adult offenders, youthful offenders, delinquents, or status offenders.

corrections A generic term that includes all government agencies, facilities, programs, procedures, personnel, and techniques concerned with the intake, custody, confinement, supervision, or treatment, or presentencing or predisposition investigation of alleged or adjudicated adult offenders, delinquents, or status offenders.

counsel See **attorney**.

count See **charge**.

court An agency or unit of the judicial branch of government authorized or established by statute or constitution, and consisting of one or more judicial officers, which has the authority to decide upon cases, controversies in law, and disputed matters of fact brought before it.

court calendar The court schedule; the list of events comprising the daily or weekly work of a court, including the assignment of the time and place for each hearing or other item of business, or the list of matters which will be taken up in a given court term.

court clerk An elected or appointed court officer responsible for maintaining the written records of the court and for supervising or performing the clerical tasks necessary for conducting judicial business; also, any employee of a court whose principal duties are to assist the court clerk in performing the clerical tasks necessary for conducting judicial business.

court disposition For statistical reporting purposes, generally, the judicial decision terminating proceedings in a case before judgment is reached, or the judgment; the data items representing the outcome of judicial proceedings and the manner in which the outcome was arrived at.

court-martial (also courts-martial) A military court convened by senior commanders under authority of the Uniform Code of Military Justice for the purpose of trying members of the armed forces accused of violations of the Code.

court of record A court in which a complete and permanent record of all proceedings or specified types of proceedings is kept.

court order A mandate, command, or direction issued by a judicial officer in the exercise of his or her judicial authority.

court probation A criminal court requirement that a defendant or offender fulfill specified conditions of behavior in lieu of a sentence to confinement, but without assignment to a probation agency's supervisory caseload.

court reporter A person present during judicial proceedings, who records all testimony and other oral statements made during the proceedings.

credit card fraud The use or attempted use of a credit card in order to obtain goods or services with the intent to avoid payment.

crime An act committed or omitted in violation of a law forbidding or commanding it for which the possible penalties for an adult upon conviction include incarceration, for which a corporation can be penalized by fine or forfeit, or for which a juvenile can be adjudged delinquent or transferred to criminal court for prosecution.

Crime Index In Uniform Crime Reports terminology, a set of numbers indicating the volume, fluctuation, and distribution of crimes reported to local law enforcement agencies, for the United States as a whole and for its geographical subdivisions, based on counts of reported occurrences of UCR Index Crimes.

crime rate The number of index offenses reported for each unit of population.

criminal homicide The causing of the death of another person without legal justification or excuse.

criminal homicide (UCR) The name of the UCR category that includes and is limited to all offenses of causing the death of another person without justification or excuse.

criminal incident In National Crime Victimization Survey terminology, a criminal event involving one or more victims and one or more offenders.

criminal justice In the strictest sense, the criminal (penal) law, the law of criminal procedure, and that array of procedures and activities having to do with the enforcement of this body of law.

criminal justice system The aggregate of all operating and administrative or technical support agencies that perform criminal justice functions. The basic divisions of the operational aspect of criminal justice are law enforcement, courts, and corrections.

criminal law That branch of modern law that concerns itself with offenses committed against society, members thereof, their property, and the social order.

criminal proceedings The regular and orderly steps, as directed or authorized by statute or a court of law, taken to determine whether an adult accused of a crime is guilty or not guilty.

criminology The scientific study of crime causation, prevention, and the rehabilitation and punishment of offenders.

culpability I. Blameworthiness; responsibility in some sense for an event or situation deserving of moral blame. II. In Model Penal Code (MPC) usage, a state of mind on the part of one who is committing an act, which makes him or her potentially subject to prosecution for that act.

custody Legal or physical control of a person or thing; legal, supervisory, or physical responsibility for a person or thing.

data encryption Methods used to encode computerized information.

deadly weapon An instrument designed to inflict serious bodily injury or death, or capable of being used for such a purpose.

decriminalization The redefinition of certain previously criminal behaviors into regulated activities, which become "ticketable" rather than "arrestable."

defendant In criminal justice usage, a person formally accused of an offense(s) by the filing in court of a charging document.

defenses (to a criminal charge) Include claims based upon personal, special, and procedural considerations that the defendant should not be held accountable for their actions, even though they may have acted in violation of the criminal law.

delinquency In the broadest usage, juvenile actions or conduct in violation of criminal law, juvenile status offenses, and other juvenile misbehavior.

delinquent A juvenile who has been adjudged by a judicial officer of a juvenile court to have committed a delinquent act.

delinquent act An act committed by a juvenile for which an adult could be prosecuted in a criminal court, but for which a juvenile can be adjudicated in a juvenile court, or prosecuted in a court having criminal jurisdiction if the juvenile court transfers jurisdiction; generally, a "felony" or "misdemeanor" level offense in states employing those terms.

delinquent child A child who has engaged in activity that would be considered a crime if the child were an adult. The term "delinquent" is applied to such a child in order to avoid the stigma that comes from application of the term "criminal."

dependent A juvenile over whom a juvenile court has assumed jurisdiction and legal control because his or her care by parent, guardian, or custodian has not met a legal standard of proper care.

dependent child A child who has no parents or whose parents are unable to care for him or her.

design capacity (or bed capacity) The number of inmates which a correctional facility was originally designed to house, or currently has the capacity to house as a result of later, planned modifications, exclusive of extraordinary arrangements to accommodate overcrowded conditions.

detainee Usually, a person held in local, very-short-term confinement while awaiting consideration for pretrial release or first appearance for arraignment.

detention The legally authorized confinement of a person subject to criminal or juvenile court proceedings, until the point of commitment to a correctional facility or until release.

detention hearing In juvenile justice usage, a hearing by a judicial officer of a juvenile court to determine whether a juvenile is to be detained, continue to be detained, or be released, while juvenile proceedings in the case are pending.

determinate sentence See **indeterminate sentence.**

deterrence A goal of criminal sentencing that seeks to prevent others from committing crimes similar to the one for which an offender is being sentenced.

directed patrol A police management strategy designed to increase the productivity of patrol officers through the application of scientific analysis and evaluation to patrol techniques.

direct evidence Evidence that, if believed, directly proves a fact. Eye-witness testimony (and, more recently, videotaped documentation) account for the majority of all direct evidence heard in the criminal courtroom.

direct supervision jails Temporary confinement facilities that eliminate many of the traditional barriers between inmates and correctional staff. Physical barriers in direct supervision jails are far less common than in traditional jails, allowing staff members the opportunity for greater interaction with, and control over, residents.

discharge In criminal justice usage, to release from confinement or supervision or to release from a legal status imposing an obligation upon the subject person.

discretion The opportunity that individual law enforcement officers have for the exercise of choice in their daily activities. The decision whether to effect an arrest or release a suspect is a primary example of discretion in law enforcement activity.

disposition In criminal justice usage, the action by a criminal or juvenile justice agency which signifies that a portion of the justice process is complete and jurisdiction is terminated or transferred to another agency, or which signifies that a decision has been reached on one aspect of a case and a different aspect comes under consideration, requiring a different kind of decision.

disposition hearing A hearing in juvenile court, conducted after an adjudicatory hearing and subsequent receipt of the report of any predisposition investigation, to determine the most appropriate form of custody and/or treatment for a juvenile who has been adjudged a delinquent, a status offender, or a dependent.

dispute resolution centers Informal hearing infrastructures designed to mediate interpersonal disputes without need for the more formal arrangements of criminal trial courts.

district attorney See **prosecutor.**

diversion The official suspension of criminal or juvenile proceedings against an alleged offender at any point after a recorded justice system intake but before the entering of a judgment and referral of that person to a treatment or care program administered by a nonjustice or private agency, or no referral.

DNA profiling The use of biological residue found at the scene of a crime for genetic comparisons in aiding the identification of criminal suspects.

docket See **court calendar.**

drug czar A cabinet-level position, originally created during the years of the Reagan presidency, that functions to organize federal drug-fighting efforts.

drug law violation The unlawful sale, purchase, distribution, manufacture, cultivation, transport, possession, or use of a controlled or prohibited drug, or attempt to commit these acts.

due process of law A right guaranteed by the Fifth, Sixth, and Fourteenth Amendments of the U.S. Constitution, and generally understood, in legal contexts, to mean the due course of legal proceedings according to the rules and forms which have been established for the protection of private rights.

element of the offense Any conduct, circumstance, condition, or state of mind which in combination with other conduct, circumstances, conditions, or states of mind constitutes an unlawful act.

embezzlement The misappropriation, or illegal disposal of legally entrusted property by the person(s) to whom it was entrusted, with intent to defraud the legal owner or intended beneficiary.

emergency searches Those searches conducted by the police without a warrant, that are justified on the basis of some immediate and overriding need, such as public safety, the likely escape of a dangerous suspect, or the removal or destruction of evidence.

ethnocentrism The phenomenon of culture-centeredness, by which one uses one's own culture as a benchmark against which to judge all other patterns of behavior.

evidence Anything useful to a judge or jury in deciding the facts of a case.

Evidence may take the form of witness testimony, written documents, videotapes, magnetic media, photographs, physical objects, and so on.

exclusionary rule The understanding, operative in contemporary American criminal justice as a result of Supreme Court precedent, that incriminating information must be seized according to constitutional specifications of due process, or it will not be allowable as evidence in criminal trials.

expert witness A person who has special knowledge recognized by the court as relevant to the determination of guilt or innocence. Expert witnesses may express opinions or draw conclusions in their testimony, unlike lay witnesses.

extradition The surrender by one state to another of an individual accused or convicted of an offense in the second state.

federal court system The three-tiered structure of federal courts, involving U.S. district courts, U.S. courts of appeal, and the U.S. Supreme Court.

federal interest computers Those that (1) are the property of the federal government, (2) belong to financial institutions, or (3) are located in a state other than the one in which the criminal perpetrator is operating.

felony A criminal offense punishable by death or by incarceration in a prison facility.

filing The initiation of a criminal case in a court by formal submission to the court of a charging document, alleging that one or more named persons have committed one or more specified criminal offenses.

fine The penalty imposed upon a convicted person by a court, requiring that he or she pay a specified sum of money to the court.

forcible rape (UCR) Sexual intercourse or attempted sexual intercourse with a female against her will, by force or threat of force.

forgery The creation or alteration of a written or printed document, which if validly executed would constitute a record of a legally binding transaction, with the intent to defraud by affirming it to be the act of an unknowing second person; also the creation of an art object with intent to misrepresent the identity of the creator.

fraud offense The crime type comprising offenses sharing the elements of practice of deceit or intentional misrepresentation of fact, with the intent of unlawfully depriving a person of his or her property or legal rights.

frivolous suit A lawsuit with no foundation in fact. Frivolous suits are generally brought by lawyers and plaintiffs for reasons of publicity, politics, or other nonlaw-related issues and may result in fines against plaintiffs and their counsel.

Fruit of the Poisoned Tree Doctrine A legal principle that excludes from introduction at trial any evidence eventually developed as a result of an originally illegal search or seizure.

good faith A possible legal basis for an exception to the exclusionary rule. Law enforcement officers who conduct a search, or seize evidence, on the basis of good faith (that is, where they believe they are operating according to the dictates of the law) and who later discover that a mistake was made (perhaps in the format of the application for a search warrant) may still use evidence seized as the result of such activities in court.

good time In correctional usage, the amount of time deducted from time to be served in prison on a given sentence(s) and/or under correctional agency jurisdiction, at some point after a prisoner's admission to prison, contingent upon good behavior and/or awarded automatically by application of a statute or regulation.

grand jury A body of persons who have been selected according to law and sworn to hear the evidence against accused persons and determine whether there is sufficient evidence to bring those persons to trial, to investigate criminal activity generally, and to investigate the conduct of public agencies and officials.

grievance procedure Formalized arrangements, usually involving a neutral hearing board, whereby institutionalized individuals have the opportunity to register complaints about the conditions of their confinement.

guilty plea A defendant's formal answer in court to the charge(s) contained in a complaint, information, or indictment, claiming that he or she did commit the offense(s) listed.

guilty verdict See **verdict.**

habeas corpus See **writ of** *habeas corpus.*

habitual offender A person sentenced under the provisions of a statute declaring that persons convicted of a given offense, and shown to have previously been convicted of another specified offense(s), shall receive a more severe penalty than that for the current offense alone.

hands-off doctrine An historical policy of nonintervention with regard to prison management that American courts tended to follow until the late 1960s. For the past 20 years the doctrine has languished as judicial intervention in prison administration has dramatically increased, although there is now growing evidence of a return to a new hands-off doctrine.

hearing A proceeding in which arguments, witness, or evidence are heard by a judicial officer or administrative body.

hearsay Something that is not based upon the personal knowledge of a witness. Witnesses who testify, for example, about something they have heard, are offering hearsay by repeating information abut a matter of which they have no direct knowledge.

hearsay rule The longstanding American courtroom precedent that hearsay cannot be used in court. Rather than accepting testimony based upon hearsay, the American trial process asks that the person who was the original source of the hearsay information be brought into court to be questioned and cross-examined. Exceptions to the hear-

say rule may occur when the person with direct knowledge is dead or is otherwise unable to testify.

hierarchy rule A standard UCR scoring practice in which only the most serious offense is counted in a multiple-offense situation.

home confinement House arrest. Individuals ordered confined in their homes are sometimes monitored electronically to be sure they do not leave during the hours of confinement (absence from the home during working hours is often permitted).

homicide See **criminal homicide.**

Hudud crimes Serious violations of Islamic law regarded as offenses against God. Hudud crimes include such behavior as theft, adultery, sodomy, drinking alcohol, and robbery.

hung jury A jury that after long deliberation is so irreconcilably divided in opinion that it is unable to reach any verdict.

illegal search and seizure An act in violation of the Fourth Amendment of the U.S. Constitution: "The right of people to be secure in their persons, houses, papers and effects, against unreasonable searches and seizures, shall not be violated, and no warrants shall issue but upon probable cause, supported by oath or affirmation, and particularly describing the place to be searched and the persons or things to be seized."

incapacitation The use of imprisonment or other means to reduce the likelihood that an offender will be capable of committing future offenses.

inchoate offense An offense that consists of an action or conduct that is a step toward the intended commission of another offense.

incident-based reporting A less restrictive and more expansive method of collecting crime data (as opposed to summary reporting) in which all the analytical elements associated with an offense or arrest are compiled by a central collection agency on an incident by incident basis.

included offense An offense that is made up of elements that are a subset of the elements of another offense having a greater statutory penalty, and the occurrence of which is established by the same evidence or by some portion of the evidence that has been offered to establish the occurrence of the greater offense.

incompetent to stand trial In criminal proceedings, the finding by a court that a defendant is mentally incapable of understanding the nature of the charges and proceedings against him or her, of consulting with an attorney, and of aiding in his or her own defense.

indeterminate sentence A type of sentence to imprisonment where the commitment, instead of being for a specified single time quantity, such as three years, is for a range of time, such as two to five years or five years maximum and zero minimum.

Index crimes See **Crime Index**.

indictment A formal, written accusation submitted to the court by a grand jury, alleging that a specified person(s) has committed a specified offense(s), usually a felony.

individual rights Those rights guaranteed to criminal defendants by the U.S. Constitution (especially as found in the first ten amendments to the Constitution, known as the Bill of Rights) facing formal processing by the criminal justice system. The preservation of the rights of criminal defendants is important to society because it is through the exercise of such rights that the values of our culture are most clearly and directly expressed.

information In criminal justice usage, a formal written accusation submitted to the court by a prosecutor, alleging that a specified person(s) has committed a specified offense(s).

infraction A violation of state statute or local ordinance punishable by a fine or other penalty, but not by incarceration, or by a specified, usually limited term of incarceration.

inherent coercion Those tactics used by police interviewers that fall short of physical abuse, but that, nonetheless, pressure suspects to divulge information.

initial appearance In criminal proceedings, the first appearance of an accused person in the first court having jurisdiction over his or her case.

initial plea (also first pleas) The first plea to a given charge entered in the court record by or for the defendant. The acceptance of an initial plea by the court unambiguously indicates that the arraignment process has been completed.

insanity defense A personal defense that claims that the person charged with a crime did not know what they were doing, or that they did not know that what they were doing was wrong. For purposes of the criminal law, insanity is a legal definition and not a psychiatric one. The differences between the psychiatric and legal conceptualizations of insanity lead often to disagreements among expert witnesses who, in criminal court, may provide conflicting testimony as to the sanity of a defendant.

institutional capacity An officially stated number of inmates that a confinement or residential facility is or was intended to house.

intake The process by which a juvenile referral is received by personnel of a probation agency, juvenile court, or special intake unit and a decision made to close the case at intake, or refer the juvenile to another agency, or place him or her under some kind of care or supervision, or file a petition in a juvenile court.

intent The state of mind or attitude with which an act is carried out; the design, resolve, or determination with which a person acts to achieve a certain result.

intermediate appellate court An appellate court of which the primary function is to review the judgments of trial courts and the decisions of administrative agencies, and whose decisions are in turn usually reviewable by a higher appellate court in the same state.

INTERPOL An acronym for the International Police Association. INTERPOL began operations in 1946, and today has 137 members.

interrogation The information-gathering activities of police officers that involve the direct questioning of suspects. The actions of officers during suspect interrogation are constrained by a number of Supreme Court decisions, the first of which was *Brown* v. *Mississippi* (1936).

jail A confinement facility administered by an agency of local government, typically a law enforcement agency, intended for adults but sometimes also containing juveniles, which holds persons detained pending adjudication and/or persons committed after adjudication, usually those committed on sentences of a year or less.

jail commitment A sentence of commitment to the jurisdiction of a confinement facility system for adults which is administered by an agency of local government and of which the custodial authority is usually limited to persons sentenced to a year or less of confinement.

judgment The statement of the decision of a court, that the defendant is acquitted or convicted of the offense(s) charged.

judgment suspending sentence A court-ordered sentencing alternative that results in the convicted offender being placed on probation.

judicial officer Any person authorized by statute, constitutional provision, or court rule to exercise those powers reserved to the judicial branch of government.

judicial review The power of a court to review actions and decisions made by other agencies of government.

jural postulates Propositions developed by the famous jurist Roscoe Pound that hold that the law reflects shared needs without which members of society could not co-exist. Pound's jural postulates are often linked to the idea that the law can be used to engineer the structure of society in order to predetermine certain kinds of outcomes (such as property rights as embodied in the law of theft do in capitalistic societies).

jurisdiction The territory, subject matter, or persons over which lawful authority may be exercised by a court or other justice agency, as determined by statute or constitution.

jury panel The group of persons summoned to appear in court as potential jurors for a particular trial, or the persons selected from the group of potential jurors to sit in the jury box, from which second group those acceptable to the prosecution and the defense are finally chosen as the jury.

juvenile In the context of the administration of justice, a person subject to juvenile court proceedings because a statutorily defined event or condition caused by or affecting that person was alleged to have occurred while his or her age was below the statutorily specified age limit of original jurisdiction of a juvenile court.

juvenile court The name for the class of courts that have, as all or part of their authority, original jurisdiction over matters concerning persons statutorily defined as juveniles.

juvenile court judgment The juvenile court decision terminating an adjudicatory hearing, that the juvenile is a delinquent, status offender, or dependent, or that the allegations in the petition are not sustained.

juvenile disposition The decision of a juvenile court, concluding a disposition hearing, that an adjudicated juvenile be committed to a juvenile correctional facility, or placed in a juvenile residence, shelter, or care or treatment program, or required to meet certain standards of conduct, or released.

juvenile justice agency A government agency, or subunit thereof, of which the functions are the investigation, supervision, adjudication, care or confinement of juvenile offenders and nonoffenders subject to the jurisdiction of a juvenile court; also, in some usages, a private agency providing care and treatment.

juvenile justice system Government agencies that function to investigate, supervise, adjudicate, care for, or confine youthful offenders and other children subject to the jurisdiction of the juvenile court.

juvenile petition A document filed in juvenile court alleging that a juvenile is a delinquent, a status offender, or a dependent, and asking that the court assume jurisdiction over the juvenile, or asking that an alleged delinquent be transferred to a criminal court for prosecution as an adult.

kidnaping Transportation or confinement of a person without authority of law and without his or her consent, or without the consent of his or her guardian, if a minor.

larceny Unlawful taking or attempted taking of property other than a motor vehicle from the possession of another, by stealth, without force and without deceit, with intent to deprive the owner of the property permanently.

larceny-theft (UCR) Unlawful taking, carrying, leading, or riding away by stealth of property, other than a motor vehicle from the possession or constructive possession of another, including attempts.

law A rule of conduct, generally found enacted in the form of a statute, which proscribes and/or mandates certain forms of behavior. Statutory law is often the result of moral enterprise by interest groups that, through the exercise of political power, are successful in seeing their valuative perspectives enacted into law.

law enforcement The generic name for the activities of the agencies responsible for maintaining public order and enforcing the law, particularly the activities of prevention, detection, and investigation of crime and the apprehension of criminals.

law enforcement agency A federal, state, or local criminal justice agency or identifiable subunit of which the principal functions are the prevention, detection, and investigation of crime, and the apprehension of alleged offenders.

law enforcement officer An employee of a law enforcement agency who is an officer sworn to carry out law enforcement duties.

lawyer See **attorney**.

lay witness An eyewitness, character witness, or any other person called upon to testify who is not considered an expert. Lay witnesses must testify to facts alone and may not draw conclusions or express opinions.

legalistic style A style of policing that is marked by a strict concern with enforcing the precise letter of the law. Legalistic departments, however, may take a "hands-off" approach to otherwise disruptive or problematic forms of behavior that are not violations of the criminal law.

mandatory sentence A statutory requirement that a certain penalty shall be set and carried out in all cases upon conviction for a specified offense or series of offenses.

maximum sentence I. In legal usage, the maximum penalty provided by law for a given criminal offense, usually stated as a maximum term of imprisonment or a maximum fine. II. In correctional usage in relation to a given offender, any of several quantities (expressed in days, months or years) which vary according to whether calculated at the point of sentencing or at a later point in the correctional process, and according to whether the time period referred to is the term of confinement or the total period under correctional jurisdiction.

mediation committees Chinese civilian dispute resolution groups found throughout the country. Mediation committees successfully divert many minor offenders from handling by the more formal mechanisms of justice.

medical model A therapeutic perspective on correctional treatment that applies the diagnostic perspective of medical science to the handling of criminal offenders. Rehabilitation is seen as a cure, and offenders are treated through a variety of programs in order to reduce their antisocial tendencies.

mens rea The state of mind that accompanies a criminal act. Also, guilty mind.

Miranda rights The set of rights that a person accused or suspected of having committed a specific offense has during interrogation, and of which he or she must be informed prior to questioning, as stated by the U.S. Supreme Court in deciding *Miranda* v. *Arizona* and related cases.

misdemeanor An offense punishable by incarceration, usually in a local confinement facility, for a period of which the upper limit is prescribed by statute in a given jurisdiction, typically limited to a year or less.

mistrial A trial that has been terminated and declared invalid by the court because of some circumstances which creates a substantial and uncorrectable prejudice to the conduct of a fair trial, or which makes it impossible to continue the trial in accordance with prescribed procedures.

mitigating circumstances the opposite of aggravating circumstances: Circumstances surrounding the commission of a crime which do not in law justify or excuse the act, but which in fairness may be considered as reducing the blame-worthiness of the defendant.

Model Penal Code A generalized modern codification of that which is considered basic to criminal law, published by the American Law Institute in 1962.

money laundering The process of converting illegally earned assets, originating as cash, to one or more alternative forms to conceal such incriminating factors as illegal origin and true ownership.[2]

moral enterprise The process undertaken by an advocacy group in order to have its values legitimated and embodied in law.

motion An oral or written request made to a court at any time before, during, or after court proceedings, asking the court to make a specified finding, decision, or order.

motor vehicle theft (UCR) Unlawful taking or attempted taking, of a self-propelled road vehicle owned by another, with the intent to deprive him or her of it permanently or temporarily.

murder and nonnegligent manslaughter (UCR) Intentionally causing the death of another without legal justification or excuse, or causing the death of another while committing or attempting to commit another crime.

narcoterrorism A political alliance between terrorist organizations and drug-supplying cartels. The cartels provide financing for the terrorists, who in turn provide quasi-military protection to the drug dealers.

NCVS An abbreviation for "National Crime Victimization Survey."

neglected child A child who is not receiving the proper level of physical or psychological care from his or her parents or guardian, or who has been placed up for adoption in violation of the law.

negligence In legal usage, generally, a state of mind accompanying a person's conduct such that he or she is not aware, though a reasonable person should be aware, that there is a risk that the conduct might cause a particular harmful result.

negligent manslaughter (UCR) Causing death of another by recklessness or gross negligence.

new police Also known as the Metropolitan Police of London, were formed in 1829 under the command of Sir Robert Peel. Peel's police became the model for modern-day police forces throughout the Western world.

nolle prosequi A formal entry upon the record of the court, indicating that the prosecutor declares that he or she will proceed no further in the action. The terminating of adjudication of a criminal charge by the prosecutor's decision not to pursue the case, in some jurisdictions requiring the approval of the court.

nolo contendere A plea of "no contest." A no contest plea may be used where the defendant does not wish to contest conviction. Because the plea does not admit guilt, however, it cannot provide the basis for later civil suits that might follow upon the heels of a criminal conviction.

not guilty by reason of insanity The plea of a defendant or the verdict of a jury or judge in a criminal proceeding, that the defendant is not guilty of the offense(s) charged because at the time the crime(s) was committed the defendant did not have the mental capacity to be held criminally responsible for his or her actions.

no true bill The decision by a grand jury that it will not return an indictment against the person(s) accused of a crime(s) on the basis of the allegations and evidence presented by the prosecutor.

occupational crime Any act punishable by law that is committed through opportunity created in the course of an occupation that is legal.

offender An adult who has been convicted of a criminal offense.

offense See **crime**.

offenses known to police (UCR) Reported occurrences of offenses, which have been verified at the police level.

opinion The official announcement of a decision of a court together with the reasons for that decision.

organized crime A complex pattern of activity which includes the commission of statutorily defined offenses, in particular the provision of illegal goods and services but also carefully planned and coordinated instances of fraud, theft, and extortion, and which is uniquely characterized by the planned use of both legitimate and criminal professional expertise, and the use for criminal purposes of organizational features of legitimate business, including availability of large capital resources, disciplined management, division of labor, and focus upon maximum profit; also, the persons engaged in such a pattern of activity.

original jurisdiction The lawful authority of a court to hear or act upon a case from its beginning and to pass judgment on the law and the facts.

parens patriae A Latin term that refers to the legal basis upon which delinquent children may be removed from the home and supervised by the state. It means, in effect, that the state assumes responsibility for the welfare of problem children.

parole The status of an offender conditionally released from a prison by discretion of a paroling authority prior to expiration of sentence, required to observe conditions of parole, and placed under the supervision of a parole agency.

parole board A state paroling authority. Most states have parole boards (also called "commissions") that decide when an incarcerated offender is ready for conditional release, and which may also function as revocation hearing panels.

parolee A person who has been conditionally released by a paroling authority from a prison prior to the expiration of his or her sentence, and placed under the supervision of a parole agency, and who is required to observe conditions of parole.

parole revocation The administrative action of a paroling authority removing a person from parole status in response to a violation of lawfully required conditions of parole including the prohibition against commission of a new offense, and usually resulting in a return to prison.

parole supervision Guidance, treatment, or regulation of the behavior of a convicted adult who is obliged to fulfill conditions of parole or conditional release. Parole supervision is authorized and required by statute, performed by a parole agency, and occurs after a period of prison confinement.

parole supervisory caseload The total number of clients registered with a parole agency or officer on a given date, or during a specified time period.

parole violation An act or a failure to act by a parolee that does not conform to the conditions of parole.

paroling authority A board or commission which has the authority to release on parole adults committed to prison, to revoke parole or other conditional release, and to discharge from parole or other conditional release status.

Part I offenses In Uniform Crime Reports terminology, the group of offenses, also called "major offenses," for which UCR publishes counts of reported instances, and which consist of those that meet the following five-part criterion: (1) are most likely to be reported to police, (2) police investigation can easily establish whether a crime has occurred, (3) occur in all geographical areas, (4) occur with sufficient frequency to provide an adequate basis for comparison, (5) are serious crimes by nature and/or volume.

Part II offenses In Uniform Crime Reports terminology, a set of offense categories used in UCR data concerning arrests.

Pennsylvania style A form of imprisonment developed by the Pennsylvania Quakers around 1790 as an alternative to corporal punishments. The style made use of solitary confinement and resulted in the nation's first penitentiaries.

peremptory challenge The right to challenge a juror without assigning a reason for the challenge. In most jurisdictions each party to an action, both civil and criminal, has a specified number of such challenges and after using all his peremptory challenges he is required to furnish a reason for subsequent challenges.[3]

perjury The intentional making of a false statement as part of testimony by a sworn witness in a judicial proceeding on a matter material to the inquiry.

perpetrator The chief actor in the commission of a crime, that is, the person who directly commits the criminal act.

petition A written request made to a court asking for the exercise of its judicial powers or asking for permission to perform some act where the authorization of a court is required.

petit jury See **trial jury**.

phenomenological criminology A perspective on crime causation that holds that the significance of criminal behavior is ultimately knowable only to those who participate in it. Central to this school of thought is the belief that social actors endow their behavior with meaning and purpose. Hence, a crime might mean one thing to the person who commits it, quite another to the victim, and something far different still to professional participants in the justice system.

plaintiff A person who initiates a court action.

plain view A legal term describing the ready visibility of objects that might be sized as evidence during a search by police in the absence of a search warrant specifying the seizure of those objects. In order for evidence in plain view to be lawfully seized, officers must have a legal right to be in the viewing area, and must have cause to believe that the evidence is somehow associated with criminal activity.

plea In criminal proceedings, a defendant's formal answer in court to the charge contained in a complaint, information, or indictment, that he or she is guilty or not guilty of the offense charged, or does not contest the charge.

plea bargaining The negotiated agreement between defendant, prosecutor, and the court as to what an appropriate plea and associated sentence should be in a given case. Plea bargaining circumvents the trial process and dramatically reduces the time required for the resolution of a criminal case.

police community relations (PCR) An area of emerging police activity that stresses the need for the community and the police to work together effectively and emphasizes the notion that the police derive their legitimacy from the community they serve. PCR began to be of concern to many police agencies in the 1960s and 1970s.

police culture (also subculture) A particular set of values, beliefs, and acceptable forms of behavior characteristic of American police, and with which the police profession strives to imbue new recruits. Socialization into the police subculture commences with recruit training, and is ongoing thereafter.

police professionalism The increasing formalization of police work, and the rise in public acceptance of the police which accompanies it. Any profession is characterized by a specialized body of knowledge and a set of internal guidelines which hold members of the profession accountable for their actions. A well-focused code of ethics, equitable recruitment and selection practices, and informed promotional strategies among many agencies contribute to the growing level of professionalism among American police agencies today.

police working personality All aspects of the traditional values and patterns of behavior evidenced by police officers who have been effectively socialized into the police subculture. Characteristics of the police personality often extend to the personal lives of law enforcement personnel.

postconviction remedy The procedure or set of procedures by which a person who has been convicted of a crime can challenge in court the lawfulness of a judgment of conviction or penalty or of a correctional agency action, and thus obtain relief in situations where this cannot be done by a direct appeal.

precedent A legal principle that operates to ensure that previous judicial decisions are authoritatively considered and incorporated into future cases.

preliminary hearing The proceeding before a judicial officer in which three matters must be decided—whether a crime was committed, whether the crime occurred within the territorial jurisdiction of the court, and whether there are reasonable grounds to believe that the defendant committed the crime.

presentence investigation The examination of a convicted offender's background prior to sentencing. Presentence examinations are generally conducted by probation/parole officers and submitted to sentencing authorities.

presentment Historically, written notice of an offense taken by a grand jury from their own knowledge or observation; in current usage, any of several presentations of alleged facts and charges to a court or a grand jury by a prosecutor.

pretrial detention Any period of confinement occurring between arrest or other holding to answer a charge and the conclusion of prosecution.

pretrial discovery In criminal proceedings, disclosure by the prosecution or the defense prior to trial of evidence or other information which is intended to be used in the trial.

pretrial release The release of an accused person from custody, for all or part of the time before or during prosecution, upon his or her promise to appear in court when required.

prison A state or federal confinement facility having custodial authority over adults sentenced to confinement.

prison argot The slang characteristic of prison subcultures and prison life.

prison capacity The size of the correctional population an institution can effectively hold.[4]

prison commitment A sentence of commitment to the jurisdiction of a state or federal confinement facility system for adults, of which the custodial authority extends to persons sentenced to more than a year of confinement, for a term expressed in years or for life, or to await execution of a death sentence.

prisoner A person in physical custody in a confinement facility, or in the personal physical custody of a criminal justice official while being transported to or between confinement facilities. A person in physical custody in a state or federal confinement facility.

prisonization The process whereby institutionalized individuals come to accept prison life-styles and criminal values. While many inmates begin their prison experience with only a modicum of values supportive of criminal behavior, the socialization experience they undergo while incarcerated leads to a much wider acceptance of such values.

prison subculture The values and behavioral patterns characteristic of prison inmates. Prison subculture has been found to have surprising consistencies across the country.

private prisons Correctional institutions operated by private firms on behalf of local and state governments.

private security Those self-employed individuals and privately funded business entities and organizations providing security-related services to specific clientele for a fee, for the individual or entity that retains or employs them, or for themselves, in order to protect their persons, private property, or interests from various hazards.[5]

private security agency An independent or proprietary commercial organization whose activities include employee clearance investigations, maintaining the security of persons or property, and/or performing the functions of detection and investigation of crime and criminals and apprehension of offenders.

probable cause A set of facts and circumstances that would induce a reasonably intelligent and prudent person to believe that a particular person had committed a specific crime; reasonable grounds to make or believe an accusation.

probation The conditional freedom granted by a judicial officer to an adjudicated or adjudged adult or juvenile offender, as long as the person meets certain conditions of behavior.

probationer A person who is placed on probation status and required by a court or probation agency to meet certain conditions of behavior, who may or may not be placed under the supervision of a probation agency.

probation revocation A court order in response to a violation of conditions of probation, taking away a person's probationary status, and usually withdrawing the conditional freedom associated with the status.

probation termination The ending of the probation status of a given person by routine expiration of probationary period, by special early termination by court, or by revocation of probation.

probation violation An act or failure to act by a probationer that does not conform to the conditions of his or her probation.

probation work load The total set of activities required in order to carry out the probation agency functions of intake screening of juveniles cases, referral of cases to other service agencies, investigation of juveniles and adults for the purpose of preparing predisposition or presentence reports, supervision or treatment of juveniles and adults granted probation, assisting in the enforcement of court orders concerning family problems such as abandonment and nonsupport cases, and such other functions as may be assigned by statute or court order.

procuratorate (also procuracy) A term used in many countries to refer to agencies with powers and responsibilities similar to those of prosecutor's offices in the United States.

professional criminal See **career criminal**.

property crime An offense category that, according to the FBI's UCR program, includes burglary, larceny, auto theft, and arson. Since citizen reports of criminal incidents figure heavily in the compilation of "official statistics," the same critiques apply to tallies of these crimes as to the category of violent crime.

property bond The setting of bail in the form of land, houses, stocks, or other tangible property. In the event the defendant absconds prior to trial, the bond becomes the property of the court.

prosecution agency A federal, state, or local criminal justice agency or subunit of which the principal function is the prosecution of alleged offenders.

prosecutor An attorney who is the elected or appointed chief of a prosecution agency, and whose official duty is to conduct criminal proceedings on behalf of the people against persons accused of committing criminal offenses. Also called "district attorney," "DA," "state's attorney," "county attorney," and "U.S. attorney" and any attorney deputized to assist the chief prosecutor.

prosecutorial discretion The decision-making power of prosecutors based upon the wide range of choices available to them in the handling of criminal defendants, the scheduling of cases for trial, the acceptance of bargained pleas, and so on. The most important form of prosecutorial discretion lies in the power to charge, or not to charge, a person with an offense.

prostitution Offering or agreeing to engage in, or engaging in, a sex act with another in return for a fee.

psychoactive drug A chemical substance that affects cognition, feeling, and/or awareness.

psychoanalysis A theory of human behavior, based upon the writings of Sigmund Freud, that sees personality as a complex composite of interacting mental entities.

psychological school A perspective on criminological thought that views offensive and deviant behavior as the products of dysfunctional personalities. The conscious, and especially the subconscious, contents of the human psyche are identified by psychological thinkers as major determinants of behavior.

public defender An attorney employed by a government agency or subagency, or by a private organization under contract to a unit of government, for the purpose of providing defense services to indigents; also, occasionally, an attorney who has volunteered such service. The head of a government agency or subunit whose function is the representation in court of persons accused or convicted of a crime who are unable to hire private counsel, and any attorney employed by such an agency or subunit whose official duty is the performance of the indigent defense function.

public defender agency A federal, state, or local criminal justice agency or subunit of which the principal function is to represent in court persons accused or convicted of a crime(s) who are unable to hire private counsel.

public safety department An agency organized at the state or local level of government incorporating at a minimum various law enforcement and emergency service functions.

radical criminology A conflict perspective that sees crime as engendered by the unequal distribution of wealth, power, and other resources which it believes is especially characteristic of capitalist societies. Also called "critical criminology."

rape Unlawful sexual intercourse with a female, by force or without legal or factual consent.

rated capacity The number of inmates that a correctional facility can house without overcrowding, determined by comparison with some set of explicit standards applied to groups of facilities.

recidivism The repetition of criminal behavior.

recidivist A person who has been convicted of one or more crimes and who is alleged or found to have subsequently committed another crime or series of crimes.

reformatory concept A late-nineteenth-century correctional model based upon the use of the indeterminate sentence and belief in the possibility of rehabilitation, especially for youthful offenders. The reformatory concept faded with the emergence of industrial prisons around the turn of the century.

rehabilitation The attempt to reform a criminal offender. Also, the state in which a reformed offender is said to be.

release on recognizance (ROR) The pretrial release of a criminal defendant on their written promise to appear. No cash or property bond is required.

reprieve An executive act temporarily suspending the execution of a sentence, usually a death sentence. A reprieve differs from other suspensions of sentence not only in that it almost always applies to temporary withdrawing of a death sentence, but also in that it is usually an act of clemency intended to provide the prisoner with time to secure amelioration of the sentence.

resident A person required by official action or his own acceptance of placement to reside in a public or private facility established for purposes of confinement, supervision, or care.

residential commitment A sentence of commitment to a correctional facility for adults, in which the offender is required to reside at night, but from which he or she is regularly permitted to depart during the day, unaccompanied by any official.

restitution A court requirement that an alleged or convicted offender pay money or provide services to the victim of the crime or provide services to the community.

restoration A goal of criminal sentencing that attempts to make the victim "whole again."

retribution The act of taking revenge upon a criminal perpetrator.

revocation The cancellation of a probationer's or parolee's freedom. Revocation usually results from the violation of at least one of the conditions of probation or parole and may be ordered only by a special hearing board constituted for that purpose.

RICO (Racketeer Influenced Corrupt Organization) A federal statute that allows for the federal seizure of assets derived from illegal enterprise.

rights of defendant Those powers and privileges which are constitutionally guaranteed to every defendant.

robbery (UCR) The unlawful taking or attempted taking of property that is in the immediate possession of another by force or threat of force.

runaway A juvenile who has been adjudicated by a judicial officer of juvenile court, as having committed the status offense of leaving the custody and home of his or her parents, guardians or custodians without permission and failing to return within a reasonable length of time.

scientific police management The application of social scientific techniques to the study of police administration for the purpose of increasing effectiveness, reducing the frequency of citizen complaints, and enhancing the efficient use of available resources. The heyday of scientific police management probably occurred during the 1970s, when federal monies were far more readily available to support such studies than they are today.

search warrant A document issued by a judicial officer which directs a law enforcement officer to conduct a search at a specific location, for specified property or persons relating to a crime(s), to seize the property or persons if found, and to account for the results of the search to the issuing judicial officer.

security The restriction of inmate movement within a correctional facility, usually divided into maximum, medium, and minimum levels.

self-defense The protection of oneself or one's property from unlawful injury or the immediate risk of unlawful injury; the justification for an act which would otherwise constitute an offense, that the person who committed it reasonably believed that the act was necessary to protect self or property from immediate danger.

sentence The penalty imposed by a court upon a person convicted of a crime. The court judgment specifying the penalty imposed upon a person convicted of a crime. Any disposition of a defendant resulting from a conviction, including the court decision to suspend execution of a sentence.

sentencing The imposition of a criminal sanction by a sentencing authority.

sentencing dispositions Court dispositions of defendants after a judgment of conviction, expressed as penalties, such as imprisonment or payment of fines; or any of a number of alternatives to actually executed penalties, such as suspended sentences, grants of probation, or orders to perform restitution; or various combinations of the foregoing.

sentencing hearing In criminal proceedings, a hearing during which the court or jury considers relevant information, such as evidence concerning aggravating or mitigating circumstances, for the purpose of determining a sentencing disposition for a person convicted of an offense(s).

sequestered jury A jury that is isolated from the public during the course of a trial and throughout the deliberation process.

service style A style of policing that is marked by a concern with helping rather than strict enforcement. Service-oriented agencies are more likely to take advantage of community resources, such as drug treatment programs, than are other types of departments.

sex offenses In current statistical usage, the name of a broad category of varying content, usually consisting of all offenses having a sexual element except forcible rape and commercial sex offenses. All unlawful sexual intercourse, unlawful sexual contact, and other unlawful behavior intended to result in sexual gratification or profit from sexual activity.

sex offenses (UCR) The name of the UCR category used to record and report arrests made for "offenses against chastity, common decency, morals, and the like," except forcible rape, prostitution, and commercialized vice.

sheriff The elected chief officer of a county law enforcement agency, usually responsible for law enforcement in unincorporated areas and for the operation of the county jail.

sheriff's department A local law enforcement agency organized at the county level, directed by a sheriff, which exercises its law enforcement functions at the county level, usually within unincorporated areas, and operates the county jail in most jurisdictions.

shock incarceration A sentencing option that makes use of "boot camp"–type prisons in order to impress upon convicted offenders the realities of prison life.

shock probation The practice of sentencing offenders to prison, allowing them to apply for probationary release, and enacting such release in surprise fashion. Offenders who receive shock probation may not be aware of the fact that they will be released on probation and may expect to spend a much longer time behind bars.

simple assault (UCR) Unlawful threatening, attempted inflicting, or inflicting of less than serious bodily injury, in the absence of a deadly weapon.

smuggling Unlawful movement of goods across a national frontier or state boundary or into or out of a correctional facility.

social control The use of sanctions and rewards available through a group to influence and shape the behavior of individual members of that group. Social control is a primary concern of social groups and communities, and it is the interest that human groups hold in the exercise of social control that leads to the creation of both criminal and civil statutes.

social–psychological school A perspective on criminological thought which highlights the role played in crime causation by weakened self-esteem and meaningless social roles. Social–psychological thinkers stress the relationship of the individual to the social group as the underlying cause of behavior.

speedy trial The right of the defendant to have a prompt trial, as guaranteed by the Sixth Amendment of the U.S. Constitution "In all criminal prosecutions, the accused shall enjoy the right to a speedy and public trial…".

split sentence A sentence explicitly requiring the convicted person to serve a period of confinement in a local, state, or federal facility followed by a period of probation.

state action doctrine The traditional legal principle that only government officials or their representatives in the criminal justice process could be held accountable for the violation of an individual's constitutional civil rights.

state highway patrol A state law enforcement agency of which the principal functions consist of prevention, detection, and investigation of motor vehicle offenses, and the apprehension of traffic offenders.

state police A state law enforcement agency whose principal functions usually include maintaining statewide police communications, aiding local police in criminal investigation, police training, and guarding state property and may include highway patrol.

state-use system A form of inmate labor in which items produced by inmates are salable only by or to state offices. Items that only the state can sell include such things as license plates and hunting licenses, while items sold only to state offices include furniture and cleaning supplies.

status offender A child who commits an act that is contrary to the law by virtue of the juvenile's status as a child. Purchasing cigarettes, buying alcohol, and truancy are examples of such behavior.

stay of execution The stopping by a court of the carrying out or implementation of a judgment, that is, of a court order previously issued.

stolen property offenses The unlawful receiving, buying, distributing, selling, transporting, concealing, or possessing of the property of another by a person who knows that the property has been unlawfully obtained from the owner or other lawful possessor.

stop and frisk The detaining of a person by a law enforcement officer for the purpose of investigation, accompanied by a superficial examination by the officer of the person's body surface or clothing to discover weapons, contraband, or other objects relating to criminal activity.

street crime A class of offenses, sometimes defined with some degree of formality as those which occur in public locations, are visible and assaultive, and thus constitute a group of crimes which are a special risk to the public and a special target of law enforcement preventive efforts and prosecutorial attention.

subculture of violence A cultural setting in which violence is a traditional method of dispute resolution.

subpoena A written order issued by a judicial officer, prosecutor, defense attorney or grand jury, requiring a specific person to appear in a designated court at a specified time in order to testify in a case under the jurisdiction of that court or to bring material to be used as evidence to that court.

supervised probation Guidance, treatment, or regulation by a probation agency of the behavior of the person who is subject to adjudication or who has been convicted of an offense, resulting from a formal court order or a probation agency decision.

suspect An adult or juvenile considered by a criminal justice agency to be one who may have committed a specific criminal offense, but who has not been arrested or charged.

suspended sentence The court decision to delay imposing or executing a penalty for a specified or unspecified period, also called "sentence withheld." A court disposition of a convicted person pronouncing a penalty of a fine or commitment to confinement, but unconditionally discharging the defendant or holding execution of the penalty in abeyance upon good behavior.

suspicionless searches Those searches conducted by law enforcement personnel without a warrant and without suspicion. Suspicionless searches are only permissible if based upon an overriding concern for public safety.

Tazirat crimes Minor violations of Islamic law, which are regarded as offenses against society, not God.

TEMPEST A standard developed by the U.S. government that requires that electromagnetic emanations from computers designated as "secure" be below levels that would allow radio receiving equipment to "read" the data being computed.

terrorism A violent act or an act dangerous to human life in violation of the criminal laws of the United States or of any state to intimidate or coerce a government, the civilian population, or any segment thereof, in furtherance of political or social objectives.[6]

theft Generally, any taking of the property of another with intent to deprive the rightful owner of possession permanently.

total institutions Enclosed facilities, separated from society both socially and physically, where the inhabitants share all aspects of their lives on a daily basis.

transfer to adult court The decision by a juvenile court, resulting from a transfer hearing, that jurisdiction over an alleged delinquent will be waived, and that he or she should be prosecuted as an adult in a criminal court.

trial The examination in a court of the issues of fact and law in a case, for the purpose of reaching a judgment. In criminal proceedings, the examination in a court of the issues of fact and law in a case, for the purpose of reaching a judgment of conviction or acquittal of the defendant(s).

trial de novo Literally, a new trial. The term is applied to cases that are retried on appeal, as opposed to those which are simply reviewed on the record.

trial judge A judicial officer who is authorized to conduct jury and nonjury trials, and who may not be authorized to hear appellate cases, or the judicial officer who conducts a particular trial.

trial jury A statutorily defined number of persons selected according to law and sworn to determine, in accordance with the law as instructed by the court, certain matters of fact based on evidence presented in a trial and to render a verdict.

UCR An abbreviation for the Federal Bureau of Investigation's "Uniform Crime Reporting" program.

unconditional release The final release of an offender from the jurisdiction of a correctional agency; also, a final release from the jurisdiction of a court.

vagrancy (UCR) The name of the UCR category relating to being a suspicious character or person, including vagrancy, begging, loitering, and vagabondage.

vandalism (UCR) The name of the UCR category used to record and report arrests made for offenses of destroying or damaging, or attempting to destroy or damage, the property of another without his consent, or public property, except by burning.

verdict In criminal proceedings, the decision of the jury in a jury trial or of a judicial officer in a nonjury trial.

victim A person who has suffered death, physical or mental anguish, or loss of property as the result of an actual or attempted criminal offense committed by another person.

victim impact statement The in-court use of victim- or survivor-supplied information by sentencing authorities wishing to make an informed sentencing decision.

victimization In National Crime Survey terminology, the harming of any single victim in a criminal incident.

violation I. The performance of an act forbidden by a statute or the failure to perform an act commanded by a statute. II. An act contrary to a local government ordinance. III. An offense punishable by a fine or other penalty but not by incarceration. IV. An act prohibited by the terms and conditions of probation or parole.

violent crime See **crime index**.

warden The official in charge of operation of a prison, the chief administrator of a prison, the prison superintendent.

warehousing An imprisonment strategy based upon the desire to prevent recurrent crime, but which has abandoned any hope of rehabilitation.

warrant In criminal proceedings, any of a number of writs issued by a judicial officer, which direct a law enforcement officer to perform a specified act and afford him protection from damage if he performs it.

watchman style A style of policing that is marked by a concern for order maintenance. This style of policing is characteristic of lower-class communities where informal police intervention into the lives of residents is employed in the service of keeping the peace.

weapons offenses Unlawful sale, distribution, manufacture, alteration, transportation, possession, or use or attempted sale, distribution, manufacture, alteration, transportation, possession, or use of a deadly or dangerous weapon or accessory.

white-collar crime Nonviolent crime for financial gain committed by means of deception by persons whose occupational status is entrepreneurial, professional, or semiprofessional and utilizing their special occupational skills and opportunities; also, nonviolent crime for financial gain utilizing deception and committed by anyone having special technical and professional knowledge of business and government, irrespective of the person's occupation.

witness In criminal justice usage, generally, a person who has knowledge of the circumstances of a case; in court usage, one who testifies as to what he or she has seen, heard, otherwise observed, or has expert knowledge of.

writ A document issued by a judicial officer ordering or forbidding the performance of a specified act.

writ of *certiorari* A writ issued from an appellate court for the purpose of obtaining from a lower court the record of its proceedings in a particular case. In some states this writ is the mechanism for discretionary reviews. A request for review is made by petitioning for a writ of *certiorari,* and granting of review is indicated by issuance of writ.

writ of *habeas corpus* In criminal proceedings, the writ that directs the person detaining a prisoner to bring him or her before a judicial officer to determine the lawfulness of the imprisonment.

youthful offender A person, adjudicated in criminal court, who may be above the statutory age limit for juveniles but is below a specified upper age limit, for whom special correctional commitments and special record sealing procedures are made available by statute.

---

[1]Michael L. Benson, Francis T. Cullen, and William J. Maakestad, *Local Prosecutors and Corporate Crime* (Washington, D.C.: National Institute of Justice, 1993).

[2]Clifford Karchmer and Douglas Ruch, "State and Local Money Laundering Control Strategies," *NIJ Research in Brief* (Washington, D.C.: NIJ, 1992), p. 1.

[3]*Federal Rules of Criminal Procedure.*

[4]See Bureau of Justice Statistics *Prisoners in 1990* (Washington, D.C.: Bureau of Justice Statistics, May 1991).

[5]See *Private Security: Report of the Task Force on Private Security* (Washington, D.C.: U.S. Government Printing Office, 1976), p. 4.

[6]See Federal Bureau of Investigation Counterterrorism Section, *Terrorism in the United States, 1987* (Washington, D.C.: FBI, December 1987).

INDEXES

ASE INDEX

NAME INDEX

SUBJECT INDEX